MW00345702

LEGAL ETHICS
AND
CORPORATE PRACTICE

By

Milton C. Regan, Jr.
Professor of Law
Georgetown University Law Center

Jeffrey D. Bauman
Professor of Law
Georgetown University Law Center

AMERICAN CASEBOOK SERIES®

THOMSON
™
WEST

Mat #40181115

American Casebook Series and West Group are trademarks registered in the U.S. Patent and Trademark Office.

© 2005 Thomson/West
      610 Opperman Drive
      P.O. Box 64526
      St. Paul, MN 55164–0526
      1–800–328–9352

Printed in the United States of America

ISBN 0–314–15013–7

 *TEXT IS PRINTED ON 10% POST CONSUMER RECYCLED PAPER*

To Nancy, Rebecca, and Ben
　　　　　— Mitt

To my parents, whose moral compass made
this possible.
　　　　　— Jeff

*

Preface

Believe it or not, we began teaching the course that is the basis for this book a few years before the recent parade of corporate scandals that began with Enron's collapse in late 2001. Why? Because a huge percentage of law students graduate and go on to represent corporate clients in either law firms or corporate legal departments—but few receive systematic guidance on the distinctive and complex ethical questions that corporate practice raises. In light of the substantial number of lawyers representing corporations, and the enormous impact that these business entities have on modern life, this seemed to us a serious omission. Convinced that it was important to fill this gap, we resolved to publish the first major casebook on ethical issues in corporate practice.

The events since Enron's fall, of course, have only strengthened our conviction. The behavior of corporations and the professionals who advise them are now the object of searching scrutiny. Why, critics ask, didn't the lawyers stop the looting, the fraud, and the manipulation of loopholes? They must have been blinded by greed, or co-opted by management, or motivated simply to look the other way. In light of this behavior, is there anything we can do to make lawyers take the role of gatekeeper more seriously?

We have no laundry list of reforms whose adoption we are certain will lead to more ethical behavior by lawyers. We believe, however things are not as simple as some critics charge. Training law students and corporate lawyers to be sensitive to ethical issues must begin with a detailed appreciation of precisely what corporate lawyers do. We need to understand the organizational and social settings in which they work, the tasks that they perform, and the judgments that they are called upon to make.

In other words, we need a feel for the texture of the corporate lawyer's daily experience, and the ways in which it shapes her understanding of the situations in which she is immersed. Focusing on these issues is crucial because ethical issues rarely come labeled as such. Awareness that any given set of circumstances has an ethical dimension instead is the product of a complicated process of perception and interpretation—in essence, the exercise of judgment.

Our firm belief that fostering ethical conduct requires helping students and lawyers develop good judgment leads us to structure this book in specific ways. First, it is organized primarily not around traditional ethical concepts but around work flow—the various kinds of work that corporate lawyers do. The questions that arise when lawyers are engaged in different tasks typically cut across a range of ethical categories. A lawyer experiences the world not as someone focused on confidentiality or conflict of interest, but as someone involved in drafting an opinion letter, or advising on disclosure for a securities filing, or conducting an internal investigation. We therefore use these and other tasks as the point of departure in most chapters.

Second, we include within the chapters extensive material on just what a lawyer does when she is engaged in a particular type of work. This ideally will make students and lawyers more sensitive to the how the lawyer's work is organized, the various parties with interest in and influence on that work, and the kinds of decisions that the lawyer must make when involved in a particular matter. Combining awareness of these considerations with knowledge of regulatory provisions relevant to the lawyer's conduct should allow the reader to imagine more vividly how events can unfold and ethical issues may arise.

Finally, most chapters close with problems that ask students to respond to a complex situation calling for the exercise of practical and ethical judgment. This requires familiarity not only with ethical rules, but often with statutory provisions and common law doctrines that are more relevant to corporate lawyers. Furthermore, fashioning a suitable response also may require taking account of organizational structures, group processes, business objectives, psychological tendencies, and other factors. Our hope is that this will enable students and lawyers to cultivate their capacity for judgment, rather than simply acquire knowledge of legal rules.

We believe that the approach we take in this book is valuable not only for those who are interested in or practice corporate law, but for anyone concerned with legal ethics. One reason is that the book covers as wide a range of functions that lawyers perform—including criminal prosecution and defense—as do most traditional casebooks. More important, as we have witnessed, learning this subject by developing an appreciation of how ethical issues arise in the course of the lawyer's work flow can be an especially powerful way of coming to "know" legal ethics. This is the case regardless of the field in which a student or lawyer ultimately practices. Knowledge acquired with sensitivity to how daily experience unfolds is valuable in any human endeavor. In legal ethics, we are firmly convinced that it is indispensable.

Acknowledgments

We are grateful for the help of several people in putting this book together. Our thanks to Ethan Yale for reviewing the Chapter on Tax Practice, and to Bill Bratton for scrutinizing the presentation of Enron transactions that is contained in the Chapter on Complex Transactions. Conversations with Donald Langevoort and Robert Haft as we have taught a course on this subject have been valuable in helping us identify and focus on important issues. Deans Judy Areen and Alex Aleinikoff, and Associate Deans Vicki Jackson and Mark Tushnet, have generously provided Writer's Grant assistance that enabled us to complete this project. Jennifer Locke of the Edward Bennett Williams Library at Georgetown Law Center, and Joe Conahan, 2004 Georgetown Law graduate, have coordinated and provided outstanding research assistance.

We also are grateful to Roxanne Birkel at Thomson/West for her considerable help in the production of the book. Roxy's steadfast patience and congeniality, along with her keen intelligence under considerable time pressure, always made clear to us that her most important objective was to help us ensure that this book would be as good as we could make it.

Finally, we want to thank the students over the past few years who have taken the course that has been the impetus for this book. They have encouraged us in the belief that this topic is of vital importance, and have pushed us to clarify ideas that were imprecise or incompletely reasoned. Most of all, they have reinforced our faith that, notwithstanding the complexity and pressures of modern law practice, students on the cusp of becoming lawyers still hope to lead lives whose sense of purpose is shaped by commitment to the profession's highest ideals.

*

Summary of Contents

*

Table of Contents

*

LEGAL ETHICS
AND
CORPORATE PRACTICE

*

Chapter 1

SETTING THE STAGE: THE CORPORATION AND ITS LAWYERS

Many modern corporations command more resources than do some countries. Their decisions on investment, product design, manufacturing activity, employment, marketing, competitive strategy, and other matters can profoundly affect the quality of life for millions of people and the natural environment. As Charles Lindblom has observed, "Corporate executives in all private enterprise systems * * * decide a nation's industrial technology, the pattern of work organization, location of industry, market structure, resource allocation, and, of course, executive compensation and status," as well as "what is to be produced and in what quantities."[1] The result is that "a large category of major decisions is turned over to businesses," and "taken off the agenda of government."[2]

In light of this, business corporations historically have been lightning rods for political debate about fundamental political, social, and economic issues. From 19th century efforts to tame the business trust to 21st century attempts to address the challenges of transnational corporations, questions have been raised about the main purposes of the corporation and the extent to which it should take into account non-economic issues in its business decisions. The answers to these questions at any historical moment are only tentative, as different perspectives continue to jostle for influence in the wake of ongoing developments.

Lawyers who represent corporations need to be aware of these dynamics in order to provide useful advice and legal services to their clients. As Model Rule of Professional Conduct 2.1 provides, "In rendering advice, a lawyer may refer not only to law but to other considerations such as moral, economic, social and political factors, that may be relevant to the client's situation." The material in this chapter is designed

---

1. Charles Lindblom, Politics and Markets 171–172 (1977).

2. *Id.* at 172.

1

to provide an overview of the main themes in the debate over the role of the corporation, in order to ensure that lawyers are sensitive to the wide range of considerations they may need to take into account in representing their corporate clients.

No less controversial have been the activities of lawyers who represent corporations. The movement from solo and small scale law offices to integrated law firms in the late 19th and early 20th centuries occurred in response to the expanding needs of corporate enterprise. Lawyers have been riding the crests of change with their corporate clients ever since. This dynamism means that corporate lawyers often are the first to confront novel questions of ethics and professional judgment. The remaining material in this chapter describes the challenges this creates both for everyday practice and the more fundamental conception of what it means to be a lawyer.

OVERVIEW OF THE CHAPTER

The first article by former Delaware Chancellor William Allen focuses on how society and law have conceptualized the corporation over the course of American history. Allen suggests that there have been two competing understandings. One is the "property" conception, which sees the corporation as owned by and run for the benefit of its shareholders. The second is the "entity" conception, which regards the corporation as having distinct interests and obligations of its own in light of its relationships with employees, consumers, and society at large. Allen notes that each conception has been influential in different historical periods. In the current era, global markets and institutional shareholders have combined to increase pressure for managers to conform to the property model by placing priority on maximizing shareholder wealth. As you read the piece, ask yourself what kinds of situations might arise in which the two conceptions of the corporation are in tension. What kind of advice from a lawyer is most useful in these instances? If the law reflects an effort to accommodate both conceptions, what is involved in counseling the corporation about "the law?"

The Regan article describes the ways in which the dynamism of the corporation continually confronts the corporate lawyer with cutting-edge legal and ethical questions for which there often is no clear answer. Law tends to lag behind economic and technological changes. As a result, lawyers for corporations may be forced to navigate unfamiliar territory, constructing guidance instruments as they go. When legal precedent offers little direct guidance, should there be any limits on a lawyer's exercise of creativity? If an arrangement can be made to fit within the literal terms of the law, does that exhaust the lawyer's responsibility?

Notice also how Regan suggests that how law practice itself is organized is shaped by the dynamism of corporate representation. Ask yourself how the changes in law practice that he describes are a result of the emerging market conditions that companies are facing. Are these changes desirable for lawyers? For their clients? Is there any tension between the two interests?

The short excerpt from Justice Potter Stewart and the second article by Chancellor Allen speak explicitly to the ethical responsibilities of the corporate lawyer. Justice Stewart maintains that the business lawyer should be guided essentially by the same maxims of enlightened self-interest that characterize the "morals of the marketplace." Does Stewart mean by this that the lawyer should not be held to standards different from those that apply to any other business actor? If so, Allen disagrees. He suggests that the corporate lawyer has a distinctive professional duty of independence. This duty requires that a lawyer advise the client to comply with the spirit, not simply the letter, of the law. Allen argues that providing such advice helps maintain the trust among parties and respect for the legal system that a market system requires in order to function. Is this rationale, however, appreciably different from Stewart's reference to "enlightened self-interest?" Can you imagine any instances in which Allen's directive that the lawyer exercise professional independence would ever conflict with the lawyer's or the client's self-interest?

William T. Allen, OUR SCHIZOPHRENIC CONCEPTION OF THE BUSINESS CORPORATION

14 CARDOZO L. REV. 261 (1992)

INTRODUCTION

* * *

My assignment is to share some of my thoughts about corporation law—that body of statutes and case precedent that governs the internal organization and functioning of the legal form within which the greatest part of our economic activity takes place. It is in that area that I have had certain experiences that occasioned my invitation.

While I want to be true to that specific purpose, I would like as well to use this occasion—and these corporate law materials—to try to make a broader point. That broader point, which will seem trite to scholars, is offered principally to the students. It is this: Corporation law and, indeed, the law generally, is not simply what it may seem at first, a comprehensive system of legal rules. While it is that, it is also a great deal more. People who think of law as a system of legal rules alone fail to understand that law is a social product, inevitably complex, at points inescapably ambiguous, and always dynamic—always becoming something new. Of course, it is essential for the student of corporation law, or of commercial law or constitutional law, to understand the legal rules that at any moment constitute the most elemental part of that body of law. But far more is necessary than that to achieve understanding of our legal order or of any part of it. In order to grasp the dynamic feature of legal rules, it is necessary to see them in their historical and social context. For while, in one sense, legal rules exist "out there," constituting shared interpretations of our common legal culture, they are, as well, continually re-created within that culture through interpretation. We cannot begin to understand the processes of law, unless we try to place law in its rich historical and social context. The evolution of the concept of the corporation can help us see that. But let me not try to state a conclusion now; I should first tell the corporation law story that I hope might suggest that conclusion.

The 1980s were turbulent years for corporation law. Twenty years earlier it had seemed that every interesting question in corporation law had been completely answered and that nothing remained to engage the wit and the energy of those with a taste for discovery and construction. The colorful statement of Bayless Manning captured the zeitgeist: "[C]orporation law, as a field of intellectual effort, is dead in the United States," Dean Manning pronounced. "When American law ceased to take the 'corporation' seriously, the entire body of law that had been built upon that intellectual construct slowly perforated and rotted away." He then added the touch of a talented rhetoritician: "We have nothing left but our great empty corporation statutes—towering skyscrapers of rusted girders, internally welded together and containing nothing but wind."

I doubt that Dean Manning's observation was far off the mark in 1962. Modern corporation law statutes were, and still are, "enabling" statutes in the broadest sense of that term. They are almost literally empty, and those few mandatory features that remain—such as the requirement of an annual meeting of shareholders, or a right to inspect the company's books and records for a proper corporate purpose—are themselves under attack from some quarters as paternalistic clogs on efficiency.

* * *

I. *Two Models*

I want to discuss this most basic question: What is a corporation? I suggest that at least over the course of this century there have been, in our public life and in our law, two quite different and inconsistent ways to conceptualize the public corporation and legitimate its power. I will call them the property conception and the social entity conception. I want to explain how these inconsistent views managed to co-exist until the tectonic forces of the 1980s takeover movement created a crisis in corporate theory. It forced us to confront the uneasy, but previously unproblematic, state of conceptual confusion.

The question, what is a corporation, has a correlative question: For whose benefit are those in control of a corporation supposed to act? That question was vividly and urgently raised by hostile cash tender offers, especially when, as frequently happened, the vast majority of a target company's shareholders wanted to accept a tender offer. When, in that setting, directors elected to resist the offer, the question unavoidably arose: Whose interests were they promoting, and whose interests were they supposed to promote? An inquiry into these vital questions exposed the fact that our law and our society had been schizophrenic on the subject of corporation law for a long time.

Two inconsistent conceptions have dominated our thinking about corporations since the evolution of the large integrated business corporation in the late nineteenth century. Each conception could claim dominance for a particular period, or among one group or another, but neither has so commanded agreement as to exclude the other from the discourses of law or the thinking of business people.

In the first conception, the corporation is seen as the private property of its stockholder-owners. The corporation's purpose is to advance the purposes of these owners (predominantly to increase their wealth), and the function of directors, as agents of the owners, is faithfully to advance the financial interests of the owners. I call this the property conception of the corporation, because it sees the corporation as the property of its stockholders. This model might almost as easily be called a contract model, because in its most radical form, the corporation tends to disappear, transformed from a substantial institution into just a relatively stable corner of the market in which autonomous property owners freely contract.

The second conception sees the corporation not as the private property of stockholders, but as a social institution. According to this view, the corporation is not strictly private; it is tinged with a public purpose. The corporation comes into being and continues as a legal entity only with governmental concurrence. The legal institutions of government grant a corporation its juridical personality, its characteristic limited liability, and its perpetual life. This conception sees this public facilitation as justified by the state's interest in promoting the general welfare. Thus, corporate purpose can be seen as including the advancement of the general welfare. The board of directors' duties extend beyond assuring investors a fair return, to include a duty of loyalty, in some sense, to all those interested in or affected by the corporation. This view could be labeled in a variety of ways: the managerialist conception, the institutionalist conception, or the social entity conception. All would be descriptive, since the corporation is seen as distinct from each of the individuals that happens to fill the social roles that its internal rules and culture define. The corporation itself is, in this view, capable of bearing legal and moral obligations. To law and economics scholars, who have been so influential in academic corporate law, this model is barely coherent and dangerously wrong.

These two, apparently inconsistent, conceptions have coexisted in our thinking over the last century. For most of the century the lack of agreement on the ultimate nature and purpose of the business corporation has not generated intense conflict. A host of macro-economic factors—secularly rising prosperity, a lack of global competition, and the absence of powerful shareholders—probably account for this placid status quo. By the 1980s however, emerging global competition, capital market innovation, and the growth and evolution of institutional investors, among other factors, made possible the takeover movement, which glaringly exposed our inconsistent thinking about the nature of the business corporation.

Let me dilate upon these different views of the nature of the corporation, and on the masking and unmasking of the conceptual conflict that is near the core of corporation law.

A. The Property Conception

At least by the mid-nineteenth century, when the movement to enact general laws of incorporation had become firmly planted, the corporation was seen in this country as an artificial creation of the state designed to enable individuals to associate together for state approved purposes. The emphasis was on the individuals—the shareholders who had been constituted a corporation. There was a sense, but only a weak sense, of a distinctive, artificial corporate entity. * * *

The dominant perception was that the corporation, while an artificial entity, was essentially the stockholders in a special form. This perception colored the way in which the role and power of the board of directors was seen. When compared to what they would become, corporations in the mid to late nineteenth century appear to have been relatively frail conceptually, with boards of directors limited in power. Directors were seen as agents of stockholders.

Thus, if towards the close of the last century one would have asked to whom directors owe a duty of loyalty, a confident answer could have been expected: The corporation is like a limited partnership; its property is equitably the property of the shareholders. The directors are elected by shareholders and it is unquestionably on their behalf that the directors are bound to act. This view, with its genesis in the mid-nineteenth century, was plainly expressed in the law and, I suppose, was the view held beyond the legal community as well.

* * * The rights of creditors, employees and others are strictly limited to statutory, contractual, and common law rights. Once the directors have satisfied those legal obligations, they have fully satisfied all claims of these "constituencies." This property view of the nature of corporations, and of the duties owed by directors, equates the duty of directors with the duty to maximize profits of the firm for the benefit of shareholders.

This model of the public corporation is highly coherent and offers several alternative arguments to support the legitimacy of corporate power in our democracy. The first argument in favor of the property concept is political and normative. It is premised on the conclusionary notion that shareholders "own" the corporation, and asserts that to admit the propriety of non-profit maximizing behavior is to approve agents spending other people's money in pursuit of their own, perhaps eccentric, views of the public good. This can be seen as morally wrong without more. On a broader level, proponents of this view assert that it is repugnant to our democratic ideals to have corporate oligarchies determining which of many competing claimants for financial support should be awarded that support.* * *

This first argument in favor of a property conception of the corporation is weakest when it asserts that shareholders "own" corporate property and that it is, therefore, normatively wrong to expend their property for the benefit of another without shareholder consent. The premise of "ownership" simply assumes but does not justify an answer. This argument is strongest, however, when it asks whence comes the authority of corporate directors to make decisions on the basis of the public good.

The second rationale for the property model is that the model, and action consistent with it, maximize wealth creation. This rationale asserts that the purpose of business corporations is the creation of wealth, nothing else. It asserts that business corporations are not formed to assist in self-realization through social interaction; they are not formed to create jobs or to provide tax revenues; they are not formed to endow university departments or to pursue knowledge. All of these other things—job creation, tax payments, research, and social interaction—desirable as they may be, are said to be side effects of the pursuit of profit for the residual owners of the firm.

This argument asserts that the creation of more wealth should always be the corporation's objective, regardless of who benefits. The sovereign's taxing and regulatory power can then address questions of social costs and re-distribution of wealth. Thus, profit maximizing behavior is seen as affording the best opportunity to satisfy human wants and is the most appropriate aim of corporation law policy. This second argument for the legitimacy of the corporation as shareholder property is not premised on the conclusion that shareholders do "own" the corporation in any ultimate sense, only on the premise that it can be better for all of us if we act as if they do.

B. The Entity Conception

* * * [T]he last quarter of the nineteenth century saw the emergence of social forces that would oppose the conception of business corporations as simply the property of contracting stockholders. The scale and scope of modern integrated business enterprise that emerged in the late nineteenth century required distinctive professional management skills and huge capital investments that often necessitated risk sharing through dispersed stock ownership. National securities markets emerged and stockholders gradually came to look less like flesh and blood owners and more like investors who could slip in or out of a particular stock almost costlessly. These new giant business corporations came to seem to some people like independent entities, with purposes, duties, and loyalties of their own; purposes that might diverge in some respect from shareholder wealth maximization.

Henry Ford's losing position in Dodge v. Ford Motor Co. reflected an idea that was in the air. Others saw these new corporate social actors as different. Owen Young, the President of General Electric, for example, stated in a public address during the 1920s as follows:

> [M]anagers [are] no longer attorneys for stockholders; they [are] becoming trustees of an institution.
>
> If you will pardon me for being personal, it makes a great deal of difference in my attitude toward my job as an executive officer of the General Electric Company whether I am a trustee of the institution or an attorney for the investor. If I am a trustee, who are the beneficiaries of the trust? To whom do I owe my obligations?

Mr. Young went on to give his answer: As the chief officer of General Electric, he acknowledged an obligation to stockholders to pay "a fair rate of return"; but he also bore an obligation to labor, to customers, and lastly to the public, to whom he saw a duty to make sure the corporation functioned "in the public interest ... as a great and good citizen should."

The secure wisdom of the nineteenth century, while convincing to the Michigan Supreme Court, was not strong enough to contain this alternative view of corporations as independent social actors who do not simply owe contract or other legal duties to those affected by its operation, but owe loyalty in some measure to all such persons as well.

This social entity conception sees the purpose of the corporation as not individual but social. Surely contributors of capital (stockholders and bondholders) must be assured a rate of return sufficient to induce them to contribute their capital to the enterprise. But the corporation has other purposes of perhaps equal dignity: the satisfaction of consumer wants, the provision of meaningful employment opportunities, and the making of a contribution to the public life of its communities. Resolving the often conflicting claims of these various corporate constituencies calls for judgment, indeed calls for wisdom, by the board of directors of the corporation. But in this view no single constituency's interest may significantly exclude others from fair consideration by the board. This view appears to have been the dominant view among business leaders for at least the last fifty years.

The principal basis for a claim to legitimacy of director power under the entity theory is premised on utility claims. According to this view, managerial expertise and discretion is the essential ingredient for the effective functioning of the large-scale, multi-division business corporation. Our need for productive business enterprise commits us to the entity view, it is claimed, because it is corporate management, with its special organizational skills, that knows how to balance the claims made on the corporation in order to make large scale enterprise productive over the long term. For the common good, those managements cannot be hobbled by a short-sighted orientation geared exclusively to stockholders.

In claiming that management's unique expertise enables it to maximize corporate performance, and that its expert judgments about long-term value creation are more dependable than market valuations reflecting investor decisions, this utility basis for the legitimacy of the entity view directly challenges the premise of many economist critics that markets in widely traded securities value future prospects more dependably than does internal management. Thus, not surprisingly, proponents of both conceptions of the corporation base a claim to the validity of their view, in part, on a claim that accepting their perspective will enhance the economic productivity of corporations.

II. *Masking and Unmasking the Conflict*

One would think that whether the corporation law endorses the property conception or the social entity conception would have important consequences. Our experience in the 1980s demonstrated that it could. But equally as interesting as that 1980s conflict is the fact that for the fifty years preceding that contentious decade, we did not share agreement on the legal nature of the public business corporation and that failure did not seem especially problematic.

The law "papered over" the conflict in our conception of the corporation by invoking a murky distinction between long-term profit maximization and short-term profit maximization. Corporate expenditures which at first blush did not seem to be profit maximizing, could be squared with the property conception of the corporation by recognizing that they might redound to the long-term benefit of the corporation and its shareholders. Thus, without purporting to abandon the idea that directors ultimately owe loyalty only to stockholders and their financial interests, the law was able to approve reasonable corporate expenditures for charitable or social welfare purposes or other actions that did not maximize current profit.

There is a utility in this long-term/short-term device. Though employment of this distinction is subject to obvious manipulation, it can nevertheless resolve the tension between these differing conceptions of the corporation in a way that offers the possibility of some judicial protection to shareholders, while affording substantial room to the multi-constituency, social entity conception to operate. With this distinction, judicial review of particular decisions is available under the fiduciary duty standard. But corporate directors are also afforded very considerable latitude to deal with all groups or institutions having an interest in, or who are affected by, the corporation. The long-term/short-term distinction preserves the form of the stockholders oriented property theory, while permitting, in fact, a considerable degree of behavior consistent with a view that sees public corporations as owing social responsibilities to all affected by their operation.

Thus, while early on much ink was spilled on the question to whom should directors be responsible, in practice the question of the nature of the corporation seemed essentially unproblematic until the emergence of the cash tender offer of the 1980s. The long-term/short-term distinction proved a serviceable, if an intellectually problematic way, for the corporation law to avoid choosing between the alpha of property and the omega of relationships.

The forces loosened by the takeover movement of the 1980s, however, could not be contained within this verbal formula. Two things made the takeover phenomenon very problematic for the legal theory of the corporation.

The first is that the takeover movement put so much at stake. The issue in the takeover cases was not whether a donation of corporate funds could be made to a museum or college; it was not whether contributions in lieu of lawful taxes could be paid to local government, or any other day to day decision, as in earlier court cases. The issue was frequently whether all of the shareholders would be permitted to sell their shares; whether a change in corporate control would occur; and often whether a radical restructuring of the enterprise would go forward, with dramatic effects on creditors, employees, management, suppliers, and communities. As the junk bond market grew in size, larger and larger enterprises were faced with these prospects.

The effects of a takeover were seen by those affected as a form of shareholder exploitation of others who had made contributions of various sorts to the corporation. In the financial setting of the 1980s, dramatically higher stock prices could often be achieved by sharply increasing the debt of the corporation and reducing or eliminating certain operations. But increasing debt substantially made the enterprise riskier and thus reduced the value of the corporation's existing bonds; and restricting operations injured workers and management, who were thrown out of work. The bondholders and employees felt that radical corporate changes made in order to increase share value breached implicit understandings that had been the basis of their participation in the organization, or so one argument went. Thus, the scale of the problems raised by the takeover movement made evasion of the fundamental question of corporate definition difficult.

A second difference between the issues of the takeover era and those of the prior sixty years was that the short-term/long-term distinction was really of little analytical or rhetorical use in resolving the takeover issues. The most pressing of these issues involved the question whether a board of directors could take action that precluded shareholders from accepting a non-coercive, all cash tender offer. That question obviously raised the further question: Whose interests is the board of directors suppose to foster or protect when substantially all of the shareholders want to sell control of the corporation? The long-term/short-term distinction could not persuasively be used to answer or evade that question when it arose in this context. It is one thing to say that an expenditure of corporate funds that benefits the community—an education grant or the installation of an unmandated pollution control device—is really for the long-term financial benefit of shareholders. Though not compelling, arguments of this type surely are plausible.

It is, however, rather a different thing to justify precluding the shareholders from selling their stock at a large immediate profit on the ground that in the long run that will be good for them. While one might of course say that, many people would find it disturbing to put such a result on the basis that directors know what is better for shareholder then they themselves do. Instead the scope and nature of the issues faced seemed to demand a facing-up to the conceptual questions: For whom are directors to act? May they act to protect others (and themselves) from claims of shareholder exploitation?

* * *

IV. Resolution or Interregnum?

* * * What might this account of conceptual conflict in corporation law teach us about how our legal system functions? Let me raise that question by asking another: When we study law, what is it that we study?

For some, when we study law, we study legal rules or, more completely, we study a system of authoritatively promulgated, comprehensive rules and the system (rules) of their administration. As a system of rules, the legal system is astonishingly complex, with an enormous variety of substantive rules regulating our conduct and other rules regulating the legal system itself. When we start out in our study of law, we think that to become a lawyer it is necessary to learn these rules, especially the rules concerning the operation of the legal machinery. We are right to think that, but we would be badly wrong to think that knowledge of legal rules is all that we need to understand the legal world.

When we study corporation law we surely must learn the content of the corporation law statutes and the rules announced in court decisions. We must learn the analytical and theoretical tools of a lawyer, so that we can manipulate these rules within the permissible zone of their ambiguity in order to guide and protect clients. But if we were to learn the content of legal rules alone we would achieve only a dry and brittle power that would quickly snap under the dynamic cross-pressures of complex and contradictory real life.

In corporation law, as in every area of law, learning the rules, and the permissible manipulation of the rules, is the crucial beginning. But it is only the beginning. We must discover and understand the principles that stand behind the rules. But even that step is not yet enough. To approach understanding, we must be able to see legal rules and principles as social constructs, affected by their internal logic, but affected even more profoundly by the social world in which they exist.

Legal ideas are not static abstractions; the legal process is not simply a deductive exercise, and the evolution of law is not an inevitable working out of anything. In the judicial process the law of each case is constructed from generalities. In explaining that process everything counts. Ideas about efficiency certainly count. But ideology also counts. And social forces that judges feel but can only vaguely articulate may be important. In this process, the internal logic of the legal system itself will serve as an important constraint, even if it is not determinative in the way our naive selves first thought.

The law, like ourselves, is always in flux, always "becoming." We accept, or invent, or reconstitute structures in the flux because we want order (some of us more than others) and predictability. The concept of the corporation is such a structure. For a long period it seemed settled, although it was not; it seemed known, even boring. The concept of the corporation became problematic only because real world economic forces changed, and those changes exerted pressures that forced legal change. But the ever-emergent quality of law suggests that the resolution of the conceptual conflict that was reached in the late 1980s by the endorsement of the entity concept, will not be a final answer to the question, what is a corporation.

We cannot of course know the future, but we can see the future stresses that the entity conception of the public corporation will generate. The entity conception inevitably will give rise to claims of inefficiency and illegitimacy; and those are claims that the blunt instruments of stakeholder statutes can neither answer nor suppress.

Each of the two dominant social trends that will exert potentially transformative power on corporate governance in the years immediately ahead—the evolution of a truly global economy and the continuing growth, and coming dominance, of institutional shareholders—is more consistent with the property conception of the corporation than with the entity conception.

As the world becomes a fiercer place for American business, corporate management is forced increasingly to consider financial performance at every stage. Thus, evolving global markets encourage efficiency and value-creating management. These developments tend to push shareholders, as residual risk bearers, back towards the center of thinking about the enterprise. Creating shareholder value, for example, is increasingly a financial measure that is used internally in the making of corporate capital budgeting decisions. Indeed while the law seems to have ringingly endorsed a managerialist or entity orientation, full-bodied statements of the managerialist philosophy appear now to be rather out of fashion, even among members of senior corporate management. Today the talk is more likely to be about creating shareholder value than about social responsibility.

In part, this is in response to the second factor that will generate problems for the entity conception. I refer to the evolution of stockholders large enough to overcome the collective action problems faced by dispersed shareholders. As institutional investors grow in importance, it is thought that the prospect of real stockholder oversight and discipline will also grow. This evolutionary factor seems, as well, to privilege the property conception of the corporation. Thus the answer to the question, what is a business corporation, that was given by the constituency statutes and implied by the Time–Warner decision, should itself be seen as provisional, not final.

I suppose that there will be no final move in defining the nature or the purpose of the business corporation. It is perhaps asking too much to expect us, as a people—or our law—to have a single view of the purpose of an institution so large, pervasive, and important as our public corporations. These entities are too important to generate that sort of agreement. Within them exists the tension that a dynamic market system creates between the desire to achieve increases in total wealth and the desire to avoid the losses and injuries—the redistribution—that a dynamic system inevitably engenders.

Thus while these entities are surely economic and financial instruments, they are, as well, institutions of social and political significance. The story of the contending conceptions of the corporation reflects that fact. Indeed, it may not be an exaggeration to imagine that this story resonates with an elemental tension that our society has endured since the days of the industrial revolution. That tension arises from the longing for stability and community in the liberal society. Business corporations may strike you as a pale, perhaps even pathetic, source of the meaning and identity people achieve through community membership and interaction. That may be as it is, and it may be as well that any instinct to preserve existing corporate structures in order to protect meaningful membership in social groups, could be satisfied only at an unacceptable cost to economic efficiency. But putting personal judgments aside, I suggest that anyone trying to understand how our law deals with corporations must have in mind that they are the locus of many conflicting claims, and not all of those claims are wholly economic.

Thus I conclude that we have been schizophrenic on the nature of the corporation, but as a society we will probably always be so to some extent. The questions "What is a corporation?" and "For whose benefit do directors hold power?" are legal questions only in the sense that legal institutions will be required at certain points to formulate or assume answers to them. But they are not simply technical questions of law capable of resolution through analytical rule manipulation. Even less are they technical questions of finance or economics. Rather in defining what we suppose a public corporation to be, we implicitly express our view of the nature and purpose of our social life. Since we do disagree on that, our law of corporate entities is bound itself to be contentious and controversial. It will be worked out, not deduced. In this process, efficiency concerns, ideology, and interest group politics will commingle with history (including our semi-autonomous corporation law) to produce an answer that will hold for here and now, only to be torn by some future stress and to be reformulated once more. And so on, and so on, evermore.

Milton C. Regan, Jr., PROFESSIONAL RESPONSIBILITY
AND THE CORPORATE LAWYER

13 GEO. J. LEGAL ETHICS 197 (2000)

I. THE WORLD OF CORPORATE PRACTICE

The dynamism of the business corporation has persistently stretched the creativity of lawyers, prompting efforts both to devise novel corporate strategy and to fashion regulatory constraints upon it. Capitalism's process of "creative destruction" continually creates the risk that legal rules will lag behind economic reality. Lawyers are called upon to exploit or to fill the gap. They have been at the center of such turbulence at least since the rise of the large corporation in the late nineteenth and early twentieth century. The specialization of lawyers in corporate practice and the emergence of the Wall Street law firm at that time precipitated intense concern that the legal profession was losing its independence and ethical compass. The result was a host of efforts designed to counter the perception that law had become less of a profession and more of a business, such as the formation of the American Bar Association and the promulgation of the Canons of Ethics. Indeed, the notion that lawyers constitute a distinct profession received perhaps its first systematic articulation at this time. The complexity of the era is reflected in the fact that members of the corporate bar were among the most vigorous proponents of professional and political reform, even as many of them in their private practice simultaneously helped to blunt its impact.

Railroads have given way to information systems as the paradigm of corporate power and innovation, but corporate law practice continues to raise important and complex questions of professional responsibility that have implications for all lawyers. In the most immediate and concrete terms, changes in corporate use of legal services in the past twenty-five years or so have dramatically altered relationships between law firms and clients, partners and associates, partners and partners, and among law firms. Increased reliance on in-house legal departments has brought inside the corporation much work that previously served as the foundation of long-term relationships between firms and clients. Corporations now tend to seek specialized expertise rather than general services from outside counsel. They also exert more vigorous controls over how those services are provided and how they are priced.

The consequences by now are well known. Competition among law firms for both clients and lawyers has intensified. Business generation has become a more significant factor in promotion and compensation decisions. Some firms have established multiple tiers of partnership, varying with respect to compensation and voice in firm governance, and also have made clear that attaining partnership is no guarantee of continued tenure at the firm. Others have expanded the ranks of permanent associates who remain at the firm without being on a partnership track. Specialization has continued apace, with many associates under more pressure to specialize at an early point in their careers so that they will be able to provide expertise for which clients are willing to pay. Large firms have merged with one another or acquired smaller firms or practice groups. The marriage of United States firm Rogers and Wells and the English firm Clifford Chance may portend a trend toward mergers of firms in different countries, as lawyers reorganize in order to meet corporate clients' needs for global representation.

These developments have consequences not only for corporate firm career patterns, training, and salaries. They also have ripple effects throughout the legal profession. Smaller firms face heightened competition from branch offices and the prospect of being acquired by larger firms, even as they also may obtain opportunities for business they did not have a generation ago. Observers are concerned about the difficulty of arranging for pro bono and public service practice in light of increasing billable hour targets and the fact that status as a law firm partner provides far less security than it once did. Legal work now tends to be performed by teams of specialists who require coordination, rather than by individual lawyers who control all aspects of the relationship with the client. We are far from being able to sort out the implications of all these developments, but it is clear that the shifting relationship between corporate clients and their attorneys has been an important catalyst for striking changes in the way that law practice is organized and conducted. Through their effects on law firm culture, practitioners' incentives, and lawyers' self-understandings, such changes also necessarily will have a complex influence on the ethical climate in which lawyers do their work.

Aside from the importance of corporate practice for the ways in which modern legal services are provided, certain features of that practice are notable for the important ethical issues that they raise. First are the complexities of representing an organization rather than an individual. That undertaking can be especially challenging because ethical provisions for the most part implicitly are premised on a relationship between an attorney and an individual client. The lawyer who represents a corporation represents an abstraction: her client is the corporate entity rather than any of the individuals who act on its behalf. Such lawyers deal daily with managers and officials who are authorized to speak for the corporation, yet they must not mistake those individuals for the entity itself. Even in the normal course of events, actors in a large organization may not be in full agreement on various matters. Lines of authority are not always clear; the organization chart may obscure as much as reveal who wields power and influence. The lawyer thus often must become familiar with the dynamics of the bureaucratic milieu in order to discern just which actors speak for the corporation on what issues.

The difficulty is compounded when there is reason to question whether an official is acting in the best interests of the corporation. Ethical provisions, along with the business judgment rule, suggest that the lawyer should defer to the manager in most instances, even when she might have charted a different course under the circumstances. That presumption of deference evaporates, however, when the lawyer knows that a corporate official is violating a duty to the entity or is acting illegally so as to threaten the corporation with serious harm. The problem is that this transformative moment can be quite difficult to recognize. One reason is that knowledge often is fragmented in large modern organizations. Information sufficient to ensure that a lawyer "knows" of misconduct may be scattered among several offices and people, no one of whom has the complete picture. It is tempting in such situations to conclude that one lacks the certitude necessary to challenge the corporate decisionmaker, even when such ignorance is the product of diligent avoidance of unpleasant facts.

Even if a lawyer for the corporation concludes that sufficiently serious misconduct is occurring, ethical rules generally give her little concrete guidance about what to do. Model Rule 1.13, typical of many state provisions, directs the lawyer to "proceed as is reasonably necessary in the best interest of the organization." . . . Such ambiguity not only makes charting a course of action difficult. It also creates the risk that the lawyer ultimately will be accused of negligence in representing the entity. Even if taking certain steps were permissive rather than mandatory under state ethical rules, one may claim with the benefit of hindsight that a reasonable lawyer under the circumstances would have taken them. Indeed, even a lawyer who has been deliberately misled by a client may be found liable in some circumstances for failing to undertake her own independent investigation of the facts notwithstanding the client's repeated assurances.

In sum, it is increasingly the case that lawyers in many kinds of modern practice represent organizations rather than individuals. Such a phenomenon calls for a more sophisticated understanding of the organizational milieu and the distinctive ethical issues that it generates. Corporate lawyers have significant experience with such representation, and often are acutely aware of how little guidance ethical rules can provide in this setting. A focus on corporate practice thus can generate insights that are becoming important for an ever larger proportion of lawyers.

A second disjunction between corporate practice and ethical rules is the fact that the latter traditionally have been formulated primarily with the litigator in mind. Yet transactional work, a staple of corporate practice, raises questions that do not always fit easily within this paradigm. Should a party with whom the lawyer is negotiating a joint venture, for instance, be regarded more as an adversary or as a cooperative partner? The answer may be important in determining the attorney's duty of confidentiality, as well as in identifying conflicts of interest that could arise from simultaneous or successive representation of other clients.

Similarly, should the fact that business negotiations typically take place outside the supervision of a court place a greater or lesser responsibility on lawyer and client to disclose information that other parties might regard as relevant to the negotiations? Litigation is marked by both judicial oversight and relatively stringent disclosure duties because of concern about the integrity of legal proceedings. By contrast, disclosure obligations are relatively relaxed in transactional settings, despite the absence of any constraining judicial involvement. They are based primarily on common law fraud standards, which in turn look to conventional expectations of typical parties engaged in negotiation. Yet reliance solely on such expectations as the touchstone of legality has the potential to create a downward spiral, as aggressive practices provoke even more aggressive responses. The cumulative effect may be to lower expectations of fair dealing, increase bargaining costs, and secure judicial validation of provisions formerly regarded as unenforceable. Corporate lawyers historically have had to navigate the transactional terrain with minimal guidance from ethical rules. This does not mean, however, that the ethical issues that arise in this form of practice are of negligible importance. Rather, it highlights the fact that law practice requires a cultivated sense of judgment that goes beyond mere rule compliance.

A third notable dimension of corporate practice is the fact that many corporate lawyers not only represent organizations, but are employed by them. The widely-noted rise in the visibility and prestige of inside counsel in the last two decades or so has fueled the continuing debate over the meaning of lawyers' professional independence. Here again, corporate lawyers have firsthand experience with a growing phenomenon: the increasing number of lawyers who are employees in various types of organizations. To what extent is it possible to preserve a sense of identification with a distinct professional legal culture while being immersed in an organizational culture as well? Is it easier to invoke ethical constraints on company conduct if the lawyer is familiar with corporate operations and is regarded as a member of the "team?" Or does her dependence on a single client who is her employer tend to make her excessively deferential toward company officials?

Many lawyers and commentators suggest that in-house counsel are in a position to provide a unique combination of business and legal advice that helps the organization plan for, rather than simply react to, a tumultuous global economy. Rather than merely passing judgment on the legality of measures that management proposes, counsel help frame strategy with an eye toward anticipating and preventing legal issues from arising in the first place. This "proactive" approach to practice expands the boundaries of legal practice to include functions not traditionally characterized as strictly legal in nature. It also calls into question the traditional assumption that the client determines the ends of representation and the lawyer selects the means to achieve those ends. This dichotomy generally is an important premise of ethical rules, which conceptualize the lawyer as distant from the substantive objectives of the client. If in-house counsel do indeed become integrally involved in formulating company goals and structuring company operations, it may be unrealistic to insist they nonetheless remain legal technicians morally unaccountable for the consequences of those activities.

Nor are business corporations the only large organizations in which corporate lawyers now practice. Corporate firms themselves are coming to resemble their clients in many respects. In addition to the greater explicit emphasis on economic considerations that I have described, these firms tend to be organized according to departments or practice groups, with managing partners, executive committees, and different strata of associates and partners. Some firms now are managed full-time by lawyers who forgo practice, while others are administered by non-lawyers with backgrounds in management. Non-legal professionals with expertise in areas such as personnel, finance, and employment benefits also may occupy positions of authority. As Marc Galanter and Thomas Palay predict, the firm of the future "will become increasingly hierarchical and will take on the characteristics of the proverbial 'corporate ladder.' "

Such developments may require that a growing number of corporate lawyers take into account organizational imperatives in their exercise of professional judgment. This "complicates ethical decision-making, because lawyers must blend issues of individual conscience with issues of organizational responsibility." Work in large-scale practice organizations also increases the necessity for lawyers to confront the distinctive ethical ambiguities and challenges that working within a bureaucracy can present, such as fragmentation of knowledge and accountability. Such a predicament is perhaps the paradigmatic ethical quandary of the contemporary era. Corporate attorneys who practice within corporations and large law firms may be those lawyers who are most likely to face this conundrum in their everyday work. Their responses could tell us much about the possibilities and limits of moral accountability in an age of bureaucratic organization.

Another development in which corporate lawyers are the advance troops is the increasingly global nature of law practice. National boundaries pose no obstacle to modern corporate activity. A parent firm may be in one country, its subsidiaries in several others, and its joint venture partners or licensees in still others. Furthermore, its products and services may well be available in most countries around the world. Corporate counsel may have her office in New York, consult long-distance about Italian law with a subsidiary in Italy that is entering into a licensing agreement with a South African company, or travel to Japan to negotiate with a Japanese bank about financing for a project that will engage in manufacturing in several Asian countries and sell its products mainly in North America and Western Europe.

Aside from the need to master the interplay among the substantive legal provisions of the different jurisdictions that may assert an interest in such corporate activities, counsel also must navigate through a thicket of differing and sometimes conflicting rules that purport to govern the conduct of lawyers. There is no common set of ethical provisions that apply to lawyers engaged in cross-border practice. Indeed, there is no uniform definition of what constitutes the practice of law in various countries, or of what is permissible activity for foreign lawyers who are authorized to practice in a jurisdiction. Once these threshold issues are resolved, the lawyer must determine which country's ethical standards— and standards of malpractice liability—are applicable. An example of the striking differences that can exist between legal regimes is the Court of Justice of the European Communities' decision that in proceedings brought by the European Commission the attorney-client privilege may not be invoked with respect to communications between a client and its in-house counsel. The difficulty of reconciling ethical obligations under different state regimes in the United States already creates unpredictability for the large number of lawyers engaged in multistate practice. That complexity is magnified exponentially in the arena of transnational practice, and corporate lawyers are the ones who increasingly must respond to it.

Corporate lawyers also tend to be in the vanguard of another emerging trend in legal practice: the subjection of lawyers to multiple sources of ethical governance. The pervasiveness of government regulation in the modern economy, the vast increase in the scope of corporate enterprise and activities, and an era of relatively modest regulatory enforcement resources have led to demands that lawyers be more attentive to the social impact of their clients' activities. One example of this is the subjection of lawyers to liability to clients under common law theories such as malpractice and breach of fiduciary duty, with ethical rules treated as evidence relevant to the issue of the propriety of an attorney's conduct. In addition, lawyers increasingly are potentially subject to liability to non-clients in actions such as suits for negligent misrepresentation. Given the number and interdependence of parties in modern business transactions, and the often plausible claims of reasonable reliance on the lawyer's work, the circle of those who are able to bring actions against corporate attorneys may well continue to widen.

Furthermore, regulatory agencies have steadfastly insisted that state ethical rules are not the sole set of standards to which attorneys must conform. The Securities and Exchange Commission has brought enforcement actions on the basis of its authority to govern the conduct of lawyers that practice before it. In doing so, it has suggested, for instance, that lawyers may have an obligation to prevent a client from consummating a transaction as to which there has been insufficient disclosure. It also has concluded that a lawyer under some circumstances may be held responsible for failing to take steps to prevent a recurrence of illegal activity by company employees. The Office of Thrift Supervision has brought charges alleging that a law firm assumed the regulatory compliance and disclosure duties of its federally insured thrift institution by interposing itself between the client and the regulatory agency. Tax lawyers are subject to a more stringent standard of good faith in presenting client positions than are other lawyers. Finally, bankruptcy rules may impose stricter disclosure requirements than ethical rules regarding potential conflicts of interest, and failure to comply with them may subject a lawyer to criminal prosecution. The fact that corporate lawyers are strategically placed in positions of influence with respect to regulated activities has led some to maintain that they have an obligation to serve as "gatekeepers" who restrain misconduct or even "whistleblowers" who report it. Such roles are in tension with the notion that the attorney's sole obligation is to the client, and the claim that self-regulation by the legal profession offers the best assurance of ethical legal practice.

This leads to a final feature of corporate law practice that has particular significance for ethical purposes. This is the fact that corporations are not simply private actors pursuing their own goals along with other interest groups in society. Rather, as Charles Lindblom has noted, a market-based economy delegates to corporations substantial authority over matters of wide-ranging social importance, such as employment, the availability of consumer goods, and investment decisions that determine how and when resources will be used. This arguably places the business firm at the intersection of private and public domains. In light of this, it is not surprising that the nature and purposes of the corporation have been fiercely contested questions since at least the latter part of the nineteenth century. The debate has taken on even greater urgency as sprawling global operations and the rapid emergence and obsolescence of new technology have intensified the dynamism of corporate enterprise at the dawn of the twenty-first century.

This generates special challenges for corporate lawyers because it requires that they play two roles that to some degree are in tension. The rapid pace of change in the corporate world demands that lawyers create new legal forms and arrangements to address unprecedented circumstances. Such creativity has always been necessary for those who represent corporations, from the lawyers who devised trusts and holding companies in the late nineteenth century to those who fashioned various "poison pills" to deter takeover activity a century later. As Michael Powell has observed, business lawyers create law "from the ground up" by developing novel legal structures and casting them in a vocabulary that confers on them the status of legitimate extensions of traditional legal categories. As activities outrun the legal paradigms meant to contain them, the alert lawyer exploits "loopholes" and pushes against the limits of the law in an effort to secure advantage for her client.

Yet the corporate lawyer must also be mindful that the integrity of the legal system is a form of social capital in a market society. A competitive economy requires cooperation and trust in order to flourish. As a study of lawyers in Silicon Valley suggests, lawyers are often strategically positioned to create and sustain this social capital. Law cannot be seen merely in instrumental terms, as an obstacle to be overcome with the help of professionals who are trained to capitalize on its ambiguity. In such a world, "abiding by the 'rule of law' is only for wimps: the smart, powerful people opt out of law by means of lawyers, and thereby provoke others to do likewise." It is difficult for legal and social norms in such a world to persist beyond the next shift in the balance of power. The effectiveness of law in a democratic polity depends heavily on voluntary compliance, and such compliance in turn requires the perception that law has at least some intrinsic normative force.

How corporate lawyers present legal provisions to their clients, and how far they are willing to push the letter of the law regardless of its spirit, cumulatively has the potential to have a profound effect on attitudes toward the legal system. Performance of this quasi-public role means that lawyers at times may have to prevail upon their clients to forbear from exploiting every possible legal advantage, for the sake of both the client's long-term interest and that of society as a whole. The distinctive function and influence of business corporations in a market democracy thus means that the corporate lawyer's work unavoidably has both private and public dimensions whose tensions are not always easily mediated.

* * *

CONCLUSION

[T]he ethical issues involved in corporate representation often require us to address fundamental questions about the roles that lawyers play and the obligations to which they are held. Indeed, as I have suggested, the transformative character of corporate enterprise virtually guarantees that corporate lawyers perpetually will be facing dilemmas for which our existing professional responsibility framework provides imperfect guidance.

... Corporate lawyers may dismiss any suggestion that their daily activity in the pragmatic world of commerce raises any deep jurisprudential issues. However, as Robert Gordon has observed:

> When a lawyer helps a client arrange a transaction so as to take maximum advantage of the current legal framework, he or she becomes one of the army of agents who confirm that framework by reinforcement and extend it by interpretation into many niches of social life. The framework is an ideological one, i.e., a set of assertions, arguments, and implicit assumptions about power and right.

... The frenetic pace of business enterprise in the contemporary world ... makes it especially difficult to understand and provide [ethical] guidance for [what] corporate lawyers [do]. Given the profound impact of corporate activity on the lives and fortunes of millions throughout the world, however, few undertakings are more important.

Hon. Potter Stewart, PROFESSIONAL ETHICS FOR THE BUSINESS LAWYER: THE MORALS OF THE MARKETPLACE

31 Bus. Law. 462 (1975)

It goes without saying, of course, that every lawyer has a duty to keep the confidences of his client, that every lawyer in whom is confided a trust must conduct himself as trustee, that every lawyer should espouse his word and deal honorably in all his associations. And it certainly is the duty of every lawyer and every association of lawyers to denounce and to eliminate from our midst those who have betrayed our profession for their own ugly or dishonest purposes.

But beyond these and a few other self-evident precepts of decency and common sense, a good case be made, I think, for the proposition that the ethics of the business lawyer are indeed, and perhaps should be, no more than the morals of the market place. The first rule for a business lawyer is to provide his total ability and effort to his client. But is this an ethical standard, or no more than a response to the economic forces of the market place? After all, the first rule in *any* occupation is to be competent. The business lawyer is in the business of providing legal advice for a businessman. If he performs that job with diligence, conscientiousness, and knowledgeable ability, his client will reap the benefits and reward him accordingly. If not, unless he is particularly lucky or married to the boss's daughter, the lawyer will find his client less than eager to retain indefinitely a professional adviser who habitually directs him down the wrong path.

In short, it can fairly be argued that many aspects of what we call "ethics" are not really ethics at all, but are merely corollaries of the axiom of the better mousetrap, an axiom that is itself derived from enlightened self-interest.

William T. Allen, CORPORATE GOVERNANCE AND A BUSINESS LAWYER'S DUTY OF INDEPENDENCE

38 SUFFOLK U. L. REV. 1 (2004)

I. INTRODUCTION

This short essay addresses a topic important to both corporate governance and, perhaps more importantly, vital to the satisfaction that we lawyers can draw from our professional lives: our conception of the duties of a lawyer when she engages in advising and assisting corporate clients.

* * * To whom do business lawyers owe duties and what is the nature of those duties? Rather than discussing external controls of the legal profession, such as licensing and lawyer disciplinary rules or processes, the topic of this essay is the internal or personal controls that a business lawyer may or should feel. In addressing the conceptions that lawyers hold of their professional identity and loyalties, the topic, in some respects, appears ephemeral. But while discussion of ideals may appear abstract and even ephemeral, it is certainly not unimportant. The ideal of our role in society that we lawyers choose to embrace will affect our behavior.

II. THE INCREASING DOMINATION OF THE ZEALOUS ADVOCACY IDEAL

The loyalty that a lawyer owes extends beyond the duties to keep client's confidences, to give honest, competent advice unaffected by conflicting interests, and to exercise energy and imagination in pursuit of clients' lawful ends. Certainly these are a lawyer's core obligations in representing a client. But there is another aspect of a lawyer's duty that we do not much notice and have not for a long time—the duty of independence. The duty of independence is the lawyer's duty to the legal system itself and to the substantive values that it incorporates. This duty has its greatest role not in the defense of clients in court, but when business lawyers advise their clients with respect to prospective compliance with regulatory or private law and in structuring and disclosing material transactions.

The value of professional independence of judgment has always been reflected in our professional identity, but it has never been central to it. As lawyers, our main and favorite identification is as the loyal, energetic, and imaginative defender of clients: as zealous advocate ...

The zealous advocacy ideal envisions the lawyer in a litigation setting. That setting, however, builds in powerful checks on the costs of the advocacy ideal. An adversary is represented by a lawyer. There are mandated discovery rights provided to both sides. Truth is tested by cross examination and a disinterested and expert judge will decide disputed questions. These factors make the costs of the zealous advocacy model in the litigation setting reasonable. But when the zealous advocacy mentality is adopted by business lawyers advising on law compliance, transaction planning, disclosure, and other advisory matters, none of these counter-balancing forces are present. In the business context, adoption of the zealous advocacy ideal is likely to give rise to unacceptable social costs.

In the short run, at least, a skilled lawyer who is willing to facilitate advantageous transactions that do not clearly and unarguably violate the law is useful to some clients. But the relative indeterminacy of many legal commands creates a very broad range over which a lawyer's imagination can roam. Unless legal advice and advocacy are rooted in principles finer than zealous advocacy, that conception can easily degenerate into socially wasteful conduct.

Once upon a time, a clearer vision of the lawyer as public citizen constrained the excesses of zealous advocacy. But the balance between the professional roles of advocate and responsible moral actor—as an independent counselor—has atrophied. The social forces shaping the environment in which lawyers now practice have reduced their capacity to act as independent counselors. Similarly, the willingness of the legal profession—as expressed through its official organs (mainly the bar associations)—to give meaningful support to a duty of moral autonomy or independence has declined.

III.   THE HISTORICAL CONCEPT OF LAWYERS AS INDEPENDENT ACTORS

Dominated as we are today by the advocacy conception of what loyalty to clients means, it probably seems strange to consider the nature or scope of a business lawyer's duty of independence. But it was not always so. The old Canons of Professional Ethics of the City Bar Association of the City of New York, for example, reflected the value of a lawyer's moral autonomy quite explicitly. They stated, for example, that "the office of attorney does not permit, much less does it demand of him for any client, violation of law or any manner of fraud or chicanery." And, in the next sentence: "[A lawyer] must obey his own conscience and not that of his client." Under this principle, a lawyer's moral scruples should affect the decision to deploy a legal strategy. It is the lawyer's moral judgment, not that of the client, that acts as the final safeguard against lawyer involvement in socially destructive activity. In the end, clients may do as they choose. They may risk breaking the law. They may engage in action that violates the discernable spirit of the law, while arguably keeping to the letter. But business clients do not deserve the assistance of a lawyer in accomplishing such actions. Of course, lawyers owe loyalty to clients. They must be kept fully informed. Client confidences must be kept inviolate. They may at any time discharge a lawyer. But, in the vision that underlies the old City Bar Association code, lawyers are seen not as amoral tools of their clients, but as professionals who are morally responsible for the results that their actions help to bring about.

This is a morally attractive view of professional responsibility. It is reflected quite powerfully in the text of Canon 32 of the original 1908 Canons of Ethics of the American Bar Association:

> "No client, corporate or individual, however powerful, nor any cause, civil or political, however important is entitled to receive, nor should any lawyer render, any service or advice involving disloyalty to the law ... or deception or betrayal to the public ... The lawyer ... advances the honor of his profession and the best interest of his client when he renders service or gives advice tending to impress upon the client, his undertaking exact compliance with the strictest principles of moral law. He must also observe the statute law, though until a statute shall have been construed and interpreted by competent adjudication, he is free and entitled to advise as to its validity and as to what he conscientiously believes to be its just meaning and extent."

This statement envisions lawyers who are not simple zealous advocates of their clients' legal interests, limited presently only by a command not to take frivolous positions. It calls upon lawyers to exercise independent judgment concerning the detectible spirit animating the law (that is, "what he conscientiously believes to be its just meaning and extent"). It also encourages a lawyer to "advance ... the best interest of his client" through impressing upon the client "exact compliance with the strictest principles of moral law." Clearly, lawyers who satisfy these ideals were seen as independent actors: counselors who conceptualized their mission as guiding clients to comply with what these experts understood to be the best interpretation of the law.

Thus, the assertion that lawyers have a duty to substantive legality that should act as a constraint upon the advice that they give has an impeccable pedigree. Today, however, the formal organs of the profession fail to recognize this history or to acknowledge a professional duty of independence ... [T]he modern rules reflect our modern perspective. Lawyers are seen as zealous advocates with few duties to the public other than refraining from deceiving the court, lying on behalf of clients, or violating or facilitating the violation of law.

IV. THE CHANGING CONDITIONS OF LEGAL PRACTICE

How do we explain this movement from the bar's acknowledgement in the early and mid-twentieth century of the moral autonomy of lawyers as a condition that co-existed with a lawyer's status as a loyal agent of her client? The answer lies not in the profession itself and its organization, but in the social conditions in which lawyers practice their craft. These circumstances differ vastly from those of forty or fifty years ago. Today, lawyers in private practice are more dependent upon their corporate clients and do not typically possess the leverage that lawyers previously had with such clients . . .

V. THE DANGER OF LEGAL PRACTICE AS COMMERCIAL ENDEAVOR

* * * [T]the legal profession has evolved into a more thoroughly commercial endeavor than it was forty years ago. No doubt much has been gained, but certainly at a cost.

We do not have to speculate to see where a profession committed only to facilitating private advantage, under even implausible interpretations of ambiguous law, might take us. Even before Enron and its complex bank-assisted financing showed us where mere technical compliance with accounting and disclosure standards could get us, the business scene provided good examples. No example is clearer or more painful than the practice of lawyers and accountants creating tax shelter "products" within large accounting firms. Congressional pressure has caused most, but not all, of these firms to finally withdraw from this business. Nevertheless, the practices that evolved in the creation and marketing of tax shelters demonstrates the kind of advice that can be expected when professionals lack a commitment to substantive legality and have an economic incentive to be "imaginative."

The major accounting firms and some investment banks created Research & Development departments to discover and exploit every ambiguity or technical flaw in the tax law in order to generate tax advantages. In principal, this is not a questionable activity. Creating securities, for example, that are tailored to the clients funding needs in a tax efficient way is productive work. What is questionable is the willingness to make extreme substantive judgments. These judgments appear sometimes to be hyper-technical and literalistic, even when it is readily apparent that the literalistic interpretation is inconsistent with the intent of the statute or regulation derived from the body of law taken as a whole. Once such a new "product" is designed by the firm, it is then actively marketed, often on a contingency fee basis.

A couple of years ago I was told by the general counsel of a Fortune 500 company that one of the then "Big 5" accounting firms had approached her firm to offer a new tax shelter opportunity with the following surprising sales pitch:

> "We have developed a tax loss opportunity. We can arrange for a legal opinion that this transaction qualifies as a legitimate business loss. We will allow you to participate only for a fee that involves our

sharing a very substantial percentage of all tax savings you realize (with a minimum). We must price this product aggressively because we believe that we can only sell a few of these as the IRS can be expected to close this opportunity down once it learns of it."

The firm wisely declined to participate in a tax shelter that it had reason to know was not intended by law and was inconsistent with the discernible policies upon which the law was based. But in doing the right thing, the firm was putting itself at a competitive disadvantage to others who were willing to act as amoral technicians.

Missing from this activity is any notion of the professional as possessing an element of loyalty to the law itself, or to the discernible spirit of the law. Abusive tax shelters result because the professionals involved exercise too little self-restraint in deploying their skills. In this instance it is not difficult to see why a lawyer might be tempted to endorse unreasonable interpretations of law. The firms that design and market these devices are financial partners, not independent professionals. Their professional judgment is subject to the extreme gravitational stress of a proprietary share of the money that the most extreme deployment of imagination can generate at whatever risk.

VI. The Lawyer's Duty of Independence

Generally, the stories of abusive tax shelters with their legal opinions designed to deflect criminal prosecutions may seem an unlikely future scenario for the business lawyer. Established law firms have been far more responsible in passing upon the legality of tax shelters than have auditing firms. But recent experiences at Enron, Adelphia, Health-South Corporation, and others certainly suggests that the commercial world in which lawyers operate today too often creates incentives for business lawyers to allow themselves to become enablers of their clients' marginal activities * * *

The conception of a lawyer independence is not canonical. It is the result of individual consideration. It is for everyone to formulate the principles that define the outer limits of your zealous advocacy. Personally, I define my conception through three chief attributes.

First, a lawyer's personal commitment to the law and to a just legal system should restrain him from giving his assistance to a project that appears to him substantially more likely than not to violate the requisites of law, even though some non-frivolous argument to the contrary may be made. As we have acknowledged, the choice to act or not belongs to the client, but at some point the independent lawyer must disassociate himself from action that he believes, in the exercise of his informed professional judgment, is quite likely to violate the applicable legal standard. Professor Geoffrey Miller and I, in some joint work undertaken with the American Academy of Arts & Sciences, have posited a test previously referred to: the discernable spirit animating ambiguous law. An independent legal professional's primary commitment should be to this discernable spirit that animates the law.

Second, because an independent legal counselor, while an agent of others, is also an autonomous moral being, she ought not associate herself with legal action that constitutes unduly harsh or oppressive behavior. It is not the office of a lawyer to be an instrument of repression, even when it is a legal right that is used to oppress. The whole of equity jurisprudence can be cited for the proposition that a legal right is not in all circumstances the ultimate value of our legal order.

Third, professional independence requires that a lawyer counsel her client on ways and means to advance their interests while satisfying the underlying goals of the law or seeking an efficient adjudication of a dispute. A lawyer exercising sound independent professional judgment, for example, will not use the machinery of law for the purpose of imposing costs on an adversary.

VII. Achieving Professional Independence

If the competitive pressures of the last forty years have indeed forced the ideal of lawyer professional independence to the deep, almost unseen, background, why should we care? And if we do care, what steps, if any, can we take? Lawyers ought to care about our ability and willingness to give independent legal advice to business clients for two reasons. First, legal advice that goes through the discipline of an independent counsel's self-critical evaluation is likely to be better legal advice to the corporate client. Second, the life of a lawyer who subjects her legal practice to this discipline will be a more satisfying and worthwhile professional life.

First, and most basically, what arguments can support the happy thought that lawyers who subject their work for business clients to the discipline of their own independent review, will, if all other factors are held constant, tend to give more useful advice to their clients? Business clients are repeat players in most of the important contexts in which they have significant legal problems. They have ongoing relationships with government regulators, customers, suppliers, partners, joint-venturers, capital markets, etc. These relationships and the firm's reputation are valuable assets. Every action or dispute that affects the future of these relationships is likely to be optimally resolved only when appropriate weight is given to that fact. The zealous advocate can get in the way of a productive long-term relationship.

A legal counsel who views herself as an independent professional adds utility by helping her client see the reasonable limits of ambient legal ambiguity so that mutual satisfaction from important relationships can be achieved. An independent counselor never abandons a commitment to substantive legality. She will therefore ask what client action would most advantageously conform the client's activity to the principles underlying the relevant legal rule and protect future utility from the legal relationship at risk. The zealous advocate, on the other hand, asks whether there is any colorable argument that can be made to support an advantageous action. This approach—call it a litigators stance—is shared, for example, by the accountant who invents abusive tax shelters, the lawyer who satisfies the aggressive opinion shopper, or the corporate lawyer who is willing to follow accounting technicality to call a loan a sale. This kind of advice may be an unavoidable stance in the one-shot litigation context, but it is dangerous to a business client in other settings.

In many instances, zealous advocacy attitudes will destroy or at least threaten states of mind that allow client firms to make relationship specific investments that produce value over time. To a substantial extent, large business corporations function on trust as well as on crisply defined legal rights. Trust is a valuable asset that emerges from a perception of shared norms of fair dealing, from patterns of prior fair practice, and from an expectation of future interactions. The diffusion of a zealous advocate mentality within a business firm, for example, would certainly erode trust and, in the long run, generate large increases in the costs of operating the firm. The detriments to the firm's relations with outside parties are not fundamentally different.

* * * In a business world in which all parties believed that their dealings were governed by the standards of zealous advocacy representation, sharply higher costs could be expected all over the place: in regulatory interactions, in commercial dispute resolution, and even in public product markets. Imagine, for example, the consequences of a zealous advocacy response to a product tampering scare.

Thus, except for the unfortunate pathologies that will arise in the one-shot litigation context, the world offers plenty of evidence that, for business clients, there is greater long-term value in legal services provided by lawyers whose zealous and loyal representation is constrained by a fundamental commitment to the finer ideals of the profession * * *

VIII. CONCLUSION

Putting aside the possible debate about the effectiveness of alternative conceptions of a lawyer's duties, different and important reasons to keep alive the self-critical capacity that an independent attorney possesses concern the personal satisfactions drawn from our lives as lawyers.

The model of an independent professional comes closer than the dominant zealous advocacy model to actually describing the greatest lawyers of this or earlier ages. Consider, for example, the case of Louis D. Brandeis. I refer not to the great Justice Brandeis but to the earlier, spectacularly successful practitioner. Brandeis' life in the law reminds us that a great business lawyer need not act as a tool of any private interest that seeks his assistance. Brandeis was committed in his work to advancing the common good of the parties and the public good. Controversially, he sometimes acted as "counsel for the situation." He undertook to counsel his clients, not to act as a mere implement in their hands. He refused to have his professional skills used in ways or for ends that he, as a citizen interested in the common good, could not endorse. Brandeis is especially eminent, of course, but the model he followed was one adopted by other great lawyers. Whether at the head of great Wall Street firms, or as trusted long-term advisors on Main Street, the role of independent counselor, not zealous advocate, is the role in which those who practice today are most likely to add value to their clients and to achieve the deeper satisfaction that seems absent from the lives of many lawyers.

Among the important sources of satisfaction that a lawyer experiences from his work is the belief that his work adds meaning to his life because it contributes to the welfare of others. Both as a judge and as a professor, I experienced the gratification that follows from a belief that one is, however modestly, advancing the cause of justice according to law.

Other lawyers should be able to derive from their work in representing others some sense that they too are contributing to the achievement of the deeper purposes of the justice system. We are too greatly invested in our professional lives to permit ourselves to merely be clever amoral agents. Certainly, we are not law enforcement officials; we serve a different role. But if we are to find our professional lives satisfying, our role as zealous advocates and loyal facilitators of legal transactions must be consistent with our role as independent professionals and moral actors dedicated to the achievement of the higher goals of the legal system. This role gives dignity and a sense of deeper meaning to our work as business lawyers.

Chapter 2

THE LAWYER'S ROLE

The economist John Maynard Keynes once wrote, "Practical men, who believe themselves quite exempt from any intellectual influences, are usually the slaves of some defunct economist."[1] So it is with many lawyers. How a lawyer approaches her practice, and the decisions that she makes on a daily basis, reflect a theory of the lawyer's role of which she may be only vaguely aware. This theory provides her with a frame of reference that shapes how she tries to reconcile obligations and demands that sometimes are in tension.

That tension comes with the territory. As the Model Rules proclaim, a lawyer is "a representative of clients, an officer of the legal system, and a public citizen having special responsibility for the quality of justice."[2] Which of these roles has priority? Does the answer differ according to the situation? Or must the lawyer try to accommodate all of them in every circumstance?

Probably most lawyers implicitly answer these questions by embracing a theory of the lawyer as a partisan advocate–a hired gun–who must advance the client's interests within an adversarial system. As a hired gun, the lawyer is not subject to the demands of ordinary morality. For instance, if she knows that her client is releasing harmful pollutants into the air, she is not obligated to persuade her client to stop at the request of the government as long as there is a non-frivolous legal argument that the client can continue. If the company has no plausible argument that what it is doing is legal, the lawyer still can take action to delay the government's enforcement on plausible procedural grounds. Furthermore, if the government or private citizens sue the corporation, the lawyer can do her best to keep these parties from obtaining information that establishes her client's liability as long as there is a colorable legal ground for doing so. An ordinary person who enabled another to continue to release harmful pollutants and to prevent others from obtaining

1. John Maynard Keynes, The General Theory of Employment, Interest, and Money 383 (1964 ed.)

2. American Bar Association, Model Rules of Professional Conduct, Preamble (2005).

information about it might well be subject to criticism that she is acting immorally. A hired gun, however, can say that she is subject to a different standard–she's just doing her job.

Few lawyers likely have thought through in detail the justifications for this model, the most important criticisms of it, or alternatives to it. This chapter provides the material to do so.

OVERVIEW OF THE CHAPTER

The first excerpt is a defense of the hired gun model by Monroe Freedman. Freedman argues that the model is justified because it is necessary to a well-functioning adversary system. Note carefully the values that Freedman claims the adversary system serves: protection of individual rights, peaceable redress of social grievances, and discovery of the truth. Ask yourself how the hired gun model ostensibly promotes these objectives and how rejecting it might threaten them.

In the first excerpt from David Luban, Luban questions whether the adversary system actually furthers the values that Freedman says it does. He concludes that Freedman's argument is persuasive only with respect to the protection of individual rights in criminal proceedings. In that setting, the criminal defense lawyer is justified in taking steps to enable a person to avoid conviction even if the lawyer believes that he is guilty. This is because making the state prove guilt beyond a reasonable doubt in every case protects citizens from government overreaching. Outside this context, Luban maintains, there is no persuasive evidence that the adversary system and the hired gun model promote the values that Freedman identifies. For Luban, this means that the lawyer should not be exempt from ordinary moral standards except in the case of criminal defense. If we accept this view, what practical effect would it have on how lawyers act?

Even if we accept Freedman's argument in its entirety, his claim only applies to litigation. Is there a defense of the hired gun model outside of that setting? Stephen Pepper argues that there is. He asserts that the model helps promote the individual autonomy of citizens who need the lawyer's assistance in achieving their goals. Respect for individuals' ability to choose the course of their lives requires that the lawyer not pass moral judgment on what a client wants to do as long as it is legal. If we don't respect this principle, Pepper claims, we effectively authorize lawyers to thwart the aims of ordinary persons that the lawyer deems unacceptable. As you read Pepper, ask yourself how much of the force of his argument depends on the assumption of an inequality of expertise and sophistication between client and lawyer. Is his argument as persuasive with respect to large business corporations?

The second excerpt from Luban takes issue with Pepper's reliance on autonomy to defend the hired gun model. Luban argues that while choosing to do something autonomously and without coercion may be morally valuable, that doesn't mean that what it is that a person chooses also is morally valuable. Many people freely choose to do bad things.

Luban also rejects Pepper's claim that lawyers should be precluded from making moral judgments about their clients' goals. Permitting lawyers to decline to help persons accomplish legal but immoral objectives does not establish lawyers as the moral gatekeepers of society, he argues. Rather, it simply allows them to act as would any other person who wishes not to help someone do something objectionable. Are you comfortable with the discretion that Luban would give lawyers to make such judgments? If not, are you comfortable with the view that says that lawyers should completely ignore their moral reactions?

Freedman, Pepper, and Luban's criticisms of each are meant to sharpen awareness of the strengths and weaknesses of the hired gun model. The excerpt from William Simon aims to set forth an alternative to that model. He calls his approach the "Contextual View." That approach advises that lawyers "should take those actions that, considering the relevant circumstances of the particular case, seem likely to promote justice." Simon is similar to Luban in his rejection of the hired gun model—indeed, he would reject it even in the criminal defense setting. He does not agree with Luban, however, that the only alternative to the model is reliance on ordinary moral standards. The Contextual View's admonition to do justice is based on a belief that the lawyer occupies a special role in society. She has special expertise that makes her responsible for upholding the integrity of the legal system as a means for achieving justice.

Simon argues that the Contextual View does not simply authorize the lawyer to rely on her own personal values. Rather, he says that there are publicly accessible standards of legal argument on which the legal community relies that constrain the lawyer's judgment. Read closely Simon's description of how the lawyer should deal with tensions between substance and procedure, and between purpose and form, in determining what course of action is most likely to serve justice. Ask yourself how you would rely on this guidance in analyzing the cases of the "innocent convict" and "agribusiness welfare." Compare this with what the hired gun model would counsel in each situation. Can you imagine any instances in which you as a lawyer would depart from or not press the literal terms of the law in order to avoid a serious injustice? Do you think that most people would do so at least in some cases? If so, does that mean that almost everyone implicitly follows the Contextual model?

Your consideration of the justifications for, and criticisms of, the hired gun model, as well as the plausibility of alternatives to it, will have prepared you for the last excerpt in the chapter: a consideration of the implications of all this for the corporate lawyer. Robert Gordon suggests why the hired gun model is inappropriate for lawyers engaged in corporate counseling and transactional work, and proposes an alternative model based on recognition of the social importance of the corporate lawyer's role.

Corporate lawyers, Gordon proposes, should have the opportunity to adopt the distinctive role of "counselor" as opposed to ordinary attorney, and clients could decide whether they wished to employ such lawyers in particular instances. A counselor would be obligated to provide a dispassionate analysis of the client's proposed conduct that took into account the impact of the conduct and the purposes of the law, rather than simply being prepared to offer whatever arguments on behalf of the client that were not manifestly frivolous. In certain kinds of transactions, Gordon suggests, corporations would be required to hire counselors because of the importance of ensuring attention to the impact of the transaction on parties such as investors or the general public.

As you read Gordon, ask yourself whether it would be feasible to distinguish between counselors and ordinary attorneys. Would there be any way to determine if counselors were actually fulfilling their responsibilities? Does Gordon's proposal amount to drafting private attorneys to do the job that government should be doing? Or would Gordon argue that the term "private" attorney is misleading and begs the question? Also, consider the global competition and increasing influence of institutional shareholders that former Chancellor Allen describes in the first chapter. Will pressure to maximize shareholder wealth make corporations reluctant to hire counselors and lawyers decline to assume that role? Does that pressure make Gordon's proposal even more important? Finally, ask yourself how Gordon's counselor would approach the agribusiness hypothetical posed by Simon. If the subsidy is challenged in court, would Simon and Gordon have the same or different views about how a lawyer should act in defending the corporation?

Unlike most of the chapters in this book, this chapter does not include a problem at the end. The most important thing in reading the materials in this chapter is to work through the steps in each defense and criticism of the hired gun model, as well as each element of the arguments for alternatives to it. Ideally, whatever you conclude about the lawyer's role, that understanding will be much richer and more subtle than before you read the material.

Monroe H. Freedman, UNDERSTANDING LAWYERS' ETHICS

(1990)

THE ADVERSARY SYSTEM

In its simplest terms, an adversary system is one in which disputes are resolved by having the parties present their conflicting views of fact and law before an impartial and relatively passive judge and/or jury, who decides which side wins what. In the United States, however, the phrase "adversary system" is synonymous with the American system for the administration of justice, as that system has been incorporated into the Constitution and elaborated by the Supreme Court for two centuries. Thus, the adversary system represents far more than a simple model for resolving disputes. Rather, it consists of a core of basic rights that recognize and protect the dignity of the individual in a free society.

The rights that comprise the adversary system include personal autonomy, the effective assistance of counsel, equal protection of the laws, trial by jury, the rights to call and to confront witnesses, and the right to require the government to prove guilt beyond a reasonable doubt and without the use of compelled self-incrimination. These rights, and others, are also included in the broad and fundamental concept that no person may be deprived of life, liberty, or property without due process of law—a concept which itself has been substantially equated with the adversary system.

An essential function of the adversary system, therefore, is to maintain a free society in which individual rights are central. In that sense the right to counsel is "the most pervasive" of rights, because it affects the client's ability to assert all other rights. As Professor Geoffrey Hazard has written, the adversary system "stands with freedom of speech and the right of assembly as a pillar of our constitutional system." It follows that the professional responsibilities of the lawyer within such a system must be determined, in major part, by the same civil libertarian values that are embodied in the Constitution.

The Adversary System and Individual Rights

There is also an important systemic purpose served by assuring that even guilty people have rights. Jethro K. Lieberman has made the point by putting forth, and then explaining, a paradox:

> The singular strength of the adversary system is measured by a central fact that is usually deplored: The overwhelming majority of those accused in American courts are guilty. Why is this a strength? Because its opposite, visible in many totalitarian nations within the Chinese and Russian orbits, is this: Without an adversary system, a considerable number of defendants are prosecuted, though palpably innocent.... In short, the strength of the adversary system is not so much that it permits the innocent to defend themselves meaningfully, but that in the main it prevents them from having to do so.

Lieberman concludes that "[o]nly because defense lawyers are independent of the state and the ruling political parties and are permitted, even encouraged, to defend fiercely and partisanly do we ensure that the state will be loathe to indict those whom it knows to be innocent." This benefit, however, is largely invisible. "We rarely see who is not indicted, we never see those whom a prosecutor, or even a governor or president might like to prosecute but cannot."

There is another systemic reason for the zealous representation that characterizes the adversary system. Our purpose as a society is not only to respect the humanity of the guilty defendant and to protect the innocent from the possibility of an unjust conviction. Precious as those objectives are, we also seek through the adversary system "to preserve the integrity of society itself ... [by] keeping sound and wholesome the procedure by which society visits its condemnation on an erring member." Professor Lawrence H. Tribe has added that "procedure can serve a vital role as . . . a reminder to the community of the principles it holds important." He goes on to explain:

> The presumption of innocence, the rights to counsel and confrontation, the privilege against self-incrimination, and a variety of other trial rights, matter not only as devices for achieving or avoiding certain kinds of trial outcomes, but also as affirmations of respect for the accused as a human being—affirmations that remind him and the public about the sort of society we want to become and, indeed, about the sort of society we are.

These rights to which Professor Tribe refers are essential components of the adversary system as it has evolved in American constitutional law.

The Adversary System in Civil Litigation

The adversary system has also been instrumental, principally in civil litigation, in mitigating the grievances of several minorities, women, consumers, tenants, citizens concerned with health and safety in our environment, and others. As one who celebrates these advances in individual rights and liberties (and those in criminal justice too), I view with concern and some suspicion the calls for basic changes in adversarial zeal. Of course, it is preferable to negotiate a satisfactory resolution of a dispute. Experience teaches, however, that those in power do not ordinarily choose to negotiate unless there is a credible threat of successful litigation.

In a report to his Board of Overseers in 1983, Harvard President Derek Bok decried "the familiar tilt in the law curriculum toward preparing students for legal combat," and called instead for law schools to train their students "for the gentler arts of reconciliation and accommodation." These are themes long associated with retired Chief Justice Warren Burger.

In response to such critics, Professor Owen Fiss has observed that they see adjudication in essentially private terms. Viewing the purpose of civil lawsuits to be the resolution of discrete private disputes, they find the amount of litigation we encounter to be evidence of "the needlessly combative and quarrelsome character of Americans." Fiss, on the other hand, sees adjudication in more public terms. That is, civil litigation is "an institutional arrangement for using state power to bring a recalcitrant reality closer to our chosen ideals." Thus, we turn to courts not because of some quirk in our personalities, but because we need to, and we train our students in the tougher arts not because we take a special pleasure in combat, but to equip them to secure all that the law promises. Fiss concludes:

> To conceive of the civil lawsuit in public terms as America does might be unique. I am willing to assume that no other country . . . has a case like *Brown v. Board of Education*, in which the judicial power is used to eradicate the caste structure. I am willing to assume that no other country conceives of law and uses law in quite the way we do. But this should be a source of pride rather than

shame. What is unique is not the problem, that we live short of our ideals, but that we alone seem willing to do something about it. Adjudication American-style is not a reflection of our combativeness but rather a tribute to our inventiveness and perhaps even more to our commitment.

For example, a case might hold for the first time that a tenant has a right, apart from the express terms of her lease, to safe and habitable premises, or that a consumer can avoid an unconscionable sales-financing agreement, or that an employee under a contract terminable at will can sue for wrongful discharge, or that an insurance company can be held liable in punitive damages for arbitrarily withholding benefits due under a policy. Such a case, establishing new rights and deterrents against harmful conduct through civil litigation, is also "a tribute to our inventiveness," using "state power to bring a recalcitrant reality closer to our chosen ideals." If the leading case is to have meaning, however, it will come to fruition in the series of every-day cases that follow and apply it, cases that will truly make the ideal into reality.

In that sense, even ordinary personal injury litigation is an expression, procedurally and substantively, of important public policies. Through the adversary system we provide a social process through which a person with a grievance against another can petition the government for redress in a peaceable fashion.

The Search for an Alternative System

Those who would either replace or radically reform the adversary system must ultimately sustain the burden of showing how their proposals can be reconciled with constitutional rights. Even before that point is reached, however, they must demonstrate, in their own utilitarian terms, that the adversary system is inferior to the proposed alternatives. To the contrary, however, the available evidence suggests that the adversary system is the method of dispute resolution that is most effective in determining truth, that gives the parties the greatest sense of having received justice, and that is most successful in fulfilling other social goals as well.

More sophisticated (and more persevering) critics have turned to the inquisitorial systems of continental European democracies for an alternative to the adversary system. The central characteristic of the inquisitorial model is the active role of the judge, who is given the principal responsibility for searching out the relevant facts. In an adversary system the evidence is presented in dialectical form by opposing lawyers; in an inquisitorial system the evidence is developed in a predominantly unilateral fashion by the judge, and the lawyers' role is minimal.

One contention of those who favor the inquisitorial model is that the adversary system limits the factfinder to two sources of data or to one of two rival factual conclusions. Frequently, of course, there is no need for more than two submissions. for example, if the sole issue is whether one car or the other ran the red light, or whether the defendant was the man who had the gun. In such a case, it is ordinarily appropriate for the factfinder to rely upon two sets of conflicting data, which may come, of course, from numerous sources.

Where there truly are more than two sides of a case, however, the adversary system provides a variety of devices for presenting them. Such procedures include joinder of plaintiffs and defendants, impleader, interpleader, intervention, class actions with more than one class representative and with subclasses, and amicus presentations.

Effectiveness in the Search for Truth

Those who favor the inquisitorial model also contend that it produces a larger body of relevant information for the decisionmaker than does an adversarial system. For example. Professor Peter Brett argues that the inquisitorial system is preferable because the judge is not limited to the material that the opposing parties choose to present. Rather, the judge "may if he wishes" actively search out and incorporate in his decision materials that neither party wishes to present. All other considerations. Professor Brett asserts, "pale into insignificance beside this one." Unfortunately, however, just as the inquisitorial system "allows the fact-finder free rein to follow all trails." it also allows the fact-finder to ignore all trails but the one that initially appears to be the most promising. It does so, moreover, without the corrective benefit of investigation and presentation of evidence by active adversaries.

This concern was expressed in a prominent thesis that was put forth by Professor Lon L. Fuller and adopted by a Joint Conference of the American Bar Association and the Association of American Law Schools.

What generally occurs in practice is that at some early point a familiar pattern will seem to emerge from the evidence; an accustomed label is waiting for the case and without awaiting further proofs, this label is promptly assigned to it. It is a mistake to suppose that this premature cataloguing must necessarily result from impatience, prejudice or mental sloth. Often it proceeds from a very understandable desire to bring the hearing into some order and coherence, for without some tentative theory of the case there is no standard of relevance by which testimony may be measured. But what starts as a preliminary diagnosis makes a strong imprint on the mind, while all that runs counter to it is received with diverted attention.

An adversary presentation seems the only effective means for combating this natural human tendency to judge too swiftly in terms of the familiar that which is not yet fully known.

As suggested by its adoption by the Joint Conference, Professor Fuller's thesis is undoubtedly shared by the overwhelming majority of American lawyers and judges, on the basis of both intuition and experience in decision-making processes.

The validity of the Fuller thesis can be considered in both theoretical and practical contexts. If the inquisitorial judge is to pursue the truth of a particular matter, where does she start? The "most sophisticated modern view" in Europe recognizes an inescapable "circularity" in the inquisitorial judge's role: "You cannot decide which facts matter unless you have already selected, at least tentatively, applicable decisional standards. But most of the time you cannot properly understand these legal standards without relating them to the factual situation of the case." In addition. "[i]t stands to reason that there can be no meaningful interrogation [of witnesses by the judge] unless the examiner has at least some conception of the case and at least some knowledge about the role of the witnesses in it."

The solution in Europe to the inquisitorial judge's "circularity" problem is the investigative file, or dossier. The dossier is prepared by the police. who, in theory, act under the close supervision of a skilled and impartial judge or examining magistrate. "The practice, however, is in striking contrast to [this] myth." The examining magistrate's investigative and supervisory role is minimal. The dossier—on which the trial judge relies to decide what facts and law are relevant to the case—is little more than a file compiled by the police. "The plain fact is that examining magistrates are no more likely than comparable American officials to leave their offices, conduct prompt interrogations of witnesses or of accused persons, or engage in searches or surveillance. For such tasks, they rely almost entirely upon the police." The trial judge, in turn, tends to rely heavily upon the police-developed dossier.

The prosecutorial bias that inevitably results from this process is confirmed by the personal experience of Bostjan M. Zupancic. Professor Zupancic clerked for several investigating magistrates in the Circuit Court of Ljubljana. Yugoslavia. "One cannot start from the presumption of innocence" under an inquisitorial system, he writes.

> In purely practical terms, if one opens a file in which there is only a police report and the prosecutor's subsequent request for investigation and develops one's thought processes from this departing point—one cannot but be partial. A clear hypothesis is established as to somebody's guilt, and the investigating magistrate's job is to verify it. But just as a scientist cannot start from the premise that his hypothesis is wrong, so the investigating magistrate cannot start from the premise that the defendant is innocent.

Professor Zupancic found that, as a result, prosecutorial bias on the part of the inquisitorial judge is not a matter of probability; it is a certainty.

Meanwhile, the prosecutor plays a distinctly secondary role to the police and the judge, and defense counsel is "particularly inactive." "Rarely does [the defense attorney] conduct his own investigation in preparing for trial. Even if his client should suggest someone who he thinks will offer testimony favorable to the defense, he often passes the name on to the prosecutor or judge without even troubling first to interview the witness himself." Very likely, European defense lawyers do not conduct the kind of thorough interview of a potential witness that is professionally required in the United States, because they could be charged with a criminal offense or with professional impropriety for obstructing justice if they did so.

Only in the rare case in which the defense lawyer assumes an active—that is, an adversarial—role, is there an exception to the typical situation in which the inquisitorial judge follows the course plotted out by the police. In those few cases, "genuine probing trials" do take place. The European experience itself seems to confirm, therefore, that adversarial presentation by partisan advocates is more effective in developing relevant material than is unilateral investigation by a judge.

Our constitutional adversary system is based in part on the premise that the adversary system is more effective in the search for truth. As the Supreme Court has reiterated in an opinion by Justice Powell:

> The dual aim of our criminal justice system is "that guilt shall not escape or innocence suffer.". . . . To this end. we have placed our confidence in the adversary system, entrusting to it the primary responsibility for developing relevant facts on which a determination of guilt or innocence can be made.

In the criminal process there are special rules, particularly the exclusionary rules, that recognize values that take precedence over truth. The adversary system should be even more effective in determining truth in the civil process, therefore, where such values are not ordinarily applicable.

There is support for that conclusion in experiments conducted by members of the departments of psychology and law at the University of North Carolina. One study tested the thesis, which I had put forward, that the most effective means of determining truth is to place upon a skilled advocate for each side the responsibility of investigating and presenting the facts from a partisan perspective. Although that proposition is related to the Fuller thesis, its focus is different. Professor Fuller was concerned with the factfinder and with her mental processes in developing a working hypothesis and then unconsciously becoming committed to it prematurely. The second thesis focuses on the adversaries and on their incentive to search out and to present persuasively all material that is useful to each side, thereby providing the factfinder with all parts of the whole.

The study produced conclusions that tend to confirm both the Fuller thesis, regarding the judge's psychological risk of premature commitment to a theory, and the second thesis, regarding the adversaries' incentive to investigate diligently. First, as soon as they become confident of their assessment of the case, inquisitorial fact investigators tend to stop their search, even though all the available evidence is not yet in. Second, with one exception of major importance, even adversary investigators have a similar but lesser tendency to judge prematurely.

Third (the crucial exception), when adversary fact investigators find the initial evidence to be unfavorable to their clients, they are significantly more diligent than are inquisitorial investigators in seeking out additional evidence. The researchers conclude, therefore, that the adversary system "does instigate significantly more thorough investigation by advocates initially confronted with plainly unfavorable evidence." That is, in those situations of "great social and humanitarian concern" the adversary system maximizes the likelihood that all relevant facts will be ferreted out and placed before the ultimate factfinder.

Another finding, which surprised the researchers, is that the opponent of an adversarial lawyer transmits more facts that are unfavorable to her own client. Apparently, awareness that one has an adversarial counterpart is a significant inducement to candor.

I do not mean to suggest that these studies prove that the adversary system is preferable as a means to determine truth. Such experimental efforts to replicate real life and to quantify it statistically are surely limited in their usefulness. On the other hand, the research that has been done provides no justification whatsoever for preferring the inquisitorial search for truth or for undertaking radical changes in our adversary system.

David Luban, The Adversary System Excuse in the Good Lawyer: Lawyers' Roles and Lawyers' Ethics

(David Luban ed. 1983)

It is not the lawyer's responsibility to believe or not to believe—the lawyer is a technician.... Law is an adversarial profession. The other side is out to get your client. Your job is to protect your client and the nonsense they hand out in these ethics courses today—if the young people listen to this kind of nonsense, there isn't going to be such a thing as an intelligent defense in a civil or criminal case.

Roy Cohn, interview, *National Law Journal,*

December 1, 1980, p. 46.

I. Introduction

Holding forth at table in 1831, Samuel Taylor Coleridge turned to the behavior of lawyers. "There is undoubtedly a limit to the exertions of an advocate for his client," he said, for "the advocate has no right, nor is it his duty, to do that for his client which his client *in foro conscientiae* has no right to do for himself." Thirteen years later, William Whewell elaborated the same point:

> [E]very man is, in an unofficial sense, by being a moral agent, a Judge of right and wrong, and an Advocate of what is right.... This general character of a moral agent, he cannot put off, by putting on any professional character.... If he mixes up his character as an Advocate, with his character as a Moral Agent ... he acts immorally. He makes the Moral Rule subordinate to the Professional Rule.

He sells to his Client, not only his skill and learning, but himself. He makes it the Supreme Object of his life to be, not a good man, but a successful Lawyer.

Whewell's position is not commonly acknowledged to be valid. George Sharswood, whose 1854 *Legal Ethics* is the great-grandparent of the current ABA Code of Professional Responsibility, wrote: "The lawyer, who refuses his professional assistance because in his judgment the case is unjust and indefensible, usurps the functions of both judge and jury." A lawyer is not to judge the morality of the client's cause; it is irrelevant to the morality of the representation. That, I think, is the official view of most lawyers: the lawyer's morality is distinct from, and not implicated in, the client's. Murray Schwartz calls this the "Principle of Nonaccountability":

> When acting as an advocate for a client ... a lawyer is neither legally, professionally, nor morally accountable for the means used or the ends achieved.

Add to this the "Principle of Professionalism":

> When acting as an advocate, a lawyer must, within the established constraints upon professional behavior, maximize the likelihood that the client will prevail.

and you get what is usually taken to be the professional morality of lawyers. Gerald Postema calls it the "standard conception of the lawyer's role"; William Simon says that these principles (which he calls the "Principle of Neutrality" and the "Principle of Partisanship") define partisan advocacy.

Shortly after introducing these principles, Schwartz raises two points about them:

> It might be argued, that the law cannot convert an immoral act into a moral one, nor a moral act into an immoral one, by simple fiat. Or, more fundamentally, the lawyer's nonaccountability might be illusory if it depends upon the morality of the adversary system and if that system is immoral. . . . If either [of these challenges] were to prove persuasive, the justification for the application of the Principle of Nonaccountability to moral accountability would disappear.

Schwartz raises these issues but does not address them. My purpose in this paper is to meet them head-on. I shall argue (1) that a lawyer's nonaccountability does depend on the adversary system; (2) that the adversary system is not a sufficient basis for it; and (3) thus, that while the Principle of Professionalism may be true, the Principle of Nonaccountability is not.

This, I believe, will defend the morality of conscience—the position of Coleridge and Whewell—against the claim that professional obligation can override it.

It is at this point that the adversary system looms large, for it provides the institutional excuse for the duty of zealous advocacy. Each side of an adversary proceeding is represented by a lawyer whose sole obligation is to present that side as forcefully as possible; anything less, it is claimed, would subvert the operation of the system. The ABA code states the matter quite clearly: "The duty of a lawyer to his client and his duty to the legal system are the same: to represent his client zealously within the bounds of the law."

Everything rides on this argument. Lawyers have to assert legal interests unsupported by moral rights all the time; asserting legal interests is what they do, and everyone can't be in the right on all issues. Unless zealous advocacy could be justified by relating it to some larger social good, the lawyer's role would be morally impossible. That larger social good, we are told, is justice, and the adversary system is supposed to be the best way of attaining it.

Indeed, it is misleading to call this Justification by the Adversary System an *argument*. It is more like a presupposition accepted by all parties before the arguments begin. Even lawyers with nothing good to say about the legal system in general believe that their current actions are justified or excused by the nature of the adversary system.

The point deserves to be labored a bit, for the universal acceptance among lawyers of the Justification by the Adversary System is a startling thing, a marvelous thing, a thing to behold. It can go something like this: one talks with a pragmatic and hard-boiled attorney. At the mention of legal ethics, he smiles sardonically and informs one that it is a joke. One presses the subject and produces examples such as the buried bodies case. The smile fades, the forehead furrows, he retreats into a nearby phonebooth and returns moments later clothed in the Adversary System, trailing clouds of glory. Distant angels sing. The discussion usually gets no further.

This portrait is drawn from life, but I do not tell the story just to be snide. It is meant to suggest that discussions of the adversary system usually stop where they ought to start, with a chorus of deeply felt but basically unexamined rhetoric.

What, then, is the adversary system? We may distinguish narrow and wide senses. In the narrow sense, it is a method of adjudication characterized by three things: an impartial tribunal of defined jurisdiction, formal procedural rules, and most importantly for the present discussion, assignment to the parties of the responsibility to present their own cases and challenge their opponents'. The attorneys are their clients' agents in the latter task. The duty of a lawyer in an adversary proceeding is therefore one-sided partisan zeal in advocating his or her client's position. This in turn carries with it familiar collateral duties, the most important of which are *disinterestedness* and *confidentiality*. Each of these is best viewed as a prophylactic designed to enhance the quality of partisan advocacy: forbidding lawyers who have conflicts of interest from advocating a client's cause is meant to forestall the possibility of diluted zeal, and forbidding lawyers from divulging clients' confidences and secrets is meant to encourage clients to give their lawyers information necessary for effective advocacy. These duties of zeal, disinterestedness, and confidentiality—which I have elsewhere called the Three Pillars of Advocacy—form the core of an attorney's professional obligations.

The structure of the adversary system, then—its fission of adjudication into a clash of one-sided representations—explains why Schwartz's Principle of Professionalism holds. But it explains the Principle of Moral Nonaccountability as well. If advocates restrain their zeal because of moral compunctions, they are not fulfilling their assigned role in the adversary proceeding. But, if lawyers must hold themselves morally accountable for what they do in the course of the representation, they will be morally obliged to restrain their zeal whenever they find that "the means used or the ends achieved" in the advocacy are morally wrong. Therefore, or so the syllogism goes, the structure of adversary adjudication must relieve them of moral accountability, and that is how the adversary system entails Schwartz's Principle of Nonaccountability—how, that is, the adversary system is supposed to provide an institutional excuse for moral ruthlessness.

All this holds (if hold it does) only within the context of adjudication. Lawyers, however, commonly act as though Schwartz's two principles characterized their relationship with clients even when the representations do not involve the courtroom. Thus, there is a *wide* sense of the adversary system in which it is defined by the structure of the lawyer-client relationship rather than the structure of adjudication. When lawyers assume Schwartz's two principles in negotiations and counseling as well as courtroom advocacy, and attribute this to the adversary system, they are speaking of it in the wide sense.

I shall ask if an institutional excuse can be based on the adversary system conceived in the narrow sense. If problems crop up even there, certainly they will be worse outside of a legitimately adversarial institution.

IV. Criminal versus Noncriminal Contexts

I have suggested that the adversary system excuse may be only as good as the adversary system. The question of how good that is, however, is often ignored by discussions that stop where they ought to start. Indeed, there is a tendency among many people to treat reservations about the adversary system as assaults on the American Way. Monroe Freedman, for example, has written what is arguably the best modern book on lawyers' ethics. He shows how the duty to put a perjurious client on the stand, or brutally cross-examine a witness known by the lawyer to be telling the truth, follows from the adversary system. But he defends the adversary system primarily by contrasting the nonadversarial systems in "totalitarian states" such as Cuba and Bulgaria, with American concern for the "dignity of the individual." Left in their bare state, phrases like these can be only slogans.

Freedman's rhetorical point still contains an important argument. That argument is that zealous adversary advocacy of those accused of crimes is the greatest safeguard of individual liberty against the encroachment of the state. The good criminal defense lawyer puts the state to its proof in the most stringent and uncompromising way possible. Better, we say, that a hundred criminals go free than that one person be wrongly convicted.

I think this is right as far as it goes, but as general defense of the adversary system, it is beside the point for two related reasons. The first is that it pertains only to criminal defense and thus is irrelevant to the enormous number of civil cases tried each year. The latter are in a way much more morally troubling. It inflicts no tangible harm on anyone when a criminal evades punishment. This is not to deny that people may be legitimately outraged (consider the Nixon pardon, the trial of Dan White in San Francisco, the acquittals of policemen that led to the 1980 riots in Miami). But no one's life is made materially worse off. However, when A wins an unjust personal injury claim against B, every dollar in A's pocket comes out of B's. A's lawyer, in my book, has a lot of explaining to do.

It is this public preoccupation with crime and criminals, I think, that leads writers like Freedman and David Mellinkoff to focus their justifications of Broughamesque advocacy on criminal defense. They are reacting to an assault from the Right, an assault that sees the rights of the accused as a liberal invention leading to anarchy. Now, emphasizing the role of lawyers in safeguarding individual liberty may indeed be the best defense against the Law and Order attack on lawyers. Criminal defense is, so to speak, the "worst-case scenario," and it might be assumed that any defense of advocacy that works there works everywhere else as well.

In fact, and this is my second point, criminal defense is a very special case in which the zealous advocate serves atypical social goals. The point is one of political theory. The goal of zealous advocacy in criminal defense is to curtail the power of the state over its citizens. We want to handicap the state in its power even legitimately to punish us. And so the adversary system is justified, not because it is a good way of achieving justice, but because it is a good way of hobbling the government and we have political reasons for wanting this. The argument, in other words, does not claim that the adversary system is the best way of obtaining justice. It claims just the opposite, that it is the best way of impeding justice in the name of more fundamental political ends, namely, keeping the government's hands off people. Nothing, of course, is wrong with that; indeed, I believe that Brougham's imperative may well hold in criminal defense. My point is merely that criminal defense is an exceptional part of the legal system, one that aims at protection rather than justice.

It seems, then, that focusing on the adversary system in the criminal context obscures the issue of how it works as a system of justice, and for this reason I shall talk only about arguments attempting to vindicate it as a system of justice.

V. Consequentialist Justifications of the Adversary System

A. *Truth*

The question whether the adversary system is, all in all, the best way of uncovering the facts of a case at bar sounds like an empirical question. I happen to think that it is—an empirical question, moreover, that has scarcely been investigated, and that is most likely impossible to answer. This last is because one does not, after a trial is over, find the parties coming forth to make a clean breast of it and enlighten the world as to what *really* happened. A trial is not a quiz show with the right answer waiting in a sealed envelope. We can't learn directly whether the facts are really as the trier determined them because we don't ever find out the facts.

Given all this, it is unsurprising to discover that the arguments purporting to show the advantages of the adversary system as a factfinder have mostly been nonempirical, a mix of a priori theories of inquiry and armchair psychology.

Here is one, based on the idea, very similar to Sir Karl Popper's theory of scientific rationality, that the way to get at the truth is a wholehearted dialectic of assertion and refutation. If each side attempts to prove its case, with the other trying as energetically as possible to assault the steps of the proof, it is more likely that all of the aspects of the situation will be presented to the fact-finder than if it attempts to investigate for itself with the help of the lawyers.

This theory is open to a number of objections. First of all, the analogy to Popperian scientific methodology is not a good one. Perhaps science proceeds by advancing conjectures and then trying to refute them, but it does not proceed by advancing conjectures that the scientist knows to be false and then using procedural rules to exclude probative evidence.

The two adversary attorneys, moreover, are each under an obligation to present the facts in the manner most consistent with their client's position—to prevent the introduction of unfavorable evidence, to undermine the credibility of opposing witnesses, to set unfavorable facts in a context in which their importance is minimized, to attempt to provoke inferences in their client's favor. The assumption is that two such accounts will cancel out, leaving the truth of the matter. But there is no earthly reason to think this is so; they may simply pile up the confusion.

Let us try another argument, this one taken from the ABA's official justification of the adversary system, the *Joint Conference Report* of the ABA-AALS. The heart of the argument is this:

> Any arbiter who attempts to decide a dispute without the aid of partisan advocacy ... must undertake not only the role of judge, but

that of representative for both of the litigants. Each of these roles must be played to the full without being muted by qualifications derived from the others. When he is developing for each side the most effective statement of his case, the arbiter must put aside his neutrality and permit himself to be moved by a sympathetic identification sufficiently intense to draw from his mind all that it is capable of giving,—in analysis, patience and creative power. When he resumes his neutral position, he must be able to view with distrust the fruits of this identification and be ready to reject the products of his own best mental efforts. The difficulties of this undertaking are obvious. If it is true that a man in his time must play many parts, it is scarcely given to him to play them all at once.

Psychologically, the argument says, a nonadversarial trial is like trying to play chess against yourself: neither white nor black pieces get played very well, and second-rate games result.

The argument, however, begs the question. True, *if* the facts are best discovered by a battle between two conflicting points of view, then one person won't do as well at it as two adversaries. But to suppose that that is how factual inquiry best proceeds is simply to take as a premise that the adversary system is best, when that was supposed to have been the conclusion.

It is not, moreover, as attractive a premise as it appears at first glance. It trades on an ambiguity in the idea that the judge in a nonadversary proceeding must be the "representative for both of the litigants." It is true that the judge must take the *interests* and *legal claims* of both litigants into account in order to grant them due process of law: in this sense he or she must "represent" both of them. But that is not to say that the judge will find the facts by somehow balancing the parties' factual claims against each other as if these were the parties' interests. Is the best way to find out about an event to ask only parties who have special interests at stake in it? The *Joint Conference Report*, assuming that truth is gotten at by making sure that both sides' versions of every aspect of the story are represented, comes close to the undergraduate fallacy of thinking that because everyone has a right to his or her opinion, everyone's opinion on any topic whatsoever is equally worthy of being taken into account. Although frequently there are versions of the truth, truth does not necessarily come in versions. Thus, there is no reason to suppose that a judge making factual inquiries must "represent" the points of view of both litigants to be fair.

No trial lawyer seriously believes that the best way to get at the truth is through the clash of opposing points of view. If a lawyer did believe this, the logical way to prepare a case for trial would be to hire two investigators, one taking one side of every issue and one taking the other. After all, the lawyer needs the facts, and if those are best discovered through an adversary process, the lawyer would be irresponsible not to set one up. That no lawyer would dream of such a crazy procedure should tip us off that the *Joint Conference Report* premise is flawed.

The *Joint Conference Report* employs two subsidiary psychological arguments as well. The first is that the adversary system will "hold the case . . . in suspension between two opposing interpretations of it," so the finder of fact will not jump to hasty conclusions. The second is that if the judge and not the lawyer had to "absorb" the disappointments of his or her theory of the case being refuted, he or she would be "under a strong temptation to keep the hearing moving within the boundaries originally set for it"; then it would not be a fair trial so much as a "public confirmation for what the tribunal considers it has already established in private."

Let me reiterate that these arguments, however plausible they sound on paper, are untested speculations from the armchair. But let us suppose for the sake of argument that they are right. They still do not show why we must have an adversary system. Consider three other possible systems: (1) a three-judge panel, two of whom investigate and present the case from the points of view of the respective litigants, making the strongest arguments they can but also pointing out weaknesses in their side's case and strengths in the other; (2) a system like our own, except that the advocates are under an affirmative duty to point out facts or arguments in the other side's favor if the adversary is unaware of them (or, perhaps, a system in which the court awards attorneys' fees on the basis of how helpful they are in the overall search for truth); (3) the French system in which one judge investigates the case beforehand and presents a dossier to the trial judge.

Now, I don't recommend any of these as a practical alternative to the existing adversary system; they have their drawbacks. But notice that (1) and (2) do just as good a job as the adversary system at holding the case in suspension, while all three do just as good a job at shifting the onus of being wrong away from the tribunal. All three, moreover, sever the search for truth from the attorney's need to win, which under the adversary system ties the attorney to the client's victory by bonds of self-interest. All three, therefore, are likely to avoid the most extravagant tactics currently employed by lawyers. The *Joint Conference Report* does not even consider this as a possibility.

Indeed, it seems to take as a premise the idea that truth is served by self-interested rather than disinterested investigation. "The lawyer appearing as an advocate before a tribunal presents, as persuasively as he can, the facts and the law of the case *as seen from the standpoint of his client's interest*" [emphasis added]. The emphasized phrase is accurate, but it gives the game away. For there is all the difference in the world between "the facts seen from X's standpoint" and "the facts seen from the standpoint of X's interest." Of course it is important to hear the former—the more perspectives we have, the better informed our judgment. But to hear the latter is not helpful at all. It is in the murderer's *interest* not to have been at the scene of the crime; consequently, the "facts of the case as seen from the standpoint of [the] client's interest" are that the client was elsewhere that weekend. From the standpoint of my *interest,* the world is my cupcake with a cherry on top; from the standpoint of yours, its streets are paved with gold. Combining the two does not change folly to truth.

All this does not mean that the adversary system may not in fact get at the truth in many hard cases. (Trial lawyers' war stories are mixed.) I suppose that it is as good as its rivals. But, to repeat the point I began with, nobody knows how good that is.

VII.   The Adversary System Excuse

A.   *Pragmatic Justification*

So far the course of argument has been purely negative, a persecution and assassination of the adversary system. By this time you are entitled to ask what I propose putting in its place. The answer is: nothing, for I think the adversary system *is* justified.

I do not, let me quickly say, have an argumentative novelty to produce. It would be strange indeed for a social institution to be justified on the basis of virtues other than the tried and true ones, virtues that no one had noticed in it before. My justification is rather a version of the tradition argument, but purged of its ideological overtones: I shall call it the "pragmatic justification" or "pragmatic argument" to suggest its affinity with the relaxed, problem-oriented, and historicist notion of justification associated with American pragmatism. The justification is this:

First, the adversary system, despite its imperfections, irrationalities, loopholes, and perversities, seems to do as good a job as any at finding truth and protecting legal rights. None of its existing rivals, in particular the inquisitorial system and the socialist system, are demonstrably better, and some, such as trial by ordeal, are demonstrably worse. Indeed, even if one of the other systems were slightly better, the human costs—in terms of effort, confusion, anxiety, disorientation, inadvertent miscarriages of justice due to improper understanding, retraining, resentment, loss of tradition, you name it—would outweigh reasons for replacing the existing system.

Second, *some* adjudicatory system is necessary.

Third, it's the way we have always done things.

These propositions constitute a pragmatic argument: if a social institution does a reasonable enough job of its sort that the costs of replacing it outweigh the benefits, and if we need that sort of job done, we should stay with what we have.

B.   *Pragmatic Justification and Institutional Excuses*

Because this is so typical of institutions it is worth asking about the effect of pragmatic argument on the moral obligations of institutional functionaries (such as lawyers). The position I want to press is roughly that a social institution that can receive only a pragmatic justification is not capable of providing institutional excuses for immoral acts. To do that, an institution must be justified in a much stronger way, by showing that it is a positive moral good. A pragmatic argument, by contrast, need show only that it is not much more mediocre than its rivals.

VIII.   Conclusion and Peroration

What does all this mean in noncriminal contexts, where this institutional excuse based on political theory is unavailable? The answer, very simply, is this. The adversary system possesses only the slightest moral force, and thus appealing to it can excuse only the slightest moral wrongs. Anything else that is morally wrong for a nonlawyer to do on behalf of another person is morally wrong for a lawyer to do as well. The lawyer's role carries no moral privileges and immunities.

This does not mean that zealous advocacy is immoral, not even when it frustrates the search for truth or violates legal rights. Sometimes frustrating the search for truth may be a morally worthy thing to do, and sometimes moral rights are ill served by legal rights. All I am insisting on is that the standards by which such judgments are made are the same for lawyers and nonlawyers. If a lawyer is permitted to puff, bluff, or threaten on certain occasions, this is not because of the adversary system and the Principle of Nonaccountability, but because, in such circumstances, anyone would be permitted to do these things. Nothing justifies doing them on behalf of a predator.

The adversary system and the system of professional obligation it mandates are justified only in that, lacking a clearly superior alternative, they should not be replaced. This implies, I have argued, that when professional and moral obligation conflict, moral obligation takes precedence. When they don't conflict, professional obligations rule the day. The Principle of Professionalism follows from the fact that we have an adversary system; the Principle of Nonaccountability does not. The point of elaborating the former is to tell the lawyer what, in this system, professionalism requires—to say that it requires zeal, for example, even when cutting corners might be more profitable or pleasant. Professionalism can tell a lawyer not to cut corners; my point is that it cannot mandate him or her to cut throats. When moral obligation conflicts with professional obligation, the lawyer must become a civil disobedient.

Stephen L. Pepper, The Lawyer's Amoral Ethical Role: A Defense, A Problem, and Some Possibilities

1986 Am.Bar. Found.Res.J. 613

The premise with which we begin is that law is a public good available to all. Society, through its "lawmakers"—legislatures, courts, administrative agencies, and so forth—has created various mechanisms to ease and enable the private attainment of individual or group goals. The corporate form of enterprise, the contract, the trust, the will, and access to civil court to gain the use of public force for the settlement of private grievance are all vehicles of empowerment for the individual or group; all are "law" created by the collectivity to be generally available for private use. In addition to these structuring mechanisms are vast amounts of law, knowledge of which is intended to be generally available and is empowering: landlord/tenant law, labor law, OSHA, Social Security—the list can be vastly extended. Access to both forms of law increases one's ability to successfully attain goals.

The second premise is a societal commitment to the principle of individual autonomy. This premise is founded on the belief that liberty and autonomy are a moral good, that free choice is better than constraint, that each of us wishes, to the extent possible, to make our own choices rather than to have them made for us. This belief is incorporated into our legal system, which accommodates individual autonomy by leaving as much room as possible for liberty and diversity. Leaving regulatory law aside for the moment (and granting that it has grown immensely, contributing to the legalization to be mentioned below), our law is designed (1) to allow the private structuring of affairs (contracts, corporations, wills, trusts, etc.) and (2) to define conduct that is intolerable. The latter sets a floor below which one cannot go, but leaves as much room as possible above that floor for individual decision making. It may be morally wrong to manufacture or distribute cigarettes or alcohol, or to disinherit one's children for marrying outside the faith, but the generality of such decisions are left in the private realm. Diversity and autonomy are preferred over "right" or "good" conduct. The theory of our law is to leave as much room as possible for private, individual decisions concerning what is right and wrong, as opposed to public, collective decisions.

Our first premise is that law is intended to be a public good which increases autonomy. The second premise is that increasing individual autonomy is morally good. The third step is that in a highly legalized society such as ours, autonomy is often dependent upon access to the law. Put simply, first-class citizenship is dependent on access to the law. And while access to law—to the creation and use of a corporation, to knowledge of how much overtime one has to pay or is entitled to receive—is formally available to all, in reality it is available only through a lawyer. Our law is usually not simple, usually not self-executing. For most people most of the time, meaningful access to the law requires the assistance of a lawyer. Thus the resulting conclusion: First-class citizenship is frequently dependent upon the assistance of a lawyer. If the conduct which the lawyer facilitates is above the floor of the intolerable—is not unlawful—then this line of thought suggests that what the lawyer does is a social good. The lawyer is the means to first-class citizenship, to meaningful autonomy, for the client.

For the lawyer to have moral responsibility for each act he or she facilitates, for the lawyer to have a moral obligation to refuse to facilitate that which the lawyer believes to be immoral, is to substitute lawyers' beliefs for individual autonomy and diversity. Such a screening submits each to the prior restraint of the judge/facilitator and to rule by an oligarchy of lawyers. (If, in the alternative, the suggestion is that the lawyer's screening should be based not on the lawyer's personal morality, but on the lawyer's assessment of society's moral views or on guidelines spelled out in a professional code of ethics, then one has substituted collective moral decision making for individual moral decision making, contrary to the principle of autonomy. Less room has been left for private decision making through a sub rosa form of lawmaking.) If the conduct is sufficiently "bad," it would seem that it ought to be made explicitly unlawful. If it is not that bad, why subject the citizenry to the happenstance of the moral judgment of the particular lawyer to whom each has access? If making the conduct unlawful is too onerous because the law would be too vague, or it is too difficult to identify the conduct in advance, or there is not sufficient social or political concern, do we intend to delegate to the individual lawyer the authority for case-by-case legislation and policing?

It is apparent that a final significant value supporting the first-class citizenship model is that of equality. If law is a public good, access to which increases autonomy, then equality of access is important. For access to the law to be filtered unequally through the disparate moral views of each individual's lawyer does not appear to be justifiable. Even given the current and perhaps permanent fact of unequal access to the law, it does not make sense to compound that inequality with another. If access to a lawyer is achieved (through private allocation of one's means, public provision, or the lawyer's—or profession's—choice to provide it), should the extent of that access depend upon individual lawyer conscience? The values of autonomy and equality suggest that it should not; the client's conscience should be superior to the lawyer's. One of the unpleasant concomitants of the view that a lawyer should be morally responsible for all that she does is the resulting inequality: unfiltered access to the law is then available only to those who are legally sophisticated or to those able to educate themselves sufficiently for access to the law, while those less sophisticated—usually those less educated—are left with no access or with access that subjects their use of the law to the moral judgment and veto of the lawyer.

David Luban, THE LYSISTRATIAN PREROGATIVE:
A RESPONSE TO STEPHEN PEPPER

1986 AM.BAR. FOUND.RES.J. 637

I

Abraham Lincoln once said to a client in his Springfield law practice:

> Yes, we can doubtless gain your case for you; we can set a whole neighborhood at loggerheads; we can distress a widowed mother and her six fatherless children and thereby get you six hundred dollars to which you seem to have a legal claim, but which rightfully belongs, it appears to me, as much to the woman and her children as

it does to you. You must remember that some things legally right
are not morally right. We shall not take your case, but will give you
a little advice for which we will charge you nothing. You seem to be
a sprightly, energetic man; we would advise you to try your hand at
making six hundred dollars in some other way.

Lincoln seems to have taken "some things legally right are not morally
right" to be an important truth. It shows that exercising one's legal
rights is not always morally acceptable. From that, Lincoln evidently
concluded that helping someone exercise their legal rights is not always
morally acceptable. And so, Lincoln rejected the lawyer's amoral ethical
role.

Pepper disagrees with this line of thinking, arguing instead that
"[t]he lawyer is a good person in that he provides access to the law."
Pepper is not the first writer to urge that—despite Lincoln's reminder
that what is legally right need not be morally right—assisting people to
do what is legally right is always morally right. Charles Fried and Alan
Donagan have also argued that legal autonomy is good, and so helping
people have their legal autonomy is good. But some things legally right
are not morally right, and so in any such argument we must ask how the
rabbit of moral justification manages to come out of the hat. And the
answer, I believe, is the one we all expected: rabbits don't come out of
hats unless they have been put in the hats to begin with. Fried gets the
rabbit in the hat by using an analogy of lawyers to friends that—as his
critics pointed out—begs the question. Donagan doesn't quite get the
rabbit out of the hat; he (rightly) imposes such stringent limitations on
the amoral role that it would be unrecognizable to its champions. And
Pepper, I believe, assumes that the morality is already in the law, that in
an important sense anything legally right *is* morally right. That, however, cannot be, or so I wish to argue.

The argument for the amoral role goes as follows: *First premise:*
"law is intended to be a public good which increases autonomy." *Second
Premise:* "autonomy [is] preferred over 'right' or 'good' conduct"; "increasing individual autonomy is morally good." *Third premise:* "in a
highly legalized society such as ours, . . . access to the law . . . in reality
. . . is available only through a lawyer." *Conclusion:* "what the lawyer
does is a social good." "The lawyer is a good person in that he provides
access to the law."

I deny the second premise, that individual autonomy is preferred
over right or good conduct: it is the point at which the rabbit gets into
the hat. Pepper appears to have blurred the crucial distinction between
the desirability of people acting autonomously and *the desirability of their
autonomous act.* It is good, desirable, for me to make my own decisions
about whether to lie to you; it is bad, undesirable, for me to lie to you. It
is good that people act autonomously, that they make their own choices
about what to do; what they choose to do, however, need not be good.
Pepper's second premise is plausible only when we focus exclusively on
the first of each of these pairs of propositions; it loses its plausibility

when we turn our attention to the second. *Other things being equal,* Pepper is right that "increasing individual autonomy is morally good," but when the exercise of autonomy results in an immoral action, other things aren't equal. You must remember that some things autonomously done are not morally right.

Pepper's subsequent argument is that since exercising autonomy is good, helping people exercise autonomy is good. Though this is true, it too is only half the story. The other half is that since doing bad things is bad, helping people do bad things is bad. The two factors must be weighed against each other, and this Pepper does not do.

Compare this case: The automobile, by making it easier to get around, increases human autonomy; hence, other things being equal, it is morally good to repair the car of someone who is unable by himself to get it to run. But such considerations can hardly be invoked to defend the morality of fixing the getaway car of an armed robber, assuming that you know in advance what the purpose of the car is. The moral wrong of assisting the robber outweighs the abstract moral goodness of augmenting the robber's autonomy.

Pepper admits that it "may be morally wrong to manufacture or distribute cigarettes or alcohol, or to disinherit one's children for marrying outside the faith, but the generality of such decisions are left in the private realm." That is true, but that doesn't imply that such exercises of autonomy are morally acceptable. On the contrary, it concedes that they are immoral. And this is simply to return to the distinction between the desirability of exercising autonomy and the undesirability of exercising it wrongly.

Pepper sees this. To make his argument work, he distinguishes between (merely) *immoral* conduct and *intolerable* conduct, and says that intolerable conduct "ought to be made explicitly unlawful"; at one point, indeed, he equates "not unlawful" conduct with conduct "above the floor of the intolerable." Using this distinction, he argues in effect that unlawful conduct *is* conduct the immorality of which does not outweigh the value of autonomous decision making. If we didn't want people to make up their own minds about such conduct, we would make it illegal, and thus the fact that we haven't shows that we do not disapprove of it sufficiently to take the decision out of people's own hands.

The conclusion does not follow, however. There are many reasons for not prohibiting conduct besides the reason that we don't think it's bad enough to take it out of people's hands. We should not put into effect prohibitions that are unenforceable, or that are enforceable only at enormous cost, or through unacceptably or disproportionately invasive means. We should not prohibit immoral conduct if it would be too difficult to specify the conduct, or if the laws would of necessity be vague or either over- or underinclusive, or if enforcement would destroy our liberties.

All these are familiar and good reasons for refraining from prohibiting conduct that have nothing whatever to do with the intensity of our disapprobation of the conduct. It is illegal to smuggle a bottle of nonduty-free Scotch into the country. It is not illegal to seduce someone through honey-tongued romancing, maliciously intending to break the lover's heart afterward (as in Kierkegaard's *Diary of a Seducer*). Surely this discrepancy does not show that we judge the smuggling (but not the seduction) "intolerable," or even that we judge the smuggling to be morally worse than the seduction. On the contrary, we judge the seduction to be worse conduct, perhaps even intolerable conduct, but we realize that prohibiting seductions would have obvious enormous social costs. The distinction between legal and illegal conduct simply does not correspond to the distinction between conduct that we think on moral grounds people should be free to engage in and conduct we find morally intolerable.

Pepper acknowledges this too, but resists its implication by posing this rhetorical question: "If making the conduct unlawful is too onerous because the law would be too vague, or it is too difficult to identify the conduct in advance, or there is not sufficient social or political concern, do we intend to delegate to the individual lawyer the authority for case-by-case legislation and policing?"

I do not treat this question as rhetorical; I answer it "yes." The reason goes, I think, to the heart of my disagreement with Pepper. What bothers Pepper the most, I believe, is the idea that lawyers should interpose themselves and their moral concerns as "filters" of what legally permissible projects clients should be able to undertake. His concern, in turn, appears to have two aspects to it, one specific to lawyers, the other more general: "Such a screening submits each to ... rule by oligarchy of lawyers." More generally, it appears to me that Pepper objects to *anyone,* lawyer or not, interposing his or her scruples to filter the legally permissible projects of autonomous agents. He objects, that is, to informal obstacles to autonomy, allowing only the formal obstacles raised by the law itself. (That seems to be the force of his argument that any conduct which is not illegal is up to "individual decision making.") I suspect that part of Pepper's worry here is that to allow informal obstacles to autonomy is to take away people's first-class citizenship as granted by the law and thus to threaten the rule of law itself.

The first of these worries is illusory, for there is no oligarchy of lawyers, actual or potential, to worry about. An oligarchy is a group of people ruling *in concert,* whereas lawyers who refuse to execute projects to which they object on moral grounds will do so as individuals, without deliberating collectively with other lawyers. The worry about a hidden Central Committee of lawyers evaporates when we realize that the committee will never hold a meeting, and that its members don't even know they are on it. An analogy will clarify this. No doubt throughout history people have often been dissuaded from undertaking immoral projects by the anger, threats, and uncooperativeness of their spouses. It would scarcely make sense, however, to worry that this amounts to subjecting autonomous action "to rule by an oligarchy of spouses." There *is* no oligarchy of spouses.

The second worry is more interesting. Unlike Pepper, I am not troubled by the existence of informal filters of people's legally permissible projects. Far from seeing these as a threat to the rule of law, I regard them as essential to its very existence.

We—people, that is—are tempted to a vast array of reprehensible conduct. Some of it can be and is tolerated; some of it we do not engage in because of our scruples; and some of it the law proscribes. But the law cannot proscribe all intolerable conduct, for human society would then be crushed flat by a monstrous, incomprehensible mass of law. And scruples—conscience, morality—will not take up all the slack.

Instead, we rely to a vast extent on informal social pressure to keep us in check. Why do people break into the line at the cafeteria so seldom? Why do they bus their own trays? Why do they keep malicious, gossiping tongues in (relative!) check at the office? Why are they civil to subordinate employees? Why do they keep their word? Why are Kierkegaardian seducers few and far between? For many people, the answer is scruples, morality; but for many people it is not. When conscience is too faint, I submit, the answer to all these questions is that people worry about what other people will say, think, and do, and guide their behavior accordingly.

Imagine now what would happen if we could no longer count on this sort of motivation, so that we would have to enforce desirable behavior legally—imprison or fine line-skippers and tray-nonbussers, gossips and rude deans and heartbreakers. Imagine policing these offenses! When we begin to reflect on the sheer magnitude of altruistic behavior we take for granted in day-to-day life, we realize that society could not exist without the dense network of informal filters provided by other people.

Among those filters is noncooperation. Many nefarious schemes are aborted because an agent's associates or partners or friends or family or financial backers or employees will have nothing to do with them. My argument is that far from this being an objectionable state of affairs, neither society nor law could survive without such filters.

And, to conclude the argument, I do not see why a lawyer's decision not to assist a client in a scheme that the lawyer finds nefarious is any different from these other instances of social control through private noncooperation. It is no more an affront to the client's autonomy for the lawyer to refuse to assist in the scheme than it is for the client's wife to threaten to move out if he goes ahead with it. Indeed, the lawyer's autonomy allows him to exercise the "Lysistratian prerogative"—to withhold services from those of whose projects he disapproves, to decide not to go to bed with clients who want to "set a whole neighborhood at loggerheads."

Autonomous decision making is valuable for two complementary reasons: metaphysically and axiologically, the exercise of freedom is one of the most important (if not the most important) components of human well-being; and psychologically, the exercise of freedom is developed in tandem with prized traits of character: rationality and prudence, adult commitment, self-actualization, and responsibility.

It is crucial to realize, however, that none of these values require *unlimited* autonomy in order to be satisfactorily realized—if they did, of course, then human autonomy would be incompatible with the very existence of law. This fact in turn implies that occasional or limited impositions pose no threat to the values underlying my autonomy, provided that my life contains plenty of other opportunities for developing and exercising the capacities associated with autonomous decision making—provided, in other words, that my life is by and large autonomous. A parent's autonomy is not jeopardized because her lawyer refuses to draft a will disinheriting her child because of the child's opposition to the war in Nicaragua: the parent still has plenty of other opportunities for free decision making (indeed, the parent probably even has plenty of other opportunities to make her child miserable). Her life is by and large autonomous.

And, since lawyers' interactions with clients are mostly occasional, lawyers' refusal to execute immoral designs of clients will not threaten the values underlying autonomy if the clients' lives are by and large autonomous in their other interactions. For this reason, in cases of conflict the threat to autonomy posed by Lincoln-like lawyers will typically be outweighed by the immorality of helping the clients.

In effect, Pepper has argued for a strong and a weak thesis. The strong thesis is that helping clients, even when they are doing bad, is good. The weak thesis is that withholding help from clients is bad. But both arguments fall: the rabbits came out of the hat only because they were waiting there to begin with.

William H. Simon, THE PRACTICE OF JUSTICE:
A THEORY OF LAWYERS' ETHICS

(1998)

INTRODUCTION

An Anxious Profession

No social role encourages such ambitious moral aspirations as the lawyer's, and no social role consistently disappoints the aspirations it encourages.

Many young people go to law school in the hope of finding a career in which they can contribute to society. They tend to come out with such hopes diminished, and the hopes often disappear under the pressures of practice. Late in their careers, especially if they achieve worldly success, they often recall their hopes with nostalgia and regret. We owe to this late-career experience a booming literature of books, after-dinner speeches, and bar association reports decrying the ethical poverty of law practice.

Some of this literature attributes ethical disappointment to recent developments in practice or theory. Practice has become more bureaucratic in some ways, more commercial in others ... Yet we know that the experience of ethical disappointment, and indeed the literature of late-career lamentation. Long antedate these developments. The current critiques are simply the latest peak in a cycle a century old. The volume of complaint has fluctuated, but complaint has been with us constantly.

We find a similar expression of anxiety about the lawyer's role, expressed at a fairly steady rate over the years, in popular culture. The heroic portrayals of lawyering consistently excise important features of both official and empirical versions of the lawyer's role. Perry Mason's clients are always innocent. Dramatic portrayals that purport to treat lawyers more realistically are usually ambivalent or downright disparaging about the role. Dickens's Jaggers and Tulkinghorn look more grotesque than more faithfully they serve their clients.

So an explanation of the moral anxiety associated with lawyering should look to conditions more longstanding than recent developments in organization and jurisprudence. My explanation focuses on a structural tension in the lawyer's role that has always been present but has become more acute during the past century. The core of the explanation is this: the dominant conception of the lawyer's professional responsibilities weakens the connection between the practical tasks of lawyering and the values of justice that lawyers believe provide the moral foundations of their role. This conception often requires that the lawyer take actions that contribute to injustice in the circumstances at hand. Of course, these actions are supposed to facilitate a greater justice in a more remote sense. But the remoteness of the ultimate moral payoff of the lawyer's conduct is a problem. At best the situation demands of the lawyer an exacting moral asceticism. Her immediate experience implicates her in violations of the values to which she is most fundamentally committed; the redeeming beneficial effects occur somewhere outside of her working life, perhaps invisibly. So in a way most readily associated with religious norms, the lawyering role demands a deferral of the ethical gratification of experiencing the good to which one's right conduct contributes.

The problem becomes more serious once we have reason to doubt the connection between the vividly perceived injustice of the here and now and the greater justice expected elsewhere and later. The connection can't be observed. It is a matter for theory, and theory has made it harder for lawyers to believe that their immediate injustices are really necessary to a more remote good * * *

The Moral Terrain of Lawyering

The kind of moral decisions that implicate the profession's most fundamental commitments to legality and justice are those that arise from conflicts between client interests on the one hand and third-party and public interests on the other. Consider some examples.

The Innocent Convict. In about 1914 Arthur Powell, a Georgia lawyer, received information from a client establishing the innocence of Leo Frank. Frank had been convicted in Atlanta of the murder a young girl a trial notoriously marred by anti-Semitism and mob hysteria. Because the client would not consent to disclosure, Powell did not communicate this information to anyone. Frank's sentence was commuted later to life imprisonment, but he was soon afterwards lynched by a mob.

Agribusiness Welfare. The Federal Reclamation Act was enacted in 1906 for the declare purpose of supporting small family farms. The fact funds projects that provide water to farmers at heavily subsidized rates. The original act limited eligibility of any farmer for subsidized water to 160 acres or less. Although it is uncontroversial that the intent of this limitation was to preclude large subsidies to wealthy farmers, over the years lawyers for such farmers, including large corporations such as the Southern Pacific Railroad, crated a series of devices to qualify their clients for billions of dollars in benefits.

An early approach was to have client disperse his holdings among various corporations. Although the shares in all the corporations would be owned by the client, together with associates and family members, and the client continued to farm the land as a unit, the lawyers then argued that since each corporation owned only 160 acres, they were collectively entitled to subsidized water for all the land farmed by the client. Another approach was to create a series of trusts for family members and assign 160 acre plots to each trust, as a separate "legal person," was entitled to subsidized water for "its" holdings . . .

The Dominant View and Alternatives

The prevailing approach to lawyer's ethics as reflected in the bar's disciplinary codes, the case law on lawyer discipline, and the burgeoning commentary on professional responsibility can be crudely but usefully summarized as the Dominant View.

The core principle of the Dominant View is this: the lawyer must–or at least may–pursue any goal of the client through any arguable legal course of action and assert any nonfrivolous legal claim. Thus, if Arthur Powell's client wants him to remain silent, Powell should do so unless some law inarguably requires that he disclose. If the agribusiness clients want subsidized water, their lawyer's manipulations are justified so long as there is a nonfrivolous argument that the law does not prohibit them . . .

Note that in the Dominant View the only ethical duty distinctive to the lawyer's role is loyalty to the client. Legal ethics impost no responsibilities to third parties or the public different from that of the minimal compliance with law that is required of everyone . . .

Of course, neither the disciplinary codes nor any court or commentator subscribes to the Dominant View *tout court*. The basic precept is nearly always qualified by some norms intended to protect third-party and public interests. But the basic precept remains the governing norm. It influences and structures discussions. It functions as both starting point and presumptive fallback position.

The critical fact of our purposes is that * * * the Dominant View * * * adopts a common style of decision-making that I call categorical. Such decision-making severely restricts the range of considerations the decision maker may take into account when she confronts a particular problem; a rigid rule dictates a particular response in the presence of a small number of factors. The decision maker has no discretion to consider factors that are not specified or to evaluate specified factors in ways other than those prescribed by the rule * * * The essence of this approach is contextual judgment—a judgment that applies relatively abstract norms to a broad range of the particulars of the case at hand.

Lawyers are so accustomed to associating contextual judgment with judges or with prosecutors and other government lawyers that they sometimes protest that the Contextual View of legal ethics collapses the lawyer's role into that of the judge or prosecutor. But that is a misunderstanding. In appealing to these other roles I mean to invoke only a style of judgment, not the particular decisions judges and prosecutors make. The Contextual View incorporates much of the traditional lawyer role, including the notion that lawyer's role has a public dimension, that assumption is grounded in the lawyer's age-old claim to be an "officer of the court" and in notions about the most effective integration of the lawyering role with other roles in the legal system.

Legal Ethics as Contextual Judgment

Lawyers should take those actions that, considering the relevant circumstances of the particular case, seem likely to promote justice. This is the maxim that the Contextual View proposes to resolve the core issue of lawyers' ethics—those in which the interests of clients conflict with those of third parties or the public.

"Justice" here connotes the basic values of the legal system and subsumes many layers of more concrete norms. Decisions about justice are not assertions of personal preferences nor are they applications of ordinary morality. They are legal judgments grounded in the methods and sources of authority of the professional culture. I use "justice" interchangeably with "legal merit". The latter has the advantage of reminding us that we are concerned with the materials of conventional legal analysis; the former has the advantage of reminding us that these materials include many vaguely specified inspirational norms.

Responsibility to justice is not incompatible with deference to the general pronouncements or enactments of authoritative institutions such as legislatures and courts. On the contrary, justice often, perhaps usually, requires such deference. Nor does such responsibility preclude deference to the adjudicatory process in the resolution of contested cases. Again, justice more often than not requires such deference. Responsibility to justice is also consistent with vigorous advocacy on behalf of client goals in a broad range of circumstances. The idea of justice invokes the lawyer's simultaneous commitments to partisan advocacy and service as an "officer of the court" to both sympathetic identification with clients and detachment from them * * *.

The Structure of Legal Ethics Problems

It will be helpful to illustrate the Contextual View by considering ethical issues in terms of certain recurring tensions: Substance versus Procedure and Purpose versus Form * * *

Substance versus Procedure

The substance-versus-procedure tension arises from the lawyer's sense, on the one hand, of the limitations of her judgment regarding the substantive merit of a matter and, on the other hand, of the limitations of the established procedures for determining the matter. We could tell the lawyer to look only to substance; we might then say that she should work to advance only the claims and goals she determined ought to prevail. The most important objection to this approach is not that the lawyer's decisions about the substantive merits would be controversial— the decisions of judges, juries, and executive officials might be controversial as well. The main objection is that judges, juries, and executive officials acting within the relevant public procedures are generally able to make more reliable determinations of the merits than are individual lawyers.

But the relative capacities of the people in these other roles depend on how the lawyer performs in her role. Moreover, even though the other actors may generally be better positioned than the lawyer to assess the merits, there may be important occasions when they are not. Perhaps an adverse party or official lacks information or resources needed to initiate, pursue, or determine a claim. Or perhaps an official is corrupt, or politically intimidated, or incompetent. Or perhaps the relevant procedures are ill designed to resolve the matter; maybe it is impossible to get jurisdiction over a necessary party or to decide the matter in a sufficiently short time to protect some urgent interest, or to find property against which to enforce a judgment.

The basic response of the Contextual View to the substance-procedure tension is this: the more reliable the relevant procedures and institutions, the less direct responsibility the lawyer need assume for the substantive justice of the resolution; the less reliable the procedures and institutions, the more direct responsibility she needs to assume for substantive justice.

The lawyer should respond to procedural defects by trying to mitigate them. By directing the lawyer to attempt first to improve the procedure, the Contextual approach respects the traditional premise that the strongest assurance of a just resolution is the soundness of the procedure that produced it. But to the extent that the lawyer cannot neutralize defects in the relevant procedure, she should assume direct responsibility for the substantive validity of the decision. She should form her own judgment about the substantive resolution and take reasonable actions to bring it about * * *

Purpose versus Form

Some instances of the Substance-versus–Procedure tension look like variations of the Purpose-versus-Form tension. When the lawyer impeaches a witness she knows to be truthful, when she objects to hearsay she knows to be accurate, when she puts the opposing party to proof on a matter the client has no legitimate reason to dispute, she takes advantage of procedural rules designed to promote accurate, efficient decision-making in ways that frustrate this purpose. When judges apply rules, we expect them to take account of the values (purposes or principles) underlying the rules. But the judge often lacks sufficient knowledge to do so. Thus it is an important objection to the Dominant View that it imposes no responsibility on the lawyer to see that the rules she invokes are applied in a manner that takes account of their purposes.

The argument so far suggests that a lawyer's choice between a purposive or formal approach to procedural rules should depend on which approach seems better calculated to vindicate the relevant legal merits. In most contexts, considerations of merit favor a purposive approach. Yet the Contextual View also requires the lawyer to remain alert for indications that a purposive approach might not further this aim * * *

The Dominant View tends to license the manipulation of form to defeat purpose * * * The Contextual View responds to the Purpose-versus-Form tension with the following maxim: the clearer and more fundamental the relevant purposes, the more the lawyer should consider herself bound by them; the less clear and more problematic the relevant purposes, the more justified the lawyers is in treating the relevant norms formally. Treating them formally means treating them the way the Dominant View prescribes for all legal norms–understanding them to permit any client goal not plainly precluded by their language * * *

The Moral Terrain of Lawyering Reconsidered

The Innocent Convict. The drama of the client who confesses to a murder for which a mistakenly convicted man awaits execution might be described as an extreme conflict of procedure (confidentiality) and substance (innocence). Clearly, the general procedural system has failed so far, and it seems unlikely that, in the absence of some intervention by the lawyer, it is likely to correct itself. The lawyer thus has some responsibility to assess substantive merit, and it seems clear that a horrendous injustice is in prospect.

Compared to the stakes for the innocent convict, the client's legitimate interest in silence seems trivial. To be sure, he has placed his trust in the lawyers, but just as "honor among thieves" shows that not all forms of honor are especially worthy, the trust of a murderer in a lawyer's willingness to remain passive in face of enormous injustice seems of small weight. The most important competing consideration is not the entitlement of the client to silence, but the effect of disclosure in deterring people with more legitimate interests in seeking legal advice * * *

I expressed skepticism about the bar's arguments that categorical confidentiality guarantees are essential to induce people to seek legal advice. The arguments seem especially weak as applied to his case. If the lawyer could make an anonymous disclosure to help the innocent convict, that would have no weakening effect on general trust in attorney confidentiality. Even a highly publicized disclosure seems unlikely to have a major effect. The most likely public interpretation of disclosure would be, not as some indiscriminate weakening of lawyers' commitment to confidentiality, but as an exception for the extreme circumstances of this case. Lay people are aware that the confidentiality norms are not absolute, and many of them already believe (incorrectly) that the norms make an exception for cases of this sort. To the extent that is so, public disclosure would have no effect at all on public willingness to seek legal advice.

If the disclosure would make a difference and the rules gave the lawyer discretion to disclose, then the case would be an easy one. It becomes difficult when we recognize that the bar's disciplinary rules, which have the force of law by virtue of their adoption by the courts forbid disclosure. This case at least is not within the explicit exceptions of the rules. Perhaps the rules could be interpreted to imply such an exception, but there are strong objections to such an interpretation. The drafters' comments to the *Model Rules* discourage implied exceptions, and commentators who have considered the Innocent Convict case have tended to interpret the rules as inflexible.

So the lawyer might have to consider disclosure as a form of nullification. It can be argued generally that the bar's confidentiality norms should be viewed as, at best, weakly binding. The bar's rationales for these norms are dogmatic and incoherent. The norms seem out of harmony with the treatment of confidentiality in analogous situations by legislatures and agencies and even by courts outside the realm of professional responsibility rules. The norms were enacted through a process strongly influenced by professional associations, which are both historically and structurally disposed toward more than occasional narrow self-interest.

Even if the arguments for categorical confidentiality safeguards are not strong, we have to acknowledge that many people, including people with authority over the matter, accept them. For the most part the norms have been recently enacted, often after substantial public debate.

Though inconsistent with some legislation on analogous matters, the bar's rules are consistent in important respects with the attorney-client privilege in the law of evidence. Notwithstanding the influence of the bar associations, professional responsibility norms are ultimately enacted by the courts.

Yet these considerations seem outweighed by the substantive absurdity of the rules' application in the particular circumstances of the Innocent Convict. If the facts are such that disclosure would probably save an innocent life without posing a demonstrable threat to important rights of others (through limiting future access to legal advice), then it would be grotesque not to disclose them. While a rule forbidding disclosure would be regarding for any actor, it is particularly so for a lawyer, since it compels him to acquiesce in a monumental violation of a core commitment of his role. The rule should not be interpreted to require such degradation. If such an interpretation is unavoidable, then the lawyer should defy the rule, not as an act of lawlessness, but as an act of principled commitment to legal values more fundamental than those that support the rule.

Agribusiness Welfare. This case is readily framed as a conflict between form and purpose. By providing for water benefits for each farmer, the statute at least arguably permits a wealthy farmer to disperse his holdings among trusts and corporations and have each of these "farmers" get benefits up to the maximum. However, this interpretation seems inconsistent with the apparent purpose, to preclude wealthy people from claiming greater benefits than nonwealthy ones. The landowners who would make these arrangements start out wealthy, and although the transfers disperse formal control and enjoyment rights, informally the transferor retains most or all of them. The purpose to limit transfers to the wealthy is not "problematical" in the sense discussed above: it does not threaten any fundamental value. So there's no reason to be wary of it.

Of course, the conflict of form and purpose becomes troubling only if we find some defect in the public enforcement process. If the process is reliable, the lawyer contributes to the elaboration of the statute by presenting the claims in a manner that facilitates determination by the authorities. Many students of agricultural policy during the period when these transactions were popular suggest that the enforcement process wan not reliable. They claim that the enforcement agencies were "captured" by the large farm organizations, which were in turn dominated by the wealthier farmers. The farm organizations controlled the flow of information to the agencies, orchestrated pressure on them both directly and through their influence on Congress, and doled out jobs to departing bureaucrats and junkets and other nonmonetary emoluments to incumbent ones in a manner well calculated to induce sensitivity to the interests of their most powerful members. These students interpret the agencies' acceptance of the transactions in questions as a function, not of dispassionate judgment on the legal merits, but of their "capture" by the people who benefited from the transactions. A lawyer who agreed with this conclusion would have an increased responsibility to assess the substantive merits of the transaction. In many cases, he should probably have concluded that the transactions should not proceed because they are inconsistent with the statutory purpose.

Of course, it might be costly for the lawyer to implement this conclusion. Once these transactions become more or less standard, lawyers who decline to go along with them will have a hard time attracting clients in this area and may even subject themselves to malpractice liability. Thus the lawyer has to weigh his own interest in earning a living against the wrong such transactions do. Neither the certainty nor the magnitude of the wrong seem so great that it would be unreasonable for him to decide to proceed.

The fact that economic pressures sometimes outweigh concerns of legal merit doesn't mean it isn't important to think about the merit, however. In other situations the pressures may not be so strong. For example, if the lawyer were considering the practice before it came into general use and the client had no expectation she would adopt it, she would probably be able to forego it without serious cost and probably should. Moreover, a lawyer who has not yet entered the relevant field but is considering doing so should view pressures that force her to engage in unmeritorious practices as a strong reason against entering it. Even the lawyer in the field who plausibly believes that she has an excuse for yielding to pressures to engage in the arrangement should be aware of its dubious merit. We might view this kind of self-awareness as a good in itself, as a constitutive feature of ethical autonomy. We might also think of the practice of assessing the moral costs of what one does as an important disposition and skill that needs to be maintained and cultivated. A lawyer who permits herself to become insensitive to the moral costs of actions she feels she must take risks losing her capacity to assess such costs in situations where she has greater discretion.

Robert W. Gordon, A New Role for Lawyers?: The Corporate Counselor After Enron

35 Conn. L. Rev. 1185 (2003)

III.   Inadequacy of the Excuses

The Enron and similar scandals illustrate the limits of * * * the standard stories as adequate accounts of the corporate lawyer's proper role * * *

The most important lessons of Enron, et al., for lawyers are the additional clouds of doubt they cast on the most common defense of the corporate lawyer's role, and the one most often invoked by the profession in the current debates over reform. That is the corporate lawyer as adversary-advocate. The usual way in which this role is framed is that the lawyer's loyalty runs to the client and only to the client. The lawyer must help the client realize its goals and desires, recognizing as hard limits only such legal constraints, the "bounds of the law," as the most ingenious interpretations he can construct of fact and law that are most favorable to his client's position. Even if the lawyer is advising the client not in an adversary proceeding but in an office, and with respect to future rather than past conduct, the lawyer is entitled to make use of any colorable justification for the client's conduct that he could use to defend it in future adversary proceedings, however unlikely such proceedings may be. Of course, the lawyer must advise the client of the risks of adventurous interpretations of law and fact, that decision-makers (if they ever find out) may not accept them and will find the client in violation of the law. But if the client is willing to take the risks, the lawyer may ethically assist the client beyond the merely conventional limits, all the way up to the arguable limits, exploiting all conceivable loopholes and ambiguities of the existing law.

This idea that the role of the corporate lawyer is really just like the role of the criminal defense lawyer has been criticized so often and so effectively that it always surprises me to see the idea still walking around, hale and hearty, as if nobody had ever laid a glove on it. I will quickly run through some of the strong objections to the analogy and then add another objection: The bar's standard construction of the corporate lawyer's role is deficient in part because it does not take the analogy seriously enough.

The most obvious objection is that legal advice given outside of adversary proceedings is not subject to any of the constraints of such proceedings. The reasons that the lawyer is given so much latitude to fight for his client in court is that the proceedings are open and public, effective mechanisms such as compelled discovery and testimony exist to bring to light suppressed inconvenient facts and make them known to adversaries and adjudicators, adversaries are present to challenge the advocate's arguments of law and his witnesses' and documents' view of facts, and there is an impartial umpire or judge to rule on their sufficiency and validity. Absent any of these bothersome conditions, lawyers can stretch the rules and facts very extravagantly in their clients' favor without risking contradiction by adversaries, or the annoyed reactions of judges or regulators to far-fetched positions.

In the trial setting, aggressive advocacy (at least in theory) supposedly operates to bring out the truth, by testing one-sided proof and argument against counter-proof and counter-argument. Ideally, it facilitates decisions of the legal validity of the parties' claims on the merits. Outside of such settings, one-sided advocacy is more likely to help parties overstep the line to violate the law, and to do so in such ways as are likely to evade detection and sanction, and thus frustrate the purposes of law and regulation.

Look at Enron for obvious examples. The legal system prescribes many rules calling for transparency of corporate activities: Disclosure of financial condition to securities markets; disclosure to the IRS of the economic purpose and substance of tax-shelter schemes; and disclosure for potential bankruptcy purposes of whether assets have been actually transferred from one entity to another, so that they may properly be considered as part of the transferor's or transferee's estate. Corporations in short are, for many legal purposes, supposed to disclose material facts about their financial situations. The lawyers treated this injunction as: Corporations may actually conceal material facts so long as we help them do it in such a way that we can later argue that, technically, they did disclose in the sense of meeting the literal requirements of disclosure laws. The purpose of their advice was to facilitate effective non-disclosure under a cover of arguably lawful action. The lawyers looked forward to a hypothetical role as counsel in adversary proceedings and the arguments they would make in that role. But the main object and real point of the help they gave to clients was to prevent anyone from ever finding out what the client was actually doing, and a fig leaf of cover in case anyone ever did find out and challenge it.

The advocacy ideology regularly and persistently confuses the managers, who ask for lawyers' advice, with the lawyers' actual client, the corporate entity. Admittedly, much corporate-law doctrine makes this easy for them because it is excessively permissive in allowing lawyers to treat the incumbent managers who consult them as the entity.

The point I want to add to these standard, but valuable, points is a simple one. Corporate lawyers could actually learn something useful from the role of the criminal defense lawyer. And that is that the adversary-advocate's role—like that of all lawyers—is in large part a public role, designed to fulfill public purposes: The ascertainment of truth and the doing of justice; the protection of the autonomy, dignity and rights of witnesses and especially of the accused; and the monitoring and disciplining of police and prosecutorial conduct. The defense lawyer is not merely or even mostly a private agent of his client, whose function is to zealously further the client's interest (which is usually to evade just punishment for his past conduct, or continue to engage in it in the future). He is assigned a specialized role in a public process in which his zealous advocacy is instrumental to the service of various public objectives. He is encouraged to make the best possible arguments for suppressing unlawfully seized evidence, not for the purpose of furthering his client's interest in freedom or getting away with crimes, but to protect third parties who are not his clients, i.e., other citizens whose freedom and security will be put at risk unless police misconduct is deterred. He is allowed to present a very one-sided, partial, and selective version of the evidence favoring the defense, in part because resourceful adversaries can poke holes in his story and present a counter-story, but even more to fulfill a public purpose—that of keeping prosecutors up to the mark, making sure they know that they have to put together a defense-proof case, deterring them from indicting where they do not have the evidence. Defense counsel's zeal is restricted precisely at the points where it might help the client at the risk of damage to the performance of his public functions and the integrity of the procedural framework that those functions are designed to serve. He may not, for example, lie to judges, suppress or manufacture real evidence, pose questions on cross-examination that he has no basis in fact for asking, or suborn or knowingly put on perjured testimony.

If you extend this analysis of the public functions of the defense bar to the corporate bar, what might you conclude? That, like the defense lawyer's, the corporate lawyer's role has to be constructed so that it serves and does not disserve its public functions as well as its private ones. I have explained the public benefits of allowing defense lawyers to suppress unlawfully seized evidence, or to refrain from volunteering inconvenient facts pointing to their clients' guilt. But what are the benefits of allowing lawyers to conceal—or hide in a maze of fine print—facts from regulators and investors that would be highly relevant to determining what the companies' real earnings were, or whether its tax shelters had some economic purpose beyond avoidance, or that managers were setting up side deals paying themselves and their cronies huge bonuses? What is the virtue of allowing lawyers to pull the wool over the eyes of the understaffed bureaucrats who monitor their transactions and try to enforce the laws? Even if all of these schemes should turn out to be (at least arguably) technically legal, what values of overall human happiness, individual self-fulfillment, or economic efficiency are served by helping clients promote them? The autonomy of clients generally is a good thing, to be sure; but there is no virtue per se in action, any old action, that is freely chosen, if it is likely to bring destruction in its wake—including, in these examples, harm to the real clients themselves, not their incumbent managements but the long-term corporate entities and their constituent stake-holders.

The real lesson from the defense lawyer's or advocate's role is simply that the lawyer is, in addition to being a private agent of his clients, a public agent of the legal system, whose job is to help clients steer their way through the maze of the law, to bring clients' conduct and behavior into conformity with the law—to get the client as much as possible of what the client wants without damaging the framework of the law. He may not act in furtherance of his client's interest in ways that ultimately frustrate, sabotage, or nullify the public purposes of the laws—or that injure the interests of clients, which are hypothetically constructed, as all public corporations should be, as good citizens who internalize legal norms and wish to act in furtherance of the public values they express.

IV. TOWARDS AN ALTERNATIVE CONCEPTION OF THE CORPORATE COUNSELOR'S ROLE

The view that I am pressing here of the corporate counselor's role is neither new nor unorthodox. It is in fact one of the traditional conceptions of the counselor's role in our legal culture, with a pedigree quite as venerable and considerably more respectable than the rival notion of the lawyer as zealous advocate or hired gun. It was regularly invoked by leading lawyers throughout the nineteenth century and surfaced as an express ethical standard in the ABA's first Canons of Ethics, promulgated in 1908:

Canon § 32: No client, corporate or individual, however powerful, nor any cause, civil or political, however important, is entitled to receive, nor should any lawyer render, any service or advice involving disloyalty to the law, whose ministers we are ... or deception or betrayal of the public.... The lawyer ... advances the honor of his profession and the best interests of his client when he renders service or gives advice tending to impress upon the client and his undertaking exact compliance with the strictest principles of moral law. He must also observe and advise his client to observe the statute law, though until a statute shall have been construed and interpreted by competent adjudication, he is free and entitled to advise as to its validity and as to what he conscientiously believes to be its just meaning and extent.

In the post World War II era, a group of lawyers and legal academics—including Lon Fuller, Willard Hurst, Hart and Sacks, and Beryl Harold Levy—theorized, from hints dropped by such Progressive lawyers as Brandeis and Adolf Berle (who disagreed on everything else but concurred on this), the role of the new corporate legal counselor as a "statesman-advisor". The counselor represents his client's interest "with an eye to securing not only the client's immediate benefit but his long-range social benefit." In negotiating and drafting contracts, collective bargaining agreements, or reorganization plans, the lawyer is a lawmaker of "private legislation" and "private constitutions", a "prophylactic avoider of troubles, as well as pilot through anticipated difficulties." The emphasis is on creative compliance with government regulators and labor unions, and on harmonious stable compromises with contract partners and the workforce * * *

Since the 1970s, this conception of the wise-counselor-lawyer-statesman has been in decay. It is no longer recognized by most corporate lawyers as a norm. It has almost no institutional support in the rules and disciplinary bodies that regulate the profession. Some academic lawyers still support some version of it; and so too do some judges and regulators. It resurfaces on occasion after business disasters such as the savings-and-loan and Enron scandals. The SEC, IRS, banking regulators, and the courts have sporadically revived it and brought enforcement actions in its spirit. Bar commissions on professionalism sometimes nostalgically evoke it. Yet even where it still has some residual influence there are no effective sanctions behind it.

The decline of the counselor's ethic has many causes: The collapse of the state-corporate-labor concords; the rise of the new social regulation and with it a newly adversary stance of companies toward regulation and regulators; the sharp rise in inter-corporate and mass-tort litigation; the consequent escalation of legal costs, which caused companies to bring operations in-house and make outside firms compete for specialized business; the reordering of law firms' priorities towards attracting business and maximizing profits-per-partner; the reorientation of professional ethics from complying with aspirational standards to following rules; the displacement of the vocation of public-regarding lawyering onto a specialized "public-interest" bar, academics and government lawyers; and the rise of the cults of market economism and shareholder-wealth-maximization as supreme goods and the vogue of contempt for government and regulation. All of these tendencies have resulted in lawyers' recharacterizing their calling as the wholly privatized business of providing consulting services aimed at legal-risk-reduction and creative law-arbitrage and law-avoidance schemes rather than the professional service of public values and the rule of law.

We cannot hope to revive the counselor's role as the profession's dominant role or self-conception or practical way of life. But events like the Enron collapse make one realize that the corporate counselor would still have a useful role to play, if one could revive it as one of the legal profession's many roles, to be deployed on occasions where clients and society would be best served by independent, public-regarding legal advice.

My idea is this: that there be established a separate professional role for a distinct type of lawyer, the Independent Counselor, with a distinct ethical orientation, institutionalized in a distinct governance regime of ethical codes, liability and malpractice rules, special statutory duties and privileges, and judicial rules of practice. Clients could for most purposes decide whether they wished to be represented by counselors or ordinary attorneys, making clear by contract and representations to the outside world which role they wanted the lawyer to occupy. For some legal purposes however, clients would be required to act through counselors. "Counselor" would be primarily an elective role that lawyers could move in and out of, could assume for particular representations or transactions or purposes, and then resume the role and function of regular lawyer. But it might also be a role regularly institutionalized in practice settings. Lawyers could organize law firms, branches, or offices within client organizations, consisting only of counselors. The counselor's role might eventually evolve into a distinct profession, one organized into separate law firms, or counselors' offices within firms or within client organizations.

This idea is only in an embryonic stage of its development. If it ever caught on as a practical possibility there would of course be many, many details to be worked out. Before that day comes, it hardly seems worthwhile to try to fill out the fine points of what is only at present a hypothetical and possibly completely utopian scheme. So I will limit my job here to trying to spell out what I think would be the essential elements of the counselor's role.

The most basic is this: That the lawyer engaged as a counselor adopt an independent, objective view of the corporate agents' conduct and plans and their legal validity. This emphatically does not mean that the counselor must take up an adversary stance to the client, or an attitude of indifference toward its welfare; indeed, as its lawyer, she ought to view the company's legitimate aims and objectives sympathetically and to give advice that will generally further those aims. Nor does it mean that her advice must be invariably conservative and obstructive, that she must be the unhelpful kind of lawyer who constantly tells managers that they cannot do what they want to do; counselors can and should be as creative as any other good lawyers in devising means to accomplish clients' objectives that will overcome and work around legal objections, and in devising innovative arguments that will alter and expand the boundaries of the existing law. But whatever advice the counselor gives, she should: (a) Construe the facts and law of the client's situation as a sympathetic but objective observer such as a judge, committed to serving the law's spirit and furthering its public purposes, would construe them; (b) impute to the corporate client the character of the good citizen, who has internalized legal norms and wishes to comply with the law's legitimate commands and purposes while pursuing its own interests and goals; and (c) be based on an interpretation and practical application of the law to the client's situation that helps the client, so constructed, to satisfy rather than subvert the purposes of the law.

When the counselor asserts facts or makes a legal claim or argument to authorities or third parties—outside the context of fully adversary proceedings where all interested parties have effective access to relevant facts and legal knowledge necessary to forming the opinion—they should generally be facts and arguments that a fair-minded and fully-informed observer could accept as plausible and correct. For example, if the counselor is giving a legal opinion on the validity of a client's proposed conduct or transaction, she cannot leave out important facts that might cast doubt on her conclusions, or slant the facts so as to obscure difficulties with the conclusions. If she is not sure that her client's agents have been giving her the important facts, or reporting them accurately, she has to ask questions until satisfied or refuse to give the opinion. In other words, she should give the kind of report that a lawyer hired to be an independent investigator and analyst of a client's situation would be expected to give. Unlike the Enron lawyers, she may not accept limits on the scope of her representation that would effectively prevent her from doing the counselor's job; nor may she permit her opinion or conclusions to be used to give cover or respectability to actions she has not really had a chance to look into.

The notion that the counselor's role has to be consistent with the law's public purposes, and should further rather than frustrate those purposes—and that she should give candid, truthful, and undistorted reports to authorities and third parties—does not mean that she must become an informer or enforcement officer. Nor does it mean that the lawyer has to accept regulators' or adversaries' construction, or an ultra-conservative and risk-averse constructions, of the law's purposes: She is perfectly entitled to present an innovative view of the law and facts that favor what her client wants to do, so long as it is a view that she thinks a judge or other competent law-maker would actually be likely to accept. But the conception of the role does pretty clearly imply that if a counselor wants to press on a client's behalf an adventurous, strained, or ingenious interpretation of existing law, or a construction of fact that an objective observer might reasonably think partial and one-sided and potentially misleading, she must do so in a way that flags the contentious nature of what she is proposing and thus permits its adequate testing and evaluation. If no effective adversary process and independent adjudicator is available to test it—not in the hypothetical distant future but here and now—the counselor has either to refrain from pushing the envelope or give intended audiences signals sufficient to inform them of the legal riskiness of getting involved with the plan. Technical, cosmetic, or literal disclosure or compliance that in practical effect is non-disclosure or non-compliance is ruled out under this conception. So is tax-evasion parading as tax-minimization. So is trying to sneak a legally-dubious transaction under the noses of regulators or third-parties whom the lawyers know are too overburdened or unsophisticated or uninformed to discover the potential problems with it * * *

In advising clients contemplating litigation, the counselor takes into account the merits or justice of the claim. She seeks to dissuade plaintiffs from pursuing plainly meritless claims and encourages defendants toward fair settlement, and away from invalid defenses, of just claims. In conducting litigation or similar adversary proceedings, the public-minded lawyer regards herself as an "officer of the court," that is, a trustee for the integrity and fair operation of the basic procedures of the adversary system, the rules of the game and their underlying purposes. She fights aggressively for her client, but in ways respectful of the fair and effective operation of the framework. In discovery, she frames requests to elicit useful information rather than to harass and inflict costs, and responds to reasonable requests rather than obstructing or delaying. She claims privilege or work-product protection only when she thinks that a fair-minded judge would be likely to support the claim independently. In deciding how ferociously to attack the credibility of a witness on cross-examination, she takes into account the likely truthfulness of the witness and the underlying merits of the case.

If the counselor perceives that her services have been or are being used to further, or even just to facilitate by providing plausible cover for, corporate strategies that could not be justified to a fully-informed objective observer as conforming to the letter, spirit, and public purposes of the law, she has to take steps to correct the problem and to try to bring the client's agents back into compliance. This means that if she has suspicions she should investigate them; if not satisfied, she should bring the problem to the general counsel, CEO, and if necessary, the board of directors to insist on compliance; and if corrective steps are not taken, she must resign. Finally, if serious damage to outside interests may result from the agents' misconduct, she must signal the problem to people such as regulatory authorities who could prevent it.

I can already hear the cries of protest: "But this is not the lawyer's role!" The obvious answer to that is, yes, I know that it is not the lawyer's role as most corporate lawyers and the bar now see that role; but that is precisely the problem that the savings-and-loan and Enron, etc. scandals have suggested needs to be solved. The legal profession already recognizes differentiated roles with special obligations. The prosecutor is supposed to be a minister of justice, with "special obligations to see that the defendant is accorded procedural justice and that guilt is decided on the basis of sufficient evidence." Government lawyers are supposed to respect the public interest, not just the position of the agency that employs them. Even private lawyers are not always expected to act as hardball adversary advocates and strategic manipulators of the legal system. For many purposes, companies already want their lawyers to act more like counselors to get the benefits of their perceived independence as reputational intermediaries—for example, to reassure regulators or prosecutors that an errant company has cleaned up its act, to reassure potential transaction partners or investors that a deal is legally safe, or to reassure governments or regulators or local communities that a proposed action is environmentally safe or a proposed reorganization is fair to the labor force. Companies mired in scandal, fraud, and mismanagement often hire law firms as independent counsel to conduct sweeping investigations and house-cleanings and recommend reforms. Companies (like divorcing couples) who want to minimize the strains and expenses of litigation hire law firms with reputations for cooperative behavior, candor and fair play in discovery, openness and a disposition to get to mutually beneficial solutions in negotiating settlements. Sometimes corporate law actually requires the use of independent counsel—for example, to assess whether the corporation should support or oppose a shareholder's derivative suit.

If the counselor's role is already available by contract, why do we need a new profession? The reason is that the counselor's role is too weakly supported by current institutional structures, incentives, statutes, and ethical rules. Ethically, the default master norm of the bar is zealous partisan representation of client interests rather than the counselor's norm of guidance of the client's desires to bring them into alignment with an objective and fair-minded construction of the public purposes of the law. Lawyers may face malpractice or disciplinary complaints if their advice is perceived as more public-regarding than client-regarding. Even if retained as counselors, they may face pressures to moderate their independence from clients' agents unhappy with their advice. Current ethical rules would preclude, or make optional, disclosures to outsiders of corporate agents' violations of law. In short, the counselor may be impeded by ethical rules regarding zeal, confidentiality and conflicts, which are not always waivable by contract.

At the very least, such obligations of partisanship and secrecy should be waivable by contract. Corporations who want to commit themselves *ex ante* to having their business dealings structured, approved, and monitored by independent counselors, with the obligation to report up and even outside the organization if they cannot get managers to comply, should be able to do so, in order to get the benefits of independent advice and objective controls on misconduct.

Giving clients the choice to hire counselors by contract would be a useful reform in itself. If the counselor-by-contract alternative were widely available and known about, there could be costs to clients for not choosing lawyers committed to act as counselors in situations where the clients wanted to assure third parties and regulators of good-faith and cooperative conduct. "If you're such good guys, how come your lawyers are hired-gun advocates?"

But counseling-by-contract is not enough. It does not ensure that lawyers will continue to give independent public-regarding advice, or candor and cooperation in bargaining and conflict situations, when the pressure is on to keep the client and prevent it from going over to more complaisant competitors. And it does not give clients enough incentives to hire counselors where—for the protection of third parties or the public—they are most needed.

So I think that the full-scale version of my proposal would have to contain at least two more components. First, there should be government mandates that for some representations and transactions, corporations must hire lawyers who have undertaken the role and accompanying obligation of counselors. For example: Lawyers certifying compliance with laws, regulations, orders, consent decrees, or reporting requirements of official agencies; lawyers giving opinions to satisfy disclosure requirements or filing proxy statements under the securities laws; and lawyers giving opinions on conformity with tax laws on tax-minimization devices. In other words, when lawyers are hired to fulfill gatekeeper obligations for the protection of third parties, investors, or the public, or to certify conformity with taxing or regulatory laws, or with official orders or decrees, they are not entitled to act as advocates, and not entitled to exploit ambiguities or loopholes in existing laws—at least not without very clearly signaling that they are doing so. Moreover, lawyers in these capacities must not conceal inconvenient material facts, must not uncritically accept facially implausible assertions of fact from their client's agents, and must inquire when a reasonable attorney would suspect material lies or violations of law and try to correct them.

Second, there should be effective institutionalization of and support for the counselor's role, incentives to perform it, and sanctions for breaches. As I picture things counselors, like lawyers, would be largely self-regulating, but with more effective monitoring and sanctions than most lawyers currently face. Counselors in each specialty (tax, securities, banking, litigation, structured-finance, etc.) would have to develop codes of best practices defining the specifics of the counselor's role for that practice. Then they would have to establish the procedures to inculcate novices into the role, and to monitor performance of it. Some law firms have already set up internal machinery to promulgate and enforce ethical standards; this could be adapted for counselors. Obviously, they would be subject to special regimes of judicial enforcement, civil liability, and malpractice; and, where practicing before agencies such as the SEC or IRS, to administrative discipline. Counselors probably should not be allowed to take equity positions in client companies, or agree to fee arrangements conditioning compensation on results. But they also need incentives to take on the role and perform it faithfully. The most effective incentives would be ones where potential counselors would receive special privileges that would benefit clients—for example, expedited and presumptively favorable regulatory action, less scrutiny and more rapid approval by courts of discovery plans, settlements of class actions, terms of consent decrees, and safe harbors from malpractice or other liability for conscientious good faith advice.

Is this idea for reviving the counselor's role an idle dream? Perhaps it is. But the status quo—a situation in which lawyers effectively facilitate, or passively acquiesce in and enable corporate frauds, in the name of a noble idea of advocacy that has been ludicrously misapplied to the context of corporate advice-giving—is not tolerable. At least some corporate lawyers may wish to revive the ideal of independent counseling which has, until very recent times, been one of the most inspiring regulative ideals of their profession. And even if they do not, a society that wants its corporations to be good citizens, as well as efficient profit-maximizers, may insist on reviving it, or something like it, against their opposition.

* * *

Reprise

You've now encountered in-depth arguments in support of and against the model of the lawyer as the "hired gun," along with suggestions of alternative models. Nonetheless, even if some of the criticisms seem to you to have considerable force and the alternatives have some appeal, there may be other less conscious influences that make you resistant to abandon the hired gun approach. The excerpt below suggests what one of those influences might be.

Kermit Roosevelt, IN THE SHADOW OF THE LAW

(2005)

* * * On the whole, Ryan very much liked being a lawyer. The lifestyle was not quite what he'd expected, not quite what television and movies had promised. There were fewer beautiful clients, mysteriously troubled, to collapse weeping into his arms, and more documents to be sorted and stamped and placed in various files. There was less pacing around the courtroom, wheeling to fire unexpected questions at cowering witnesses, and more solitary research and tedious memo-writing. But there was one thing that television and movies hadn't even hinted at: there was certainty.

As a lawyer, Ryan was realizing, as a litigator, you had a license to say anything. You're not responsible. In a way it was like being crazy, being given a free pass for whatever came out of your mouth, but it was better, because people didn't try to pretend you weren't in the room or lock you away in an attic. Instead they praised you for zealous advocacy, for doing your duty to the client. Duty to the client made things wonderfully clear. Is a promise enforceable if made in gratitude for a benefit already conferred? That was the sort of question professors had tortured him with in law school, and the answer was always that it depended on a maddeningly complex set of factors. But once you were out of law school, it depended only on one thing: what outcome favored the client. That was the answer you were duty-bound to give, and no one could reproach you for it.

This gave him a confidence and clarity he wished he could bring other areas of his life. Duty to the client propelled him ever forward. Argue as forcefully as you can, it told him; never doubt. And if you're judged wrong in the end, your arguments broken and thrown back in your face, you just say: we caught a bad break with the judge. We're considering an appeal. You never have to admit that you're wrong, and if other people think you are, they also have to concede that you're supposed to be wrong—supposed to be a zealous advocate, supposed to be occasionally on the far side of the accurate. Law is the license to be always in the right, Ryan thought; law means never having to say you're sorry. Things were much simpler when you didn't have to worry about the truth.

Chapter 3

WHO IS THE CLIENT?

What does it mean to say that a lawyer represents a corporation or another business organization? A corporation includes a variety of constituents–employees, shareholders, executives, directors, and subsidiaries, to name a few–but itself is a legal fiction. Representing such an abstraction poses distinctive challenges for a lawyer, especially when these constituencies are at odds with one another.

The issue of who speaks for the client recurs in the representation of corporations and other business entities, and we will examine it in more detail in other chapters in contexts such as internal investigations, close corporations, regulatory compliance, and shareholder derivative litigation. This chapter, however, is intended to expose you to the general contours of the issue and to frameworks that might be used to analyze it.

OVERVIEW OF THE CHAPTER

The chapter begins with a short excerpt from Ralph Jonas, which vividly expresses the anomalies involved in representing a corporation. As Jonas observes, lawyers serve at the pleasure of individuals who are not formally their clients, and they owe no duty to the shareholders who supposedly own the entity.

You should read carefully the longer excerpt from William Simon that follows, which suggests that there are at least three general approaches to determining to whom the corporate lawyer should look for guidance and instruction. The first is what he calls the Control Group approach. This directs the lawyer to defer to the persons who hold positions of authority in the corporation. Such an approach closely mirrors day-to-day practice, in which the lawyer typically deals with these officials on corporate matters. It is natural for the lawyer to identify these persons effectively as speaking for the corporate entity that is her formal client.

Simon calls the second theory the Authority Structure approach. This looks for guidance to those corporate officials who are acting in accordance with duly granted authority within the company. By contrast, the Control Group approach defers to those in authority without regard to any allegations of lack of authority or breach of duty. Simon suggests that the Authority Structure principle appears to correspond to ABA Model Rule of Professional Conduct 1.13, which says that the lawyer for an organization represents "the organization acting through its duly authorized constituents." He argues that this approach is problematic when the corporation's highest authority has a serious conflict, and when officials take duly authorized action that nonetheless violates substantive rights of constituents.

A Framework of Dealing approach, argues Simon, recognizes that officials may act in accordance with prescribed decision-making procedures but still breach their fiduciary duties. He asserts that the corporation is constituted by a background framework that expresses the expectations of various constituents that they will be treated fairly vis-à-vis one another. On occasion, he suggests, a lawyer will need to determine which constituent's claim best reflects this fundamental understanding. In such cases, it is this constituent that most legitimately speaks on behalf of the corporation. When the lawyer cannot make such a judgment, she should remain neutral among the contending parties.

Ask yourself if you find persuasive Simon's typology of when each approach is most appropriate. Are lawyers in a position to make the kinds of judgments that are necessary to choose among these approaches? Is it appropriate for the lawyer to pass judgment on the substantive merits of various constituents' claims before deciding who speaks for the corporation? Should there be any presumptions that the control group is acting in accordance with it authority, or that duty authorized officials are taking the position that is most justified? Do you agree with how Simon argues that his Founder Freeze–Out problem should be analyzed?

The final excerpt in the chapter is an American Bar Association Opinion that establishes the presumption that a lawyer for a partnership represents the partnership as an entity rather than any of its individual partners. Is this a realistic approach in all circumstances, or are there situations in which individuals should be able reasonably to assume that the lawyer represents them personally? That is, should we treat partnerships just as we do corporations? Notice the complications that the Opinion points out can arise if the lawyer does undertake to represent both the partnership and its individual partners.

Finally, the Problem at the end of the chapter presents a case of potential, but not actual, conflict among constituents of the corporation. It asks that you consider each of the approaches that Simon has identified and discuss which is best suited to provide guidance to the lawyer in this situation.

MODEL RULES: 1.4, 1.6, 1.7, 1.13

Ralph Jonas, WHO IS THE CLIENT?: THE CORPORATE LAWYER'S DILEMMA

39 HASTINGS L.J. 617 (1988)

It is axiomatic that a corporation is a distinct, discrete legal entity that exists separate and apart from its officers, agents, directors, and shareholders. It is almost equally axiomatic that a lawyer who is retained to represent a corporation owes his allegiance solely to that legal entity, and not to the corporation's officers, directors, and shareholders.

These simple predicates, however, mask a morass * * * A corporation is a legal fiction. Its independent existence has been created out of statutory "whole cloth." Only by reason of legislative fiat has this "entity" been separated from its owners and its managers.

Therefore, we have the perverse situation in which the lawyer who represents a publicly held corporation is selected and retained by, and reports to and may be fired by, the principal officers and directors of the corporation—*who are not his clients.* Moreover, the shareholders of a corporation, who, collectively, are the owners of the mythical beast, typically do not participate in the process by which the lawyer is selected, retained, or fired. Furthermore, the attorney who represents the corporation does not consult nor owe any duty or allegiance of any kind whatsoever to the shareholders.

The arguments underlying this seemingly preposterous result appear very straightforward:

    A.   A corporation is separate and distinct from its shareholders, directors, and officers and has an independent existence.

    B.   The legal and economic interests of a large, diverse group of shareholders may be internally adversarial.

    C.   The legal and economic interests of one or more groups of shareholders may conflict with the best interests of the corporation, when that entity is looked upon as a discrete, independent entity having a perpetual life of its own.

    D.   The officers of a publicly held corporation may have legal and economic interests directly adverse to the corporate entity which employs them.

    E.   The directors, although selected by the corporation's shareholders, may have legal and economic interests adverse to and conflicting with both the shareholders (or one or more groups of shareholders) and the corporation.

* * * [I]n the corporate arena, the lawyer [thus] lives in an "Alice in Wonderland" world. The client to which he owes undivided loyalty, fealty, and allegiance cannot speak to him except through voices that may have interests adverse to his client. He is hired and may be fired by people who may or may not have interests diametrically opposed to those of his client. And finally, his client is itself an illusion—a fictional

"person" that exists or expires at the whim of its shareholders, whom the lawyer does not represent.

It is not surprising, therefore, that to a great extent lawyers simply do not concern themselves with these ethical considerations, or if they do, become so frustrated in their application that they throw up their hands in despair. In the main, the Bar seems to position itself so as to avoid criticism or claims of unethical conduct by "papering" its position with the requisite legal formalities. The substance of the problem, however, remains untouched and untreated. Similarly, the Bench gives the lawyer little guidance in this area. The limited number of cases that refer to the issues pretend that corporate clients have a reality separate and apart from a corporation's officers, directors, and shareholders and should be treated as "natural persons" for purpose of the lawyer's ethical standards.

Thus, illusion appears to have overcome reality.

William H. Simon, Whom (Or What) Does the Organization's Lawyer Represent?: An Anatomy of Intraclient Conflict

91 Calif. L. Rev. 57 (2003)

* * *

A large fraction of the bar spends its time representing organizations. The law tends to characterize these organizations as unitary "entities" or "legal persons" and to suggest that lawyers' duties to such clients are analogous to their duties to individual clients. In fact, however, these organizations consist of multiple individuals with potentially differing interests, and hence they are prone to internal conflicts that do not arise in individual representation.

For most of the bar's history, there was little discussion of such conflicts, but a substantial body of authority has emerged in recent years applying both substantive corporate law doctrine and professional responsibility norms to lawyers in situations of what might be called "intraclient" conflict. For the most part, this authority responds to three broad categories of claims:

> (1) Breach of Duty: The lawyer is charged with breach of duty, as a matter of either professional discipline or tort liability, for assisting or acquiescing in conduct by some organizational constituents that allegedly wrongfully injures others.

> (2) Disqualification: Either the organization or a constituent argues that the lawyer is subject to disqualification on conflict-of-interest grounds.

> (3) Privileged Communications: An organizational constituent alleging management wrongdoing seeks access to privileged communications between management and counsel.

Doctrinal responses to these claims have been incoherent and implausible. This Article offers some suggestions to clarify thinking about organizational representation and some specific solutions for current controversies. It criticizes a common tendency to invoke the idea of entity representation in an unreflective and question-begging way. Often the interests of the organization are conflated with those of management. A more sophisticated approach, exemplified by the ABA Model Rules of Professional Conduct ("Model Rules") and the Restatement of the Law Governing Lawyers ("Restatement"), treats the organization as a structure of authority. Even this approach is inadequate in many situations, however. This Article argues that a satisfactory approach would understand the corporation as a "Framework of Dealing," a set of procedural and substantive terms grounded in the understandings of the organization's constituents and supplemented by publicly provided default and mandatory terms. These terms generate convergent expectations that make it possible to treat the organization as a unitary client.

... I begin with a hypothetical to illustrate the issues. It uses a close corporation because the problems with present doctrine are most visible in this context, but I will later suggest that the analysis developed in response to this situation also applies to larger organizations.

* * *

The Founder Freeze–Out

Founder, the principal entrepreneur and technical spirit of Hi–Tech, Inc., is an engineer who developed a new gizmo—a critical component of various electronics products. Shortly after Founder set up the corporation, Investor, a venture-capital partnership, became a major shareholder. Investor owns preferred stock, and under relevant terms of the Articles of Incorporation, it is entitled to take control of the board of directors ("board") if specified financial milestones are not met, including one regarding revenues.

Product development and marketing have exceeded expectations, but the enterprise encountered unanticipated production problems. Soon thereafter, Investor asserted that the revenue milestone had not been met, and with Founder's acquiescence, assumed control. The Investor-controlled board then informed Founder that his services as an employee were no longer needed by the firm. The board exercised the firm's option to repurchase Founder's stock on his departure from the firm. Half of these shares were unvested and hence were subject to repurchase at the price Founder paid for them, which was a small fraction of their market value. At the next shareholder meeting, Founder was replaced as a director.

One of the Investor directors has told Hi–Tech's corporate counsel that, according to the firm's accountant, the claim that the milestone has not been met—the basis for Investor's assumption of control of the board—rests on a debatable accounting judgment (about, say, when orders should be booked). "It could have gone either way," the accountant said. Founder is unaware of the accountant's view, and neither the accountant nor the directors have any intention of telling him of it. What should corporate counsel do?

The position most strongly supported by judicial authority is probably that counsel has no duty to inform Founder and may have an affirmative duty not to do so. There is also ample support for the proposition that counsel may represent the corporation in litigation against Founder over his separation. And there is authority that the board will be able to invoke attorney-client privilege to preclude Founder from deposing counsel in subsequent litigation. As we will see, there is also differing authority with respect to each of these issues, and indeed the last position on attorney-client privilege appears to be a minority one. But few cases or commentators have confronted the flawed logic that pervades this body of doctrine.

The holdings against the shareholder usually are supported with the claim that corporate counsel represents the corporation, not its constituents. This precept is typically invoked without elaboration as if it were sufficient on its face to dispose of the shareholders' claim. In fact, this precept merely raises the question of what the corporation's interests are in the circumstances of the case.

* * * Most lawyers think it uncontroversial that corporate counsel can represent the corporation in a dispute with a constituent such as Founder, assuming that she has never represented him individually. If the only client has been the corporation, then Founder is neither a present nor a former client, and there is no conflict that might disqualify.

This analysis * * * it assumes that representing the corporation is fundamentally different than representing Founder when Founder is its only shareholder (prior to Investor's investment). Lawyers representing start-up companies looking for venture financing routinely ask the founders to sign letters acknowledging that counsel represents the corporation and not the founders individually and suggesting that the founders consider seeking separate individual representation. In fact, the founders never seek separate representation, and were they to do so, no one has any idea what the additional lawyer would do. At this stage, it seems impossible to draw any distinction between individual and corporate interests. Lawyers' insistence on the distinction seems to serve little purpose other than to preserve their ability to align themselves against the founders should a dispute arise after the outside investment.

* * *

III.   *Entity Representation I: The Organization as Control Group*

The first interpretation of entity representation conflates the corporation with those who have de facto control of it and the corporation's interests with the interests of the control group. The control group will usually be the group of officers or inside directors with whom the lawyer routinely deals.

The "Control Group" view gives definite answers to most of the questions raised by the Founder Freeze–Out scenario. After Founder has been squeezed out, Investor is in control. Investor's interests become the corporation's interests. It is in Investor's interests for the lawyer to defend against any claims Founder might make, so the lawyer is not disqualified. It is against Investor's interests for Founder to find out about the accountant's statements, so confidentiality forbids disclosure. And the Investor-controlled board can invoke the attorney-client privilege against Founder.

A case that comes close to explicit espousal of the Control Group model is Bell v. Clark, in which the Indiana Supreme Court held that a lawyer for a limited partnership had no duty to inform limited partners of wrongdoing by the general partner. The court held that a partnership lawyer is answerable only to the partners who have managerial authority:

> "To the extent that a partnership agreement places responsibility for the management of the partnership in the hands of less than all the partners, those partners to whom management responsibilities have been given become the "duly authorized constituents' [entitled to instruct the lawyer]."

Since both the agreement and the statute gave managerial responsibility to the general partner, the lawyer was answerable only to him. The opinion is indifferent to the fact that the general partner allegedly violated limitations on his conduct imposed by both the agreement and the statute. Its use of "authorized" is thus a term of art. According to this view, holding office, rather than authority, characterizes the organization.

This view is grounded in powerful psychological forces. An organizational lawyer can only deal with her client through agents. If she has recurring dealings with particular agents, she is likely to develop personal relations with them * * * Other corporate constituents are faceless and silent. Relations with particular managers will be the most concrete, vivid, and emotionally engaging dimension of the lawyer's work for the client. There is thus a natural psychological tendency to identify the client with these personal relations.

This psychological disposition is reinforced by other factors. If the managers are senior officers, they will have broad authority over corporate affairs, so the psychological identification substantially overlaps the legal one. More than likely, these officers will have chosen to employ the lawyer and will make decisions about her future employment. Self-interest encourages the lawyer to identify these officers as the entity. Finally, professional responsibility rhetoric tends to speak of clients as persons and, even when it distinguishes organizational clients, to speak of them as unitary entities, thus obscuring possible conflict.

This tendency is also reinforced by the fact that personifying the corporation in terms of its agents is a useful cognitive and legal device across a broad range of situations in which the lawyers assist managers in dealing with outsiders on behalf of the corporation. In these situations, the legal fiction that treats the corporation as a unified, organic entity rests in part on the shared interest of its constituents in enhancing its value. There is good reason to presume in this situation that those in control will act on behalf of this interest * * * [W]here there is no manifest disagreement and no apparent conflict of interest, it is reasonable to presume that those in control are serving the shared interest.

* * * However, the grounds for the identification erode when the managers are dealing, not with an outsider on behalf of an apparently unified group of constituents, but with or on behalf of insiders in situations of conflict. Managerial self-interest is less likely here to coincide with legitimate constituent interests.

In the intracorporate situation, the Control Group perspective is subject to the obvious objection that it confuses power with right. It is unreasonable to view the interests of those with de facto control as those of the corporation without regard to how they attained control or how they are using it.

... There may, however, be a range of situations involving conflict where the application of something like the Control Group principle would be supportable. Perhaps the most important candidates involve control contests in public corporations—either proxy battles or hostile tender offers. Corporate counsel routinely assists managers in fighting proxy challenges and hostile takeovers. It seems to be taken for granted that such practice serves legitimate corporate interests. It is just as commonly assumed that it would be improper for corporate counsel to assist the challenger, even if she felt that the corporation would be better off if the challenge succeeded * * *

The promanagement default position might be grounded on a corporate law presumption that continuity of management serves corporate interests. * * *

The pro-management policy has limits, however. If a presumption is warranted, it has to be a rebuttable one. First, it is routinely conceded that counsel must not assist where management is pursuing a course that is plainly unlawful. This is not a demanding standard in the control contest area, however, where standards are vague and management has a good deal of discretion. Second, substantial authority requires that corporate counsel remain neutral in some derivative suits. Where the individual defendants include incumbent officers, joint representation is deemed permissible in the early stages of the suit, while the nature of the claims is explored, or where the claims seem patently without merit. In other situations, however, courts have insisted on separate representation ... [C]ourts [often] insist that corporate counsel represent the corporation and that they remain neutral or "passive" toward the derivative officers. * * *

What differentiates many proxy or acquisition contests from derivative suits is that the latter necessarily involves a specific allegation of breach of fiduciary duty on the part of management. Where such an allegation is not patently without merit, it suffices to overcome the promanagement presumption.

A harder case arises in situations like the Founder Freeze–Out example, where the breach is not clear, and there has been no constituent claim, but there probably would be a claim if material information were available to an affected constituent. If Founder knew the accountant's statement, he likely would make a claim. If the claim were nonfrivolous, it might be desirable from the point of view of the organization as a whole for it to be asserted, since it would trigger a more reliable process for the resolution of the issue than would otherwise occur. Current management has a strong and specific conflict of interest here, so it makes no sense to accord them the benefit of any presumption.

Some kind of pro-Control Group presumption may help explain why corporate counsel has broad latitude to assist incumbent management in control disputes, but the presumption is only plausible if subject to strong limits. Those limits will have to be supplied by principles of authority and fiduciary duty. These form the basis of the second and third interpretations of the entity idea * * *

IV. Entity Representation II: The Organization as Authority Structure

The second perspective equates the corporation with its authority structure. One way in which a formal organization differs from a collection of individuals is that its constituents have adopted arrangements for allocating power and making decisions. Thus, we could say that the lawyer's duty is to this structure.

A. Model Rule 1.13

ABA Model Rule 1.13 seems to adopt the Authority Structure perspective in providing that "[a] lawyer employed or retained by an organization represents the organization acting through its duly authorized constituents." Control is not enough; authority is the touchstone. * * *

* * *

B. Beyond the Board?

* * * In corporations, [the highest authority] is usually the board. Many lawyers tend to conflate the authority structure with the board and operate on the general principle that, when they encounter intracorporate conflict, they should look to the board for instruction. This can be a useful presumption, but it is not categorically valid. As the rule's comments acknowledge, "applicable law may prescribe that under certain conditions highest authority reposes elsewhere." The comments mention as an example that special responsibility for some corporate decisions is conferred on independent directors.

Curiously, the comments do not mention shareholders as potentially the "highest authority," although they have responsibility for some important decisions. The question thus arises whether the "highest authority" should include shareholders when the relevant course of conduct could only be authorized by shareholders.

We might * * * elaborate on the Authority Structure principle by suggesting that, where no one with authority is available to instruct the lawyer, her job is to facilitate the processes of authoritative decision. This would usually entail providing information likely to prompt them to trigger the relevant processes to key participants.

This approach would be more difficult to apply with large publicly held corporations, where informing shareholders would often be tantamount to public disclosure. There might be important corporate interests that would weigh against this. Perhaps the information would trigger government prosecution or damage suits by private outsiders or give some advantage to competitors. Yet, even with public corporations, going to shareholders may be an appropriate course * * *

C. Limits of the Authority Structure Perspective

* * * In general, cases where all or most of the board has a serious conflict will pose difficulties under the Authority Structure principle. The authority of a board in this situation is often ambiguous. A decision by an interested board is usually voidable on the complaint of shareholders unless either ratified by shareholders after full disclosure or proven "fair." Suppose, however, that management does not seek ratification by the board, and the shareholders do not have enough information to complain. Is such a decision "authorized"? The decision is not clearly unauthorized, at least it is not per se ultra vires. Moreover, the statutes do not require shareholder authorization; they simply make that one mode of authorization. The transaction is also legitimate if it is "fair," but here authority depends not on procedures, but on the substantive merits of the decision. It seems likely that in some situations of this type it would be desirable for managers to make disclosures to shareholders. The reasons for this, however, are not fully captured by the Authority Structure idea.

If the Authority Structure perspective is ambiguous where the dispute is about authority, it is incomplete in circumstances where an act that seems procedurally authorized arguably violates substantive rights. An important category of cases involves constituents without control rights. Minority shareholders, for example, often lack both board representation and veto rights in a shareholder vote. Nevertheless, they have a right to fair treatment by the corporation and the board.

If nonshareholders are considered corporate constituents, then some of their claims would also not be reached. Internal-control rights are presumptively accorded to shareholders, but some argue that nonshareholder groups such as creditors or workers or local communities should be considered corporate constituencies to which substantive duties are owed. To the extent that procedural norms do not provide control rights parallel to these substantive ones, the Authority Structure approach does not reach them.

V. Entity Representation III: the Organization as Framework of Dealing

A. Introduction

The third understanding of entity representation identifies the corporation with its entire legal framework, including norms about both authority and substantive norms. The corporation derives its unity from a legal structure designed to reconcile the interests of its constituents. The Authority Structure is only part of the full legal structure. In particular, it omits much of the range of fiduciary duties. Understood in terms of its full legal structure, the corporation's identity includes, in addition to a set of decision-making procedures, a substantive commitment that its constituents be treated fairly. Thus, a corporation has an interest in the fair treatment of its constituents.

The Framework of Dealing and Authority Structure approaches overlap and will often lead to the same result. Where a particular issue is clearly committed to the discretion of a particular constituent or body within the corporation (such as the board), both approaches counsel deference to that constituent. But the Framework of Dealing approach suggests that the lawyer's responsibilities sometimes turn on substantive norms.

For example, in the Founder Freeze–Out scenario, the lawyer might resolve the conflict-of-interest issue by aligning herself with the constituent who had the more meritorious claim. If Founder's claim is valid, the lawyer should represent him; if not, she should continue to represent the incumbent board. Her goal in either case is to represent the corporation. She decides which among the competing claimants speaks for the corporation by determining which claim is most consistent with the Framework of Dealing.

Similar considerations might bear on confidentiality. If the board's substantive position is consistent with the Framework of Dealing, its claim to control the attorney-client privilege is strong. If not, the attorney might feel obliged to make her own judgment as to whether confidentiality is in the corporation's interest. The same applies to fiduciary duties. The lawyer's duties to the corporation should extend to a constituent who has a claim well grounded in the Framework of Dealing. If Founder's claim is valid, and disclosure of the accountant's statement to him will facilitate its assertion, then this approach supports a duty to disclose.

Of course, in many, perhaps even most, situations, the lawyer will not be able to determine reliably the substantive merits. In these circumstances, the Framework of Dealing approach favors neutrality. With respect to the conflict-of-interest issue, this means that the lawyer cannot speak for any of the disputing constituents. She must withdraw * * * The Framework of Dealing approach requires withdrawal because the client's interests cannot be determined. If the lawyer cannot determine the organization's interests, then the premise of treating its constituents as a unity is absent.

With respect to confidentiality, neutrality implies no confidentiality as among constituents. If it is not apparent which constituent speaks on behalf of the corporation, then none of them are in a position to invoke confidentiality against the others. With respect to fiduciary duties, neutrality implies no active duties to constituents, including the board, except for ongoing duties of confidentiality vis-a-vis outsiders, and fiduciary duties to protect undisputed corporate interests would continue. Neutrality applies only to the intracorporate dispute.

* * * The Framework of Dealing perspective thus adopts the best theoretical understanding of why the law speaks of the organization as an entity. This does not necessarily mean, however, that it has value as a practical guide to professional responsibility decisions. Some will be disturbed by the notion that the lawyer has responsibility for determining the merits of an intracorporate dispute. Some will think she will so seldom be able to make such a judgment that the approach will require neutrality too often. In fact, however, something like the Framework of Dealing approach seems already presumed by current doctrine in a variety of situations, and it seems to be workable in these and other situations.

B. Jurisprudential Basis

1. The Framework of Dealing

The Framework of Dealing approach provides the most plausible understanding of the "corporation," or more generally, "organization," as we conventionally personify it in legal discourse. The starting point is the recognition that the corporation is a legal fiction. It has no psychology of its own and no moral status of its own. Thus, it cannot have interests of its own. We use the fiction as convenient proxy for the interests of its constituents. We may regard these constituent interests as forming a whole that transcends its parts (an "entity" rather than an "aggregate"), but it remains the case that a corporation's interests are entirely dependent on those of its constituents.

Thus, it makes no sense to speak of corporate interests that are unrelated or contrary to shared constituent interests. Courts are mistaken, for example, when they say, in characterizing actions to compel dissolution as direct rather than derivative, that "an action for dissolution of a corporation cannot possibly benefit the corporation." If a corporation were a natural person, the analogy to dissolution would be suicide, which one might plausibly think is never, or virtually never, in a natural person's interest. But when we think about organizations this way, we have lost our moorings. The only meaningful benefit a corporation can produce is for people, and there are many situations in which the relevant people might benefit from dissolution (notably, shareholders will benefit when there are significant assets but no going concern value). It makes as much sense to speak of a corporation benefiting from dissolution as it does to speak of a corporation benefiting from a tax refund. In both cases, the corporation stands as a proxy for interests of its human constituents.

The second point is that, when we reify or personify the corporation, it is usually to segregate a particular subclass of the interests associated with it. These are the interests associated with ownership. In the business corporation, ownership claims are associated with the provision of capital, but there may be other bases through which shareholders acquire ownership (and in some other organizational forms, such as charitable nonprofits or cooperatives, capital supply is usually not a basis for ownership claims). The critical distinction—the one that motivates organizational personification—is between residual claims and ordinary contract claims. Ownership claims are residual. Residual claims and ordinary contract claims can be either for financial or control rights. In the business corporation, residual financial claims tend to go with (but do not always coincide with) residual control claims.

Residual claims tend to be less specified than ordinary contract claims. Ordinary contract is more likely to specify a fixed return, a defined performance, or a set of particular protective covenants. But the critical distinction is that residual claims are secondary or "junior" to contract claims. This does not mean that they are less important. It means that scope can be defined only after ordinary contract duties have been delineated. The residual rights apply to what is left over (control or economic surplus) after ordinary contract claims have been given their due.

The personified corporation is a proxy for these residual claims. We tend to speak of these residual claims as "fiduciary" and to contrast them to "contract" claims. Residual claims by their nature are harder to specify. Moreover, residual claims typically entail both greater risk and greater possibility of exceptional gain, and both possibilities lead those who hold such claims to look for greater trust in their collaborators than the law provides for arm's length contract relations. Thus, fiduciary or residual-claim duties often require more initiative in pursuing shared ends, more forbearance in pursuing selfish ends, and more candor than ordinary contract duties * * *

2.   The Importance of Distributive Norms

The residual-claim contract that constitutes the corporation as an entity is a Framework of Dealing. It consists of both procedural and substantive norms. It includes specific negotiated terms, implied agreed terms, and background default and mandatory terms supplied by law. These terms appear in a variety of sources, including articles, bylaws, contracts, statutes, and cases.

One further distinction that can be made among the norms of the Framework of Dealing is between allocative and distributive norms. Allocative norms concern the pursuit of aggregate benefits. The ultimate allocative norm is "maximize constituent welfare," but there are a variety of subnorms that may specify the meaning of such welfare (for example, short term or long term) and the means that can be used to attain it (for example, levels of risk, lines of business). The other type of norm is distributive. Distributive norms specify how control and financial benefits in the firm are divided among constituents.

It is easy to think of the allocative interests of constituents as converging on a continuing basis. As long as distributive norms give each constituent a fraction of the corporation's net assets and income, all share an interest in maximizing these assets and income * * * At the time the constituents join together (or a later-arriving constituent joins an established organization) the distributive norms make collaboration possible. As the collaboration proceeds, a constituent will have an interest in getting a larger share than she bargained for, but like ordinary contracts, the organizational Framework of Dealing is designed both to resolve conflict and to preserve the integrity of the general organizational structure by holding constituents to their distributive commitments * * *

Virtually all intracorporate disputes are distributive. This is literally true in the sense that the distribution of control is always at issue in a dispute among corporate constituents. It is virtually true in the sense that nearly all tenacious disputes involve economic conflicts of interest. Corporate disagreements rarely become disputes and almost never reach the courts when they are simply matters of disinterested differences of opinion over how to maximize aggregate benefits to residual claimants.

From the perspective of both client and lawyer, the organization can only be regarded as a unity if it appears to reconcile the interests of its participants. No one would become a corporate constituent if he did not envision arrangements that promised both an aggregate return to the group and a fair share of it for him. Professional responsibility doctrine could not permit simultaneous representation of the constituents if there were not some set of norms under which collaboration would be mutually beneficial. From both perspectives, the distinction between allocative and distributive norms is unimportant. Both are fundamental to the Framework of Dealing that constitutes the organization.

It is dangerous to think of this framework as a contract because the word connotes arm's length relations and literalistic interpretations that are inappropriate here. But the techniques through which the framework of dealing is elaborated and applied are contractual * * *

Conventional doctrine, in a largely tacit and unreflective way, treats the corporation as a set of norms that promote a collaborative effort to maximize joint gains but invite a Hobbesian free-for-all with respect to how they are divided. In fact, distributive norms are just as fundamental and integral as allocative ones to the coherence and viability of the organization.

* * *

VI. The Entity Approach Summarized and Compared

A. An Integrated Entity Approach

It is possible, but not defensible, to apply either the Control Group or the Authority Structure models alone as a comprehensive guide to the responsibilities of the organizational lawyer. The Framework of Dealing approach, however, presupposes both of them.

The Control Group view contributes a presumption that senior management and the board represent the organization. It is based in part on management's authority to make ordinary business decisions and the board's authority to make policy decisions. (To this extent, it overlaps the authority-structure approach.) It is also based on the fact that across a broad range of decisions, management's incentives are well aligned with those of other constituents, and management is likely to be better informed than any other decisionmaker. This range consists mainly of allocative decisions—those that affect shareholders in equal proportion to their distributive shares. Finally, the presumption is based on the psychological tendency of lawyers to identify the organization with the agents with whom they work, and the fact that this tendency facilitates valuable communication and collaboration.

The Control Group presumption should not be a strong one, however. It clearly should not survive indications that management is violating authority or fiduciary norms. Moreover, it should not apply in situations involving distributive issues where management might have a conflict of interest. This includes situations of actual constituent conflict as well as situations of potential constituent conflict, in particular, situations in which it seems likely that there would be conflict if material information not available to constituents were provided to them.

Where the Control Group presumption is not dispositive, attention should shift to procedural norms, the focus of the Authority Structure perspective. The lawyer asks to which agents the corporate legal structure confers ultimate responsibility over the issue. Where the lawyer has substantial doubts that a particular course of corporate conduct is in the interest of the organization, and the conduct has not received informed consideration by the agents with ultimate authority, the lawyer ought not to assume that those engaged in the conduct speak for the corporation. In this instance, the lawyer should facilitate review by the agents with authority. In the most common case, this would involve urging management to seek board authority. In a more extreme case, it would involve bypassing management and going to the board. A still more extreme course would be to make direct contact with shareholder constituencies and, at the limit, with public authorities.

Where authority is ambiguous or disputed, the authority-structure perspective implies that the lawyer ought to try to facilitate clarification of it. This would most commonly mean assuring that all the relevant constituents have material information. It would be consistent with this principle, for example, for counsel representing the corporation in a derivative suit to oversee the corporation's response to discovery requests with a view toward insuring the availability of material information. (Whether it is realistic to expect counsel to do this in a manner independent of incumbent management is another question.)

Some cases require that analysis proceed beyond authority considerations. Although perhaps not often, it will sometimes happen that the lawyer can say confidently that the decision of the highest authority violates an important duty. Clear violations will most likely occur when the duty protects interests that are not represented in the authority structure—for example, minority shareholders or creditors. In such circumstances, the lawyer has to make a substantive judgment about the corporation's interests and responsibilities. Disclosure to the affected constituent or a public authority might be the most plausible remedy.

With respect to conflicts, in intracorporate disputes where the lawyer cannot confidently make a judgment on the merits, the Framework of Dealing approach implies that neutrality is appropriate. On the other hand, in situations where the lawyer can make such a decision, she probably should be authorized to take sides with the meritorious claim, whether management or dissident. Current doctrine already provides this option in derivative suits with frivolous plaintiff's claims. It may be that an apparent lack of merit that does not rise (descend) to frivolousness should be sufficient. In any event, the doctrine should be symmetrical so that lawyers can ally with dissidents when their claims are strong. To be sure, it may be hard to police the reasonableness and good faith of lawyers' judgments of merit, but there is no reason to think that lawyers are more likely to be wrong when they side with dissidents than when they stick with management.

As for attorney-client privilege, the current Garner rule seems well adapted to the Framework of Dealing perspective. It defines the scope of confidentiality in terms of an assessment of organizational interests of exactly the sort that this perspective recommends.

Finally, where the lawyer has dealings regarding corporate matters outside the Authority Structure, the Framework of Dealing perspective prescribes duties of disclosure and fair dealing to constituents. These duties are consistent with specific prescriptions of current doctrine, for example, the insider-trading prohibitions of the securities laws, but the Framework of Dealing view provides a better explanation of these prescriptions than do the alternative models of organizational representation.

* * *

Conclusion

How can we treat separate individuals with both common and conflicting interests as a unity—a single "client"—for the purposes of representation? The only plausible answer is that these individuals have adopted or developed, explicitly or implicitly, a structure that reconciles their differing interests and facilitates potential mutually beneficial collaboration. If this is the answer, then the lawyer's professional responsibilities should be defined in relation to this structure.

Conventional doctrine is excessively preoccupied with formality. It tends to assume that such a structure exists just because legal formalities of organization have been satisfied, and it often ignores that such structures are present in relations without formal organization. It draws elaborate and often implausible inferences from the fact of formal organization * * *

Once conventional doctrine identifies a client as an "entity," it tends to either ignore its normative structure for purposes of ethical decision making or to focus on only part of it. The Control Group approach ignores the structure; the Authority Structure looks at just part of it.

This Article has argued that the focus of ethical analysis should be, not on formality, but on the normative structure of the collaborative relationships * * * When there is a sufficiently rich structure—a Framework of Dealing—she should define her professional responsibilities in terms of this structure. She should look first to its authority norms, and in many situations, she will not need to look farther. But authority norms will not resolve all cases. Substantive fiduciary norms form an important part of the Framework of Dealing. Where authority norms are indeterminate, or where they are in conflict with fiduciary norms, the lawyer needs to look also to the substantive norms in defining her obligations.

AMERICAN BAR ASSOCIATION STANDING COMMITTEE ON ETHICS AND PROFESSIONAL RESPONSIBILITY, FORMAL OPINION NO. 91–361

REPRESENTATION OF A PARTNERSHIP

A partnership is an organization within the meaning of Rule 1.13. Generally, a lawyer who represents a partnership represents the entity rather than the individual partners. Confidential information received by the lawyer while representing the partnership is "information relating to the representation" of the partnership that normally may not be withheld from the individual partners.

The question has been raised whether partnerships are "organizations" within the meaning of Rule 1.13, ABA Model Rules of Professional Conduct, so that a lawyer who represents a partnership represents the entity rather than the individual partners. Two related questions frequently arise: (1) When does a partnership's lawyer have an attorney-client relationship with an individual partner? (2) Under what circumstances does information received by the partnership's lawyer from an individual partner constitute "information relating to representation" of the partnership within the meaning of Rule 1.6(a) so as to give the partnership a right of access to that information; and conversely, to what extent is each partner entitled to know whatever information has been conveyed on the partnership's behalf to the partnership's lawyer?

The pertinent provision of the Model Rules with respect to representation of an entity is Rule 1.13(a):

(a) A lawyer employed or retained by an organization represents the organization acting through its duly authorized constituents. * * *

The entity concept upon which Rule 1.13 is based, broadly stated, rests on two notions. The first is that an organization of persons, often in corporate form, is a separate jural entity having distinct rights and duties and capable, among other things, of entering into contracts and either bringing suit or being sued in its own name. Second, under the law of agency, a lawyer is an agent of the employing organization and it is the organization, as principal, to which the lawyer is professionally responsible, not its directors, officers, owners or other agents.

Ultimately, the rationale behind the Rule is that an organization will have goals and objectives that may, or may not, be consistent with the goals and objectives of all or some of its members or other constituents. A lawyer ordinarily cannot be expected to represent differing interests, but must exercise fidelity to the person, or entity, that engaged his or her services. However, because a partnership is a unique legal entity, where the individual members comprise the whole, there may be confusion as to which interests the lawyer represents.

There is no logical reason to distinguish partnerships from corporations or other legal entities in determining the client a lawyer represents * * * Both case authority and commentary support the treatment of partnerships as entities separate from their owners.[1]

Accordingly, the Committee is of the opinion that a partnership is an organization within the meaning of Rule 1.13.

Turning to the first of the related questions posed—when does a partnership's lawyer have an attorney-client relationship with an individual partner—the Committee is of the view that a lawyer who represents a partnership represents the entity rather than the individual partners unless the specific circumstances show otherwise. Furthermore, whether a lawyer representing a partnership has an attorney-client relationship with any individual partner depends on the facts of the particular situation, discussed more fully infra. A lawyer who represents a partnership must take care to avoid the creation of an attorney-client

---

1. It should be noted that because the structural organization of limited partnerships, in which only the general partners have managerial responsibility and limited partners are usually passive investors, differs from that of general partnerships, the application of the Model Rules to the two forms of partnership may not be the same in all circumstances. Judicial decisions dealing with the responsibility of an attorney who represents a limited partnership, or its general partner, to the limited partners have not been wholly consistent. One court, interpreting § 10(1)(b) of the Uniform Limited Partnership Act, a provision which gives certain informational rights to limited partners, held that an attorney for a general partner had no duty, in connection with the preparation of an offering memorandum, to disclose to investing limited partners information received from the general partner. Buford White Lumber Co. v. Octagon Properties, Ltd., 740 F.Supp. 1553 (W.D. Okla. 1989). Other cases, however, have held that the attorney for a limited partnership may not withhold information from the limited partners on the basis of attorney-client privilege. McCain v. Phoenix Resources, Inc., 185 Cal.App.3d 575, 230 Cal.Rptr. 25, 26 (1986).

relationship with individual partners unless the lawyer is satisfied that it is ethical to do so and intends to create such a relationship.

Representation of the partnership does not necessarily preclude the representation of individual partners in matters not clearly adverse to the interests of the partnership, nor preempt such an individual representation previously undertaken. However, simultaneous representations of partnerships and of individual partners, even on basically unrelated matters, may result in the lawyer possessing confidences of one client that may not be revealed to another, a circumstance which could effectively prevent continued representation of the other client. See Rule 1.7(a). In such a case the lawyer may have to withdraw from one or both of the representations.

Because Rule 1.13(e) authorizes a lawyer to represent both an organization and one or more of its representatives or owners, the difficulties inherent in multiple representation are close to the surface for a lawyer who undertakes to advise both a partnership and one or more of its partners. Thus, before accepting the representation of one or more partners individually in addition to the partnership, a lawyer should consider whether it would be possible to discharge his or her responsibilities to the partnership under Rule 1.13(b) (requiring disclosure to the entity of acts of individual officer, employee or other agent that may harm the entity), if an individual partner client were to take or contemplate taking action adverse to the partnership.

The lawyer should also consider whether the dual representation may compromise the lawyer's duties of fidelity, candor and independent professional judgment either to the partnership or to the individual partner clients.

Finally, the lawyer should assess whether the dual representation may impair the lawyer's ability to maintain the confidentiality of communications from an individual partner or made on behalf of the partnership.

Because these important issues are sometimes overlooked, lawyers who represent partnerships face serious problems when litigation arises affecting both the partnership and the individual partners. An attorney-client relationship does not automatically come into existence between a partnership lawyer and one or more of its partners.

Whether such a relationship has been created almost always will depend on an analysis of the specific facts involved. The analysis may include such factors as whether the lawyer affirmatively assumed a duty of representation to the individual partner, whether the partner was separately represented by other counsel when the partnership was created or in connection with its affairs, whether the lawyer had represented an individual partner before undertaking to represent the partnership, and whether there was evidence of reliance by the individual partner on the lawyer as his or her separate counsel, or of the partner's expectation of personal representation.

Once the legal nature of the lawyer's relationship, or lack thereof, to the partnership and the individual partners has been determined, Rule 1.13 and its companion rules are readily applied. Where the attorney for a partnership also represents one or more individual partners, explicitly or as a result of the close relationship between the partnership and its members, the obligations and limitations of Rule 1.7 apply, as Rule 1.13(e) expressly recognizes. Thus it is clear, under Rule 1.7(a), that the partnership's attorney could not, without the informed consent of the partnership, represent the interests of one partner against the partnership. It is also clear that, under Rule 1.7(a), the partnership's attorney could not, without the informed consent of both the partnership and all adverse partners, represent the interests of one partner against other partners with respect to a matter involving the partnership's affairs. However, a lawyer undertaking to represent a partnership with respect to a particular matter does not thereby enter into a lawyer-client relationship with each member of the partnership, so as to be barred, for example, by Rule 1.7(a) from representing another client on a matter adverse to one of the partners but unrelated to the partnership affairs.

As to the second related question posed above—in what circumstances may or must information regarding the partnership or individual partners relating to the representation of each be kept confidential from the other—the Committee believes that information received by a lawyer in the course of representing the partnership is "information relating to the representation" of the partnership, and normally may not be withheld from individual partners.

Questions with respect to client confidences under Rule 1.6(a) will often arise when the lawyer for a partnership also represents an individual partner, or a client adverse to the interests of an individual partner * * *

The mandate of Rule 1.6(a), not to reveal confidences of the client, would not prevent the disclosure to other partners of information gained about the client (the partnership) from any individual partner(s). Thus, information thought to have been given in confidence by an individual partner to the attorney for a partnership may have to be disclosed to other partners, particularly if the interests of the individual partner and the partnership, or vis-a-vis the other partners, become antagonistic ...

PROBLEM

You are general counsel of the Financial Affairs Unit of the Waldorf Corporation. Waldorf is interested in generating a greater cash flow, both to meet its revenue projections to analysts and to fund attractive business projects. One way to do so is periodically to sell some of its physical and financial assets to a third party. Waldorf has found this difficult to do on a regular basis, however. First, the company often desires to sell an asset quickly near the end of a quarter in order to meet its revenue target for that quarter. Prospective purchasers, however, often cannot move quickly enough for Waldorf to accomplish this. Second, Waldorf's financial assets consist in large measure of investments in volatile high-tech companies. Purchasers sometimes are reluctant to pay a price that reflects the current share price of these companies because of concerns that the stock later will plummet. In addition, some of the companies in whom Waldorf invests are not publicly traded. Establishing a market price thus requires the use of mathematical models that necessarily contain speculative assumptions.

Bill Brooks, the Waldorf CFO, has proposed to help establish and run investment funds that can serve as purchasers of Waldorf assets. If 3% of the money in these funds comes from investors with no connection to Waldorf, transactions between them and Waldorf will be regarded as conducted at arms-length. This will allow Waldorf to book the results of these sales as revenue and cash flow from operations. Brooks indicates that he will round up the other 97% of the money from himself, his wife's family, and selected persons who are "friendly" to Waldorf. Because he will manage the funds, Brooks maintains that his familiarity with the assets that Waldorf wants to sell will make it possible for the funds to move quickly to purchase assets and avoid wrangling over the purchase price.

Waldorf's by-laws prohibit any Waldorf executive officer from participating in a transaction with the company that produces personal benefits for him or her. The Board of Directors, however, has authority to waive this conflict of interest prohibition if it concludes that doing so is in the best interest of the company. Brooks asks you to prepare material in support of a request for such a waiver. You believe that the arrangement he proposes involves creates significant risks for Waldorf because Brooks will be serving both as company CFO as well as the person who bargains with Waldorf on behalf of the investment funds. This, along with Waldorf's need to make some sales quickly, could result in transactions that unfairly benefit the funds at the expense of the company.

For these reasons, you suggest that the arrangement contain several forms of control and monitoring by Waldorf internal auditors, risk management officers, and the Board. Both Brooks and Waldorf Chief Operating Officer Dan Berlin, however, argue that this would be too complicated and time-consuming. They propose that agents of Waldorf and the investment funds fill out a checklist for each transaction that attests to the fair price of the asset and the inability to find a better deal. These will be submitted to the Chief Risk Officer, who must sign off on them. Brooks and Berlin insist that their business judgment is that this will be sufficient. You disagree with Brooks and Berlin that the controls they plan to suggest to the Board will adequately protect Waldorf. The two men indicate, however, that this is the proposed form of control that they will submit to the Board in connection with the waiver request.

If you have serious misgivings about the waiver proposal in this form, what does the Control Group model that Simon discusses indicate that you should do? The Authority Structure model? The Fair Dealing model? Which approach do you think is most justified?

Suppose that the proposed waiver contains all the controls that you suggest, but that the Board requires only Chief Risk Officer review of the checklist filled out by the agents who negotiated the transaction on behalf of Waldorf and the investment funds. What, if anything, does the Control Group model suggest that you should do? The Authority Structure model? The Fair Dealing model? Which do you think is most justified?

Chapter 4

MORAL ACCOUNTABILITY

As we saw in Chapter 2, there is disagreement about the extent to which lawyers should be exempt from accountability to ordinary moral standards. Whatever one's view on that issue, it raises the question: what does it mean to be morally accountable? If a lawyer is subject to moral criticism for following a legal or ethical rule, what does it matter if there is no sanction for the moral violation?

The answer is that it seems to matter to most people quite a lot. It is striking how tenaciously human beings want to be able to claim that they are acting morally and how much they resist the accusation that they are not. As the recent book *Talk of the Devil* indicates, for instance, former dictators under whom massive atrocities were committed nonetheless steadfastly insist that they were engaged in socially necessary or patriotic endeavors, rather than in wrongdoing.[1] To ignore this powerful human impulse thus is to miss an important component of the lawyer's sense of personal and professional well-being.

Furthermore, for many, perhaps most, people acting morally means more than just following rules. Determining what an ethical rule or a rule of liability permits and prohibits thus may be only a small part of a lawyer's ethical deliberations. Not taking this into account thus risks adopting a narrow and inadequate account of how lawyers identify, confront, and resolve ethical questions. Even those who equate morality with rule compliance must implicitly rely on some theory of why rule compliance in itself is morally praiseworthy.

Finally, we need to look closely at the concept of moral accountability because some may be skeptical in the modern age about the possibility of reasoned argument about moral matters. One potential result of such skepticism is a radical relativism that maintains that morality reduces simply to personal preference if there is no objective scientific basis for moral judgments. If this view is warranted, it effectively prevents us from justifying any evaluation of behavior in moral terms. From this perspective, any sanctions for ostensibly immoral behavior ultimately

1. Riccardo Orizio, Talk of the Devil: Encounters with Seven Dictators (2004).

97

rest only on brute power—a conclusion that has bleak implications for social and political life. This possibility ought to be of particular concern for lawyers, because it undermines the very notion that law serves as a civilized alternative to the war of all against all.

OVERVIEW OF THE CHAPTER

The material in this chapter is designed to explore how we arrive at judgments of moral accountability. It includes two conceptual pieces on moral judgment, an excerpt that addresses the moral accountability of corporate lawyers in particular, and a case that squarely raises the issue of moral accountability apart from legal liability. The Problems then ask you to draw on the material in the chapter to determine if and when you would feel any moral accountability for the actions of your corporate client. This Chapter Overview is longer than others, since we assume that many students will not have as much familiarity with the material in this chapter as they will with the more traditional legal material in the rest of the book.

The excerpt from Deborah Rhode and David Luban discusses what we might call a "top down" approach to moral judgment. That approach begins with a particular moral theory and then attempts to apply it to a particular situation. As they note, probably the two most influential moral theories are consequentialism deontological theory. Consequentialism maintains that the morally superior course of action is the one that maximizes the benefits, and minimizes the costs, to everyone affected by the action. Imagine, for instance, that during World War II I am hiding Anne Frank and her family in my attic. A Nazi soldier knocks on my door and asks if I know the whereabouts of any Jews. We might think that it's wrong to lie, but consequentialism would say that lying is justified under the circumstances. It saves the lives of Anne Frank and her family, while simply denying the Nazis more Jews to send to their deaths. Consequentialism thus seems to tap into a powerful intuition that we must judge the morality of an action not in the abstract, but by the results that it produces.

Consider now a proposal to enslave ten members of exceptional intellectual capacity in order to provide significant benefits to a population of one million. Assume that any plausible calculation reveals that the costs incurred by the ten slaves are vastly outweighed by the benefits that the one million will enjoy. Notwithstanding this calculation, most people would not regard enslavement as morally justified. Why? Implicitly because they accept "deontological" theory, which asserts that some actions are intrinsically right or wrong regardless of their consequences.

Rhode and Luban suggest that each theory seems to capture something of moral importance, but that neither adequately governs all situations. Instead, perhaps we should accept moral pluralism: the idea that the moral concerns in certain areas of experience may be especially amenable to expression in terms of one theory or the other. As you read the excerpt, see if you can think of other examples in which one theory or the other seems especially appropriate.

In contrast to Rhode and Luban, the excerpt from Paul Tremblay discusses what we might call a "bottom up" approach to moral judgment. This is casuistry. It takes its name from the fact that it proceeds by analyzing particular cases, from which it tries to extract tentative moral principles that reflect our judgments about those cases. Our analysis is guided by awareness of "paradigm" cases, which represent situations that elicit general agreement about right or wrong conduct. When we confront a situation, we first ask how close it is to a paradigm case.

Suppose, for instance, that we are asked to judge whether someone should have stopped to rescue a person drowning in a lake. The paradigm case for a duty would be if one person intentionally pushes another into the lake knowing that the latter person can't swim. Do we still find moral accountability for failure to rescue if the person negligently pushed the other into the lake? Probably, on the ground that he bears some responsibility for the other being in the lake. What if the person who refuses to rescue played no part in the other's fall into the lake? We might still find a duty if he could easily rescue the other. What if he couldn't swim? Would that be enough to avoid moral accountability? Or would we say that he is still responsible if he could easily have summoned help?

The factual variations can be almost infinite. The important point is that we determine moral accountability not by consulting consequentialist or deontological theory and then asking how that theory applies to the facts at hand. Rather, we begin with the facts at hand, try to determine how closely those facts resemble the paradigm case, and draw a conclusion based on an assessment of the moral salience of the ways in which the situation differs from the paradigm case. Based on our judgment in the case, we posit a tentative moral principle that we can apply to other cases, always open to the possibility of revising either the principle or our intuitive moral judgments about certain facts.

This process should sound familiar to lawyers. It resembles the development of the common law, which begins with particular cases and reasons from them to more general propositions. By contrast, to oversimplify a bit, moral assessment that begins with a certain moral theory and then applies it to specific cases resembles the application of statutory criteria to a set of facts. The difference in practice is not quite as stark as this, but the contrast helps illuminate what is distinctive about casuistry.

The excerpt from Richard Painter moves from the realm of moral theory to the ground of corporate practice. It asks when lawyers may be held morally responsible for the actions of their corporate clients. The claim that this is never the case, says Painter, assumes that the client determines what objectives it wants to accomplish and the lawyer simply selects the best means to do so. In this situation, as long as the objective is legal, it is the client who bears full moral responsibility for choosing it. In real practice, however, Painter suggests, it is often difficult to make such a distinction. Lawyers influence clients by shaping general desires into specific goals, which the clients may not have considered but for the lawyer's involvement. Furthermore, nowadays corporate lawyers provide advice that draws on both legal and business considerations, and are participants in a collective process of determining a corporation's direction.

Painter argues that moral interdependence is especially pronounced in two instances. The first is when lawyer serve as liaisons between management and other constituencies, such as shareholders, creditors, and employees. Each of these parties is dependent to some degree on the lawyer to monitor management's behavior with reference to contractual, statutory, and common law standards. The second is when the lawyer serves as a "dealmaker" who drafts language that both reflects and shapes clients' understandings of their rights and relationships vis-à-vis other parties. Corporate lawyers, according to Painter, thus are not mere technicians who choose the best instrument to achieve pre-selected ends. Instead, "[c]orporate lawyers cannot deny that they often have a substantial role in both the choices their clients make and the way those choices are implemented."

As you read Painter, ask yourself whether acknowledging moral accountability in the way that he suggests would undermine, or enhance, the lawyer's representation of the client. If a lawyer concludes that she bears partial responsibility for a course of action that is legally permissible but morally problematic, what should she do? Does Painter's argument suggest that corporate lawyers should adopt the Contextual View that Simon describes in Chapter Two: do what would further justice under the circumstances? Note that Painter acknowledges that lawyers have obligations to clients that may justify acting contrary to their broader moral obligations, but says that in these cases "moral responsibility for such actions" still "is unabated." Do you agree? Or does your belief that your professional obligation overrides your more general moral responsibility absolve you of any moral culpability?

The chapter then turns to the case of *Doe v. Unocal.* The issue before the court is whether Unocal can be liable under the Alien Tort Claims Act for atrocities committed by others with whom it is associated. The case is included not for this purpose, however. Rather, it is designed to be a springboard for discussion of whether a company such as Unocal has any moral accountability even if it has no legal liability.

The first problem is intended to make you consider at what point, if any, you would feel any moral complicity in such atrocities. Approach it by asking first what would be a paradigm case of moral accountability that elicits wide agreement that there is such complicity. Then ask yourself about other situations that differ to varying degrees from this case. At what point would you believe that it was no longer appropriate to find moral accountability? Where does the assignment described in the Problem fit along that spectrum?

Finally, the second problem asks you to consider if you have any concerns about pursuing a colorable legal strategy to block government enforcement of environmental laws that could result in the company emitting harmful pollutants for another three years.

MODEL RULES: 1.2(b), 1.16(b), 2.1

Deborah L. Rhode & David Luban

LEGAL ETHICS (4th ed. 2004)

[E]ven in cases that are clearly covered by formal ethics rules or other law, moral issues inevitably remain.

First, and most fundamentally, there is always the question whether to comply with the law or to engage in conscientious disobedience. That issue is philosophically controversial and continues to be debated—but no serious theory on the question denies that disobedience is sometimes morally justified. On those (hopefully rare) occasions when settled legal rules clearly demand a course of action that the lawyer finds morally repugnant, serious soul-searching is necessary. To dismiss the issue simply because the law is clear is a rationalization, not a reason, for decision. Second, even in less serious dilemmas, when conscientious disobedience to formal rules is unwarranted, moral deliberation remains necessary to decide whether to comply to the bare minimum degree that the letter of the rules requires, or whether to comply more fully.

In any event, many of the formal ethics rules leave the ultimate decision to the lawyer's discretion. Thus, for example, the ABA's Model Rules of Professional Conduct permit, but do not require, a lawyer to reveal confidential client information "to prevent reasonably certain death or substantial bodily harm."[12] Bar ethical rules permit, but do not require, a corporate lawyer to reveal confidences if the corporation's highest authority insists on violating the law in a way that is likely to injure the corporation.[13] They permit, but do not require, a lawyer to withdraw from representation if the client insists on taking an action that the lawyer finds "repugnant."[14] They permit, but do not require, lawyers to include "moral, economic, social and political factors" in the advice they offer clients.[15] They recommend, but do not require, that lawyers perform fifty hours annually of pro bono service.[16] For these as well as many other issues that arise in legal practice, the law itself invites lawyers to consider their own moral values.

Indeed, * * *, a prominent characteristic of legal practice is the complex, discretionary nature of the judgments that lawyers make in daily practice. Some of those judgments will inevitably implicate ethical

---

12. Model Rule 1.6(b)(1).

13. Model Rule 1.13(c).

14. Model Rule 1.16(b)(3).

15. Model Rule 2.1.

16. Model Rule 6.1.

principles. * * * [L]awyers' definition of their professional role and the responsibilities that it entails is heavily influenced by moral values.

MORAL THEORIES

Moral philosophy is concerned with what makes an action right or wrong. That inquiry has given rise to three basic approaches: those that focus on the consequences of the action; those that emphasize the intrinsic nature of the action itself; and those that center on the character of the actor.

Consequentialism judges the rightness or wrongness of actions based on their consequences. The most familiar consequentialist theory is *utilitarianism*, primarily as developed by Jeremy Bentham, John Stuart Mill, and Henry Sidgwick. In its most familiar form, utilitarianism evaluates actions on the basis of the pleasure they create or the pain they inflict: utilitarians attempt to sum up the pleasure and pain, and recommend the action that creates the "greatest good for the greatest number." From this perspective, an individual's moral obligation is to maximize utility.

However, consequentialist theories need not focus on pleasure and pain, which are, after all, hard to measure with any precision. Some economists treat total social wealth as the "good" to be maximized, and judge actions or policies according to their economic effects. Closely related to this approach is the framework of many welfare economists. They identify utility as the satisfaction of individual preferences. Since it is difficult to make interpersonal comparisons of utility in the absence of some common standard of measure, economists generally rely on money; they assess the strength of preferences by reference to how much individuals would be willing to pay to reach a certain result. Money is thus treated as a stand-in or surrogate for utility (preference-satisfaction). One other prominent consequentialist theory, "ideal utilitarianism," includes less tangible outcomes, such as ideals of fairness, among the goods to be maximized.

Such approaches have two major limitations. One involves indeterminacy; it will often be extremely difficult to predict and weigh all relevant costs and benefits. A second limitation concerns utilitarianism's inability to distinguish legitimate from illegitimate preferences or to protect rights. Individuals' expressed desires are in some measure socially constructed and constrained, and many preference-maximizing approaches provide no basis for challenging those desires, however self destructive. Moreover, since consequentialists simply add together the gains and losses of society's members, they can justify policies that benefit the many at the expense of the few. For this reason, critics often object that consequentialism cannot safeguard the rights of minorities against overreaching by a majority, a deficiency that other ethical theories seek to address.

The most prominent of those other theories are *deontological*. The term, derived from the Greek word for duty, refers to approaches that view right action in terms of discharging responsibilities, independent of their consequences. Those responsibilities typically are grounded on universal, generalizable principles.

In a famous passage in *The Brothers Karamazov*, one of Dostoyevsky's characters poses this challenge:

> Imagine that you are creating a fabric of human destiny with the object of making men happy in the end, giving them peace and rest at last. Imagine that you are doing this but that it is essential and inevitable to torture to death only one tiny creature—that child beating its breast with its fist, for instance—in order to found that edifice on its unavenged tears. Would you consent to be the architect on those conditions? Tell me. Tell me the truth.

For a utilitarian, this question is easy: to achieve happiness for millions of individuals one would of course torture a single child. But perhaps there is something suspect about a theory that makes this an easy question. Would we be morally comfortable about enslaving a minority to provide greater wealth and leisure to the majority? Deontologists focus on the intrinsic character of the action—slavery or torture—and argue that some actions are right or wrong quite apart from their consequences. Kant's categorical imperative is a deontological formula: it forbids us from using other individuals as a means, no matter how compelling the end.

Kant is the best-known deontological philosopher. His writings focused heavily on moral duties, which he believed could be deduced from the categorical imperative. These included such obligations as fidelity (keeping promises and avoiding deception); benevolence (helping others and avoiding harm); and cultivating our own abilities. Among contemporary deontologists, however, the focus has shifted from an emphasis on duties to an emphasis on rights, in their moral not legal sense. A modern proponent of deontological approaches would argue that the innocent child in Dostoyevsky's fable has a moral entitlement not to be tortured—an entitlement that overrides the gain in utility to humanity at large. In the words of Ronald Dworkin, whose book title *Taking Rights Seriously* might be seen as a formula for modern deontologists, rights "trump" utility.

Of course, there is plenty of room for debate about what our moral rights are. Moreover, some deontologists believe that in defining rights, it is appropriate to take account of consequences. Thus, it is most accurate to think of deontology as a family of theories rather than as a single theory, which all rest on the view that consequences are not determinative.

Critics argue that the strength of deontological approaches is also the source of their limitations. A rule that one is prepared to universalize will often need to be framed at such a level of abstraction that it cannot resolve particular cases. Some formulas, such as the categorical imperative, are devoid of specific content, and cannot decide cases where principles are in conflict. Moreover, many critics, including communitarians and feminists, have underscored the inadequacies of frameworks that elevate abstract individual rights over concrete responsibilities and over relationships with family, friends, and communities.

A third group of theories are generally grouped together under the label *virtue ethics*. These theories focus on the character of the actor, rather than on the nature of the act or on its consequences. Aristotle's *Ethics* offered the first systematic expression of this approach. His focus was neither on the nature of obligations nor on the consequences of action. Rather, Aristotle discussed the virtues and vices of the actor: what it is to be courageous or cowardly, moderate or immoderate, wise or foolish. In the Middle Ages, Christian moralists followed Aristotle's approach, although they also recognized certain virtues, such as mercy, that were quite foreign to Greek thought. A number of contemporary moral philosophers have attempted to revive the Aristotelian tradition, and have insisted that the most important questions of ethics concern our character.

Alasdair MacIntyre's 1981 book *After Virtue* has played a central role in this revival. According to MacIntyre, we argue endlessly about moral issues because we no longer share a moral language. Enlightenment and post-Enlightenment developments eroded the Greek and Christian teaching about virtues from which our moral vocabulary evolved. We now face the problem of "ethics after Babel": the language of our disputes—rights and duties, acts and rules, responsibilities and consequences—has become detached from the traditions that gave it force. Individuals who focus on rights talk past those who focus on consequences, and the possibilities for consensus have become increasingly remote. In a society where "there is no longer any shared concept of the community's good ... there can be no very substantial concept of what it is that contributes more or less to the achievement of that good."

To focus on virtue in legal ethics is to shift emphasis from the nature of particular actions and their consequences and to center attention instead on the character of the lawyers who perform these actions. Under this approach, conduct is subject to praise or condemnation primarily on the grounds of what it reflects about the person; acts may be dishonest or forthright, extortionate or generous, disloyal or decent. Yet to critics, this approach yields no more determinate conclusions than other frameworks. As subsequent discussion will note, the central question for legal ethics is often what the good lawyer should do under circumstances of moral complexity or competing values. An approach that focuses on character as a unitary concept may not be helpful in addressing the demands of particular roles under such circumstances. Nor is such a unified concept of character consistent with much contemporary research in psychology and organizational behavior, which documents the situational nature of moral conduct and the extent to which contextual pressures can undermine individuals' ethical commitments.

THE POSSIBILITY OF PLURALISM

All of these approaches have something to recommend them; all are subject to significant limitations. To choose among them, it is helpful to reflect on what would make them useful under particular circumstances. The eminent philosopher John Rawls suggests that a moral theory should be tested by our "moral intuitions": the moral judgments we would be inclined to make before we begin to theorize. A useful moral framework offers principles that accommodate our considered moral intuitions. These principles can then help revise our intuitions. Our intuitions thus modified may then assist in further refining our principles, and so on. Eventually, Rawls suggests, we should arrive at a "reflective equilibrium" between principles and intuitions, in which neither requires further adjustment.

In practice, it may well be that different areas of our moral experience will fall into reflective equilibrium with different moral principles; some judgments may be best systematized by consequentialist theories, some by deontological theories, and some by theories of virtue. Although the objective of traditional philosophy was to produce unified theoretical frame-works, we have no reason to believe that our individual moral worlds are that tidy. According to many contemporary philosophers, our moral experience is, at its deepest level, *pluralistic;* no single framework is adequate to encompass all aspects of our-moral-life. In the final analysis, we will often have to rely upon a kind of second-order intuition. While we may look to moral theories for guidance, we still need to make intuitive judgments about which moral theory is most appropriate to the case at hand.

Paul R. Tremblay, THE NEW CASUISTRY

12 GEO. J. LEGAL ETHICS 489 (1999)

* * *

I. PRACTICING PHILOSOPHY

Let us suppose, just for the moment, that "plain people" care about ethics, that they would prefer, everything else being equal, to do the right thing, or to lead the good life. And let us imagine that lawyers share that sentiment—they too would prefer to practice law in an ethical manner, by and large. We could also assume, further, that "ethics" for lawyers means something different from, and more than, simply following a set of rules established by the legal profession, rules with obligatory qualities implying penalties for their violation. Many within the profession seem to think of "legal ethics" as such rule-obligations, but it is fair for us to assume that ethics can and does mean a lot more.

We can readily accept these premises, but doing so implies some benchmark, or standard, or similar criterion to differentiate "better" decisions from "worse" ones. Without some identifiable method by which to evaluate ethical choice, "caring" about ethics is meaningless. Unless we defend the proposition that *any* choice is acceptable so long as it violates no outstanding rule (a proposition with few defenders), we implicitly accept the reality of normative standards. This, of course, comes as no surprise, but the nature and source of those standards remain remarkably elusive, especially in the discourse of legal ethics. This Article represents an effort to identify sources of moral agreement without descending into the meta-discussions of the philosophers.

The most conventional approach to questions about moral authority is to suggest some version of moral theory as the underpinning of ethical choice. Those suggestions intimate a deductive reasoning process. Moral theory serves as the major premise in a syllogism; the facts of any given case might then be "applied" to arrive at a conclusion. This theory conception not only introduces many misgivings, including its frequent inaccessibility and the problem of competing theories, but it also misunderstands our practices. We may not be entirely sure about the process we use to resolve moral dilemmas, but deducing answers from a coherent theory is unlikely to be high on the list for most of us * * *

In the pages below, this Article argues that these dominant approaches fail to inform practicing lawyers—plain persons usually lacking philosophical training—about how best to resolve their tensions. This Article introduces here and seeks to defend an alternative insight about ethical choice, one grounded in the wisdom of the Jesuits of the Middle Ages, the clinical experiences of modern bioethicists, and the practical judgments of plain persons. This alternative is casuistry. Casuistry accepts the central truths of such grand theories as consequentialism and Kantianism. It acknowledges the importance of virtue and character, with special emphasis on practical wisdom and judgment. It melds these insights, though, with a recognition of the importance of cases and context in moral thinking, in a process that offers better concrete guidance to those who must "practice philosophy."

Casuistry represents a case-based, particularized, context-driven method of normative decisionmaking. Casuistry starts with *paradigm cases*, examples upon which most observers will readily agree, and reasons analogically from those agreed-upon cases to more complex cases representing ethical conflict. By understanding and emphasizing sources of agreement, casuistry elides the all-too-common stalemate in ethics talk, where "the only alternatives [are] dogmatism and relativism." The lawyer as casuist need not decide, nor know, whether she is a Kantian, a utilitarian, or a Rawlsian. Indeed, in one case a lawyer might act "deontologically," and in a different circumstance act "consequentially," and be right in both instances. Casuistry leaves the deep and difficult philosophy debates to the philosophers, and aims its insights to the clinician, the practitioner, and the plain person * * *

II.   Dominant Paradigms of Moral Reasoning: Theories, Principles, and Virtues

A.   *A Tale of Discretionary Ethics*

The reasoning and insight underlying casuistry have relevance for law practice or legal ethics broadly defined, but the scope of the argument here is a more limited one. This part explores the implications of casuistry for "discretionary ethics"—that part of the ethics of law practice in which the regulatory schemes now in place have conferred full discretion on lawyers to act in the best way they can.

This part begins with an example. A young lawyer, Mark, works in a legal services office in a very poor community. Mark represents Edna, who came to Mark's office with a notice from the Department of Public Welfare (DPW) terminating the TANF welfare benefits on which she relies to support her three children. According to the DPW notice, Edna did not provide adequate documentation or "verifications" necessary to maintain benefits for another year. Mark's research shows that, while the welfare administrators were correct in their determination, the verifications are easily acquired, and the regulations permit Edna to submit these verifications at an appeal hearing, with no penalty. These are among the "easy" cases in a poverty law practice.

Edna's case has a complication, however. Mark's interview of Edna discloses that her uncle routinely gives her money for food and clothes for her children. That money is regular and, by Mark's reading of the state welfare regulations, reportable and "countable." Edna also baby-sits on a predictable schedule but has never informed the welfare office about that money, which is also reportable and countable by Mark's reading of applicable law. The reporting and counting of these two sources of income would leave Edna eligible for a very small amount of welfare benefits. She would not be barred from participation in the program, but the level of her benefits would be affected significantly if she were to report the income.

Mark is in a dilemma. He has a lawful, non-frivolous, and indeed quite promising defense to DPW's effort to terminate Edna's welfare benefits. In doing so, though, he participates, arguably, in a form of "welfare fraud," for Mark's success at the hearing will advance Edna's unlawful procurement of TANF funds. While Mark's research shows that no substantive law *forbids* him from working on this hearing, his representation of Edna raises moral concerns that need to be justified.

If an ethicist were to buttonhole Mark before his hearing and ask him to explain or justify his choices here, the ethicist might encounter something like the following:

"I know this is a tough call. Edna will received a lot of money that she does not "deserve" in a substantive sense, and I play a part in that result. But there are legal arguments on her behalf supporting her continued eligibility, so it's not *illegal* for me to do what Edna asks. But not everything that's legal is moral, I understand."

So how do I justify this on a moral level? I worry a lot about that. On the one hand, there's my commitment to Edna as my client, and my agreement to be her advocate. I confess I am also swayed by her need for the money. Edna finds it very hard, literally impossible perhaps, to survive on what the welfare officials offer her for a monthly grant. The money comes from this large government agency which has never been too friendly to our clients, and they'll never miss this few thousand dollars per year given their multi-million dollar budgets. There are political arguments persuading me that welfare grants are never set at subsistence levels, so it's not as though Edna is being greedy or anything.

On the other hand, I am taking advantage of an agency and a hearing officer who will decide this case without knowing the true implication of his or her decision. Edna has no *right* to this money, and it is only my careful lawyering that keeps the money in her pocket. I hate it when big firm lawyers use those tactics to take advantage of the IRS, or bankruptcy debtors, or consumers. I am sure that they all think that their particular case justifies their sharp tactics, just as I'm trying to do here.

In the end, I will make the arguments for Edna because she is my client and because she is poor. I would not *violate* the law for those reasons, but, again, everything I do in this case is legal, and that makes it harder for me to opt for a path that my client doesn't want. The fact that it is my *role* to make the best legal arguments for Edna also persuades me a great deal. This is, after all, what lawyers are hired to do."

Mark seems to be reasonably thoughtful here, and considerate of the appropriate moral implications. His sentiments probably exemplify how lawyers tend to think about discretionary ethics matters. At the same time, his deliberation is *ad hoc*—it lacks reference to evaluative standards or benchmarks by which to judge the success of the endeavor, other than its ultimate reliance on the role obligations, which, as the ethicist would teach us, cannot serve as an operative trump in this kind of moral reasoning.

The pertinent question, of course, is whether some method or process might serve Mark better in his struggle through discretionary ethics. That inquiry ought to have meaning for most practitioners, even if its goals seem rather elusive. Either one believes that there are coherent ways to understand moral disagreement, or one does not. For the latter individuals, there is no such method of practical ethics that can ever "work," and we can safely ignore them. The rest of us, while not denying that moral reality is controversial and that objective answers about moral reality are, at the very least, debatable, nevertheless accept that *some* basis exists by which to discuss questions of value * * *

III. A Pragmatic Alternative: Casuistry, Clinical
Ethics, and Case-Based Reasoning

A. *The New Casuistry*

* * * Casuistry does not pursue universal truths and it does not rely on foundations of moral belief derived from some developed intellectual scheme. It instead looks more modestly, if not intensely, at the circumstances of the particular case that demand moral inquiry, resisting abstract or formal theories in favor of identifying paradigm cases from which one can reason analogously and contextually. Casuistry then arrives at "probable certitude" through the exercise of reflective, prac-

tical judgment. * * * [I]t builds upon shared moral sentiment; like virtue ethics, it discerns that sentiment in the particulars of cases.

This Article explores the underpinnings of casuistry in the following Part, and takes up, in Part IV, a comparison of casuistry to its alternatives, through the use of some examples from clinical law practice. This analysis reveals that casuistry, while different in its approach from much of conventional ethical discourse, is surprisingly evocative of common law reasoning with its reliance on precedent and analogical reasoning. It is also quite illustrative of the actual *practice* of ethics, if not of the structured discussion of ethics. In this respect, it can claim affinity with the traditions of feminism, pragmatism, that part of postmodern thinking that resists the abstracting effects of theory, and early twentieth-century legal realism.

B. Casuistry's Component Understandings

1. The "Wellsprings question": cases as the source of moral knowledge

Casuistry's most critical premise is that moral knowledge develops incrementally through the analysis of concrete cases. * * * Casuists credit theories and principles as developed insights formed from considered reactions to individual cases. A lawyer understanding that insight can more readily accept conflict between theories or among principles by looking more particularly at the cases that account for the competing sentiments. In the end, the cases drive the sentiment * * *.

The casuists observe that moral theory seldom has contributed meaningful insights to the resolution of practical problems; instead, the "locus of moral certitude" remains with the particular cases. What moral theory can do well, at times, is summarize what we know about moral truth from our encounters with concrete cases * * *.

* * * It is therefore not at all implausible for lawyers to accept the critical premise of casuistry—that moral insight stems from the particularities of concrete cases. This is not meant to deny theory an important place in moral deliberation, nor to ignore the insights of theoretical moral philosophy. Each competing moral theory represents sentiments derived from paradigm cases, and can summarize those sentiments in effective ways. A welcome benefit of casuistry, in fact, is that one can accept the arguments of competing theories selectively, without concluding that the theory is defective when a counter-example appears for which the theory cannot account.

2. The Role of Paradigm Cases and Analogical Reasoning

Theories and principles, despite their faults, offer a semblance of comfort. The worry is that their absence leaves only relativism, or perhaps nihilism. The casuists avoid despair by recognizing the centrality of paradigm cases, "in which the actions to be taken are clear and agreed on by virtually anyone familiar with the case and its particulars." The force of paradigm cases is largely intuitive. Once she identifies one or more paradigm cases, a casuist proceeds in a fashion quite familiar to lawyers: she employs a common law reasoning style, comparing the case at hand with a collection of available easy cases. Through "moral triangulation," she reasons by analogy from the exemplars, identifying the morally relevant features of the paradigm cases, the features of the cases which account for their ready acceptance, and comparing the newer, less certain case with each paradigm case to discern which comes closest to the case under consideration * * *.

[Moral] conflict is the result of two competing but incompatible "principles" (to borrow from the earlier discussion) seeming to apply to a new case. Each of those principles represents an easier case where no such conflict exists. It is inconceivable—literally so—that one can respect a principle without acknowledging an easy case where that principle would fit. It would be an odd principle indeed that could not be described by an example demonstrating it. In Mark's case, for illustration, he easily concludes that he would never ethically lie to a welfare official in order to obtain benefits to which he was not entitled. He equally easily concludes that he would never refuse to make a direct argument applying law to facts as a legal advocate for a client who had hired him to respect her rights. He may call these conclusions "principles," but they really arise from cases. His current dilemma arises because he cannot use either of these cases as a simple analogy for his current plight.

It makes sense, then, at least in the pragmatic way described here, for lawyers to work from the paradigm cases they readily recognize. Like their use of precedent in common law jurisprudence, paradigm cases establish a common shared basis from which to craft moral arguments and to make moral choices.

3. "Fallibilism" and "Probable Certitude"

Casuists claim that their approach to moral deliberation differs from that of the theorists and the principlists in an important way. The respective methods vary in the way they utilize shared agreements arising from considered judgments. One touted difference is that casuists do not pretend to secure certainty about the case before them, accepting instead what they call "probable certitude." Casuistry's goal is the best solution, all things considered. . . .

4. The Role of Phronesis and the Importance of Context

Casuistry is impatient with "thin" descriptions of moral dilemmas and with simple hypothetical examples. It resists abstraction, claiming that appropriate judgments are only found when all of the relevant circumstances are understood. * * * Lawyers acting in good faith will understand and learn not by carefully deducing propositions through chains of reasoning, but instead by the faculty of judgment, prudence, or Aristotle's *phronesis*. Here the casuists and the virtuists meet. Good ethical judgment takes into consideration relevant relationships, roles, power imbalances, emotional needs, community expectations, vulnerabilities, and so forth, just as the virtue ethics adherents profess. * * *

VI. CASUISTRY IN ACTION

A. Introduction to the Examples

* * * To model the casuist method, I choose to revisit two of the examples discussed and explored in Susan Kupfer's important article. * * * Using these examples provides certain benefits. Her stories are real ones arising from her clinical practice. She has publicly discussed them, both from her students' perspective as well as from the perspective of her ethical model. And, I happen to think that her resolution is different from what might occur using the casuistry approach. As I review each case, I shall note not just the casuist perspective, but I shall also compare the other "competing" methods as well. After my discussion of the Kupfer examples, I briefly return to our earlier story of Mark and his dilemma about "welfare fraud."

B. The First Example: "The Zealous Advocate"

1. The Case

In this case, a student attorney represented a nineteen year-old man in his claim for unemployment insurance benefits after the client was discharged from his work. The client's employer objected to his collecting benefits because, it alleged, the man's conduct amounted to "intentional misconduct in willful disregard of the employer's interest." The employer bears the burden of proving that set of facts, which includes the requisite state of mind for "willfulness." The student, in his preparation for the appeal, had learned that the man was mentally retarded and, with his client's consent, had obtained school records evidencing borderline I.Q.

The client, however, refused to permit the student to argue a theory that would characterize him as retarded or disabled. To overcome this resistance, the student arranged to have the client "called out of the room during the hearing," at which time the student presented his evidence and arguments on the mental impairment theory. The client was awarded unemployment benefits by the hearing officer, who apparently cited to the evidence in the favorable decision. After the case was completed, the student defended his choice, in class, by characterizing it as one "raising strategic considerations," presumably placing it within the realm of the lawyer's discretion and not a choice requiring client consent. If the student is right about the scope of obligation, then this choice qualifies as a discretionary ethics matter. * * *

3. A Casuistry Approach

The casuist's approach to the unemployment case would look different from the deductivist's approach. She will not search for a theory or a principle, or a lexical ordering of principles, to decide how to proceed, or to evaluate the law student's choice to proceed as he did. She will instead rely on the principles available as orienting points, develop paradigm cases from those principles, consider carefully the relevant moral factors present in the paradigm cases, and then explore the specifics of those factors in the case at hand. Then using analogical reasoning and the practice of "moral triangulation," she will assess whether the case at hand better resembles one paradigmatic case or another. She will then make her best judgment of that conclusion, all things considered, understanding that she has at best probable certitude for her choices. Carson Strong calls this the "case comparison" method.

Two principles apply in this case, as noted: beneficence and autonomy. Each principle can be stated as a "maxim": "Advance your client's legal interests" and "Follow your client's wishes." Carson Strong suggests first that, where it is apparent that more than one principle has moral applicability, we identify clear cases representing each principle. Note that for this process to unfold, the practitioner must acknowledge each competing consideration. A law student who *only* saw the beneficence factor here could not use the "case comparison" method, of course, but such a student would not perceive ethical conflict at all (and would thus have no use for any of the methods we have explored). Any deliberative method, then, will call for some minimal ability to recognize ethical tension in practice.

Here, Kupfer's student *does* recognize the tension between the principles. He reported to his Professional Responsibility class that "the cost to client autonomy was quite high." The student obviously saw the costs as worth the candle, though, given how he proceeded. The fact that his actions also implicate a possible conflict of interest—his need to be a successful lawyer with a "win" on his record might affect his decision-making—means that he will need to include a third principle, that of loyalty. That principle ought also to be represented by a paradigm case, as well as a maxim—say, "Never let your interests interfere with your duty to your client."

The casuist would need to call upon paradigm cases to stand for each of the conflicting principles that come to bear on this dispute. Because casuistry is not yet an established practice within legal ethics, these cases are not yet part of the lore or "stock stories" of the profession, at least not explicitly. Such a collection of precedential stock stories would arise from the "special topics" within law practice, and can, in time, be represented by maxims. Legal ethicists have not yet mastered this method as well as bioethicists have. For present purposes, though, we can imagine the cases and maxims, as well as the special topics identified earlier.

A paradigm case for the autonomy principle ought to be reasonably accessible to the casuist. The principle stands for the proposition that a person's choices about his life ought to be respected. His conception of what is good is one of the choices deserving of respect. A client who chooses to settle a case for emotional satisfaction, closure, avoidance of litigation, and a small amount of money rather than to proceed to trial for a chance to win more money at greater emotional risk represents a clear, evocative paradigm case that captures the principle of autonomy. A casuist could work with the law student to have him identify cases where the principle he accepts would be exemplified.

Cases capturing beneficence might be harder to locate, especially those that are not trite. The reason for this is that the value of autonomy is so privileged within American moral philosophy, and certainly within law. Beneficence is certainly a value, no doubt, and easily represented by everyday cases in which the lawyer's obligation is to act zealously. For the stock story to have weight as a paradigm case, though, it ought to serve as a clear case in which beneficence trumps other competing interests.

Two such "beneficence" cases come to mind. One is the case of the disabled client. We could construct a paradigm case in which a lawyer opts not to follow the express choices of a client because it is very apparent that the client is not able to understand the available choices *and* it is equally clear that the client would, if competent, choose the option that maximizes her interests. The second case would be a variation on the present case, where the interest of the client to be protected is less central and the harm to the client, and to his immediate family, is patent and direct. We could achieve consensus on these stories, that in these cases it would be morally appropriate to act against what otherwise would be autonomy interests.

The casuist would then, following Carson Strong's model, proceed to identify the morally relevant ways in which the cases of the type in question can differ from one another. This step is not hard in our case. The "autonomy" stock stories differ from the "beneficence" stories in these morally relevant ways: the paradigm case for autonomy reflects clear understanding by the client of the risks, and/or no egregious harm to the client or to others. The case for beneficence reflects either no clear choice by the client or such grave harm to those around him, or to himself, that respecting his choice, even if freely adopted, is unacceptable.

The next step consists of moral triangulation, the comparison between the case at hand and the two or more paradigm cases, looking at the morally relevant factors just identified and the very specific details of the case at hand. This step should immediately reveal why Kupfer seems right and her student wrong *as she describes the case to us*. I read the story as one where the nineteen year-old will not suffer grave harm by losing his unemployment case. I see no family, no minor children, and no other factors that might alter the resemblance of this case to the autonomy stock story. He appears to understand the choice before him, and the injury to his dignity seems plausible. If we add in the two other factors I have not explored—the student's deceptive manipulation of the client and his possible conflict of interest—and quickly imagine the paradigm cases for each of these principles, the case becomes even clearer.

Yet, there are two important insights from the casuists embedded in this assessment. The first is that *the details count for a lot*. We have not developed a "rule" that holds that clients always deserve respect in settings like this unemployment case. Make this man forty-five, give him sick, young children and a disabled wife, and the result is not necessarily the same. The second point is that the conversation with the client, so central to the discursive method, does not end matters in the casuist world. Kupfer employs the dialogue to nudge her student to respect his client more, and that is a laudable goal. But the casuists will warn that, even after such reciprocal conversation, this student may have to do the same thing as he did before. It all depends on the results of the conversation and the specific circumstances of the case.

C.   The Second Example: "The Proceduralist"

In much briefer fashion, I now attempt a similar casuist assessment of a second of Professor Kupfer's cases. In this case, a law student faces a tactical choice to use a court process instrumentally or substantively. The student represents an elderly couple in an eviction proceeding. The *pro se* landlord filed a complaint in court too soon under prevailing law. If the student were to object to the misfiling quickly, the case could be refiled by the landlord, and then heard on the merits. If the student deliberately delayed his objection, the landlord would lose his right to sue once the present case was dismissed for its procedural impropriety. The student's clients would then win, but not on the merits. The student perceived this to be a true dilemma.

* * * My purpose here is * * * to visit the case as would a casuist. Kupfer implies that there are no conflicting principles here, but I think that view misunderstands her description of her student's angst and the level of moral complexity in her story. There are, indeed, conflicting moral principles here, even if observers might see the conflict as quite one-sided: the commitment to zealous advocacy (a variation of the beneficence norm described above) and a commitment to fairness. The former is so well-established that it requires no discussion. The latter, though, is gaining respectability. It even has its stock stories. * * * [Certain] cases * * * find their way into professional responsibility texts because they represent, or at least conjure up, paradigm cases in which winning by a technicality offends our moral conceptions.

The question for the lawyer in the eviction case, then, is to identify the morally relevant differences between the two sets of paradigm cases and to use those factors to analogize to the eviction case. Once again, we see that Kupfer's judgment about the morally preferable choice is right, but it is important to understand why she is right, and how dependent that sentiment is on the context of the case. We can assume certain facts here—facts the law student would need to know. What is the relevant harm to the landlord in this case? He is described as a college professor, thus not too poor and not too unsophisticated. What are his remedies once this proceeding is dismissed with prejudice? Because this is a setting requiring administrative proceedings to be held before any formal eviction complaint may be brought, the landlord impliedly will get at least part of the monthly rent during the period of delay (and maybe all, if this is not a non-payment case). We do not know the harm to the tenants, or the fairness of the procedures which the tenants must endure in order to have their rights adjudicated.

All of these factors would need to be explored and understood for a proper casuist assessment to occur. In many cases, the moral qualms presented by the student in this eviction case would be determined to be entirely legitimate ones. No simple principle can decide when the fairness concerns will override the obligations of advocacy. As we are wont to do implicitly, casuistry allows us to build upon our intuitive judgments to make those kinds of calls in as rigorous a fashion as this reality can permit. John Arras is right—"we've all been 'practicing casuistry' all along." We just did not realize we were doing so.

D. A Third Example: Casuistry and Welfare Fraud

We return now to the example with which I introduced the idea of discretionary ethics. In this case, Mark, the legal services lawyer, represents a woman who is not eligible for a full welfare grant, but who needs the money to raise her family, and, through Mark's instrumental and lawful tactics, can maintain all of her grant. Mark experiences tension in this representation; he is not comfortable using procedural tactics to obtain goods not covered by the applicable administrative scheme. At the same time, his professional role obligation suggests that he "win" his client's case, and the prospect of Edna lacking funds to feed her children is an unpleasant one. Hence his dilemma. Because both acting and not acting are *legal*, the law of lawyering does not help Mark here.

* * * Mark's resort to casuistry does not promise any simple or formulaic solution, nor a universal one. But * * * the casuists can offer an opportunity for some reasoned consideration or discussion about Mark's plight. In fact, his deliberation will resemble that of the preceding example, as it involves similar competing considerations.

Mark's dilemma can be represented by two principles, or maxims, or paradigm cases: (1) using sharp legal tactics to obtain benefits not intended by substantive law is presumptively wrong; and (2) failing to assist a mother to feed her family by means of legal means is also presumptively wrong. Whether Mark ought to violate the first or second of these turns not on questions of moral preferences or some kind of lexical ordering, but rather on predictions about facts. Will Edna's family suffer if Mark refuses to assist her in her deception? Is her welfare grant truly a last resort? Is the legislative or regulatory scheme a fair one? Does the scheme intend to deny money to women like Edna, or are the rules developed more for administrative or bureaucratic convenience or efficiency?

Sometimes, then, Mark ought to assist his client, despite his commitment not to use law instrumentally. At other times, Mark ought to refuse to do so. Mark will arrive at a decision in any given circumstance in much the same way that a judge will decide a contested question of law—by analogical reasoning from the fixed and accepted precedents.

CONCLUSION

This Article's purpose has been to introduce to the world of legal ethics the conception of casuistry, and to borrow from the rich world of bioethics insights about case-based reasoning and clinical ethics that can inform the practice of law. In many ways the ideas developed here are nearly self-evident. * * * We are all casuists, as we use analogies and easy cases to make the best sense of ethical conflict. The "new casuistry" helps us to identify the processes we use and to offer a structure and some governing themes for those processes.

In other ways, though, the model expressed by casuistry undercuts much of the rules-and principles-based syllogistic thinking that pervades much thinking and writing within legal ethics. Those ordinary ways of confronting ethics are in great need of refinement and rethinking, and this Article has shown how the wisdom of the casuists might guide us in that task of refinement and rethinking. If the casuists are right, this effort can aid plain persons to confront ethical complexity in a meaningful way without needing to resolve, or even understand, more sophisticated debates about moral philosophy.

If casuistry seems promising in these important ways, it also invites much more reflection by critics and supporters within the legal profession. Central to a critical assessment of casuistry are questions about conservatism and self-interested decisionmaking. Crafting a method of ethical deliberation grounded in considered judgments arising from cases risks privileging the status quo, and seems to discourage innovative or progressive ethical thinking. It also permits, in its resistance to blanket theories and principles, arguments about ethical propriety that are intended to produce certain identified results—the very abuse that the common understanding of "casuistry" has so often invoked in the past. These risks of casuistry seemingly will not trump its apparent benefits, but they must be confronted head-on if casuistry is to play a meaningful role in lawyers' ethical decisionmaking.

Richard W. Painter, THE MORAL INTERDEPENDENCE
OF CORPORATE LAWYERS AND THEIR CLIENTS

67 SOUTHERN CALIFORNIA LAW REVIEW 507 (1994)

I. INTRODUCTION

Lawyers have claimed, since at least the days of John Adams, that they are "independent" from their clients in that they are not morally responsible for their clients' actions. Although lawyers' actions may assist clients' conduct or assist clients in escaping consequences of their conduct, the clients are the only ones responsible. Lawyers can thus represent criminals without being criminals and can defend tort actions without being tortfeasors. Such is the "moral independence theory."

An important premise underlying this theory is that the actions of a lawyer and client are distinguishable. If conduct results from concerted action by both, attributing responsibility for that conduct to only one would not make sense. On the other hand, if the actions of lawyer and client are distinct, the responsibilities of lawyer and client are also distinct. A criminal, for example, has in many cases already committed a crime before consulting a lawyer and a tortfeasor has already committed a tort before seeking to escape liability. In these situations, the lawyer's task is to assist their client through the scrutiny of the adversarial process, and the lawyer is not responsible for the client's actions.

* * *

The moral independence theory is not the only important ideological principle of the bar. Another related principle—the loyalty principle—is that, once a client finds a lawyer, the client is entitled to that lawyer's loyal adherence to their cause. * * *

This Article will suggest an alternative to this moral independence theory—a moral interdependence theory. The moral interdependence theory is premised on the assumption that actions of lawyers and clients are not always easily distinguished. Often, lawyers and clients accomplish objectives together, not separately. They each exercise some independent judgment, but they work together and not always in distinct roles; lawyers do more than render discrete legal advice or advocacy. Lawyers therefore cannot always deny moral responsibility for their clients' conduct.

This Article seeks to demonstrate that the premise to the moral independence theory, that actions of lawyers are easily distinguishable from actions of their clients, is problematic in the context of corporate representation. Two characteristics of modern corporations have undermined this premise by blurring the distinction between lawyers' actions and clients' actions. * * * [M]ost publicly held corporations are characterized by a separation of ownership from control. Law and lawyers bridge the gap between the two, as well as bridge a similar gap between management and other corporate constituencies. Furthermore, * * * many corporations engage in complex transactions with extensive legal ramifications. Corporate clients thus will demand lawyers who perform functions summarized * * * under the labels "monitor" and "dealmaker" respectively. When lawyers act as monitors and dealmakers, they often lend their reputations to clients and their actions are sometimes difficult to distinguish from actions of their clients. Clients can be as dependent upon lawyers to frame and carry out their business objectives as lawyers are dependent upon clients for employment.

* * * Although this Article is not about morality or identifying normative rules, this Article is about moral responsibility, or who is responsible for conduct contrary to a lawyer's own principles. If a corporate lawyer believes that a leveraged buyout with adverse consequences for employees or financing a company domiciled in a dictatorship violates the lawyer's own sense of right and wrong, to what extent can the lawyer assist a client in such conduct and still rationally believe that the lawyer is not responsible for the conduct?

It is also important to distinguish this discussion of moral responsibility—responsibility for adherence to ones own moral principles—from two related topics: legal responsibility, whether a person is responsible for conduct incurring criminal or civil liability, and professional responsibility, whether a person is responsible for violating agreed upon standards of professional ethics. Legal and professional responsibility, however, are not irrelevant to this discussion—the same monitor and dealmaker functions that increase a lawyer's exposure to legal liability or disciplinary sanctions can also make a lawyer morally responsible for participation in client conduct which violates the lawyer's own moral principles. Conversely, a lawyer who understands what they actually do for a client before determining moral responsibility for client conduct will also make better judgments about potential exposure to civil or criminal liability and professional sanctions. The question may be different, but the analytical framework is similar.

* * * The cornerstone of exhortations that lawyers should exert more control over clients' conduct is often an ideal of lawyer independence whereby lawyers are "independent professionals" capable of exercising judgment apart from clients' interests. Indeed, scholarly debates often juxtapose this lawyer independence ideal with an alternative client independence ideal fostered by vigorous advocacy and minimal lawyer interference with autonomous client decisions. To the extent lawyers think independently from their clients and act on what they think, lawyer independence restrains excessive client independence and is a worthy goal. This Article suggests, however, that in practice—at least in the corporate arena—lawyers often fall short of this goal, and the lawyer independence ideal becomes an ideology of independence recited by lawyers whether or not they act independently of their clients. Presumed lawyer independence thus distances lawyers from client conduct but does nothing to restrain clients' excesses. Lawyers embracing this ideology do not become independent but succeed only in segregating their own moral beliefs from actions closely involved with their day to day work. Their "moral activism" might be directed at bar association and political activities where they advocate their own moral beliefs, but is rarely directed at their clients. These lawyers also may protect themselves as much as possible from receiving client information which might accentuate conflict between their real and perceived roles—they look the other way when their clients use their assistance to do wrong. Lawyers in this scenario become people who believe one thing, do another, and are convinced that they are not responsible.

There is, however, another ideal: lawyers who recognize that decisions, particularly within business organizations, are often made collectively and that lawyers do not always play subordinate roles in this process. These lawyers recognize that, although they contract to perform services for clients, theirs are not discrete contracts in which parties perform obligations independently. Rather their contracts are relational; neither lawyers nor clients can effectively perform without cooperation from each other.

These lawyers will also recognize that debate over the relative merits of lawyer and client autonomy may be moot. Corporations are not autonomous, but rather corporate decisions are made by people standing behind the corporate entities: directors, officers, employees, and lawyers. Lawyers' choice is not whether to participate in making clients' decisions, but what type of participation theirs will be. Lawyers also are not autonomous, rather their decisions and actions are determined in part by business objectives of their clients. Lawyers who thus recognize that they can be participants in corporate decisionmaking, instead of independent advisors to it, are more likely to believe that their moral principles deserve to influence clients' conduct and to ensure that they do.

II. The Lawyer as Monitor

Corporate lawyers' clients make decisions through the process of corporate governance. The dominant corporate governance model in the United States—which I will call the Berle–Means model—separates ownership from legal control (or shareholders from management) and separates lender, labor, and public interests from shareholders and management. American corporations are governed by managers constrained primarily by legal relationships with the other constituencies, not by consensus among these different constituencies.

* * * As discussed below, in the "Berle–Means" corporation, lawyers' role in monitoring corporate governance has been expanded because corporate constituencies rely on legal mechanisms to influence management.

A. The Berle–Means Corporation and the Monitoring Role of Lawyers

1. Lawyers as Monitors of Management Relations with Government

* * *

Today, corporations depend more than ever on lawyers to advise management and to lobby government concerning regulation. * * * Even apart from industry-specific regulation, regulation of almost every aspect of economic life such as the environment, health and safety, employment, and securities ensures that legal and business components of corporate decisions are often intertwined. As Robert Swaine of Cravath, Swaine & Moore put it when describing his firm's emerging practice at the turn of the century: "the problems were more intricate, requiring much more concentration and effort; and frequently the line between a legal question and a business question was difficult to draw." This blurring of legal and business issues has caused not only the explosive growth of law firms and in-house counsel departments, but has also led many lawyers to become directors of clients. Joint decisiomnaking by lawyer and client has become both efficient and prudent.

2. Lawyers as Monitors of Management Relations with Shareholders

The salient feature of the Berle–Means corporation is separation of ownership from control: shareholders, who theoretically own the corporation, and managers, who control the corporation, are not the same. * * * Managers, whether seeking to acquire a controlling block of shares, to influence shareholder voting, or to fulfill fiduciary duties to shareholders, seek assistance from lawyers. Lawyers are monitors of the manager-shareholder relationship.

* * *

[The growth of fiduciary duties] brought with it, however, side effects that stimulated growth in the legal profession. * * * Corporate decisionmaking revolved almost exclusively around management and shareholders, reinforcing demand by other constituencies for regulatory and contractual control, which in turn reinforced the dependence of all corporate constituencies on lawyers.

Second, mechanisms for enforcing fiduciary duties—principally shareholder derivative suits and direct actions against managers by minority shareholders—coupled with the complexities of the judicially created "out" for management known as the "business judgment rule," have made lawyers the principal monitors of management-shareholder relations. Shareholders have relied on lawyers to monitor management; management has relied on lawyers not only in control contests with other managers but also in monitoring their relations with passive investors.

* * *

Despite [the] legal obligations to investors, managers can still shirk, or at least minimize, performance of fiduciary and disclosure duties to the extent they, or their lawyers, are sufficiently familiar with legal standards to manipulate the standards to their advantage. Self-interested conduct and helping oneself to the corporate "cookie jar" are possible but require sophisticated maneuvering. More scrupulous managers who seek to meet their obligations to investors also must do so within the confines of legal standards, usually interpreted and explained to them by lawyers.

* * *

Management and shareholders are unique among the corporate constituencies in that one owes a fiduciary duty to the other. However, like the other constituencies, management and shareholders use lawyers to monitor their relationship, and lawyers have some responsibility for how that relationship turns out.

3. Lawyers as Monitors of Management Relations with Creditors

In American corporations, creditors, like government and labor, usually cannot elect directors or vote on major transactions. This is so even though many corporations depend on debt, and many investors can only contribute debt capital.

* * *

Creditors not only lack voting control, they also have little access to other means of influencing corporate governance absent the contracts that lawyers provide for them. * * * The contracts that lawyers draft thus become the principal means by which these creditors control corporate conduct.

Lawyers have a crucial role in this process because contractual control of a corporation by its creditors requires detailed negotiation and drafting that usually cannot be done by creditors and borrowers alone. Negotiators and drafters of contracts must understand legal rights and responsibilities and, perhaps even more important, drafters should have experience drafting, and access to precedents of, contracts for similar transactions. * * * Creditors' reliance on contractual control thus creates new opportunities and new responsibilities for the private bar.

4. Lawyers as Monitors of Management Relations with Labor

Another constituency is a corporation's employees. Like creditors, employees do not have voting power. Unlike creditors, most individual employees have limited contractual control; the standard at-will employment contract is often not even in writing and gives the employee little control over the conduct of management other than the right to quit. Organized labor, however, empowers employees to do collectively what they probably would not do individually: enter into detailed contractual relations with management.

* * *

Management, and ultimately shareholders, control the boardroom, while labor unions have the right to strike and negotiate settlements. Despite some recent movement toward developing a "cooperative workplace," an "adversarial psychology" still dominates collective bargaining. Each side uses lawyers to exert whatever contractual control it can over the other. Furthermore, labor and management both have incentives to engage in "strategic behavior" such as boycotts and lockouts, during the collective bargaining process and, because of legal restrictions on such behavior, usually design their strategies with the help of lawyers.

* * *

B. The Power of Lawyers

* * *

At this point, it is important to discuss how these mechanisms of the law are uniquely, if not intentionally, designed to confer substantial power on lawyers. Whether or not regulatory and contractual control are more efficient than participatory models of corporate governance, the regulatory/contractual model does require each constituency's rights and obligations to be phrased in precise legally operative language. Lawyers are intermediaries trained in the task of interchanging this complex language with clients' concrete objectives. Exertion of political and economic power through regulatory and contractual control thus allows corporate conduct to be influenced by legal language and by lawyer intermediaries who construct and interpret that language.

* * *

First, lawyers who draft regulations or contracts control translation of communications made to them in a layperson's words into legally operative language. These lawyers can draft language that will be interpreted by a court or administrative body to have a different meaning than what laypersons agreed upon. Second, lawyers who interpret regulations or contracts to clients, nonclients, or to other lawyers less familiar with the language than they are, control conversion of legal language back into a layperson's explanation of the regulatory and contractual control that the language was intended to articulate. Needless to say, lawyers' translations and interpretations can influence the way corporate constituencies, both clients and nonclients, view their rights and responsibilities. Through control of legal language, lawyers thus can encourage clients to adhere to the letter, but not the purpose, of the law, or to take advantage of loopholes in the law. Lawyers can also induce nonclients to give up legal rights they did not intend to give up or to fail to exercise whatever rights they have. In these legal language games, lawyers have a substantial role in determining who ends up with what.

Furthermore, the same lawyers often participate in drafting and interpreting legal language. Lawyers draft and interpret contracts, and many lawyers have either drafted government regulations or been involved in enforcing regulations. Lawyers with such experience are often most in demand by clients. For example, when in 1933 the Senate Banking Committee investigated its business practices, The House of Morgan retained John W. Davis, a former Democratic nominee for President and drafter of New York's statute exempting private banks like Morgan from state inspection. While Davis' government experience is more extensive than that of most lawyers, many have worked for government agencies, participated in bar association projects which propose legislation, or have contact, through their firms or other professional associations, with lawyers responsible for drafting and enforcing laws and regulations about which clients seek advice. Perhaps more importantly, experienced lawyers understand the thought processes fellow lawyers used when they created legally operative language. The contractual and regulatory game has rules made in large part by lawyers and is a game that lawyers will, for a fee, play for their clients.

* * *

To the extent economic relationships are cast as legal relationships, lawyers will exert extraordinary power. As Justice Stone observed:

> The intricacies of business organization are built upon a legal framework which the current growth of administrative law is still further elaborating. Without the constant advice and guidance of lawyers business would come to an abrupt halt. And whatever

standards of conduct in the performance of its function the Bar consciously adopts must at once be reflected in the character of the world of business and finance. Given a measure of self-conscious and cohesive professional unity, the Bar may exert a power more beneficent and far reaching than it or any other non-governmental group has wielded in the past. This beneficent and far reaching power is, in part, the power to be monitors of corporate conduct.

* * *

III. The Lawyer as Dealmaker

A. *The Dealmaking Role*

Corporate constituencies ordinarily function within preexisting relationships: regulator and regulated, shareholder and management, debtor and creditor, and employee and employer. Each of these relationships has legally defined borders that are monitored by lawyers. At times, however, these borders come down and new relationships are created, such as when a new owner takes over a regulated business, a public company buys back its shares in a leveraged buyout, a corporation takes on a substantial amount of new debt, or employees unionize. Lawyers participate in building these new relationships for the same reasons they monitor preexisting ones: regulatory control, fiduciary duty, and contractual control define relationships between corporate constituencies. Because these new relationships are built in transactions sometimes referred to as "deals," I will use the term "dealmaker" to describe lawyers' role in the process. Justice Benjamin Cardozo described this type of corporate lawyer:

> He is a creative agent just as truly as the advocate or the judge.
> In our complex economic life, new problems call from day to day for
> new methods and devices. The lawyer in his office formulates a trust
> receipt, or stock certificates with novel incidents, or bonds, munici
> pal or corporate, with privileges or safeguards till then unknown to
> the business world. . . . the courts do no more than set the imprima
> tur of regularity upon methods that have had an origin in the
> creative activity of an adviser, working independently of courts in
> the quiet of an office.

Corporate lawyers can conduct their practice in two ways. First, they can allow clients to make proposals which lawyers subsequently evaluate within a statutory and regulatory framework. Lawyers tell clients how these proposals can be accomplished and of legal risks that should be balanced against economic rewards. Lawyers and clients together then make decisions that are usually acceptable to both. Second, lawyers can act as creative agents, as Justice Cardozo points out, and participate in the formative stage of transactions, designing proposals to fit within legal parameters and then taking these proposals to clients for approval. Once again, lawyers and clients usually make final decisions together. The first approach, or "evaluative" lawyering, is prevalent when lawyers monitor corporate conduct. The second approach, or "creative" lawyering, becomes more prevalent when lawyers move beyond their monitoring role to become dealmakers.

The amount of dealmaking lawyers do depends on the transactions involved. All transactions involve legal problems, but the legal component is more important in some transactions than in others. In more routine transactions, * * * evaluative lawyering often suffices and clients will initiate most business decisions. * * * However, in transactions with a substantial legal component, whether it be tax issues or complex corporate structures, lawyers will also engage in creative lawyering. Asset purchase agreements, leveraged buyouts, tender offers, and most other forms of merger activity, for example, are legally driven to a greater extent than simpler transactions. As clients expect lawyers to construct and coordinate transactions, the line between legal questions and business questions becomes even more difficult to draw. Lawyers initiate client conduct themselves, and the premise to the moral independence theory—that lawyer and client conduct are empirically distinct and separable—becomes even more problematic.

Dealmaking not only erodes lawyers' independence from clients, but also erodes lawyers' independence from themselves; lawyers cease to objectively evaluate transactions that are often their own creations. Objectivity is lost, first, because lawyers invest their time and professional prestige in transactions they want to see completed. Second, lawyers, like investment bankers and other intermediaries, have a financial interest in closing transactions, which usually increases, or facilitates collecting their fees. Whereas other corporate constituencies—management, the community, shareholders, lenders, and employees—contribute money or human capital to ongoing businesses and are affected by the underlying economics and other merits of transactions, lawyers and other intermediaries contribute human capital to transactions themselves, and acquire an economic interest therein. During the period between initial planning and closing, when the fates of transactions may hang in the balance, lawyer intermediaries thus become part of the multitude of constituencies seeking to influence corporate governance. Lawyers, however, may not recognize, or be willing to admit, the extent their dealmaking role gives them an interest in, as well as influence over, client conduct.

B. The Practice of Business

* * *

1. The Relationship Between Purchaser and Seller—Contract Negotiation

Contract negotiation requires lawyers to put on the hats of businesspeople and assume their clients' objectives. * * *

Economic risk can be shifted to, and return extracted from, other parties by shifting legal rights and obligations. Lawyers' skills are required to recognize where legal advantages can be found and to determine what they are worth.

Such advantages might include contractual loopholes unrecognized by opponents, unenforceable contractual provisions, and other misperceptions of law or fact relied on by opponents. Furthermore, if lawyers cannot extract favorable terms in negotiations, they may intentionally insert ambiguous language into contracts. Later, the same lawyers may assist their clients in taking advantage of the ambiguous language. Finally, clients may take advantage of credibility they gain from lawyers to make misrepresentations in negotiations while their lawyer "reputational intermediaries" stand by and do nothing. This can all be done without lawyers making any explicit misrepresentations themselves.

Opposing parties in these situations may have remedies against lawyers' clients under tort, contract, or securities law. The lawyers, however, even if they discovered and alerted their clients to loopholes in contracts or opposing parties' misapprehensions of law or fact, probably have no similar legal duties to those opposing parties. Indeed, lawyers' options for alerting opposing parties even to affirmative misrepresentations by their clients may be limited by restrictions on disclosure of client information. Having legally picked the lock and opened the door, lawyers can in most cases sit back and watch clients go in and loot the store. If, however, clients' actions violate lawyers' own moral principles, lawyers' moral responsibility does not vanish merely because they may not have legal responsibility. It is illogical for lawyers to argue that acts of subterfuge accomplished with their assistance, and their reputation, are exclusively acts of their clients and not in any part their own.

* * *

3. Restructuring Relationships with Other Constituencies—The Leveraged Buyout as a Case in Point

Restructuring relationships among corporate constituencies confronts lawyers with the moral and possibly legal dilemmas that confront managers when transactions have unwanted social consequences or harm inadequately represented constituencies. Because there are so many different types of corporate restructurings, this Article will examine the leveraged buyout ("LBO") as a case in point.

LBOs require massive debt and use more than the usual amount of contractual control over management conduct. Because lenders and purchasers of junk bonds must accept substantial risk, often without any voting control, onerous indentures and loan agreements are necessary. These documents can minimize risk or maximize expected return for various participants, and skilled lawyering in the preparation of indentures and loan agreements is important to realizing equity and debt providers' economic objectives. Lawyers therefore often structure LBOs, create documents, and help with strategic planning. These transactions, driven by debt, and thus dependent on contractual control, cannot help being influenced by lawyers.

Financial studies and academic literature support and oppose LBOs. It is, however, difficult to generalize; some LBOs probably increase efficiency and employment and are fair to all corporate constituencies, whereas others do none of these. Among the decisions LBO designers, including lawyers, may be responsible for, are whether management shares risks as well as rewards (perhaps by contributing something more than nonrecourse notes to capital), whether employees are likely to be laid off to preserve cash flow for debt payments, and what disclosures are made to other constituencies. Distinguishing between the well being of management and that of the corporation is also important. Finally, LBOs that use employee stock ownership plans ("ESOPs") as financing vehicles present difficult legal and moral issues where employees could lose both their jobs and their pensions if the venture fails.

One factor that sometimes undermines whatever independence lawyers have in LBOs and other corporate restructurings is legal fees dependent upon successfully completing transactions. Lawyers may use "premium billing" for successful transactions or merely know that they will have to reduce their fees if transactions fail to close. Such contingent fee structures enhance the interdependence of lawyers and clients by creating a strong parallel between economic incentives of lawyers and transactional objectives of clients. This correlation may increase the return side of lawyers' risk/return analysis of assisting behavior that violates their own moral principles, and perhaps even the law.

* * *

IV. THE MORAL RESPONSIBILITY OF THE LAWYER

A. *Moral Responsibility*

1. Moral Interdependence

* * *

Legal responsibility for their actions can be attributed to lawyers by courts, administrative agencies, and bar disciplinary committees. Moral responsibility, however, whether attributed by lawyers themselves or by others, can also result from relationships between lawyers and their clients. Person A (client) can be dependent on Person B (lawyer) in that A needs B's assistance to implement or make moral choices. If B provides assistance to implement A's choices, B shares moral responsibility for the implementation. If B provides assistance to A in making the choices, B shares moral responsibility for making the choices. Furthermore, if B is compensated for this assistance, B is in fact acting to benefit B as well as A. If the amount of B's compensation or the likelihood that B will receive future compensation from A is determined in part by what A's moral choices are and how they are implemented, B is even more obviously acting on B's own behalf.

Corporate clients and their lawyers perform roles analogous to A and B respectively. Principles of agency law affirm that client A is responsible for the conduct of lawyer B. Clients give consultation and sometimes consent before their lawyers make choices, and clients are legally responsible for most of their lawyers' conduct. Clients also usually believe themselves morally responsible for what lawyers do on their behalf "My lawyer did it" is rarely an acceptable excuse, in law or in ethics. Although lawyers sometimes assist clients in implementing moral choices, and lawyers' assistance can be critical to clients' making choices, "my client did it," is nonetheless a common excuse. Such an excuse is, however, unacceptable where lawyers and clients are interdependent, where they in fact influence each others' conduct.

This lawyer-client interdependence affects consequences of actions as well as actions themselves * * * Consequences of lawyers' actions will differ depending on the actions of other persons, including clients. To analogize, selling guns to hunters causes a different result than selling guns to criminals. Knowingly selling guns to criminals is still another matter. Providing factually and legally correct opinion letters, or other assistance, to clients engaged in fraudulent transactions has clear consequences. If these consequences are foreseeable, they are consequences for which lawyers are morally, if not legally responsible. As monitors and dealmakers, corporate lawyers will face situations in which they may be responsible for such consequences resulting from their clients' actions combined with their own.

2. *Moral Justification*

Lawyers, however, have obligations to clients that gun salespersons do not have to customers. Do these obligations constrain lawyers' capacity for moral choice and therefore absolve them of moral responsibility?

Lawyers are not absolved of responsibility for moral choices because lawyers' obligations to clients or even to their profession are not their only obligations. All persons have some obligations to other human beings, although each person will develop their own moral principles which define what these obligations are. These "human" obligations coexist with role-specific obligations such as the obligation of soldiers to obey commanding officers, of corporate directors to observe duties of loyalty and care, and of lawyers to represent clients "zealously within the bounds of the law." Lawyers are free from human obligations no more than soldiers and directors. Indeed, lawyers have more obligations than other persons, not fewer, and are responsible for conduct that infringes upon either clients' rights to zealous representation or the human or legal rights of others whom lawyers and their clients may harm. Obligations unique to lawyers supplement rather than supplant the moral obligations of human beings.

Often, human and role-specific obligations will conflict in that actors have to choose between them. Certain obligations in particular circumstances may be more important than others, and arguments for some obligations may be more compelling than for others. None of these obligations, however, go away merely because actors must choose between them. Responsibility for disregarding obligations does not go away either.

Although lawyers have obligations to clients that may justify actions contrary to lawyers' human obligations, moral responsibility for such actions is unabated. This distinction is important because justification is proportional in balancing competing obligations rather than categorical in negating obligations or absolving actors of responsibility. Circumstances dictate whether departure from either human or role-specific obligations is justified. Lawyers are sometimes justified, as Lord Brougham argues, in bringing alarm, torments, and destruction on others in order to zealously represent their clients. Sometimes, however, they are not.

* * *

VII. UNDERSTANDING THE MORAL INTERDEPENDENCE OF LAWYER AND CLIENT

A. *Allocating Responsibility*

The purpose of this Article is not to resolve debates over legal responsibility of lawyers for clients' actions, but rather to demonstrate that lawyers cannot categorically deny moral responsibility for conduct of their clients. As I have pointed out, consensus on standards for legal liability and standards of professional ethics will be difficult unless there is more consensus on the broader issue of moral responsibility. Furthermore, consensus will be difficult when a substantial number of lawyers are ideologically committed to the categorical assumption that lawyer and client conduct are distinct and separable, an assumption that others, including some government agencies, are insisting must be supported by facts. If lawyer and client conduct are not always independent of each other, lawyers must sometimes accept moral responsibility for client conduct.

Denying any moral responsibility is particularly irrational in situations where conduct would not have been possible without the lawyer's assistance. In other words, the lawyer is the "but for" cause of the conduct. Denial is also irrational where the lawyer had a formative role in a transaction, or was the "proximate" cause of client conduct. Although the SEC specifically alluded to "but for" causation and found it lacking in Carter and Johnson, that case is an example of "proximate cause" in that the lawyers rendered substantial assistance to their client over a time period of more than a year while the client defrauded its investors. Although these categories of causation should not themselves become a basis for rigid categorical allocation of moral responsibility for client conduct, they are at least a starting point.

* * *

B. *Accepting Responsibility*

When should corporate lawyers accept moral responsibility for client conduct? First, lawyers should accept responsibility when the facts of lawyer participation in client conduct make any other conclusion illogical. Corporate lawyers cannot deny that they often have a substantial role in both the choices their clients make and the way those choices are implemented. * * *

Second, lawyers should accept moral responsibility when they are paid to accept actual responsibility. The roles of monitor and dealmaker, like the more narrowly defined roles of "reputational intermediary" and "transaction cost engineer," are roles that lawyers willingly assume and the performance of which justifies a significant portion of their fees. Monitoring conduct often means monitoring the flow of information provided by clients to investors and regulators who trust the accuracy of clients' information because they trust the clients' lawyers. Responsibility not to betray trust that comes with these roles is part of the bargain. Corporate lawyers are not soldiers, and they are certainly not conscripts required to launch sneak attacks on unsuspecting victims at the whim of their clients.

Finally, lawyers should accept moral responsibility when they perform functions in corporate governance that they have chosen collectively as well as individually. The Berle–Means corporation that gives lawyers so much responsibility and so many opportunities to earn fees is the product of law as well as economics. Regulations, many of which have been drafted by lawyers, severely limit participation in corporate governance by nonshareholder constituencies and by many institutional shareholders, leaving these constituencies with primarily legal levers to control corporate conduct. Management, not to be outdone, has been provided with legal levers of its own. For lawyers to deny any responsibility when they pull these levers for clients is self serving to say the least.

The corporate bar has, however, been prone to a pattern of denial reinforced by the belief that lawyers for large corporations do not have to confront moral or ethical problems to the extent that other "lower status" practitioners do. Corporate lawyers earn more than many other parts of the bar and may believe themselves to be more ethical as well. In many of the law firm histories cited throughout this Article, corporate lawyers also boast of their influence over the world of business and government. It is time that lawyers abandon the notion that they are mere scriveners and acknowledge their own power.

C. *Interdependent Lawyering*

Briefly, how is interdependent lawyering, or practicing law knowing that lawyers can be morally responsible for client conduct, different from the presumably independent lawyering illustrated by so many of the unfortunate examples discussed in this Article? First, if lawyers believe that ethical dilemmas of their clients can become their own, some lawyers may change the way they choose their clients. Legal representation might be allocated in part by moral commitments of lawyers in addition to by the market. Lawyers might also consider the merits of a particular client's transactional objectives relative to the objectives of others whom the lawyer could represent instead. Finally, the impact on lawyers' own moral character, and that of their partners and associates, from representing a particular client might be considered. A learning experience for some lawyers, such as representing a Charles Keating, Jr., might be a corrupting experience for others. Despite Lord Erskine's dire prediction, our liberties are unlikely to be threatened by the notion that everybody is not entitled to a lawyer for every purpose.

Interdependent lawyering might also involve giving more than legal advice. If clients contemplate leveraged buyouts, for example, lawyers could inform them of moral, political, and economic advantages of deals that increase long-term goodwill with the community, employees, and regulatory authorities, instead of deals that exclusively emphasize short-term profits. If clients contemplate discharging pollutants that Congress intended to prohibit but agency regulations arguably allow, lawyers could explain to clients that taking advantage of regulatory loopholes involves moral dilemmas, legal risk, and loss of reputation. They could also urge clients to consider the purpose as well as the letter of the law. When lawyers participate in client conduct and acknowledge that they are morally, if not legally, responsible for that conduct, such advice cannot rightfully be regarded as unwarranted intermeddling.

Finally, wider acceptance of the moral interdependence theory should enhance lawyer communication with clients. As pointed out above, some clients may not understand or accept the moral independence theory. Others may embrace the crudest form of the moral independence theory, the notion that moral decisions are exclusively theirs and that a lawyer's role is to tell them what they can get away with, get paid, and go away. In either case, lawyers who do not believe they are justified in assuming moral responsibility narrower in scope than their actual contribution to a transaction should say so. Enhanced communication about responsibility by lawyers who do so much on behalf of their clients but sometimes say too little would be a significant accomplishment.

DOE v. UNOCAL CORPORATION
395 F.3d 932 (9th Cir. 2002)

PREGERSON, CIRCUIT JUDGE:

This case involves human rights violations that allegedly occurred in Myanmar, formerly known as Burma. Villagers from the Tenasserim region in Myanmar allege that the Defendants directly or indirectly subjected the villagers to forced labor, murder, rape, and torture when the Defendants constructed a gas pipeline through the Tenasserim region. The villagers base their claims on the Alien Tort Claims Act, and the Racketeer Influenced and Corrupt Organizations Act, as well as state law.

The District Court, through dismissal and summary judgment, resolved all of Plaintiffs' federal claims in favor of the Defendants. For the following reasons, we reverse in part and affirm in part the District Court's rulings.

I.

FACTUAL AND PROCEDURAL BACKGROUND

A. *Unocal's Investment in a Natural Gas Project in Myanmar*

Burma has been ruled by a military government since 1958. In 1988, a new military government, Defendant–Appellee State Law and Order Restoration Council ("the Myanmar Military"), took control and renamed the country Myanmar. The Myanmar Military established a state owned company, Defendant–Appellee Myanmar Oil and Gas Enterprise ("Myanmar Oil"), to produce and sell the nation's oil and gas resources.

In 1992, Myanmar Oil licensed the French oil company Total S.A. ("Total") to produce, transport, and sell natural gas from deposits in the Yadana Field off the coast of Myanmar ("the Project"). Total set up a subsidiary, Total Myanmar Exploration and Production ("Total Myanmar"), for this purpose. The Project consisted of a Gas Production Joint Venture, which would extract the natural gas out of the Yadana Field, and a Gas Transportation Company, which would construct and operate a pipeline to transport the natural gas from the coast of Myanmar through the interior of the country to Thailand.

Also in 1992, Defendant–Appellant Unocal Corporation and its wholly owned subsidiary Defendant–Appellant Union Oil Company of California, collectively referred to below as "Unocal," acquired a 28% interest in the Project from Total. Unocal set up a wholly owned subsidiary, the Unocal Myanmar Offshore Company ("the Unocal Offshore Co."), to hold Unocal's 28% interest in the Gas Production Joint Venture half of the Project. Similarly, Unocal set up another wholly owned subsidiary, the Unocal International Pipeline Corporation ("the Unocal Pipeline Corp."), to hold Unocal's 28% interest in the Gas Transportation Company half of the Project. Myanmar Oil and a Thai government entity, the Petroleum Authority of Thailand Exploration and Production, also acquired interests in the Project. Total Myanmar was appointed Operator of the Gas Production Joint Venture and the Gas Transportation Company. As the Operator, Total Myanmar was responsible, *inter alia*, for "determining . . . the selection of . . . employees [and] the hours of work and the compensation to be paid to all . . . employees" in connection with the Project.

B. *Unocal's Knowledge that the Myanmar Military Was Providing Security and Other Services for the Project*

It is undisputed that the Myanmar Military provided security and other services for the Project, and that Unocal knew about this. The pipeline was to run through Myanmar's rural Tenasserim region. The Myanmar Military increased its presence in the pipeline region to provide security and other services for the Project.[1] Unocal memoran-

---

1. Although anti-government rebels were active elsewhere in Myanmar, the record indicates that there was in fact little to no rebel activity in the region where the pipeline construction occurred, and that the center of the Myanmar civil war was 150–200 miles distant from the pipeline project.

dum documenting Unocal's meetings with Total on March 1 and 2, 1995 reflects Unocal's understanding that "four battalions of 600 men each will protect the [pipeline] corridor" and "fifty soldiers will be assigned to guard each survey team." A former soldier in one of these battalions testified at his deposition that his battalion had been formed in 1996 specifically for this purpose. In addition, the Military built helipads and cleared roads along the proposed pipeline route for the benefit of the Project.

There is also evidence sufficient to raise a genuine issue of material fact whether the Project *hired* the Myanmar Military, through Myanmar Oil, to provide these services, and whether Unocal knew about this. A Production Sharing Contract, entered into by Total Myanmar and Myanmar Oil before Unocal acquired an interest in the Project, provided that "[Myanmar Oil] shall . . . supply[]or make available . . . security protection . . . as may be requested by [Total Myanmar and its assigns]," such as Unocal. Unocal was aware of this agreement. Thus, a May 10, 1995 Unocal "briefing document" states that "according to *our contract*, the government of Myanmar is responsible for protecting the pipeline." (Emphasis added.) Similarly, in May 1995, a cable from the U.S. Embassy in Rangoon, Myanmar, reported that Unocal On–Site Representative Joel Robinson ("Unocal Representative Robinson" or "Robinson") "stated forthrightly that *the companies have hired* the Burmese military to provide security for the project." (Emphasis added.)

* * * Furthermore, there is evidence sufficient to raise a genuine issue of material fact whether the Project directed the Myanmar Military in these activities, at least to a degree, and whether Unocal was involved in this. In May 1995, a cable from the U.S. Embassy in Rangoon reported:

> [Unocal Representative] Robinson indicated . . . Total/Unocal uses [aerial photos, precision surveys, and topography maps] to show the [Myanmar] military where they need helipads built and facilities secured. . . . Total's security officials meet with military counterparts to inform them of the next day's activities so that soldiers can ensure the area is secure and guard the work perimeter while the survey team goes about its business.

* * *

C.   Unocal's Knowledge that the Myanmar Military Was Allegedly Committing Human Rights Violations in Connection with the Project

Plaintiffs are villagers from Myanmar's Tenasserim region, the rural area through which the Project built the pipeline. Plaintiffs allege that the Myanmar Military forced them, under threat of violence, to work on and serve as porters for the Project. For instance, John Doe IX testified that he was forced to build a helipad near the pipeline site in 1994 that was then used by Unocal and Total officials who visited the pipeline during its planning stages. John Doe VII and John Roe X, described the construction of helipads at Eindayaza and Po Pah Pta, both of which were near the pipeline site, were used to ferry Total/Unocal executives and materials to the construction site, and were constructed using the forced labor of local villagers, including Plaintiffs. John Roes VIII and IX, as well as John Does I, VIII and IX testified that they were forced to work on building roads leading to the pipeline construction area. Finally, John Does V and IX, testified that they were required to serve as "pipeline porters"—workers who performed menial tasks such as such as hauling materials and cleaning the army camps for the soldiers guarding the pipeline construction.

Plaintiffs also allege in furtherance of the forced labor program just described, the Myanmar Military subjected them to acts of murder, rape, and torture. For instance, Jane Doe I testified that after her husband, John Doe I, attempted to escape the forced labor program, he was shot at by soldiers, and in retaliation for his attempted escape, that she and her baby were thrown into a fire, resulting in injuries to her and the death of the child. Other witnesses described the summary execution of villagers who refused to participate in the forced labor program, or who grew too weak to work effectively. Several Plaintiffs testified that rapes occurred as part of the forced labor program. For instance, both Jane Does II and III testified that while conscripted to work on pipeline-related construction projects, they were raped at knife-point by Myanmar soldiers who were members of a battalion that was supervising the work. Plaintiffs finally allege that Unocal's conduct gives rise to liability for these abuses.

The successive military governments of first Burma and now Myanmar have a long and well-known history of imposing forced labor on their citizens. ... As detailed below, even before Unocal invested in the Project, Unocal was made aware—by its own consultants and by its partners in the Project—of this record and that the Myanmar Military might also employ forced labor and commit other human rights violations in connection with the Project. And after Unocal invested in the Project, Unocal was made aware—by its own consultants and employees, its partners in the Project, and human rights organizations—of allegations that the Myanmar Military was actually committing such violations in connection with the Project.

Before Unocal acquired an interest in the Project, it hired a consulting company, Control Risk Group, to assess the risks involved in the investment. In May 1992, Control Risk Group informed Unocal that "throughout Burma the government habitually makes use of forced labour to construct roads." Control Risk Group concluded that "in such circumstances UNOCAL and its partners will have little freedom of manoeuvre." Unocal's awareness of the risk at that time is also reflected in the deposition testimony of Unocal Vice President of International Affairs Stephen Lipman ("Unocal Vice President Lipman"):

"In our discussions between Unocal and Total [preceding Unocal's acquisition of an interest in the Project], we said that the option of having the [Myanmar] Military provide protection n7 for the pipeline construction and operation of it would be that they might proceed in the manner that would be out of our control and not be in a manner that we would like to see them proceed, I mean, going to excess."

* * * On January 4, 1995, approximately three years after Unocal acquired an interest in the Project, Unocal President Imle met with human rights organizations at Unocal's headquarters in Los Angeles and acknowledged to them that the Myanmar Military might be using forced labor in connection with the Project. At that meeting, Imle said that "people are threatening physical damage to the pipeline," that "if you threaten the pipeline there's gonna be more military," and that "*if forced labor goes hand and glove with the military yes there will be more forced labor.*" (Emphasis added.)

Two months later, on March 16, 1995, Unocal Representative Robinson confirmed to Unocal President Imle that the Myanmar Military might be committing human rights violations in connection with the Project. Thus, Robinson wrote to Imle that he had received publications from human rights organizations "which depicted in more detail than I have seen before the increased encroachment of [the Myanmar Military's] activities into the villages of the pipeline area." Robinson concluded on the basis of these publications that "our assertion that [the Myanmar Military] has not expanded and amplified its usual methods around the pipeline on our behalf may not withstand much scrutiny."

* * * Shortly thereafter, on May 10, 1995, Unocal Representative Robinson wrote to Total's Herve Madeo:

> From Unocal's standpoint, probably the most sensitive issue is "what is forced labor" and "how can you identify it." I am sure that you will be thinking about the demarcation between work done by the project and work done "on behalf of" the project. Where the responsibility of the project ends is *very important*.

This statement is some evidence that Unocal knew that the Myanmar Military might use forced labor in connection with the Project.

In June 1995, Amnesty International also alerted Unocal to the possibility that the Myanmar Military might use forced labor in connection with the Project. Amnesty International informed Unocal that comments from a Myanmar Department of Industry official "could mean that the government plans to use 'voluntary' labor in conjunction with the pipeline." Amnesty International went on to explain that "what they call 'voluntary' labor is called forced labor in other parts of the world."[2]

2. Also in 1995, Human Rights Watch informed Unocal that forced labor was so pervasive in Myanmar that Human Rights Watch could not condone any investment that would enrich the country's current regime. That same year, the General Assembly of the United Nations "strongly urged the Government of Myanmar ... to put an

Later that year, on December 11, 1995, Unocal Consultant John Haseman ("Unocal Consultant Haseman" or "Haseman"), a former military attache at the U.S. Embassy in Rangoon, reported to Unocal that the Myanmar Military was, in fact, using forced labor and committing other human rights violations in connection with the Project. Haseman told Unocal that "Unocal was particularly discredited when a corporate spokesman was quoted as saying that Unocal was satisfied with ... assurances [by the Myanmar Military] that no human rights abuses were occurring in the area of pipeline construction." Haseman went on to say:

> Based on my three years of service in Burma, my continuous contacts in the region since then, and my knowledge of the situation there, my conclusion is that egregious human rights violations have occurred, and are occurring now, in southern Burma. The most common are forced relocation without compensation of families from land near/along the pipeline route; forced labor to work on infrastructure projects supporting the pipeline ...; and imprisonment and/or execution by the army of those opposing such actions.... Unocal, by seeming to have accepted [the Myanmar Military]'s version of events, appears at best naive and at worst a willing partner in the situation.

Communications between Unocal and Total also reflect the companies' shared knowledge that the Myanmar Military was using forced labor in connection with the Project. On February 1, 1996, Total's Herve Chagnoux wrote to Unocal and explained his answers to questions by the press as follows:

> By stating that I could not *guarantee* that the army is not using forced labour, I certainly imply that they might, (and they might) but I am saying that we do not have to monitor army's behavior: we have our responsibilities; they have their responsibilities; and we refuse to be pushed into assuming more than what we can really guarantee. About forced labour used by the troops assigned to provide security on our pipeline project, let us admit between Unocal and Total that we might be in a grey zone.

* * *

II.

ANALYSIS

A. *Liability Under the Alien Tort Claims Act*

* * *

end to ... the practices of torture, abuse of women, forced labour ..., and ... disappearances and summary executions...."

2. Forced Labor

* * * Viewing the evidence in the light most favorable to Plaintiffs, we conclude that there are genuine issues of material fact whether Unocal's conduct met the *actus reus* and *mens rea* requirements for liability under the ATCA for aiding and abetting forced labor. Accordingly, we reverse the District Court's grant of Unocal's motion for summary judgment on Plaintiffs' forced labor claims under the ATCA * * *

3. Murder, Rape, and Torture

* * * Viewing the evidence in the light most favorable to Plaintiffs, we conclude that there are genuine issues of material fact whether Unocal's conduct met the *actus reus* and *mens rea* requirements for liability under the ATCA for aiding and abetting murder and rape. Accordingly, we reverse the District Court's grant of Unocal's motion for summary judgment on Plaintiffs' murder and rape claims under the ATCA. By contrast, the record does not contain sufficient evidence to support Plaintiffs' claims of torture. We therefore affirm the District Court's grant of Unocal's motion for summary judgment on Plaintiffs' torture claims.

* * *

III.

Conclusion

For the foregoing reasons, we REVERSE the District Court's grant of summary judgment in favor of Unocal on Plaintiffs' ATCA claims for forced labor, murder, and rape. We however AFFIRM the District Court's grant of summary judgment in favor of Unocal on Plaintiffs' ATCA claims for torture. We further AFFIRM the District Court's dismissal of all of the *Doe*-Plaintiffs' claims against the Myanmar Military and Myanmar Oil. We also AFFIRM the District Court's grant of summary judgment in favor of Unocal on the *Doe*-Plaintiffs' RICO claim against Unocal. We REMAND the case to the District Court for further proceedings consistent with this opinion * * *

After the panel decision in *Unocal*, the Ninth Circuit voted to hear the case en banc. Doe v. Unocal Corporation, 395 F.2d 978 (9th Cir. 2003). Unocal eventually settled with the plaintiffs on confidential terms that it said would "in principle ... compensate plaintiffs and provide funds ... to improve living conditions, health care and education" and "provide substantial assistance to people who may have suffered hardships in the region." Robert Horn, Paying for It, Time Asia, December 27, 2004, at 14.

PROBLEMS

1. You are one of three Assistant General Counsels for TransEnergy Corporation (TEC), a large international energy company. TEC is in the

final stages of negotiating a joint venture with the government of Lotustan to build a natural gas pipeline for several hundred miles through the country. Lotustan is a central Asian country that is wracked by civil unrest and violence. The Lotustan government has been accused by human rights organizations of widespread activities similar to those alleged in *Doe v. Unocal*, namely the use of the military to conscript people into slave labor, and murder, rape, and torture of the civilian population by government soldiers. Lotustan plans to use the military to provide security services for joint venture activities in unstable parts of the country.

After the Unocal settlement, TEC's general counsel asks you to begin drafting suggestions about how the TEC pipeline joint venture with the Lotustan government might be structured to avoid TEC liability for any of the actions of the Lotustan military or other government employees.

How do you respond to this request?

2. You are a lawyer at a law firm that does regulatory work for Exogen, a company that manufactures components for the engines of automobiles and other vehicles. One of the solvents used in the manufacturing process, Durasol, has been implicated as a potential carcinogen in recent scientific studies. The data from this research is consistent with internal information and reports about the dangers of Durasol that Exogen has in its possession. The Occupational Health and Safety Administration (OSHA) has begun to consider the possibility of banning the use of Durasol because of its effect on workers who come in contact with it or breathe in its fumes. OSHA officials have approached the company about the possibility of voluntarily discontinuing the use of the solvent.

Exogen officials privately have concluded that they eventually will have to discontinue the use of Durasol. They are concerned, however, that doing so will significantly increase the costs of manufacturing, since the substance that would have to be used in its place is considerably more expensive. The company is in the process of moving its major manufacturing operations to Indonesia, and expects those operations to be up and running within three years. Indonesia regulates substances used in the manufacturing process more leniently than does the United States, and Exogen would be able to use Durasol in its operations there. If the company could delay OSHA efforts to ban the solvent for three years, Exogen would be able to sustain its profits by continuing to use Durasol in its United States plants during that period. At the end of that time, its major manufacturing activities would take place in Indonesia, where it would not have to worry about the OSHA ban.

Company officials meet with you to discuss a legal campaign that could accomplish this goal. This campaign could consist of a number of strategies. First, rather than voluntarily cease using Durasol, Exogen could insist that OSHA institute formal procedures to prohibit use of the solvent. This would require hearings, the opportunity for Exogen to present data that question whether the harms of Durasol have been adequately established, the chance to respond to adverse testimony, and other elaborate procedural measures. In addition, Exogen has learned that the daughter of the OSHA official who would play a major role in the OSHA proceedings works for an insurance subsidiary of Panoply Corporation. Panoply is a multinational holding company that has just purchased a small corporation that manufactures a solvent that some companies might use if Durasol were banned. Exogen plans to hold on to this information until OSHA formally prohibits use of Durasol, then challenge the OSHA action on the ground that the lead agency official has a conflict of interest because of his daughter's employment with Paroply. If it loses, Exogen plans to appeal to the U.S. Court of Appeals and, if necessary, seek review by the Supreme Court. All these steps should comprise a legal strategy that would delay OSHA prohibition of Durasol for about three years.

How do you proceed?

Chapter 5

THE WORK OF THE CORPORATE LAWYER: WHAT DO CORPORATE LAWYERS DO?

Kurt Vonnegut, God Bless You, Mr. Rosewater 1965

"In every big transaction, * * * there is a magic moment during which a man has surrendered a treasure, and during which the man who is due to receive it has not yet done so. An alert lawyer will make that moment his own, possessing the treasure for a magic microsecond, taking a little of it, passing it on. If the man who is to receive the treasure is unused to wealth, has an inferiority complex and shapeless feelings of guilt, as most people do, the lawyer can often take as much as half the bundle, and still receive the recipient's blubbering thanks."

What, exactly, does a corporate lawyer do? Put simply, a corporate lawyer does what all lawyers do: negotiate, litigate, draft, advise, counsel. A moment's reflection suggests a more complex answer. A corporate lawyer's client is, by definition, an entity, a corporation. It may be large or small, public or closely held, domestic, foreign or multi-national, but it is an entity rather than an individual or group of individuals. And the advice that the corporation seeks often inextricably blends legal and business questions. And as the line between them blurs, the ethical issues become harder to identify and resolve. This chapter introduces some of those issues in order to give you a deeper understanding of what, exactly, a corporate lawyer does.

THE WORK OF THE CORPORATE LAWYER:
A SIMPLE ROADMAP

Before studying the materials in this chapter, consider the following roadmap which, although necessarily incomplete, summarizes much of a corporate lawyer's work. Many of the subjects listed below will be treated in subsequent chapters.

Transactional Work

- Negotiating
- Drafting
- Advising as to form and structure of transaction
- Rendering legal opinions

Litigation

- Drafting litigation documents
- Discovery
- Interviewing and preparing witnesses
- Negotiating settlements
- Court arguments
- Defending government civil, criminal and administrative actions

Regulatory Work

- Advising about regulatory compliance
- Drafting SEC disclosure documents
- Drafting other regulatory documents
- Communicating with regulatory bodies (e.g., SEC no-action letters, IRS rulings)

General Corporate Work

- Drafting corporate announcements
- Filing corporate documents with state agencies
- "Corporate housework" (e.g., preparing minutes of meetings, maintaining shareholder records)
- Counseling on related legal issues (e.g., intellectual property, employment, etc.)

Advising Corporate Management

- Preparing codes of conduct relating to legal compliance
- Advising corporate management as to fiduciary duties
- Conducting internal investigations of possible law violations
- Advising as to federal and state legal duties and obligations
- Advising as to regulatory compliance (e.g., insider trading, Section 16 reports and transactions)

OVERVIEW OF THE CHAPTER

Although business lawyers do many things in the course of their practice, this chapter deals entirely with transactional work rather than litigation. It explores how lawyers create value for their clients. It also examines the concept of what it means to be a business lawyer and suggests that it involves a great deal more than simply knowing the law with respect to the particular transaction with which the lawyer is involved.

In the first article, Ronald Gilson's hypothesis is that a business lawyer is fundamentally a transaction cost engineer whose job, when done correctly, is to lower the costs of a particular venture. In so doing, the lawyer creates value for the client that would not have been available without the lawyer's work. To illustrate his point, he focuses on an acquisition transaction, and particularly on the acquisition agreement that sets out the terms of the transaction and the rights and obligations of the parties to the transaction. With capital asset pricing theory as his starting point, Gilson contends that in a world of perfect markets and information, a lawyer would not be needed. In the real world, however, because the parties do not have homogeneous expectations or the same time horizons, a lawyer can create structures that minimize these differences. It is these structures that create value and justify the use of lawyers.

James Freund expands this idea through a broader perception of the role of a transactional lawyer. For Freund, the line between advising a client on legal or business matters is fuzzy at best, particularly if the lawyer is experienced and the client accepts the lawyer in a more non-traditional role. You will study this dichotomy again when you consider the the attorney-client privilege in Chapter 12 and the lawyer as a director of a corporation in Chapter 14. By casting his ideas in the form of a play, Freund is able to demonstrate the potentially wide range of choices that a lawyer has when advising a client and how easy it is to move back and forth between business and legal advice. He also shows, without explicitly saying so, that a transactional lawyer by virtue of being a repeat player, even with different clients, acquires an expertise that can be transferred to new clients and subsequent transactions. It is that expertise that helps to explain the high fees that some business lawyers charge.

The articles by Friedman, Gordon, Pirie & Whatley and Suchman & Cahill dealing with lawyers in Silicon Valley representing high-tech start-up companies bring the business lawyer into an entrepreneurial role far beyond what Gilson and Freund contemplate. The ethical implications of this expansion are profound. As you read these articles, consider the extent to which professional standards are bent or broken in an attempt to create the economic value that Gilson has described. Can the value system that the Silicon Valley lawyers have constructed in order to facilitate capital raising to develop new technologies be exported into different business settings? Is the Silicon Valley culture transferable to other locales with other cultural expectations. Consider whether, as a young lawyer in a Silicon Valley firm, you would be comfortable in negotiating and drafting an acquisition agreement of the type that Suchman and Cahill describe. Do you believe that such an agreement adequately protects your client if the transaction falls apart. If not, how would you handle your concern?

The last article in the chapter may seem strange, focusing as it does on accounting, but it is extremely important and provides the introduction for the material in Chapter 19 which is devoted to accounting and financial reporting issues. It also provides some background for the securities law questions in Chapters 16 and 17.

Lawrence Cunningham's basic point is quite simple. In today's complex financial world, a business lawyer must know something about the accounting consequences of the transactions in which the client is involved. In so doing, the lawyer will be creating value for the client (an extension of the ideas that Gilson and Freund develop earlier in the chapter) as well as helping the client avoid accounting fraud. As with the article by Robert Rosen that you will read in Chapter 9, Cunningham uses Enron as the starting point for his analysis although he carefully avoids blaming the lawyers for what went wrong in Enron. Rather, he argues that because Enron is fundamentally an accounting scandal, the lawyers in such a transaction were required to know some accounting in the course of advising their client.

For Cunningham, the need to know some accounting is a part of a lawyer's basic duty of competence, whether dictated by Model Rule 1.1 or the fiduciary duty that a lawyer owes to the client. He notes that a lawyer's duty of competence is usually thought of as limited to legal matters. He argues, however, that the intersection of law and accounting today is so powerful that the duty can no longer be confined solely to questions of law. He points out that the obligation to be informed about accounting matters is no different from a lawyer's duty to be informed about the basic subject matter of any transaction in which she is involved. Although a lawyer may satisfy that duty by relying on experts (for example, a geologist in a mineral exploration transaction), Cunningham believes that such reliance will not suffice when financial and accounting matters are involved. He is not dogmatic about how a lawyer should obtain the requisite knowledge (although, in a part of the article not included here, he argues that law schools have a duty to include accounting as a required part of the curriculum); it is simply something that is now a part of a lawyer's basic duty of competence.

Ronald J. Gilson, VALUE CREATION BY BUSINESS LAWYERS: LEGAL SKILLS AND ASSET PRICING

94 YALE L.J. 239 (1984)

What do business lawyers *really* do? Embarrassingly enough, at a time when lawyers are criticized with increasing frequency as nonproductive actors in the economy, there seems to be no coherent answer * * *

Clients have their own, often quite uncharitable, view of what business lawyers do. In an extreme version, business lawyers are perceived as evil sorcerers who use their special skills and professional magic to relieve clients of their possessions * * *

Clients frequently advance other more charitable but still negative views of the business lawyer that also should be familiar to most practitioners. Business lawyers are seen at best as a transaction cost, part of a system of wealth redistribution from clients to lawyers; legal fees represent a tax on business transactions to provide an income maintenance program for lawyers. At worst, lawyers are seen as deal killers whose continual raising of obstacles, without commensurate effort at finding solutions, ultimately causes transactions to collapse under their own weight * * *

[T]he unfavorable views ascribed to the client reflect the view that business lawyers *reduce* the value of a transaction, while both the quite favorable view held by business lawyers themselves and the more neutral but still positive view offered in the academic literature assume that business lawyers *increase* the value of a transaction. But both sides do seem to agree on the appropriate standard by which the performance of business lawyers should be judged: *If what a business lawyer does has value, a transaction must be worth more, net of legal fees, as a result of the lawyer's participation.* And the common failure of all of these views is not their differing conclusions. Rather, it is the absence of an explanation of the *relation* between the business lawyers' participation in a transaction and the value of the transaction to the clients. In other words, precisely *how* do the activities of business lawyers affect transaction value?

I recognize that I may appear to have shifted the focus of my inquiry—from what business lawyers really do to whether whatever they do increases the value of a transaction. But this emphasis on the business lawyer's effect on transaction value should not shift attention from examination of the particular activities in which business lawyers engage. Rather, my goal is to develop a mode of analysis that allows identification of those activities that have value; in the absence of a tie to transactional value, a particular legal function is simply besides the point.

I.   THE IDEA OF VALUE CREATION

My simple assertion—that what business lawyers do has value only if the transaction on which the lawyer works is more valuable as a result—requires both clarification and some means by which the lawyer's performance can be measured against the standard. Because clarification of the standard is by far the more straightforward of the two problems, I begin there.

A.   *Conceptual Clarification*

My point in clarifying the value creation standard is to make it significantly more difficult to meet. I have in mind two familiar functions—distributive bargaining and manipulation of a regulatory system—which, depending on your perspective, support an argument that business lawyers create value. For each function, however, the potential for value creation depends on a critical assumption. In the case of distributive bargaining, it depends on the assumption that lawyers will be used at all; in the case of manipulation a regulatory system, on the assumption that such a system exists. Examining each situation will clarify the rigorous standard I set: Can business lawyers create value even when use of their services is truly voluntary, when there is nothing that, in effect, artificially requires the use of a business lawyer?

Consider first the case of distributive bargaining. Imagine that a client has had the good fortune to retain a very talented business lawyer when the other party is represented by a dullard. Assuming that the lawyers can have *any* impact on the value of a transaction, we might anticipate that it would be to alter the allocation of gains from the transaction between the parties. Here the claim would be merely that one lawyer's greater skill in distributive bargaining results in that client's receiving a greater share of the gain than would have been the case if the lawyers were more evenly matched. One might then argue that the performance of the talented lawyer meets the value-creation standard. From the perspective of that lawyer's client, the transaction is worth more than if that lawyer had not participated.

One reaches a different conclusion if the transaction is viewed from the perspective of *both* clients. Then the value of the transaction has not changed as a result of participation by business lawyers; rather, resources have been expended to alter the *distribution* of gains that, by definition, would have been forthcoming even without the lawyers' participation. And for purposes of evaluating whether the participation of business lawyers increases the transaction's value, the appropriate perspective is not that of the client with the more talented lawyer, but the joint perspective of both clients * * *

We can thus add one condition to the proposition that business lawyers have potential to add value to a transaction: The increase must be in the overall value of the transaction, not merely in the distributive share of one of the parties. That is, a business lawyer must show the potential to enlarge the entire pie, not just to increase the size of one piece at the expense of another.

A business lawyer's skill at negotiating a regulatory system presents a more compelling case for value creation. In these settings, the business lawyer's function is to convince the regulatory authority that the client's activities are not subject, or only minimally subject, to the regulatory system. Because compliance is typically costly, the lawyer's effort may well increase the value of the transaction in precisely the sense that the value creation standard contemplates.

I suppose no one would be surprised if clients greeted this explanation with little enthusiasm. A client suspicious of the lawyer's role in the first place may not be reassured by the explanation that lawyers minimize regulatory interference with the client's activities. The same client may also have noticed, with some justification, that lawyers are often the source of much of the current regulatory jungle confronting those doing business. From this perspective, a client may be less than grateful for salvation from the very problems the savior originally created.

Moreover, even if we ignore the lawyer's original sin with respect to the imposition of regulation, the regulatory explanation remains unsatisfactory. A more important failing of the regulatory justification for business lawyers is that it simply does not get us far enough. Although it may help explain the potential for Washington lawyers, or regulatory lawyers generally, to create value, business lawyers frequently function in a world in which regulation has made few inroads. For these lawyers the critical rule of law is that a court will enforce whatever the lawyer writes. Thus the hard problem that remains, my principal focus here, is to determine whether *these* business lawyers can meet the value-creation standard. Can business lawyers create value even when there is virtually no law to apply? Is there a purely *private ordering* role for business lawyers?

* * *

II. The Relationship Between Legal Skills and Transaction Value

Framing a hypothesis that explains the relationship between the participation of business lawyers in a transaction and the transaction's value requires recognition that the subjects of these transactions are typically capital assets: assets whose value is determined solely by the income, whether in cash flow or appreciation, they are expected to earn. What we normally think of as a transaction, then, is simply the transfer of a capital asset from one party to another. Characterizing transactions as the transfer of capital assets is important, because over the last fifteen years, financial economists have developed a substantial body of theory to explain how capital assets are valued. If capital asset pricing theory can identify the factors that determine transaction value, then these factors can be examined to determine whether business lawyers can influence them in a way that will alter transaction value.

A. Capital Asset Pricing Theory

The modern development of capital asset pricing theory began with the insight of Harry Markowitz that risk-averse investors will always hold a diversified portfolio of capital assets. This conclusion follows from two premises: that investors prefer more return to less, given the same level of risk, and that investors prefer less risk to more given the same level of return. By holding a number of assets—a portfolio—an investor can reduce risk without reducing return. A rational investor thus will select the portfolio of assets that offers the most return for the desired level of risk.

The next step in the theory's development is a closer look at what kind of risk is reduced by diversification, *i.e.,* by holding a portfolio of assets as opposed to a single asset. The risk consists of two components:

unsystematic and *systematic* risk. Unsystematic risk is that associated with holding a *particular* asset. For example, if the capital asset in question is a specialized machine tool, the risk of a reduction in the demand for the particular product it makes is unsystematic. In contrast, systematic risk is that associated with holding *any* asset. For example, increases or decreases in GNP or changes in the level of inflation affect the value of all assets, and thus present systematic risk. Diversifying one's portfolio eliminates unsystematic risk; as long as the investor holds a sufficient number of assets, the impact of one event on a particular asset will be balanced both by that event's different impact on other assets in the portfolio, and by the occurrence of other events affecting other assets in the portfolio. On balance, the value of the portfolio as a whole will be unaffected. Thus, a diversified portfolio is not subject to unsystematic risk.

The only risk that remains in a diversified portfolio, then, is systematic risk: the risk of events that will alter the value of all assets. And the final step in the development of capital asset pricing theory is the recognition that investors will not be paid to bear risk that can be avoided by diversification. As a result, the return on, and therefore the price of, a capital asset depends on how much systematic risk is associated with it. If an asset is subject to a great deal of systematic risk, an investor will require a higher return, and the asset will sell at a lower price, than would be the case with a less sensitive asset. As long as the capital market is relatively efficient in informational terms, arbitrageurs who identify an asset whose market price is different from what would be expected based on the asset's systematic risk would push prices toward the predicted level.

Although there have been important criticisms of this formulation of capital asset pricing theory, they do not blunt its central insight for our purposes: *In a world in which assets are valued according to any version of capital asset pricing theory, there is little role for business lawyers.* Because capital assets will be priced correctly as a result of market forces, business lawyers *cannot* increase the value of a transaction. Absent regulatory-based explanations, the fees charged by business lawyers would *decrease* the net value of the transaction.

Like many economic models, capital asset pricing theory can be derived only after a number of important simplifying assumptions are made * * *

The difference between the simple world of capital asset pricing theory and the complex world in which transactions actually take place provides the focus for developing a hypothesis concerning the potential for a business lawyer to increase a transaction's value. In the world described by capital asset pricing theory's simplifying assumptions, the lawyer has no function; in my terms, the business lawyer really *does* nothing. What happens, however, when we relax the assumptions on which capital asset pricing theory is based? Is there a role for the business lawyer in this less orderly world?

At this point we need to look more carefully at the assumptions on which capital asset pricing theory is built. Of particular importance to our inquiry are four:

1. All investors have a common time horizon—*i.e.*, they measure the return to be earned from the asset in question over the same period of time.

2. All investors have the same expectations about the future, in particular, about the future risk and return associated with the asset in question.

3. There are no transaction costs.

4. All information is costlessly available to all investors.

These assumptions, of course, do not describe the real world. Investors do not have the same time horizons; indeed, it is often precisely because they do not—for example, an older person may wish to alter the composition of his portfolio in favor of assets whose earnings patterns more closely match his remaining life span—that a transaction occurs in the first place. Similarly, investors do not have homogeneous expectations; the phenomenon of conflicting forecasts of earnings or value even among reputed experts is too familiar for that assumption to stand. Transaction costs, of course, are pervasive. Finally, information is often one of the most expensive and poorly distributed commodities. In short, the world in which capital assets are priced and transactions actually carried out differs in critical respects from the world of perfect markets in which capital asset pricing theory operates.

For a business lawyer, however, the unreality of these perfect market assumptions is not cause for despair. Rather, it is in the very failure of these assumptions to describe the real world that I find the potential for value creation by lawyers. When markets fall short of perfection, incentives exist for private innovations that improve market performance. As long as the costs of innovation are less than the resulting gains, private innovation to reduce the extent of market failure creates value. It is in precisely this fashion that opportunity exists for business lawyers to create value.

B. A Hypothesis Concerning Value Creation: Business Lawyers as Transaction Cost Engineers

The basic assumptions on which capital asset pricing theory is built can be reduced to the simple statement that there are no costs of transacting; there are neither informational disparities between the parties nor any of the more traditional forms of transaction costs. In such a setting, even one unfamiliar with capital asset pricing theory hardly would be surprised that assets would be correctly priced. In this Coasean world, private outcomes are always optimal, and capital asset pricing theory is no more than the inevitable result of the investor's ability costlessly and thoroughly to diversify his portfolio in a frictionless would. The accuracy of capital asset prices, however, is reduced to the extent there are deviations from capital asset pricing theory's perfect market assumptions. For assets to be correctly priced, the real-world deviations from these assumptions must be constrained. This insight is the first step toward a hypothesis explaining how business lawyers might create value.

The next step, then, is to focus on the mechanisms which reduce real world deviations from the capital asset pricing theory's central assumptions. From this perspective, the variance between assumption and reality is, in effect, a form of market failure. My concern here is with the character of the market response to that failure. Just as competitive conditions create incentives that encourage reduction of production costs, the market also encourages private efforts to reduce transaction costs. A service that reduces the net cost—transaction or other—of a good will earn a positive return. To the extent that private economizing successfully reduces transaction costs, the deviation between the real world in which assets are transferred and the frictionless world of the capital asset pricing theory is minimized. The continued presence of a voluntary social convention—for example, the pervasive use of business lawyers—raises an inference that it is a cost-saving, in my terms value-creating, phenomenon.

Formulating a hypothesis about how business lawyers create value, however, requires more than establishing the importance of private innovation as an important method of reducting transaction costs. Two steps are necessary: the specification of precisely how business lawyers can reduce transaction costs, and the tie between their activities and transaction value.

It is useful at this point to return to the idea that a business transaction is the transfer of a capital asset in which the central aspect of the transaction is the asset's valuation * * *

I suggest that the tie between legal skills and transaction value is the business lawyer's ability to create a transactional structure which reduces transaction costs and therefore results in more accurate asset pricing. * * * My hypothesis about what business lawyers *really* do—their potential to create value—is simply this: Lawyers function as *transaction cost engineers,* devising efficient mechanisms which bridge the gap between capital asset pricing theory's hypothetical world of perfect markets and the less-than-perfect reality of effecting transactions in this world. Value is created when the transactional structure designed by the business lawyer allows the parties to act, *for that transaction,* as if the assumptions on which capital pricing theory is based were accurate.

The central role of transaction cost economizing in private ordering is, by now, no longer surprising. What has received less attention is the link between capital asset pricing theory and transaction cost economics, and the institutional framework in which transaction cost economizing takes place. My hypothesis—the business lawyer as transaction cost engineer—thus asserts the dual claim that skilled structuring of the transaction's form can create transaction value *and* that business lawyers are primary players at the game.

III. Testing the Hypothesis: Examination of the Work Product of Business Lawyers

* * * I intend now to examine a standard form of corporate acquisition agreement. If the hypothesis is correct, the traditional contractual approaches reflected in the agreement should be explainable by their relation to one or more of the perfect market assumptions on which capital asset pricing theory is based. And if major elements of a corporate acquisition agreement can be understood by by reference to their impact on these assumptions, then this discovery would constitute substantial empirical evidence of business lawyers' potential to create value. Moreover, we would not only better understand the function of different portions of the agreement but also be better able to draft and negotiate them.

Before examining a standard form of acquisition agreement, I should explain briefly why I selected this form of transaction for study in preference to, for example, a complex real estate transaction or joint venture formation. First, a corporate acquisition is obviously the transfer of a capital asset; indeed, the valuation of corporate securities—the indicia of ownership of a corporation—has dominated the empirical tests of capital asset pricing theory. Second, the business lawyer's role in corporate acquisitions is pervasive. This pervasiveness gives the lawyer the opportunity to play the hypothesized role, and also makes the strongest case for the inference that because the lawyer's role in the transaction has survived, it serves a useful function. Third, negotiation and preparation of the acquisition agreement is the lawyer's principal charge in the transaction. There is thus a fairly complete set of "tracks" of the lawyer's activity * * *

A. An Overview of the Acquisition Agreement

Using an acquisition agreement as the data sample for my examination is desirable not only because it covers a form of transaction particularly appropriate to the lens of theory through which I view the problem, but also because of the very development of a *form* of agreement. Without having become boilerplate—enormous amounts of time still are spent on their negotiation—the general contents of the agreement have by now become pretty much standardized. This is not to say that the distributive consequences of acquisition agreements are likely to be the same. Rather, it is that the problems confronted and the mechanics of the solutions adopted are similar, even if the impact of the specific application of the solution to the parties will differ from transaction to transaction. Because the overall approach and coverage of typical acquisition agreements, and the types of contractual techniques they contain, are largely the same, they can be taken fairly to reflect not merely an individual lawyer's inspired response in a particular situation, but the collective wisdom of business lawyers as a group ...

A description of the subject necessarily precedes an examination of the functional significance of its parts. A skeletal outline of the form of a typical agreement provides a representative picture.

Description of the Transaction. The initial, and usually most straightforward, portion of the agreement provides an overall description of the transaction. The parties are identified, the structure of the transaction—for example, a purchase of stock or assets, or some triangular variation—is described, and details concerning such matters as the timing and location of the closing of the transaction are set forth.

Price and Terms of Payment. The next portion of the agreement typically focuses on the price to be paid and the medium and timing of payment. The text is most straightforward when the medium of payment is cash and the entire amount is to be paid on closing. But where the transaction contemplates other than immediate payment of the entire purchase price, the document inevitably becomes a great deal more complicated. For example, at the time the agreement is prepared, it may be possible to describe the purchase price only by reference to a formula because its amount depends on the performance of the business over some period following the agreement's execution. * * * Similarly, when the medium of payment is other than cash, the need to address valuation issues—for example, if the consideration will be shares of the buyer's stock, how the effects of pre-closing changes in the market price of the stock will be shared—also expands the document's text. Of course, if the timing of the payment will be delayed—for example, if the medium of payment will be the buyer's note—the agreement must cover what is, in effect, an additional transaction: a loan from the seller to the buyer.

Representations and Warranties. The next major portion of the agreement consists of representations and warranties made by the seller and, typically to a much lesser extent, by the buyer. These provisions consist of a series of detailed statements of fact concerning the relevant business. The seller commonly will warrant, *inter alia,* the accuracy of its financial statements; the absence of any liabilities for taxes or other matters accruing after the date of its most recent audited financial statements including, most importantly, the absence of contingent liabilities; the ownership and condition of various assets of importance to the operation of the seller's business; the existence of litigation against the seller, whether actual or threatened; and the extent to which the seller's operations are unionized. Thoroughly done, this portion of the acquisition agreement paints a detailed picture of the seller—the capital asset that is being acquired.

Covenants and Conditions. The two final steps in our survey of the major portions of a typical acquisition agreement result from the fact that many acquisition transactions contemplate a significant gap between the date on which the acquisition agreement is signed and the date on which the transaction is closed. Whether delay is caused by regulatory necessity, such as the requirement that a proxy statement seeking the approval of the transaction by the seller's shareholders be filed and reviewed by the Securities and Exchange Commission, by regulatory convenience, such as the need for an Internal Revenue Service ruling as to the income tax consequences of the transaction, or simply by the buyer's need for additional time to complete its investigation of the seller, the temporal gap between execution and closing requires contractual bridging. This is accomplished by two complementary techniques: *covenants* governing the operation of the business during the gap period, and *conditions* which, if not satisfied, relieve a party of its obligation to complete the transaction. Typically these two techniques combine with the representations and warranties to operate as a unit, providing a hierarchy of obligations and the potential for a hierarchy of remedies if one or more of the other party's obligations are not met. Thus a covenant may require that the seller maintain working capital above a specified level pending closing. At the same time, the seller may also have warranted that working capital was, and at closing will be, above the specified level, and the buyer's obligation to close the transaction may be conditioned generally on the accuracy of the seller's representations and warranties as of the date of closing, on the seller's satisfaction of all covenants during the pre-closing period, and, specifically, on the required level of working capital at the closing date. A failure to maintain adequate working capital will then constitute both a breach of warranty and a violation of a covenant, as well as providing the buyer with a number of justifications for not completing the transaction.

In formal terms, then, the acquisition agreement is simply a more complicated version of what one would expect in any sales agreement: It states the form and terms of the transaction, describes the asset to be transferred, and specifies the manner in which the asset will be preserved pending the completion of the transaction. The possibility that this contractual structure has the potential to create value, however, arises not from a formal overview, but from the manner in which different elements of the agreement respond to the problem of constraining the effect of real world deviations from capital asset pricing theory's perfect market assumptions. For this purpose, it is necessary to focus attention directly on the assumptions themselves, particularly the assumptions that all investors have homogeneous expectations, that they share a common time horizon, that information is costlessly available to all, and that there are no other transaction costs. It is in response to the potential impact of this unholy host that my hypothesis holds out the potential for a value-creating role for business lawyers.

B. *The Failure of the Homogeneous–Expectations Assumption: The Earnout Response*

I want to begin with the assumption that can be most clearly examined from my perspective: The assumption that all investors have homogeneous expectations. The critical place in asset pricing theory of the assumption that all investors share the same beliefs about the future risk and return associated with owning the asset in question, in our case a business, is obvious: As long as we all agree about the future income stream associated with owning the business and about the systematic risk associated with that income, there is no reason to expect potential buyers and sellers of the business to disagree about its price. But it is also obvious that buyers and sellers often *do not* share common expectations concerning the business future.

Imagine a negotiation between the presidents of a buyer and seller concerning the price at which the transaction will take place. Imagine further that the negotiations have progressed to the point where agreement has been reached on an abstract, but nonetheless important, pricing principle, that the appropriate way to value the seller's business is $1 in purchase price for each $1 in annual sales. The critical nature of the homogeneous-expectations assumption should be apparent. Even after agreement on a valuation principle, the parties will agree on price *only* if they share the same expectations about the seller's future sales. The problem, of course, is that they will not. The negotiating dance that results is familiar to practitioners.

Now suppose that the buyer's president, having done his homework, believes that there is a 50% chance the seller will do $10 million in sales next year and a 50% chance that it will do only $5 million. The expected value of the alternatives is $7.5 million which the buyer's president offers as the purchase price which the agreed-upon valuation principle dictates. The president of the seller, not surprisingly, has different expectations. He is much more optimistic about the probabilities associated with next year's sales. His homework suggests an 85% chance of $10 million in sales and only a 15% chance of sales as low as $5 million. These figures yield an expected value, and a purchase price under the agreed valuation principle, of $9.25 million. The result is inaccurate pricing at best and, because of the resulting conflict over the purchase price, at worst no transaction at all if the parties are unable to resolve their differences.

It is important to emphasize at this point that the problem which "kills" our hypothetical deal is not distributional conflict—disagreement over sharing the gains from the transaction. The distributional principle in the form of a valuation formula has already been approved. Rather, the problem is an example of the failure of the homogeneous-expectations assumption: The parties simply have different expectations concerning the future performance of the business. If this problem could be solved, a deal could be made. Tautologically, the value of the transaction would be increased. And if my hypothesis about what business lawyers do is correct, a particularly inviting opportunity then exists for value creation by a business lawyer. The lawyer can increase the value of the transaction if he can devise a transactional structure that creates homogeneous expectations.

As my hypothesis predicts, there is a familiar remedy, commonly called an "earnout" or "contingent price" deal, for this failure of the homogeneous-expectations assumption. It is intended, as a prominent practitioner has put it, to "bridge the negotiating gap between a seller who thinks his business is worth more than its historical earnings justify and a purchaser who hails from Missouri." The solution that business lawyers resort to for this problem is one that economists refer to as state-contingent contracting. Its central insight is that the difference in expectations between the parties as to the probabilities assigned to the occurrence of future events will ultimately disappear as time transforms a prediction of next year's sales into historical fact. If determination of the purchase price can be delayed until next year's sales are known with certainty, the deal can be made. The solution, therefore, is to formulate the purchase price as an initial payment, here $7.5 million, to be followed by an additional payment at the close of the next fiscal year equal, in this case, to $1 for each $1 of sales in excess of $7.5 million. The problem of non-homogeneous expectations is avoided by making the failure irrelevant. Only uncertainty concerning the future forced the parties to rely on expectations about the future; the earnout solution allows the purchase price to be set after that uncertainty has been resolved. That is, each party is allowed to act *as if* his expectation were shared by the other. In effect he bets on the accuracy of his expectation, with a settling up only after the uncertainty has been eliminated and the parties really do have homogeneous beliefs concerning the matter.

The business lawyer's traditional response to failure of the homogeneous-expectations assumption can thus create value by allowing a transaction to go forward that might otherwise not have occurred. But the technique's potential for value creation is greater than just allowing the deal to be made; it also may increase the total value of the deal beyond that which would have resulted even if the parties were capable of compromising their differences. Recall that under capital asset pricing theory the value of the business turns on both the expected return—the weighted average of the possible sales for the next year in our hypothetical—and the systematic risk associated with that return. The effect of the contingent price arrangement is to reduce the buyer's risk by transforming the price from a function of expected—risky—returns to one of certain returns. Thus, the buyer should be willing to pay a higher price per unit of sales because there is no risk associated with that return.

Thus far, my hypothesis about what business lawyers do and how they create value seems confirmed. At least with respect to the failure of the homogeneous-expectations assumption, business lawyers create a transactional structure which bridges the gap between the perfect market assumptions of capital asset pricing theory and the imperfect reality of transacting.

C. The Failure of the Common–Time–Horizon Assumption: Conduct of the Business During the Earnout Period

The failure of a second assumption—this time that investors measure risk and return over the same period-provides an additional opportunity for business lawyers to create value. This can be seen most easily by pursuing discussion of the earnout solution just considered. The earnout concept responds to the failure of the homogeneous-expectations assumption. Efforts to make the concept operational, however, highlight the absence of a common time horizon and the resulting potential for strategic, opportunistic behavior. Where the parties do have different time horizons, each has an incentive to maximize value in the period relevant to it, even at the expense of a decreased in value in the period relevant to the other party. This conflict reduces the value of the transaction.

Consider first what behavior we would expect during the earnout's one-year measuring period if the seller's original management were allowed to run the company for that time. From the seller's perspective, the earnout formula reduces to one year the relevant period over which asset value is to be determined; at the end of that year the seller's shareholders will receive whatever payment is due under the earnout formula. At least for them, the asset will cease to exist. To the seller's shareholders, therefore, the asset is worth only what it can earn for them in a year's time. Their goal is to maximize value over that short period. The buyer, in contrast, is concerned with the value of the business over a much longer period: the entire time it expects to operate the seller's business. Accordingly, the buyer's behavior will differ substantially from that which would be dictated by the seller's short-term orientation.

Returning to the terms of the hypothetical earnout formula—an additional $1 in purchase price for each $1 in sales over $7.5 million— the seller would maximize sales during the one-year measuring period. For example, prices might be cut and advertising expenditures substantially increased, even if these actions meant that the company actually suffered a loss. In contrast, the buyer, which would ultimately bear the loss because it continues to own the company after the one year period, has a very different interest. and the conflict is not merely the result of a poorly specified earnout formula. Stating the formula in terms of profits rather than sales, thus eliminating the seller's incentive to maximize sales at the expense of the buyer's long term interest in earnings, would be a possible improvement. But even then the different time horizons would create an incentive for the seller's management to behave opportunistically. Short term profits could be maximized by eliminating research and development expenditures, cutting maintenance, and, in general, deferring expenses to later periods.

This failure of the common-time-horizon assumption reduces the value of the transaction. So long as the buyer anticipates that the seller's management will behave opportunistically—which hardly requires a crystal ball—it will reduce its offer accordingly. The business lawyer then has the opportunity to create value by devising a transaction structure that constrains the seller's ability to maximize the value of the business over a period different from that relevant to the buyer. The typical earnout agreement responds to precisely this challenge.

Stated most generally, a complete earnout formula is a complicated state-contingent contract that, by carefully specifying in advance the impact on the purchase price of all events that might occur during the earnout period, substantially reduces the incentives and opportunity for the parties to behave strategically. For example, the perverse incentives growing out of a formula specifying either earnings or sales as a sole measure of performance might be reduced by a measure that combines them: *e.g.,* a $1 increase in purchase price for each $1 increase in sales provided that profits remain above a specified percentage of sales. Similarly, where the earnout period is greater than one year, incentives to manipulate the year in which particular events occur can be minimized by provisions which specify whether shortfalls or overages in one year carry forward or backward to other years.

A thoroughly specified earnout formula is extraordinarily complex and, in any event, cannot entirely eliminate the potential for strategic behavior. To be fully effective, a formula would have to specify not only the complete production function for the business, but all possible exogenous events that might occur during the earnout period and the impact of such events on the formula. Neither, of course, is possible. Moreover, the cost of detailed contracting—not just in lawyers' fees, but in the time and goodwill of the parties—will be substantial and in many cases prohibitive. There will be times, then, where the gain in transaction value resulting from ameliorating the failure of the homogeneous-expectations or common-time-horizons assumptions will be outweighed by the cost of the cure. But this possibility merely constrains, rather than eliminates, the potential for value creation by business lawyers. That transaction costs are, at some level, irreducible hardly diminishes the value of efforts to keep costs at that level. It is value creation of the sort the reflects what I understand clients to mean by the comment that a particular lawyer has good "judgment," to know when the game is not worth the candle.

D. The Failure of the Costless–Information Assumption: Representations, Warranties, Indemnification, and Opinions

Perhaps the most important assumption of all is that information is costlessly available to all parties. Its central importance derives in part because it is, in a sense I will consider shortly, a *master* assumption that controls the other assumptions we have considered, and in part because it is in response to its failure that business lawyers have been most creative.

The relation between the costless-information assumption and the homogeneous-expectations assumption illustrates the central role for information problems in our analysis. For our purposes, information is data that can alter the parties' beliefs about the price of an asset * * *

The portion of the acquisition agreement dealing with representations and warranties—commonly the longest part of a typical acquisition agreement and the portion that usually requires the most time for a lawyer to negotiate—has its primary purpose to remedy conditions of asymmetrical information in the least-cost manner. To understand the way in which the device of representations and warranties operates to reduce information asymmetry between the buyer and seller, it is helpful to distinguish between the costs of acquiring new information and the costs of verifying previously acquired information. I consider first the contractual response to information-acquisition problems.

1. Costs of Acquiring Information

During the negotiation, the buyer and seller will face different costs of information acquisition for two important reasons. First, as a simple result of its prior operation of the business, the seller will already have large amounts of information concerning the business that the buyer does not have, but would like to acquire. Second, there usually will be information that neither party has, but that one or both would like and which one or the other can acquire more cheaply. The question is then how both of these situations are dealt with in the acquisition agreement so as to reduce the informational differences between the parties of the lowest possible cost.

At first, one might wonder why any cooperative effort is necessary. Assuming that the seller did not affirmatively block the buyer's efforts to acquire the information the buyer wanted (and the seller already had), nothing would prevent the buyer from independently acquiring the desired information. Similarly, assuming both parties had the opportunity to acquire the desired new information, nothing would prevent both parties from independently acquiring it.

Actually, however, it is in the seller's best interest to make the information that the seller already has available to the buyer as cheaply as possible. Suppose the seller refused to assist the buyer in securing a particular piece of information that the seller already had. If the information could have either a positive or negative value on the buyer's evaluation of the worth of the business, a rational buyer would infer from the seller's refusal to cooperate that the information must be unfavorable. Thus, the seller has little incentive to withhold the information. Indeed, the same result would follow even if the information in question would not alter the buyer's estimate of the value of the business, but only increased the certainty with which that estimate was held. Once we have established that the seller wants the buyer to have information, the only issue that remains is which party can produce it most cheaply. The total price the buyer will pay for the business is the sum of the amount to be paid to the seller and the transaction costs incurred by the buyer in effecting the transaction. To the extent that the buyer's information costs are reduced, there simply is more left over for division between the buyer and seller.

Precisely the same analysis holds for information that neither party has yet acquired. The seller could refuse to cooperate with the buyer in its acquisition. To do so, however, would merely increase the information costs associated with the transaction to the detriment of both parties.

There is thus an incentive for the parties to cooperate both to reduce informational asymmetries between them and to reduce the costs of acquiring information either believes necessary for the transaction. As a result, we would expect an acquisition agreement to contain provisions for three kinds of cooperative behavior concerning information acquisition costs. First, the agreement would facilitate the transfer of information the seller already has to the buyer. Second, the agreement would allocate the responsibility of producing information that neither the seller nor the buyer already has to the party who can acquire it most cheaply, thereby both avoiding duplication of costs and minimizing those that must be incurred. Finally, the agreement would try to control overspending on information acquisition by identifying not only the type of information that should be acquired, but also how much should be spent on its acquisition.

a. *Facilitating the Transfer of Information to the Buyer*

In the course of negotiating an acquisition, there is an obvious and important information asymmetry between the buyer and the seller. The buyer will have expended substantial effort in selecting the seller from among the number of potential acquisitions considered at a preliminary stage and, in doing so, may will have gathered all the available public information concerning the seller. Nonetheless, the seller will continue to know substantially more than the buyer about the business. Much detailed information about the business, of interest to a buyer but not, perhaps, to the securities markets generally, will not have been previously disclosed by the seller.

It is in the seller's interest, not just in the buyer's, to reduce this asymmetry. If the seller's private information is not otherwise available to the buyer at all, the buyer must assume that the undisclosed information reflects unfavorably on the value of the seller's business, an assumption that will be reflected to the seller's disadvantage in the price the buyer offers. Alternatively, even if the information could be gathered by the buyer (a gambit familiar to business lawyers is the seller's statement that it will open all its facilities to the buyer, that the buyer is welcome to come out and "kick the tires," but that there will be no representations and warranties), it will be considerably cheaper for the seller, whose marginal costs of production are very low, to provide the information than for the buyer to produce it alone. From the buyer's perspective, the cost of acquiring information is part of its overall acquisition cost; amounts spent on information reduce the amount left over for the seller.

This analysis, it seems to me, accounts for the quite detailed picture of the seller's business that the standard set of representations and warranties presents. Among other facts, the identity, location and condition of the assets of the business are described; the nature and extent of liabilities are specified; and the character of employee relationships—from senior management to production employee—is described. This is information that the buyer wants and the seller already has; provision by the seller minimizes its acquisition costs to the benefit of both parties.

b. *Facilitating the Production of Previously Nonexistent Information*

A similar analysis applies when the buyer needs information that the seller has not already produced. For example, the buyer may desire information about aspects of the seller's operation that bear on the opportunity for synergy between its own business and that of the seller and that, prior to the negotiation, the seller had no reason to create. Alternatively, the buyer may be interested in the impact of the transaction itself on the seller's business; whether the seller's contracts can be assigned or assumed; whether, for example, the transaction would accelerate the seller's obligations. Like the situation in which the buyer has already produced the information desired by the seller, the only issue here should be to minimize the acquisition cost of the information in question.

While the analysis is similar to the situation in which the seller had previously produced the information, the result of the analysis is somewhat different. Not only will the seller not always be the least-cost information producer, but there will also be a substantial role for third-party information producers. Returning to the synergy example, a determination of the potential for gain from the combination of the two businesses requires information about both. The particular character of the businesses, as well as the skills of their managers, will determine whether such a study is better undertaken by the seller, which knows its own business but will be required to learn about the buyer's business, or by the buyer, which knows about its own business and is in the process of learning about the seller's.

The more interesting analysis concerns the potential role for third-party information producers. This can be seen most clearly with respect to information concerning the impact of the transaction itself on the seller's business. As between the buyer and the seller, the seller will usually be the least-cost producer of information concerning the impact of the transaction on, for example, the seller's existing contracts. Although there is no reason to expect that either party routinely will have an advantage in interpreting the contracts, it is predictable that the seller can more cheaply assemble the facts on which the interpretation will be based. The real issue, however, is not whether the seller is the lower-cost producer out of a group of candidates artificially limited to the seller and buyer. Rather, the group of candidates must be expanded to include third parties.

The impact of including third-party information production in our analysis can be seen by examining the specialized information production role for lawyers in acquisition transactions. Even with respect to the production of information concerning the seller's assets and liabilities, the area where our prior analysis demonstrated the seller's prominence as an information producer, there remains a clear need for a specialized third party. Production of certain information concerning the character of the seller's assets and liabilities simply requires legal analysis. For example, the seller will know whether it has been cited for violation of environmental or health and safety legislation in the past, but it may require legal analysis to determine whether continued operation of the seller's business likely will result in future prosecution.

The need for third-party assistance is even more apparent with respect to information about the impact of the transaction itself on the seller's business. Again, however, much of the information requires legal analysis; there exists a specialized information-production role for third parties. For example, it will be important to know whether existing contracts are assignable or assumable: The continued validity of the seller's leasehold interests will depend on whether a change in the control of the seller operates—as a matter of law or because of the specific terms of the lease—as an assignment of the leasehold; and the status of the seller's existing liabilities, such as its outstanding debt, will depend on whether the transaction can be undertaken without the creditor's consent.

In both cases, the seller's lawyer appears to be the lowest-cost producer of such information. As a result, I would expect typical acquisition agreements to assign lawyers this information-production role. And it is from this perspective that important elements of the common requirement of an "Opinion of Counsel for the Seller" are best understood.

Any significant acquisition agreement requires, as a condition to the buyer's obligation to complete the transaction, that the buyer receive an opinion of seller's counsel with respect to a substantial number of items. Consistent with my analysis, most of the matters on which legal opinions are required reflect the superiority of the seller's lawyer as an information producer. For example, determination of the seller's proper organization and continued good standing under state law, the appropriate authorization of the transaction by seller, the existence of litigation against the seller, the impact of the transaction on the seller's contracts and commitments, and the extent to which the current operation of the seller's business violates any law or regulation, represent the production of information which neither the buyer nor the seller previously had, by a third party—the lawyer—who is the least-cost producer.

Just as was the case in our examination of the function of representations and warranties, this focus on the information-production role for lawyers' opinions also provides a non-adversarial approach to resolving the conflict over their content. Because reducing the cost of information necessary to the correct pricing of the transaction is beneficial to both buyer and seller, determination of the matters to be covered by the opinion of counsel for seller should be in large measure a cooperative, rather than a competitive, opportunity. Debate over the scope of the opinion, then, should focus explicitly on the cost of producing the information. For example, where a privately owned business is being sold, the seller often retains special counsel to handle the acquisition transaction, either because the company has had no regular counsel prior to the transaction, or because its regular counsel is not experienced in acquisition transactions. In this situation, recognition of the informational basis of the subject matter usually covered by legal opinions not only suggests that a specialized third-party producer is appropriate, but also provides guidance about *whose* third party should actually do the production.

From this perspective, seller's counsel typically will be the least-cost producer of the information in question. Past experience with the seller will eliminate the need for much factual investigation that would be necessary for someone who lacked a prior professional relation to the seller. Similarly, seller's counsel may well have been directly involved in some of the matters of concern—such as the issuance of the securities which are the subject of an opinion concerning the seller's capitalization, or the negotiation of the lease which is the subject of an opinion concerning the impact of the transaction on the seller's obligations. Where the seller has retained special counsel for the transaction, however, the production-cost advantage in favor of seller's counsel will be substantially reduced, especially with respect to past matters. In those cases, focus on the cost of information production provides a method for cooperative resolution of the frequently contentious issue of the scope of the opinion.

c. *Controls Over What Information to Look for and How Hard to Try*

Emphasis on the information-production role of the seller's representations and warranties and the opinion of counsel for the seller leads to the conclusion that determination of the least-cost information producer provides a cooperative focus for negotiating the content of those provisions. The same emphasis on information production also raises a related question. The demand for information, as for any other good, is more or less price elastic. Information production is costly even for the most efficient producer, and the higher the cost, the less the parties will choose to produce. Thus, some fine tuning of the assignment of information-production roles would seem to be necessary. We would expect some specific limits on the kind of information required to be produced. And we would also expect some specific limits on how much should be spent even for information whose production is desired.

Examination of an acquisition agreement from this perspective identifies provisions which impose precisely these kinds of controls. Moreover, explicit recognition of the function of these provisions, as with our analysis of representations and warranties and opinions of counsel, can facilitate the negotiation of what have traditionally been quite difficult issues.

* * *

2. *Costs of Verifying Information*

Problems of information cost do not end when the information is acquired. Even if cooperative negotiation between the buyer and seller minimizes the costs of reducing the informational asymmetry confronting the buyer, another information-cost dilemma remains: How can the buyer determine whether the information it has received is accurate? After all, the seller, who has probably provided most of the information, has a clear incentive to mislead the buyer into overvaluing the business.

Just as the market provides incentives that offset a seller's inclination to withhold unfavorable information, the market also provides incentives that constrain a seller's similar inclination to proffer falsely favorable information. If, before a transaction, a buyer can neither itself determine the quality of the seller's product nor evaluate the accuracy of the seller's representations about product quality, the buyer has no alternative but to treat the seller's product as being of low quality, regardless of the seller's protestations. To avoid this problem, a high quality seller has a substantial incentive to demonstrate to a buyer that its representations about the quality of its product are accurate and can be relied upon. And because it is in the seller's interest to keep all information costs at a minimum, there is also an incentive to accomplish this verification in the most economical fashion * * *

a. *Economizing by the Parties*

Perhaps the cheapest verification technique is simply an expectation of future transactions between the buyer and seller. When the seller's misrepresentation in one transaction will be taken into account by the buyer in decisions concerning future transactions, whether by reducing the price to reflect lowered expectations, or, at the extreme, by withdrawing patronage altogether, the seller will have little incentive to mislead. In a corporate acquisition, however, the seller has no expectation of future transactions; for the seller, a corporate acquisition is, virtually by definition, a one-shot transaction. Thus, the expectation of future transactions is simply not available as a constraint on the seller's incentive to misrepresent the information provided.

Nonetheless, the insight gleaned from understanding how an expectation of future transactions serves to validate a seller's information can be used to create an inexpensive verification technique that will work even in the one-period world of a corporate acquisition. The expectation technique works because of the existence of additional periods; the insight is simply to devise what Oliver Williamson has called a "hostage" strategy, *i.e.,* an artificial second period in which misrepresentations in the first period—the acquisition transaction—are penalized. If any of the seller's information turns out to be inaccurate, the seller will be required to compensate the buyer; in effect, the seller posts a bond that it has provided accurate information. This technique has the advantage of being quite economical: Beyond the negotiating cost involved in agreeing to make the buyer whole, there is no cost to the seller *unless* the information proves inaccurate.

This technique is among the most common approaches to verification that appear in corporate acquisition agreements. The seller verifies the accuracy of the information it has provided through its representations and warranties by agreeing to indemnify the buyer if the information turns out to be wrong, *i.e.,* if a breach of a representation or warranty occurs. And the hostage metaphor rings especially true because the seller's promise to indemnify the buyer is frequently backed by the buyer's or a neutral third party's retention of a portion of the consideration as a fund to assure the seller's performance of its indemnification obligation * * *

E. Summary and Evaluation

The analysis of a typical acquisition agreement in this Part was intended to provide some empirical verification for the hypothesis that business lawyers serve as transaction cost engineers and that this function has the potential for creating value. If business lawyers do act to bridge the gap between the perfect market assumptions of capital asset pricing theory and the drastically less-than-perfect market conditions of the world in which transactions actually take place, this activity should be visible from examination of a by now standardized document—the acquisition agreement—that creates the structure for the transfer of a significant capital asset. From this perspective, the traditional contractual approaches reflected in the agreement should act to ameliorate the failure of one or more of the key perfect market assumptions.

Although my examination of the contents of a typical corporate acquisition agreement has not been exhaustive, and although aspects of the agreement can be explained in terms different from mine, I think the core of my hypothesis has been established: Important elements of the acquisition agreement serve to remedy failures of the perfect market assumptions on which capital asset pricing theory is based. Earnout or contingent-pricing techniques respond to the failure of the homogeneous expectations assumption; controls over operation of the seller's business during the period in which the determinants of the contingent price are measured respond to the failure of the common-time-horizon assumption; and the panoply of representations and warranties, together with provisions for indemnification and other verification techniques, respond to the failure of the costless-information, or as I have characterized it, the homogeneous-retrospection assumption.

IV. WHY LAWYERS? IMPLICATIONS OF THE HYPOTHESIS FOR THE LEGAL PROFESSION

* * * There is nothing traditionally "legal" about the role I have described business lawyers as playing, nor are there any special requirements peculiar to lawyers necessary to play this role. One need not be able to recite ancient Latin incantations to bless the union of the parties' interests through exchange and * * * there is precious little in traditional legal education that gives lawyers any obvious competitive advantage in assuming this role. The question then naturally arises: Why lawyers?

A. The Academic Perspective: Understanding
the Allocation of Professional Roles

* * * In our society, the transfer of significant capital assets is surrounded by substantial regulatory structures. As seemingly straightforward a transaction as the simple transfer of real estate must be effected through a regulatory system that, in essence, actually determines ownership of the property. A more complex transaction, like a corporate acquisition, touches a host of different regulatory systems, each of which can have an important impact upon the form taken by the transaction. Tax law, antitrust law, labor law, products liability law, ERISA, securities law, and corporate law do not exhaust the spectrum of regulatory oversight that may influence the format of a particular acquisition. And it is the existence of these regulatory influences on the structure of a transaction that seems to me to explain a significant part of the dominance of lawyers as transaction cost engineers.

Most regulatory systems express the boundaries of their application and the detail of their requirements in formal terms: Transactions which take a particular outward form are covered. So, for example, Subchapter C of the Internal Revenue Code treats a corporate acquisition that takes the form of a statutory merger differently than one that takes the form of a sale of assets, and many state corporation laws draw a similar distinction. This approach to regulation inevitably draws a response. Capital assets, in the end, are only generic streams of future income with a particular systematic risk. So long as actual cash flows are not altered, the formal trappings of the transaction can be altered almost endlessly without altering its financial substance. The regulatory system itself then serves as an invitation to the targets of the regulation to structure transactions so that their form falls outside the terms of the regulation. This eternal triangle is completed by the courts which, in the end, must determine whether to credit the form in which the parties cast a transaction, or look beyond the formal terms of the regulatory structure to its purpose, and through the formal structure of the transaction to its financial substance. Indeed, I would argue that this tension—between transaction form and regulatory purpose—is really the central dilemma for most traditional business law; the form versus substance doctrine in tax law and the de facto merger doctrine in corporate law are only the most familiar examples.

The critical importance of transactional structure for purposes of regulation provides the core of an explanation for lawyers' domination of the role of transaction cost engineer. Because the lawyer must play an important role in designing the structure of the transaction in order to assure the desired regulatory treatment, economies of scope should cause the nonregulatory aspects of transactional structuring to gravitate to the lawyer as well. Knowledge of alternative transactional forms and skill at translating the desired form into appropriate documents are as central to engineering transactions for the purpose of reducing transaction costs as for the purpose of reducing regulatory costs; indeed, if these purposes in one or another way conflict, facility at both tasks should result in more

optimal trade-offs between them. Viewing the matter from this perspective, it would have been surprising if lawyers had not dominated the field
* * *

James C. Freund, ADVISE AND INVENT

(1990)

THE PROBLEM

Joe Top, the president of your client, Big Corp. (a public company), comes to your office one day with his chief financial officer. Here's the story, in Joe's words:

"Counselor, I need your help on a problem we're facing.

"We've made a corporate decision to dispose of our Stove division, if we can get a decent price for it. Only a few people at corporate headquarters know about this, plus our investment banker, Quincy Adams & Co., and now you. We've said nothing to the management of Stove, although they may sniff that something is up.

"I had a surprise visit the other day from Bob Burner, the president of Stove. Without referring to *our* intentions, he came right out and said that he and his key managers would like to buy Stove from us. He said they had been in touch with some sources of financing and felt they could raise the money for a leveraged buyout of the division.

"I was taken aback by this, not realizing it was the purpose of his visit. Fortunately, I was saved by the bell—my secretary rang to say an important call was coming in from London—so I told Burner that I couldn't talk further just then, but that I would get back to him in a few days.

"Now, the sense we get from initial discussions with our financial adviser, Quincy Adams, is that the maximum price for Stove is unlikely to be raised in a leveraged buyout by management (or by anyone else, for that matter), but rather will come from an industrial buyer—using its own cash—for whom Stove is a good fit. As a matter of fact, the prime opportunity is probably with Mix Inc., which has a similar operation and has alluded in the past to its interest in Stove.

"But the real problem here is, what do we do about Bob Burner and his management group? From the tone of his voice, I got the impression that Burner wants to buy Stove badly; he's certainly going to be unhappy if it's sold to someone else—particularly to an entity like Mix, which will merge the operations with its own and probably shed a number of Stove's managers and employees to achieve the synergies needed to justify the high price. Yet, Burner and his team will be key players if we get involved in negotiating a deal with Mix or anyone else. Mix will ask to meet with them on an operating level to understand the business better; Mix will want to see all kinds of financial information, including projections which Stove management is in the process of preparing; and Mix may even want employment contracts from certain key guys.

"Burner and his men have a real conflict of interest here. *We* want to display Stove in the best light; *their* interests might be served by portraying Stove to others in the worst light—either to drive away the competition or to get the price down into an area where Burner and his financial backers can compete. I don't think Bob Burner is a bad man, but the temptation to undermine our plans could be enormous.

"If we let them get in on the bidding for the business, this will exacerbate the conflict of interest. If we forbid them from bidding, it could infuriate them—and we need Burner and his guys to continue to operate Stove and make money; it would be a disaster if they all walked out on us.

"How can I keep them in line? What should we do to handle this situation? And, by the way, counselor, keep in mind that whatever we do may have broader implications later on with other of Big's divisions and key employees."

* * *

Easy on the Oracular

So there it is—a problem not unlike those many of us have encountered in recent years. There's no strictly legal aspect to the situation, although certain facets touch on possible issues—disclosure, fiduciary obligation, conflict of interest—as to which lawyers possess expertise. What the client is looking for here is good judgment; he came to his lawyer to figure out the best method of proceeding.

But Joe Top has undoubtedly put the same question to other executives within the Big organization whose judgment he values; so, it's possible that he also likes the idea of having someone who's *not* inside the Company—who is more detached than an officer with a closer interest in the outcome—make a recommendation.

Quite often, the question isn't posed to you exclusively, but is directed to a larger group of which you're a member. In such circumstances, you have to proceed with some caution, making sure that your probing and analysis aren't viewed as meddling in what is essentially a corporate business decision. It's important to know that the client wants *you* to get involved in the solution of the problem—as is the case in our hypothetical.

In this type of strategy question, the lawyer doesn't have any particular *expertise* to bring to bear on its solution—at least, any expertise certified by his admission to the Bar. As contrasted with a legal question, there's no reason that one of the others involved—Joe Top, who asked the question; his chief financial officer, who listened to it; other Big executives, who have already wrestled with it; Quincy Adams, the investment bankers who have been consulted—can't come up with an equally sound response. And that's important for you to keep in mind, as you deal with these kinds of issues.

When you discourse on legal matters—pontificating on what the courts have done, or what a statute means—in a sense, you're a bit of an oracle; everyone listens because you're clearly the expert on this subject, and they are not. But with questions of strategy, you're on the same ground as everyone else. So, if you tend to sound oracular here, it can create a backlash effect when the views of the audience differ from yours; and, of course, you're wide open to second-guessing if they take your opinionated advice and it doesn't turn out well. On the other hand, if you approach the question like Casper Milquetoast, your counsel probably won't be given much value. It's a difficult line to walk: you have to appear confident, be sensible, and avoid pomposity.

Favorable Working Conditions

Yet, you do have some things in your favor. The fact is that many of the "working conditions" here closely parallel the practice of business law. For example:

- Operating as a lawyer-strategist involves a tantalizing mix of intellectual and practical concerns—the very mix that has always appealed to me in the practice of law. A professor, by contrast, exercises his intellect, but rarely deals with real world matters. Some operating types, rooted in the practicalities of everyday business, seldom face problems with real intellectual content. The lawyer-strategist is right in the middle, dealing with tough analytical situations, yet realizing that it's not enough to analyze them, to write them up, to think "What a nice question this one is!"—rather, he has to try to solve them.

- The lawyer-strategist has the ability, within limits, to shape what he's doing to achieve the outcome he seeks. Contrast this with a traditional litigator, who gets the case after the damage is done; all the facts he has to deal with have already happened. But a business lawyer can affect the likely legal results by inserting (or deleting) a certain clause in an agreement, in order to put his client's best foot forward. (This process, which might be termed "legal strategizing," goes beyond telling the client whether a certain proposed action is lawful, to the point of advising him *how* to do it so as to achieve the optimal legal position.) The lawyer-strategist operates in analogous territory.

- What makes strategizing—as well as legal practice—both fascinating and frustrating is that, so often, things work at cross-purposes. As a lawyer, the recurring irony is that what the client should do to achieve a better *legal* result makes it a worse *business* deal, and vice versa. The more absolute the acquisition "lock-up" option is, for instance, the more inclined the courts are to strike it down as unfair. So, how far should you go? With no black letter guides at hand, good lawyers—calling on their experience and judgment—operate on a sort of touch, feel and smell basis. This can be a little difficult to explain to clients, and often leaves the lawyer wondering whether he's been too conservative (or too liberal). With strategy questions, where there are no touchstones of precedent or expectations of judicial rationality— where the criteria are such amorphous considerations as, "How will it be perceived on the Street?" or "Would this influence their board to come out the other way?" or "What's the best way to reach our goal without attracting attention?"—where the risks and rewards are all relative and changing from day to day, as new concerns and opportunities present themselves—well, you really have that cross-purposes syndrome in spades.

- In strategizing, as in the practice of law, we are often called upon to act on an imperfect set of facts. Rarely is everything in hand at the time the decision must be made. What's important is that we make every effort to get at the relevant facts, that we not be paralyzed into inaction by their inaccessibility, and that we reach decisions and take actions that will stand up no matter which reasonable way the facts turn out.

All of which positions the lawyer-strategist in the midst of a familiar and fascinating—albeit mine-strewn—landscape.

The Spontaneous Response

There is, however, one significant contrast I find between handling difficult legal and strategic issues. When a legal question is posed, the lawyer usually declines to furnish a definitive answer off the top of his head. He may well give some indication of where he thinks it's likely to come out, but he'll also refer to the need for legal research, checking some documents or source materials, talking to others in the firm with particular expertise, or even running it by the applicable administrative agency on an informal basis—all with a view to getting back to the client at some later date with an answer. When the legal question is a hard one, the lawyer doesn't want to appear as a hip-shooter; and there's a certain value in taking it "back to the shop"—to be labored over lovingly by a flock of attorneys representing various disciplines—in terms of impressing the client with the institutional nature of the expert advice.

But, with one of these strategy questions, where no amount of "hitting the books" will matter a great deal, there's a real advantage in being able to produce an answer—or at least the framework of a response—in the very session in which the issue is posed. (I'm excluding here the kind of questions, often asked over the phone, where the client does not expect an immediate reaction but just wants you to reflect on the situation prior to a meeting being held on the subject later in the week.) In this more individualized setting, spontaneity—as contrasted with an amalgam of your colleagues' views—becomes a virtue. And since, as we'll see in dealing with the example, so much of the analysis of strategic problems lies in your asking the pointed questions to elicit responses that guide the direction of your advice, you might as well do this while the persons who can answer those queries are right there in the room.

(The same-day reaction, I should add, is particularly effective when you have something helpful to offer! If, in probing the matter, you can't come up with anything decent, then just tell everybody you'd like to "sleep on it"—in hopes that tomorrow may produce a more imaginative response....)

SIX KEY STEPS

Notwithstanding the goal of providing an answer to the strategic question in the same session it's posed, it's a rare case where the optimum solution is apparent right off the bat—and even when it is, you need to work your way through a process in order to evaluate its soundness. Often, the procedure is akin to solving a legal problem; as you probe and elicit information, as you eliminate options and rank priorities, the solution—almost like a Polaroid picture, gradually developing in front of your eyes—just seems to appear.

So, before attempting to answer the question, you're well advised to undergo the discipline of proceeding through at least the following half-dozen steps.

1. Specifying the Question. Make sure you understand the precise question being asked. It's not always as readily apparent as in the hypothetical. At times, the client himself isn't sure what he's asking. He might come to you with a legal question ("If Burner makes a specific dollar offer, must we disclose its existence publicly?"), not realizing that a strategic issue lurks in the background. Or, the client may put a different strategy question—in this case, the manner of handling the disposition of Stove ("Should we conduct an auction, or would it be better to approach Mix to see if they're willing to make a preemptive offer?") Then, as you probe the situation and the Burner conflict begins to loom as a threshold matter, you may find yourself posing it to the group as a complication calling for specific attention.

Sometimes, in the course of defining the question, you can make it easier to answer. For example, it may be possible to convert a tough legal question—like the subtle conflict of interest issues raised for management buyers in an LBO situation—into a more practical issue ("How do we discourage Burner?"), thereby ducking the harder call.

2. Getting the Facts. Just as with a thorny legal question, you need all the material facts that are relevant to the situation. After all, good judgment often comes down to assigning varying weights to conflicting factors; if you don't know all the factors, you can't assign the proper weights.

In this regard, you cannot assume that the executive will provide you with all the information required to answer the question. For example, Joe Top related his encounter with Bob Burner without any mention of price for the Stove division; that's clearly one of the first areas I would explore. Did Burner offer a price? If not, did he hint at a price level or range? If not, can anything about the price Burner has in mind be inferred from his other remarks? Do you think Burner realizes that he may not be in a position to offer top dollar? In this fashion, you can often jog the executive's memory about something that didn't seem significant at the time, but in retrospect provides useful information.

The related issue is whether any of the facts provided by Joe Top were misstated, or given inappropriate emphasis, so as to throw you off in pursuing a solution. This can be the case with an executive who isn't too precise—who tends to oversimplify or "round up." If you sense this to be the case, proceed cautiously—you don't want to embarrass the executive, and this isn't the forum for vigorous cross-examination. But, by asking for a reiteration ("just to clarify it in my own mind") and probing gingerly around the fringes, you may discover that an unwarranted nuance was conveyed.

Let's say, for example, that Joe Top "quoted" Burner as saying that Stove management "had the necessary financing in place and was prepared to bid." Now, that conveys a certain sense of urgency to the proceedings—for all you know, a written offer from Burner might be waiting on Top's desk when he returns from your office. It might even call for a crisis strategy, at variance with what you would advise if the matter seemed less pressing. Well, it's worth poking around to see if, perhaps, Burner wasn't quite so ready—that, in fact, his message was more that Stove management was *interested* in buying Stove, and had received *preliminary* indications from an institutional source that the deal was financable—a quite different emphasis which could definitely affect the ultimate strategy you devise.

3. Understanding the Context. Next, you have to broaden your focus to the context in which the question arises. Strategy questions inevitably involve a particular path to be taken; you have to make sure you're in sync with the overall direction in which the company is moving. A solution that works for the narrow strategic issue posed might be unfavorable in the larger picture. Make it your business to comprehend that context, although it may not automatically be volunteered by the client.

In the hypothetical, the immediately broader picture is the sale of the Stove division. It could provide the key to how to handle Mr. Burner. We'll see in a moment what questions regarding the divestiture should be asked.

This aspect can sometimes be a little delicate, as where your firm is not handling the overall situation, or there's some sensitivity to revealing the company's plans. If, however, you can show the client that this is essential to devising the strategy for your piece of the puzzle, there's usually no trouble. But don't go into the context in great detail; it makes people uneasy, and all you need is a sketch of the pertinent information.

4. Knowing the Personalities Involved. It's fair to say that there are few strategic-type issues in which the personalities, characteristics and idiosyncracies of the individuals concerned don't play a significant role. So, I always try to find out something about who we're dealing with. Here, you probably don't know Bob Burner at all; but since he's the potential source of trouble—the object of any strategy you devise—you've got to become better acquainted with him. What are you up against? Is he the type who, when all is said and done, will follow the company line? If so, that's much different from a rebellious sort who's likely to cause trouble if he doesn't get his own way. Is he stubborn and opinionated, or open to arguments based on reason? Does he speak his mind or is he evasive? Does he understand matters of corporate finance? Is he a good negotiator?—and so on, all with a view towards fitting the strategy to the person at whom it's aimed.

5. Ascertaining the Client's Objective. It's not just Burner you need to know about; there's also your own client. How does Joe Top, the president of Big, want this strategic issue to come out? (Not *how to* accomplish the result, because that's what he came to you for, but what is the *result* he wants to achieve?) With legal dialogue flows readily, because the client has usually done some thinking on the subject before the meeting.) You learn that, in their view, the critical factor is realizing the best price for Stove. Other considerations—the impact of the sale on Stove's management, precedent value, the morale of the Big troops—while not unimportant, are definitely secondary.

That being the key, and with Burner and his team itching to buy, the threshold question then becomes whether or not Burner is a viable buyer—the sort who could pay the best price for Stove, or challenge someone else to do so. You can pose this issue to Joe Top and his colleague, along the following lines:

> "Given the prime importance of obtaining the best price for Stove, if you think that Burner is a viable buyer, then your strategy should be aimed at keeping him in the contest—even to the extent of encouraging his participation. This doesn't come without cost, as you've clearly recognized, but first things first; you need to manage the situation to get the most out of Burner.

> "But, if you believe that Burner is unlikely to be a top bidder for Stove, and that his presence in the bidding isn't necessary to insure the proper auction fervor, then your strategy in dealing with him should be completely different. Here, the negatives of his continuing involvement in the chase begin to greatly outweigh the positives; so your goal should be, how do we gracefully ease Burner out of active participation as a buyer?"

Fine. You've posed the first issue squarely. Now what? To answer it yourself—as some lawyers do—would be improper; this is definitely a business judgment. But to simply sit back and await a reaction—which so many lawyers also do—is not a terribly helpful approach, either. In my view, the lawyer-strategist should assist the executives in figuring out what they ought to review in order to achieve a reasoned response.

How should management make this particular determination? Well, the executives need as much information as can be gleaned on two points: how much is Bob Burner able to pay, and what are others likely to pay? With respect to the latter, the surest reading would come from soliciting actual bids, but that's premature at this point—particularly since the Burner problem isn't solved, and Bob might sabotage any other deal before it gets off the ground. Secondarily, Big could turn to its investment banker for advice on what price Stove is likely to fetch, and whether there is a sufficient universe of potential bidders (other than Burner) to assure that the competitive juices will flow.

How about Burner's price? Joe Top could ask him for a specific number, but to do so prior to deciding on a strategy might close off options—such as undercutting the rationale for the approach of not letting Burner bid as a matter of corporate policy. Alternatively, Quincy Adams may be able to arrive at the practical limits to Burner's price by calculating the maximum amount of leverage feasible in this type of debt-driven buyout—in contrast to a transaction with a corporate buyer, flush with its own funds, where the price isn't limited to what can be raised on the assets and cash flow of Stove itself.

At this point, Joe Top breaks in to say that Quincy Adams has actually been working on this question in recent days. Great!—let's find out what the story is by placing a call to the investment banker. It's a safe start, which doesn't compromise Big in any way or reduce its options in dealing with Burner. And the message from Quincy Adams is that, indeed, a much better price than Burner can afford to pay will likely be available from Mix; moreover, Mix will perceive the need to "beat the competition" without the necessity of using Burner to keep Mix honest.

So, Top is now in a position to decide—at least tentatively—that he doesn't want or need Burner in the middle of a bidding contest. In fact, he makes the decision on the spot. Now, given that premise, what's the best way to handle Burner?

FIAT OR DEMONSTRATION?

Well, after analyzing the various possibilities, you ascertain that there are two basic alternatives: acting by fiat, or demonstrating to Burner his inability to compete on price.

Take the fiat route. Joe Top could tell Burner that, as a matter of company policy, Big simply doesn't permit its managers to buy their divisions. "No offense, Bob, and we're not aiming this at you, but our hands are tied...." The problem here, though, is that Big's past activities may have been inconsistent with this policy—in which case, the argument wouldn't ring true. Or, Joe Top may want the flexibility to be able to sell other divisions to management in the future; creating a hard-and-fast policy now could hamstring Big later on. Top is also concerned how other divisional management would react to this—since, even if the policy isn't publicized, it could be expected to make the rounds throughout the company.

A different fiat might be to tell Burner that we don't want him to compete *here*—not as a matter of company policy, but because of the inherent conflict of interest in a case where so many other logical buyers exist. But this smacks of unfairness; Burner could say, "Why am I (a valued employee), of all the potential buyers in the world, being penalized by not being allowed to compete?" It also might be seen as casting an aspersion—that Burner won't deal fairly in the situation—which he may take in the wrong spirit.

Alternatively, the fiat could be that Bob Burner simply won't be able to compete on price, so why bother? But is Burner likely to accept that determination, without having had an opportunity to propose a price— and with no evidence of what someone else would be willing to pay? I suppose Joe Top could specify a high price, identify it as what he expects to obtain, and state that he wouldn't take less; but then, if other offers fail to materialize at that level, he may be placed in the embarrassing position of having to accept a lesser bid.

None of these fiats are particularly satisfactory. On the other hand, if there were a way to actually *demonstrate* to Burner that he can't compete on price—demonstrate it so decisively that, although disappointed, he is forced to bow to the inevitable—it would be far preferable. After all, you say to Top, isn't that the real key: to stop Bob Burner from thinking like a buyer, and enlist him to work as a key member of the selling team?

I agree with that analysis, says Joe Top; but how can we demonstrate it to Burner? Well, the clearest showing would be to obtain Burner's maximum price, and then reveal the existence of another firm offer 25% above his. But this may prove trouble-some to accomplish— will anything short of it do the trick?

Could we, for example, make an assumption as to Burner's maximum number and then have Quincy Adams tell him how much higher a price they expect to get? Would Burner accept that? Since this depends in part on what kind of person Burner is, you now delve a bit into that subject. And let's assume you learn that Bob Burner is feisty and cynical, unlikely to accept a valuation lecture from Quincy Adams at face value— particularly since, at this juncture, he may not even know how high his own financing source is willing to go.

THE SELLING STRATEGY

Along about now, you can begin to see the outline of how to proceed, but there's still a missing piece. To give good advice, you need to understand the larger picture. And the remaining question is, assuming Burner were out of the way, what's the best way to sell Stove? Should it be auctioned off publicly to the highest bidder? Would the investment banker conduct a private auction among selected likely prospects? Might they approach just one or two buyers to elicit a preemptive bid? The answer to this feeds directly into the question of how to deal with Burner.

So, at this point another call is placed to Quincy Adams, to confer on the selling strategy. And, let's say you all concur that the best technique is the preemptive bid. Here's how it would play out.

We approach Mix and also one other likely prospect. We tell Mix (with a similar story to the other buyer) that Big is preparing to dispose of Stove, has hired Quincy Adams to take on the task, and will shortly be exposing the property to a broad circle of likely buyers. However, we can see the excellent fit that Stove would make with the existing Mix operations. Accordingly, we want to give Mix and one other unnamed buyer a chance to preempt the field. *[We tell Mix about the other buyer, so that Mix will feel the pressure of simultaneous, as well as sequential, competition.]* If Mix makes a bid that is both higher than that of the second party and at a level we're unlikely to better in the auction, then we won't feel the need to shop the property. If, on the other hand, the Mix offer is only middling, then we'll have to open it up to all comers. So, come on, Mix; put your best foot forward right now.

All right. Given this sales strategy, what's the best way to handle Burner? Assume we discourage him from putting in a bid. Keep in mind, we may not be able to provide Mix and the second buyer with the information or access they need to make a preemptive bid without involving Burner and his people. Even if we could, Burner would be very upset when we suddenly announce a contemplated deal with Mix— furious that he wasn't given a chance to better the Mix price. Although it may then be too late for him to upset the deal, the process can leave behind feelings of bitterness and betrayal that aren't salutary for the Big organization.

On the other hand, if we let Burner actually put in an informal bid (which, as expected, falls way short of what Mix is ultimately prepared to pay), then, although Burner will be disappointed over not capturing the prize, our decision to sell to Mix will appear a lot more rational and less unfairly directed against him.

And there's one more thing—which illustrates the importance of *listening* carefully when your client is talking. Remember when Joe Top mentioned at the outset that the management of Stove is currently in the process of preparing financial projections? Now, it's important to Big, in trying to sell Stove, that these estimates of future earnings— which, by their nature, contain elements of subjectivity—not be understated. If Burner is trying to raise the money for his own group to buy Stove, you can bet that the numbers he prepares for his financial backers—which Big intends to use later on with Mix and the others— will be properly aggressive.

GIVE US A BID

And so, if I were you, I'd advise Joe Top to tell Burner to consult with his financial advisers and let Big know what price he has in mind for Stove.

Now, the way in which this is conveyed to Burner should be an important part of the strategy, too. It's not enough to decide *what* to do; the technique of *how* to do it is equally critical, and can't just be left to chance.

Here, since you know in advance that Big will probably spurn the price Burner is likely to bid—but obviously can't tell him that now—you need to soften Burner up for what's going to happen, so that he won't be caught off guard by your response and react irrationally. Here are the points that Joe Top (or whoever else might handle the task) should make to Burner, as soon as possible:

1. *We may be interested in selling Stove if the price is right.*

To pretend otherwise is not only untrue but flies in the face of the process that will be under way; it can only damage Top's credibility. On the other hand, there's no need to state Big's intention unequivocally; you might as well keep open the option of pulling back at a later date— if, for instance, no one bids up to the desired level and management is unwilling to part with Stove at Burner's price.

2. *If you think you can obtain financing, talk to your financing source—we assume it's someone reputable who can deliver the goods— and then come back to us with your price.*

We don't want Burner to simply pick a price out of the blue; we want him to undergo the discipline of having a reputable financing source tell him how much he can afford to pay.

3. *This ought to be done promptly and under conditions of total confidentiality; we don't want any leaks, and there shouldn't be any letter or other writings.*

The need for speed and confidentiality is obvious.

4. *You understand, Bob, that for the company to sell a large division to its managers leaves us open to a charge of favoritism. Therefore, unless we consider your offer to be clearly better than what we might expect to get elsewhere—and, in that regard, it makes sense for you to come up with as high a figure as you can justify—we'll have to take some steps to satisfy our board of directors that we're getting top dollar.*

This is a good way of introducing the subject of potential competition to Burner. He would be hard-pressed to disagree with the analysis; yet, it's not put in a way that makes Big seem determined to sell to someone else. And the importance of Burner putting his best figure on the table—which you'll want to use against his interest later on—has been adequately stressed.

My sense is that no specific price, or even range of prices, should be transmitted to Burner, nor should any reference be made to consultations with Big's investment bankers—since we *don't* want Burner to infer that the sale of Stove has been under serious consideration for some time now. I think you should advise Joe Top that, if Burner asks what price we have in mind, Top should reply that we have an open mind and will be interested to see what Burner comes up with.

That's the first part of the strategy. The second part involves how to handle matters when Bob Burner returns with his price—and includes the issue of how to incentivize Burner and his people to act constructively during the ensuing negotiations with other bidders.

The matter of incentives may or may not have been brought up by the Big executives in your meeting; but if they don't mention it, then you should. After all, Big wants something from Burner—a favorable outcome can be very valuable to the company—so Big should be prepared to ante up.

Such incentives usually fall into the two key areas of money and security. In terms of money, the idea is that Burner and his cohorts—key members of the team to sell Stove—should be entitled to something special if the business is sold at a high price. This could take the form of a flat bonus, or even better, a payment keyed to the ultimate price. A really imaginative approach would be to give them a small percentage of every dollar over *Burner's own price* that the Company is able to obtain from the sale—which neatly serves to emphasize the disparity between the Burner and Mix values.

In terms of security, if Stove is sold to a competitor, Stove's top managers may be out of work once the deal takes place. Perhaps Joe Top can offer them good positions elsewhere within the Big organization. If that's not in the cards, then generous severance packages—golden parachutes, if you will—which assure the top Stove executives of being well-treated financially if they're fired after the sale (or if the basic terms of their employment become untenable), are the next best thing.

So, spend some time—either at this or a later session—preparing Joe Top for Burner's return with a dollar figure. Let's assume that the investment bankers have told Top that, if all goes well, he can expect to get something over $120 million for Stove. Say that Bob Burner comes back from his financial sources with a figure of $95 million—"and that's really a stretch for us, Joe." Here are some points you can suggest that Top make to Burner at this juncture:

1. Since our first talk, we've had some discussions with Quincy Adams, our investment bankers, about the price we could expect to realize on Stove; and I'm sorry to have to tell you, Bob, that it's way in excess of your "stretched" $95 million—as a matter of fact, it's over $120 million.

Might as well give it to Burner straight, so he can see what he's up against.

2. We've also refined our own thinking to the point that we do intend to pursue the disposition of Stove at the higher price. We would not, however, be willing to sell Stove at your price.

This makes it clear that the sale is going forward, but it won't be to Burner.

3. In view of the price disparity and, frankly, the potential for conflict of interest, I'm going to ask you to withdraw from the bidding, so that you can concentrate on helping us realize the best price for Big.

This means, Bob Burner, that from now on you're a seller, not a buyer.

4. Now, we realize how important your support is to us in this venture, Bob ...

And here, Top can segue into the arrangements to incentivize Burner and his troops.

After this conversation, the company should move swiftly to implement its preemptive offer strategy with Mix, having reasonable assurance that Burner—who now knows the company is expecting a price 25% above his own stretched number—won't try to interfere. Nothing's certain, of course, but at least we've positioned things as well as possible under the circumstances.

* * *

Now, let's see what lessons about strategizing of more general applicability might be derived from the Stove saga, in terms of the process, the client, and particularly, the solution.

THE PROCESS

The process of getting to an acceptable solution was typical of the way that I find works best for me in these matters.

- As you can see, I like to pose questions to the client that isolate key issues—Is Burner a viable buyer? What kind of person is Burner?—and then take my cue from his answers, whichever way they lead.

- I feel it's important to get involved in helping the client to *answer* some of my own queries—as in determining *how* to reach the conclusion of whether Burner's bid was likely to be competitive.

- The process itself serves the function of having the solution bubble up to the surface. For instance, examining the various fiat solutions, and finding each of them unsatisfactory for different reasons, practically forced us to conclude that *demonstrating* to Burner the inadequacy of his bid was the best solution. This points up a more general dictum: Don't become so involved in your own train of thought that you fail to listen closely to the replies, which often convey more information than might be apparent at first.

- Make sure you are in possession of all the available salient facts *before* venturing a solution—even if you sense you're getting close. I felt that closeness at one point, but realized we needed information on the overall sales strategy of Stove before proffering a course of action on Burner.

THE CLIENT

Strategizing usually takes place in the presence of your client, and this interplay prompts the following observations.

- Never forget that the ultimate strategy is the client's decision to make. You recommend; he decides.

- Make sure that the rationale behind your recommendation is fully spelled out, so that the client—if he disagrees with that rationale—can overrule your advice and proceed in a way that makes him comfortable. Don't overpower the client with conclusions; rather, concentrate on making him understand your reasoning.

- At some point along the way, I like to utter the caveat that this is a matter of business judgment (as contrasted with law), on which I don't profess any particular expertise. I want the client to realize that he shouldn't feel intimidated by the advice (as he might, if it were of a legal nature) and is perfectly free to disregard it.

- In this same vein, there's a fine line to walk—but it's the groove you should strive for—between pronouncing your judgments with the requisite degree of self-assuredness (without which, your views have less chance of being accorded maximum weight), yet not sounding cocksure and omniscient on what are essentially intuitive matters.

- Finally, as I've stressed previously, if the client doesn't buy your advice, and you're satisfied that he understands your reasoning, then back off. It's his call; you've given it your best shot. Don't display pique or any sense of your superiority or his ingratitude. Instead, be constructive; go back to the drawing board and come up with another approach.

THE SOLUTION

Finally, here are a few thoughts about solutions to strategy issues.

- As with so much else in our practice, useful solutions to strategic questions—whether the lawyer is *advising* or *inventing*—tend to be simple rather than complex. It's the *problem* that's complicated—or at least the client considers it so. The idea is to fuss around in the complexities, sorting out what is really important and what isn't, and then, all of a sudden, everything falls into place with a certain clarity. This impresses clients much more than your ability to spin webs. And it makes good sense, because simple solutions can be more readily explained within an organization and are usually easier to implement than complex ones.

  (I can't provide a sure fire formula for this kind of resolution, but it usually requires overcoming some blockage. The other day, I was listening to a Walkman cassette player through headphones. I also had on a pair of sunglasses, attached to one of those shoestring-type holders behind my head. In a moment of clumsiness, the shoestring and the headphone cord became hopelessly entangled. I wrestled with the resulting disorder for a few seconds, then uttered a cry for help. My wife whisked over and, without even hesitating—without wasting one second trying to disentangle the two cords—she yanked the headphone plug out of the Walkman. *Voilà!* In no time, the mess was cleared up. What I can't seem to handle with headphones is precisely what we should strive for on strategic problems.)

- Often, with questions of strategy, there is no single answer. If you let yourself get trapped in the box of coming up with a single answer, it may well be the wrong one, since it depends on what different people consider important. A recurring characteristic of strategic solutions is that there are greater risks if you proceed down a particular path, but correspondingly greater benefits should you attain your objective. It's not always apparent, however, whether your client is a risk-taker—or even, if he is one generally, whether he wants to take the risk inherent in this particular situation. So, your advice is often stated in these terms: "If obtaining A [the reward] is more important to you than enduring B [the risk], then you probably should take the C course; whereas if you're more concerned about risking B than gaining A, then you ought to go the D route." (This can also be utilized when the imponderable is how another person will act: "If you think A will act in B manner, then X seems like the proper course; but if you think A will act in C manner, then Y would be the path to take.")

- So often I find that the key to a good solution is the sequencing of moves: what comes first, what comes next, what comes last? If the sequence is out of whack, the solution doesn't work. Sequencing is important for various reasons: you may need to know a particular item of information at the time you'll be making a certain decision, but you won't get that knowledge until some time has passed; or conversely, you'd rather hold a certain conversation *before* you know something for sure; or you need to accomplish something first before it makes sense to move on to the next item.

  (In the Stove saga, for example, it would have been wrong to ask Burner for his price prior to working out the strategy—since that might have foreclosed some options that hadn't yet been ruled out—but it made sense to do so at a later point when the strategy was set.)

- When suggesting a course of action that involves meetings with other people, it's not enough to say *what* should be accomplished; you also have to demonstrate *how* it ought to be handled—if not the precise words to use, then at least the concepts to get across. (We saw this in the summaries of how Top should deal with Burner in the before-and-after conversations.)

- An important feature of any solution is, who does what—particularly for your listeners, who are trying to visualize this happening and who may be involved in the execution. Depending on the situation, you can leave this part out on the first go 'round, to be added later; or you might decide to include it right from the outset. Sometimes, the safest course is to allude to the issue, but say you'll come back to it later—*after* you've seen the reaction to your solution. If, for example, a key executive reacts favorably, it might be sensible to suggest that *he* initiate the action; whereas, if you sense there's some trepidation, the wise course might be to offer to take the burden on yourself. Be careful, though, of emphasizing your own role, since you don't want to appear self-aggrandizing. Still, there are times when the client would like you to handle the dirty work. I usually phrase this in the alternative: "So, then, you would make the call—or, if you prefer, I could do it. . . ."

• Always prepare the client, not only for his own part in the process, but to be able to answer questions and to counter moves that the other party can be expected to ask or make. (Thus, we prepped Top for what he should say if Burner inquired about price.) Every encounter is a two-way street; it's not enough to make the opening argument.

* * *

So, there's the business lawyer as strategist—an important facet of his counseling function—utilizing many of the thought processes and techniques that serve him well in his regular practice, but with a few extra twists on the ball as he ventures into less familiar territory.

And that concludes our examination of the lawyer's role as a resourceful counselor. But, just in case you're beginning to feel omniscient in the area, let me leave you with a tough one—which calls on every bit of learning you've assimilated in the preceding pages.

Bernardo, your longtime client (the two of you first met on the beach during the Bay of Pigs evacuation), is accompanying you to a football game. The radio has forecast a remote chance of showers, so naturally you're carrying an umbrella. Bernardo tells you of his concern over being in breach of a contract with a supplier—a contract that *you* had drafted—due to a blatant ambiguity in a crucial clause. At the gate, when you take out your wallet, the tickets are missing; within moments, a scalper comes by, hawking seats at an exorbitant price. Bernardo, ignoring your plight, seeks advice on the best means of disposing of a stove.

What now, counselor?

Lawrence M. Friedman, Robert W. Gordon, Sophie Pirie & Edwin Whatley, LAW LAWYERS, AND LEGAL PRACTICE IN SILICON VALLEY: A PRELIMINARY REPORT

64 INDIANA L.J. 555 (1989)

What do lawyers contribute to technological change and economic development? Much popular opinion assumes that the contribution is mostly negative, that the vast amounts of legal time billed to corporate enterprise ($38 billion worth annually, according to a recent estimate) are the pathological symptoms of an over-regulated, excessively litigious culture that diverts resources from productivity and innovation into wasteful paperpushing. Other, more sanguine observers—usually lawyers—argue to the contrary that legal services are valuable, even indispensable parts of the infrastructure that support the efficiency of transactions, even if their value is not always appreciated by clients or the general public. The debate has been chiefly at the level of assertion, because there has been so little serious research since James Willard Hurst's monumental study in 1964 of the ways in which lawmakers and lawyers designed and operated the legal-institutional frameworks for the growth and organization of the lumber industry in nineteenth century Wisconsin. Studies of the 'legal profession' tend to focus on the organization, entry policies, education and ethics of the bar. Although some excellent work has recently appeared on the social structure of the bar and the internal organization and cultures of law firms, there is still almost no scholarly research into lawyers' actual work tasks. So before approaching the grand questions of how lawyers facilitate or parasitically feed off economic growth, we need to have reliable pictures of their practices, of the ordinary jobs they do for their business clients.

Inspired by the example of Hurst's work, the authors have begun to study the lawyers who work in Palo Alto, California—the legal hub of the computer products industries of the Silicon Valley. As a subject of study, the Silicon Valley is nearly ideal. It has a dense concentration of lawyers, and a dense concentration of new industry. The lawyers claim that their role in the Valley's boom has been extremely influential. The industry and the legal practice that has grown up around it are both young; their entire histories are within the grasp of living memories. The explosive pace of growth gives us the chance to watch basic changes in form unfold even as the study progresses. This brief paper describes, in general terms, some of the observations and hypotheses arrived at after preliminary work on the project.

* * *

II. Legal Services Required by New Businesses

Before we suggest some reasons why a flourishing local bar emerged to handle the legal business of high-tech industries, it might be useful to specify more generally the types of legal services that new industries ordinarily seem to need. Historical experience suggests the following loose sketch that describes the evolving demand for legal skills.

In the start-up phase, small businesses, especially those run by scientists and engineers without business experience, need access to elementary advice about such matters as record-keeping for tax and accounting purposes, and such basic legal services as the drafting of partnership agreements and secured financing documents. Lawyers in this society have often also been used as repositories of general knowledge of business practices, for advice that the client can neither generate internally nor afford to buy from other outside sources. A business must also hire and pay lawyers for services only they can legally perform. Thus, the added cost of general business advice is low, especially when lawyers can draw upon experience with similar clients who have faced similar problems. Lawyers in this phase also function as all-purpose intermediaries, as links between entrepreneurs and financial sources, as well as between business and government agencies at all levels. When giant enterprises formed in the late nineteenth and early twentieth centuries, lawyers made key links between management of railroad and manufacturing corporations, on the one hand, and, on the other, the investment banking houses of Wall Street and Europe, which underwrote the vast consolidations of 1898–1906. Lawyers designed the risk-reward-and-security structures to attract different types of investment and often acted as salesmen of new issues of securities.

The maturing of an enterprise, in the regulatory environments that have been constructed in this country starting with the Progressive movements and New Deal, has called for a different, and much more specialized, range of legal services. Companies usually identify the stage at which their consumption needs for lawyers sharply changes as the decision to 'go public.' The legal job of registering the company's stock issues under the federal and state securities laws calls for disclosure of company information and preparation of incredibly detailed forms, specialists in securities law, a staff of paralegals and secretaries to do the routine state 'Blue Sky' registrations, and, perhaps most important, enough experience with similar transactions to have produced files full of forms to copy. Mistakes in these transactions can be very costly, exposing companies to civil damage actions and heavy fines.

The decision to go public usually also entails changes in management and organization that call for other new legal tasks: design of executive compensation plans, employee pension plans, tax plans, and the like. City law firms with divisions of specialists and established reputations in corporate work have an obvious edge in their ability to attract such business. At this stage, it is not efficient for these companies to hire an internal legal staff that can handle 'going public.' But neither can the companies continue to rely on solo practitioners and small partnerships for this complicated, specialized work. At this stage—which many industries in Silicon Valley have reached—mid-sized companies tend to use mid-sized firms, although the biggest downtown firms, who are afraid of losing business to in-house counsel, have tried to move in on the mid-sized market as well.

If the company continues to prosper and grow, and avoids the need for the ghoulish services of bankruptcy specialists (another booming Silicon Valley legal field), its legal needs may change yet again. It may reach a third stage in which the company may want to take over or merge with other companies, or, conversely, defend itself against takeover attempts. It may wish to acquire foreign subsidiaries, or to engage in joint ventures or arrangements to cross license its technology. It may need legal help with union recognition or collective bargaining negotiations (although unions have not gotten a firm foothold in the Valley so far). It will probably need antitrust advice. It is likely to be dealing constantly with regulatory authorities on health, safety, and environmental matters. It is likely to be embroiled in litigation to protect its intellectual property rights and market share. And finally, it may, through its trade association or on its own account, see itself as having a major stake in or entitled to a major influence over the information of public policies regarding taxes, labor, intellectual property, tariffs, trade, and regulation.

For such needs as these, companies tend to adopt a two-tiered strategy. They are likely to bring an increasing amount of work in-house—not only the more routine legal work that they formerly contracted out to firms, but also the general business advising function. The company's general counsel's office assumes the important function of deciding when to stay inside and when to contract outside, with whom, and on what terms; it also serves as the chief monitor of the outside work. House counsel will draw on outside legal and business counsel only for specialized and non-routine matters, and will spread such transactions—a new stock offering, a piece of litigation business, the job of designing an employee stock-option plan—around different outside firms rather than placing all their eggs in a single firm. The outside firms capable of such specialized work are usually either the very largest downtown metropolitan firms, who can muster large forces of specialized manpower at short notice to counter a takeover bid or an antitrust suit, or else smaller, super-specialized 'boutique' firms.

III.   Legal Services and High Tech in Silicon Valley

How does this very general model of the phases of the evolution of corporate needs for legal services map onto the Silicon Valley experience? Many of the high-tech companies began as tiny outfits—twentieth century analogs to bakeries or dry cleaning shops. When they found themselves, often to their surprise, with revenues in the millions, they needed lawyers who could provide the same services, especially in fields like securities regulation, that big-city lawyers were providing large, established clients elsewhere. So naturally, in the early years of the high-tech boom, companies entering the second phase thought of going to San Francisco for legal services, rather than to local lawyers who had chosen to practice in the provincial backwaters of Palo Alto. The resulting division of labor between San Francisco and the Peninsula bar was, in the main, acceptable to Palo Alto lawyers. Most were solo practitioners, each with a mix of civil and criminal work. A few had banded together into loose associations, sharing common office space; a few had formed two-man partnerships, in which one partner concentrated on litigation, and the other on corporate work. Local lawyers tended to believe that only big firms, staffed with experts, could handle public offerings of stock. The accounting firms, which figure in any major financing, hesitated to let their clients use Peninsula lawyers: they too preferred legal opinions from brand name firms.

Ultimately, two Peninsula lawyers—John Wilson and Leo Ware—decided, independently of each other, to take the plunge. They saw no reason why they could not cope with public offerings. After all, securities work is not the only form of practice that takes skill and experience. Ware and Wilson were general practitioners. They were used to learning new legal skills on short notice. They had stood on the sidelines while their clients went public. They had observed and felt ready to participate; they did not think of themselves as country bumpkins. And, significantly, they found some indulgent clients, guinea pigs willing to resist the 'Go North' tradition.

> Because [we] had been in big law firms . . . we did think that given an opportunity we could develop whatever expertise necessary. . . . [O]ur first client that wanted to go public, we didn't think about sending it out to somebody else. We took it public ourselves. When it became important to struggle with complicated tax matters, why we recruited people out of the NYU graduate tax program. . . .

The crucial decision was far-reaching; but it was perhaps idiosyncratic. Other lawyers, who had equal stature in the legal community, and clients ready for large infusions of capital, chose not to join the bandwagon. Today, the firms of Wilson and Ware are the two biggest, most successful Silicon Valley firms. One contemporary of Wilson and Ware, who chose to stay put, is still a general practitioner, in a small, three lawyer office, modern only in that the other two partners are women. This lawyer is not a failure; he has a thriving practice. After all, Silicon Valley is not just the location of a spectacular industrial boom. Real people live there, with real if mundane legal problems—people who marry and divorce, buy property and sell it, make out wills, and even die. Not everyone works for IBM or Apple or Genentech; and for those who do, these companies do not define all aspects of their existence. But the lawyers who 'stayed behind' were nonetheless affected by the high-tech boom. It brought them work, simply by increasing the need for building permits, drafts of condominium agreements, and the incorporation of sushi bars and car washes. These lawyers were and are busy at their usual jobs—as pervasive facilitators in society. Their ranks have been swelled by a new generation of solos and small-firm lawyers, some of whom have deliberately turned their back on high-tech practice. These lawyers, almost totally neglected by scholarship and the media, are worth a closer look.

For present purposes, however, high-tech firms like Wilson, Sonsini, or Ware & Friedenrich, are the more interesting story. As the high-tech clients grew in number and size, hired more employees, and increased their revenues, the law firms grew as well; they acquired more clients, hired more associates, and raised their fees. In one sense, they were merely riding the waves. Or did the firms help make the waves? Did they make the boom possible by clearing away legal obstacles, by finding and brokering the union of brains and money, and by structuring arrangements?

There is no way, as yet, to answer these questions. But the two opposing perspectives on practice are each important. They influence the way the lawyers perceive themselves, and perhaps they influence the practice as well. To understand law and lawyers in Silicon Valley, it is probably best, paradoxically, to accept both perspectives as reasonably accurate: Lawyers reacted to the high-tech boom, but they also helped to shape it. It is interesting to ask how they reacted, how they shaped events, and what effect their actions had on their rhetoric, their practice, and their social utility.

Some of the leading lawyers themselves, pressed to describe their contribution to the high-tech industries' growth, tend to stress those aspects of their practice roles and styles that in their view distinguish them from big downtown firms of corporate lawyers, especially in New York. They can offer their clients, they claim, service that business lawyers outside the high-tech regions cannot offer: general business advice based on local industry-specific knowledge, access to local sources of venture-capital financing, a facilitative, or 'engineering' approach to the client' problems, and, very notably, a style of law practice—informal, practical-result-oriented, flexible and innovative, keyed to high-trust business relations—that matches the business culture of Silicon Valley.
* * *

Mark C. Suchman & Mia L. Cahill, THE HIRED GUN
AS FACILITATOR: LAWYERS AND THE SUPPRESSION OF
BUSINESS DISPUTES IN SILICON VALLEY

21 LAW SOC. INQUIRY 679 (1996)

Lay discourse often criticizes the legal profession for generating disputes and for introducing adversarial bias into "naturally cooperative" social relations. Many academic observers, too, suggest that attorneys foster an inflated "rights consciousness" that disrupts more flexible and consensual extralegal relationships. Often, lay discussions and scientific analyses alike move from initial observations regarding lawyers' disputatious impact on bilateral relationships to more speculative assertions regarding lawyers' chilling effects on larger systems of economic activity. The underlying assumption seems to be that self-interested attorneys goad their clients into an excessively punctilious awareness of legal rights and that such an awareness, in turn, drains the reservoir of trust and good faith that would otherwise lubricate the wheels of commerce.

Despite the pervasiveness of this jaundiced view, recent years have witnessed a persistent trickle of evidence that the lawyer's economic role may be somewhat more positive than the prevailing imagery would suggest. This alternative perspective is particularly visible in the growing social-scientific literature on corporate legal practice. As researchers have turned their attentions to the high-priced business attorney, they have had to confront the vexing question of why apparently rational executives would be willing to pay such large sums of money for the services of an unproductive trouble-maker. While one could perhaps explain the demand for legal counsel entirely in terms of corporate self-defense, the empirical evidence suggests that lawyers may be earning their keep as more than simply hired guns.

In this regard, at least two general themes seem to be emerging: First, several researchers have highlighted lawyers' potentially significant contributions to the "engineering" of complex transactions. By designing and implementing innovative legal devices, attorneys assist their clients in minimizing transaction costs, circumventing regulatory constraints, escaping encumbering liabilities, and pursuing various strategic objectives. * * *

A second, less well-developed theme in the recent literature addresses the contributions that lawyers make by deploying evocative symbols rather than by providing concrete technical services. In this view, clients face a complex, turbulent, and unpredictable social environment, and they seek legal counsel primarily as a way of fending off cognitive chaos. Thus, lawyers are rewarded for performing rituals that persuasively symbolize certainty and order, even when those rituals produce few material benefits. * * *

The present essay adds to this emerging body of evidence on corporate lawyers' positive contributions to commerce; however, it should not be read as an unconditional assault on earlier, more critical assessments. Our analysis does not dispute the claim that lawyers occasionally inject elements of rights consciousness into arenas previously governed by informal norms of reciprocity and good faith. Nor does it question the assertion that such a transformation, were it to occur, might well disrupt preexisting extralegal business practices. Rather, the following pages advance the more limited contention that neither an elevation of rights consciousness nor a disruption of commercial conviviality are inevitable consequences of an assertive legal profession. The argument, here, takes the form of a detailed empirical counterexample, constructed from qualitative interview data on the role of lawyers and law firms in California's Silicon Valley.

Contrary to the popular image of lawyers as purveyors of discord, Silicon Valley attorneys see themselves (and are seen by others) as key players in an informal apparatus of socialization, coordination, and normalization that serves to avert potential disputes between members of the local business community. This integrative role becomes most notable in interactions between Silicon Valley lawyers and the region's high-technology entrepreneurs and venture capitalists, and it is on this central aspect of Silicon Valley legal practice that the present essay focuses. By virtue of their distinctive location within the Silicon Valley community, lawyers quite literally produce and reproduce the social structures underpinning the local high-risk capital market. Through their relations with both entrepreneurs and investors, they identify, create, transmit, and enforce the emerging norms of the community. In so doing, Silicon Valley lawyers absorb and control some of the central uncertainties of encounters between venture capitalists and entrepreneurs, facilitating what might otherwise be prohibitively costly, complex, and unpredictable transactions. They accomplish this in at least three distinct ways, at three distinct levels of analysis: (1) Silicon Valley lawyers directly absorb some of the uncertainties of individual transactions through their day-to-day professional activities; (2) Silicon Valley lawyers help to define the informal norms of the local business community through their overall pattern of relations with their clienteles; and (3) Silicon Valley lawyers work to formally incorporate these local norms into the national legal regime through their activities in courtrooms, in professional education projects and in regulatory arenas. After briefly outlining the distinctive challenges of high-technology financing, this paper will examine each of these three legal contributions, in turn.

The Uncertainties of Venture Capital

* * *

Taken broadly, the terms "venture capital" and "venture finance" refer to the external funding of a wide range of high-risk business activities. In the context of Silicon Valley, the most important of these high-risk activities is the formation of new technology-based corporations. The difficulty of funding such start-ups through bank loans or other conventional financial vehicles becomes clear when one considers a few "vital statistics" on these enterprises: According to one Silicon Valley consultant, over 60% of the start-up companies in an average venture capital portfolio will enter bankruptcy before the investors can recoup their original stake; less than 10% will ever reach the most desirable "liquidity event," an initial public offering (IPO). Further, even the most successful new companies often take several years to show a profit and substantially longer to offer positive returns on investment.* * * Given these considerations, new technology-based companies are often unable to secure commercial loans at any price. Moreover, even when such backing is available, most start-ups find themselves poorly positioned to assume the burdens of regular debt service or to accept the strictures of heavily covenanted borrowing agreements.

In contrast to conventional lending institutions, venture capital funds address these risks through specialized intra-and interorganizational social structures rather than through the elaborately crafted protective provisions of individual financial instruments. In particular, venture capitalists attempt to manage the risks inherent in high-tech start-ups by (1) emphasizing long-term equity investment, (2) adopting a patient capital-gains-oriented financial strategy, and (3) replacing inflexible covenants with direct oversight of corporate operations.

* * *

Despite these specialized organizational structures, however, the financial market in Silicon Valley faces substantial challenges that are absent even from venture capital investing in many other settings. In particular, high-technology start-ups confront investors not only with high failure rates and dramatically variable returns but also with large elements of sheer guess-work. Markets for new technologies are notoriously difficult to predict, with the performance of any given start-up often depending on technological developments that postdate the firm's founding. These market-shaping developments, themselves, often pivot on essentially random elements of timing and serendipity—both within the start-up's own R & D, production and marketing efforts, and within the R & D, production and marketing efforts of its actual and potential competitors. Consequently, the commercialization of new technologies is highly "path-dependent," and even the most knowledgeable analysts cannot forecast long-run outcomes with any degree of certainty. Further, when the rate of new innovation is rapid and when the mix of commercially available technologies in the future will reflect the mix of investment decisions in the present, high-technology investors may have difficulty even identifying a relevant universe of technologies from which to construct a balanced portfolio.

Equally formidable cognitive hurdles plague high-technology entrepreneurs, as well. Lacking recourse to conventional lenders, innovators face the challenge of raising start-up funding at a reasonable cost in a time-sensitive environment where even small delays may (or may not) prove commercially disastrous. The average venture capital fund finances only 6 out of every 1000 business plans that it receives each year, and founders must invest substantial time and effort into a start-up long before they know whether their search for capital will ultimately pay off. Further, with no solid baseline for judging company valuations, entrepreneurs are often hard-put to evaluate the fairness of those few funding offers that they do receive. Moreover, since most venture capitalists demand a relinquishment of corporate control, founders may have difficulty predicting whether the "post-money" corporation will make effective use of their intellectual property and "sweat equity"—particularly since a majority of board seats are likely to be held by investors with substantial stakes in various competitors, buyers, and suppliers. Finally, all these problems are further compounded by the fact that many high-technology entrepreneurs come from engineering, hobbyist and academic backgrounds and thus lack either independent financial resources or relevant business experience. * * *

On the whole, then, high-technology start-up financing poses challenges not only of risk but also of uncertainty. Although lay parlance often employs these terms interchangeably, the organizational decision-making literature uses them to describe two distinct conditions. Under conditions of "risk," decision-makers may not be able to predict the future deterministically, but at least they can describe it probabilistically: With a little effort, individuals can identify the full range of options and outcomes, and they can determine roughly how likely it is that any given option will produce any particular outcome. Consequently, despite the presence of risk, decision-makers can still make rational choices based on expected-value calculations, and markets can still produce efficient coordination based on contingent-claims contracts.

Uncertainty, on the other hand, arises when decision-makers cannot determine either (1) the full menu of alternative behavioral options or (2) the relative probability of alternative possible outcomes. Unlike risk, uncertainty is deeply incompatible with the neoclassical model of fully rational decision-making. Instead of producing a careful expected-utility analysis of all lines of action, conditions of uncertainty tend to produce "boundedly rational" decision strategies, involving "good enough" choices, gut feelings, and rules of thumb. At a more macroscopic level, uncertainty elevates transaction costs and exacerbates intra-organizational strains and power struggles. Consequently, unresolved uncertainty poses a fundamental cognitive and organizational obstacle to the formation and maintenance of stable markets for high-technology start-up capital.

In a turbulent environment such as this, large-scale economic activity depends heavily on the emergence of social structures capable of managing relevant uncertainties. Significantly, organizations theory speaks of "managing" uncertainty (rather than of "eliminating" uncertainty) in order to allow for the fact that uncertainty can be resolved in at least three distinct ways: Most obviously, social structures may develop that reduce the actual level of environmental turbulence—by, for example, formulating industry standards, establishing barriers to entry, or regulating competitive activities. Somewhat more restrictively, social structures may evolve that localize uncertainty within certain parts of the environment or that allow the costs of uncertainty to be absorbed by certain specialized organizations or subunits—by, for example, establishing stockpiles and other structural buffers, creating insurance schemes, or chartering brokers and arbitrageurs. Finally, social structures may arise that moderate the cognitive challenges of uncertainty without eliminating environmental turbulence, itself—by, for example, propounding "normalizing" cultural accounts, enacting simplified representations of reality, or institutionalizing ritualized practices whose efficacy is assumed rather than tested. All these responses are visible to a greater or lesser extent in the activities of Silicon Valley lawyers.

The Role of Law Firms in Managing Uncertainty

For the reasons outlined above, the uncertainties of high-technology finance persistently threaten to render transactions between entrepreneurs and venture capitalists costly, unstable, and cognitively intractable, even when such exchanges might, in the abstract, seem mutually beneficial. In Silicon Valley (and perhaps in other regions as well), the local legal community shoulders a substantial share of the responsibility for managing such challenges. In contrast to the conventional image of lawyers as sources of disruptive litigiousness, Silicon Valley law firms seem to be active facilitators of local economic development—both through their efforts to absorb some uncertainties and to subject these to collective control, and through their parallel efforts to symbolically downplay other uncertainties and to render these less paralyzing. Indeed, by reducing both perceived and actual levels of cognitive disorder, the local bar may substantially moderate pressures toward disputatiousness in the community as a whole.

Specifically, Silicon Valley's legal practitioners appear to foster market development and to suppress business disputes in three distinct but interrelated ways: First, and most simply, Silicon Valley lawyers often interpose themselves as third-party buffers in particular transactions. While such active intervention may be ethically problematic from the standpoint of the larger legal profession, it allows attorneys to directly absorb transactional uncertainties, facilitating agreements that might otherwise prove unattainable. Second, Silicon Valley lawyers also stabilize the local capital market in general, by transmitting community norms to their clients and by embodying those norms within standardized contractual structures and practices. In so doing, attorneys reduce the transaction costs of negotiating agreements, creating a cooperative climate in which the dangers of opportunism and uncertainty fade from view: Tutored in community norms, contracting parties know which demands are (or are not) "legitimate" and "reasonable"—which concessions they may expect of others, and which concessions others may expect of them in return. Third, Silicon Valley lawyers increasingly act to insulate the local community against exogenous regulatory shocks and competitive challenges, by transforming parochial norms into national legal standards. This "double-institutionalization" of local expectations further reduces the uncertainty of high-technology start-up finance, once again facilitating economic expansion. The following pages will examine each of these market-building activities, in turn.

Absorbing Uncertainty in Individual Transactions

At the simplest level, Silicon Valley law firms reduce the uncertainties of new-company finance by directly interposing themselves into otherwise-problematic corporate transactions. Rather than standing aloof from their clients' operations, as prescribed by conventional legal ethics, many law firms in Silicon Valley display a striking willingness to absorb elements of transactional uncertainty into the law firm's own operations if this will facilitate an endangered deal. This practice appears most vividly in the selection of fee structures and in the drafting of "opinion letters." Each of these activities serves to mitigate some of the uncertainty inherent in the founding and funding of high-technology start-ups.

Fee Structure

Long before a new venture secures financial backing, the founders must engage in a number of relatively hazardous and costly activities, such as leaving jobs with former employers, developing a business plan, and approaching potential investors. Consequently, one of the primary sources of uncertainty for the potential high-technology entrepreneur is the possibility that these efforts may never pay off—either in funding commitments from investors or in a successful enterprise. In this context, Silicon Valley lawyers can facilitate new-company formation by assuming a portion of the risk that financial backing will fail to materialize. In particular, since one of the start-up's primary pre-financing costs is the cost of hiring legal counsel, law firms can absorb a portion of the founders' entrepreneurial uncertainty by foregoing conventional billing and by substituting a payment scheme conditioned on the start-up's subsequent success. Historically, two such contingent-payment schemes predominate: deferred billing and equity compensation.

Often, Silicon Valley law firms offer their corporate clients a deferred-billing structure that amounts, essentially, to a "contingency fee" for business transactions. As a partner in one of the core Silicon Valley law firms explains:

Normally, we will take on start-up companies and make an effort to keep the billable hours down, without compromising the legal issues involved. Frequently we will hold, delay or suspend billing until financing can be obtained. In effect, we become partners with the start-up client. With most of our start-up companies, either by express agreement or by some tacit understanding, there is an attempt made to either completely suspend billing or to go forward on the billing on a very limited basis.

By delaying or waiving billing, a law firm assumes the risk that if its client fails to secure financing, the law firm will, in effect, have provided free legal work. Most unfunded start-ups are essentially judgment-proof, and most successful Silicon Valley attorneys "realize that if a company doesn't get funded, we're not going to look to the founders, personally, to pay." This downside is balanced, of course, against the possibility that a client will successfully locate financing and will then pay the law firm's premium fees out of the newly obtained capital reserves.

Another common payment structure among lawyers with start-up clients is the acceptance of corporate stock in lieu of monetary compensation. Like deferred billing, this strategy, too, involves a gamble on the law firm's part: The corporation could fail, leaving the stock virtually worthless, or the corporation could eventually go public, dramatically increasing the value of the law firm's holdings. Since the cost of pre-financing legal services is, in effect, pegged to the company's stock price, the uncertainty of the funding search is shared (in part) between the start-up and its outside counsel.

Significantly, stock compensation provides entrepreneurs with important symbolic reassurances, as well as with economic risk spreading: Equity compensation schemes (particularly employee stock options) are an important element of Silicon Valley culture, and by accepting payment in stock, a law firm can express confidence in its entrepreneurial clients and in their products. Indeed, in addition to accumulating common stock as equity compensation during the funding search, local law firms often augment their holdings by purchasing preferred stock alongside the venture capital investors in the first-round financing. * * *

Clearly, contingent fee structures—including both deferred payment and equity compensation—can fulfill a number of interrelated purposes. In addition to reducing entrepreneurial uncertainty and serving as important cultural symbols, creative fee arrangements accomplish the far more mundane task of increasing access to (and demand for) legal services within the community. Since small garage-based enterprises can rarely afford traditional hourly legal bills, charges tailored to the start-up life cycle may substantially increase the pool of potential clients. Even if some of the clients thus acquired are not, in themselves, "worth the risk," an expanded client base may have substantial appeal for law firms operating in a rapidly developing, network-oriented community such as Silicon Valley. Among other things, Silicon Valley lawyers are selling their practical start-up experience and their community connections, and these attributes are enhanced by every additional client that comes through the law firm's doors—even those clients that eventually fail.

Before moving on, it is perhaps worth noting that Silicon Valley's favored payment schemes are not entirely unproblematic. In particular, both deferred payment and equity compensation tread near the boundaries of professional ethics, as defined by the California Business and Professions Code and the California Rules of Professional Conduct. When lawyers are to be paid from the proceeds of a financing, their own interests in prompt payment may conflict with their client's interest in securing the best overall funding package. More significantly, when lawyers accept stock in a client, they may be compromising their professional detachment and objectivity. In particular, attorneys who receive equity compensation run the risk of developing interests (as shareholders) that are adverse to the interests of the corporation or to the interests of other stakeholders, including the founders. This problem becomes particularly severe when company counsel participates as a stock purchaser in a financing, alongside the investor syndicate. Technically, all of these issues can be remedied by the informed consent of the various affected parties. Nonetheless, it seems clear that Silicon Valley law firms tend to read the profession's ethical strictures somewhat less restrictively than would their counterparts in other settings.

* * *

Opinion Letters

In addition to absorbing some of the uncertainties facing entrepreneurs, Silicon Valley law firms also absorb some of the uncertainties facing investors. Just as Silicon Valley lawyers contrast their "entrepreneurial" fee arrangements against the more restrictive practices of big-city lawyers, many local attorneys also pride themselves on a willingness to assume investorside risks in order to bridge the gap in imperiled financing transactions.

This facilitative orientation becomes most visible in the distinctive attitude of Silicon Valley lawyers toward the "opinion letters" that they write in support of their clients' representations in venture capital financing agreements. Technically, opinion letters report a law firm's assessment of the veracity and validity of claims contained in contractual documents, and in this sense, these letters would appear to be primarily informational in purpose. Yet, since the vast majority of Silicon Valley opinion letters merely restate the client's pre-negotiated representations and warranties, their actual informational value would seem to be slight—particularly given the fact that venture capital investors are hardly naive buyers. Thus, a more plausible framework for understanding these informationally superfluous writings would be to see them as devices for managing the uncertainties inherent in financing untested, judgment-proof start-ups: Since a law firm is legally responsible for the veracity of its opinion letters, even a simple reiteration of the client's representations would place the law firm's resources on the line as a kind of insurance against deception.

* * *

Traditional legal ethics, of course, would look askance at the idea of knowingly drafting representations and opinion letters that "might not be totally 100% right"; however, by exposing itself to liability for misrepresentation (or for lack of due diligence), the Silicon Valley law firm is able to lift some of the hazards of a failed investment off the shoulders of the venture capital fund. Essentially, the law firm interposes its own deep pockets between the concerned investor and the judgment-proof client, facilitating completion of what might otherwise be a prohibitively uncertain transaction.

While the "insurance" aspects of Silicon Valley legal practice may be clearest in the case of opinion letters, a heightened tolerance for uncertainty appears in other arenas, as well. Thus, for example, this attitude fosters a generalized antipathy toward traditional "belt-and-suspenders" documentation—despite the ability of such writings to protect the drafting law firm against potential malpractice claims. * * *

On the whole, then, Silicon Valley attorneys see themselves as facilitators rather than as voices of caution in the venture financing process. Admittedly, from an external perspective, the facilitative effects of local legal norms might not necessarily outweigh the ethical and professional considerations underlying more traditional models of law-firm behavior. Nonetheless, it is easy to understand how, in a close-knit and dynamic interorganizational environment, conventional professional strictures might come to be seen as deal-killing catechisms rather than as useful components of a smoothly functioning capital market. Indeed, metaphorically, many venture capital financings in Silicon Valley look less like careful apportionments of legal rights than like a collection of parties—founders, investors, attorneys, etc.—standing in a circle, with each agreeing to indemnify the party on his or her left against any damage caused by the party on his or her right, as the entire circle slowly edges its way over a cliff. The desirability of such a social structure depends, of course, on the desirability of encouraging people to jump off cliffs. But it seems clear that, in the absence of such arrangements, high-technology entrepreneurship would be substantially less common.

Suppressing Uncertainty through Community Norms

In addition to accompanying their clients over the cliffs of new-company finance, Silicon Valley law firms also seem to be working to make the drop a bit less precipitous. In particular, the region's attorneys employ their distinctive interorganizational position to create, transmit, sustain, and enforce a normative and cognitive order that increases both the stability and the predictability of the local venture capital market. Years of vicarious experience with the start-up process give Silicon Valley lawyers unusual credibility as business advisors; and years of close contact with the local financial community give Silicon Valley lawyers unusual power as venture capital deal makers. Together, these roles place the region's law firms in an excellent position to shape client behaviors and to set client expectations. This influence emerges most strongly in three major activities: gatekeeping, proselytizing, and sorting.

Gatekeeping

As a result of their status as repeat players and reputational brokers in the venture capital financing process, Silicon Valley law firms play a substantial role in determining which clients gain access to which investors, and vice versa. Local attorneys both accept and refer clients selectively, and as a result, they can use their capacity as "deal makers" to screen out entities that challenge the community's taken-for-granted assumptions or that threaten the community's social cohesion. * * *

Gatekeeping activities such as these help to establish normative boundaries around the Silicon Valley community, albeit perhaps at the risk of stifling structural innovation. The resulting increase in community cohesion reduces the costs associated with choosing business partners and assures that all parties to a transaction will share a common framework of basic values and assumptions. In essence, gatekeeping moderates the uncertainty of anonymous market relations, protecting the cultural underpinnings of the local economy.

Proselytizing

In addition to screening out potential deviants, Silicon Valley lawyers can also reduce uncertainty in the venture capital market by affirmatively encouraging clients to adopt the community's preferred models for action. In contrast to the traditional image of detached professionalism, local start-ups often turn to their attorneys not only for legal advice but also for general business guidance. In this expanded counseling capacity, lawyers have the ability to foster and reinforce community norms by promoting certain types of financing transactions over others. Thus, beyond evaluating the legal implications of proposed contracts, a robust Silicon Valley legal practice often involves educating inexperienced entrepreneurs in the less formal aspects of Silicon Valley's venture capital market. As one prominent attorney put it:

The lawyers in Silicon Valley who are experienced in venture financing provide a very important service. If it's the entrepreneurs' first company, experienced lawyers make them very comfortable with venture financing and, in a very professional way, provide them with the guidance that they need. After all, the venture capitalist on the other side of the table has been through it many, many times. One of the major contributions, then, that experienced lawyers make is to level the playing field and to provide supplements for the entrepreneur with a lack of experience in this process.

Significantly, these "supplements" appear to consist primarily of reassurance and tutelage in community norms, rather than of conventional adversarial representation. Silicon Valley law firms participate in a culture that depicts venture capital transactions as being natural and desirable rather than as being "evil" (in the words of one entrepreneur-turned-venture capitalist) and oppositional. Consequently, a nonadversarial orientation toward venture finance represents an essential element of the outlook that local attorneys seek to inculcate in their clients. In the words of one senior attorney:

> It is not an adversarial process. People who view it properly, who have a lot of experience in venture financing, realize that they are creating a very long-term partnership between the venture capitalists on the one hand and the entrepreneurs on the other. So it's important that it be very fair, that parties can live with each other for a long time.

Another attorney contrasts this collaborative approach with a more traditional image of the legal profession:

> Silicon Valley legal practice is really defined by common understandings of how things should be, and by a sense that lawyers are facilitators and ought to do things pretty efficiently—as opposed to an antagonistic style where you fight for every nickel on the table, and you take extreme positions and engage in hard-knocks negotiating. That's not accepted very much in this area.

Anti-adversarialism, however, is not the only lesson imparted by Silicon Valley's lawyer-evangelists. In addition to preaching cooperation, local business attorneys also promote the sorts of clear and stable expectations that make such cooperation possible. Thus, for example, when entrepreneurs are relatively inexperienced or when a particular type of deal is relatively new, lawyers may serve as a crucial source of information about the range of "reasonable" terms and valuations. As an attorney who specializes in "corporate partnerships" states:

> The markets for these deals are very inefficient and people don't have a good idea of what kind of payments are involved. So as lawyers who see a lot of these deals, we're sort of a repository of information about how these deals get done. Even though we don't,

obviously, tell clients what others are charging, we can influence what they might ask for.

* * *

Thus, as proselytizers, Silicon Valley lawyers work to "civilize" their clienteles, indoctrinating new entrants into the routines and vocabularies of the local business community. In a setting where the rapid influx of companies and technologies threatens to undermine social coherence, law firms help to define and communicate the socially constructed boundaries of "reasonable" behavior. In contrast to the traditional "hired-gun" stereotype, such ministrations increase the likelihood that financial transactions will reflect the cultural norms of the community rather than the individual interests of the client. Once again, this treads near the boundaries of conventional legal ethics. Yet, such social regulation may be the price for a viable market: In spreading the venture capital gospel, Silicon Valley lawyers suppress both the appearance and the reality of decision-making uncertainty, permitting the routinization of what would otherwise be prohibitively complex and costly transactions. * * *

Sorting

Both gatekeeping and proselytizing call on law firms to standardize their clients' activities by enforcing the norms of the Silicon Valley business community; yet such regulatory efforts are not the only routes to reduced uncertainty. Uncertainty is fundamentally a cognitive condition, and in addition to constraining the overall range of behavioral variation, law firms can also manage uncertainty by developing conceptual schemata that make sense of whatever variability remains. Thus, in a third set of community-building activities, lawyers formulate and apply simplifying cultural typologies, both to steer start-ups to "appropriate" investors and also to select "appropriate" contractual structures for specific transactions.

* * *

Averting Uncertainty through Legal Standards

In addition to establishing community boundaries, promoting normative transactions, and categorizing recurrent situations, Silicon Valley law firms also reduce the uncertainty of local capital markets by translating the region's informal norms into the currency of the larger legal system. As gate-keepers, proselytizers, and sorters, attorneys build and transmit common understandings within the surrounding organizational community. However, the routinizing influence of Silicon Valley lawyers does not end there. In their professional capacities, the region's attorneys shape both the interpretation and the regulation of their preferred financing instruments, both locally and nationally. Increasingly, the Silicon Valley bar appears to be embedding the community's distinctive business practices not only in individual contracts but also in the local and national legal discourse, through standardized trade practices, professional formbooks, judicial doctrines, and administrative regulations.

Local Legal Standards

Locally, lawyers' adherence to community norms has the effect of homogenizing financing structures, making contracts increasingly similar across transactions. Such isomorphism both limits the range of plausible models and restrains debate over specific provisions. As one Palo Alto attorney observes:

> If there's a transaction with one of the other Silicon Valley law firms, the transaction costs tend to be minimal. Very often, they've adopted our forms or vice versa. Usually, the forms that are used representing the investor are the same as were used representing the company, because they follow well-defined molds. There's no negotiating on it really. I remember one attorney at another firm saying that a couple of years ago, he had this whole set of negotiating responses to my firm's forms. But in the last few deals that I did with them, their forms were virtually identical to ours, and there wasn't anything to argue over.

The consequences of this transition are twofold: First, as the preceding quotation suggests, standardization reduces the cost of individual transactions, since parties need not expend resources arguing over issues that have already been "worked out." Thus, simple economics would predict that both the overall number of transactions and also the ratio of standard to nonstandard terms will rise. Second, the emergence of standard forms may have normative and cognitive effects that further reinforce the trend toward institutionalization. In particular, as contracts come to routinely incorporate clauses that have been "decided" years before, lawyers may hesitate to rock the boat by overzealously promoting client interests on specific issues. Indeed, excessively partisan advocacy can itself come to be seen as a mark of bad citizenship:

> It's very hard to argue against a provision that you, yourself, insisted on in some other transaction. During the early days, negotiation was much more contentious. But the lawyers who were contentious—who lost sight of the fact that the goal was to achieve a long-term harmonious relationship between the investors and the entrepreneur—really dropped out. There were a number of lawyers who over-negotiated agreements and created their own work as part of the process. Sooner or later, those lawyers stopped getting business.

The more pervasive the standard, the more normatively and cognitively difficult will be the task of enunciating an opposing perspective. And the more often attorneys must "cool out" their clients by justifying dominant conventions, the more likely these attorneys are to perceive such conventions as not only "common," but also "right," "fair," "effective" and ultimately "legal." In this sense, by homogenizing and routinizing venture capital transactions, Silicon Valley lawyers help to construct a de facto "local law."

Initially, the binding character of these emergent contractual standards rests primarily on the extralegal pressures that attorneys encounter in establishing and protecting positions within the local community. Under certain circumstances, however, local norms can take on the force of official law: In the unlikely event that a financing agreement were to actually end up in court, the "trade practices" of the community could be invoked to guide the judicial interpretation of ambiguous contractual terms. Thus, by standardizing contracts and by categorizing transactions, Silicon Valley attorneys help the community to construct a "law of its own"—facilitating the region's favored practices by selectively modifying the strictures of the larger legal regime.

Lawrence A. Cunningham, SHARING ACCOUNTING'S BURDEN: BUSINESS LAWYERS IN ENRON'S DARK SHADOWS

57 BUS. LAW. 1421 (2002)

"[T]o paraphrase Clemenceau on war and generals, accounting has become just too important to be left to the accountants." So said Jim Freund, renowned mergers and acquisitions (M & A) lawyer at Skadden, Arps in his classic 1975 book Anatomy of a Merger. Though accounting had become important to law and society by the mid–1970s, it is now more important than ever, as Enron and a parade of accounting debacles attest. Accounting concepts so directly affect the structuring of deals, their disclosure, the form and amount of consideration, and other aspects of negotiations and compliance, that the Clemenceau quip has become more apt in the three decades since Freund penned it. Lawyers now more than ever must assume roles of diplomats and statesmen when working in the trenches or vineyards of business practice. The focus of this Article is on the need for business lawyers to know more about accounting, and for law schools to teach more about it. Enron figures prominently but not exclusively in this discussion.

The lawyerly sharing of accounting's burden is not one of the leading lessons to learn from the Enron debacle and the problems it epitomizes. Instead, dozens of other lessons are drawn by a wide variety of critics, regulators, and legislators, who offer a stunning range of incompatible prescriptions. Enron's cacophonous commentators share the trait of the proverbial man with a hammer, to whom every problem looks like a nail. Advocates of stricter auditing standards see a system-wide breakdown in audit quality; devotees of corporate social responsibility cite Enron to support their cause. Those on the left use it to bolster their case that more regulation is needed, while those on the right point to insufficient market competition as the cause of the failure.

A charitable view of this phenomenon—seeing what we want to see—is based on the fact that it is a natural cognitive bias, perhaps the sensible recognition of competency. Even so, care must be taken not to overemphasize the significance of one's field or preexisting viewpoint in assessing new events. Bearing this wisdom in mind, any lawyer remotely interested in corporate governance and accounting must be able to appreciate that lawyers play a significant role when accounting fraud occurs and should consider the nature of that role and duties attendant to it. This appreciation shows that an important lesson from Enron is the danger that prevailing professional cultures create a crack between law and accounting that resolute fraud artists exploit, not cultures that emphasize the intersection of law and accounting that should foil would-be fraudsters.

* * *

Enron in Perspective

* * *

There is no question that Enron is an accounting scandal and no doubt that accounting scandals have been on the rise. Whether reforms of accounting and auditing are overdue or other responses warranted, there is one other thing that is certain: business lawyers are present during most accounting frauds. That presence, coupled with a credible dose of accounting sense, will often enable a lawyer to discourage accounting fraud—and perhaps even, on rare occasions, prevent it. While lawyers face delicate issues of ethics relating to the preservation of client confidences in such settings, lawyers may not simply stand on the sidelines and allow accounting frauds to go forward.

In Enron's case, lawyers played a central role in the formation, structuring, and reporting of various partnerships treated as off-balance sheet to Enron and involving related parties. But under applicable accounting rules, these special purpose entities were required to be shown on Enron's consolidated balance sheet (and therefore also subject to disclosure under federal securities laws). Questions concerning who knew what when remain unanswered, but with Enron in this perspective, prudence suggests that before regulating by adding new layers and monitors, active professionals should be required to beef up their accounting skills.

The Practice of Business Lawyers

The incentive for lawyers to become part-time accountants is by no means limited to helping clients steer clear of accounting irregularities or fraud, though that adds value. It is an asset at the bargaining table and should be used as such.[56] * * *

56. The emphasis on the importance of accounting to the business lawyer should not disguise the broader significance of accounting to lawyers. Accounting is pervasive in law, and life, and must be familiar to lawyers in a wide variety of practice areas: litigators calculating damages and structuring settlements, tax lawyers in virtually every professional setting, environmental lawyers handling cost allocations, labor lawyers dealing with profit sharing agreements, domestic relations lawyers addressing asset settlements and maintenance and alimony arrangements, regulatory lawyers involved with antitrust, health care, insurance, and public utilities, and so on.

Failure of lawyers to understand accounting can produce disastrous results. For example, a statute settling disputes among Alaska natives specified a resource sharing arrangement that pooled and reallocated resources based on "revenues" of each cooperative rather than based on "income"—as no doubt was intended. But failure to appreciate the difference led the legislation to continue rather than settle the dispute.

[C]onsider a deal to sell a corporate division. A threshold legal issue is whether the division sale constitutes the sale of all or substantially all the assets of the corporation requiring a shareholder vote. The standard approach to analyzing whether an asset sale triggers statutes requiring shareholder votes for the sale of "all or substantially all" a corporation's assets considers quantitative and qualitative characteristics of the transaction.

Different judges have applied a bewildering array of metrics for the quantitative assessment. These range from the book, market or transaction value of the assets to the revenue, gross or net income or cash flows generated by the assets. Each of these concepts is a term of art. They can mean different things, within a range, so long as it is reasonable. Knowing this, as well as the boundaries, is essential for a lawyer to reach an informed opinion concerning whether shareholder approval is required—or at least and more likely to advise a client of the probability that a judge would decide on a preliminary injunction or summary judgment motion that it was.

The question of whether a division sale constitutes all or substantially all a corporation's assets can call for refining the numbers even further; a refinement of the numbers that also calls for close cooperation between lawyers and accountants in designing suitable representations and warranties. Major questions arise due to the difficulty of deriving reliable historical or projected operating results at the division level. The two broadest questions are the feasibility of the buyer's accounting post-closing and the sense of its purchase price.

Divisions are typically run as integrated operations within a corporation. Intra-company transactions may not be recorded in accordance with generally accepted accounting principles (GAAP). They may be invisible. Funds flowing from headquarters to the division may have been assigned a cost (an interest rate), but how that was determined (not using market rates), and how the division is going to be charged when it is freestanding or part of the buyer, are different matters. Moreover, headquarters would have provided a range of back office services, such as legal, accounting, and insurance, whose costs will not burden the division's books either.

Lawyers obviously are not the prime professionals to assess these matters. But they must understand them to assure that a due diligence team staffed with accountants gains access to required information and draft agreements reflecting adjustments required by these accounting realities. These representations are intended, in part, to elicit information from the seller about variances and ultimately to provide adjustments to the purchase price or representations that everyone is happy with (the seller can stand by and the buyer can look to if things go awry).

* * *

A lawyer asked to give an opinion concerning whether a company has the legal power to pay a distribution to its shareholders must know some accounting. Such distributions are often made in connection with transactions involving a substantial role for business lawyers, ranging from spin-offs and split-ups to joint ventures and other cooperative enterprises.

Rules in most states forbid shareholder distributions that would render assets less than liabilities or produce equity insolvency (the inability to pay debts as they come due). No one can form a judgment about these matters without knowing basic accounting. Likewise, without such knowledge no one can assess whether certain adjustments to the accounts are lawful for the purpose of enabling the making of the distribution.

Loan agreements contain private arrangements to afford creditor protection like that offered by statutes restricting distributions to shareholders. They invariably are tighter than the statutes and are defined expressly in terms of financial ratios that depend on accounting information. A typical covenant requires a lender to maintain a minimum level of working capital, defined in turn as current assets less current liabilities (themselves further defined).

Remedies for breach of these financial covenants may include acceleration of the principal amount of the loan. Some agreements contain cross-default provisions under which the agreement is deemed breached upon the breach of another agreement. Lawyers negotiating and drafting these documents obviously must be competent to create legal definitions using accounting concepts, and sufficiently understand the variety of these definitions to ensure harmonization of triggers in various agreements.

Beyond knowledge of basic definitions, a business lawyer's familiarity with a few technical accounting rules is important. For example, if the remedy on default is acceleration of the principal, accounting rules require that the entire principal amount be treated as a current liability. That treatment can trigger defaults under other agreements that contain ratio tests requiring minimum working capital levels.

Accounting rules also provide, however, that a lender's waiver of default for at least one year from a balance sheet date enables the borrower to treat the defaulted obligation as a long-term liability. If so reducing the borrower's working capital would trigger a default on senior debt, it may be in the lender's best interest to waive the breach rather than accelerate. A lawyer who is also a part-time accountant can explain this to the lender and its other lawyers in a way that many cannot—sometimes preventing a financial cascade in no one's interest.

Many terms in loan agreements and other corporate documentation incorporate by reference the definition of GAAP. It is common for first drafts of agreements to include as a "rule of construction" a provision such as, "an accounting term not otherwise defined has the meaning assigned to it in accordance with generally accepted accounting principles" in effect from time to time.

Innocuous, fair, and even-handed as an appeal to "generally accepted" principles sounds, this is not always in a client's bests interest and only an accounting-savvy lawyer will know or understand why. GAAP is a set of conventions, rooted in historical cost accounting, and conservative in its philosophy, that tends to understate the fair value of vast asset classes, including particularly intellectual property. A shareholder buyout agreement of a high-tech company with enormous intellectual property rights using unadorned GAAP to set the price would be disastrous for the selling shareholder.

Untutored lawyers sometimes face arguments from seasoned counterparts that a position is necessary or desirable because it accords with GAAP. The unwashed may find this stance convincing, but it invariably is not. GAAP's conventions authorize a wide variety of treatments for identical economic events, from relatively standard contexts such as inventory and depreciation to more challenging contexts such as derivatives and leases. Accounting requires choices and judgments entailing substantial subjectivity, making compliance with GAAP insufficient. It rarely mandates particular treatments and by no means forecloses massaging numbers, or even committing fraud. Seasoned advocates working with accounting data know this about GAAP.

The framework of the federal securities laws relating to the disclosure of forward looking information is teeming with the law and accounting overlap. The Private Securities Litigation Reform Act of 1995 defines various categories of forward looking information, two of which pose substantial mixed questions of law and accounting (fact): predictions that must be disclosed if created and those that may voluntarily be disclosed. The cautious advice is to resist creating projections in these two categories, advice that must conform with legal standards and accounting principles.

Suppose two firms plan to merge. Rules require a joint proxy statement governing shareholder approval of the deal to include pro forma financial statements showing how the combined entity's financials would look if they had been combined previously. That suggests what is called for is historical information and to that extent there is no major problem (though the activity is by no means simple addition, but calls for reconciling the accounting used by the combining firms that may have differed when they stood alone).

More critical is whether the resulting picture presents a reasonably accurate one or whether it is deficient or misleading in some way that requires adjustment. SEC regulations say that when this occurs the pro forma presentation must "give effect to the range of possible results."

While lawyers may read this to require detailed presentation and foot-note analysis of the range, the standard response of accountants is not to disclose such details but offer a broad and strict disclaimer emphasizing that pro forma presentation is a "mechanical exercise" bearing no relation to actual results or any measurement or aggregation of synergy or other gains to be generated from the combination. No lawyer can advise in this process without knowing what these sorts of terms are intended to convey, why accountants are concerned about them, or how to negotiate with the SEC if that becomes necessary to convince it to approve proxy materials prepared this way.

Similar conversations between lawyers and auditors arise concerning loss contingencies resulting from litigation risks. These are disclosed as a line item on the balance sheet with cross-references to footnotes. Lawyers and auditors must confer to prepare the appropriate disclosure. That discussion is more productive when each side understands that the other has different professional objectives and duties. The concern of lawyers is confidentiality, while that of auditors is disclosure; lawyers are advocates for their clients, while auditors are watchdogs for the public. But understanding different professional roles is hardly enough.

The law and accounting professions use different vocabulary to discuss the subject of loss contingencies. Auditing rules provide that losses that are remote need not be disclosed at all, those that are possible call for such descriptive disclosure, and those that are probable (and can be estimated in amount) must be recorded on the books in those amounts. The two professions define these terms remote, possible, and probable differently. Lawyers negotiating with auditors over which risks and amounts must be disclosed or kept confidential will be far more successful armed with an understanding of these differences and will be able to find a middle ground that meets the professional duties of both sides.

* * *

The Fiduciary Duties of Business Lawyers

Lawyers owe clients a series of duties in discharging professional responsibilities. One is competence. This section addresses whether a business lawyer's duty of competence includes some level of accounting knowledge. The preceding discussion of what business lawyers do and what law students must know to grasp corporate law may suggest that they do. The professional literature concerning legal ethics offers a more equivocal answer. An analysis of that literature informed by the context of a business law practice suggests that whatever the duty's precise technical content, a business lawyer's professional ethics should command them to master accounting basics.

* * *

Lawyers think of competency in terms of "general technical proficiency." Competency means ability, in fact, to accomplish objectives with the capacity of an ordinarily able professional in similar circumstances. This normally concerns legal knowledge, skill, and preparation, in light of the legal and factual context of a representation. Knowledge relates to identifying, assessing, and dealing with legal problems; skill relates to advising, negotiating, and planning a course of action; and preparation is the thinking through on both lines of professional activity.

The professional literature and ethics codes speak of legal competence. On its face, therefore, competency in distinctly non-legal areas of accounting would not be required. Yet the intersection of law and accounting is clear, as the practice and classroom examples given suggest. So questions of mixed law and fact arise because of that intersection. The facts or factual context of a business law representation include financial realities and the manner of their accounting reporting. Competence encompasses an understanding of that relationship and an analysis of the degree to which differences exist that affect legal relations.

Reinforcing this common-sense view are prudential factors that stem from two kindred duties, the duty of diligence and the duty of candor. The duty of diligence may compel business lawyers, as a matter of legal ethics, to gain a little accounting competency. Advising a corporate client concerning the disposition of sixty percent of its "net book assets" may require brushing up on the meaning of the terms assets, sales, and earnings. Failing that, the duty of candor probably compels lawyers to inform clients of limited capabilities.

As an outer limit, finally, and apparently an issue implicated by Enron, lawyers must advise clients so that they avoid any violation of the law and may not "counsel . . . or assist a client, in conduct that . . . is criminal or fraudulent." Lawyers cannot further a client's criminal or fraudulent purpose nor continue representation that is known to assist the client in the design. These mandates call for active rather than passive attention to client actions and purposes. They encompass the capacity to address non-legal matters, in the business law setting including ways accounting facts may indicate when fraud or criminality is afoot. Cynicism is obviously not required, but healthy professional skepticism and curiosity is.

* * *

If a business lawyer's duty of competence encompasses matters of accounting, however, this by no means requires direct or prior knowledge of accounting. That is only one way to discharge the duty. Lawyers may discharge the duty of competence by learning on the spot. Lawyers can also meet their duty of competence by leaning on other professionals with the requisite expertise. So the duty of competence can be discharged by knowing, learning, or affiliating. In the case of affiliation, moreover, relying upon trained accountants would ordinarily meet the requirements of the duty.

Even if the duty of competence can be met by associating with accountants possessing the core competency, there remains a substantial professional and practical necessity for business lawyers to have a working knowledge of relevant accounting standards. This view of the duty of competence means only that failure of business lawyers to understand accounting issues involved in transactions they are structuring and advising upon do not, as a technical matter, breach their professional responsibility or constitute malpractice.

This is not saying much. In practice, after all, enforcement of competency standards by professional discipline is rare, limited to the "blatant bungler." Legal malpractice claims can be defeated even for failure to master legal principles taught in basic first-year law classes, such as the rule against perpetuities. Failure to master accounting matters, even in the intersection of law and accounting, is less likely to result in successful malpractice claims. For these, a good defense would be the hardy "mere error in judgment" doctrine, strong so long as a lawyer can show good faith.

Should this excuse business lawyers from the effort? All lawyers know that just because something is legal does not mean it is right. In the area of legal ethics, just because a duty can be technically discharged in a painless way, does not mean client interests are served. This is particularly the case when rival lawyers are masters of the competency. Clients without such lawyers are twice disadvantaged.

Rather than examining the technical content of the duty of competence and doing the bare minimum to meet it, the more ethical and prudential question is how best to meet client needs in the realistic context of business law practice. The answer is akin to the knowledge lawyers in other fields must command though no formal legal or ethical demand is imposed on the lawyer: environmental lawyers knowing a little geology; medical malpractice lawyers knowing a little medicine; constitutional lawyers knowing some political theory; agents who are lawyers knowing something about publishing, music, or sports; and criminal defense lawyers having some street smarts.

Business lawyers may also be required to have a core competency in such related fields as antitrust, environmental law, intellectual property, regulatory, tax, even zoning. To the extent these arise less frequently than accounting issues, however, it is far easier for business lawyers to discharge the duty of competence through affiliation rather than using direct knowledge. For example, suppose an M & A lawyer represents a buyer of a manufacturing facility with numerous underground storage tanks. As part of his due diligence in assessing risks of assuming environmental liabilities he may retain a geologist to conduct ground water tests and rely on that expert to discharge the duty of competence.

Certainly he can do the same thing as to the financial statements furnished about the facility—hire an accountant (or have the client hire an accountant). However, one difference in thinking about this context is that the M & A lawyer will face the accounting questions in every deal he advises on. Environmental and other matters do not routinely arise. Also, buyers and sellers invariably have or retain accountants to work on just about every deal. Relying on accountants hired by the client or the other side is not the same as hiring a geologist to investigate an environmental risk.

* * *

THE COMPETENCY OF BUSINESS LAWYERS

A familiar pass-the-buck pas de deux in deal meetings and conference calls occurs when the accountant says, after an impasse, "that's a legal problem" while the lawyer says "that's an accounting problem." Frequently the truth is what's not said: both are right. Each should be more willing to venture into the other's territory—and the good news is Enron may accelerate what was already emerging as a trend in that direction.

The collapse of Enron arises from related party transactions that were improperly accounted for and inadequately disclosed. Many hinged on the SEC's minimum equity rule for special purpose entities. Was this a matter of law, given its origin in an SEC position, or a matter of accounting, given its impact on the financial statement presentation? The answer is both, underscoring the accounting and law link.

For any business transaction, there is an accounting consequence and in turn or simultaneously a disclosure consequence. They are related. The captain of the accounting team may be a different person from the captain of the disclosure team, but the two go hand in hand, they must harmonize, the one must know what the other is doing and understand why. They cannot ignore what the other is doing, as may have occurred at Enron.

Consider then a very different professional outlook and culture offered throughout the Enron ordeal by one of Enron's main outside law firms, Vinson & Elkins. In briefs supporting the firm's motion to dismiss Enron shareholder lawsuits against it, the lawyers took the position that they were neither responsible for accounting matters nor competent to assume any responsibility for them. They argued that these matters were "largely a matter of the application of not within the purview of lawyers." In response to criticism of the law firm's role in the debacle, its senior partner is quoted in an interview by The New York Times as saying: " 'There is a misunderstanding of what outside counsel's role is. . . . We would have no role in determining whether, or what, accounting treatment was appropriate' for a client."

If this statement is true, it suggests a wedge between the professional cultures of lawyers and accountants that is dangerous. If true, it may help to explain, in part, the accounting transgressions that occurred at Enron. This is not to argue that had Vinson & Elkins's deal lawyers working on Enron matters understood accounting they would have been able to hold credible discussions about relevant rules to prevent the accounting shenanigans or (much less) Enron's collapse. The cautionary tale is more modest, yet still quite meaningful. Lawyers with such capabilities will be in a position to do so and, at least some of the time, that capability will pay off.

Nor is this to argue that Vinson & Elkins breached any such duty in its representation of Enron. As a technical matter, the duty of competence may not call for a law firm's involvement in discussing appropriate accounting treatment. But the statement attributed to the senior partner still defies reality. The interplay between accounting questions and the overall deal environment is such that the accounting issues cannot be ignored. They are often a central part of a deal and negotiations. It would be astonishing if business lawyers at Vinson & Elkins did not seek to understand, discuss, and negotiate the accounting treatment of transactions in the ordinary course of events. The quoted statement sounds more like post hoc advocacy.

The degree of accounting knowledge required or appropriate will vary with a business lawyer's professional role. The role and responsibility of inside general counsel concerning internal controls is likely to be far greater than that of outside counsel. The role of outside counsel is likely to be far greater than inside general counsel in structuring major transactions. Yet a different role is played by lawyers representing adverse parties, as underwriters, lenders, other investors, or buyers/sellers on the other side of a business combination. * * *

Requisite accounting knowledge among lawyers may also vary with the stage of a business transaction calling for representation. In the early stages of a deal—and further into them for smaller operations—greater facility is likely to be required because the lawyer may be the only professional involved in the early planning phases. There is often no accountant yet on the participant's list.

Equally, however, accounting is as specialized a field as law, so that a business lawyer experienced in acquisitions or public offerings, say, may have a better feel for accounting problems and issues in doing those deals than an accountant experienced in tax matters or liquidations. When the expert accountant is present, moreover, the lawyer must be able to speak his language—to reach a deal that achieves the many competing objectives of any complicated transaction—corporate governance, tax, accounting, securities, regulatory, antitrust, and so on.

A business lawyer's competency as a part-time accountant does not entail that a lawyer become a certified public accountant (CPA) or even hold an undergraduate degree in accounting, nor to read everything available about accounting. Rather, it means a basic familiarity with the landscape—the basic financial statements and their relationships to each other, the major categories of accounts that appear in these statements, the sources of accounting authority in the professional literature, and the range of discretion and judgment accounting rules allow and require (and the temptations this creates for massaging the numbers)—pretty much what is provided in a traditional law school course introducing law students to accounting.

Beyond such a handle on the basics, lawyers should make it a professional habit to stay abreast of the top handful of hot topics of debate within the accounting profession and also understand the accounting aspects of transactions they are involved with (e.g., true sale rules, leasing rules, and derivatives rules). This calls for a commitment to develop an evolving base of professional experience—the opposite of the attitude reflected in the conference-call buck passing.

It is not generally necessary to research issues in the accounting literature, but to read the leading release or position. Nor is it necessary, as it is with reading legal materials, to master all the accounting jargon—it is sufficient to get to the heart of the document. Business lawyers should get on the mailing list of leading accounting firms that periodically prepare and distribute newsletters on current topics of interest.

When a lawyer's practice leads to repeat representation in the same type of deal—M & A or underwriting or high-tech venture capital—prudence calls for learning the special accounting issues that arise in those kinds of deals. The business lawyer should become familiar with the interpretations of principles produced by the FASB and AICPA on the relevant subjects. For lawyers routinely drafting transactional documents involving accounting concepts, there are a number of reliable practice aids that should be consulted.

Tips for business lawyers on how to develop simple core competencies in basic accounting thus overlap with tips for staying abreast of relevant court precedents, administrative rule making, legislation, market contexts, and other matter relevant to the effective representation of clients. The list could include more general advice such as attending bar meetings and lectures concerning law and accounting, attending panels where business lawyers or SEC representatives discuss accounting, subscribing to professional literature addressing the subject, and so on.

PROBLEMS

1. Universal Products, Inc. is one of the ten largest American corporations, engaged in world-wide businesses involving a wide range of products. It has been a client of Durbin & Rollins, a major Washington D.C law firm, for a number of years on a variety of matters, principally antitrust and tax. It is one of the firm's ten largest clients. Universal uses a number of law firms throughout the country on its business, including several in Washington.

In early December, as the culmination of an extensive advertising campaign, Universal's razor blade division arranged for samples of a new blade to be placed in the Sunday supplements of newspapers throughout the country. The division had the blades placed in a container especially designed to prevent injuries to children and pets. No one in the top management was aware of the advertising campaign until the first newspaper supplement was published, nor was Universal's general counsel consulted as to Universal's possible liability from the distribution of the razor blades.

No injures resulted from the first supplement. Nevertheless, immediately after its publication, the Federal Trade Commission advised Universal's general counsel that it would seek to enjoin publication of future supplements on the ground that it constituted "deceptive advertising" as prohibited by the relevant statutes. The general counsel, in turn, asked the senior partner at Durbin & Rollins in charge of Universal's matters to represent Universal in the FTC action.

Without doing any legal research, the partner was aware that courts had refused to extend the "deceptive advertising" language of the FTC statute to cover solely dangerous devices and that Congress had explicitly declined to amend the statute to include such devices. Thus, however undesirable the distribution of razor blades might be, the partner believed that Universal could defeat the FTC's efforts to obtain an injunction. The partner also knew that, even if a court were to grant an injunction, it would be too late to stop publication of the second supplement.

What factors should Durbin & Rollins consider in deciding whether to accept the representation?

In answering that question, consider how the following variables might affect your analysis.

a) Rather than being one of Universal's regular law firms, this is the first time that Universal has come to the firm for legal advice.

b) Universal has paid Durbin & Rollins a substantial retainer every year for any business it may choose to bring to the firm. A large amount of that retainer remains unspent.

c) Would your analysis change if Universal were a start-up Corporation that believes that the supplements are the best way of entering an industry that is dominated by two other companies?

2. Consider the following excerpt that describes the difficulties that Enron encountered with a foreign power project that was not involved in any of the misconduct that occurred at the company.[1] If you are a senior lawyer in Enron's Legal Department, what recommendations do you have about what Enron should do next? What information would be useful in arriving at your recommendations, and from what sources would you obtain it? Is there anything you might have advised Enron to do beforehand that could have avoided problems?

Bethany McLean & Peter Elkind, The Smartest Guys in the
Room: The Amazing Rise and Scandalous Fall of Enron

(2004)

[I]n early 1992 * * * [a]n Indian delegation, led by the country's power secretary, came to the United States touting the government's program of economic reforms, and seeking investors to help India

---

1. For a discussion of that misconduct and questions about Enron's attorneys, see   Chapter 20: Complex Transactions.

address its chronic energy shortages. Many American companies, wary of the problems that came with doing business in India, held only cursory meetings with the delegation. Not Enron. * * * Eventually, [Enron] told [the officials] that it would be the company's first investor, but only if India were willing to meet three conditions. It would have to work with Enron on an expedited basis, it would have to commit to using natural gas, and it would have to back up any deal with ironclad government guarantees.

On June 30, Enron signed a letter of intent with the electricity board in Maharashtra, India's wealthiest and most heavily industrialized state, which was desperately in need of power * * * The spot that [the parties] chose [for the project, Dabhol,] was so remote that the project would have to develop its own roads, hospital, housing, and port. Enron was awarded the right to develop the site without competing bids.

Eighteen months later, in December 1993, [Enron] inked a 20-year power-purchase contract with the Maharashtra State Energy Board (MSEB). The terms called for Enron to build an enormous, 2015 megawat plant * * * The construction would be done in two phases at an estimated cost of $2.8 billion. The two sides agreed that power prices in the region would rise once the plant was up and running, in part because, for environmental and reliability reasons, the fuel would be imported liquefied natural gas, and expensive fuel. The bill for the power would be calculated in dollars, so that the MSEB, not Enron, bore the currency risk. Finally, the MSEB promised to buy 90 percent of the power Dabhol produced for the entire 20-year period. Its ability to pay was guaranteed by both the state and the central government.

* * * [N]o one * * * could envision the kind of resentment and backlash that [the] agreement would engender. To many Indians, the deal came to represent nothing less than a huge give-away to a rapacious multinational corporation * * * [In addition, there were risks to Enron]. If the MSEB was ever going to be able to pay for the power on its own, the Indian government would have to push through serious economic reforms, reforms that would put state electricity boards such as the MSEB on a firm financial footing. But such reforms were politically contentious because they would mean increasing the price of power for some consumers. On top of the normal economic risk was a frightening amount of political risk.

* * * [T]he World Bank had held a near monopoly on financing infrastructure investments in India. But the bank objected to the project, warning that Dabhol was "to large" and "not economically viable" and would "place a heavy financial burden on Maharashtra." * * * [I]n February 1995, after two government reviews, nine court cases, and reviews by over hundred outside lawyers, advisers, and bankers, * * * Dabhol received a total of $643 million for Phase I of the project from sources as varied as OPIC, a syndicate of Indian banks, and Bank of America.

* * * [Shortly after groundbreaking on the project,] there was an ominous development. In Indian state elections that took place in March 1995, the ruling Congress Party in Maharashtra lost to a nationalist coalition that had campaigned on an anti-foreign investment platform and a promise to "push Enron into the Arabian Sea."

Suddenly, questions that had been bubbling in the background erupted. * * * Why had the Enron contract been negotiated in secrecy, without a competitive bidding process? How was MSEB ever going to be able to afford all that power? "India's status will be enhanced, not lowered, if it tells the world that it is no pushover, no banana republic ready to accept an atrocious deal," opined the *Times of India*. The new ruling party immediately began a review of Dabhol.

The situation soon got uglier. In May, hundreds of protesting villagers swarmed over the site, and a riot broke out. Human Rights Watch and Amnesty International eventually charged security forces guarding Dabhol for Enron with human rights abuses; Human Right Watch blamed Enron for being "complicit." Meanwhile, various Clinton administration officials, including Treasury Secretary Robert Rubin, weighed in on behalf of Enron; in June, the Department of Energy issued a statement saying that canceling Dabhol could have an adverse effect on India's ability to attract foreign investment.

On August 3, the Maharashtra state government ordered the project halted because of "lack of transparency, alleged padded costs, and environment hazards." Construction ground to a halt; by then, some $300 million had been spent on the project. [An Enron official told the press], "What we are experiencing here is every investor's worst nightmare."

Chapter 6

IN–HOUSE COUNSEL

Perhaps the most significant change in the legal profession over the past generation has been the increase in the size, responsibilities, and prestige of in-house corporate legal departments. Many functions that traditionally performed by law firms have now been assumed by in-house lawyers. Furthermore, the work that law firms now do for corporations tends to be closely monitored by the company's legal department.

These developments mean that many in-house counsel now are more involved than ever before in decision-making that involves both legal and business considerations. Lawyers may participate in top management's discussion of business strategy, hold positions within the company in addition to that of legal counsel, and may work on project teams where most, if not all, of the other members are not lawyers. This greater integration of the lawyer into the fabric of the company can enhance the contributions that in-house counsel makes to the success of the company. It also, however, can raise questions about the ability of the lawyer to retain professional independence while serving as a corporate employee.

OVERVIEW OF THE CHAPTER

The chapter from Michael Kelly's book offers a case study of a legal department at the Standish Development Company. As you read this material, you should focus on certain issues. First, how do the company's in-house lawyers see themselves as different from lawyers in law firms? What features of their work environment do they believe contribute to and reinforce this difference? Are they accurate in their perception of the differences and the reasons for them?

Second, pay close attention to how the work of the lawyers is organized. How is their work assigned, and who supervises it on a day-to-day basis? In any given work week, how much contact are the lawyers likely to have with other lawyers as compared to business people? What are the advantages of this arrangement? What are the risks? What role does the company general counsel play in their work lives? Considering these questions should make you sensitive to the fact that choices of organizational structure that on their face don't seem to raise ethical questions nonetheless may have subtle implications for the kinds of ethical issues that lawyers may face.

Finally, ask yourself what the satisfactions and dissatisfactions of life in the Standish legal department are likely to be? How do these compare to the experience of colleagues in law firms? With non-lawyers in the company? What sorts of people are likely to thrive in this setting?

The excerpt from Nelson and Nielsen explores the kinds of roles that lawyers fashion for themselves inside the corporation. They suggest that there are three general roles. A given lawyer may play one of these roles exclusively, or may shift from role to role depending on the circumstances. The first is the "cop," who ensures that the company complies with the law. Lawyers report that a willingness to say "no" is a crucial attribute for playing this role. Another term for a cop is a "gatekeeper," a concept that we will discuss in more detail in the chapters on securities regulation.

A second role, which Nelson and Nielsen find is the most common, is that of "counsel." A counselor offers advice to the company that often reflects a mixture of legal and business considerations. The excerpt suggests that the more a lawyer departs from providing strictly legal advice, the more influence she is likely to exert within the company. The final role that the authors identify is the in-house lawyer as "entrepreneur." This lawyer seeks to market legal services to other departments in the company for use as an instrument to help the company meet its financial objectives. The entrepreneurial use of law, for instance, may result in structuring a business transaction so as to avoid regulatory constraints, or to enable the company to lower its effective tax rate.

Read closely the authors' account of AlphaCorp for a small case study of how lawyers and business managers negotiate these different roles for lawyers in different situations. In particular, note the discussion of the implications of having lawyers work within a centralized legal department or within functional business units. This is an issue that also is relevant to the Standish Development Company in the excerpt from Kelly in this chapter.

As you read Nelson and Nielsen, take note of how in-house lawyers often feel the need to shape their roles so as to be perceived as team players rather than as nay-sayers. Traditionally, departments like the general counsel's office have been seen within the corporation as "cost centers," which mainly impose constraints on other departments that pursue ways to generate profits. The authors posit that modern lawyers have a strong incentive to portray legal work as "adding value" to corporate activities, rather than simply as a drag on profits. Ask yourself what implications, both practical and ethical, might flow from lawyers conceptualizing what they do in this way. Also consider to what extent some of the corporate scandals in the past few years might have been connected to this trend. Nelson and Nielsen describe the "entrepreneur" as coming to overshadow the "cop" role for in-house lawyers. Do responses to recent scandals suggest that the "cop" role may be making a comeback?

The final excerpt in the chapter is from an excellent study of corporate life by Robert Jackall. The situation faced by the in-house lawyer Reed is the basis for the Problem that closes the chapter. It reflects the ways in which large organizations often avoid clear-cut assignment of responsibilities and resolution of issues. This can give rise to an unsettling sense of uncertainty for lawyers who are trying to fulfill their obligations to the company.

MODEL RULES: 1.2(a), 1.2(d), 1.3, 1.6, 1.13, 1.16 and Comment 4.

Michael J. Kelly, Lives of Lawyers: Journeys
in the Organizations of Practice

(1994)

Chapter Four: Corporate and Professional
Life at Standish Development Company

A Small Matter of Fees

Robert McGill and his senior management group in the Legal Division of Standish Development Company were incensed. They had just received a bill for legal services for the previous seven months for $580,000. The text of the bill ran about six single-spaced pages, listing in finely crafted detail various activities and discussions ("it probably took an associate two days to write this thing!"). The bill contained no mention of a date of service, who in the law firm worked on the matter, how much time the person spent, or the billing rates for those who did work. McGill and his colleagues felt the bill offered no useful information to evaluate the basis of a charge in excess of half a million dollars. The bill was sent from the firm of Butler Stern Wellington and Yeats for their services to the First Midwest National Bank and Trust Company, permanent lender on a ninety-million-dollar office complex being developed by Standish Development Company. All loan commitments by Midwest, as is customary at financial institutions nationwide, require the borrower to pay the lender's legal fees in connection with the negotiations, drafting of documents, and other matters related to the permanent financing. Midwest always used the Butler firm. Their relationship dated back decades to the origins of both the bank and the law firm.

The Butler bill was the latest in a series of bills over three years that totaled close to $1 million. Worse, there was no end in sight. The deal was not closed. Standish was paying close to $20,000 a day in interest costs for their construction loan, which they had taken out when interest rates were astronomical. The office complex was built and open, and still the lawyers from Butler were haggling over permanent loan documents. The lawyers for Standish knew the Butler lawyers were aware of how desperate Standish was to close the permanent financing.

The company was over a barrel, and the Butler lawyers were in control of the roll.

The deal was extraordinarily complicated, involving a renewal project in which county government, a state financing agency, and a nonprofit development corporation had important interests, amplified by lawyers and bankers associated with each of these groups. Initially the most difficult party had been the county or, to put it more accurately, the lawyer representing the county, Jack Ericson, a cigar-chomping Jimmy Cagney type said to be very close to the county executive. Ericson insisted on drafting the entire agreement between the county and Standish, which led to a tough set of negotiations because Ericson was not an experienced real estate lawyer nor, to say the least, an artful draftsman. During those rocky early negotiations, lawyers for Standish considered the possibility of going over Ericson's head to the county executive, but the pressure to close the deal took precedence. They knew, however, there would be a reckoning when the documents reached Angus Hawkins, a younger partner at Butler Stern Wellington and Yeats who did most of the real estate financing work for Midwest.

Hawkins was notorious. He was a compulsive nitpicker in whom stubbornness, a volatile temper, and general insecurity in understanding complicated deals combined to make negotiations with a lender carrying the clout of Midwest preposterously difficult. The young business people at Midwest who cut the original deal with Standish had no interest in supervising Hawkins. They were generally inexperienced, "hotshot MBAs" working at the bank to gain experience in order to move up or out to greener pastures. During the time between the initial commitment and the final settlement on the financing there were three complete turnovers in the Midwest personnel who dealt with Standish. More important, the business people had no muscle. They knew that senior lawyers of Butler had long-standing and close relationships with the senior officers of Midwest, and in effect had higher rank than they did in the bank. Hawkins spoke for Midwest. For all practical purposes he was Midwest, and he was impossible.

The concern among the lawyers for Standish—that Hawkins might have difficulty with the Ericson-drafted documents—soon ripened into a reality worse than their fears. Relations between Ericson and Hawkins—Jimmy Cagney battling with David Niven—grew so acrimonious that Standish lawyers and the outside law firm representing the company were reduced to serving as arbitrating gobetweens. Niven and Cagney refused to meet in the same room together.

The Butler firm was well aware of Standish's unhappiness, because the company had refused to pay the bills. Receipt of a Butler bill marked the commencement of a small ritual. Standish lawyers would request backup information about hourly rates and hours spent by lawyers who worked on the matter. The Butler firm would refuse to provide the information because it was "against firm policy" to do so. Time would pass, and Butler would press for payment and Standish would refuse to do so in the absence of backup documentation. Butler would agree to provide the information as to hours spent to their client, Midwest. Midwest business people would promptly relay the information to Standish. Billing rates for various people, despite Butler's policy against providing such information, could eventually be obtained, and thus Standish could piece together the basis for the billing. After reviewing the bill, the project lawyer, and eventually McGill, would express outrage to Midwest about both the size of the bill and the horrendous costs being run up as a result of Hawkins's behavior. Finally, Standish would wait until some partial closing when Butler would demand payment, and Standish would negotiate payment of the cumulative interim bill less a discount of $100,000 or so.

Meanwhile, in a separate ring, another bout was taking place between Butler and Standish. The company's development of an industrial building in another city led to negotiations with Midwest over permanent financing. On the basis of its prior experience, Standish insisted they would not deal with Midwest unless there was a cap placed on the cost of Butler's legal work. Agreement was reached on a $100,000 "upset" figure for the Midwest legal fee related to the $35 million financing.[1] However, the deal for the industrial building had to be recast for crucial tax reasons, and Standish acknowledged that it was appropriate for the cap to be taken off. Once the cap was off, the flood began, and midway through the industrial building project legal bills from Butler had accumulated to a total of $450,000. The ritual resumed.

After consultation with his senior management group and the officers of Standish, McGill finally precipitated what he describes as a summit meeting with the head of the Midwest Real Estate Department, the in-house general counsel of Midwest, and the Butler partners in charge of the Midwest account. He argued that Standish was being victimized by overlawyering, ineffective negotiating, and outlandish costs in view of the size of the projects being financed by Midwest. To illustrate the company's position, he pointed to the fact that Butler had thus far billed $125,000 for the utterly ineffective work of one junior associate on the industrial building financing for which the total legal work was originally meant to cost no more than $100,000. Charges for secretarial work on the office complex financing documents had already reached $140,000.[2] The Butler pattern of charges was in sharp contrast with those of another firm of comparable quality that represented Standish during the complex negotiations and transactions with all of the parties to the office development. And the hourly rates for the Butler lawyers were exceptionally high, rising over a three-year period from an *average* of $212 to $282 per hour for partners, $143 to $182 for associates, and $25 to $45 for legal assistants.[3] McGill also alluded to the major bank that issued the construction financing for the office develop-

---

1. An *upset* price is a ceiling price.

2. Traditionally, lawyers' billing rates include overhead costs, which include secretarial services. The unbundling of these costs through separate categories of billing is a method of increasing fees.

3. These are 1986 figures.

ment. This bank used a small, highly capable specialty firm charging $165 an hour for partners and $100 for associates, but more important, their lawyers knew what they were doing and engaged in no overlawyering, so that the total charges to Standish were less than $250,000. Finally, McGill insisted they would pay no more than $1.3 million for the office development legal work.

Ultimately, permanent financing with Midwest was settled, and Butler received a 1.3 percent fee on the eventual $100 million transaction after discounting bills by a total of $300,000. The Butler firm never budged from their position that their fees were completely appropriate given the complexity of the transactions and the importance of protecting Midwest's interests.

Stories of the Butler fracas are not uncommon around Standish Development Company. A business person characterizes the incident as a "legal root canal." Jack Newman, a senior real estate partner in the large Pittsburgh law firm that handles more of the outside real estate work for the company than any other firm, knows the story of the Butler fee dispute and hopes that it will be put on record, because of his feelings that vultures like Butler give responsible corporate law firms (such as his) a bad name.

Like most popular stories in an organizational setting, the telling is a parable. Although the numbers are not widely known or generally cited, it seems clear that the memory of Butler is vivid because Butler actions hurt—hurt where it counts—by escalating, along with a number of other factors, the capital costs of the office development project close to unprofitable heights. Thus the story is often told with sequels to illustrate how the company learned from the disaster and took steps to prevent its recurrence.

After settlement of the permanent financing and paying off Butler, McGill and the chief financial officer of the company paid a visit to Midwest to state that the company would never do another financing with them if they used Butler in the deal. They argued that the costs of using Butler, in terms of rates, charges, and delays they cause, alter the economics of a project so significantly that the company could not afford to finance through Midwest. Midwest agreed not to use Butler for future Standish projects. They chose a boutique real estate firm for Standish loans, never informing Butler of their decision.

The successful skirmish with Midwest has spread to a larger front. Legal fees, due to the practices of law firms like Butler, have now become an element in negotiations over every major Standish financing. McGill describes a recent equity financing in which the bank insisted on using a law firm with the same policy of nondisclosure of backup information for bills as Butler. McGill demanded an upset price for the bank's legal fees payable by his company. He thought this would be totally unacceptable to the law firm, but to his surprise, they agreed to the cap. The bank's business person managed the law firm so successfully that the fee came in $10,000 document that also had a warmth and thoughtfulness perfectly crafted to suit the problem. Mullan was convinced no outside firm could have done it.

Frank Tuoey is enthusiastic about the quality of his in-house legal support. He immodestly characterizes his lawyers as having "very sophisticated clients" for whom they do cutting-edge work. The company lawyers are probably as expert as anyone in the country on floating zones, and a recent financing with convertible subordinated securities in the Eurodollar market was handled by the in-house staff. The company's lawyers compare extremely well with many private practitioners, who may be well-known but cannot put a cogent document together. Legal Division people typically gain control of the preparation of documents on deals, a way of controlling the transaction.

Rich Francis, a man fully capable of submitting devastating evaluations to McGill of the lawyers with whom he works, is convinced that the quality of his lawyers has improved enormously. The deals are far more complicated than they were four or five years earlier, and he has in-house people now that are as good as, if not better than, any private lawyer, making it possible for him to put together deals in what might seem impossible time frames. Francis raves about Frank Leyman, who he says can "draft like lightning, understands the dynamics of a deal, and always seems to be able to think six or eight moves ahead." He is taking Leyman out to dinner for the best lobster in town for his absolutely invaluable role in helping him pull off a recent miracle.

The clients are not uncritical of the legal side. One of Tuoey's concerns is costs. Unlike many real estate companies, Standish has chosen to put its development capabilities under one roof, which creates a large fixed overhead. And Tuoey feels the lawyers are expensive, although McGill claims it costs less than going outside. Of course, to the extent the lawyers are hardworking (that is, putting in more than a forty-hour standard workweek), the company may be getting sixty hours of time for the forty-hour basis of allocating costs to a project, a savings to the developer client.

Francis mentions that several years ago "McGill's law firm" had some mediocre people on the development side and was unresponsive as well. "This is a 'no shit, Sherlock' kind of business," says Francis. "I don't have time to wait around, so I'd say, 'Fuck this—let's go get Jack'" (Newman, formerly of the Legal Division, in private practice). Fred Whitney confirms there was a period in the late 1970s when some of the younger company lawyers were not as client-oriented as outside attorneys. At the same time, Mark Knowles, head of the development group, felt that neither he nor his lawyers were getting clear communications from their clients as to priorities and expectations. In an effort to deal with these mutual concerns, Knowles set up monthly meetings with the business people to work out ninety-day forecasts of needs and deadlines that are fundamental to risk management in the commercial development process.

Thomas Mullan feels the Legal Division is not as well equipped as outside law firms to provide dispassionate advice in major litigation. Company lawyers are by and large transactional lawyers, and there is no substitute for having veteran warriors from the trenches provide sound and deliberate analyses of the possibilities in a lawsuit.

Bill Evans, a development director who left the Legal Division, offers a different perspective on the changes that have occurred in it. One of his reasons for leaving was a growing perception that the lawyers were less in charge. During the 1970s the Legal Division played a greater role in development, both because the business people were less experienced and the Legal Division was a real repository of talent. They were counted on to take charge; documentation lends itself to this. As the deals became more complex and the business people became more experienced and asserted more control of the process, the lawyer took a more professional role, responding more like a lawyer from a large firm to demands made by more sophisticated business people. On the operating side, where the lawyer is involved more with questions of immediate and short duration, division lawyers play a somewhat larger role because of the influx of new business people, an expansion that continued through the 1980s.

Compensation

Despite McGill's care in recruiting people who fit the organization and for whom the bottom line is not the highest professional priority, a general undercurrent of dissatisfaction over compensation is a fact of life in the Legal Division. As one lawyer puts it, there is a natural frustration associated with being in a company where top levels of management, including CEO Mullan and McGill, are making big money. Mullan was paid $900,000 in annual salary and bonus in the early 1990s, plus stock compensation worth approximately $500,000; McGill's annual salary and bonus at the same time was $425,000, with stock compensation valued at $175,000.

The compensation of division lawyers is a mixture of salary, bonus, benefits, and incentive payments. Cash compensation in the early 1990s ran from $70,000 for junior lawyers up to $180,000 for experienced people. The benefits program amounts to an additional 20 percent of salary and is comprised of cafeteria-style, mostly tax-free, programs that the individual can tailor to his or her own needs. McGill argues that the benefits setup is superior to that of most private firms, which tend to distribute higher income but give lower total value because the individual must pay for benefits from after-tax dollars. The company offers a 401k retirement plan, matching a portion of the individual's retirement funds with stock. For a company like Standish, which has experienced growth in the market for its stock, the increased value to the employee can be substantial. Most of the lawyers of the division have access to another incentive compensation program, periodic stock options. According to McGill's calculations, lawyers who receive options under this program have historically added about $12,500 to $15,000 to their annual compensation for each grant of stock options. Lawyers with seniority who have received several stock-option grants have realized a multiple of this value.

Top-level compensation in the company is less disturbing to Legal Division lawyers than are peer comparisons. Lawyers at the company are proud of the challenging nature of the law they practice, its pressure, excitement, and demands on their time, energy, and ingenuity. They feel their practice is superior to what most young partners and many senior partners experience in large corporate law firms. Many of the lawyers in their thirties are acutely aware of the passage to partnership of their friends and law-school classmates. While they acknowledge the pay scale of the company is not out of line with Pittsburgh compensation scales, they feel large firms in the District of Columbia, Cleveland, New York City, or Philadelphia are the more appropriate measure. Compared to their peers in these other cities, they feel underpaid. McGill acknowledges that more experienced lawyers in the division are probably earning between 20 and 30 percent less than their peers in the best major firms, but that the company can compete "on a career basis" through its benefits and stock plans.

When the argument shifts to the perspective of a career with the company, the comparison with colleagues on the business side emerges as an aggravation. A system of quality review applies to all personnel in the company, including the Legal Division. This system is based on defined job levels and individualized objectives agreed upon by subordinate and supervisor. Performance is measured in terms of these objectives at salary-setting time. The range of bonuses varies from year to year, depending on the performance of the company as a whole. This "management by objectives" program works best with quantitative measures, but the Legal Division tries to adapt the system to accommodate quality-of-performance measures. Line personnel such as development-project managers have the potential for higher bonuses (from 20 to 30 percent in good years) than the people of staff departments like the Legal Division (from 15 to 20 percent for outstanding performance). To the management of the company, the rationale for this distribution is that entrepreneurs are the heart of the company, and the people who bear the risks of failure should receive larger bonuses when their work leads to financial success. But the effectiveness of the company's teamwork networks of people from different departments leads staff personnel to conceive of themselves as responsible entrepreneurs, particularly the lawyers who play a crucial role in structuring deals and, in some cases, guiding rather inexperienced business people. The result is that some lawyers in the division feel the potential for higher bonuses of their business peers means the company undervalues their own efforts.

An important factor in the calculus of compensation is the potential for advancement. McGill is a man in his forties. The associate general counsels and group leaders are the same age. The likelihood of members of this management group leaving seems remote to most lawyers in the division. McGill is aware of how constrained are the possibilities of advancement when most of the rungs on the Legal Division corporate ladder are filled. He has recently developed senior attorney and senior assistant general counsel positions in order to justify higher compensation for some of his best people, and to make improvements in supervision and management of the groups. He is also conscious of how difficult and delicate is the task of promoting two or three people from a group of a dozen highly competent and ambitious people. Inevitably, these moves generate the potential of yet another comparison that may seem arbitrary or unjustifiable to division lawyers.

One of the most serious crises of McGill's leadership of the division occurred in the mid-1980s, when the company considered extension of stock-bonus compensation beyond the leadership group to senior-level management. Under this program the company makes restricted stock grants available and provides loans to pay for the stock. The loans are gradually forgiven over a period of time if the individual is still working for the company. The intent of the program is to provide financial incentives to key personnel to stay with Standish, as well as financial disincentives for leaving. McGill argued vigorously that all lawyers in his division should be eligible for these benefits. The initial decision went against him, and after relaying the information to his staff, his senior people, Jack Simon and Mark Knowles, were enraged enough to make moves to leave. Simon received an offer from a large Los Angeles law firm and openly threatened to accept it. Knowles, who had tentative offers from three leading Pittsburgh firms, lobbied his principal development "clients" within the company. Faced with the loss of two experienced real estate lawyers representing over three decades of understanding of the company and its business, senior management agreed to extend the stock bonus plan to the group-leader level of the Legal Division, insuring compensation levels competitive with the private market for senior real estate specialists in private firms. The result, while satisfying the group leaders for the time, added yet another invidious comparison for many of the lawyers in the division.

Except to the extent supervisors are involved in the evaluation of their subordinates, salary information is guarded carefully by the management of the company. But the informal sharing process within the Legal Division is sufficiently widespread that discontent has a factual basis. At division retreats McGill sometimes talks about compensation issues but remains uncomfortable talking salaries or salary policy outside a one-to-one setting. To some extent, McGill and his three group managers have become inured to the insolubility of the problem.

A Different Practice

Whatever may be their complaints about the Legal Division, most lawyers appreciate the difference between their professional lives and those of lawyers in private firms. Lawyers of the division do not consider private practice a desirable option in thinking of possible next steps in their careers. Their feeling of satisfaction involves the professional pride of members of an organization who know they are successful, and a measure of contempt for shoddy work in the profession that they see on a fairly regular basis. But the sense of fulfillment includes a conviction that work at the company is harder, more interesting, more satisfying, and more relevant than that of the best of private practice.

With the exception of a few lawyers who emigrated from notorious sweatshops, most feel that the company commands more hours from them than did private firms. But these hours are different, less burdensome, more "natural," less "artificial." There is not the relent-less pressure of the time sheet to record billable hours. Work is driven solely by what is needed to get the job done satisfactorily.

For most lawyers at the company, the pressure to perform is heavier than what they experienced in private practice, if only because most were associates, not responsible billing partners in private law firms. They also perceive that the lean character of the Legal Division precludes the specialist support characteristic of large firms. They may now and then be able to draw on the head of their group for some advice or help in controlling a skeptical client, but essentially they are solo performers on the line with the development or operating team of which they are a part. Part of the tension and exhilaration of this position of responsibility is that negotiating opponents are usually senior real estate partners of major private firms.

McGill seeks to emulate the private law firm in one respect. His concept of professionalism includes the traditional encouragement given to lawyers at many of the best private firms to engage in outside activities, such as community or civic associations, bar associations, and continuing education or law school teaching. A firm believer that he must model what he says if the message is to have any force to it, McGill is active in the Pennsylvania Bar Association, the American Corporate Counsel Association, and boards of civic and community organizations. Several other lawyers engage in similar professional and community activities. Division lawyers feel free to undertake outside activities without explicit counterpressures from the company. In fact, a large number are not active outside of their work and home lives probably due to the demands of their young families, commuting time from their homes in the Pittsburgh area, and their sense of obligation to the company under heavy workloads. McGill expresses regrets about this, wonders whether the group leaders are reinforcing this message sufficiently, and then concludes that all he is in a position to do is to explain by word and example that such activity is encouraged.

Atmosphere or style is a factor often cited by many of the division lawyers as a favorable factor attracting them to the company. They say the division is a good place to work. Although old timers maintain that morale is lower than in previous years (more of a "corporate" atmosphere, they say), the general feeling is that the division is comprised of good, hardworking, and helpful colleagues who engage in virtually none of the internal politics or climbing over backs to get ahead that is said to characterize many law firms.

Most of the Legal Division's recruits were attracted to the company by the nature of the legal work, which they conclude is more challenging than work in private firms. Lawyers and clients within the company allude to the increasing complexity of development activity. One young lawyer keeps a diagram handy of one of his projects, in which there are twelve major corporate and governmental participants, five property owners in addition to the company, three different permanent lenders in addition to a federal Urban Development Action Grant, a score of interlocking long-term leases of land and building levels, and a variety of joint-venture and equity-sharing arrangements. The division lawyers are proud of being at the cutting edge of national real estate practice.

Division lawyers also talk about the variety of their practices. They are close to *being* business people, engaged in a stimulating range of technical development issues of modern real estate practice. They need to be familiar with partnership and joint-venture law, accounting, securities and corporate law, and (in their supervisory as well as preventive law functions) a wide variety of litigation. The sophisticated real estate transaction lawyer must be a generalist to be a successful deal maker in a world of more intricate deals.

Close relationships with the business people are pleasures that most of the division lawyers did not experience in private practice. It is important to the lawyers to have genuinely grateful clients. It is the gratitude of a fellow team member. McGill talks of his "client-driven environment" as a more fulfilling practice than the sometimes remote and often episodic relationships with clients that characterize modern large-firm specialists, particularly associates. Company lawyers are grateful to be free from that special large-firm impracticality, or "blindness," or obsessive focus on minutiae out of proportion to the worth of issues. But McGill argues there is a deeper level of fulfillment involved— identifying with, and caring about, what the lawyer is contributing to the client—that is often lacking in private practice, where lawyers may have deep personal reservations about the ends or policies of the client. The company's lawyers are proud of their client. It is satisfying to work for something you believe in.

Robert L. Nelson and Laura Beth Nielsen, Cops, Counsel,
and Entrepreneurs: Constructing the Role of Inside
Counsel in Large Corporations

34 Law & Soc'y Rev. 457 (2002)

I. Introduction

Lawyers who are employed in major business corporations play an important role in the legal affairs of business. Although inside counsel once were relegated to routine tasks and were the clear status inferiors of partners in corporate law firms, they have assumed new power and status within the legal profession. Inside counsel now make decisions about allocating legal work to outside law firms, with the result that outside law firms largely have lost the function of general counsel and instead focus increasingly on the provision of specialized services on a case-by-case, transaction-by-transaction basis. Inside counsel typically are the first lawyers contacted concerning a potential legal problem; they are the lawyers who monitor the legality of myriad corporate operations; and even in cases in which outside lawyers are retained, they often are crucial participants in developing legal strategies and acting as intermediaries to the corporation.

* * * [D]ebates about corporate lawyers, both those working in law firms and in the legal departments of corporations, have focused on the question of their professional autonomy from business. [Some] analyses of the legal profession have asserted that inside lawyers lack independence to act as agents of social control within the corporation. Scholars who study the decisionmaking of corporate lawyers in particular organizational and historical contexts have suggested that corporate lawyers have considerable room for maneuver in how they interpret law for corporate management * * *

[T]here have been dramatic changes in the [last two decades] in the management of major corporations and in their legal environment * * * which may well have altered the role of law and lawyers in corporations. [We are now in an era] of what [some] call the financial conception of control in the corporation, in which corporations [tend] to be seen as a bundle of potentially diversified investments and in which corporate functions of all forms [are] subject to rigorous financial analysis for their impact on profit and loss * * * [T]his conception of the corporation has fueled the trend toward downsizing and reorganization that has swept major corporations in the 1980s and 1990s and fundamentally altered previous understandings between corporations and their managers. The law has become a more salient feature of the corporate environment in the past three decades. Large corporations confront sweeping regulation of personnel, environmental, and financial practices, and more frequently are involved in major litigation. As a result of these and other changes, the legal expenditures of business have grown dramatically.

It is unclear a priori how these changes might affect inside counsel. Corporate downsizing might put additional pressures on corporate lawyers to tailor their legal advice to support managerial efforts at short-term profit maximization. But the pervasiveness of legal issues in corporate operations might afford inside lawyers greater power and status in the corporation, and thus make them more professionally autonomous from their business peers.

This article reassesses the role of inside counsel in major American corporations in light of these changes. We analyze in-depth interviews with corporate counsel and a case study of the relationships between inside lawyers and non-lawyer executives in one large corporation conducted in the mid–1990s. We frame our analysis in terms of how inside lawyers construct their roles in the corporation. This * * * approach allows us to address many of the questions conventionally posed about the professional autonomy of corporate lawyers, while also allowing us to move beyond those questions * * * [I]t is not enough to ask who has power in the relationship [between lawyer and client]. Instead, it is important to begin to analyze how power is constructed, resisted, and subverted in their relationships, and what the implications are for law as a cultural and institutional force in society. We not only are interested in whether inside lawyers have power in the corporation but also of what kind, under what circumstances, and with what implications for the role of law in corporate governance * * *

After discussing our methods, we present the three ideal types of lawyers' roles in the corporation—cops, counsel, and entrepreneurs. We then analyze four dimensions of the work, professional ideologies, and careers of inside counsel, which are fundamental to how they construct their roles: (1) the gatekeeping functions of corporate counsel; (2) how lawyers and executives view each other within the corporation; (3) the blending of legal and business advice; and (4) the distinctiveness of lawyers' identities. Finally, we examine the relationships between inside counsel and corporate executives in one large financial corporation to better understand how the roles of inside counsel are constructed out of the interactions of lawyers with their organizational environment * * *

III.   THREE IDEAL TYPES OF CORPORATE COUNSEL: COPS, COUNSEL, AND ENTREPRENEURS

It is useful in beginning to examine the roles of inside counsel to construct a set of categories that captures the range of lawyering styles in corporations. Our analysis of the interviews suggested that lawyers played three ideal typical roles: some spoke of their role as narrowly legal, some spoke of mixing legal and business advice, and some emphasized entrepreneurial or profit-generating uses of law. Bearing in mind that the ways lawyers describe their tasks are complex and sometimes contested by others in the organization, we attempted to devise a conceptual scheme that would allow us to classify individual lawyers by role type: [as cops, counselors, and entrepreneurs]. The scheme is useful analytically. Some individuals vividly represented the cop, the counsel, and the entrepreneur. And with some decision rules, it is possible to categorize cases. Yet the interviews also made clear that inside counsel play different roles in different circumstances. The interviews are full of seemingly contradictory statements, until one realizes that the lawyers are describing a repertoire of responses to different situations. In this section we describe the key dimensions of the ideal types, present respondents who exemplify each type, and discuss the results of our attempt to classify lawyers by type.

Cops

When corporate counsel are playing the "cop" role, they are primarily concerned with policing the conduct of their business clients * * * They interact with business people almost exclusively through legal gatekeeping functions, such as approving contracts, imposing and implementing compliance programs, and responding to legal questions. Cops are less willing to offer non-legal advice, even when they have the opportunity.

The vice president for legal affairs for a major chemical firm exemplified the role of lawyer as cop. He was hired for the position from outside the corporation after a distinguished career in government and private practice. He interpreted his hiring as an effort by the corporation to bring in someone who would be independent within the corporate environment.

"I think that the thought is when you get somebody who has an independent stature, apart from his or her position in the corporation, that the person is also more likely to be independent and give you that independent professional judgment that is so essential."

Even though he was a member of the corporation's Board of Directors and the corporation's Executive Committee, he characterized his work "principally as a lawyer." We asked whether he took a managerial approach to the legal function:

"Q. Do you see the management of legal costs and legal risks as your major job?

A. I think it is a major job and increasingly important ... but I think that that can't be subordinated to the need to provide independent legal judgment and counsel to the company."

A theme that consistently emerged in this interview, despite some discussion of lawyers attempting to act as part of the management team in the various subsidiaries of the corporation, was the need for lawyers to say no.

"I mean there are [business] people who want to do something and they just simply can't do it, they can't understand why, and then I say, 'Well, that's just the way the law is.'"

And later, after recounting such an incident, he said,

"So, the businessmen had quite a lot of trouble with that, and I don't blame them; I do too. I have to say, 'That's the law. You can't do it'; I would never say they can't do anything. I can't forbid it. I can say, 'If you do it, you run the risk and you're going to go to prison; you don't have any defense. You've been advised you are in violation of the law.'"

Our exemplar of the cop was unusual also in his lack of commitment to, indeed his disdain for, certain aspects of his employer. When asked how strongly he identified with Bigchem (a pseudonym), he said, "My identity was pre-Bigchem; and I'm identified some with Bigchem, but I am that person who works with Bigchem and not the Bigchem person who does these things." In response to a question about what he found frustrating about his work, he answered:

"The frustration is in a corporate culture where they speak in sort of a code or certain agreed words. We're going through a big thing now called continuous quality improvement. It's patterned after all these gurus of [management] ... They talk about ... employee empowerment. But you're giving [employees] an impression I think, a false one at that, that people, that someone ... is going to be playing greater roles in running the organization. And that's not it! So I have a lot of problems with that kind of corporate stuff we have ... American companies are running hard and all scared to death ... The only thing under their control is cost, so it just scares everybody."

Counsel

The role that corporate lawyers most often play is the counsel. Legal gatekeeping plays an important part in inserting these lawyers into business activities, but it is not the only basis on which they relate to management. Counsel most often confine their advice to legal questions and legitimate their suggestions or demands based on legal knowledge. Yet the counsel role implies a broader relationship with business actors that affords counsel an opportunity to make suggestions based on business, ethical, and situational concerns.

Our exemplar of this type, a general counsel in a bank, described this mixture of legal and business functions.

"Forty percent of my time is spent managing the legal position, ... 20% of my time is as the bank's chief compliance officer: dealing with regulators, overviewing the auditing process within the bank, [overseeing] training done by the legal division ... Another 30% of my time is as consigliere of executive and senior management: I am the counselor; I am the guy who is asked to draft letters; to advise on particular issues, which can overlap with the first two primarily because it relates to the regulators ... The remaining 10% of my time I practice law."

"Q. The consigliere role, you distinguish that from the law practice?

A. Yes, because when I think of practicing law ... it's more taking a particular legal problem and finding out what the law is, and then applying the law to the facts ... That's not what I do most of the time when I am dealing with senior management ... The law has very little to do with it. An example would be, the regulators have found what they believe to be a regulatory violation. Well, I've got either a member of my staff or outside counsel who confer with me on whether it is or isn't. That's practicing law. My consigliere role is how I am going to interface between the executive management and the regulators to convince the regulators that it's not [a violation]. And that has nothing really to do with the law. It's negotiating; it's common sense; ... it's how it's communicated."

This corporate counsel clearly goes beyond merely giving legal advice, although it appears that it is the law and potential legal problems that bring him into business decisions.

"I believe that it's my role to make the decision and to make sure the business person goes along with it. Now that's contrary to everything I'd say on the outside or any general counsel would say, because we'd say, 'It's not our role to make business decisions.' We lay out the risks and the alternatives to our clients and then they make an informed business decision. Well, if they are making an informed business decision, in my mind there is only one decision they can make, the one I want them to make or I think they ought to make—because that's my job. I don't conceive it to be just laying out the risks, but I have to know enough about the company and enough about the situations and circumstances to weigh those risks . . . If I think they are doing something that is legal, that is stupid, it's my job to say to them, 'That's stupid,' or to convince them in such a way that they come around to my point of view, thinking it's their point of view. So there are some people that I've had to use that deceptive type of process on more than others.

Our ideal typical counsel appears to be quite broadly involved in important managerial decisions; he draws on both legal and other forms of knowledge, and, according to his own account, he is highly influential. He is remarkable within our sample for his suggestion that he is willing to deceive non-lawyers about the law in order to get them to make what he terms a correct decision. Several other informants indicated directly and indirectly that there are often grey areas in the advice they give, but virtually no one else admitted that they actually deceived clients about legal issues.

Entrepreneurs

Although the ideal typical "counsel" is still primarily concerned with the legal aspects of business, entrepreneurs emphasize business values in their work. Entrepreneurial lawyers say law is not merely a necessary complement to corporate functions, law can itself be a source of profits, an instrument to be used aggressively in the marketplace, or the mechanism through which major transactions are executed. Our exemplar of the entrepreneur is the general counsel of a holding company, not yet 40 years old at the time of the interview, with a law degree from Harvard. He had been a securities specialist in a large corporate law firm before moving to his corporate employer, where he had worked his way up from being an inside transactional lawyer to general counsel of several subsidiaries, until reaching one of the top two law positions in the corporation. He became most animated in the interview when talking about the size of the "deals" he had put together, such as taking various subsidiaries public, the "phenomenal multiple" they had achieved in an especially large public offering, and the major acquisitions he had worked on for the corporation. His role, and that of many of the lawyers in the corporation, went well beyond giving legal advice.

"The chairman and the chief financial officer consult me, as part of the strategic planning process that we go on. On matters outside of the legal function, I think probably because of the credibility I've gained in representing them over the last ten years in a variety of contexts, they've never expected, and we don't expect, our attorneys to limit their advice and input to pure legal advice. The client here has never found that to be the most valuable type of relationship. There are some clients that certainly expect the lawyers to limit their input to legal advice, but those folks have not succeeded well and don't represent the mainstream of our business management."

This informant, and at least some of the other lawyers in his corporation, present themselves as offering advice "beyond the legal function," in large part because the executives of the corporation expect him to do so. These comments demonstrate that lawyers' roles in the corporation are not fixed choices among discrete categories, but evolve according to the needs of business.

Our entrepreneurial general counsel offered a telling contrast between his approach to his job and that of another general counsel in the corporation, a lawyer who was more senior than our informant, whom our informant had reported to prior to assuming a parallel position in the corporation. Our informant described why he thought he would eventually rise above his former superior.

"I knew his background; his background was litigation and antitrust. I never believed he was an effective business counselor to the Board of Directors. That wasn't his style, his style was to manage contentious issues. That probably is why he and I succeeded so well together, because that's what I like to do the least. Anything that's negative, the criminal investigations that we've had, anti-trust litigation ... If I never had to deal with them, the better. I was more interested in what I consider the positive side: raising money, buying companies, selling companies. I mean, at the end of the day your client was happy, or at least knew why the deal wasn't done ... And Bill's background also was that he was personally kind of the conscience of the company in its formative years, when it was going from mom's and dad's and entrepreneurs into [a] professionally managed [firm]. And it's a role he was personally suited for, but it made him quite unpopular ... He was the guy who had always played the devil's advocate ... As the company's evolved and gotten older and become more professionally managed at the operating level, that role hasn't been that necessary; it wasn't one that I desired. [A senior executive] told me that Bill was never considered a candidate for corporate secretary ... [even though] it was natural for that position to have gone to Bill ... I was always very positive in my outlook, in my ability to succeed ... And frankly I expect ... who could possibly run this company in perhaps 15 or 20 years if it [isn't] me?"

From these comments, it appears that Bill is a "cop" who was more influential in the corporation in an earlier era, when it "needed" a corporate conscience. According to our informant, the need for that role has diminished as the management of the corporation has become more professionalized. He attributes his own rise to influence to his ability to be a business counselor. Indeed, he expects to run the company some day in the future.

What is the motivating force in our informant's career?—his interest in making money and growing the company. He describes himself as part of the second-generation management of the corporation.

" I think the [senior management] group is extremely motivated by financial returns. Certainly the professional challenges are there too. The ability to take the business the next step, to take it from 10 [billion in revenues] to 20 [billion], which is very doable given the marketplace opportunities ... It's a huge challenge. It's very exciting."

When we asked him how strongly he identified with the corporation, he made it clear that what he loved about it was the financial opportunities that it presented, rather than the functions it served.

"What was so attractive to me about [the corporation] was, it was a fabulous venture capital firm, or a fabulous merchant banking firm. We had access, in fact we still do have access, to tremendous amounts of capital. We could stop growing the basic X business today, stop investing in X facilities, and the cash flow would be so tremendous that we would have to either go buy some other business ... or buy our own stock back, in which case I'll make a fortune because the stock price will go up. What excites me about any of these opportunities ... is the financial dynamic."

This entrepreneur derives great personal meaning from the contemporary managerial conception of the corporation: it is, above all, a financial institution. Our informant used his legal expertise to gain entree to the world of corporate finance. He continues to hold the title of General Counsel, which denotes continuing legal responsibilities. Yet it is clear that business objectives, rather than legal accomplishments, motivate his work.

Distribution of Respondents by Ideal Type

* * * To gain some preliminary sense of the relative frequency of these roles, it is necessary to classify and count individuals by role * * * We measured the scope of advice and the nature of knowledge claims, respectively, by involvement in business decisions and the invocation of economic values to legitimate the decisions of lawyers (what we call marketing the legal function). We treated counsel as the default category; that is, to be classified as a cop or an entrepreneur, a respondent's interview had to clearly meet certain criteria. If it did not, the respondent was coded as a counsel. A respondent was classified as a cop if he or she indicated that (a) they offered only legal advice and avoided giving business advice, (b) they played an active gatekeeping role (marked by an affirmative obligation to monitor compliance, the ability to say no to business clients, and the ability to go over the head of management), and that (c) they did not market the legal function within the corporation. A

respondent was coded as an entrepreneur if he or she (a) offered non-legal advice on business decisions, and (b) marketed the legal function. Though the classification of respondents was based on specific criteria, our decisions were confirmed by our overall assessment of the interview.

Only a relatively small proportion of our sample, some 17%, approximate the role of the cop within their organization. Twice as many (33%) meet our definition of the entrepreneurial role. Half of the lawyers we interviewed fall into the counsel category. The numerical predominance of the counsel role to a certain extent is a product of our coding scheme * * * [Nonetheless, our sample] contains a variety of corporations and a variety of inside lawyers within the corporate hierarchy. Hence, we think this distribution of cases is a plausible, if preliminary, portrait of the prevalence of different kinds of lawyerly roles among corporate counsel. The majority of corporate counsel hew to a traditional role in which they primarily are called on for legal advice, rather than for business judgments. Relatively few corporate counsel totally avoid involvement in business decisions and primarily are engaged in cop-like functions. A significant minority of corporate counsel are deeply involved in business decisions and in marketing their own lawyerly role in terms they hope their business peers will understand. Not only do entrepreneurs outnumber cops by two to one, but also the center of gravity within the counsel category is closer to entrepreneurs than to cops.

Thus we detect what may be a significant difference in the orientations of inside counsel from that reported in earlier research. Donnell and Rosen found the close equivalent of our "cops" and "counsel" among the corporate attorneys they studied in the 1960s and 1970s. Lawyer-entrepreneurs, in contrast, seem to represent a different breed. Although we lack direct data on change over time, if we compare the discourse of our informants to that reported by Donnell and Rosen, we see a much more explicitly entrepreneurial discourse in many interviews. This entrepreneurial discourse reflects the efforts of corporate counsel to use their legal knowledge to serve the ideology and prerogatives of corporate management * * *

IV. CONSTRUCTING THE ROLE OF INSIDE COUNSEL

Our typology of roles maps variation in how individual attorneys approach their work, but does not fully capture the challenges lawyers confront as they attempt to define their roles in corporations. In this section of the article, we examine four salient axes around which lawyers construct their roles, as well as the organizational forces that shape these constructions. First, how do inside lawyers manage their gatekeeping functions? Second, how do inside counsel attempt to shape their images within corporations, taking into account the attitudes of executives toward law and lawyers? Third, what is the relationship between the legal expertise and the business objectives of corporate lawyers? Fourth, what happens to the professional identities of inside counsel in the corporate milieu?

A. The Gatekeeping Function: Pervasive but Circumscribed

When the corporate attorney acts as a gatekeeper, he or she monitors legal compliance and serves as a final hurdle or "gate" through which business ideas must pass prior to implementation. The ability to "trump" a business decision has been identified by researchers as a source of contention and confusion for both lawyers and their business clients * * * Cops and counsel continue to confront such tensions.

One lawyer put it this way:

"When individuals in the organization come to me and say, "will you help me execute my deal?" if I come across to them or the lawyers on my staff come across to them as cops, they are not going to come to us. They are ... either going to go elsewhere or operate in the dark without lawyers."

This lawyer identifies two possible negative outcomes of behaving too much like a cop. The business people will simply go without legal advice, or they will engage in an intra-organizational version of "forum shopping," bringing their problems to the lawyer in the company who is least likely to challenge the business-person's project. A number of lawyers identified forum-shopping as a problem resulting from active gatekeeping:

"There are some businesspeople who try and play games with the lawyers ... they run between us and do forum shopping ... They know some people have a reputation as stricter or more liberal ... I have a reputation for being a strict constructionist."

Lawyers and business executives recognize that without some level of autonomy, counsel would not be able to guard the corporation from unwise legal risks. The interviews have a somewhat schizophrenic character in this respect. Lawyers indicated that they have the autonomy required to act independently and to be "deal-stoppers," but several claimed that their companies are "very ethical." When they observed clear cases of legal problems, informants were sure that their company would do everything required to ensure legal compliance. When questioned, almost every attorney could imagine a situation in which he or she would go over the head of management to become a deal-stopper, but few could recall situations in which they had actually done so. It seemed to us that if our respondents found themselves in a John Grisham-like tale of corporate intrigue, they would know how to get help. Most day-to-day business activity does not rise to this level, however.

Yet some attorneys acknowledged that their autonomy is constrained by the need to "get the deal done." Although their "official" role is to advise on legal risks, the business-people would prefer it if the lawyers gave only business-friendly legal advice. One lawyer explained, "Every business manager says they want honesty. They don't mean it, none of them mean it." In fact, this lawyer said that in his corporation, "it's a no-no to say no." According to this informant, inside lawyers are caught between their obligation to the law and their obligation to the company. This struggle for autonomy can have implications for lawyers' careers. The same lawyer said, "I will be honest, to the best of my ability ... if my boss doesn't like it then let him get rid of me. Which almost happened a few years ago."

Another general counsel indicated that to whom lawyers report was very significant to him. He said that

"lawyers ... report to the General Counsel, they do not report to business. That was a deliberate decision. I mean, that might even become, for me, a "resignation" kind of decision, but I don't think there's any prospect of it turning into that kind of issue. But I feel strongly about that—it's my job to protect their independence."

Apparently this general counsel would oppose decentralizing the legal function by placing lawyers under the authority of business units. Attorneys in centralized departments sometimes have difficulty learning what is happening throughout the corporation. An attorney who practiced in a centralized legal department complained that sometimes he had to "hunt down and chase and spy on [the business executives] in order to try to keep them in line."

Deploying lawyers in a decentralized structure, by housing them in functional units such as Human Resources or Engineering, allows lawyers to "stop [legally questionable] things earlier and know about those things earlier." Yet * * * nesting attorneys in functional divisions exposes them to more intense pressure to agree with their business colleagues rather than offer objective legal advice.

No matter how much a lawyer may wish to be the moral compass of the organization and provide expert legal advice all the time, there are practical constraints on his or her ability to do so. The practical constraints most often mentioned by our respondents were lack of resources and profit pressures. One lawyer spoke of the bind between providing quality legal advice and keeping the costs associated with the legal department within a range that is acceptable to the businesspeople. She said,

"There simply aren't enough lawyers. There's enormous pressure to control costs and yet there's an inconsistent pressure ... They have simultaneously said," You've got to control expenses and you can't hire and in fact, you have to cut ... "So you know that you're not doing the job all that well. You know you don't have enough people; you know you can't get any more."

Inside counsel, like their business peers, are under intense pressure to meet business objectives. The lawyers working in these conditions are, like the business professionals with whom they work, held responsible for the bottom line of their division. One attorney explained that the "bottom line results are really what make or break [a career] ... the bottom line—success—is how everybody is judged." Another lawyer conceded that his responsibility is to the stockholder and that his job is first and foremost "to make sure that investment grows." These constraints and pressures affect all three types of inside counsel. They render the gatekeeping functions, and indeed other advisory functions, more difficult to perform. Although the external legal environment may impose more legal obligations on corporations, lawyers are not exempt from the resource and profit pressures with which other corporate managers and professionals must deal.

Obviously some of our respondents interpose legal opinions that frustrate the plans of the business executives. Even the attorneys who claim to have the power to be deal-stoppers admit that they must use this power judiciously, however. Half of the lawyers in our sample acknowledge that, most of the time, the businesspeople in the company make the final determination regarding whether to assume a legal risk. The lawyer's role is reduced to informing business executives about the legal risks associated with different actions.

The blending of law and business makes it sometimes difficult for one to establish exactly who is making final decisions regarding business matters. Who makes the final decision is a function of the nature of the issue at hand, the personalities of the people involved, and the complexity of the legal matter involved. One lawyer explained it this way:

> "Our job is to assess risks, and it's the businessperson's job to make decisions about risks, what risks they are willing to assume. Now, having said that, I also think of it as my job to make sure that the decision about what risks to assume is being made at the appropriate level. So, if somebody was prepared to assume a risk which I felt was inappropriate, I would say, 'I don't think this is a decision for you to make. I need to talk to your boss.' "

In these comments the lawyer reveals a recognition of the distinction between business decisions and legal decisions, a preference to make only "legal" decisions, and a desire for the businessperson to make the "business" decision. Nonetheless, the lawyer retains the power to ensure that the business decisions are being handled appropriately.

Corporate counsel who participate in the top management of their companies are different in this respect, however. Ten of 11 respondents who were part of the corporate or divisional management (91%) indicated that they made the final decision about whether to incur a legal risk, whereas only 35% of other lawyers claimed to make the final decision about legal risk. If all questions of legal risk percolated to a legal officer in top management, lawyers would be making such judgments. The clear impression from the interviews, however, is that not all questions go up the legal chain of command. Moreover, corporate counsel in top management contain the same proportions of cops, counsel, and entrepreneurs as the entire sample. They appear, therefore, to confront the same tensions as other lawyers in balancing gatekeeping and entrepreneurial roles.

B. Views Across the Law/Business Divide: A Mixture of Suspicion and Appreciation

Lawyers' attitudes about the businesspeople in their organization may affect how these lawyers approach their work. Several informants reported altering the legal advice they provide according to how they think business executives view them, as well as how they assess business executives' knowledge of the law and business ethics. Inside counsel often noted the legal sophistication of higher levels of management.

Yet a substantial minority of informants criticized businesspeople for poor business judgment and for failing to understand basic legal principles. For example, one inside counsel complained that "the low-I.Q. club is well-represented" among the businesspeople in his department. More substantively, he said that certain businesspeople are "so in love with [a particular] project, [that they] would do anything to get the deal done. They would compromise the integrity of the bank." Another lawyer expressed a similar sentiment when he said that at least some of the businesspeople "just want to get their deal done and get their bonus," without regard to "basic integrity, documentation, follow-through, responsibility, and accountability." Less insidious, but no less problematic, a number of lawyers indicated that the businesspeople were simply ignorant regarding the importance of the law and lawyers within the organization. One lawyer complained of businesspeople who are "bumpkins ... who literally tell you they want to violate the law." Inside counsel also occasionally were critical of the way management works. They complained that the corporate culture was little more than nonsense, that businesspeople were often slow to make decisions and to take action.

Conversely, lawyers recognize that businesspeople do not always think highly of lawyers' roles within the company. Inside counsel report that businesspeople "do not really want to have them around," think of them as a "necessary evil," "don't associate lawyers with creative solutions," and do not view them as "team players." More than one-third of inside counsel suggested that they encountered a negative view of lawyers in the corporation. Despite these negative images, many attorneys believe that their work is appreciated by at least some of their clients.

All three types of inside counsel must deal with tensions between lawyers and non-lawyers, although they appear to use different strategies with respect to such tensions. Attorneys as cops are less likely than counsels or entrepreneurs to soft-pedal their advice. They risk being characterized as inflexible, or worse. In at least one instance a "cop" was characterized by a manager as "not very smart ... in a meeting this guy is like two pages behind, metaphorically." Counsel attempt to minimize conflicts with business people. Entrepreneurs market the law to nonlawyers.

C. Blending Law and Business

In a sense, all the lawyer roles we identify blend legal and business objectives. When a lawyer acts as a cop, he or she serves business by ensuring that the company meets its legal obligations. When a lawyer acts as a counsel, he or she tries to find legal means for doing business. When a lawyer acts as entrepreneur, his or her service to business is more obvious because the lawyer's goals and the businessperson's goals are the same—only the expertise is different. Here we discuss two ways in which inside lawyers explicitly pay deference to business objectives in practice: in their substantive legal advice and in the marketing of law to business.

1. Substantive Advice

Although much of the discussion here and elsewhere concerns the social control functions of law within corporations, much of what corporate lawyers do as they ply their substantive expertise is to invent ways to make (or save) money for corporations. This function may be more apparent in certain substantive fields or activities than others. The tax lawyers among our respondents, for example, although they also spoke about their role in tax compliance, thought their duties were very much appreciated by business executives because they directly contributed to profits. When we asked whether the businesspeople she worked with had a negative view of lawyers, one tax lawyer commented:

> "As a tax lawyer I look less like a lawyer than a lot of . . . those do-nothing regulatory lawyers, and I don't say that facetiously. Because potentially in this corporation the business managers are measured on an after-tax basis: they look at their tax line . . . Last year we . . . had one very specific objective in mind for the corporation. We had to lower our effective tax rates; they had just gotten too high. We had a lot of pressure and we brought [them] way down. The numbers were very significant . . . These guys knew about it and acknowledged it . . . So tax lawyers sometimes do good things."

. . . Informants in other legal fields discussed highly creative applications of legal expertise to advance the economic interests of their employers. A lawyer in a bank described his success in establishing an insurance subsidiary in another state, even though banking regulations largely prohibit the entry of banks into insurance. After detailing his accomplishments in getting legislation passed in a state legislature and winning an appellate court case to protect various state banking operations from federal regulations, he described how his blend of legal and business expertise was essential to giving his employer the "powers" needed to enter such a venture.

> "I guess . . . every lawyer has a different role in every different business. In this particular business it's so complex from a legal and regulatory perspective in that we have two regulated industries, banking and insurance. We are trying to meld them together, coupled with all the various nuances that go with it, and the fact that the powers came not directly, but indirectly, that I can't think of many more businesses that really need the lawyer to give the road map and the guide to getting it done. Certainly new businesses, like telecommunications, they suffer from the same thing, but you would never think two old businesses, banking and insurance, to still be muddling around trying to figure out who can do what. Yet what happened when we passed the law, and with some of the court cases,

is 100 years of history were thrown out the window and it is a whole new ball game now."

This informant used his knowledge of insurance and banking law, combined with the lobbying capacity and litigation capacity of his corporate employer, to invent "a whole new ball game." Other informants offered similar stories. One lawyer at a large corporation that developed highly sophisticated information systems for its own operations took the lead in developing intellectual property claims over the corporation's business systems. His work laid the basis for the sale of the business system to other corporations. Another corporate counsel led a quiet campaign to subsidize litigation filed by third parties against a leading competitor of his corporation, in which the third parties charged that the competitor had engaged in unfair trade practices.

Lawyers for corporations constantly use their legal expertise to advance the corporation's financial interests. Much of this activity involves the rather mundane application of existing law. But in large corporations that command huge resources and sophisticated legal talent, inside lawyers are constantly pushing to expand law and legal practices to generate new sources of corporate growth or to gain a new edge in economic competition. This brand of lawyering, which some scholars have referred to as "penumbra lawyering" (Piciotto 1991) or "professional innovation" (Powell 1993), goes far beyond the Brandeisian ideal of counsel-for-the-situation. In many of these instances lawyers are developing creative institutional devices. But in intent and effect, these are not the sorts of devices that Brandeis would have seen as progressive. Their primary purpose is to generate profits and competitive advantages for particular corporations. Although at least some informants suggested that gains for particular corporations brought general benefits to society by generating new wealth, such beliefs are only part of a general ideology and quite clearly did not inspire the actions of these lawyers in these specific instances.

2. Marketing Law to Business

Of the 42 attorneys interviewed, 18 (43%) indicated that they market the law and lawyers to others in the corporation. Of those 18, 13 (31%) also acknowledged that such marketing affects the way they give legal advice. In other words, in order to ensure that business professionals will continue to consult them, lawyers try to make their advice more palatable to businesspeople. This marketing of the legal function is a response to a perceived threat. Many respondents indicated that there is a danger that the Legal Department may come to be viewed as expendable. The very existence of the Legal Department depends on lawyers' ability to change their image in the corporation.

As one lawyer-entrepreneur explained, "We need to make [the business executives] feel as though, by and large, our overall outlook is to try to help them accomplish the things they are trying to do, and, by and large, that's true and it's fine." Another informant cited with pride the fact that the lawyers of his division "have the best reputation in [the company] because we are so close to the businesspeople in getting the deal done." Another lawyer, who told us he convinces managers in his functional department to use his expertise, said, "I just want to be value-added; I want to be helpful. Mostly that's a pretty easy sell." This attorney indicated that he not only has to convince the business executives to use his services but also accomplishes this goal by using the business language of "value added." Other general counsel related that they were trying to change how their departments were perceived in their respective corporations. "I think there was a sense a couple of years ago that the lawyers . . . just weren't players. I'm trying to make it players." Another said,

> "[A] significant part of our department was conceived, or seen, by the business people as a barrier to getting the job done, something to be gotten around, or past, or through, or whatever, and . . . we really needed to do some work to reestablish ourselves as counselors or partners."

Lawyers are now eager to be seen as part of the company, rather than as obstacles to getting things done. To do so, it appears that inside counsel are themselves interested in discounting their gatekeeping function in corporate affairs.

D. Maintaining Professional Identity

The foregoing does not mean that lawyers have completely abandoned their professional identities. Indeed, inside counsel still strongly identify themselves as lawyers and are reluctant to consider changing to a non-legal executive position, for various reasons. When we asked if they would be interested in moving from the law to the business operations within the company, most of the lawyers said they would be willing to listen to an offer; but only 12 (29%) said they would consider moving to the business side, and only two of these respondents expressed an explicit desire to move from law to a suitable business position. Thus, even though they see themselves as performing a business-oriented role, they do not want to leave the law to become businesspeople * * *

Despite the fact that they frequently are involved in business decisions, that they must promote their role based on business values, and that they often report deriving great satisfaction from seeing business projects through from start to finish, lawyers recognize that their professional status carries certain rewards . . . Even an inside counsel, the lawyer most directly embedded in business, retains a self-image as a legal professional. Like accountants, engineers, or human resources professionals who are employed in corporations, inside lawyers retain a dual identity—as employees of a corporation and members of a professional (or at least expert) group.

V. ALPHACORP: A CASE STUDY OF INSIDE LAWYERING

We can gain a better appreciation of the role of inside counsel in business through an in-depth investigation of relationships between lawyers and managers in a particular organization. Here we report on a case study of a major financial corporation, Alphacorp, in which we conducted multiple interviews in the course of ten days of fieldwork.

Alphacorp is a major financial institution that enjoys a powerful, if not dominant, position in some aspects of consumer financial markets in the United States. The corporation as a whole employs well over 50,000 employees, has billions in assets, and over $100 million a year in net income. Its position in the industry makes it a highly influential actor in government policies affecting financial markets. In 1993, the year of our interviews, Alphacorp was still struggling to overcome setbacks it had sustained in various components of its business in the 1980s, as well as the effects of the recession of the early 1990s. The effects of corporate downsizing were obvious. As we wandered the corridors of the corporate complex, we walked past numerous empty reception areas, which we imagined were once bustling business centers but now seemed like deserted outposts in a shrinking empire. Informants told us of 40% cuts in some staff areas. The cuts had weakened employee morale. According to one source, an annual survey of employee attitudes had recorded a drop in the percentage of employees who believed Alphacorp cared about their well-being from 56% in 1990 to 27% in 1993.

We conducted interviews with 34 informants in Alphacorp. We concentrated the interviews in one of the major business divisions, where we interviewed the entire divisional legal staff and several non-lawyer managers just below the small top strata of divisional management. We also spoke to some non-lawyer staff and inside lawyers scattered throughout the entire corporation; these included informants in human resources, tax, litigation, government affairs, and various business units

. . .

The interviews revealed that within one large corporation it is possible to find the full range of lawyering roles presented above. Although these roles sometimes are identified with certain fields and functions, they again appear to reflect individual and situational variations that cannot be summarized simply. It also is obvious that executives are aware of variations in lawyering style, and that they choose different kinds of lawyers for different kinds of problems. Our comparisons of non-lawyers and lawyers working in Alphacorp underscore the fact that important differences remain between business lawyers and business managers.

A. *Structure of the Law Department*

The legal function in Alphacorp is largely decentralized. Most lawyers work in operating divisions or in corporate-wide functional groups (such as Human Resources). The Litigation Division is the one exception; there is one litigation unit for the corporation overall. Although it appears that entrepreneurial lawyering is prevalent in Alphacorp, that does not mean the corporation has forsaken traditional ties to outside law firms. A telling indication of this fact is that the General Counsel of Alphacorp, who had assumed the position just a few years before, previously was a partner in the outside law firm that historically was strongly associated with the corporation * * *

Below the General Counsel, the leading lawyers in this division had a distinctly entrepreneurial orientation. The General Counsel of the corporate subsidiary that contained the division we studied had started in Alphacorp on the business side and had gone to night law school. He saw himself as a bridge between law and business and ran seminars to help the lawyers in the corporation "understand the business guys." He thought management had an essentially negative view of lawyers. The division General Counsel fit our ideal type of an entrepreneurial lawyer, although, like many informants, how he characterized his role defied easy classification. Our respondent is circumspect about the proper role of lawyers vis-a-vis businesspeople.

"The most common debate I have with the staff here ... is you folks [staff] have to understand what is a business decision and a legal decision. You [as counsel] constantly have to resist the idea that your business judgment is better than theirs ... You may think that their judgment stinks on it, but at the end of the day, they are going to make a zillion dollars in this business and pay your salary. And if you are running the busness, it would be in bankruptcy."

Yet, in virtually the same breath, this respondent pointed out how he and his lawyers were "a steady rock in this business" because they dealt with every facet of the division's operations. The lawyers are a "repository of everything that's happening in the business," have a "historical continuity," and are seen as having "good judgment." The result is that their business judgments are consulted.

"You're asked from time to time ... 'What do you think we ought to do with this?' You don't stand there and say, 'I'm not going to tell you what I think, that's a legal decision.' It doesn't happen as cleanly as I said because you're just part of the flow and you're there. I have been involved in deals where it's right before we're going to decide whether we're going to do the deal. And they'll go around the room and say, 'What do you think, what do you think?' Everybody will raise their hand, you know [and say], 'I think it's solid.' Come to me and I'll say you shouldn't do the deal. It's purely business. This is my comment, 'It's not going to make money.' Now, should I keep my mouth shut?"

At least two of the attorneys under this informant's immediate supervision fit our characterization of lawyers acting as cops. The divisional legal staff as a whole, however, quite clearly functioned in entrepreneurial fashion, because the divisional General Counsel exercised control over staffing, and he could make the final decisions on legal strategy when conflicts emerged between lawyers and non-lawyers. The hierarchical positioning of entrepreneurs over other lawyers at Alphacorp also appeared in the litigation and the tax units and one of the other business units in which we did more than one interview. Thus it appears that in Alphacorp the higher-ranked lawyers are more entrepreneurial than their subordinates.

B.   *Managerial Strategies for Using Inside Counsel.*

Alphacorp's executives are sophisticated in how they use lawyers to accomplish transactions with other corporations and shape decisions in the corporation. One manager spoke of how she chose between a "hard-line" lawyer in the department and another "management-oriented" attorney for different transactions. In one instance she was involved in contract negotiations with another large corporation, which turned difficult.

> "They would be like arguing about this stuff to the point where I really felt like I had to protect my back. The lawyer that I had working on it, as it happens, is a very hard-line guy, and it was exactly the right thing for him to be doing."

She continued that this "hard-line guy" would not have been right for a different deal, with a different company. For that transaction, she brought in an attorney who she knew had a different style.

> "Meanwhile ... we did a renewal of ... a good, solid, successful business ... We just needed to sort of clean it up and renew it. It would have been wrong to have that guy work on this; because this was a noncontentious, friendly situation. I had a very soft attorney working on it ... somebody who is much more relationship, management oriented, much more low key in her approach to things and stuff."

Note that this manager had the ability to select the attorney she preferred. Although the interviewee suggested there was an element of chance in which lawyers got assigned a certain matter, when it is particularly important to an executive at Alphacorp, he or she can influence the assignment process.

Another manager revealed that he used a particular division counsel to find "empowering" solutions. He said that he called on Attorney X when

> "I really want to do something different ... It's not that the others don't do things differently, but Attorney X truly spearheads creative solutions. I call them empowering versus limiting. So if I want empowerment I go to see Attorney X, if I want limiting, I can find lots of people who will give me a reason why I can't do things."

When we asked for a concrete example, the manager described an instance in which he wanted to create a subsidiary that could take a more aggressive commercial posture than the parent corporation. In his words, the parent corporation evoked a "Walt Disney"-like image. He wanted a subsidiary that could appear more like the "John Gotti Collection Agency." Previous legal advice had suggested that such an arrangement was not legally possible. Attorney X figured out a way to establish the subsidiary.

Another manager also spoke of Attorney X as different.

> "He is different from some of the other lawyers I have dealt with in our organization . . . He is much more proactive in trying to change law and apply it so that it fits with what he thinks is fair for our business and that we obviously support and is probably favorable for our business. A lot of other lawyers I've worked with tend to quote law as opposed to trying to manage legislation and things like that."

This manager cited Attorney X's willingness to argue against various regulatory limitations on accessing a customer's financial information for purposes unrelated to the original reason it was collected.

> "One set of lawyers would argue, and argued in fact, . . . 'You can't, so don't even bother [to try to change the regulations].' Attorney X and his folks challenge it and go back to the [government regulator] and ask for a different interpretation."

These lawyers are attractive to divisional management because they are willing to push the envelope in grey areas of the law. This is creative lawyering with a morally ambiguous edge—creating subsidiaries with "Gotti-like" images or moving to broader corporate access to putatively private consumer information. The "creative" or entrepreneurial role for lawyers in this corporation is a construction by lawyers in response to the needs of business. When they pick and choose the lawyers more likely to engage in this kind of lawyering, business executives ensure the prominence of entrepreneurial lawyers. Lawyers who tend to act as cops must change or be left behind. They may eventually be forced out of the corporation.

Yet * * * inside lawyers can be deployed by managers to produce corporate decisions that are more socially responsible even if not strictly dictated by the law. A midlevel executive in a major subsidiary of Alphacorp reported a situation in which he thought as a matter of business ethics that they should disclose to a third party corporation that they were negotiating a deal with another corporation. He brought the issue to the President of the subsidiary. When the executive proposed disclosing this information, the President

> "slapped me right down and said no! It was very much a hierarchical thing of—[I] made the recommendation [and] got told no. But I still felt like this was . . . I really felt he was wrong. So then what do you do? . . . So I went to [Attorney Y]. He wrote a memo and then eventually we did tell them. And he wrote it as a sidebar, not as a . . . it's not a legal opinion, it's more like these things are happening. I don't know; he sort of insinuated it into some process that he was working on. And it worked out great and it was really very useful to me."

These examples reveal some of the complexities in how different managers use law and lawyers in their work. Several of the "creative" lawyering solutions described here have a hard instrumental edge—lawyers are seen as pushing the boundaries of business taste, if not legal regulations. The last example, however, serves at least one manager's view of a higher form of business ethics. The lawyer he involved advanced this manager's approach, not by creating a legal opinion to support it, but by reshaping how the decision was made . . .

C. *Professional Autonomy in the Corporate Context*

The foregoing suggests that both lawyers and non-lawyers frequently engage in strategic calculations about the roles they play in a corporate structure. For the reasons we already have elaborated, inside lawyers probably more often experience a tension between fidelity to a formal body of rules and norms (the law and the complex of professional obligations it imposes on lawyers) and allegiance to corporation objectives than to other businesspersons. Yet there are variations in how these tensions are resolved both within the category of inside counsel and across the categories of non-law jobs (especially other professional groups).

We have already noted that many of the inside lawyers who are most popular with executives at Alphacorp are "can do" types who champion aggressive legal approaches to management projects. A human resources (or employment) lawyer, practicing in a centralized Human Resources Department, had a different orientation. She described the inherent tension between lawyers and non-lawyers within Human Resources. Non-lawyer Human Resource staff

"want employees to believe . . . that this is a good place to work and that the policies are there to assist and protect and encourage [employees]. And we on the other hand want to make sure that they are not written in a way that guarantees anybody a bonus, that guarantees them a job for any time certain."

As a result of the lawyers' role in manuals and contracts, there are provisions where "it's obvious that the lawyers have insisted that that language be in there." Here the lawyer is guarding the corporation from a potential risk. Lawyer and non-lawyer may disagree over specific language, but they share an overall objective.

In other situations, however, the Human Resources lawyer may be in the position of telling management that employees have certain rights. The same Human Resources lawyer had practiced in a public interest organization before moving to Alphacorp. When she discussed how she was recruited, she described how she reconciled a move from public interest to employment law for management.

"I would not have accepted a position if I had to only be what I would call a corporate mouthpiece. The department head was also very amenable to allowing the position to be one that ensured that employees' rights were not being trampled on, and gave the position enough autonomy that I was able to ensure that the right thing was done by the employee if a wrong had occurred."

"Q. I assume that's still the case, you still very much feel that way.

A. Oh, absolutely, absolutely."

This informant explicitly recognized that she had "switched sides" in her career. Though she insisted she was still very autonomous in terms of professional decisions, she also acknowledged that her values had changed during the course of her time at Alphacorp.

> "I wouldn't have stayed if I didn't feel comfortable with the values of the company and all of that. I do think your values somewhat change as you grow older and your view on the world somewhat changes. I mean you take with you all of your prior experiences."

Lawyers are not unique in occasionally finding themselves at odds with management. A non-lawyer Human Resources staff person provided a graphic account of how she had intervened to prevent a manager from firing an employee who had become disabled.

> "This was before the days of ADA laws. His manager was very upset because he was being held accountable for the productivity of his staff, that this guy was ... bringing down his numbers. He needed assistance getting into and out of the building ... So he put forth a decree that nobody was any longer allowed to help this person to come and go, because then he would be forced to leave ... We did not allow it. We told him that we ... overruled his order and that [that] was unacceptable."

Some of the tensions inside lawyers experience in the corporation result from their position as "staff." An accounting officer in Alphacorp reported experiencing many of the same difficulties in dealing with business managers that our lawyer informants had reported. Accountants also struggle with the image among executives of being "obstructionist" because occasionally they must deliver the "bad news" that structuring a deal a certain way may lead "to [the corporation] losing a favorable accounting treatment." Indeed, this informant thought lawyers were more powerful than accountants in business decisions because executives tend to back off if a lawyer says there is a legal problem, but will argue with an accountant's interpretation. This informant's approach to the tension between accounting concerns and business concerns sounded quite similar to the approach of many inside counsel: get closer to business.

> "Why I moved into this particular job recently was to get closer to the business and to ... you know, it was sort of a bridge to move somewhat out of accounting policy and into business. It served a purpose here because they needed someone closer in the organization, to be closer to transactions that were occurring from the inception, so that there would not be any sort of accounting blowups or at least fewer accounting blowups. So it served a need for me to move here. And at the same time I have a desire to move from the accounting policy, accounting theory, accounting practice, more into the business transactions."

Inside lawyers are not the only professionals in corporations who are actively pursuing more involvement in, and alignment with, business goals.

D. *A Difference Between Lawyers and Non–Lawyers*

The Alphacorp interviews provide an opportunity to compare lawyers and non-lawyers within the same organization. One distinction between the two groups that comes through very clearly is that all the non-lawyer executives we interviewed were interested in moving up the corporate ladder to division-wide, indeed corporate-wide, positions. When we asked the inside counsel about their career desires, some mentioned moving up inside the legal function at Alphacorp or elsewhere. But only a few seemed to seriously entertain the possibility of shifting to a business job. The Human Resources staff person for the legal function confirmed this pattern. She indicated that even though the corporation left it to individuals and had no policy to encourage or discourage these moves, very few inside lawyers sought a job change to the business side.

The Alphacorp interviews deepen our understanding of how lawyers and managers interact within a given corporate structure. Although individual lawyers can be classified as cops, counsel, or entrepreneurs, it is valuable to see how these roles are arranged and negotiated in an organizational setting. Alphacorp is a corporate environment that encourages aggressive entrepreneurialism on both the business and the legal side. In the division we studied most closely, power and prestige rested with the entrepreneurial lawyers. The hard-line guys were seen as useful for a delimited set of problematic negotiations, and, occasionally were denigrated by business executives as "not very smart." Staff lawyers in Human Resources and other technical specialties were accorded autonomy and deference to their expertise. Yet the Divisional Counsel and the General Counsel for the larger subsidiary were seen as lawyers who came up with "empowering" solutions to management's problems. The lawyer-entrepreneurs were in turn "empowered" by management.

VI. CONCLUSION

* * * First, it is clear that inside counsel are subservient to managerial prerogatives. We find that inside lawyers work hard to avoid conflicts with business executives; they typically leave the final call on acceptable levels of legal risk to the businesspersons involved; and managers can exercise control over which lawyers work on their matters and thus influence the very style of lawyering employed inside the corporation.

In some sense this is an unsurprising, commonplace observation. All lawyers are obliged to be zealous advocates for clients within the bounds of professional ethics. Despite claims of professional autonomy, corporate lawyers—whether in law firms or in corporate counsel's offices—have been reported to be closely aligned with client interests throughout the twentieth century * * *

In another sense our finding is significant because subordination to management continues in the contemporary period, despite profound changes in the structural position of inside counsel, in the presence of law in the corporate environment and the ideology of management itself.

Inside counsel have gained power relative to their peers in outside law firms, but this apparently has not resulted in a fundamentally different role within the corporation. Law almost certainly has become a more salient concern for American business as a result of increased exposure to litigation, the rise of regulatory structures in the 1970s, and the increasing reliance on legal expertise in corporate governance, financing, and transactions. It appears that lawyers are indeed involved in many corporate functions, yet they report similar sorts of pressure to conform to executives' preferences as the lawyers that Donnell and Rosen described from the 1960s and late 1970s.

One significant reason may be the changed ideology of corporate management and a general corporate climate that devalues legal regulation. The inside counsel we interviewed reported dealing with extremely aggressive business executives who are interested in maximizing short-term results and cutting corporate costs. This managerial style is the hallmark of contemporary conceptions of the corporation. Staff functions such as the law are under pressure to reduce costs and reduce the drag on the velocity of business transactions. Hence our lawyer informants have attempted to craft a new image within the corporation in which lawyers are team players, rather than cops. Inside counsel have not abandoned their roles as monitors of corporate legality and analysts of legal risk, but they have adopted the current idiom of corporate management as they play those roles. Corporate lawyers, like the management they serve, attempt to be lean and mean.

Second, in the contemporary period corporate counsel have taken on an explicitly entrepreneurial orientation. In our sample of inside counsel (which is not a random sample, but was chosen in an effort to avoid bias), "cops" are significantly outnumbered by "entrepreneurs." More importantly perhaps, even "counsel" often speak in entrepreneurial terms. A sizeable minority of inside counsel are engaged in attempting to use the law to generate new sources of revenue for the corporation, by taking advantage of loopholes in regulations to enter new fields of business, by creating new forms of intellectual property, by creating new business entities. Others "market" the law to business executives, attempting to portray the law as adding value to the business, rather than only cost.

* * * [T]he apparent rise of entrepreneurialism among inside counsel appears to be part of a general movement toward marketization within the legal profession, as well as a product of changes specific to corporate management. Several commentators have noted the shift toward increased entrepreneurialism in various precincts of the legal profession, beginning with the Supreme Court's decisions in the mid–1970s to strike down restraints on lawyer advertising and minimum fee schedules * * * In the 1980s, the Reagan administration narrowed antitrust regulation, creating new opportunities for corporate mergers and acquisitions. This shift, in conjunction with deregulation in the financial markets, spurred a new wave of corporate restructuring and downsizing, as management began to emphasize short-term stock price and performance. In the marketplace for corporate legal services, the rapid increase in the cost of legal services led corporations to move away from a model of relying on one law firm to a model of parceling legal work to various law firms. Moreover, they began to closely monitor the costs of legal services and to demand highly detailed accountings of services rendered. Law firms reacted by developing self-conscious strategies for increasing profits in a more uncertain and competitive market.

It is no wonder that inside counsel were deeply affected by these changes. As inside counsel began to insist that outside law firms become accountable for the value of the legal services they rendered, they must have begun to think of their own role in corporate affairs in similar, economistic terms. But the entrepreneurialism of corporate counsel is also in part unique to the corporate context itself. As corporate management turned from relying on fixed institutional arrangements for conducting business to frequently reorganized, project based teams, which were evaluated for economic return, inside lawyers appear to have done the same (generally, see Leicht 1998). There is at least the suggestion in several interviews that in an earlier era corporate management asked for something different from their lawyers (both inside counsel and outside law firms). Management expected their lawyers to more often function as cops to protect the corporation from legal risks in a regulated corporate environment. The new generation of management began to ask their lawyers to be more entrepreneurial, in line with the loosening of regulation in corporate governance and business transactions. The "cops" declined in influence within the corporation; the "entrepreneurs" rose to take their place.

Third, despite the embrace of entrepreneurialism by inside counsel, we find that inside lawyers overwhelmingly cling to a self-image as lawyers * * * Even the most entrepreneurial amongst our respondents could not ignore the significance of their professional status for what they did. Many of our informants were happy to offer non-legal advice, but none would deny that the reason they were at the management table in the first place was their function as a legal advisor. And many of these informants admitted that they were not sure they wanted to be, or would be good at, making business decisions.

* * * Inside counsel embody a joint identification with business and legal knowledge. They are an example of corporate professionals who combine technical expertise and a kind of portable or commodified commitment to their work. We were struck over the course of our interviews that inside counsel seemed to very quickly develop loyalty to their employer. Just as a star athlete who is traded to a new team develops instant commitment to make his or her new team win, corporate professionals have been socialized in dedicated service to clients. Indeed, part of their professionalism lies in the practiced art of embracing their new clients' objectives as their own. In the corporate context, professionalism reinforces dedication to the profitmaking objectives of business. The lawyers we interviewed, for the most part, were not

alienated from their business peers, but were enthusiastic partners in their profit-generating enterprise ...

Fourth, * * * [t]he lawyers in our study negotiate multiple tensions and questions. Should I be involved in a particular business decision? What should my role be? Should I act as cop, counsel, or entrepreneur? These relationships are undergoing constant transformation and recreation, not only because of the choices the lawyers make, but as a result of the ongoing decisions of businesspersons concerning law and lawyers. A lawyer's behavior is shaped by past experiences in the corporation. When lawyers are criticized by businesspeople or when businesspeople resist legal advice in various ways (by not going to lawyers at all, or by choosing to go to a different lawyer within the corporation, or by complaining to higher ups that the lawyers are not "team players") it affects how the lawyer will behave the next time. Although we have emphasized the ways corporate counsel "construct" their roles, it is important to recognize that this is a reciprocal process among the lawyers, their "clients," and other members of top management. These roles are not fixed either historically or organizationally by field or by individual (i.e., they can vary across and within each of the above). Lawyers and their business clients can exercise individual choice within structural constraints.

It is this realm of discretion that Gordon and Simon hail as providing corporate lawyers with an opportunity to act according to a higher ethical and civic code. We are less sanguine about how corporate lawyers in fact choose to use their discretion. With a few notable exceptions, the lawyers we interviewed (like their non-lawyer peers) were literally absorbed in a high-pressure corporate environment. They appeared far more concerned with pursuing corporate profits than with pursuing the public good. But we agree that corporate lawyers retain a zone of discretion that allows them to shape the role of law and lawyers within the corporation.

Robert Jackall, MORAL MAZES: THE WORLD OF CORPORATE MANAGERS

(1989)

Drawing lines when information is scarce becomes doubly ambiguous, a problem that often emerges in shaping relationships with one's colleagues. For instance, Black, a lawyer at Covenant Corporation, received a call from a chemical plant manager who had just been served with an order from the local fire department to build retaining dikes around several storage tanks for toxic chemicals so that firemen would not be in danger of being drenched with the substance should the tanks burst if there were a fire at the plant. The plant manager indicated that meeting the order would cause him to miss his numbers badly that year and he wondered aloud if the fire chief might, for a consideration, be persuaded to forget the whole thing. Black pointed out that he could not countenance even a discussion of bribery; the plant manager laughed and said that he was only joking and would think things over and get back to Black in a few weeks. Black never heard from the plant manager about this issue again; when they met on different occasions after that, the conversation was always framed around other subjects. Black did inquire discreetly and found out that no dikes had been built; the plant manager had apparently gone shopping for a more flexible legal opinion. Should he, Black wondered, pursue the matter or in the absence of any firm evidence just let things drop, particularly since others, for their own purposes, could misconstrue the fact that he had not acted on his earlier marginal knowledge? Feeling that one is in the dark can be somewhat unnerving.

More unnerving, however, is the feeling that one is being kept in the dark. Reed, another lawyer at Covenant, was working on the legal issues of a chemical dumpsite that Alchemy Inc. had sold. He suddenly received a call from a former employee who had been having trouble with the company on his pension payments; this man told Reed that unless things were straightened out in a hurry, he planned to talk to federal officials about all the pesticides buried in the site. This was alarming news. Reed had no documentation about pesticides in the site; if Alchemy had buried pesticides there, a whole new set of regulations might apply to the situation and to Covenant as the former owner. Reed went to the chemical company's director of personnel to get the former employee's file but was unable to obtain it. Reed's boss agreed to help, but still the director of personnel refused to release the file. After repeated calls, Reed was told that the file had been lost. Reed went back to his boss and inquired whether it might be prudent for Covenant to repurchase the site to keep it under control. This was deemed a good idea. However, the asking price for the site was now three times what Covenant had sold it for. Everyone, of course, got hesitant; another lawyer became involved and began working closely with Reed's boss on the issue. Gradually, Reed found himself excluded from discussions about the problem and unable to obtain information that he felt was important to his work. His anxiety was heightened because he felt he was involved in a matter of some legal gravity. But, like much else in the corporation, this problem disappeared in the night. Eventually, Reed was assigned to other cases and he knew that the doors to the issue were closed, locked, and bolted.

PROBLEM

Suppose that you are Reed in the excerpt from Jackall's *Moral Mazes*? What would you do? How much guidance do you get from Model Rules 1.2(a), 1.2(d), 1.3, 1.6, 1.13, and 1.16, and Comment 4 to Rule 1.16?

Chapter 7

THE CORPORATE LAW FIRM: CHARACTERISTICS AND TRENDS

It's impossible to appreciate fully the kinds of ethical questions that outside lawyers for corporations face without understanding the setting in which most of those lawyers work: the large law firm. As this chapter makes clear, large law firms have become major business enterprises in the past quarter century, adopting many of the features that their corporate clients adopted long ago. This chapter provides an overview of this transformation, and then traces the evolution of one large firm as it has gone through it. The next chapter will describe how dramatic changes in the large law firm have affected the career opportunities available in this practice setting. The material in these two chapters is intended to give you gain a deeper understanding of the workplaces that a large percentage of law school graduates will enter. Ideally, it will help you make more intelligent choices about you career by illuminating the rewards, pressures, and trade-offs that lawyers encounter in the large law firm.

OVERVIEW OF THE CHAPTER

This chapter begins with an excerpt from Galanter and Palay that offers an overview of the changes that have occurred in the large law firm since the 1980s or so. The most succinct way to describe these changes is that law firms have moved from a world in which they faced little competition for either clients or lawyers to one in which they face fierce competition for both. A good way to grasp the impact of these changes is to compare the law firm of a generation ago with today's firm along two dimensions: its relationship with clients and its relationship with lawyers in the firm.

With respect to the first, consider how much business each client provides, whether the client belongs to the firm or individual lawyers in it, the type of work done for clients, the degree of specialization in practice, how clients are billed, and where clients are located. Regarding the relationship between the firm and the lawyers within it, focus on the hiring process, establishment of associate salaries, where partners come from, criteria for promotion to partner, the amount of movement of lawyers among firms, the size of the firm and the number of its offices, the administration of the firm, and the firm's stability.

As you focus on these issues, consider the claim in some quarters that the law firm a generation enjoyed a "golden age." Do you agree? Who benefited most from the way that practice was organized during this period? Who has benefited from the change? Who has been hurt? Note also that Galanter and Palay observe that the law firm of a generation ago reflected changes that emerged around the beginning of the 20th century. How does today's law firm compare to how law practice was organized before that time? Do changes in the law firm reflect broader changes in the market economy? If so, can we anticipate ways in which law firms will change further?

Four articles from the *American Lawyer* follow, which provide a case study of how a particular law firm, Rogers & Wells, has taken steps to effect the kind of transformation that Galanter and Palay describe. Note carefully the measures that the firm has taken to accomplish this, culminating in a merger with a major English law firm. What have been the challenges that the firm has faced as it has evolved? How well do you think the firm has anticipated and responded to the problems that it has faced? What have been the benefits from the changes that have occurred? What have been the costs? What kinds of questions would you ask, and of whom, if you were considering working at the firm?

Finally, the Problem for the chapter asks you to consider how, if at all, your law firm should respond to a significant increase in associate salaries from a major national firm. Ask yourself what the consequences would be if your firm chose not to follow the other firm's lead. If you feel the need to respond by increasing salaries, what alternatives are available to pay for the increase? How might the adoption of each affect the firm? How much choice do you feel you really have once the other firm announces its decision?

* * *

Marc Galanter & Thomas Palay, *The Transformation of the Big Law Firm* in Lawyers' Ideals/Lawyers' Practices

(Robert L. Nelson, David M. Trubek, & Rayman L. Solomon, eds. 1992)

The Emergence of the Big Firm

The big firm and its distinctive style of practice emerged around the turn of the century. The break from earlier law practice can be discussed under the six headings; (1) partner, (2) other lawyers, (3) relations to clients, (4) work, (5) support systems, and (6) new kinds of knowledge. Any of these indicia of the big firm can be found apart from its distinctive institutional character–a character that is changing as these features are rearranged.

Partners: In the big law firm the loose affiliation of lawyers, sharing offices and occasionally sharing work for clients, is replaced by the office in which clients "belong to" the firm rather than to an individual lawyer. The entire practice of these lawyers is shared by the firm. The proceeds, after salaries and expenses, are divided among the partners pursuant to some agreed upon formula.

Other lawyers: Unpaid clerks and permanent assistants are replaced by salaried "associates" (as we have come to call them) who are expected to devote their full efforts to the firm's clients. A select group of academically qualified associates, chosen on grounds of potential qualification for partnership, are given a prospect of eventual promotion to partnership after an extended probationary period during which they work under the supervision of their seniors, receive training, and exercise increasing responsibility.

Clients: Firms represent large corporate enterprises, organizations, or entrepreneurs with a need for continuous (or recurrent) and specialized legal services that could be supplied only by a team of lawyers. The client "belongs to" the firm, not to a particular lawyer. Relations with clients tend to be enduring. Such repeat clients are able to reap benefits from the continuity and from the economies of scale enjoyed by the firm.

Work: The work involves specialization in the problems of particular kinds of clients. It involves not only representation in court, but services in other settings and forums. The emergence of the firm represents the ascendancy of the office lawyer and the displacement of the advocate as the paradigmatic professional figure.

Litigation no longer commanded the energies of the most eminent lawyers. By 1900, Robert Swaine concludes, "the great corporate lawyers of the day drew their reputations more from their abilities in the conference room and facility in drafting documents than from their persuasiveness before the courts." In 1908 Roscoe Pound remarked this shift and apprised its consequences for reform: "The leaders of the American bars are not primarily practitioners in the courts. They are chiefly client caretakers...Their best work is done in the office, not in the forum. They devote themselves to study of the interests of particular clients, urging and defending those interests in all their varying forms, before legislatures, councils, administrative boards and commissions quite as much as in the courts. Their interest centers wholly in an individual client or set of clients, not in the general administration of justice."

Support Systems: The emergence of the big firm is associated with the introduction of new office technologies. The displacement of copying, clerks, and messengers by the typewriter, stenography, and the telephone greatly increased the productivity of lawyers.

New Kinds of Knowledge: The proliferation of printed materials—reporters, digests, treatises–rendered obsolete the earlier style of legal research and required mastery of new areas of specialized knowledge. The acquisition of legal skills changed too. Between 1870 and 1910 the portion of those admitted to the bar who were law school graduates rose from one-quarter to two-thirds.

The blending of these features into the big law firm as we know it is commonly credited to Paul D. Cravath, who in the first decade of this century established the "Cravath system" of hiring outstanding graduates straight out of law school on an understanding that they might progress to partnership after an extended probationary period, requiring them to work for the firm only, eschewing practices of their own, paying them salaries, providing training and a "graduated increase in responsibility".

The core of the big firm, we submit, is the "promotion to partnership." This is our shorthand for the organization of the firm around the expectation that the junior lawyer can cross the line by promotion and become a partner. Partners and juniors are not equals, but form a hierarchy with command and supervision exercised by partners. But the junior lawyers are neither transient apprentices nor permanent employees. They are peers, fellow professionals of presently immature powers, who have the potential to achieve full and equal stature.

Firms can offer this promise only when they are confident that they will attract sufficient work to keep these young lawyers busy. That is, the senior lawyers must have either clients who produce more work than the senior lawyers can handle themselves or a reputation that will attract such clients. Typically, association with a corporation or "super-capitalist" provided the necessary stream of work and "the publicity from serving such clients and the expansive contacts of these clients resulted in a growing network of contacts for the emergent firm."

The big law firm—and with it, the organization of law practice around the promotion to partnership pattern—became the industry standard. Gradually, the older patterns of fluid partnerships, casual apprenticeship, and nepotism were displaced. Law firms grew. In every city, the number of big firms (as big was then defined) increased at an accelerating rate, and over time there were ever-bigger firms. As firms grew, the lawyers in them became more specialized and firms began to departmentalize.

Through ascendant in the profession, these successful lawyers were subservient to and dependent on their business clients. From its origins the big firm was haunted by a sense that the profession had compromised its identity and had itself become a branch of business.

CIRCA 1960: The Golden Age of the Big Law Firm

Before the Second World War the big firm had become the dominant kind of law practice. It was the kind of lawyering consumed by the major economic actors. It commanded the highest prestige. It attracted many of the most highly talented entrants to the profession. It was regarded as the "state of the art," embodying the highest technical standards. In the postwar years this dominance was solidified.

To get a reading on the changes over the past generation, we will develop as a baseline a portrait of the big firm in its "golden age" before the transformation that it is now undergoing. This golden age of the big firm, the late 1950s and the early 1960s, was a time of stable relations with clients, of steady but manageable growth, of comfortable assurance that an equally bright future lay ahead—which is not to say that its inhabitants did not look back fondly to an earlier time when professionalism was unalloyed.

Hiring: Firms were built by "promotion to partnership." Lateral hiring was almost unheard of, and big firms did not hire from one another. Partners might leave and firms might split up, but it didn't happen very often. Hiring of top law graduates soon after their graduation was one of the building blocks of the big firm. Most hiring was from a handful of law schools, and walk-in interviews during the Christmas break were the norm. Starting salaries at the largest New York firms were uniform—$4000 in 1953, rising to $7500 in 1963. The "going rate" was fixed at a luncheon, attended by managing partners of prominent firms, held annually for this purpose.

Historically, the big firms had confined hiring to white Christian males. Few African–Americans and women had the educational admission tickets to contend for these jobs. But there were numerous Jews who did and, with a few exceptions, they too were excluded. This exclusion began to break down slowly after the Second World War. Jewish associates were hired, and some moved up the ladder to partner. The lowering of barriers to Jews was part of a general lessening of social exclusiveness. But African–Americans and other minorities of color were still hardly visible in the world of big law firms. In 1956 there were approximately eighteen women working in large New York firms— something less than one percent to the total complement of lawyers.

Promotion and Partnership: Only a small minority of those hired as associates achieved partnership. Of 454 associates hired by the Cravath firm between 1906 and 1948, only 36 (just under 8 percent) were made partners. Cravath may have been the most selective but it was not that different from other firms. In 1956 Martin Mayer reported that the "chance of becoming a partner ... varies from one in seven to one in fifteen, depending on the firm and the year in which he joins it". The "average chance at a partnership ... is only one in twelve" Spencer Klaw, writing two years later, provides the more optimistic assessment that partnership is achieved by "perhaps one out of every six or seven"

One of the basic elements of the structure of the big firm is the up or out rule that prescribes that after a probationary period, the young lawyer will either be admitted to the partnership or will leave the firm. In this model, there can be no permanent connection other than as a partner. Many firms had an explicit up or out rule—in some cases quite recently minted—but there was at work a competing and powerful norm that it was not nice to fire a lawyer. Termination tended to be drawn out and disguised. "Failure ... is carefully disguised by the firms with the knowing help of their members and associates."

For associates who did not make partner, firms undertook outplacement, recommending them for jobs with client corporations and with smaller firms. Ties might be maintained as the firm referred legal work to them or served as outside counsel to the corporation.

Although departure from the firm was decreed by the up or out norm, there were some lawyers who were permanent but not partners. These included managing clerks and a few specialists who because of a low-status origins had no expectation of being considered for partnership, although they were professionally respected and well paid. But most permanent associates were "failure," "second-class citizens" who had not been promoted but stayed on and were assigned routine work—especially "back office" work that did not involve dealing with clients.

In the course of the 1960s, there was a decline in the number of permanent associates; or, to put it another way, the up or out norm was enforced more vigorously. In his epilogue, Smigel notes the "reduction in the number permanent associates. The firms...no longer consider the permanent associate desirable." He suggests a number of possible reasons for this: the firms' work may have become more complex; the work formerly done by permanent associates was now being done by in-house corporate counsel; the permanent associate was viewed as an undesirable model of failure for associates.

Partners were chosen by proficiency, hard work, and ability to relate to clients. In many cases there was some consideration of the candidate's ability to attract business. And selection depended on the perceived ability of the firm to support additional partners.

Achieving partnership, the "strongest reward," meant not only status but security and assurance of further advancement: "They ... know that they have tenure and feel certain that they will advance up the partnership ladder". There was certainly pressure to keep up with one's peers, but competition between partners was restrained. In this environment, "admission to the partnership of a leading firm was a virtual guarantee not only of tenured employment but of a lifetime of steadily increasing earnings unmatched by a lawyer's counterparts in the other learned professions".

Work and Clients: The work of the big firm was primarily office work in corporate law, securities, banking, and tax with some estate work for wealthy clients. Litigation was not prestigious, and it was not seen as a money-maker. Where big firms were involved in litigation, it was typically on the side of the defendant. Big firms usually represented dominant actors who could structure transactions to get what they wanted; it was the other side that had to seek the help of courts to disturb the status quo. Disdain of litigation reflected the prevailing attitude among the corporate establishment that it was not quite nice to sue.

As they grew, many firms broadened their client bases, becoming less dependent on a single main client. Relations with clients tended to be enduring. "A partner in one Wall Street firm estimated its turnover in dollar volume at 5 percent a year, mostly in one-shot litigation". Corporations had strong ties to "their" law firms. Many partners sat on the boards of their clients—a practice that had been viewed as unprofessional earlier in the century—and would lose favor again later. A 1959 Conference Board survey on the legal work of 286 manufacturing corporations found that "three fourths of them retain outside counsel on a continuing basis ... Companies most frequently report that "present outside counsel has been with us for many, many years," or that "we are satisfied with the performance of our outside counsel and have never given any thought to hiring another".

We have no evidence about how many hours were actually worked or billed. Smigel reports that "some firms believe an associate should put in 1800 chargeable hours a year and a partner 1500, with the hours decreasing as the partner gets older". It was widely believed, perhaps with some basis, that lawyers (especially associates) were not working as hard as they had in earlier times.

For big firms, circa 1960 was a time of prosperity, stable relations with clients, steady but manageable growth, and a comfortable assumption that this kind of law practice was a permanent fixture of American life.

Big law firms enjoyed an enviable autonomy. They were relatively independent vis-à-vis their clients; they exercised considerable control over how they did their work; and they were infused with a sense of being in control of their destinies.

THE TRANSFORMATION OF THE BIG FIRM

The more numerous and more diverse lawyers of the late 1980s were arrayed in a very different structure of practice than their counterparts a generation earlier. There has been a general shift to larger units of practice. The number of lawyers working in sizable aggregations, capable of massive and coordinated legal undertaking has multiplied many times over.

Work and Clients: The kinds of work big firms do have changed. The mix of work coming into big firms has been changed by a surge of corporate litigation since the 1970s and by the increase in the number, size, and responsibility of in-house legal departments. Long-term retainer relations have given way to comparison shopping for lawyers on an *ad hoc* transactional basis. Corporations that view legal expenses as ordinary costs of doing business rather than singular emergencies have monitored legal costs, set litigation budgets, required periodic reporting, and awarded new business on the basis of competitive presentations from competing outside firms.

The practice of law has become more specialized. Within large firms, specialization has become more intense and the work of various levels more differentiated. Much routine work has been retracted into corporate law departments, shifting the work of large outside firms away from office practice toward litigation and deals. With more deals, higher stakes more regulation to take into account, and more volatile fluctuations of interest and exchange rates there is greater demand for intensive lawyering. The large contested and/or risk-prone one-of-a-kind, "bet your company" transactions—litigations, takeovers, bankruptcies, and such—make up a larger portion of what big law firms do. Since few clients provide a steady stream of such matters and those that have them increasingly shop for specialists to handle them, firms are under ever greater pressure to generate a steady (or increasing) supply of such matters, by retaining the favors of old clients and securing new ones.

Competitiveness: The new aggressiveness of in-house counsel, the breakdown of retainer relationships, and the shift to discrete transactions has made conditions more competitive. The practice of law has become more openly commercial and profit-oriented, "more like a business". Firms rationalize their operations; they engage professional managers and consultants; their leaders worry about billable hours, profit centers, and marketing strategies. "Eat what you kill" compensation formulas emphasize rewards for productivity and business-getting over "equal shares" or seniority. There is more differentiation in the power partners wield and the rewards they receive; standing within the firm depends increasingly on how much business a partner brings in. Rising overhead costs and associate salaries put pressure on partners. In many firms, partners work more hours, but their income has not increased correspondingly.

The need to find new business has led to aggressive marketing. Some firms have taken on marketing directors, a position that did not exist in 1980. Those lawyers who are responsible for bringing in business enjoy a new ascendancy over their colleagues. The need to find new business has shaken the traditional structure of the big firm. A description of big firms in the Southeast reports that the "shift from a traditional reliance upon a small number of rainmakers to the aggressive stance that everyone must make rain has resulted in a reduction in numbers of associates receiving a vote for partnership as well a in— many cases—a redivision of partners' profit pie. Many firms also go a step further by eliminating non-producing partners and restructuring or jettisoning non-productive departments".

The search for new business has been directed not only toward would-be clients, but to existing ones. In a setting where corporations are more inclined to divide their custom among several law firms, firms engage in "cross-selling" to induce the purchaser of services from one department to avail itself of the services offered by other departments.

Lateral Hiring and Mergers: In the classical big firm, almost all hiring was at the entry level. Partners were promoted from the ranks of associates. Those who left went to corporations or smaller firms, not to similar large firms since these adhered to the same no lateral hiring norm. But starting in the 1970s, lateral movement became more frequent. At first, firms made an occasional lateral hire to meet a need for litigators or to fill some other niche. But soon lateral hiring developed into a means of systematically upgrading or enlarging the specialties and localities they could service and of acquiring rainmakers who might bring or tract new clients.

The flow of lateral movement widened from individual lawyers to whole departments and groups within firms and to whole firms. Mass defections and mergers became common, enabling firms at a stroke to add new departments and expand to new locations. Mergers were not only a way to grow; they also provided a convenient device to shake out or renegotiate terms with less productive partners.

Firms hired laterally not only by mergers but by inducing specific lawyers to change firms, "cherry picking" as it came to be called in the late 1980s. Lateral movement was not confined to the partner level. The same survey found that one quarter of the responding firms reported that more than half their associates were hired laterally. Increasingly, associates move from one big firm to another.

The other side of this movement was splits and dissolutions of firms. As firms grew larger the task of maintaining an adequate flow of business often became more difficult. Firms were more vulnerable to defections by valued clients or the lawyers to whom those clients are attached. Size multiplies the possibility of conflicts of interest resulting in tension between partners who tend old clients and those who propose new ones that can induce a breakaway. Surrounded by other firms attempting to grow by attracting partners with specials skills or desirable clients, firms are vulnerable to the loss of crucial assets. So dissolution may be catalyzed by lateral movement and merger activity and such break-up in turn stimulates a new round of lateral movement.

Hiring: As firms grew, thus requiring larger numbers of qualified associates, recruitment activity intensified. Recruiting visits to an increasing roster of law schools, extensive summer programs, brochures, and expense-paid "call-backs" of candidates have become familiar parts of the big law firm scene. Starting salaries have increased dramatically, beginning with a great contraction of the supply of associates in the late 1960s.

Firms responded to their supply problem not only by accommodating their recruits' public-interest impulses but by sharply increasing their compensation. In 1967, the staring salary for associates at elite firms in New York was $10,000; scheduled to increase to $10,500 for 1968 recruits. In February 1968, the Cravath firm, breaking with the "going rate" cartel, raised the salaries for incoming associates to $15,000, setting in motion a new competitive system of bidding for top prospects. Firms that wanted to be considered in the top stratum had to match the Cravath rate. The change in new York staring salaries reverberated through out the upper reaches of the profession. The salaries of more senior associates had to be raised to preserve differentials; the take of junior partners had to be adjusted accordingly; firms outside New York, though paying less, had to give corresponding raises to maintain parity with their New York rivals. Unlike later increase in compensation, the one in the late 1960s was not accompanied by pressure to bill more hours. In fact, it appears that hourly billings were dropping during this period.

In 1968, when the highest-paid beginning associates were getting $53,000, Cravath administered a second shock by unilaterally raising salaries to $65,000. At the time of the first "Cravath shock" the big firm "going rate" referred primarily to a few dozen firms, most which were located in New York; by the time the second occurred the big-firm world consisted of several hundred geographically dispersed firms, many national in scope. Long-accepted city differentials have been eroded by branching, especially by recent moves by New York firms into other legal markets, causing some firms in those localities to match the higher New York salaries.

As the number and size of large firms has increased, recruitment has become competitive and more meritocartic, leading to changes in the social composition of the new recruits. The range of law schools from which the big firms recruit had widened, and recruitment has gone "deeper" into each graduating class. Religious, racial, and gender barriers have been swept away. The social exclusiveness in hiring that was still a feature of the world of elite law practice in 1960 has receded into insignificance. Performance in law school and in the office counts for more; social connections for less.

Leverage: Firms have become more highly leveraged—that is, the ratio of associates to partners has risen. Using the date from our Group I set of fifty of the largest firms in 1986 we calculated the change in associate to partner ratios at five year intervals from 1960, the midpoint of golden age, to 1985. During that period these firms grew from an average size of 48 to 239 and the ratio of associates to partners increased 28 percent from 1.16 to 1.49. The ratio rose consistently during the successive five year intervals, with the exception of the period from 1965 to 1970.

Promotion and Partnership: Over the two decades preceding 1980 the period during which lawyers served as associates before becoming partners became shorter. A National Law Journal survey of thirty-five firms in seven localities found that some two-thirds of associates hired in the late 1970s had spend seven to eight "years to partner". Many partners anticipated further increases.

Generally, increases in leverage suggest that a smaller percentage of associates will be promoted to partner.

A constriction of promotion to partnership, anticipated elsewhere, seems to have arrived already in New York's largest firms.

We noted earlier that in the 1960s firms applied the up or out norm with increasing stringency. Permanent associates were described as a "dying breed". But before the end of the decade, the institution was reinvented. Firms modified the promotion to partnership model by creating a new stratum of permanent salaried lawyers. This is done under various names: nonequity partner, special partner, senior attorney, senior associate, participating associate, etc. As a Washington legal headhunter recently observed, "Everyone is studying this because everyone is running against the same economic realities. The larger classes of associates are coming up, and there is just not enough room at the top". But permanent associates need not be those who failed to make partner. The managing partner at Cravath noted in 1983 that "we now have about 24 what we call "permanent associates", who almost all were specialists in one sort of work or another. Most, but not all, had been hired laterally with their specialties already in hand".

As the firm copes with the exigencies of its new competitive environment, the situation of the junior lawyer is more precarious and more pressured, although it is also more lucrative. But the partnership core is even more affected. Partners are under mounting pressure to maintain a high level of performance—and performance that fits the business strategy of the firm. Many new features of the law firm world such as mergers and lateral movement amplify the power of dominant lawyers within a firm to sanction their errant colleagues—and the prevalent culture endorses such sanctions. So partners worry about having their prerogatives or shares reduced or even being "pushed off the iceberg" or "de-partnerized". There are now real possibilities of downward movement. The unassailable security of partnership is no longer assured. "Partnership used to be forever, but it no longer".

CONCLUSION

For a long time, those who inhabited the world of the big firm could expect that the years to come would not be terribly different from the years just past. But this sense of stability has been shaken.

Susan Hansen, THE YOUNG AND THE RESTLESS

THE AMERICAN LAWYER, September 1995

Alan Gosule, the head of Rogers & Wells's real estate securities practice group, doesn't think of himself as a conspicuous consumer. He just likes to live well—and in the past year the 54–year-old Gosule has done just that, flying off to the Caribbean isle of Saint Barthelemy, touring the south of France, and skimming the waters off of Long Island's Atlantic Beach in his 22–foot blue and white Baja speedboat.

"Rogers & Wells," declares Gosule, a 1991 arrival from the now defunct Gaston & Snow, "has been very, very good to me."

Gosule, who earned roughly $750,000 last year as head of the $10 million real estate securities group, has been equally good to Rogers & Wells. Thanks to Gosule and a score of other new laterals, over the past two years a younger, more aggressive Roger & Wells has been pulling in record profits. In 1994 the firm posted an all-time firm high of $510,000 in profits per partner. And to hear James Asher, the firm's no-nonsense 46–year-old managing partner tell it, there are higher earnings to come.

It's a far cry from the mid–1980s, back when then-firm chair and former secretary of State William Rogers admonished younger partners to be patient. Wait, Rogers was quoted as saying in a 1984 American Lawyer article: If you work hard, in 20 years you'll be making "more than the president of the United States." (The president's salary that year was $200,000.)

The instructions didn't exactly take. Throughout the eighties, as profits languished, Asher and other younger partners pressed for a greater say in governance. After taking control in 1988 of the firm's governing body, a seven-member executive committee, the new generation of mostly forty-something leaders wasted no time in ushering in change.

In 1990, as part of a three-year plan to climb above the median level of profitability for New York law firms, Rogers & Wells hired Deloitte & Touche management consultant Richard Killian as executive director. By the end of the year, some 15 of the firm's then–105 partners were cut.

A year later, the firm's compensation system, which had been partly seniority-based, received its own workover: Partners now are expected to meet new, explicitly defined goal for billable hours and business generation—and are paid according to how well they measure up.

At the same time, Asher and other managers have been shaking up the once sleepy Rogers & Wells with lateral hires. Since 1990 six new practice areas have been added—including white-collar criminal defense, antitrust, project finance, and intellectual property—the last by scooping up a 26–lawyer group from the defunct Shea & Gould.

The changes have made their mark. After slogging through the late 1980s with profits per partner of about $300,000, the 400–lawyer Rogers & Wells has been roaring ahead. In 1994, after three years of steady improvement, profits soared by 28 percent over the previous year to $53 million, out of $158 million in gross revenue.

Not surprisingly, the improved numbers are doing wonders for the firm's self-image. "Frankly, we had too many partners who were not practicing up to today's standards," admits corporate department chair David Bernstein, who at 57 is the oldest (and only fully silver-haired) member of the executive committee. "Our reputation was that we were uneven."

"We just made a decision in terms of how we saw ourselves," adds managing partner Asher.

The debate, recalls Asher, who took over as managing partner in 1990, boiled down to "What are we? Are we going to be a top second-tier firm or are we going to be a top-tier firm?"

"The clear consensus," says Asher, "was that we saw ourselves as a firm that ought to be in the top tier, and partners have to fit in with that. If they don't, it doesn't work."

The new hard-nosed management style has had its downside. Virtually all of the 45 partners and expartners and 25 present and past associates interviewed for this story agreed that Rogers & Wells is no longer the homey family-style place it was in the 1980s. Partners and associates say they work harder. And while they insist that collegiality is still strong, even executive committee members Bernstein, Asher, and Laurence Cranch admit that the new performance-based compensation system has led to fighting over credit for clients.

"Its a lot more Darwinian," says one current partner. "You're either a rainmaker or a potential rainmaker," agrees a former Rogers & Wells lawyer, "or you're out the door."

Harsh, perhaps. But Asher, Cranch, and other firm leaders say they're comfortable with the course they've taken—and, indeed, the talk now is of taking profits to an even higher level. So far the new management team has accomplished what it set out to do. The question for the long haul, though, is what price the colder competitive climate will exact on firm unity—and how well the new survival-of-the-fittest culture will hold up.

Generation Gap

* * * The firm Asher and Cranch joined as associates in the mid–1970s was dominated by its two name partners: Rogers, the tall, polished ex-secretary of State, and Jack Wells, the portly, gravelly voiced, cigar-smoking former confidant of New York Republican governor Nelson Rockefeller.

The firm did have an executive committee. But Rogers and Wells picked its members, and when it came to critical decisions such as compensation, the two name partners—along with long-reigning managing partner Caesar Pitassy—largely called the shots.

Back then, Pitassy ran Rogers & Wells without a formal budget, recalls corporate department chair Bernstein. "Caesar did not understand, strangely, about accounting," asserts Bernstein, who still recalls his horror the day he says Pitassy confessed, "Frankly, I don't understand how these capital accounts work."

(Pitassy, now retired, declines to comment, saying only that that assertion is "Mr. Bernsteins opinion.")

By the early 1980s, the firm had a hefty group of junior partners (late thirties, early forties), a heavy concentration of older partners (fifty-and sixty-something), and not much in between. Clearly, a generational clash was waiting to happen. The younger group—including Cranch, Bernstein, and litigator James Weidner—were increasingly frustrated at being shut out of firm governance. After Wells's death in 1980, they began lobbying for a greater say in management. "There was a sense that the firm should be more democratic," recalls Cranch.

In 1983, at the behest of younger partners, Rogers and other senior executive committee members agreed to make half of the committee's six seats elected positions. The same year, a formal budgeting process was put in place for the first time. Two years later, again at the urging of younger partners, Pitassy stepped down as managing partner.

Discontent grew, however. Despite the rainmaking talents of Rogers, profits remained flat through much of the 1980s. A 1984 article in The American Lawyer that dubbed Rogers & Wells as one of "four firms in trouble" drove home the point. According to the article, the average Rogers & Wells partner that year was making roughly $125,000 to $150,000, well below the median of $232,000 at similarly sized New York firms.

Events on the West Coast didn't help relieve any feelings of economic insecurity. Besides trying to stem a steady stream of its defections in its money-losing Los Angeles office, the firm in the mid–1980s also had to battle dozens of suits over the involvement of former San Diego partner Norman Nouskajian in a fraudulent investment scheme cooked up by convicted securities felon J. David Dominelli * * *

The rest of the decade didn't get much easier. Despite further management changes, such as the hiring of the firm's first full-time executive director in 1987, younger partners continued to complain that the firm was not doing enough to boost profits ...

By 1988 rumors of a power struggle were rumbling through the firm, and according to one former partner, that summer, word reached the Los Angeles office that some of the most productive younger partners were threatening to leave unless the partnership was cut.

Both Rogers and four current executive committee members deny there was any such showdown, though all do say that in 1988 the partnership agreement was amended: All members of the executive committee were to be elected; the managing partner would be elected by that committee. By the end of the year younger partners were in control of four of the seven committee seats.

At the same time, the then–75–year-old Rogers agreed to defer to the new majority's management initiatives. And though he retained his seat on the executive committee (as well as the title of chairman of the firm), he soon took a less active role in committee meetings, according to Bernstein, and began phasing out of firm management. Today, seven years later, the stately Rogers maintains that the transition "was not at all difficult.... I think it has worked out exceptionally well."

Executive committee member Cranch, though, recalls that period as a "painful" time. "[Rogers] had gone from being leader of the firm to a situation where he couldn't make all the decisions," says Cranch, who was elected to the executive committee in 1989. "But in the end he was the kind of person who, once he got over that, saw that the most important thing was the firm and that some of the ideas [such as the need to improve productivity] were not bad ideas."

FUTURE SHOCK

The 82–year-old Rogers today retains his corner office at the Met Life building. He still talks of generating new matters, still talks of cases—including a $400 million settlement he won last February on behalf of Italy's Banca Nazionale del Lavoro against the U.S. government—and still holds an emeritus seat on the firm's executive committee.

But there's not much resemblance between the Rogers & Wells of today and the firm he built.

The changes, when they happened, were dramatic. In early 1989, under the newly reconstituted executive committee, Rogers & Wells hired consultant Ronald Cullis of the management consulting firm Pensa (independent of Altman Weil Pensa) to lead its first ever firmwide planning effort. When the process was over, the upshot was clear. A clear majority of partners, claims Asher, were seeking change. They wanted a more select client base, they wanted higher-end business, and they believed the firm had too many unproductive partners.

With the help of newly hired executive director Killian, the executive committee that year reviewed the performance of all the firms partners—including billable hours and business generation. In late 1990, according to Bernstein, roughly 15 of Rogers & Wells's then 105 partners were either forced into early retirement, made of counsel, or asked to leave the firm.

"It was wrenching," recalls litigation department deputy chair James Benedict. "In some cases these were people who had spent a lifetime at the firm."

"It was a soul-searching process," adds Asher, "and implicit in the process was that the firm was going to move in a direction that was going to leave some partners behind."

LATERAL HIRING SPREE

Besides lending support for the cuts, the planning effort, as it turned out, didn't provide much specific guidance for the future. Corporate department chair Bernstein recalls that he and other executive committee members at the time believed the firm needed to rebuild. How to do that was another question.

In 1991 and 1992, in an effort to shore up the firm's struggling Los Angeles office and establish a stronger bicoastal presence, Asher, Bernstein, and then—litigation department chair John Sheehy initiated merger talks with Los Angeles's now-defunct McKenna & Fitting and San Francisco's Orrick, Herrington & Sutcliffe . . .

Corporate department chair Bernstein today claims he's happy the merger talks didn't pan out. The firm has grown well on its own. All told, in fact, Rogers & Wells has picked up some 30 new laterals—almost one-third of its current partnership—and opened offices in Frankfurt and Hong Kong. That growth, though, asserts Asher, has been gradual and carefully targeted.

On the corporate side, both Asher and Bernstein say they're looking to develop greater depth in key practice areas while giving the firm a higher international profile.

For example, partner Roberto Danino, a 1993 arrival from the Washington-based Interamerican Investment Corporation, has helped Rogers & Wells's cross-border finance group develop a stronger Latin American niche, says Asher. The cross-border group last year was among the corporate side's hottest practice areas, he says, generating some $14 million out of total corporate revenue of some $69 million. Among the deals the group handled were a $51 million global offering brought in by Danino, a native Peruvian, on behalf of issuer Banco Wiese in Peru, as well as a $26 million transaction on behalf of Peruvian food processor La Fabril.

* * * On the litigation side, meanwhile, department chair James Weldnet says he has been stressing diversification beyond the firm's traditional financial services client base. Through much of the 1980s and early 1990s, says Weidner, the litigation department had been dependent on securities-related class action suits from Merrill Lynch & Co. Inc. and other financial services clients for as much as half of its work.

Today, however, after an aggressive shopping spree—during which Sheehy and Weidner picked up the white-collar criminal defense, intellectual property, and antitrust groups—the balance is shifting. "It's a much healthier department," asserts Asher, who projects that in the next few years intellectual property, antitrust, and securities litigation will each contribute an equal share of revenue, roughly 80 percent of the department's overall billings.

None of the recent acquisitions, of course, compare to the 26–lawyer intellectual property group from Shea & Gould. "It was," recalls Asher, "the biggest thing we had ever done."

The Shea & Gould lawyers were not exactly short on other offers . . . But Kidd says his group was already on friendly terms with Rogers & Wells, since Nicholas Coch, Kidd's longtime partner at Shea & Gouold, had served in the Navy with Rogers & Wells media partner Richard Winfield. And, Kidd notes, the Rogers & Wells partners who courted him—including Weidner, Bernstein, and Asher—tried hard to be accommodating. For example, unlike several other firms that made offers, recalls Kidd, Rogers & Wells understood that the Shea & Gould partners "wanted to remain as a family" and agreed to take in the entire 26–lawyer intellectual property group.

In addition, says Kidd, department chair Weidner was willing to promise the group autonomy. "At some firms it looked like I was going to be reporting to committee upon committee upon committee," says

Kidd, noting that he instantly related to Weidner's "low-key, jacket off, sleeves rolled up" style.

Kidd admits that Rogers & Wells also threw in a few other important sweeteners—notably the promise that Kidd would immediately be among the firm's highest-paid partners. (Last year, according to two partners, Kidd earned just over a million dollars.)

Asher says that Kidd and his group—whose clients include biotech giant Genentech, Inc. and Pfizer Inc., the New York-based pharmaceutical conglomerate—have more than paid off. In 1994 the intellectual property group pulled in roughly $10 million in billings, according to Asher.

The now–35–lawyer Kidd group brought in another major new client last fall, when E.I. du Pont de Nemours and Company decided to send all its outside intellectual property work to just two firms: Rogers & Wells and New York-based Morgan & Finnegan. Du Pont corporate counsel Barty Estrin says he was impressed by Kidd's willingness to offer financial incentives—such as volume discounts—as well as his inclination to do value billing. "They were a pretty lean and mean operation," Estrin observes.

Growing Pains

While Kidd's group joined the firm with a readymade stable of clients, new antitrust partner Kevin Arquit had no such luxury. Before Arquit arrived in late 1992, Rogers & Wells had only a small antitrust practice, and Arquit, the former head of the Federal Trade Commission's Bureau of Competition, came in with no clients.

Under the 40–year-old Arquit, however, the antitrust group has since landed matters from Johnson & Johnson, The SherwinWilliams Company, and the Major League Baseball Players Association, among other big-name clients, and now boasts some 30 lawyers. Last year the antitrust practice generated roughly $5 million in billings, according to Asher, and is on track for at least double that amount this year.

Arquit, for his part, credits Rogers & Wells, noting that Weidner and other executive committee members were willing to let him spend almost his entire first year attending seminars and making speeches to build the practice up. According to Asher, Arquit logged just 700 billable hours in his first ten months at the firm. "There's not many places that would be willing to put that much capital up front," says the personable, all-American-looking Arquit, pulling out a stack of speeches and promotional materials to make his point. "Here they said, 'Don't worry about it. Do what you think needs to be done.' Now I'm buried in real work."

The antitrust group has also been bringing in work for other Rogers & Wells lawyers. When Sherwin–Williams was looking for a mergers and acquisitions specialist earlier this year, senior corporate counsel Richard Legenza says he called Arquit for a referral. Arquit recommended Rogers & Wells partner John Healy—leading to the firms representation of

Sherwin–Williams in its recent (ultimately unsuccessful) attempt to acquire New York-based paint manufacturer Grow Group, Inc.

Besides opening new cross-selling opportunities, the new antitrust and intellectual property groups are also helping the firm's once-dominant litigation department get back on more equal footing with the corporate side. If projected collections hold up, litigation will have pulled in roughly $61 million in revenue last year, according to Asher, while corporate work will have contributed roughly $69 million, thanks to a strong year in real estate investment trust and derivatives work, as well as cross-border finance.

Not all of the firm's lateral hiring has been perfect, however. After a rash of defections, the once–45–lawyer Los Angeles office shrank to about 15 lawyers by 1993 and had so much extra space, say two former lawyers, that associates had taken over partners' offices . . .

The situation in L.A. certainly got no better in late 1993, when a long-time client, insurance giant Chubb & Son Inc., quit the firm. The company's departure, says one current partner, came after Chubb claimed that Rogers & Wells had overbilled. One former partner says he understood the overcharge to be between $1 million and $2 million—a figure that one executive committee member says is "not dimensionally wrong."

. . . Asher allows that the L.A. office had been handling a "significant amount" of the company's work—and says L.A. "continues to be a thorn in our side." Closing the now–25–lawyer L.A. office has been an ongoing topic of discussion, according to Asher. But he says the firm is now intent on using L.A. (along with a new Hong Kong outpost) as the base for a new project finance group. In May Rogers & Wells signed on project finance specialist John Forry (a former partner at Morgan, Lewis) for the Los Angeles office, and this summer dispatched New York corporate partner Jonn Keitt, Jr., to manage the L.A. office in an effort to bolster ties with New York.

"We've tried so hard out there," says former executive committee member John Christian, "that we don't want to give up."

Performance Counts

If there's any doubt that Rogers & Wells today has moved in a different direction, one has only to look at the firm's entirely revamped compensation system. In contrast to the old system, under which Rogers and other executive committee members would mete out partner draws based on a loose mix of seniority and performance, the current system leaves no question about who will be most handsomely compensated. To put it simply, performance counts. And if partners hope to take home all the dollars for which they are eligible, they'd better perform up to expectations.

The new compensation scheme combines a range of base salaries with "performance units." Partners are now divided among five levels, depending on their expected contributions to the firm, and receive a fixed number of base points, determined by their level, each year. Last year, for example, level one partners had 6 base points, worth $42,000 each; level five partners had 15.5 base points. To earn a greater share of profits—through "performance units" (also worth $42,000 each last year)—partners must meet the billing and business generation goals the executive committee sets for each level. The committee, says Asher, also factors in client servicing and "profitability"—realization and leverage— in awarding performance units.

Last year, a level two partner, with 8.25 base points worth about $346,500, would have needed $1.7 million in business origination credit and 1,950 billable hours to receive an additional 2.25 performance points worth $94,500. To meet their targets—and thereby earn 2.75 performance units worth $115,500—level four partners would have had to bring in $4 million in business and tally up 1,700 billable hours. The firm's eight level five partners were also expected to bill 1,700 hours, in addition to bringing in $5.5 million in new business—a feat that would have earned them 3.25 performance units worth $136,500.

Asher claims that four of the eight level five partners substantially exceeded their goals last year, and thereby earned a total of nine performance units each. Those four, according to two current partners, were Asher, litigation chair Weidnor, cross-border group head Cranch, and Kidd, the intellectual property head. Each brought home just over $1 million last year.

Depending on an individual partner's level and earnings the previous year, says Asher, his or her compensation could theoretically go up or down by nearly $400,000 in a given year—although Asher points out that such extreme swings are unlikely.

Given the new emphasis on hard numbers, it's no surprise that when the executive committee unveiled the system in 1992, partners didn't exactly warm to it. "Everyone was terrified," recalls retired partner Joseph Levie.

"Was there universal acceptance? No, there wasn't universal acceptance," allows executive committee member Weidnor. Still, Weidner and other firm leaders claim that the new system is immeasurably fairer, since all partners are now fully aware of what they must do to earn their keep, and since it gives partners at the lowest level the potential almost to double their pay.

Firm leaders also note that the new system takes an expansive view of what constitutes business generation. Thus partners get credit for bringing in new matters from existing clients as well as for bringing in new clients. That approach, they say, is supposed to discourage hoarding of clients, since when it comes to assigning credit for new business, both the "lead client contact," the partner in charge of the client, and the "matter generator," the partner who brought in the new work, receive equal credit. That means that on a piece of business worth $500,000, for example, both partners would get $500,000 counted toward business generation. "It gives every incentive for other partners to get involved," says executive committee member James Benedict.

Younger partners particularly benefit, adds Weidner, since, while they "might not have time to go out and beat the bushes for new clients," they can earn business development credit and performance points just for generating new matters from existing clients.

The new system, claim Weidner and other executive committee members, has proven to be an effective carrot. "It's amazing," says Cranch. "It really does motivate people to go out and sell."

One 35–year-old partner who racked up about $3.8 million in billings—and took home roughly $500,000 last year—agrees. Unlike many other firms, where junior lawyers might spend years paying dues, this partner says hungry younger partners at Rogers & Wells can make a swift climb up the earnings scale. "It's pretty impressive that you can do it here so quickly," he adds.

While managing partner Asher says that it's difficult to measure the direct impact of the new compensation scheme, he claims that Rogers & Wells today is a markedly more entrepreneurial place. In contrast to the 1980s, when Rogers alone accounted for more than a third of the business, Asher contends that now more than half of the firm's partners generate over a million dollars of business a year. Forty percent, he says, bring in more than $2 million in business annually.

A NECESSARY EVIL?

The new system does have its drawbacks, however.

With compensation so closely tied to business generation, even the biggest boosters of the new system admit that partners have become more territorial in regard to clients and that there is much more bickering over how credit is assigned. Big clients such as Merrill Lynch, which accounted for about a tenth of Rogers & Wells's $158 million in business last year, have been particularly problematic, according to one partner, because there are often several partners who handle various aspects of those clients' work.

"If you have a transaction that comes in with two different parts [such as tax and corporate], where does that really come from?" asks this partner. "One partner will say it came in because of me. Another will say it came under me. You can't very well go ask the client. There are inevitably fights about who brought it in. It only gets worse when there are three people involved."

One former partner also claims that members of the firm became so focused on earning business credit that when partners brought in a new matter it was often a challenge to find help. "People began negotiating whether they would work on your matters based on if they would get credit," he says. "It came down to negotiating fee splits."

Cranch admits that he sometimes worries that in promoting entrepreneurialism the firm has gone too far. For example, he says that he has seen partners making a pitch to clients and wondered, "Why didn't they include So-and-So" in the sales effort?" and "Why did they play it so close to the vest?"

"It's not," he says, "what we'd like to see our partners doing."

Rogers & Wells has been trying to address the problem. Cranch notes that earlier this year he and corporate department head Bernstein talked informally to partners to promote more teamwork. He also says the executive committee last year announced that it will begin factoring such hard-to-quantify phenomena as team spirit and general cooperation into its compensation decisions—and will be further reviewing the compensation system this fall to see how it can be improved. But, Cranch adds, more competition is probably a "necessary evil" in the drive to get more partners to produce business.

Cranch may be right about that. Yet it's still not clear how the new more cutthroat environment will affect firm unity over the long haul—especially now that there are so many new laterals at the firm.

One former lawyer, for instance, claims that the Washington, D.C., office had so many new arrivals in the past few years that partners there had little idea who all their colleagues were. "They would ask me, 'Who is So-and-So and who is So-and-So?'" this lawyer recalls. "Each of the little groups just didn't need to talk to each other. There was no cohesion whatsoever." Asher agrees that the D.C. office in particular had to absorb a lot of new laterals in a short time, but says the office is now coming together.

Few would dispute that Rogers & Wells, which has grown from 265 lawyers to 400 lawyers in the past five years, has become a more impersonal place. "There used to be going-away parties for everybody," says one partner. "Now you don't even know when somebody's left until the departure memo comes around." Nor do partnership meetings appear to be an occasion for much bonding. "The idea of a good partners meeting here is if nobody asks a question and you're in and out in fifteen minutes," says another partner, in a typical comment.

This partner claims that the firm's new leaders, after having pushed for greater democracy while Rogers was in charge, are now keeping decision-making power in a relatively small number of hands. Even executive committee member Mark Pomerantz (head of the white-collar criminal practice) agrees that Rogers & Wells "is not all that democratic. "It's not a real-free-for-all," says Pomerantz, who asserts that for the most part the executive committee and the managing partner make the decisions and "the partners have tended to go along."

Weidner, though, maintains there is still "a strong glue holding the partnership together." And while he agrees that the firm is not as homey as it used to be, he claims the improvements have been worth the price.

For one thing, asserts corporate partner David Bernstein, there has been a marked upgrading of Rogers & Wells's lawyers. "It used to be that anyone around here for eight years was likely to become a partner, and why not," says Bernstein. Now, says corporate partner Robert King, the litmus test for new partners is, "Are they capable of being a brand name in their field?"

A Repeat Performance

Asher agrees that standards for all lawyers at the firm are tougher. And that's not likely to change. Indeed, Asher claims that, having surpassed the $500,000 per-partner profit mark, Rogers & Wells is now out to reach $650,000 profits per partner by 1998. Getting there won't be easy. Since executive director Killian's arrival in 1990, the firm has cut support staff by some 10 percent, according to Asher. Many of those cuts, including a wholesale firing of the proofreading department, are said to be taking a toll. "It's ridiculous," scoffs one former associate, who claims secretaries are now covering phones for up to five attorneys. "You spend a lot of time having to track down who the hell took your message."

Asher, while insisting that the cuts on the whole have made Rogers & Wells more efficient, does say that squeezing out more savings will be difficult. Nor will new revenue be easy to come by. The cross-border group, which accounted for 20 percent of the corporate department revenue last year, has seen business slow considerably since the fall of the Mexican peso last year. And corporate partner and former executive committee member John Christian contends that "it will be virtually impossible" for the cross-border group to match last year's record results.

The litigation side is also facing a slowdown, now that one mammoth matter for Merrill Lynch, the Guaranteed Security Life Insurance Company case, recently settled * * *

Asher agrees that the firm this year will be hard-pressed to repeat last year's record performance. "If we can equal last year, I think we will have done well," he says. But he notes that the firm is not abandoning its new goal of $650,000 profits per partner. To get there, says Asher, Rogers & Wells, among other things, is now seeking to build on recent deal work for Sherwin–Williams and German chemical and pharmaceutical conglomerate E. Merck and build up a new transactional practice.

"Clearly we're not Wachtell or Skadden," says Asher. He adds, though, that because Rogers & Wells does not have the luxury of having one or two huge institutional clients, the firm now has a "strong entrepreneurial group of partners. "We've had to scrap and fight for all our transactional practice," says Asher, who claims that entrepreneurialism is helping Rogers & Wells build a name.

In fact, Rogers & Wells did earn several mentions in this year's "Corporate Scorecard," a ranking compiled by The American Lawyer of firms involved in the biggest M & As, bankruptcies, and stock and bond issues in 1994. Corporate partner Christian concedes, though, that the firm is currently "involved in few of the major deals" and still "has a way to go."

In the meantime, the big question is how well this new entrepreneurial assemblage of partners will hold together.

One former partner, noting the huge influx of laterals, points out that any number of groups at the firm could survive as independent profit centers. "At the end of the day, there's not much of an institutional presence," asserts this former partner, who says he wonders if the desire to increase profits is the only real common denominator at the firm.

Even Christian allows that the identity of the firm has changed, but he claims the "partnership is pulling together." He concedes that that's "easy when things are going well." Yet he says he's convinced Rogers & Wells has "done the right thing" in overhauling its culture. "We wanted the firm to be better," agrees partner Peter Williams. "It's clearly what we've done."

The new hard-nosed approach to profitability may strike some as ruthless. But, as partner Paul Hopkins suggests, it's only a reflection of a harsher marketplace. After all, shrugs Hopkins, "it ain't the fifties."

John E. Morris, THE NEW WORLD ORDER

THE AMERICAN LAWYER, August, 1999

The normally contained Larry Cranch becomes animated as he describes the sensation of rowing his scull on the lake near his weekend home in Pennsylvania. Tennis and running are fine, but Cranch, the managing partner of New York's Rogers & Wells, lives for that feeling of gliding across the water. It's best when a light breeze ripples the water; you feel like you're moving faster, explains Cranch, a short, compact man with the gaunt look of the compulsive athlete. There's just one problem: He has to get on the lake at the crack of dawn, before the water-skiers arrive.

It's an apt metaphor for his firm. After drifting in the 1980s, a wrenching turnaround in the early 1990s set the firm back on course. It has cruised on a steady heading since, with profits up each year. But with a strong international focus, 40 percent of its work is for foreign clients or for U.S. clients overseas, the 400–lawyer firm was always at risk of being swamped, if not sunk, in the wake of bigger competitors.

"We thought of ourselves as a global law firm and had an international focus," Cranch explains. Rogers & Wells has offices in London, Paris, Frankfurt, and Hong Kong. But, he says, for the best international work, "we found it harder and harder to compete with the Clifford Chances of the world."

Cranch won't have to compete with Clifford Chance anymore. On July 9–10 he and his partners overwhelmingly approved a January 1 merger with the 2,050–lawyer London firm, which they hope will become the leading global law firm, a $1 billion leviathan with more lawyers and a better reputation than Baker & McKenzie, more corporate finance depth than White & Case, and far more depth in the U.S. than its big

U.K. competitors. Add 262–lawyer P nder, Volhard, Weber & Axster, one of Germany's top five firms, which is finalizing details to make it a three-way merger, and Clifford Chance will have clout in all four of the world's biggest financial centers: New York, London, Frankfurt, and Hong Kong.

It took 14 months to put the Rogers & Wells deal together and get it approved. There were issues of culture and expectations. "I think people have a hypothetical image of their bride. But when your bride comes along, she doesn't always look like your image," says Stuart Popham, head of Clifford Chance's finance practice, summing up his partners' first reactions to the news that management was talking to Rogers & Wells. "But then you realize that the bride is attractive. It is a firm I'd known for years, but it was not necessarily the one I would have thought of."

There were client conflicts issues, among other things, and there were issues of compensation, with Clifford Chance's lockstep firm pitted against Rogers & Wells's eat-what-you-kill scheme. But the firms think they've finessed that issue, one that is often cited as a barrier to a big Anglo-American merger, with a simple compromise. Rogers & Wells partners will merge into the English lockstep, except that a handful of key Americans will be eligible for extra partnership units that could boost their pay to more than twice what top Clifford Chance partners make. The merger is not the one that Clifford Chance and other London firms have fantasized about, with a first-tier New York firm like Sullivan & Cromwell or Davis Polk & Wardwell. But it may be the only deal that can be done today. Partners at the two firms hope that, with their shared client base of financial institutions, they will get the jump in the race to globalize the law business, while wedging their way into the top ranks of New York firms. Here's the story of the deal of the year.

It is a match of two born-again firms. Clifford Chance itself was the product of a 1987 merger between two second-tier London firms. The firm has been on an unrelenting quest to make itself global ever since, sacrificing profits through much of the 1990s to build a network of offices across Europe, Asia, South America, and the United States.

The strategy has paid off on the bottom line in the last several years: Profits are sharply up, and the firm is far ahead of its English rivals in international reach. Rogers & Wells, meanwhile, had spent the 1990s instilling an entrepreneurial ethos among partners and building a phenomenally successful antitrust practice from scratch.

The two firms crossed paths almost by chance in March 1998, when Cranch flew to San Francisco to speak about Rogers & Wells's turn-around. Another speaker, Stephen Hood, then the head of Clifford Chance's New York office, took note as Cranch trotted out one statistic after another, charting the firm's financial improvement. For three years Hood had been pondering how to beef up his firm's American practice. "I sat there listening to Larry Cranch ... and I began to think that I hadn't paid enough attention to this firm," says Hood.

At a dinner for the panelists that night, Hood introduced himself to Cranch. Walking back to their hotel afterward, the two compared their firms' strategic challenges. For Rogers & Wells, they were overseas. "The investments that were required to really make our international practice viable weren't really possible," says Cranch, unless partners settled for much lower profits. And key partners were pushing to refocus the firm on its domestic practice. Clifford Chance, meanwhile, had been struggling to make inroads in the U.S. market. It had three dozen lawyers practicing American securities law, but "we'd run up against the incredible resistance from the New York firms to our doing anything beyond 144A private securities offerings," says Hood. "There were incredible scare stories fed to clients. To get beyond that was going to be very difficult." It would take a merger with an American firm, he had concluded, for his firm to win SEC-registered deals.

Neither of the men explicitly mentioned a merger that evening. But they caught each other's drift. "When you get back to New York, 'we should have lunch,' " Hood recalls Cranch saying. "I said, Larry, I think we should." Actually, it was breakfast. In early April, Hood met Cranch and Rogers & Wells's executive director, Richard Killian, at the Sky Club atop the Metropolitan Life Building, where Rogers & Wells is located. Killian "was pretty tough in terms of questioning the strategy and whether it was doable," recalls Hood. But the meeting was positive. "Within two or three weeks ... I told Larry and Dick that we have enough interest, and we're not talking to anyone else," says Hood. "I wanted the same assurance from them, and they gave it to me."

Soon Keith Clark, Clifford Chance's senior partner (chairman, in American parlance), came to New York, and he and Hood met with Killian again. Only a few partners on either side knew about the talks, which they soon dubbed "Project Water." Project Water didn't begin to bubble until July, however, when practice group leaders, about ten partners from each firm, assembled in New York to see how their groups might fit. Corporate finance was the rationale for the merger. But partners discovered other possible synergies. Rogers & Wells has an extremely successful antitrust practice, which would dovetail with Clifford Chance's M & A and competition practices in Europe. And clients would benefit from worldwide advice about their intellectual property rights from a single firm. More surprisingly, there even seemed to be potential in litigation, where antitrust, securities, and regulatory cases increasingly spill across borders.

In the meetings and over dinner at La Cote Basque, the partners found themselves quite comfortable with one another. So far, so good, but things moved slowly after the July meeting. Clifford Chance's executive committee had other things on its mind, namely, merger talks with firms in Germany and Australia. They hadn't expected to do a U.S. merger so soon, and were focused on the other moves, according to Hood, who was frustrated because he felt the U.S. market deserved to be the top priority.

Building The Business Case Three more months went by before there was another major meeting. By that point, both sides had appointed negotiating teams. On the American side, it consisted of executive director Killian and five partners: Robert King, Jr., a young corporate partner who had risen to the upper ranks in compensation; John Healy, an English-born M & A lawyer; Richard McDermott, a senior corporate lawyer; John Carroll, a litigator who specializes in white-collar and regulatory defense; and David Moldenhauer, a young international tax specialist. Healy and Killian took the lead.

On the English side, the lineup was: COO Garth Pollard; litigator Christopher Perrin; M & A partner Jeremy Brownlow; Michael Bray, a banking lawyer; and Kevin Geary, the firm's nonlawyer head of business development. Taking the lead were Bray and Pollard, both of whom had hands-on roles in putting together the Coward Chance–Clifford Turner merger in 1987 that created Clifford Chance. That track record reassured Rogers & Wells partners. "The fact that they had done that gave these guys a lot of credibility in my eyes," says McDermott. The heads of the two firms, Cranch and Clark (another veteran of the 1987 merger), took backseats.

There was no shortage of issues to be settled if the two firms were to be combined: who would run the firm, how profits would be divided, how to resolve client conflicts, what the name should be, and what a partnership agreement should look like. But both sides wanted to focus first on whether there was a good business case for a merger and whether the firms were culturally compatible.

After the July meeting, they exchanged lists of their 100 biggest clients, and were surprised to see how similar their businesses were. Both lists were dominated by financial services firms, and there was an enviable roster of bank clients that they shared: The Chase Manhattan Corporation; Citigroup Inc.; Merrill Lynch & Co., Inc.; and Morgan Stanley Dean Witter & Co. The negotiating teams sat down together for the first time at the end of October and explored more systematically what a merged firm would look like. In a three-day session at the Hyatt Regency in Greenwich, Connecticut, they began to see in more detail what they thought were true synergies, areas where the merged firm would be able to attract business neither firm could alone.

In litigation, for instance, "we are very strong on the regulatory side," says Clifford Chance litigator Perrin. "We've increasingly found that the large problems that arise ... tend to be international, the same issue is generally investigated in other jurisdictions." His firm also has a large international arbitration practice, which should fit with the commercial litigation practice in the U.S. On the other side, Rogers & Wells litigator John Carroll had seen an ever-growing share of his work coming from foreign clients, so he was enthusiastic about a merger. They also found that their average profits per partner were much closer than they first thought when they factored in differences in accounting methods.

A detailed discussion of compensation was put off. But they reached agreement on one point right away: There should be just one profit pool. Clifford Chance partners saw that as essential to integrating the operations. That was fine with the Americans, whose Paris office is a separate profit center. "Nobody was happy with that," says Healy. Beyond the substance, the meeting also helped both sides move past stereotypes and fears about culture clashes: The Brits were not too stuffy and the Yanks not too pushy. Some of the Americans were worried that Rogers & Wells would simply be swallowed up by a London-centered giant. But Bray allayed those fears. Clifford Chance was exploring possible mergers with large firms in Australia and Germany, too, he explained. Inevitably, Clifford Chance would have to change itself, Bray assured them. No concrete agreements emerged from Greenwich, but it was a turning point for both sides. "It was from that meeting on that I really became convinced that this would really produce benefits," says Perrin, the Clifford Chance litigator.

MONEY TALKS

That meant they had to tackle compensation in earnest. Rogers & Wells's system was merit-based with a vengeance. Ninety percent of compensation is allocated according to a formula, based on billings, collections, client origination, and hours worked. Even among American firms, it was on the each-partner-for-himself end of the scale, and left unusually little room for discretionary adjustments. Moreover, the spread from top to bottom was wide. The highest-paid partner, antitrust maven Kevin Arquit, took home $2.3 million in 1998, about eight times the $290,000 that first-year partners drew.

Clifford Chance is much more egalitarian, with the spread from $430,000 to $1.1 million. There partners move up the ladder quickly, so they top out early in their careers. And switching to an American-style system wasn't an option for them. "As a firm, we're very wedded to lockstep," says Hood, the partner who launched the talks last year. "It's a very emotional issue." Fortunately for Clifford Chance, there was widespread dissatisfaction at Rogers & Wells with its formula. "It's a system that has served us well over the last seven or eight or nine years," says corporate partner McDermott. "But ... it has its shortcomings. It can put strain on the institutional glue." At times, partners were forced to horse-trade credits to get their matters staffed, litigator Carroll recounts: "You've got a big litigation and you need three partners, and you have to pay them to do that."

One of the appeals of the merger, Cranch says, was that it would force a change in the compensation system. Clifford Chance indicated early on that it would discuss modifying its lockstep, as long as it remained essentially intact. But it was one thing to be open-minded, another to reach agreement on the specifics. To bridge the gap, the firms had to figure out what to do with the Rogers & Wells partners who made much more than the top-paid people under Clifford Chance's scheme, most notably, Arquit and Steven Newborn, who head up the antitrust practice and who each drew more than $2 million last year. The group is on track to take in $60 million in revenue this year, and there is only one other partner in the group, so the firm could ill-afford to have these two walk.

The issue came to a head at the next meeting, December 10–12, at the Cannizaro House, an inn on large, grassy grounds in Wimbledon, outside London, where the two teams spent the first day in frustrating talks. At several points, discussions broke off so the negotiators could cool off by walking the grounds. The Americans thought they were getting nowhere. But after breaking for the night, the Rogers & Wells lawyers started to feel that the two sides weren't that far apart, Killian says.

The next day they returned and went through Clifford Chance's last proposal step by step and came to agreement on the fundamentals of a new, hybrid compensation process. The plan was simple at its core: Almost all Rogers & Wells partners will switch over to the Clifford Chance lockstep. They will be ranked based on seniority, past perform-ance, and historical compensation, so they won't necessarily be at the same level as Clifford Chance partners of the same seniority. But high-paid Americans who would lose out even at the top of the Clifford Chance ladder, five to eight partners if the switchover were made this past year, will be eligible for "additional units," and could make up to two-and-a-half times what a partner does at the top of the lockstep.

Thus, if the system had been in place last year, when partners at the top of Clifford Chance's lockstep made almost $1.1 million, top American partners could in theory have drawn up to $2.5 million, conveniently, just about what Arquit made. In addition to Arquit and Newborn, the candidates would include corporate partner L. Martin Gibbs (who earned $1.4 million in 1998), IP heavyweight John Kidd ($1.3 million), negotiat-ing team member and corporate partner King ($1.2 million), litigator James Benedict and Cranch (both $1.1 million), and possibly German specialist Klaus Jander ($1 million). "It's a relatively small number of people," says Bray. "That reflects the realities of the New York market."

Rogers & Wells suggested that partners in all offices be eligible for the extra units, but Clifford Chance partners wanted the exceptions to their cherished lockstep limited to the U.S. The switch will take place over a 28–month transition period, during which the former Rogers & Wells partners will get a pool of partnership units, slotting themselves into the lockstep and moving up and down as they see fit. Over time, partners' positions should converge toward their future lockstep levels.

Management on both sides insists that the Americans can be shifted to lockstep without goring anyone's ox. "We're comfortable from the models we've constructed that we can do that without disadvantaging anyone at Rogers & Wells, or diluting people elsewhere in the firm," says Clifford Chance managing partner Anthony Williams. (The drafters labored to avoid a separate profit center or incentives that would benefit one part of the firm over another. Thus the number of units assigned to the old Rogers & Wells partners will be fixed at the outset, and their side's profit will rise and fall with the entire firm's.)

A fortuitous accounting twist will help smooth the switch. Rogers & Wells, which has used cash-basis accounting, booking income only when it is received, will switch to Clifford Chance's accrual bookkeeping. Because partners keep the profits accrued by their respective firms through December 31, Rogers & Wells partners will catch up on past profits and get a modest bonus. "Inventory will move into income," as Killian puts it. Then into partners' pockets.

Partners will have to take much on trust. The inch-and-a-half-thick prospectus handed out just before the July 4 holiday weekend laid out only the broad mechanism; it didn't say who will make how much. Even Arquit says he doesn't know what he will make. In London, the hope is that with time the American partners will change the way they look at compensation. "Their practice going forward is going to be much less dependent on the individual partners and their client base," says Hood. "It will be a much more institutional client base." And there are hints of an attitude shift already: You can't talk to a Rogers & Wells partner these days without hearing the word "platform", the new "platform" they will have to attract business, and the "platform" to attract talent. It's a term that focuses attention on what the individual derives from the institution. The more the Americans think like that, the easier it will be to appreciate lockstep.

Before the Wimbledon proposal could get to a vote, however, management needed to woo some key players. Gibbs, Rogers & Wells's third-highest-paid partner, was initially skeptical of lockstep. And Arquit, the antitrust head, was a problem. He had been lobbying to refocus the firm domestically. He was concerned about client conflicts in a bigger firm, and he worried that in a huge firm he wouldn't be able to run a conflicts check at any hour of the day or night, as he sometimes has to in quick-moving mergers. As the highest-paid partner, he also had the most to lose in a lockstep pay system.

Michael Bray from Clifford Chance took a stab at bringing Arquit around. The two met over dinner at Bobby Van's steakhouse in New York in December, a few weeks after the Wimbledon meetings. There Arquit outlined his concerns. "I think that was where my thinking changed," says Arquit. "When you don't know people, you look for little signs. He conveys the strong sense that he's thought things through." One factor that tipped the balance: Arquit's group refers millions of dollars of antitrust work every year to English and European firms, most of which could be kept within the merged firm. Gibbs, too, got over his concerns: "I asked, 'What incentive do you have in lockstep?'" Then I found the answer: a lot of peer pressure.... I'm impressed with their lockstep because their people seem very hardworking ... and motivated."

On the other side, Clifford Chance convened an all-partners meeting in January where the merger, including the deviation from lockstep, was outlined in some detail. Some partners were unhappy about paying the Americans outside the lockstep. Some sniffed at their betrothed. "A lot of them had heard of Rogers & Wells," says Hood. "But the knee-jerk reaction was, We're one of the top two or three firms in London. Why aren't we merging with one of the top two or three firms in New York?" Others were upset that they might not be able to work with their usual New York firms, which refer them work. But at the end, the partners voted to move forward.

Meanwhile, the negotiators were hammering out technical details such as the partnership agreements and tax structures. And the slow process of conflicts checking was moving forward. Because Clifford Chance has no litigation practice in the U.S., there were few direct conflicts. And, because so much of the firms' business comes from financial institutions, which typically use multiple firms and don't object to their firms working for competitors, there were relatively few business conflicts. But there was one difficult client conflict: an intellectual property case of John Kidd's, Rogers & Wells's chief IP rainmaker, where Clifford Chance had a noncourtroom role on the other side. (Both firms are tight-lipped about details of the case, including the clients.) And the talks dragged out, which worried Rogers & Wells, because word of them had leaked to the press after the Clifford Chance partners meeting.

The Americans told the British that things had to move faster. "We felt exposed in the marketplace," says Killian. There was the danger of "a zillion headhunters trying to destabilize the partnership," says one partner. But the talks were further complicated when Punder, Volhard popped up on the scene. The Frankfurt-based firm had had informal discussions with several British and American firms last year, but it was only at a partners meeting in April that the Germans resolved to seek an Anglo–Saxon partner. Clifford Chance's talks with Rogers & Wells piqued the Germans' interest. "Our firm was split on whether to pursue a U.S. or a U.K. firm," says Peter Nagele, Punder's co-managing partner who favored an American connection. "When Clifford Chance spoke of hooking up in a tripartite merger, it was the best of all possible worlds for us."

By the full partnership votes in July, enough details had been settled with the Germans that the British and American partners were able to vote in principle on that as well as giving final approval to their bilateral merger. In a stroke of luck, by the time of the partners' votes, the IP case that created the toughest conflict had settled as a result of a corporate reorganization. They approved a merger for January 1, after which the firm will be known as Clifford Chance worldwide, except in the U.S., where it will be Clifford Chance Rogers & Wells, and in Germany, where it will be Clifford Chance Punder. The top three management positions will go to the British. Clark will head the firm, his title changed to chairman; Pollard will remain as COO; and Bray will become CEO. Cranch will be managing partner for the Americas, and James Benedict, the deputy chair of Rogers & Wells's litigation department, will head the worldwide litigation practice. Williams, who had been managing partner of the British firm, will return to practice.

Can 2 + 2 = 5? The two firms are betting that clients, particularly financial institutions, want one-stop shopping for legal advice around the world, and that the firm will be able to increase their market share by offering that before competitors can. Clients confirm that it's a good idea in principle.

Michael Ross, deputy general counsel of Citigroup in New York, cites a recent syndicated loan that posed legal issues in the U.S., Mexico, Spain, Holland, and the Cayman Islands. "Having one firm able to operate in all those jurisdictions is attractive," says Ross, whose bank has used both firms. Similarly, a Clifford Chance Rogers & Wells-like firm would have an edge with The Prudential Insurance Company of America for international "real estate merchant banking" and private equity work, says its general counsel, John Liftin, a former Rogers & Wells partner, even though Rogers & Wells hasn't done much work for the company.

Having depth in both English and American law under one roof would be an advantage in many deals where it isn't clear at the beginning which law will be most advantageous, says William McDavid, general counsel of Chase Manhattan Corporation, another mutual client. If you start with English lawyers, they'll lean toward English law, he complains, while an American firm has a stake in using New York law.

But Rogers & Wells, despite its many bank clients, is not a major player in corporate finance in the U.S. Only in a few niches, mutual fund work, real estate investment trusts, and derivatives, is it among the top firms. And clients make it clear that they aren't going to switch their prime cross-border assignments to the merged firm just because it has more American lawyers. After all, Rogers & Wells is not a powerhouse securities or M & A firm. "It's a question of getting comfortable, and our investment banking committee getting comfortable with the quality of Rogers & Wells, or any other U.S. firms that ties up with an English firm," says a client at one major investment bank. On the M & A side, Rogers & Wells is even weaker than in securities, handling very few large mergers. "We wouldn't necessarily go to Rogers & Wells for a cross-border M & A transaction," says one client.

The firms acknowledge they will need to beef up their American practice. "In an ideal world, we would have liked a big swinging corporate group," says Hood. They say they will probably look for lateral partners in New York in M & A, high-yield bonds, and restructuring. They contend that the combined firm, the new platform, will be much more appealing to top candidates. So the synergies are unlikely to be realized immediately. "I don't think it's anything that the rest of us need to fall on our swords about," says Ned Stiles, chairman of New York's Cleary, Gottlieb, Steen & Hamilton.

Aside from the challenge of winning over the clients, there will be internal issues. Just making the gargantuan institution function will be a challenge. Management will be spread thin over the next year with a three-way merger, and rank-and-file partners will be forced to adapt to big changes. (Australia is on the back burner.) And it remains to be seen if the compromise on compensation will retain the top stars on the American side. Will English, German, French, and Hong Kong partners be willing to shell out what it takes to keep the likes of Arquit and Newborn if business slows? Or will they decide in the end that they can afford to sacrifice a few partners to preserve the concept of their lockstep? (Partners in Rogers & Wells's Paris office are planning to split off before the merger, but the firms say that will not hurt because Clifford Chance has a large French practice. Two other partners left in June, apparently for reasons unrelated to the merger.)

For outside observers, the most interesting question is how competitors, particularly Clifford Chance's three big, internationally minded London competitors, Allen & Overy, Freshfields, and Linklaters & Alliance, will respond. Will they continue to add American lawyers incrementally, despite Clifford Chance's huge lead in the U.S.? Or will they try to pull off a similar merger?

Alan Hodgart, a London-based consultant with Hildebrandt International, says that at the moment, the only firm that would deliver the New York-based securities practice they want and that might consider a merger appears to be Brown & Wood, which was in merger talks with White & Case earlier this year. But a deal with a firm like that might make it impossible to merge with a first-tier Wall Street firm later, he says. The other London firms profess not to be concerned. "How many top European firms are there going to be?" asks Tony Angel, managing partner of Linklaters & Paines, who seems to be waiting for that ideal bride. "Clifford Chance has chosen its partner. . . .

The interesting thing to see is whether this changes the views of the major Wall Street firms about merging themselves. "Plainly, it remains for Clifford Chance and Rogers & Wells to demonstrate that they really can deliver what clients want on a global scale." But there is no shortage of ambition. "We'd like to be, if not in the Magic Circle in New York in five years, at least knocking at the door," says Stuart Popham, the head of Clifford Chance's finance group, borrowing the term for the top five London firms. "No, we'd like to be in the Magic Circle." That's a tall order. The world is filled with law firms that aspire to move upmarket. But, if Popham's aim sounds implausible, consider this: His firm was born of a merger 12 years ago of two firms that were outside the inner circle of top-tier firms. No one questions that they are in London's Magic Circle today.

Krysten Crawford, A MARRIAGE OF CONVENIENCE

THE AMERICAN LAWYER, November, 2001

Standing in a conference room high above Manhattan's Grand Central Terminal last May, James Benedict tried to mollify his partners. "Lockstep," he told them, "isn't communism." To the assembled former

Rogers & Wells partners, it might as well have been. Nearly 18 months had passed since their merger with London's Clifford Chance, but only now were they coming to grips with an end to their eat-what-you-kill compensation system.

Benedict, the newly ensconced head of Clifford Chance's U.S. operations and himself a former Rogers & Wells partner, knew that his colleagues were anxious. They had indicated as much during a retreat in late March. Although the official transition to Clifford Chance's lockstep, seniority-based pay model wasn't scheduled to occur until spring 2002, their concern was understandable. Rogers & Wells, with its roots in the insurance morass that grew out of the great Chicago fire of 1871, had been a ruthless meritocracy, rewarding partners based on individual contributions to the bottom line.

Although Clifford Chance and Rogers & Wells shared comparable profitability at the time of their merger, there was a big difference in the spread between the highest-and lowest-paid partners at the two firms. Switching to the British model would mean compressing Rogers & Wells's pay scale. In theory, that meant that some American stars were facing steep pay cuts, while some lesser lights would more than double their draws. Everyone knew that that wouldn't work. Something had to give.

On May 17, it did. Benedict, in his address to roughly 100 partners in New York, described a series of complex changes to the lockstep model. Most Rogers & Wells partners would move into compensation levels based on several factors, seniority being just one of them. But even at the top of Clifford Chance's lockstep, as many as eight high performers would end up taking pay cuts (in Benedict's case, by about half). A tiny group most likely including antitrust partners Kevin Arquit and Steven Newborn, would continue to be paid well above the top of the lockstep's maximum, in recognition of their market heft. (Arquit and Newborn each took home about $4 million last year, more than three times Clifford Chance's top earner in London.) At the opposite end of the pay spectrum, roughly a dozen Rogers & Wells partners would not make the transition to lockstep. To avoid diluting equity, the firm would compensate them at levels below the lockstep minimum.

A year and a half earlier, Clifford Chance had boldly absorbed 400–lawyer Rogers & Wells and Germany's 262–attorney Punder, Volhard, Weber & Axster as part of a grand plan to build the world's premier law firm. The integration had been difficult, and was further complicated by the looming compensation switch that hung over the heads of the former Rogers & Wells partners. Now, with their pay levels spelled out, Benedict was urging the lawyers to move forward. "The transition is over," he declared. "We need to be thinking about implementing our strategy for the future instead of worrying about the past."

That could be wishful thinking. In the short run, Benedict's communique triggered a wave of negative publicity on both sides of the Atlantic. News reports spoke of a "bloodbath" and a sizable "de-equitization" characterizations that Benedict angrily rejects. He also denies claims by several former partners and two current partners that the leviathan is pushing out about a dozen former Rogers & Wells partners who practice in tax, real estate, and other areas deemed undesirable.

The bad press has come amid other signs of a rocky transition. Although some partners rave about the benefits of an international platform, others gripe that the rate of internal referrals has been unspectacular. Conflicts of interest, as expected, have been treacherous in certain growth areas. What's more, all three of the firm's senior management posts are now in flux. Last month, longtime chairman Keith Clark announced plans to step down before his term expires next year and take over as international general counsel at client Morgan Stanley Dean Witter & Co. The news came six months after a stormy partners' retreat outside London. At that March meeting, there was "open revolt," in the words of one attendee, as several malcontents mostly British partners blasted management for lack of communication and imposition of bureaucratic constraints. Although Clark, 56, says that no one "directly" asked him to leave, he says that he recognized the firm needed an infusion of fresh blood. After nine years on the job, he says, you "risk growing stale."

Now all eyes are on Peter Cornell, the incoming chief executive officer. Cornell, a popular partner based in Madrid, edged out a competing candidate backed by management during an election earlier this year. It would be an overstatement to interpret Cornell's election, along with Clark's exit and the retirement this summer of the firm's third-in-command, as a no-confidence vote for the firm's global strategy. But the changes are symptomatic of the challenges from clients to culture to compensation faced by a firm hell-bent on world preeminence. The broad issue at play is how to balance traditional notions of partnership with the pressures of running a global business. As Clifford Chance management has discovered, there are limits to the sacrifices partners are willing to make. Whether the firm can continue to increase profits and expand its client base while giving partners a sense of control remains to be seen. But it is clearly the debate of the day. Cornell's campaign message? Give the partnership back to the partners.

The Clifford Chance Rogers & Wells union was born of mutual ambition. In the late nineties, Rogers & Wells was facing an uncertain future in an increasingly competitive market. Efforts to internationalize by opening offices in London, Paris, Frankfurt, and Hong Kong had been largely unsuccessful, current and former partners say. The partnership recognized that it had a choice: Either shrink and focus on select areas, or do something big and bold.

Clifford Chance, known for its banking and finance prowess, had been globetrotting too, investing heavily in Europe and, to a lesser extent, in Asia. But it had failed in its concentrated effort to build a formidable New York operation from the ground up. By 1998, a decade after it had arrived in the U.S., the outpost was among the least profitable in Clifford Chance's 20–office empire. Recognizing the need to establish a foothold in New York, the firm directed six partners to hunt full-time for a U.S. mate.

Rogers & Wells wasn't Clifford Chance's first or even second or third choice ["The New World Order," August 1999]. But Clifford Chance, like its top British rivals, had discovered that the most desirable New York shops spurned suitors. In Rogers & Wells, Clifford Chance saw profitability comparable to its own, as well as strong litigation and antitrust practices and an attractive securities group. Taken together, Clifford Chance concluded, these practices could provide a platform from which it could build a sizable U.S. capability, particularly in mergers and acquisitions. The firm's overarching goal is to combine high-end corporate and litigation work around the world with strong regional practices.

Together with a synchronous deal to absorb Punder, one of Germany's top five firms, the January 2000 combination is the largest law firm merger ever. It gave Clifford Chance a sizable presence in some of the world's biggest financial centers, including New York, London, Frankfurt, and Hong Kong. For the firm, it is a source of considerable pride that all of this has derived from a 1987 merger between two middling British firms. That union defied critics' skepticism as Clifford Chance clawed its way into the Magic Circle Britain's top five firms. "We're writing the book on global mergers," chortles Michael Bray, the incumbent CEO and a veteran Clifford Chance partner.

Nearly two years after the Clifford Chance Rogers & Wells Punder combination, some progress has been made. The core infrastructure technology, conflicts-checking systems, and now compensation is more or less in place. The firm, though perhaps not the world's best, is certainly the biggest. Some 3,200 lawyers in 19 countries brought in revenues last year of $1.4 billion, a 24 percent jump over the aggregate billings of the three predecessor firms. Average per partner profits topped $1 million.

What's more, partners say that clients are taking notice. They point to the merged firm's early assignment as IPO counsel to European Aeronautic Defense and Space Company, the parent of airplane manufacturer Airbus, S.A.S. More recently, the firm handled worldwide antitrust issues arising from PepsiCo, Inc.'s acquisition of Quaker Oats. Partners involved in both assignments credit the merger with giving them the cross-border capability necessary to land the jobs. Billings to the firm's top four banking clients Merrill Lynch & Co., Inc.; Citigroup Inc.; J.P. Morgan Chase & Co.; and Morgan Stanley Dean Witter & Co. doubled in the first full year of operation. George Schieren, the associate general counsel at Merrill Lynch and a long-standing client of both Clifford Chance and Rogers & Wells, says he likes what he's seeing. The firm is "penetrating deeper into the [bank's business]," he says.

Still, Schieren's not ready to call the Clifford Chance strategy a success. "It's still early," he says. Adding to his hesitation are doubts that a global, full-service firm is even necessary, despite Merrill Lynch's own worldwide expansion. "I didn't feel myself suffering beforehand," he says. Clifford Chance is gambling that clients like Schieren will change their minds, sooner rather than later. When if that happens, the theory goes, it will touch off a wave of copycat deals between American and British firms. By then, Clifford Chance hopes to be way ahead of the competition.

But growth presents plenty of difficulties aside from questions of partnership autonomy. How does a firm cultivate a blue-chip clientele and manage conflicts effectively? How do managers ensure that partners in Dubai are taking on desirable work? As one former Clifford Chance partner puts it, merging is actually the easy part: "It's what happens afterwards that matters."

Some of the adjustments have been minor. London-based Rogers & Wells partners got used to sharing offices with their colleagues, a common British tradition. British lawyers, meanwhile, learned that Americans like ice cubes in their drinks. Both sides discovered that they formatted their electronic documents differently.

But other challenges are more difficult. Conflicts the bane of many law firm courtships have been hard to navigate. A big plus for the merger was the overlap of financial institutions served by both firms; investment banks tend to be more relaxed than other types of businesses about conflicts of interest. One conflict involving a pharmaceuticals company, however, almost killed the merger, and others had to be resolved either by getting waivers or by dropping the client. For instance, Microsoft Corporation, a Clifford Chance client, had to go, because Rogers & Wells's Kevin Arquit was, and still is, embroiled in the antitrust case against the software giant.

To deal with the sheer volume of daily client inquiries, the firm took the power to conduct conflicts checks away from the partners and built a multimillion-dollar conflicts center in London. All new matters even new work for existing clients must first pass through the checkpoint. With 45 staffers in four locations around the world, the operation handles a few hundred inquiries a day, according to deputy chief operating officer Christopher Perrin. There's also the so-called Black Box, a highly secure database containing the names of hundreds of hands-off companies such as PepsiCo, which is verboten because Clifford Chance represents the Coca–Cola Company. It also includes companies that the firm has reason to think will send it work in the future.

The system, says Perrin, is neither foolproof nor beloved by all. In the beginning, conflicts checks were a disaster, in large part because of software glitches, he says. Now the main obstacles are the $2.7 million annual price tag and the risk of human error, according to Perrin. Still, he estimates that only three mistakes were made in the past year, far fewer than if partners had been running checks on their own.

The conflicts center also helps ensure that partners are doing work that fits into the firm's overall strategy. If a project submitted for a check doesn't fit in with long-term goals, partners are told to turn it down, says Perrin, whose job is to monitor the firm's intake. In the effort to attract blue-chip corporations and the high-value work they offer, managing assignments effectively is especially critical and involves extensive analysis of industries and the companies in each sector that are likely to be on the move in the coming years. (Sometimes it means placing bets. The firm recently turned down a small piece of a multibillion-dollar merger in the hopes of landing a bigger role in the deal, but the strategy didn't pay off.) Partners don't always react well to edicts commanding them to turn down assignments. Globalization, it turns out, has its price.

As the firm increases its roster of corporate clients, while maintaining a sizable litigation practice, conflicts have become a bigger problem. That's especially the case in M & A, where one former partner says that the firm had to turn down two out of three possible assignments in a recent week because of conflicts. "The major problem we've faced isn't that Clifford Chance is an international company but that it's a big firm," says one partner.

Adding to frustration over conflicts is the slow rate at which practices are cross-selling services to clients, this partner says. The partner notes that the merger has caused a drop-off in referrals from other firms, who are now worried about handing clients over to a major competitor. The expectation was that a boost in internal client referrals would help offset the lost business. But that hasn't happened, according to Robert King, Jr., the New York based head of the firm's capital markets practice and former Rogers & Wells partner: "The expectation was that things would come flying over the transom." But King is quick to add that the expectation was unrealistic. Cross-selling takes time, he says.

The firm's struggles with conflicts and client marketing aren't out of the ordinary, given the magnitude of Clifford Chance's brazen mission. Though less than thrilled, partners say they recognize that opportunity costs are necessary. That said, neither the unhappiness over communication nor the ongoing debate over the compensation is so easily excused.

What irked some British partners and led to their criticism of management at the March meeting was the high price of rapid, aggressive global growth. Lockstep, they fear, could become its biggest casualty. To make the deal work, Rogers & Wells had agreed to abandon performance-based compensation, a system that many viewed as flawed and deeply corrosive. But the system had effectively rewarded top performers. Shifting to the Clifford Chance model would result in drops in income for several American stars. Antitrust star Arquit, for instance, was earning over $2.3 million a year by 1999. That same year, the top of the Clifford Chance lockstep paid about $1.1 million.

The short-term solution was to designate about eight top Rogers & Wells earners, including Benedict and Arquit, and pay them additional units, up to 250, on top of the maximum 100 allowed under the Clifford Chance system. According to two partners, the special treatment was sold to Clifford Chance partners many of whom were intent on keeping their prized lockstep system pure as onetime exceptions. According to management, the extra money would come out of the 23 percent in profits that Clifford Chance agreed to transfer to the Americans in the first two years of the merger. It was unclear to the partners, however, how many of these exclusions would survive the start of Clifford Chance's 2002 fiscal year, or even where individual partners would end up on the lockstep ladder.

The payment of the extra units, a first for Clifford Chance, were not easy to take. To many, the lockstep system works because it's rigid and egalitarian. Deviations, the purists fear, only undermine the system and the firm culture. The exceptions, according to former partners and the merger prospectus, have been portrayed as interim, U.S. only deals aimed at keeping top talent until firm profits reached market levels, at which time the need for exceptions would disappear. Instead, more exceptions have been made. Earlier this year Clifford Chance absorbed its longtime Italian affiliate, 134–lawyer Grimaldi e Associati, one of that country's leading corporate firms. To lure Grimaldi into the fold, management agreed to pay several Grimaldi partners above the top of lockstep. And to accommodate Vittorio Grimaldi, the firm's 60–year-old senior partner, Clifford Chance agreed to extend the firm's mandatory retirement age by five years, to age 70. The deal was struck without input from Clifford Chance partners.

A few months later partners from around the globe gathered in Hammersmith, on the outskirts of London, for their second all-hands meeting. At one point, partners were divided into small groups and given topics to discuss (for example: "What headline would you like to see about the firm in 2010?"). British partners balked at the exercise and openly criticized firm leaders for keeping them in the dark on key issues and "whitewashing" others. Another sore point was lower-than-expected profits in New York. According to firm managers and partners, profits there were lagging because of soaring associate salaries and a sizable increase in merger-related administrative costs. But as part of the merger agreement, Clifford Chance handed over nearly a quarter of the firm's profits to the Americans. "People were pretty unhappy," says one attendee. The message, he says, was simple: Stop putting a gloss on issues. Be straightforward with us. Clark says he wasn't surprised by the outburst. A merger of this magnitude, he says, produces "a lot of uncertainty and insecurity."

If partners wanted candor, they got it. Less than two months later, Benedict stood before his former Rogers & Wells partners and detailed the compensation switch that he knew was causing them anxiety. A 52–year-old litigator from upstate New York who is known for 14–hour workdays and an affinity for Tab soda, Benedict was a prime beneficiary of the eat-what-you-kill system and someone who could make tough calls regarding compensation. He landed the role as head of the firm's Americas practice this spring, when Laurence Cranch, the former Rogers & Wells managing partner, stepped down amid criticism that he wasn't a strong enough leader. Cranch, who's still practicing at the firm, declined a request for an interview for this article.

The system that Benedict described to his colleagues this spring was a muddled version of lockstep. The foundation was unchanged: Partners move onto lockstep with 40 units, advancing a notch each year until they top out at 400 units, after about nine years. But for the former Rogers & Wells partners, seniority would be just one determinant of placement on the lockstep ladder. Consider Arquit and Newborn, both former Federal Trade Commission officials. They oversee a vibrant antitrust regulatory practice that brought $70 million into the firm last year. Because Clifford Chance hopes to use its antitrust practice to lure M & A work, it's clear that the firm needs to keep them happy. Though Arquit and Newborn deny they're looking to leave, both are rumored to be talking to other firms. Upping the ante is Clifford Chance's loss of competition partner Christopher Bright to the London office of New York's Shearman & Sterling. Bright had wanted to head Clifford Chance's global competition practice, a job that instead went to Arquit and Newborn.

Decisions about which partners will receive special compensation treatment will be made in the next few months, although Arquit and Newborn appear to be the only shoo-ins. Assuming there are no others, about six partners who were also paid extra units during the two-year transition will have to give up the added income to move to the top of the lockstep.

At the bottom of the pay scale, the problem was brutally simple: By the late 1990s, the lowest-paid Rogers & Wells partners made just under $300,000, while their Clifford Chance counterparts drew roughly $430,000. Moving to the first rung on the Clifford Chance ladder, then, would have risked diluting the firm's equity. As a result, fewer than a dozen Rogers & Wells equity partners would be paid below lockstep.

Nonequity partnership is a concept that is not foreign to either Clifford Chance or Rogers & Wells, both of which had tiers for salaried partners before their merger. For Clifford Chance, the need to keep profits per equity partner high and to pay partners in remote locations based on the local cost of living has been a key element of its march around the globe. By 1999, some 70 partners or about 20 percent of the total partnership were nonequity. Today that figure has swelled to about 200 out of 650 partners. Rogers & Wells contributed to the increase, but most of the additions actually came from Germany's Punder, where most of the firm's 100–plus partners signed on with nonequity status.

Benedict is baffled that compensation has generated so much controversy. Partners understood all along that these steps were inevitable and that the firm was looking "to change the mix" of practices to focus on high-end work for multinational firms, he says. Arquit, who also serves as deputy chairman, agrees that the changes were not a shock: "Lockstep operates on the assumption that everybody is providing the same value added," says Arquit. "I think there are few things that have occurred that were not anticipated [during merger negotiations]."

But the compensation debate isn't over. Firm leaders have sold their patchwork to partners on the grounds that profits are bound to grow, eventually equaling those of the richest U.S. firms. At that point enticements would no longer be necessary. But until that happens and it could take a few years the tension between partners who see a need to keep the system flexible in order to attract top talent, particularly in M & A, and the purists who want to safeguard lockstep will only increase. "If Clifford Chance's culture is clearly collectivist, and I'm someone who's entrepreneurial," says one partner, "there's bound to be a clash."

If partners crave a great communicator to help bridge these gaps, they may have found one in Peter Cornell, an affable partner and extreme skier who considers moments of physical danger to be good for the soul. The 49–year-old banking lawyer has spent nearly a quarter-century practicing at Clifford Chance, having spent time in London and Singapore before he ventured to Madrid in 1989 to resurrect the firm's ailing Spain practice and help run the firm's European operations. More than for his management experience, current and former partners praise Cornell for being straightforward and for bringing the firm a perspective that reaches far beyond London.

Although Cornell won't take the reins until late next year, he's already setting his agenda. Among his priorities are a top-to-bottom review of the firm's management structure. The future of the chairman's job, for instance, is unclear: Clark could be replaced by Cornell or someone else, or the position could be eliminated altogether.

In the seven months since his election, Cornell already has shown himself to be a skilled politician. "We need to strike a balance between achieving the right business discipline and retaining partnership values," he told partners at the March 31 retreat. "Partners should not be taken for granted." Months later, Peter Chaffetz, a reinsurance lawyer who joined the New York office in early 2000 and says he doesn't know Cornell that well, was astounded to discover that Cornell had left a voicemail message at his home a day or two after the September 11 terrorist attacks on the United States. "He asked me if I was okay, if my family was okay and if there was anything he could do," says Chaffetz.

Perhaps that level of hand-holding is more necessary now than it ever has been, as the firm sets out to show the marketplace that the combination with both Rogers & Wells and Punder was not only sound but also prescient. Until then, detractors abound, many of whom speculate that Rogers & Wells won't be the last large-scale U.S. merger for Clifford Chance. The notion is audacious. But that's exactly the kind of move that the partners relish.

Remember: Clifford Chance has been down this road and silenced its critics before.

Susan Beck, Clifford Chance Makes Push for Profits

LEGAL TIMES, December 6, 2004

Faced with seemingly endless turmoil in the United States, Clifford Chance is attempting to right its ship with some worldwide deck swabbing. Since its 2000 merger with New York's Rogers & Wells, the London-based firm has lost more than 30 partners in the United States, including such standouts as Kevin Arquit, Kenneth Gallo, and, most recently, James Benedict. Most left because of tension over Clifford Chance's lockstep compensation system, which limits flexibility to reward overachievers.

This year, aiming to improve its profitability and stop desirable partners from leaving, the world's largest law firm has been conducting more-rigorous partner reviews. Clifford Chance won't say it's pruning deadwood; instead, managing partner Peter Cornell explains that the firm is reinforcing its standards: "We must have an obsession with quality. It must be nonnegotiable."

But will anything short of a radical attitude readjustment be enough?

COMPROMISING POSITION

Before the merger, the firms knew they'd have to resolve two different compensation systems: Clifford Chance's lockstep, and Rogers & Wells' model that rewarded business generation. With neither side willing to give up its system right away, they cobbled together a short-term compromise that allowed a handful of stars in New York and the District to be paid above the top lockstep rate.

For the U.S. lawyers, there was another key element to the deal. To assure American partners that a lockstep-dominated system would be fair, the British firm agreed to conduct "rigorous" partner reviews and enforce an "intolerant" lockstep. [These conditions were stated in the merger agreement.] That, theoretically, would weed out underperforming partners or drop them down the scale. "It was a way to come up with a common set of expectations," says one former partner. "Do we aspire to be the worldwide equivalent of Sullivan & Cromwell, or not? ... You can't bill 1,500 hours and say you want to be Sullivan & Cromwell."

Management underestimated the resistance it would face from old-line partners in London, where the culture is not as driven by the bottom line. Cornell, who took over as managing partner in 2002, confirms that these reviews didn't happen. "We tried and failed about three years ago to introduce a partner assessment procedure," he says.

The firm's failure to impose high expectations on all partners led to frustration in the United States. For the firm's last full fiscal year, which ended April 30, a partner at the top of Clifford Chance's lockstep made less than $1 million. The firm ranked 40th in profitability on The American Lawyer Global 100 list. One problem is that most partners rise to the top lockstep level after nine years. As a result, nearly half of Clifford Chance's partners sit at the top rung, diluting the profits at that level. [The firm has also recently been reminded that it's vulnerable to poaching abroad. In November, Paris corporate partner Dominique Bompoint was lured to Sullivan & Cromwell.]

Cornell says that to succeed in the United States and globally, Clifford Chance needs to improve its profitability. The firm has been cutting costs, but also is focusing on getting partners to generate more revenue. For the current fiscal year, the firm has targeted an increase in profits of 25 percent, which would raise the top lockstep rate to $1.25 million. This would at least elevate it to the level of the most lucrative British firms.

Cornell says the partner reviews have been focused on quality, with billable commitments secondary. Does the process aim to weed out underperformers? "Not really," Cornell responds. "That's an issue that has to be dealt with, but [the reviews] are not actually related to that. It's more focused on whether [partners'] personal goals are aligned with what the group is doing."

The reviews didn't appease at least one New York partner. In late October, Clifford Chance suffered arguably its most significant loss in the states when New York partner Benedict left for Milbank, Tweed, Hadley & McCloy. Benedict, a 55–year-old litigator, was not just a tireless worker with a huge book of business. He had led the firm's management team in the United States and had been a visible booster for the merger.

Benedict, who started his career at Rogers & Wells 30 years ago, bluntly states his reasons for leaving. "The British playbook doesn't work [in the United States], or at least it needs to be modified," he says, referring to lockstep. "I think that any change to lockstep is a huge threat to a big part of Clifford Chance."

For Benedict and others, the turning point came last year when Cornell urged partners to approve a compensation system that would allow a handful of U.S. partners to be paid above lockstep for another five years. A majority of partners backed it, but it fell short of the two-thirds vote required under the partnership agreement. Instead, the firm continued to require the few New York partners above lockstep to be reconsidered every two years. Shortly after, Benedict told the U.K. publication Legal Business that a "Taliban" of partners was holding the firm hostage.

"I looked at the vote last fall as saying that the purity of lockstep was more important than success in the U.S.," says Benedict, who was compensated above the top lockstep level. "It is really that [proposal] being voted down by a dissident minority that really triggered the exodus in [the] U.S.," he says. After the vote, a stream of top litigators left the firm, including U.S. litigation head Gallo to Paul, Weiss, Rifkind, Wharton & Garrison, and Leora Ben–Ami to Kaye Scholer. [Both had extra points above lockstep.] "I spent 15 years building what I thought was one of the very leading U.S. litigation practices, and I watched it blow apart in a very short time," says Benedict.

"When we did the merger, I don't think enough thought was given on either side—either side—to compensation," concedes managing partner Cornell. "We didn't understand how different the markets are. We did not think it out as thoroughly as we should have."

Keith Clark, who was managing partner of Clifford Chance during the merger, and Laurence Cranch, the last managing partner of Rogers & Wells, declined to comment. Both have taken positions with clients.

ROCKY ROAD

"It's been a bit more turbulent than I'd like, but we have made progress," says Cornell about the integration. He notes that the firm averaged a 20 percent increase in U.S. revenue from its top 20 clients in its last fiscal year. Cornell declines to name clients, but they include Citigroup Inc., Morgan Stanley, and Merrill Lynch & Co. Cornell also points to the firm's rise in some of Thomson Financial Capital Markets "league tables," which track deals handled by a firm. In M & A, it ranks fifth in the United States, with deals valued at $88 billion. Still, Cornell says he'd like to see the firm pick up the pace in the United States, especially in M & A and tax. [The firm declined to break out U.S. revenue numbers.]

But the firm still needs to resolve compensation issues. In addition to reviews, it has formed a committee to address pay—again.

Cornell says he believes the New York partners support lockstep: "I think just about all of them accept it now." But in New York, John Carroll, managing partner of the Americas, says the firm must be more flexible. "We have to evolve to a place where our basic lockstep system is more sensitive to the competition," he says.

PROBLEM

You are a partner at Brown & Bergen, a Chicago law firm that aspires over the next ten years to move into the top tier of national corporate law firms. Your firm currently has 350 lawyers in Chicago, and 400 more in offices in Los Angeles, Washington, DC, Boston, and Houston. It has just achieved its longstanding goal of entering the New York market by acquiring Parker Dutton & Amos, a firm of 250 lawyers that has a substantial practice in major corporate transactions.

Shortly after the acquisition, the top tier Wall Street firm of Woodworth & Hayes announces that it will be increasing starting salaries for associates by $20,000, with commensurate increases throughout its associate ranks. Brown & Bergen starting associate salaries already are about $10,000 less than those at Woodworth & Hayes. Some Brown & Bergen lawyers believe that the firm should match the Woodworth & Hayes starting salary in light of the firm's recent entry into the New York market and its goal of becoming a top tier national law firm. Others, however, maintain that doing so would impose excessive costs on a firm with the large majority of its lawyers outside New York, and are concerned about what measures the firm would have to adopt to pay for the increase. You are on a committee that has been asked to consider how, if at all, Brown & Bergen should respond to Woodworth & Hayes. What, if any, other information would you want before making a recommendation? What should your committee ultimately recommend?

Chapter 8

THE CORPORATE LAW FIRM: CAREER PATHS

As the previous chapter describes, law firms no longer offer the relatively fixed and predictable career path that they did a generation ago. A more robustly competitive market for lawyers has created more mobility and opportunity, as well as more risk and uncertainty. Can we discern any patterns in this new state of affairs? Is it possible to identify any characteristic career paths, or is there too much variety and instability? What kinds of factors are likely to shape the course of a lawyer's professional life? This chapter attempts to shed some light on these issues by focusing on three categories of law firm lawyers: associates, partners, and permanent lawyers who are in neither category.

OVERVIEW OF THE CHAPTER

The excerpt from Wilkins and Gulati analyzes how law firms tend to distribute salaries, work assignments, training, mentoring, and opportunities for partnership among associates. It suggests that law firms decisions on these issues reflect a variety of organizational concerns, only one of which is the desire to evaluate associates for promotion to partner. Furthermore, Wilkins and Gulati suggest that firms often sort associates onto separate tracks in a way that belies the notion of a completely meritocratic competition.

The article by Martha Neil explores how life as a law firm partner has become both more lucrative and more hazardous. Many firms have established different levels of partnership, only some of which entitle the partner to a share of the firm's profits or a voire in its operations. In addition, making partner typically subjects the lawyer to increasing responsibility for generating revenues. Falling short of the target can result in cuts in compensation and even in termination from the firm. The excerpt from Gorman then describes reasons for the resurgence of a category of lawyers who are neither associates nor partners, but salaried employees of the firm. Finally, the problem at the end of the chapter asks you to assess the possible employment law implications of the charging structure of law firm career paths.

The material in this chapter is designed to provide greater depth and detail about various career paths in the law firm. This is valuable for its own sake. It also should help you anticipate how lawyers in different positions in the firm may confront distinctive incentives and pressures when they encounter ethical issues.

David B. Wilkins and G. Mitu Gulati,
RECONCEIVING THE TOURNAMENT OF LAWYERS: TRACKING, SEEDING, AND INFORMATION CONTROL IN THE INTERNAL LABOR MARKETS OF ELITE LAW FIRMS

84 VA. L. REV. 1581 (1998)

Tournament theory has become the dominant academic model for analyzing the institutional structure of large law firms. In the most influential of these accounts, Marc Galanter and Thomas Palay argue in their justly celebrated book, Tournament of Lawyers: The Transformation of the Big Law Firm, that the core institutional characteristic of large law firms is the "promotion-to-partner tournament." This tournament, Galanter and Palay contend, is structured around a simple promise made by senior lawyers (partners), who have excess human capital, to junior lawyers (associates), with little human capital but an abundant supply of labor. In return for the associates' promise to work diligently and competently on the firm's business, partners promise that at the end of a probationary period, they will promote a fixed percentage of these junior lawyers to partnership * * *

Galanter and Palay contend that the dynamics of the competition for these limited partnership slots accounts for the current size and institutional structure of contemporary elite firms ... [They] assert that the firm's promise to promote a fixed percentage of every associate class to partnership provides an efficient mechanism for associates and partners to prevent each other from behaving opportunistically with respect to the quality of an associate's work. With respect to associates, the lure of the financial rewards and other benefits that are supposed to come with partnership (and the corresponding fear of not making partner) reduces an associate's incentive to "shirk" (by producing inferior work or failing to invest in firm-specific capital), "grab" (by stealing the partners' clients), or "leave" (before the firm has recouped its investment in the associate's development). At the same time, the firm's ex ante commitment to promote a fixed percentage of each associate class reduces its incentive to "shark" (i.e., refusing to pay for services received) by failing to promote those who have exerted the most effort.

Galanter and Palay's claim that the tournament of lawyers is a response to the mutual monitoring problems of partners and associates is expressly premised on the more general economic model of tournament theory * * *

Our critique of tournament theory proceeds along two seemingly paradoxical lines. First, we argue that a theory of law firm internal labor markets must take account of the ways in which the promotion-to-partnership tournament differs from a standard rank-order economic tournament. Specifically, we argue that theorists such as Galanter and Palay fail to account for six differences between the economic tournament model and the actual practices of elite law firms: (1) Many associates are not competing in the tournament; (2) firms do not give every associate an equal chance of winning; (3) the interests of individual partners diverge from those of the firm; (4) the tournament is not divided into two (and only two) distinct stages; (5) partnership is not awarded as a reward for past performance; and (6) firms do not seek to make the tournament's rules and outcomes transparent to associates. Once we account for these differences, we contend, it is clear that the standard economic model is not an appropriate tool for analyzing the internal labor markets of large law firms.

Nevertheless, we do not advocate abandoning tournament theory altogether * * * Although elite firms are not structured as rank-order tournaments, the competition among certain associates for the limited number of available partnership slots does play a crucial role in structuring the hiring, promotion, and retention practices of these institutions. As a result, although we reject the basic tournament model used by Galanter and Palay and others, we contend that the tournament metaphor remains a valuable aid for constructing a model that accurately describes elite firms. We therefore propose a model of law firm internal labor markets that acknowledges the importance of the competition for partnership without assuming that this competition proceeds along the lines of a standard economic tournament * * *

II. The Rules of the Game

Galanter and Palay's model of the promotion-to-partner tournament rests on a number of interconnected assumptions about the internal labor practices of elite firms, and the motivations and actions of those who participate in and help to shape these practices. Not surprisingly, these assumptions track the foundational assumptions underlying standard economic tournament theory. We group these assumptions into seven categories. First, Galanter and Palay assume that every associate is competing in the tournament, and that the tournament is the primary motivational tool used by the firm. Second, by emphasizing that associates can be confident that partnership decisions will be made on the basis of merit, Galanter and Palay implicitly assume that firms give every associate an equal chance of winning the tournament, or to put the point somewhat differently, that firms will not favor some associates over others. Third, by describing these firms as operating in accordance with a single economic model where the rewards to any one person are a function of his or her rivals not performing quite as well, the implicit assumption is that cooperation among associates is not crucial, i.e., that sabotage is not an important problem. Fourth, by modeling their theory on a hypothetical contract between a single partner and her associates, Galanter and Palay implicitly assume that the interests of individual partners are synonymous with those of the firm. Fifth, the promotion-to-partner tournament Galanter and Palay describe has two, and only two, distinct periods: associateship and partnership. Sixth, they assume that victory in the tournament is a reward for production as an associate. Finally, Galanter and Palay assume that firms seek to make both the rules of the tournament and its results transparent to associates.

These assumptions do not accurately describe the internal practices of contemporary elite law firms. The following seven Sections discuss the limitations of each of these model-based assumptions.

A. Not Everyone Is Competing

It is impossible to spend time talking to law students about their career goals without coming to the conclusion that many of the young women and men who join large law firms have no intention of staying long enough to become partners. Ironically, the very pervasiveness of this sentiment among law students makes it difficult to quantify exactly how many entering associates fall into this category. At law schools like Harvard, it is now considered slightly unfashionable, or perhaps more accurately, egotistical, to declare publicly that one is interested in braving the long odds and demanding hours of the modern promotion-to-partner tournament. As a result, even students with a relatively strong commitment to participating in the tournament may disavow any interest in doing so for fear of alienating their peers. Nevertheless, anecdotal evidence, including our own barefoot empiricism, strongly suggests that a large number of associates have opted out—or, more accurately, never opted into—the tournament.

The fact that some significant percentage of entering associates do not see themselves as participating in the tournament creates two important problems for firms. First, firms must find other ways to motivate those associates who do not intend to compete in the race to make partner. This motivation includes convincing young lawyers to join firms initially, since it is at least plausible that a firm's employment needs will outstrip the number of associates committed to participating in the tournament. Relatedly, firms must find ways to prevent non-participating associates from shirking or engaging in other forms of opportunistic behavior once they arrive.

Second, firms must develop ways of identifying those associates who are interested in winning the tournament. This might seem like an insignificant issue; firms can simply rely on self-selection. The reality, however, is more complex. Those associates who initially identify themselves as tournament players might not be the ones that the firms view as the best potential partnership candidates. Although qualities such as confidence and assertiveness are highly valued by firms, it is not always true that those who declare themselves to be the most interested in a given job are actually the best candidates. This is particularly true given that firms, for reasons that we elaborate below, have an incentive to value partnership candidates from elite law schools where social mores discourage students from publicly (or perhaps even privately) admitting their ambitions. Finally, many associates who might want to compete in the tournament will be discouraged from doing so, or quickly persuaded to abandon their quest, by the sheer size of the firm's entering class of associates. Many associates are likely to ask themselves, "What makes me think that I will be the one out of all the talented members of my class to grab the partnership prize?"

Collectively, these distortions between the expressed preferences of entering associates and the needs of firms suggest that the simple promotion-to-partner tournament does not resolve all of the firm's monitoring problems. These motivational problems are exacerbated once we take into account that even those lawyers who see themselves as participating in the tournament do not have an equal chance to succeed.

B.   The Playing Field Is Not Level

One of the appeals of tournament theory is that it seems to confirm what law firms have always said about themselves: Firms are meritocracies in which every associate has an equal chance to succeed. The problem with this characterization is that it fails to account for differences in the work done by particular associates. These differences have a profound influence on a given associate's chances of winning the tournament.

Large law firms produce two categories of work that must be done by associates. The first category consists of work that provides valuable training in the skills and dispositions of lawyering. Although law school (one would hope) teaches students to "think like a lawyer," virtually all of the skills and dispositions that associates need to be good lawyers must be learned on the job. Training, therefore, is an essential part of the bargain that Galanter and Palay posit between partners and associates in which the latter trade their labor for the chance to develop human capital. More important, it is essential to the long term survival of the firm.

Training work encompasses a wide variety of tasks. Examples include writing a draft motion or brief and then going over the draft with the partner, watching a partner negotiate a contract or conduct a strategy session with a client, and writing a comprehensive report of a new regulatory development that will be distributed to clients. As these examples make clear, training work increases an associate's firm-specific and general human capital.

In addition, however, training work also enables an associate to develop strong relationships with particular partners. This relational capital is crucial to an associate's partnership chances. Associates depend on their partner-mentors to give them good work (and to protect them from bad assignments), to pass on important client relationships, and ultimately to push for their promotion among their fellow partners. Without strong advocates in the partnership, an associate's chances of winning the tournament are substantially diminished.

Contrary to the implicit uniformity suggested by tournament theory, training work is not the only work produced by large law firms. Instead, these entities produce a substantial amount of "paperwork." Examples of paperwork range from writing, answering, and supervising discovery requests, to proofreading and making slight modifications to pre-existing corporate documents, to writing legal memos to the file or for review by senior associates, to faxing important documents to the client. Once again, this work can lead to the development of both firm-specific (e.g., knowledge of a particular client's document retention policy) and general (e.g., careful proofreading skills and the abilities to take orders and work long hours on a regular basis) human capital. Paperwork is unlikely, however, to develop the kind of higher order skills and judgment that partners look for when evaluating associates for partnership. Nor does this work typically result in an associate developing relational capital, since partners rarely have much contact with those who are only doing paperwork and tend to notice these unlucky associates only when something goes wrong. Given this division of labor, every associate who wants to have a chance of winning the promotion-to-partner tournament needs to gain access to training work.

Unfortunately, this essential good, which we have elsewhere analogized to the "royal jelly" that allows worker bees to develop into queens, is in short supply. This is true for three reasons. First, because of the sheer volume of paperwork generated by many areas of legal practice, firms must deploy a substantial number of associates to satisfy this demand. Firms therefore have strong incentives not to provide training work to those associates who are performing paperwork for fear of diverting their attention from completing these uninteresting, but nevertheless critically important, tasks. More important, training work requires the firm to commit a substantial amount of uncompensated (or, at best, undercompensated) partner time because much of this valuable training can only be transmitted in the one-on-one, on-the-job context (e.g., being with the partner at a negotiation or at a client meeting). Partner time, which can be billed out at high rates, is extremely valuable. Finally, firms do not need to provide—nor do they want to provide—all of their associates with significant firm-specific training. Paperwork associates only require minimal training. Moreover, firms realize that most associates will leave before the firm can reap the benefits of its investment in their development.

Once again the importance and scarcity of training work undermines the effectiveness of the promotion-to-partner tournament as a method for resolving the mutual monitoring problems of partners and associates. Two problems are significant.

First, those not receiving training work have strong incentives to shirk or to leave. Diligently performing paperwork is unlikely to result in partnership. Therefore, an associate who finds herself doing mostly paperwork has an incentive to shirk while she investigates other job possibilities. Moreover, she has an incentive to begin this job search sooner rather than later. Not only does an associate doing primarily paperwork have limited partnership prospects (because the associate has not been trained), but the kind of general human capital produced by paperwork is likely to be of diminishing value to employers the longer an associate stays at the firm. A general knowledge of legal practice and careful proofreading skills are valuable in junior lawyers. Senior lawyers, however, are only valuable to the extent that they bring higher order skill and judgment to their work. As a result, paperwork associates face strong pressures to leave while their marketability is still relatively high.

Tournament theory implies that firms should be concerned about these early departures. In a standard tournament model, a firm wants its employees to stay at the firm until the end of the probationary period. Galanter and Palay endorse this general view on the ground that partners want to recoup their investment in an associate's human capital development.

The reality of law firm economics, however, suggests that firms have a more complex interest in the longevity of paperwork associates. Paperwork attorneys are not receiving the kind of partner investment that tournament theory implies all associates receive. Consequently, the marginal productivity of paperwork associates (as measured by the firm's ability to bill the associate's work to clients at the appropriate rate) remains relatively constant throughout their tenure; hence we have elsewhere described these associates as "flatlining." After a certain number of years, the flatline of a paperwork associate's marginal utility will drop below the marginal cost (measured in terms of the associate's salary and benefits) of keeping that lawyer at the firm. When that happens, the firm has every incentive to let the associate go.

Before that time, however, firms need paperwork associates to do the enormous amount of paperwork that firms generate. In an associate's early years, this work can be billed to clients. Not only do clients recognize the need for a certain amount of paperwork, but a paperwork associate's cost to the firm is significantly less than that of a training associate precisely because partners are not investing in his development to the same extent that they are investing in the development of the training associate. Firms therefore need to keep a sufficient number of paperwork lawyers in their employ to cover this important demand.

Of course, no associate does only paperwork. Indeed, some might object to our division between training and paperwork on the ground that every associate does a certain amount of both. Randomly distributing training and paperwork throughout the associate pool, however, is inefficient. As we noted, there is substantially more paperwork than training work, particularly in an associate's early years. Consequently, a random distribution of these two kinds of tasks ensures that associates who leave because they think they are getting too much paperwork will also take with them some amount of valuable firm-specific training. To the extent that this departure occurs early in the associate's career, the firm may very well have not yet recouped its cost in providing this training. Firms have strong incentives to minimize the loss of unrecouped training expenses through associate attrition. This has important implications for the model we construct.

The scarcity of training work creates a second problem for firms seeking to use the promotion-to-partner tournament as a means of creating the right mix of incentives for their associates. Whereas the first problem focuses on associates who are likely to leave if they are not getting sufficient training work, the second highlights problems for those who decide to stay and attempt to win the tournament. If associates recognize that their chances for succeeding at the firm are directly tied to their ability to gain access to training work, then those who want to win the tournament are likely to engage in fierce struggles to obtain this scarce good.

As with the first problem, this second phenomenon may at first look like no problem at all. After all, the whole point of the tournament is to give associates an incentive to outcompete their peers in the hopes of capturing the brass ring of partnership. This characterization of law firms as a Hobbesian world of all against all, however, ignores the degree to which these institutions rely on lawyers to work in teams.

C. It Is a Team Sport

* * * [A] significant percentage of the work done by lawyers at elite firms is done in teams on projects that respond to client emergencies. Taken together, these characteristics of elite firm work suggest that firms must structure themselves in ways that foster cooperation as well as competition.

A firm structured entirely as a tournament would not be an environment that fostered cooperation simply because one's success in the standard tournament is a direct function of others not performing as well. If associates see themselves as directly competing against a substantial number of their peers—for scarce training resources or client contact, for example—they may act in ways that disturb the delicate balance between competition and cooperation. Thus, associates might refuse to share important information about clients or legal developments with their peers. In the worst case scenario, associates might seek to sabotage work done by other associates, for example, by spreading rumors or giving misleading advice. Behavior of this kind creates problems for firms—problems that are exacerbated where work has to be done in cooperative teams. Put simply, the higher the rewards of the tournament, the higher the incentive to engage in sabotage for those who want these rewards.

Large law firms, however, do not appear to be characterized by high levels of employee sabotage. There are few reports of junior lawyers refusing to cooperate with their peers. To the contrary, it is our sense that these young lawyers frequently share information about both substantive legal issues and the internal workings of the firm. The situation with senior associates is more complex. It is not uncommon, for example, to hear a junior associate accusing his senior of taking credit for the junior's work, or blaming the junior for the senior's mistake. As we indicate below, the fact that many senior associates (unlike the majority of junior associates) are competing for partnership helps to explain such reports. Nevertheless, the absence of many visible problems suggests that, for the most part, associates work well together on teams. This observation is at odds with the claim that law firms are organized as standard economic tournaments.

Nor is it plausible that the high levels of cooperation typically reported in these institutions are the result of direct monitoring and control by partners. Partners, of course, can seek to minimize the dangers of excessive competition by making clear that an associate's ability to work well with his or her peers plays an important role in partnership decisions—in other words, by setting up a competition in cooperation. Although partners undoubtedly seek to convey this message, its effect is muted by one of the monitoring problems that we identified in Part I, the difficulty of measuring cooperation (and the corresponding difficulty of detecting sabotage) when lawyers are working in teams. In addition, while the partnership as a whole has strong incentives to detect and sanction sabotage, individual partners are likely to have suboptimal incentives to participate in this joint enterprise—at least when the sabotage does not directly affect their own practices. The existence of widespread competition within the partnership itself, as we shall see, creates its own problems for the promotion-to-partner tournament.

D. *Individual Umpires Have a Stake in Who Wins the Tournament*

Tournaments work, in part, because a firm's commitment to promote a fixed percentage of associates sends a credible signal to these young lawyers that the "best" of their ranks will be selected for partnership. In essence, tournament theory analogizes partners to neutral umpires whose only interest is to select (albeit in a non-mechanistic way) those competitors who have performed the best during the competition. This image of partners as neutral decisionmakers fails to capture the fact that partners are players as well as judges.

Partners are players with vested interests, as opposed to neutral decisionmakers, because partnership no longer means tenure. With tenure and lockstep compensation, existing partners face relatively few threats to their privileged positions. This security, in theory, frees partners from self-interest and enables them to vote to promote the best qualified associates. When one takes away tenure and makes compensation variable, partners inevitably begin asking questions such as: "If we make this person partner, will he someday vote to have my compensation reduced, or worse, to have me fired?" It is a reality of today's competitive environment that if new partners find that they are generating the lion's share of the partnership's profits, they may well decide to terminate some of their older, less productive colleagues. Further, in addition to fighting to retain their hard-earned partnership positions, partners also compete to move up within the hierarchy of partners. This competition between partners is most visible where people compete for positions on the committees (executive, management, compensation, etc.) that run most large firms. As such, individual partners are likely to have interests that are at least in tension, and potentially at odds, with the interests of the firm as a whole.

Consider, for example, the issue of training raised in the prior Section. Firms have an incentive to ensure that every associate receives a basic level of training, both as a means of improving the overall quality of the firm's work, and to minimize the risk that those who do not receive training will leave while they are still economically profitable to the firm. Individual partners, however, have suboptimal incentives to contribute to the production of this firm-wide benefit. Training is costly to individual partners—time spent training is time that the partner cannot spend either producing revenue or consuming leisure. The benefits of training, on the other hand, are diffuse. To be sure, every partner needs a certain number of well-trained associates to do his or her work. Time spent training these associates produces private gains for the partner—assuming that the associate continues to work for that partner. Associates, however, typically work for multiple partners, and therefore no individual partner will be able to capture fully the time invested in training. As a result, partners have an incentive to ration time spent on training and to invest only in those associates who are most likely to provide direct benefit to their practices (i.e., the one or two associates for whom an individual partner can provide a steady stream of billable assignments).

One can tell a similar story about the behavior of partners when it comes to selecting tournament winners. As tournament theory predicts, with respect to an associate's past contributions, it is in the firm's interest to promote those associates who have demonstrated their commitment to the firm by exerting more effort than their peers. Individual partners, however, have strong incentives to favor their own proteges over the arguably better qualified proteges of others. By the time an associate is considered for partnership, he or she will have worked closely with a small number of partners over a number of years. These partner-mentors will frequently come to believe that their proteges (who in many cases will also have become their friends) are better qualified to become partners than associates with whom the partner-mentor has not worked.

More important, in the increasingly competitive world of large law firms, senior partners depend upon junior partner proteges for more than friendship. In the early years, senior partners need junior partners who will do their work (without trying to steal their clients) while the senior lawyers go out to look for additional business. In later years, senior partners depend on their proteges to support them (perhaps by referring clients in the other direction) when the senior lawyers are no longer able to protect their own interests in the partnership. Given these realities, we should expect tournament winners to be selected as much on the basis of politics as on firm efficiency.

The fact that partners are both adjudicators and participants raises two further difficulties for the tournament. First, the skewed incentives of individual partners are likely to skew the incentives of associates away from those that would be optimal for the firm. From the firm's perspective, associates should be willing to work for whichever partners are most in need of help. Given the importance of building relational capital with powerful partners, however, associates (particularly good associates) will seek to avoid working for partners who are less able to promote a given associate's career.

Second, partners have strong incentives to encourage this behavior by attempting to monopolize the services of star associates (even if they have to create "make-work" to do so) and by overvaluing their protege's contributions. Firms must develop mechanisms for policing this kind of opportunistic behavior. This task is made more difficult by the fact that partners are both formally and presumptively autonomous.

E.   Of Shirking Umpires and Absent Players

Galanter and Palay treat the partnership decision as the end of the tournament. One might seek to justify this conclusion on the ground that once a lawyer becomes a partner, she no longer has an incentive to shirk or to engage in other forms of opportunistic behavior since she is now a part owner of the firm. We do not believe, however, that Galanter and Palay hold this view. As two of the most trenchant observers of the legal profession, these authors are well aware that controlling opportunistic behavior by partners has become perhaps the single greatest preoccupation of large law firms. Instead, we believe that the authors' assumption that the tournament is divided into two and only two distinct phases—associateship and partnership—reflects the fact that their model is premised on a simple economic model in which there are only two categories of workers.

Characterizing the tournament as a single-round game masks two issues that have a direct bearing on how law firms structure their internal labor markets. The first issue relates to the firm's need to retain senior associates, who have been given valuable firm-specific human capital. Not all associates are fungible. Firms need both senior associates, who are capable of supervising junior lawyers and of relieving partners of many of their day-to-day responsibilities, and junior associates who can turn out the large volume of paperwork (and smaller volume of training work) required to service the needs of corporate clients. Due to the scarcity of training work, however, only a relatively small number of associates who start at a given firm are likely to "graduate" to the level of senior associates. As the years go by and senior associates confront the fact that their prospects for moving laterally may diminish the closer they get to the partnership decision, this number declines further. The net result is that firms can end up with too few senior associates.

The second issue bearing on law firms' internal labor markets is the danger that partners will shirk in ways that their fellow partners will find difficult to detect. Partners are even less supervised than associates and therefore have an even greater opportunity to shirk. Given their greater level of responsibility, the costs of a partner shirking are likely to be particularly high. For example, a partner may fail to bring his fair share of business into the firm, or may work less-than-diligently on matters that are generated by others.

Collectively, these two phenomena—the need to retain senior associates and to prevent shirking by partners—raise two additional problems for the standard promotion-to-partner tournament. First, firms must motivate junior associates to become senior associates, and motivate senior associates to stay with the firm, even though some of them will neither win the tournament nor easily find alternative employment with a comparable employer. Second, these firms must design ways to prevent shirking by partners. This last point underscores the need to make partnership decisions based on a prediction about the future as opposed to a reward for the past.

F. Choosing the Best Representatives, Not the Best Performers

In the standard tournament model, winners are selected solely on the basis of their past contributions to the firm. This selection criterion makes sense because the point of the tournament is to induce employees to exert high levels of effort and care at their current jobs by promising that those who perform the best will be rewarded in the future.

In their account of the promotion-to-partner tournament, Galanter and Palay qualify this standard assumption by suggesting that an additional criterion for selecting partners is the associate's development of his or her own human capital. Since excess human capital is what allows partners to employ additional associates, Galanter and Palay assume that by rewarding associates for their past accumulation of human capital, firms also ensure their own future growth and development.

We agree that human capital accumulation is a crucial element in the final partnership decision. This modification of the standard economic model, however, undermines tournament theory's usefulness as an explanatory model for the internal labor markets of elite firms.

One of the main virtues of tournament theory is that it provides employees with a measurable commitment that the firm will not cheat on its promise to reward those workers who have performed the best during the probationary period. In order for this commitment to be credible, however, the firm must clearly signal that tournament rewards will be given on the basis of past performance and not on the basis of the firm's prediction about future performance in the higher level job.

Two effects underlie this intuition. First, at the time the firm chooses tournament winners, it has already acquired all the benefits of the employee's work during the probationary period. As a result, it has the incentive to shark by ignoring this work and awarding tournament prizes on the basis of what is in the firm's best interest in the future, to wit, selecting employees that the firm believes will perform better at the higher level job regardless of how these employees performed as juniors. At the same time, associates, recognizing that what will ultimately be rewarded is their capacity to do the higher level job, have strong incentives to divert their energies into acquiring the skills associated with the higher level job rather than in diligently doing the work of a junior level employee. Since the point of a standard economic tournament is for the firm to cut down on the cost of preventing shirking by junior level workers by giving them a reason to work hard with little supervision, a system that hands out tournament rewards on the basis of predictions about future performance undermines the tournament's original purpose, namely to induce people to work hard while they are associates. As a result, by including—correctly, as we will argue—the firm's assessment of an associate's accumulated human capital as part of the partnership decision, Galanter and Palay's model no longer explains why associates work so hard with relatively little supervision on the large amount of routine paperwork that has little if any effect on their accumulation of the kind of human capital that will enable them to become partners.

One might respond to this objection by arguing that in the law firm context, the difference between choosing tournament winners on the basis of their past performance and choosing them on the basis of predictions about their future ability is unimportant because an associate's past performance is highly correlated to his or her future abilities as a partner. There are good reasons to believe, however, that this is not the case. At the most elementary level, firms need associates to bill a substantial number of hours, many of which will be spent, as we have already indicated, on paperwork. Although the inclination and willingness to work hard as an associate may signal the same willingness as a partner, it is the acquisition of human capital that is crucial for the partner. If a partner does not acquire a sufficiently high amount of human capital, there will not be enough to rent out to the associates. As a result * * * partners do not rank "hours worked" highly on the list of criteria that are important to the partnership decision.

Moreover, partners need a substantially different kind of human capital than good associates need—even associates who do primarily training work. The most important work done by today's large law firm partners is bringing in business. Associates do virtually no rainmaking. Although accumulating the kind of general and firm-specific human capital that comes from being a good associate undoubtedly plays a role in whether a given lawyer is likely to become a rainmaker, even the best associate may not have the different mix of personal and professional qualities that enable someone to attract significant corporate business.

Finally, as critics of tournament theory as a method for explaining law firm growth have noted, partnership decisions are beholden to the business cycle. Even if firms feel substantial pressure to make the same number of partners every year (regardless of swings in demand), the location of these partners (i.e., corporate, litigation, tax, etc.) will depend upon the amount of business that the firm believes each of these departments is likely to produce in the future. Thus, the fundamental issue with respect to both the individual candidate and the firm's needs is one of prediction, not reward.

Given these three differences between "associate" work and "partner" work, it is not surprising that, in a recent study of large New York law firms, O'Flaherty and Siow found only a loose correlation between "past performance" as an associate and "future performance" as a partner. As they conclude, "performance as an associate is not an especially informative signal about whether a lawyer will make a good partner." Given that "the costs of mistaken promotion [to partnership] are relatively high," firms have an incentive to focus on future performance as a partner, rather than past performance as an associate, when making partnership decisions.

The focus on prediction raises complications for the basic tournament model, both for the firm and for associates. Although assessing an associate's past efforts and investment is undeniably difficult, it is less difficult than predicting whether the associate will perform well in an area where she has so far not been tested, and whether she will be loyal to the incumbent partners. Moreover, the stakes resting on this predictive judgment are quite high, especially if one argues, as do Galanter and Palay, that partnership is not only the end of the tournament, but essentially equivalent to tenure.

From the associate's perspective, the fact that partnership is more of a prediction about the future than a reward for past service makes it difficult to evaluate the fairness of the firm's partnership choices. This is particularly true given the emphasis that firms place on issues such as the strength of future demand for a particular department's or office's services. Existing partners have the incentive to understate future demand in order to cut down on the number of partners who are entitled to share in future revenues. Because associates are rarely given access to information about either partner compensation or the firm's revenues, they will have a difficult time evaluating whether the firm's projections are realistic or opportunistic. This last point raises the final problem with the application of standard tournament theory to elite firms: the issue of transparency.

G. Who's on First?

Galanter and Palay assert that the promotion-to-partner tournament solves the mutual monitoring problems of associates and partners by making the rules of the game visible to all parties. Firms therefore need to give credible signals of their commitment to abide by the rules of the tournament game that can easily be monitored by associates.

Galanter and Palay argue that a firm's promotion rate provides a sufficient signal. According to their model, by promoting a fixed percentage of associates to partnership every year, the firm demonstrates that it has no incentive to shark by failing to promote the best associates from the available pool. Even assuming that firms promote a fixed percentage of associates every year—a contestable proposition—standing alone, this signal is unlikely to reassure associates that the firm is fulfilling its obligations in the tournament.

Two features of law firm life support this conclusion. First, the growing importance of lateral hiring makes it difficult for associates to determine whether firms are abiding by their commitment to promote those associates who have produced the most during the probationary period. Although associates can monitor how many partners were brought in as lateral associates, they will still have difficulty determining whether the firm was justified in bringing in these senior associates to meet demand, or whether this kind of hiring is simply a way to avoid having to reward the firm's "own" associates for work during their junior years.

Moreover, to the extent that existing associates have difficulty detecting whether firms are behaving opportunistically, law students, whom Galanter and Palay rely on to boycott firms who fail to fulfill their partnership commitments, are likely to be even less well informed. Although law students can observe whether a firm has made partners in a given year, they are unlikely to know whether these new members came up through the ranks or were added laterally. Nor are the statistics indicating the percentage of a given law school class who make partner at a firm particularly useful. Consistent with our first qualification to Galanter and Palay's assumptions, law students know that many of the associates who start work at a given law firm have no intention of making partner. Depending upon exactly how large this group of non-participants is, even a small partnership percentage may look relatively attractive if one assumes that most of the other associates who did not become partners left of their own volition.

The second problem firms have with displaying adherence to tournament rules arises from our discussion in the preceding Section about "past" versus "future" performance. To the extent that associates know that firms will consider an associate's likely future performance as a partner (as well as her past performance as an associate) when making partnership decisions, they can no longer rely on the total number of associates who made partner in any given year as a reliable barometer of whether the firm is sharking on its commitment to promote on the basis of past performance. To reach accurate judgments about the relative weighting of past versus future performance, associates would need to know how partners assessed these different criteria in specific cases.

If firms were structured as simple economic tournaments, one would expect to see firms attempting to provide associates with this kind of information. In essence, the firm would do everything possible to make the partnership process an open book so that associates (and law students) could see that the process was indeed a fair one in which those who performed best were promoted. For example, one might expect to see firms permit associates to sit in on partnership meetings, allowing them to ask questions and to make comments, although probably not to vote. Or, to the extent that the partnership meetings involve discussions of trade secrets, one might expect to see law firms hire external verifiers, such as accounting firms, to make sure that the process involved a fair and accurate evaluation and ranking of associate past performance.

Needless to say, these standard tournament theory predictions never fail to draw laughter from associates and partners at elite firms. Why? Because the partnership decisions at these firms are explicitly structured to be a black box, i.e., to provide as little external visibility as possible. Associates have little or no information about what goes on at partnership or committee meetings, and the partnerships at these firms do not see disclosing the details of these meetings as a way to increase efficiency. In the next Part, we offer some reasons why this is so. For the moment, however, we want to emphasize that standard tournament theory would predict that firms would respond to the ambiguity in the signal provided by their yearly partnership percentages by making the internal workings of their promotion practices more visible to associates. The fact that firms appear to be doing the opposite, i.e., making their promotion practices even less visible, suggests that these firms are not structured as simple economic tournaments.

In sum, none of Galanter and Palay's seven assumptions about the operation of the promotion-to-partner tournament hold up under scrutiny. Since these assumptions are consistent with standard tournament theory, the fact that they do not correspond with our observations of elite firm practices suggests that these institutions are not structured as standard economic tournaments * * *

III. THE TOURNAMENT RECONCEIVED: WHY THIS IS NOT YOUR FATHER'S PARTNERSHIP TOURNAMENT

Contemporary elite law firms continue to follow many of the traditional practices that led scholars to characterize the promotion policies of these organizations as tournaments. Firms continue to hire the majority of their associates out of law school and, after a relatively fixed number of years, promote some to partnership and dismiss the rest. For all of the fanfare surrounding the introduction of "contract lawyers," "permanent associates," "professional managers," and other similar innovations, these developments remain at the margin.

As we demonstrated in the last Part, however, beneath the surface of this important continuity, the pressures exerted by the changing market conditions in which big firms compete for labor and clients have taken their toll on the traditional promotion-to-partner tournament. Thus, although the process may look the same as it did in the golden age, and in many important respects is the same, firms have made significant modifications to their internal labor practices to take account of their new environment ...

B. Multiple Incentive Systems

Tournament theory assumes that associates are motivated by the desire to make partner (and the fear of being terminated if they do not get that reward). In Part II, we argued that this assumption fails accurately to capture the motivations of many associates. Standing alone, this suggests that if firms are going to keep their direct monitoring costs within reasonable limits, these institutions must find additional ways to motivate associates with weak commitments to partnership to work hard with relatively little supervision. For this reason alone, firms are likely to adopt a multiple incentive strategy.

Our observations in Part II suggest, however, that firms have reasons for adopting a multiple incentive strategy that go beyond the expressed preferences of associates. For example, contrary to Galanter and Palay's model, under current conditions, elite firms cannot afford for every associate to be strongly motivated to win the tournament. As we noted, the kind of training work and relational capital that associates need to win the tournament are scarce commodities. If every associate were to compete fiercely to acquire these goods, firms would have to expend substantial resources to guard against sabotage and other forms of costly strategic behavior by associates.

More important, because firms select partners in part on the basis of which associates have acquired the greatest amounts of firm-specific and relational capital during their probationary period, it is in the best interest of these institutions if these scarce goods end up being concentrated in the small pool of senior associates from which the firm will ultimately make its selection. The smaller the number of associates competing for scarce and valuable training and mentoring opportunities, the more of these forms of capital each of those who are competing are likely to acquire. Assuming that these valued associates can be induced to stay long enough to be considered for partnership—a subject about which we will have more to say later—limiting the number of associates competing for partnership is likely to raise the average quality of the pool from which the firm ultimately selects its partners.

These advantages of limiting the number of associates actively competing for partnership underscore the need for firms to implement a multiple incentive strategy. In addition to training work, firms have large amounts of paperwork that also must be done by associates. Given that this work is unlikely to lead to partnership, paperwork associates need more than the tournament to motivate them to do this tedious but necessary work competently and effectively with relatively little supervision by partners. Firms appear to be succeeding at this task. As we observed at the outset, even associates doing primarily paperwork exert high levels of effort and care in their work. The question is what is motivating these lawyers to do so.

We suggest that firms rely on three additional motivational tools (beyond the chance for partnership) to either supplement or supplant the incentive effects of the tournament: high (above market) associate wages, associate reputational bonds, and the promise of general (as opposed to firm-specific) training. We discuss each one in turn.

1. High Wages. High wages offer incentives for employees to exert high levels of effort where the wage paid is significantly higher than that paid at an alternative job. These high or "efficiency" wages serve as sufficient incentives because workers fear losing these scarce high-wage jobs; by definition, those who lose these coveted positions will have difficulty finding similarly high-paying jobs in the marketplace. At the same time, workers know that employers can easily find replacement workers who will gladly take their high-paying jobs. This fear induces employees to exert high levels of effort and care even where monitoring is low. Employers, in turn, use part of the gains from increases in worker productivity and decreases in monitoring costs to pay for the above market wages * * *

[O]nce an associate joins a corporate firm, the wages paid by these employers create a substantial inducement to stay and to continue to work hard. For some associates, deferred gratification makes the prospect of acquiring a lifestyle that is at least commensurate to (if not in excess of) their high salaries virtually irresistible. Others may decide to stay at high-paying firm jobs simply to pay back student loans. Moreover, as we indicated firm leaders might predict at the hiring stage, the lure of continued high salaries (not to mention the super bonus that accompanies partnership) induces some associates to opt into the tournament once they have spent a few years at the firm.

2. Reputational Bonds. Associates risk losing something potentially even more valuable than their salaries if they lose their elite law firm jobs: They risk losing the market value of their hard-earned educational and employment related credentials. The value of this reputational "bond" is an important deterrent to shirking.

The mechanism by which this incentive structure operates is straightforward. The large law firms hire primarily from elite law schools and from the top part of the classes of non-elite law schools. These students, therefore, enter law firms with a valuable reputational credential—the signal that they attended and succeeded at an elite law school, or some other comparable signal (such as finishing first in their class at a regional law school or obtaining a prestigious clerkship). This signal is valuable because it suggests that the person who possesses it has the skills and disposition to become a good lawyer. Because prestigious academic credentials are only a signal of whether the individual is likely to be a good lawyer—and, as we have already suggested, a loose signal at that—the value of these credentials can always be undermined by evidence of the real thing, i.e., evidence of whether the bearer of the signal is in fact a good lawyer. To the extent that there is convincing evidence that an associate is not as good as her academic credentials would suggest, she risks forfeiting much of the value of her education. Given both the price of an elite education and the overwhelming evidence that prestigious academic credentials (if untainted) pay handsome long-term dividends, forfeiting this reputational bond constitutes a substantial penalty.

Law firms rely on the fear of this potential loss to motivate their associates to work carefully and hard even in the absence of direct monitoring. Because monitoring lawyer quality is inherently difficult, and because an associate's current employer will always have more information than potential employers upon which to base qualitative judgments, both firms and associates know that the firm's judgment about the quality of an associate's work is likely to carry significant weight in the marketplace. Consequently, being fired from an elite law firm job is likely to diminish substantially the value of an associate's prestigious educational credentials. Although other employers will take the fact that the fired associate graduated from a top school like Harvard into consideration when making employment decisions, that signal is likely to be swamped by the negative signal of having been terminated * * *

3. *Training.* Law students know that they need to develop their general human capital if they are to become successful lawyers. Law school offers little instruction in how to be a lawyer. Students, therefore, have good reason to seek out jobs that they believe will train them in the skills and dispositions that they need to become competent practitioners. Firms, in turn, have strong incentives to cater to this need by promising these aspiring professionals that in addition to their high salaries, associates will receive significant training that will be of value to them wherever they work.

The promise of general, as opposed to firm-specific, training helps firms to reduce their monitoring expenses for those associates who are not participating in the tournament. Like high wages, the promise of general training gives lawyers with low partnership aspirations a reason to join firms as opposed to working for other legal employers. This increase in the applicant pool is important to firms. In addition, law students who join firms in the hope of receiving general training will also be motivated to exert high levels of effort and care in their work as associates to the extent that they believe that hard work improves their own development * * *

In sum, elite firms pursue a multiple incentive strategy. Consistent with tournament theory, firms continue to hope that some lawyers will be motivated by the chance of making partner. For those who are not, firms create additional incentives through high wages, reputational bonds, and the promise of general training. Moreover, these four incentive systems (including the tournament) are interconnected. The less credible a firm's partnership promises, the more it is likely to rely on high wages or promises of providing valuable external signals * * *

C. Multiple Tracks and Multiple Rounds: Why Sampras and Agassi Never Meet before the Final Round

As a formal matter, firms maintain few distinctions between associates in a given class. This formal uniformity, however, masks fundamental differences between the experiences and opportunities of particular associates. In order to ensure that they have adequate supplies of senior associates and partners, firms have to train some of their associates. For reasons previously discussed, however, it is inefficient for a firm to invest in training all of its associates. Given the confluence of high leverage ratios and low levels of commitment by many associates to winning the tournament, the majority of associates who join a given large firm will leave, most before reaching the rank of senior associate. Moreover, as we noted, firms generate an enormous quantity of paperwork which can be done by associates with little or no training. Taken together, these two factors—high associate attrition and the abundance of paperwork—give firms strong incentives to separate associates into two informal, but nevertheless quite real, groups: training-work associates and paperwork associates * * *

Firms create a multiround tournament by the manner in which they distribute and evaluate training work. Associates who do well on their initial training assignments are given preferential access to additional training opportunities. Those junior associates who successfully complete a number of such assignments move up to become senior associates, giving them even greater access to training opportunities, and, equally important, helping them build strong relationships with partners.

These relationships, in turn, further improve a training associate's prospects when he or she enters into the actual promotion-to-partner tournament: the competition among senior associates for one of the firm's limited number of partnership slots. Although training does not guarantee partnership, it is the ticket that allows training associates to compete for the reputational capital that winning the tournament requires. As we argued, the interests of individual partners are not necessarily the same as those of the firm. Although the firm has an interest in partners spreading training opportunities to all associates who plausibly might be considered on the partnership track, individual partners in a large firm will primarily focus only on training associates who will benefit their practices. As a result, "once partners find associates they like who can do the work, they're more than happy to continue delegating work only to those associates."

Finally, once associates are firmly on the training track, they are likely to be further protected in the evaluation process. Given that the firm has already made a substantial investment in the development of these associates' careers (in the form of unreimbursed and unrecouped training costs), partners are likely to see it as in the firm's interest to help training associates learn from their mistakes, thereby inducing them to stay at the firm and continue to work * * *

Tracking, therefore, helps firms solve the dilemma created by the fact that many entering associates have only a weak commitment to winning the tournament. As we have repeatedly stated, only a handful of the associates begin their careers at an elite firm with a strong commitment to making partner. Most other associates are uncertain about their future plans, i.e., whether they will attempt to make partner, or will leave the firm after a few years. Through tracking, firms strengthen the commitments of associates whom they want to stay while simultaneously giving those not receiving training reason to seek rewards other than winning the tournament. Associates who continue to get good work are more likely to be happy and to stay at the firm. Not only are they satisfying their desire to develop human capital, but they are also receiving a tangible signal from the firm that their chances of winning the tournament are better than the many associates who are only receiving paperwork * * *

At the same time, those associates who consistently receive only paperwork are likely to realize that their partnership chances are limited and leave voluntarily (as soon as they have earned enough money or obtained enough general training for an in-house or other job). Firms benefit from these "voluntary" departures in two ways. First, at a human level, firing someone is not easy. No matter how much the decision is dressed up, the decision to turn an associate down for partnership or to ask an associate to leave is unpleasant. Second, at the institutional level, "voluntary" departures make it easier for firms to tell both remaining associates and law students that the odds for those who "really want" to become partners are substantially better than the naked statistics showing the percentage of each entering class that actually obtains this goal would lead one to believe ...

With each passing "round," more and more associates decide (partly in response to actions taken by the firm and its partners) to abandon thoughts of being on the partnership or training track. For these associates, the shadow of the tournament as a motivational device recedes, replaced (for as long as they stay at the firm) by their desire to keep their high wages, protect their reputational bonds, or acquire general (as opposed to firm-specific or relational) capital. As a result, they are unlikely to engage in the kind of fierce competition for training work that would, as we argued in the last Part, undermine collegial working relationships. At the same time, those associates who continue to aspire to partnership—those on the training track—are increasingly motivated by the prospect of winning the tournament.

Tracking, therefore, is an important feature of the internal labor markets of firms, including the final promotion-to-partner tournament among senior associates. The question remains, however, how some associates seem to be "tracked" from their first day at the firm. To answer this question, we turn our attention to [a] standard feature of the kind of sporting events upon which tournament theory is loosely based: seeding.

* * *

F. *Information Management: Why Agassi Is Sometimes Seeded Higher at the U.S. Open than at Other Tournaments*

Tournament theory assumes that it is in the firm's interest to make the rules of the game transparent to all concerned. However, once we understand the complexity of an elite firm's internal labor market, including those aspects that are structured as a tournament, it is clear that firms have strong incentives to manage the flow of information to associates and law students in order to maximize the system's overall incentive effects. In order to accomplish this objective, firms must pay attention to the effects of various kinds of information on the effort levels exerted by associates at different stages in their careers. To understand this point, it is once again useful to look at real tournaments.

Information management systems, although not the norm, exist in some tournaments. For example, in certain debate tournaments, teams are not told whether they have won or lost their preliminary rounds until after all of these rounds have been completed. By withholding this information, tournament officials hope to induce maximum effort by all participants, since even those with poor records will believe that they have a chance to get into the elimination rounds. Similarly, until recently, in soccer only the referee knew exactly how much time was left in the game. Once again, controlling this information helps to induce "end-of-game" effort at an earlier point than would otherwise occur, as teams seek to minimize the risk that they will run out of time. Even tennis officials often refuse to disclose how they arrive at their initial seedings and brackets.

Elite firms utilize a similar information control policy. As we indicated in Part II, firms do not have an open door policy about how they make their partnership decisions. Instead, firms pursue a "black box" approach in which associates are provided only a vague idea about the criteria for making partner and almost no information about how these criteria are applied in particular cases. Notwithstanding the fact that junior associates are formally reviewed at least once a year, most of these lawyers have relatively little information about their partnership chances. As a preliminary matter, virtually every firm we have looked at vehemently denies that there is a separate "partnership" (or training) track. Moreover, to the extent that associates are told about their own performance, they are rarely given information about the performance of their peers. As a result, although many associates know that there is a training track, and that some associates are seeded on that track, they are expressly denied official information about how or why this has occurred * * *

[F]irms are * * * likely to engage in a strategy of selective disclosure, designed both to get the "right" information to the "right" people while minimizing the effects of the "wrong" information. As a preliminary matter, this involves distinguishing between senior associates who are fighting to win one of the finite number of partnership slots and the associate pool in general.

1. Information Management for the Senior Associates: Signals, Skills, and Relational Capital. Firms use a "black box" approach in making new partners. Much like the information control strategies in debate and soccer, this approach maximizes the "end-of-game" effort by senior associates. Recall that these lawyers are primarily motivated to work hard with little supervision by the desire to make partner. Having no more than a minimal amount of information about how they rank against their competitors and what weights are going to be given to different aspects of their performance/capital-acquisition, these lawyers have strong incentives to work hard at everything possible. From the firm's perspective, therefore, the black box approach—not the open door policy suggested by standard tournament theory—maximizes the incentive effects of the tournament for these lawyers.

In contrast, look at what might happen if associates knew both their relative rankings and the exact criteria (signals) used to rank them. If associates at the top knew that they were far enough ahead of those at the bottom, these front runners would have an incentive to exert less effort since they would already know that they will win. At the same time, those at the bottom might give up and leave before the partnership decision is made.

* * * The black box approach, however, does create one important problem for the overall operation of the tournament for senior associates. Galanter and Palay correctly argue that one reason why firms gravitate toward a tournament structure is to provide associates with a mechanism (the number of partners made in any given year) that will help them guard against sharking by the firm. If partnership is a black box rather than the open book implicitly envisioned by tournament theory, what assurances do associates have that the firm will treat them fairly? This question is especially urgent, since, as Galanter and Palay also note, if associates have no assurances that the process will reward their efforts in acquiring firm-specific capital, they have strong incentives not to do so.

The tournament structure we have described suggests three possible answers. First, since partnership is not a reward for past performance, but instead is a prediction about who will be the most productive in the future, firms have less incentive to cheat. When partnership is a reward for past performance, cheating allows firms to avoid paying for the benefits already acquired while leaving the institution free to optimize its future returns. When a firm "cheats" by failing to promote those associates most likely to bring in future revenues, it reduces its future returns * * *

Politics * * * can also help protect senior associates. The senior associates competing for partnership, in large part, have acquired substantial relational capital. They have reached this stage in the tournament, because there are partners who have invested in their success. These partners, as we have suggested, can act as a check on whether other partners are acting opportunistically in seeking to promote the interests of their protégés * * *

Finally, firms can try to induce senior associates to bear the risk that the firm will behave opportunistically through the same high wage strategy that they use to induce associates to join firms in the first instance. Firms profit handsomely from the black box approach. Senior associates—arguably the most valuable lawyers in any law firm—are induced to work extremely hard on virtually every facet of their jobs with almost no supervision, thereby freeing partners to bring in the new business that the firm needs to survive. Firms therefore have sufficient resources to pay these valuable lawyers a risk premium to compensate them for bearing the additional uncertainty produced by the black box * * *

2. *Information Management for the General Pool.* With respect to those who gain access to the training track after their initial projects, these favored associates need only know that they are favored. For the most part, this involves conveying accurate information. Thus, firm leaders need to tell training associates that they will continue to get good work and that realistically, they are only competing for partnership against the relatively small number of other associates who also have been given this privileged status.

Firm leaders, however, must be careful to convey this information quietly. Just because an associate is not on the training track does not mean that he does not consider himself to be competing in the tournament. The less that associate knows about the opportunities afforded those on the training track (or, to put the point somewhat differently, the harder it is for a paperwork associate to evaluate the difference between the work he is doing and training work) the more likely it is that he will be motivated to work hard in order to increase his chances of making partner. This is one reason, we suspect, why firms keep the evaluations of associates in their first few years vague and generally upbeat * * *

IV. CONCLUSION: TOWARD A NEW SYNTHESIS

* * *Although firms must find ways to motivate their associates to work hard with relatively little supervision, with the exception of those senior associates who are within a short distance of partnership, *the tournament is not the primary means by which firms accomplish this objective.* For the most part, junior associates who join large law firms are motivated primarily by high salaries, reputational bonds, and the promise of general training. For these lawyers, the promise of partnership is at best a distant shadow of a reward. Based upon their impressions of the lives of the firm's current partners, furthermore, many entering associates are quite unsure about whether they would even want partnership if it were offered to them. To be sure, firms attempt to nurture this ambiguous spark in some associates through seeding and tracking. With respect to the rest, however, firms are content to trade high salaries and the promise—although in most cases, not the reality— of general training for a few years of paperwork before these associates redeem their reputational bonds and move on.

If monitoring were the firm's only problem, this might be the end of the story. But in addition to supervising its associates, law firms must also train the next generation of senior associates and partners. Firms have responded to this need by creating a de facto training track for certain associates. The existence of a separate training track, ironically, helps firms solve part of their monitoring problems. Associates who are being trained are also likely to be monitored. More important, the training track provides the gateway to the real promotion-to-partner tournament, since only those associates who have been trained will have the firm-specific and relational capital that it takes to have a realistic chance of becoming partners in the firm.

The real tournament, therefore, only begins when a lawyer becomes a senior associate * * *

[The] differences between standard tournament theory and the reconceived model we present here have important practical and theoretical implications. As a practical matter, law students and young associates have much to gain from puncturing some of the myths surrounding the promotion-to-partner tournament. These aspiring lawyers are typically presented with one of two stories about their future careers in large law firms. The first is decidedly upbeat: Large law firms are the ultimate meritocracies in which the "best" lawyers rise to the top and the rest work on interesting and rewarding cases before walking away with the best training that any lawyer can receive. It is a testament to the changes documented in Part II that it is almost impossible for anyone—even law firm partners—to recount this happy story with a straight face. As a result, the optimistic traditional story has been replaced by one of unremitting pessimism. According to this account, the work of lawyers today is all drudgery, depressing, and too specialized. There is neither any meaningful mentoring by partners nor the type of long-term relationships that developed in the "golden age" of lawyering.

The reality of the modern elite firm falls somewhere in between these two accounts. While we agree that much of the work that associates do is highly specialized, qualifies as drudgery, and involves fewer client relationships and much less mentoring, these characterizations do not define "all" of associate work. For associates on the training track, the work is not drudgery, it is not over-specialized, there is mentoring, and the associates do develop relationships with clients. Both standard accounts—the traditional optimistic one preferred by firms, and the pessimistic one that has become the ordinary religion of law students—overlook this diversity.

Martha Neil, Brave, New World of Partnership

90 ABA Journal 31 (2004)

Once upon a time—but easily within the memory of many attorneys still in practice—typical young law school graduates took jobs as associates at firms with the intention of spending their entire professional lives at that one place—perhaps with an eventual detour into the judiciary.

If they worked hard and did good work, most associates could expect to become partners with equity stakes in their firms. Once they did, it was highly unusual to be forced out of the partnership, even if they became less productive than their peers. Likewise, it was practically unheard of for star partners to be lured away by better offers from competing law firms.

Today, that scenario seems almost like a fairy tale.

Now, new associates at many major firms are expected to bill 1,800 to 2,000 hours a year, or more. And they often start working at a firm with the assumption that they may well be moving on after two or three years, or less. Only a small fraction of associates are eventually offered partnerships. And for those who do grasp the brass ring, the prize of partnership isn't what it used to be.

Many law firms now have two-tiered partnerships: equity partners on one level, and, below them, salaried partners without equity stakes in the firm. The result is, in effect, an extended partnership track—eight years, say, to become a junior nonequity partner, then perhaps another five until full equity partnership is offered to those who make the grade.

But even for them, partnership doesn't offer the kind of job security it once did. Increasingly, partners are finding themselves demoted or forced into early retirement if they don't meet today's tougher productivity standards, as younger colleagues fill their spots in the partnership ranks.

Certainly, things can work both ways. Valued rainmakers are like free agents on sports teams, routinely looking for more lucrative partnerships elsewhere. When they find them, they often take along not only their clients but also well-regarded colleagues, potentially decimating the firms from which they're departing.

As a result of this sea change, many lawyers are asking themselves what once was the unthinkable: Is making partner worth the trouble?

"Associates voiced strong reservations about their desire to achieve partnership status, observing that the lifestyles of partners and the necessary sacrifices partners make in their personal lives led associates to question whether that professional goal meshed with their own goals," states a report on attrition among associates who graduated from law school between 1998 and 2002. The report was issued in 2003 by the NALP Foundation, a research affiliate of the National Association for Law Placement in Washington, D.C.

Within the first two years of practice, nearly a quarter of the associates at law firms of all sizes have moved on, according to the NALP report, titled *Keeping the Keepers II: Mobility and Management of Associates*. After nearly five years, more than half of those hired out of law school have left their original firms.

While the five-year attrition rate for women, 54.9 percent, was only slightly higher than for men, 52.3 percent, attrition rates jumped more significantly for minorities. The five-year attrition rate for minority male lawyers was 68.0 percent, and the attrition rate for female minority lawyers was 64.4 percent.

The NALP study found that firms of 500 lawyers or more generally had lower attrition rates than smaller firms. The highest attrition rates generally occurred at firms with between 251 and 500 attorneys. (Other studies have identified higher attrition rates at larger firms.)

In recent programs sponsored by the ABA on diversity in the legal profession, both women lawyers and lawyers of color said they continue to face barriers to advancement in law firms and other practice settings.

"I think a lot of people, they're looking at the partner they're working for, they're looking ahead, and they're observing, questioning whether that's what they really want," says Mark Harris of New York City. He left after several years as a law firm associate to establish Axiom Legal, which sends lawyers to work in-house at corporate legal departments.

Nice Work if You Can Get It

But Others Say Law Partnership Is Still a Great Gig

"Frankly, I think it is as attractive and in some ways more attractive" than it used to be, says John R. Sapp, managing partner of Michael Best & Friedrich in Milwaukee and the author of *Making Partner, A Guide for Law Firm Associates,* published by the ABA Section of Law Practice Management.

Sapp says law firm partners enjoy many advantages today, including higher compensation and greater opportunities to do interesting work. These benefits were created by efficiencies of computerization and the trend toward lawyer specialization.

Another managing partner agrees. "It's one of those jobs where you get to work consistently with committed, intelligent people—your clients, your colleagues at the firm—and you get challenged to solve problems," says Debora de Hoyos of Mayer, Brown, Rowe & Maw in Chicago. "Those of us who stick with it find that very gratifying."

One thing that has changed in recent years is the number of desirable alternatives to partnership, says de Hoyos. She cites in-house corporate counsel work as an example. These jobs offer more interesting work and higher pay than they used to, and more partners now find them appealing.

Another alternative is to pass up the ultra-competitive environment of the nation's largest law firms and join a smaller law practice, says Carol Kanarek, a New York City lawyer who works as a career counselor.

"There are many, many high-quality smaller law firms out there that are competing with large law firms in many areas," she says. "That's not something that you used to see."

At the same time, Sapp says, "We've had a significant increase in the number of folks who do not want to make the time commitment" required of partners, particularly when they and their spouses both have professional careers. He thinks the financial flexibility created when both spouses have professional jobs may be one reason for this change.

Meanwhile, the financial payoff is a major motivation for lawyers who do pursue partnerships at larger firms, says de Hoyos. "Whether you are male or female, if you stay with practicing law at this level, chances are the money is a significant part of it."

David M. Neff agrees that the money is a big motivator. "Typically, people would not want to give up equity partnership unless they want to work fewer hours," he says. "And that would be pretty rare."

Neff, a bankruptcy lawyer, has been a partner at two different law firms. In 1993, he became an equity partner at Jenner & Block in Chicago. In 2002, he made a lateral move to become an equity partner in the Chicago office of Piper Rudnick. Still, he thinks it is harder to become a partner today than it was even a decade ago.

"There are just a heck of a lot more lawyers around," Neff says. "That means there are probably a heck of a lot more talented lawyers around. And when you combine that with the mobility of lawyers, there's just a lot more competition to get into the capital partner ranks."

As a result, "There is a greater requirement that you have your own business" to improve your chances at becoming an equity partner, Neff says.

Fighting the Odds

Neff is not alone in citing changes within recent decades in what it takes to become a partner.

When Kanarek graduated from law school in 1979 and went to work as an associate at a large Manhattan law firm, the number of partners there and at many other firms was roughly equal to the number of associates, and it was generally expected that associates who worked hard and did a good job would be made partner. "There was a presumption when you were going in that there would be a partnership for you," she recalls.

Now, those presumptions are practically reversed, she says, as "a whole constellation of factors" weigh against an associate's chances of eventually making partner.

Those factors include a trend toward specializing early in one's career on a narrow practice area that may or may not still be hot when a particular lawyer is considered for partnership, Kanarek says. Moreover, now there often is "leverage" of as many as four or five associates—and sometimes even more—for every one partner at big firms, she says. This ratio greatly increases the competition among associates for partnership slots and greatly decreases the opportunity to work closely with partners and learn from them.

"It's not enough to be just a really good lawyer" in competing for partnerships, Kanarek says. "You have to be a really good lawyer, in the right practice area, in the right time in the economy. There are so many variables that are just beyond anyone's control."

In some cases, a lawyer's choice of law firm can significantly affect his or her chances at making partner several years later, Sapp says.

"Assuming your goal is to be a partner, you should recognize that your choice of firm is one of the most important decisions you will make," Sapp writes in *Making Partner*. "The reality is that firms vary enormously in how many partners they make, what is required and what being a partner entails."

Rather than simply focus on firm prestige and associate pay when deciding where to work, it is important to read trade publications and "ask a lot of tough questions of the people who are there already," Sapp advises. Information worth seeking includes the ratio of associates to partners, the firm's partnership structure, the firm's criteria for achieving partnership, and the percentage of associates selected for partnership.

It also can be illuminating to get a picture of the firm's finances, although firm managers may be reluctant to share that information, says Frank McClain–Sewer, who formed his own firm in New York City after leaving a midsize Manhattan firm where he was a junior partner.

"To the extent that you're allowed to look at the financials to see the debt distribution ratios for those partners with power versus the nonequity junior partners," he says, "that would be the kind of document that would allow you to make an informed decision whether you want to become a partner or whether you can live with that level of inequity."

The challenge today isn't just becoming a partner. Thriving and even surviving in the partnership ranks isn't as easy as it once was.

"There is still, I think, a romanticized notion of being an equity partner in a large firm," Neff says. "And then, when people get there, they see that it's an awful lot of hard work—a lot of demands on your time, and a lot of pressures to perform," he says, citing the need to bring in business, and the need to keep busy despite a higher billable rate that discourages colleagues from assigning work to their partners. "Pressures can be even more intense when you become a capital partner than when you were a noncapital partner or an associate."

Shannon L. Spangler, managing partner of the San Francisco office of Shook, Hardy & Bacon, says there is more pressure on existing partners to generate business compared to just a few years ago.

Spangler attributes the increase to changing attitudes on the part of corporate clients, who bring in new lawyers—both in-house and outside counsel—more frequently than they used to. "The longtime relationships that we used to count on, you can't take those for granted," she says.

There was a time when partners stayed at their firms until they retired or died.

"Moving from Firm A to Firm B, and taking a client group, was basically unheard of, at least in New York," recounts Joseph Hinsey, who was a partner at White & Case in New York City for more than 20 years until he left in 1987 to teach at Harvard University.

In those days, once you became a partner, a uniform compensation scheme applied in which all partners at the same seniority level received the same increases, recalls Hinsey, a professor emeritus at Harvard Business School.

Today, both lifetime job security and lockstep compensation are long gone from most U.S. law partnerships, Kanarek says. Because of more stringent law firm productivity demands, "You find that people are billing enormous numbers of hours right up until the time they retire," she says.

New Focus on the Bottom Line

The tendency in a competitive business environment is to emphasize law practice as a business. With that mind-set, the need—or desire—to maximize profits trumps traditional professional values that include loyalty to one's partners, even in the face of their failings.

"In the past, if some partners were very good at business development and others were less so, law firms tended to take a relatively tolerant view of that and just say, 'Ah well, people play different roles,' " says David H. Maister, a legal consultant in Boston. "Now, there's a lot more follow-up that takes place, and the extremes of performance on the downside are not accepted."

Partners who don't meet present-day productivity standards can be—and often are—expelled or demoted, forced into nonequity partnerships or senior counsel positions, Maister says.

Such actions, however, can pose risks for firms and the partners who remain.

In 1999, for instance, Chicago-based Sidley & Austin (which has since become Sidley Austin Brown & Wood) announced the demotion of 32 partners, most of them over 50 years old.

The demotions triggered an investigation by the U.S. Equal Employment Opportunity Commission for possible age discrimination.

Workplace anti-discrimination laws do not apply to partners because they are not employees. But many of the partners at Sidley were treated like employees and had virtually no voice in running the firm, the EEOC contended in pleadings filed in U.S. district court. Therefore, they should be considered employees for purposes of enforcing anti-discrimination laws, the commission maintained.

The pleadings were made in support of a subpoena seeking discovery of relevant information from the firm. The Chicago-based 7th U.S. Circuit Court of Appeals ruled that the commission was entitled to obtain some of the information it was seeking. The EEOC's investigation is continuing, but there are no court proceedings on the matter at this time.

The implosion in early 2003 of Brobeck, Phleger & Harrison, a onetime San Francisco-based powerhouse, provides another cautionary tale about the risks of partnership.

When Brobeck closed its doors, it left a number of long-time partners without promised retirement benefits. Now, a group of retired Brobeck partners along with other plaintiffs, including the firm itself, is seeking to recoup their losses in court. The suit was filed in early October in California state court. Defendants are Brobeck's former managing partner, Tower Snow, who was expelled in 2002, and his new firm, London-based behemoth Clifford Chance Rogers & Wells.

The suit contends that Snow and Clifford Chance improperly encouraged the departure in 2002 of some 16 Brobeck lawyers and their clients to establish a new San Francisco office of Clifford Chance. The suit seeks more than $100 million in damages based on allegations including breach of fiduciary duty, unfair competition and tortious interference. Clifford Chance says the allegations are without merit.

Law firms in recent years have been adopting organizational structures intended to insulate partners, especially equity partners, from liability for legal claims and other obligations.

In traditional general partnerships, such obligations were difficult to avoid because partners were personally liable for the firm's debts. Today, growing numbers of law firms are set up as limited liability partnerships or companies—LLPs and LLCs—to protect partners' personal assets.

These new forms of corporate structure, however, are still largely untested in the courts.

At firms that do suffer financial setbacks, it isn't certain whether LLP and LLC organizational structures will shield partners from personal liability. Because law firms rarely go bankrupt, there is little decisional law on point. Also, even though most law firms are now LLPs and LLCs, it isn't unusual for partners to personally guarantee certain firm debts, such as office leases.

Nonequity partners may view one of the few advantages of their status as a lack of personal liability for firm debts. That's because nonequity partners are likely to be characterized as the equivalent of employees, Neff notes.

But a potential pitfall awaits nonequity partners if they are represented to firm creditors as indistinguishable from equity partners. This is at least arguably the case, since business cards, firm letterheads and the like ordinarily do not make clear which "partners" in fact have no stake in the firm. If creditors rely on such alleged misinformation to their detriment, nonequity partners might be included in any claim in which equity partners can be held personally liable, Neff suggests.

Neff says he is not aware of any cases that have litigated the issue. But he notes that section 16 of the Uniform Partnership Act states that an individual who holds himself or herself out as a partner may be estopped from denying liability for the partnership's debts to another party who relies on those representations.

In some ways, law firms have become their own worst enemies, suggest some legal management experts.

One of the chief villains is the billable hour, which some view as an arbitrary and inaccurate measure of the true worth of an associate or partner. The ceiling for billable hours has risen steadily for decades.

While billable hours offer some quantifiable standard for measuring a lawyer's performance, they also tend to treat legal skills as commodities, Hinsey says. And since many law firms have become much larger through the 1980s and 1990s, often with many far-flung offices, partners may not be familiar with other attorneys in the firm and their work except through billable hours.

"In a very large firm, if a young associate bills 2,800 hours and another associate bills 1,900, which is the better associate?" Hinsey says. "Well, if you know the two, it may very well be that the second is the star. But if the decision-maker in the very large organization does not know the first lawyer or the second lawyer, is the right decision going to be made? Hopefully, someone up the line has the access to the expertise of the low-billing person. But analytically, each billable hour, it's a commodity if you're just looking at billable hours."

Others say the emphasis on billable hours signals the deterioration of law practice as a profession. Maister says, "We've turned what should have been an incredibly noble, meaningful profession—we've turned everybody in it into viewing what they do as burdensome labor."

Elizabeth H. Gorman, MOVING AWAY FROM "UP
OR OUT": DETERMINANTS OF PERMANENT
EMPLOYMENT IN LAW FIRMS

33 LAW & SOC'Y REV. 637 (1999)

Since the early 1980s, large law firms have increasingly implemented permanent employment arrangements alongside traditional probationary ones. Some permanent employees hold titles that clearly indicate the permanent nature of their employment such as "senior attorney," "principal attorney," "counsel," "of counsel," "senior counsel," and "special counsel." Other permanent employees hold the title "associate," as probationary employees do; they are referred to informally as "permanent associates." Permanent employees may be former probationary associates of the firm who have been rejected for partnership, or they may have been hired directly into their current positions. In some firms, permanent employees remain eligible for possible promotion to partnership; in others, they do not. Even if they do remain eligible, they have no guarantee of consideration, and no fixed time period within which it must occur.

This new pattern represents a marked departure from the employment model that was dominant in large law firms for much of the twentieth century. Under traditional "up-or-out" arrangements, associates are employed on a probationary basis for a fixed period, usually between 6 and 10 years from law school graduation. Through on-the-job training, associates are expected to develop practical skills that are not taught in law school. Upon the expiration of the probationary period, firm partners consider the associate for admission to the firm's partnership. If the associate is "passed over," or rejected, he or she is expected to leave the firm within a reasonable period of time.

The spread of permanent employment arrangements has important consequences for lawyers' careers, the organization of legal practice, and the cohesion of the bar. Some lawyers are likely to welcome the opportunity for permanent employment, emphasizing the relative security of such positions and the freedom they offer to focus on law practice rather than on management or client development. Others are likely to view a permanent-employee position as a signal of career failure. Whether viewed positively or negatively, permanent-employee positions necessarily rank below partners in status and authority, and they thus conflict with lingering professional norms of autonomy and formal equality among professional colleagues. Permanent-employee positions also add a layer of hierarchy within large firms, thus advancing the bureaucratization of the organizational settings in which law is practiced. In addition, as part of the proliferation of status distinctions among lawyers, permanent employment arrangements contribute to the growing stratification of the bar.

Despite a general increase in the use of permanent employment, law firms vary considerably in the extent to which they have created permanent positions. Which firms make greater use of permanent employment? Organizational theory directs us to look in organizations' environments for factors that influence their structures and practices. Important changes have occurred in the legal environment during the same period that has witnessed changes in firms' employment practices. I begin by examining three changes that have attracted a great deal of scholarly and journalistic commentary: the increase in the complexity of legal work, the weakening of ties between law firms and clients, and the fading of social norms of collegiality. I then propose that these factors be treated as variables that can explain cross-sectional variation in firms' use of permanent employment. I argue that firms that have been more heavily exposed to these new features of the legal environment— firms where work is more complex, ties to clients are weaker, and lawyers place less emphasis on collegiality—make greater use of permanent employees. I test this argument using a nationwide sample of law firms.

The Changing Environment of Law Firms Legal Work

In the 1950s and 1960s, corporations turned to their law firms for legal guidance on day-to-day, routine business activities, such as commercial contracts and bank loans. Firms with a major bank as a client usually established banking departments that processed loan agreements and operated almost as a unit of the bank. Corporate clients also turned to lawyers for their social contacts and perceived general knowledge of business and politics. Although the dispensing of general business advice bolstered the image of the lawyer as a "wise counselor", it called for practical wisdom and experience rather than analytical skill or knowledge of the law.

Beginning in the 1970s, several factors combined to bring about a substantial increase in the complexity and knowledge-intensity of large law firms' work. The sheer amount of law and law-related information grew dramatically, fed by increases in federal and state statutes, regulations, and administrative and judicial decisions and by an expansion in the amount of legal commentary offered by law journals and newsletters. Technological advances—such as electronic legal databases, overnight delivery services, and the Internet—have made all this information more easily and rapidly available. As new types of actors and controversies have arisen, the variety of issues regulated by law has increased. Perhaps most important, corporate clients now direct most of their routine work to their in-house legal departments. They turn to outside counsel only when they encounter an unusually complex problem requiring special expertise, such as a major lawsuit, a large public offering of securities, or a merger. Such complex problems have become more frequent as corporate clients' have become increasingly willing to engage in litigation, hostile takeovers, and other forms of adversarial and transactional behavior involving high stakes

Client Relationships

At the middle of the twentieth century, large firms' relationships with their clients tended to be strong and enduring. Clients rarely shifted from one firm to another, and new generations of corporate managers were often content to pass along their legal business to the new partners of the same law firm that had served the company in the past * * *

In recent decades, ties between law firms and their clients have become less close. When clients retain outside lawyers only episodically to handle special problems, clients and lawyers interact less frequently. Moreover, as sophisticated corporate legal departments have assumed responsibility for directing and monitoring the work of outside lawyers, the importance of trust between clients and firms has diminished. Guided by in-house lawyers, corporations have become more willing to shop around for quality and price in outside legal services, creating a much more competitive business environment for large law firms. Indeed, large-firm failures, once unthinkable, began to occur in the 1980s and 1990s.

SOCIAL NORMS

At midcentury, behavior in large law firms was governed by a clear set of social norms revolving around the concept of collegiality. Partners at large firms valued the sense of community that arose from personal relations among equals. Partnership was viewed as a lifelong commitment involving mutual dependence among lawyers with different talents and specialties. Indeed, firms sometimes refused to assess the relative profitability of different areas of legal practice, fearing that such information would lead to "unprofessional" status and power distinctions among lawyers. Decisions concerning firm policies and actions were reached through consensus, and powerful partners often made an effort to obscure their leadership roles.

In the 1970s and 1980s, a new set of values began to challenge the older ideal of collegiality. In particular, many large-firm lawyers began to place a candid emphasis on financial success. Money became important not solely for the material comforts it could bring, but as a way of "keeping score," of identifying the most successful lawyers and firms. Lawyers—including partners—who did not produce at expected levels began to find that old loyalties mattered little as their compensation was reduced or their firm affiliations terminated. Although some lawyers applaud the new culture as refreshingly honest, others are dismayed by what they perceive as increasing commercialization and declining professionalism.

FROM CHANGES TO VARIABLES: IMPACTS ON THE USE OF PERMANENT EMPLOYMENT

Law firms are differentially exposed to general environmental trends. Work complexity, the strength of client relationships, and the collegiality of social norms vary across firms. It is reasonable to think that variation in these factors may be associated with variation in the use of permanent employment arrangements. Prior research has shown that the knowledge and skill involved in an organization's work influences the duration of its employment relationships. The nature of client ties shapes firms' organizational structures, which in turn are likely to affect employment practices. Organizational norms and values also play important roles in determining employment arrangements.

WORK COMPLEXITY

The complexity of legal work varies across areas of practice. Legal work is more difficult and challenging when it requires specialized knowledge, or in other words, dense knowledge relating to a narrow topic with little application to other topics. Knowledge in a particular practice area of law is more specialized when it involves a greater number of classifications and rules unique to that practice area. A second dimension of complexity is the extent to which legal work requires the exercise of professional judgment. Professional judgment involves a kind of tacit knowledge, embedded in experience rather than articulated in rules. In legal practice, professional judgment comes into play when a statute or court decision is not clear on its face and cannot be applied directly to the case at hand. The lawyer must then engage in a process of legal reasoning, drawing on his or her familiarity with prior cases and judicial modes of logic to predict how a court would rule. A third element of complexity is the extent to which work calls for skill in communicating with others, such as in advising clients or negotiating with other parties.

Law firms with more complex work are likely to need more lawyers with high levels of experience and skill. Firms can, of course, respond to this need by increasing the ratio of partners to associates, but the severe financial disadvantages of this course of action are likely to lead them to search for an alternative. Probationary associates do not provide a satisfactory solution. Law school teaches abstract legal rules and the process of legal reasoning, but provides little or no training in dealing with the messy reality of clients and their problems. In firms with more complex work, a longer-than-average period may be required before associates are able to function at the required level of skill. Junior lawyers may not be willing to remain in a probationary status for the necessary time. Associate attrition is, indeed, a problem for many large law firms. If a high proportion of probationary employees leave before the expiration of the partnership track period, a firm may find it has few skilled employees. To avoid this outcome, it may be necessary for firms to offer lawyers permanent employment arrangements.

Even if a firm could be assured of a steady supply of senior associates, there is a second point to consider. Associates usually spend only 1 or 2 years functioning at a high skill level before they become partners or—in most cases—leave the firm. Firms with more complex work have a special interest, however, in maintaining long-term employment relationships. Over time, an employer and its employees make "match-specific" investments in their relationship. Employees develop skills relating to their organization's specific production processes. They also learn to navigate within their firm's culture, and they build networks of ties to others who can provide information and help. Their skills, knowledge, and social ties enable long-term employees to function more effectively than new employees, making them more valuable to the firm. The firm, for its part, becomes familiar with long-term employees' strengths, weaknesses, and personality traits. As a result, the firm is better able to assign such employees to tasks and teams where they will be most productive.

In the legal context, such match-specific investments should be especially valuable in firms where work is complex and highly knowledge-intensive. For both firms and lawyers, the relevant knowledge takes longer, and thus is more costly, to acquire when work is more complex. Lawyers must learn a greater variety of skills and customs and must form ties to a greater number of people. Firms find it more difficult to monitor and evaluate employee performance. Moreover, when work is more challenging, match-specific investments are likely to have a greater impact on lawyers' productivity. Match-specific investments by both employee and firm facilitate rapid, accurate communication and promote interpersonal trust. As Kanter points out, smooth communication and trust are especially vital when work involves high levels of uncertainty and discretion, as it does in a large securities offering or antitrust action, for example. Finally, more complex work tends to involve higher stakes for clients and firms, and thus individual productivity is likely to have more significant consequences. With a deadline looming for registering a major securities offering, it can be crucial for a lawyer to know which tax partner can answer a last-minute question or to be on good terms with the firm's most reliable messenger. This reasoning leads to the following hypotheses:

Hypothesis 1a: Firms where work involves more specialized knowledge make greater use of permanent employees than other firms.

Hypothesis 1b: Firms where work involves more professional judgment make greater use of permanent employees than other firms.

Hypothesis 1c: Firms where work requires greater negotiating and advising skill make greater use of permanent employees than other firms.

CLIENT RELATIONSHIPS

Two factors contribute to the strength of a law firm's client relationships: their stability over time and the average proportion of the firm's business associated with each client. In a stable, enduring relationship, a client sends a regular flow of work to the firm over a long period. Transitory relationships, in contrast, typically involve a single engagement for an unusual problem that may or may not recur. Even longstanding relationships may not be strong, however, if the firm has a large number of clients and each one represents only a small fraction of the firm's revenues. The two dimensions should interact: the stability of a client relationship matters more when that client is the source of a large volume of business, and the amount of business brought to the firm by a client matters more when the firm's relationship with that client is enduring rather than transitory.

When a law firm's client relationships are strong, firms are likely to develop a client-based division of labor. Relatively small work groups, consisting of junior lawyers working under the supervision of one or more senior partners, serve the needs of a limited number of clients. The senior partners cultivate the relationship with the client, and the work group handles the full range of the clients' legal problems. This form of organization is likely to be more efficient for the law firm, which makes a considerable investment in client-specific knowledge: the client's structure and history, its personnel and their political dynamics, its industry, and its customer and supplier markets. When a law firm's client relationships are weak, on the other hand, firms are likely to develop specialized departments defined by legal skills and tasks, such as tax, litigation, real estate, and securities. When a client retains the firm for an engagement requiring multiple skills, the firm assembles a temporary team of lawyers drawn from these departments. This more bureaucratic form of organization is likely to be more efficient, because it facilitates the development of the cutting-edge substantive expertise that tenuously attached clients expect when they retain a firm for an unusual problem. Moreover, if client business volume is small, the firm's investment in client-specific knowledge is likely to be minimal; if the client approaches the firm with a massive but temporary crisis, the firm's investment can be billed to the client at steep rates.

Pfeffer and Baron have argued that task-based, bureaucratic organizational structures tend to go hand in hand with permanent employment arrangements. In this view, permanent employment arrangements are part of a larger employment system that also encompasses task-based roles, hierarchical structures for coordination and control, and internal labor markets. This view is supported by empirical studies finding that more bureaucratically structured organizations make less use of short-term or contingent employment, and, implicitly, greater use of permanent employment. This reasoning leads to the following hypotheses:

Hypothesis 2a: Firms with more enduring client relationships make less use of permanent employees than other firms.

Hypothesis 2b: Firms whose client relationships involve a larger business volume make less use of permanent employees than other firms.

Hypothesis 2c: The two dimensions of client relationships interact so that the effect of each is stronger when the level of the other is greater.

COLLEGIALITY NORMS

Traditionally, collegiality has been an important value among lawyers and other professionals, amounting to an ideology about the way professional firms ought to be organized. The collegial mode of organization centers on the possession and use of knowledge or skill. In a collegial organization, all members have control over their own work, all are formally equal in status, and all participate in organizational governance. Only apprentices, who have not yet met the required standard of expertise, are subject to limitations on autonomy, equality, and participation. The collegial mode of organization is consonant with traditional professional values, which include individual autonomy and formal equality among colleagues. Firms vary, however, in the strength of their commitment to the collegial ideal.

Permanent employment relationships cannot be easily reconciled with norms of collegiality. Lawyers who are permanent employees are subject to the supervision of partners and thus are not fully autonomous. Permanent employees are not the status equals of partners, nor do they participate to the same extent in organizational governance. The disadvantaged situation of permanent employees, unlike that of associates, cannot be justified on the ground of professional immaturity. Most permanent employees are experienced lawyers, and the few who are not are generally ineligible for the training that might qualify them for partnership. Organizations that adhere more strongly to an ideology are less likely to make use of practices inconsistent with that ideology. Thus, firms that place a high value on collegiality should be less comfortable with permanent employment arrangements. This argument leads to the following hypothesis:

Hypothesis 3: Firms that value collegiality more highly make less use of permanent employees than other firms.

RESEARCH METHODS SAMPLE AND DATA

The sample I use is drawn from the 1996–1997 National Directory of Legal Employers prepared by the National Association for Law Placement (the NALP Directory) * * * The unit of analysis is the establishment, which can be a single-office law firm or an office of a larger firm with multiple locations. The NALP Directory contains information on more than 900 establishments. My theoretical population consists of large law firms that primarily serve large corporate clients ...

DISCUSSION

The increasing prevalence of permanent employment arrangements in large law firms raises questions about the determinants of firms' use of permanent employees. Starting from the premise that organizations shape their employment practices in response to environmental forces, I examined three major recent changes in the environment surrounding large law firms—the increasing complexity of work, the attenuation of client relationships, and the weakening of social norms of collegiality—and developed hypotheses about their effects on the use of permanent employed lawyers. [I] tested these hypotheses on a nationwide sample of law firm establishments.

Four major conclusions can be drawn from the results. First, the results indicate that firms with more complex and challenging work than other firms make greater use of permanent employees. Three dimensions of work complexity were examined—the specialized nature of the knowledge involved, the amount of professional judgment required, and the need for skill in advising and negotiating with others—and, on balance, each of these dimensions increased firms' use of permanent employment. This finding is consistent with the argument that firms with more complex work need more lawyers with high levels of skill and find that they need to offer permanent employment to attract or retain those lawyers. It is also consistent with the view that firms with more challenging work rely more heavily on the development of "match-specific" in-depth knowledge by each party to the employment relationship and consequently place a greater premium on long-term employment arrangements.

Second, law firms that enjoy stronger ties to their clients than other firms make less use of permanent employees. Both the duration of the relationship and the proportion of the firm's time devoted to the client are important. This finding is consistent with the argument that firms with weaker client relationships are more likely to adopt a task-based, bureaucratic division of labor, which in turn tends to foster the use of permanent employment arrangements.

Third, law firms that place a higher value on collegiality than other firms are more reluctant to make use of permanent employees. Permanent employment arrangements are incompatible with traditional collegial norms, which hold that professional colleagues should have autonomy over their own work, enjoy formally equal status, and participate in organizational governance.

Finally, the results suggest that law firms employ two distinct categories of permanent lawyers: experienced lawyers with nontraditional titles such as "senior attorney" and "senior counsel," on the one hand, and permanent associates, on the other. The effects of the key predictors are larger in magnitude and attain higher levels of statistical significance in the case of the first group. There is even a clear negative association between one aspect of work complexity—professional judgment—and the use of permanent associates.

Because the sample used in this study is limited to medium-sized and large law firms, the findings here are not necessarily generalizable to small firms ... The extensive differences between small and large firms are likely to be reflected in different employment practices.

On the whole, although permanent lawyers are often well rewarded in terms of pay and job security, the results here hint at less desirable aspects of their work experience. Senior attorneys appear to practice in complex, challenging areas of law, but this is not the case for permanent associates, whose work appears to be more routine. Both types of permanent lawyers are likely to be found in firms with more tenuous client relationships than other firms, due to more rapid client turnover or the smaller size of client matters, which implies that they have fewer opportunities to build ties to client personnel or to develop the overall understanding of the client's situation necessary to participate in broad, strategic decisionmaking. Kronman argues that the lawyer's role is shrinking; whereas lawyers once deliberated with clients about ends, they now merely provide technical expertise about means. Permanent employees, in particular, seem likely to be experiencing this narrowing of the scope of their work, and with it a loss of intrinsic interest and meaning. Nor is unfulfilling work likely to be offset by rewarding relationships with colleagues, as permanent lawyers tend to work in firms where norms of collegiality have faded.

From an organizational point of view, permanent employment arrangements seem to reflect a further step in the trend ... toward the bureaucratization of large law firms. Whereas the ideal-typical model of professional organization involves the concentration of multiple tasks and skills within one individual trained to coordinate and control his or her own work, the bureaucratic model involves the vertical and horizontal division of tasks among different workers Permanent nonpartner positions contribute to vertical differentiation by creating an additional layer of hierarchy between partners and probationary associates. They increase horizontal differentiation as well, insofar as permanent employees specialize in relatively narrow tasks and areas of law (for example, "blue sky" work or employee benefits law). Permanent positions mesh easily with other aspects of firm bureaucratization, such as formal departments, full-time managerial positions, and the use of nonlawyer personnel to handle administrative and marketing functions.

Permanent employment arrangements also contribute to the growing stratification of the bar, a trend taking place both across law firms and within them. Across firms, there is an increasing social separation of lawyers who practice in different specialties and serve different clients. Within firms, there is growing inequality along the dimensions of earnings, status, and power. At midcentury, it was relatively easy for large-firm associates to accept their disadvantaged status, due to "the knowledge that ... associates whose work was of high quality would in due course become partners." As partnership prospects have grown increasingly remote and permanent employment arrangements have proliferated, however, the gulf between owners and employees appears to be widening.

PROBLEM

The Equal Employment Opportunity Commission (EEOC) has filed suit against the large law firm McKinney & Doyle, claiming that the firm has violated the Age Discrimination in Employment Act (ADEA). The EEOC's complaint is based on M&D's action in requiring 25 partners in their fifties to accept demotion from partner to "counsel" or "senior partner" or leave the firm. The firm stated that it took such action in an effort to expand opportunities for younger partners and associates.

M&D's main defense to the lawsuit is that the ADEA addresses discrimination only against "employees," and that law firm partners are effectively "employers" or managers. The EEOC concedes that the ADEA protects only "employees," but argues that the M&D partners effectively were employees of the firm.

In support of its defense, M&D notes that partners at the firm, including the 31 on whose behalf the EEOC is suing, have made capital contributions to the partnership and are responsible for the firm's liabilities in proportion to those contributions. The firm also notes that partners' income is determined by a number of percentage points of the firm's overall profits that the firm's executive committee assigns to each partner. In addition, partners have the authority to hire, fire, promote, and determine the compensation of subordinates. The firm also maintains that its partnership agreement establishes that the firm's executive committee has absolute authority to run the firm, so that the committee effectively acts in furtherance of the power delegated to it by all partners. Finally, the firm argues that a partnership is akin to a private association, whose personal relationships would be distorted by authorizing some members to sue others for decisions regarding the best interests of the partnership.

The EEOC argues that M&D has over 500 partners, but the firm is run by the executive committee, whose decisions can be made unilaterally and are not subject to appeal. While partners can exercise control over subordinates, their own tenure and compensation is completely at the mercy of the executive committee, whose decisions are final. Aside from no recourse with respect to their own situations, the EEOC asserts, partners not on the executive committee also have no voice on major firm decisions, such as who becomes a partner, who is removed from the partnership, how the profits of the firm are distributed, and who serves on the executive committee (whose members are chosen by existing members). In short, the EEOC argues that while partners in the traditional law firm may not have been "employees," partners in firms such as M&D Austin are not.

Which side do you think should prevail in the EEOC suit against McKinney & Doyle? What would be the implications of this? What if the EEOC filed suit against a firm that took similar action with respect to its non-equity partners?

Chapter 9

THE ORGANIZATIONAL SETTING

The ethical issues that a lawyer faces do not arise in a vacuum nor can they be simply resolved by looking at a series of rules and judicial decisions. Indeed, one of the skills that a lawyer must develop is to recognize when there is an ethical problem. When faced with such a problem, a lawyer often must ascertain and interpret a complex set of facts. And that interpretation, as behavioral and organizational theory has taught us, is influenced by factors that make it more difficult for a lawyer to render "objective" or "independent" advice. Put differently, when advising a client, a lawyer must recognize her own individual biases as well as those of the organizational worlds in which she operates and the extent to which those biases affect her own decision-making, interpretation and advice. The materials in this chapter explore some of the behavioral and organizational forces that operate in a lawyer's work. Keep these ideas in mind in later chapters in which you are asked to evaluate the ways in which lawyers resolved the dilemmas they faced.

OVERVIEW OF THE CHAPTER

The first article in the chapter by Dennis Gioia is a fascinating exploration of why a person actively involved in the Ford Motor Company's recall program did not take action to recall the Ford Pinto before the tragedies that ultimately caused Ford to stop manufacturing the Pinto.

Gioia believes that his conduct throughout the crisis was both legal and ethical because his decisions accorded with accepted professional standards. In his article, he is concerned with the more difficult question of whether that conduct was "moral," which he defines as being consistent with a higher inner standard of conscience. Ultimately he concludes that he failed his own ethical test. As you read the article, consider whether you are as harsh on him as he is on himself.

Gioia's article focuses on the way in which people process the huge flow of information with which they are confronted. Drawing on behavioral theory, he argues that to deal with this flow, people create "scripts" or "schemas" in which information is organized into categories and patterns that enable people to react without analyzing the information as if they were receiving it for the first time. Because the early data on the Pinto problems did not fit the existing scripts, because Gioia had many other more immediate recall problems, and because Ford's organizational culture stressed lowering costs, Gioia did not recognize the dangers with the Pinto until it was too late. His difficulties were compounded by his desire to advance within the Ford hierarchy and thus not to be seen as a trouble-maker.

In a later article that draws on Gioia and an expanding body of behavioral and organizational literature, Donald Langevoort examines some of the factors that may make it difficult for a lawyer to exercise independent judgment when advising a client on disclosure issues under the federal securities laws. Langevoort notes that in giving such advice, the lawyer will be highly dependent on the client in obtaining the facts on which the advice will be based. He argues that in ascertaining those facts, the lawyer is likely to be affected, often unconsciously, by biases that are present within the client's organizational structure. Foremost among those biases are the need for simplification through the types of schemas that Gioia described, a tendency toward excessive optimism and a commitment to decisions that have already been made. It can be difficult for a lawyer to recognize those biases and to evaluate their strength. That difficulty is exacerbated by the lawyer's own concerns, the strongest of which is the need to be accepted within the client's "in group" so as to be able to continue generating fees from the client.

Langevoort does not suggest that all corporate lawyers will be caught up in organizational biases to the extent that they will lose their cognitive independence and be unable to give objective advice. Rather, he argues that a corporate lawyer must play a mediative role with the client in which the lawyer points out the risks to the client and permits the client to make its own judgment as to its course of action. Langevoort notes that the lawyer's own self-interest and her desire to be perceived as having given correct advice in order to obtain future business, may cause the lawyer to be over-threatening when detailing the risks to the client. Langevoort does not propose ways in which a lawyer should act to overcome the behavioral world in which she operates. For Langevoort, success begins by recognizing the forces that are at work when the lawyer is called on for advice.

In the last article, Robert Rosen uses the Enron collapse as a vehicle for examining how the changing nature of corporate decision-making has affected the role of auditors and lawyers. Rosen argues that the corporation has been "redesigned" to give greater importance to self-managing project teams. One of the principal tasks of such teams is to engage in risk management. In the redesigned corporation, the legal, accounting and finance departments are no longer cost centers with the potential to raise objections to a project that might cause the project not to come to fruition. Rather, these departments are now viewed as profit centers which engage in risk evaluation and monitoring whose purpose is ultimately to add value to the corporation.

Rosen contends that Enron illustrates the danger of using lawyers and accountants for such monitoring. Their changed roles lessens the likelihood that outside independent professionals will act to stop activities that may turn out to be both illegal and financially disastrous. If non-compliance becomes a decisional option that is subject to risk analysis, both lawyers and accountants are faced with the conflict between being independent advisers and the sellers of risk compliance.

As you read these articles, ask yourself how you would handle the next Pinto or Enron before they become crises. Do the materials change your view of how a lawyer should act when faced with an ethical dilemma when time will not permit reflection on the behavioral forces that operate on the lawyer's own decision-making?

MODEL RULES: 1.2(d), 1.6, 1.13, 1.16(a)–(b), 2.1

Dennis A. Gioia, PINTO FIRES AND PERSONAL ETHICS: A SCRIPT ANALYSIS OF MISSED OPPORTUNITIES

11 J.BUS. ETHICS 379 (1992)

In the summer of 1972 I made one of those important transitions in life, the significance of which becomes obvious only in retrospect. I left academe with a BS in Engineering Science and an MBA to enter the world of big business. I joined Ford Motor Company at World Headquarters in Dearborn Michigan fulfilling a long-standing dream to work in the heart of the auto industry. I felt confident that I was in the right place at the right time to make a difference. My initial job title was "Problem Analyst"—a catchall label that superficially described what I would be thinking about and doing in the coming years. On some deeper level, however, the title paradoxically came to connote the many critical things that I would not be thinking about and acting upon.

By that summer of 1972 I was very full of myself. I had met my life's goals to that point with some notable success. I had virtually everything I wanted, including a strongly-held value system that had led me to question many of the perspectives and practices I observed in the world around me. Not the least of these was a profound distaste for the Vietnam war, a distaste that had found me participating in various demonstrations against its conduct and speaking as a part of a collective voice on the moral and ethical failure of a democratic government that would attempt to justify it. I also found myself in MBA classes railing against the conduct of businesses of the era, whose actions struck me as ranging from inconsiderate to indifferent to simply unethical. To me the typical stance of business seemed to be one of disdain for, rather than responsibility toward, the society of which they were prominent members. I wanted something to change. Accordingly, I cultivated my social awareness; I held my principles high; I espoused my intention to help a troubled world; and I wore my hair long. By any measure I was a prototypical "Child of the '60s."

Therefore, it struck quite a few of my friends in the MBA program as rather strange that I was in the program at all. ("If you are so disappointed in business, why study business?"). Subsequently, they were practically dumbstruck when I accepted the job offer from Ford, apparently one of the great purveyors of the very actions I reviled. I countered that it was an ideal strategy, arguing that I would have a greater chance of influencing social change in business if I worked behind the scenes on the inside, rather than as a strident voice on the outside. It was clear to me that somebody needed to prod these staid companies into socially responsible action. I certainly aimed to do my part. Besides, I liked cars.

INTO THE FRAY: SETTING THE PERSONAL STAGE

Predictably enough, I found myself on the fast track at Ford, participating in a "tournament" type of socialization, engaged in a competition for recognition with other MBA's who had recently joined the company. And I quickly became caught up in the game. The company itself was dynamic; the environment of business, especially the auto industry, was intriguing; the job was challenging and the pay was great. The psychic rewards of working and succeeding in a major corporation proved unexpectedly seductive. I really became involved in the job.

Market forces (international competition) and government regulation (vehicle safety and emissions) were affecting the auto industry in disruptive ways that only later would be common to the wider business and social arena. They also produced an industry and a company that felt buffeted, beleaguered, and threatened by the changes. The threats were mostly external, of course, and led to a strong feeling of we-vs-them, where we (Ford members) needed to defend ourselves against them (all the outside parties and voices demanding that we change our ways). Even at this time, an intriguing question for me was whether I was a "we" or a "them." It was becoming apparent to me that my perspective was changing. I had long since cut my hair.

By the summer of 1973 I was pitched into the thick of the battle. I became Ford's Field Recall Coordinator—not a position that was particularly high in the hierarchy, but one that wielded influence for beyond its level. I was in charge of the operational coordination of all of the recall campaigns currently underway and also in charge of tracking incoming information to identify developing problems. Therefore, I was in a position to make initial recommendations about possible future recalls. The most critical type of recalls were labeled "safety campaigns"—those that dealt with the possibility of customer injury or death. These ranged from straight-forward occurrences such as brake failure and wheels falling off vehicles, to more exotic and faintly humorous failure modes such as detaching axles that announced their presence by spinning forward and slamming into the startled driver's door and speed control units that locked on, and refused to disengage, as the care accelerated wildly while the spooked driver futilely tried to shut it off. Safety recall campaigns, however, also encompassed the more sobering possibility of on-board gasoline fires and explosions * * *

THE PINTO CASE: SETTING THE CORPORATE STAGE

In 1970 Ford introduced the Pinto, a small car that was intended to compete with the then current challenge from European cars and the ominous presence on the horizon of Japanese manufacturers. The Pinto was brought from inception to production in the record time of approximately 25 months (compared to the industry average of 43 months), a time frame that suggested the necessity for doing things expediently. In addition to the time pressure, the engineering and development teams were required to adhere to the production "limits of 2000" for the diminutive car: it was not to exceed either $2000 in cost or 2000 pounds in weight. Any decisions that threatened these targets or the timing of the car's introduction were discouraged. Under normal conditions design, styling, product planning, engineering, etc., were completed prior to production tooling. Because of the foreshortened time frame, however, some of these usually sequential processes were executed in parallel.

As a consequence, tooling was already well under way (thus "freezing" the basic design) when routine crash testing revealed that the Pinto's fuel tank often ruptured when struck from the rear at a relatively low speed (31 mph in crash tests). Reports (revealed much later) showed that the fuel tank failures were the result of some rather marginal design features. The tank was positioned between the rear bumper and the rear axle (a standard industry practice for the time). During impact, however, several studs protruding from the rear of the axle housing would puncture holes in the tank; the fuel filler neck also was likely to rip away. Spilled gasoline then could be ignited by sparks. Ford had in fact crash-tested 11 vehicles; 8 of these cars suffered potentially catastrophic gas tank ruptures. The only 3 cars that survived intact had each been modified in some way to protect the tank.

These crash tests, however, were conducted under the guidelines of Federal Motor Vehicle Safety Standard 301 which had been proposed in 1968 and strenuously opposed by the auto industry. FMVSS 301 was not actually adopted until 1976; thus, at the time of the tests, Ford was not in violation of the law. There were several possibilities for fixing the problem, including the option of redesigning the tank and its location, which would have produced tank integrity in a high-speed crash. That solution, however, was not only time consuming and expensive, but also usurped trunk space, which was seen as a critical competitive sales factor. One of the production modifications to the tank, however, would have cost only $11 to install, but given the tight margins and restrictions of the "limits of 2000," there was reluctance to make even this relatively minor change. There were other reasons for not approving the change, as well, including a widespread industry belief that all small cars were inherently unsafe solely because of their size and weight. Another more prominent reason was a corporate belief that "safety doesn't sell." This observation was attributed to Lee Iacocca and stemmed from Ford's earlier attempt to make safety a sales theme, an attempt that failed rather dismally in the marketplace.

Perhaps the most controversial reason for rejecting the production change to the gas tank, however, was Ford's use of cost-benefit analysis to justify the decision. The National Highway Traffic Safety Association (NHTSA, a federal agency) had approved the use of cost-benefit analysis as an appropriate means for establishing automotive safety design standards. The controversial aspect in making such calculations was that they required the assignment of some specific value for a human life. In 1970, that value was deemed to be approximately $200000 as a "cost to society" for each fatality. Ford used NHTSA's figures in estimating the costs and benefits of altering the tank production design. An internal memo, later revealed in court, indicates the following tabulations concerning potential fires:

COSTS: $137000000

(Estimated as the costs of a production fix to all similarly designed cars and trucks with the gas tank aft of the axle (12500000 vehicles x $11/vehicle))

BENEFITS: $49530000

(Estimated as the savings from preventing (180 projected deaths x $200000/ death) + (180 projected burn injuries x $67000/injury) + (2100 burned cars x $700/car))

The cost-benefit decision was then construed as straightforward: No production fix would be undertaken. The philosophical and ethical implications of assigning a financial value for human life or disfigurement do not seem to have been a major consideration in reaching this decision.

PINTOS AND PERSONAL EXPERIENCE

When I took over the Recall Coordinator's job in 1973 I inherited the oversight of about 100 active recall campaigns, more than half of which were safety-related. These ranged from minimal in size (replacing front wheels that were likely to break on 12 heavy trucks) to maximal (repairing the power steering pump on millions of cars). In addition, there were quite a number of safety problems that were under consideration as candidates for addition to the recall list. (Actually, "problem" was a word whose public use was forbidden by the legal office at the time, even in service bulletins, because it suggested corporate admission of culpability. "Condition" was the sanctioned catchword.) In addition to these potential recall candidates, there were many files containing field reports of alleged component failure (another forbidden word) that had led to accidents, and in some cases, passenger injury. Beyond these existing files, I began to construct my own files of incoming safety problems.

One of these new files concerned reports of Pintos "lighting up" (in the words of a field representative) in rear-end accidents. There were actually very few reports, perhaps because component failure was not initially assumed. These cars simply were consumed by fire after apparently very low speed accidents. Was there a problem? Not as far as I was concerned. My cue for labeling a case as a problem either required high frequencies of occurrence or directly traceable causes. I had little time for speculative contemplation on potential problems that did not fit a pattern that suggested known courses of action leading to possible recall. I do, however, remember being disquieted by a field report accompanied by graphic, detailed photos of the remains of a burned-out Pinto in which several people had died. Although that report became part of my file, I did not flag it as any special case.

It is difficult to convey the overwhelming complexity and pace of the job of keeping track of so many active or potential recall campaigns. It remains the busiest, most information-filled job I have ever held or would want to hold. Each case required a myriad of information-gathering and execution stages. I distinctly remember that the information-processing demands led me to confuse the facts of one problem case with another on several occasions because the tell-tale signs of recall candidate cases were so similar. I thought of myself as a fireman—a fireman who perfectly fit the description by one of my colleagues: "In this office everything is a crisis. You only have time to put out the big fires and spit on the little ones." By those standards the Pinto problem was distinctly a little one.

It is also important to convey the muting of emotion involved in the Recall Coordinator's job. I remember contemplating the fact that my job literally involved life-and-death matters. I was sometimes responsible for finding and fixing cars NOW, because somebody's life might depend on it. I took it very seriously. Early in the job, I sometimes woke up at night wondering whether I had covered all the bases. Had I left some unknown person at risk because I had not thought of something? That soon faded, however, and of necessity the consideration of people's lives became a fairly removed, dispassionate process. To do the job "well" there was little room for emotion. Allowing it to surface was potentially paralyzing and prevented rational decisions about which cases to recommend for recall. On moral grounds I knew I could recommend most of the vehicles on my safety tracking list for recall (and risk earning the label of a "bleeding heart"). On practical grounds, I recognized that people implicitly accept risks in cars. We could not recall all cars with potential problems and stay in business. I learned to be responsive to those cases that suggested an imminent, dangerous problem.

I should also note, that the country was in the midst of its first, and worst, oil crisis at this time. The effects of the crisis had cast a pall over Ford and the rest of the automobile industry. Ford's product line, with the perhaps notable exception of the Pinto and Maverick small cars, was not well-suited to dealing with the crisis. Layoffs were imminent for many people. Recalling the Pinto in this context would have damaged one of the few trump cards the company had (although, quite frankly, I do not remember overtly thinking about that issue).

Pinto reports continued to trickle in, but at such a slow rate that they really did not capture particular attention relative to other, more pressing safety problems. However, I later saw a crumpled, burned car at a Ford depot where alleged problem components and vehicles were delivered for inspection and analysis (a place known as the "Chamber of Horrors" by some of the people who worked there). The revulsion on seeing this incinerated hulk was immediate and profound. Soon afterwards, and despite the fact that the file was very sparse, I recommended the Pinto case for preliminary department-level review concerning possible recall. After the usual round of discussion about criteria and justification for recall, everyone voted against recommending recall—including me. It did not fit the pattern of recallable standards; the evidence was not overwhelming that the car was defective in some way, so the case was actually fairly straightforward. It was a good business decision, even if people might be dying. (We did not then know about the pre-production crash test data that suggested a high rate of tank failures in "normal" accidents or an abnormal failure mode.)

Later, the existence of the crash test data did become known within Ford, which suggested that the Pinto might actually have a recallable problem. This information led to a reconsideration of the case within our office. The data, however, prompted a comparison of the Pinto's survivability in a rear end accident with that of other competitors' small cars. These comparisons revealed that although many cars in this subcompact class suffered appalling deformation in relatively low speed collisions, the Pinto was merely the worst of a bad lot. Furthermore, the gap between the Pinto and the competition was not dramatic in terms of the speed at which fuel tank rupture was likely to occur. On that basis it would be difficult to justify the recall of cars that were comparable with others on the market. In the face of even more compelling evidence that people were probably going to die in this car, I again included myself in a group of decision makers who voted not to recommend recall to the higher levels of the organization.

CODA TO THE CORPORATE CASE

Subsequent to my departure from Ford in 1975, reports of Pinto fires escalated, attracting increasing media attention, almost all of it critical of Ford. Anderson and Whitten revealed the internal memos concerning the gas tank problem and questioned how the few dollars saved per car could be justified when human lives were at stake. Shortly thereafter, a scathing article by Dowie attacked not only the Pinto's design, but also accused Ford of gross negligence, stonewalling, and unethical corporate conduct by alleging that Ford knowingly sold "firetraps" after willfully calculating the cost of lives against profits. Dowie's provocative quote speculating on "how long the Ford Motor Company would continue to market lethal cars were Henry Ford II and Lee Iacocca serving 20 year terms in Leavenworth for consumer homicide" was particularly effective in focusing attention on the case. Public sentiment edged toward labeling Ford as socially deviant because management was seen as knowing that the car was defective, choosing profit over lives, resisting demands to fix the car, and apparently showing no public remorse.

Shortly after Dowie's expose, NHTSA initiated its own investigation. Then, early in 1978 a jury awarded a Pinto burn victim $125 million in punitive damages (later reduced to $6.6 million, a judgment upheld on an appeal that prompted the judge to assert that "Ford's institutional mentality was shown to be one of callous indifference to public safety"). A siege atmosphere emerged at Ford. Insiders characterized the mounting media campaign as "hysterical" and "a crusade against us" (personal communications). The crisis deepened. In the summer of 1978 NHTSA issued a formal determination that the pinto was defective. Ford then launched a reluctant recall of all 1971–1976 cars (those built for the 1977 model year were equipped with a production fix prompted by the adoption of the FMVSS 301 gas tank standard). Ford hoped that the issue would then recede, but worse was yet to come.

The culmination of the case and the demise of the Pinto itself began in Indiana on August 10, 1978, when three teenage girls died in a fire triggered after their 1973 Pinto was hit from behind by a van. A grand jury took the unheard of step of indicting Ford on charges of reckless homicide. Because of the precedent-setting possibilities for all manufacturing industries, Ford assembled a formidable legal team headed by Watergate prosecutor James Neal to defend itself at the trial. The trial was a media event; it was the first time that a corporation was tried for alleged criminal behavior. After a protracted, acrimonious courtroom battle that included vivid clashes among the opposing attorneys, surprise witnesses, etc., the jury ultimately found in favor of Ford. Ford had dodged a bullet in the form of a consequential legal precedent, but because of the negative publicity of the case and the charges of corporate crime and ethical deviance, the conduct of manufacturing businesses was altered, probably forever. As a relatively minor footnote to the case, Ford ceased production of the Pinto.

CODA TO THE PERSONAL CASE

In the intervening years since my early involvement with the Pinto fire case, I have given repeated consideration to my role in it. Although most of the ethically questionable actions that have been cited in the press are associated with Ford's intentional stonewalling after it was clear that the Pinto was defective—and thus postdate my involvement with the case and the company—I still nonetheless wonder about my own culpability. Why didn't I see the gravity of the problem and its ethical overtones? What happened to the value system I carried with me into Ford? Should I have acted differently, given what I knew then? The expenence with myself has sometimes not been pleasant. Somehow, it seems I should have done something different that might have made a difference.

As a consequence of this line of thinking and feeling, some years ago I decided to construct a "living case" out of my experience with the Pinto fire problem for use in my MBA classes. The written case description contains many of the facts detailed above; the analytical task of the class is to ask appropriate questions of me as a figure in the case to reveal the central issues involved. It is somewhat of a trying experience to get through these classes. After getting to know me for most of the semester, and then finding out that I did not vote to recommend recall, students are often incredulous, even angry at me for apparently not having lived what I have been teaching. To be fair and even-handed here, many students understand my actions in the context of the times and the attitudes prevalent then. Others, however, are very disappointed that I appear to have failed during a time of trial. Consequently, I am accused of being a charlatan and otherwise vilified by those who maintain that ethical and moral principles should have prevailed in this case no matter what the mitigating circumstances. Those are the ones that hurt.

Those are also the ones, however, that keep the case and its lessons alive in my mind and cause me to have an on-going dialogue with myself about it. It is fascinating to me that for several years after I first conducted the living case with myself as the focus, I remained convinced that I had made the "right" decision in not recommending recall of the cars. In light of the times and the evidence available, I thought I had pursued a reasonable course of action. More recently, however, I have come to think that I really should have done everything I could to get those cars off the road.

In retrospect I know that in the context of the times my actions were legal (they were all well within the framework of the law); they probably also were ethical according to most prevailing definitions (they were in accord with accepted professional standards and codes of conduct); the major concern for me is whether they were moral (in the sense of adhering to some higher standards of inner conscience and conviction about the "right" actions to take). This simple typology implies that I had passed at least two hurdles on a personal continuum that ranged from more rigorous, but arguably less significant criteria, to less rigorous, but more personally, organizationally, and perhaps societally significant standards: (Equation omitted)

It is that last criterion that remains troublesome.

Perhaps these reflections are all just personal revisionist history. After all, I am still stuck in my cognitive structures, as everyone is. I do not think these concerns are all retrospective reconstruction, however. Another telling piece of information is this: The entire time I was dealing with the Pinto fire problem, I owned a Pinto (!). I even sold it to my sister. What does that say?

What Happened Here?

I, of course, have some thoughts about my experience with this damningly visible case. At the risk of breaking some of the accepted rules of scholarly analysis, rather than engaging in the usual comprehensive, dense, arms-length critique, I would instead like to offer a rather selective and subjective focus on certain characteristics of human information processing relevant to this kind of situation, of which I was my own unwitting victim. I make no claim that my analysis necessarily "explains more variance" than other possible explanations. I do think that this selective view is enlightening in that it offers an alternative explanation for some ethically questionable actions in business.

The subjective stance adopted in the analysis is intentional also. This case obviously stems from a series of personal experiences, accounts, and introspections. The analytical style is intended to be consistent with the self-based case example; therefore, it appears to be less "formal" than the typical objectivist mode of explanation. I suspect that my chosen focus will be fairly non-obvious to the reader familiar with the ethical literature (as it typically is to the ethical actor). Although this analysis might be judged as somewhat self-serving, I nonetheless believe that it provides an informative explanation for some of the ethical foibles we see enacted around us.

To me, there are two major issues to address. First, how could my value system apparently have flip-flopped in the relatively short space of 1–2 years? Secondly, how could I have failed to take action on a retrospectively obvious safety problem when I was in the perfect position to do so? To begin, I would like to consider several possible explanations for my thoughts and actions (or lack thereof) during the early stages of the Pinto fire case.

One explanation is that I was simply revealed as a phony when the chips were down; that my previous values were not strongly inculcated; that I was all bluster, not particularly ethical, and as a result acted expediently when confronted with a reality test of those values. In other words, I turned traitor to my own expressed values. Another explanation is that I was simply intimidated; in the face of strong pressure to heel to company preferences, I folded—put ethical concerns aside, or at least traded them for a monumental guilt trip and did what anybody would do to keep a good job. A third explanation is that I was following a strictly utilitarian set of decision criteria and, predictably enough, opted for a personal form of Ford's own cost-benefit analysis, with similar disappointing results. Another explanation might suggest that the interaction of my stage of moral development and the culture and decision environment at Ford led me to think about and act upon an ethical dilemma in a fashion that reflected a lower level of actual moral development than I espoused for myself. Yet another explanation is that I was co-opted; rather than working from the inside to change a lumbering system as I had intended, the tables were turned and the system beat me at my own game. More charitably, perhaps, it is possible that I simply was a good person making bad ethical choices because of the corporate milieu.

I doubt that this list is exhaustive. I am quite sure that cynics could match my own MBA students' labels, which in the worst case include phrases like "moral failure" and "doubly reprehensible because you were in a position to make a difference." I believe, however, on the basis of a number of years of work on social cognition in organizations that a viable explanation is one that is not quite so melodramatic. It is an explanation that rests on a recognition that even the best-intentioned organization members organize information into cognitive structures or schemas that serve as (fallible) mental templates for handling incoming information and as guides for acting upon it. Of the many schemas that have been hypothesized to exist, the one that is most relevant to my experience at Ford is the notion of a script.

My central thesis is this: My own schematized (scripted) knowledge influenced me to perceive recall issues in terms of the prevailing decision environment and to unconsciously overlook key features of the Pinto case, mainly because they did not fit an existing script. Although the outcomes of the case carry retrospectively obvious ethical overtones, the schemas driving my perceptions and actions precluded consideration of the issues in ethical terms because the scripts did not include ethical dimensions.

Script Schemas

A schema is a cognitive framework that people use to impose structure upon information, situations, and expectations to facilitate understanding. Schemas derive from consideration of prior experience or vicarious learning that results in the formation of "organized" knowledge—knowledge that, once formed, precludes the necessity for further active cognition. As a consequence, such structured knowledge allows virtually effortless interpretation of information and events. A script is a specialized type of schema that retains knowledge of actions appropriate for specific situations and contexts. One of the most important characteristics of scripts is that they simultaneously provide a cognitive framework for understanding information and events as well as a guide to appropriate behavior to deal with the situation faced. They thus serve as linkages between cognition and action.

The structuring of knowledge in scripted form is a fundamental human information processing tendency that in many ways results in a relatively closed cognitive system that influences both perception and action. Scripts, like all schemas, operate on the basis of prototypes, which are abstract representations that contain the main features or characteristics of a given knowledge category (e.g., "safety problems"). Protoscripts serve as templates against which incoming information can be assessed. A pattern in current information that generally matches the template associated with a given script signals that active thought and analysis is not required. Under these conditions the entire existing script can be called forth and enacted automatically and unconsciously, usually without adjustment for subtle differences in information patterns that might be important.

Given the complexity of the organizational world, it is obvious that the schematizing or scripting of knowledge implies a great information processing advantage—a decision maker need not actively think about each new presentation of information, situations, or problems; the mode of handling such problems has already been worked out in advance and remanded to a working stock of knowledge held in individual (or organizational) memory. Scripted knowledge saves a significant amount of mental work, a savings that in fact prevents the cognitive paralysis that would inevitably come from trying to treat each specific instance of a class of problems as a unique case that requires contemplation. Scripted decision making is thus efficient decision making but not necessarily good decision making.

Of course, every advantage comes with its own set of built-in disadvantages. There is a price to pay for scripted knowledge. On the one hand, existing scripts lead people to selectively perceive information that is consistent with a script and thus to ignore anomalous information. Conversely, if there is missing information, the gaps in knowledge are filled with expected features supplied by the script. In some cases, a pattern that matches an existing script, except for some key differences, can be "tagged" as a distinctive case and thus be made more memorable. In the worst case scenario, however, a situation that does not fit the characteristics of the scripted perspective for handling problem cases often is simply not noticed. Scripts thus offer a viable explanation for why experienced decision makers (perhaps especially experienced decision makers) tend to overlook what others would construe as obvious factors in making a decision.

Given, the relatively rare occurrence of truly novel information, the nature of script processing implies that it is a default mode of organizational cognition. That is, instead of spending the predominance of their mental energy thinking in some active fashion, decision makers might better be characterized as typically not thinking, i.e., dealing with information in a mode that is akin to "cruising on automatic pilot". The scripted view casts decision makers as needing some sort of prod in the form of novel or unexpected information to kick them into a thinking mode—a prod that often does not come because of the wealth of similar data that they must process. Therefore, instead of focusing what people pay attention to, it might be more enlightening to focus on what they do not pay attention to.

PINTO PROBLEM PERCEPTION AND SCRIPTS

It is illustrative to consider my situation in handling the early stages of the Pinto fire case in light of script theory. When I was dealing with the first trickling-in of field reports that might have suggested a significant problem with the Pinto, the reports were essentially similar to many others that I was dealing with (and dismissing) all the time. The sort of information they contained, which did not convey enough prototypical features to capture my attention, never got past my screening script. I had seen this type of information pattern before (hundreds of times!); I was making this kind of decision automatically every day. I had trained myself to respond to prototypical cues, and these didn't fit the relevant prototype for crisis cases. (Yes, the Pinto reports fit a prototype—but it was a prototype for "normal accidents" that did not deviate significantly from expected problems). The frequency of the reports relative to other, more serious problems (i.e., those that displayed more characteristic features of safety problems) also did not pass my scripted criteria for singling out the Pinto case. Consequently, I looked right past them.

Overlooking uncharacteristic cues also was exacerbated by the nature of the job. The overwhelming information overload that characterized the role as well as its hectic pace actually forced a greater reliance on scripted responses. It was impossible to handle the job requirements without relying on some sort of automatic way of assessing whether a case deserved active attention. There was so much to do and so much information to attend to that the only way to deal with it was by means of schematic processing. In fact, the one anomaly in the case that might have cued me to gravity of the problem (the field report accompanied by graphic photographs) still did not distinguish the problem as one that was distinctive enough to snap me out of my standard response mode and tag it as a failure that deserved closer monitoring.

Even the presence of an emotional component that might have short-circuited standard script processing instead became part of the script itself. Months of squelching the disturbing emotions associated with serious safety problems soon made muffled emotions a standard (and not very salient) component of the script for handling any safety problem. This observation, that emotion was muted by experience, and therefore de-emphasized in the script, differs from Fiske's widely accepted position that emotion is tied to the top of a schema (i.e., is the most salient and initially-tapped aspect of schematic processing). On the basis of my experience, I would argue that for organization members trained to control emotions to perform the job role, emotion is either not a part of the internalized script, or at best becomes a difficult-to-access part of any script for job performance.

The one instance of emotion penetrating the operating script was the revulsion that swept over me at the sight of the burned vehicle at the return depot. That event was so strong that it prompted me to put the case up for preliminary consideration (in theoretical terms, it prompted me cognitively to "tag" the Pinto case as a potentially distinctive one). I soon "came to my senses," however, when rational consideration of the problem characteristics suggested that they did not meet the scripted criteria that were consensually shared among members of the Field Recall Office. At the preliminary review other members of the decision team, enacting their own scripts in the absence of my emotional experience, wondered why I had even brought the case up. To me this meeting demonstrated that even when controlled analytic information processing occurred, it was nonetheless based on prior schematization of information. In other words, even when information processing was not automatically executed, it still depended upon schemas. As a result of the social construction of the situation, I ended up agreeing with my colleagues and voting not to recall.

The remaining major issue to be dealt with, of course, concerns the apparent shift in my values. In a period of less than two years I appeared to change my stripes and adopt the cultural values of the organization. How did that apparent shift occur? Again, scripts are relevant. I would argue that my pre-Ford values for changing corporate America were bona fide. I had internalized values for doing what was right as I then understood "rightness" in grand terms. They key is, however, that I had not internalized a script for enacting those values in any specific context outside my limited experience. The insider's view at Ford, of course, provided me with a specific and immediate context for developing such a script. Scripts are formed from salient experience and there was no more salient experience in my relatively young life than joining a major corporation and moving quickly into a position of clear and present responsibility. The strongest possible parameters for script formation were all there, not only because of the job role specifications, but also from the corporate culture. Organizational culture, in one very powerful sense, amounts to a collection of scripts writ large. Did I sell out? No. Were my cognitive structures altered by salient experience? Without question. Scripts for understanding and action were formed and re-formed in a relatively short time in a way that not only altered perceptions of issues but also the likely actions associated with those altered perceptions.

I might characterize the differing cognitive structures as "outsider" versus "insider" scripts. I view them also as "idealist" versus "realist" scripts. I might further note that the outsider/idealist script was one that was more individually-based than the insider/ realist script, which was more collective and subject to the influence of the corporate milieu and culture. Personal identity as captured in the revised script became much more corporate than individual. Given that scripts are socially constructed and reconstructed cognitive structures, it is understandable that their content and process would be much more responsive to the corporate culture, because of its saliency and immediacy.

Donald C. Langevoort, THE EPISTEMOLOGY OF CORPORATE-SECURITIES
LAWYERING: BELIEFS, BIASES AND ORGANIZATIONAL BEHAVIOR

63 BROOKLYN LAW REVIEW 629 (1997)

In this lecture, I want to draw connections from underutilized literature on organizational behavior to the domain of corporate lawyering, especially on matters of disclosure and legal compliance. Theory and research on predictable biases in managerial judgment have much to say to us about the problems that lawyers face when counselling organizational clients. Drawing from these materials, my primary goal is to add something new to the literature on lawyers' professional responsibility and the often-discussed (if dimly understood) virtues of lawyerly independence.

We tend to think of the problem of independence as the one that faces the corporate lawyer when the client's management is bent on fraud or some other form of legal or moral wrongdoing. My argument here is that the hazards are more subtle and banal, that some of what passes for deliberate fraud and failure to supervise is often more a question of managerial misperception—in good faith, perhaps, but potentially just as harmful to the client corporation and its external constituencies. If such bias is a robust phenomenon, then not only are there important implications for corporate-securities law, but the common understanding of the challenges associated with good corporate-securities lawyering needs to change.

I. COGNITION AND INDEPENDENCE

There are two spheres of knowledge that lawyers must bridge when giving legal advice. One is knowledge of the law: an amalgam of information and insight drawn from precedents, other forms of authority and practical experience. The other is knowledge of the facts: a broad understanding of the situation in which the client finds itself. Volumes have been written about the former kind of knowledge, the process of legal reasoning. In contrast, my interest here is in the latter form of epistemology and its relationship to professional responsibility. I speak here not in the disciplinary sense, but in the aspirational terms of what it means to be a "good" business lawyer. Lawyers are often told, with commonplace attribution to Louis Brandeis, that they cannot offer sound advice unless they thoroughly understand their client as well as the problem it wants to solve. But apart from some clinical "interviewing and counselling" literature, most of which relates to (often unsophisticated) people as clients, the question of what it means to know the client and the situation remains largely unexplored.

The knowledge problem is especially challenging in my special field of interest, securities law. Lawyers are frequently asked to create documents, filings or press releases that portray the company's business, managerial and financial situation. The client, of course, is a fictional entity, embodied in a large and diffuse collection of people and information. The disclosure will be used by investors whose aim is to predict the issuer's future financial performance. There must be attention to material risks and adverse trends: factors that may affect the business, but which fall far short of certainty, thereby requiring complex and subjective probability assessments.

At the risk of venturing into postmodern rhetoric, it should be plain that discovering the "truth" about an issuer—especially when the truth is reflected in a mosaic of probabilistic and forward-looking data—is an exercise in social constructionism. There are always multiple meanings that can be drawn from all the little bits of data that go into the total mix of materiality. The process of arriving at a single meaning cannot be divorced from the collective perceptions and interests of the people engaged in the process; and in business organizations, those people are large in number and far from single-minded. The aggregation and assessment of information from diffuse sources is an extraordinarily difficult task for a lawyer. Yet law schools and law firms largely assume that securities lawyers will confront this interpretive task intuitively, or through training and experience drawn from others who, though considered experts, have not developed a systematic theory of what they do either. To be sure, many lawyers do their job well, exercising what Donald Schon describes as the practitioner's reflective wisdom. What is missing is both a candid acknowledgement of the epistemological difficulty of corporate-securities practice and a rigorous effort to study it in context to aid the profession as a whole.

* * *

II. THE RISK OF PROXIMITY: COGNITIVE BIAS AND CORPORATE DISCLOSURE

Lawyers learn about their entity clients and their situations in many ways. Some of it is documentary: reading files, letters and accounting reports. But putting aside the formal exercise of due diligence, most learning comes from talking to people associated with and usually employed by the company. Those people have the first-hand knowledge of the business and problems that require legal assistance, and hence the lawyer's "schema"—the term psychologists use to describe mental roadmaps that people use to make sense of a situation—is initially driven by theirs'. During interviews and more informal (even gossipy) conversations, savvy lawyers will try to figure out who seems reliable and trustworthy, and weigh their accounts accordingly. The schema will evolve and become more elaborate as the lawyer has more and more contact with people and information. But its largely derivative nature will persist.

In pursuing the concept of cognitive independence, I recognize that there is a vast array of postures that lawyers assume vis-a-vis the client in the course of information-gathering. Some of this is a matter of choice, some of circumstance. A lawyer called into to advise a new client on a discrete, short-term matter rarely has the opportunity to come to know the client well—one or two interviews (sometimes over the phone), perhaps a lunch or dinner, will have to suffice. But continuous disclosure questions under the federal securities laws and comparable high-level legal judgments are usually answered by lawyers with a close, on-going relationship with the company. For purposes of discussing the risk of proximity, therefore, I simply want to posit a relationship in which the lawyer successfully "blends into" the clients' management group culture. This is most likely the case with respect to some in-house counsel, or outside counsel that has built a long-term working relationship with an important client, where key lawyers in the firm spend a significant amount of their time on that client's business and interacting both socially and professionally with the client's managers. To be sure, no blending is ever absolute. As we shall pursue later on, lawyers do have a self-interest that is subtly at odds with their clients', and competing claims to their time and attention. I am sure, however, that there are commonplace situations where the lawyer does blend in to the corporate culture for all practical purposes.

If so, we can assume that the lawyers' perceptions of the client and its circumstances will be influenced heavily by the prevailing corporate belief system. That is not to say that the lawyer will always think like everyone else: disagreements within groups are natural and often testy. Still, as discussed below, group bonding processes create centripetal pressures toward shared perceptions and explanations. Remember that what the lawyer knows about the clients' business will usually be highly derivative: the lawyer who has blended well into the group may accept those perceptions and explanations fairly willingly. He is committed to the client, and wants to be a team player. Psychologists have shown that commitment heavily influences attitudes; we are also motivated to like and believe those upon whom our success depends.

This, then, describes a lawyer who is cognitively dependent on the client. And it follows that assessing the risks associated with cognitive dependence is first a matter of identifying the biases commonly associated with management groups as they interpret the risks and realities of their business. In other words, we must temporarily shift our focus away from the lawyer as such, and turn to corporate inference generally.

A. Managerial Inference, Client Bias

Most litigation involving corporate concealment or misrepresentation in the secondary markets—i.e., when the issuer is not buying or selling its own stock and thus has nothing directly to gain from deceit— involve situations where information is available to the company that indicates that finances are deteriorating, a particular product or strategy is failing, or that some key executive is acting improperly, yet the company's disclosure fails to take candid account of it. * * *

I am sure that some of the time, these kinds of deceptions (assuming they did occur) are indeed deliberate, whether in management's self-interest or in order to preserve some corporate confidentiality. But I want to pursue here the professional responsibility implications of an alternative possibility; that cognitive biases lead managers to unrealistic causal explanations for events and an underestimation of risk. These biases can be sharpened in institutional settings, becoming part of the company's belief system. In turn, the disclosure—which at least sometimes will affect the market for the stock—is skewed by relatively sincere but unrealistic beliefs. To perceptive lawyers who have worked closely with business people, their presence will not be too surprising.

One well recognized phenomenon, for instance, is the process of cognitive simplification. Psychologists emphasize that human beings (and organizations) must simplify their thought processes in order to manage daily affairs. There is too much to think about otherwise. And one way we do this is to develop stock explanations for what is happening. Once established, these "schemas" are naturally resistant to revision: to rethink our assumptions constantly results in cognitive paralysis. This tendency to resist evidence of change is enhanced in group settings, where there is a well-recognized "groupthink" tendency not to introduce the stress that comes from challenging established common understandings. * * *

Another such phenomenon is optimism. Put simply, there is much reason to believe that corporate cultures that subconsciously promote a pervasively optimistic frame of view are the most adaptive, leading to harder work and more long-term commitment by employees and other stakeholders (and dampening through self-deception the awareness of danger that might otherwise trigger a cascade of selfishness). In a "can do" kind of organizational culture, there will be a natural tendency to deflect or rationalize emerging evidence of problems or risks, leading to the obvious potential for distorted disclosure. Faced with some evidence that a product under development is failing, or an erosion of market share, managers in many companies will honestly but mistakenly believe that these are minor challenges that can readily be overcome. They will draw on inflated schemas of past successes, and underrate their competitors ability to capitalize.

* * *

A third well-recognized trait has to do with commitment. Once people have made some voluntary commitment to a person or course of behavior, there is a strong subconscious need to maintain consistency in the face of subsequent events, to justify the commitment to themselves and others. This underlies the well-known concept of cognitive dissonance. Thus, managers who make an investment are motivated to focus on the project's upside potential more than its downside risks, to bolster the wisdom of the choice. The most dramatic form this takes in business settings is the escalation of commitment. A bank official who makes a bad loan may well foolishly make an additional loan to the borrower to try to cause a turn-around, motivated largely by the inability to admit a mistake in the first place—a reason that some banks carefully separate their work-out teams from the original lenders.

* * *

The three motivational forces described above hardly operate separately. In most organizations, it is their confluence that can produce the most severe distortions of reality in the corporate belief system. A company that faces some external risky shift in its environment wants to avoid the stress of acknowledging the threat—with the accompanying destabilization of group cohesion should change be needed—especially if the external threat calls into question the commitments made by the organization as a whole or its senior management. And it may well trivialize the most salient of the red flags by drawing on collective and individual myths of power and control. Much of the literature on episodes of organizational failure in the 1980s and 90s invokes some combination of these accounts in telling their stories. Companies that have successfully weathered such crises are often those that resisted the biases and accepted the reality of the imminent risk of loss, often engaging in wholesale dismissals of senior executives in order to facilitate the necessary cognitive readjustment. No doubt the public disclosures by companies in crisis reflected the way they dealt with the threats internally, unless their lawyers intervened both carefully and vigorously.

Of course, the behavioral accounts here gradually merge into ones that fit the more orthodox economic story as well: management buying time through more deliberate concealment and deception in an effort to take one last shot at saving their jobs. But that may come relatively late in the process, after the managers have underestimated the problem and committed themselves to a course of action (or inaction) that they are highly motivated to rationalize both to themselves and external constituencies. Once realization finally does set in, they are already in very deep. In other words, the last period problem may be a serious concern, but it is probably more delayed in its onset and shorter in its duration—and thus all the more intense when it does emerge—than the standard rational-actor account would suggest.

From the foregoing, we can predict that the cognitive challenges to the lawyer will vary depending on the age and circumstances of the company in question. Younger firms have less well developed internal cultures, and hence less rigid belief systems. Those beliefs are more likely to be dominated by the personalities of the company's founders. With fewer cognitive commitments, there is greater flexibility. No doubt the greatest threat to accurate disclosure for young companies comes from overoptimism. These firms have grown quickly, overcoming the obstacles that face all start-ups through some combination of skill and luck. They often rely heavily on the cohesiveness and enthusiasm of a small group of executives, often dominated by a single charismatic founder, with an extraordinarily high sense of skill and ability that is untempered by time and experience. These managers will place great weight on hiring new managers with similar traits and transmitting their "can do" optimism throughout the firm, resisting the enthusiasm-draining acknowledgement of uncontrollable risk. This is probably part of the story underlying many of the high tech fraud allegations that, meritorious or not, are the subject of so many securities class actions.

In contrast, aging firms are frequently more rigid. Here, leadership by top management may often be more an illusion rather than a reality. Their response to external risks are more likely to be affected by the pressure to preserve existing norms and commitments. Indeed, in many cases—once external threats are finally acknowledged—the first response of top management is to increase the centralization of control and decision-making authority, which has the unintended and dangerous effect of reducing the flow of useful information to the top. Lower level managers abet this by distancing themselves from crucial decisions, lest they be tainted completely by the ensuing failure. This further narrows the focus and range of options considered by the top managers, leaving them to draw excessively on their own (and now misleading) past experiences, thereby making decline all the more likely. Moreover, if the initial response is too conservative, that commitment by itself will bias the managers subsequent perceptions, making it hard to reverse the effects of the judgmental error. * * *

B. The Lawyer's Place

Once we acknowledge the possibility of corporate bias, we can plainly see a vexing challenge to the corporate lawyer who must guide her organizational client through the process of disclosure: she must worry about contagious bias. That lawyer may find herself cognitively overdependent on the client for factual inferences, and thus unable to exercise the kind of objective legal judgment necessary to arrive at sound disclosure decisions. She can become so much a part of the client "team" that she shares all the motivations and attitudes that affect the management group.

This is especially the case if the lawyer has actually been involved in a decision or assisted a course of action, so that she, too, is motivated by commitment to bolster the choice. The well-connected lawyer assumes in-group status, and the various in-group biases follow. There are strong temptations pushing the lawyer in this direction. Team players are highly valued, and can expect continued business from the client. As negotiators and advocates (in contrast to the purely advisory function), internalizing the company's belief system probably results in greater loyalty and zealousness—highly adaptive traits for an ambitious lawyer or firm. Here, the optimism and sense of control that can enhance managerial performance bolsters the lawyer's performance as well, albeit with the same kinds of risks that are the unavoidable by-product of too much comfort and confidence. And, frankly, many lawyers want to be "in-group" for reasons of personality, status and sociability.

Nor is it likely that this loyalty and zealousness will be any more a cynical act of dramaturgy for lawyers than it is for managers. Cognitive dissonance theory suggests the strong need to maintain consistency between adaptive attitudes and beliefs and the lawyer's commitment to the representation. The commitment dominates, and the beliefs and attitudes migrate toward conformity. Anxiety is diminished and effectiveness enhanced if the lawyer believes what the client believes rather than carrying the baggage of nagging, distracting doubts. In sum, there are ample conformity pressures that incline the lawyer toward the internal, self-deceptive acceptance of the organization's positive belief system that defines cognitive dependence.

III. COGNITIVE INDEPENDENCE AND THE DILEMMA OF DISTANCE

Now that we have defined and explored the risks of managerial bias and cognitive dependence, the notion of cognitive independence follows naturally. A securities lawyer is cognitively independent when he has effected sufficient separation from the inferential biases of the corporation's belief system so that it is possible to exercise good judgment relating to materiality and the duty to disclose. Such independence, of course, is important to all corporate lawyers in their counselling function, far beyond disclosure matters.

Cognitive independence is not a question of status or physical proximity, but of state of mind. It involves a sophisticated understanding of the risks of bias, and a recognition that judgments of the accuracy of the perceptions of individual managers cannot be made simply by estimating whether they are good, trustworthy people. Lawyers probably overestimate the extent to which they can make such credibility judgments anyway, but honesty is never the whole question. Fortunate corporate lawyers will have as clients companies with thoughtful managers who do see things realistically and without bias. Although biases may be pervasive, distortion that has a material effect on corporate disclosure is the exception, not the rule. But the skilled corporate lawyer must be sensitive to the frequency with which good people (and good organizations) distort reality, the circumstances that exacerbate such tendencies, and the unconscious pressure that she faces to follow those inferences. She should be prepared to question managerial perceptions in light of these predictable biases and try to reorient the disclosure.

* * *

A.   The Difficulties and Burdens of Distance

Unfortunately, there is far more to the problem, causing me to see the question of cognitive independence in terms of both necessity and dilemma, and thus I want to extend the discussion further. We have already established one reason that cognitive independence is difficult to achieve. Usually, the lawyer is motivated to believe what the client's management group believes, and the tendency to conform will occur subconsciously. The egocentric attributions that can distort managers' self-evaluations can also taint lawyers. A lawyer may well consciously embrace the need for independence: proclaiming its virtue to others, convinced that she lives out the professional ideal of sympathetic detachment. But in practice, her perception may still be distorted in order to reduce the stress of dissonance. Probably far more lawyers pride themselves on independence and good judgment than consistently exhibit it. It becomes easy to see cognitive dependence as other lawyers' problem.

Such hubris is not easy to overcome. People rarely learn well from their own mistakes of judgment because they either fail to acknowledge them or externalize much of the blame. Learning from the mistakes of colleagues, assuming that these mistakes are publicized at all, is difficult as well. It is probably better to intervene early, allowing young lawyers to glimpse situations where honest, decent lawyers (hypothetical or real) fell prey to distorted judgment, and let them recognize both the breadth and depth of the difficulty, hopefully generating a "There but for the grace of God ..." response. This debiasing is a job for legal scholars, law schools and bar associations. Law firms might use senior lawyers not involved with a particular client as independent sounding boards on fact perception, though this is probably of limited utility given the contextually complex nature of such judgments.

Suppose, however, that a lawyer acknowledges the pressure toward dependence and the resulting need for careful self-monitoring. A strong message of the previous section is of the need for some skepticism of management's optimistic assessment or dismissal of risk. But there are also costs associated with too much questioning. First, it is distracting. If materially-significant cognitive distortions are the exception rather than the rule, as suggested earlier, then questions and demands for independent assessment by a lawyer who is a step removed from the business situation both in terms of familiarity and expertise will introduce an unnecessary burden most of the time. This burden comes both in the form of time and expense in responding to the lawyer, as well as the introduction of doubt and stress—the very things that these biases are adaptively designed to avoid. In some sense, the "realistic" lawyer may debilitate the group by threatening its solidarity and optimism.

There is also an informational risk to the quality of legal advice associated with too visible a posture of detachment and skepticism. Management teams no doubt test their lawyers for loyalty, and may well use the lawyer's willingness to conform to their perceptions as a proxy. The lawyer who repeatedly expresses doubt hardly endears herself to the client's managers; failure to show loyalty to the group, and the group's beliefs, is likely to result in exclusion from the inner circle and hence loss of access to key information and insight. She becomes part of the out-group rather than the in-group, and information blockage may well follow—assuming that the representation is even allowed to continue.

B.   The Uneasy Techniques of Mediation

Being a cognitively independent lawyer is difficult and stressful enough internally. But ultimately, the client's management is in control of both the underlying facts and the output of corporate disclosure, and the lawyer's professional responsibility offers her little leverage over the management group. When factual assessments are subjective and hence multiple good faith interpretations possible, the lawyer is not barred from rendering assistance. Usually, the lawyer will only suspect, not know, that the managers are being unrealistic. In the end, then, the good lawyer—the one who does not simply suffer a failure of will when faced with the challenge—must effectively negotiate with the managers for both undistorted access to information and influence over the disclosure process. She must also do so in a way, as noted above, that does not jeopardize her in-group status or result in diminished access to information.

If legal requirements are clear enough, this will not be difficult. But most forms of risk disclosure are subjective and probabilistic, and here, the difficulty is plain. When a lawyer challenges management's overly optimistic assessment or dismissal of some risk, the natural reaction is rarely one of welcome. Because of its adaptive nature, managers will not easily drop their optimism simply because a lawyer has a different point of view. Just as likely, if not more, they will dismiss the lawyer's view as inexpertly alarmist, lacking in sufficient business experience or acumen. Like many people, their reaction to a threatening message will, in essence, be to "shoot the messenger" (i.e., deflect the message by challenging the credibility or competence of the source). The right response is a persistent, tactful assessment of the risk of litigation, bad publicity and other adverse consequences from potential nondisclosure, emphasizing the risks of hindsight. For many clients, especially those where the securities law compliance function has become well-routinized, this will be enough. But sometimes, management may have too much at stake in its own belief system.

If management balks, there are two conventional, but problematic, responses short of giving in and washing one's hands of the consequences. One is to draft the disclosure in a way that discloses a risk but talks about it in distant, hypothetical terms. I suspect that one explanation for the prevalence of boilerplate disclosure is that it represents an easy compromise between the lawyer's insistence on disclosure and management's refusal to acknowledge, publicly or to themselves, that the risk is a real one that they may not be able to control.

Boilerplate, however, is hardly the best solution, for it is too easy for a judge or jury to disregard later on. * * * The independent lawyer needs to push harder if she can.

Another conventional response is to overthreaten. If it seems necessary, the lawyer can skew a presentation by dramatically inflating the risk either a lawsuit or a judgment, trying to instill the sharp fear that even if they are right in trivializing or ignoring the risk, the chance of being second-guessed wrongly is simply too great. The problem here, of course, is that the lawyer must essentially be dishonest with the client, albeit with the best of intentions. And that, as we shall see in the next subsection, can become a very slippery slope. I do have a suspicion that the apparent misperception among corporate managers and boards of directors of the relatively high risk of a securities class action (or SEC investigation)—statistics notwithstanding—may be due at least in part to the way some corporate lawyers have portrayed those risks to them in an effort to overcome their natural reluctance or apathy with respect to disclosure obligations.

C. The Lawyer's Own Self–Serving Bias

A third problem inherent in the notion of cognitive independence mirrors a discussion found in the debate over lawyers' independence generally. Once the lawyer accepts the need to sometimes second-guess the managers' perception of the facts and circumstances and exercise independent judgment, there is an inevitable risk that this judgment will itself be distorted by the lawyer's own self-interest. * * *

Lawyers have a strong self-interest in the advice they give. Even conceding the importance of not cheating in the short-run if it would jeopardize repeat business from a client relationship, some advice leads to more billable hours on a project than others. As we have just seen, questioning the client is time-consuming. Just as important, however, is the reputational asymmetry. A lawyer loses far more by giving the go ahead to a course of action that is later subject to legal sanction than she gains from advice that is not challenged. On the other hand, there is frequently no reputational penalty from too much caution because the client lacks the knowledge and expertise to second-guess the lawyer's judgment. In sum (and subject to some predictable exceptions), lawyers are motivated to overstate legal risk. James Freund observes this in his book on client counselling. Also apt along these lines is a fascinating study by Edelman, Abraham and Erlanger of the way both business lawyers and human resource specialists have seemingly inflated the threat posed by wrongful discharge law, with a resulting gain to them in power and resources within client organizations. And just as managers can distort reality when believing that they are acting in the corporation's best interests, so can lawyers dwell excessively on risk while considering themselves fully loyal to their client's interests.

This inclination will be offset when the lawyer bonds too completely with the client's management group. Once the lawyer internalizes the group's motivation to deflect or rationalize risk, her interest in solidarity and whatever other needs are met by inclusion may come to dominate the tendency to spot and dwell on disclosure risks. This is especially so if the lawyer has some means of avoiding apparent responsibility for the final disclosure judgment calls.

A deliberate posture of cognitive independence, on the other hand, permits this self-interest to surface. To a limited extent, this is probably a good thing—self-interest boosts the lawyer's motivation to resist management's biases. However, when the lawyer becomes too independent of the client's way of thinking, the anchor of client interest may be displaced in favor of one that is based too much on the lawyer's reputational and pecuniary interests. The problem then becomes lawyer involvement in the disclosure process that overcompensates for managerial bias and results in a risk of excess disclosure and a chilling of useful impression management techniques above what a rational cost-benefit analysis would require. This, too, may be an explanation for the seemingly excessive fear of litigation and enforcement that has been inculcated in many corporate officers and directors. * * *

For all these reasons, we cannot embrace cognitive independence without also acknowledging its subtle dangers. The truly good corporate lawyer must seek independence, but recognize the difficult terrain of its path and the sometimes selfish temptations lawyers face along the way. Our profession should at least be willing to provide a map and a compass.

Robert Eli Rosen, RISK MANAGEMENT AND CORPORATE
GOVERNANCE: THE CASE OF ENRON

35 CONN. L. REV. 1157 (2003)

The Role of the Board of Directors in Enron's Collapse, which was prepared by the United States Senate's Permanent Subcommittee on Investigations (the "Subcommittee") found that the Enron Corporation's ("Enron") Board of Directors (the "Board") "failed to monitor . . . or halt abuse." Sometimes the Board "chose to ignore" problems, other times it "knowingly allowed Enron to engage in high . . . risk practices." In so doing, the Board breached its duties "to safeguard Enron shareholders."

[T]hese findings [reflect] more general problems of corporate governance. These problems derive from the now dominant strategies of "progressive" corporate organization, which I will name the "redesigned corporation." Enron was a redesigned corporation.

First, in corporations that are redesigned, projects flow bottom-up, not top-down. In such companies, executive monitoring means analyzing risk management reports. The Powers Report concludes that Enron's Board "can and should be faulted for failing to demand more information, and for failing to probe and understand the information that did come to it." If so, the Board is being faulted for its reliance on risk management reports. It is not that Enron's Board was not a monitoring board, but that it poorly monitored risk management reports.

Second, companies are redesigned to foster innovation. Such companies will take high risks, hedge or retain others risks, and seek unprecedented projects. Enron was "consistently voted the most innovative large company in America in *Fortune's* Most Admired Companies survey." The governance project for redesigned companies is to manage "high risk . . . practices." With the benefit of hindsight, some of Enron's projects were too risky. "Too risky", in the redesigned company, means that project risks were either improperly mitigated or unfortunately retained. It does not mean that risks, including legal risks, are eliminated. Enron poses the question of what duty of care attaches to the choices of mitigating and retaining risks . . .

Enron is not the best evidence for these arguments. At Enron, looting, bribery, egotism, and other dramas of greed appear to such an extent that Enron may be a distinctive organization . . . [T]his Article addresses how the redesign of corporations challenges corporate governance, even when it is not manipulated by evil-doers . . .

Corporate law contains an organizational focus. It focuses on a chain of command. Its corporation is a bureaucracy. Corporate law is concerned with Generals and leaves it to the Generals to command the troops. Corporate law's focus does not capture the governance structures of innovative corporations. Corporate redesign attacked bureaucracies for stifling innovation. Redesigned corporations flatten hierarchy. Rather than directing the troops, redesigned corporations energize the zeal of the troops. In such corporations, Generals will find hierarchical commands insufficient to govern their troops.

In the redesigned corporation, management and the board do not review, let alone direct, the substance of most transactions. They review risk-management reports on the transactions. Good governance means getting the right information to the actors charged with decision-making. That did not happen at Enron. Good governance also means creating mechanisms of accountability. In redesigned corporations, risk management is the key internal control mechanism . . .

I. ACCOUNTABILITY IN THE REDESIGNED CORPORATION

"Managers cannot bring out the intelligence of everyone in the organization if they pretend they can do better thinking in a few hours than a project team that has wrestled with the problem for months. Instead of issuing arbitrary orders, they need to raise concerns and trust the project team to find a way of handling them that integrates with all the other issues guiding the design."

Gifford Pinchot & Elizabeth Pinchot, The End of Bureaucracy and the Rise of the Intelligent Organization 34 (1994). Redesigned corporations are among us. "Throughout much of the economy, and especially among new firms, hierarchies are flatter, headquarters staff smaller . . . [and employees experience] more fluid job definitions, and more ambiguous reporting relationships." An objective of redesign is to free innovation from the constraints of hierarchical control. Redesigned organizations lack "the rules of clarity and commitment" of "bureaucratic organizations."

There is a worldwide cultural and political movement attacking bureaucracy. In the public sector, governments are privatizing and dismantling bureaucracies. Corporate groups and networks are utilizing markets instead of hierarchies. Within corporations, headquarters' staffs and "middle-management" are downsized. In redesigned corporations, instead of bureaucrats, employees are innovators.

Proponents of redesign disparage specialization, the self-sufficiency of technical competence, uniform policies as well as standardized procedures. They also target a hierarchical accountability structure, where "coordination" is "done from a level or more above the work being coordinated" * * *

Corporations are redesigned to better realize "the obligation of an employee to deliver all elements of the value that he or she is being compensated for delivering." Corporate redesign accepts that agents will engage in opportunistic behaviors. Unlike bureaucracies, redesign does not reduce agency costs by supervision. In redesigned corporations, agent opportunism is managed indirectly and covertly.

First, incentive structures are established to align employee and corporate interests. Employees learn the operating rule of redesigned corporations: "You will be employed by us as long as you add value to the organization, and you are continuously responsible for finding ways to add value." Management by objectives is one strategy for this control: Management supplies numbers to hit and compensation is based on hitting these numbers. Such forms of hierarchical control are indirect mechanisms of control. For example, Enron's management may have set targets, but teams and employees initiate, plan, and implement projects to hit the numbers.

Second, redesigned corporations utilize various motivational strategies. For example, redesigned companies develop "fired up, highly cohesive" teams. Rather than imposing hierarchical controls, redesigned corporations heavily rely on horizontal (e.g., peer) controls. In the redesigned company, managers have a hands-off attitude toward teams. The "transmission belt" delegation of powers from principal to agent is replaced by one that emphasizes "network coordination." Instead of transparent bureaucratic controls, redesigned companies employ covert motivational controls.

Business transactions in redesigned companies are not managed hierarchically, but typically by self-managing project teams. Standardized procedures and policies are replaced by a commitment to aligning incentives. Coordination by the hierarchy is constrained by a commitment to the teams being self-managing.

Hierarchical supervision of the projects that are developed is conducted through reviews of risk-management reports, which project originators write, at least in part. In redesigned companies, teams develop "risk management plans ... to deal with unresolved issues and project risks, negotiate their allocation and sharing, and create ways to deal with them so as to mitigate the impact or eliminate the risks completely." Senior executives decide on whether or not to go forward with the project by assessing these risk management plans, sometimes requiring that independent assessments be made.

In sum, in the redesigned corporation, markets are created within firms and competition occurs through risk management reports. In many respects, redesigned firms are combinations of intrapreneurial teams. A sociologically accurate, but legally metaphorical, image of the redesigned corporation is that of a holding company of intrapreneurial teams (metaphorically, dominated subs). The incentive structure is manipulated so that to each team, their project is a bet-your-company deal * * *

III. RISK MANAGEMENT

A. *Law and Accounting as Profit Centers*

Traditionally, corporate funds expended for legal and auditing services were seen as losses, payments for side-constraints on the corporate mission. Today, tax departments, accounting firms, corporate legal departments, and law firms claim they are profit centers. They "add value" to the corporation * * *

The Subcommittee [report on Enron] found that high risks were assumed because of "Enron's ordering its tax department to produce billions of dollars in company earnings through the use of complex tax shelters." More accurately, Enron's tax department developed and bought, from accounting and law firms, products to increase company earnings. In redesigned companies, tax departments will seek innovations to add value (produce earnings) to the company. The problem is not that they do so, but that these innovations may not be adequately assessed. The problem is not that "Enron was using accounting practices that 'push limits' and were 'at the edge' of acceptable practices" and "approved an unprecedented arrangement." That is called innovation. The problem is that the risks of these innovations to Enron were not properly addressed.

Enron's financial team was composed of the firms that sold themselves as leaders (and innovators) in the use of derivatives and other complex financial solutions to corporate problems. Vinson & Elkins marketed themselves as "in the forefront of . . . capital markets, project finance and structured finance solutions for . . . energy initiatives." Arthur Andersen also emphasized its technical expertise, innovative approach and commitment "to help the client emphasize the best strategies" to succeed in the energy and utilities market. In particular, Arthur Andersen's energy and utilities group praised Enron for "rethinking business models" and for developing a "value dynamics" model for "the valuation of a company's assets." Enron was the "leading edge."

Beyond the self-dealing, a lesson of Enron [is] the dilemma of monitoring risks when finance and law are seen as profit centers. In the redesigned company, such monitoring is especially difficult because professionals work on and for teams. As an outside lawyer put it, "We were giving advice to the people we were instructed to give it to under their protocol" and they were aware of the risks. The lawyers were there to help teams develop projects so their exposures were reduced. For risk management purposes, at least, teams treat lawyers like hired guns. They are there to advance the project by mitigating, transferring, and hedging risks. As one energy and utilities company senior executive said: "From a [*transactional*] lawyer, what I want is quality of work: bringing up good issues and pertinent points *to defend our side of the equation.*"

In the redesigned corporation, not all risks are eliminated. Projects will be funded that have legal risks. Executives confront many risks and legal risks are just one among many others. Legal non-compliance is a possibility. The corporate decision depends on the management of risks, not only the removal of risks * * *

Professionals in redesigned corporations add value by advancing projects that may realize benefits, while mitigating the projects' risks. Professionals also add value by using their expertise to develop projects that increase corporate earnings * * * Their projects, as well as the projects of the teams for whom they work, are monitored by risk management reports * * *

B. The Raptor Project and Enron's Board

* * * Two * * * subtle problems emerge from considering the Enron case. First, there are moral hazard problems. Teams have incentives to shape risk management reports so that their project will be selected. When bad business deals result, officers and directors will say, "We were aware of this moral hazard problem and responded to it, albeit inadequately as this legal action demonstrates. But, we are able to respond to agency costs. If not, the market will. No second-guessing is needed from outsiders. For the current case, we have no liability because we didn't order it nor did we fail to respond to clear signals which were (not) present."

Officers and directors are unlikely to mention the moral hazard problem that emerges from their "empowerment" of workers. In a bottom-up strategy, executives attain plausible deniability. "We treated them like adults and they betrayed us." In shifting responsibility down the line, executives are all too likely to engage in risky behavior.

Consider a director's or officer's testimony that, "We knew there were these very significant risks, but we did it anyway. It was a cost-benefit weighing." This is music to a tort lawyer's ears. On the other hand, in a corporation with a properly functioning risk management system, this is a choice that officers and directors must make for the benefit of the shareholders. For officers and directors, this creates a double-bind. The redesigned corporation, in allowing executives to attain plausible deniability through self-managing employees, resolves this double-bind. But, it imposes agency costs on shareholders when the corporation is liable or suffers financial losses from actions that were never directed, but worked their way up from the bottom.

Second, as a result of corporate redesign, compliance officers have become risk-managers. Compliance officers' zeal is re-shaped. A crucial consequence is that noncompliance becomes an option. Risks are not always eliminated; they often are transformed, hedged, and insured.

This change in the understanding of corporate compliance is reflected not only within the corporation, but also in multi-disciplinary auditing firms. Post–Enron, the big news is that consulting partners exited from their partnerships with auditors. This news fails to emphasize that compliance consultants, and tax consultants, stayed with the auditors. That compliance and tax consultants remained with the auditors reflects that these consultants' added value derives in large part from their organizational link with auditors. A tax product, for example, is easier to sell when your partners are going to audit the books. Compliance decisions similarly increase in value when your audit partner decides what needs to be reported. As compliance decisions are understood as risk management decisions, serious conflicts of interest emerge between the normative idea of auditors and the reality of their business, in which compliance partners sell risky compliance.

PROBLEM*

During the 1970s, one of Ford Motor Company's design experts approaches in-house counsel and expresses a concern that Ford, in its rush to market a model competitive with small foreign cars, has been unwilling to make certain safety improvements in the fuel tank placement of Pinto automobiles. Based on counsel's preliminary investigation, management undertakes a full review of safety test results and alternative design plans for the Pinto fuel system. After extensive consultation with the engineering and legal staff, Ford's chief executive officers determine that the system, although susceptible to explosion if punctured from the rear, nonetheless meets federal safety standards and that the cost of liability in foreseeable tort litigation. The benefits and costs of improving the system are set out in the table below. Accordingly, the officers determine not to recall the model and there is no reason to believe that the Board of Directors would arrive at a different conclusion.

Assume that you are a member of the in-house legal staff and that you are aware of the preceding information. What would you do? If you disagree with the chief executive officer's decision, but are unable to alter his views, what would be your possible courses of action? What factors would be relevant to your judgment?

BENEFITS AND COSTS RELATING TO
FUEL LEAKAGE ASSOCIATED WITH THE
STATIC ROLLOVER TEST PORTION OF FMVSS 208

Benefits:	*Savings*—180 burn deaths, 180 serious burn injuries, 2100 burned vehicles.
	Unit Cost—$200,000 per death, $67,000 per injury, $700 per vehicle.
	Total Benefit—180 x ($200,000) + 180 x ($67,000) + 2100 x ($700) = $49.5 million.
Costs:	*Sales*—11 million cars, 1.5 million light trucks.
	Unit Cost—$11 per car, $11 per truck.
	Total Cost—11,000,000 x ($11) + 1,500,000 x ($11) = $137 million.

Source: Strobel, Lee, "How Ford put a price tag on auto's safety," *Chicago Tribune,* October 14, 1979, p. 18. [Table taken from Ford's study]

* This problem is adapted from Deborah L. Rhode & David J. Luban, LEGAL ETH-   ICS (2d ed. 1995).

Chapter 10

ATTORNEY DISCIPLINE
AND LIABILITY

Like all other lawyers, attorneys in corporate practice are subject to discipline for ethical misconduct by the bar association of the states in which they are admitted to practice. Each state has adopted rules that mirror to varying degrees the American Bar Association (ABA) Model Rules of Professional Conduct. Violation of these provisions can subject the lawyer to sanctions such as private reprimand, public reprimand, suspension, and disbarment.

As a practical matter, however, state bar associations tend to prosecute actions against corporate lawyers only in the most extreme cases. To a large extend, this pattern reflects the limited resources typically available to state bar disciplinary committees. It often is a more efficient use of those resources to pursue actions against attorneys who have engaged in misconduct while representing individuals than against lawyers in large law firms or corporate legal departments who represent corporations.

In addition, as this chapter describes, corporations have a variety of legal responses available when they believe that lawyers representing them have misbehaved. The typical corporate lawyer is more concerned about the possibility of liability in these actions than about state bar discipline. Lawsuits can be brought not only by clients, but in some cases by non-clients who have been affected by the lawyer's work. A lawyer's violation of a state ethical rule can be used as evidence of misconduct in these cases, although it alone is not dispositive with respect to liability. The material in this chapter describes the elements of a variety of potential causes of action against lawyers. This body of law effectively serves as a form of ethical regulation that is at least as important, if not more so, than state bar rules of professional conduct.

OVERVIEW OF THE CHAPTER

The chapter first provides a short description of the system of bar admission and discipline, which is administered by bar associations on a state-by-state basis. The bulk of the Chapter is then organized around some of the most common types of liability that lawyers can incur. The first is malpractice—the tort of negligence in the practice of law. The excerpt from the Harvard Law Review "Developments in the Law" issue sets for the elements of this tort, while the excerpt from John Leubsdorf situates legal malpractice within the doctrine relating to fiduciary duties. *FDIC v. Clark* makes clear that even being misled by a client will not automatically protect a lawyer from a malpractice claim, if the circumstances were sufficiently suspicious that a reasonable lawyer under the circumstances would have taken steps independently to confirm the truth of the client's representation. Ask yourself what a reasonable lawyer might have done under the facts in *Clark* to avoid liability. How aggressive must a lawyer be in verifying what a client tells her? What kinds of considerations must a lawyer balance in answering this question?

The second cause of action is breach of fiduciary duty. *Milbank, Tweed v. Boon* illustrates the willingness of some courts to adopt a more lenient standard of causation for such claims than for allegations of malpractice. Make sure that you understand how this tort differs from malpractice, and why a court might apply a different standard. *Hendry v. Pelland* reflects the common rule that a client suing a lawyer for breach fiduciary duty need not show causation or even injury if the client is suing for return of legal fees. Ask yourself why this is the case, and whether such a rule is likely to achieve the purpose that it is supposed to serve.

Section 552 of the Restatement of Torts, dealing with negligent misrepresentation, reflects the expanding realm of lawyer liability to non-clients. Make sure that you understand both the traditional reasons for resistance to liability to non-clients, and the criteria and rationales for recognizing it with respect to negligent misrepresentation. How foreseeable should harm to a third party be before a cause of action is available? Does Section 552 adopt a sensible approach, or are there better alternatives?

A claim that may be asserted against corporate lawyers is that they aided and abetted a company official's breach of his fiduciary duty. *Chem-Age Industries v. Glover* exemplifies a common standard that courts use to determine whether a lawyer may be liable for rendering such assistance. Be sure to note the concerns that lead the court to frame the test in the way that it does. Is the test responsive to those concerns? *Austin v. Bradley, Barry & Tarlow* addresses the issue of when a lawyer may be liable for aiding and abetting simply by failing to disclose information. The court comes close to saying that mere silence cannot constitute providing such assistance—but then it seems to back away from this proposition. Is the court clear about whether and when a lawyer can aid and abet a client's wrongdoing by failing to disclose it?

Finally, the chapter includes a short note on the regulation of lawyer conduct by specialized agencies with which specialists deal, and mentions one case in which violation of a bankruptcy rule resulted in a lawyer's criminal conviction. Keep in mind that there is another important source of lawyer liability that we do not discuss in this chapter—liability under the federal securities laws. We will cover material on that topic in Chapter 17.

The Problems for the Chapter ask you to work through short fact patterns that touch upon each of the forms of liability included in the Chapter. You should be able to consult in straightforward fashion the materials under each topic in analyzing each of these Problems.

A. BAR ADMISSION AND DISCIPLINE

The highest court in each state is deemed to have inherent authority to regulate the conduct of lawyers practicing in that state. Courts typically delegate the responsibility of formulating and enforcing standards of conduct to state bar associations, subject to review by the court. Since 1908, the American Bar Association has promulgated proposed model rules of ethics, which state bar associations are free to accept, adoption with revisions, or ignore. Currently, most state ethical rules are variations of the ABA's Model Rules of Professional Conduct. These Rules were first adopted in 1983, and were designed to supercede the ABA's Model Code of Professional Responsibility, which had been established in 1970. The Rules have been amended periodically since 1983, with amendments adopted by the states to varying degrees. A few states, most notably New York, still pattern their ethical rules on the ABA Model Code, and California has its own distinct set of ethical provisions.

In order to practice in a state, a lawyer must be admitted by the bar association on the basis of an examination or, in some states, recognition of the lawyer's membership in another bar association. Lawyers generally must be members of the state bar in order to be subject to discipline by that bar, with limited exceptions in some states for lawyers temporarily practicing in the state (a subject that will be discussed in more detail in the next Chapter). A client, another lawyer, or any other person may file a complaint against a lawyer with the state bar disciplinary committee. The committee then conducts investigations and, if necessary, hearings, that provide various measures of procedural protection for the lawyer who is the subject of the complaint. If a lawyer is deemed to have violated a rule, the committee has a range of sanctions available, including private reprimand, published reprimand, suspension, and disbarment. In several states, a lawyer who has been disbarred may apply for readmission after a certain period of time. A lawyer may seek review of disciplinary decisions from the state's highest court.

State bar disciplinary organizations for the most part have only minimal funding. Furthermore, many critics have pointed out their close connections to the practicing bar. For these and other reasons, only a low percentage of grievances ever reach the bar, and only a small percentage result in sanctions. Disciplinary committees overwhelmingly focus on complaints against solo or small firm lawyers who represent individuals. This means that state bar discipline for most corporate lawyers is only a remote possibility.

The rules are relevant to corporate lawyers for another reason, however. They are admissible as evidence in lawsuits against lawyers as an indication of what a reasonable lawyer would have done under the circumstances. A fact-finder cannot regard violation of an ethical rule as dispositive evidence that a lawyer is liable for torts such as malpractice, breach of fiduciary duty, or negligent misrepresentation, all of which will be discussed in more detail below. The fact that a lawyer violated a conflict of interest rule, for instance, does not automatically mean that her representation of a client was actually compromised by allegiance to another. Nonetheless, for juries charged with determining subtle matters such as whether a lawyer acted loyally toward a client, evidence of such a violation can have a powerful impact.

B. LIABILITY

1. MALPRACTICE

DEVELOPMENTS IN THE LAW: LAWYERS' RESPONSIBILITIES AND LAWYERS' RESPONSES

107 Harv. L. Rev. 1547, 1557 (1994)

II. Lawyers' Responsibilities to the Client: Legal Malpractice and Tort Reform

A. The Elements of a Legal Malpractice Claim

Legal malpractice litigation primarily involves allegations of professional negligence. A plaintiff who seeks to establish such a claim must typically prove that the relevant statute of limitations has not expired, that the defendant attorney owed him a duty of professional care that was breached, and that the breach proximately caused quantifiable damage. This Section sketches some of the rules that govern these elements of a legal malpractice claim and, in the process, identifies an evolutionary pattern common to several doctrinal areas. In most areas, either judges have relaxed the barriers to plaintiff recovery, or commentators have argued that revisions should be made. These developments are often justified as necessary to compensate more fully the victims of legal malpractice.

The story does not end, however, with these revisions. Observers generally agree, that partly as a result of changes in legal doctrine, both the frequency of claims and the size of awards have increased. During the professional insurance "crisis" of the mid–1980s—when many lawyers' legal malpractice insurance premiums doubled or tripled—these trends captured political attention. In response to the problem of high-cost insurance, a number of state legislatures passed laws that counter-act the general pro-plaintiff trend.

1. The Statute of Limitations.—Statutes of limitations, under which a claim is barred if not filed within a certain time, provide the most common and effective affirmative defense to allegations of legal malpractice. When the defense is asserted, a court must first decide which limitations period to apply. Once this threshold question is answered, a court must then determine when the particular claim accrued—that is, when the limitations period began to run. Accrual doctrine was, until the 1960s, extremely favorable to legal malpractice defendants, because statutes of limitations ran from the *occurrence* of the essential facts constituting the claim. In some cases, this "occurrence rule" barred the plaintiff's claim before he had any chance to discover the alleged negligence in question.

The "injustices and frequently illogical results" of the occurrence rule have led many courts during the last twenty-five years to adopt instead both the "damage rule" and the "discovery rule." Under the damage rule, a plaintiff must have suffered actual injury before the limitations period will begin to run. For example, the statute of limitations on a negligently drafted will would be tolled until the death of the testator. In some cases, the discovery rule delays the accrual of a case for an even longer period than the damage rule. The discovery rule tolls the statute of limitations for malpractice until a client discovers, or reasonably should have discovered, the facts underlying the claim. * * *

2. The Duty of Care.—Duty is generally the next element of a legal malpractice claim. The question is whether the lawyer owed a duty to the particular individual suing for malpractice. Prior to the 1960s, the "American rule" was that attorneys would be liable for professional negligence only to those individuals with whom they established contractual privity—or, in other words, an attorney-client relationship. Courts feared that a more expansive duty to third parties would in some cases require an attorney to choose between advocating his client's position and protecting a third party. The privity rule, however, sometimes operated to deny a cause of action to the only party affected by the attorney's negligence. This result might happen if, for example, the attorney was hired to draft a will for the express benefit of a third party not in privity of contract with the attorney. Faced with this unappealing result, courts slowly overcame their concerns regarding third-party liability and instead focused on "providing a remedy to the victim, placing losses on the responsible attorney, and deterring culpable behavior."

Hence, the privity rule is now generally not followed in cases involving a third party who is a clearly intended beneficiary of the attorney's services. Because they often involve parties who were clearly intended to benefit by a client's retention of an attorney, the paradigmatic circumstances in which liability has been extended involve beneficiaries of negligently drafted wills or lenders who relied on improperly drafted title certifications. Among courts that have recognized a legal duty without strict privity, a decided majority has in fact explicitly adopted an intended-beneficiary test to determine whether an attorney owed a duty to a third party. The intended-beneficiary test requires that both the attorney and the client expressly intended the plaintiff to benefit from the legal services, and that this [*1562] benefit was the "primary or direct purpose of the transaction or relationship." * * *

3. The Standard of Care.—Once the plaintiff establishes that the defendant lawyer owed him the professional duties of an attorney, the question becomes—what are those duties? As is generally the case in other areas of tort law, the standard of care for attorneys is an objective one. Rather than a general "reasonable person" standard, however, lawyers are typically held to a "reasonable attorney" standard which requires them to exercise the degree of diligence, care, and skill ordinarily or commonly demonstrated by attorneys in the relevant geographical area. In some cases, this generalized standard of care insulates particular attorneys against malpractice liability. Sophisticated tax lawyers, for example, could argue that they had performed as proficiently in handling a tax question as an ordinary general practitioner would.

However, because specialization has become increasingly accepted as a reality of law practice, the trend is toward imposing a more stringent, particularized standard of care on specialists. Accordingly, lawyers who hold themselves out as specialists must generally measure up against "other specialists of ordinary skill and capacity specializing in the same field." In fact, a generalist may also be compared to specialists in a given field when he handles a matter within a complex area of the law, and one court has explicitly held that a general practitioner should either refer such a case to a specialist or consult with one. This trend toward heightened standards for attorneys practicing in specialized areas significantly increases the likelihood that they will be found in breach of their professional duty.

4. Proving Breach.—Whether the standard of care is defined in terms of the ordinary lawyer or similarly situated specialists, jurors are left with a fairly general yardstick against which to measure the specific conduct of a particular attorney. Because jurors are often unfamiliar with the standard practice of lawyers, courts have developed several ancillary legal rules to aid juries in their attempts to apply this general standard of care to specific factual circumstances.

(a) The Use of Expert Witnesses to Determine the Standard of Care and Whether Breach Occurred.—Before a jury can decide whether a defendant breached his standard of care, someone must define that standard. Prior to the 1960s, judges generally did so in jury instructions. Whether the defendant breached the standard of care was then a question of fact for the jury to decide. * * *

Since the 1960s, however, views on who should define the standard of care have changed dramatically; every jurisdiction that has addressed the issue has held expert testimony admissible to establish the standard of care in legal malpractice cases. In fact, courts in a majority of jurisdictions now *require* that a malpractice plaintiff present testimony from a qualified expert on the particular requirements of the standard of care and the defendant's fulfillment of those obligations. Several concerns led to this acceptance of expert testimony. Courts worried, for example, that judges were not sufficiently versed in all areas of legal practice to provide reliable guidance, that the parties to a case would not have an opportunity to test the judge's credibility through cross-examination, and that juries would give undue credence to statements from a judge. Furthermore, to allow a judge to decide whether the defendant breached his duty could be taken as a violation of the right to due process guaranteed in a particular state's constitution. * * *

(c) Ethical Rules and Negligence Per Se.—In addition to deciding who could testify, courts had to consider what expert witnesses would be permitted to say in court. The evolution of detailed ethical codes complicated this question. The codes could conceivably have made it easier for a plaintiff to prove that her attorney breached the relevant standard of care. A violation of an ethical provision, much like a violation of a statutory prohibition, might plausibly be considered negligence per se, eliminating the need for sophisticated, particularized expert testimony. The drafters of the Model Rules of Professional Conduct and the Model Code of Professional Responsibility, however, recognized the possibility that plaintiffs would try to use the codes to prove that their lawyers were negligent. In response, both the Model [*1567] Rules and the Model Code were drafted with disclaimers intended to forestall their use in legal malpractice cases as definitive statements of the appropriate standard of care. Because of the disclaimers, states are divided on what role, if any, these ethical guidelines should play in establishing the standard of care in legal malpractice cases.

Most courts do not hold that violation of the ethical guidelines creates a presumption of negligence, although they do permit discussion of such a violation at trial as some evidence of negligence. * * *

5. Causation.—After proving breach, the plaintiff must next prove that the lawyer's inadequacy proximately caused a particular, quantifiable loss. The rules for causation in legal malpractice have remained remarkably static given the acceptance of new theories of causation in other areas of tort law. Courts apply a "but-for" test to determine whether the defendant's negligence injured the plaintiff. In other words, the plaintiff must prove that injury would not have occurred but for the defendant's negligence. * * *

The appropriate methods for proving causation vary greatly depending on the substantive backdrop for the malpractice claim. A rough line can be drawn, however, between cases that arise in a litigation and those that arise in a transactional setting. Transactional cases often involve a fairly straightforward causal inquiry, such as whether an attorney's failure to adequately secure title in real property caused injury to the client. As a result, little controversy surrounds the but-for test used in such cases.

By contrast, cases involving the alleged mishandling of litigation have engendered lengthy debate regarding how causation should be established. The "hypothetical or counterfactual nature of the [but-for test]" requires plaintiffs to prove what *might* have happened had their attorney handled matters differently. To establish causation, then, "the client may be required to prove that he or she would have been successful in prosecuting or defending the underlying action, if not for the attorney's negligence or other improper conduct." This means that the plaintiff would have to conduct a "trial within a trial" in which both the malpractice and the underlying claims are tried to the same jury, with the malpractice defendant forced to represent the opponent in the underlying action. * * *

* * * Plaintiffs and commentators alike have argued that plaintiffs should be allowed to prove causation through expert testimony regarding the value of the mishandled claim—that is, either the settlement value of the lost claim or the value of the lost chance to prevail. Underlying the idea of settlement value is the realization that most cases are settled prior to trial. The injury to the plaintiff, then, is not the loss of a valid claim, but the loss of a reasonably calculable settlement amount. Proof of causation would thus involve the presentation of expert testimony on the likely settlement amount of the underlying claim based on prior cases in the jurisdiction. * * *

6. *Damages.*—The issues of proximate causation and damages are linked, because in both phases of the trial the plaintiff must identify a particular injury caused by the defendant. In the damages phase of the trial, the plaintiff must show how that injury should be valued. Like the but-for test, the rules concerning the proof of damages have undergone little judicial revision in recent years. Despite this continuity, however, the issue of damages received considerable attention during the malpractice reform debate.

A client generally can recover all economic losses that flow directly and naturally from his attorney's malpractice. The difficulty in distinguishing between direct and consequential damages, however, potentially exposes lawyers to expansive liability. The mishandling of an incorporation might, for example, result in a claim for a considerable amount of lost profits, which might be characterized as the direct result of attorney negligence. To protect lawyers from such expansive, and potentially crippling, liability, courts usually "reject attempts to recover for the 'ripple effect' of a negligent act," such as unforeseen lost profits. Although it is difficult to generalize the approaches taken by courts, they tend to uphold recovery for injuries that could have been foreseen at the time the plaintiff retained the defendant. * * *

John Leubsdorf, LEGAL MALPRACTICE AND
PROFESSIONAL RESPONSIBILITY

48 RUTGERS L. REV. 101 (1995)

* * *

B.   BREACH OF FIDUCIARY DUTY

One part of the law regulating lawyers with which legal malpractice should be integrated is the law defining and enforcing lawyers' fiduciary duties. Unfortunately, this integration has not yet been accomplished.

There can be no question, of course, that lawyers are fiduciaries. Regardless of whether the ground for this classification is the importance of the matters confided to lawyers, the trust that clients are encouraged to place in them, or the difficulty of monitoring their performance, lawyers are and should be subject to special rules for the protection of their clients. Likewise, lawyers are clearly subject to civil liability for failure to fulfill fiduciary duties such as the duty to preserve client confidences, to safeguard client property, and to avoid certain conflicts of interest. * * *

The study of fiduciary duties should provide a useful bridge between traditional malpractice law and disciplinary rules and foster the integration of the two. Fiduciary duties are like traditional malpractice law in that they are enforced through civil actions by injured parties: the beneficiaries of the fiduciary relationship. They are like the obligations to clients set forth in the disciplinary rules in that they articulate a relatively detailed regulatory scheme, based on the vulnerability of clients. At the same time, the invocation of fiduciary duty summons up the law and scholarship that deals with the duties of fiduciaries other than lawyers, such as trustees, corporate officers and directors, and agents.

Ultimately, legal malpractice in the narrow sense should be considered just one form of actionable breach of fiduciary duty; breach of fiduciary duty should not be viewed as a peripheral subject area that must somehow be squeezed into legal malpractice. The action for legal malpractice in the narrow sense enforces duties of diligence and competence. These duties are themselves fiduciary in nature, classifiable as duties of care. But lawyers also owe duties of loyalty that are likewise enforceable by injured clients. Although distinctions between the enforcement of different duties will sometimes make sense, in general duties of care and of loyalty should be treated similarly for purposes of civil liability. From a client's point of view, it makes little difference whether a lawyer lost the case by failing to obtain vital information or by disclosing protected information to the opposing party. . . .

FEDERAL DEPOSIT INSURANCE CORPORATION v. CLARK

978 F.2d 1541 (10th Cir. 1992)

BROWN, SENIOR DISTRICT JUDGE

This action was brought by the Federal Deposit Insurance Corporation against two attorneys, defendants Clark and Swanson, and their law firm, to recover damages sustained by the Aurora Bank, a Colorado state bank, which was closed on November 1, 1985, when the Colorado State Bank Commissioner determined that it was insolvent.

The losses to the bank arose from a fraudulent conspiracy, known as the "heist money scheme," which involved the purchase of stolen money through bank loans procured from the Aurora bank. The defendant attorneys were not personally involved in the fraud, but the jury found them to be liable for negligence in their capacity as attorneys for the bank.

The claims against the defendant attorneys were brought under Colorado state law for professional negligence and/or for breach of an implied warranty of professional capacity and ability.

In a bifurcated trial, the jury first found that both defendants Swanson and Clark were "negligent or at fault by breach of implied warranties," and that such "negligence or fault" was a cause of loss to the bank, and that both were acting in their authority as partners in the defendant law firm.

In addition, the jury fixed proportionate liability among defendants and others not named in the case, finding that Clark should be charged with 14% and Swanson with 5% of the damages arising from negligence.

In the second phase of the trial, the jury found that the damages sustained by the bank between October 18, 1984, and December 20, 1984, were in the total sum of $914,013.19. In accordance with the verdicts of the jury, judgment was entered against the defendant Clark in the sum of $127,961.80, against Swanson in the sum of $45,700.00, and against their firm, Hamilton, Myer, Swanson, Faatz & Clark, jointly and severally.

In this appeal, the defendant attorneys claim that, [*inter alia*] * * * they are not responsible for damages because their client, the Aurora Bank, by and through its dishonest agent, Nowfel, provided them with false information [and that] * * * they were not negligent and breached no duty[.] * * *

FACTS

Turning to the question of defendants' liability in this action, we note that the FDIC claimed that the defendants negligently failed to uncover and prevent a fraud perpetrated against the bank by third parties. In particular, plaintiff alleged that defendants breached four duties owed by counsel to the bank—first, to exercise independent judgment without compromising loyalties of joint representation; second, a duty to investigate allegations of fraudulent activities; third, a duty to fully disclose the allegations of fraud to the board of directors; and fourth, a duty to advise the board of the legal significance of the allegations of the Rizzo complaint.

Under the evidence submitted at trial, the jury was entitled to find that the bank's losses arose from the following described factual situation:

The defendant attorneys represented the Aurora Bank in a number of matters from the time of its opening until the time it was closed by state regulators. Defendant Clark represented the organizers in establishing the bank; and, afterwards, represented the bank in its corporate affairs. He was a shareholder in the bank and served as its corporate secretary and as the bank's registered agent.

Defendant Swanson, with Clark, represented the bank in the lawsuit, described subsequently, which gave rise to this malpractice action— that is a federal lawsuit referred to by the parties as the "Rizzo case".

Clark and Swanson were partners in the firm of Neef, Swanson, Myer & Clark, that became the firm of Hamilton, Myer, Swanson, Faatz & Clark on January 1, 1986. Neef, Swanson, Myer & Clark were designated as the Bank's legal counsel at the annual meeting of the bank's shareholders in February, 1984.

The "heist money scheme" began in May, 1984. This involved the sale of $9 million of stolen currency, or "heist money," for payment of $2 million in "clean money." One John A. Napoli, Jr., assisted by others connected to organized crime, acted as the representative for the heist money seller and negotiated the terms of sale. The buyers were to be Dennis Nowfel, president of the Aurora Bank; Bill Vanden Eynden, the bank's vice-president; and Faud Jezzeny and Henrich F. Rupp, who worked together to obtain the $2 million purchase money from the Aurora Bank.

The vehicle used for defrauding the bank was a checking account there owned by Swiss American, Ltd., a company in which Rupp was the sole principal. Money from the Aurora Bank was fraudulently obtained in three ways:

 a. Nowfel and Vanden Eynden approved fraudulent loans to out-of-state borrowers, including Anthony Del Vecchio and Jilly Rizzo, who were involved in the heist money scheme. These loans were made without collateral or adequate documentation and their proceeds were deposited to the Swiss American account and used to make payments on the $2 million purchase price for the "heist" money.

 b. Forged checks or checks drawn on nonexistent accounts were deposited in the Swiss American account. Nowfel or Vanden Eynden approved the immediate withdrawal of these funds, which were paid over to Napoli. This ultimately created large overdrafts in the Swiss American account.

 c. Some loans were made by the Aurora Bank directly to Napoli.

The entire scheme lasted seven months, and included numerous transactions by which Nowfel and his conspirators attempted to drain $2 million from the Aurora Bank.

Between July and October, 1984, the bank and its directors had no information about the scheme. Defendant Clark was the first to learn of it. On October 3, 1984, Clark, as the registered agent for the Aurora Bank, was served with a civil summons and complaint brought by Rizzo and Del Vecchio in the United States District Court for the District of Colorado against the bank, Nowfel "individually, and in his capacity as President and Chief Executive Officer of The Aurora Bank," and Jezzeny and Rupp, who were bank customers. By this suit, plaintiffs Rizzo and Del Vecchio sought to cancel their obligation to repay the $350,000 they had borrowed from the bank in July, 1984.

The jury could find that in their complaint, Rizzo and Del Vecchio accurately alleged that Nowfel had approved loans to them without financial affidavits, financial information or collateral; that the loans were collateralized by 500,000 shares of "World Wide Venture" stock which, due to restrictions, had no present value; that the loan to Rizzo was made without his presence and without an adequate power of attorney; that Jezzeny, as a part of the scheme, executed $600,000 in promissory notes payable to Rizzo and Del Vecchio; that $275,000 of the loan proceeds were deposited into the Aurora Bank account of Swiss American; that Rupp removed $300,000 in cash from this account, and that shortly thereafter Rupp informed Del Vecchio and Rizzo that he had been robbed of the loan money thus preventing plaintiffs' investment in Swiss American. The Rizzo complaint specifically alleged that the real purpose of the transactions was to provide a nominee loan by the bank to Rupp, without incurring any liability on his part, and that Nowfel was at all times acting as Rupp's agent. In particular, Paragraph 51 of the complaint described Nowfel's actions in this manner:

51. Said conspiracy to defraud the plaintiffs was furthered by defendant Nowful's (sic) intentional violation of federal statute and regulations designed to protect the Bank and its shareholders, including but not limited to loaning out sums in excess of reserve requirements of *12 U.S.C. 84* (a)(1) and *12 C.F.R. Section 32.3*, thereby rendering the Bank's board of directors potentially liable and *12 U.S.C. 936*(b)(1) and rendering the Bank's franchise susceptible of forfeiture under *12 U.S.C. 93* (a).

The Rizzo plaintiffs sought $300,000 actual and $300,000 consequential damages in addition to $1,000,000 punitive damages against the bank and Nowfel and others for "their acts of fraud attended by conduct that was wilful, wanton and recklessly in disregard of the rights and feelings of plaintiffs."

After defendant Clark was served with the complaint, he called Nowfel about it and Nowfel told Clark that it was simply a misunderstanding between borrowers and would be resolved. Clark did not inquire further, and neither Clark nor Swanson asked Nowfel any other questions about the Rizzo case.

On October 18, 1984, Clark made the following report to the board of directors of Aurora Bank, summarizing the facts in this manner:

Mr. Clark explained that the case primarily involves a dispute between customers of the Bank. However, the Plaintiffs are also seeking actual and punitive damages against the Bank and Dennis Nowfel as conspirators. Apparently the Plaintiffs' attorney has joined the Bank and

Dennis Nowfel in order to put additional pressure on the other Defendants to clear up the case. It now appears that the loans of the Plaintiffs at the Aurora Bank will be paid in full by the Defendants and the case will be dismissed. Mr. Clark will keep the Board advised of progress in obtaining dismissal of the case.

The jury could find from the evidence that the board was not informed of the specific allegations of the complaint concerning the irregularities in making the loan, the inadequacy of the collateral, the disbursement of loan proceeds to Rupp and Rupp's withdrawal of $275,000 in cash. In this manner, the directors heard only Nowfel's version of the suit from the bank's attorney, Clark. The jury could also find that Clark did not apprise the board of the potential conflict of interest presented in view of the allegations made against the bank president.[3] There was evidence that the directors, had they been fully informed of the situation on October 18, would have undertaken a thorough investigation into the allegations of the Rizzo complaint, and would have discovered the fraud at that time.

Instead, the board saw no need for further action, and it received no additional information about the Rizzo suit until its meeting on November 15, 1984, when the board was informed that the case had been settled.

An entry of appearance was filed by the Neef, Swanson, Myer & Clark firm in the Rizzo suit, whereby the firm entered its appearance "on behalf of Defendants The Aurora Bank ... and Dennis L. Nowfel, individually and in his capacity as President and Chief Executive Officer of The Aurora Bank." Both Clark and Swanson signed this entry of appearance.

Defendant Swanson negotiated the settlement of the Rizzo suit, and under the evidence the jury could find that he, too, negligently failed to make an appropriate inquiry into the serious allegations raised in the complaint in that action.[4]

Because the board did not know the true facts, the fraudulent scheme continued. On October 29, 1984, Vanden Eynden approved a draw by John Napoli, Jr., for $80,000 against a line of credit. In late October, 1984, the defendant Swanson and the attorney for Rizzo and Del Vecchio reached a settlement of the Rizzo suit, which provided that all claims would be dismissed, that the Rizzo and Del Vecchio loans would be paid, and that the bank would cancel their notes.

---

3. It appears that Clark gave a copy of the Rizzo complaint to Whitlock, the chairman of the board. By special verdict, the jury found that Whitlock's negligence was responsible for 8% of the bank's loss.

4. While Swanson testified that he had studied the Rupp loan file before negotiating the settlement, there was evidence that had he examined the loan file, in the light of allegations made in the Rizzo suit, he would have been put on notice that all was not right, since the stock used as collateral had a restrictive covenant on its face, there was no power of attorney in the file which would authorize Del Vecchio to sign the note for Rizzo, there were no financial statements or credit reports in the file, etc.

On November 1, 1984, the loans were "paid off" by debiting the Swiss American account. This increased that account's overdraft by $362,471.20. Later, the notes were canceled and returned to Rizzo and Del Vecchio.

On November 8, 1984, John Napoli, Jr.'s friend, Michelle Propato, and his father, John Napoli, Sr., were given loans in the amount of $190,000 and $210,000, respectively. The proceeds of these loans were used to buy cashier's checks drawn to the order of Swiss American, signed by Vanden Eynden, and deposited to the Swiss American account. The entire sum was then withdrawn and delivered to Napoli, Sr., and Propato for delivery to Napoli, Jr.

On December 11, 1984, Rupp received another unsecured loan for $75,000; and on December 17, 1984, Napoli, Jr. drew a final $20,000 against his line of credit at the Aurora Bank.

The scheme began to unravel on December 12, when defendant Clark, and Whitlock, the chairman of the board of the bank, were advised by a bank competitor of a huge overdraft in one of the bank's accounts. The bank took immediate action to investigate the overdraft, confirmed it existed in the Swiss American account, and attempted to recover the amount of the overdraft from Rupp. The bank placed Nowfel under close supervision, and after an initial investigation, fired him.

The FDIC alleged that between the board meeting on October 18, and December 20, 1984, the bank sustained losses of $1,756,484.39 on account of the fraudulent activity.

In November, 1986, the FDIC brought an action in the United States District Court for the District of Colorado to recover funds diverted from the Aurora Bank through a scheme to defraud the bank in violation of the Racketeer Influenced and Corrupt Organization Act (RICO) and the Colorado Organized Crime Act. In this action twenty-nine claims were made against twenty-one defendants. Among these defendants were Del Vecchio, Napoli, Jr., Rizzo, Rupp, and William Vanden Eynden. * * *

Liability

Defendants contend that they cannot be liable in this action because if a client lies and defrauds its own attorney, then the client cannot recover from that attorney for negligence. In this manner, defendants seek to impute the fraud and dishonesty of Nowfel to the bank itself so that the FDIC, as successor to the bank, is barred by the fraudulent activities of the bank's employees. The trial court rejected this theory of imputed liability and estoppel because the bank had no contractual or fiduciary duty to protect the defendant attorneys from Nowfel's fraud. In this respect, the trial court explained that "this is not a case ... where a principal liable for the fraudulent acts of its agents is attempting to profit from the fraud by suing innocent third parties."

In June, 1992, the Ninth Circuit reached a decision in *FDIC v. O'Melveny & Meyers, 969 F.2d 744 (9th Cir. 1992),* which involved the nature of the professional relationship between attorneys and their corporate clients. Under California law, an attorney is required to perform with such "skill prudence and diligence as lawyers of ordinary skill and capacity commonly possess." There, the FDIC, as successor to an insolvent financial institution filed an action against legal counsel for professional negligence and breach of fiduciary duties, in connection with the firm's representation of the bank.

In ruling that the district court improperly sustained the law firm's motion for summary judgment, the Ninth Circuit noted that the presence of fraud did not cancel an attorney's duty of due care; that the firm had a duty to make a "reasonable independent investigation" in order to detect and correct false information in the materials it reviewed; and that, in the face of wrongdoing by bank officers, the attorneys were not justified in assuming that the facts presented by those officers were true, since an attorney was required to make a "reasonable effort" to independently verify facts on which an opinion is based. In O'Melveny, the court likewise held that the FDIC was not estopped from recovering by reason of the bank officers' fraud, since the FDIC did not stand in the shoes of the bank. The court pointed out that the bank was the client, not the officers of the bank, and that there could be no attribution of fault to the bank because the insiders were working to benefit themselves and not the bank. * * *

Defendants forcefully present the argument here that they were in fact the victims of Nowfel's fraud, that they were in no way responsible for the fraudulent scheme, and that they had no duty to ferret out and discover its nature. In this manner they misconstrue the nature of their professional duty under Colorado law.

Under Colorado law, "an attorney owes his client a duty to employ that degree of knowledge, skill, and judgment ordinarily possessed by members of the legal profession." *Myers v. Beem, 712 P.2d 1092, 1094,* (Ct. App. Colo. 1985). * * *

The jury was instructed that an attorney is negligent:

"... when he does an act within his profession which a reasonably careful attorney would not do, or fails to do an act which a reasonable careful attorney would do.

An attorney's conduct in this regard must be measured against what an attorney having and using that knowledge, skill and care of attorneys practicing law at the same time would or would not do under the same or similar circumstances."

These instructions follow Section 15:19, Colorado Jury Instructions 2d. Standard instructions on causation were also given to the jury.

We agree that the court's instructions "adequately placed the applicable law before the jury." Ibid.

Under the evidence recited above, there was ample proof for the jury to find that defendants were negligent in their professional duties to the bank, and that their negligence was a cause of loss to the Aurora Bank.

2. BREACH OF FIDUCIARY DUTY

MILBANK, TWEED, HADLEY & McCLOY v. BOON

13 F.3d 537 (2d Cir. 1994)

REAVLEY, CIRCUIT JUDGE:

The New York law firm of Milbank, Tweed, Hadley & McCloy ("Milbank") appeals from a judgment awarding Carol Sui–Han Leo ("Mrs. Leo") $2,000,000 on her claim that Milbank breached its fiduciary duty to her. After representing Mrs. Leo through her agent, Chan Cher Boon ("Chan"), Milbank represented Chan alone without Mrs. Leo's consent in completing the same transaction. A jury found that Milbank's representation of Chan constituted a breach of fiduciary duty to Mrs. Leo that was a substantial factor in preventing her from obtaining assets she sought in the transaction. We affirm. * * *

DISCUSSION

A.

Milbank asserts that the district court erred by denying its motion for judgment after trial pursuant to *Rule 50(b) of the Federal Rules of Civil Procedure.* A motion for judgment notwithstanding the verdict should be denied unless the jury reached a verdict reasonable jurors could not have reached. It is improper to grant a j.n.o.v. unless there is "such a complete absence of evidence supporting the verdict that the jury's findings could only have been the result of sheer surmise and conjecture. . . .". Although "judgment as a matter of law" now encompasses pre-verdict and post-verdict motions, the standard for granting what used to be known under Rule 50 as a j.n.o.v. has not changed.

Milbank first claims that even if it did breach a duty owed Mrs. Leo, no harm was caused to her, because no evidence sustains the jury's determination that Milbank's representation of Chan impeded Mrs. Leo from acquiring the second stage assets. Milbank contends that its actions caused no harm to Mrs. Leo because she would not have been able to acquire the assets without bidding on them, and this she failed to do by her own choice. The fact remains, however, that the original agreement conditionally entitled Mrs. Leo to all of the assets, and she was prevented from obtaining the second stage assets by her former agent, assisted by her former attorney, and apparently with the attempted use of her own $8.5 million.

A fiduciary unsuccessfully advanced a similar causation argument in *ABKCO Music, Inc. v. Harrisongs Music, Ltd., 722 F.2d 988, 995–96 (2d Cir. 1983).* In ABKCO, certain business affairs of the Beatles, including those of George Harrison and Harrison Interests, had been handled by

ABKCO and Allen Klein, the president of ABKCO. Harrison Interests claimed that Klein later interfered with settlement negotiations between Harrison Interests and another company in a dispute. The district court found that Klein's status as former business manager added special credibility to the advice and information that he gave to the hostile company, making it less willing to settle with Harrison Interests. Although it was unclear whether Harrison Interests would have settled with the company without ABKCO's interference, Klein's intrusion made the settlement less likely.

On appeal ABKCO argued, in part, that there was no causal relationship between its actions and Harrison Interests' failure to obtain settlement. We disagreed and affirmed, reasoning that "an action for breach of fiduciary duty is a prophylactic rule intended to remove all incentive to breach—not simply to compensate for damages in the event of a breach." Having found that ABKCO's conduct constituted a breach of fiduciary duty, "the district judge was not required to find a 'but for' relationship between ABKCO's conduct and lack of success of Harrison Interests' settlement efforts."

Although we stated in ABKCO that the facts of that case were "novel" and unique, we indicated that the situation was similar, "although not wholly analogous" to side-switching cases involving attorneys and their former clients. There is an even more compelling reason to apply a prophylactic rule to remove the incentive to breach when the fiduciary relationship is that of an attorney and former client because of the attorney's unique position of trust and confidence. Furthermore, breaches of a fiduciary relationship in any context comprise a special breed of cases that often loosen normally stringent requirements of causation and damages. See *Northwestern Nat. Ins. Co. v. Alberts, 769 F.Supp. 498, 506 (S.D.N.Y. 1991)* ("[A] plaintiff alleging breach of fiduciary duty . . . is not required to meet the higher standard of loss or proximate causation."); *Diduck v. Kaszycki & Sons Contractors, Inc., 974 F.2d 270, 284 (2d Cir. 1992)* (a third party participating in a fiduciary's breach need not profit from the breach and liability may attach for acts or omissions that are a "substantial factor" in the sequence of causation); *Zackiva Communications Corp. v. Horowitz, 826 F.Supp. 86, 88 (S.D.N.Y. 1993)* (to state a claim for a breach of fiduciary duty, "a plaintiff need not allege damages to itself"); *Diamond v. Oreamuno, 24 N.Y.2d 494, 498, 248 N.E.2d 910, 912, 301 N.Y.S.2d 78, 81 (1969)* (a corporate fiduciary entrusted with information may not appropriate that asset for his own use even if he causes no injury to the corporation).

Milbank promised in writing not to represent Chan or Mrs. Leo after Chan's agency was terminated. Milbank then turned around, without consent, to pursue on behalf of Chan an amendment to the same transaction that it had previously negotiated on behalf of Mrs. Leo. This conduct was more serious than the case where an attorney later represents a party with interests adverse to a former client in a similar yet wholly new transaction. This constitutes a serious breach of fiduciary duty where a "prophylactic rule" should apply; Mrs. Leo does not have to show strict "but for" causation or proximate cause. She has to show that Milbank's representation of Chan was at least a substantial factor in preventing her from acquiring the second stage assets. Milbank cannot enjoy impunity by showing that Mrs. Leo's losses *might* have resulted from other possible causes.

The jury could have reasonably inferred from the evidence that Milbank's representation of Chan was a substantial factor in preventing Mrs. Leo from acquiring the second stage assets. Similar to ABKCO, the jury could have found that Milbank's presence gave Chan added credibility, which could have been critical to his success in completing the transaction. This is especially true where Milbank and Chan were the ones who had negotiated the stock transaction from the beginning. The jury could have decided that, by taking advantage of their prior position and Mrs. Leo's escrow funds, Milbank and Chan substantially enhanced their prospects during the November and December negotiations with Deak. The jury could have concluded that the second stage was ultimately completed because Milbank improperly negotiated the deal on behalf of Chan using Mrs. Leo's $8.5 million, regardless of whether or not someone actually intended to replace the money at some point. Furthermore, this conduct on the part of Milbank interfered with Mrs. Leo's negotiating posture, because (a) she was more concerned with protecting the $8.5 million and avoiding a threatened lawsuit by the creditors' committee than she was with staying abreast of the maneuvers of Chan, (b) because she was not sure the $8.5 million would be available to close a transaction on her behalf, and (c) because she was deprived of the tactical option of offering the Deak creditors' committee the $8.5 million on a take-it-or-leave-it basis before Chan could demonstrate plausible independent financial capacity. * * *

D.

Milbank's objections to the court's instruction to the jury on the essential elements of an agency relationship are also rejected. The jury heard uncontested evidence that Chan signed a document which was requested by the Leos' attorney and notarized by a Milbank attorney, specifically stating that Chan was acting on behalf of Mrs. Leo in negotiating the transaction. The jury was told by the court that it was necessary for them to find that Chan was acting at that time at the behest of Mrs. Leo, which finding the jury must have necessarily made.

There being no error, the judgment of the district court is affirmed.

HENDRY v. PELLAND

73 F.3d 397 (D.C. Cir. 1996)

TATEL, CIRCUIT JUDGE:

Three clients sued their former attorney and his law firm for breach of fiduciary duty, seeking punitive damages, compensatory damages, and disgorgement of the legal fees they had paid. The attorney's law firm counterclaimed for unpaid legal fees. Applying District of Columbia law, we address three district court rulings made during the jury trial. First, because we agree with the district court that the record contained insufficient evidence for a reasonable jury to find that the attorney wilfully disregarded his clients' rights, we affirm the judgment denying the clients' request for punitive damages. Second, concluding that clients seeking disgorgement of legal fees for a breach of their attorney's fiduciary duty of loyalty need only prove that their attorney breached that duty, not that the breach injured them, and finding that the clients here presented sufficient evidence for a jury to conclude that their attorney breached his duty of loyalty, we set aside the district court's judgment for the lawyer and his law firm on the fiduciary duty claim. Finally, because the clients had a valid claim for breach of fiduciary duty, we set aside the court's ruling precluding them from using that breach as a defense to the law firm's counterclaim for unpaid fees. We therefore remand for a new trial on the clients' breach of fiduciary duty claim and the law firm's counterclaim for legal fees.

I.

Five members of the Hendry family—the mother, her son and daughter, and the daughter's two infant children—owned an historic twenty-acre parcel of land in Arlington County, Virginia as tenants in common. The adult owners of the property, as well as the spouses of the son and daughter, who held rights of dower and curtesy, signed an agreement to sell the property for $4.5 million to a developer who planned to build a retirement home on the land. According to the agreement, if county officials failed to approve zoning changes needed to build the retirement home, the parties would undertake "good faith" negotiations to restructure the transaction. When county officials turned down the retirement home project, the developer proposed amending the agreement to provide for the construction of a 56–unit residential development. Under the proposed amendment, the $4.5 million price was unchanged. Although the son told the developer that he objected to the proposed amendment, his mother and the developer signed the amendment while the son was away on vacation.

Discovering what his mother had done, the son and his wife retained Francis Pelland, a partner in the Washington, D.C. law firm of Sadur, Pelland & Rubinstein. The son explained to the lawyer that he was opposed to the residential development and concerned about his mother's mental capacity. Relying on the agreement's "good faith" clause, Pelland advised his clients not to oppose the residential development. Although the county ultimately approved the site plan for the residential development, all of the owners—now including the mother—refused to sell. Claiming breach of contract and unjust enrichment, the developer sued them in a Virginia state court.

While Pelland originally represented only the son and his wife, he represented all the owners of the property in defending the lawsuit. At a conference shortly before trial, the presiding judge told the parties that although the developer's contractual claims were meritless, the unjust enrichment claim had merit because the developer's efforts in securing county approval of the residential site plan increased the value of the Hendrys' property. He advised the litigants to negotiate a settlement on the unjust enrichment claim. Following Pelland's advice, the family settled with the developer for $1.5 million.

Unhappy with this result, three of the clients—the mother, the son, and his wife—sued Pelland and his law firm in the United States District Court for the District of Columbia based on diversity of citizenship, claiming both professional negligence and breach of fiduciary duty. The Hendrys sought identical relief on both claims: punitive damages; $2,069,000 in compensatory damages (representing the $1.5 million settlement plus amounts for interest, additional property taxes, and remodeling costs); and return of $86,538.62 in legal fees they had paid. The law firm counterclaimed for $37,504.38 in unpaid legal fees.

* * * At the close of all the evidence, the court granted Pelland's motion for judgment as a matter of law on the breach of fiduciary duty claim for compensatory damages and disgorgement of legal fees, finding that the Hendrys had failed to present any evidence as to the applicable standard of conduct. Finally, because the Hendrys no longer had a claim for breach of fiduciary duty, the court prohibited them from arguing breach of fiduciary duty as a defense to the law firm's counterclaim for legal fees. Accordingly, only the Hendrys' negligence claim (minus their request for punitive damages) and the law firm's counterclaim for legal fees went to the jury. The Hendrys lost on both counts. Entering judgment for Pelland and his law firm, the court awarded the firm its unpaid legal fees. * * *

II.

* * * Turning to the principal question before us—whether the district court erred in granting judgment to Pelland and his law firm on the Hendrys' claim for breach of fiduciary duty—we begin by noting the limited nature of the parties' arguments on appeal. First, in challenging the judgment, the Hendrys contend only that they presented sufficient evidence to justify a favorable jury verdict on their fiduciary duty claim *insofar as they sought disgorgement of legal fees*. They do not argue that they presented adequate evidence to support their $2 million claim for *compensatory damages*. Second, the parties agree that in order to prevail in a fiduciary duty claim for disgorgement of legal fees, clients need to present evidence establishing that their lawyer breached a fiduciary duty to them. The parties disagree about only two issues: whether the Hendrys presented such evidence; and whether, in addition to establishing that their attorney breached his duty, the Hendrys also needed to prove that the breach caused them injury.

As for the first issue, we agree with the Hendrys that their evidence that Pelland violated one of the rules of the District of Columbia Code of Professional Responsibility was sufficient to support their claim that he violated his common law fiduciary duty. While not holding that the ethical rules are co-extensive with an attorney's fiduciary duties, the District of Columbia Court of Appeals in *Griva v. Davison, 637 A.2d 830 (D.C. 1994)* clearly ruled that "a violation of the Code of Professional Responsibility or of the Rules of Professional Conduct *can* constitute a breach of the attorney's common law fiduciary duty to the client." *Id. at 846–47* (emphasis added). In particular, and significantly for this case, the court treated an alleged violation of Disciplinary Rule 5–105— prohibiting a lawyer from representing multiple clients "if the exercise of his independent professional judgment * * * would be likely to involve him in representing differing interests" unless "it is obvious that he can adequately represent the interest of each [client] and * * * each consents to the representation after full disclosure," D.C. CODE OF PROFESSIONAL RESPONSIBILITY DR 5–105(B) to (C)—as equivalent to a breach of an attorney's fiduciary duty. The *Griva* court's ruling that a conflict of interest may violate not only ethical rules, but also an attorney's common law fiduciary duties, is far from novel. As Pelland recognizes, a basic fiduciary obligation of an attorney is the duty of "undivided loyalty," which is breached when an attorney represents clients with conflicting interests.

The Hendrys' expert testified that Pelland violated DR 5–105 because his representation of all five owners of the property put him in the "impossible" position of serving individuals with conflicting interests: the mother, anxious to reach a settlement with the developer that would allow her to keep a house on the land; the son and the daughter, opposed to the plan to build a residential development because it would destroy the trees on the property; and the two infant grandchildren, whose primary interest was in maximizing the long-term value of the property. The son testified that the lawyer never discussed the possible conflicts of interest with him. Viewed most favorably to the Hendrys, this evidence was sufficient for a reasonable jury to find that Pelland violated DR 5–105, thereby breaching his fiduciary duty of loyalty.

We also agree with the Hendrys that, to the extent they sought disgorgement of legal fees, they needed to prove only that Pelland breached his duty of loyalty, not that his breach proximately caused them injury. Although we have found no District of Columbia cases precisely on point, courts in other jurisdictions have held that clients must prove injury and proximate causation in a fiduciary duty claim against their lawyer if they seek *compensatory damages,* not if, as here, they seek only *forfeiture of legal fees.* Even courts that sometimes *do* require a showing of injury and causation in claims seeking only forfeiture of legal fees have stated that it is not necessary when the clients' claim is based, again as here, on a breach of the duty of loyalty.

Recent opinions of the District of Columbia Court of Appeals lend support to this distinction between claims for compensatory damages and claims for disgorgement of legal fees. In one case where clients sought *compensatory damages,* the court described the elements of the clients' negligence claim as including "a causal relationship between the violation and the harm complained of," stating that its disposition of the negligence claim "applied with equal force to the [clients'] claim of *breach of fiduciary duty.*" In another case, where the clients sought not compensatory damages but *forfeiture of legal fees,* the court relied upon decisions where the clients did *not* need to prove injury or causation.

The different treatment of compensatory damages and forfeiture of legal fees also makes sense. Compensatory damages make plaintiffs whole for the harms that they have suffered as a result of defendants' actions. Clients therefore need to prove that their attorney's breach caused them injury so that the trier of fact can determine whether they are entitled to any damages. Forfeiture of legal fees serves several different purposes. It deters attorney misconduct, a goal worth furthering regardless of whether a particular client has been harmed. It also fulfills a longstanding and fundamental principle of equity—that fiduciaries should not profit from their disloyalty. And, like compensatory damages, it compensates clients for a harm they have suffered. Unlike other forms of compensatory damages, however, forfeiture reflects not the harms clients suffer from the tainted representation, but the decreased value of the representation itself. Because a breach of the duty of loyalty diminishes the value of the attorney's representation as a matter of law, some degree of forfeiture is thus appropriate without further proof of injury.

We thus conclude that, under District of Columbia law, clients suing their attorney for breach of the fiduciary duty of loyalty and seeking disgorgement of legal fees as their sole remedy need prove only that their attorney breached that duty, not that the breach caused them injury. Because the Hendrys presented evidence that Pelland breached his duty of loyalty by violating DR 5–105, they were entitled to have their fiduciary duty claim for disgorgement of legal fees go to the jury. The district court therefore erred in granting judgment for Pelland and his firm.

In reaching this conclusion, we have not addressed two issues of District of Columbia law relating to the Hendrys' fiduciary duty claim. Because the testimony regarding DR 5–105 is adequate to support our holding, we have not considered whether violations of two other ethical rules mentioned by the Hendrys' expert—DR 6–101, requiring an attorney to act competently, and DR 7–101, requiring an attorney to represent clients zealously, *see* D.C. CODE OF PROFESSIONAL RESPONSIBILITY DR 6–101, 7–101—can also constitute breaches of an attorney's common law fiduciary duties. Nor have we addressed the extent of forfeiture to which the Hendrys might be entitled if, at a new trial, they succeed in proving that Pelland breached his duty of loyalty. Some courts have suggested that attorneys must forfeit all fees earned in their tainted representation of a client; others have ruled that lawyers must forfeit all fees earned in the such representation *after* the breach occurred; while still others have held that the extent of forfeiture depends upon the facts and circumstances of the case.

The final issue in this case—the court's ruling on the law firm's counterclaim—turns on the proposition that clients may defend a claim by their lawyer for unpaid legal fees by proving that their attorney breached a fiduciary duty. Because the Hendrys presented sufficient evidence for a jury to find that Pelland violated his fiduciary duty, the district court erred in prohibiting them from using this argument as a defense to the counterclaim.

III.

We affirm the district court's ruling on punitive damages, vacate the court's ruling granting judgment as a matter of law to Pelland and his firm on the Hendrys' fiduciary duty claim, and vacate its ruling and judgment on the counterclaim for legal fees. We remand to the district court for a new trial on the Hendrys' fiduciary duty claim and on the law firm's counterclaim.

3. NEGLIGENT MISREPRESENTATION

RESTATEMENT OF THE LAW, SECOND, TORTS

§ 552 Information Negligently Supplied for the Guidance of Others

(1) One who, in the course of his business, profession or employment, or in any other transaction in which he has a pecuniary interest, supplies false information for the guidance of others in their business transactions, is subject to liability for pecuniary loss caused to them by their justifiable reliance upon the information, if he fails to exercise reasonable care or competence in obtaining or communicating the information.

(2) Except as stated in Subsection (3), the liability stated in Subsection (1) is limited to loss suffered

    (a) by the person or one of a limited group of persons for whose benefit and guidance he intends to supply the information or knows that the recipient intends to supply it; and

    (b) through reliance upon it in a transaction that he intends the information to influence or knows that the recipient so intends or in a substantially similar transaction.

(3) The liability of one who is under a public duty to give the information extends to loss suffered by any of the class of persons for whose benefit the duty is created, in any of the transactions in which it is intended to protect them.

Comment:

    a. * * * The liability stated in this Section is likewise more restricted than that for fraudulent misrepresentation stated in § 531. When there is no intent to deceive but only good faith coupled with negligence, the fault of the maker of the misrepresentation is sufficiently less to justify a narrower responsibility for its consequences.

The reason a narrower scope of liability is fixed for negligent misrepresentation than for deceit is to be found in the difference between the obligations of honesty and of care, and in the significance of this difference to the reasonable expectations of the users of information that is supplied in connection with commercial transactions. Honesty requires only that the maker of a representation speak in good faith and without consciousness of a lack of any basis for belief in the truth or accuracy of what he says. The standard of honesty is unequivocal and ascertainable without regard to the character of the transaction in which the information will ultimately be relied upon or the situation of the party relying upon it. Any user of commercial information may reasonably expect the observance of this standard by a supplier of information to whom his use is reasonably foreseeable.

On the other hand, it does not follow that every user of commercial information may hold every maker to a duty of care. Unlike the duty of honesty, the duty of care to be observed in supplying information for use in commercial transactions implies an undertaking to observe a relative standard, which may be defined only in terms of the use to which the information will be put, weighed against the magnitude and probability of loss that might attend that use if the information proves to be incorrect. A user of commercial information cannot reasonably expect its maker to have undertaken to satisfy this obligation unless the terms of the obligation were known to him. Rather, one who relies upon information in connection with a commercial transaction may reasonably expect to hold the maker to a duty of care only in circumstances in which the maker was manifestly aware of the use to which the information was to be put and intended to supply it for that purpose.

By limiting the liability for negligence of a supplier of information to be used in commercial transactions to cases in which he manifests an intent to supply the information for the sort of use in which the plaintiff's loss occurs, the law promotes the important social policy of encouraging the flow of commercial information upon which the operation of the economy rests. The limitation applies, however, only in the case of information supplied in good faith, for no interest of society is served by promoting the flow of information not genuinely believed by its maker to be true.

b. The rule stated in this Section applies not only to information given as to the existence of facts but also to an opinion given upon facts equally well known to both the supplier and the recipient. Such an opinion is often given by one whose only knowledge of the facts is derived from the person who asks it. As to the care and competence that the recipient of such an opinion is justified in expecting, see Comment *e.*
* * *

e. Reasonable care and competence. Since the rule of liability stated in Subsection (1) is based upon negligence, the defendant is subject to liability if, but only if, he has failed to exercise the care or competence of a reasonable man in obtaining or communicating the information. (See §§ 283, 288 and 289). What is reasonable is, as in other cases of negligence, dependent upon the circumstances. It is, in general, a matter of the care and competence that the recipient of the information is entitled to expect in the light of the circumstances and this will vary according to a good many factors. The question is one for the jury, unless the facts are so clear as to permit only one conclusion.

The particulars in which the recipient of information supplied by another is entitled to expect the exercise of care and competence depend upon the character of the information that is supplied. When the information concerns a fact not known to the recipient, he is entitled to expect that the supplier will exercise that care and competence in its ascertainment which the supplier's business or profession requires and which, therefore, the supplier professes to have by engaging in it. Thus the recipient is entitled to expect that such investigations as are necessary will be carefully made and that his informant will have normal business or professional competence to form an intelligent judgment upon the data obtained. On the other hand, if the supplier makes no pretense to special competence but agrees for a reward to furnish information that lies outside the field of his business or profession, the recipient is not justified in expecting more than that care and competence that the nonprofessional character of his informant entitles him to expect. When the information consists of an opinion upon facts supplied by the recipient or otherwise known to him, the recipient is entitled to expect a careful consideration of the facts and competence in arriving at an intelligent judgment. In all of these cases the recipient of the information is entitled to expect reasonable conversance with the language employed to communicate the information in question and reasonable care in its use, unless he knows that his informant is ignorant of the language in question or peculiarly careless in its use. * * *

h. Persons for whose guidance the information is supplied. The rule stated in this Section subjects the negligent supplier of misinformation to liability only to those persons for whose benefit and guidance it is supplied. In this particular his liability is somewhat more narrowly restricted than that of the maker of a fraudulent representation (see § 531), which extends to any person whom the maker of the representation has reason to expect to act in reliance upon it.

Under this Section, as in the case of the fraudulent misrepresentation (see § 531), it is not necessary that the maker should have any particular person in mind as the intended, or even the probable, recipient of the information. In other words, it is not required that the person who is to become the plaintiff be identified or known to the defendant as an individual when the information is supplied. It is enough that the maker of the representation intends it to reach and influence either a particular person or persons, known to him, or a group or class of persons, distinct from the much larger class who might reasonably be expected sooner or later to have access to the information and foreseeably to take some action in reliance upon it. It is enough, likewise, that the maker of the representation knows that his recipient intends to transmit the information to a similar person, persons or group. It is sufficient, in other words, insofar as the plaintiff's identity is concerned, that the maker supplies the information for repetition to a certain group or class of persons and that the plaintiff proves to be one of them, even though the maker never had heard of him by name when the information was given. It is not enough that the maker merely knows of the ever-present possibility of repetition to anyone, and the possibility of action in reliance upon it, on the part of anyone to whom it may be repeated.

Even when the maker is informed of the identity of a definite person to whom the recipient intends to transmit the information, the circumstances may justify a finding that the name and identity of that person was regarded by the maker, and by the recipient, as important only because the person in question was one of a group whom the information was intended to reach and for whose guidance it was being supplied. In many situations the identity of the person for whose guidance the information is supplied is of no moment to the person who supplies it, although the number and character of the persons to be reached and influenced, and the nature and extent of the transaction for which guidance is furnished may be vitally important. This is true because the risk of liability to which the supplier subjects himself by undertaking to give the information, while it may not be affected by the identity of the person for whose guidance the information is given, is vitally affected by the number and character of the persons, and particularly the nature and extent of the proposed transaction. On the other hand, the circumstances may frequently show that the identity of the person for whose guidance the information is given is regarded by the person supplying it, and by the recipient, as important and material; and therefore the person giving the information understands that his liability is to be restricted to the named person and to him only. Thus when the information is procured for transmission to a named or otherwise described person, whether the maker is liable to another, to whom in substitution the information is transmitted in order to influence his conduct in an otherwise identical transaction, depends upon whether it is understood between the one giving the information and the one bringing about its transmission, that it is to be given to the named individual and to him only.

Illustrations:

* * * 5. A is negotiating with X Bank for a credit of $50,000. The Bank requires an audit by independent public accountants. A employs B & Company, a firm of accountants, to make the audit, telling them that the purpose of the audit is to meet the requirements of X Bank in connection with a credit of $50,000. B & Company agrees to make the audit, with the express understanding that it is for transmission to X Bank only. X Bank fails, and A, without any further communication with

B & Company, submits its financial statements accompanied by B & Company's opinion to Y Bank, which in reliance upon it extends a credit of $50,000 to A. The audit is so carelessly made as to result in an unqualified favorable opinion on financial statements that materially misstates the financial position of A, and in consequence Y Bank suffers pecuniary loss through its extension of credit. B & Company is not liable to Y Bank.

6. The same facts as in Illustration 5, except that nothing is said about supplying the information for the guidance of X Bank only, and A merely informs B & Company that he expects to negotiate a bank loan, for $50,000, requires the audit for the purpose of the loan, and has X Bank in mind. B & Company is subject to liability to Y Bank.

7. The same facts as in Illustration 5, except that A informs B & Company that he expects to negotiate a bank loan, but does not mention the name of any bank. B & Company is subject to liability to Y Bank.

4. AIDING AND ABETTING

CHEM–AGE INDUSTRIES, INC. v. GLOVER

652 N.W.2d 756 (S.D. 2002)

KONENKAMP, JUSTICE.

We are confronted with the question whether a lawyer who incorporates a business on behalf of an individual client owes any duty of care to the corporation thus created and to its director-investors who have no contractual relationship with the lawyer. While obtaining substantial funds and credit from two investors, the client had his attorney incorporate a business, naming the two investors as incorporators and directors. Then the client misappropriated the investors' funds and gave some money and property to the lawyer. The investors and the corporation sued the lawyer, his client, and others to recover all the funds and property, alleging * * * [*inter alia,*] breach of fiduciary duty. The circuit court granted summary judgment to the lawyer on all issues, ruling, among other things, that no privity of contract existed between anyone other than the lawyer and his individual client. We conclude that there are material questions of fact on whether the lawyer * * * (3) knowingly assisted his client in breaching a fiduciary duty to the director-investors and the corporation. We affirm in part, reverse in part, and remand for trial.

A. BACKGROUND

In the past twenty years, attorney Alan F. Glover of Brookings, South Dakota, has represented Byron Dahl, a Watertown entrepreneur, in various transactions and lawsuits around the country. In March 1997, Dahl interested two Watertown businesspersons, Roger O. Pederson and Garry Shepard, in investing in a start-up firm, under the name Chem–Age Industries. Dahl would contribute equipment and expertise; Pederson, and, to a lesser extent, Shepard, would contribute capital. According to attorney Glover's deposition, Dahl had told him "that [Dahl] had basically started up a business in Watertown with the assistance of some people who had chosen to invest their money with him in this business." That is, Chem–Age as a brand new business did not preexist the agreement made by Dahl, Pederson, and Shepard.

Sometime during their business engagement (the exact timing is disputed), Pederson obtained a report from a private investigator warning him that Dahl was a "crook." According to Pederson, the report indicated that Dahl had done this all over the country. He had done it on the east coast, he done it in Las Vegas. Guy lost his home in Las Vegas. The guy out east lost 300,000.

Pederson executed two "Stock Agreements" and a "Subscription Agreement and Letter of Investment," and despite this report continued to invest thousands of dollars in Dahl's enterprise. According to the terms of the stock agreements as prepared by Dahl, Pederson was to receive 48 shares of common stock in exchange for his investments. Pederson had originally given Dahl $25,000, but both Pederson and Shepard wanted the business to be incorporated before they invested more money. They pressed Dahl to get an attorney involved to set up the corporation. At some point between March and October 1997, Pederson, Shepard, and Dahl decided that Chem–Age Industries would be incorporated under the name "Chem–Age Industries, Inc." Pederson and Shepard agreed to serve as incorporators and directors of the corporation; Dahl agreed to serve as chief executive officer. With this understanding, Dahl engaged Glover to draw up articles of incorporation.

Glover prepared the articles and faxed them, either to Dahl alone or to both Pederson and Shepard: the parties disagree on this point. In either case, Dahl secured the signatures of Pederson and Shepard. The articles were dated October 30, 1997. When Dahl delivered the signed articles to him, Glover notarized Pederson's and Shepard's signatures, despite the fact that they had not signed the document in his presence. On the same day, Glover signed a Consent of Registered Agent, agreeing to act as registered agent for "Chem–Age Industries, Inc." Soon thereafter, at Dahl's request, Glover filed the articles with the South Dakota Secretary of State. On November 6, 1997, the Secretary of State issued a Certificate of Incorporation. Glover then sent a letter to the company, attaching an application to obtain a federal tax identification number for the corporation.

On November 7, 1997, the day after Chem–Age Industries, Inc., was issued its Certificate of Incorporation, Sam's Club approved a "Business Membership–Credit Application" for "Chem–Age Industries" as a corporation. Pederson, in his capacity as President of Chem–Age, had completed and signed the document on the previous day, listing Dahl as "Billing Representative." By that date, Chem–Age had obtained a "Resale–Tax ID number." Soon thereafter, Pederson had acquired for the company a Bank One credit card, an American Express Optima card, and a charge account at Office Max. Pederson also obtained loans from Norwest Bank to provide operating capital for Chem–Age Industries, Inc. These amounted to some $140,000. It was the understanding of the Bank's representatives that the money was to be used by the corporation. With the number of judgments and liens against Dahl, the bankers would not have loaned him the money.

By early fall of 1998, Pederson and Shepard became suspicious that they were being swindled: Dahl had accumulated large balances on the company's credit cards for what appeared to be personal items. They engaged attorney John L. Foley of Watertown for legal advice. According to Foley's affidavit, a meeting was held in his office in October 1998. Present were plaintiffs Pederson and Shepard as well as defendants Glover and Dahl. At that meeting, Glover stated that he was representing "the corporation, Chem–Age Industries, Inc.," and that Dahl owned that entity. Foley also reported that Glover and Dahl were negotiating the sale of "the business" to New Age Chemical, Inc., a Wisconsin corporation. In Glover's presence, Dahl told Pederson and Shepard that "they would be paid out of the sale of the business." Pederson and Shepard claim that Glover led them to believe that he would be representing Chem–Age in this sale. Nonetheless, in a document entitled "License Agreement," dated November 11, 1998, the Chem–Age assets were sold to the Wisconsin business, under the name "Byron Dahl d/b/a BMD Associates, a South Dakota sole proprietorship." Glover represented Dahl in that transaction. When later questioned, Glover was not sure of the relationship between Chem–Age Industries, Inc., and BMD Associates.

* * * Thereafter, in October 2000, plaintiffs Chem–Age Industries, Inc., Pederson, and Shepard sued Dahl, Glover, and certain others who were later released by stipulation.... Glover moved for summary judgment on all claims against him. Plaintiffs, in turn, moved for summary judgment on two questions: whether Glover owed them a duty, and whether he had breached a fiduciary duty to them. The trial court denied plaintiffs' motion and granted summary judgment to Glover on all plaintiffs' claims.

* * *

E.

BREACH OF FIDUCIARY DUTY

1. *Direct Breach of Fiduciary Duty to Nonclients*

To ascertain a fiduciary duty, we must find three things: (1) plaintiffs reposed "faith, confidence and trust" in Glover, (2) plaintiffs were in a position of "inequality, dependence, weakness, or lack of knowledge" and, (3) Glover exercised "dominion, control or influence" over plaintiffs' affairs. *Garrett v. BankWest Inc., 459 N.W.2d 833, 838 (SD 1990).*

* * * Plaintiffs Pederson and Shepard have submitted no evidence to show how they were in a confidential relationship with Glover, where they depended on him specifically to protect their investment interests, and where Glover exercised dominance and influence over their business affairs. On the contrary, they never consulted with Glover during the time he is alleged to have breached a fiduciary duty to them. Aside from simple avowals that they believed Glover was watching out for their interests, their claim that Glover was entrusted with explicit responsibility for their investments is "factually unsupported." Likewise for the corporation: outside the existence of an attorney-client relationship, we detect no facts justifying a fiduciary duty owed to the company. We conclude that there was no direct fiduciary relationship between Glover and plaintiffs.

2. Aiding and Abetting Breach of Fiduciary Duty

Although he may not have directly breached a fiduciary duty, if Glover assisted Dahl in a breach of Dahl's fiduciary duty, Glover may still be subject to liability. Plaintiffs' complaint alleges that both Dahl and Glover breached their fiduciary duties. The Restatement provides:

"For harm resulting to a third person from the tortious conduct of another, one is subject to liability if he knows that the other's conduct constitutes a breach of duty and gives substantial assistance or encouragement to the other so to conduct himself."

Restatement (Second) of Torts § 876(b) (1977). When they participate in their clients' tortious acts, lawyers are not exempt from liability under this theory.

"Legal authorities ... are unanimous in expressing the proposition that one who knowingly aids another in the breach of a fiduciary duty is liable to the one harmed thereby. That principle readily extends to lawyers. None of those authorities even implies that liability for participants in the breach of fiduciary duty is confined to those who *themselves* owe such duty."

Granewich v. Harding, 329 Or. 47, 985 P.2d 788, 793–94 (Or 1999).

In *Granewich*, the defendant attorneys provided substantial assistance to the controlling shareholders to squeeze out the minority shareholder in breach of the fiduciary duties the majority shareholders owed to the minority shareholder. Unlike the fraud allegations against Glover, which require proof of misrepresentations, liability for aiding and abetting breach of a fiduciary duty requires only the giving of substantial assistance and encouragement. *See Restatement (Second) of Torts § 876* cmt b (1979) (one who gives advice or encouragement to a tortfeasor is also a tortfeasor).

Dahl, as the operating officer of the corporation, owed a fiduciary duty to the company and to its investors. Like controlling shareholders, officers and directors possessing discretion in the management of a company have a fiduciary duty "to use their ability to control the corporation in a fair, just, and equitable manner...." For summary judgment purposes, the evidence that Dahl breached his fiduciary duties to the corporation and the investor-directors remains wholly uncontradicted. He used corporate funds for personal expenditures; he failed to deliver promised stock issues; he sold corporate assets and kept the proceeds. Now the question is whether his lawyer may be subject to liability for assisting Dahl in his breach of fiduciary duties.

Holding attorneys liable for aiding and abetting the breach of a fiduciary duty in rendering professional services poses both a hazard and a quandary for the legal profession. On the one hand, overbroad liability might diminish the quality of legal services, since it would impose "self protective reservations" in the attorney-client relationship. Attorneys acting in a professional capacity should be free to render advice without fear of personal liability to third persons if the advice later goes awry. On the other hand, the privilege of rendering professional services not being absolute, lawyers should not be free to substantially assist their clients in committing tortious acts. To protect lawyers from meritless claims, many courts strictly interpret the common law elements of aiding and abetting the breach of a fiduciary duty.

The substantial assistance requirement carries with it a condition that the lawyer must actively participate in the breach of a fiduciary duty. *See Spinner v. Nutt, 631 N.E.2d 542, 546 (Mass 1994)* (allegation that trustees acted under legal advice of defendants, without more, is insufficient to give rise to claim that attorney is responsible to third persons for fraudulent acts of clients). Merely acting as a scrivener for a client is insufficient. A plaintiff must show that the attorney defendant rendered "substantial assistance" to the breach of duty, not merely to the person committing the breach. In *Granewich*, the lawyers facilitated the squeeze-out, not just by providing legal advice and drafting documents, but by sending letters containing misrepresentations and helping to amend by-laws eliminating voting requirements that protected the minority shareholder's interest.

Another condition to finding liability for assisting in the breach of a fiduciary duty is the requirement that the assistance be "knowing." *Restatement (Second) of Torts § 874* cmt c (1979). Knowing participation in a fiduciary's breach of duty requires both knowledge of the fiduciary's status as a fiduciary and knowledge that the fiduciary's conduct contravenes a fiduciary duty. Although in some instances actual knowledge may be required, constructive knowledge will often suffice. Constructive knowledge is adequate when the aider and abettor has maintained a long-term or in-depth relationship with the fiduciary.

In accordance with these principles, we hold that to establish a cause of action for aiding or assisting in the breach of a fiduciary duty, a plaintiff must prove that (1) the fiduciary breached an obligation to plaintiff; (2) defendant substantially assisted the fiduciary in the achievement of the breach; (3) defendant knew that the fiduciary's conduct constituted a breach of duty; and (4) damages were sustained as a result of the breach.

Glover recounts that shortly after incorporation, Dahl told him that the two investors, Pederson and Shepard, had decided not to proceed and that the business would be solely controlled by Dahl as a proprietorship. Because no shares were issued, Glover took the position that the company had no official existence. But we think that what Glover actually knew and what he should have known are questions of credibility. After all, Glover notarized Pederson's and Shepard's signatures on corporate documents without having them in his presence. If he did not know his client was in the midst of a swindle, he certainly knew Dahl had several questionable investment schemes in the past, leaving unhappy investors in his wake. Thus his decision to notarize these signatures may or may not have been an altogether innocuous act. Perhaps if Glover had met with Pederson and Shepard at that time, instead of simply notarizing their signatures unseen, and heard their expectations, he could have disabused them of any misunderstanding or encouraged them to seek independent legal advice.

Pederson and Shepard allege that this was part of a pattern in which Glover allowed Dahl to use his legal services as a means to allow Dahl to misappropriate investor funds. The creation of a corporation with the assistance of an attorney gave a patina of authenticity to Dahl's otherwise rogue activities. Moreover, Glover listed himself as registered agent for the company. Pederson and Shepard claim that they began investing more heavily once they learned the company had been incorporated and an attorney was onboard. They say that they felt reassured upon incorporation that the business would proceed with all the formalities required of corporations.

Four months after the business was incorporated, Glover received a "gift" of office furniture from Dahl, bought with the company credit card. Glover claimed he did not know how the furniture was paid for. Accepting such a "gift" from a client like Dahl, who Glover knew had longstanding financial problems, raises a question of constructive knowledge and exposes the problem of improper, personal financial gain in assisting Dahl.

We think it also significant that Glover assisted Dahl in selling assets that were obtained with investor funds in the corporation. In a meeting with the investors and their lawyer, Glover was present when Dahl assured the investors that upon the sale, they would be receiving their money back. The next month, with Glover's help, the company's assets were sold to a Wisconsin business. Dahl and Glover had taken the position that Chem–Age Industries, Inc., was not a corporation but a proprietorship owned solely by Dahl. Yet Glover helped to arrange the sale of Chem–Age assets through another entity: "Byron Dahl d/b/a BMD Associates, a South Dakota sole proprietorship." Glover later testified that he did not know the relationship between BMD and Chem–Age.

Although Glover may not have taken any active role in defrauding the investor-directors and may not have owed any direct fiduciary duty to them, Dahl did owe such a duty, and a material question of fact exists on whether Glover substantially assisted Dahl in breaching that duty. It may be that Glover, as much as Pederson and Shepard, was duped by Dahl's conniving business dealings, but that is for a jury to decide.

F.

CONCLUSION

* * * Because there are genuine issues of material fact, we reverse and remand for trial the claim[ ] of aiding and abetting the breach of fiduciary duty.

5. LIABILITY FOR SILENCE

AUSTIN v. BRADLEY, BARRY & TARLOW, P.C.

836 F.Supp. 36 (D. Mass. 1993)

SKINNER, S.D.J.

This case and three related actions were brought by four investors in a fall 1982 yacht sale and management offering by Ocean Limited. The defendants, the law firm Bradley, Barry & Tarlow, P.C. and two of its partners, Edward T. Tarlow and Richard P. Breed, III (collectively referred to as BB & T), served as legal counsel to Ocean and prepared a significant portion of the allegedly fraudulent offering memorandum. The crux of the plaintiffs' claims against BB & T is that the offering memorandum was misleading because it failed to disclose material information regarding Ocean's insolvency and inability to fulfill future obligations under the management plan. The defendants move for summary judgment, asserting that the plaintiffs are unable to establish a material element of their remaining claims—that BB & T was under any duty to disclose.

DISCUSSION

1. Primary Liability

Our court of appeals has made eminently clear that "even if the information is material, there is no liability under [Securities and Exchange Commission] Rule 10b–5 [prohibiting securities fraud] unless there was a duty to disclose it." The plaintiffs here do not contend that BB&T's duty to disclose arose from any prior affirmative misrepresentation, insider trading, or violation of any statutory or regulatory disclosure requirements. Instead, the plaintiffs assert that the offering memorandum was misleading because BB&T remained silent, failing to disclose its knowledge of Ocean's insolvency. The plaintiffs further allege that BB&T was obliged to disclose this material information because, by preparing significant portions of the fall 1982 offering memorandum, BB&T assumed a duty to third party investors who BB

& T knew would reasonably and detrimentally rely on the completeness and accuracy of BB & T's professional services.

Under Massachusetts law, "an attorney owes a duty to nonclients who the attorney knows will rely on the services rendered." However, courts will not infer a duty to nonclients if to do so would impose "conflicting duties on attorneys." The record here reveals that imposing a duty on BB&T to disclose Ocean's insolvency to nonclient investors like the plaintiffs would conflict directly with BB&T's concurrent obligation of confidentiality to its client. Accordingly, I decline to infer such a duty in this case.

* * * [T]he plaintiffs here do not allege that BB & T made any prior affirmative misrepresentations or misleading disclosures giving rise to a * * * duty to speak. *See Backman v. Polaroid Corp., 910 F.2d at 16–17* (duty to disclose arises only to correct or update what would otherwise be a materially misleading prior statement by the defendant). The plaintiffs premise BB&T's duty to speak on the allegedly misleading nature of the offering memorandum, which they allege was misleading only because BB&T remained silent. [This argument], however, is not a persuasive basis for abandoning the well-settled rule that "silence, absent a duty to disclose, is not misleading under Rule 10b–5."

In short, the plaintiffs are unable to establish an element essential to their federal securities law claims and BB & T is entitled to summary judgment on Count I of the complaint. Absent any "fiduciary or other similar relation of trust and confidence between [the parties, BB&T had no duty to speak].

2. *Secondary Liability*

[Editors' Note: After this case was decided the United States Supreme Court held in Central Bank of Denver v. First Interstate Bank of Denver, 511 U.S. 164 (1994) that a cause of action for aiding and abetting is not available in claims under the federal securities laws. Congress thereafter made such a cause of action available in actions brought by the Securities and Exchange Commission (SEC), although private actions are still barred. The analysis of aiding and abetting that follows therefore is relevant both for claims brought by the SEC under the securities laws, and by plaintiffs in private actions based on claims that actors are primary violators or assertions that rest on other sources of liability, such as fraud under other statutes or the common law].

To establish liability as an aider and abettor * * * the plaintiffs must establish the following three elements:

    1. the commission of a violation * * * by the primary party;

    2. the defendant's general awareness that his role was part of an overall activity that is improper; and

    3. knowing and substantial assistance of the primary violation by the defendant.

BB&T asserts that, as a matter of law, it cannot be held secondarily liable as an aider and abettor of securities law violations because, absent a duty to disclose, its silence cannot constitute "knowing and substantial assistance" of the primary violation.

The defendants' argument is overstated. Several courts have held that inaction or silence may constitute knowing and substantial assistance of the primary violation where the "defendant recklessly violates an independent duty to act or manifests a conscious intention to further the principal violation." Since I have already determined that BB & T was under no independent duty to act, that is, to speak, BB & T can only be liable as an aider and abettor if its silence was consciously intended to further the principal violation.

In determining whether silence was accompanied by a conscious intent to assist the primary violation, courts query whether the "defendant has thrown in his lot with the primary violators." Crucial to this determination is "whether the alleged aider-and-abettor benefitted from such silence." In making these determinations, courts have been "particularly exacting."

Viewed against these standards and in the light most amiable to the plaintiffs, the record here fails to support a finding that BB&T's silence was "consciously intended" to assist the primary violation. First, there is no allegation that BB&T benefitted from its silence. While presumably BB&T received a fee for its legal services, this economic motivation alone is too remote and minimal to demonstrate that BB&T's silence was " 'designed intentionally to aid the primary fraud.' " *National Union Fire Ins. Co. v. Turtur, 892 F.2d 199, 207 (2d Cir. 1989)* (premiums received by insurance company insufficient to demonstrate conscious intent) (quoting *Armstrong v. McAlpin, 699 F.2d 79, 91 (2d Cir. 1983)); see also DiLeo v. Ernst & Young, 901 F.2d at 629* (accountant fees received over a two-year period found insufficient to demonstrate conscious intent on part of alleged aider and abettor). Second, the plaintiffs have failed to refute BB&T's assertion that its silence was motivated solely by its professional obligation of confidentiality * * *

Accordingly, the defendants are entitled to summary judgment as to Count II of the complaint. *See Cleary v. Perfectune, Inc., 700 F.2d at 778–79* (affirming entry of summary judgment against plaintiffs who failed to introduce any evidence demonstrating that defendants' silence was consciously intended to further fraudulent scheme).

3. State Law Claims

In light of the foregoing finding that BB&T was under no duty to disclose Ocean's insolvency to the plaintiffs, BB&T is also entitled to summary judgment on the plaintiffs' common law negligence (Count IX) and fraud (Count VII) claims. Absent a duty to disclose, there can be no negligence or fraud arising from BB&T's silence.

Similarly, the plaintiffs' failure to demonstrate that BB&T's silence substantially assisted the primary violation mandates that judgment be entered in BB&T's favor on the plaintiffs' state law claim of aiding and abetting fraud (Count VIII). This is because under Massachusetts law liability for aiding and abetting a tort attaches where: (1) the defendant provides "substantial assistance or encouragement to the other party;" and (2) the defendant has "unlawful intent, i.e., knowledge that the other party is breaching a duty and the intent to assist that party's actions."

CONCLUSION

The clerk is directed to enter final judgment in favor of the defendants on all counts of the complaint, the defendants to recover their costs.

C. PRACTICE SPECIALTY RULES

As lawyers' practices become more specialized, increasing numbers of practitioners will be subject to rules of conduct established by regulatory bodies. Chapter 22, for instance, describes some of the rules that the Internal Revenue Service has issued to govern persons who practice before that agency, while Chapter 16 discusses the rules for securities lawyers that the Securities and Exchange Commission has adopted pursuant to the Sarbanes–Oxley legislation.

A particularly striking example of the consequences of violating a practice specialty rule is in *United States v. Gellene*, 182 F.3d 578 (7th Cir. 1999). That case upheld the conviction of a partner in a Wall Street law firm for making false statements under oath in a bankruptcy proceeding (18 U.S.C. 152(3)), and for knowingly using a false document under oath (18 U.S.C. 1623). The bases for the conviction were the lawyer's application to the bankruptcy court to represent a corporate debtor and his subsequent application to the court for compensation for that work, while failing to disclose under Bankruptcy Rule 2014 that his firm also represented in other matters parties with interests in the bankruptcy. The lawyer was sentenced to fifteen months in prison and fined $15,000. He also was expelled from his law firm and disbarred. For an account of these events that examines them in the broader context of the changes in law firm practice discussed in Chapter 7, see Milton C. Regan, Jr., Eat What You Kill: The Fall of a Wall Street Lawyer (1994).

PROBLEMS

Malpractice

Duty of Care

1. You are a partner in a law firm that does general commercial litigation and transactions that has been invited to participate in a "beauty contest" in which Messenger, a large telecommunications company, will choose a firm to represent it in a possible antitrust suit against a competitor, Obelisk. In your meeting with the company's general counsel, she provides information about Messenger and describes the facts about Obelisk's behavior that would

be the basis for the suit. You provide your analysis of the strength of Messenger's company's case, sketch out the tentative litigation strategy that your firm would adopt, and indicate how the firm would handle administrative details such as staffing and billing. Ultimately, Messenger selects another firm to handle the case for it.

2. A few months later, your firm is approached by Obelisk to represent it in a lawsuit against Messenger for patent infringement. The information that you obtained from Messenger about its operations is helpful in your becoming familiar with the case, although it does not include any patent information. When you file the complaint and commence discovery, Messenger sues your firm for malpractice and moves to disqualify you from the case. What basis would there be for Messenger's lawsuit and motion, and what are the chances of it succeeding?

3. If your firm is disqualified, what steps could you have taken to avoid it?

4. Suppose that you are preparing an opinion letter on the validity and enforceability of contracts to sell material to an electric company, which are to serve as collateral for a loan to your client from a bank. You learn from a middle-level manager that the electric company has exercised an option to rescind, and has rescinded two of the forty contracts that form the collateral for the loan. You check on this with a vice-president of the company. He assures you that this reflects an isolated problem brought on by an unexpected temporary cash-flow problem with the electrical manufacturer. All the remaining contracts, he insists, will be performed. In fact, the vice-president knows that the manufacturer is in serious financial trouble and has withdrawn its commitment on the majority of its contracts with your client. Based on his assurance, however, you remove the two contracts from the appendix, prepare the opinion letter, and the loans are made. The bank then becomes aware of the larger problem about six months later when the client cannot make its periodic payment.

The bank then sues the company for fraud, seeking compensatory and punitive damages. It prevails in the suit. Shareholders of the company then on behalf of the company sue management for fraud and sue you for malpractice. What result in the malpractice suit?

Causation

1. Suppose that you represent Obelisk in the patent case mentioned in question two. You use in that lawsuit information that you had obtained from Messenger about its general operations, although none of it relates to patent matters. Your client wins the case, on the ground that the technology used in a portion of the defendant's manufacturing process is in violation of your client's patent.

The defendant Messenger then sues you for malpractice, contending that you were negligent in failing adequately to maintain the confidentiality of its information. If the company can establish that you have breached your duty to it, will it prevail in the suit?

Liability to Non–Clients

1. Let's return to the opinion letter relating to the enforceability of the contracts serving as collateral for the bank's loan. Could the bank successfully sue you for negligence in preparing the letter?

2. Suppose that you prepared the opinion letter at a time when the client was not yet certain which bank it would approach for the loan. You therefore did not know to which institution the letter would be provided. Could the bank that eventually provided the loan successfully sue you for negligence in preparing the letter?

Breach of Fiduciary Duty

1. Let's return to the case in which you use confidential information gained about a company's finances and market share in a patent suit against it. Suppose that the plaintiff sues you for a breach of fiduciary duty rather than for malpractice. Any different result?

2. You represent both parties in a business transaction involving the sale of some real estate to a partnership. You have a small investment in the partnership, but do not disclose this to the seller. After the sale, the seller learns of your interest and sues you for breach of fiduciary duty. Assume that the seller cannot show that he received any less than full market value for the real estate. Does he have any recourse against you?

Aiding and Abetting

1. You are the head of the legal department of Willoway Corporation, a company in the energy industry. A periodic review of Willoway's financial controls by the company's internal audit team has led Willoway's internal auditor to raise questions about documentation for three transactions in which Willoway sold $25 million worth of assets near the end of a recent fiscal quarter. The gains from these sales contributed $11 million in revenue for that quarter. Over the next two months, Willoway repurchased substantially all of these assets in six different transactions with the original purchaser in return for Willoway stock. These facts raise the question whether Willoway ever engaged in a genuine sale of the assets. If not, then the company was not entitled to recognize revenue from these transactions and will need to restate its financials to reflect $10 million less in revenue for the relevant quarter.

You are asked to participate in a meeting with the internal auditor and Willoway's Chief Financial Officer (CFO). The auditor says that he has not been satisfied with the explanations for the transactions that have been offered by the employees involved in them. He asks some pointed questions of the CFO. You are not an accountant, but it seems to you that the officer is not able to provide answers that are entirely responsive to the auditor's concerns. The CFO vehemently insists that the transactions were genuine sales of assetsk and is quite defensive when the auditor raises any suggestion otherwise. The meeting ends with the CFO asking the auditor to review the documentation for the deals one more time and to reconsider his position.

Two days later, you receive a call from the CFO. He tells you that, upon further reflection, the auditor has concluded that there was no problem with the transactions about which he had raised questions. In addition, the CFO says, the company and the auditor have agreed that the auditor will leave Willoway to pursue other career opportunities. In connection with his departure, the company would like to provide the auditor with a generous severance package to compensate him for his years of valuable service. Under the terms of this package, the auditor will receive a combination of cash and company stock worth $5 million. The CFO tells you that the CEO has asked that you draft a severance agreement that reflects the understanding of the parties for their signature.

Is there any reason for concern if you draft the agreement?

2.   You are an attorney in the general counsel's office of a major bank. You conduct an internal investigation that indicates that a bank vice-president has conspired with a depositor who operates a drug ring to engage in money laundering. You report your findings to the chief executive officer (CEO) of the bank, who orders the immediate termination of the vice-president. You then bring to the attention of the CEO a Federal Deposit Insurance Corporation regulation, 12 C.F.R. 353, that requires the bank to make a criminal referral to the F.B.I., U.S. Attorney, and F.D.I.C. when it appears that a crime has been committed involving or affecting the assets or affairs of a federally-insured bank. In addition to the risk of agency sanctions, if the bank fails to make the referral and takes any steps that constitute affirmative concealment of the crime, it would be liable for misprision of a felony under 18 U.S.C. 4 and possibly conspiracy to violate the Currency Transactions Reporting Act under 18 U.S.C. 371.

The CEO tells you that he does not want to make the referral because the bank is about to merge with another major financial institution and such news could jeopardize the deal. He believes that he has taken care of the problem by firing the offending vice-president. He directs you to send your report to storage and not to provide any criminal referral to the relevant agencies.

Federal banking laws provide that any employee of a federally insured bank who violates any statute or regulation, or aids and abets another in doing so, can be barred from any further employment in an insured financial institution. Such debarment will be ordered if the violation is willful and the bank is likely to suffer financial loss or other damages because of it.

Are you at risk of being barred from ever working for a federally insured financial institution?

Do you face this risk if you also are working on the merger?

Chapter 11

MULTISTATE LAW PRACTICE

As the previous chapter describes, lawyers generally must be members of the bar in a particular state in order to provide legal services in that state. With the national expansion of both law practice and corporate operations, however, it now is quite common for lawyers to provides legal services in more than one state, including in states in which they are not a member of the bar. A lawyer with a firm in New York, for instance, may meet with and provide legal advice to a client in Texas, in a matter that requires an interpretation of California law and a trip to a manufacturing plant in Alabama. If the lawyer is a member only of the New York bar, has she engaged in the unauthorized practice of law in Texas, California, and Alabama?

As the material below describes, litigators traditionally have been able to avoid such concerns through temporary, or *pro hac vice*, admission for the purpose of representing a client in a particular proceeding. Lawyers engaged in other type of legal work, such as transactional practice, however, have not had such an arrangement available. This can pose a problem both for lawyers in law firms and lawyers in corporate legal departments who may have to respond to legal issues on a nationwide basis.

An additional concern that arises from multistate practice is that the ethical rules of the states in which a lawyer practices may differ—sometimes dramatically. To which rule must a lawyer look for guidance in this situation? What if the rules conflict? Because of the nature and scope of their practice, corporate lawyers therefore experience acutely the mismatch between a state-based system of bar regulation and the reality of an increasingly national practice.

OVERVIEW OF THE CHAPTER

The Chapter begins with an excerpt from the report of the American Bar Association (ABA) Commission on Multijurisdictional Practice. The excerpt underscores that cross-border law practice is common in the United States, even though practicing in a state in which one is not a member of the bar can constitute the unauthorized practice of law.

Every state has a prohibition on such activity, but when such provisions will be invoked and how they will be interpreted is highly uncertain. The Commission suggests that much unauthorized practice is occurring without any penalty. The ever-present possibility of enforcement, however, may make some lawyers cautious about representing clients even when doing so would be efficient and advantageous for the client. The current situation of underenforcement of what lawyers regard as outmoded rules also may create a more general disregard for ethical provisions that lawyers find inconvenient.

The Chapter continues with three cases—*Birbower, Condon,* and *Fought*—that illustrate the variation in how courts go about interpreting unauthorized practice rules. What constitutes the "practice of law" and when such practice occurs "in" a state are not necessarily questions with straightforward answers. As the cases indicate, considerations such as the location of the attorney, the residence of the client, that state law that governs the matter that is the subject of the representation, and various policy concerns all influence how courts resolve these issues. As you read the cases, ask yourself what purposes unauthorized practice rules are designed to serve. How relevant are those purposes with respect to corporate clients?

The Chapter returns to the ABA Commission report, focusing on the recommendations issued by the Commission. Read this excerpt in conjunction with Model Rule 5.5(c), which has been amended to reflect these recommendations. That Rule now contains a provision that permits lawyers under certain conditions to engage in the temporary practice of law in states in which they are not admitted to the bar. Note also Model Rule 8.5, which has been amended to permit states to discipline lawyers engaged in temporary practice in their jurisdictions.

The first problem asks you to apply new Model Rule 5.5(c) to a set of facts. It then asks you to analyze the same facts assuming that the state in question has not adopted the new Model Rule. This requires that you draw on the three cases in the Chapter in determining how a state court is likely to rule on an unauthorized practice claim when the state has made no provision for temporary practice. The second problem focuses on conflicting ethical provisions between two states, requiring application of Rule 8.5's provision on conflicts of rules.

MODEL RULES: 5.5, 8.5

CLIENT REPRESENTATION IN THE TWENTY–FIRST CENTURY

REPORT OF THE COMMISSION ON MULTIJURISDICTIONAL PRACTICE 2002

* * *

INTRODUCTION

The predicate for this national study undertaken by the American Bar Association was the dynamic change and evolution in nature and scope of legal practice during the past century, facilitated by a transformation in communications, transportation and technology. In the early twentieth century, states adopted "unauthorized practice of law" (UPL) provisions that apply equally to lawyers licensed in other states and to nonlawyers. These laws prohibit lawyers from engaging in the practice of law except in states in which they are licensed or otherwise authorized to practice law. UPL restrictions have long been qualified by *pro hac vice* provisions, which allow courts or administrative agencies to authorize an out-of-state lawyer to represent a client in a particular case before the tribunal. In recent years, some jurisdictions have adopted provisions authorizing out-of-state lawyers to perform other legal work in the jurisdiction.

Jurisdictional restrictions on law practice were not historically a matter of concern, because most clients' legal matters were confined to a single state and a lawyer's familiarity with that state's law was a qualification of particular importance. However, the wisdom of the application of UPL laws to licensed lawyers has been questioned repeatedly since the 1960s in light of the changing nature of clients' legal needs and the changing nature of law practice. Both the law and the transactions in which lawyers assist clients have increased in complexity, requiring a growing number of lawyers to concentrate in particular areas of practice rather than being generalists in state law. Often, the most significant qualification to render assistance in a legal matter is not knowledge of any given state's law, but knowledge of federal or international law or familiarity with a particular type of business or personal transaction or legal proceeding. Additionally, modern transportation and communications technology have enabled clients to travel easily and transact business throughout the country, and even internationally. Because of this globalization of business and finance, clients sometimes now need lawyers to assist them in transactions in multiple jurisdictions (state and national) or to advise them about multiple jurisdictions' laws.

Although client needs and legal practices have evolved, lawyer regulation has not yet responded effectively to that evolution. As the work of lawyers has become more varied, specialized and national in scope, it has become increasingly uncertain when a lawyer's work (other than as a trial lawyer in court) implicates the UPL law of a jurisdiction in which the lawyer is not licensed. Lawyers recognize that the geographic scope of a lawyer's practice must be adequate to enable the lawyer to serve the legal needs of clients in a national and global economy. They have expressed concern that if UPL restrictions are applied literally to United States lawyers who perform any legal work outside the jurisdictions in which they are admitted to practice, the laws will impede lawyers' ability to meet their clients' multi-state and interstate legal needs efficiently and effectively ...

THE BASIS FOR CHANGE

Background: State Licensing and Jurisdictional Restrictions

State admissions and regulation. Lawyers in the United States are not licensed to practice law on a national basis, but are licensed by a state judiciary to practice law within the particular state. In general, state admissions processes are intended to protect the public by ensuring that those who are licensed to practice law in the state have the requisite knowledge of that state's laws and the general fitness and character to practice law.

The state-based licensing process originated more than two centuries ago when the need for legal services was locally based and often involved the need for representation in court. Over time, the nature of law practice has expanded. Increasingly, lawyers counsel and assist clients outside the courthouse. Although understandings differ about the extent to which a law license gives lawyers exclusive authority to render legal services in addition to litigation, it is generally understood that a state license to practice law permits a lawyer to offer a range of legal services, including but not limited to courtroom advocacy, and that some of those legal services may not be rendered in the state either by nonlawyers or by lawyers who are licensed to practice law only in another jurisdiction. * * *

Geographical Boundaries. In general, a lawyer may not represent clients before a state tribunal or otherwise practice law within a particular state unless the lawyer is licensed by the state or is otherwise authorized to do so. Jurisdictional restrictions promote a variety of state regulatory interests. Most obviously, by limiting law practice in the state to those whom the state judiciary, through its admissions process, has deemed to be qualified to practice law in the state, they promote the state interest in ensuring that those who represent clients in the state are competent to do so. Jurisdictional restrictions also promote the state interest in ensuring that lawyers practicing law within the state do so ethically and professionally. Lawyers licensed by the state are thought to be more conversant than out-of-state lawyers with state disciplinary provisions as well as with unwritten but understood expectations about how members of the local bar should behave, and lawyers in the state may be disciplined more easily and effectively than out-of-state lawyers when they engage in professional improprieties. By strengthening lawyers' ties to the particular communities in which they maintain their offices, jurisdictional restrictions may also help maintain an active and vibrant local bar, which in many communities serves a crucial public role, because lawyers serve voluntarily on court committees, in public office, and on boards of not-for-profit institutions in the community.

States give effect to jurisdictional restrictions through UPL statutes and proscriptions in the rules of professional conduct such as those based on ABA Model Rule 5.5. Although UPL provisions are most often applied to nonlawyers, they have also been applied to lawyers. They subject lawyers to the risk of sanction (in some states, criminal sanction) for practicing law within a state where they are not licensed. Besides being enforced directly, these provisions may be invoked in disciplinary proceedings based on disciplinary rules that prohibit lawyers from engaging in, or assisting others in, the unauthorized practice of law, in fee forfeiture actions or other civil actions by clients against their lawyers or by opposing parties in the context of disqualification motions.

Today, no state categorically excludes out-of-state lawyers and there is general agreement that, as a practical matter, lawyers cannot serve clients effectively unless accommodations are made for multijurisdictional law practice, at least on a temporary or occasional basis. For example, every jurisdiction permits *pro hac vice* admission of out-of-state lawyers appearing before a tribunal, although the processes and standards for *pro hac vice* admission differ.

For transactional and counseling practices, and other work outside court or agency proceedings, there is no counterpart to *pro hac vice* admission, but, as discussed below, multijurisdictional law practice is common for certain types of practitioners. The laws of two states, Michigan and Virginia, specifically authorize occasional or incidental practice by out-of-state lawyers. Michigan's UPL statute provides that it does not apply to an out-of-state lawyer who is "temporarily in [Michigan] and engaged in a particular matter." The Virginia rules permit an out-of-state lawyer occasionally to provide legal advice or services in Virginia "incidental to representation of a client whom the attorney represents elsewhere." * * * California now specifically authorizes out-of-state lawyers to represent clients in arbitrations. Some state courts have identified similar exceptions in judicial decisions.

Some states also accommodate certain out-of-state lawyers who seek to establish a law office in the state or to practice law in the state on a regular basis. For example, states have adopted provisions permitting in-house corporate lawyers, or lawyers employed generally by organizational clients, to provide legal services on behalf of the organization from an office located in a state where the lawyer is not licensed. Typically, the lawyer is required to register and to submit to the state's regulatory authority * * *

The Increasing Prevalence of Multijurisdictional Practice

Testimony before the Commission was unanimous in recognizing that lawyers commonly engage in cross-border legal practice. Further, there was general consensus that such practice is on the increase and that this trend is not only inevitable, but also necessary. The explosion of technology and the increasing complexity of legal practice have resulted in the need for lawyers to cross state borders to afford clients competent representation.

In connection with litigation, it is not uncommon for parties to retain lawyers in whom they have particular confidence, or with whom they have a prior relationship, to represent them in lawsuits in jurisdictions in which the lawyers are not licensed, and for these lawyers to be admitted *pro hac vice* to appear on behalf of the client. However, lawyers also perform work outside their home states for which they cannot obtain *pro hac vice* admission, which is not available prior to the filing of a lawsuit or to authorize work that is not related to a judicial proceeding in the particular state. For example, litigators commonly go to states other than those in which they are authorized to practice law in order to review documents, interview witnesses, enter into negotiations, and conduct other activities that are either ancillary to a lawsuit pending in a state in which they are authorized to practice or that are performed before a lawsuit is filed.

In ADR proceedings as well, it is common for lawyers to render services outside the particular states in which they are licensed. Sometimes, the parties choose to conduct the ADR proceeding in a state that has no relation to the parties or the dispute, because they prefer a neutral site. Because particular knowledge of state law and procedure is not necessary, the parties often select lawyers based on other considerations, such as the lawyers' prior knowledge of the relevant facts or a preexisting client-lawyer relationship.

Lawyers who provide legal advice or assistance in transactions also commonly provide services in states in which they are not licensed. Like litigators, transactional lawyers who are representing clients in the state in which they are licensed travel outside the state in order to conduct negotiations, gather information, provide advice, or perform other tasks relating to the representation. Lawyers also travel outside their home states in order to provide assistance to clients who are in special need of their expertise. For example, lawyers who concentrate their practice in federal law—such as securities, antitrust, labor, or intellectual property law—are often retained by clients outside their home states because of the clients' regard for their particular expertise. The same is true of foreign lawyers whose expertise in foreign law is sought, as well as of other lawyers, such as bond lawyers or mergers-and-acquisition lawyers, who practice in specialized areas. For some lawyers, multijurisdictional practice grows out of an ongoing relationship with a client. Sometimes, the work is for a client who resides in the lawyer's home state but who has business dealings outside the state. Other times, the work is for a client who has moved out of state. A lawyer who drafts a will for a client in one state may be asked by that client to draft a codicil to the will after the client has moved to another state. For in-house lawyers in particular, ongoing work for a corporate employer commonly involves travel to the different states where the corporation has offices or business interests.

The Impact of Jurisdictional Restrictions on Legal Practice

* * * The existing system of lawyer regulation is and should be a matter of serious concern for many lawyers. Even in contexts where jurisdictional restrictions clearly apply, as in state-court proceedings, problems are caused by the lack of uniformity among the *pro hac vice* provisions of different states, unpredictability about how some of the provisions will be applied by the courts in individual cases, and, in some cases, the provisions' excessive restrictiveness. Of even greater concern, however, is that, outside the context of litigation, the reach of the jurisdictional restrictions is vastly uncertain as well as, potentially, far too restrictive. Lawyers may recognize that UPL enforcement proceedings are infrequent, and that when UPL laws are invoked, courts have the ability to interpret them realistically to accommodate the interests of clients with interstate or multi-state legal problems. Nevertheless, some lawyers will turn down clients or take other steps to avoid or reduce the risk of having to defend against UPL charges or of appearing to violate rules of professional conduct.

The existing system of lawyer regulation has costs for clients. For example, out of concern for jurisdictional restrictions, lawyers may decline to provide services that they are able to render skillfully and ethically. In doing so, they may deprive the client of a preferred lawyer including, at times, a lawyer who can serve the client more efficiently and economically than other available lawyers by drawing on knowledge gained in the course of prior work for the particular client or by drawing on expertise in the particular subject area * * * Cautious lawyers may deny both institutional and individual clients the benefit of an ongoing client-lawyer relationship. Alternatively, lawyers may insist that the client engage local counsel or co-counsel in situations where doing so adds unnecessarily to the expense of the representation, because the out-of-state lawyer possesses all the necessary knowledge and expertise and would represent the client competently and ethically.

BIRBROWER, MONTALBANO, CONDON & FRANK, P.C., ET AL. v. THE SUPERIOR COURT OF SANTA CLARA COUNTY

17 Cal.4th 119, 70 Cal.Rptr.2d 304, 949 P.2d 1 (1998)

OPINION: CHIN, J.

Business and Professions Code section 6125 states: No person shall practice law in California unless the person is an active member of the State Bar. We must decide whether an out-of-state law firm, not licensed to practice law in this state, violated section 6125 when it performed legal services in California for a California-based client under a fee agreement stipulating that California law would govern all matters in the representation.

Although we are aware of the interstate nature of modern law practice and mindful of the reality that large firms often conduct activities and serve clients in several states, we do not believe these facts excuse law firms from complying with section 6125. Contrary to the Court of Appeal, however, we do not believe the Legislature intended section 6125 to apply to those services an out-of-state firm renders in its home state. We therefore conclude that, to the extent defendant law firm Birbrower, Montalbano, Condon & Frank, P.C. (Birbrower), practiced law in California without a license, it engaged in the unauthorized practice of law in this state. We also conclude that Birbrower's fee agreement with real party in interest ESQ Business Services, Inc. (ESQ), is invalid to the extent it authorizes payment for the substantial legal services Birbrower performed in California. If, however, Birbrower can show it generated fees under its agreement for limited services it performed in New York, and it earned those fees under the otherwise invalid fee agreement, it may, on remand, present to the trial court evidence justifying its recovery of fees for those New York services * * *

I. BACKGROUND

The facts with respect to the unauthorized practice of law question are essentially undisputed. Birbrower is a professional law corporation incorporated in New York, with its principal place of business in New York. During 1992 and 1993, Birbrower attorneys, defendants Kevin F. Hobbs and Thomas A. Condon (Hobbs and Condon), performed substantial work in California relating to the law firm's representation of ESQ. Neither Hobbs nor Condon has ever been licensed to practice law in California. None of Birbrower's attorneys were licensed to practice law in California during Birbrower's ESQ representation.

ESQ is a California corporation with its principal place of business in Santa Clara County. In July 1992, the parties negotiated and executed the fee agreement in New York, providing that Birbrower would perform legal services for ESQ, including "All matters pertaining to the investigation of and prosecution of all claims and causes of action against Tandem Computers Incorporated [Tandem]." The "claims and causes of action" against Tandem, a Delaware corporation with its principal place of business in Santa Clara County, California, related to a software development and marketing contract between Tandem and ESQ dated March 16, 1990 (Tandem Agreement). The Tandem Agreement stated that "The internal laws of the State of California (irrespective of its choice of law principles) shall govern the validity of this Agreement, the construction of its terms, and the interpretation and enforcement of the rights and duties of the parties hereto." Birbrower asserts, and ESQ disputes, that ESQ knew Birbrower was not licensed to practice law in California.

While representing ESQ, Hobbs and Condon traveled to California on several occasions. In August 1992, they met in California with ESQ and its accountants. During these meetings, Hobbs and Condon discussed various matters related to ESQ's dispute with Tandem and strategy for resolving the dispute. They made recommendations and gave advice. During this California trip, Hobbs and Condon also met with Tandem representatives on four or five occasions during a two-day period. At the meetings, Hobbs and Condon spoke on ESQ's behalf. Hobbs demanded that Tandem pay ESQ $15 million. Condon told Tandem he believed that damages would exceed $15 million if the parties litigated the dispute.

Around March or April 1993, Hobbs, Condon, and another Birbrower attorney visited California to interview potential arbitrators and to meet again with ESQ and its accountants. Birbrower had previously filed a demand for arbitration against Tandem with the San Francisco offices of the American Arbitration Association (AAA). In August 1993, Hobbs returned to California to assist ESQ in settling the Tandem matter. While in California, Hobbs met with ESQ and its accountants to discuss a proposed settlement agreement Tandem authored. Hobbs also met with Tandem representatives to discuss possible changes in the proposed agreement. Hobbs gave ESQ legal advice during this trip, including his opinion that ESQ should not settle with Tandem on the terms proposed.

ESQ eventually settled the Tandem dispute, and the matter never went to arbitration. But before the settlement, ESQ and Birbrower modified the contingency fee agreement. The modification changed the fee arrangement from contingency to fixed fee, providing that ESQ would pay Birbrower over $1 million. The original contingency fee arrangement had called for Birbrower to receive "one-third (1/3) of all sums received for the benefit of the Clients ... whether obtained through settlement, motion practice, hearing, arbitration, or trial by way of judgment, award, settlement, or otherwise...."

In January 1994, ESQ sued Birbrower for legal malpractice and related claims in Santa Clara County Superior Court. Birbrower removed the matter to federal court and filed a counterclaim, which included a claim for attorney fees for the work it performed in both California and New York. The matter was then remanded to the superior court. There ESQ moved for summary judgment and/or adjudication on the first through fourth causes of action of Birbrower's counterclaim, which asserted ESQ and its representatives breached the fee agreement. ESQ argued that by practicing law without a license in California and by failing to associate legal counsel while doing so, Birbrower violated section 6125, rendering the fee agreement unenforceable.

* * * [T]he Santa Clara Superior Court * * * concluded that: (1) Birbrower was "not admitted to the practice of law in California"; (2) Birbrower "did not associate California counsel"; (3) Birbrower "provided legal services in this state"; and (4) "The law is clear that no one may recover compensation for services as an attorney in this state unless he or she was a member of the state bar at the time those services were performed" * * *

Birbrower petitioned the Court of Appeal for a writ of mandate directing the trial court to vacate the summary adjudication order. The Court of Appeal denied Birbrower's petition and affirmed the trial court's order, holding that Birbrower violated section 6125. The Court of Appeal also concluded that Birbrower's violation barred the firm from recovering its legal fees under the written fee agreement, including fees generated in New York by the attorneys when they were physically present in New York, because the agreement included payment for California or "local" services for a California client in California. The

Court of Appeal agreed with the trial court, however, in deciding that Birbrower could pursue its remaining claims against ESQ, including its equitable claim for recovery of its fees in quantum meruit.

II. Discussion

A. *The Unauthorized Practice of Law*

The California Legislature enacted section 6125 in 1927 as part of the State Bar Act (the Act), a comprehensive scheme regulating the practice of law in the state. Since the Act's passage, the general rule has been that, although persons may represent themselves and their own interests regardless of State Bar membership, no one but an active member of the State Bar may practice law for another person in California. The prohibition against unauthorized law practice is within the state's police power and is designed to ensure that those performing legal services do so competently * * *

A violation of section 6125 is a misdemeanor. Moreover, "No one may recover compensation for services as an attorney at law in this state unless [the person] was at the time the services were performed a member of The State Bar."

Although the Act did not define the term "practice law," case law explained it as " 'the doing and performing services in a court of justice in any matter depending therein throughout its various stages and in conformity with the adopted rules of procedure.' " (*People v. Merchants Protective Corp. (1922) 189 Cal. 531, 535 [209 P. 363] (Merchants).)* *Merchants* included in its definition legal advice and legal instrument and contract preparation, whether or not these subjects were rendered in the course of litigation * * *

In addition to not defining the term "practice law," the Act also did not define the meaning of "in California." In today's legal practice, questions often arise concerning whether the phrase refers to the nature of the legal services, or restricts the Act's application to those out-of-state attorneys who are physically present in the state.

Section 6125 has generated numerous opinions on the meaning of "practice law" but none on the meaning of "in California." In our view, the practice of law "in California" entails sufficient contact with the California client to render the nature of the legal service a clear legal representation. In addition to a quantitative analysis, we must consider the nature of the unlicensed lawyer's activities in the state. Mere fortuitous or attenuated contacts will not sustain a finding that the unlicensed lawyer practiced law "in California." The primary inquiry is whether the unlicensed lawyer engaged in sufficient activities in the state, or created a continuing relationship with the California client that included legal duties and obligations.

Our definition does not necessarily depend on or require the unlicensed lawyer's physical presence in the state. Physical presence here is one factor we may consider in deciding whether the unlicensed lawyer has violated section 6125, but it is by no means exclusive. For example, one may practice law in the state in violation of section 6125 although not physically present here by advising a California client on California law in connection with a California legal dispute by telephone, fax, computer, or other modern technological means. Conversely, although we decline to provide a comprehensive list of what activities constitute sufficient contact with the state, we do reject the notion that a person *automatically* practices law "in California" whenever that person practices California law anywhere, or "virtually" enters the state by telephone, fax, e-mail, or satellite. (See e.g., *Baron v. City of Los Angeles (1970) 2 Cal.3d 535, 543 [86 Cal.Rptr. 673, 469 P.2d 353, 42 A.L.R.3d 1036] (Baron)* ["practice law" does not encompass all professional activities].) * * *

Exceptions to section 6125 do exist, but are generally limited to allowing out-of-state attorneys to make brief appearances before a state court or tribunal. They are narrowly drawn and strictly interpreted. For example, an out-of-state attorney not licensed to practice in California may be permitted, *by consent of a trial judge*, to appear in California in a particular pending action.

In addition, with the permission of the California court in which a particular cause is pending, out-of-state counsel may appear before a court as counsel pro hac vice. A court will approve a pro hac vice application only if the out-of-state attorney is a member in good standing of another state bar and is eligible to practice in any United States court or the highest court in another jurisdiction. The out-of-state attorney must also associate an active member of the California Bar as attorney of record and is subject to the Rules of Professional Conduct of the State Bar * * *

B. The Present Case

The undisputed facts here show that neither *Baron*'s definition *(Baron, supra, 2 Cal.3d at p. 543)* nor our "sufficient contact" definition of "practice law in California" would excuse Birbrower's extensive practice in this state. Nor would any of the limited statutory exceptions to section 6125 apply to Birbrower's California practice. As the Court of Appeal observed, Birbrower engaged in unauthorized law practice *in California* on more than a limited basis, and no firm attorney engaged in that practice was an active member of the California State Bar. As noted, in 1992 and 1993, Birbrower attorneys traveled to California to discuss with ESQ and others various matters pertaining to the dispute between ESQ and Tandem. Hobbs and Condon discussed strategy for resolving the dispute and advised ESQ on this strategy. Furthermore, during California meetings with Tandem representatives in August 1992, Hobbs demanded Tandem pay $15 million, and Condon told Tandem he believed damages in the matter would exceed that amount if the parties proceeded to litigation. Also in California, Hobbs met with ESQ for the stated purpose of helping to reach a settlement agreement and to discuss the agreement that was eventually proposed. Birbrower attorneys also traveled to California to initiate arbitration proceedings before the matter was settled. As the Court of Appeal concluded, " ... the Birbrower firm's in-state activities clearly constituted the [unauthorized] practice of law" *in California* * * *

* * * Birbrower urges us to adopt an exception to section 6125 based on the unique circumstances of this case. Birbrower notes that "Multistate relationships are a common part of today's society and are to be dealt with in commonsense fashion." (*In re Estate of Waring (1966) 47 N.J. 367 [221 A.2d 193, 197].*) In many situations, strict adherence to rules prohibiting the unauthorized practice of law by out-of-state attorneys would be " 'grossly impractical and inefficient.' "*(Ibid.*; see also *Appell v. Reiner (1964) 43 N.J. 313 [204 A.2d 146, 148]* [strict adherence to rule barring out-of-state lawyers from representing New Jersey residents on New Jersey matters may run against the public interest when case involves inseparable multistate transactions].)

Although, as discussed, we recognize the need to acknowledge and, in certain cases, to accommodate the multistate nature of law practice, the facts here show that Birbrower's extensive activities within California amounted to considerably more than any of our state's recognized exceptions to section 6125 would allow. Accordingly, we reject Birbrower's suggestion that we except the firm from section 6125's rule under the circumstances here.

C.   Compensation for Legal Services

Because Birbrower violated section 6125 when it engaged in the unlawful practice of law in California, the Court of Appeal found its fee agreement with ESQ unenforceable in its entirety * * * We agree with the Court of Appeal to the extent it barred Birbrower from recovering fees generated under the fee agreement for the unauthorized legal services it performed in California. We disagree with the same court to the extent it implicitly barred Birbrower from recovering fees generated under the fee agreement for the limited legal services the firm performed in New York.

It is a general rule that an attorney is barred from recovering compensation for services rendered in another state where the attorney was not admitted to the bar.

* * * Because Birbrower practiced substantial law in this state in violation of section 6125, it cannot receive compensation under the fee agreement for any of the services it performed in California. Enforcing the fee agreement in its entirety would include payment for the unauthorized practice of law in California and would allow Birbrower to enforce an illegal contract.

* * * Birbrower seeks to recover under its contract for those services it performed for ESQ in New York that did not involve the practice of law in California, including fee contract negotiations and some corporate case research.

We agree with Birbrower that it may be able to recover fees under the fee agreement for the limited legal services it performed for ESQ in New York to the extent they did not constitute practicing law in California, even though those services were performed for a California client. Because section 6125 applies to the practice of law in California, it does not, in general, regulate law practice in other states * * *

The fee agreement between Birbrower and ESQ became illegal when Birbrower performed legal services in violation of section 6125. It is true that courts will not ordinarily aid in enforcing an agreement that is either illegal or against public policy. Illegal contracts, however, will be enforced under certain circumstances, such as when only a part of the consideration given for the contract involves illegality. In other words, notwithstanding an illegal consideration, courts may sever the illegal portion of the contract from the rest of the agreement * * *

In this case, the parties entered into a contingency fee agreement followed by a fixed fee agreement. ESQ was to pay money to Birbrower in exchange for Birbrower's legal services. The object of their agreement may not have been entirely illegal, assuming ESQ was to pay Birbrower compensation based in part on work Birbrower performed in New York that did not amount to the practice of law in California. The illegality arises, instead, out of the amount to be paid to Birbrower, which, if paid fully, would include payment for services rendered in California in violation of section 6125.

Therefore, we conclude the Court of Appeal erred in determining that the fee agreement between the parties was entirely unenforceable because Birbrower violated section 6125's prohibition against the unauthorized practice of law in California. Birbrower's statutory violation may require exclusion of the portion of the fee attributable to the substantial illegal services, but that violation does not necessarily entirely preclude its recovery under the fee agreement for the limited services it performed outside California.

Thus, the portion of the fee agreement between Birbrower and ESQ that includes payment for services rendered in New York may be enforceable to the extent that the illegal compensation can be severed from the rest of the agreement * * *

III. Disposition

We conclude that Birbrower violated section 6125 by practicing law in California. To the extent the fee agreement allows payment for those illegal local services, it is void, and Birbrower is not entitled to recover fees under the agreement for those services. The fee agreement is enforceable, however, to the extent it is possible to sever the portions of the consideration attributable to Birbrower's services illegally rendered in California from those attributable to Birbrower's New York services.

ESTATE OF CONDON v. McHENRY

65 Cal.App.4th 1138, 76 Cal.Rptr.2d 922 (1998)

OPINION: WALKER, J.

Michael R. Condon and his attorneys, Michael Katz and his firm (the Elrod firm), appeal an order of the probate court denying Katz attorney fees for services rendered to the estate of Evelyn J. Condon. Michael, Evelyn's son, was appointed co-executor of her will with his sister, Caroline M. McHenry, the respondent to this appeal. Michael lives in Colorado; Caroline lives in California, as did their mother. The Elrod firm, which Evelyn J. Condon had retained to prepare her will and other documents effectuating her estate plan, n1 is in Colorado, where the will was prepared, and where Katz is licensed to practice law. Katz is not a member of the California State Bar.

Michael retained Katz and the Elrod firm to advise him as co-executor in the probate proceedings. Caroline retained counsel in California, James Cody and his firm (the Carr firm), to represent her as co-executor in the same proceedings. The record reflects that Katz did most of his work in Colorado, where Michael resides, communicating by telephone, mail, and fax with Cody and with other of the Condon siblings in California. Michael also retained California counsel, Dominic Campisi and his firm (the Evans firm), to file papers and make appearances on his behalf in the probate court in San Mateo County.

In January 1996, fully three acrimonious years after the will was admitted to probate, the parties scheduled a hearing to approve the account, distribute the estate's assets, and award the fees owed the executors and their attorneys. Michael, through Campisi, filed a petition seeking compensation from the estate for Katz's ordinary and extraordinary legal services. Caroline challenged the petition, asserting that some of the work for which Katz sought payment was done for Michael and their brother, Eugene, individually, not for the estate. She also contended that the sums Katz claimed were unreasonable.

The probate judge never reached the issues Caroline raised. Once he determined that Katz was not a member of the California State Bar and had not applied to appear *pro hac vice* he expressed his view that Katz was not an "attorney" within the meaning of *Probate Code section 10810*: "[A]s far as this court is concerned he's not a licensed legal practitioner. . . ." The judge adjourned the hearing, telling Campisi, "I will give you [two hours] to come up with some authority [for me] to order payment out of a California estate to a nonmember of the California bar for attorney's fees[.]"

When the hearing resumed, the judge denied Katz's hastily assembled application for leave to appear *pro hac vice*. After hearing argument, he concluded that, by serving as counsel for the co-executor of a will written for a California decedent, which devised California property, and was subject to California probate proceedings, Katz, a nonmember of the

State Bar, had "practice[d] law in California" in violation of Business and Professions Code section 6125. The court therefore refused to authorize payment of his legal fees. Michael and the Elrod firm timely appealed.

In our June 25, 1997, opinion, we reversed the probate court's order, holding that *California Probate Code section 8570* et seq. allowed for such fees and that section 6125 did not proscribe them. Following our denial of a petition for rehearing, the Supreme Court granted review and ordered action on the cause deferred until disposition of *Birbrower, Montalbano, Condon & Frank v. Superior Court (1998) 17 Cal.4th 119 [70 Cal.Rptr.2d 304, 949 P.2d 1] (Birbrower)* then pending before it. Following its decision, the Supreme Court transferred review to us with directions to vacate our prior decision and to reconsider that case in light of *Birbrower*.

Following our review we conclude that Katz did not violate section 6125. He is therefore entitled under the Probate Code to ordinary statutory fees and to extraordinary fees in whatever amount the court deems reasonable for the services he rendered to Michael in his capacity as co-executor.

THE LEGAL QUESTION

Section 6125 provides that "[n]o person shall practice law in California unless the person is an active member of the State Bar." Section 6126 states that "[any] person advertising or holding himself or herself out as practicing or entitled to practice law or otherwise practicing law who is not an active member of the State Bar, is guilty of a misdemeanor." Our courts have spun from these prohibitions a policy against awarding attorney fees to unlicensed practitioners of law.

It is well settled in California that "practicing law" means more than just appearing in court. "' ... [T]he practice of the law ... includes legal advice and counsel and the preparation of legal instruments and contracts by which legal rights are secured although such matter may or may not be []pending in a court.'" The parties agree that Katz "practic[ed] law" for Michael in his capacity as co-executor of his mother's will.[5]

We must decide whether an out-of-state law firm, not licensed to practice law in California, violated section 6125 when it performed legal services by either physically or virtually[6] entering California on behalf of a Colorado client who was an executor of a California estate.

---

5. By appellants' uncontradicted account, Katz "represented his client—negotiating transactions, drafting agreements, researching law and giving legal advice[]—from his office in Colorado[, while r]outine probate administration filings were handled by [Caroline] and her California counsel." All filings made on behalf of Michael as co-executor of the estate were filed by the Evans firm, retained California counsel on behalf of Michael.

6. We define virtual presence as used in our opinion as entry into the State of California by telephone, fax, e-mail, satellite or any other means of communication when a person outside of the State of California communicates with one within.

ANALYSIS

1. *The Probate Code Allows the Payment of Attorney Fees to an Out-of-state Attorney Rendering Services on Behalf of a California Estate.*

The Probate Code makes specific allowance for a nonresident, such as Michael, to serve as executor of a will subject to probate in California, and our courts have made clear that "[t]he executor[] has the right to choose independent counsel to perform the necessary legal services on behalf of the estate." Here, Michael's choice was not only his to make, it was also reasonable; the Elrod firm did business where he lived and its principals had originally prepared his mother's estate plan.

* * * [I]t is common practice for California probate judges to award fees to out-of-state attorneys rendering legal services in "ancillary" matters.... [T]hough out-of-state attorneys have undoubtedly served California estates before this, and their services have surely entailed professional communications with people in California, there is nothing in the Probate Code or prior cases to suggest that they are disqualified from receiving statutory compensation.

2. *Section 6125 Does Not Proscribe an Award of Attorney Fees to an Out-of-state Attorney for Services Rendered on Behalf of an Out-of-state Client Regardless of Whether the Attorney Is Either Physically or Virtually Present Within the State of California.*

[The court here describes the facts and the Court's holding in the *Birbower* case]

Implicit in the court's formulation of the rule is the ingredient that the client is a "California client," one that either resides in or has its principal place of business in California. This conclusion is not only logical, it comports with the reason underlying the proscription of section 6125.

In the real world of 1998 we do not live or do business in isolation within strict geopolitical boundaries. Social interaction and the conduct of business transcends state and national boundaries; it is truly global. A tension is thus created between the right of a party to have counsel of his or her choice and the right of each geopolitical entity to control the activities of those who practice law within its borders. In resolving the issue of the applicability of section 6125 it is useful to look to the reason underlying the proscription of section 6125. *Birbrower* instructs that the rationale is to protect California citizens from incompetent attorneys stating: "California is not alone in regulating who practices law in its jurisdiction. Many states have substantially similar statutes that serve to *protect their citizens* from unlicensed attorneys who engage in unauthorized legal practice. Like section 6125, these other state statutes protect local citizens 'against the dangers of legal representation and advice given by persons not trained, examined and licensed for such work, whether they be laymen or lawyers from other jurisdictions.' Whether an attorney is duly admitted in another state and is, in fact, competent to practice in California is irrelevant in the face of section 6125's language and *purpose*.

It is therefore obvious that, given the facts before us, the client's residence or its principal place of business is determinative of the question of whether the practice is proscribed by section 6125. Clearly the State of California has no interest in disciplining an out-of-state attorney practicing law on behalf of a client residing in the lawyer's home state.[3]

3. *The Applicability of the Birbrower Guidelines to This Case.*

It is apparent that both the facts and the issues in *Birbrower* are distinguishable from those presented in this case. Most significantly Michael R. Condon was a resident of the State of Colorado. Thus, the issue was not "whether an out-of-state law firm, not licensed to practice law in this state, violated section 6125, when it performed legal services in California for a *California-based client* ..." (*Birbrower, supra, 17 Cal.4th at p. 124),* but whether an out-of-state law firm practicing law on behalf of a resident of the lawyer's home state violated section 6125 when that lawyer either physically or virtually entered the State of California and practiced law on behalf of that client. Adopting the premise, as articulated in *Birbrower*, that the goal of section 6125 is to protect California citizens from incompetent or unscrupulous practitioners of law we must conclude that section 6125 is simply not applicable to our case.

The Elrod firm was retained by Michael to represent him in his capacity as coexecutor of the estate of Evelyn J. Condon. The firm's primary representation involved the implementation of the buy/sell agreement which was part of an estate plan drafted by the firm in Colorado. Its services involved the negotiation, settlement and drafting of documents resolving the dispute among the heirs of the estate leading to the sale of the estate's principal asset, the family business. The negotiation and discussion with beneficiaries of the estate and their attorneys in California occurred for the most part by phone, fax and mail while the attorneys were physically located in Colorado. It appears that communication between Michael and the Elrod firm took place entirely within Colorado.

Under *Birbrower* one of the factors to be considered by the court in determining the applicability of section 6125 is whether the practitioner is plying "California law." Nevertheless, our Supreme Court instructs that a person does not automatically practice law "in California" whenever that person practices "California law" anywhere. (*Birbrower, supra, 17 Cal.4th at p. 129.)* In the matter before this court there is no record reflecting that Katz was practicing "California law." Furthermore, that factor is not relevant to our holding. If indeed the goal of the statute is to protect California citizens from the incompetent and unscrupulous

3. This, of course, does not apply to attorneys physically coming into California to practice law in our courts.

practitioner (licensed or unlicensed), it simply should make no difference whether the out-of-state lawyer is practicing California law or some other breed since the impact of incompetence on the client is precisely the same.

* * * Furthermore, it is insular to assume that only California lawyers can be trained in California law. Surely the citizens of states outside of California should not have to retain California lawyers to advise them on California law. Finally, the fact that California law was not implicated in the Elrod firm's representation of Michael R. Condon provides us additional impetus to conclude that the policy of protecting California citizens from untrained and incompetent attorneys has not been breached.

For the reasons stated herein we hold that Katz and the Elrod firm (licensed to practice law in Colorado) did not practice law "in California" within the meaning of section 6125 when its members entered California either physically or virtually to practice law on behalf of Michael (a Colorado citizen).

In light of the foregoing, we conclude that appellants did not violate our Business and Professions Code. Katz and the Elrod firm are, therefore, entitled under the Probate Code to ordinary statutory fees and to extraordinary fees in whatever amount the court deems reasonable for any services he rendered to Michael in his capacity as co-executor.

[Respondent's petition for review by the Supreme Court was denied November 4, 1998].

FOUGHT & COMPANY, INC. v. STEEL ENGINEERING AND ERECTION, INC.

87 Hawai'i 37, 951 P.2d 487 (1998)

OPINION OF THE COURT BY LEVINSON, J.

* * *

I.   BACKGROUND

The lawsuit underlying the present requests for attorneys' fees and costs arose out of the construction of a new terminal building, phase I, unit 2, at the Kahului Airport, Kahului, Maui, designated as project No. AM1042–13 (the project). Kiewit was general contractor for the project. Kiewit subcontracted with Steel for the supply and erection of structural steel components for the project. Steel in turn contracted with Fought to supply materials pursuant to Steel's subcontract with Kiewit.

After a dispute arose pertaining to the correct interpretation of provisions in the project specifications, the [Hawaii Department of Transportation (DOT)] claimed that Fought, Steel, and Kiewit had all breached their respective contracts by providing and/or utilizing nonconforming steel and, accordingly, withheld $312,000.00 in compensation for the alleged breach from its payments to Kiewit. As a result, Kiewit withheld $312,000.00 under its subcontract with Steel, and Steel with-held the same amount from its payment to Fought.

Fought then filed suit, seeking payment of the $312,000.00 from Steel. Steel cross-claimed against Kiewit, and Kiewit cross-claimed against the DOT. As a result of motions for summary judgment filed by Fought, Steel, and Kiewit, judgments were entered in favor of Fought and against Steel, in favor of Steel and against Kiewit, and in favor of Kiewit and against the DOT.

* * * [T]his court affirmed all of the orders and judgments of the circuit court in a summary disposition order[.] , which was filed on July 28, 1997. Having been mooted, Kiewit's and Steel's cross-appeals were not addressed * * *

In opposition to Fought's request for fees, Steel argues that [,*inter alia,*] fees for the services of Fought's retained general counsel, who [is] licensed to practice law in Oregon where Fought is headquartered and assisted Fought's attorneys in Hawai'i in the preparation of the appeal, are not recoverable pursuant to the provisions of *HRS § 607–14* [,which authorizes the award of attorneys' fees to prevailing party in legal proceeding] * * *

II.   DISCUSSION

[We must address the issue] whether, pursuant to the provisions of *HRS § 607–14*, a prevailing party may recover the fees of attorneys who, although licensed in another jurisdiction, assist local attorneys in con-ducting litigation in the courts of Hawai'i * * *

A.   Fees Of Attorneys Who Are Licensed And Perform Services In Other Jurisdictions And Who Assist Attorneys Licensed In Hawai'i In The Prosecution Of Litigation In The Courts Of Hawai'i Are Recoverable Pursuant To The Provisions Of *HRS § 607–14*.

Both Steel and the DOT argue that Fought's request for taxation of the fees of Kobin and Kobin (Kobin), its retained general counsel, must be denied, inasmuch as no member of that firm is licensed to practice law in this jurisdiction, and such an award would therefore violate the public policy embodied in *HRS §§ 605–14* (1993) and 605–17, which respectively prohibit and criminalize the practice of law without a license, except in instances in which an attorney licensed to practice in some other jurisdiction has been admitted pro hac vice for the purpose of participating in a specific case. It is uncontested that Kobin did not appear in any Hawai'i court on Fought's behalf. However, it is not apparent that "the practice of law," as contemplated by *HRS §§ 605–14* and 605–17, is limited to court appearances. Accordingly, in order to determine the merits of this argument, we must first determine whether the attorneys' fees sought for Fought's general counsel were incurred for the performance of services that comprise "the practice of law," as that phrase is contemplated in the relevant statutes * * *

In the present matter, Kobin was engaged in such activity as consultation with Fought and Fought's Hawai'i counsel regarding the appeal, preparation of Fought's statement of position in anticipation of mediation, assisting Fought's Hawai'i counsel with legal research, analysis of briefs and papers submitted by other parties to the litigation, resolution of issues pertaining to the posting of Steel's supersedeas bond, planning Fought's strategy for the appeal, and reviewing and critiquing the briefs and other papers prepared by Fought's Hawai'i counsel. It is apparent that Kobin was "practicing law" when it engaged in these activities.

However, this determination does not end our inquiry. *HRS § 1–4* (1993) provides in relevant part that "the laws [of Hawai'i] are obligatory upon all persons ... within the jurisdiction of the State." Hence, the restrictions of *HRS §§ 605–14* and 605–17 are applicable to legal services rendered Kobin only if those services were rendered "within the jurisdiction." The question as to what constitutes the practice of law "within the jurisdiction" is one of first impression, the resolution of which must adequately address "the tension that exists between interjurisdictional practice and the need to have a state-regulated bar." *Birbrower, 17 Cal.4th 119, at 129 (Cal. 1998).*

The foregoing consideration [is] germane to ascertaining the scope of *HRS §§ 605–14* and 605–17, particularly in light of the legislature's expressed disinclination to define the "practice of law" in the face of "new developments in society, whether legislative, social, or scientific in nature, [which] continually create new concepts and new legal problems." While the scope of these statutes must be expansive enough to afford the public needed protection from incompetent legal advice and counsel, the transformation of our economy from a local to a global one has general compelling policy reasons for refraining from adopting an application so broad that a law firm, which is located outside the state of Hawai'i, may automatically be deemed to have practiced law "within the jurisdiction" merely by advising a client regarding the effect of Hawai'i law or by "virtually entering" the jurisdiction on behalf of a client via "telephone, fax, computer, or other modern technological means." See *Birbrower, 17 Cal.4th at 128–129.* A case such as this—involving parties domiciled in at least five different jurisdictions—only emphasizes what seems intuitively obvious: a commercial entity that serves interstate and/or international markets is likely to receive more effective and efficient representation when its general counsel, who is based close to its home office or headquarters and is familiar with the details of its operations, supervises the work of local counsel in each of the various jurisdictions in which it does business. Undoubtedly, many Hawai'i corporations follow the same practice.

A blanket rule prohibiting the taxing of fees for the services of extrajurisdictional legal counsel who assist local counsel in the conduct of litigation among parties, who are themselves domiciled in different jurisdictions, would be an imprudent rule at best. At a minimum, the result would be to increase the total cost of legal representation and to magnify the difficulty of controlling multijurisdictional litigation. Moreover, such a rule might also create an incentive for ethical violations, inasmuch as Hawai'i Rules of Professional Conduct (HRPC) Rule 1.1 mandates that "[a] lawyer shall provide competent representation to a client." In many instances involving complex litigation among parties domiciled in different jurisdictions, competent representation undoubtedly requires consultation with legal counsel licensed to practice in another jurisdiction. To prohibit an award of fees for these services would only undermine the policies underlying *HRS §§ 605–14* and 605–17, which were enacted to protect the public against incompetence ...

In fashioning a test for what constituted the practice of law "in California," the court in *Birbrower* court reasoned that

> the practice of law "in California" entails sufficient contact with the California client to render the nature of the legal service a clear legal representation. In addition to a quantitative analysis, we must consider the nature of the unlicensed lawyer's activities in the state. Mere fortuitous or attenuated contacts will not sustain a finding that the unlicensed lawyer practiced law "in California." The primary inquiry is whether the unlicensed lawyer engaged in sufficient activities in the state, or created a continuing relationship with the California client that included legal duties and obligations.

17 Cal.4th at 128.

Considering Kobin's activities in light of the factors suggested by Birbrower, we hold that it did not practice law "within the jurisdiction," that is, "in Hawai'i," and, therefore, that it was not subject to the restrictions imposed by *HRS §§ 605–14* and 605–17. Fought and Kobin are both located in Oregon. Hence, Kobin did not represent a "Hawai'i client." Furthermore, all of the services rendered by Kobin were performed in Oregon, where the firm's attorneys are licensed. Kobin did not draft or sign any of the papers filed during the appeal, did not appear in court, and did not communicate with counsel for other parties on Fought's behalf. Finally, Kobin's role was strictly one of consultant to Fought and Fought's Hawai'i counsel. We are convinced that Fought's Hawai'i counsel were at all times "in charge" of Fought's representation within the jurisdiction so as to insure that Hawai'i law was correctly interpreted and applied. While Kobin undoubtedly contributed to the successful completion of the litigation in this case by its collaborative effort with Fought's Hawai'i counsel, we cannot say, on the record before us, that Kobin rendered any legal services "within the jurisdiction." Because Kobin's law practice in Oregon is not regulated by Hawai'i law, it is apparent that Kobin did not violate *HRS §§ 605–14* and 605–17 or the public policy embodied by those statutes in rendering legal services to Fought. Accordingly, the statutes do not bar Fought's recovery of fees for services rendered by Kobin in the present matter.

AMERICAN BAR ASSOCIATION, CLIENT REPRESENTATION IN THE TWENTY-FIRST CENTURY

REPORT OF THE COMMISSION
ON MULTIJURISDICTIONAL PRACTICE

2002

* * *

Summary of Recommendations

"Multijurisdictional practice" ("MJP") describes the legal work of a lawyer in a jurisdiction in which the lawyer is not admitted to practice law. As this report discusses, a wide variety of practices falling within this rubric have been called to the attention of the MJP Commission. The guiding principle that informs the Commission's recommendations is simple to state: we searched for the proper balance between the interests of a state in protecting its residents and justice system, on the one hand; and the interests of clients in a national and international economy in the ability to employ or retain counsel of choice efficiently and economically. A key word here is "balance." Our challenges did not lend themselves to mathematical solutions. Rather, accommodating our state-based system of bar admission, which we fully support, with the realities of modern life and our tradition of respect for client choice required the exercise of informed judgment. Our judgment was informed not only by the diverse experience and perspectives of the members of the Commission and its liaisons, but also by the wealth of testimony, written and spoken, of which we have been the most fortunate beneficiary.

Following is a summary of the Commission's recommendations:

1. The American Bar Association affirms its support for the principle of state judicial regulation of the practice of law. (*See* Recommendation 1, *infra*.)

2. The American Bar Association amends the title of Rule 5.5 of the ABA *Model Rules of Professional Conduct* as "Unauthorized Practice of Law; Multijurisdictional Practice of Law".

The American Bar Association amends Rule 5.5(a) of the ABA *Model Rules of Professional Conduct* to provide that a lawyer may not practice law in a jurisdiction, or assist another in doing so, in violation of the regulations of the legal profession in that jurisdiction.

The American Bar Association adopts amended Rule 5.5(b) to prohibit a lawyer from establishing an office or other systematic and continuous presence in a jurisdiction, unless permitted to do so by law, or another provision of Rule 5.5; or holding out to the public or otherwise representing that the lawyer is admitted to practice law in a jurisdiction in which the lawyer is not admitted.

The American Bar Association adopts Rule 5.5(c) to identify circumstances in which a lawyer who is admitted in a United States jurisdiction, and not disbarred or suspended from practice in any jurisdiction, may practice law on a temporary basis in another jurisdiction. These would include:

- Work on a temporary basis in association with a lawyer admitted to practice law in the jurisdiction, who actively participates in the representation;

- Services ancillary to pending or prospective litigation or administrative agency proceedings in a state where the lawyer is admitted or expects to be admitted *pro hac vice* or is otherwise authorized to appear;

- Representation of clients in, or ancillary to, an alternative dispute resolution ("ADR") setting, such as arbitration or mediation; and

- Non-litigation work that arises out of or is reasonably related to the lawyer's practice in a jurisdiction in which the lawyer is admitted to practice.

The American Bar Association adopts Rule 5.5(d) to identify multijurisdictional practice standards relating to (i) legal services by a lawyer who is an employee of a client and (ii) legal services that the lawyer is authorized by federal or other law to render in a jurisdiction in which the lawyer is not licensed to practice law.

3. The American Bar Association adopts amended Rule 8.5 of the ABA *Model Rules of Professional Conduct* in order to clarify the authority of a jurisdiction to discipline lawyers licensed in another jurisdiction who practice law within their jurisdiction pursuant to the provisions of Rule 5.5 or other law.

PROBLEMS

1. Omnicorp is a manufacturer of household products that is based in Atlanta and has offices throughout the United States. About two years ago, Omnicare was involved in a dispute with one of its senior managers about the compensation and benefits to which the manager was entitled upon his departure from the company. Omnicare hired the law firm of Reese & Ahmed (R&A) to represent it in the litigation that ensued. R&A is a law firm based in Dallas, with offices in Washington, D.C. and Chicago. R&A litigators drew upon advice from the firm's Employment Law Practice Group in brokering a settlement that the company regarded as very favorable.

In the course of the dispute, R&A advised Omnicare executives that Alabama law is especially favorable to employers with respect to their employment contracts with managerial personnel. The firm suggested that the company relocate its Human Resources Department to Birmingham, Alabama, and provide that henceforth employment contracts with its 250 or so senior managers would be governed by Alabama law. Omnicare did so. The company also decided to retain R&A's Dallas office to negotiate all its new senior manager employment contracts and to represent the company in any disputes over contracts of managers who leave the company. This requires occasional visits by R&A lawyers to Birmingham and Atlanta. None of the R&A lawyers are members of the bar in either Alabama or Georgia.

The Birmingham law firm of Cash & Burns recently has filed a petition with the Alabama Bar Association alleging that R&A is engaged in the unauthorized practice of law in Alabama.

Assume that Alabama has adopted Model Rule 5.5. How should the case be decided?

Assume that Alabama has not adopted Model Rule 5.5. How should the case be decided under *Birbower*? Under *Condon*? Which approach is preferable?

Omnicare plans to enter negotiations to license a company in California to distribute a line of its products. Omnicare wants R&A's Dallas office to handle the negotiations. None of the lawyers in that office are members of the California bar. If California has adopted Rule 5.5, would R&A violate it if the licensing agreement were to be governed by California law? What if Omnicare wants its deputy general counsel, who is in the headquarters office and is a member of the Georgia bar, to negotiate the agreement?

2. You work for the Los Angeles office of a law firm with offices in several cities in the United States. You are a member of both the California and New Jersey bars, since you previously practiced in the firm's New Jersey office.

You are representing Mediastream, a small California electronic entertainment company, in a deal involving the sale of Mediastream to IdKing, a company based in New Jersey. Another lawyer from your firm's New Jersey office is working with you on the transaction. At a meeting in New Jersey with Mediastream officials prior to closing the deal, Mediastream's Chief Financial Officer (CFO) mentions to you privately that the company is likely to default on some of its major contracts because of problems with some of its new software. Such defaults would reduce Mediastream's future stream of revenues and lower the value of the company, and therefore could materially affect the price at which the company is sold to IdKing. Nonetheless, the CFO indicates that Mediastream plans to proceed with the sale without disclosing this information.

California bar rules provide that a member of the bar is permitted to disclose confidential information only in order to "prevent a criminal act that the member reasonably believes is likely to result in death of, or substantial bodily harm to, an individual." New Jersey requires that a bar member disclose confidential information to prevent a client "from committing a criminal or fraudulent act" likely to result in, *inter alia*, "substantial injury to the financial interest or property of another." Assume that both California and New Jersey have adopted Model Rule 8.5 as written.

What, if anything, should you do?

Chapter 12

CONFIDENTIALITY

The circumstances in which a lawyer has a duty of confidentiality, and the occasions on which that duty may or must give way to other concerns, evokes perhaps the most vigorous discussion of any issue in legal ethics. Those who argue for expansive confidentiality claim that assuring it encourages clients to be candid with their lawyers. In the litigation context, this can be important because a client reluctant to trust his lawyer may withhold information that the client does not realize is legally relevant to his defense.

In settings outside of litigation, such as providing legal advice, the argument is that strict confidentiality furthers legal compliance. Clients who need not fear disclosure of what they tell their lawyers are likely to let lawyers know of all courses of action they are contemplating—including those that may run afoul of the law. This gives the lawyer the opportunity to dissuade the client from illegal behavior and to suggest alternative ways to accomplish the client's goals. The lawyer might not have this opportunity, proponents claim, if the client were concerned that the lawyer might report what he said to the authorities. Such a concern is especially important for lawyers advising corporations about their legal obligations.

Those who argue for a narrower duty of confidentiality maintain that the duty too often is used as a shield that effectively protects those who engage in wrongdoing. They question the assumptions of those who maintain that the duty should be only narrowly qualified. In corporate representation in particular, they suggest, companies must constantly consider the legal ramifications of the actions that they take. As a result, they cannot afford to be less than candid with their lawyers, because doing so risks suffering significant adverse legal consequences. This claim has some support in the few empirical studies of the privilege in corporate representation.

Proponents of greater disclosure authority also assert that lawyers will be more effective in ensuring legal compliance if corporate clients know that their lawyers have the option of blowing the whistle. The large percentage of companies who intend to comply with the law will be candid with their lawyers because they have nothing to fear. Those who are contemplating illegal conduct, however, either would not consult their lawyers in the first place, or are unlikely to be dissuaded unless the threat of disclosure is in the background.

As the Overview indicates, the material in this Chapter is designed mainly to make clear when information can be protected from disclosure, and to highlight the special considerations that come into play in determining this in the corporate context. Problems in other Chapters throughout the book will present situations in which the corporate lawyer must weigh confidentiality concerns along with other considerations in deciding how to proceed.

OVERVIEW OF THE CHAPTER

The material in this Chapter clarifies that a lawyer may have a duty to keep information confidential based on three different bodies of law. First is the *attorney-client privilege,* which is part of the law of evidence. The privilege protects from disclosure in a legal proceeding communications between attorney and client. Outside of a legal proceeding, the lawyer's obligation is to preserve the ability of the client to assert the privilege, by ensuring that all privileged information remains confidential. The classic statement of the elements of the privilege is by John Wigmore:

> (1) Where legal advice of any kind is sought (2) from a professional advisor in his capacity as such, (3) the communications relating to that purpose (4) made in confidence (5) by the client (6) are at his instance permanently protected (7) from disclosure by himself or the legal advisor, (8) except the privilege be waived.[1]

As the excerpt from John Villa describes, the U.S. Supreme Court in *Upjohn Co. v. United States,* 449 U.S. 383 (1981), held that corporations are entitled to assert the attorney-client privilege for certain communications between its employees and counsel for the corporation. In such instances, it is the entity, rather than any of its employees, that holds the privilege.

The client is deemed to waive the privilege if it acts in a way that suggests that it does not regard the communication as confidential, such as disclosing it to a third party. In addition, communications are not privileged if the client seeks legal advice with the intention to use the lawyer's services to commit a crime or fraud in the future. In such an instance, it is the intent of the client, not the lawyer, that determines if the privilege is available.

---

1. John H. Wigmore, 8 Wigmore on Evidence section 2292 at 554 (John T. McNaughton rev. ed. 1961).

Recall the material in Chapter 6 on in-house counsel that describes how corporate lawyers commonly provide a mixture of business and legal advice. The *Simon* case underscores that the attorney-client privilege protects only communications conducted for the purpose of obtaining legal advice. Communications relating to business matters are not privileged. Routing regular company reports to lawyers therefore does not by itself bring them within the privilege. Is it feasible to distinguish between business and legal advice in the course of lawyers' communications with corporate managers and employees? Should courts adopt a rebuttable presumption that mixed advice is or is not protected by the privilege?

A second excerpt from Villa makes clear that the corporation may not be able to assert the privilege against shareholders who are plaintiffs in certain shareholder derivative actions. The *Valente* case illustrates how courts have expanded this doctrine beyond derivative cases. Ask yourself what general principle seems to explain the expansion, and what its limits might be.

The second basis for protecting information from disclosure is the *work product doctrine*, recognized by the Supreme Court in *Hickman v. Taylor*, 329 U.S. 495 (1947) and codified in Federal Rule of Civil Procedure 26. This doctrine applies to material that is prepared in anticipation of litigation, by the lawyer or by someone at her behest. The test for waiver of work product protection is more stringent than for waiver of the attorney-client privilege. The issue is whether disclosure of the work product enhances the ability of an adversary to gain access to the information.

A second excerpt from the *Simon* case illustrates how courts may distinguish between work product and records kept for the purpose of business planning. The *Adlman* case reflects a decision by the Second Circuit, over a dissent, that grants work product protection to an analysis of the outcome of possible litigation that is used to make a business decision. Ask yourself how common this scenario is likely to be, and what the implications are of treating such analyses as work product.

Finally, state ethical rules impose a duty of confidentiality on lawyers. With limited exceptions that vary from state to state, a lawyer is prohibited from disclosing any information gained from any source during representation of a client. Unlike the attorney-client privilege and work product protection, this obligation applies in all settings, not simply in legal proceedings.

The first problem asks you to apply the reasoning in cases such as *Garner* and *Valente* to determine if the corporation should be entitled to assert the privilege against the plaintiff. The second problem requires you to analyze the facts to decide whether the report in question should be given work product protection in light of the decision in *Adlman*.

MODEL RULES: 1.6, 1.13(c)

A. ATTORNEY–CLIENT PRIVILEGE

John K. Villa, 1 CORPORATE COUNSEL GUIDELINES

(1999)

CHAPTER 1: THE ATTORNEY-CLIENT PRIVILEGE AND IN-HOUSE CORPORATE COUNSEL

§ 1.03 The Client—Who Speaks for the Client?

When a corporate employee walks into the office of in-house corporate counsel to ask about, or give information about, a legal problem, one of the first questions counsel should consider is whether the ensuing communications are likely to be covered by the attorney-client privilege—that is, is the employee, in this context, speaking for the corporation?

[B] Upjohn v. United States

The Supreme Court weighed in on this issue with its opinion in *Upjohn Co. v. United States. Upjohn* concerned an investigation by both in-house and outside counsel of payments by a foreign corporate subsidiary to foreign government officials. The company's general counsel sent questionnaires to corporate employees and then interviewed them. The IRS later sought discovery of both the questionnaires and memoranda of the interviews. The Supreme Court held that these documents were protected by the privilege because the employees were "acting as [employees], at the direction of corporate superiors in order to secure legal advice from counsel." The Supreme Court eschewed a strict control group test, or indeed any bright-line test at all. Rather, the Court held that the applicability of the privilege must be determined on a case-by-case basis, finding the following factors persuasive:

- the communications were made by employees to corporate counsel in order for the corporation to secure legal advice;

- the employees were cooperating with corporate counsel at the direction of corporate superiors;

- the communications concerned matters within the employees' scope of employment;

- the information was not available from upper-echelon management.

Upjohn does not, therefore, definitively resolve the issue of whose communications are protected, nor was that the Court's aim. While an objective test would prove a useful tool for counsel seeking to predict whether the privilege applies in any given situation, the Court chose a case-by-case approach to ensure the closest fit between the communications protected and the interests meant to be protected by the privilege. By using such an approach, the Court necessarily opted to trade a certain measure of predictability in the application of the law for an increased likelihood that the values underlying the privilege would be upheld. It is worth noting, though, that the list of factors considered by thé Court in its decision matches the key elements of the subject-matter test the Court ostensibly rejected. *Upjohn* is thus based on a model of the corporate attorney-client privilege that assumes that corporations will voluntarily comply with their legal responsibilities, and should be given the room to do so.

For in-house counsel hoping to determine the boundaries of the privilege, *Upjohn* unfortunately leaves many questions unanswered. Are the elements cited by the *Upjohn* court necessary predicates for the existence of the privilege in all cases, or simply factors to be considered when making a determination of privilege? It is clear, for example, that to ensure the protection of the privilege, counsel asked to conduct an investigation must document, with respect to each employee interviewed, that the corporation is seeking legal advice, and that management has expressly requested the cooperation of corporate employees. Yet, although a requirement that the communication concern matters within the employee's scope of employment has been called "the real heart of the *Upjohn* standard," few courts have explicitly held that the privilege is so limited. Neither is it clear whether a communication is privileged *only* if counsel can establish that the information is not available from higher level management.

Further, since *Upjohn* was specifically concerned with the extent of the privilege in corporate investigations, it says nothing directly applicable to the myriad other occasions in which in-house counsel deals with other corporate employees. On many of these occasions, there is no formal investigation, and no formal directive from management authorizing employees to speak to counsel. It would be reasonable to suppose that corporate employees have implied authority to speak to in-house counsel when they believe it is in the corporations's best interest to do so. The Ninth Circuit, for example, applies the privilege "to communications by any corporate employee regardless of position when the communications concern matter within the scope of the employee's corporate duties and the employee is aware that the information is being furnished to enable the attorney to provide legal advice to the corporation." Not all courts, though, have been willing to make this supposition. Perhaps eager to establish some clear bounds for the corporate privilege, some courts have denied the privilege to communications not made at the specific direction of corporate superiors. The Restatement takes a broad view, holding such a requirement unnecessary, as long as the communication concerns a legal matter of interest to the corporation.

Upjohn's holding is also limited to its forum, the federal courts; many states have not adopted the *Upjohn* test. Other states follow some form of the "control group" test. In yet other states, the extent of the privilege is governed by different common law rules, or by statute. If the corporation does considerable business in a state that still uses the control group test, counsel should consider that in a state court proceeding, it is highly unlikely that communications with anyone outside the control group will be deemed privileged. Even in a jurisdiction following *Upjohn,* when an employee acting alone walks into counsel's office without any direction from a corporate superior, counsel should be alert to the possibility that the ensuing communication may someday be discoverable.

To maximize chances that a given communication will be protected, counsel should strive to satisfy both the control group test and the *Upjohn* test wherever possible by meeting only with those who are authorized decision-makers within the corporate structure.

SIMON v. G.D. SEARLE & CO.

816 F.2d 397 (8th Cir. 1987)

WOLLMAN, Circuit Judge.

G.D. Searle & Co. appeals the district court's order permitting discovery of certain Searle documents. * * *

Searle manufactures an intrauterine contraceptive device known as the "Cu–7." Approximately forty products liability actions pending against Searle in the United States District Court for the District of Minnesota and seeking damages for injuries alleged to have resulted from use of the Cu–7 were consolidated for discovery and have generated this appeal. The district court appointed a special master to supervise the discovery process in these cases.

The district court originally ordered Searle to produce "each and every document contained in its files which relates to the Cu–7 IUD." Although Searle produced approximately 500,000 documents to appellees and has continued to provide documents, it resisted the discovery of certain documents from its risk management department. Searle's risk management department monitors the company's products liability litigation and analyzes its litigation reserves, apparently utilizing individual case reserve figures determined by the legal department's assessment of litigation expenses. The risk management department also has responsibility for the company's insurance coverage. * * *

The questions certified for appeal are as follows:

    1. To what extent, if any, should Searle's "Risk Management" documents, prepared by nonlawyer corporate officials in an attempt to keep track of, control and anticipate costs of product liability litigation for business planning purposes (including budgetary, profitability and insurance analysis), be protected from discovery by the Work Product Doctrine or the Minnesota attorney-client privilege because some portions of the documents reveal aggregate case reserves and aggregate litigation expenses for all pending cases when each individual case reserve is determined by Searle's lawyers on a confidential basis in anticipation of litigation?

* * *

III

ATTORNEY-CLIENT PRIVILEGE

Searle * * * argues that its risk management documents are protected by the attorney-client privilege. *Rule 501 of the Federal Rules of Evidence* provides that evidentiary privileges are to be determined in accordance with state law in diversity actions. Consequently, the Minnesota attorney-client privilege, codified at *Minn. Stat. Ann. § 595.02 subd. 1(b)* (West Supp. 1987), is applicable here.

The risk management documents reflect attorney-client communications running in two directions. First, the aggregate reserve information contained in the documents incorporates the individual case reserve figures communicated by the legal department to the risk management department—an attorney-to-client communication. Second, the record indicates that some of the risk management documents themselves were delivered to Searle attorneys—a client-to-attorney communication.

Assuming *arguendo* that the attorney-client privilege attaches to the individual case reserve figures communicated by the legal department to the risk management department,[1] we do not believe the privilege in turn attaches to the risk management documents simply because they include aggregate information based on the individual case reserve figures. For the reasons that we have already stated in relation to the work product doctrine, we do not believe that the aggregate information discloses the privileged communications, which we are assuming the individual reserve figures represent, to a degree that makes the aggregate information privileged.[2] The attorney-to-client communications reflected in the risk management documents are therefore not protected by the attorney-client privilege.

Although the aggregate reserve information does not confer attorney-client privilege protection to the risk management documents, those documents that were given to Searle attorneys may still be privileged client-to-attorney communications. The special master devoted only a very brief discussion to this matter. * * * [T]he special master stated: "A business document is not made privileged by providing a copy to counsel. * * * Thus, those documents from one corporate officer to another with a copy sent to an attorney do not qualify as attorney client communications." We perceive no error in this statement of the law, which appears to have been carefully applied by the special master to the

1. We state no view whether the attorney-client privilege in fact attaches to the individual case reserve figures, other than to note that such a determination would require analysis of whether the individual reserve figures are based on confidential information provided by Searle. We need not decide whether the individual case reserve figures are protected in the light of our determination that even if they are it does not follow that the aggregate informa-tion in the risk management documents also is protected.

2. When a client acts on privileged information from his attorney, the results are protected from discovery to the extent that they disclose the privileged matter, directly or inferentially. Our holding is faithful to this principle. As we have discussed, the individual case reserve figures cannot be traced or inferred from the aggregate information.

point of redacting sections of privileged material from within individual documents.

Minnesota adheres to Professor Wigmore's classic statement of the attorney-client privilege, which requires that an attorney-client communication relate to the purpose of obtaining legal advice before it is protected. Moreover, a number of courts have determined that the attorney-client privilege does not protect client communications that relate only business or technical data. *See First Wis. Mortgage Trust v. First Wis. Corp., 86 F.R.D. 160, 174 (E.D. Wis. 1980); SCM Corp. v. Xerox Corp., 70 F.R.D. 508, 515* (D. Conn.) ("legal departments are not citadels in which public, business or technical information may be placed to defeat discovery and thereby ensure confidentiality"), *appeal dismissed, 534 F.2d 1031 (2d Cir. 1976).* Just as the minutes of business meetings attended by attorneys are not automatically privileged, business documents sent to corporate officers and employees, as well as the corporation's attorneys, do not become privileged automatically. Searle argues, however, that the special master formulated a *per se* rule barring privilege claims where a document is sent to corporate officials in addition to attorneys. We do not read the special master's report as establishing such an approach. Client communications intended to keep the attorney apprised of business matters may be privileged if they embody "an implied request for legal advice based thereon." Based on this view of the special master's report, we do not understand the district court to have taken an errant position on the law of the attorney-client privilege. Having stated the applicable law, and noting that there are only six sample documents before us, we decline any invitation to determine the applicability of the privilege to individual documents.

John K. Villa, 1 Corporate Counsel Guidelines

(1999)

§ 1.27   Waiver and Loss of Privilege—The *Garner* Doctrine

For the most part, courts have applied the attorney-client privilege to the corporate client using the same model they use for individual clients, and accommodating the unique problems posed by such an application by tinkering with, but not changing that basic model. In 1970, the Fifth Circuit stepped outside this paradigm to confront head-on some of the concerns raised by applying the privilege to the corporate client in *Garner v. Wolfinbarger. Garner* concerned a shareholder derivative suit charging management with fraud, and a direct suit charging fraud and violations of security laws. When the shareholders sought discovery of communications between management and the corporation's attorneys, the corporation asserted the privilege. Recognizing the tension between protecting the integrity of managerial decision-making and the interests of the shareholders, who ultimately own the client, the court went back to basics:

The privilege must be placed in perspective. The beginning point is the fundamental principle that the public has the right to every man's evidence, and exemptions from the general duty to give testimony that one is capable of giving are distinctly exceptional.

The court noted that such an exception requires a balancing of "the injury that would inure to the relation by the disclosure of the communications" with the benefit gained "for the correct disposal of litigation." In balancing those interests, the court identified the following non-exclusive list of factors as worthy of consideration:

> the number of shareholders and the percentage of stock they represent; the bona fides of the shareholders; the nature of the shareholders' claim and whether it is obviously colorable; the apparent necessity or desirability of the shareholders having the information and the availability of it from other sources; whether, if the shareholders' claim is of wrongful action by the corporation, it is of action criminal, or illegal but not criminal, or of doubtful legality; whether the communication related to past or to prospective actions; whether the communication is of advice concerning the litigation itself; the extent to which the communication is identified versus the extent to which the shareholders are blindly fishing; the risk of revelation of trade secrets or other information in whose confidentiality the corporation has an interest for independent reasons.

Several policy considerations provide the underpinning for *Garner*. *Garner* is an attempt to ensure that corporate information not be kept from the shareholders who are, in principle, the owners of the corporation, and that questions of when it is appropriate to waive the privilege are decided by a disinterested tribunal. Since this decision, *Garner* has become the accepted law, and has even been applied to permit discovery by employees of a former subsidiary of a defendant corporation in an action under the Employee Retirement Income Security Act (ERISA). *Garner* applies equally to communications with an outside corporate law firm or with house counsel. "Public disclosure of the existence of an internal corporate investigation, or the results of such an investigation, frequently gives rise to shareholder litigation. Ironically, it is this predictable consequence of investigative activity that renders the attorney-client privilege most vulnerable. This weakness is created by the *Garner* rule."

How many shareholders, owning how much stock, are suing?

The first factor to consider in determining whether there exists "good cause" for disregarding the privilege is the size of the plaintiff class, both in terms of the percentage of shareholders, and the percentage of stock they own. A small percentage, though not necessarily fatal to the claim, will certainly weigh against a finding of good cause. Courts have held that a plaintiff class owning 15 or 40 percent of stock supports a finding of good cause to overcome the privilege.

What are the bona fides of the shareholders, the nature of their claim, and is it obviously colorable?

Garner was based on a recognition that there is a "sufficient mutuality of interest between management and shareholders in communications with attorneys to bar any assertion by management alone of an absolute privilege against the shareholders." In any shareholder suit, there is a possibility that the interests of the shareholders will not align perfectly with the interests of the corporation; *Garner* is not limited to cases where those interests are perfectly aligned. Even in a derivative action against management charging the corporation with illegal acts,

> the interests of the corporation at such time are not necessarily coincidental with shareholder plaintiffs complaining of past misconduct. The Plaintiff class is frozen when corporation wrongdoing ends. From that time on, the class interest are adverse to the corporation which has allegedly defrauded it, and possibly adverse to nonparty shareholders as well.

For such a derivative claim, the strength of plaintiffs' "bona fides" may allow for a finding of good cause even though other factors are only marginally established.

For other claims, the tension between the plaintiff class' interests and those of the corporation appear in greater relief. Thus, when shareholder-plaintiffs bring a non-derivative action, seeking recovery for themselves only, their motives are more suspect than if they bring a derivative action, and *Garner* requires the court to subject such claims to "careful scrutiny." Although the non-derivative nature of the claim weighs heavily against a finding of good cause, not all courts consider it fatal; it is still just one factor to be considered in determining whether the privilege should be upheld in any particular case.

Is there a legitimate need for the information and is it available from other sources?

Another factor that weighs heavily in the good cause determination is whether the information is both needed and unavailable from other sources. Merely alleging a claim that includes the element of scienter—for example, that a corporation acted in bad faith—is insufficient to establish a need for the information under *Garner*; "[o]therwise all fraud claims would pry open the privilege for shareholder indulgence."

Further, if the information is available from other sources, it is unlikely that a court will find good cause to pierce the privilege. To establish the unavailability of the information, the plaintiff class must at least make an effort to obtain the information from other sources, particularly where it may have been known by other corporate employees or contained in other business documents. Nor is relevance of the privileged communication the correct criteria—where the plaintiff class has obtained a final corporate report, earlier drafts of that report, though relevant, are not "necessary."

Are there allegations of criminal or illegal behavior?

Allegations of criminal or illegal behavior give some support to finding of good cause, but allegations that do not rise to the level of statutory violations will probably not be enough.

Do the communications concern past or prospective actions?

Communications between a corporation alleged to have committed an offense and an attorney acting in his professional capacity to represent the corporation in proceedings involving that offense deserve particular solicitude. Such after-the-fact communications with counsel are not subject to disclosure under *Garner* because "[f]orced disclosure of counsel's remedial advice would do great injury to the corporation's interest in self-investigation and preparation for litigation." Where the communications concern future actions, this factor supports a finding of good cause, particularly where the communication is "strongly related to the breach of fiduciary duties at issue."

Do the communications include advice concerning the litigation itself?

If the sole purpose of a communication is to consult regarding litigation strategy concerning the same proceedings in which the *Garner* claim is made, this factor weighs strongly against a finding of good cause. Otherwise, "a corporation and its directors could never effectively defend themselves in legal proceedings commenced by shareholders since they could not obtain confidential legal advice." In this way, *Garner* recognizes the legitimate interest of an organization in resisting a derivative or similar claim, but this factor does not reach beyond this situation to reach all communications that might be immunized under the attorney work product doctrine.

Is this a fishing expedition?

If a court feels that the plaintiffs are merely "fishing," it is unlikely to find good cause to set aside the privilege.

What is the risk of revelation of trade secrets or other comparable information?

The risk that piercing the privilege will reveal trade secrets, or other analogous information in whose confidentiality the corporation has an interest for independent reasons, is a factor that militates against a finding of good cause.

Additional considerations

Some courts have identified another factor significant to a finding of good cause beyond those explicitly set forth in *Garner*. In *Sandberg v. Virginia Bankshares, Inc.,* the Fourth Circuit considered a claim of privilege for communications made during a meeting between officers of a corporation and its counsel, at which the counsel and officers for a third party corporation were also present. The meeting was called to discusses a shareholder's action to stop a proposed merger between the corporation's subsidiary and the third party. Assuming that the corporate parties had common interest sufficient to permit such a meeting without loss of the privilege, the court nevertheless held that *Garner* required the production of the notes taken at the meeting. In addition to the factors listed in *Garner,* the court found that "[t]he shareholders' interest is particularly strong" where the communications at issue were shared with counsel for a third party "whose interests are potentially adverse to those of the executive's shareholders."

VALENTE v. PEPSICO, INC.

68 F.R.D. 361 (D. Del. 1975)

WRIGHT, SENIOR JUDGE.

This is a class action brought by plaintiffs, who represent the minority shareholders and warrant holders of Wilson Sporting Goods Co. ("Wilson"). The case arises from the efforts of the plaintiffs originally to enjoin, and presently to seek damages, arising from the merger of Wilson into the defendant PepsiCo. ("PepsiCo"). PepsiCo became, in February, 1970, the majority shareholder in Wilson, by the purchase of a block of stock amounting to approximately 74% of the outstanding shares. Between that time and December, 1972, PepsiCo, through its officers, considered various methods and took various actions resulting in the eventual merger of Wilson into PepsiCo under the Delaware Short Form Merger Statute. As part of the accomplishment of the merger, the minority shareholders in Wilson were offered $17.50 in cash for their shares. In addition, outstanding obligations of Wilson included a series of warrants, giving the holder the right to purchase a share of Wilson for $20.50, the option period running through 1978. As part of the merger proposal, the holders of the warrants were offered $3.50 for each warrant. The minority shareholders and warrant holders brought this action claiming that certain representations made by the defendant PepsiCo and its officers were untrue; that the arrangement offered to the plaintiffs was unfair; and otherwise charging violations of SEC Rule 10(b)(5) and the Securities Act of 1934, as well as pendent claims of fraud.

This motion is brought by the plaintiffs to compel the production in discovery of certain documents to which the defendant objects, raising grounds of relevance and attorney-client privilege. * * * For the reasons discussed, *infra,* this Court holds that the documents are relevant, and that due to the circumstances of this case, the attorney-client privilege does not attach. The documents are therefore discoverable by the plaintiffs.

A. FACTS NECESSARY TO DECISION.

Prior to discussing the issues of relevancy and privilege, it is important to note the complex intertwining of relationships which make up this case. The Court notes initially that at the time of the events in

question, PepsiCo owned some 74% of the stock, and through that
ownership exercised some control over the affairs of Wilson. It is
undisputed that various officers of PepsiCo sat on the Board of Wilson,
and that Wilson's officers were appointed at the direction of PepsiCo as
controlling shareholders. During this time, the general counsel of Pepsi-
Co, was among the PepsiCo officials who sat on the Board of Wilson.

As a result of its ownership of a controlling interest in Wilson,
PepsiCo owed a fiduciary obligation to Wilson and to the minority
shareholders. A similar fiduciary duty was, of course, also borne by the
members of the Board of Wilson including those who were PepsiCo
officers. Such a fiduciary obligation runs necessarily to protect the
interests of the minority from domination and overreaching by the
controlling shareholder.

The documents in issue here arise from efforts by PepsiCo, through
its house counsel, outside counsel and others, to determine the consequences of various alternative forms of merger of the two corporations.
Of particular relevance to PepsiCo were the tax consequences, since not
only did PepsiCo wish to keep its own tax burden as a result of the
merger as light as possible, but also sought to preserve certain tax
benefits which Wilson had. In so doing, PepsiCo had originally sought a
tax ruling from the IRS on one form of the merger, which it preferred. A
favorable ruling was not forthcoming, and the various opinions, communications and studies herein at issue seemingly arose from PepsiCo's
attempts to develop and select an alternative method.

Relevance

Among the information sought by plaintiffs herein are certain
studies undertaken by PepsiCo of the tax consequences of various forms
of merger * * *

Here the tax studies conducted by PepsiCo are relevant insofar as
they indicate the price considerations being used by PepsiCo and the
effect of the tax advantages to PepsiCo in determining what a fair price
for the Wilson minority would be. They are also relevant insofar as they
describe the information possessed by PepsiCo at the time when it was
its duty to make disclosures of necessary information on a subject which
the minority shareholders and warrant holders were entitled to consider
prior to making their decision.

Since the information contained in the tax studies is relevant to
whether the defendant PepsiCo misrepresented facts in its tender offer,
and to whether the terms of the offer made to the minority shareholders
and warrant holders were not unduly disadvantageous to them, Pepsi-
Co's objection is not well taken. Insofar as PepsiCo objected to the
discovery of the documents here at issue on grounds of relevancy, the
documents are to be produced.

Attorney–Client Privilege

As to six documents sought by the plaintiffs, PepsiCo has objected
on the grounds that the documents are covered by the attorney-client

privilege, and, therefore, may not be disclosed. The documents cover a period of several years, and are from several different individuals acting as house or outside counsel for the defendant PepsiCo.[1]

Plaintiffs claim that the attorney-client privilege ought not to attach here, because as to some documents it was allegedly waived by deposition testimony concerning their contents, and because, under the principles enunciated in *Garner v. Wolfinbarger, 430 F.2d 1093 (5th Cir. 1970)*, a corporation ought not to be able to withhold this information from persons in the position of the plaintiffs.

The Court finds this issue to be more complex than a mere waiver problem, or the situation presented in *Garner*. It has instead required an examination of the function of the rule, and of the role of attorneys and other fiduciaries in light of the requirements of the law.[2]

* * * This Court has long adhered to the rule that house counsel are to be treated in the same fashion as outside counsel with respect to activities in which they are engaged as attorneys. Where house counsel is engaged in giving business advice or mere technical information, no privilege attaches. Where he acts as an attorney, however, the confidences revealed in the process of communication as to those issues should be treated in the same manner as those to any other attorney.

Garner v. Wolfinbarger, 430 F.2d 1093 (5th Cir. 1970), on remand, *56 F.R.D. 499 (S.D. Ala. 1972)*; and *Bailey v. Meister Brau, Inc., 55 F.R.D. 211 (N.D. Ill. 1972)*, stand generally for the proposition that where a corporation seeks advice from legal counsel, and the information relates to the subject of a later suit by a minority shareholder in the corporation, the corporation is not entitled to claim the privilege as against its own shareholder, absent some special cause. The rule of *Garner* as followed in *Meister Brau* is of some relevance here, but is not controlling since we deal here with the application where a minority shareholder seeks information not from his own corporation, but from a separate corporation which was a controlling shareholder in his. More important is the basis of those decisions, resting in each case on the understanding that a corporation is, at least in part, the association of its

---

1. Six documents are claimed to be within the attorney-client privilege:

1. A memorandum from house counsel to a corporate official in charge of tax planning concerning alternative methods of acquiring stock in the event of an unfavorable revenue ruling.

2. A memorandum from outside counsel to PepsiCo concerning one method of acquiring shares of Wilson.

3. A memorandum from house counsel to the same official as in document 1 *supra,* concerning a particular alternative following an unfavorable revenue ruling.

4. A memo from general counsel and outside counsel to the President of Pepsi-Co concerning acquisition of minority interests.

5. A formal legal opinion by Delaware counsel to New York counsel concerning rights of the minority warrant holders under Delaware law.

6. A formal legal opinion from outside counsel to PepsiCo concerning a merger plan and the rights of various parties.

2. In the present situation, the suit is brought subject to a federal cause of action under the securities laws, with pendent state law claims. The Court, therefore, treats the issue as one involving a determination under the federal rule of privilege and not the state rule as would be necessary under diversity jurisdiction.

shareholders, and it owes to them a fiduciary obligation which is stronger than the societal policy favoring privileged communications.

The documents in question here must, therefore, be seen in light of the obligations which are part of the circumstances of this case. The Court makes no general rule regarding discovery as to corporations in general: it is willing to assume that corporations are ordinarily entitled to the attorney-client privilege, and that they may claim that privilege, especially against the outsider who seeks information. Nonetheless, where the documents are produced in situations which involve other obligations of attorneys or shareholders, the applicability of the privilege must be determined in light of the obligations and policies to be served.

With respect to Documents Numbers 4 and 6, both memoranda from counsel to PepsiCo or officers of PepsiCo, the decision is clear. At the time Document Number 4 was drafted, its author, Peter DeLuca sat as a member of the Board of Directors of Wilson. He was, in addition, General Counsel to PepsiCo. In those positions, he owed separate fiduciary obligations to two separate entities and their interests. He could not subordinate the fiduciary obligations which he owed to Wilson and the minority shareholders of Wilson to those of his client PepsiCo. The fact that Wilson may not have had an attorney-client relationship with him is of no import. His knowledge in one capacity cannot be separated from the other, nor can his duties as a fiduciary be lessened or increased because of professional relationship. It is a common, universally recognized exception to the attorney-client privilege, that where an attorney serves two clients having common interests and each party communicates to the attorney, the communications are not privileged in a subsequent controversy between the two. The source of the rule is not clear, whether based on an assumption that where an attorney serves two different clients in relation to the same matter, neither anticipates that communications will have the same degree of confidence; or, as is more likely, the court will not allow the attorney to protect the interest of one client by refusing to disclose information received from that client, to the detriment of another client or former client. The fiduciary obligations of an attorney are not served by his later selection of the interests of one client over another.

The situation here is more complex. There can be no doubt, however, that Mr. DeLuca owed fiduciary duties to both Wilson and PepsiCo. Just as importantly as a director of Wilson, his obligations ran to the shareholders of Wilson, and the protection of their best interests. PepsiCo cannot now claim a privilege as to his communications with PepsiCo officials concerning the interests of the Wilson shareholders. Document Number 4 is therefore discoverable.

Document Number 6 consists of a memorandum from Mudge, Rose, Guthrie & Alexander, evidently outside counsel to PepsiCo, concerning the various recommended forms of the merger. At the time of the drafting of the memorandum, a general partner of Mudge, Rose, Mr. James Frangos, had replaced Mr. DeLuca on Wilson's board. Mr. Frangos, therefore, owed to Wilson and Wilson's shareholders and warrant holders the same obligation which Mr. DeLuca had. Through Mr. Frangos' seat on the Board, Mudge, Rose, as his partnership, carried those same obligations. Once again, the fact that the firm carried additional professional responsibilities to PepsiCo is unimportant. For the reasons discussed *supra,* the memorandum listed as Document Number 6 is discoverable by the Wilson minority.

Documents Numbers 1, 2, 3 and 5 present a somewhat different situation. Documents 1 and 3 are memoranda from house counsel to a Vice President in Charge of Tax Administration for PepsiCo. Whatever fiduciary obligations are attached are therefore only those which attach to PepsiCo and its officers: there is not in this situation the representation of two interests discussed *supra.* Document Number 2 is a memorandum from Mudge, Rose, Guthrie & Alexander, evidently signed by Mr. Frangos prior to the time when Mr. Frangos joined the Wilson Board. Since it does not appear that Mr. DeLuca was a partner in the Mudge firm, this document also appears to be in a category different than those described *supra* involving the representation of two interests.

Document Number 5 is an opinion from Delaware counsel as attorneys of PepsiCo to Mudge, Rose, evidently describing certain rights of the Wilson minority under Delaware law. At this time, Mr. Frangos was sitting on the Wilson Board, but it does not appear that any member of the Delaware firm was in a similar conflicted position. The memorandum appears to be one between co-counsel, and not one from the Delaware firm to the New York firm as attorney and client. It, therefore, appears to be in a category different than that described previously.

These latter four documents do have a common element, however. In each instance, the recipient of the advice or the client whose interest is being ascertained, had fiduciary obligations which ran to Wilson and the Wilson minority. It is no longer open to question that a majority shareholder who controls a corporation must not use his position to the undue disadvantage of the minority: his obligation is to the corporation and not simply to himself.

These documents are the result of inquiries by the controlling shareholder, as to matters which touch upon the interests of the minority shareholders, and from their titles appear to be directly concerned with the duties which the controlling shareholder and its controlled corporation owed to the minority.

This Court holds that under these circumstances, the documents presented are discoverable. The attorneys whose opinions were written to PepsiCo could not avoid PepsiCo's own obligations as a fiduciary. Where the fiduciary has conflicting interests of its own, to allow the attorney-client privilege to block access to the information and bases of its decisions as to the persons to whom the obligation is owed would allow the perpetration of frauds. A fiduciary owes the obligation to his beneficiaries to go about his duties without obscuring his reasons from the legitimate inquiries of the beneficiaries.

There are, of course, limits on such an obligation. Were the claim here one made in bad faith, or one where the interests of the great majority of the beneficiaries would be better served by the privilege, the case would be different indeed. Similarly, if the information sought were a trade secret, or otherwise covered by other public policies which would give added weight to a need for secrecy, the obligations of the fiduciary might have entirely different circumstances. But those situations are not this situation. The power of courts to determine such matters individually, in light of their facts, will adequately protect the interest of both fiduciaries and beneficiaries.

The defendant urges that the Court should not allow discovery in the situation of the fiduciary with conflicted obligations, in order to foster the seeking of professional advice by the fiduciary who finds himself in that position. A fiduciary will not be less likely in this situation to either seek advice or fully disclose the facts, since it is in his interest to be aware of adverse consequences of his conflicted position, which is or will be obvious prior to the issuance of any discovery order.

For these reasons, the Court orders the production of the documents listed as Numbers 1–6 in Defendant's Memorandum, and those documents pertaining to certain tax studies as described in the papers before the Court.

So Ordered.

Delaware courts since the *Valente* decision have accepted the court's conclusion that plaintiffs may be entitled to otherwise privileged documents in the kind of dispute involved in that case. They have rejected, however, the suggestion in *Valente* that the defendant may not assert the privilege against plaintiffs in those circumstances absent special cause. Instead, they have said that the burden is on the plaintiff in a situation ostensibly controlled by *Garner* to show cause why the privilege should not attach. See, e.g., *Deutsch v. Cogan*, 580 A.2d 100, 105–106 (Del. Ch. 1990).

B. WORK PRODUCT DOCTRINE

SIMON v. G.D. SEARLE & CO.

816 F.2d 397 (8th Cir. 1987)

Wollman, Circuit Judge.

[For a statement of the facts, see the excerpt from this case earlier in this Chapter in the section on attorney-client privilege]

* * *

II

Work Product Doctrine

Searle's first argument is that its risk management documents are protected from discovery by the work product doctrine. That doctrine was established in *Hickman v. Taylor, 329 U.S. 495 (1947),* and is now expressed in *Rule 26(b)(3) of the Federal Rules of Civil Procedure,* which provides that "a party may obtain discovery of documents and tangible things * * * prepared in anticipation of litigation or for trial by or for another party or by or for that other party's representative * * * only upon a showing that the party seeking discovery has substantial need of the materials." Our application of the work product doctrine to specific documents is guided by the purposes of the doctrine set out in *Hickman.* The work product doctrine was designed to prevent "unwarranted inquiries into the files and mental impressions of an attorney," and recognizes that it is "essential that a lawyer work with a certain degree of privacy, free from unnecessary intrusion by opposing parties and their counsel."

The special master found that the risk management documents at issue were generated in an attempt to keep track of, control, and anticipate the costs of Searle's products liability litigation; the documents have been so identified in the district court's first certified question. Many of the documents include products liability litigation reserve information that is based on reserve estimates obtained from Searle's legal department. When Searle receives notice of a claim or suit, a Searle attorney sets a case reserve for the matter. Case reserves embody the attorney's estimate of anticipated legal expenses, settlement value, length of time to resolve the litigation, geographic considerations, and other factors. The individual case reserves set by the legal department are then used by the risk management department for a variety of reserve analysis functions, which the special master found were motivated by business planning purposes including budget, profit, and insurance considerations.

The work product doctrine will not protect these documents from discovery unless they were prepared in anticipation of litigation. Our determination of whether the documents were prepared in anticipation of litigation is clearly a factual determination:

> The test should be whether, in light of the nature of the document and the factual situation in the particular case, the document can fairly be said to have been prepared or obtained because of the prospect of litigation. But the converse of this is that even though litigation is already in prospect, there is no work product immunity for documents prepared in the regular course of business rather than for purposes of litigation.

8 C. Wright & A. Miller, *Federal Practice and Procedure* § 2024, at 198–99 (1970) (footnotes omitted. * * * The advisory committee's notes to Rule 26(b)(3) affirm the validity of the Wright and Miller test: "Materi-

als assembled in the ordinary course of business * * * or for other nonlitigation purposes are not under the qualified immunity provided by this subdivision." *Fed. R. Civ. P. 26(b)(3)* advisory committee notes. Applying this test, we do not believe it can be said that the risk management documents were prepared for purposes of litigation. We are no better qualified to evaluate the facts of this case than the special master and the district court, and we believe their conclusion that the risk management documents are in the nature of business planning documents is a reasonable factual conclusion. The risk management department was not involved in giving legal advice or in mapping litigation strategy in any individual case. The aggregate reserve information in the risk management documents serves numerous business planning functions, but we cannot see how it enhances the defense of any particular lawsuit. Searle vigorously argues that its business is health care, not litigation, but that is not the point. Searle's business involves litigation, just as it involves accounting, marketing, advertising, sales, and many other things. A business corporation may engage in business planning on many fronts, among them litigation.

Although the risk management documents were not themselves prepared in anticipation of litigation, they may be protected from discovery to the extent that they disclose the individual case reserves calculated by Searle's attorneys. The individual case reserve figures reveal the mental impressions, thoughts, and conclusions of an attorney in evaluating a legal claim. By their very nature they are prepared in anticipation of litigation and, consequently, they are protected from discovery as opinion work product. We do not believe, however, that the aggregate reserve information reveals the individual case reserve figures to a degree that brings the aggregates within the protection of the work product doctrine. The individual figures lose their identity when combined to create the aggregate information. Furthermore, the aggregates are not even direct compilations of the individual figures; the aggregate information is the product of a formula that factors in variables such as inflation, further diluting the individual reserve figures. Certainly it would be impossible to trace back and uncover the reserve for any individual case, and it would be a dubious undertaking to attempt to derive meaningful averages from the aggregates, given the possibility of large variations in case estimates for everything from frivolous suits to those with the most serious injuries. The purpose of the work product doctrine—that of preventing discovery of a lawyer's mental impressions—is not violated by allowing discovery of documents that incorporate a lawyer's thoughts in, at best, such an indirect and diluted manner. Accordingly, we hold that the work product doctrine does not block discovery of Searle's risk management documents or the aggregate case reserve information contained therein. * * *

UNITED STATES v. ADLMAN

134 F.3d 1194 (2d. Cir. 1998)

LEVAL, CIRCUIT JUDGE:

This appeal concerns the proper interpretation of *Federal Rule of Civil Procedure 26(b)(3)* ("the Rule"), which grants limited protection against discovery to documents and materials prepared "in anticipation of litigation." Specifically, we must address whether a study prepared for an attorney assessing the likely result of an expected litigation is ineligible for protection under the Rule if the primary or ultimate purpose of making the study was to assess the desirability of a business transaction, which, if undertaken, would give rise to the litigation. We hold that a document created because of anticipated litigation, which tends to reveal mental impressions, conclusions, opinions or theories concerning the litigation, does not lose work-product protection merely because it is intended to assist in the making of a business decision influenced by the likely outcome of the anticipated litigation. Where a document was created because of anticipated litigation, and would not have been prepared in substantially similar form but for the prospect of that litigation, it falls within Rule 26(b)(3).

The district court ruled that the document sought by the IRS in this case did not fall within the scope of Rule 26(b)(3) and ordered its production. Because we cannot determine whether the district court used the correct standard in reaching its decision, we vacate the judgment and remand for reconsideration.

BACKGROUND

Sequa Corporation is an aerospace manufacturer with annual revenues of nearly $2 billion. Prior to 1989, Atlantic Research Corporation ("ARC") and Chromalloy Gas Turbine Corporation ("Chromalloy") were wholly-owned Sequa subsidiaries. Appellant Monroe Adlman is an attorney and Vice President for Taxes at Sequa.

In the spring of 1989, Sequa contemplated merging Chromalloy and ARC. The contemplated merger was expected to produce an enormous loss and tax refund, which Adlman expected would be challenged by the IRS and would result in litigation. Adlman asked Paul Sheahen, an accountant and lawyer at Arthur Andersen & Co. ("Arthur Andersen"), to evaluate the tax implications of the proposed restructuring. Sheahen did so and set forth his study in a memorandum (the "Memorandum"). He submitted the Memorandum in draft form to Adlman in August 1989. After further consultation, on September 5, 1989, Sheahen sent Adlman the final version. The Memorandum was a 58–page detailed legal analysis of likely IRS challenges to the reorganization and the resulting tax refund claim; it contained discussion of statutory provisions, IRS regulations, legislative history, and prior judicial and IRS rulings relevant to the claim. It proposed possible legal theories or strategies for Sequa to adopt in response, recommended preferred methods of structuring the transaction, and made predictions about the likely outcome of litigation.

Sequa decided to go ahead with the restructuring, which was completed in December 1989 in essentially the form recommended by Arthur Andersen. Sequa sold 93% of its stock in ARC to Chromalloy for $167.4 million, and the remaining 7% to Bankers Trust for $12.6 million. The reorganization resulted in a $289 million loss. Sequa claimed the loss on its 1989 return and carried it back to offset 1986 capital gains, thereby generating a claim for a refund of $35 million.

In an ensuing audit of Sequa's 1986–1989 tax returns, the IRS requested a number of documents concerning the restructuring transaction. Sequa acknowledged the existence of the Memorandum, but cited work-product privilege as grounds for declining to produce it. On September 23, 1993, the IRS served a summons on Adlman for production of the Memorandum.

When Adlman declined to comply, the IRS instituted an action in the United States District Court for the Southern District of New York to enforce the subpoena. Adlman defended on the grounds that the Memorandum was protected by both the attorney-client and work-product privileges. The district court * * * rejected Adlman's claim that the Memorandum was protected by attorney-client privilege, finding that Adlman had not consulted Arthur Andersen in order to obtain assistance in furnishing legal advice to Sequa * * *

On remand, Adlman argued that the Memorandum was protected by Rule 26(b)(3) because it included legal opinions prepared in reasonable anticipation of litigation. Litigation was virtually certain to result from the reorganization and Sequa's consequent claim of tax losses. Sequa's tax returns had been surveyed or audited annually for at least 30 years. In addition, the size of the capital loss to be generated by the proposed restructuring would result in a refund so large that the Commissioner of Internal Revenue would be required by federal law to submit a report to the Joint Congressional Committee on Taxation. Finally, Sequa's tax treatment of the restructuring was based on an interpretation of the tax code without a case or IRS ruling directly on point. In light of the circumstances of the transaction, Adlman asserted there was "no doubt that Sequa would end up in litigation with the IRS." Sequa's accountant at Arthur Andersen concurred, opining that "any corporate tax executive would have realistically predicted that this capital loss would be disputed by the IRS" because of the "unprecedented and creative nature of the reorganization, the fact that Sequa was continually under close scrutiny by the IRS and the size of the refund resulting from the capital loss."

The district court again rejected the claim of work-product privilege, concluding that the Memorandum was not prepared in anticipation of litigation. Adlman appeals.

DISCUSSION

The work-product doctrine, codified for the federal courts in *Fed. R. Civ. P. 26(b)(3)*, is intended to preserve a zone of privacy in which a lawyer can prepare and develop legal theories and strategy "with an eye toward litigation," free from unnecessary intrusion by his adversaries. Analysis of one's case "in anticipation of litigation" is a classic example of work product, and receives heightened protection under *Fed. R. Civ. P. 26(b)(3)*.

This case involves a question of first impression in this circuit: whether Rule 26(b)(3) is inapplicable to a litigation analysis prepared by a party or its representative in order to inform a business decision which turns on the party's assessment of the likely outcome of litigation expected to result from the transaction. Answering that question requires that we determine the proper interpretation of Rule 26(b)(3)'s requirement that documents be prepared "in anticipation of litigation" in order to qualify for work-product protection.

I.

In *Hickman v. Taylor, 329 U.S. 495 (1947),* the Supreme Court held that notes taken by the defendant's attorney during interviews with witnesses to the event that eventually gave rise to the lawsuit in the case were not discoverable by the plaintiff * * *

Rule 26(b)(3) codifies the principles articulated in Hickman. The Rule states that documents "prepared in anticipation of litigation or for trial" are discoverable only upon a showing of substantial need of the materials and inability, without undue hardship, to obtain their substantial equivalent elsewhere. Even where this showing has been made, however, the Rule provides that the court "shall protect against disclosure of the mental impressions, conclusions, opinions, or legal theories of an attorney or other representative of a party concerning the litigation."

II.

The first problem we face is to determine the meaning of the phrase prepared "in anticipation of litigation." It is universally agreed that a document whose purpose is to assist in preparation for litigation is within the scope of the Rule and thus eligible to receive protection if the other conditions of protection prescribed by the Rule are met. The issue is less clear, however, as to documents which, although prepared because of expected litigation, are intended to inform a business decision influenced by the prospects of the litigation. The formulation applied by some courts in determining whether documents are protected by work-product privilege is whether they are prepared "primarily or exclusively to assist in litigation"—a formulation that would potentially exclude documents containing analysis of expected litigation, if their primary, ultimate, or exclusive purpose is to assist in making the business decision. Others ask whether the documents were prepared "because of" existing or expected litigation—a formulation that would include such documents, despite the fact that their purpose is not to "assist in" litigation. Because we believe that protection of documents of this type is more consistent with both the literal terms and the purposes of the Rule, we adopt the latter formulation.

1. "Primarily to assist in" litigation.

* * * We believe that a requirement that documents be produced primarily or exclusively to assist in litigation in order to be protected is at odds with the text and the policies of the Rule. Nowhere does Rule 26(b)(3) state that a document must have been prepared to aid in the conduct of litigation in order to constitute work product, much less primarily or exclusively to aid in litigation. Preparing a document "in anticipation of litigation" is sufficient.

The text of Rule 26(b)(3) does not limit its protection to materials prepared to assist at trial. To the contrary, the text of the Rule clearly sweeps more broadly. It expressly states that work-product privilege applies not only to documents "prepared . . . for trial" but also to those prepared "in anticipation of litigation." If the drafters of the Rule intended to limit its protection to documents made to assist in preparation for litigation, this would have been adequately conveyed by the phrase "prepared . . . for trial." The fact that documents prepared "in anticipation of litigation" were also included confirms that the drafters considered this to be a different, and broader category. Nothing in the Rule states or suggests that documents prepared "in anticipation of litigation" with the purpose of assisting in the making of a business decision do not fall within its scope.

In addition, the Rule takes pains to grant special protection to the type of materials at issue in this case—documents setting forth legal analysis. While the Rule generally withholds protection for documents prepared in anticipation of litigation if the adverse party shows "substantial need" for their disclosure and inability to obtain their equivalent by other means, even where the party seeking disclosure has made such a showing the Rule directs that "the court shall protect against disclosure of the mental impressions, conclusions, opinions, or legal theories of . . . [a party or its representative] concerning the litigation." Where the Rule has explicitly established a special level of protection against disclosure for documents revealing an attorney's (or other representative's) opinions and legal theories concerning litigation, it would oddly undermine its purposes if such documents were excluded from protection merely because they were prepared to assist in the making of a business decision expected to result in the litigation.

In addition to the plain language of the Rule, the policies underlying the work-product doctrine suggest strongly that work-product protection should not be denied to a document that analyzes expected litigation merely because it is prepared to assist in a business decision. Framing the inquiry as whether the primary or exclusive purpose of the document was to assist in litigation threatens to deny protection to documents that implicate key concerns underlying the work-product doctrine.

The problem is aptly illustrated by several hypothetical fact situations likely to recur:

(i) A company contemplating a transaction recognizes that the transaction will result in litigation; whether to undertake the transaction and, if so, how to proceed with the transaction, may well be influenced by the company's evaluation of the likelihood of success in litigation. Thus, a memorandum may be prepared in expectation of litigation with the primary purpose of helping the company decide whether to undertake the contemplated transaction. An example would be a publisher contemplating publication of a book where the publisher has received a threat of suit from a competitor purporting to hold exclusive publication rights. The publisher commissions its attorneys to prepare an evaluation of the likelihood of success in the litigation, which includes the attorneys' evaluation of various legal strategies that might be pursued. If the publisher decides to go ahead with publication and is sued, under the "primarily to assist in litigation" formulation the study will likely be disclosed to the opposing lawyers because its principal purpose was not to assist in litigation but to inform the business decision whether to publish. We can see no reason under the words or policies of the Rule why such a document should not be protected.

(ii) A company is engaged in, or contemplates, some kind of partnership, merger, joint undertaking, or business association with another company; the other company reasonably requests that the company furnish a candid assessment by the company's attorneys of its likelihood of success in existing litigations. For instance, the company's bank may request such a report from the company's attorneys concerning its likelihood of success in an important litigation to inform its lending policy toward the company. Or a securities underwriter contemplating a public offering of the company's securities may wish to see such a study to decide whether to go ahead with the offering without waiting for the termination of the litigation. Such a study would be created to inform the judgment of the business associate concerning its business decisions. No part of its purpose would be to aid in the conduct of the litigation. Nonetheless it would reveal the attorneys' most intimate strategies and assessments concerning the litigation. We can see no reason why, under the Rule, the litigation adversary should have access to it. But under the Fifth Circuit's "to assist" test, it would likely be discoverable by the litigation adversary.

(iii) A business entity prepares financial statements to assist its executives, stockholders, prospective investors, business partners, and others in evaluating future courses of action. Financial statements include reserves for projected litigation. The company's independent auditor requests a memorandum prepared by the company's attorneys estimating the likelihood of success in litigation and an accompanying analysis of the company's legal strategies and options to assist it in estimating what should be reserved for litigation losses.

In each scenario, the company involved would require legal analysis that falls squarely within Hickman's area of primary concern—analysis that candidly discusses the attorney's litigation strategies, appraisal of likelihood of success, and perhaps the feasibility of reasonable settlement. The interpretation of Rule 26(b)(3) advocated by the IRS Imposes an untenable choice upon a company in these circumstances. If the company declines to make such analysis or scrimps on candor and completeness to avoid prejudicing its litigation prospects, it subjects Itself and its co-venturers to ill-informed decisionmaking. On the other hand, a study reflecting the company's litigation strategy and its assessment of its strengths and weaknesses cannot be turned over to litigation adversaries without serious prejudice to the company's prospects in the litigation.

We perceive nothing in the policies underlying the work-product doctrine or the text of the Rule itself that would justify subjecting a litigant to this array of undesirable choices. The protection of the Rule should be accorded to such studies in these circumstances. We see no basis for adopting a test under which an attorney's assessment of the likely outcome of litigation is freely available to his litigation adversary merely because the document was created for a business purpose rather than for litigation assistance. The fact that a document's purpose is business-related appears irrelevant to the question whether it should be protected under Rule 26(b)(3) * * *

2. Prepared *"because of"* litigation.

The formulation of the work-product rule used by the Wright & Miller treatise, and cited by the Third, Fourth, Seventh, Eighth and D.C. Circuits, is that documents should be deemed prepared "in anticipation of litigation," and thus within the scope of the Rule, if "in light of the nature of the document and the factual situation in the particular case, the document can fairly be said to have been prepared or obtained because of the prospect of litigation." The Wright & Miller "because of" formulation accords with the plain language of Rule 26(b)(3) and the purposes underlying the work-product doctrine. Where a document is created because of the prospect of litigation, analyzing the likely outcome of that litigation, it does not lose protection under this formulation merely because it is created in order to assist with a business decision.

Conversely, it should be emphasized that the "because of" formulation that we adopt here withholds protection from documents that are prepared in the ordinary course of business or that would have been created in essentially similar form irrespective of the litigation. It is well established that work-product privilege does not apply to such documents. Even if such documents might also help in preparation for litigation, they do not qualify for protection because it could not fairly be said that they were created "because of" actual or impending litigation. Furthermore, although a finding under this test that a document is prepared because of the prospect of litigation warrants application of Rule 26(b)(3), this does not necessarily mean that the document will be protected against discovery. Rather, it means that a document is eligible for work-product privilege. The district court can then assess whether the party seeking discovery has made an adequate showing of substantial need for the document and an inability to obtain its contents elsewhere without undue hardship. The district court can order production of the portions of the document for which a litigant has made an adequate showing. The court can focus its attention on whether the document or any portion Is the type of material that should be disclosed, while retaining the authority to protect against disclosure of the mental impressions, strategies, and analyses of the party or its representative concerning the litigation.

In short, we find that the * * * "because of" test appropriately focuses on both what should be eligible for the Rule's protection and what should not. We believe this is the proper test to determine whether a document was prepared "in anticipation of litigation" and is thus eligible for protection depending on the further findings required by the Rule.

III.

We cannot determine from the district court's opinion what test it followed in concluding that the Memorandum was ineligible for protection * * *

The order enforcing the IRS summons is vacated, and the matter is remanded to the district court for further findings under the standard prescribed in this ruling.

KEARSE, CIRCUIT JUDGE, dissenting:

I respectfully dissent. It does not appear to me that the district court applied an erroneous standard in this case. Accordingly, I would affirm.

The attorney work product privilege accords limited protection for materials that were "prepared in anticipation of litigation or for trial." Where the only prospect of litigation is what would be anticipated if the party undertakes a contemplated transaction but not otherwise, and the materials in question were prepared in connection with providing legal advice to the party as to whether or not to undertake that transaction, I do not regard the materials as having been prepared "in anticipation of litigation." I regard the majority as having extended the work product privilege to a stage that precedes any possible "anticipation" of litigation.

This does not mean, as suggested by the majority opinion, that such materials will normally be discoverable. Documents in which a party's attorney assesses the legal advisability of contemplated business transactions, including the possibility and efficacy of litigation if the client elects to proceed with the transaction, will normally be protected from discovery, by the attorney-client privilege, so long as the client meets the usual requirements of, inter alia, maintaining confidentiality and showing that it was seeking legal advice. The assertion of attorney-client privilege in the present case was rejected only because the client had failed to make any record that distinguished the present consultation of its accounting firm from its normal business consultations.

I disagree with the majority's expansion of the work-product privilege to afford protection to documents not prepared in anticipation of litigation but instead prepared in order to permit the client to determine whether to undertake a business transaction, where there will be no anticipation of litigation unless the transaction is undertaken.

C. ETHICAL DUTY OF CONFIDENTIALITY

MODEL RULE 1.6: CONFIDENTIALITY OF INFORMATION

(a) A lawyer shall not reveal information relating to the representation of a client unless the client gives informed consent, the disclosure is impliedly authorized in order to carry out the representation or the disclosure is permitted by paragraph (b).

(b) A lawyer may reveal information relating to the representation of a client to the extent the lawyer reasonably believes necessary:

(1) to prevent reasonably certain death or substantial bodily harm;

(2) to prevent the client from committing a crime or fraud that is reasonably certain to result in substantial injury to the financial interests or property of another and in furtherance of which the client has used or is using the lawyer's services;

(3) to prevent, mitigate or rectify substantial injury to the financial interests or property of another that is reasonably certain to result or has resulted from the client's commission of a crime or fraud in furtherance of which the client has used the lawyer's services;

(4) to secure legal advice about the lawyer's compliance with these Rules;

(5) to establish a claim or defense on behalf of the lawyer in a controversy between the lawyer and the client, to establish a defense to a criminal charge or civil claim against the lawyer based upon conduct in which the client was involved, or to respond to allegations in any proceeding concerning the lawyer's representation of the client; or

(6) to comply with other law or a court order.

Comments

* * *

[3] The principle of client-lawyer confidentiality is given effect by related bodies of law: the attorney-client privilege, the work product doctrine and the rule of confidentiality established in professional ethics. The attorney-client privilege and work-product doctrine apply in judicial and other proceedings in which a lawyer may be called as a witness or otherwise required to produce evidence concerning a client. The rule of client-lawyer confidentiality applies in situations other than those where evidence is sought from the lawyer through compulsion of law. The confidentiality rule, for example, applies not only to matters communicated in confidence by the client but also to all information relating to the representation, whatever its source. A lawyer may not disclose such information except as authorized or required by the Rules of Professional Conduct or other law. See also Scope.

* * *

Disclosure Adverse to Client

[6] Although the public interest is usually best served by a strict rule requiring lawyers to preserve the confidentiality of information relating to the representation of their clients, the confidentiality rule is subject to limited exceptions. Paragraph (b)(1) recognizes the overriding value of life and physical integrity and permits disclosure reasonably necessary to prevent reasonably certain death or substantial bodily harm. Such harm is reasonably certain to occur if it will be suffered imminently or if there is a present and substantial threat that a person will suffer such harm at a later date if the lawyer fails to take action necessary to eliminate the threat. Thus, a lawyer who knows that a client has accidentally discharged toxic waste into a town's water supply may reveal this information to the authorities if there is a present and substantial risk that a person who drinks the water will contract a life-threatening or debilitating disease and the lawyer's disclosure is necessary to eliminate the threat or reduce the number of victims.

[7] Paragraph (b)(2) is a limited exception to the rule of confidentiality that permits the lawyer to reveal information to the extent necessary to enable affected persons or appropriate authorities to prevent the client from committing a crime or fraud, as defined in Rule 1.0(d), that is reasonably certain to result in substantial injury to the financial or property interests of another and in furtherance of which the client has used or is using the lawyer's services. Such a serious abuse of the client-lawyer relationship by the client forfeits the protection of this Rule. The client can, of course, prevent such disclosure by refraining from the wrongful conduct. Although paragraph (b)(2) does not require the lawyer to reveal the client's misconduct, the lawyer may not counsel or assist the client in conduct the lawyer knows is criminal or fraudulent. See Rule 1.2(d). See also Rule 1.16 with respect to the lawyer's obligation or right to withdraw from the representation of the client in such circum-

stances, and Rule 1.13(c), which permits the lawyer, where the client is an organization, to reveal information relating to the representation in limited circumstances.

[8]   Paragraph (b)(3) addresses the situation in which the lawyer does not learn of the client's crime or fraud until after it has been consummated. Although the client no longer has the option of preventing disclosure by refraining from the wrongful conduct, there will be situations in which the loss suffered by the affected person can be prevented, rectified or mitigated. In such situations, the lawyer may disclose information relating to the representation to the extent necessary to enable the affected persons to prevent or mitigate reasonably certain losses or to attempt to recoup their losses. Paragraph (b)(3) does not apply when a person who has committed a crime or fraud thereafter employs a lawyer for representation concerning that offense.

* * *

[12]   Other law may require that a lawyer disclose information about a client. Whether such a law supersedes Rule 1.6 is a question of law beyond the scope of these Rules. When disclosure of information relating to the representation appears to be required by other law, the lawyer must discuss the matter with the client to the extent required by Rule 1.4. If, however, the other law supersedes this Rule and requires disclosure, paragraph (b)(6) permits the lawyer to make such disclosures as are necessary to comply with the law.

[13]   A lawyer may be ordered to reveal information relating to the representation of a client by a court or by another tribunal or governmental entity claiming authority pursuant to other law to compel the disclosure. Absent informed consent of the client to do otherwise, the lawyer should assert on behalf of the client all nonfrivolous claims that the order is not authorized by other law or that the information sought is protected against disclosure by the attorney-client privilege or other applicable law. In the event of an adverse ruling, the lawyer must consult with the client about the possibility of appeal to the extent required by Rule 1.4. Unless review is sought, however, paragraph (b)(6) permits the lawyer to comply with the court's order.

[14]   Paragraph (b) permits disclosure only to the extent the lawyer reasonably believes the disclosure is necessary to accomplish one of the purposes specified. Where practicable, the lawyer should first seek to persuade the client to take suitable action to obviate the need for disclosure. In any case, a disclosure adverse to the client's interest should be no greater than the lawyer reasonably believes necessary to accomplish the purpose. If the disclosure will be made in connection with a judicial proceeding, the disclosure should be made in a manner that limits access to the information to the tribunal or other persons having a need to know it and appropriate protective orders or other arrangements should be sought by the lawyer to the fullest extent practicable.

[15] Paragraph (b) permits but does not require the disclosure of information relating to a client's representation to accomplish the purposes specified in paragraphs (b)(1) through (b)(6). In exercising the discretion conferred by this Rule, the lawyer may consider such factors as the nature of the lawyer's relationship with the client and with those who might be injured by the client, the lawyer's own involvement in the transaction and factors that may extenuate the conduct in question. A lawyer's decision not to disclose as permitted by paragraph (b) does not violate this Rule. Disclosure may be required, however, by other Rules. Some Rules require disclosure only if such disclosure would be permitted by paragraph (b). See Rules 1.2(d), 4.1(b), 8.1 and 8.3. Rule 3.3, on the other hand, requires disclosure in some circumstances regardless of whether such disclosure is permitted by this Rule. See Rule 3.3(c).

PROBLEMS

1. Six years ago David Ball founded Hornet Corporation, a firm that develops software programs for use in military satellite intelligence systems. Two years ago, Hornet became a subsidiary of Hercules Corporation, a major defense contractor, when Ball sold 80% of the shares to Hercules. Ball retained the other 20% of the shares, but withdrew from active involvement in Hornet.

Hornet recently developed new software that greatly enhances the range and accuracy of certain types of military surveillance. Hercules then entered into a licensing agreement with Hornet that gives Hercules the exclusive right to use this software. Since the Hercules legal department serves as counsel for all its subsidiaries, Kelly Burke, an assistant general counsel for Hercules, worked with Hercules and Hornet management to put the agreement together. It provides that Hornet is entitled to royalties from sale of the software once revenues exceed $4 million. This figure represents Hercules' calculation of the support that it provided to Hornet for research and development of the software, which includes an estimate of the intellectual contribution that two Hercules engineers made to the project. Hercules also has the option to obtain licensing rights to any new software devoted to the same type of surveillance, as long as it is willing to provide compensation within 10% of that offered by any other company.

Ball has now brought a shareholder derivative suit on behalf of Hornet against its directors and officers. The suit claims that they breached their duty to the subsidiary by entering into a licensing agreement with terms that greatly favor Hercules to the detriment of Hornet. It alleges that Hornet management agreed to such terms in return for the recent receipt of additional stock options in the parent corporation. In connection with the suit, Ball seeks discovery of all material reflecting Burke's communications with both Hercules and Hornet that deal with the licensing agreement. Is he entitled to obtain such material?

Suppose that Ball were bringing suit against Hercules alleging that Hercules bought out his share in Hornet in a cash-out merger at an unfairly low price. Would Ball be entitled to obtain communications between Hercules and its attorneys regarding the terms of the merger?

2. You are a lawyer in a firm that represents Electric Age Corporation (EA), which manufactures a variety of electronic systems and components. A year ago, EA entered into Project Soundwave, a joint venture agreement with airplane manufacturer Jetway to develop a supersonic aircraft that would be comparable in price to jet airplanes. EA is contributing the electronic control system for the aircraft, while Jetway is responsible for building the frame. The joint venture team is working on integrating the two functions to produce a prototype affordable supersonic plane, which eventually will lead to mass production of the aircraft. Jetway is the world's fourth largest airplane manufacturer, with sales mostly in North America and Western Europe.

Section Four of the joint venture agreement provides that neither party may provide the technology and trade secrets that it contributes to Soundwave to any competitor of either EA or Jetway. Section Eight provides that the two companies will share such technology and trade secrets, but that neither may use such intellectual property for any purpose other than development of aircraft under the Soundwave project. Section Twelve of the agreement provides that either party may withdraw from the joint venture upon a material breach of it by the other party. If either party alleges such a breach, a jointly selected arbitrator will have binding authority to determine the validity of this claim. In such arbitration, normal rules of evidence will be relaxed in various ways, but each party is entitled to claim any privilege that would be available in a state or federal court proceeding.

The EA Vice–President for International Markets approaches you with the information that Megair Corporation, the world's largest aircraft manufacturer, is interested in exploring the possibility of developing an affordable supersonic plane. Megair sells aircraft all over the world, and has an especially dominant share of the fast-growing Asian market. Its overall market share is three times that of Jetway. Megair has indicated that it is especially interested in working with EA because of the company's reputation for innovation and quality control. If that is not possible, it will turn to other companies for the electronic control system for the aircraft.

The Vice–President tells you that EA top management would love to be able to work with Megair. He says, however, that he fears that the Soundwave agreement could preclude EA working with Megair on the project. He asks that you advise him on the feasibility of entering into a joint venture agreement with Megair, including whether it is worth it for EA to try to withdraw from the Soundwave project if necessary.

After conducting research and several interviews with EA managers and engineers, you prepare and submit your memo to the Vice–President. You first indicate that an arbitrator almost certainly would interpret Section Four of the Soundwave agreement to preclude EA working with Megair as long as the joint venture is in place.

You then offer $450 million as an estimate of what Jetway might accept from EA as payment for being able to terminate the joint venture. Based on consultation with EA's business development team and an assessment of Megair's sales and production capacity, your best estimate of the revenues from participating in a project with Megair is about $550 million.

An alternative that might enable EA to enjoy most or all of the estimated $550 million revenues would be for EA to withdraw from Soundwave on the ground that Jetway has breached the agreement. The best basis for this claim probably is that Jetway has violated Section Eight by using EA trade secrets in developing some of its own components not related to the Soundwave project. Although the evidence is ambiguous at best, you suggest that EA could make at least a colorable claim that Jetway has used EA trade secrets in developing the Jetway components, and that Jetway therefore is in breach of the joint venture agreement. As a result, EA would have the right to withdraw without making any payment to Jetway.

You estimate that EA would have a 40% chance of prevailing on this claim with an arbitrator, which means that estimated damages would be 60% x $450 million, or $270 million. That would leave net benefits to EA of $280 million from entering into a joint venture with Megair. Withdrawing on the basis of an alleged breach of the agreement thus could be a more profitable alternative than paying Jetway to get out of it.

Additional costs that EA needs to consider from claiming breach and withdrawing, you indicate, are damage to EA's relationship with Jetway and injury to EA's reputation in the industry more generally. You admit that quantifying each of these considerations is difficult, but suggest some ballpark numbers. On balance, you conclude, EA has more to gain than to lose by claiming that Jetway has breached the Soundwave agreement and seeking to withdraw from the joint venture.

You give your memo to the Vice–President, who thanks you for your work. Over the next several days, EA's top management considers what to do. Finally, they conclude that EA will notify Jetway that it plans to withdraw from the Soundwave project because Jetway has breached Section Eight of the agreement. Jetway files for arbitration, claiming that EA has withdraw from the joint venture in bad faith. Will EA be able to protect your memo from disclosure in the arbitration proceeding?

Chapter 13

CONFLICTS OF INTEREST

Conflicts of interest arise when there is a danger that a lawyer's representation of one client may be compromised by representation of another current or former client, another person whom the lawyer might be tempted to favor at the expense of a client, or the lawyer's own personal interest. If a lawyer is in violation of the rules relating to conflicts of interest, she may be disqualified from representing a certain client. If one lawyer in a law firm is disqualified from representing a party because of a concurrent or successive conflict, all members of the firm in most cases are disqualified as well. In addition, if a client later learns that its lawyer had an undisclosed conflict of interest, the client may bring an action for malpractice or breach of fiduciary duty.

It is important to recognize that having a conflict of interest does not in itself constitute wrongdoing. Rather, it means that certain relationships that the lawyer has creates the *potential* that the lawyer may not whole-heartedly pursue the interest of a particular client. Rules that prevent lawyers from representing clients because of conflicts of interest are meant to be prophylactic—to avoid placing the lawyer in a situation in which a person might be tempted to favor one person over another.

One form of conflict arises by virtue of the lawyer's concurrent representation of different clients. In this instance, the concern is that the lawyer may not represent one or both clients with unqualified diligence, and that the lawyer might disclose to one client confidential information gained from another that could disadvantage the latter. Another type of conflict can occur as a result of successive representation—that is, between a lawyer's current and former clients. Of particular concern in this case is that the lawyer not use or disclose to the disadvantage of the former client any confidential information that she obtained from that client.

Conflicts of interest have become a major concern in corporate representation. They have proliferated because of the expansion and consolidation of corporations and their affiliates around the globe, along with the rise of large multi-office law firms and the increasing rate at which lawyers move from one firm to another. Corporations may acquire or divest themselves of various affiliates, which create new alignments of either common or conflicting interest that lawyers must take into account. Merger negotiations between law firms necessarily require a review of the extent to which there is any conflict between the clients that each firm represents and the matters in which they are involved. Conflict issues also arise between or among lawyers in the same firm, as potentially lucrative new clients may have interests that conflict with existing clients.

The result is that conflicts of interest are the ethical issue to which law firms, and the corporate legal departments that hire them, devote most of their attention. The material in this chapter will acquaint you with the most important conflict of interest issues that lawyers must confront in the course of corporate representation.

OVERVIEW OF THE CHAPTER

The chapter begins with an article by John Villa that describes how conflicts can arise in modern corporate practice. The article also lays out the basic provisions of Model Rule 1.7, dealing with concurrent representation, and Rule 1.9, which relates to conflicts with former clients. Make sure that you understand how each Rule can operate to disqualify a lawyer.

The Villa article also provides a short description of two issues that will receive more lengthy treatment in the chapter. The first is whether corporate affiliates such as subsidiaries should be considered for conflicts purposes as part of a single entity or as separate entities. The second is the conditions under which clients can waive objection to conflicts of interest in advance. Consider also what Villa describes as the "hot potato" rule, and the rationale for preventing a lawyer from terminating representation of one client in order to represent a more lucrative one. Make sure that you are clear about how permitting a lawyer to do this can convert the conflict from one governed by Rule 1.7 to one governed by Rule 1.9.

American Bar Association (ABA) Opinion 95–390 on "Conflicts of Interest in the Corporate Family Context" that follows Villa provides that a lawyer who represents a corporation is not automatically precluded from representing another party adverse to an affiliate of that corporation in another matter. The Opinion sets forth several considerations that are relevant in determining whether the affiliate and the corporation should be treated as a single client. Ask yourself how much guidance these factors provide, and what is likely as a practical matter to influence what a lawyer chooses to do in this situation. Consider also whether you agree with the Dissent that corporations and their affiliates should always be regarded as a single client because they are economically interdependent. What would be the impact on law practice if this rule were adopted?

Make sure also that you understand the three steps of analysis that the Opinion says the lawyer must go through in determining whether representation adverse to a corporate affiliate violates Rule 1.7. First, should the affiliate be treated as the equivalent of the corporation, and thus as a current client? Second, if not, would representation against the affiliate be directly adverse to the corporation? Finally, if not, would the lawyer's representation of the party adverse to the affiliate be materially limited by the lawyer's representation of the corporation, or vice versa?

ABA Opinion 93–372, dealing with "Waivers of Future Conflicts of Interest," sets forth the criteria for such waivers to be effective. The lawyer first must make the threshold determination that it is reasonable to ask the client to execute such a waiver. If it is, the waiver must be as specific as possible about the kinds of future conflicts that might arise. Note that even if a prospective waiver is presumptively enforceable, the lawyer must revisit the issue of the reasonableness of seeking a waiver once a conflict covered by the waiver actually arises. Ask yourself the rationale for this. Does it render largely irrelevant the original prospective waiver?

The first problem is meant to illustrate when the disqualification of one lawyer in a firm can result in the disqualification of all it lawyers. The Problem reflects the kinds of scenarios that can result because of the increasing mobility of lawyers among firms. The second problem requires you to apply the principles set forth in the ABA Opinions on conflicts in the corporate family context and advance waivers of conflicts.

MODEL RULES: 1.7, 1.9, 1.10, 1.13

John K. Villa, CONFLICTS OF INTEREST ISSUES INVOLVING OUTSIDE COUNSEL

19 ACCA DOCKET 56 (2001)

Your company now consists of several divisions of what had been two separate companies before a merger. Your primary outside law firm is the product of several recently merged practices: a national firm; a small, boutique specialty firm; and a large, non-U.S. firm with a general practice. Ah, isn't consolidation grand. In its effort to clarify its relationship with its outside counsel, your company has scheduled a meeting with the firm to develop principles on certain conflicts of interest issues involving outside counsel. Before reaching agreements, shouldn't you review the basic legal and ethical principles?

FORMER CLIENT CONFLICTS

Although perhaps a reflection of what's going on in the business world generally, today's legal profession is becoming an increasingly mobile market. Whether motivated by career interests or necessitated by new trends in law firm mergers or downsizing, lawyers are moving among firms at an accelerating pace.

Even though it has become a commonplace occurrence, the lateral movement of lawyers is not without its risks, especially when a client of the lawyer's previous firm raises conflict of interest allegations that threaten the lawyer's and the lawyer's new firm's representation of an existing or a prospective client. Such a claim raises several competing considerations: the lawyer's continuing duty of loyalty to a client, the lawyer's right to practice the profession of law, and a person's right to choice of counsel. Of these considerations, loyalty and professional freedom are particularly complex matters to reconcile. As one court remarked with respect to a similar former-client situation, this type of conflict "goes to the very heart of a lawyer's ethics: the continuing and sacrosanct duty of fidelity to a client, versus the right to be emancipated from that client and to go off to do lawyering elsewhere."

In order to reconcile these competing interests, many jurisdictions have adopted a "substantial relationship" test, such as that set forth in Rule 1.9 of the *Model Rules of Professional Conduct,* to determine whether a former representation conflicts with a current representation so as to require disqualification of the lawyer. Under Rule 1.9, representation of a new client is prohibited in those cases in which the new client's interests are materially adverse to those of a former client whom the lawyer or the lawyer's firm represented in the same or a substantially related matter, unless the former client consents. In cases in which only the firm had represented the former client, the lawyer may still be disqualified from representing a different client in a substantially related matter, but only if the lawyer acquired protected information that is material to the new matter.

The term "substantially related" has been described as having attained "the status of a term of art in the general law of attorney conflicts of interest." Because the term is not defined in the *Model Rules,* its application in a given case necessarily requires a factual comparison between the two representations. As a general rule, in cases in which the relationship between the issues in the prior and current representation is shown to be "patently clear," "identical," or "essentially the same" and the lawyer's involvement in the prior representation is shown to have been direct or fairly extensive, courts have found that the substantial relationship test has been satisfied.

Although application of the substantial relationship test is relatively straightforward when the lawyer was directly involved in a prior representation that is factually similar to the new representation, its application when the lawyer's involvement was anything less than direct is not always so clear. For this reason, one court has applied the test in connection with Rule 1.9(a) by focusing on the quality of the information received by the lawyer in connection with the prior representation: in cases in which the information falls within a general knowledge category for a corporate client, such as the "subtle criteria" for selecting personnel, the subsequent representation of a different client with adverse interests would not be precluded; on the other hand, in cases in which the knowledge consists of specific, valuable, and confidential information that, if disclosed, could cause irreparable economic harm to the former client, subsequent representation of a different client with adverse interests would be barred. Both the ABA and the *Restatement* concur with this view.

In cases in which only the lawyer's previous firm had represented a client in a matter found substantially related to a matter with which the lawyer is involved in the lawyer's new firm, the lawyer may be disqualified if the lawyer personally acquired material, confidential information. Although courts differ on what information constitutes such protected information, it is clear that disqualification is required only upon a showing that the lawyer had actual knowledge of this information. Knowledge, however, may be imputed to the lawyer based upon whether the lawyer had access to the protected information, a question that requires "a fact-specific inquiry considering all relevant aspects of the case." Essentially, the court must determine whether confidential information "would normally have been imparted to the attorney during his tenure at the old firm." In cases in which no reasonable probability of access is shown to have existed, disqualification is not necessary. Even in cases in which access to protected information is established, some courts take the position that a presumption of knowledge merely arises, which may be rebutted by the lawyer's sworn assertions to the contrary.

Disqualification of a lawyer based on a former-client conflict ordinarily brings with it the disqualification of the lawyer's entire firm unless the firm has implemented screening programs. Although the *Model Rules* do not provide for the use of screening devices with respect to former-client conflicts involving lateral movements among private firms, several jurisdictions recognize that the existence or implementation of sufficient screening devices will insulate the firm from the taint of the disqualified lawyer, thereby protecting the firm against disqualification. Whether particular screening procedures and devices are adequate necessarily depends upon the facts of the particular case, but courts are willing to protect firms against disqualification in cases in which effective screening programs have been timely and fully implemented.

The reality of the legal marketplace requires the application of ethical rules in a manner that preserves client confidentiality without penalizing the law firm. Firms can assist in this endeavor by implementing screening programs in the hiring process to identify potential conflicts from a lateral hire. Depending upon the jurisdiction, firms may also implement effective screening procedures after hiring to eliminate the risk of disclosure of confidential information.

Corporate Family Conflicts

Corporate consolidation has become an increasing phenomenon in today's business world and, like lawyer mobility, implicates serious conflict of interest issues for law firms that represent sophisticated corporate enterprises. What once had been a single corporate client entity at the commencement of the representation subsequently becomes one of several affiliated companies, threatening the firm's representation of other corporate clients whose interests may now be adverse. When considered in conjunction with the expansion in the geographic scope of many firms' practices, the need for vigilance in ensuring compliance with the law and the ethical rules in order to prevent the ultimate sanction of disqualification becomes ever more urgent. But what, exactly, are those laws and ethical rules? Are those affiliates of a corporate client now clients, as well? Is your outside counsel ethically barred from being adverse to any affiliate of your company?

Rule 1.7 of the *Model Rules of Professional Conduct* prohibits a lawyer from undertaking the representation of a client whose interests are directly adverse to those of an existing client unless each client consents after consultation and the lawyer reasonably believes that the representation will have no adverse effect on the existing client. Although the rule is clear in what is prohibited, it does not expressly address the question of whether an affiliate and its parent may be considered a single entity and thus one "client" for purposes of the rule. A review of case law and ethics opinions discloses that a definitive answer to this question is yet to be reached.

According to the ABA, a lawyer is not ethically prohibited from undertaking a representation that may be adverse to a corporate client's affiliate where the representation involves an unrelated matter. In an opinion on this question, the Ethics Committee noted that the *Model Rules* do not prohibit a representation under these circumstances and concluded that "[t]he fact of corporate affiliation, without more, does not make all of a corporate client's affiliates into clients as well."

Although some courts concur with the ABA's position, a few courts take the opposite position and hold that, when resolving conflicts issues, an affiliate of a corporate client is to be considered a client of the firm. Other courts, rejecting such a *per se* rule, use a fact-specific approach in determining whether corporate affiliates constitute a single entity or distinct entities for purposes of applying the conflicts rules.

In applying the fact-specific approach, a court find may the corporate structures of the two entities determinative of the question. Another court, on the other hand, may focus on whether there is a substantial relationship between the subject matters of the two representations. The degree of control exerted by the parent over the legal affairs of its subsidiary may also be a decisive factor in the court's inquiry. Thus, even though the courts may apply the same approach in resolving the question, the factors that they consider may vary, thereby producing results that are not predictable and are sometimes conflicting.

Notwithstanding this lack of clarity as to whether an affiliate of an existing client should be considered a client, as well, certain red flags should alert counsel to the need to consider the affiliate of a corporate client as a client of the firm, such as in cases in which one corporation is merely the alter ego of the other or in cases in which there is considerable overlap in the corporate structures of the entities. In this situation, consent of the corporate client will probably be required before undertaking a representation adverse to the affiliate. Even if the representation is not directly adverse, consultation with the client, although not ethically required, may be an advisable option.

Corporate family issues are totally unpredictable and often result without warning from a corporate merger. When hiring outside counsel, the most sensible course for both lawyer and client may be to consider including specific language in the engagement letter identifying which entity or entities the firm represents. Both at the outset and during the course of existing representations, firms should also have in place adequate screening measures (1) at the outset to identify potential conflicts and (2) during the representation to minimize the risk of disclosure of confidential information.

WAIVERS OF FUTURE CONFLICTS

With the increase in lawyer mobility, the rise of law firms with multijurisdictional practices, and the ever changing composition of the corporate client, law firms can rest assured that a potential conflict of interest involving a future client is just waiting around the corner. But not all potential conflicts will be related to the firm's representation of existing corporate clients. Can an outside firm have its corporate clients execute a waiver before the conflict appears and thereby avoid the inevitable disruption caused by a subsequent conflicts dispute?

With the increase in lawyer mobility, the rise of law firms with multijurisdictional practices, and the ever changing composition of the corporate client, law firms can rest assured that a potential conflict of interest involving a future client is just waiting around the corner.

Waivers of objections to prospective conflicts of interest that a future representation might raise are neither a new phenomenon nor unethical. Both the ABA and the authors of the *Restatement* endorse their use, though the ABA does so somewhat guardedly, and the courts have generally upheld their validity and enforceability. In order to be effective, however, the waivers must conform to the requirements governing client consent to contemporaneous conflicts of interest, such as those set forth in Rule 1.7 of the *Model Rules of Professional Conduct.*

Model Rule 1.7 permits a client to consent to a conflict of interest in cases in which the representation will be directly adverse to the client and in cases in which the representation, although not adverse, may be materially limited because of the lawyer's responsibilities to another client. In both types of situations, there are two prerequisites to an effective consent: (1) a reasonable belief on the part of the lawyer that the representation will not have an adverse effect either on the lawyer's relationship with the client or on the representation and (2) consultation before the giving of consent.

Application of the first requirement of Rule 1.7 to a prospective waiver requires the lawyer to make an independent judgment at the time of the second representation as to the potential adverse effect of the second representation on both clients from whom the waiver had been obtained. As explained by the ABA, it is only at the time of the second representation that the lawyer will know both what has transpired since having secured the prospective waiver and what the second representation will entail. In cases in which such an assessment discloses a fact that would adversely affect the initial representation, the prospective waiver probably cannot be relied upon as a basis for undertaking the second representation.

The requirement that the consent be given "after consultation" requires that the consent be informed. Thus, there must be disclosure of the legal implications and possible effects of the future representation. The client should be informed that consent to a future conflict does not constitute a waiver of the client's rights of confidentiality under Rule 1.6. What constitutes a sufficient disclosure depends on the particular facts, including the sophistication of the client, the client's familiarity with the potential client, and the length of the relationship between client and lawyer. Thus, although a prospective waiver that identifies the potential adverse client may be satisfactory with respect to some clients, it might not be sufficient as to other clients if they did not appreciate the nature and potential effect of the representation on their interests.

Although a corporate client may understandably be reluctant to execute an agreement waiving its objections to a future conflict of interest, the execution of such an agreement may be advantageous for both client and lawyer. It may, as the ABA acknowledges, "represent a total concordance of the present interests of attorney and client," securing to the client its right to choice of counsel, while at the same time protecting the lawyer from subsequent challenges to prospective, not-yet-identified conflicts. Moreover, in view of the ethical considerations implicated by such a waiver, compliance with the requirements of Rule 1.7 ensures that even the most sophisticated client will be protected (1) from waivers that in the lawyer's judgment may adversely affect or materially limit the continued representation of the client, (2) from an adverse representation resulting in a loss of confidentiality, or (3) from an adverse representation that was wholly unanticipated. Of course, some clients may not be persuaded as to the benefits of a future waiver, and its prudence is doubtful in cases in which clear loyalty or confidentiality concerns exist.

ACCOMMODATION CLIENTS

Corporate clients often want outside counsel to represent individual directors and officers, as well as the entity itself. Although sometimes joint representation in a particular matter presents no problems, at other times conflicts subsequently emerge between the entity and the individuals that threaten the lawyer's ethical responsibilities to the lawyer's clients. Can the lawyer avoid the consequence of disqualification by getting the corporate client to agree at the time of engagement that, in the event of a conflict between the entity and an individual, the lawyer will represent only the entity?

To put the question in a better perspective, let's look at the principles underlying the issue. A lawyer who undertakes the representation of a client must ordinarily continue the representation until its contemplated end, despite the possibility of unforeseen difficulties, in cases in which the failure to do so would impose burdens on the client. In the absence of justification, a withdrawal from representation that prejudices the client not only violates the lawyer's duty of loyalty owed to the client, but also may constitute a breach of the employment contract between the lawyer and the client. The same prohibition against withdrawal applies to representations of two clients on the same matter. Known as the "hot potato" rule, it precludes a lawyer from dropping one client in favor of another client, "especially if it is in order to keep happy a far more lucrative client."

Despite the "hot potato" rule, there is growing precedent for the rule that a lawyer may ethically withdraw from representing one of two or more joint clients, if the "dropped" client can be characterized as a secondary or an "accommodation" client. Under the *Restatement,* a lawyer may with the informed consent of each client undertake the representation of one client "as an accommodation to the lawyer's regular client." If adverse interests subsequently develop between the clients, even if relating to the matter involved in the common representation, the accommodation client may be found to have impliedly consented to the lawyer's continued representation of the regular client in the matter.

At least one court has applied the *Restatement's* accommodation client theory to the joint representation of a corporate entity and one of its officers. In *In re Rite Aid Corporation Securities Litigation,* in-house counsel retained a single firm to represent both the corporation and its CEO in a securities class action lawsuit based on the CEO's representations that the suit was without merit. When an investigative audit subsequently disclosed serious breaches of fiduciary duty on the part of the CEO, which had been concealed by the CEO from both the corporation and outside counsel, outside counsel advised in-house counsel that he could no longer represent the CEO, who had recently resigned, and that the CEO should be instructed to retain his own counsel. In a subsequent motion by the CEO to disqualify the firm, based on Model Rule 1.9(a)'s prohibition against representing a person in the same or a substantially related matter that is materially adverse to the interests of a former client, the court found that the CEO was an "accommodation" client under the terms of the *Restatement.* Accordingly, it denied the motion.

In finding that the CEO was an accommodation client who had impliedly consented to the outside lawyer's withdrawal as his counsel and the lawyer's continued representation of the corporation, the court focused on two factors: (1) the fact that all contact with the outside lawyer was made through in-house counsel, including the initial engagement of the firm, and (2) the fact that the outside lawyer in his engagement letter had clearly identified his responsibilities in the event of a subsequent conflict between the interests of the corporation and those of the CEO. Other factors that may warrant the inference that an officer is an accommodation client who has understood and consented to such qualified representation include the fact that outside counsel has represented the regular or "primary" client for a long period of time before its representation of the other client, the limited duration and scope of the representation of the other client, and the understanding that outside counsel "was not expected to keep confidential from the regular client any information provided to the lawyer by the other client."

Rite Aid instructs that an initial agreement that provides for outside counsel's withdrawal upon the subsequent development of a previously unforeseen conflict may be a permissible way for outside counsel to continue representation of the corporate client without risking disqualification. Because, however, such an agreement implicates the ethical proscriptions against representing materially adverse interests, the agreement must sufficiently establish that the individual client had given an informed consent to counsel's subsequent withdrawal from representation.

* * *

Now that you know the rules, go get 'em, Tiger.

THE ASSOCIATION OF THE BAR OF THE CITY OF NEW YORK COMMITTEE ON PROFESSIONAL AND JUDICIAL ETHICS

FORMAL OPINION 2005–05

UNFORESEEABLE CONCURRENT CLIENT CONFLICTS

1. QUESTION

When unforeseeable conflicts develop between clients in the course of ongoing representation of both, without fault of the lawyer, and the clients refuse to consent to simultaneous representation, which, if any, client may the lawyer continue to represent? If the lawyer may continue to represent one but not both clients, how does the lawyer decide which client to continue representing?

2. INTRODUCTION

Conflicts that arise through no fault of the lawyer may develop in the course of representing two or more clients in unrelated matters as a result of corporate acquisitions or other unforeseeable circumstances. In those situations, lawyers typically seek conflict waivers from the affected clients, but in some instances a client may withhold consent to the multiple representation. This opinion examines the lawyer's ethical duties when confronted with such so-called "thrust upon" conflicts, which are illustrated by the following two scenarios.

Scenario 1: A law firm represents Client A in a breach of contract suit against Company B. During the pendency of that suit, Client C, a longtime ongoing client of the law firm, acquires Company B in a stock sale, and Company B becomes a wholly owned subsidiary of Client C. The law firm (which does not represent Client C in the acquisition of B) informs Clients A and C that it wishes to continue to represent each of them in their respective matters. Client A consents to a conflict of interest waiver, but Client C does not. May the law firm continue to represent at least one client, and if so, may the law firm choose which client to represent?

Scenario 2: A law firm has advised Client A for several years regarding various intellectual property licensing issues. The law firm has also advised Client B for several years on general corporate transactional matters not involving intellectual property licensing, including current negotiations with Company C to form a joint venture. During the course of those negotiations, Client A acquires Company C. Upon learning of the merger, the law firm seeks to obtain conflict of interest waivers from Clients A and B so that it may continue to represent both clients in their respective matters. Client A agrees to provide the necessary conflict of interest waiver, but Client B does not. May the law firm continue to represent at least one of the clients, and if so, may the law firm choose which client to represent?

As these scenarios suggest, "thrust upon" conflicts often, but do not always, arise as a result of changes in corporate ownership. Also, they may arise in both litigation and transactional practice. While in litigation a disqualification motion may as a practical matter resolve the question, in any case a lawyer's ethical duties exist independent of court disqualification jurisprudence and a lawyer will have to guide him or herself based on analysis of ethical obligations under the Code. A lawyer faced with an unforeseen conflict that arises through no fault of his or her own, the lawyer should be guided by the factors set forth in this opinion when deciding from which representation to withdraw.

3. DISCUSSION

Lawyers have a duty to consider potential conflicts at the outset of an engagement and to decline proffered employment when such conflicts are likely. DR 5–105(A). Even careful conflicting-checking, however, will not eliminate the risk of unforeseeable conflicts arising after the lawyer or firm has commenced multiple representations. Under the New York Code of Professional Responsibility (the "Code"), a lawyer may not *continue* the concurrent representation of multiple clients "if the exercise of independent professional judgment on behalf of a client will be or is likely to be adversely affected by the lawyer's representation of another client, or if it would be likely to involve the lawyer in representing differing interests," DR 5–105(B), unless the conflict is capable of being, and is, consented to under DR 5–105(C). This opinion addresses the requirements of DR 5–105(B) in the case of "thrust upon" concurrent client conflicts. For purposes of this opinion "thrust upon" conflicts are defined as conflicts between two clients that (1) did not exist at the time either representation commenced, but arose only during the ongoing representation of both clients, where (2) the conflict was not reasonably foreseeable at the outset of the representation, (3) the conflict arose through no fault of the lawyer, and (4) the conflict is of a type that is capable of being waived under DR 5–105(C), but one of the clients will not consent to the dual representation. Although the "thrust upon" conflict may be unforeseeable and arise through no fault of the lawyer or law firm affected, when it gives rise to a concurrent conflict under DR 5–105, the lawyer must nevertheless take action to avoid violation of DR 5–105(B). The customary response to such conflicts is for the lawyer to withdraw as necessary to avoid the conflict. *See* DR 2–110(B)(2). The Code does not, however, expressly address the case of "thrust upon" conflicts, nor does it specify under DR 2–110 from *which* representation(s) the attorney should withdraw in order to cure the conflict.

Nor has this dilemma been addressed directly by New York ethics opinions construing the Code. A growing body of case law, however, has dealt with "thrust upon" conflicts in litigation, applying a flexible approach that is consistent with the Code and should be used as a guide to resolving such conflicts, within the limits set forth in this opinion.

A. A lawyer faced with an apparent "thrust upon" conflict should first determine whether a concurrent conflict under DR 5–105 exists

When client relationships change during the course of a representation, the lawyer should first determine whether the changed circumstances create an actual conflict. As Scenarios 1 and 2 above, as well as case law suggest, corporate transactions are often sources of apparent "thrust upon" conflicts. In such cases, an apparent conflict may arise during the representation of two formerly unrelated clients when one becomes a member of the same corporate family (e.g., an affiliate, subsidiary, parent, or sister corporation) as another client's adversary. Representation of one member of a corporate family, however, does not automatically constitute representation of another member of the same corporate family. For the purposes of the ethics rules, a current client's adversary that, due to a merger or acquisition, has become the parent or subsidiary of another client, may not be considered a "client" at all. And if the apparent conflict does not actually involve two current clients, there is no conflict of interest under DR 5–105, and the attorney does not need to obtain consent from both clients in order to continue representing both.

Previous opinions have articulated the circumstances under which an apparent conflict involving a member of a current client's corporate family will be considered an actual conflict of interest requiring consent to continue representing both parties. This determination is based on several factors, including the relationship between the two corporate entities, and the relationship between the work the law firm is doing for the current client and the work the law firm wishes to undertake in opposition to the client's corporate family member. *See Eastman Kodak Co. v. Sony Corp.*, 2004 WL 2984297 at *3 (W.D.N.Y. Dec. 27, 2004) ("[t]he relevant inquiry centers on whether the corporate relationship between the two corporate family members is 'so close as to deem them a single entity for conflict of interest purposes'"); *Discotrade Ltd v. Wyeth–Ayerst Int'l, Inc.*, 200 F.Supp.2d 355, 358–59 (S.D.N.Y. 2002) (concluding that a corporate affiliate was also a client for conflict purposes because, among other things, the affiliate was an operating unit or division of an entity that shared the same board of directors and several senior officers and used the same computer network, e-mail system, travel department and health benefit plan as the client) * * *

In "thrust upon" conflict situations, application of the factors articulated in the cited ethics opinions will often lead to the conclusion that no conflict exists. For example, in Scenario 1 above, Company B has become a subsidiary of a long-time firm Client C. If the firm has no pre-existing relationship with Company B, is not representing Company B at the time the purported conflict arises, was not involved in the transaction whereby Company B became a subsidiary of Client C, and the firm has not acquired confidences of Company B that are relevant to the litigation, then, absent other factors, it may be that the firm will be able to conclude that it does not have an attorney-client relationship with Company B. As a result, there is no concurrent conflict and it would be permitted to continue to represent Client A in litigation without the consent of Company B or Client C.

The remainder of this opinion assumes that the unforeseen change of circumstances does result in a concurrent conflict within the purview of DR 5–105.

B. General rule requiring withdrawal where a consentable conflict of interest exists between concurrent clients, and one or both clients will not consent to the conflict.

Under the Code, a lawyer may not take on or continue the concurrent representation of multiple clients if the representation would "involve the lawyer in representing differing interests" or if "the exercise of independent professional judgment in behalf of a client will be or is likely to be adversely affected," unless the lawyer obtains the consent of each client affected by the conflict. DR 5–105. It is well settled that this means a lawyer may not oppose a current client in any matter, even if the matter is totally unrelated to the firm's representation of the client, without consent from both clients * * * When faced with a thrust upon conflict under DR 5–105, therefore, a lawyer would be unable to continue representing both clients without violating the disciplinary rule, if the lawyer is unable to obtain consent. Pursuant to DR 2–110(B)(2), a lawyer must withdraw from representing a client where the representation would violate a disciplinary rule. Therefore, ordinarily, when two clients will not consent to a conflict of interest, and the conflict requires consent, the law firm must withdraw from representation of at least one of the clients.

The New York disciplinary rules do not, on their face, indicate whether an attorney must withdraw from both representations in conflict situations, or whether the attorney may withdraw from representing only one client, and if so, which one. The disciplinary rule that governs withdrawal, DR 2–110(B)(2), merely states that a lawyer shall withdraw from employment if ("[t]he lawyer knows or it is obvious that continued employment will result in violation of a Disciplinary Rule." It sheds no light on situations where the withdrawal to avoid violation of a disciplinary rule involves more than one client * * *

The New York disciplinary rules governing former client conflicts also do not directly state whether a lawyer may, in order to avoid a material conflict between two current clients, withdraw from representing one client (thereby creating a "former client") and continue to represent the other. Under DR 5–108(A), a lawyer may not represent a client adverse to a former client without consent in the same or substantially related matter, where the current client's interests are materially adverse to the interests of the former client. If the matters are not substantially related, however, the lawyer may continue to represent a client even if that client is directly adverse to a former client, as long as the representation does not violate the lawyer's duty of confidentiality to the former client.

C. Determining which matter to withdraw from

Since the ethics rules do not instruct lawyers how to determine from which client to withdraw when faced with a current client conflict that violates DR 5–105, lawyers confronting this situation must be guided by the duties of confidentiality and loyalty to the client. Under the Code, the duty of confidentiality extends to both current and former clients. DR 4–101(B); DR 5–108(A)(2). If the conflict of interest between two current clients arises because the lawyer possesses confidential information, and consent cannot be obtained, the lawyer normally must withdraw from the affected representation * * * In circumstances where material confidential information is involved, or there is a substantial relationship between the two matters, a lawyer probably cannot solve the conflict merely by withdrawing from representing one client and continuing to represent the other, because the continuing representation would most likely still violate the rules regarding former client conflicts.

The duty of loyalty is also central to the ethical rules in Canon 5 prohibiting a lawyer from representing multiple clients with differing interests. "Maintaining the independence of professional judgment required of a lawyer precludes acceptance or continuation of employment that will adversely affect the lawyer's judgment on behalf of or dilute the lawyer's loyalty to the client." EC 5–14. And as explained by EC 5–1, "[t]he professional judgment of a lawyer should be exercised, within the bounds of the law, solely for the benefit of the client and free of compromising influences and loyalties. Neither the lawyer's personal interest, the interests of other clients, nor the desires of third persons should be permitted to dilute the lawyer's loyalty to the client." * * *

Concurrent representation in particular "presents the risk of divided loyalty to each client, portending constrained vigor and impeding independent judgment on the lawyer's part." ABA Annotated Model Rules of Professional Conduct 1.7 (5th ed. 2003) at 116.

While the Code may not expressly prevent a lawyer from dropping one client in order to represent another, it is well-settled that the duty of loyalty prevents an attorney from doing so opportunistically. For example, under the so-called "hot-potato" rule, a lawyer or law firm should not ordinarily be permitted to abandon one client in order to take on the representation of a more lucrative client, where representing both would create a conflict of interest. This approach has been followed in several court cases involving attorney disqualification motions, where courts have articulated the need to protect confidential client information, as well as to protect the disfavored client from being "cut adrift" simply because a more lucrative client comes along with a claim against it.

The "hot potato" rule prohibiting the abandonment of a current client to take on a more lucrative representation is a salutary one, but it is not commanded by the text of the Code or the ABA Model Rules and should not apply to situations where its underlying rationale would not be served. The rule condemns affirmative self-interested acts of disloyalty by an attorney to an existing client in order to switch allegiance to a new one. In circumstances where an attorney is representing two clients, and an unforeseeable conflict between the two arises during the ongoing representation of both, concerns about opportunistic attorney activity are less evident: by definition, the problem was "thrust upon" the lawyer.

Many courts have also found that the duty of loyalty concerns underpinning the "hot potato" rule are not present in the "thrust upon" situation where the lawyer has not instigated the conflict or deliberately sought to abandon a client. In addition, in the current business climate, corporate mergers and acquisitions occur with sufficient regularity that conflicts of interests between two clients will often arise unexpectedly and through no fault of the lawyer, creating conflict situations that are not governed by the "hot potato" rule. Consequently, many courts have applied a flexible approach to "thrust upon" situations that focuses on balancing the interests of all affected parties rather than mechanically applying the "hot potato" rule to prevent a lawyer from withdrawing from one client in order to continue representing the other * * *

Nothing in the Code bars an attorney from employing similar reasoning in carrying out the obligations of Canons 2 and 5. When confronted with a "thrust upon" concurrent client conflict, lawyers should balance several factors in deciding whether they may withdraw from one representation and continue the other, and if so, which client to continue representing. Of course, absent consent, an attorney should not simply withdraw from a representation and continue an adverse one where doing so would compromise material confidences and secrets of what would become the former client. *See* DR 5–108. Because thrust upon conflicts typically involve totally unrelated matters, however, the requirement of protecting confidences of an ex-client will not always command a particular result. Where confidences will not be placed at risk, the overriding factor should be the prejudice the withdrawal or continued representation will cause the parties, including whether representation of one client over the other would give an unfair advantage to a client. The lawyer must also consider other factors, for example, the origin of the conflict (*i.e.*, which client's action caused the conflict to arise); whether one client has manipulated the conflict to try to force a lawyer off the matter and is using the conflict as leverage; the costs and inconvenience to the party being required to obtain new counsel, including the complexity of the representation; whether the choice would diminish the lawyer's vigor of representation toward the remaining client; and, the lawyer's overall relationship to each client.

The commentary to the Model Rules supports this approach. As under the New York Code, the ABA Model Rules generally prohibit a lawyer from continuing to represent a client where that representation would be directly adverse to another client, or where a significant risk exists that the representation would be materially limited by the lawyer's responsibilities to the other client. Model Rule 1.7(a). However, the commentary to Model Rule 1.7 suggests that in cases in which a conflict arises during the course of representation, and where the conflict was the result of "[u]nforeseeable developments, such as changes in corporate and other organizational affiliations," the lawyer may have the option to withdraw from one of the representations in order to avoid the conflict. Model Rule 1.7 Comment [5] * * *

The Restatement also supports a lawyer's ability to withdraw "in order to continue an adverse representation against a theretofore existing client when the matter giving rise to the conflict and requiring withdrawal comes about through initiative of the clients" so long as the situation causing the conflict was not "reasonably foreseeable" by the lawyer when the lawyer first undertook the representation of the client. Restatement (Third) of the Law Governing Lawyers § 132 cmt. J * * *

* * * [An] example is *Gould, Inc. v. Mitsui Mining & Smelting Co.* In *Gould*, a conflict of interest for plaintiff's counsel arose several years after litigation had commenced, when the defendant acquired a company, IGT, that plaintiff's counsel represented in unrelated matters. The defendant moved to disqualify plaintiff's counsel, but the court rejected the motion. In doing so, the court refused to mechanically apply the "hot potato" rule, and took a more flexible approach that balanced the various interests involved. First, the court found that the defendant had not been prejudiced because confidential information had not passed to the plaintiff as a result of plaintiff's firm's representation of IGT. Second, disqualifying plaintiff's firm would cost plaintiff a great deal of time and money in retaining new counsel and would significantly delay the progress of the case, which involved complex technological issues. Finally, the court found that the conflict was created by defendant's acquisition of IGT several years after the current litigation commenced,

and not by any affirmative act of plaintiff's law firm. *Gould, Inc. v. Mitsui Mining & Smelting Co.,* 738 F. Supp. 1121, 1126–27 (N.D. Ohio 1990) * * *

The scenarios set forth at the outset of this opinion illustrate how these factors may be applied in specific situations. Scenarios 1 and 2 involve situations where a current client has, through a merger or acquisition, become adverse to another client that is a member of the same corporate family. Depending on, among other things, the relationship between Company B and Client C in Scenario 1, and Company C and Client A in Scenario 2, the adversary may or may not be considered a "client" for conflicts purposes * * *

Assuming that a conflict does exist between the clients, however, the law firm would need to balance the factors outlined above in determining which client to represent. For example, in Scenario 1, the law firm would first need to determine who would be most prejudiced by the withdrawal. This would depend in part on the complexity of the breach of contract suit against B and how close to trial the suit is. The closer the suit is to trial, the more Client A would be prejudiced if the law firm withdrew from representation. In contrast, if the law firm had only recently been retained to represent Client A in the breach of contract suit and had yet to engage in extensive discovery, the prejudice to Client A from withdrawal would not be as great. Other factors that would determine which client would be most prejudiced involve, for example, the financial costs to each and whether the lawyer has acquired material confidential information that could be used against the client from whom the lawyer withdraws. In addition, because Client C created the conflict, the law firm should question whether Client C is seeking to use the conflict as leverage to force the law firm off the case involving Client A. As noted in *Installation Software*, a "conflict by acquisition" should not give the acquiring client a means to strategically disadvantage Client A, who is in effect an innocent bystander with respect to Client C's acquisition of Client A's adversary (Company B). More broadly, we believe that it will generally appear fairer and more understandable to a client whose lawyer withdraws because of a conflict if the client's action gave rise to the conflict in the first place.

At the same time, if Client C is a large, important client of the firm, the law firm must be wary in applying the balancing test that it is not motivated by purely economic factors to retain Client C. After weighing all of the factors, if the law firm decides that the balancing test favors Client C, it should inform Client A that due to a conflict of interest it must withdraw from representing that client in the law suit against Company B. If the law firm concludes that the factors weigh in favor of Client A, it should inform Client C that it will not withdraw from representing Client A in the breach of contract suit. At that point, it will be up to Client C to decide whether it wishes to consent to the conflict after all, or terminate its relationship with the law firm.

D. Limitations to Opinion

This opinion is not intended to apply other than in cases of a "thrust upon" conflict as defined above.

First, the conflict must truly be unforeseeable. This requirement will often be satisfied in the merger and acquisitions context, as in Scenarios 1 and 2, as long as the law firm represented both clients before the corporate transaction occurred or before the law firm knew it was under consideration. It could be satisfied in other contexts when, for example, a current client unexpectedly appears in an adverse capacity in a government investigation.

Second, the conflict must truly be no fault of the lawyer. So, for example, if the conflict arose because the lawyer did an inadequate conflicts check originally by, for example, failing to check necessary individuals or entities, failing to spell the names of the clients accurately when putting information into a database or by other conduct that is negligent, this opinion does not apply * * *

Third, the conflict must be between concurrent clients. The rules governing when a current client becomes a former client for conflicts purposes are beyond the scope of this opinion but in determining whether this opinion applies the lawyer must consider whether even a client for whom the lawyer has done no work for a significant period of time is, in fact, a current client under the conflicts rules. This analysis involves a delicate fact-specific inquiry. *See, e.g. International Business Machines Corp. v. Levin*, 579 F.2d 271, 281 (3d Cir. 1978) ("[a]lthough CBM had no specific assignment from IBM on hand on the day the antitrust complaint was filed . . . the pattern of repeated retainers, both before and after the filing of the complaint, supports the finding of a continuous relationship") * * *

Of course, attorneys must keep in mind that the continued representation of one client after withdrawing from the other must still satisfy DR 5–108, the rule governing former client conflicts. See DR 5–108; Restatement (Third) of the Law Governing Lawyers § 132 cmt. j (continuing an adverse representation against a theretofore existing client "must be otherwise consistent with the former-client conflict rules"). In particular, the confidences and secrets of the former client must be protected, and no attorney may continue an adverse representation, without court approval, even in a "thrust upon" situation, in which material confidences and secrets of either client (or former client) will be placed at risk.

Finally, implementation of the balancing test for thrust upon conflicts must be performed in good faith. Where the attorney's decision regarding withdrawal appears opportunistic, for example the retained client generates significantly more fees than the dropped client and there are no other factors that weigh in favor of retaining that client, any insistence that the conflict was thrust upon the lawyer, or protestations of prejudice to the major client, may be viewed skeptically. On the other hand, a lawyer who does balance the relevant considerations in good faith should not be subject to discipline for getting it wrong in hindsight.

E. Prophylactic Measures

Lawyers may take several steps to anticipate and potentially avoid concurrent client conflicts. In particular, some conflicts may be avoided by obtaining advance consents from clients to waive conflicts that may come up in the future. Of course, the fact that "thrust upon" conflicts by definition are not reasonably foreseeable may make it particularly difficult in some cases to obtain enforceable advance waivers. Nonetheless, in appropriate instances clients can give informed and therefore effective waivers in advance to a sufficiently described set of circumstances without necessarily knowing all details or the identity of the other client * * *

In addition, attorneys may be able to draft the letter of engagement to avoid uncertainty as to whether the representation is ongoing or not, and who is the client. For example, the lawyer could clarify that he or she only represents the client in a particular area or for a particular matter, and representation in any other matter would necessitate a separate agreement. Similarly, the lawyer could clarify that he or she represents only specified entities within the corporate family, and not current or future affiliates.

4. CONCLUSION

When, in the course of continuing representation of multiple clients, a conflict arises through no fault of the lawyer that was not reasonably foreseeable at the outset of the representation, does not involve the exposure of material confidential information, and that cannot be resolved by the consent of the clients, a lawyer is not invariably required to withdraw from representing a client in the matter in which the conflict has arisen. The lawyer should be guided by the factors identified in this opinion in deciding from which representation to withdraw. In reaching this decision, the overarching factor should be which client will suffer the most prejudice as a consequence of withdrawal. In addition, the attorney should consider the origin of the conflict, including the extent of opportunistic maneuvering by one of the clients, the effect of withdrawal on the lawyer's vigor of representation for the remaining client, and other factors mentioned in this opinion.

AMERICAN BAR ASSOCIATION STANDING COMMITTEE ON ETHICS AND PROFESSIONAL RESPONSIBILITY FORMAL OPINION 95–390 CONFLICTS OF INTEREST IN THE CORPORATE FAMILY CONTEXT (1995)

* * * The Committee has been asked whether a lawyer who represents a corporate client may undertake a representation that is adverse to a corporate affiliate of the client in an unrelated matter, without obtaining the client's consent.

The issue is one that has arisen with increasing frequency because of "[t]he proliferation of national or multi-national public corporations owning or partially owning subsidiaries which may also be national or multi-national [and] the spawning of varied types of corporate affiliates...." *Pennwalt Corp. v. Plough, Inc.*, 85 F.R.D. 264, 267 (D. Del. 1980). Although, in the sense described in *Pennwalt*, the problem has been "created" by modern corporations, the onus is squarely on the lawyer to anticipate and resolve conflicts of interest involving corporate affiliates. *Id.* at 273. As stated in the Comment to Rule 1.7 of the Model Rules of Professional Conduct (1983, amended 1994):

> The lawyer should adopt reasonable procedures, appropriate for the size and type of firm and practice, to determine in both litigation and non-litigation matters the parties and issues involved and to determine whether there are actual or potential conflicts of interest.

> In addition to the ethical questions that a lawyer may face in undertaking a representation adverse to an affiliate of an existing corporate client, the lawyer also faces a potential motion to disqualify. Indeed, these circumstances have been considered most often in the context of such a motion.

* * * Clearly, the best solution to the problems that may arise by reason of clients' corporate affiliations is to have a clear understanding between lawyer and client, at the very start of the representation, as to which entity or entities in the corporate family are to be the lawyer's clients, or are to be so treated for conflicts purposes. This Opinion is principally addressed to those circumstances where there are not such clear governing terms to the engagement. Such circumstances will frequently obtain simply because the relationship with the client is of long standing, antedating the time when letters of engagement came into common use; or because there is a change in the identity or the corporate affiliations of the client, through acquisitions, mergers and the like.

Even in circumstances where there is no established understanding about the lawyer's obligations toward affiliates of the client, considerations of client relations will ordinarily dictate the lawyer's course of action, without the occasion even arising to consider whether the Model Rules forbid the contemplated new representation. Nonetheless, there will sometimes be circumstances where the requirements of the Model Rules rather than considerations of client relations will govern: for example, where by virtue of merger or acquisition the corporate affiliation of the client changes.

It is the Committee's opinion that the Model Rules of Professional Conduct do not prohibit a lawyer from representing a party adverse to a particular corporation merely because the lawyer (or another lawyer in the same firm) represents, in an unrelated matter, another corporation that owns the potentially adverse corporation, or is owned by it, or is, together with the adverse corporation, owned by a third entity.[2] The fact

---

2. We here principally address, for simplicity of analysis, situations where the subsidiaries in the corporate family are wholly owned by the corporate parent. Corporate affiliations involving lesser degrees of ownership may of course present the same issues, and involve in some degree the same analysis, as those involving whole ownership * * *

of corporate affiliation, without more, does not make all of a corporate client's affiliates into clients as well. Nonetheless, the circumstances of a particular representation may be such that the corporate client has a reasonable expectation that the affiliates will be treated as clients, either generally or for purposes of avoidance of conflicts, and the lawyer is aware of the expectation.

In any event, although the ethical propriety of a given representation will depend on the particular circumstances, the Committee believes that as a general matter, in the absence of a clear understanding otherwise, the better course is for a lawyer to obtain the corporate client's consent before the lawyer undertakes a representation adverse to its affiliate.

The Requirements of Rule 1.7

* * * Rule 1.7 is a rule of general applicability, governing lawyers' conduct whether they represent individuals or entities. The touchstone of the Rule, as the Comment to it makes clear, is loyalty to the client.

When requested to undertake a new representation that may adversely affect the interests of an existing client, a lawyer must first consider Rule 1.7(a). Under that provision, representation of a party "directly adverse to another client" is prohibited unless a lawyer concludes that his relationship with the existing client will not be "adversely affected" by the new representation, and both clients consent. The use of the term "directly adverse" in Rule 1.7(a) clearly differentiates the more general or indirect adverseness which is addressed in paragraph (b) of the Rule, discussed below. The Comment to Rule 1.7 confirms this interpretation of the term "directly," noting that "a lawyer ordinarily may not act as advocate against a person the lawyer represents in some other matter, even if it is wholly unrelated," but "simultaneous representation in unrelated matters of clients whose interests are only generally adverse, such as competing economic enterprises, does not require consent of the respective clients."

Where there is direct adverseness, so that Rule 1.7(a) applies, the lawyer may not take on the new representation unless two tests are met. First, the lawyer must reasonably believe that his new assignment will not adversely affect his relationship with his existing client. The lawyer's subjective judgment is not necessarily dispositive: his belief must be a reasonable one.

Second, both clients must consent after "consultation," which means that there has been "communication of information reasonably sufficient to permit the client to appreciate the significance of the matter in question." Model Rules, Terminology.

If the provisions of Rule 1.7(a) do not apply because the affiliate is not a client, the lawyer must nonetheless consider, under Rule 1.7(b), whether either the subsisting representation or the prospective one may be "materially limited by the lawyer's responsibilities to another client or to a third person." Loyalty to a client is impaired not only when a lawyer undertakes a representation directly adverse to the client, but also "when a lawyer cannot consider, recommend or carry out an appropriate course of action for the client because of the lawyer's other responsibilities or interests." Comment to Model Rule 1.7.... [T]he lawyer must also consider under Rule 1.7(b) whether the lawyer's representation of his existing client would be materially limited by his duties to the new client.[3] By its terms, Rule 1.7(b) requires the consent only of the client whose representation may be materially limited by the lawyer's other duties, but the lawyer must consider the effect of the simultaneous representation of two clients on each of them, and obtain consent where required by the Rule.

* * *

The application of these provisions in the circumstances before us can best be addressed in relation to three questions: (1) Is the corporate client's affiliate also a client, or entitled to be so treated for purposes of Rule 1.7? (2) If the affiliate is not a client, is the representation adverse to the affiliate also "directly adverse" to the corporate client, so as to bring it under Rule 1.7(a)? (3) If Rule 1.7(a) is not applicable, will the lawyer's responsibilities to one or the other client nonetheless materially limit the lawyer's representation so as to bring Rule 1.7(b) into play?

(1) Is the Corporate Client's Affiliate Also a Client?

Since a lawyer owes a duty of loyalty only to the lawyer's client, it is necessary to determine at the outset of analysis whether the affiliate of the lawyer's corporate client is also a client. As explained below, we conclude that the fact of corporate affiliation, without more, does not necessarily make the affiliate of a corporate client also a client. Nonetheless, the particular circumstances may be such that the affiliate also should be considered a client. It may also be the case that the corporate client has an expectation, binding on the lawyer in the circumstances, that its affiliates will be treated as clients for purposes of addressing conflicts under Rule 1.7, even though there is not a full-fledged client-lawyer relationship with the affiliates.

As to whether the fact of corporate affiliation *ipso facto* creates a client-lawyer relationship with every member of a corporate family when one of its members is formally represented by the lawyer, the Model Rules are silent.

* * * Rule 1.13 squarely states that when a lawyer represents an "organization"—a term that clearly includes corporations—it is the organization that is the lawyer's client. Its constituents, including its stockholders, are not also the lawyer's clients solely because of their relationship to the client. Rule 1.13(e) contemplates that a client-lawyer relationship between a constituent, including a stockholder, and corpo-

---

3. As the Comment makes clear, Rule 1.7 applies not merely to new representa- tions but also to conflicts arising after a representation has commenced.

rate counsel, must be specifically formed, rather than arising automatically by virtue of the client-lawyer relationship with the organization.

To be sure, Rule 1.13 does not directly address the question of when an affiliate of a corporate client is also a client, for the thrust of the Rule is to require the lawyer to distinguish between the corporation or other organization, which is his client, and the human representatives of the corporation, with whom the lawyer works and often forms personal relationships.

* * * We conclude, therefore, that whether a lawyer represents a corporate affiliate of his client, for purposes of Rule 1.7, depends not upon any clearcut per se rule but rather upon the particular circumstances.

The Model Rules do not directly address the question of when or how a client-lawyer relationship has been established: that is a matter governed by substantive law outside the Model Rules. *See* Model Rules, Scope Section:

> [F]or purposes of determining the lawyer's authority and responsibility, principles of substantive law external to these Rules determine whether a client-lawyer relationship exists.... Whether a client-lawyer relationship exists for any specific purpose can depend on the circumstances and may be a question of fact.

The client-lawyer relationship is principally a matter of contract, and the contract may be either express or implied. Thus, the entities within a corporate family that are to be considered clients may have been expressly identified as clients, or they may have become entitled to be so treated by reason of the way the representation of one of the members of the corporate family has been handled. In addition, it may be one of the terms of the engagement that the corporate client expects some or all of its affiliates to be treated as clients *for purposes of Rule 1.7*—i.e., that the lawyer will not accept engagements that would be prohibited by that Rule if the affiliates were clients.[7]

Clearly, a corporate affiliate must be treated as a client, whether generally or only for purposes of Rule 1.7, if the lawyer has agreed so to treat it, regardless of whether any actual work has been or is to be performed for the affiliate. Clearly also, it is important that lawyer and client share an understanding as to whether the client expects the lawyer to observe obligations to persons or entities other than the client itself, for that information is necessary for the lawyer to make the appropriate inquiries under Model Rule 1.7 to determine whether he can undertake the representation. Moreover, a client that has such an expectation has an obligation to keep the lawyer apprised of changes in the composition of the corporate family. While competent general counsel can be expected to be familiar with the corporate family and the

---

7. Such an understanding between the lawyer and the corporate client that the lawyer will refrain from representations adverse to the corporate affiliates of the client does not in itself establish a full-fledged client-lawyer relationship with the affiliates.

expectations of one member as to the treatment of other members, outside lawyers who are performing only a limited role for a single aspect of the business, no matter how well-intentioned, should not be expected to be current on all of the names, relationships and ownership interests among a client's varied and sometimes far-flung business interests. A lawyer who has no reason to know that his potential adversary is an affiliate of his client will not necessarily violate Rule 1.7 by accepting the new representation without his client's consent.

A client-lawyer relationship does not, however, require an explicit agreement, let alone a written letter of engagement: it may come into being as a result of reasonable expectations and a failure of the lawyer to dispel those expectations.

* * * Thus, when a lawyer is considering whether he can assume the representation adverse to a corporate affiliate of a client, he must consider not merely the terms of his engagement to that client but in addition whether the circumstances are such that the affiliate has reason to believe, on the basis of the nature of the lawyer's dealings with it, that it has a client-lawyer relationship with the lawyer.

* * * Thus, the nature of the lawyer's dealings with affiliates of the corporate client may be such that they have become clients as well. This may be the case, for example, where the lawyer's work for the corporate parent—say, on a stock issue or bank financing—is intended to benefit all subsidiaries, and involves collecting confidential information from all of them.

Even if the subject matter of the lawyer's representation of the corporate client does not involve the affiliate at all, however, the lawyer's relationship with the corporate affiliate may lead the affiliate reasonably to believe that it is a client of the lawyer. For example, the fact that a lawyer for a subsidiary was engaged by and reports to an officer or general counsel for its parent may support the inference that the corporate parent reasonably expects to be treated as a client.

A client-lawyer relationship with the affiliate may also arise because the affiliate imparted confidential information to the lawyer with the expectation that the lawyer would use it in representing the affiliate. Additionally, even if the affiliate confiding information does not expect that the lawyer will be *representing* the affiliate, there may well be a reasonable view on the part of the client that the information was imparted in furtherance of the representation, creating an ethically binding obligation that the lawyer will not use the information against the interests of any member of the corporate family.

Finally, the relationship of the corporate client to its affiliate may be such that the lawyer is required to regard the affiliate as his client. This would clearly be true where one corporation is the alter ego of the other. It is not necessary, however, for one corporation to be the alter ego of the other as a matter of law in order for both to be considered clients. A disregard of corporate formalities and/or a complete identity of managements and boards of directors could call for treating the two corporations as one. As stated by the court in *Teradyne, supra* (quoting Formal Opinion No. 1989–113 of the State Bar of California Standing Committee on Professional Responsibility and Conduct):

> In determining whether there is a sufficient unity of interests to require an attorney to disregard separate corporate entities for conflict purposes, the attorney should evaluate whether corporate formalities are observed, the extent to which each entity has distinct and independent managements and boards of directors and whether, for legal purposes, one entity could be considered the alter ego of the other.

> The fact that the corporate client wholly owns, or is wholly owned by, its affiliate does not in itself make them alter egos. However, whole ownership may well entail not merely a shared legal department but a management so intertwined that all members of the corporate family effectively operate as a single entity; and in those circumstances representing one member of the family may effectively mean representing all the others as well. Conversely, where two corporations are related only through stock ownership, the ownership is less than a controlling interest and the lawyer has had no dealing whatever with the affiliate, there will rarely be any reason to conclude that the affiliate is the lawyer's client.

(2) Is the Representation Affecting the Affiliate "Directly Adverse" to the Client?

Even though the corporation against which the lawyer is considering an adverse representation clearly is not the lawyer's client (or entitled for purposes of Rule 1.7 to be treated as such), the corporation that *is* a client may argue that the representation is nonetheless "directly adverse" to it, because any potential economic impact on the affiliate entails an impact on the corporation itself.

The paradigm situation here is presented by a lawyer's bringing a lawsuit, unrelated in substance to the lawyer's representation of a corporate client, seeking substantial money damages against a wholly owned subsidiary of the client: if the suit is successful, this will affect adversely not only the subsidiary but the parent as well, in the sense that one of its assets is the equity in the subsidiary, and its consolidated financial statements may (unless the subsidiary has applicable insurance coverage) reflect the impact of material adverse judgments against the subsidiary. *See Stratagem Dev. Corp. v. Heron Int'l N.V.*, 756 F.Supp. 789, 792 (S.D.N.Y. 1991) ("the liabilities of a subsidiary corporation directly affect the bottom line of the corporate parent."). It may also be the case, although less often, that a suit against a *parent* corporation will have a similarly direct economic impact on a wholly owned subsidiary (absent an "alter ego" situation), or that a corporation will be directly affected by a suit against a sibling corporation.

* * * The critical question is whether, in any of the situations referred to above, the representation is, as to the corporate client, *directly* adverse, so as to fall under Rule 1.7(a); or only *indirectly*

adverse, so that Rule 1.7(b) is the only potentially applicable provision. Although there is room for dispute on the point, we believe the better view is that the adverseness in such circumstances is indirect, and not direct.

The Committee has not previously addressed this question ... In Formal Opinion 93–377 (Positional Conflicts) (1993) ... we held that representation of two clients in different suits, where one suit may create a legal precedent that materially undercuts the position being advanced for the client in the other suit, presents a conflict under Rule 1.7(b), not a "directly adverse" representation under Rule 1.7(a). We there explained (in footnote 4):

> "Where there is such a conflict between separate representations, in the Committee's view the provision of Rule 1.7 that is potentially applicable is not paragraph (a), but paragraph (b). The former, in referring to a representation that is "directly adverse" to another client, contemplates litigating, or maintaining a position, in a given matter, on behalf of one client against a person or entity which is a client of the lawyer (or her firm) in another matter. The test under paragraph (b), on the other hand, is whether the representation of a client in one matter may be "materially limited" by the lawyer's responsibilities to another client in another matter, and the Committee views the impairment of a representation as a material limitation within the meaning of that paragraph."

> Thus, we have interpreted "directly adverse" to refer not merely to the practical impact (on the adversely affected client) but also to the circumstances in which the conflict arises, and specifically the closeness of the connection between the lawyer's actions and the adverse effect on the client. As a prominent treatise observes in this connection,

> The direct-remote distinction ... calls attention not simply to the clients' general economic interests, but specifically to the transactions in which the clients employ the lawyer's services.

1 Geoffrey C. Hazard & William W. Hodes, *The Law of Lawyering* § 1.7.203 (2d ed. 1990).

Simultaneous representation of clients in different lawsuits but which involve a related matter can also give rise to the direct, impermissible conflict proscribed by Rule 1.7(a).

We conclude, then, that although in situations involving an unrelated suit against an affiliate of a corporate client, the client may be adversely affected, that adverseness is, for purposes of Rule 1.7, indirect rather than direct, since its immediate impact is on the affiliate, and only derivatively upon the client. The phrasing of Rule 1.7(a) is not ambiguous: the reference to a representation that is "directly adverse" clearly draws a distinction between direct and indirect adverseness, and thereby draws a bright line striking a balance between the interests of lawyer and client ... [W]e see no principled way otherwise to draw a line short of the point where *any* discernible economic impact on a client arising from another representation (however slight or remote) must be treated as direct adverseness, requiring application of Rule 1.7(a) rather than Rule 1.7(b).

We recognize that there is some authority for a broader reading of "directly adverse." However, we think the foregoing analysis represents a sounder approach to Rule 1.7.

(3) If Rule 1.7(a) Is Not Applicable, Is the Representation Nonetheless Barred by Rule 1.7(b)?

As has been discussed above, even if it is determined that Rule 1.7(a) does not bar a particular representation adverse to an affiliate of a corporate client, because the affiliate is not also a client and the representation is not directly adverse to the corporate client, the lawyer must also be sure that the representation does not fall afoul of Rule 1.7(b). The lawyer must consider whether the representation that is adverse to the affiliate may be materially limited by the lawyer's responsibilities to the corporate client, or, correlatively, the representation of the corporate client may be materially limited by the representation of the client adverse to the affiliate; and if so in either case, the lawyer may not take on the adverse representation unless the lawyer reasonably concludes that the representation will not be adversely affected, and the potentially affected client consents.

What triggers Rule 1.7(b) is a lawyer's recognition of the possibility that a particular representation *may be materially limited* by the lawyer's responsibilities to another client. As the Comment to the Rule makes clear, the reference is to situations "when a lawyer cannot consider, recommend or carry out an appropriate course of action for the client because of the lawyer's other responsibilities or interests." Such a material limitation on the lawyer's ability properly to represent a client could arise, for example, if the lawyer's concern for remaining in the good graces of client A was likely to impair the independence of judgment or the zeal that the lawyer could bring to bear on behalf of client B. Thus, Rule 1.7(b) might come into play if the lawyer had reason to believe that, even though there was no understanding as to how the corporate client's affiliates were to be treated, nonetheless the corporate client would resent the lawyer's undertaking any representation that threatened, even indirectly, any adverse effect on either the financial well-being or the programmatic purposes of the corporate client; and if, because of this belief, there was a significant risk that the lawyer's diligence or judgment on behalf of his new client would be adversely affected by his awareness of the corporate client's displeasure.

The foregoing discussion recognizes that Rule 1.7(b) must be considered by the lawyer whenever a representation adverse to a corporate client is considered; it should not, of course, be taken to imply that Rule 1.7(b) requires the lawyer to seek consent from either the new client or the existing corporate client whenever a proposed representation is adverse to an affiliate of a corporate client. It is only when there is a threat of material limitation on the lawyer's ability properly to represent a client because of his responsibilities to another client that the Rule requires the lawyer to seek consent.

CONCLUSION

The provisions of both paragraphs of Rule 1.7 emphasize the paramount importance of preserving a lawyer's relationship with his client. In that light, doubts about whether one or another requirement of the Rule applies should be resolved by a presumption that favors the client who will be adversely affected by the prospective representation.

A lawyer should not strain to conclude that a proposed representation will not adversely affect his relationship with that client.[14] Where it is difficult to ascertain whether a matter will be directly adverse to an existing client, or to judge whether taking on the matter will affect the lawyer's relationship with the client, a lawyer ordinarily would be well advised as a matter of prudence and good practice to discuss the matter with his existing client before undertaking a representation adverse to an affiliate of the client, even though consent may not be ethically required. We hasten to add that the fact that the lawyer has as a matter of prudence and good practice sought consent where consent was not ethically required does not make the lawyer's undertaking the new representation in the absence of consent a disciplinable ethical violation. However, in any instance where the lawyer concludes that no client consent is required, under either paragraph of Rule 1.7, the lawyer should be prepared to show how he was able to make the various determinations required without contacting the client for information or consent—particularly determinations (a) that the client does not have an expectation that the corporate affiliate will be treated as a client, and (b) that the proposed representation adverse to the affiliate will not have a material adverse effect on the representation of the client.

Assuming that obtaining client consent is the preferable course would have several practical benefits. Loyalty is an essential element in a lawyer's representation of any client. Disloyalty is easily perceived by a client, whether or not that perception is well-founded. As this Committee noted in Formal Opinion 91–361 (Representation of a Partnership) (1991), if a lawyer explains the implications of a dual representation and obtains the informed consent of both parties, "the likelihood of perceived ethical impropriety on the part of the lawyer should be significantly reduced."

DISSENT

* * *

The majority's opinion starts from a premise that is so flawed it can only be explained by the fact that its proponents imagine its conclusion

---

14. * * * Where disqualification is not available, of course, a client can simply choose to discharge counsel.

only to apply to the largest of America's corporate conglomerates; then the majority compounds this error by assuming that companies that are part of these very large conglomerates do not very much care what happens to other members of the corporate family who are in different lines of business or in different geographical areas or led by different management, but just happen to be part of the same corporate enterprise.

The first problem with this approach is that the opinion as written applies to all corporate families regardless of their size or the nature of their businesses. Thus, even if one could imagine a special rule for "nasty" big companies, a possibility this writer rejects out of hand, that is not what the majority has crafted. The second problem is that the majority opinion fails to recognize the fact that corporate families are financially totally inter-dependent and that the sole purpose for the existence of these corporate families is economic success. Thus, when the majority opinion argues that an event economically adverse to subsidiary "A" only indirectly affects subsidiary "B," it clearly ignores the fact that for members of a corporate family the location of a corporate family's losses are totally irrelevant to the impact on the bottom line. Parents are directly dependent on the health of their subsidiaries; subsidiaries are directly dependent on the health of the parent; and subsidiaries are directly dependent on the health of other subsidiaries. For the last proposition one need look no further than the drastic effects on General Electric Credit Corporation of the widely publicized events at Kidder, Peabody.

* * * Taking the profession where no prior opinion has ever tread, the majority today condones lawyers taking positions adverse to the parents, subsidiaries and siblings of their corporate clients on the ground that doing so is only indirectly adverse because it involves economic harm to a subsidiary, parent or sibling. The sole reason for corporate existence is the maximization of economic success. Thus, when a corporation is harmed economically it is being hurt in the only way that counts. Yet somehow because the corporation has decided to, been forced to or, indeed, been counseled by its own lawyer to conduct its affairs through subsidiaries, it has lost the protection the majority concedes it would enjoy if its various businesses were organized as divisions. Why a corporation with subsidiaries may be so "punished" is nowhere explained by the majority. Nor is it explained why the suit against the Ford Division of Ford, even if it is for $100, results in direct adverseness while the suit against Jaguar, even if it is for $100,000,000, is indirect.

It is the conclusion of the majority opinion that the way a client chooses, is advised or is forced to organize its business is determinative of how the company should be treated for conflict of interest purposes. Yet every lawyer knows that there will be almost no cases where, *from the client's perspective,* that should be so. And it is clients, not lawyers, that the conflict of interest rules are supposed to protect.

The existence of subsidiaries often reflects regulatory requirements, historical accidents or considerations of limiting liability. They will almost never reflect a client judgment that what happens to the subsidiary, parent or sibling is not a matter that it cares about very much indeed. Just as Ford undoubtedly cares as much about what happens at its Jaguar subsidiary as it does about what happens at its Lincoln Mercury Division, so, too, is this the case in virtually every wholly owned corporate family. In the final analysis the enterprise is simply one economic conglomerate whose sole reason for being is earning profits for its shareholders * * *

CONCLUSION

It is the view of this writer that the majority opinion misinterprets Model Rule 1.7(a) when it concludes that the rule's interdiction of conduct directly adverse to a client does not include taking a position directly adverse to a corporate affiliate of the client. Perhaps another Standing Committee on Ethics and Professional Responsibility on another day will see the error of the majority's ways and correct it. Until then, this dissent is offered as a call to the profession to follow the dissent's bright line rule whenever the profession approaches conflicts of interest in the corporate family context. The last thing our profession needs is another black eye caused by jettisoned client loyalty in the name of economic expediency.

Lawrence J. Fox

AMERICAN BAR ASSOCIATION STANDING COMMITTEE ON ETHICS AND PROFESSIONAL RESPONSIBILITY

FORMAL OPINION 05–436

INFORMED CONSENT TO FUTURE CONFLICTS OF INTEREST; WITHDRAWAL OF FORMAL OPINION 93–372

The Model Rules contemplate that a lawyer in appropriate circumstances may obtain the effective informed consent of a client to future conflicts of interest. General and open-ended consent is more likely to be effective when given by a client that is an experienced user of legal services, particularly if, for example, the client is independently represented by other counsel in giving consent and the consent is limited to future conflicts unrelated to the subject of the representation. Rule 1.7, as amended in February 2002, permits a lawyer to obtain effective informed consent to a wider range of future conflicts than would have been possible under the Model Rules prior to their amendment. Formal Opinion 93–372 (Waiver of Future Conflicts of Interest) therefore is withdrawn.

This opinion applies the ABA Model Rules of Professional Conduct to the subject of a lawyer obtaining a client's informed consent to future conflicts of interest. The Committee concludes, for the reasons discussed below, that ABA Model Rule of Professional Conduct 1.7 permits effective informed consent to a wider range of future conflicts than would have been possible under the Model Rules prior to their amendment.

Model Rules 1.7, 1.6, and 1.9

Rule 1.7 addresses concurrent conflicts of interest and the circumstances in which a lawyer may, with the informed consent of each affected client, represent a client notwithstanding a concurrent conflict. Rule 1.6, regarding confidentiality of information, and Rule 1.9, regarding duties to former clients, are relevant with respect to the confidentiality issues relating to obtaining such consent.

In 1993, when the Committee issued Opinion 93–372, the Model Rules did not expressly address a client's giving informed consent to future conflicts of interest. Moreover, no Rule or Comment provided express guidance as to when an earlier matter for a former client and a later matter for a different client should be considered substantially related. In 2002, that changed in both respects.

In February 2002, Model Rule 1.7 was restructured and revised. Rule 1.7(a) defines a "concurrent conflict of interest." Rule 1.7(b) addresses the circumstances under which a lawyer may undertake or continue representation of a client in reliance upon the client's informed consent to a conflict:

> Notwithstanding the existence of a concurrent conflict of interest under paragraph (a), a lawyer may represent a client if:
>
> > (1) the lawyer reasonably believes that the lawyer will be able to provide competent and diligent representation to each affected client;
> >
> > (2) the representation is not prohibited by law;
> >
> > (3) the representation does not involve the assertion of a claim by one client against another client represented by the lawyer in the same litigation or other proceeding before a tribunal; and
> >
> > (4) each affected client gives informed consent, confirmed in writing.

The Comments to Model Rule 1.7 were also revised. New Comment [22] expressly addresses the subject of a client's giving informed consent to future conflicts:

> Whether a lawyer may properly request a client to waive conflicts that might arise in the future is subject to the test of paragraph (b) [of Model Rule 1.7]. The effectiveness of such waivers is generally determined by the extent to which the client reasonably understands the material risks that the waiver entails. The more comprehensive the explanation of the types of future representations that might arise and the actual and reasonably foreseeable adverse consequences of those representations, the greater the likelihood that the client will have the requisite understanding .. Thus, if the client agrees to consent to a particular type of conflict with which the client is already familiar, then

the consent ordinarily will be effective with regard to that type of conflict. If the consent is general and open-ended, then the consent ordinarily will be ineffective, because it is not reasonably likely that the client will have understood the material risks involved. On the other hand, if the client is an experienced user of the legal services involved and is reasonably informed regarding the risk that a conflict may arise, such consent is more likely to be effective, particularly if, e.g., the client is independently represented by other counsel in giving consent and the consent is limited to future conflicts unrelated to the subject of the representation. In any case, advance consent cannot be effective if the circumstances that materialize in the future are such as would make the conflict nonconsentable under paragraph (b).

The Committee believes that the term "waiver," as used in the first part of Comment [22], is intended to mean the same thing as the term "informed consent," as used in Rule 1.7 and elsewhere in the Comments.

We interpret the meaning of the term "unrelated to the subject of the representation" in Comment [22] by referring to Comment [3] to Model Rule 1.9, also added in February 2002. Comment [3] provides guidance on when an earlier matter for a former client and a later matter for a different client are to be considered "substantially related." The Comment, which is lengthy, begins with the general principle that "matters are substantially related' for purposes of this Rule if they involve the same transaction or legal dispute or if there otherwise is a substantial risk that confidential factual information as would normally have been obtained in the prior representation would materially advance the client's position in the subsequent matter." We are of the opinion, therefore, that the term "unrelated to" as used in Comment [22] should be read as meaning not "substantially related to," as that term is used in Rule 1.9 and its Comment [3], i.e., that the future matters as to which the client's consent to the lawyer's conflicting representation is sought do not involve the same transaction or legal dispute that is the subject of the lawyer's present representation of the consenting client, and are not of such a nature that the disclosure or use by the lawyer of information relating to the representation of the consenting client would materially advance the position of the future clients.

Opinion 93–372

As noted above, when the Committee issued Opinion 93–372 no Model Rule or Comment expressly addressed informed consent to future conflicts of interest, and none provided express guidance on when successive matters for different clients are to be considered substantially related. Opinion 93–372 cites Model Rules 1.7 and 1.6, Disciplinary Rule 5–105(c) of the predecessor Model Code of Professional Responsibility, and authorities that pre-date (with the exception of one decision) the Model Rules. Opinion 93–372 does not cite Model Rule 1.9.

Opinion 93–372 concludes that the effectiveness of a client's "consent after consultation" is generally limited to circumstances in which the lawyer is able to and does identify the potential party or class of parties that may be represented in the future matter(s). Opinion 93–372 also concludes that, in some instances, the lawyer may need to identify the nature of the likely future matter(s). Although Opinion 93–372 acknowledges that clients differ in their level of sophistication, the opinion does not vary its conclusions as to the likely effectiveness of informed consent to future conflicts when the client is an experienced user of legal services or has had the opportunity to be represented by independent counsel in relation to such consent. Also, although Opinion 93–372 is based to a considerable degree on concerns about the possibility of disclosure or use of the client's confidential information against it in a later matter,[6] it does not address those concerns in the context of the lawyer's seeking informed consent that is limited to future matters that are not substantially related to the client's matter. An informed consent that is limited to future matters that are not substantially related should not raise the concerns regarding the disclosure and use of confidential information that were among the central considerations underlying Opinion 93–372, given the criteria, discussed earlier, for determining whether successive matters are substantially related.[7]

Opinion 93–372's limitation of the scope of effective consent to future conflicts, which is its central conclusion, is inconsistent with the amended Model Rules. Hence, we withdraw Opinion 93–372 in its entirety. The Committee notes that other conclusions in Opinion 93–372 on related points are consistent in whole or in part with the Model Rules as amended; those other conclusions are incorporated in this opinion.

Additional Limitations and Requirements

The Committee notes the following additional limitations and requirements relating to a client's giving informed consent to a future conflict of interest. First, under Rule 1.7(b)(2) and (3), some conflicts are not consentable. An informed consent to a future conflict (like an informed consent to a current conflict) cannot alter that circumstance. Second, under Rule 1.7(b)(4), the client's informed consent must be confirmed in writing. Third, as noted earlier, a client's informed consent to a future conflict, without more, does not constitute the client's informed consent to the disclosure or use of the client's confidential information against the client. Finally, a lawyer, when considering taking on a later matter covered by an informed consent given in

---

6. Opinion 93–372 stated that consent to waive a future conflict of interest does not have the effect of authorizing the lawyer to reveal or use confidential client information. That remains the case. *See also* Rules 1.6(a) and 1.9(b)(2) and (c)(1). Opinion 93–372's reliance on confidentiality concerns as a basis for limiting the scope of the effectiveness of consent to future conflicts seemed to be based on the risk that the lawyer later may violate Rules 1.6 or 1.9. The Committee does not view the hypothetical risk that the lawyer later might violate the Model Rules as a sufficient basis for proscribing the sort of informed consent to future conflicts contemplated by Rule 1.7 cmt. 22.

7. Opinion 93–372's limitation of the scope of effective consent to future conflicts, which is its central conclusion, is inconsistent with the amended Model Rules. Hence, we withdraw Opinion 93–372 in its entirety. The Committee notes that other conclusions in Opinion 93–372 on related points are consistent in whole or in part with the Model Rules as amended; those other conclusions are incorporated in this opinion.

advance, even if the conflict is consentable, still must determine whether accepting the engagement in impermissible for any other reason under Rules 1.7(b) and 1.9, or any other Model Rule. The lawyer also must determine whether informed consent is required from the client that is to be represented in that later matter.

PROBLEMS

1.[1] Senior Partner, an attorney at the law firm of Adams & Adams, represents Telecom Corp. in its defense of a suit brought by Media Enterprises. The suit alleges that Telecom has engaged in discriminatory pricing of its telecommunications equipment. Junior Partner, another attorney in Adams & Adams, has acquired confidential information about Telecom and the lawsuit, although she has done no work on the case. Associate, a third attorney at Adams & Adams, has researched a purely legal issue connected with the suit, but has acquired no confidential information about it.

Using Model Rules 1.9 and 1.10, answer the following questions:

1. (a) Suppose that Senior Partner moves to law firm Baker & Baker. That firm wishes to represent Oxymoron, Inc. in a lawsuit against Telecom. The suit alleges that Telecom has violated antitrust law by requiring that purchasers of its telecommunications equipment also purchase installation contracts from Telecom. May Senior Partner undertake the representation of Oxymoron after he has moved to Baker & Baker? May any lawyer in Baker & Baker do so?

(b) Suppose instead that Junior Partner moves to Baker & Baker. May she represent Oxymoron in its suit against Telecom? May any lawyer in Baker & Baker?

(c) Finally, suppose instead that Associate moves to Baker & Baker. May he represent Oxymoron in its suit against Telecom? May any lawyer in Baker & Baker?

Suppose instead that Senior Partner and Junior Partner both move to Baker & Baker. They were the only lawyers in their firm who acquired confidential information from Telecom relating to the lawsuit filed by Media Enterprises. Their former firm, Adams & Adams, wishes to represent Oxymoron in a suit against Telecom alleging that Telecom has failed to make its communications equipment available on fair terms to companies that are not engaged in joint ventures with Telecom. May Adams & Adams represent Oxymoron in this lawsuit?

2. Your law firm, Rosetti and Caplan, regularly does legal work for Escapes, Inc., a corporation that operates resort hotels around the world. Escapes recently acquired an 80% interest in Travelink, an on-line travel booking service. Travelink seeks to provide "one-stop" on-line reservation services for all aspects of travel, both for business and for pleasure. It permits customers to make reservations for transportation, lodging, rental cars, entertainment, side trips, tours, amusement parks, and any other needs that may arise in the course of travel.

---

1. Adapted from Deborah L. Rhode & David J. Luban, *Legal Ethics* 526 (2d ed. 1995).

Escapes regards Travelink as an opportunity to expand its reach within the travel industry, as well as to add electronic services to its brick and mortar operations. Travelink will provides its services to a wide range of customers, including those who book vacations at resorts other than those operated by Escapes. Prospective Escapes customers will be directed to Travelink to make their reservations, which will make it possible for them to arrange in one session all the features of the vacation that they desire at Escapes resorts, such as skiing in Switzerland or a safari in Kenya.

Four of Travelink's five directors are also directors of Escapes. Travelink's CEO will remain in his position, while one of Escapes' three vice-presidents will become the vice-president of Travelink. Legal work for Travelink has been integrated into the Escapes legal department. Escapes also will perform a variety of "back office" functions for Travelink, such as work on billing and accounts receivable, payroll, pensions, and purchasing.

About six months after the acquisition, your law firm adds six partners from an intellectual property boutique. One of the clients for whom the partners do work is Yeehaw, an Internet search engine company. A month after the new partners arrive, Yeehaw asks that the firm represent it in a lawsuit against Travelink for infringement of its property rights in its search engine. Escapes gets wind of the prospective lawsuit, and informs you that it will move to disqualify Rosetti and Caplan if it seeks to represent Yeehaw in the suit against Travelink.

You and two other partners comprise the conflicts committee for your firm. You meet to discuss how to proceed. One piece of information relevant to your deliberations is a memorandum of understanding that the firm and Escapes signed a couple of years ago when Escapes began to increase its reliance on Rosetti and Caplan for legal services. The memorandum reads:

"Because of the large size of our law firm and our representation of many clients, it is possible that there may arise from time to time in the future an engagement in which another client represented by the firm has interests that do not coincide with those of Escapes, Inc. Escapes agrees that representation of it by Rosetti and Caplan on any matter will not preclude the firm from representing another client in such a situation. This agreement does not permit the firm to disclose, use, or rely on in any way confidential information that it gains during the course of its representation of Escapes, Inc."

How do you proceed?

Chapter 14

INCORPORATION AND CLOSE CORPORATIONS

INTRODUCTION

If three people were to ask a lawyer to incorporate their business, why should the lawyer not do so? If incorporation simply involved compliance with the few requirements found in most corporate statutes, there might be no reason why the lawyer should not perform the work. Unfortunately, life is not that simple. Often, a standard form of incorporation will not suffice and greater detail will be required at the beginning of the corporation's life. Corporate statutes require little in the organic documents, and enable the parties, relatively free from legal requirements, to engage in a complex system of private ordering that can deal with fundamental issues of organization, governance, finance and the allocation of control profit and risk.

If a simple incorporation will not suffice, the potential for conflict between the parties is present throughout the formation of the corporation. Thus, when they consult a lawyer, the first question that the lawyer must answer before accepting the representation is "who is the client." The question is important because the lawyer has specific duties to clients that she does not have to non-clients. Under Model Rule 1.4, a lawyer has the duty to promptly inform the client of any situation requiring the client's informed consent, to consult with the client about her objectives and how they will be accomplished, to keep the client reasonably informed and to promptly comply with information requests. Model Rule 1.6 forbids the lawyer from revealing information about a client without the client's informed consent. And Model Rule 1.7 requires a lawyer to get informed consent before representing one or more clients who may have a conflict of interest or to decline the representation altogether.

At first glance, determining who is the client would not seem to be a difficult task. An attorney-client relationship is either formed explicitly by a formal contractual agreement or implicitly by the client requesting, and the attorney performing, legal services for the client. RESTATEMENT

(THIRD) THE LAW GOVERNING LAWYERS, § 14. In practice, however, where there are multiple parties to a transaction, it is not always easy to determine whether each of the parties is a client, whether the corporation is (or will be) a client, and whether the lawyer's prior representation of one or more of the parties will raise a conflict of interest in the current representation that will make such representation impossible.

The potential for conflict is present whenever there is multiple representation. In the corporate setting, the potential is stronger when the enterprise is a closely held corporation where the same parties will be officers, directors and shareholders, each with differing goals. Multiple representation means that no party will have her own advocate in that process. If the parties do not know what form of business is most desirable, each will look to the lawyer to guide them through the choices they must make. They will need to agree upon the choice of securities, voting rights, and the way in which control will be exercised. At the outset, the actual or potential conflicts may be clearer to the lawyer than to the parties themselves and once the conflicts have been identified, the parties may expect the lawyer to suggest the most desirable way of resolving them. The lawyer as planner may find it difficult to maintain a neutral role since every solution involves tradeoffs. How does the lawyer respond? To whom, if anyone, at this stage (before there even is a corporation), does the lawyer owe her loyalty?

There are, of course, arguments in favor of multiple representation. Although the parties may have divergent interests, they start with a common goal, going into business together, and divergent interests do not always rise to the level of conflicts of interest. Thus, Model Rule 1.7 permits multiple representation, albeit with informed consent after full disclosure of the consequences. The parties also are likely to want to minimize their organizational expenses before the business has begun, and the cost of each party retaining her own lawyer at this stage may seem excessive. Finally, there is distinguished precedent. As you will read later in this chapter, Justice Brandeis, when a private practitioner, often became what he called "lawyer for the situation," representing what most of us would consider to be conflicting interests in a variety of transactions. Most of us, however, are not Justice Brandeis, and there is an element of playing God when assuming the role of the lawyer for the situation that may be difficult, attractive as that role may be.

Keep in mind the practical consequences determining who is the client. Once a lawyer-client relationship is established, the lawyer must "comply with obligations concerning the client's confidences and property, avoid impermissible conflicting interests, deal honestly with the client, and not employ advantages arising from the client-lawyer relationship in a manner adverse to the client." RESTATEMENT (THIRD) THE LAW GOVERNING LAWYERS § 16. Only clients can assert the attorney-client privilege, seek disqualification of the attorney in litigation because of the attorney's conflict of interest, or sue for malpractice.

OVERVIEW OF THE CHAPTER

The chapter is divided into three sections. The first, dealing with identifying the client, is limited in scope, arising primarily with respect to close corporations. The second and third sections which deal with the lawyer as a director of a corporation and a lawyer accepting stock of the corporate client as a fee for services rendered clearly are relevant to representing a close corporation but also relate to other aspects of corporate practice that you will study in subsequent chapters.

Who is the Client?

Rule 1.7 is the starting point for answering the question of the identity of the client, but how much guidance does it give? *Jesse* and the opinion of the State Bar of Arizona consider the issue in the context of the confidentiality requirement of Rule 1.6 and the attorney-client privilege. Does the retrospective test that they adopt or Rule 1.7 itself help answer the threshold question raised in the Introduction: can the lawyer incorporate the business of the three people in her office? Or who is to be considered the client if the business is never incorporated?

Banks and the District of Columbia Bar opinion consider the conflict question as it arises in litigation. If under Rule 1.13, the corporation rather than any of its constituents is the client, who, if anyone can a lawyer represent when there is a dispute among the constituents involving the corporation's business? The question is more difficult when, as is often the case, the disputing parties are both shareholders and managers, are the ones who have retained the lawyer to organize and advise the corporation and who, before the dispute, were receiving the lawyer's advice in a way that made it difficult to separate out the personal from the business. The answer here (which we will revisit in Chapter 29 when considering shareholder derivative litigation separately) often is that the lawyer should represent neither the corporation nor its constituents. If that is correct, how should the lawyer be acting as the dispute unfolds?

In returning to the question of the initial representation, Geoffrey Hazard thinks that the answer lies with former Justice Brandeis who contended that in such circumstances, he was "lawyer for the situation." In fact, many lawyers with lesser credentials do assume that role today, recognizing as they do so, that at some point, the parties are likely to need their own lawyers to represent their own individual interests. In permitting multiple representation, the comments to Rule 1.7 may be read as implicitly accepting the concept of lawyer for the situation provided that it has the protection of full disclosure by the lawyer and the client's informed consent after that disclosure.

Lawyer as Director

The question of a lawyer becoming a director of a client corporation often occurs at the time of the formation of a close corporation. The parties will want the lawyer who has helped organize the corporation and who often may be a friend of one or more of the parties to be a director. In some cases, the lawyer may be the only director who also is not active in the daily operation of the business.

The Model Rules do not explicitly prohibit the lawyer from being a director, notwithstanding the potential conflict of interest problems that are likely to arise in doing so. The American Bar Association opinion identifies the principal dangers as relating to the lawyer's professional independence when advising the corporation, the potential for corporate management to be unsure whether the lawyer is giving legal or business advice, and the need to protect confidential information and particularly to protect the attorney-client privilege. As you read the opinion, consider whether these problems are more likely to arise with a public than a close corporation even though the opinion itself does not draw that distinction.

As Craig Albert's article suggests, a lawyer may have strong economic and psychological reasons for being a director, notwithstanding the conflict of interest problems she may face. Albert reviews the advantages to both the lawyer and the corporation from the dual role and the arguments that can be raised against such service, ultimately concluding the risks are not serious enough to warrant a blanket prohibition.

The articles at the end of this section suggest that there has been a decline in lawyers serving on their client's board in the last few years. Some of this decline is attributable to the fallout from the recent corporate scandals. Another reason may be found in recent stock exchange rules requiring a majority of the board of directors of a listed corporation to be "independent." and defining "independent" so as to preclude many lawyers from serving even though the rules themselves do not explicitly prohibit the dual role.

After reading these materials, what factors—legal, economic, psychological, ethical, practical—would make you more or less likely to accept or decline the offer to be a director of your corporate client?

Stock for Services

Another issue that lawyers face in their representation of close corporations is the propriety of taking the corporation's stock as payment for some of their fees. In many cases, a start-up corporation may not have the capital to pay these fees and the lawyer will risk nonpayment to enable the client to get its business started. In the late 1990s, however, the picture changed as a number of lawyers representing high tech start-up companies made huge amounts of money by investing in their clients' stock, apart from the client's own economic needs.

The opinions of the American Bar Association and the Association of the Bar of the City of New York in this section address the problems that stock for services raise. Both conclude that despite the potential conflicts of interest that a lawyer faces when deciding to accept a client's stock in payment of the fee, the practice should not be prohibited. Both opinions stress the need for a fair valuation of the stock at the time of its issuance. Of equal (or possibly greater) importance is the lawyer's duty to disclose to the client the various conflicts that may arise from the lawyer's being a stockholder when the lawyer advises the client on matters that may affect the value of the lawyer's own stock.

Again, as you read these materials, consider what factors—legal, economic, psychological, ethical, practical—would make you more or less likely to accept your client's stock as payment for your services?

MODEL RULES: 1.4, 1.5, 1.6, 1.7 and Comments 28–35; 1.8, 1.13, 2.1

A.   WHO IS THE CLIENT?

Scott Thomas FitzGibbon, PROFESSIONAL ETHICS,
ORGANIZING CORPORATIONS, AND THE IDEOLOGY
OF CORPORATE ARTICLES AND BY-LAWS

(1982)

Organizing a business corporation is regarded by the corporate bar as the most prosaic of tasks; it is often delegated to a young associate who completes it in a few hours. The by-laws and the articles of incorporation may be the only formidable documents involved. Forms for these are usually retained in the law firm's files. The associate often does little more than have them retyped with proper names and addresses filled in, have them adopted at a brief meeting of the incorporators and directors, and make the necessary filings with state officials.

These nearly automatic procedures merit greater attention. Organizing a corporation falls squarely in the intersection of two areas of augmented concern. First, there is a move towards reconsideration of "corporate governance": the standards and structures according to which corporations are run. Second, professional ethics: there is a marked trend towards scrutinizing the behavior and revising the ethical standards governing corporate lawyers, especially those applicable where disputes or divergences arise among constituents of the corporate client such as directors, officers, and shareholders.

I.   ETHICAL CONSIDERATIONS AS TO PRESENT PRACTICES

The major ethical difficulty that the corporate lawyer is likely to encounter is that of conflict of interest. He usually sets to work at the behest of a few individuals who normally intend to be among the shareholders, directors, and officers. The interests of these individuals will often diverge according to their intended roles. Provisions in the corporate documents that serve the interests of the majority shareholder, for example, may disserve those of the minority. Similarly, provisions that extend more leeway to management correspondingly constrict those who are not part of management.

During the organization process, the corporation passes through several stages, sequentially acquiring incorporators, by-laws, articles of organization, directors and officers, stockholders, funds, and a business. The lawyer normally represents the new corporation and he may eventually work more for it than for the individuals. Representation of some or all of the individuals may continue along with representation of the new corporation. Additional divergences of interest can now be identified. Conflicts may arise between the new corporation and the individuals, or between the individuals acting as individuals and the individuals acting in some corporate capacities, for example, as officers. Provisions in the documents which advance the interests of the corporate client in some respect—by restricting indemnification payments, for example, or by limiting interested transactions—may do so at the expense of some of the individual clients.

The ABA Model Code of Professional Responsibility prohibits the lawyer from continuing to represent more than one client where "the exercise of his independent professional judgment in behalf of the client will be or is likely to be adversely affected . . . or if it would be likely to involve him in representing differing interests." An exception is made where consent has been obtained after "full disclosure of the possible effect of such representation on the exercise of [the lawyer's] independent professional judgment," provided that "it is obvious that he can adequately represent the interests of each."

The principle of client autonomy also raises ethical questions. Inexperienced clients often enter the lawyer's office with no views on the proper allocation of corporate rights and powers, beyond the desire to do the decent thing by one another. Ethical Consideration 7–7 states:

> In certain areas of legal representation not affecting the merits of the cause or substantially prejudicing the rights of a client, a lawyer is entitled to make decisions on his own. But otherwise the authority to make decisions is exclusively that of the client and, if made within the framework of the law, such decisions are binding on his lawyer.

Ethical Consideration 7–8 provides:

> A lawyer should exert his best efforts to insure that decisions of his client are made only after the client has been informed of relevant considerations. A lawyer ought to initiate this decision-making process if the client does not do so. . . . A lawyer should advise his client of the possible effect of each legal alternative. . . . In the final analysis . . . the lawyer should always remember that the decision whether to forego legally available objectives or methods because of non-legal factors is ultimately for the client and not for himself.

That the lawyer must comply with the informed decision of the client is fundamental to the concept of "representation" and reflects the fact that the interests at stake are those of the client. Unfortunately, the implications of the principle of client autonomy have not been much clarified by the authorities. In view of the importance and complexity of corporate articles and by-laws, the lawyer cannot be sure that adequate respect has been paid to the organizers' decision-making authority unless he informs them adequately, affords them an opportunity for reflection, and prepares documents reflecting the conclusions they reach.

The conflict of interest and client autonomy provisions are subject to strict interpretation, and in the present climate they may lead to a hard look at the customary practices of the bar, however disposed regulatory authorities may have been in the past to defer to established corporate practices. Present practices may not survive such scrutiny. Frequently the articles and by-laws which the lawyer pulls out of the form file are thoroughly onesided. The literature of corporate law takes much note of "managerialism," the state of independence from the owners which corporate management often enjoys. But the commentators have not recognized that a significant cause of managerialism is the preparation by the corporate bar of managerialist organizational documents—documents containing broad purposes and powers clauses, providing for indemnification of management out of corporate assets to the maximum permissible extent, and conferring on directors and officers almost as many powers as the law allows. Provisions are often included giving the directors the power to amend the by-laws or to expand the board and fill the resulting vacancies themselves. "Shark repellent" provisions designed to help management deter or repulse takeovers are another example, as are provisions intended to validate transactions in which officers or directors have an interest and to shelter the officers and directors from liabilities arising from them.

It is not the practice of the bar to identify the ideology behind the documents or to suggest alternate approaches to clients. Nor is it the practice to explain the implications of the documents to minority shareholders—to point out, for example, how they may permit or prevent freeze-outs, alteration of shareholder rights, or other changes that can be used to oppress minorities. Nor is it the practice to warn minority shareholders that the lawyer's own interest lies with management, as it very likely does. Not is it the practice to suggest that the minority consider retaining other counsel. It is not the practice of all of the bar to obtain any explicit consent to joint representation. The hard look may lead, then, to the hard conclusion.

It is an indication that the ethical standards should be revised when the bar departs from them not only in instances of haste or dereliction, but as a matter of settled practice. It is also an indication that the settled practices need change.

II.   The Lines Along Which the Ethical Precepts Should Be Improved

The rigidity of the Model Code in the area of corporate organization stems in large measure from its uniform treatment of all joint representation. No distinctions are made between the representation of strangers and that of allies. The major exception applies where the parties have allied themselves to the point of forming a corporation or similar entity. The ethical precepts which govern in that case are vague, but the outlines of a reasonable approach to the problem can be discerned.

A similar approach is taken by the proposed Model Rules which provide that "[a] lawyer employed or retained to represent an organization represents the organization as distinct from its directors, officers, employees, members, shareholders, or other constituents."

This approach can best be understood by a look at two alternative approaches which clearly have *not* been adopted. One approach is to regard the corporate constituents as the primary clients, so that when the interests of some conflict with those of others, joint representation must cease. One commentator has suggested that there might then be "a corporation with three retained law firms: one to represent the outside directors, one to represent the officers, and one to represent the stockholders." Another approach is to abandon altogether, for some joint representation circumstances, the concept of attorney duties to particular clients, and to view the attorney as "counsel for the situation," with a mandate to act, like a mediator, in the interests of justice and the good of all.

Instead, the Model Code considers the attorney as the servant of a particular client, and identifies that client not as any of the constituents, but as the corporation. The "fiction" of the corporate personality is taken seriously, and the lawyer is within his rights—in fact is obliged—to act as directed by the corporation, despite resulting harm to corporate constituents. The question of what the corporation has directed is answered in the same manner as any other question about what the corporation has "done": it has directed whatever its shareholders, directors, and officers have caused it to direct within their powers and in compliance with the stipulated formalities. When the corporation so instructs the attorney, he may, and sometimes must, comply as fully as when instructed by a human client, restrained only by rules, such as those relating to frauds and other illegal activities, which apply whomever he represents. There are exceptions for corporate deadlocks, battles for corporate control, and disputes about the propriety of management's behavior in office. Arguably there is an exception where the corporation is the *alter ego* of an individual. One recent case goes much further and holds that where an attorney represents a closely held corporation he represents the shareholders as well as the corporation unless "other arrangements are clearly made." It has been suggested that there should be an exception where corporate management is acting unethically. And certainly where the purported instructions come from a corporate officer whose authority to speak for the corporation is clouded, as a matter of corporate law, by self-interest or by his exceeding his authority, the lawyer's duty is far harder to determine. Absent some such special circumstance, the lawyer should be justified in taking seriously the clear implication of the Model Code that he may establish an attorney-client relationship with a corporation without establishing a similar one with its constituents. When he does establish such a relationship, however, he must seek and act in accordance with the informed instructions and consent of the corporation, but need not inform its constituents separately or seek their instructions or consent even when acting to their disadvantage. A similar approach should be taken to problems involving client confidences and secrets: that is, the lawyer should be justified in treating communications from the corporation as its confidences and secrets. He should not reveal them except with the consent of the corporation or in certain other circumstances such as where illegalities are involved; but when directed to do so by the corporation he should reveal them, even when to do so is to the disadvantage of nonclient corporate constituents.

The rationale underlying this approach must be that the constituents of a corporation are in a very different posture than strangers or antagonists. The constituents have chosen to bind their fates together. Their interests may differ but they have freely chosen to join them, and their judgments that a mutual subordination of goals will benefit all is entitled to respect. Furthermore, insofar as the constituents have embraced documents such as articles of incorporation and by-laws which establish who speaks for whom and when, they have provided the lawyer with a means of knowing how to act for all of them. The lawyer can follow the directions of those authorized to speak for the entity.

When the corporation is in the organizational stage neither the Model Code nor the proposed Model Rules afford a clear basis for adopting a similar approach. For some time, no corporation is in existence. Under state law, the organizers who retain the lawyer may be deemed partners, but frequently they will not have any written pre-incorporation agreement or even be aware of their partnership status. To conclude that the lawyer may resolve his concern about the divergence of interests by deciding he owes his loyalty to the "entity to be formed" or to the "partnership" requires a strained interpretation of the Model Code and only a slightly less strained interpretation of the proposed Model Rules.

Nevertheless, many of the considerations which militate in favor of the "lawyer-for-the-entity" approach apply. The organizers are not strangers. They have determined to throw in their lots with one another. They contemplate a system of decision making by some for all, and may already be acting in accordance with such a system. Those who are not decision makers are likely to be protected by fiduciary duties running from those who are, since partners are fiduciaries to one another. Much of the lawyer's work will affect them only if the incorporation process is completed. They therefore may have no real need for separate lawyers. Where separate lawyers are not needed and not sought, it is better not to require them because of the extra expense. Some potential clients might prefer to forego legal representation altogether. Furthermore, the introduction of opposing counsel would likely give the whole matter an adversarial cast, to the detriment of the planning and mediating side of the lawyer's work.

III.   THE LINES ALONG WHICH CURRENT PRACTICES SHOULD BE IMPROVED

A.   The Lawyer Should Make Express Disclaimers to Parties with Whom He deals But Who Are Not to Be Represented

Recent decisions have made it easier for lawyer-client relationships to be established inadvertently. The corporation's lawyer may easily slip into representation of those individuals who work with him as corporate insiders. Once established such a relationship may be difficult to terminate. The Model Code imposes restrictions on withdrawal. Furthermore, it is likely that no attempt to withdraw will be made because the relationship, having been entered into inadvertently, is likely to be inadvertently perpetuated. Even after termination, such a relationship can cause serious difficulty because of the attorney's duties to former clients. * * * Duties may exist even where the terminated relationship was not fully that of an attorney and client. * * * In 1969, the law firm of Cahill, Gordon, Sommett, Reindel & Ohl was disqualified from representing its client, E.F. Hutton, in a lawsuit against a former Hutton officer because Cahill, Gordon lawyers had accompanied the officer to hearings in related proceedings and, no doubt inadvertently, led him to believe they were protecting his individual interest. In 1978, the law firm of Kirkland and Ellis was disqualified from representing its client, Westinghouse, in a major antitrust action against several oil companies because the firm also represented the American Petroleum Institute, and in that capacity had gathered confidential information from the oil companies. Episodes of this sort can embarrass the law firm, disappoint the client, and lead to prosecution for ethics violations. In addition, they can impose unnecessary expense on the client and expose corporate insiders to liability.

To diminish these dangers, the lawyer should clearly explain who is being represented, in what matters, and for what purposes and which communications will be treated as confidential and which will not; and he should explain these limits in advance. This should be done, for example, when the lawyer who intends to represent only the new corporation is called upon to explain legal matters to its shareholders.

B.   The Lawyer Should Obtain, from All Parties He Is to Represent, Informed Consent as to the Nature of the Representation

In complex situations, the lawyer involved in organizing a corporation should furnish, at the outset, a "representation letter" to all parties with whom he will have an attorney-client relationship. In most cases, these persons will be the organizers and the corporation.

This letter should be a careful and complete document. "Full disclosure" is a condition to informed consent in attorney-client relations, and the trend, as with informed consent doctrine in medicine and disclosure requirements in the law generally, is to make this requirement more stringent. This is particularly true where consent is sought to the representation of differing interests. There, as Justice Cardozo said, "the disclosure to be effective must lay bare the truth, without ambiguity or reservation, in all its stark significance." At a minimum, the letter should set forth the subject matter of the representation, the time period, the identities of the other clients, and the scope and nature of the representation of them. When the matter is delicate or complex, it should also include descriptions of how joint representation operates, how it might divide the loyalties of the lawyer, and how it might jeopardize client confidences, and it should put the clients on notice that separate counsel may eventually become necessary. The letter should remind the client of his option to retain separate counsel. An explanation of the nature of loyalty to an "entity" client is also in order, including an explanation of how and through whom the entity gives instructions to the lawyer, and an explanation of how the lawyer's duties to an entity may conflict with his loyalty even to its constituents. An explanation of how client confidences will be treated should be included, together with disclosures as to how privilege doctrines will apply.

When the client receives a letter of this sort at the outset, his continued employment of the attorney ought to be regarded by courts as entailing informed consent to the potential conflicts described in the letter, unless the client lacks the intelligence or sophistication necessary to understand the matter, or unless he is under special pressure such as might arise, for example, where the joint representation was of a corporation and a member of management. In the latter case, the lawyer is safer if he obtains express consent from the corporate client by action of a body higher than or at least independent of the one to be represented individually—consent of independent directors or of the shareholders. If he obtains express consent from the individual client after having made clear that selecting other counsel would be acceptable to the corporation and would not result in disadvantageous treatment with respect to indemnification or payment of attorneys' fees.

C. The Lawyer Should Obtain Further Consent When Acting to the Disadvantage of Any of His Clients

Even the lawyer who has taken care to obtain initial informed consent to the joint representation should carefully inform his clients when adjusting their respective interests, taking the precautions mentioned above for instances of special pressure such as on employees. Drafting charter documents eminently illustrates such adjustments. Before securing the adoption of the standard managerialist by-laws and articles, for example, the lawyer should explain to his clients, and especially to the nonmanagement constituents, that alternative provisions, more to their advantage, are available. In some instances, where the documents are to be exceptionally onesided or depart greatly from the expectations of some clients, it will be far from "obvious" that the lawyer can adequately represent the interests of each and he must therefore withdraw from representation of some clients.

D. The Lawyer Should Avoid Joint Representation When One Potential Client Is Perpetrating Substantial Unfairness upon Another

Even after the precautions proposed above have been taken, a lawyer should avoid joint representation where one of the clients is substantially overreaching in dealings with another. For example, he should avoid representing both a dominant promoter and one who is, as a result of lack of sophistication or general passivity, prepared to accept substantially unfair treatment. To be sure, there is no provision in the Model Code explicitly requiring that the lawyer generally ensure fair results (although some have suggested that professional ethical standards should be developed in that direction). But where the unfair results would occur within the context of joint representation—where one client would impose them on another—serious ethical problems do arise. The lawyer is likely required to explore the facts with the intended victim. The principles of zealous representation and client autonomy and the requirements of informed consent to joint representation demand at least that much. The lawyer may be required to warn and even perhaps to argue with the client. But such activities might violate the lawyer's duties to the perpetrator of the unfairness; they may violate his confidences and secrets and constitute less than zealous representation of him. Furthermore, an instance in which unfairness is being perpetrated is always an instance of a latent dispute. When, as may eventually happen, the latent dispute becomes an active one, a lawyer will probably have to withdraw from representing both parties, thereby likely harming each of them and himself as well. Thus the practical consequences are no more appealing than the ethical problems. The future is bleak for the clients' relations with one another and for each client's relationship with the lawyer. Therefore, the lawyer should avoid joint representation under such circumstances.

JESSE BY REINECKE v. DANFORTH

169 Wis.2d 229, 485 N.W.2d 63 (1992)

[In 1985, Drs. Danforth and Ullrich were part of a group of twenty-three physicians who retained Douglas Flygt (Flygt), an attorney with the law firm of DeWitt, Porter, Huggett, Schumacher & Morgan, S.C. (DeWitt). The physicians asked DeWitt to assist them in creating a corporation for the purpose of purchasing and operating a magnetic resonance imaging machine (MRI). Flygt incorporated MRIGM in 1986 and continued to serve as its corporate counsel. The twenty-three physicians became the shareholders of MRIGM, and Dr. Danforth became president of the corporation.

In May 1988, the Jesse family sued Drs. Danforth and Ullrich for medical malpractice unrelated to the activities of MRIGM. The plaintiffs retained Eric Farnsworth, also an attorney with DeWitt. Farnsworth had conducted an internal conflict of interest check at DeWitt, but had not found the defendants listed as clients of the firm. Drs. Danforth and Ullrich moved to disqualify DeWitt, alleging that the firm had a conflict of interest. They argued that they were clients of DeWitt because of Flygt's pre-incorporation of the twenty-three physicians and because of other advice that Flygt had provided to the defendants.]

Day, Justice:

We begin with SCR 20:1.7, the conflict of interest rule [which parallels the 1983 Model Rule 1.7]. Subsection (a) states: "A lawyer shall not represent a client if the representation of that client will be directly adverse to another, unless. * * * "Thus, the question is, who did or does DeWitt represent, *i.e.,* who were and are DeWitt's clients?

It is undisputed that DeWitt, through Farnsworth, represents Jean Jesse in this case. What remains disputed is whether Drs. Danforth or Ullrich were ever or are currently clients of DeWitt.

The entity rule contemplates that where a lawyer represents a corporation, the client is the corporation, not the corporation's constituents. * * *

[T]he clear purpose of the entity rule was to enhance the corporate lawyer's ability to represent the best interests of the corporation without automatically having the additional and potentially conflicting burden of representing the corporation's constituents.

If a person who retains a lawyer for the purpose of organizing an entity is considered the client, however, then any subsequent representation of the corporate entity by the very lawyer who incorporated the entity would automatically result in dual representation. This automatic dual representation, however, is the very situation the entity rule was designed to protect corporate lawyers against.

We thus provide the following guideline: where (1) a person retains a lawyer for the purpose of organizing an entity and (2) the lawyer's involvement with that person is directly related to that incorporation and (3) such entity is eventually incorporated, the entity rule applies retroactively such that the lawyer's pre-incorporation involvement with the person is deemed to be representation of the entity, not the person.

In essence, the retroactive application of the entity rule simply gives the person who retained the lawyer the status of being a corporate constituent during the period before actual incorporation, as long as actual incorporation eventually occurred.

This standard also applies to privileged communications under SCR 20:1.6. Thus, where the above standard is met, communications between the retroactive constituent and the corporation are protected under SCR 20:1.6. And, it is the corporate entity, not the retroactive constituent, that holds the privilege. This tracks the Comment to SCR 20:1.13 which states in part: "When one of the constituents of an organizational client communicates with the organization's lawyer in that person's organizational capacity, the communication is protected by Rule 1.6."

However, where the person who retained the lawyer provides information to the lawyer not directly related to the purpose of organizing an entity, then it is the person, not the corporation which holds the privilege for that communication.

Applying the above standard to the case at hand, we observe that the evidence cited and quoted by the defendants demonstrates that the above standard is met and that DeWitt represented MRIGM, not Drs. Danforth or Ullrich.

For example, defendants Drs. Danforth and Ullrich point to Flygt's affidavit wherein Flygt states that he was contacted *"to assist a group of physicians in Milwaukee in organizing an entity to own and operate one or more * * * facilities * * *."* (Emphasis added.)

Dr. Danforth points to a January 29, 1986 letter from Flygt to Dr. Danforth wherein Flygt stated:

I would suggest that the *corporation* come to a quick resolution of the subchapter S corporation question. * * * (Emphasis added).

Drs. Danforth and Ullrich point to a May 5, 1986 letter from Flygt to Dr. Danforth which states that "to the extent that there are common expenses of the partnership, such as drafting documents, etc., *it would be appropriate to have the entity pay those fees while the attorneys fees of each individual group are its own cost."* (Emphasis added).

[Drs.] Danforth and Ullrich point to a May 13, 1987 memorandum Flygt wrote to the "Shareholders" of MRIGM. This memorandum begins, "The purpose of this letter is to advise you as to a decision *which must be made by the corporation* at this time." (Emphasis added). * * *

This evidence overwhelmingly supports the proposition that the purpose of Flygt's pre-incorporation involvement was to provide advice with respect to organizing an entity and the Flygt's involvement was directly related to the incorporation. Moreover, that MRIGM was eventually incorporated is undisputed.

In addition, with respect to Flygt's advice concerning the structure of the entity, the fact that a particular corporate structure may benefit the shareholders or the fact that there was communication between Flygt and the shareholders concerning such structuring does not mean that Drs. Danforth and Ullrich were the clients of the law firm. Again, the very purpose of the entity rule is to preclude such automatic dual representation.

Drs. Danforth and Ullrich also contend that they provided certain confidential information to attorney Flygt that should disqualify DeWitt under SCR 20:1.6, the confidential information rule. Defendants point to questionnaires Flygt provided to the physicians involved in the MRI project which inquire, in part, as to the physicians' personal finances and their involvement in pending litigation.

Because MRIGM, not the physician shareholders, was and is the client of DeWitt, and because the communications between Drs. Danforth and Ullrich were directly related to the purpose of organizing MRIGM, we conclude that Drs. Danforth or Ullrich cannot claim the privilege of confidentiality.

STATE BAR OF ARIZONA, OPINION NO. 02–06

(September 2002)

1. Can a lawyer represent an entity that does not yet exist?

Yes, as long as the incorporators understand that they are retaining counsel on behalf of the yet-to-be-formed entity and will need to ratify this corporate action, *nunc pro tunc,* once the entity is formed. According to ER 1.13(a), a lawyer may represent an "organization." The Comments to the Rule explain that an "organizational client is a legal entity, but it cannot act except through its officers, directors, employees, shareholders and other constituents.... The duties defined in this comment apply equally to unincorporated associations." Under this statute, a corporation does not exist as a separate legal entity until its articles of incorporation are filed with the Corporation Commission. [2] Section 10–204 of the Arizona Revised Statutes further cautions that individuals who attempt to transact business as a corporation, knowing that no corporation exists, will be jointly liable for their actions. Presumably, however, a newly formed corporation may ratify pre-incorporation acts of the corporation, *nunc pro tunc.*

A decision from Wisconsin specifically holds that a lawyer hired to form an entity can represent the to-be-formed entity, not the incorporators, and the "entity" rule applies retroactively. *Jesse v. Danforth,* 485 N.W.2d 63 (Wis. 1992). This view would be consistent with the "entity" theory of representation, under ER 1.13(a). The "entity" theory holds that a lawyer may represent the corporation and does not, necessarily, represent any of the constituents that act on behalf of the entity–even if it is a closely held corporation.

An alternative view is the "aggregate" theory in which the lawyer is found to represent the incorporators/constituents collectively as joint clients. *See Griva v. Davison,* 637 A.2d 830 (D.C. 1994). Under the aggregate theory, a lawyer represents multiple co-clients during formation of the corporation and then once the entity is formed, the clients must determine whether the lawyer will continue to represent all of the constituents *and* the entity, or just the entity. Who a lawyer *may* represent depends upon whether the lawyer's independent professional judgment would be materially limited because of the lawyer's duties to another client or third person.

Thus, a lawyer may represent an entity during the formation process, as long as the constituents who are acting on behalf of the yet-to-be-formed entity understand and agree to the entity being the client.

2. Can a lawyer represent *only* the yet-to-be-formed entity and not the constituents?

Who a lawyer represents depends upon the reasonable perceptions of those who have consulted with the lawyer. *In re Petrie,* 154 Ariz. 295 (1987). When two or more individuals consult with a lawyer about forming an entity, it is the responsibility of the lawyer at that initial meeting to clarify who the lawyer will represent. ER 1.13 provides that a lawyer may represent an entity and the Rule suggests that the lawyer will not automatically be considered counsel for the constituents * * *

* * * [U]nless a lawyer *wants* to be counsel to all of the incorporators and the entity, the lawyer should specify that the lawyer does *not* represent the constituents collectively—the lawyer only represents the entity. If an engagement letter or oral representation by the lawyer suggests that the constituents are represented as an aggregate, then the lawyer will have ethical obligations to *each* constituent. Aggregate representation also is ethically proper if the disclosure to each client includes an explanation that the lawyer may have to withdraw from representing *each* client if a conflict arises *among* the clients.

3. What disclosures should a lawyer make to the incorporating constituents to obtain their informed consent to the limited representation of the entity?

The underlying premise of the conflict Rules is loyalty to clients. Where a lawyer's independent professional judgment for a client is materially limited due to *anything or anyone,* a conflict may exist. Thus, in order to avoid inadvertent conflicts caused by misunderstandings of constituents in corporate representations, it is crucial for lawyers to specify exactly who they represent, who they do *not* represent, and how information conveyed to the lawyer by constituents of an entity client will be treated, for confidentiality purposes.

Therefore, it is crucial that a lawyer specify in the engagement agreement if the lawyer is not representing the constituents of an entity client.

Even if the engagement letter specifies that the constituents are not clients, lawyers still should regularly caution constituents that they are not clients—particularly when they consult with counsel. Lawyers who represent entities also must be aware of the *entity's* potential fiduciary duties to the constituents, so that the lawyer does not run afoul of those statutory or common law obligations. For instance, there are cases that have held that lawyers may have fiduciary duties to non-clients, depending upon whether the *entity* represented had fiduciary duties to the third parties.

With respect to confidentiality obligations, lawyers should specify how information conveyed to the lawyer will be treated for confidentiality purposes. If the firm is representing only the entity, constituents must be advised that their communications to the lawyer will be conveyed to the other decision-makers for the entity and are not confidential as to the entity. The information is confidential, however, according to Rule 1.6(a), to the "outside world." Similarly, information shared by one co-client that is necessary for the representation of the other joint clients will be shared with the other co-clients because there is no individual confidentiality when a joint representation exists.

Finally, if the lawyer has chosen to represent multiple clients, including the constituents and the entity, the lawyer should explain, at the beginning of the joint representation, that in the event that a conflict arises among the clients, the lawyer most likely will need to withdraw from representing *all* of the co-clients. However, some commentators, including the *Restatement Third,* note that the engagement agreement may provide that in the event of a conflict, the lawyer may withdraw from representing one of the co-clients and continue to represent the remaining clients.

IN RE BANKS

283 Or. 459, 584 P.2d 284 (1978)

PER CURIAM.

This is a combined disciplinary proceeding brought by the Oregon State Bar against two of its members. The accuseds are partners in a large firm, the accused Thompson being in the firm's business department, and the accused Banks being in its litigation department. The charges against both arise out of legal business transacted for United Medical Laboratories, a corporation (UML), its board of directors, its officers, the members of the family who owned the corporate stock, and a corporation competing with UML. As would be anticipated, the facts are complicated.

UML was engaged in operating a medical testing laboratory, a large amount of whose business was done by mail. Its creator, organizer, founder, chief executive, and driving force was R. S. Michel. The stock was originally owned solely by Michel and his wife, but, through subsequent estate planning, successive gifts of stock were made to two daughters, resulting ultimately in 29 shares each being owned by Michel and his wife and 21 shares each being owned by the daughters. However, Michel was a completely dominating force and ran the business as his private fief.

The business was tremendously successful. From its start in the basement of a private home, it grew to employ in excess of 1,500 people and to become the largest user of the mails in Oregon and one of the larger users of the telephone. The accuseds' firm began its representation of the Michels and their business in 1965. Most of the transactions out of which the present charges arise occurred in 1972. At that time the legal business of both the corporation and the Michel family was one of the substantially lucrative accounts possessed by the firm of which the accuseds are members. Thompson did estate planning, will drawing and other private business for Mr. and Mrs. Michel, as well as representing the corporation in its business transactions; Banks handled UML's litigation. Because of the identity of interests, corporate and private, all legal services were billed to the corporation regardless of whether the work performed was corporate or private.

The board of directors of UML was composed of Mr. and Mrs. Michel and their two daughters. Michel was president and Mrs. Michel held various offices in the corporation. There is no record of any dividends ever having been paid. Michel had a 10–year employment contract with the corporation whereby he received a percentage of the Gross income of the corporation. There is no evidence of any income to anyone else except for the possibility of a salary to Mrs. Michel. Michel was thus in a position to assure himself of substantially all immediate benefits from the operation of the corporation. The employment agreement between Michel and the corporation was entered into in 1967 and was drawn by Thompson. By 1972 both daughters were grown and married. One lived in Seattle, where her husband was a professor at the University of Washington, and the other lived in Portland, where her husband was employed by UML.

UML's equipment was owned by a separate corporation, UML Leasing (Leasing), which leased it to UML. Leasing was owned by the Michel family and was controlled by Michel in the same manner as was UML. The real property used by UML was owned by a UML employee profit sharing trust which leased it to UML. Thompson was a trustee of the profit sharing trust, as was Michel.

UML had non-competition contracts with its salesmen and with most of its administrative personnel. The contracts were not originally drawn by the accuseds' firm. However, Banks engaged in considerable litigation for the corporation in the enforcement of these contracts and from time to time would suggest changes in the form of the contracts as his experience in their enforcement dictated.

Because of the rapid growth of the corporation, some unsuccessful ventures, and difficulty in operating an expensive computer effectively, the corporation became short of operating funds. By 1972 it was in debt to a bank for approximately $3,000,000 and was dependent upon the continued advancement of operating funds from the bank. In addition, it had many past-due bills. The bank was becoming progressively more demanding about a refinancing of the corporation or its sale so it could be reimbursed for the money it had advanced.

In an effort to relieve the pressure and to break the logjam caused by the computer, Michel directed the computer technicians to remove certain limits or safeguards from the computer which had been set by the medical directors employed by the corporation. As a result, 60,000 test results were spewed out, the accuracy of which was doubted by the medical directors. As a consequence of this action, high level employees became concerned about the moral aspect of the accuracy of the published test results as well as their personal responsibility therefor and were threatening to go to the federal agencies which licensed and regulated medical testing laboratories. Mrs. Michel's and her daughters' concerns about the removal of the computer safeguards and about the solvency of the company and its ability to meet its debts caused, for the first time, a confrontation between Michel and the members of his family. For the first time his absolute control was questioned. As a result, Michel made the tactical mistake of physically assaulting his wife.

On the morning of July 4, 1972, after having been assaulted by her husband, Mrs. Michel promised to assign her stock to him. As a result, Michel called Thompson to his home early in the morning to have him arrange the stock transfer. Before Thompson arrived Mrs. Michel had slipped away from her husband and had gone to the home of the daughter who lived in Portland. Also present there were the other daughter, who had come down from Seattle, and an attorney from New York City, who had been called for consultation by the daughter from Seattle. Michel, having missed his wife, went to the daughter's home and, in the ensuing imbroglio, made a physical assault upon the Seattle daughter. Michel then returned to his home and directed Thompson, who in the meantime had arrived, to go to the daughter's home to see what was going on. Thompson went to the daughter's home and spent considerable time with the New York lawyer and the other members of the Michel family talking over the difficulty which was presented. The creation of a voting trust for the corporate stock was discussed, but there was no indication at that time that such a trust, if created, would not include all the stock of the corporation.

Subsequently, on July 6, at a stockholder's meeting, the New York attorney presented the right to vote the stock of both Mrs. Michel and the two daughters pursuant to an irrevocable voting trust which they had created, and a new board of directors was elected which retained Michel as a member of the board but substituted new directors in place of the other members of the family. This was an attempt by the other members of the family to curb Michel and at the same time to isolate themselves from constant confrontation with him, since they did not feel they could emotionally withstand such confrontation. Mrs. Michel went into hiding. The new board permitted Michel to remain as president and executive officer but attempted to institute stringent controls on his authority. A voting trust without the inclusion of Michel's stock came as a surprise to both Michel and Thompson.

This status existed about a month, with Michel and the board at odds and with the situation gradually deteriorating. Thompson continued to advise Michel as the executive head of the organization, and he also advised other members of the board regarding their problems, which Michel took as a display of disloyalty to him. On August 2, the board put Michel on a leave of absence. Thompson then told Michel he could no longer advise him and that he would have to secure other counsel for this purpose.

The bank requested, as a condition of continuing to advance operating money, that Leasing subordinate its claims against UML for rent on equipment to the indebtedness of the bank. Michel still controlled Leasing, as it had not been made subject to the voting trust created by the other members of the family; he refused to so subordinate the debt. Pursuant to a request of the board, Banks rendered an opinion to it that

Michel's failure to cooperate in subordinating Leasing's claim for rent constituted a violation of Michel's employment contract with UML. Ultimately, Michel did subordinate Leasing's claims to the bank's loans.

After Michel was relieved as executive officer, he made up with his wife who, as a result, had a change of heart and decided she had made a mistake in establishing the voting trust. Though the accuseds claim otherwise, the plain inference is that under Michel's guidance she sought separate legal counsel and commenced litigation challenging both the legality of the voting trust and the election of the new board of directors. This put her in conflict with her daughters, who had joined with her in the formation of the voting trust. The defendants in the litigation were the daughters, the trustees of the voting trust and the new board of directors for UML. UML was not a defendant. At the request of the board, the accuseds' firm, in the person of Banks, undertook the defense of the suits. Michel expressed outrage that Banks would do this. Upon being told by Mrs. Michel's attorney of Michel's objections, Banks withdrew and had an associate attorney of the firm handle the defense thereafter.

Although extensive depositions, including a deposition of Mrs. Michel, were taken by the accuseds' firm, the cases were never tried because the bank put on additional pressure for liquidation of its indebtedness and it was decided by all concerned to sell the corporation, if possible. As a result all agreed that Michel should be designated to attempt to sell the business. He was successful in selling it for $10,000,000. When it was sold, the board of directors resigned and Michel was retained by the purchasers to run the business. He immediately fired all administrative personnel and officials of the corporation who, in his opinion, had been disloyal to him. He also terminated the accuseds' firm as attorneys for the corporation.

About a dozen of the discharged personnel of UML decided they would put their expertise to work and form a business in competition with UML. Thus was born Lancet Medical Industries (Lancet). The accuseds' firm was engaged as legal counsel for Lancet. Thompson became a director during its formation and both he and Banks became stockholders and investors in the company. Banks was asked by the founders of the new business for a legal opinion as to the enforceability of non-competition contracts. This was thought to be important by the founders of Lancet because they would necessarily be engaging salesmen throughout the country who might have previously worked for competing businesses. The founders of Lancet put out a prospectus for the purpose of raising funds to finance the new business and Banks' memorandum in response to the founders' request was included therein. Thompson helped edit the prospectus. * * *

After UML terminated Thompson's services as its attorney and after he invested in and undertook to represent Lancet, Thompson remained as a trustee of the profit sharing trust for several years. During that time the trust had under lease to UML the real property upon which it operated its business, and questions arose concerning the enforcement of a provision for an increase in rental of that property. There is no evidence that Thompson took advantage of his position as trustee to the detriment of UML.

We point out, prior to delineating the specific charges against the accuseds, that they were absolved of all unethical conduct by a determination of the trial board, which determination was concurred in by the Disciplinary Review Board. However, the Disciplinary Review Board expressed some uneasiness, as indicated by a part of their statement:

> The Review Board, however, is of the opinion that a gray area exists with respect to who (sic), as successive clients, an attorney can properly represent when a business split-up or division occurs. * * *

All of the charges made against both accuseds are in the nature of claims of conflict of interest. The first charge made against both accuseds questions whether, after having drawn Michel's contract of employment for the parties, they could with propriety advise UML that Michel's conduct in refusing to subordinate UML's debt to Leasing to the indebtedness of the bank was a breach of his employment contract with UML. Thompson drew the contract and Banks gave the advice. It is the accuseds' position that the firm represented the corporation not Michel, that the contract was drawn for UML in the course of the firm's representation of UML, that UML paid for the firm's work in drawing the contract, that the firm's sole duty was to UML, and that, pursuant to such duty, it was obligated to advise the corporation in accordance with its request concerning the contract's possible breach by Michel.

The general rule relative to a corporate attorney's conduct is in accordance with the accuseds' contention. The corporation usually is considered an entity and the attorney's duty of loyalty is to the corporation and not to its officers, directors or any particular group of stockholders.

* * *

No one has cited any authority, nor have we been able to find any, on the question of whether this general rule should be applicable to a closely held family corporation which is substantially controlled and operated by one person and where the corporation's attorneys have been that person's personal attorneys as well. For example, suppose Michel had owned 100 per cent of the stock and subsequently sold all of it to another and continued to operate the corporation under his contract. In such a situation, if a dispute concerning his possible breach of his employment contract erupted, would the accuseds ethically be able to represent the corporation in that dispute? Would there not be an inherent conflict of interest because of the original identity of the corporate and private interests? Under the hypothetical facts just stated, the corporate interests and the individual interests would subsequently become disparate. At the time the contract was drawn, the individual interests would really dictate what was done because the corporate form would be only a method of doing business chosen by the individual for the purpose of promoting his private interests. In such a situation, as in many other fields, common sense dictates that the corporate entity should be ignored.

Moving from the hypothetical situation to the present one, are there material differences in the present situation which dictate a different result? There are differences in degree, but we consider them insufficient to change the result. At the time of the drawing of the contract Michel was the corporation. As he expressed himself when, at the beginning of the difficulty, he was asked to resign by an employee, "I told him that I had made the company and that I could destroy the company." The stock had been distributed among the members of the family, but, for practical purposes, it was his corporation. He was in absolute control and substantially all the immediate benefits of the business could be made to flow to him through his contract for compensation. Nor can we differentiate between Michel and his wife. He was the completely dominant marital partner at the time the contract was drawn. Until the events which precipitated the confrontation, the participation of the other members of the family in corporate activities was whatever Michel wanted it to be. It is small wonder that as a layman Michel was completely outraged when he found that the attorneys he thought he had hired to protect his interests, both personal and corporate, which interests were substantially identical, were opposing him in a dispute calling into question the application of the legal work he had hired them to do.

Subsequent to the sale of the corporation, Michel and his wife sued the purchaser. Called into question were the records of UML during the time the accuseds' firm represented UML. * * *

The relationship at the time the contract was drawn was inherently ambiguous, as demonstrated by Thompson's uncertainty as to whether, in that transaction, he had represented the corporation or "both sides." Because of that inherent ambiguity, the firm should not thereafter have taken sides when the contract came into question.

The accuseds urge upon us Ethical Consideration 5–18 of the American Bar Association Code of Professional Responsibility * * *

This ethical consideration is part of the rationale behind the entity theory which we have previously set forth and to which we believe the present situation is a logical exception. The ethical consideration implies that if a corporate officer is represented by a corporate attorney at a time when no conflict exists as we believe was the fact in the present case, and then a conflict arises between the officer and the corporation about the subject of the representation, the attorney is in an untenable position if he represents either one.

The accuseds also point to the necessity that the interests of the corporation be protected by a continuity of legal service by someone who is familiar with the particular problems of the corporation at a time of extreme corporate stress as exhibited by the facts in this case. In weighing the interests of the corporation and the desirability of avoiding conflicts of interest, it seems to us that the balance should be struck the other way in closely held family corporations where the operator of the corporation either owns or controls the stock in such a manner that it is reasonable to assume that There is no real reason for him to differentiate in his mind between his own and corporate interests. In such a situation all the reasons are in existence which give rise to the rule against conflicts of interest because there is no basis for the individual to believe that the attorney has or ever will have other than his individual interest at heart. It is our conclusion that the only ethical position for an attorney to adopt when substantially identical interests which he has represented become divergent is to represent neither the individual nor the corporation. * * *

We realize that whether, at the time of the original representation, the interests of the individual and the corporation were sufficiently identical to justify ignoring the corporate entity is a question of degree, and there will be many cases close to that non-exact line between the permissible and the impermissible. However, this is a common problem and is not singular to ethical considerations involving conflicts of interest.

In each instance the Bar has alleged the possession by the accuseds of confidential information secured by their firm in its representation of Michel's interests. However, the possession and disclosure of confidential information by attorneys in their representation of another party is unnecessary to the existence of a conflict of interest. Although the disclosure of such confidences is one of the probable consequences of representing adverse interests, such disclosures are unnecessary to a charge of conflict of interest. * * *

The Oregon Code of Professional Responsibility does not directly dispose of the issue. However, no code of ethics can establish unalterable rules governing all possible eventualities. Therefore, the ultimate resolution of problems like the present rests in the reasoned discretion of the court. * * *

We believe the only realistic view that can be taken is that the accuseds' firm represented both Michel and the corporation at the time the contract was drawn and that it could not subsequently, when the interests of its clients were in opposition, represent either one in a dispute over the application of the contract without the consent of both.

The next two charges, although not identical, will be treated together. The first one, against Thompson, charges him with unethical conduct in continuing to represent the corporation and its new board of directors after Michel lost control and at a time when Michel's interests and the board's interests were opposed. The second charge, against Banks, alleges unethical conduct in representing the daughters, the new board of directors and the voting trust in the law suits brought against them by Mrs. Michel. Contrary to the accuseds' contention, the evidence plainly indicates that Mrs. Michel was bringing the suits at the request of Michel and in his interests as opposed to those of the board. Most of what has been said in disposing of the previously discussed charge is applicable here. The firm's relations with Michel and his prior identity of interest with the corporation made involvement on behalf of the daughters, the new board and the voting trust improper. We believe this to be so despite the request by the board, which was the governing body of the corporation, that Banks represent the defendants in the suits. By such a holding we do not intend to include the usual situation where, in the beginning of the representation, the corporate and individual interests are not, for practical purposes, substantially identical.

Michel testified that after the new board took over early in July and before the board relieved him of his duties as executive officer early in August, he and Thompson would have conferences concerning how best "to forestall a complete take-over by this group ." This is verified by Thompson's responses, found in the same deposition from which we have quoted, when asked to differentiate between personal representation of Michel and representation of the corporation in relation to the firm's files which reflected its activity during the summer of 1972:

* * *

In fairness to Thompson, it must be remembered that he was, while testifying, in a position in which he did not wish to be accused of disclosing any information which could possibly be claimed to be subject to the attorney-client privilege; nevertheless, his reasonable indecision as to whom he was representing at the time demonstrates that the firm's relationship with Michel made its position sufficiently equivocal to indicate that the firm should not have been representing both sides after Michel lost control.

* * *

It is the court's conclusion that the accuseds are guilty of the charges as above indicated and that, because of the novel aspects which have caused us to plow some new ground, only a public reprimand is required. This opinion will stand as that reprimand.

LEGAL ETHICS COMM. OF THE D.C. BAR, Op. 216 (1991)

REPRESENTATION OF CLOSELY HELD CORPORATION IN ACTION AGAINST CORPORATE SHAREHOLDER

Applicable Rules Provision

- Rule 1.13(a) (Organization as Client)

A and B were each 50% shareholders of C, a close corporation organized under Maryland law which did business in the District of Columbia.

C had a banking relationship with U, which also extended personal loans to A and B, individually. A and B have defaulted on their loan payments to U. C has filed an action in the District of Columbia against U, alleging a wrongful termination of the banking relationship.

Following the filing of C's action against U, U obtained a judgment against A and, as the result of a Sheriff's execution sale, U became the owner of A's 50% interest in C. A, however, maintains that he is still President of C, since C's two shareholders, B and U are deadlocked and a majority vote is needed to remove him. U has filed an action in the Maryland courts to dissolve C because of shareholder deadlock. This action is still pending.

B's widow, who has succeeded to B's interest in C, wishes to maintain C's action against U. U, of course, wishes to discontinue the action. The question in this Inquiry is whether C's corporate lawyer, retained when C was controlled by A and B, may continue to represent C in its action against U, now one of its 50% shareholders, and in U's action to dissolve C.

Discussion

The Inquiry is governed by Rule 1.13 of the District of Columbia Rules of Professional Conduct. Under Rule 1.13(a), "[a] lawyer employed or retained by an organization represents the organization acting through its duly authorized constituents." This rule embodies the well-established principle that a lawyer retained by a corporation, or by any other organization recognized as a separate legal entity, represents the entity. As stated in EC 5–18 of the former Code of Professional Responsibility, "[a] lawyer employed or retained by a corporation or similar entity owes his allegiance to the entity and not to a shareholder, director, officer, employee, representative, or other person connected with the entity." *See,* Opinion 159 (1985); Opinion 186 (1987); *Egan v. McNamara,* 467 A.2d 733, 738 (D.C. Ct. of App. 1983).

The principle that a lawyer representing a corporation represents the entity and not its individual shareholders or other constituents applies even when the shareholders come into conflict with the entity. Courts have generally held, therefore, that a corporation's lawyer is not disqualified from representing the corporation in litigation against its constituents. *See, e.g., Bobbitt v. Victorian House, Inc.,* 545 F.Supp. 1124 (N.D. Ill. 1982); *Dalrymple v. National Bank and Trust Co. of Traverse City,* 615 F.Supp. 979 (W.D. Mich. 1985); *U.S. Industries, Inc. v. Goldman,* 421 F.Supp. 7 (S.D. N.Y. 1976); *Wayland v. Shore Lobster & Shrimp Corp.,* 537 F.Supp. 1220 (S.D. N.Y. 1982). A different result may sometimes be required where the shareholders of a closely held corporation reasonably might have believed they had a personal lawyer-client relationship with the corporation's lawyer. *See, e.g., Rosman v. Shapiro,* 653 F.Supp. 1441 (S.D. N.Y. 1987); *In re Brownstein,* 288 Or. 83, 602 P.2d 655 (1979); *In re Banks,* 283 Or. 459, 584 P.2d 284 (1978). This is not such a case, however, since under the circumstances U, the bank, could not reasonably believe it has or had a personal lawyer-client relationship with C's lawyer.

Since C's lawyer is not disqualified from continuing to represent C in its litigation with one of its 50% shareholders, the question arises how the lawyer is to carry out his ethical duties in this representation. On the one hand, the corporate lawyer owes a duty of loyalty to the corporation, as distinct from its owners and managers, and he or she must act in the best interests of the corporation as an entity.

On the other hand, the lawyer must normally follow the direction of those duly appointed or elected to act on behalf of the corporation. *See, e.g., Financial General Bankshares, Inc. v. Metzger*, 523 F.Supp. 744, 764 (D. D.C. 1981), vacated for lack of jurisdiction, 680 F.2d 768 (D.C. Cir. 1982) ("... both practically and theoretically, the corporate attorney should consider himself as representing the entity interests articulated by those in current control of the management"); ABA Informal Opinion 1056 (1968); Comment, *Conflicts of Law in the Legal Profession*, 94 Harv. L. Rev. 1244, 1336 (1981). Rule 1.13 expressly recognizes that a lawyer represents an organization such as a corporation "through its duly authorized constituents." Comment [4] further states that "[w]hen constituents of the organization make decisions for it, the decisions ordinarily must be accepted by the lawyer even if their utility or prudence is doubtful."

The difficulty here is that the corporation's President, A, may continue to hold office only because of the shareholder deadlock; moreover, because of his own dispute with U, A may have reason to disregard the corporation's interest in determining the corporation's course of action in its dispute with U. These difficulties notwithstanding, the corporation's lawyer may continue to take direction from A until the dispute over control of the corporation is resolved by the courts or the parties. If, however, the lawyer should become convinced that A's decisions are clearly in violation of A's own fiduciary duties to the corporation, the lawyer may be forced to seek guidance from the courts as to who is in control of the corporation, there being no higher authority within the corporation to whom the lawyer can turn. Throughout the representation, the lawyer must continue to recognize that the interests of the corporation must be paramount and that he must take care to remain neutral with respect to the disputes between the present shareholders, B and U, and between A and U. *See,* ABA Opinion 86 (1932) ("In acting as the corporation's legal adviser [an attorney] must refrain from taking part in any controversies or factual differences which may exist among stockholders as to its control"), quoted with approval in *Financial General Bankshares, Inc. v. Metzger*, 523 F.Supp. at 765.

Geoffrey C. Hazard, Jr., ETHICS IN THE PRACTICE OF LAW

(1978)

The problem of deciding who is the client arises when a lawyer supposes that a conflict of interest prevents him from acting for all the people involved in a situation. That is, if the interests of the potential clients were in harmony, or could be harmonized, no choice would have to be made between them and the lawyer could act for all. When the lawyer feels that he can act for all, it can be said simply that he has several clients at the same time. When the clients are all involved in a single transaction, however, the lawyer's responsibility is rather different from what it is when he represents several clients in transactions that have nothing to do with each other. This difference is suggested by the proposition that a lawyer serving more than one client in a single transaction represents "the situation."

The term is the invention of Louis D. Brandeis, Justice of the United States Supreme Court and before that practitioner of law in Boston. It emerged in a hearing in which Brandeis's professional ethics as a lawyer had been questioned.

* * *

The objections to Brandeis's conduct in all these situations were twofold. One was that his conduct was unethical per se because he represented conflicting interests. The other was that he had not adequately made clear to the clients that their interests were in conflict. On the second point, Brandeis acknowledged that at least in some instances he may not have adequately explained the situation to the clients and adequately defined his role as he saw it. Having acknowledged this, he defended his conduct not only on the ground of its being common practice but also on the ground that it was right. In the instances questioned, he said, he did not regard himself as being lawyer for one of the parties to the exclusion of the others, but as "lawyer for the situation." Eventually, the charge did not so much collapse as become submerged in concessions from other reputable lawyers that they had often done exactly as Brandeis.

The transactions complained of included the following: First, Brandeis had at one time represented one party in a transaction, later represented someone else in a way that impinged on that transaction. Second, he had acted in situations where those he served had conflicting interests, for example by putting together the bargain between parties to a business deal. Third, he had acted for a family business and continued so to act after a falling out among the family required reorganization of the business arrangement. Fourth, over a course of several years he had mediated and adjusted interests of the owners and creditors of a business in such a way as to keep the business from foundering.

* * *

"Situations" can arise in different ways. Two or more people who have not been clients may bring a "situation" to a lawyer. Sometimes a client who has a lawyer will become involved in a transaction with a third party who does not, and the transaction is one that ought to be handled as a "situation." Most commonly, perhaps, a lawyer may find himself in a "situation" involving clients that he has previously served in separate transactions or relationships. In this circumstance the lawyer, if he properly can, will intercede before the transaction between his clients reaches counterposed positions. Doing so is in his interest, because that way he can retain both clients.

Having a lawyer act for the situation is also in the clients' interests, if adjustment on fair terms is possible, because head-on controversy is expensive and aggravating. A lawyer who failed to avoid a head-on controversy, given reasonable opportunity to do so, will have failed in what his clients generally regard as one of his chief functions—"preventive" legal assistance.

If Brandeis was wrong, then "lawyering for the situation" is marginally illicit professional conduct because it violates the principle of unqualified loyalty to client. But if Brandeis was right, and the record of good practitioners testifies to that conclusion, then what is required is not interdiction of "lawyering for the situation" but reexamination of what is meant by loyalty to client. That is, loyalty to client, like loyalty to country, may take different forms.

It is not easy to say exactly what a "lawyer for the situation" does. Clearly, his functions vary with specific circumstances. But there are common threads. The beginning point is that no other lawyer is immediately involved. Hence, the lawyer is no one's partisan and, at least up to a point, everyone's confidant. He can be the only person who knows the whole situation. He is an analyst of the relationship between the clients, in that he undertakes to discern the needs, fears, and expectations of each and to discover the concordances among them. He is an interpreter, translating inarticulate or exaggerated claims and forewarnings into temperate and mutually intelligible terms of communication. He can contribute historical perspective, objectivity, and foresight into the parties' assessment of the situation. He can discourage escalation of conflict and recruitment of outside allies. He can articulate general principles and common custom as standards by which the parties can examine their respective claims. He is advocate, mediator, entrepreneur, and judge, all in one. He could be said to be playing God.

Playing God is a tricky business. It requires skill, nerve, detachment, compassion, ingenuity, and the capacity to sustain confidence. When mishandled, it generates the bitterness and recrimination that results when a deep trust has been betrayed. Perhaps above all, it requires good judgment as to when such intercession can be carried off without unfairly subordinating the interests of one of the parties or having later to abort the mission.

When a relationship between the clients is amenable to "situation" treatment, giving it that treatment is perhaps the best service a lawyer can render to anyone. It approximates the ideal forms of intercession suggested by the models of wise parent or village elder. It provides adjustment of difference upon a wholistic view of the situation rather than bilaterally opposing ones. It rests on implicit principles of decision that express commonly shared ideals in behavior rather than strict legal right. The basis of decision is mutual assent and not external compulsion. The orientation in time tends to be a hopeful view of the future rather than an angry view of the past. It avoids the loss of personal autonomy that results when each side commits his cause to his own advocate. It is the opposite of "going to law."

One would think that the role of "lawyer for the situation" would have been idealized by the bar in parity with the roles of partisan advocate and confidential adviser. The fact that it has not been may itself be worth exploring.

It is clear that a "lawyer for the situation" has to identify clearly his role as such, a requirement that Brandeis conceded he might not always have fulfilled. But beyond saying that he will undertake to represent the best interests of all, a lawyer cannot say specifically what he will do or what each of the clients should do in the situation. (If the outcome of the situation were clearly foreseeable, presumably the lawyer's intercession would be unnecessary.) Moreover, he cannot define his role in the terms of the direction of his effort, for his effort will not be vectored outward toward third persons but will aim at an interaction among the clients. Hence, unlike advocacy or legal counselling involving a single client, lawyering for a situation is not provided with a structure of goals and constraints imposed from outside. The lawyer and the clients must create that structure for themselves, with the lawyer being an active participant. And like the other participants he cannot reveal all that is on-his mind or all that he suspects the others may have on their minds, except as doing so aids movement of the situation along lines that seem productive.

A lawyer can proceed in this role only if the clients trust him and, equally important, he trusts himself. Trust is by definition ineffable. It is an acceptance of another's act without demanding that its bona fides be objectively provable; to demand its proof is to confess it does not exist. It is a relationship that is uncomfortable for the client but perhaps even more so for the lawyer. Experienced as he is with the meanness that people can display to each other, why should the lawyer not doubt his own susceptibility to the same failing? But trust is involved also in the role of confidential adviser and advocate. Why should lawyers regard their own trustworthiness as more vulnerable in those roles than in the role of "lawyer for the situation"?

Perhaps it is because the legal profession has succeeded in defining the roles of confidential adviser and advocate in ways that substantially reduce the burden of being trustworthy in these roles. The confidential adviser is told that he may not act to disclose anything about the client, except an announced intention to commit a crime. Short of this extremity, the rules of role have it that the counsellor has no choices to make between the interests of his client and the interests of others. His commitment is to the client alone. Correlatively, the advocate is told that he may assert any claim on behalf of a client except one based on fabricated evidence or one empty of any substance at all. Short of this extremity, the advocate also has no choices to make.

The "lawyer for the situation," on the other hand, has choices to make that obviously can go against the interest of one client or another, as the latter perceives it. A lawyer who assumes to act as intercessor has to evoke complete confidence that he will act justly in the circumstances. This is to perform the role of the administered justice itself, but without the constraints inherent in that process (such as the fact that the rules are written down, that they are administered by independent judges, and that outcomes have to be justified by references to reason and precedent). The role of lawyer for the situation therefore may be too prone to abuse to be explicitly sanctioned. A person may be entrusted with it only if he knows that in the event of miscarriage he will have no protection from the law. In this respect, acting as lawyer for the situation can be thought of as similar to a doctor's "authority" to terminate the life of a hopeless patient: It can properly be undertaken only if it will not be questioned afterwards. To this extent Brandeis's critics may have been right.

Yet it seems possible to define the role of intercessor, just as it has been possible to define the role of the trustee or guardian. The role could be defined by contrast with those of confidential counsellor and advocate, perhaps to the advantage of clarity in defining all three. At minimum, a recognition of the role of lawyer for the situation could result in a clearer perception by both clients and lawyers of one very important and socially estimable function that lawyers can perform and do perform.

B. LAWYER AS DIRECTOR

AMERICAN BAR ASSOCIATION FORMAL ETHICS OPINION 98–410 (1998)

LAWYER SERVING AS DIRECTOR OF CLIENT CORPORATION

The Model Rules of Professional Conduct do not prohibit a lawyer from serving as a director of a corporation while simultaneously serving as its legal counsel, but there are ethical concerns that a lawyer occupying the dual role of director and legal counsel should consider. The lawyer should reasonably assure at the outset of the dual relationship that management and the other board members understand the different responsibilities of legal counsel and director; understand that in some circumstances matters discussed at board meetings with the lawyer in her role as director will not receive the protection of the attorney-client privilege; and understand that conflicts of interest could arise requiring the lawyer to recuse herself as a director or to decline representation of the corporation in a matter. During the dual relationship, the lawyer should exercise reasonable care to protect the corporation's confidential information and to confront and resolve conflicts of interest that arise. From the discussion of these ethical concerns, the Committee derives general guidelines that a lawyer, once having agreed to serve on the board of a corporate client, should follow in order to minimize the risk of violations of the Model Rules.

* * *

We emphasize that not every lawyer will confront the same ethical challenges when serving as a member of a client's board of directors. The issues to be faced will differ depending on the nature of the legal services to be provided by the lawyer-director or her firm, the nature of the client's business, and the nature of the representation which could range from serving as general counsel to handling a few discrete transactions. Thus, the advice that follows is general in nature and does not attempt to reflect the specific facts of every contemplated dual relationship.

* * *

I. Advice to Clients Regarding the Dual Role

There are several broad categories of ethical concerns that exist when corporate counsel agrees to serve as director of her corporate client: (1) concerns that conflicts of interest will arise, causing reasonable parties to question the lawyer's professional independence and sometimes requiring the lawyer-director to decline representation in a matter or resign as a director; (2) concerns that the lawyer, other directors, and management will be confused whether the lawyer's views on a matter are legal advice or are expressed as the business or practical suggestions of a board member; and (3) concerns with protecting the confidentiality of client information, especially protecting the attorney-client privilege. While these concerns are real, many of the problems can be cured, or at least ameliorated, by full, free and frank discussions by the lawyer with the corporation's executives and the other board members. Ideally this discussion will occur before the lawyer becomes a board member. It is at this stage that the ethical lawyer should reasonably assure herself that those in authority understand the ethical and practical pitfalls that lie along the way. When in-house corporate counsel employed as a corporate executive is available, a discussion with him often will suffice. In other situations, the lawyer should take the time to explain the risks to the executive officers and other board members herself.

The explanation should describe the potential for conflicts of interest and how they might disable the lawyer from acting as either a director or a lawyer at some particularly critical time or require safeguards, such as engaging the services of counsel other than the lawyer or her firm. Similarly, the lawyer also should reasonably assure herself that the possible threat to the attorney-client privilege and consequent disclosure of confidential information are understood, either by discussions with employed corporate counsel or with the executive officers and other board members. In situations where a substantial likelihood exists that a disabling conflict of interest will arise or that the attorney-client privilege will be lost in a pending matter, the lawyer should offer to continue as counsel, attend board meetings and preserve her role solely as corporate counsel until the risk abates.

If there is reasonable assurance that the client is informed of the potential issues that might arise and still wishes the lawyer to serve as a director, and if the lawyer concludes that no current disqualifying conflict of interest or other ethical impediment bars the dual role, then the lawyer may accept the directorship. This initial decision about the continuing role of lawyer as lawyer and lawyer as director must nevertheless be revisited as situations arise that call for further consultation with the client, and the lawyer may have to consider withdrawing from one position or the other if necessary. See infra Part III.

Because of the need for the lawyer and the corporation's management and board to give ongoing attention to potential conflicts, attorney-client privilege protection and other issues that may arise as a result of the dual role, the lawyer-director should consider providing a written memorandum in addition to an oral explanation. A written memorandum is of particular assistance in describing the lawyer's role as counsel for the corporate entity and not for its constituent officers or directors and in explaining the differences between serving as a director and serving as counsel. It is, of course, imperative that any standards specified in such a written memorandum be followed in practice.

II. The Lawyer–Director Must Exercise Reasonable Care to Protect the Corporation's Attorney–Client Privilege

Lawyers serving as directors have the same obligation as other lawyers to maintain confidentiality and avoid compromising the attorney-client privilege of the corporation. A lawyer's duty of confidentiality under Model Rule 1.6 is consistent with a director's duty of confidentiality that arises from her role as a fiduciary for the corporation, although the scope of these two duties is not precisely the same.

A problem arises, however, as the result of the inconsistent responsibilities of director and lawyer in the application of the attorney-client evidentiary privilege. Because the lawyer-director provides the management and board with business advice as well as legal assistance, the lawyer, management and board members could find themselves forced to testify about conversations that would not be involuntarily disclosed if the lawyer-director had been acting only as a lawyer.

* * *

Given the stricter limitations applied by some courts on the privilege for communications with a lawyer-director, it is vital that the lawyer who also serves as a director be particularly careful when her client's management or board of directors consults her for legal advice. The lawyer-director should make clear that the meeting is solely for the purpose of providing legal advice. The lawyer should avoid the temptation of providing business or financial advice, except insofar as it affects legal considerations such as the application of the business judgment rule. When appropriate, the lawyer-director should have another member of her firm present at the meeting to provide the legal advice.

These procedures not only will provide the best support for a claim of privilege for the conversations, but also will alert board members who otherwise might mistakenly believe the lawyer-director is giving them business advice. The procedures also alert all involved to treat the information with the utmost care that normally is associated with confidential attorney-client communications.

The lawyer-director also should bear in mind that, although only the client (or a lawyer acting with the client's express consent) can waive the attorney-client privilege, the lawyer, because she also is director, may be found to have waived the privilege on behalf of the corporation without need of any further client consent. In [United States v]. Vehicular Parking, [52 F.Supp. 751 (D.Del. 1943)] for example, the court found that a lawyer-director's voluntary disclosure of memoranda to the government in an antitrust case effected a waiver of the lawyer-client privilege because he produced the documents in his role as a "business manager" and not while "wear[ing] his lawyer suit."

Finally, a director, who also is the corporation's lawyer, may be under a duty to disclose information to third parties (such as in response to an auditor's request) that in her role as legal counsel to the corporation she could not disclose without specific consent. Acts of a lawyer-director and her knowledge as a director may prove inseparable from the lawyer's acts and knowledge as member of a law firm. The director's fiduciary obligations as a director and her professional obligations as a lawyer cannot "be placed in convenient separate boxes." The knowledge of a corporate director and officer, with respect to transactions in which she is authorized to act, is imputed to the corporation. Similarly, the knowledge of a partner in a law firm gained during confidential relationships with clients is imputed to the other partners in the law firm. There is a risk in some circumstances that the files and work processes of the law firm could become as available for discovery as are the files and records of the corporation itself.

III. The Lawyer–Director Must Confront and Resolve Ethical Issues that Arise During the Dual Role

* * *

A. Conflict in Pursuing Client Objectives that the Lawyer, as a Director, Opposed.

An ethical issue arises when a lawyer-director is asked to represent the corporation in an undertaking that she, as a director, has unsuccessfully opposed. Should the lawyer undertake the representation? If the lawyer should not, may other lawyers in her law firm represent the corporation in the matter? Are there circumstances when the lawyer and her firm are precluded under the Model Rules from representing the corporation?

In this situation, the lawyer must determine whether her representation of the corporation may be "materially limited" by her opposition to the action the corporation has decided to undertake, such that Model Rule 1.7(b) applies. Generally, when a lawyer counsels any client against a given course of action, but the client rejects that advice, the client's decision once made must be accepted by the lawyer. A lawyer by representing a client does not endorse "the client's political, economic, social or moral views or activities." Model Rule 1.2(b). And even after offering an opinion on such matters, it may be easy for a lawyer to conclude that, once the client has decided to pursue its chosen course, the lawyer can remain the lawyer for the client.

However, for the lawyer-director, who is required as a director to make a business judgment, this calculus may be different, a fact the lawyer should recognize before she undertakes representing the corporation in the matter. When a lawyer has participated in the decision-making as a client, there may be an increased risk that she will be tempted to "pull her punches" as she represents the corporation in going forward, or may be perceived by others as providing less than diligent representation. See Model Rule 1.3.

If representation of the corporation may be materially limited by these factors, the lawyer then must also determine whether she reasonably believes the representation will not be adversely affected. See Model Rule 1.7(b). If she reaches that conclusion, which applies objectively, and the client consents after consultation, then the lawyer is not disqualified from the representation. Even so, if the lawyer continues to believe that the corporation's chosen course of action is imprudent, she may be unwise to undertake the representation personally; another lawyer in her firm would be permitted to represent the corporation under Model Rules 1.7(b) and 1.10(a).

If, however, the lawyer-director concludes that under Rule 1.7(b) she personally is disqualified, her conflict is imputed under Model Rule 1.10(a) to the rest of her firm's lawyers, who also are disqualified from the representation. This could occur, for example, were she to conclude that she will face personal liability as a result of the course chosen by a majority of the directors over her objection. If so, she should consider resigning from the board if necessary for self-protection. Whether or not she resigns, the situation may create a nonconsentable conflict of interest under Rule 1.7 (b) because the representation would be adversely affected, thus disqualifying her law firm as well as herself from the representation. This would be true even if the corporation's actions are not criminal or fraudulent, and do not violate a legal obligation owed by the directors or management to the corporation that is likely to result in substantial injury to it.

B. Conflict in Opining on Board Actions in which the Lawyer–Director Participated.

A lawyer who serves as a director could be disabled from rendering opinions or offering her best legal judgment with respect to a specific matter because of her role as a director. For example, when the lawyer-director is asked to provide advice to the corporation on matters involving prior actions of the board, such as whether an incentive pay arrangement is lawful, she may in effect be advising on the legality of actions in which she herself has participated as a director. Under these circumstances, it may prove difficult for the lawyer to speak independently as counsel to the corporation in light of her own interest as a director.

Moreover, seeking a waiver of the potential conflict is problematic because the very directors who would need to provide the waiver are themselves directly concerned by the question that is being raised. Finally, if the opinion is sought in order to justify an action the board currently has before it, the advice-of-counsel defense to a later lawsuit may be undermined by the lack of independence of the lawyer-director and her firm. In some cases these concerns can be mitigated by the participation of other counsel to advise on the issue, without compelling the complete withdrawal of the lawyer-director as counsel.

C. Conflict Regarding Corporate Actions Affecting Lawyer or Her Firm.

A conflict issue may also arise when a matter comes before the board of directors that will significantly affect the corporation's use of lawyers. For example, the corporation might consider a major purchase or merger, an initial public offering, or launching a new product that requires major regulatory approval. Is the lawyer-director able to exercise sound business judgment as a director when participating in the board's decision in circumstances where it is clear, e.g., that (i) her firm will be engaged to perform the legal services, or (ii) her firm will be a candidate to do so, or (iii) another firm will be engaged to perform the services?

The analysis here differs from the conflict regarding legal advice discussed above. To the extent that the lawyer is taking action as a director, the question here is whether she is able to exercise independent judgment as a director when the board's decision could significantly affect the director's law firm. The lawyer-director should consider whether, under the law of corporate governance, she should recuse herself as a director from consideration of the matter, or remove her firm from consideration to perform the legal services, or both, or whether she may participate after noting to the other board members (or to employed corporate counsel) her personal interest and its potential effects.

* * *

* * * [T]he prudent lawyer should at a minimum abstain from voting as a director on issues which directly involve the relationship of the corporation with her law firm, such as issues of engagement, performance, payment or discharge.

If the lawyer-director's firm has been pre-selected to perform the services that will be necessary if the course of action is approved, the lawyer-director also should consider abstaining as a director from voting on the action, although the law of corporate governance requires to validate the corporate action only disclosure of such a conflict of interest, following which the director may participate. If the board is closely divided on a matter of serious consequence to the corporation, however, the lawyer-director's recusal as a director could interfere with the corporation's selection of the best course to follow. In such a case, the lawyer-director may decide to withdraw her firm from consideration as counsel in the matter and participate fully in the board's decision-making process. We emphasize that, in our opinion, no violation of any Model Rule would result if the lawyer participates in corporate action as a result of which she or her firm is employed to perform legal services.

* * *

Craig C. Albert, THE LAWYER-DIRECTOR: AN OXYMORON?

9 GEO. J. LEGAL ETHICS 413 (1996)

INTRODUCTION

The Board awaits your vote. The CEO of the Company, your good friend and the person who invited you to join the Board, has just completed a presentation outlining a possible takeover bid by the Company for its foremost competitor. Management staunchly believes that the proposed acquisition would cut costs, increase profit margins and boost the Company's lagging market share. Most importantly, management favors the acquisition because it will eliminate its chief competitor.

As a business matter, the proposal sounds promising, and you are inclined to support it. Yet as the Company's outside counsel, you are concerned that the proposed takeover could catch the ire of the Antitrust Division of the Department of Justice or the Federal Trade Commission. While you think the purchase would eventually achieve regulatory approval, the process would be costly and time-consuming. Complicating matters even further, the acquisition and the accompanying regulatory review would generate hundreds of thousands of dollars of legal fees for your law firm. How do you vote? Can you wear both hats—lawyer and director—simultaneously?

In 1949, influential attorney Robert Swaine of New York's Cravath, Swaine & Moore stated that while "most of us would be greatly relieved if a canon of ethics were adopted forbidding a lawyer in substance to become his own client through acting as a director ... of a client ... [t]he practice is too widespread to permit any such expectation." Forty-five years later, the practice shows no signs of abating. Studies indicate that outside counsel serve as directors of more than one in six public companies in the United States. Recent increases in shareholder activism and demands for increased director independence suggest that it is just a matter of time before the bar will address the question of whether to prohibit lawyers from serving as directors of their corporate clients.

* * *

I. *Benefits of the Dual Role*

A. *Benefits to the Client*

Supporters of the dual role argue that clients receive superior legal service when outside counsel serves on a client's board. Several reasons are frequently mentioned. First, the attorney-director acquires insight into the "ins-and-outs" of the client's business, enabling the attorney-director and his or her law firm to render more meaningful legal advice. By virtue of a director's increased access to management, the attorney-director should be more informed about the company's day-to-day affairs than ordinary outside counsel. Further, the attorney-director may recognize legal issues that management or other directors may fail to identify, thereby permitting the client to nip potential problems in the bud. These factors can facilitate the rendering of timely "legal advice when a transaction is first proposed or when a problem begins to develop." These benefits inure directly to the client, particularly because "the hardest counseling decisions often arise where inattention has allowed a situation to deteriorate."

Commentators have also suggested that the dual role fosters trust between counsel and management because counsel is perceived as a partner in the corporate purpose. While opponents of the dual role contend that the benefits resulting when outside counsel is also a director can be attained by asking counsel to attend board meetings, proponents contend that a board may be more reluctant to follow the advice of outside counsel who is not a director, especially if the advice is counter to the board's wishes. If members of management are more likely to heed the advice of a lawyer when they know that he shares their responsibility as a director, clients and shareholders are the beneficiaries of the dual role.

Another frequently cited benefit, and a major reason why corporations request their outside counsel to join the board, is that lawyers make good directors. As one lawyer put it, "the questioning nature of the attorney in scrutinizing proposed plans and his analytical skills in studying and examining matters before the board are of much value to a corporation." Moreover, the attorney-director's ability to identify the legal implications of a matter assists the board as a whole in fulfilling its fiduciary obligations to the corporation and its shareholders. Particularly in today's complex legal environment, where virtually every major corporate decision is influenced by a mix of federal, state and local laws and regulations, it is not surprising that clients and their non-lawyer directors seek to include attorneys on the board. In fact, clients "are often reassured when a lawyer joins the board." One client, in recruiting outside counsel to accept a nomination, explained:

I would like you to go on the board because I know that if you are on the board you are going to worry about liability, your own liability as well as our liability; and if you are worried about your own liability, I know you will try to get us to do the right thing. So I want you there, worrying. If you yourself are worrying, I will feel a lot better about it.

If, as this client suggests, attorney-directors will be more committed to serving their clients than ordinary outside counsel because they know that they, too, are subject to personal liability, corporations and shareholders benefit when outside counsel is also a director.

Lastly, proponents of the dual role argue that an attorney-director can be a more effective monitor of management than a director who is not counsel to the corporation because, through legal services rendered to the client, the attorney-director often will be more familiar with a company's operations than its outside directors, who generally have limited contact with a company's day-to-day affairs.

B.   Benefits to Lawyers and Law Firms

For law firms and law firm partners, one incentive for supporting and, in fact, encouraging the firm's partners to serve as directors of the firm's clients is, not surprisingly, money. Gone are the days when a corporation used one law firm exclusively. Today, large corporations commonly retain several law firms. As a result, competition between law firms for business—and accompanying fees—has escalated. Given the transactional nature of today's legal practice, law firms relish any opportunity to solidify the firm's position as outside counsel. The presence of one of the firm's lawyers on a client's board is a particularly effective method of maintaining the attorney-client relationship because the dual role enables the attorney-director to cement personal alliances with the board and with the members of senior management who generally select outside counsel.As one lawyer aptly put it, the attorney-director "may be friendly and sympathetic to management—he probably would not be the lawyer or a director if he were not."

Another explanation for the relative frequency of the practice is that corporate clients often insist that outside counsel join the board. While an attorney can deny the invitation, few attorneys are able to resist their client's request. In light of the intense competition among law firms for business, lawyers and law firms are understandably wary of disappointing a client by refusing an invitation. One attorney, whose firm has a strong policy against serving on the boards of clients, stated that when a fellow attorney in his firm refused a client's request to be a director, the client contacted a lawyer in another firm who said he would accept only if the company shifted its business to the other firm. As this example illustrates, the perception among many lawyers and law firms is that if you refuse an invitation, your competitor will accept.

Lastly, yet not to be underestimated, directorships are prestigious. An impressive list of directorships is not only an indicator of professional success and achievement, but also a valuable marketing tool for securing new business.

II.   Arguments Against the Lawyer–Director

*   *   *

A.   Loss of Independent Professional Judgment

Justice Potter Stewart cited "the need for the brightest possible line of demarcation between the function of a lawyer in giving professional counsel to his client and the function of corporate management in carrying on the corporation's business in the profit-making interests of its stockholders." While both corporate lawyers and directors have duties to the corporation, their responsibilities differ. In broad terms, the primary responsibilities of directors are to monitor management and to exercise business judgment in determining appropriate business risks for the corporation. Outside counsel ordinarily is retained by management to advise the corporation on the legal implications and risks of business decisions made by management and the board. When these positions are merged, the lawyer-director may be unable to simultaneously fulfill the obligations that each demands. While the dual role will not always result in disabling conflicts under a state's rules of professional responsibility, the attorney-director's independent judgment may nevertheless be impaired. The concern with independence is twofold—independence as an attorney, discussed below, and independence as a director, which is addressed in Part II.C.

1.   Independence as an Attorney

As an attorney, the issue for the lawyer contemplating a board nomination is whether the dual role will adversely impact his or her ability to provide objective legal advice to the corporation. Justice Brandeis stated that "a man who is his own lawyer has a fool for a client." Echoing Brandeis' theme, opponents of the dual role have argued that an attorney-director is effectively his own client, that clients are best advised by a lawyer who maintains an objective point of view and that such objectivity will be compromised by participation in management. Accordingly, they question whether an attorney-director can possibly provide independent legal advice to a board of which he is a member.

Those who believe lawyers should never serve as directors of their clients also claim that it is impossible for the attorney-director to serve adequately in both roles. They contend that while both positions require that the individual be objective and prepared to disagree with management as circumstances require, the responsibilities of lawyers and directors are not identical. The dual role would appear to create inconsistent obligations, for example, where a corporation asks its attorney-director and his or her law firm to formulate defenses to a takeover attempt. Under the ethical rules, the attorney must implement the defenses unless the attorney "knows" such measures are illegal. Because the legality of defensive measures is rarely free from doubt—particularly since board decisions are protected by the business judgment rule—in many cases the attorney will have an ethical obligation to prepare the requested defenses even though the measures may later be found to have been adopted in violation of his or her fiduciary obligations as a director. As a result of these ethics rules, the attorney-director may, as a practical matter, be restricted in his right, and possibly his obligation, as a director to voice his disagreement.In such a situation, it would appear impossible for the lawyer-director to simultaneously satisfy his ethical and fiduciary obligations.

Opponents of the dual role also note that the Code of Professional Ethics for Certified Public Accountants (the CPA Code) prohibits accountants from serving as directors of their clients. Rule 101 of the CPA Code prohibits an accountant from opining on the financial statements of an enterprise unless the accountant and his firm are "independent" with respect to the enterprise. Rule 101 states that the independence requirement is not satisfied if the accountant served as a director of the enterprise either during the period covered by the financial statements, during the period of professional engagement or at the time of expressing an opinion. Given that the accounting profession has effectively adopted an ethical prohibition, an obvious question follows:

> Why should everybody expect the accountant not to have stock in the client, nor to be on the board, to have all this independence, when the lawyer is giving opinions and being relied upon by the public or affecting the public, but he does not have all of those prohibitions?

Are accountants distinguishable from attorneys such that the need for independence is greater with respect to accountants?

Perhaps. Lawyers are quick to note that unlike accountants, who generally serve only as independent auditors of an entity's financial statements, attorneys serve in many roles for their clients, functioning as, among other things, advisors, advocates and negotiators. Moreover, while corporate attorneys, like accountants, express opinions on their clients' actions, independence concerns may be less significant with respect to attorneys because fewer people rely on legal opinions provided by corporate attorneys. Conversely, the investing public, in making investment decisions, relies heavily on audited financial statements and the accompanying auditors' opinions.

2. Is Independence a Realistic Goal?

Notwithstanding the foregoing concerns and claims that a lawyer-director whose law firm receives large legal fees from a corporation cannot possibly maintain his or her independence, query whether lawyers or directors can ever be truly independent. As stated earlier, the attorney-director probably never would have been asked to serve as counsel or as a director if he or she did not have a good relationship with management. Given this reality, in examining the propriety of the dual role and an ethical ban, we should ask instead whether the dual role compromises independence in any additional manner.

Is a lawyer who receives large fees from a corporation likely to be any more independent in advising that company than the same lawyer who also serves as a director? Arguably not. While a lawyer-director may have a pre-conditioned management view, so too does ordinary outside counsel. Both are paid by the corporation. Both are asked by management to serve the corporation. Both have an equal incentive to preserve the attorney-client relationship. Lastly, all attorneys, directors or otherwise, have at least some incentive to advise clients to take actions that produce the largest legal fees. For these reasons, the risk that a directorship will make counsel less independent and more pro-management may be overstated. That being said, an obvious difference exists between the two: the lawyer-director may vote on matters affecting the client, whereas ordinary outside counsel will not. Moreover, as intimated above, the lawyer-director may encounter situations in which his or her obligations as a lawyer are inconsistent with his or her duties as a director. In such situations, the lawyer-director would lack the independence that the legal professional demands.

* * *

C. Independence as a Director

3. An Issue of Corporate Governance, Not Ethical Responsibility

This Article does not challenge the independence concerns raised above, but rather questions whether such concerns justify an ethical rule completely barring the dual role. Normatively, the arguments against the dual role make sense. However, one should not overlook the benefits to corporations and shareholders when outside counsel is also a director.

Despite the recent trend toward greater board independence, the chief executive officer, the ultimate insider, is also chairman of the board of almost twenty-five percent of all public corporations. The fact that corporations have not excluded management entirely from the boardroom indicates that corporate America profits from having those most knowledgeable about a particular corporation on its board of directors.

The Principles of Corporate Governance have recognized this benefit. "[P]ermitting senior executives to serve on the board ensures knowledgeable and detailed board discussion about the business, and encourages management to take important issues to the board." The Principles also acknowledge that allowing other persons with significant dealings with the corporation's senior executives (for example, outside counsel) to serve on the board enables persons who may be useful directors to serve in that capacity.

Those who nevertheless advocate a complete ban are reminded that shareholders, as owners of the corporate enterprise, have the sole power to elect directors and to replace them if they are performing poorly. As the Delaware Court of Chancery recently affirmed, "[A]ssuming full disclosure of the relevant facts, 'it would be improper' for a court to pass judgment on the fitness of a person to serve as a director ...; that question is for stockholders, not courts."

As intimated by the Delaware Court of Chancery, conflicts are not per se improper. An attorney-director concerned about an apparent or actual conflict generally can safeguard the validity of a board decision and avoid personal liability by disclosing his or her self-interest and not participating in the discussion or the vote. In fact, even if it is judicially determined that a lawyer-director participated improperly in a board discussion or vote, one director's self-interest, standing alone, generally will not invalidate a board decision.

Those who question the independence of the lawyer-director should also consider whether outside counsel who is not a director would be more willing to challenge management than the lawyer-director given that both have an equal incentive to maintain the attorney-client relationship. In fact, one could argue that, by virtue of the responsibilities imposed on lawyers by the ethics rules, lawyer-directors have greater incentive to act in the best interests of the corporation than directors constrained only by state law. Further, many purported "outside" directors, not just lawyers, have a pre-existing relationship with management, and even those that do not have such a relationship have some incentive to side with management because of the often-lucrative compensation and benefits accompanying many directorships.

Each of the independence concerns raised above are legitimate and should be considered by lawyers, law firms and clients alike when evaluating whether outside counsel should serve on the board. In analyzing the propriety of an ethics prohibition, however, one should also consider whether an attorney-director's ability to be an effective board member is a matter more properly addressed by state corporate law, stock exchange requirements and SEC rules rather than professional responsibility rules. As one commentator put it,

I would be in favor of [counsel not serving as directors of their corporate clients] as a general proposition, but I question whether it should be in the Code of Ethics. * * * I think it would be a mistake to mandate that as a rule for all companies. It seems to me this is a business judgment.

In fact, opponents of the adoption of an ethical ban argue that the interjection of a complete prohibition into a principal area of corporate governance would constitute an act of disservice to clients.

[I]f lawyers should elect to disqualify themselves, the profession would be depriving companies, particularly smaller companies, of the service of a whole class of persons who * * * are among the best kind of directors companies should have * * * [T]he quality of corporate governance would suffer.

In the end, the important question relating to director independence remains the same: Does the dual role harm the client? Admittedly, if a significant percentage of a corporation's directors are "insiders" who are unable to participate in discussions or vote on important matters, the corporation, in effect, loses the benefit of their presence on the board. At the same time, however, so long as corporations recognize that an attorney-director may be unable to participate in certain decisions or serve on certain committees, corporations arguably should not be deprived of the right to request their outside counsel to be a director. For these reasons, any discussion of an ethical prohibition should focus on whether the dual role will impair the service that the lawyer-director renders to the corporation as a lawyer rather than on outside counsel's ability to be an effective director.

* * *

III. Arguments Against Complete Prohibition

A. Scope of the Inquiry

Should the legal profession adopt an ethical rule prohibiting lawyers from serving as directors of their corporate clients? A logical response would be to simply balance the advantages and disadvantages of the dual role discussed in this Article. However, such a reaction would be misplaced. Questions of liability are for lawyers and law firms to consider individually and as institutions, and concerns regarding the impact of both positions on a lawyer-director's independence as a director are better left to shareholders, state corporate law and stock exchange and SEX rules. The proper question for the ethical codes is whether serving simultaneously in both capacities impairs the quality of professional legal service provided to the client.

B. An Ethical Ban Would Be Over–inclusive

As an ethical matter, the fundamental argument raised against the dual role is the risk that the lawyer's independence, objectivity and judgment will be impaired. This Article does not challenge the above contention. In fact, this Article concedes that, due to the risk of conflict, serving in both capacities will be inadvisable in many instances. Clearly, to the extent a lawyer-director's obligations as a director are inconsistent with his or her ethical obligations as a lawyer, the lawyer-director cannot maintain the independence that the legal profession demands.

At the same time, however, this Article questions whether the risk of conflict is significant enough to justify the adoption of a blanket rule prohibiting all lawyers, in all circumstances, from serving as directors of their clients. As discussed in Part II.B. above, the dual role ordinarily will not create additional conflicts or aggravate those that confront all corporate attorneys because the duties of corporate attorneys and directors are generally consistent. Occasionally, a conflict will arise that will require the attorney-director to recuse himself or herself from participating in a board decision, obtain advice from another attorney or resign from the board. However, this risk is insufficient to justify a blanket prohibition. Where such conflicts develop, the conflict rules adequately guide a lawyer's response. Thus, while this author would support a rule prohibiting the practice in certain enumerated circumstances, such as in the takeover context or in other situations where the obligations of directors and lawyers clearly differ, this Article concludes that the foregoing independence concerns do not, in and of themselves, justify a blanket rule prohibiting the dual role in all circumstances.

Similarly, neither the risk of disqualification nor loss of privilege justifies an absolute ban. While these risks should not be discounted, disqualification and privilege issues arise only in litigation and will never prevent an attorney-director from continuing to handle transactional work for the client.

C. Disservice to Clients

In addition, this Article submits that such a ban would constitute a disservice to clients. When management invites a lawyer from its outside law firm to join the board, it does so presumably because it believes that the attorney's presence on the board will benefit the corporation. As one lawyer stated, "some of the best ... [lawyers] are not only damn good lawyers, but damn good businessmen; and the deprive the business community of the opportunity to use those people's services in both roles ... would be a terrible mistake."

As detailed throughout this Article, the competence, diligence and loyalty demanded of lawyers by the legal profession arguably equals or exceeds the requirements imposed on directors under state corporate law. Corporations and shareholders benefit when attorneys bound by these high standards are enlisted to serve the corporation. To deprive corporations and shareholders of these benefits in the absence of a serious systemic problem seems unwise and unnecessary.

In fact, such a rule conceivably could deprive non-clients, as well as clients, of a valuable source of talented directors. Were a complete prohibition enacted, it is possible that some law firms would not permit their attorneys to accept board nominations because the board position would, in effect, preclude the lawyer-director's law firm from performing legal work for the corporation.

Laura Pearlman, WHEN LAWYERS SIT ON BOARDS: IT'S A COMMON PRACTICE, BUT TODAY'S CORPORATE SCANDALS COULD CALL IT INTO QUESTION

LEGAL TIMES (July 1, 2002)

With corporate scandals abundant, this much is clear: When it comes to corporate governance, gray areas aren't good. In the past few months, the Securities and Exchange Commission has called upon the New York Stock Exchange, Nasdaq, and the professional organization Financial Executives International to recommend stricter governance standards for officer and director qualifications, among other things. The result has been a flurry of opinions and proposals about shoring up board ethics, structures, and procedures. There's no assurance that lawyers who serve as directors of client corporations will escape scrutiny.

Sitting on a client's board is a common practice. According to recent SEC proxy statements, partners from 69 of the AmLaw 100 firms sit on boards of NYSE-listed companies; 61 of those lawyer-directors' firms have performed legal services for the companies. While the practice may be widespread, it's also risky. The American Bar Association's Model Rules of Professional Conduct do not bar lawyers from sitting on clients' boards, but the ABA Standing Committee on Ethics and Professional Responsibility has discouraged the practice in a series of reports, says Lawrence Fox, a former committee chairman. Fox, a partner at Philadelphia's Drinker Biddle & Reath, frames the problem as a conflict: How can a lawyer claim to be an independent director while profiting from legal work performed for management? "Ninety percent of the time it all works out fine," Fox says. "But when everything hits the fan, this is another black eye."

Kenneth Bialkin, a corporate securities partner at New York's Skadden, Arps, Slate, Meagher & Flom who served on the boards of Citigroup Inc. and several other companies before reaching the boards' retirement age, has a contrary view. "You're never totally independent," he says. "But am I less independent than another director who's a friend of the CEO? The world is full of conflicts." Bialkin says that lawyers' training and integrity make them very good directors. But even he doesn't suggest that his partners rush out to join boards en masse: "There are dangers," he acknowledges. At worst, a firm with a partner on the board of a public company could be held liable in shareholder litigation.

The hazards lie in the difference between the roles of company lawyer and independent director. The lawyer's allegiance is to the company. In contrast, an outside director should be independent from management. Discussions that other directors have with the lawyer-director do not enjoy attorney-client privilege, and the line between business advice and legal advice can be blurred.

In some cases—primarily bankruptcies—a firm can be conflicted out of legal work for a company if one of its partners belongs to the company's board. That is one reason New York bankruptcy powerhouse Weil, Gotshal & Manges rarely allows its partners to serve on boards. "It's not a blanket rule," says Richard Davis, a member of the firm's ethics committee. But partners are required to get the management committee's approval, which Davis says is rarely given to lawyers in the United States. "It's generally disfavored," Davis says. (Since boards are structured differently in Europe, the firm's restriction on its lawyers there is not as stringent.)

Of the dozen big firms surveyed for this article, all said they make decisions about board membership on a case-by-case basis. Weil Gotshal comes closest to having a hard-and-fast rule against allowing partners to serve on boards. Of the other firms, New York's Cadwalader, Wickersham & Taft requires partners who want to join boards to obtain permission from the firm's management committee. At Dallas' Akin, Gump, Strauss, Hauer & Feld, membership on a public company's board is limited to corporations;700;700 that have a market capitalization of at least $500 million; partners who want to join the boards of such companies must obtain approval from a committee of three partners.

At San Francisco's Pillsbury Winthrop, a partner who wants to accept a board seat must apply in writing for the firm's permission and be interviewed by the firm's professional responsibility committee before receiving approval. The firm also asks the partner for a certificate of directors and officers insurance. If that partner has been working on securities offerings for the client, then a different partner takes over the work. And that's not the end of the firm's oversight. Every year partners must update the status of the relationship with board and client. A staffer tracks the procedure on a centralized database.

Not every large firm has such a structured process. Los Angeles' Munger, Tolles & Olson, for instance, doesn't have a formal process like Pillsbury Winthrop's, but nonetheless reviews each case carefully. "As Enron has so clearly pointed out, it isn't a free lunch," says Ronald Olson, a name partner who is a director of Berkshire Hathaway Inc. Lawyer-directors must understand the responsibility and knowledge required for the director's job, Olson says.

Lawyers have been serving on boards since the birth of the American corporation, and the ethical issues have probably been debated since then. In the 1860s George Templeton Strong, a founding partner at Cadwalader, reportedly gave up his share of earnings from a firm client, the Bank for Savings, when he joined its board. It's not known whether Strong was acting on his personal code of ethics or his firm's, but his decision would hardly be common today. (These days, Cadwalader has no formal policy about such fees, according to a spokeswoman for the firm.)

In fact, compensation for lawyers from boards is a hot topic. Generally, directors are compensated in equity or with a combination of cash and stock options. At some firms, lawyer-directors are required to share such compensation (which can reach $150,000 at a Fortune 100 company) with the rest of the partnership. In addition, board work takes a lawyer away from billable client matters. Finally, partners who serve on the boards of public clients are required to disclose fees paid by the client to the lawyer-director's firm in proxy filings—a prospect that makes some firms uncomfortable.

One area where there appears to be consensus, at least at first glance, is audit committee membership. About two years ago the NYSE adopted a rule saying that the audit committee must be made up entirely of independent directors. The rule defines directors who have a business relationship with the company as nonindependent. But there's a loophole—a big one—that makes it possible for lawyers to serve on the audit committee. The rule allows the board to determine that the lawyer's relationship does not interfere with his independent judgment as a director. Among the lawyers who have been allowed to join audit committees under the provision are Akin, Gump's Rick Burdick and Dechert's Barton Winokur. Both lawyers say they know the companies in question very well and have financial expertise that makes their audit committee membership appropriate.

Given all the hassle, why do lawyers bother joining boards in the first place? For one thing, says Mark Stevens, a former Fenwick & West partner, serving on a board tends to seal a lawyer's relationship with a client. For another, outside counsel who fantasize about going in-house often find that sitting on a board is the next best thing, says Stevens, who now spends time serving on boards and is no longer a practicing lawyer. "You learn what it's like to sit in the hot seat," Stevens says. "It gives you a taste of business."

"It's helpful, acting as a principal," says Akin, Gump's Burdick, who sits on the boards of Cleveland's Century Business Services Inc. and Fort Lauderdale, Fla.'s AutoNation Inc. Because it provides a front-row view of life on the inside of the company, "it better qualifies me to represent and advise my clients in corporate governance matters," he says. Burdick stresses that both companies are relatively small clients and that he doesn't provide legal advice to either. When a lawyer both sits on the board of a company and provides it with legal advice, he says, "it's not a very good dynamic."

Given that truth—and the increased attention to corporate governance—it's possible that fewer lawyers will seek to join clients' boards, at least for the short term. Says Munger Tolles' Olson: "Enron was a wake-up call for directorships generally." Will lawyers sleep through the alarm?

Michael H. Trotter, Exodus of Outside Counsel Leaves Hole in Corporate Boards

Fulton County Daily Reporter (May 21, 2003)

It used to be commonplace for a lawyer who served as the principal outside legal adviser to a company also to serve on its board of directors. It is far less common today.

That's because the in-house general counsel is likely to occupy the lawyer's chair on the board and there is no logical candidate among the many outside lawyers providing limited services to the company. It also is because stock exchange rules classify such lawyer-directors as "not independent" and therefore not eligible to sit on audit and other committees or be counted as a part of the required independent majority.

Unfortunately, true independence is not the test because it's hard to determine. Rather, the test is the existence of an interest that "might" compromise the ethics of an outside lawyer-director.

As a result, it is far less likely today that a lawyer whose firm represents a corporation will serve on the corporation's board. When I became an associate of the Alston firm in the early 1960s, I believe that every publicly owned client for which the firm served as primary outside legal counsel had elected to its board the partner responsible for its legal work at the firm.

By 1987, based on a National Law Journal annual survey, there were only 91 private practice lawyers serving on the boards of the 250 largest publicly owned service or industrial companies in the United States. Of these 91 lawyer-directors, 38 served on the boards of companies that used the director's law firm for significant amounts of the legal services. Of these, 33 served on the boards of companies that identified the lawyer-director's firm as the first among those law firms providing significant amounts of legal services. Twenty-three of the outside lawyer-directors served on the boards of companies that named their firm as the only firm supplying significant services or as the company's primary outside counsel. That same year, 60 of the largest 250 corporations indicated that they used only one firm for their legal services.

By 1999, the number of private practice lawyers serving on the boards of the 250 companies in The National Law Journal survey (this time including financial companies as well as service and industrial companies) had dropped from 91 to 77. Some served on more than one board. For instance, Sam Nunn of King & Spalding served on the boards of General Electric Co., Texaco and The Coca–Cola Co.

The number of outside lawyer-directors whose law firms were identified as a major supplier of services had dropped from 38 to 36, and the number of companies that listed a director's law firm as the only significant supplier of legal services or as primary outside counsel had dropped from 23 to 5. The number of corporations that indicated that they had only one law firm that provided significant services had dropped from 60 in 1987 to 24 in 1999.

As a result, we can see a clear trend. Fewer private practice lawyers are serving on corporate boards, even fewer are serving on the boards of companies represented by their law firms and the number whose firms serve as primary or exclusive outside legal counsel has dropped dramatically from 23 to 5. These significant changes do not come as a surprise to any of us who have been practicing corporate law these past 15 years.

Of course, most large companies these days have in-house general counsel and these general counsel often are serving on the boards of directors of their companies. In addition, large companies increasingly are hiring outside lawyers they think have the right skills and experience instead of the lawyers provided by firms that have partners sitting on their boards.

Since the in-house general counsel have become the dominant players on the field, it is natural that they would want to determine the lawyers working for their companies. Indeed, why should any of them have to compete with an influential outside lawyer-director for the control of the company's legal policies and budget? Not surprisingly, the relative strength and influence of outside counsel has declined along with the participation by senior private practice lawyers on the boards of directors of their larger clients.

A significant number of the private practice lawyer-directors serving on the boards of large companies are retired politicians-former U.S. cabinet members, senators, congressmen and governors.

I identified without research 20 former political or U.S. government administrators on a 1988 National Law Journal list of outside lawyers serving on boards. (The list surveyed firms in 1987.) They included William T. Coleman, Nicholas Katzenbach, Joseph A. Califano Jr., Griffin B. Bell, Edward W. Brooke, Stuart E. Eizenstat, George D. Busbee and Newton N. Minow.

On the 1999 list, I identified 16 prominent political names including those of Sam Nunn, James A. Baker III, Walter F. Mondale, George

Deukmejian, Newton N. Minow and Robert P. Forrestal, the former President of the Federal Reserve Bank of Atlanta. I'm sure in both years there were other political figures that I didn't recognize.

We can assume reasonably that in most of these cases the political figures were selected to serve as directors because of their special knowledge of government and politics and for whom they knew, rather than for their skill or knowledge as lawyers. They are important to the boards on which they serve for what they bring to the table personally rather than for the law firms they represent or the legal services the firms provide.

INDEPENDENCE OF OUTSIDE COUNSEL

Some folks think it is a good thing for shareholders that so few lawyers serve on the boards of their clients today, but I disagree. Some of the best and most independent directors that I have seen in my 40 years of practice have been directors who were the principal outside legal counsel for the companies on whose boards they served.

Why is this the case? For one thing, they knew the legal requirements under which the corporation operated and they knew that the enterprise was their client and not its executive officers. For another, they had careers that were not entirely dependent on the client on whose board they served. And they had a comprehensive knowledge of the company's operations, usually more knowledge than any other director outside of management. The outside lawyer-director carried the additional burden of legal responsibility for the company's conduct, and in some cases was held to a higher standard of care and conduct than a nonlawyer director of the same company.

Consequently, any outside lawyer-director faced with a decision about how to address a problem involving the company's legal conduct had to decide if it was better to confront the issue and lose the future income represented by the representation or lose his reputation and capital in a shareholder suit.

Practicing lawyers were and are usually much more attuned to these risks than nonlawyer directors. I also suspect that many lawyers today are unwilling to serve as directors of companies represented by their firms and are encouraged not to serve by the firms' malpractice insurance carriers.

As a member of the board, the outside lawyer-director has a different relationship with the other directors and management than does the nondirector lawyer for the company. It would be rare for a nondirector lawyer with limited access to the board, limited access to information about the company and limited opportunity to establish a relationship of trust to develop as good a working relationship with the company's directors as an outside lawyer serving on the board.

As a result, the outside lawyer-director is better able to advise his client and to make it stick than a lawyer who does not serve on the company's board. A private practice lawyer serving on the board of a client company can be a much more effective advocate for proper corporate governance than one who does not so serve, and they often have been.

STANDING UP TO MANAGEMENT

One must wonder if Sen. John Edwards, D–N.C, the self-appointed defender of shareholder interests against the malfeasance of lawyers, knows what he is talking about. Edwards was recently quoted from a speech he made on the Senate floor as saying: "We have seen corporate lawyers sometimes forget who their client is. What happens is their day-to-day conduct is with the [chief executive officer] or the chief financial officer because those are the individuals responsible for hiring them. So as a result, that is with whom they have a relationship. When they go to lunch with their client, the corporation, they are usually going to lunch with the CEO or the chief financial officer. When they get phone calls, they are usually returning calls to the CEO or the chief financial officer."

Edwards obviously hasn't been representing any of the large corporations in America in the last 20 years because his description of how corporate representations works is hopelessly out of date. If he knew more about corporate legal practice today, he would know that far more often than not the outside lawyer is dealing with the in-house general counsel or another lawyer lower down on the organization chart who hired him and his firm. In many cases the outside lawyer will not have met the CEO or the CFO, much less conversed with them over lunch at the CEO's club.

Edwards also apparently does not understand that the outside lawyers (and they are usually many and from different firms) are less likely to know what is going on than the in-house lawyers. It is unlikely that any serious and important issue of law has failed to come to the attention of the in-house general counsel, and the integrity of corporate governance systems now rest heavily on their shoulders.

The virtual elimination of the private practice lawyers from the boards of public companies they represent has caused the public often to lose a valuable defender of the interest of the shareholders. This is an inevitable result of rules that eliminate board candidates based on their formal relationships rather than on other more important but harder to apply criteria such as character and independence. The existing rules do not result in the identification of those individuals who would make the best directors.

I don't think that any of the negative screens existing or proposed will by themselves lead to the selection of a proper board of directors. The list of disqualifications can grow as long as Rip Van Winkle's beard without leading to the selection of a proper director.

Unfortunately for the reputation of the legal profession, lawyers' obligations of client confidentiality prevent them from telling the world about all the times they stood up to management and achieved a proper result for the company and its shareholders.

In addition, any lawyer that wants to retain the good will of his clients will go about his work quietly and effectively to avoid any unnecessary publicity or embarrassment to his fellow directors or management. As a result, the public hears only of the instances when a lawyer fails to live up to his obligations.

Consequently, those lawyers who have done their jobs, and the profession as a whole, are not getting credit for the good work done by the bar to assure proper corporate governance. Regrettably, they are not going to get it, and we will have to make the best of a bad situation.

C. STOCK FOR SERVICES

AMERICAN BAR ASSOCIATION FORMAL ETHICS OPINION 00–418 (2000)

ACQUIRING OWNERSHIP IN A CLIENT IN CONNECTION WITH PERFORMING LEGAL SERVICES

With growing frequency, lawyers who provide legal services to start-up businesses are investing in their clients, sometimes accepting an ownership interest as a part or all of the fee. Some representatives of the organized bar have questioned this practice. Many lawyers nevertheless believe that acquiring ownership interests in start-up business clients is desirable in order to satisfy client needs and also, because of growing competition with higher paying venture capital and investment firms, to attract and retain partners and associates. From the client's perspective, the lawyer's willingness to invest with entrepreneurs in a start-up company frequently is viewed as a vote of confidence in the enterprise's prospects. Moreover, a lawyer's willingness to accept stock instead of a cash fee may be the only way for a cash-poor client to obtain competent legal advice. Frequently, this may be the determining factor in the client's selection of a lawyer.

The Committee in this Opinion examines the issues that must be addressed under the ABA Model Rules of Professional Conduct when a lawyer or law firm acquires an ownership interest in a client in connection with performing legal services. A typical situation might be one in which the client business is a corporation that the law firm is organizing at the request of the founding entrepreneurs. The latter already have a few friends and family members who are eager to invest funds to start up the corporation. The founders may allow the lawyer working with them to invest the firm's fee for legal services in stock of the corporation. The organizers expect the law firm to introduce them to the firm's venture capital contacts and to continue representing the corporation, eventually performing the services necessary to take it public.

A.   Compliance with Rules 1.8(a) and 1.5(a)
When Acquiring Ownership in a Client

In our opinion, a lawyer who acquires stock in her client corporation in lieu of or in addition to a cash fee for her services enters into a business transaction with a client, such that the requirements of Model Rule 1.8(a) must be satisfied. In determining whether Rule 1.8(a)'s first requirement of fairness and reasonableness to the client is satisfied, the general standard of Rule 1.5(a) that "[a] lawyer's fee shall be reasonable" and the factors enumerated under that Rule are relevant.

For purposes of judging the fairness and reasonableness of the transaction and its terms, the Committee's opinion is that, as when assessing the reasonableness of a contingent fee, only the circumstances reasonably ascertainable at the time of the transaction should be considered. It seems clear that "[i]n a discipline case, once proof has been introduced that the lawyer entered into a business transaction with a client, the burden of persuasion is on the lawyer to show that the transaction was fair and reasonable and that the client was adequately informed." Accordingly, it is incumbent upon the lawyer to take account of all information reasonably ascertainable at the time when the agreement for stock acquisition is made.

Determining that the fee is reasonable in terms of the enumerated factors under Rule 1.5(a) does not resolve whether the requirement of Rule 1.8(a) that the transaction and terms be "fair and reasonable to the client" has been met. Determining "reasonableness" under both rules also involves making the often difficult determination of the market value of the stock at the time of the transaction. As Professors Hazard and Hodes state, "[o]ne danger [to the lawyer who accepts stock as a fee] is that the business will so prosper that the fee will later appear unreasonably high." Of course, instead of increasing in value, the stock may become worthless, as occurs frequently with start-up enterprises. The risk of failure and the stock's nonmarketability are important factors that the lawyer must consider, along with all other information bearing on value that is reasonably ascertainable at the time when the agreement is made.

One way for the lawyer to minimize the risk noted by Professors Hazard and Hodes is to establish a reasonable fee for her services based on the factors enumerated under Rule 1.5(a) and then accept stock that at the time of the transaction is worth the reasonable fee. Of course, the stock should, if feasible, be valued at the amount per share that cash investors, knowledgeable about its value, have agreed to pay for their stock about the same time.

A reasonable fee also may include an agreed percentage of the stock issued or to be issued when the value of the shares is not reasonably ascertainable. For example, if the lawyer is engaged by two founders who are contributing intellectual property for their stock, it may not be possible to establish with reasonable certainty the cash value of their contribution. If so, it also would not be possible to establish with reasonable certainty the value of the shares to be issued to the lawyer retained to perform initial services for the corporation. In such cases, the percentage of stock agreed upon should reflect the value, as perceived by the client and the lawyer at the time of the transaction, that the legal services will contribute to the potential success of the enterprise. The value of the stock received by the lawyer will, like a contingent fee permitted under Rule 1.5(c), depend upon the success of the undertaking.[16]

In addition to assuring that the stock transaction and its terms are fair and reasonable to the client, compliance with Rule 1.8(a) also requires that the transaction and its terms must be fully disclosed and transmitted in writing in a manner that can be reasonably understood by the client. Thus, the lawyer must be careful not only to set forth the terms in writing, but also to explain the transaction and its potential effects on the client-lawyer relationship in a way that the client can understand it. For example, if the acquisition of stock by the lawyer will create rights under corporate by-laws or other agreements that will limit the client's control of the corporation, the lawyer should discuss with the client the possible consequences of such an arrangement.

At the outset, the lawyer also should inform the client that events following the stock acquisition could create a conflict between the lawyer's exercise of her independent professional judgment as a lawyer on behalf of the corporation and her desire to protect the value of her stock. She also should advise the client that as a consequence of such a conflict, she might feel constrained to withdraw as counsel for the corporation, or at least to recommend that another lawyer advise the client on the matter regarding which she has a personal conflict of interest.

Full disclosure also includes specifying in writing the scope of the services to be performed in return for receipt of the stock or the opportunity to invest. The scope of services should be covered in the written transmission to the client even though the stock is acquired by the firm's investment partnership as an opportunity rather than by the firm directly as a part of the fee in lieu of cash. If the client's understanding is that the lawyer keeps the stock interest regardless of the amount of legal services performed by the lawyer and solely to assure the lawyer's availability, it is important to set forth this aspect of the transaction in clear terms. Otherwise, a court might regard the stock acquisition as being in the nature of an advance fee for services and require part of the stock to be returned if all the work originally contemplated as part of the services for which the stock was given has not been performed.

16. The Committee is aware that sometimes the lawyer will ask the corporation to issue her a percentage of the shares initially issued to the founders as a condition to the lawyer agreeing to become counsel to the new enterprise. We take no position on the ethical propriety of this practice. We caution, however, that in this circumstance, and especially if the cash value of the shares is not reasonably ascertainable, the lawyer should take special care to be in a position to justify the reasonableness of the total fee should it later be questioned as a violation of Rule 1.5(a).

Although it is better practice to set forth all the salient features of the transaction in a written document, compliance with Rule 1.8(a) does not require reiteration of details that the client already knows from other sources. Indeed, too much detail may tend to distract attention from the material terms. Nonetheless, the lawyer bears the risk of omitting a term that seems unimportant at the time, but later becomes significant because she has the burden of showing reasonable compliance with Rule 1.8(a)(1). A good faith effort to explain in understandable language the important features of the particular arrangement and its material consequences as far as reasonably can be ascertained at the time of the stock acquisition should satisfy the full disclosure requirements of Rule 1.8(a).

The client also must have a reasonable opportunity to seek the advice of independent counsel in the transaction and must consent in writing to the transaction and its terms. In addition, although not required by the Model Rules, the written documentation of the transaction should include the lawyer's recommendation to obtain such advice. This serves to emphasize the importance to the client of obtaining independent advice. The client's failure to do so then is his own deliberate choice. The lawyer has complied with Rule 1.8(a) in this respect because actual consultation is not required.

The best way to comply with the requirements of Rule 1.8(a) is to set forth the salient terms of the transaction in a document written in language that the client can understand and, after the client has had an opportunity to consult with independent counsel, to have the document signed by both client and lawyer.

B.   Conflicts Between the Lawyer's Interests and Those of the Client

On rare occasions the acquisition of stock in a client corporation will amount to acquiring, in the language of Rule 1.8(j), "a proprietary interest in the cause of action or subject matter of litigation the lawyer is conducting." As Comment [7] under Rule 1.8 explains, the prohibition "has its basis in common law champerty and maintenance [and] is subject to specific exceptions developed in decisional law and continued in these Rules, such as the exception for reasonable contingent fees set forth in Rule 1.5...." The modern rationale for the rule is the concern that a lawyer acquiring less than all of a client's cause of action creates so severe a conflict between the lawyer's interest and the client's interest that it is nonconsentable.

In our view, when the corporation has as its only substantial asset a claim or property right (such as a license), title to which is contested in a pending or impending lawsuit in which the lawyer represents the corporation, Rule 1.8(j) might be applicable to the acquisition of the corporation's stock in connection with the provision of legal services. If the acquisition of the stock constitutes a reasonable contingent fee, however, Rule 1.8(j) would not prohibit acquisition of the stock. Rule 1.7(b) prohibits representation of a client if the representation "may be materially limited ... by the lawyer's own interests," unless two requirements are met. The lawyer must reasonably believe that "the representation will not be adversely affected," and the client must consent to the representation after consultation.

A lawyer's representation of a corporation in which she owns stock creates no inherent conflict of interest under Rule 1.7. Indeed, management's role primarily is to enhance the business's value for the stockholders. Thus, the lawyer's legal services in assisting management usually will be consistent with the lawyer's stock ownership. In some circumstances, such as the merger of one corporation in which the lawyer owns stock into a larger entity, the lawyer's economic incentive to complete the transaction may even be enhanced.

There may, however, be other circumstances in which the lawyer's ownership of stock in her corporate client conflicts with her responsibilities as the corporation's lawyer. For example, the lawyer might have a duty when rendering an opinion on behalf of the corporation in a venture capital transaction to call upon corporate management to reveal material adverse financial information that is being withheld, even though the revelation might cause the venture capital investor to withdraw. In that circumstance, the lawyer must evaluate her ability to maintain the requisite professional independence as a lawyer in the corporate client's best interest by subordinating any economic incentive arising from her stock ownership. The lawyer also must consider whether her stock ownership might create questions concerning the objectivity of her opinion. She must consult with her client and obtain consent if the representation may be materially limited by her stock ownership.

The conflict could be more severe. For example, the stock of the client might be the lawyer's major asset so that the failure of the venture capital opportunity could create a serious financial loss to her. The lawyer's self-interest in such a case probably justifies a reasonable belief that her representation of the corporation would be affected adversely. This would disqualify her under Rule 1.7(b) from providing the opinion even were the client to consent.

In order to minimize conflicts with the interests of the clients such as those described, some law firms have adopted policies governing investments in clients. These policies may include limiting the investment to an insubstantial percentage of stock and the amount invested in any single client to a nonmaterial sum. The policies also may require that decisions regarding a firm lawyer's potential client conflict be made by someone other than the lawyer with the principal client contact (who also may have a larger stock interest in the corporate client) and may also transfer billing or supervisory responsibility to a partner with no stock ownership in the client. Even though a lawyer owns stock in a corporation, she, of course, has no right to continue to represent it as a lawyer if the corporate client discharges her.Were the lawyer to challenge the decision duly made by the authorized corporate constituents to discharge her, she would violate Rule 1.7(b) because it is clear that her own interests adversely affect the representation of the corporation.

CONCLUSION

When a lawyer accepts stock or options to acquire stock in a client corporation in connection with providing legal services to it, she must comply with the requirements of Rule 1.8(a) because the stock acquisition constitutes a business transaction with a client and, if applicable, with the requirement of Rule 1.5(a) that the lawyer's fee shall be reasonable. Under Rule 1.8(a), the stock transaction and its terms must be fair and reasonable to the client. This is satisfied if the fee, including receipt of the stock, is reasonable applying the enumerated factors under Rule 1.5(a), and if the transaction and its terms in other respects are fair and reasonable to the client under the circumstances that are reasonably ascertainable at the time the arrangement is made.

The terms of the transaction also must be fully disclosed in writing to the client in a manner that can be reasonably understood by the client. Full disclosure includes, for example, discussions of the consequences of any rights by virtue of the lawyer's stock ownership that may limit the client's control of the corporation under special corporate by-laws or other agreements and the possibility that the lawyer's economic interests as a stockholder could create a conflict with the client's interest that might necessitate the lawyer's withdrawal from representation in a matter. The client also must be afforded a reasonable opportunity to consult independent counsel concerning the transaction and its terms. Finally, the client's consent must be in writing.

Although a lawyer's representation of a corporation in which the lawyer owns stock creates no inherent conflict of interest, circumstances may arise that create a conflict between the corporation's interests and the lawyer's economic interest as a stockholder. In such event, the lawyer must consult with the client and obtain client consent if, as a result of her ownership interest, the representation of the corporation in a particular matter may be materially limited. The lawyer may in some circumstances be required under Rule 1.7(b) to withdraw from representing the client in a matter if her financial interest in the client is such that she cannot reasonably conclude that the representation would not be adversely affected.

THE ASSOCIATION OF THE BAR OF THE CITY OF NEW YORK

FORMAL OPINION 2000-3

THE ACCEPTANCE OF SECURITIES IN A CLIENT COMPANY IN EXCHANGE FOR LEGAL SERVICES TO BE PERFORMED

Question

May an attorney accept securities in a corporate client for legal services to be rendered, and, if so, what ethical concerns are presented by an agreement by an attorney to accept securities in a client company instead of a cash fee?

Opinion

As high technology and internet companies have continued to spawn throughout the country from Silicon Valley, California to Silicon Alley, New York, the legal profession has been prompted to examine and adopt alternatives to the conventional hourly billing rate arrangement that has been traditionally applied to more mature companies. In response to the attitudes and concerns of the "new age" entrepreneurs who are often strapped for cash, normally risk-averse attorneys increasingly are accepting securities, including options or equity stakes, in startup companies, instead of their customary cash retainers and monthly payments for legal services. These relatively new and novel, business-driven fee arrangements, which provide the attorney with an additional interest in the business success of the client, raise important questions of professional and ethical concern to attorneys in private practice and have generated a new arena for critical review and analysis.

Among the ethical issues raised by a lawyer's acceptance of securities in a corporate client in exchange for legal services to be rendered are those relating to the reasonableness of the fee charged to the client, the potential conflicts of interest with the client and the effect on the attorney's independence and judgment. Given the increasing frequency with which lawyers are accepting securities and the wide-spread interest by members of the Bar in the ethical propriety of these arrangements, we take this opportunity to examine and address the ethical issues raised by acceptance of securities in exchange for legal services to be rendered.

Before turning to these specific ethical concerns, for the sake of clarity, we state here our conclusion that there is no *per se* ethical prohibition on the acceptance of shares or other securities, including options, as compensation for legal services to be rendered. We hasten to add, however, our caution that such arrangements can present thorny ethical and other issues that must be resolved prior to entering into an arrangement in which a lawyer is to be compensated in client company securities.

A.   *Entering into a Business Transaction with a Client*

As a threshold matter, whenever an attorney is considering accepting securities in a client company as a fee for services to be rendered, DR 5–104(A) may be implicated. This rule outlines the parameters under which it is ethically permissible for an attorney to enter into a business transaction with her client. DR 5–104 provides:

> (A) A lawyer shall not enter into a business transaction with a client if they have differing interests therein and if the client expects the lawyer to exercise professional judgment therein for the protection of the client, unless:

(1) The transaction and terms on which the lawyer acquires the interest are fair and reasonable to the client and are fully disclosed and transmitted in writing to the client in a manner that can be reasonably understood by the client;

(2) The lawyer advises the client to seek the advice of independent counsel in the transaction; and

(3) The client consents in writing, after full disclosure, to the terms of the transaction and to the lawyer's inherent conflict of interest in the transaction.

On its face, DR 5–104(A) requires a two part inquiry. First, the attorney must determine if the transaction is one in which the attorney and her client have differing interests and in which the client expects the lawyer to exercise professional judgment on the client's behalf. If these questions are answered in the affirmative, then the attorney must demonstrate that the terms of the transaction are fair and reasonable to the client and have been transmitted to the client in clear written form, that the attorney has advised the client that the client may consult independent counsel and that the client has consented in writing after full disclosure.

In other jurisdictions, ethics committees considering arrangements in which an attorney accepts securities in a client instead of a cash fee consistently have concluded such transactions may withstand ethical scrutiny provided that the obligations to provide full disclosure, to advise the client of the client's right to obtain independent counsel and to obtain written consent of the client are satisfied.

However, the text of N.Y. DR 5–104(A) differs from that of the rules under which these opinions were issued. Unlike these other rules, the New York rule interposes a threshold inquiry before requiring the lawyer to undertake the disclosure and other prescribed remedial measures. On its face, DR 5–104 applies only to business transactions where "the client expects the lawyer to exercise professional judgment therein for the protection of the client," and absent a specific requirement imposed by disciplinary rule, requirements such as those imposed by DR 5–104(A) would not be mandated.

In Opinion 88–7, we concluded that an attorney's acceptance of a mortgage interest in a client's home to secure payment of a fee constituted a "business transaction with a client" within the meaning of DR 5–104(A). In reaching this conclusion, we stated:

A mortgage and related agreements may well contain highly technical language raising important legal obligations readily ascertained by the lawyer but imperceptible to the untrained eye. People whose situation requires the assistance of counsel may be particularly vulnerable.

In certain circumstances, these concerns may also apply to the fee arrangements considered here. Principals in startup companies typically entering into "securities for fees" arrangements may be legally unsophisticated and may be relying on the attorney with respect to the transaction.

In our opinion, the application of DR 5–104(A) can, and should, be resolved by the text of the rule, which extends its mandates to all those situations in which the client expects the lawyer to exercise independent judgment for the protection of the client. Consistent with Opinion 88–7, we conclude that DR 5–l04(A) does not exclude from its ambit fee agreements between lawyers and clients.

This same textual analysis also leads the Committee to the ineluctable conclusion that New York's DR 5–104(A) does not automatically impose any consent or disclosure requirements on all transactions in which an attorney accepts securities in a client company for legal services to be rendered, at least where such an agreement is reached at the outset of the representation. This is not to say that DR 5–104(A) will never apply to such a fee arrangement. Whether the rule applies in specific circumstances will necessarily turn on whether the lawyer is expected to provide independent advice in the specific transaction by which the securities for services exchange is made. If the lawyer is expected to play any role in advising the client, especially if a client lacks sophistication, the mandates of DR 5–104(A) must be followed. *See* N.Y. City 88–7. In performing this analysis, we note, however, that there is a crucial difference between bargaining with the client, a function that puts the lawyer squarely on the other side of the table, and providing advice to the client relating to a transaction, including a transaction involving fees, where the client expects to rely on the attorney's judgment.

B. *Conflicts of Interest*

An attorney's inquiry into her potential ethical obligations arising out of a transaction in which the attorney accepts securities for fees does not end with DR 5–104. Unique issues of potential conflicts of interest also may arise as a result of such arrangements.

At the outset of the representation, the acceptance of securities in a client corporation as part of the consideration for legal services to be rendered may implicate the standard of independent professional judgment that is embodied in DR 5–101(A):

> A lawyer shall not accept or continue employment if the exercise of professional judgment on behalf of the client will be or reasonably may be affected by the lawyer's own financial, business, property, or personal interests, unless a disinterested lawyer would believe that the representation of the client will not be adversely affected thereby and the client consents to the representation after full disclosure of the implications of the lawyer's interest.

DR 5–101(A)

Under this rule, if the lawyer accepts securities from a client in exchange for legal services to be rendered, as a threshold matter, she must determine whether this ownership interest in the client would, or reasonably may, affect the exercise of her independent professional judgment on behalf of the client. If the answer is affirmative, the lawyer must then determine whether a "disinterested lawyer" would believe that the effect on the lawyer's exercise of professional judgment will be *adversely* affected because the lawyer stands to be paid in securities of her client. If the effect is determined to be adverse, then the conflict is non-consentable and the representation on those terms must be declined. On the other hand, if a reasonable determination is made that the effect on the representation would not be adverse, then the arrangement can proceed if the client consents to the representation after the implications of the lawyer's interest are fully disclosed.

It is this Committee's opinion that an arrangement by which a lawyer accepts securities in a client corporation as compensation for legal services to be rendered reasonably may affect the professional judgment of the lawyer on behalf of her client. By way of example, when a lawyer has agreed to accept securities in a client corporation as a fee for negotiating and documenting an equity investment, or for representing it in connection with an initial public offering, there is a *risk* that the lawyer's judgment will be skewed in favor of the transaction to such an extent that the lawyer may fail to exercise independent professional judgment. It is possible that the lawyer's interest in the securities *may* create economic pressure to "get the deal done," which pressure in turn *may* impact the lawyer's independent judgment on disclosure issues. In this respect, the risk is not significantly different than that presented when the lawyer's cash fee depends (in whole or in part) on a business transaction's successfully closing. In both cases, the lawyer is "invested" in the transaction. The contingent fee arrangement has long been accepted as ethical if the fee is appropriate and reasonable and the client has been fully informed as to alternative billing arrangements. We see no ethical distinction between the transactional contingent fee and agreeing to take client securities instead of cash fees.

Although such an arrangement may affect the lawyer's independent professional judgment, it still can pass muster under the "disinterested lawyer" test of DR 5–101(A). DR 5–101(A) would preclude any arrangement if there exists a reasonable probability (viewed objectively) that the lawyer's interests will affect adversely the advice to be given or the specific services to be rendered to the client. This Committee believes that, standing alone, acceptance by a lawyer of a "stake in the action," is not sufficient to warrant the conclusion in every case that a lawyer's exercise of professional judgment on behalf of his client will be adversely affected by accepting securities in her client's company for legal services to be performed.

The determination of whether a reasonable probability of such an adverse effect exists is factually driven and demands an analysis of the nature and relationship of the particular interest and the specific legal services to be rendered. Some salient factors to be considered may be the size of the investment in proportion to the holdings of other investors, the potential value of the investment in relation to the law firm's earnings or assets, the possible impact on the lawyer of levels of risk involved, and whether the investment is active or passive. The Committee can envision situations in which there exists a likelihood, when viewed objectively, that the lawyer's interest in "getting the deal done" will adversely affect the lawyer's independent professional judgment. The risk of such an adverse effect would be especially high, for example, in the case of a potentially very large fee paid in client securities which represents both a significant portion of the law firm's revenues and a substantial stake in the client's business. In these circumstances, it is conceivable that the desire to obtain such a fee might diminish the willingness of the attorney, albeit unconsciously, to advise the client company to disclose negative information or increase the lawyer's willingness to issue a questionable legal opinion required to close the deal. In such situations, the conflict would be non-consentable and the fee arrangement ethically prohibited.

If, however, a determination is made under the "disinterested lawyer" test that the lawyer's representation of the client will not be adversely affected by an agreement to accept client securities as payment for legal services to be rendered, DR 5–101(A) allows the representation, but only if full disclosure is made to the client and the client's consent is obtained. Although not required under the Disciplinary Rule, the Committee recommends that the disclosure and consent be in writing for the same reasons we believe it is prudent under DR 5–104(A).

Disclosure should include, among other things: (1) the risks inherent in representation by a lawyer with a financial, business, property, or personal interest in the company, including the possible effects upon the lawyer's actions and recommendations to the client; (2) the possible conflicts that might arise between lawyer/shareholder and client or its management and the range of possible consequences stemming from them; and (3) any potential impact on the attorney/client privilege and confidentiality rules, particularly in communications between the client and the attorney in his role as investor rather than as counsel.

C. Excessive Fees

A lawyer must also consider whether accepting securities in a client as payment for legal services to be rendered constitutes the charging or collection of an excessive fee in violation of DR 2–106.

An agreement to accept securities in satisfaction of legal fees is not prohibited by DR 2–106(A). However, DR 2–106(A) prohibits a lawyer from agreeing to charge an excessive fee for his or her legal services as well as collecting such a fee. An arrangement by which an attorney is to be paid wholly or partly in securities must satisfy this requirement.

DR 2–106(B) provides a test for determining whether a fee is "excessive" by asking whether it would be the "definite and firm conviction" of "a lawyer of ordinary prudence" that "the fee is in excess of a reasonable fee." This test (eliminated from comparable Rule 1.5(a) of the ABA's Model Rules of Professional Conduct) is intended to be an objective one.

A determination of whether a fee is excessive is not always easily made. In the case of an arrangement in which securities are received for legal services, the decision is more complex, and there are additional factors which should be considered, especially where the securities to be received are those of a "start up" business, or are part of or in connection with a public offering of the securities. Examples of additional such "factors" are:

> ... (1) The likelihood the transaction in question will or will not close and whether there are any contingent plans for payment of legal fees; (2) the estimated current and future value of the equity [i.e. securities] interest considering all the normal risks of a start-up business and any specific risks to the business or its assets; (3) the liquidity of the interest, including whether it is now or may in the future be publicly traded; (4) any restrictions on transfer of the interest, whether by agreement with the client ... or by law; (5) the percentage amount of the interest, and what, if any, degree of control it provides the lawyer over the business; and (6) what restrictions, if any, are placed on the money used to pay for the equity interest—for example that it must be used to pay future legal bills.

Many of these factors, especially in the case of securities in a startup company, obviously cannot be determined with any degree of assurance, at least until the transaction or matter is completed. As such, a crucial question in determining whether a fee in the form of securities is "excessive" is the time at which the value is measured. An equity stake in a corporation that turns out to be successful might seem excessive in relation to the services rendered if the value is determined only after the success is achieved. But to make this evaluation at that end point—and with the wisdom of hindsight—would not value the fee that the client agreed to pay or the lawyer accepted, because it would eliminate the risk that the lawyer undertook that the venture would fail and the securities, *i.e.* the fee, would have little or no value. Accordingly, we conclude that a determination of whether a fee accepted in the form of securities is excessive requires a determination of value be made at the time the agreement is reached. To be sure, this test may allow attorneys to receive fees that *turn out* to be spectacular windfalls in relation to the compensation that would normally be received on a cash basis. But as long as the reward stems from the investment risk accepted, not from an excessive fee, the result will equate to a lawyer's investing cash, not services, in the venture. We hasten to add that not all payments in the form of client securities will pass muster under this test. In cases where the risks are minimal and the amount of securities received by the lawyer is excessive in relation to the services to be rendered, the fee would not cease to be "excessive" merely because the venture was not a sure thing.

The importance of estimating the value of the arrangement whereby payment is made in the form of client securities instead of cash is not limited to issues of professional responsibility. In addition to being subject to professional discipline under DR 2–106(A) if a fee were found to be excessive, a lawyer might also face possible civil liability or a justified refusal on the part of the client to make payment of the agreed-upon fee. The problem is compounded by the rule that an attorney, as a fiduciary, bears the burden of proving that the transaction entered into with a client is reasonable and not the fruit of undue influence.

A lawyer accepting payment in the form of client securities should seriously consider engaging an investment professional to advise as to the value of the securities so given. The attorney and client can then make their own advised decisions as to the reasonableness of the transaction.

PROBLEMS

1. You have represented Jane Cox on personal legal matters over the last ten years. She has come to you and told you that she and two friends, Bob Anderson and Jim Burton, want to set up a corporation to manufacture components for electrical equipment.

Anderson, who is in his sixties, will be investing most of the capital in the business. He is particularly interested in receiving a steady stream of income, although he also wants the opportunity to realize large gains if the business takes off. Unlike Burton and Cox, he does not contemplate being involved in the business on a daily basis although he has made clear that he wants "some voice" in order to protect his substantial investment.

Burton is a recent business school graduate who wants to get in on the ground floor of a business and aggressively build it. He comes from a financially modest background, is married, has two young children and owns his own home. Aside from the amount he will invest in the new corporation, he has little capital. He has ideas for attaining a significant market share as soon as possible by adopting measures such as discounting prices to attract customers, establishing a Web site, and mounting legal challenges to rivals' business practices.

Cox is a writer and researcher for business publications, specializing in high technology corporations. She has a substantial stock portfolio, comes from a wealthy family and stands to inherit a large amount of money on the death of her elderly father. She has been married for ten years; her husband was laid off a year ago and has been unable to find permanent employment since then. She sees the corporation as a chance to attain some professional independence after being an employee for fifteen years. She hopes that starting a business with two other people will enable her to travel less and give her some flexibility to find more time to raise her two children.

The three parties believe that their new venture may be profitable from the beginning. They recognize, however, that because it is new, there is a real possibility that it will experience losses in the first few years because of start-up costs, borrowing at higher than prime interest rates and sowing some marketing seeds that will not bear fruit immediately.

a) They have asked you to form a corporation for them. What might you have to do before you agree to do so?

b) If you accept the representation, who is your client?

2.   As a result of your recent representation of Cox, you have learned that she and her husband are considering a divorce. Because he has significantly less earning power and fewer assets than she does, she is afraid that the financial settlement will require her to be responsible for child support and, conceivably, for spousal maintenance payments.

May you disclose this information to Anderson and Burton? Must you? Would it make a difference if you had never represented Cox and discovered this information in a private conversation with her?

3.   Anderson, Burton and Cox have told you that they would like to have a five person board Each of them will be a director and Anderson will designate a fourth director. They have asked you be the fifth director, as Cox put it, "to be the tie-breaker."After pointing out the need for the new business to conserve cash, they have asked whether your firm would take stock in lieu of, or as a part of its fee. How do you respond? To what extent would your answer change if, for many years, your firm had had a policy forbidding its lawyers from owning any stock in a client corporation (absent a waiver from the firm's Ethics Committee) on the ground that such abstention would remove many conflicts of interest that the lawyers might otherwise face.

4.   Standard Electronics Corp. is one of the largest manufacturers of electronic equipment in the United States. In recent years, however, it has experienced a number of severe business setbacks arising primarily because of its inability to anticipate developments in rapidly changing technology. Three years ago, in a major management upheaval, Stanley Black was chosen from outside the company to be its CEO after a rapid rise to fame as an entrepreneur in Silicon Valley.

You are a partner in a major multi-city law firm specializing in corporate law. You were Black's college roommate and have remained on close terms with him. Shortly after Black's became CEO, he asked you to become a director of Standard, suggesting that your firm would receive considerable legal business thereafter. Black also made clear that one of the reasons he wanted you on the board was because he valued your business acumen.

One year ago, Black presented the board with the possible acquisition of a large corporation whose product mix seemed to be highly complementary to that of Standard but which was also one of Standard's major competitors in several important areas. The board established a committee consisting of four outside directors and Black to examine the business and legal implications of the acquisition. The board selected you as one of the committee members and retained your firm to advise as to the corporate, tax and antitrust aspects of the acquisition.

After considerable investigation and analysis, the committee concluded that, although the acquisition was not without considerable business risk, the risk was worth taking because of Standard's increasingly shaky financial condition. Your firm rendered an opinion that there was a material possibility that the acquisition would be challenged by the Federal Trade Commission or the Antitrust Division of the Department of Justice and that Standard's chances of success in such a challenge were less than 50%. The opinion noted the amount of regulatory review that would be required to obtain antitrust clearance and the possibility of additional legal costs if there were to be litigation.

The matter is now before the board for a final decision. Consider the following questions.

a) What disclosures to Black and the board should you have made before (or immediately upon) becoming a director?

b) What limits were there on your ability to be a member of the committee? How should you have voted in the committee with respect to the acquisition? How should you vote now?

c) To what extent are the discussions between lawyers in your firm and corporate executives protected by the attorney-client privilege?

d) What duties, if any, did you have with respect to the choice of counsel to advise Standard either at the committee or the board level?

e) To what extent, if any, might/should your answers affect your decision to become a director of Standard? To what extent, if any, do the answers change if you were not a director?

Chapter 15

LEGAL OPINIONS

One of the most important things that a lawyer does is to give an opinion as to the legality of a proposed or completed transaction. "Opinion" as used in the corporate setting is a term of art and does not have its usual colloquial meaning. It does not mean "in my opinion, it will rain today." Rather it expresses a lawyer's conclusion as to how the relevant law applies to a given state of facts. Parties entering into a transaction with a corporation often will require the corporation's outside lawyer to provide an opinion on legal matters affecting the transaction. This opinion may cover relatively routine matters such as the corporation's existence, its good standing under state corporate law, its power to enter into the transaction, and a corporate official's authority to act on behalf of the corporation. Similarly, the opinion may state that an agreement to which the corporation is a party is legal, valid, binding, and enforceable against the corporation in accordance with its terms. Finally, lawyers will opine as to whether a transaction will violate applicable securities laws or regulations.

Legal opinions have developed into highly stylized documents. Bar associations have developed guidelines for the methodology and language employed in giving opinions together with standards for interpreting an opinion. These guidelines describe how an opinion should be dated, to whom it should be addressed, how its scope should be limited, the documents that should be examined, and whether the lawyer may rely on facts supplied by third parties of opinions of other counsel. Recently there also have been attempts to standardize the form of opinion letters and the meaning of terms they regularly use. *See* ABA Committee on Legal Opinions, *Legal Opinion Principles,* 53 Bus. Law. 831 (1998); ABA Committee on Legal Opinions, *Third-Party Legal Opinion Report, Including the Legal Opinion Accord,* 47 Bus. Law. 167 (1991).

Legal opinions serve as a hedge against business risks. If the transaction fails, the disappointed party will look to the lawyer on whose assurances the party relied. Whether the party can recover, however, is far from clear. A lawyer is not liable simply because the opinion was mistaken. Instead, it must be shown that the opinion was negligently rendered and that any losses were proximately caused by the lawyer's failure to meet the relevant professional standards. Although there is little case law, lawyers are most likely to face liability where the opinion assists a client in a fraud or the commission of a crime.

OVERVIEW OF THE CHAPTER

This chapter introduces the issues that arise when a lawyer is asked render an opinion in connection with a transaction. Because this book deals with corporate and securities law, the materials focus on transactions that arise in those contexts although lawyers give opinions in many other settings that are not considered here.

The first part of the chapter describes the nature of a legal opinion and the process by which such an opinion is prepared and given. The excerpt from John Sterba's treatise explores the various types of opinions that lawyers are asked or required to give and the procedures that they generally follow in preparing those opinions. Richard Howe's article then examines different types of financial opinions and how the context in which they are given will dictate both the scope of the opinion and the matters on which a lawyer is able to opine. Howe also analyzes the theories under which a lawyer can face liability in rendering an opinion either to a client or to a third party.

The next set of materials deals with one of the most difficult problems facing a lawyer who must give an opinion: what must the lawyer do to determine the facts upon which her legal opinion will be based. As you read the opinion of the American Bar Association and the article by Glazer and Macedo, ask yourself the extent to which a lawyer can rely on the facts that her client tells her and how much independent investigation of those facts (and other facts that may arise from that investigation) must she do? Because it is always possible to find new facts, when can she stop asking questions? In a transaction involving a relatively small amount of money, how does or should the cost of a lawyer's investigation affect her determination of how far that investigation should extend? In that connection, recall Langevoort's behavioral analysis in Chapter 9.

Finally, since a legal opinion is based on the lawyer's knowledge of the facts, what does "knowledge" mean? Does your answer to that question change if you are talking about the knowledge of an individual lawyer or the knowledge that should be imputed to the law firm in which she is a partner? Your study of Model Rule 1.2(d) has already introduced you some aspects of these questions. How far does your analysis of that Rule help you decide what "knowledge" mean in a very different context?

The last part of the chapter consists of two cases involving a lawyer's duties in rendering an opinion. As you read them, ask yourself what you would have done in each transaction. Are you persuaded by the court's suggestion in *Schatz* v. *Rosenberg* that a lawyer need not disclose adverse facts if all she is doing is "papering the deal?" What does it mean to "paper the deal" and why should it excuse a lawyer from further action? Keep in mind your answer to the questions that this chapter raises when you study the materials in Chapter 17.

MODEL RULES: 2.3

M. John Sterba, Jr., LEGAL OPINION LETTERS

(3d ed. 2002)

§ 1.1 WHAT CONSTITUTES AN OPINION

In the United States, lawyers either perform certain tasks on behalf of a client in order to accomplish the client's objectives or advise the client (or others) of their opinion or view as to what the law is with respect to a particular factual situation. Appearing in court or preparing and filing a financing statement pursuant to the Uniform Commercial Code are examples of the former. One could say of the latter that the most purely legal task that an office lawyer is called on to do is to interpret the law for a client. The essence of the office lawyer's job is to guide by informing the client (or, with the client's consent, someone the client is dealing with) of the content of the applicable law. In rendering legal advice, a lawyer applies the law to a particular set of facts in order to reach a legal conclusion or conclusions regarding those facts.

The advice of a lawyer may be communicated in a number of ways and settings. Most advice is undoubtedly given orally. Indeed, much of the professional conversation between lawyers and clients is sprinkled with the lawyer's opinion as to what the relevant law is and how it might apply to the situation under discussion. The same might be said of correspondence, memoranda, and other writings flowing from lawyer to client.

Ordinarily, the lawyer's oral or other informal advice (either off the top of his head or after some study) will suffice. In some situations, however, it is appropriate for the lawyer to state formally an opinion in writing. Such situations tend to be ones in which the exact legal consequences of some action, inaction, or state of affairs are deemed to be important, for instance, those involving significant sums of money. The form these opinions take is usually that of a letter containing certain traditional elements.

Black's Law Dictionary (7th ed. 1999 at 1120) defines *opinion letter* as a "a document, usually prepared at a client's request, containing a lawyer's understanding of the law that applies to a particular case."

This book is about formal, written legal opinion letters. As used herein, unless the context otherwise requires, the word "opinion" refers to either an entire opinion letter or to any one or more of the individual operative elements of opinion contained in such a letter. Memoranda of law, prepared by a lawyer for delivery, usually to his client, may in certain instances be the functional equivalent of opinion letters. Other types of writings regarding legal judgment may be useful for comparative purposes and vice versa. Examples include lawyer's letters to accountants, legal opinions expressed in requests for Securities and Exchange Commission no-action letters, Internal Revenue Service private letter rulings, state attorneys general opinions, bar ethics opinions, and judicial and alternate dispute resolution opinions.

§ 1.3 REASONS WHY OPINIONS ARE SOUGHT

Lawyers do not render formal written opinions without a specific external stimulus. Typically they are requested to do so by their clients or by third parties dealing with their clients. A third party may request the opinion directly or by way of a contractual or regulatory requirement; a typical third party is a present or prospective investor in, lender to, or licensee from a client; a client's accountant or outside counsel in another jurisdiction; or a government agency. Because formal opinions require a high level of diligence in their preparation, because malpractice liability and/or professional embarrassment may attach to an incorrect opinion, and, in some cases because of the possibility of disclosure of client confidences to third parties, lawyers prefer to render oral advice to written opinions.

Many opinions are sought as statements of the legal consequences (or lack thereof) of some particular proposed or past action or inaction: "The execution, delivery and performance of the Agreement have been duly authorized by all requisite corporate action." Other opinions are sought to obtain assurance that a certain legal state of affairs has been achieved or otherwise exists: "XYZ corporation is an existing corporation under the laws of the State of Delaware." Still others are sought to resolve a dispute as to the legal interpretation of a document: "In conclusion, in our opinion the better view is that X owes Y, Z dollars."

Some laws, regulations or administrative bodies require that certain legal opinions be delivered. Examples include, in the securities area, opinions as to the legality of securities being registered pursuant to the Securities Act of 1933 or listed on a national securities exchange, and opinions used by the staff of the Securities and Exchange Commission ("SEC") as bases for issuing no-action letters. It is virtually impossible to list all the categories of purposes for which legal opinions are sought.

There are also what we might call ulterior or secondary reasons for seeking a legal opinion. In order to reach a legal conclusion concerning a factual situation, the opining lawyer must carefully investigate the facts. Not infrequently, these investigations uncover states of affairs that the relevant party or parties did not contemplate and need either to change or at least take into consideration. Stated another way, and in a particular context, a legal opinion "provides an independent check of the accuracy of the representations and warranties" made by, for instance, the opining lawyer's client to a third party. Furthermore, not only is that check independent, it is performed by someone (the opining lawyer) with higher professional standards than might prevail in the average commercial marketplace. Many institutional opinion recipients have a policy of requiring certain legal opinion letters for their files as a matter of diligence.

It is possible that opinion letters have been misguidedly requested in order to have the opining lawyer, in effect, warrant certain facts with, perhaps, the ultimate security being the lawyer's net worth or malpractice insurance. Needless to say, this is not a reason that lawyers counsel their clients to seek opinions either from themselves or other lawyers, and the ABA Legal Opinion Principles contradict any such motivation. Other secondary, and usually inappropriate, reasons for seeking opinions include establishing another party's legal position from which it may become difficult to deviate, allocating legal fees to another party, or (in the case of the opinion giver) advocating a particular legal position that may be in doubt.

§ 1.4 TYPES OF OPINIONS

Legal opinions may be classified in several ways. An opinion may be unqualified (sometimes called flat or clean), qualified, or reasoned (sometimes called explained). An "unqualified" opinion is one in which the lawyer, applying the law to the facts, is able to reach a clear legal conclusion that is essentially free from doubt. For example, "The Shares have been duly authorized and validly issued and are fully paid and nonassessable" is an unqualified opinion. The standard of legal conclusion for an unqualified opinion has been said to be "how the highest court the jurisdiction whose law is being addressed would appropriately resolve the issues covered by the opinion on the date of the opinion letter." In order to meet that standard in an unqualified opinion, the opiner may have to condition or limit his opinion with some *customary* assumptions or exceptions (for that type of opinion); but, so limited, the legal conclusion is without reservation or explanation. "Qualified" opinions contain exceptions or limitations that are *not customary* for the particular type of opinion. Various exceptions, assumptions, qualifications, and other ways of limiting the expression of opinions are discussed in § 1.5.

In a "reasoned" or explained opinion, the lawyer feels the need to explain his reasoning in addition to stating his view as to a legal conclusion. Such an explanation may be advisable either because the law itself is unclear, the facts are not entirely straightforward, or the lawyer believes there are reasonable arguments that might lead to a different legal interpretation than the one the opining lawyer favors. The reasoned opinion may have the appearance of a brief or memorandum of law, containing citations to relevant case law or legislative history and arguments regarding various sides of an issue. Reasoned opinions are therefore longer than comparable unqualified or qualified opinions. Before reaching its conclusion, the reasoned opinion might contain phrases such as "although the matter is not free from doubt," "I believe the better view is that," "notwithstanding that the stated views of the [regulatory agency] are to the contrary," "while no controlling authority exists as to this matter," and "although the X and Y cases would appear to reach a contrary conclusion." Sometimes a lawyer's reasoned opinion is stated in terms of a prediction of the probable judicial result if the issue were appropriately presented to a court.

More frequently, reasoned opinions are presented to one's own client to apprise him of the legal uncertainty of a situation, and, if to a third party, usually not as a standard condition in closing a business transaction. There are certainly benefits to confining advice as to uncertainties within the attorney-client privilege. Reasoned opinions are often given in matters of intellectual property, antitrust, and bankruptcy law. Reasoned opinions are undoubtedly given much less frequently than the other types of opinions.

Another grouping of opinions issued by lawyers might exaggeratedly be called non-opinions because they contain less of an element of legal opinion. "Factual" opinions are expressions regarding facts more than laws, for example, a statement by a lawyer that his client has not breached certain covenants or warranties contained in applicable instruments. Arguably, there may be others who are more conversant with the facts and more easily and less expensively able to make such statements. As observed in Section 1.3, however, lawyers are often called on to give predominantly factual opinions on the pretext that there is or may be some law involved and because the opinion seeker wishes to obtain the reliability associated with the high professional standards of lawyers involved in opinion practice. It has been suggested that, when confronted with requests for essentially factual opinions, lawyers might deliver such statements in a separate letter from the one containing their legal opinions or at least in a segregated section of their opinion letter emphasizing the essentially factual nature of the statements. Some subjects for opinion, although essentially factual, are nevertheless ones with respect to which a lawyer is in the best position to express a view. The most prominent example is probably the lawyer's response to an auditor's request for information regarding litigation and potential liabilities. Auditors believe, with some justification, that lawyers for an auditee will be particularly aware of pending and threatened litigation and sensitive to potential liabilities. In any event, issues involving this type of response letter came to a head in the mid-1970s with governing bodies of both professions settling on guidelines for requesting and expressing such letters.

Another category of "non-opinion" is the tautological or conclusion-assuming opinion. If too many of the relevant facts are simply assumed or, even worse, if the applicable law is to a significant extent assumed, the opinion element evaporates. An example is the opinion by counsel for a seller that a buyer is receiving shares free and clear of all liens when it is assumed that the buyer is acquiring the shares in good faith without notice of any claim.

Yet another category of "non-opinion" is one that is so highly qualified or limited that it amounts to no opinion at all. Some of these non-opinions are essentially expressions of belief. Because of the similarity among many of these opinions and the accountants' so-called cold comfort letter used in the securities underwriting process, this category is sometimes referred to as *comfort opinions*. A common example of this sort of negative assurance lawyer's opinion, also in the securities underwriting setting, is the conclusion that the lawyer "has no reason to believe that either the registration statement or the prospectus contains an untrue statement of a material fact or omits to state a material fact required to be stated therein or necessary to make the statements therein not misleading." In the case of this sort of opinion or statement, the lawyer will want to state clearly the extent of his participation, investigation and independent verification of facts. He may also want explicitly to limit reliance on his opinion to the addressee and no other.

Legal opinions may be categorized in other ways: (1) by whether they are addressed to the opining lawyer's client (to whom greater duties may be owed) or to a third party; and (2) by their subject matter. This book generally organizes its discussion of legal opinions by their subject matter for ease of reference. Some opinion letters will contain individual opinions that are dealt with in more than one subject area in the book.

§ 1.5 NEGOTIATION AND QUALIFICATION OF OPINIONS

In some cases the content of an opinion letter is not the subject of negotiation between the opiner and the addressee. Opinions of lawyers to their clients for the client's own purposes often are not negotiated as to form or content. (The form may simply be that of a memorandum speaking to the legal matter in question.) Opinion letters to third parties, however, are more frequently the subject of negotiation between the opining lawyer and the lawyer for the opinion recipient.

The first matter to be considered before the form and content of an opinion are determined is whether an opinion should be given at all, and, if so, whether by the lawyer in question. Sometimes this primary issue is not accorded appropriate consideration because of the increasingly habitual use of legal opinions in this country. It may be that because the matter in question is largely factual, a particular nonlawyer is able to provide more readily the necessary comfort, perhaps in the form of a corporate officer's certificate. Another possibility that should be considered is whether there might be another lawyer in as good or better a position to render the desired opinion—for example, whether the client's own counsel might more effectively opine instead of a third party's lawyer. To a certain extent this may simply be a question of allocation of costs of counsel, and that allocation could be adjusted as a separate matter and still have the most logical counsel render the opinion.

Perhaps the economic interests of the opinion-requesting party could be satisfied by appropriate representations and warranties from another party; or perhaps there is some other way to meet the requesting party's objectives without a legal opinion. The diligence and preparation necessary to render a particular legal opinion can result in a substantial cost to the lawyer's client. The actual benefit to be gained by the proposed opinion should always be weighed against its cost.

Sometimes most or all of the benefit from the receipt of a legal opinion can be retained and the cost significantly diminished by negotiating various qualifications of and exceptions to the opinion. Such negotiations should take place sooner rather than later. The content of an opinion is often contained, with more or less specificity, in an agreement between parties to a business transaction. The exact form and content of the opinion should be negotiated, if possible, along with the other terms and conditions of the agreement. If the agreement is negotiated and executed without an exact specification of the legal opinion, the exact text of the legal opinion should be agreed on as soon thereafter as possible. An agreement provision to the effect that a lawyer will deliver "such [other] opinions as [the third party] may reasonably request" is perhaps the least desirable specification. There is a tendency for lawyers to leave the consideration of (and back-up work for) their opinions until the last minute, perhaps on the unconscious theory that "the client's work" in connection with the transaction should come first. The pressures to complete a transaction often increase in inverse proposition to the length of time until a scheduled closing. The less pressure, the more rationally differences over opinion language can be resolved. It is most embarrassing when clients find their attorneys haggling over opinion language and even delaying the closing of a transaction over apparently useless nit-picking for which, to add insult to injury, the clients are paying.

It has been often observed that attorneys negotiating legal opinions should follow the Golden Rule: Ask not of opposing counsel an opinion you would not yourself give. Notwithstanding the lip service given to this rule, some attorneys, in effect, have two files of opinions: one for themselves and a harsher one for opinions requested of others. While the two-files approach might be appropriate for negotiating the other provisions of business agreements, it is not appropriate for negotiating the scope and content of professional legal opinions. A lawyer should not use his client's greater economic bargaining power to attempt to force another lawyer, in his opinion, to address unreasonable or inappropriate issues or to reach a legal conclusion that is not justified.

The negotiation process may involve a wide variety of factors, such as the type of opinion the opinion recipient has received from others in prior similar instances, what opinion the opining attorney gave in prior similar instances, what opinions other lawyers have given in the past under similar circumstances, the relative bargaining power of the lawyers' clients, whether the requesting party can receive economic comfort from representations and warranties or other means, whether the law on the subject is free from doubt, the difficulty and cost of any necessary factual investigation, the economic benefit to the receiving party of the opinion and the prior expertise of the opining attorney in the subject area.

Because of the nature of the legal system, lawyers probably tend to give more weight to precedent than do businesspeople, doctors or scientists. In the opinion letter negotiation process, however, it is appropriate that we keep an open mind, be creative and let reason be our guide.

Once the hurdles of whether an opinion is to be given, and by whom, are overcome, the next task is to tailor the opinion with various limitations and qualifications. While some of the qualifications will be expressed in a general section of a formal opinion letter, frequently various qualifications are included as a part of the operative opinion language. The latter may be preferable when the qualification may be expressed in few words and applies only to the enumerated opinion paragraph. The qualification may be introduced by the words "except" or "subject to." Examples of this type of qualification are (1) the so-called bankruptcy exception, regarding an opinion as to the enforceability of an agreement: "except as may be limited by bankruptcy, insolvency, or other similar laws affecting the enforcement of creditors' rights in general;" and (2) the equitable remedies exception thereto: "subject to general equity principles."

One common way of limiting the breadth of an opinion dealing primarily with factual matters is by qualifying it with the phrase "to [the best of] our knowledge" or similar phrases such as "known to me," "nothing has come to our attention," or "We have no knowledge of any pending or threatened suits or claims." Sometimes the knowledge phrase is modified with words such as "after due inquiry" or "after reasonable investigation." Questions naturally arise as to what knowledge is properly imputed to the opining lawyer, for example, that of his law partners or that in his firm's files. The bar reports have covered these topics well. The trend is toward defining the meaning of knowledge in the opinion letter itself.

The concept of materiality may also modify an opinion that would otherwise be impossible or impractical for a lawyer to give. Materiality is used as a scope-narrowing device in the following ways:

> There are no actions, suits, claims, investigations, or proceedings ... which if decided adversely to XYZ Co. would have a materially adverse effect on the financial position of XYZ Co.

> No consent, permit, license, approval or authorization of, or registration, filing or declaration with, or action by any governmental body ... is required to be made in connection with the execution, delivery, or performance of the contract except for routine filings which, if not made, will not render XYZ Co. liable for any material penalties.

Other techniques for limiting the scope of opinions include:

1. In addition to those, such as the antitrust laws, generally excluded from the scope of a legal opinion by custom, limiting the laws or regulations covered: "We express no opinion, however, with respect to any state or federal environmental law;"

2. Specifying the limited nature of counsel's (a) participation in the transaction that is the subject of the opinion, (b) investigation of the facts underlying his opinion, or (c) general familiarity with the affairs of his client; and

3. Basing the opinion on specified assumed facts or reliance on only specified documents for factual information.

The use of limitations and qualifications in opinion letters, although a positive device to aid in the rendering of desired opinions, can also hold dangers. Because of the complexity of some scope-narrowing techniques when applied in particular instances, convolution, misunderstanding and even deception may result. Certain non-opinions alluded to in Section 1.4 may be deceptive—for example, the tautological opinion, or a "legal, valid, and binding" opinion, when limited to laws other than those governing the agreement in question. If opining lawyers expressly assume facts they know to be untrue or inapplicable, the opinion is likely to be misleading. It has been suggested that legal opinions, like financial statements, should "fairly present" their subject matter.

§ 1.6 PROCEDURES FOR ISSUANCE OF OPINIONS

Once a lawyer agrees to render an opinion, he must then perform the work necessary to actually give the opinion. In agreeing to give an opinion, a lawyer ordinarily has a reasonable idea of its outcome. If the situation is one in which the text of the agreed-on opinion has been outlined or specified, the opining lawyer must have already undertaken most if not all of the requisite investigation of the relevant facts and the applicable law. The latter knowledge he should have from prior practice or from at least preliminary research, and the former should result from his prior work with the client, his participation in the transaction or matter in question, or some level of prior factual investigation. The foregoing amounts to no more than the rather obvious proposition that one should not agree to give an opinion that one cannot give. Having agreed to give a specified opinion prior to a conclusive investigation, attorneys ought to complete the necessary investigation as soon as possible in order to lessen the embarrassment or other consequences of having agreed to do the impossible.

As alluded to in Sections 1.3 and 1.4, the applicable standard of care and diligence in issuing legal opinions is as high as in any professional activity in which a lawyer might engage. The necessity for high standards is evidenced in Chapter 12 regarding malpractice and other liability for faulty opinions. The appropriate extent of investigation depends, of course, upon the particular opinion and the extent to which its scope may be limited factually or as to the law. An opinion which is limited to the securities laws of Wisconsin or limited by reliance on only certain stated facts would ordinarily require less investigation or research than the same opinion without such qualifications.

The high standards required in opinion giving are reflected in the organizational procedures that many individuals or law firms or departments, particularly the larger ones, follow in issuing opinions. The firm may, as a practical matter, want to consider whether taking a particular legal position in an opinion may conflict with other positions taken by the firm in representing the same or other clients, or whether such a position may have the effect of precluding certain possible future legal engagements. Typically, a firm's opinion policy will require that only certain persons or classes of persons may sign opinion letters and that a record be kept of the person who signed each opinion issued by the firm.

Many attorneys and firms have formally or informally adopted and attempt to use certain forms of opinion or opinion language. Such forms often have been carefully considered by a legal opinion committee of the firm, and are revised and maintained as a part of a firm's opinion policy. The forms may be annotated with explanations for particular language, and specific factual and legal investigation procedures may be required or suggested before the opinion may be issued. Deviations from an applicable form may, as a matter of firm policy, require review and authorization by a designated lawyer or committee.

In some cases, lawyers set forth the factual and legal investigations performed by them in one or more back-up memoranda for their files. In case the opining lawyer or another finds it useful to review the work done, it is most convenient to have a written record available. Such a record may, for instance, save time in providing the results of investigations necessary for other opinions in the future. Virtually the only instance in which such a record's usefulness is questionable is when the work performed was inadequate or the opinion is being challenged. Back-up memoranda may be organized in a variety of ways; one method is to set forth the factual and legal research performed as to each enumerated opinion following a copy of the opinion paragraph.

Sizable law departments or firms usually have established internal peer review procedures that must be adhered to before an opinion is issued. The purpose of peer review is to provide a second look or an independent overview of the opinion in question. Even without formal procedures, opining lawyers often informally consult with others on difficult issues in their opinions. The particular procedures vary among different legal organizations. In some cases the reviewer is simply another lawyer in the opining lawyer's practice specialty. In others, a committee of lawyers undertakes the review. While two heads are better than one, and three better than two, a committee that is too large produces diminishing returns and inefficiency. The more independent of the client and subject matter of the opinion the reviewing lawyer or lawyers are, arguably the more objective and useful the review will be.

The review may be conducted at varying levels of thoroughness, depending on a number of factors such as potential liability, or the level may in all cases be the same. If a firm's policy requires complete and detailed back-up memoranda, the review may be of those memoranda as well as of the proposed opinion. Records are often kept of the review.

A peer review system may aid a lawyer in negotiating his opinion, helping to combat pressures to give an opinion that is unreasonably broad. Assuming that an opinion review is properly carried out, it ought to also help in defending against claims of lack of diligence on the part of the opiner.

The extent and nature of opinion issuance policies and procedures are not generally well known, and they evolve over time. The authors are aware of no widely published, broad-based, systematic studies of the subject. Several informal surveys touching on the subject of law firm opinion policies and procedures have been conducted by questionnaire. The following is an attempt to summarize, with approximate figures, some of the results of the most complete of the surveys.

Of the firms surveyed, 80 percent allowed only a partner to sign firm opinions; 57 percent required a second partner or similar review of all opinions issued by the firm. Fifty-five percent of the firms surveyed had an opinions committee. Of firms with an opinions committee, 74 percent of the committees prescribed procedures and 66 percent prescribed forms for issuing opinions. One-half of the committees acted only upon inquiry, presumably with respect to review of or advice on opinions. Of the firms surveyed, 74 percent had developed forms of opinions. In those firms with prescribed forms, use was mandatory in 27 percent of the firms and optional in 73 percent. Of the firms surveyed, 60 percent had some rules for specific diligence as to particular opinions, and 40 percent had no such rules; 59 percent of firms surveyed had no prescribed rules as to preparation of a due diligence *file* regarding opinions, and 41 percent had such rules.

In the more recent survey, only 5 percent of the survey respondents require a partner to sign or approve firm opinion letters, but 60 percent require a second partner to review all firm opinion letters. Approximately 63 percent of firms "have a standardized approach to legal opinions across the firm," and 87 percent "primarily provide opinions based on forms submitted to it, with some internal rules." Only 50 percent of responding firms required a centralized record of all opinion letters. Finally, only 58 percent required disclosure of partner directorships or other interests in opinion letters.

Richard R. Howe, The Duties and Liabilities of
Attorneys in Rendering Legal Opinions

1989 Colum. Bus. L. Rev. 283 (1989)

Introduction

Attorneys in the United States have established themselves as central advisers to the participants in planning and executing business transactions, and their advice is often followed both by their clients and by the other participants in the transaction. An attorney is expected to be a zealous advocate for his or her client's best interests and to endeavor to obtain every legitimate advantage that his or her client is entitled to in the negotiation and implementation of a transaction. Consequently, when a legal opinion is given by an attorney to a third party—i.e., the other side of the transaction—it is narrowly crafted to contain only the minimum assurances necessary to induce the third party to proceed. In order to appreciate the standards which have been developed to measure the duties and liabilities of attorneys associated with legal opinions in business transactions, it is useful to begin with an overview of the role of attorneys and legal opinions. This article focuses upon the attorney's duties and liabilities as the giver of a legal opinion, and it explores the tension between his or her role as advocate, negotiator, and implementer on the one hand, and as opinion giver on the other.

I. The Variety of Opinion Letters

There are a number of rather common, recurring situations in corporate finance in which lawyers render legal opinions. Although the following discussion is not comprehensive, it will illustrate the types of opinions which are involved in the cases that are discussed below. The discussion will also focus on the persons who are expected and entitled to rely upon opinions, and on those who are not but who may nevertheless be affected by opinions.

A. Bank Loan

Perhaps the most straightforward situation is a simple, two-party transaction such as a bank loan in which the borrower's attorney gives an opinion to the bank. Such opinions will generally cover the due organization of the borrower and the validity of the securities issued to the bank—i.e., that the note issued to the bank has been duly authorized, executed, and delivered by the borrower and constitutes a valid and legally binding obligation of the borrower, enforceable in accordance with its terms, with the customary bankruptcy and equitable principle exceptions. Often additional opinions are given covering such matters as the due incorporation of subsidiaries, the absence of any liens or encumbrances, the absence of conflicts with other agreements and instruments affecting the borrower, and the absence of pending or threatened litigation. For the most part, these additional opinions only amplify and strengthen the basic conclusion that the note issued to the bank is valid and legally binding upon the borrower. The bank is usually the only recipient of the opinion although it may be addressed to the borrower as well. However, the lawyer's duty is generally understood to extend only to the bank and the borrower, and no further.

B. Private Placement of Debt

A slightly more complex transaction would be a private placement of debt with institutional investors such as insurance companies. Here the lawyer's opinion will cover the same topics as in the two-party bank loan transaction, and the opinion will also usually state that it is not necessary to register the securities under the Securities Act of 1933 (the "1933 Act"). In traditional private placements, the lenders were not concerned with reselling the securities in the future and would hold them to maturity. Although this practice is changing, and may change dramatically if the Securities and Exchange Commission (the "SEC") adopts proposed Rule 144A, there are still some examples of traditional private placements with no expectation of resale. In such cases the attorney's duty is generally regarded as extending only to the borrower and the lenders.

C.   Private Placement of Equity

A more complex transaction is a private placement of equity securities where there is every expectation of resale. As in the case of the bank loan, the lawyer will traditionally give an opinion covering the due organization of the borrower and the validity of the securities—in the case of common stock, that the shares are duly authorized, have been validly issued and are fully paid and nonassessable. The opinion will also cover the exemption from registration under the 1933 Act, but it may also specifically address the ability of the purchasers to resell the securities in the future under specified conditions; e.g., not in excess of certain volume limitations, in brokers' transactions so long as the issuer has filed all required reports under the Securities Exchange Act of 1934 (the "1934 Act"). However, since equity securities usually represent "permanent" capital, there is never any expectation of their retirement. Thus, although the attorney's opinion may be addressed only to the initial purchasers of the securities, all persons who acquire the securities in the future will be affected if the attorney's opinion is not correct. Moreover, the attorney may not only have potential liability to the holders of the securities but may also face disciplinary proceedings brought by the SEC in the event that the securities are resold to the public.

D.   Registered Public Offerings

In contrast to private placements, in registered public offerings of debt and equity securities the securities are sold to the public and are expected to be resold from time to time thereafter, but it is uncommon for attorneys to give opinions to the public as such. Most opinions are given to the underwriters, who are the initial purchasers of the securities, and often cover not only the validity of the securities, but also the absence of conflicts with specified agreements and instruments, of defaults under any other outstanding securities, and of violations of law in connection with the issuance of the securities. Generally speaking, though, the only opinion that the public should see is the opinion of the issuer's counsel filed with the registration statement. Such opinions are generally limited to the minimum necessary to satisfy the requirements of the 1933 Act and cover only the validity of the securities.

At the same time, it is customary for both counsel to the issuer and counsel to the underwriters to give opinions to the underwriters (sometimes separate from the opinion as to the validity of the securities) to the effect that, in the course of their participation in the preparation and review of the registration statement and prospectus, the attorneys did not become aware of any misstatement of a material fact or omission to state any material fact required to be stated in the registration statement or necessary to make the statements therein not misleading. Although it is widely known by purchasers of securities in public offerings that such opinions are given, these opinions are not addressed to the public and the public is not entitled to rely upon them. In a way, such opinions are not really "legal opinions" at all in that they do not state any legal conclusion but only say that the attorney believes certain facts to be true. The purpose of such opinions is to assist the underwriters, and sometimes also the directors of the issuer if addressed to them, in establishing their "due diligence" defense under section 11 of the 1933 Act.

There are no generally established procedures which lawyers may follow with assurance in order to determine whether they should give such opinions, nor will the underwriters satisfy their due diligence obligations if they do nothing but receive such opinions. At the same time, the fact that reputable law firms are making investigations of the affairs of issuers of securities sold accompanied by registration statements is undoubtedly relied upon by many purchasers in assessing the quality of the securities, just as purchasers of securities rely upon underwriters' express or implicit recommendations.

E. Public Offerings of Exempt Securities

In offerings exempt from registration under the 1933 Act, such as municipal bonds, legal opinions are often more comprehensive. Because of the absence of review of such offerings by the SEC and state Blue Sky examiners, attorneys may have a somewhat greater responsibility to ensure that their clients' conduct meets appropriate standards. The opinions that are disclosed to the purchasers of the securities generally cover not only the validity of the securities, but also the exemption from taxation of interest on the securities under the Internal Revenue Code. Usually lawyers' opinions also cover the absence of need to register the securities under the 1933 Act, which generally follows from the tax-exempt character of the securities. Often, municipal securities are revenue bonds or other limited obligations payable solely from particular sources. In such cases legal opinions also cover the validity of the separate agreement, lease or other arrangement that supports the payments on the bonds. In addition, because the SEC has developed the position over the years that underwriters of exempt securities have essentially the same obligations of due diligence as underwriters of registered securities, attorneys usually give further opinions to the effect that they are not aware of any misstatements or omissions in the offering statement. These opinions, as in the case of registered public offerings, are not intended to be shown to or relied upon by investors.

Because of the development of municipal securities underwriting practices in the United States, most municipal securities cannot be sold without an approving opinion of "bond counsel," which is frequently printed directly on the bonds. Bond counsel generally view themselves not as counsel to the issuer but as counsel to the holders of the bonds, and the opinion printed on the bonds is intended to be relied upon by all persons who may invest in the bonds. This is very different from the role of lawyers in registered public offerings, whose opinions are not printed on the bonds and are generally intended for the benefit only of the initial purchasers. As the following discussion illustrates, many cases involving lawyers' opinions have involved bond counsel and reflect the rather unique responsibility of bond counsel.

The foregoing discussion of the function of legal opinions in business transactions involving the sale of securities ignores the role of lawyers in facilitating and implementing transactions. In the course of working on a transaction, lawyers give advice and counsel to their clients in making business decisions. Lawyers are often in a position where they can prevent a transaction from going forward—for example, by refusing to deliver an opinion, even when they may be satisfied that the opinion would be correct if delivered, or by controlling the flow of documents. Many of the cases involving lawyers' opinions are not based upon the language of the opinions, or even brought by the persons entitled to rely upon the opinion, but rather are based upon the attorney's role in the transaction.

II.   *Theories of Attorneys' Duties and Liabilities*

The basic theories that have been developed to judge legal opinions alleged to be incorrect fall into three broad categories: traditional malpractice, aiding and abetting a violation by another person of her legal duties, and acting as a participant in a fraudulent scheme. The focus of the following discussion will be upon the consequences of rendering an incorrect opinion rather than upon how the correctness or incorrectness of a legal opinion is determined.

A.   *Justifiable and Foreseeable Reliance by Third Parties Upon the Attorney's Opinion*

The liabilities of attorneys in connection with opinion letters are generally based upon general principles of tort liability, and where breach of contract analysis is applied, the courts reach the same results. At common law, a negligence standard is applied to legal opinions; a lawyer is expected to exercise the standard of care that would be exercised by another attorney of ordinary skill performing a similar task. A lawyer is not an insurer or a guarantor of the opinion so long as he has not been negligent in rendering it. In giving legal opinions, lawyers are judged not as participants in a transaction but rather as advisors to the participants.

The liability of attorneys is similar to that of other professionals, except for one major difference: in general, only the addressee of the opinion or the attorney's own client—i.e., a person in privity with the attorney—is entitled to bring suit. The most fundamental reason for this development is probably the attorney-client privilege: the need for the attorney to maintain almost absolute confidentiality of communications with his client in order to be able to provide effective representation. If a third party were permitted to sue the attorney, he might be compelled to reveal client confidences or act in a manner adverse to his client in order to defend himself. Knowing these consequences, the client will not communicate fully with the attorney, and the attorney will not be able to provide effective representation.

From the discussion above of the function of legal opinions in corporate finance transactions, it should be apparent that the attorney-client privilege has to be alive and well for the attorney to be able to give correct and useful legal opinions. While this is especially true in the context of disclosure opinions in public offerings it is also important in the case of opinions on the validity of securities. The attorney must have unfettered access to the client's records, thoughts and fears in order to be confident that all material facts have been disclosed and that the Board of Directors and stockholders have knowingly provided all necessary authorizations. She must understand the client's objectives in pursuing the transaction and be satisfied that they are lawful and proper. Finally, she must be in a position to defend the client in the future from claims that may arise out of the transaction.

Nevertheless, where the client, in order to accomplish a business transaction, acquiesces in the attorney's rendering a legal opinion to a third party, the statements made to the third party—i.e., the legal opinion—are not subject to the attorney-client privilege, and the client has waived the privilege to the extent of this communication. Accordingly, there is no policy reason for not holding the attorney liable to the third-party recipient of the opinion under traditional principles of tort liability if the attorney is negligent in performing this service. At the same time, it does not necessarily follow that all parties who may be affected by the fact that the attorney has rendered an opinion should have the right to sue the attorney. What the cases tend to focus on are which parties the attorney reasonably foresaw would reasonably and justifiably rely upon the rendered opinion and whether he intended the opinion for their benefit even if he did not address the opinion to them.

* * *

* * * [T]here are few examples in which attorneys have been held liable for allegedly incorrect opinions to persons other than the addressees of their opinions. Nevertheless, attorneys' opinions have a significant effect upon a much wider group of people, even where the attorneys are not liable for damages. As will be discussed below, there are many cases in which the attorney's role in the transaction has led to disciplinary proceedings to suspend the attorney from further practice, particularly in cases brought by the SEC.

B.   Aiding and Abetting

* * *

Two * * * cases that have involved aiding and abetting allegations against attorneys in connection with legal opinions are SEC v. Spectrum,

Ltd., and SEC v. Universal Major Industries Corp. Both were suits for injunctions against further violations alleging that an attorney had rendered an opinion as a part of a scheme to distribute securities to the public in violation of the registration provisions of the 1933 Act. Spectrum involved shares issued in a merger with a shell corporation, which at the time had to be registered under the 1933 Act only in connection with resales by affiliates of the acquired corporation. The court found that the attorney was negligent in not having appreciated that his opinion would be used in connection with resales by affiliates, and it noted that he had been retained only because another lawyer had refused to give the opinion and should have suspected what would happen. There was a question as to whether he had actual knowledge, although the court found that he did not. The opinion by Judge Kaufman contains the interesting observation that "an attorney can prevent the illicit use of his opinion letter by prohibiting its utilization in the sale of unregistered securities by a statement to that effect clearly appearing on the face of the letter."

Universal Major Industries involved an attorney who advised his client as to the general requirements for a private placement of convertible debentures. Whether his advice was correct was not an issue, but in any event the company did not comply with it and proceeded to issue almost $4 million of convertible debentures to 451 persons. The attorney then told the company to register the debentures with the SEC, and the company retained another attorney to process the registration, but it was never accomplished. Although his advice may have been sloppy, the lawyer would probably not have been charged had he stopped there. But what then happened was that holders of the debentures converted them into stock and started to sell the shares to the public. The company's transfer agent requested an opinion letter stating that these transfers were legal. The attorney wrote 118 letters stating that he "renders no opinion as to the original sale or issuance of the debentures" and was relying upon the enclosed opinion of the other attorney "to the effect that the conversion of the debentures and the issuance of the stock upon conversion, in and of itself, does not constitute a violation of the Securities Act." However, the enclosed opinion of the other attorney was simply to the effect that although the debentures "were in our opinion, sold in transactions violative of section 5 of the Securities Act of 1933, the conversions at this time, as proposed, would not constitute additional violations of the Act." It should have been obvious to both attorneys that their opinions were being utilized to facilitate the distribution of unregistered securities, and the court issued an injunction against further violations.

* * *

C. Participation in a Fraudulent Scheme

The line between aiding and abetting and being a participant in a fraudulent scheme is sometimes very thin. In general, in rendering opinions, lawyers are not thereby changing their role from advisers to participants with an interest in the outcome of the transaction. The one common situation in financing transactions where lawyers do perform such a role is when they act as bond counsel.

Bond counsel is an essential participant in a municipal securities transaction, and in many cases, bond counsel's fees are dependent upon the consummation of the transaction. Whether or not the fees are contingent, it is the practice for bond counsel to supervise and coordinate the legal activities of all the participants in the financing and, usually, to draft all of the papers as well. * * *

* * *

D. Cases Which Have Exonerated Attorneys: Lack of Reliance upon Attorney's Opinions

In order to end on a more positive note, it is useful to review some cases in which attorneys were not held liable for opinions which they rendered in business transactions. If there is a common element in these cases, it is that there was no reliance by the plaintiffs upon the attorneys' opinions.

* * *

First Interstate Bank of Nevada, N.A. v. Chapman & Cutler was a suit by bond purchasers for federal securities and racketeering violations in connection with several public bond offerings. Chapman & Cutler was asked to act as bond counsel in connection with a proposed offering to finance construction of a nursing home. After brief investigation, they declined to act out of concern about the not-for-profit status of the issuing corporation. The promoters then went ahead with other counsel, obtained a tax ruling and presented the bond issue to the Cook County Board, which was represented by Chapman & Cutler. The Board requested Chapman & Cutler to issue an opinion to it prior to adopting a resolution approving the bond issue. Chapman & Cutler then rendered a hypothetical opinion, stating that, assuming certain facts, the bond issue would be tax-exempt. As it turned out, some of the assumed facts were not consistent with the actual facts, and so a suit against Chapman & Cutler was brought upon the theory that it knew, based upon its earlier investigation, that the issuing corporation had not complied with the requirements necessary to be a not-for-profit corporation. The Court dismissed the complaint, reading it to find that it did not even allege that Chapman & Cutler took part in an overall conspiracy to defraud the bond investors.

This kind of suit raises difficult questions regarding the attorney-client privilege. Chapman & Cutler did not undertake, in issuing its opinion to the Cook County Board, to make an investigation of the facts and was not asked to do so. It was only asked to render an opinion based upon hypothetical facts. The fact that it had made a preliminary investigation with a view to representing another client should have no effect upon its duty to the Board, because that investigation would not have been expected to be thorough and complete at the time, and, moreover, information gained by a firm in the course of representing one client should not be presumed to be available for utilization by or for the benefit (or detriment) of another client. The Court's opinion is supportable on the basis that the opinion letter that Chapman & Cutler did render was not addressed to the bond purchasers, was not intended to be relied upon by them and disclosed on its face that they had not assumed any responsibility for the facts. But the case also serves to illustrate the pitfalls of legal opinions that are based upon hypothetical facts. Lawyers must be ever-vigilant to appreciate the uses which their clients intend to make of their legal opinions, and that if the facts they have assumed are not correct, the participants in the transaction may reach incorrect conclusions.

Abell v. Potomac Insurance Co. was a suit by bond purchasers against a developer, the law firm of Wright, Lindsey & Jennings ("WLJ"), which acted as counsel to the underwriters, and others for securities fraud, racketeering and pendent state law claims. The suit against WLJ was based upon the opinion they rendered to the underwriters which concluded, after detailing the procedures they had followed, that nothing had come to their attention which indicated that there was any misstatement or omission in the official statement. A complicating factor was that, as WLJ knew, the original counsel for the underwriters and the original bond counsel had resigned their representations, although for understandable reasons (i.e., the departure of the principal associate working on the matter from the firm). But WLJ nevertheless did little to investigate why the original counsel had resigned. Moreover, they readily acquiesced in several material changes to the final official statement without inquiring as to why these changes were being made. Finally, the complaint alleged that WLJ had failed to investigate properly the truth of the statements in the official statement, in breach of its duty to its own client.

Nevertheless, the Court overturned a jury verdict against WLJ, viewing the evidence as insufficient to support a finding of actual participation in a fraudulent scheme. The Court found that an action against WLJ under Rule 10b–5 required the plaintiffs to allege and prove reliance upon misstatements made by the firm, and since no statements at all had been made by the firm to the plaintiff, the Court dismissed this count as well. Finally, the Court held that the bondholders could not sue counsel to the underwriters under Louisiana law since its opinion was rendered to the underwriters and was not intended to be relied upon by the plaintiffs. The Court noted that the allegations of the complaint might be sufficient to state a claim against WLJ brought by its client, the underwriters, but not by a third party.

In my view, the outcome of this case, and of other suits against counsel to the underwriters, is in accordance with substantial justice. This is not just because of the traditional rules of privity and reliance upon legal opinions, but also because the result seems so intuitively fair and reasonable. Lawyers' opinions to the effect that in the course of their representation they did not become aware of any misstatement or omission should not be understood by third parties to mean that the lawyer necessarily investigated every fact and pursued every conceivable inference that could be made; there is always an allocation of responsibility between the underwriters and their counsel in their review of registration statements and official statements, as well as budgetary limitations upon the amount of investigation which can be done by an outside law firm that the underwriter will have to pay. Moreover, the purpose of the opinion is to protect the underwriter and not the purchasers of the bonds, and the underwriter must make its own investigation as well. If the lawyer actually believes his opinion to be true, he should not be held accountable to third parties, for the opinion is not addressed to third parties, is not relied upon by third parties and is not rendered for their benefit. The lawyer performed the only duty he undertook-to the own client-and only his own client should be able to hold the lawyer accountable for negligence.

* * *

AMERICAN BAR ASSOCIATION FORMAL OPINION 335 (1974)

IN WRITING OPINIONS AS THE BASIS FOR TRANSACTIONS INVOLVING SALES OF UNREGISTERED SECURITIES, A LAWYER SHOULD MAKE ADEQUATE PREPARATION INCLUDING INQUIRY INTO THE RELEVANT FACTS IN A MANNER CONSISTENT WITH THE GUIDELINES SET OUT IN THIS OPINION, BUT, WHILE HE SHOULD NOT ACCEPT AS TRUE THAT WHICH HE DOES NOT REASONABLY BELIEVE TO BE TRUE, HE DOES NOT HAVE THE RESPONSIBILITY TO 'AUDIT' THE AFFAIRS OF HIS CLIENT OR TO ASSUME, WITHOUT REASONABLE CAUSE, THAT THE CLIENT'S STATEMENT OF THE FACTS CANNOT BE RELIED ON.

Release #5168 of the Securities and Exchange Commission (SEC) under the Securities Act of 1933 (Release #9239 under the Securities Exchange Act of 1934) was published on July 7, 1971. It set forth certain basic standards of conduct required of broker-dealers to meet their responsibilities in connection with sales of unregistered securities. In a footnote to the next-to-last paragraph of the Release, dealing with the obligation of a broker-dealer to review the surrounding facts and obtain the opinion of competent disinterested counsel concerning the legality of sales, it referred to Securities Act Release #4445 (Securities Exchange Act Release #6721), published on February 2, 1962, in the following manner:

> "In this regard, the Commission has stated that 'if an attorney furnishes an opinion based solely on hypothetical facts which he has made no effort to verify, and if he knows that his opinion will be relied upon as the basis for a substantial distribution of unregistered securities, a serious question arises as to the propriety of his professional conduct.' "

The Commission's repetition of this language led to inquiries of this Committee as to the circumstances under which and the extent to which the Code of Professional Responsibility might require that a lawyer make some effort to verify or supplement the facts submitted to him as the basis for an opinion that certain sales of securities need not be registered under the Securities Act of 1933. The question is of such importance to so many lawyers that this Committee has issued this Formal Opinion in an effort to clarify the existence and extent of a lawyer's responsibility in writing such opinions.

At the outset it should be made clear that we are concerned only with opinions written as the basis for transactions involving sales of unregistered securities. The scope of this opinion does not include legal or other services of lawyers rendered in securities transactions or their participation therein beyond the rendering of such opinions. Furthermore, opinions written in connection with securities registrations or other matters are not within the scope of this opinion. We should also make it clear that, having no specific facts before us and being in a position only to provide guidelines rather than standards, this opinion is not concerned with what constitutes negligence—an issue for the trier of fact under a particular set of facts.

Section 5 of the Securities Act of 1933 broadly prohibits the use of the mails or facilities of interstate commerce to sell a security unless a registration statement is in effect covering such security. However, important exemptions from the requirements of registration are provided, inter alia, by Section 4 of the Act, which, as supplemented by rules thereunder, e.g., Rule 144, exempts transactions by an issuer not involving a public offering, transactions not involving an issuer, underwriter or dealer, and certain transactions by dealers and brokers.

Where an exemption is claimed it has been common for the principals to rely on opinions of attorneys who recite the facts, and then say that on the basis of such facts the transaction is entitled to the exemption.

It is, of course, important that the lawyer competently and carefully consider what facts are relevant to the giving of the requested opinion and make a reasonable inquiry to obtain such of those facts as are not within his personal knowledge. Depending upon the circumstances, the lawyer may or may not need to go beyond directing questions to his client and checking the answers by reviewing such appropriate documents as are available.

Before going into more detail on the matter of the extent of any required further inquiry, we should point out the important of avoiding mistakes in communication between the client and the lawyer. In cases turning upon whether or not registration of securities is required, the facts are likely to be important and a lack of proper communication between the client and the lawyer could cause grave difficulties. Therefore, before a lawyer signs an opinion based on facts furnished by his client, he should take reasonable steps to make sure that the client understands exactly what facts he has requested and that he accurately understands what the client has told him.

We turn now to the precise question presented, namely, the circumstances under which, and the extent to which, a lawyer should verify or supplement the facts presented to him as the basis for such an opinion.

In any event, the lawyer should, in the first instance, make inquiry of his client as to the relevant facts and receive answers. If any of the alleged facts, or the alleged facts taken as a whole, are incomplete in a material respect; or are suspect; or are inconsistent; or either on their face or on the basis of other known facts are open to question, the lawyer should make further inquiry. The extent of this inquiry will depend in each case upon the circumstances; for example, it would be less where the lawyer's past relationship with the client is sufficient to give him a basis for trusting the client's probity than where the client has recently engaged the lawyer, and less where the lawyer's inquiries are answered fully than when there appears a reluctance to disclose information.

Where the lawyer concludes that further inquiry of a reasonable nature would not give him sufficient confidence as to all the relevant facts, or for any other reason he does not make the appropriate further inquiries, he should refuse to give an opinion. However, assuming that the alleged facts are not incomplete in a material respect, or suspect, or in any way inherently inconsistent, or on their face or on the basis of other known facts open to question, the lawyer may properly assume that the facts as related to him by his client, and checked by him by reviewing such appropriate documents as are available, are accurate.

Preliminarily, we state two examples as a means of defining the extremes of the problem in giving an opinion to a security holder who wishes to sell securities to the public without registration. On the one extreme, if a lawyer is asked to issue an opinion concerning a modest amount of a widely traded security by a responsible client, whose lack of relationship to the issuer is well known to the lawyer, he may ordinarily proceed to issue the opinion with considerable confidence. On the other extreme, if he is asked to prepare an opinion letter covering a substantial block of a little known security, where the client (be it selling shareholder or broker) appears reluctant to disclose exactly where the securities came from or where the surrounding circumstances raise a question as to whether or not the ostensible sellers may be merely intermediaries for controlling persons or statutory underwriters, then searching inquiry is called for.

As a further example, suppose that a broker client requests a legal opinion that a proposed sale of shares of X Company would comply with Rule 144, and thus be exempt from registration, and supplies the lawyer with a statement of the facts that allegedly would support such an opinion and a copy of Form 144 proposed to be filed, if any. Assuming that the broker is known to the lawyer to be of good repute, that the lawyer has read the proposed or executed Form 144, if any, and that the alleged facts do not require further inquiry for any of the reasons stated above, the lawyer may properly give the opinion. If on the other hand the alleged facts do require further inquiries for any of the reasons stated above, the lawyer should either make such inquiries until satisfied or refuse to give an opinion if he concludes that reasonable inquiry would still not satisfy him. It is difficult to state a formula for determining how far a lawyer must go to satisfy the requirement that he make a reasonable effort to verify particular facts in such a case. However, it would seem that, for example, the verification from the issuer or its counsel of the number of shares of the class outstanding and the verification (perhaps through financial journals) of the relevant trading volume, an attempt (by checking through a quotation service and/or the relevant 'pink' quotation sheets) to determine whether or not the broker is making solicitations of offers to buy the securities, and the inspection of a written statement from the issuer of the securities that it has complied with the reporting requirements mentioned in Rule 144 should normally be sufficient where verification is indicated.

Another example would be where a corporate client requests an opinion as to whether a proposed transaction would be within the private offering exemption furnished by Section 4(2) of the Securities Act of 1933. In this situation, the lawyer should obtain from the client information, preferably in writing, from which the lawyer may reach the legal conclusion that the exemption is (or is not) available. Here again, the lawyer may properly rely upon the information furnished by a client well known to him, assuming that it is not inconsistent, suspect, otherwise open to question, or incomplete in a material respect.

If the lawyer has some reason to believe that one or more of the statements of fact furnished him as a basis for the opinion may not be correct, he should make a determination as to whether to refuse to give an opinion or whether to attempt to verify one or more of the relevant facts. This matter was discussed in connection with the example dealing with Ruling 144. If he does determine that he will proceed, he should decide on the extent of verification in the light of the particular situation. If, for example, the lawyer has any reason to doubt the reliability of the information relevant to whether the offerees have the requisite sophistication to meet the standard applicable to the Section 4(2) exemption, he should reasonably satisfy himself that the client correctly understands the concept of 'sophistication' and he might appropriately obtain from his client further information on each offeree and his background in order to determine that each was sufficiently 'sophisticated' to be able to fend for himself and did not need the protection of a registration statement. Where information which may be relevant to a determination of whether or not the exemption provided by Section 4(2) is available may be quite difficult, if not impossible, to verify, it might in fact be necessary to rely completely on the client, but this necessity does not decrease the lawyer's ultimate responsibility to exercise his independent judgment in determining whether the client had a reasonable basis for his determination that each client was sufficiently 'sophisticated' and whether, in view of all the facts developed, the Section 4(2) exemption is available. If the lawyer considers that there is any material deficiency in that information, he should simply refuse to give an opinion in the subject.

A properly drafted opinion will recite clearly the sources of the attorney's knowledge of the facts. Where verification is otherwise called for, an attorney should make appropriate verification and should not rely on the use of such phrases as 'based upon the facts as you have given them to me' or 'apart from what you have told me, I have not inquired as to the facts.'

The essence of this opinion, the scope of which has been set forth in the third paragraph, supra, is that, while a lawyer should make adequate preparation including inquiry into the relevant facts that is consistent with the above guidelines, and while he should not accept as true that which he should not reasonably believe to be true, he does not have the responsibility to 'audit' the affairs of his clients or to assume, without reasonable cause, that a client's statement of the facts cannot be relied upon.

The steps reasonably required of the lawyer in making his investigation must be commensurate with the circumstances under which he is called upon to render the opinion, but he must bear in mind that his responsibility is to render to the client his considered, independent opinion whether, having made at least inquiries such as those suggested by the above guidelines, the claimed exemption is or is not available under the law. While the responsibility of the lawyer is to his client, he must not be oblivious of the extent to which others may be affected if he is derelict in fulfilling that responsibility. A good lawyer is a conscientious lawyer who strives to fulfill, not only the obligations imposed by the Code's Disciplinary Rules, but also the higher responsibilities contained in the Code's Ethical Considerations.

Donald W. Glazer & Charles R.B. Macedo, DETERMINING THE UNDERLYING FACTS: AN EPISTEMOLOGICAL LOOK AT LEGAL OPINIONS IN CORPORATE TRANSACTIONS

1989 COLUM. BUS. L. REV. 343 (1989)

INTRODUCTION

This article discusses a subject that has received very little attention in the literature—how lawyers deal with facts in legal opinion letters.
* * *

I. When Is an Assumption Appropriate?

The legal opinion customarily delivered at the closing of a business transaction relates to a real life transaction. The facts on which the opinion is grounded are there for the finding. Counsel usually investigates some of the facts himself by reviewing, for example, the charter, by-laws and records of corporate action of stockholders and directors. For other facts, counsel typically obtains a factual representation, often from an officer of the corporation or a government official. As for still other facts, counsel commonly does nothing, choosing instead to rely on assumptions—stated and unstated—as to what the facts are.

* * *

A. Facts That Are Always Assumed

Lawyers always assume the genuineness of signatures. They may state it. They may not. Yet it is understood that lawyers are not expected to confirm that the signatures on the documents furnished to them have not been forged. Similarly, lawyers always assume the authenticity of the documents furnished to them as originals and the conformity with the originals of documents furnished to them as copies.

Lawyers also always make assumptions as to the capacity of the other party to enter into the agreement. Lawyers always assume that the other party has duly authorized and executed the agreement and that the agreement is binding on the other party.

Because of the difficulty of determining whether an interested transaction is fair, lawyers ordinarily assume the fairness of transactions between a corporation and its officers or directors. Courts generally will invalidate such transactions if they are unfair to the corporation. As a result, whether stated expressly or not, every opinion on an interested transaction necessarily is grounded on an assumption as to fairness.

Finally, lawyers commonly rely on assumptions when opining on transactions that are to take place in the future. If a lawyer is opining on the validity of stock to be issued at some future date under a stock option plan, for example, the lawyer will base the opinion in part on an assumption that the shares will be issued pursuant to the provisions of the plan.

B. Facts That Are Never Assumed

At the opposite end of the spectrum are facts that are never assumed. Lawyers, for example, almost always obtain a certificate from the Secretary of State of the jurisdiction in which the company is incorporated, confirming the filing in his office of charter documents. An assumption as to the filing of those documents would ordinarily be regarded as inappropriate.

Lawyers also rarely rely on assumptions as to the facts relating to outstanding stock—an instructive contrast with our earlier example concerning stock that is to be issued in the future. When opining on outstanding stock, a lawyer will obtain an officer's certificate concerning compliance with the authorizing resolution and receipt of the requisite consideration.

Finally, lawyers opining that shares being issued are "duly authorized" will not assume the number of authorized shares (or, for that matter, obtain a factual certificate to that effect). Instead, lawyers will themselves personally confirm a company's authorized capital by reviewing its charter documents.

C. *Principles Derived*

Do these examples, at both ends of the spectrum, reveal any general principles? We think they do. One principle is that assumptions are appropriate in circumstances where it is not practical for a lawyer to confirm the facts himself or when a representation from someone else is not obtainable, prohibitively expensive, inherently unreliable or for some other reason adds nothing of value. Another more controversial principle—and one that is the converse of our first principle—is that assumptions ordinarily are inappropriate when a lawyer can, without undue difficulty, confirm the facts himself or obtain a third-party representation. It is important to note that these principles are subject to the overriding qualification that opining counsel ordinarily should be free, where the parties are sophisticated and represented by knowledgeable counsel, to make any assumption requested by the parties, even an assumption counsel and the parties know to be contrary to the actual facts.

How do these principles measure up against our examples? Consider first the assumptions concerning the genuineness of signatures and authenticity of documents. On those subjects an officer's certificate would be no more reliable than an assumption and would add nothing of value to the opinion. Even after obtaining such a certificate, neither the opining lawyer nor the opinion recipient would have any greater certainty since the basic question, whether addressed implicitly by delivery of the documents or expressly in a certificate, is whether corporate officials are telling the truth.

A representation as to the capacity of the other party to the agreement (usually the opinion recipient) would add nothing of value. When facts are peculiar to the opinion recipient, they are properly its responsibility and not that of the opining lawyer. * * *

The third example, fairness of an interested transaction, raises the issues of both cost and reliability. Here, an investment banker's opinion as to fairness is often prohibitively expensive, and an officer's certificate inherently unreliable. Under those circumstances an assumption is likely to be the only reasonable alternative.

As for future stock issuances under a stock option plan, it goes without saying that no one can certify today what will happen tomorrow. This is another case where a representation would be inherently unreliable. Accordingly, an assumption is again appropriate.

Our examples of matters as to which assumptions are never used also support this principle. In the first two cases, the filing of charter documents and past issuances of stock, ordinarily the facts are easily ascertainable and certificates readily obtainable—in the former case, from the Secretary of State, and in the latter from an officer of the corporation. Under those circumstances, it is hard to justify an assumption. As for the number of authorized shares, a lawyer can easily confirm the facts himself. Accordingly, the appropriate action for a lawyer is to conduct that review.

II. Factual Representations

If an assumption is not appropriate, a lawyer will be required to base the opinion on a factual investigation. * * *

A. Representations Commonly Requested

Consider again the filing of a company's charter documents with the Secretary of State. Lawyers do not ordinarily ask a corporate officer for a representation that the documents were filed. Instead, as previously suggested, the standard procedure is to obtain a Secretary of State's certificate to that effect.

Consider also the standard opinion clause that the corporation is in good standing in a particular jurisdiction. Generally, this opinion will be based on a certificate from the Secretary of State and, in some states, from state tax authorities. However, if the opinion relates to good standing in a state, such as Massachusetts, in which a certificate of tax good standing may be difficult if not impossible to obtain by the closing date, the lawyer may rely instead on an officer's certificate confirming that state tax returns have been filed.

A third example relates to the representation as to stock issuances discussed in Part I. Ordinarily, counsel will seek a certificate from the treasurer or chief financial officer as to the receipt of consideration and from the secretary of the corporation, not the treasurer, as to the adoption of the authorizing board resolution.

* * *

B. Principles Derived

These examples suggest a principle to guide counsel in deciding from whom a representation should be sought: subject to considerations of cost and practicality, the lawyer should seek a representation from the person, inside or outside the company, who is the most reliable source of the information or, if that person is an employee of the company, from the officer or other employee to whom that employee reports. This principle (like the other principles suggested in this article) is not intended to bind counsel or, somehow, subject counsel to liability: a lawyer should be entitled to rely on a representation from any competent officer regardless of his formal title. This principle is intended, however, to provide guidance to counsel in deciding from whom to seek a representation. Applying the principle to the foregoing examples will illustrate how it works.

First, for a representation as to the filing of charter documents, lawyers obtain a Secretary of State's certificate because it is readily available and because no one is in a better position than the Secretary of State to confirm that the documents were filed with his office. Under such circumstances it is hard to justify obtaining a certificate from anyone else. * * *

The circumstances may be different for a good standing opinion. While a lawyer's first choice will ordinarily be a certificate from a state official, such a certificate, at least in the case of tax good standing, may not be readily available, as in Massachusetts. Under those circumstances, the lawyer may properly turn to the next most reliable person available, usually a company officer, for a representation that state tax returns have been filed.

The third group of examples deals with the question of which employee within a company should be asked to make a representation. In the stock issuance example, counsel ordinarily will seek a representation as to receipt of consideration from either the treasurer or the chief financial officer, not the secretary. Why? Because the treasurer has direct responsibility for such matters and the chief financial officer, as the person to whom the treasurer reports, has indirect responsibility. Either will do. The secretary will not do because he has no responsibility (direct or indirect through the corporate chain of command) for financial matters. By way of contrast, the treasurer and chief financial officer ordinarily would have no responsibility for keeping track of actions taken by the board. Accordingly, as to the board resolution authorizing issuance of the stock, the secretary is the officer who should make the representation.

As an alternative to obtaining a certificate from a lower level officer, a lawyer may choose to obtain a certificate from the president. This is appropriate because of the president's position at the top of the corporate hierarchy. Care should be taken, however, to make sure that the president understands what he is representing, particularly in technical areas requiring reliance by the president on those reporting to him. If the president prefers, he may properly ask counsel to obtain the representations from the person directly responsible for the subject area.

III. Knowledge

Each opinion clause in an opinion letter necessarily is grounded on the facts known to counsel. Some of those facts will be determined directly by counsel, but most will be based on an assumption or on a representation by someone else. In each instance a lawyer must filter those facts through what he already knows and, in the case of a law firm, what others in the firm know. If those facts are inconsistent with other facts known to the lawyer, a lawyer is not entitled to rely upon them.
* * *

A. How the Concept of Knowledge Arises

The concept of knowledge arises in legal opinions in two very different ways. In one way it is used to describe when a lawyer is entitled to rely on a factual representation of someone else. In the other it is used expressly to qualify certain standard opinion clauses.

As discussed above, when a lawyer renders an opinion, he necessarily relies on factual representations by others. A lawyer is not, however, entitled to rely on representations he knows to be untrue. For example, if a corporate secretary represents that the minute books are complete, a lawyer is not entitled to accept that representation if he knows that the minute books fail to include the minutes of an important meeting. Consider, however, whether a lawyer may properly rely on such a representation if he has no actual knowledge of an unrecorded meeting but has reason to suspect that such a meeting has taken place. Does knowledge for this purpose extend beyond actual recognition to what a lawyer should reasonably be deemed to know? Are there circumstances when what a lawyer knows requires that he inquire further? We address those questions later. Our purpose for now simply is to illustrate that one way the issue of knowledge arises in a legal opinion is in the context of a lawyer's ability to rely on facts that are represented to him by others. Knowledge matters in this context, even though the word itself does not appear for that purpose in the opinion.

Knowledge also arises in a different context, a context in which the phrase "to our knowledge" or "known to us" is used expressly to qualify a specific opinion clause. Company counsel, for example, typically opine that performance of a loan agreement will not conflict with any other contracts to which the company is a party. Company counsel may also opine that there are no pending or threatened law suits or claims against the company except as set forth in a specified schedule. These opinions typically are qualified by a "to our knowledge" limitation. This express use of the term "knowledge" as a method of limiting counsel's responsibility for certain facts is the second way in which the concept of knowledge arises for opinion purposes.

B. How the Problem Arises in Practice

What a lawyer and his firm know for opinion purposes cannot be analyzed as an abstract proposition. Rather, such an analysis requires an examination of the many ways in which the issue can arise in actual practice. Suppose, for example, that many years ago the partner in charge of a loan transaction was, as a young associate, involved tangentially in a transaction governed by an agreement that is violated by the loan agreement. Suppose, however, that he barely remembers the earlier transaction and has no recollection of the terms of the agreement. Should he be deemed to have knowledge of the earlier agreement? Should the firm? Suppose that everybody who worked on the transaction, except the associate-turned-partner, has left the firm but the agreement is preserved somewhere in the firm's files. Or suppose that another partner who worked on the earlier transaction remembers the agreement well but has done no work for the client for many years and no one remembers his earlier involvement or would think to ask. Or suppose that a lawyer in the firm knows of the conflicting agreement as a result of his representation of the client while employed by another firm or while serving on the client's inside legal staff. What if it is not a lawyer who knows, but a legal assistant or a secretary?

Consider a related example. Suppose the firm did not work on the earlier agreement but it is listed as one of the many exhibits to a Securities Act registration statement the firm is preparing for the same company at about the same time. However, the firm's SEC lawyers, not its bank lawyers, are working on that transaction. In rendering an opinion on the new loan agreement, should the firm be deemed to know of the existence of the conflicting agreement? Would it matter if the firm did not work on the registration statement (perhaps it was prepared by inside counsel) but received a copy? Would it matter that the firm did not receive a copy from the client but that a partner in the firm was given a copy in his capacity as a director of the company?

Finally, consider whether the answers to the foregoing questions should be affected by inclusion of a "to our knowledge" limitation. What if the opinion does not contain such a limitation but instead rests entirely on an officer's certificate that fails to identify the agreement at issue?

1. The Law Firm Problem

At one time, when law firms were smaller and had regular and intimate relationships with client companies, knowledge may have meant the knowledge of the lawyers working on the client's affairs or perhaps that of the entire firm. There was not much difference. Today, however, law firms are bigger and more departmentalized, the relationship between outside law firms and their clients are less regular and more specialized and companies often have their own inside legal staffs. Under these circumstances, whose knowledge counts makes a big difference.

Defining knowledge to mean what is known by the partner who signs the opinion letter is an easy but unsatisfactory solution. An opinion recipient can reasonably expect that the firm is accountable for some knowledge of the client beyond that of the opining partner. A law firm's name not (or in some firms not just) the name of the signing partner appears on the bottom of an opinion letter. Other lawyers are likely to have worked on the transaction. Still other lawyers are likely to have worked on other matters for the client.

To take the other extreme, does knowledge comprehend everything known to everyone in the firm? In a large or even medium size law firm, no lawyer or small group of lawyers is likely to know everything about a client's affairs. Moreover, it would be impractical for the lawyers responsible for the transaction to find out what everyone else in the firm knows about the client, much less determine how that collective knowledge bears on the transaction. The lawyers whom those responsible would have to consult may include not only lawyers who currently are working for the client but also those who previously have represented the client, even perhaps many years ago.

Time adds another dimension. Should it matter when a fact came to the attention of the firm? If a lawyer learned of it five years ago, should he be deemed to have knowledge of it today? What if the lawyer learned of it ten years ago? Or twenty? Memories dim. Is there a period beyond which a lawyer ought not to be responsible for remembering?

How the facts came to the firm's attention adds still another dimension. Lawyers may learn something while working on a client's affairs. But they may also learn it by reviewing documents prepared for the client by another firm, through service as a director or, perhaps, in some entirely non-professional capacity, such as reading the daily newspaper. Should it matter how a lawyer learned of the facts in question?

2.   The Files Problem

Memories are fallible. Is knowledge only what the people in the firm—however that group is defined—remember, or does it also include what resides in their files? If files are included, then whose files count and how far back must they be searched? One year? Five years? Twenty years? The answer may depend upon what is within the firm's capabilities. However, what is possible and what is practical are two different things.

If a firm has a good file management system and a limited number of files for the client in question, a file check might not be too difficult. However, as the quality of the file management system diminishes or the number of records increases, a file search may be impractical if not impossible.

C.   A Possible Solution

As noted, the concept of knowledge arises in two very different ways in the context of a legal opinion. One way is to define the extent to which a lawyer is entitled to rely on factual representations by third parties. The other is to limit expressly counsel's responsibility for certain facts-i.e., the existence of conflicting contracts or adverse litigation—that are central to certain standard opinion clauses. A failure to distinguish between these two uses of the concept of knowledge has resulted in some heated debates—debates that have generated much smoke but little light. Distinguishing between the ways knowledge is used, and analyzing them each separately, is, we believe, the best and perhaps the only way to clear the air.

1.   Knowledge for Reliance Purposes

Experienced lawyers all agree that a lawyer is not entitled to rely on a representation the lawyer knows to be untrue. While various definitions are possible, we believe knowledge for this purpose is best defined as "current consciousness" or, perhaps even better, "clear recognition." Such definitions are intended to convey the concept that what is known should be in the forefront of a lawyer's mind, not in the deep recesses of his memory.

Experienced lawyers do not all agree on whether a lawyer is entitled to rely on a representation the lawyer should know to be untrue but, for whatever reason, does not. Some lawyers have framed this issue as whether a lawyer has an obligation to add two plus two. When put that way, the question seems to cry out for the answer, yes. However, putting the question that way is too simplistic. In practice each lawyer is aware, more or less clearly, of many facts about a client, facts that are analogous not to simple numbers but to pieces of a puzzle or, more accurately, to pieces of many different puzzles. Which pieces fit together, and how, may be obvious—but only with the benefit of hindsight after they are assembled. Before an opinion is rendered, the lawyer is likely to be focusing on other things, wholly unaware that he even has a puzzle in his possession, much less one that if solved would lead to a conclusion that a representation is untrue.

In the context of a law firm, a yes answer to the question whether a lawyer should be expected to add two plus two is even more problematic. In the case of an individual all the pieces are, at least, in the possession of one person. In the case of a law firm, those pieces are likely to be held by many different lawyers, no one of whom is aware of the pieces held by the others or even for that matter that anyone else holds a piece. Under those circumstances, even adding a two held by one lawyer to a two held by another may be more than can reasonably be expected. Because it often is so easy with hindsight to see the obvious and so hard in the thick of a transaction, we favor an actual knowledge standard for reliance purposes so as to protect lawyers from being unfairly second-guessed about the factual underpinnings of their opinions.

Defining knowledge for this purpose as actual knowledge solves the problem of determining which lawyers within a firm should be counted. A firm would have no obligation to educate everyone who has worked for the client about the transaction or everyone who has worked on the transaction about the client. Instead, the lawyers whose knowledge would count would be those lawyers working on the transaction who, on the basis of what they already know about the opinion, the transaction and the client without any special briefing, are in a position to recognize that a factual representation is wrong. Lawyers who are not in the ordinary course familiar with the opinion and back-up documentation would not have to be consulted. This accords with what law firms do in practice. No firms we know attempt to communicate the terms of a complex transaction and the related legal opinion to everyone in the firm. Not only is such an effort impractical, but clients would be unwilling to pay for it even if it were. The merits of meshing what is required with what lawyers actually do are obvious—and should help those lawyers who have worried whether they have been doing enough to sleep better at night.

2. Knowledge as an Express Limitation

Use of knowledge as an express limitation presents a different problem. Here, an actual knowledge standard may be inconsistent with the reasons opinion recipients request opinions on the matters typically qualified by a "to our knowledge" limitation. Those opinions—no conflicts with contracts, orders, judgments or decrees, no adverse litigation—are highly fact-oriented, and their purpose is to tap the reservoir of knowledge contained in the opining firm. If knowledge included only what is known about the client by the lawyers working on the transaction, those opinions could lose most of their significance. For example, if a firm's mergers and acquisitions group is representing a company in the disposition of an important division, the lawyers in that group may have little, if any, knowledge of the credit agreements to which the company is a party (and which might be violated by a sale of a substantial portion of the company's assets). Once one departs, however, from a requirement that only those familiar with the transaction be consulted, one is faced with the hard problem of determining exactly where to draw the line.

Two knowledge limitations that, at least theoretically, might provide some help would be to excuse lawyers from accountability for facts that came to their attention prior to some specified time period or apart from their representation of the client. The first of these limitations would acknowledge that knowledge is not a black or white proposition but over time takes on various shades of gray. The second would acknowledge that lawyers are not always on duty, that their clocks are not always running. The objection to both of these limitations, however, is their inherent arbitrariness. There is no good reason why a lawyer should not be accountable for facts within his current consciousness regardless of how or when the lawyer learned them.

As we have previously seen, it is unfair to the opinion recipient to restrict knowledge to what is known by the lawyer signing the opinion and impractical from the standpoint of a law firm to extend it to what is—or once was—known by every lawyer in the firm. Thus, we are left again with the problem of where to draw the line.

We start with the proposition that knowledge for purposes of an express knowledge limitation should cover at least the same territory as knowledge for reliance purposes. Thus, knowledge should, at the very least, comprehend what is actually known by the lawyers in the firm who are familiar with the transaction. In some cases that should be sufficient, for example, where the partner in charge of the transaction himself has a good overview of all the work the firm has performed for the client or where the partner in charge of the client has such an overview and is working on the transaction (perhaps in a supervisory capacity). We believe, however, that an inquiry beyond the working group is needed if a firm is to be prevented from hiding behind an actual knowledge standard in those instances where the lawyers working on the transaction are not familiar with the subject matter of areas dealt with by the opinion clause that is qualified by the knowledge limitation. Such a situation could arise, for example, where work for a client is spread among many lawyers, in many departments and in many offices, and no one partner is on top of everything that is being done. In those circumstances, we propose that the lawyer responsible for preparing the opinion be required to consider who in the firm has a good overview of the work the firm has performed for the client in each subject area and to review the requested opinion with each of those persons. If the knowledge limitation relates to agreements for money borrowed, for example, the responsible lawyer would determine whether there is a specific lawyer who is familiar with the company's borrowing arrangements; if litigation, whether any one litigator has a good grasp of all the litigation handled for the client by the firm. If no one person meets that standard in a particular area, the responsible lawyer would be required to check with the two or three lawyers who know the most in that area. The responsible lawyer should not, however, be required to check with all the lawyers who have worked in each of those areas. A reasonable inquiry under the circumstances is all that should be required.

A final question is whether the lawyers who are consulted should be required to review the firm's files or to consult with anyone else. Clearly, a comprehensive file review is not normally practical and hence should not be required. However, if the firm maintains a computer listing of the factual matters in question, for example a litigation docket, it would not be unreasonable to expect someone to consult it. Similarly, if another lawyer is exceptionally knowledgeable about a company's activities in sub-area, such as borrowing arrangements by foreign subsidiaries, it might make sense to consult with him as well. A strong bias should exist, however, toward keeping any such inquiry within manageable limits. While drawing hard and fast lines is difficult, it is important that the duty of inquiry be kept well within the range of what is practical.

Those who share the concerns we have outlined and would like to adopt our solution face the practical problem of how to implement it. The Business Law Section of the American Bar Association has taken some preliminary steps toward developing a convention that could be incorporated by reference in legal opinions. If such a convention is ever adopted and includes a definition of knowledge along the lines we have suggested (as we think it should), it would clarify what is now a murky area. Until that day arrives, however, lawyers will have to resort to self-help. Opinions are negotiated documents and whatever the parties agree should control. Accordingly, we believe the best way for lawyers to implement the approach we propose is for them to include in their opinions an express statement that the firm shall be deemed to know only those facts that are in the current consciousness of (or are clearly recognized by) (i) lawyers in the firm who are familiar with the transaction and (ii) in the case of opinions qualified by an express knowledge limitation, lawyers having an overview of the subject areas qualified by that limitation, in each case without any independent inquiry or file review (except as may be specifically identified).

Would such a limitation be acceptable to opinion recipients? In most cases, we think it should. The problems we have outlined are real, and even a rigorous analysis of what a firm should be deemed to know does not provide assurance that lines will be drawn in a way that produces a practical result. The statement we have suggested, on the other hand, is consistent with how law firms really work, drawing lines that provide reasonable assurance to the opinion recipient that key lawyers in the firm are not aware of inconsistent facts without burdening those lawyers with the time consuming and most likely unproductive task of checking with everyone else and searching the firm's files . . .

SCHATZ v. ROSENBERG

943 F.2d 485 (4th Cir. 1991)

CHAPMAN, SENIOR CIRCUIT JUDGE:

* * *

I.

On December 31, 1986, MER purchased an eighty percent (80%) interest in two companies the plaintiffs owned, Virginia Adjustable Bed Manufacturing Corporation ("VAMCO") and Advanced Bed Concepts ("ABC"). MER is a holding company which Mark Rosenberg created to purchase the VAMCO and ABC stock. As payment for their eighty percent (80%) interests in VAMCO and ABC, Mr. and Mrs. Schatz received $1.5 million in promissory notes issued by MER, which Rosenberg personally guaranteed. The plaintiffs relied on a financial statement dated March 31, 1986 and an update letter delivered at closing on December 31, 1986 which indicated that Rosenberg's net worth exceeded $7 million. These financial documents contained several misrepresentations obscuring the fact that Rosenberg's financial empire had crumbled between April and December of 1986. Rosenberg's largest business, Yale Sportswear Corporation ("Yale"), filed for bankruptcy in September 1987, and Rosenberg filed for personal bankruptcy thereafter. The law firm of Weinberg & Green represented Rosenberg and his entities throughout this period.

The plaintiffs never received payment on their promissory notes and lost an additional $150,000 when they made a "bridge loan" to BBC, the company which was formed when VAMCO and ABC merged with the Back Center, Inc. ("BCI"), another of Rosenberg's companies. To add insult to injury, Rosenberg paid Weinberg & Green's legal fees for the transaction out of VAMCO and ABC's cash reserves. Rosenberg siphoned off operating capital from VAMCO and ABC to prop up Yale. By the time Rosenberg and Yale filed for bankruptcy, VAMCO and ABC were essentially worthless, and plaintiffs had no control over the businesses. Thereafter, plaintiffs filed a seven-count complaint asserting: a violation of the Racketeer Influence and Corrupt Organizations Act ("RICO") against defendants Rosenberg and Jaeger (Count I), violations of section 10(b) of the Securities Exchange Act of 1934 against Rosenberg and Jaeger (Count II), and Weinberg and Green (Count III), violations of section 12 of the Securities Act of 1933 against Rosenberg and MER (Count IV), common law fraud against Rosenberg and Jaeger (Count V), aiding and abetting liability under the securities laws against Weinberg & Green (Count VI), common law misrepresentation against Weinberg & Green (Count VII), and declaration of non-dischargeability in bankruptcy of debts owed by Rosenberg (Count VIII)...

* * *

On March 8, 1990, the district judge issued an opinion in which he accepted the recommendations to dismiss the counts against Weinberg & Green, but rejected the recommendation that plaintiffs be granted leave to amend these counts. Although the district judge noted that leave to amend should usually be freely granted, he concluded that since plaintiffs had amended the complaint twice, they did not deserve another opportunity to cure their defective pleadings. The judge noted that the plaintiffs never claimed that they could allege that Weinberg & Green had made any affirmative misstatements or other misrepresentations. Therefore, he doubted whether plaintiffs could ever plead a viable cause of action against these defendants.

On September 12, 1990, the Schatzes moved for reconsideration based on an opinion they had obtained from the Maryland State Bar Association's Committee on Ethics. The district court denied this motion, and the Schatzes appeal.

* * *

III.

Plaintiffs argue that Weinberg & Green committed fraud by remaining silent even though it knew that its client, Rosenberg, was financially insolvent. Plaintiffs allege in their second amended complaint that:

—Weinberg & Green provided legal services to Rosenberg in the past and in connection to the purchase of plaintiffs' business;

—Weinberg & Green had a copy of Rosenberg's financial statement, which it knew to be false as a result of legal services to Rosenberg and his various companies;

—Weinberg & Green prepared draft closing documents for the purchase of plaintiffs' business, which Weinberg & Green then delivered to plaintiffs' lawyers;

—Weinberg & Green gave plaintiffs a letter from Rosenberg at closing in which Rosenberg stated that no material adverse changes had occurred in his financial condition; and

—Weinberg & Green and plaintiffs' lawyers jointly agreed on language in the purchase agreement stating that Rosenberg had delivered his 1986 financial statement and an update letter to the plaintiffs, and that the letters were accurate in all material respects.

Based on these facts, plaintiffs argue that Weinberg & Green is liable (1) for violating section 10(b) of the 1934 Securities Act, (2) for aiding and abetting a violation of the securities laws, and (3) for knowingly perpetrating or assisting in misrepresentations under Maryland tort law.

b. *Duty of Disclosure Based on Maryland Law*

Plaintiffs also claim that the Maryland Rules of Professional Conduct obligated Weinberg & Green to either withdraw from representing

Rosenberg or to disclose his financial misrepresentations to the plaintiffs. In support of this claim, plaintiffs' counsel submitted to the Maryland State Bar Committee on Ethics an anonymous request for an ethics ruling on the facts of the present case. The committee concluded that a law firm in Weinberg & Green's position had an ethical duty to either withdraw from representation or disclose the misrepresentations to the third person. This ethical responsibility, plaintiffs argue, establishes a legal duty to disclose and subjects Weinberg & Green to section 10(b) liability.

We reject this argument. An ethical duty of disclosure does not create a corresponding legal duty under the federal securities laws. Courts have consistently refused to use ethical codes to define standards of civil liability for lawyers... More specifically, courts have refused to base a legal duty of disclosure for section 10(b) on a disciplinary rule...

The rationale for these rulings is clear. The ethical rules were intended by their drafters to regulate the conduct of the profession, not to create actionable duties in favor of third parties. The preliminary statement to the Model Code, upon which the Maryland code is patterned, warns that the Code does not "undertake to define standards for civil liability of lawyers for professional conduct." Preliminary Statement, Model Code of Professional Responsibility. We believe this statement accurately reflects the goals and purposes of the Maryland Code of Professional Responsibility. Thus, we hold that the ethical rules do not create a legal duty of disclosure on lawyers and that plaintiffs cannot base a securities fraud or other misrepresentation claim on a violation of an ethical rule.

We also hold that Maryland common law does not impose a duty to disclose under these circumstances. In the negligence context, Maryland courts have held that a lawyer only owes a duty to his clients or third party beneficiaries of the attorney-client relationship... Applying such rule to the facts of this case, we hold that because plaintiffs were neither clients nor third party beneficiaries of the attorney-client relationship, Weinberg & Green had no duty to disclose.

Plaintiffs rely on *Crest Investment Trust, Inc. v. Comstock*, 23 Md.App. 280, 327 A.2d 891 (1974), to establish a common law duty of disclosure for lawyers. However, this case says nothing about whether an attorney owes a duty of disclosure to persons who are not his clients. *Comstock* involved a lawyer who had a conflict of interest because he tried to represent both sides in a transaction, and, therefore, the lawyer owed a duty of disclosure to both sides. Thus, *Comstock* does not impose a duty of disclosure on a lawyer to a third party the lawyer does not represent. In this case, plaintiffs do not allege that Weinberg & Green represented them; in fact, plaintiffs admit that they were represented by their own chosen lawyers. Thus, the facts of *Comstock* are not analogous to this case.

c. *Duty of Disclosure Based on Public Policy*

Precedent aside, plaintiffs also argue that, as a matter of public policy, lawyers should not be permitted to perpetrate or assist in a fraud without being held responsible for their wrongdoing. Plaintiffs' counsel urges the court to rule that a lawyer has a duty to disclose misrepresentations to innocent third parties on the basis of public policy. While we sympathize with plaintiff's position and certainly do not condone lawyers making misrepresentations, we find that public policy counsels against imposing such a duty. Attorney liability to third parties should not be expanded beyond liability for conflicts of interest. Any other result may prevent a client from reposing complete trust in his lawyer for fear that he might reveal a fact which would trigger the lawyer's duty to the third party. Similarly, if attorneys had a duty to disclose information to third parties, attorneys would have an incentive not to press clients for information. The net result would not be less securities fraud. Instead, attorneys would more often be unwitting accomplices to the fraud as a result of being kept in the dark by their clients or by their own reluctance to obtain information. The better rule—that attorneys have no duty to "blow the whistle" on their clients—allows clients to repose complete trust in their lawyers. Under those circumstances, the client is more likely to disclose damaging or problematic information, and the lawyer will more likely be able to counsel his client against misconduct.

Other federal courts have arrived at similar conclusions in addressing the policy concerns of this identical issue. The Fifth Circuit explained that

> It is well understood in the legal community that any significant increase in attorney liability to third parties could have a dramatic effect upon our entire system of legal ethics. An attorney required by law to disclose "material facts" to third parties might thus breach his or her duty, required by good ethical standards, to keep attorney-client confidences. Similarly, an attorney required to declare publicly his or her legal opinion of a client's actions and statements may find it impossible to remain as loyal to the client as legal ethics properly require.

Abell v. Potomac Ins. Co., 858 F.2d 1104, 1124 (5th Cir.1988), *vacated on other grounds*, 492 U.S. 914, 109 S.Ct. 3236, 106 L.Ed.2d 584 (1989) (footnotes omitted).

Likewise, the Seventh Circuit, in the accounting context, refused to impose a duty of disclosure based upon policy reasons:

> Such a duty would prevent the client from reposing in the accountant the trust that is essential to an accurate audit. Firms would withhold documents, allow auditors to see but not copy, and otherwise emulate the CIA, if they feared that access might lead to destructive disclosure—for even an honest firm may fear that one of its accountant's many auditors would misunderstand the situation and ring the tocsin needlessly, with great loss to the firm.

DiLeo v. Ernst & Young, 901 F.2d 624, 629 (7th Cir.), *cert. denied,* 498 U.S. 941, 111 S.Ct. 347, 112 L.Ed.2d 312 (1990) (accountant under no legal duty to blow whistle on client upon discovery that client was in financial trouble). Therefore, we hold that public policy interests protected by the attorney-client relationship outweigh any public policy interests served by imposing a duty of disclosure like the one urged by the plaintiffs in this case.

2.   Affirmative Misrepresentations by Weinberg & Green

Plaintiffs also claim that Weinberg & Green violated section 10(b) by making various affirmative misstatements. Plaintiffs complain that Weinberg & Green informed plaintiffs' attorney that it would supply an update letter which would state that Rosenberg's financial position had not materially changed as of December 31, 1986. Weinberg & Green then presented the update letter to plaintiffs' counsel. The letter misrepresented Rosenberg's financial position, and the agreement and closing documents drafted by Weinberg & Green contained representations made by Rosenberg that the financial statement was "true, correct, and complete in all material respects."

Plaintiffs never contend that Weinberg & Green made any representations other than those made by Rosenberg. In fact, plaintiffs only claim that Weinberg & Green stated that Rosenberg would supply an update letter and that Weinberg & Green forwarded the Rosenberg letter to plaintiffs' attorneys. Since Weinberg & Green made no independent affirmative misstatements, Weinberg & Green did not commit a primary violation of section 10(b). *See Friedman v. Arizona World Nurseries, Ltd.,* 730 F.Supp. 521 (S.D.N.Y.1990) (lawyers who drafted an offering which included an offering memorandum, a legal opinion, and a tax assistance letter not liable for misrepresentations in the offering memorandum since it was not a representation from the law firm). Weinberg & Green's drafting of closing documents which contained representations by Rosenberg does not mean that they warranted or promised that Rosenberg had been honest.

Plaintiffs also argue that Weinberg & Green should be liable for the affirmative misrepresentations that Rosenberg made under principles of agency law. *See* Restatement (Second) of Agency § 348 ("[a]n agent who fraudulently makes representations, . . . or knowingly assists in the commission of tortious fraud . . . by his principal . . . is subject to liability in tort to the injured person although the fraud or duress occurs in a transaction on behalf of the principal."). Plaintiffs apparently believe that, under general principles of agency law, whenever a lawyer incorporates a representation by a client into a letter, contract, or other document, the representation becomes the lawyer's as well as the client's. This argument inherently presents two issues: first, as a matter of law, whether an attorney-client relationship should be treated as a typical agent-principal relationship governed by the general laws of agency; and second, as a matter of fact, whether Weinberg & Green "knowingly assisted" Rosenberg in his fraud in its status as his agent as required by the Restatement section. We are reviewing only the legal sufficiency of the complaint, we, therefore, will only consider the first issue which requires a ruling of law.

There are numerous similarities between an attorney-client relationship and an agent-principal relationship, and a lawyer may act as an agent for a client in various financial transactions, such as when the lawyer negotiates the terms of the transaction for the client. However, the fact that an attorney is an agent in that he represents his client does not automatically make the attorney liable under agency law for misrepresentations his client makes. Regardless of what plaintiffs wish the law required of lawyers, lawyers do not vouch for the probity of their clients when they draft documents reflecting their clients' promises, statements, or warranties. Thus, Weinberg & Green's alleged transmission of Rosenberg's misrepresentations does not transform those misrepresentations into the representations of Weinberg & Green.

In *Friedman v. Arizona World Nurseries*, Ltd., 730 F.Supp. 521 (S.D.N.Y.1990) the court considered whether to dismiss a complaint under Section 10(b) and Rule 10b–5 against a law firm that drafted an offering memorandum and a legal opinion and tax assistance letter included in the memorandum. The court determined that, with respect to "the only parts of the memorandum which arguably contain representations from [the law firm] to the limited partners"—the legal opinion and the tax assistance letter—plaintiffs failed to identify any misrepresentations. Id. at 533–34. As for the remainder of the offering memorandum, the court declared that "counsel who merely draft [an offering memorandum] cannot be held liable for the general statements in the offering memorandum not specifically attributed to them." Id. at 533.

We find this reasoning persuasive and therefore hold that a lawyer or law firm cannot be liable for the representations of a client, even if the lawyer incorporates the client's misrepresentations into legal documents or agreements necessary for closing the transaction. In this case, Weinberg & Green merely "papered the deal," that is, put into writing the terms on which the Schatzes and Rosenberg agreed and prepared the documents necessary for closing the transactions. Thus, Weinberg & Green performed the role of a scrivener. Under these circumstances, a law firm cannot be held liable for misrepresentations made by a client in a financial disclosure statement.

* * *

Weinberg & Green substantially assisted the fraud by "participating in negotiations, drafting documents and conducting the Closing at its offices."

* * *

The plaintiffs also allege that Weinberg & Green provided substantial assistance to Rosenberg by representing him in the transaction. They argue that a lawyer provides "substantial assistance" in aiding and abetting tortious conduct if he prepares or disseminates documents containing material misrepresentations or omissions. However, the "substantial assistance" element requires that a lawyer be more than a scrivener for a client; the lawyer must actively participate in soliciting sales or negotiating terms of the deal on behalf of a client to have "substantially assisted" a securities violation. In other words, a plaintiff must prove that a defendant rendered "substantial assistance" to the primary securities law violation, not merely to the person committing the violation.

If a lawyer, for example, is a member of the investment group, acts as an general agent for the investment group and not merely its attorney, or actively participates in the transaction by inducing or soliciting sales or by negotiating terms of the deal, the lawyer may be held liable for substantially assisting a securities violation. However, when a lawyer offers no legal opinions or affirmative misrepresentations to the potential investors and merely acts a scrivener for the investment group, the lawyer cannot be liable as a matter of law for aider and abettor liability under the securities laws without an allegation of a conscious intent to violate the securities laws...

In this case, Weinberg & Green did no more than "paper the deal" or act as a scrivener for Rosenberg. These activities cannot form the basis for a securities violation since plaintiffs never allege any facts tending to show an intent on Weinberg & Green's part to violate the securities laws. While it is true that some of Rosenberg's documents prepared by Weinberg & Green (on the basis of information provided by Rosenberg) were misleading, this fact alone does not meet the "substantial assistance" threshold. Otherwise, there would be a per se rule holding attorneys liable in every securities fraud case, because in virtually every transaction, attorneys draft the closing documents. Clearly, the fact that an attorney drafts a closing document does not automatically create a warranty that every statement and agreement made by the client is true. Any other result would make attorneys co-guarantors and co-signatories, along with their clients, in every securities transaction.

C. Liability for Knowingly or Recklessly Perpetuating a Misrepresentation under Maryland Tort Law

IV.

The extent of a law firm's liability for knowingly incorporating a client's misrepresentations into closing documents for a financial transaction presents troubling legal issues. However, we do not sit as an ethics or other attorney disciplinary committee, but as a civil court with a duty to interpret the securities laws, and the solution to these legal issues cannot be found in the securities laws. As the Seventh Circuit stated in *Barker v. Henderson, Franklin, Starnes & Holt*, 797 F.2d 490 (7th Cir.1986):

> We express no opinion on whether the [law firm] did what [it] should, whether there was malpractice under state law, or whether the rules of ethics ... ought to require lawyers and accountants to

blow the whistle in equivalent circumstances. We are satisfied, however, that an award of damages under the securities laws is not the way to blaze the trail toward improved ethical standards in the legal and accounting professions. Liability depends on an existing duty to disclose. The securities laws therefore must lag behind changes in ethical and fiduciary standards.

Id. at 497 (emphasis in original). We agree with this statement of policy and affirm the order of the district court.

AFFIRMED.

SECURITIES AND EXCHANGE COMMISSION v. SPECTRUM, LTD.

489 F.2d 535 (2nd Cir. 1973)

IRVING R. KAUFMAN, CHIEF JUDGE:

The securities laws provide a myriad of safeguards designed to protect the interests of the investing public. Effective implementation of these safeguards, however, depends in large measure on the members of the bar who serve in an advisory capacity to those engaged in securities transactions. The standard of diligence demanded of the legal profession to meet this responsibility is a matter on which we are required to comment in the resolution of this appeal.

On April 2, 1971, the Securities and Exchange Commission (SEC) filed a complaint charging twelve defendants, including the appellee, Stuart Schiffman, with participation in a partially successful scheme to distribute over one million unregistered shares of the common stock of Spectrum, Ltd. in violation of the registration provisions of the Securities Act of 1933 (the 1933 Act) and the antifraud provisions of that Act and of the Securities Exchange Act of 1934 (the 1934 Act). Although the Commission has obtained permanent injunctions against at least ten of the defendants, it was unsuccessful in its effort to gain preliminary injunctive relief against Schiffman, an attorney who allegedly prepared an opinion letter on the basis of which some of the unregistered securities were sold. Judge Tenney, after reviewing the affidavits, cross-affidavits, exhibits, and depositions filed by the SEC and by Schiffman, denied the SEC's request for an evidentiary hearing, on the grounds that there were no material facts in dispute, and concluded that Schiffman's conduct, although perhaps negligent, did not rise to a violation of the securities laws. Upon a careful examination of the record, we find the existence of a highly material factual conflict. Accordingly, we reverse and remand to Judge Tenney for an evidentiary hearing in which the disputed issues can be resolved.

I.

* * *

In September, 1969, Louis Marder, representing the Westward Investment Corporation, and Bernard Goldenberg and Joseph Dye, representing Spectrum, Ltd., agreed to a merger of Westward into Spectrum. The purpose of this merger was to provide a vehicle for the distribution of unregistered Spectrum securities which could later be sold to an unwitting public.

Section 5(c) of the 1933 Act states that 'it shall be unlawful for any person, directly or indirectly ... to sell ... any security unless a registration statement has been filed as to such security.' To avoid this registration requirement, a plan was devised, principally by Marder and Goldenberg, which relied on a two-step procedure for securing exemption from Section 5. First, a large block of unregistered Spectrum common stock would be issued to the shareholders of Westward in the merger of Westward into Spectrum. This stock would be exempt from the registration mandate of Section 5 pursuant to Commission Rule 133 [now repealed and replaced by Rule 145], which provided that the exchange of shares between a surviving corporation and the shareholders of a disappearing corporation in the course of a merger would not be considered a 'sale' within the purview of Section 5. Second, under Section 4(1) of the 1933 Act, the recipients of this unregistered Spectrum stock would be able to dispose of these securities, again without the filing of a registration statement as a predicate to the transaction, as long as the seller was not deemed to be 'an issuer, underwriter or dealer' under the Act.

For Marder, who controlled Westward, successful implementation of this plan presented one obvious stumbling block—Rule 133 classified a controlling shareholder of the 'constituent corporation' (Westward) as an 'underwriter' and, therefore, a person not qualified for exemption under Section 4(1). Accordingly, prior to the merger Marder commenced distributing some of his Westward shares to various friends, many of whom, as the court below found, were in fact unaware of their status as Westward shareholders. Following the merger, Marder intended to effect the sale of the Spectrum stock received by his acquaintances in transactions which, because of the stock's nominal ownership by non-controlling former Westward shareholders, would appear to satisfy the criteria for a Section 4(1) exemption.

The stage was set for the successful charade upon consummation of the Spectrum–Westward merger on November 10, 1969. Of the 4,596,465 shares of Spectrum stock issued in the exchange, approximately one million shares went to Marder's corps of nominees. By obtaining the necessary stock powers from these individuals, Marder was in a position to begin the illicit sale of unregistered Spectrum securities.

On the day of the merger, November 10, Spectrum's general counsel, Morton Berger, wrote an opinion letter to Spectrum's transfer agent in which he instructed the agent on the proper classification of the Spectrum shares then being issued. Berger's letter, based upon representations by Goldenberg and Marder, included his opinion that the merger complied with the requirements of Rule 133 and that certain recipients of the newly-issued Spectrum stock should receive shares labelled 're-stricted'—i.e. not for public sale—because these former Westward share-holders, whom Berger listed, were considered to be 'underwriters' pursu-ant to Rule 133(c). Berger concluded his letter by opining that the remaining former Westward shareholders, whose names Berger did not recite, could be issued Spectrum securities without a restrictive legend.

On November 25, 1969, Berger wrote a second letter, this time to the president of Spectrum, in which he listed those persons who had received unrestricted shares of Spectrum stock pursuant to the merger. This letter, however, was not in the form of an opinion letter

Retracing our steps, on November 13 and November 28, 1969, Marder delivered for sale a total of 125,000 shares of unrestricted Spectrum stock, nominally owned by William and John Doyen, to Mi-chael Gardner, a principal at the registered broker-dealer firm of Gard-ner Securities. Gardner balked at the sale of these unregistered securi-ties, despite their unrestricted nature, insisting upon an opinion letter which stated that these shares were considered exempt from the regis-tration requirements of Section 5. Although Marder possessed the Ber-ger letters of November 10 and November 25, Gardner viewed them as insufficient, apparently because the November 10 letter failed to specify the individuals entitled to exemption, while the November 25 letter did not purport to be an opinion letter.

Although Gardner called Berger about preparing the requisite opin-ion letter, Berger refused to issue such a letter on behalf of any shareholder. Because of this refusal, Gardner communicated with Schiff-man stating that he wished to discuss a securities matter the details of which Gardner failed to provide on the telephone. Schiffman responded by meeting Gardner at his office.

It is at this juncture—Schiffman's debut so to speak—that the crucial factual controversy arises. According to Schiffman's affidavit submitted in opposition to the motion for a preliminary injunction, he visited Gardner's office twice in late November. On the first occasion, he and Gardner spoke in general terms about Gardner's securities business and Gardner introduced him to James Morse, one of Gardner's clients. At the second meeting, several days later, Morse was again present at Gardner's office. On this occasion, Morse mentioned that a friend of his, a Mr. Doyen, was in need of some help and asked Schiffman if he would speak to Doyen. After Schiffman agreed, Morse telephoned Doyen. Morse handed the instrument to Schiffman and Doyen proceeded to explain to Schiffman that he owned some unregistered stock in Spectrum, Ltd. for which he wanted an opinion letter that would indicate that the securities could be sold without registration. Schiffman allegedly responded that since he had no knowledge of the underlying transactions, he would be hesitant to write such a letter. But, Schiffman claims that his reluctance was overcome when Morse showed him the two Berger letters. Schiffman then proceeded to advise Doyen that he would prepare an opinion letter which would 'verify' Berger's opinion.

Schiffman's version of these meetings at Gardner's office is sharply in conflict with Gardner's recollection of the events, as described in his affidavit submitted by the SEC. Gardner recalls only one meeting with Schiffman at which not only Morse was present but Louis Marder as well. Gardner's affidavit then notes, quite specifically, that

I (Gardner) introduced Schiffman to Marder and Morse for the purpose of Schiffman representing Marder and Morse. Marder and Morse asked Schiffman, in my presence, to prepare an opinion letter for securities of Spectrum that were going to be sold by Marder an Morse.

The affidavit concludes with the statement:

I do not recall at any time ... Morse telephoning one William Doyen, giving the telephone to Schiffman, and Schiffman speaking to Doyen about an opinion letter to be prepared by Schiffman concerning either Doyen's stock, or any other stock.

In any event, Gardner was evidently satisfied that Schiffman would write the opinion letter because, sometime before its preparation, he proceeded to sell 50,000 shares of Spectrum stock jointly owned by the Doyens. As for Schiffman, he claims to have arranged a conference with Berger so that he could learn more about the Spectrum stock for which he had agreed to write an opinion letter.

What transpired at this meeting between Schiffman and Berger is also the subject of conflicting documentary versions. Both men agree that Berger gave Schiffman the two letters dated November 10 and November 25. Berger, however, in his affidavit submitted in the preliminary injunction proceeding, added that he warned Schiffman that he 'suspected that this stock (the unregistered Spectrum securities) was going to be traded by a control person and therefore the stock should not be freely traded.' This account did not appear in Berger's two prior depositions, also part of the record below. Schiffman, on the other hand, in his reply affidavit, denied that Berger uttered any warning whatsoever.

It is uncontroverted that following this meeting Schiffman prepared an opinion letter which closely paralleled the Berger opinion letter of November 10 with one key addition—it contained the names of those shareholders, mentioned only as a group by Berger, who could sell their Spectrum stock in a transaction exempt from the registration requirement of Section 5. Although Schiffman's letter, dated December 4, was addressed to Doyen, Schiffman delivered it to Gardner's office because Schiffman had never received Doyen's address. Subsequently, on December 8, Schiffman sent a second letter to Doyen, again through Gardner's office, in which Schiffman stated that his opinion letter of December 4 was not to be used for the sale of unregistered Spectrum stock. No such caveat, however, was incorporated in the December 4 letter.

The use to which Schiffman's opinion letter of December 4 was put is a matter of some uncertainty. The SEC has alleged that in January, 1970, Marder showed the Schiffman letter to 'Canadian citizen #1' in order to assure this anonymous Canadian that the Spectrum shares that he had agreed to purchase from Marder could be traded without registration. The SEC charges that 'Canadian citizen #1' subsequently sold 15,000 shares of this unregistered Spectrum stock in the Canadian market. Although these allegations were never contested by Schiffman, they also remain unsupported by any independent evidence.

Eighteen months after this documentary joust commenced, Judge Tenney, on October 10, 1972, denied the SEC's request for a preliminary injunction to enjoin Schiffman from further violations of §§ 5(a), 5(c) and 17(a) of the 1933 Act and § 10(b) of the 1934 Act. He concluded that there was no evidence, apart from the bare allegations by the SEC, that any unregistered Spectrum stock had been sold on the basis of Schiffman's opinion letter. Recognizing that Schiffman might still have violated the securities laws as an aider and abettor, the district court, after pronouncing a standard of liability which required actual knowledge of the illegal scheme, found a dearth of credible evidence in the papers before him to sustain a finding of such knowledge on Schiffman's part. Judge Tenney finally noted that even if Schiffman were considered negligent in preparing his opinion letter, there had been no showing that, unless enjoined, he would be likely to run afoul of the law in the future.

II.

* * *

* * * Examination of this record discloses a sharp factual conflict bearing heavily on the critical question of Schiffman's actual knowledge of the scheme to illicitly distribute unregistered Spectrum stock at the time he agreed to draft the December 4 opinion letter.

On Schiffman's part, he has steadfastly maintained that he was ignorant of the Marder plan. Yet, these protestations of innocence are met squarely on two fronts—by the affidavits of Gardner and Berger. Although we do not disagree with the district court that the Berger affidavit would seem to be incredible on its face in light of Berger's failure to make any mention of his alleged warning to Schiffman in the course of two prior depositions, we cannot overlook the dispute between Gardner and Schiffman over the events and participants at the crucial meeting at Gardner's office in late November, 1969. If Gardner's statement that Marder personally asked Schiffman for an opinion letter so that Marder could sell unregistered Spectrum stock is true—and only a hearing could determine this—then Schiffman's claim of unawareness of the scheme would appear thin. To be sure, Gardner's veracity may be questioned, but no more nor less than Schiffman's, in view of Schiffman's stake in the outcome of this lawsuit. Accordingly, since oral testimony is a medium far superior for evaluating credibility than the cold written word, we consider an evidentiary hearing essential to the proper disposition of this case. See SEC v. Frank, 388 F.2d 486 (2d Cir.1968).

III.

* * *

We do not believe, moreover, that imposition of a negligence standard with respect to the conduct of a secondary participant is overly strict, at least in the context of this case. The legal profession plays a unique and pivotal role in the effective implementation of the securities laws. Questions of compliance with the intricate provisions of these statutes are ever present and the smooth functioning of the securities markets will be seriously disturbed if the public cannot rely on the expertise proffered by an attorney when he renders an opinion on such matters. Schiffman, himself, realized that his opinion letter of December 4 could be used in due course to sell unregistered securities and sought to prevent that use by his subsequent letter to Doyen of December 8. This belated effort was ineffectual, however, since the limitation expressed in the second letter could hardly affect the potency of the December 4 opinion letter which remained unrestricted on its face.

We do not find persuasive the argument by one recent commentator that since 'the alleged aider and abettor will merely be engaging in customary business activities, such as loaning money, managing a corporation, preparing financial statements, distributing press releases, completing brokerage transactions, or giving legal advice, (a requirement that he) investigate the ultimate activities of the party whom he is assisting (may impose) a burden ... upon business activities that is too great.' Ruder, Multiple Defendants in Securities Law Fraud Cases: Aiding and Abetting, Conspiracy, In Pari Delicto, Indemnification and Contribution, 120 U.Pa.L.Rev. 597, 632–633 (1972). In the distribution of unregistered securities, the preparation of an opinion letter is too essential and the reliance of the public too high to permit due diligence to be cast aside in the name of convenience. The public trust demands more of its legal advisers than 'customary' activities which prove to be careless. And, to be sure, where expediency precludes thorough investigation, an attorney can prevent the illicit use of his opinion letter by prohibiting its utilization in the sale of unregistered securities by a statement to that effect clearly appearing on the face of the letter.

Nor does Professor Ruder's analogy to the strict scienter requirement for criminal liability of an aider and abettor seem appropriate to gauge the quality of conduct sufficient to warrant injunctive relief in a civil action. The disparate consequences cannot be glossed over when striking the balance between private rights and the public interest.

* * *

For the reasons stated, the order of the district court is reversed and the case remanded for further proceedings. * * *

PROBLEMS

1. TechPub, Inc. is a Delaware corporation that publishes a wide range of on-line specialty technology magazines. It was formed in 1997 by Lewis,

Monroe and Peterson who were its sole stockholders. The company sold additional stock in private placements in 1999 and 2000, using the funds to expand its highly successful business. In early 2005, it agreed to be acquired by International Press, a large multi-national publishing corporation for $300 million.

You are a partner in the law firm that TechPub has retained in connection with the acquisition. Your firm has never done any previous work for the company. In connection with the closing of the transaction, scheduled to be held in one month, your firm has been asked to give a legal opinion that includes the following provision:

> The company is duly incorporated, validly existing and in good standing under the laws of the state of Delaware. All of its capital stock has been duly authorized, validly issued and is fully paid and non-assessable.
>
> a) What must you do in order to make sure that this provision is correct?
>
> b) Assume that during your investigation, you discover that Lewis and Monroe had not fully paid for their stock at the time it was issued to them although the company had sufficient funds to begin operating. How do you proceed?

2. Robbins and Greenberg is a law firm whose principal office is in Philadelphia. It also has offices in Washington, Miami and San Diego. It has approximately 100 lawyers in its Philadelphia office and a total of 80 lawyers in its other offices. One of the clients of the Miami office is Collins Stores, Inc. ("Collins"), a chain of department stores in the Southeast. The firm has represented Collins since its inception in 1953.

In October 2000, Collins received a federal grand jury subpoena asking for records relating to certain payments that might be considered commercial bribery. Albert Devere, a partner in the Miami office, a former federal prosecutor and an experienced white collar criminal lawyer, was in charge of Collins' compliance with the subpoena. Two weeks later, Collins delivered documents pursuant to the subpoena. A week later, the Assistant United States Attorney advised Devere that the response was incomplete. Collins provided no further documents and for almost a year, there was no communication between the U.S. Attorney's office and Devere.

In June 2001, Collins agreed to be acquired by Stansbury, Ltd., a large English corporation with department stores throughout the world. Because the Miami office of the firm had little experience with large acquisition transactions, Susan Lester, a senior transactional partner in the Philadelphia office, represented Collins in the negotiations. As part of the acquisition agreement, Collins made the following representation:

> *Absence of Litigation.* Except as set forth in Schedule 2.10 of the Company Disclosure Schedule, there is no claim, action, suit, litigation, proceeding, arbitration or investigation of any kind, at law or in equity (including actions or proceedings seeking injunctive relief), pending or, to the Company's knowledge, threatened against the Company or any of its subsidiaries, and neither the Company nor any of its subsidiaries is subject to any continuing order of, consent decree, settlement agreement or other similar written agreement with or continuing investigation by,

any Governmental Entity, or any judgment, order, writ, injunction, decree or award of any Governmental Entity or arbitrator, including, without limitation, cease-and-desist or other orders.

In connection with preparing the disclosure schedule, Devere told Lester about the grand jury subpoena that Collins had received. At a meeting with Richard Harrison, the chief executive officer of Collins to discuss whether the subpoena should be disclosed in the schedule, Devere told Lester that he had not heard from the U.S. Attorney's office in eight months and that he believed that the investigation had been completed with no action taken against Collins. He also told Lester that several of Collins' suppliers had been indicted as a result of the investigation. Lester strongly advised Harrison to disclose but Harrison refused because of his fear that several large Collins shareholders who opposed the transaction might use the disclosure to try and break up the deal. At the closing, the schedule did not disclose the subpoena.

As a part of the closing, Robbins and Greenberg has been asked to deliver the following opinion:

> To our knowledge, except as set forth in Schedule 2.10 of the Company Disclosure Schedule, there is no claim, action, suit, litigation, proceeding, arbitration or investigation of any kind, at law or in equity (including actions or proceedings seeking injunctive relief), pending or, to the Company's knowledge, threatened against the Company or any of its subsidiaries, and neither the Company nor any of its subsidiaries is subject to any continuing order of, consent decree, settlement agreement or other similar written agreement with or continuing investigation by, any Governmental Entity, or any judgment, order, writ, injunction, decree or award of any Governmental Entity or arbitrator, including, without limitation, cease-and-desist or other orders.

How should the firm respond to this request? What additions or deletions should it ask for before agreeing to provide the opinion? In order to give the requested opinion, what investigation should the firm undertake? What internal procedures should the firm have with respect to rendering such an opinion?

Chapter 16

SECURITIES REGULATION: THE DISCLOSURE SYSTEM

The federal securities laws are an integral part of many business lawyers' practice. Whether representing public or closely held corporations, a lawyer must have a basic understanding of how those laws affect the business transactions in which the client engages.

Although the securities laws in their totality cover a wide range of subjects, most lawyers are primarily concerned with the Securities Act of 1933 and the Securities Exchange Act of 1934. The former deals primarily with the sale of securities by the issuing corporation and the resale of such securities by the purchasers. The latter, insofar as relevant here, deals with trading transactions in organized securities markets and the disclosure obligations of public corporations.

The heart of both statutes is disclosure. Whatever the context, the statutory regime contemplates that a corporation will disclose all the material information necessary for a reasonable investor to make an informed investment decision. Thus a critical role for a securities lawyer is to advise corporations on how to comply with the disclosure requirements to which they are subject. As you will see, that task is made more difficult when the corporation does not want to accept the lawyer's advice.

The materials on the federal securities laws are divided into two chapters. This chapter gives an overview of the securities laws and examines the role of the lawyer in the disclosure system. The next chapter treats the ways in which a lawyer may face liability for her conduct in securities transactions. These chapters do not deal with the conduct of the lawyer when defending a client who is accused of violating the securities laws. Although that is an important part of a lawyer's practice, it is no different than representing any client who is accused of violating the law. That representation is covered extensively in other chapters in the book.

OVERVIEW OF THE CHAPTER

Introduction

The first part of the chapter is an overview of the federal securities laws, focusing primarily on the Securities Act of 1933, the Securities Exchange Act of 1934 and the Sarbanes–Oxley Act of 2002 (SOX). If you have taken a course in securities regulation, this is a useful review. If you have not taken such a course, it is a good introduction to the material that will be covered in the next two chapters.

Attorney as Gatekeeper

The materials in this section present a conceptual framework for thinking about the role of the securities lawyer, in the disclosure system.

The phrase "gatekeeper" colloquially means that the lawyer stands between the corporation and the completion of a transaction. Whether giving an opinion or advising on disclosure, the lawyer is viewed as the means for stopping illegal conduct. Unless the lawyer opens the gate, the conduct cannot occur. As you read this chapter, consider whether that is an accurate description of the lawyer's role and the extent to which the lawyer voluntarily has accepted this role.

Former Commissioner A.A. Sommer Jr.'s speech is as relevant today as it was in 1974 when he gave it. Sommer contends that a lawyer is often closely involved in the substantive decision of her client. He is skeptical of undue reliance on the traditional view that a lawyer's function is limited to protecting the client's interests. Thus he maintains that a lawyer, without giving up that view, must exercise greater independent judgment when giving her advice, however uncomfortable that may be. It is scarcely necessary to note the prescience of his warning that lawyers' independence would be increasingly scrutinized in the years following his speech.

Reinier Kraakman's article is more theoretical and is not limited to securities lawyers. He argues that a gatekeeper is appropriate where enforcement against both the corporation and the individual wrongdoer fails to "elicit sufficient compliance at an acceptable cost." He notes that gatekeepers will face liability for performing their services and that it is important both to choose the correct people to be gatekeepers and to design their duties without imposing undue costs. For Kraakman, the success of gatekeeper liability turns on developing legal duties that will encourage the detection of illegal conduct without endangering the relationships that make gatekeeping possible in the first place. He concludes his analysis by looking at both directors and outside counsel as potential gatekeepers, noting the strengths and weaknesses of both. He does not accept the idea that securities lawyers always are, or ought to be, gatekeepers. Rather, he notes the nuanced relationships that may or may not make gatekeeping desirable.

John Coffee, on the other hand, after analyzing the history of the attorney as gatekeeper, urges the SEC to institutionalize the concept, at least with respect to the disclosure documents that the lawyer has assisted in drafting. Drawing on the certification requirements of SOX to which corporate executives are subject, he suggests that the SEC require a lawyer to certify that she believes the statements made in the disclosure document are true in all material respects and that she does not know of any material information that would make the disclosure not misleading. How likely is it that the SEC would adopt such a rule? What factors would affect the SEC's decision? As you read the remainder of the chapter, consider whether the rule would be consistent with what you believe the role of the lawyer in the disclosure process should be.

The last two pieces in this section show how strongly the SEC believes in the gatekeeper theory. Thirty years separate *Fields* and *Isselman* but the SEC continues to view the bar as owing some duty to enforce the securities laws while simultaneously representing clients. It is certainly true that the SEC does not have the personnel to enforce the securities laws against every violation. Does that mean that it is appropriate to conscript the lawyer into the agency's enforcement process? If not, where and how should the line be drawn? In answering those questions, don't forget the Model Rules and particularly Rule 1.2(d).

Materiality

If the disclosure system is the heart of the federal securities laws, materiality is the heart of the disclosure system. Other than specific SEC disclosure requirements, a corporation must disclose information only if it is material. Absent materiality, there is no duty to disclose.

Whether information is material is one of the questions most asked of a securities lawyer. The test of *TSC Industries* v. *Northway*, what a reasonable investor would want to know is easy to state but hard to apply, particularly when, as the Supreme Court said in *Basic, Inc.* v. *Levinson*, "the event is contingent or speculative in nature." In such a case, the Court adopted the "probability/magnitude" test, requiring balancing "the probability that the event will occur and the anticipated magnitude of the event in light of the company activity."

Materiality is almost always a question of fact rather than something to be determined on a motion for summary judgment. For the lawyer, the factual nature of the determination creates a problem when the client refuses to disclose information that the lawyer believes is material. If a court subsequently decides that the information was material, it is the client rather than the lawyer who will be liable. On the other hand, Model Rule 1.2(d) prohibits a lawyer from participating in conduct that the lawyer "knows" is unlawful. If materiality is a factual question, how much can the lawyer "know?" The SEC's rules adopted under SOX Section 307 that require a lawyer to go up the corporate ladder if the lawyer believes there has been a "material violation" of the securities laws simply complicate the lawyer's task.

Preparation of a Registration Statement

For a corporation that has never made a public offering of its securities, the process can be long and difficult. The registration statement used in such an offering is an extensive disclosure document covering every aspect of the corporation, its business, financial condition and management. Schneider, Manko and Kant make clear that the lawyer plays a central role in drafting the registration statement, and coordinating the various sources of information that the corporation must disclose and advising the corporation as to what that information must be. Not surprisingly, the advice often includes many determinations of materiality of the type described in the previous section.

In preparing the registration statement, the lawyer necessarily depends on the client to provide the relevant factual information. How much independent verification of those facts must the lawyer do? The report of the Association of the Bar of the City of New York concludes that the lawyer's role should be limited both as to factual investigation and determinations of materiality. Many securities lawyers would agree with this conclusion and it has a good deal of force. In evaluating the report, however, consider the biases that may underlie the report which appeared at a time when the role of securities lawyers was very much under fire (Commissioner Sommer's speech is contemporaneous with the report). Who were likely to have been the authors of the report? Given the potential for liability if lawyers were required to play an expanded role, how likely is it that the report would have reached a different conclusion? If you are troubled by the report's conclusions, consider the cost of greater factual investigation. No increased duty, after all, is costless. But to what extent should costs enter into a determination of a lawyer's duties?

The last part of this section deals with the due diligence defense available to defendants in an action involving material misstatements or omissions in a registration statement. The *BarChris* case is a landmark opinion, in part because it was written by a judge who had been an experienced securities lawyer before going on the bench. Although the facts are complex, consider what a lawyer preparing a registration statement should do to minimize the risk of liability for the various defendants. More important, note what Judge McLean says about whether the lawyer is an "expert" for purposes of liability and the consequences that would arise if he had reached a different conclusion. Does the fact that he removes the risk of securities law liability lessen the lawyer's duties when preparing the registration statement?

Continuous Disclosure

Most corporate disclosure occurs either in connection with the quarterly and annual reports that public corporations are required to file with the SEC or the press releases that corporations regularly issue. Disclosure is less likely to occur for most public corporations in registration statements because these corporations rarely make public offerings.

Although outside counsel does not always prepare such documents, their participation is not infrequent and the client often does not want to make the disclosures that the lawyer believes to be required.

The *Carter & Johnson* case raises the conflict between lawyer and client most directly. Although it is not the usual way to study a case, try and read the case as if you were the lawyers involved, faced with the disclosure questions as they arise rather than looking at the totality of the facts. How would you act at each point that the client disregarded your advice? Keep in mind that it is the client's decision rather than the lawyer's that usually governs. At what point, if at all, would you have withdrawn from representation? What would have been the consequences of withdrawal? Does the SEC give sufficient guidance to lawyers going forward in the last part if its opinion? Professor Painter clearly doesn't think so. This excerpt from the article you previously have read demonstrates his argument that a lawyer cannot completely distance herself from the client's conduct.

The last part of this section, the report of the examiner in the Spiegel bankruptcy raises similar questions. What should Kirkland & Ellis have done and when? How do you assess the role of White & Case in deciding not to file the required disclosure documents?

Sarbanes-Oxley

One of the most important provisions of Sarbanes–Oxley is Section 307 which mandates the SEC to adopt rules requiring securities lawyers to report violations up within the corporate hierarchy. Those rules, which the Commission adopted in January 2003, represent a major incursion of federal law into the regulation of lawyers' conduct, an area that traditionally had been left to the states. The rules make mandatory what Model Rule 1.13 had made optional (the last piece in this section compares the SEC and Model Rules) . They produced the final impetus that caused the American Bar Association to amend Model Rule 1.6 to permit disclosure of financial fraud. And they have created enormous controversy about the extent to which they will deter clients from freely talking to their lawyers.

The first part of this section is a detailed outline of the SEC rules by Simon Lorne, a former SEC general counsel. Because the rules themselves are complex, not easy to read, and not always in the sequence in which they would apply, Lorne has reorganized them so as to make clearer the stages at which events will happen and how the rules apply at each stage. He has also annotated the rules to identify the interpretative and practical issues that each rule presents. In addition to Lorne's outline, you should, of course, read the rules in the order in which they actually appear.

One of the arguments in favor of SEC regulation is that the SEC is more likely to bring enforcement actions against lawyers than are state bar authorities. Professor Perino questions that conclusion. He contends that the same institutional constraints that hamper state enforcement are likely to be present with the SEC. He argues that apart from budgetary limitations, the SEC will be reluctant to bring actions against large law firms either for fear of losing an important case, because SEC lawyers often go to such firms after leaving the Commission, and because the SEC is very much aware of the indeterminate contexts in which securities lawyers advise their clients. While the law may be clear in hindsight, it is often less clear when the advice is being given. That is why we suggest that you read *Carter & Johnson* and *NSMC* prospectively from the perspective of the lawyers giving the advice to their clients. It is too early to know how vigorously the SEC will enforce its rules, but Perino's critique is worth keeping in mind as you evaluate the rules themselves.

MODEL RULES: 1.2, 1.6, 1.7, 1.13, 1.16, 2.1

A. INTRODUCTION TO SECURITIES LAWS

James D. Cox, Robert W. Hillman & Donald C. Langevoort,
SECURITIES REGULATION: CASES AND MATERIALS

(4th ed. 2004)

THE FRAMEWORK OF SECURITIES REGULATION

A. SECURITIES TRANSACTIONS

The securities laws exist because of the unique informational needs of investors. Unlike cars and other tangible products, securities are not inherently valuable. Their worth comes only from the claims they entitle their owner to make upon the assets and earnings of the issuer, or the voting power that accompanies such claims. Deciding whether to buy or sell a security thus requires reliable information about such matters as the issuer's financial condition, products and markets, management, and competitive and regulatory climate. With this data, investors can attempt a reasonable estimate of the present value of the bundle of rights that ownership confers.

Securities are bought and sold in two principal settings: issuer transactions and trading transactions. As we shall see, the federal securities laws are structured differently for each of these settings.

1. Issuer Transactions

Issuer transactions are those involving the sales of securities by the issuer to investors. They are the means by which businesses raise capital—to develop, to grow, or simply to survive. The successful business is one that grows. Growth in sales, assets, and earnings can occur without the issuance of additional securities that would add new claimants to the firm's assets and earnings beyond those of its founders, but, frequently, in order to grow a firm must expand its ownership base. The sole proprietorship may take on a partner, the partnership may add partners, the close corporation may become publicly owned, and the public corporation may issue more stock or bonds to become an even larger company.

By far the most expedient form of issuer transaction is the private placement of securities. This entails the issuer selling securities to a select number of investors. On the small scale, a private placement includes a partnership or closely held corporation adding new owners. Large public corporations also engage in private placements when they raise large sums of capital through negotiated sales of securities to one or more financial institutions, such as an insurance company. In either case, special exemptions exist under the securities laws that enable private placements to escape the rigors of regulation.

On the other hand, the firm may not be able to raise all the capital it needs from a small number of investors. In this case, it must make a public offering of securities to a large number of diverse investors. We shall refer to such a public offering as a *primary distribution*. Whenever a large amount of securities is to be offered to the public, the selling effort usually occurs through a syndicate of broker-dealers, known as underwriters. An offering on behalf of a company going public for the first time is called an *initial public offering* (IPO).

2. Trading Transactions

In contrast to primary distributions, *trading transactions* are the purchasing and selling of outstanding securities among investors. Resales of securities may either be privately negotiated or occur through public markets. Those who hold securities in a small firm for which no public market exists generally can only dispose of their shares by privately negotiating with an interested buyer. An exception to this statement occurs when the amount of securities to be resold is so great as to support a public offering. This is called a *secondary distribution* and most frequently occurs when individuals who control the securities' issuer wish to sell some of their shares.

Resales of outstanding securities are much more easily accomplished when there is a pre-existing public market for those securities. The facilities through which outstanding securities are publicly traded are known as *securities markets*. The trading of equities in public markets in 2001 totaled $23.4 trillion (compared with $170 trillion in issuer transactions of stock that was publicly offered). SIA, Securities Industry Yearbook 2002–2003 at 834–836. It should be apparent that investors engaged in trading transactions are in need of information just as are those who purchase securities in a primary distribution. The considerations of whether and at what price to purchase IBM common shares on an exchange are identical to the considerations investors ponder when offered IBM shares in a primary distribution. As will be seen, the mechanics, practices, and rules for disclosure, as well as other activities, differ significantly for primary distributions and trading transactions.

B. THE LEGAL FRAMEWORK OF SECURITIES REGULATION

1. The Federal Securities Laws

a. The Securities Act of 1933[1]

Debate on the merits of a mandatory disclosure system began early in this century, but it was the Great Depression and the market collapse in October 1929 that provided the political momentum for congressional action that would over the course of a decade produce a collection of acts known as the federal securities laws. The first of the federal securities laws enacted was the Federal Securities Act of 1933 ('33 Act), which regulates the public offering and sale of securities in interstate commerce. The abuses prompting the legislation were legion:

> During the postwar decade some 50 billion of new securities were floated in the United States. Fully half or $25,000,000,000 worth of securities floated during this period have been proved to be worthless. These cold figures spell tragedy in the lives of thousands of individuals who invested their life savings, accumulated after years of effort, in these worthless securities. The flotation of such a mass of essentially fraudulent securities was made possible because of the complete abandonment by many underwriters and dealers in securities of those standards of fair, honest, and prudent dealing that should be basic to the encouragement of investment in any enterprise.
>
> Alluring promises of easy wealth were freely made with little or no attempt to bring to the investor's attention those facts essential to estimating the worth of any security. High pressure salesmanship rather than careful counsel was the rule in this most dangerous enterprise.

H.R. Rep. No. 85, 73d Cong., 1st Sess. 2 (1933).

Disclosure is the remedy the Securities Act embraces for this malady. The '33 Act and much of the federal securities laws are influenced by the regulatory philosophy championed by Justice Brandeis: "Sunlight is said to be the best of disinfectants; electric light the most efficient policeman." L.D. Brandeis, Other People's Money 62 (1914). The Act's disclosure demands apply to public offerings of securities that occur through the process of "registering" such an offering with the Securities and Exchange Commission (SEC). The following is a broad overview of the Securities Act's registration process * * *

Through the preparation of a registration statement, the Securities Act seeks to assure full and fair disclosure in connection with the public distribution of securities. The information issuers are compelled to disclose in their registration statements is set forth in the SEC regulations and covers all significant aspects of the issuer's business. The

---

1. In June 2005, the SEC adopted sweeping reforms for regulating the public offering process to take accord of the dissemination of information through electronic media. In reading the description of this process in this chapter, keep in mind some aspects have been changed by the new rules.

precise disclosure requirements are somewhat industry sensitive. In general, the registration statement must provide a thorough description of the issuer's business, property, and management. Extensive financial information must be disclosed, including certified financial statements for the current and several previous years as well as revenues and earnings for each significant product line. Management must also provide its analysis and review of the issuer's capital needs, solvency, and financial performance, including analysis of any variances in revenues or profits from the preceding year. A detailed description of the rights, privileges, and preferences of the offered security, as well as the existing capital structure of the firm, must be set forth in the registration statement.

Paternalism toward investors is evident throughout the SEC's instructions and guides to its disclosure regulations as it seeks to paint a somber picture on the issuer's prospects. This dimension of the '33 Act disclosure process is underscored by information appearing in the first section of the registration statement, where any "risk factors" that make the offering speculative must be described. Examples of such special risks are that there is no pre-existing market for the security (i.e., it is an IPO), that the issuer has recently experienced substantial losses, and that the nature of the business the issuer is engaged in or proposes to engage in poses unusual risks. The information filed by an "unseasoned" issuer with the SEC undergoes several drafts and reviews under the watchful and demanding eye of the SEC's Corporate Finance staff. Most of the registration statement's substantive information is also required to be disclosed in the *prospectus*. The need for care and honesty in the preparation of the registration statement is underscored by the exposure of the issuer's underwriters, officers, directors, and certain experts to civil liability for omissions and misstatements in the registration statement.

As can be seen from the above, the objective of the registration process is the production of a prospectus that includes most of the information disclosed in the registration statement. The prospectus is designed to provide all material information necessary for investors to fully assess the merits of their purchase of the security; the prospectus is the vehicle for stationing investors on as nearly an equal footing with the issuers and their underwriters as possible, with the hope their purchase is neither worthless nor overpriced.

The underwriters' selling efforts cannot commence until the registration statement has been filed with the SEC, and no sales or deliveries of securities may occur until the registration statement is effective. Nevertheless, extensive selling efforts commence after the registration statement is filed, at which time investor interest is orally solicited. Written offers during this period can only be made through a preliminary prospectus that embodies all the substantive information then contained in the registration statement. Once the registration statement becomes effective, written offers must be accompanied or preceded by a final prospectus that embodies the information current as of the date the registration became effective. Also, once the registration statement is effective, actual sales can be made, and the purchased securities can be delivered. The Securities Act's objective of full disclosure for public offerings of securities occurs through the registration process and the Act's compulsion for the distribution of a prospectus.

As will be seen in later chapters, Section 3 exempts numerous categories of securities from the Act's registration requirements, the most significant being those issued by governmental bodies, banks, and insurance companies, and Section 4 exempts securities sold in certain types of transactions. Importantly, the Act provides both private and public remedies to assure compliance with its provisions. Thus, Section 11 provides a private right of action for materially false statements in the registration statement, and Section 12 imposes civil liability upon those who sell securities in violation of Section 5's registration requirement as well as upon anyone who sells any security in a public offering by means of a materially misleading statement. The SEC's enforcement powers include the power to issue administrative cease-and-desist orders under Section 8A as well as to prosecute violations civilly in the federal courts under Section 20.

b.   The Securities Exchange Act of 1934

History and Philosophy. The disastrous market effects of the Great Depression were, of course, not borne solely by the purchasers of new issues. The decline in value of outstanding securities was dramatic and painful. For example, the total value of all New York Stock Exchange listed securities declined from a precrash 1929 high of $89 billion to $15 billion in 1932. Investor interest and confidence in markets evaporated overnight, and for many stocks, trading halted completely.

The causes of the crash were many, and most were unrelated to abusive practices. The precrash market was driven not by fundamentals, but by speculative frenzy. Speculating in stocks was something of a national pastime. For example, 55 percent of all personal savings were used to purchase securities. E.R. Willet, Fundamentals of Securities Markets 211 (1968). A significant amount of all investment was on margin, in which an investor borrowed most of the stock's purchase price. There was no limit on the amount of credit that could be extended to an investor for margin trading. Typically, the lender was the brokerage firm, which in turn borrowed the funds from a bank. So long as the stock price did not decline, substantial margin trading posed no harm to the investor or markets generally. However, once steam began to run out of the market in late 1929, lenders began making calls upon the investor to cover the amount that the securities' market value had declined below its purchase price. This produced a chain reaction as margin calls triggered sales of securities owned by overextended customers; sales made in response to margin calls further depressed stock prices, so that even more margin calls were made upon other investors, and so on.

Much of the hearings leading up to Congress' enactment of the securities laws was devoted to accounts of trading practices by unscrupulous market manipulators. The hearings produced reports that the bull market of the 1920s was the heyday of the crooked stock pools. These were devices used by brokers and dealers to create a false appearance of trading activity by simultaneously buying the same security they were selling. Innocent investors were attracted to the manipulated stock by its price and volume changes. Eventually, unwitting investors' orders provided all the upward momentum to the stock's price. And, as the price rose, the broker and dealers behind the scheme dumped their holdings at the higher price created by the unwitting investors' interest. More recent examination of market practices in the 1920s suggests that the congressional hearings greatly exaggerated the effect and existence of such abusive schemes, perhaps doing so for political purposes. *See* Mahoney, The Stock Pools and the Securities Exchange Act, 51 J. Fin. Econ. 343 (1999).

There also was plenty of evidence that stock prices were adversely affected by false and misleading information and that corporate insiders took advantage of their access to confidential inside information to further their own trading profits. Related to this was the absence of legal compulsion for publicly traded firms to make timely disclosures of material information or to publish even annual financial reports. A further problem was the belief that public corporations were not sufficiently responsive to their owners due to weaknesses in the proxy solicitation process.

An inventory of these market abuses is summarized in Section 2 of the Securities Exchange Act ('34 Act), which captures the popular and congressional view that stock prices reflected the actions of speculators, manipulators, and inside traders, as well as the gullible, but not the astute and the sophisticated. *See* Thel, The Original Conception of Section 10(b) of the Securities Exchange Act, 42 Stan. L. Rev. 385, 409 (1990). One of the great ironies of securities regulation is that, even though Congress when it enacted the '34 Act had a dim view of the overall sophistication of market participants, today many of the Commission's regulatory initiatives under the '34 Act are premised on the assumption that trading markets are dominated by sophisticated, resourceful investors. The irony of this underscores the breadth and flexibility of the '34 Act's provisions.

There is an important difference in style between the Securities Act and the Exchange Act. In the Securities Act, Congress empowered the Federal Trade Commission (FTC) to discharge a specific and well-defined task: the registration of public offerings of securities not otherwise exempt from the Act. The means, as well as the end result, are clearly and unequivocally defined in the Securities Act. In contrast, the Exchange Act is in large part a laundry list of problems for which Congress articulated neither the means nor the end objective. Instead, Congress, through Section 4 of the Act, created the Securities and Exchange

Commission and delegated to it the task of grappling with the problem areas.

The contrast in style between the two acts bears witness to the fact that compromises were necessary to assure passage of the Exchange Act whereas that was not the case for the Securities Act. Recall that the Congress that enacted the Securities Act also enacted in those heady first hundred days of Roosevelt's first term other legislative packages that greatly centralized the federal government's control over the economy, the most prominent piece being the National Recovery Act. Many of Roosevelt's advisers were urging upon him a similar approach to the regulation of securities practices. For example, then-Professor William O. Douglas, who would later become the second Chairman of the SEC before being appointed to the Supreme Court, was one who openly counseled Roosevelt that a disclosure-oriented approach was inadequate and that legislation was needed that directly involved the federal government in identifying the firms that should be permitted to approach investors with their public offerings and thus gave it an active role in channeling capital into industries the government preferred to nurture. *See, e.g.*, Douglas, Protecting the Investor, 23 Yale L.J. (N.S.) 521 (1934).

Despite the willingness of the New Dealers to embrace modes of direct government involvement in the economy's private sector, the Securities Act's exclusive orientation was disclosure, a clear victory for those who embraced a less intrusive federal role in capital markets. Landis, The Legislative History of The Securities Act of 1933, 28 Geo. Wash. L. Rev. 29 (1959). On the other hand, the Exchange Act as originally proposed envisioned strong federal control of the trading markets as well as important structural changes for the securities industry and its participants. The radicalism of these proposals energized the securities industry, and its representatives came to Washington with their own proposals. In the end, the '34 Act reflects the many compromises necessary to assure its passage. Indeed, the creation of the Securities and Exchange Commission itself was a concession to the industry, which felt it would fare better under an agency whose energies were focused exclusively on capital markets and the securities industry— the industry had found the leading regulators at the FTC to be formidable and devoted regulators. In the end, many of the pressing regulatory issues were unresolved in the '34 Act and were instead dumped into the lap of the newly created Commission, where the debate and compromise would continue. *See generally* J. Seligman, The Transformation of Wall Street, chs. 2 & 3 (3d ed. 2003).

Continuous Disclosure and Other Disclosure Provisions.

Whereas the Securities Act grapples with the protection of investors in primary distributions of securities, the Exchange Act's concern is trading markets and their participants. An important contribution to efficient trading markets is the '34 Act's system of continuous disclosure for companies required to register under its provisions. Three categories of companies are subject to the '34 Act's continuous disclosure requirements: companies that have a class of securities listed on a national securities exchange (Section 12(b)), companies that have assets in excess of $10 million and that have a class of equity securities held by at least 500 persons (Section 12(g) and Rule 12g-1), and companies that have filed a '33 Act registration statement that has become effective (Section 15(d)). Companies meeting any one of these requirements are called reporting companies.

Reporting companies are required to register with the SEC and thereafter make timely filings of the reports required by Section 13 of the '34 Act. Unlike the '33 Act's disclosure requirements, there is no additional requirement that '34 Act filings be forwarded to investors or market professionals. All registrants (domestic and foreign) are required to file with the SEC their '33 Act registration statements and their periodic reports under the '34 Act in electronic format (i.e., submissions occur through e-mail or the physical delivery of diskettes or magnetic tapes). This system is called EDGAR (Electronic Data Gathering, Analysis, and Retrieval System). Such filed information is available to anyone through the SEC's web site (www.sec.gov).

The most significant of the compelled reports is the annual report on Form 10-K, which is required to include an extensive description of the company's business, audited financial statements for the fiscal year, and management's discussion and analysis of the position and performance of the company. Quarterly reports on Form 10-Q are also required to be filed with the SEC. The disclosures on Form 10-Q include unaudited interim financial statements for the company as well as management's analysis of financial operations and conditions. A further report compelled by Section 13 is Form 8-K, which must be filed within a few days of the occurrence of a material development of the type specified in the form, for example, a change in control, credit downgrade, the acquisition or disposition of a significant amount of assets, the commencement of insolvency proceedings, a change in auditors, or the resignation of a director in a dispute over policy.

The SEC in the early 1980s adopted the process of "integrated disclosure," whereby certain companies registering securities under the Securities Act could fulfill many of the '33 Act's disclosure demands by incorporating into the Securities Act registration statement information from their Exchange Act (e.g., Form 10-K) filings. As we see in Chapter 4, integrated disclosure is limited to relatively large companies that have been reporting companies under the Exchange Act for at least one to three years. Integrated disclosure was the first step toward melding the Securities Act and Exchange Act so that their disclosure demands are complementary and their registrants' burdens lightened. Under integrated disclosure, issuers are required to file a registration statement with the SEC in advance of their offering, and there is a period of delay before the issuer can sell the registered securities. As will be seen, integrated disclosure reduces greatly the delay and costs that normally accompany registering securities.

The Act also requires those companies that are subject to the continuous reporting requirements because they fall within either Exchange Act Section 12(b) or Section 12(g), discussed above, to make full and fair disclosure whenever soliciting their stockholders' proxies and to otherwise comply with the numerous proxy rules the Commission has promulgated under Section 14(a). Through the Williams Act Amendments in 1968, disclosure by an outsider is required when more than 5 percent of a class of registered equity securities is or will be owned as a result of a tender offer or purchase. Other tender offer practices are also regulated as a consequence of the Williams Act Amendments.

Regulation of Exchanges, Broker-Dealers, and Market Abuses. Continuing its emphasis on regulating trading markets, the Exchange Act embraces a strong, active role for a variety of self-regulatory organizations (SROs). Two important types of SROs are each of the national securities exchanges and the National Association of Securities Dealers (NASD). * * *, [T]he SRO's regulatory role is played under the Commission's watchful eye. * * * The Exchange Act also seeks to protect the integrity of capital markets and investors by arming the SEC, as well as private litigants, with its antifraud and anti-manipulation provisions. * * *

c. Federal Regulation Beyond Disclosure: The Sarbanes-Oxley Act of 2002

In July 2002, the Sarbanes-Oxley Act was enacted and ushered in a new era of financial regulation for U.S. capital markets. As is seen throughout this book, with Sarbanes-Oxley Congress departed radically from its historical preoccupation of addressing investor protection via disclosure. Among other features, the Act sets forth broad prescriptions for corporate governance, authorizes the SEC to develop rules for professional conduct for lawyers, and regulates areas that have always been the province of the states, such as loans to officers and directors. The events that prompted Congress to act were many and are collectively referred to as the accounting and financial scandals of 2002. The scandals actually began in 2001 with the sudden collapse of Enron Corporation, the seventh largest American corporation.

Enron was a high-flying energy trading company whose aggressive management style consistently impressed Wall Street with ever-increasing profits and reports of an even brighter future. For five consecutive years before its collapse Fortune 500 executives had voted Enron as one of America's most innovative companies. But all that glitters is not gold. In early December 2001, Enron filed for bankruptcy protection, at that time the largest bankruptcy filing in American history. It was soon revealed that Enron's profits were fabricated by its executives, that its Big Five accounting firm, Arthur Andersen, had acquiesced in clear violations of accounting and reporting principles, that it appeared that two national law firms that advised it had not appropriately advised their clients of possible misconduct by senior management, and that financial analysts were co-opted by pressures from their investment banking colleagues to support Enron with "strong buy" recommendations as a means to garner lucrative investment banking business from Enron. *See generally* Report of the Staff to the Senate Committee on Governmental Affairs, Financial Oversight of Enron: The SEC and Private-Sector Watchdogs (Oct. 8, 2002). * * *

Sarbanes-Oxley would not have been enacted if Enron had been an isolated event. Enron's bankruptcy was soon followed by the financial collapse of approximately a dozen large public companies where there was also strong evidence of reporting violations and audit failures even more egregious than that which occurred in Enron. Moreover, over the course of the five preceding years the number of earnings restatements by public companies quadrupled. The final culminating event propelling the enactment of Sarbanes-Oxley was the revelation in late June 2002 that WorldCom's chief financial officer had overstated earnings over several quarters by several billions of dollars. Soon after making its own earnings restatements, WorldCom itself entered bankruptcy, supplanting Enron for the honor of the largest company ever to seek the protection of the bankruptcy laws. With the enactment of Sarbanes-Oxley the focus of the securities laws and the SEC is today significantly broader than disclosure. Sarbanes-Oxley does not alter the core features of the U.S. securities laws, but the Act introduces important procedural and substantive requirements for public companies as additional safeguards to protect investors. It is also apparent from this book's review of the regulatory initiatives ushered in by Sarbanes-Oxley that important areas of corporate governance are no longer solely a matter controlled by state law.

On the financial frauds leading up to the enactment of Sarbanes-Oxley and assessments of the Act, *see* Bratton, Enron and the Dark Side of Shareholder Value, 76 Tulane L. Rev. 1275 (2002); Cunningham, The Sarbanes-Oxley Yawn: Heavy Rhetoric, Light Reform (And It Just Might Work), 35 Conn. L. Rev. 915 (2003); Ribstein, Market vs. Regulatory Responses to Corporate Fraud: A Critique of the Sarbanes-Oxley Act of 2002, 28 J. Corp. L. 1 (2002).

* * *

e.   *The Organizational Structure of the SEC*

The SEC is an independent, nonpartisan agency created by the Securities Exchange Act of 1934; the '33 Act, until the creation of the Commission, was administered by the FTC. The Commission is composed of five commissioners appointed by the President to five-year terms, the terms are staggered so that one expires each June, and not more than three commissioners may be of the same party as the President. One of the commissioners is designated by the President to serve as the chairman of the Commission. The commissioners meet frequently as a deliberative body to resolve issues raised by the staff. The Commission's staff is organized into divisions and offices.

The SEC operates through four principal divisions. The Division of Corporate Finance has overall responsibility for administering the federal securities laws' disclosure requirements through its review of the registration statements for public offerings, quarterly and annual reports, proxy statements, tender offer statements, and other documents required to be filed with it. The Division of Market Regulation has responsibility to oversee the operation of secondary trading markets, including the registration and behavior of exchanges and broker-dealers. Responsibility for administering the Investment Company Act and the Investment Advisers Act is with the Division of Investment Management. The Enforcement Division is to the general public the most visible of all the divisions because of the publicity that frequently accompanies its investigations and prosecutions. Enforcement actions can occur via an administrative proceeding or in the courts. Criminal prosecutions, however, are within the exclusive authority of the Department of Justice attorneys, usually through the appropriate U.S. Attorney's Office, with assistance of the SEC enforcement staff.

B. THE ATTORNEY AS GATEKEEPER

Commissioner A. A. Sommer, Jr., THE EMERGING
RESPONSIBILITIES OF THE SECURITIES LAWYER

(1974)

For many years the sponsors of securities institutes and programs have been blessed with innumerable occasions to promote their wares: attorneys have flocked to programs on Rule 10b-5, then the *Texas Gulf Sulphur* complaint (at this point we all ceased to wait for the decisions and spent endless hours and days discussing simply the *charges*) was the focus, then *Bar Chris*, accountants' liabilities, and innumerable subtopics and variations of these. All of these and others have now been subordinated in interest to a single topic: the legal exposures of lawyers under the securities laws administered by the Securities and Exchange Commission. Anyone organizing a program to which he expects to entice lawyers in substantial numbers cannot safely omit this topic. The topic is, in the vernacular, hot, a best seller.

The event which triggered this interest, of course, was the filing of the complaint by the Commission against National Student Marketing Corp., its accountants, several of its executives, and most importantly from the standpoint of attorneys, two outstanding and prestigious law firms, one in New York, and the other in Chicago, and partners in the firms.

It was not just the filing of a complaint naming attorneys that triggered this intense and tense interest, for, after all, other attorneys had been named in Commission complaints, frequently because of conduct during their representations of clients and not because of other roles—director, officer, and so on. Clearly, the interest was heightened by the fact that for the first time old firms of recognized competence and integrity were named as defendants. I think many attorneys had read the travails of other less well-known counsel with the thought that these were not really relevant because of their obscurity and the absence of recognition of their firms as expert and knowledgeable, whereas the naming of firms of national prominence hinted that no one was immune. Everyone who worked in securities law suddenly felt vulnerable and exposed. Lawyers began to experience the trepidation and concern and uneasiness that began to afflict their accounting brethren many years ago as they began to realize that prestige, name, proud history, did not afford immunity against civil and even criminal action.

Attorneys have since the earliest days of the federal securities laws been at the heart of the scheme that developed in response to those laws. While their formal participation mandated by the '33 and '34 Acts was limited—the only reference to counsel was in Item (23) of Schedule A to the 1933 Act which required the inclusion in registration statements of "the names and addresses of counsel who have passed on the legality of the issue . . ."—nonetheless, the registration statement has always been a lawyer's document and with very, very rare exceptions the attorney has been the field marshall who coordinated the activities of others engaged in the registration process, wrote (or at least rewrote) most of the statement, made the judgments with regard to the inclusion or exclusion of information on the grounds of materiality, compliance with registration form requirements, necessities of avoiding omission of disclosure necessary to make those matters stated not misleading. The auditors have been able to point to clearly identifiable parts of the registration statements as their responsibility and they have successfully warded off efforts to extend their responsibility beyond the financial statements with respect to which they opine. With the exception of the financial statements, virtually everything else in the registration statement bears the imprint of counsel.

Counsel have been involved in many other ways with the federal securities laws. They are frequently called upon to give opinions with respect, principally, to the availability of exemptions from the requirements for registration and use of a statutory prospectus. None would deny the importance of these opinions: millions upon millions of dollars of securities have been put into the channels of commerce—not just sold once, but permanently into the trading markets—in reliance upon little more than the professional judgment of an attorney. In many, perhaps most, instances these opinions have been confined to questions concerning the technical availability of the exemption and have not been concerned with questions of disclosure, compliance with the somewhat amorphous mandates of Rule 10b-5 and other anti-fraud provisions of the federal securities laws.

Attorneys' opinions have played other roles as well. They are customarily rendered in connection with the closing of registered public offerings, both by issuer and underwriter counsel, and in those opinions conclusions with respect to disclosure begin to emerge. In opining that a registration statement complies as to "form" with the requirements of the Securities Act of 1933, often counsel may be saying more about the contents of the statement than he realizes and if his opinion goes to the question of the legality of the offering as distinguished from the securities, certainly clear questions concerning the adequacy of disclosure are raised.

In a word, and the word is Professor Morgan Shipman's, the professional judgment of the attorney is often the "passkey" to securities transactions. If he gives an opinion that an exemption is available, securities get sold; if he doesn't give the opinion, they don't get sold. If he judges that certain information must be included in a registration statement, it gets included (unless the client seeks other counsel or the attorney crumbles under the weight of client pressure); if he concludes it need not be included, it doesn't get included.

Securities lawyers have since the adoption of the 1933 Act stoutly urged that they play a limited role in this process, even to the point of continuing to insist, despite the requirement of Form S-1, among others, that there be submitted as a part of the registration statement an opinion of counsel concerning the legality of the securities being registered, that they are in no way "experts" within the meaning of Section 11. Beyond that, they have gloried in the occasional judicial acknowledgment of the limitations of their role.

We are consistently reminded that historically the attorney has been an advocate, that his professional ethics have over the years defined his function in those terms, that such a role includes unremitting loyalty to the interests of his client (short of engaging in or countenancing fraud). Whenever the effort is made to analogize the responsibilities of the attorney to those of the independent auditor, one is reminded that the federal securities law system conceives of the auditor as independent and defines his role specifically, whereas the attorney is not and cannot be independent in the same sense in which an auditor is independent. It has been asserted by very eminent counsel that, "The law, so far, [this was in 1969] is very clear. The lawyers' responsibility is exclusively to their own client." If this distinction is clear to lawyers, it is less clear to others.

I would suggest that the security bar's *conception* of its role too sharply contrasts with the *reality* of its role in the securities process to escape notice and attention—and in such situations the reality eventually prevails. Lawyers are not paid in the amounts they are to put the representations of their clients in good English, or give opinions which assume a pure state of facts upon which any third year law student could confidently express an opinion.

I would suggest that in securities matters (other than those where advocacy is clearly proper) the attorney will have to function in a manner more akin to that of the auditor than to that of the advocate. This means several things. It means he will have to exercise a measure of independence that is perhaps uncomfortable if he is also the close counselor of management in other matters, often including business decisions. It means he will have to be acutely cognizant of his responsibility to the public who engage in securities transactions that would never have come about were it not for his professional presence. It means he will have to adopt the healthy skepticism toward the representations of management which a good auditor must adopt. It means he will have to do the same thing the auditor does when confronted with an intransigent client—resign.

This may seem shocking to many ears, but I would suggest that these conclusions are already implicit in what the courts and the Commission have already said; more important, their foundations lie deep in the past.

Quite obviously the implications of the cases being decided and the convictions of the Commission being expressed through complaints which it files, even though, as I suggest, these are but manifestations of broad social trends, raise a host of questions concerning the manner in which attorneys should conduct their representation of clients. How does this affect the traditional attorney-client privilege? Does it undermine the relationship of confidence between attorney and client that has been so important to the bar in doing its work? Must the attorney "welsh" on his client when he discerns an illegal direction to his activities? Must the attorney, in short, become another cop on the beat?

I would suggest that the bar will make a serious error if it seeks to defend itself against the emerging trends by reliance upon old shibboleths and axioms. Society will not stand for it, any more than it will stand for the accounting profession saying that all it does is determine whether financial statements are prepared in accordance with generally accepted accounting principles and that it has no professional concern with their overall fairness or the adequacy of their portrayal of economic reality. Everyone has been shocked by the massive betrayal of public investors in recent years and inevitably the focus is upon the people and the process through which these debacles came about. This spotlight will, I predict, increasingly focus upon the role of attorney who is invariably a keeper of the stop and go signal.

I would not have you understand that I believe the attorney must become the guarantor of his client's probity any more than I would suggest that the auditor is the guarantor of the accuracy of his client's financial statements. Attorneys and auditors can be the victims of unprincipled clients as can the public and even regulatory agencies. And I would not suggest that whenever there is a financial collapse there is necessarily or invariably involved derelictions on the part of the attorney or auditor. But I do suggest that the role of the attorney, the conduct of the attorney, the competence of the attorney, the integrity of the attorney, and yes, in some measure, the independence of the attorney will be increasingly scrutinized.

Notwithstanding the efforts of the private bar and others to alleviate the uncertainties of the members of the bar who practice securities law, notwithstanding the discomfort and dangers of cancelled and sharply restricted insurance policies, I cannot help but conclude somewhat pessimistically that there will be several years ahead before the clouds begin to separate and the outlines of the landscape amid which we will practice for the remainder of our lives become clear. Society in general, the securities law in particular, is in a period of revolution and usually efforts to hasten the conclusion of a revolution are unavailing. The courts, and to some extent the Commission, are the conduits through which the forces causing change bring it about—and these instrumentalities move somewhat cautiously—case by case, problem by problem.

The Commission cannot remain quiescent in the face of the changes of our society and the demands which that society is making on all those who occupy positions of responsibility and learning. Furthermore, the Commission has the responsibility of constantly reexamining the standards which it demands of those involved in securities matters so that the interests of investors can be steadily advanced. Thus, conduct which might have been tolerable in other ages becomes unacceptable in these times. The accountants' conduct clearly comes under new, more urgent, more searching scrutiny. The standards by which directors carry out their responsibilities in publicly-held companies are similarly undergoing critical reexamination. It is not given to any group in society, and certainly not lawyers, to be insulated from the trends.

However, the Commission and its staff must be cautious in the steps it takes in realizing this enhancement of responsibility. All of us know of the dramatic and unfortunate impact any litigation questioning the conduct of a professional can have on his career, as well as his finances. Corporations can withstand legal attacks and go forward to thrive and not infrequently corporate executives can do the same. However, it is far more difficult for a professional to retain his community standing, his self-respect and his financial security after questions have been raised publicly concerning his integrity or his competence. The Commission and its staff must be extremely cautious when it is confronted with a seeming involvement of counsel in securities misconduct. It is too easy, too tempting to believe that an attorney always has knowledge or awareness sufficient to rouse inquiry into the misshapen schemes of his client. It is too facile to conclude that the presence of counsel is a necessary ingredient of every witches' brew. It is too easy to confuse vigorous, even commendable, representation of a client with countenancing misconduct. Before the Commission files a complaint, institutes a Rule 2(e) proceeding or makes a criminal reference, it must be as certain as it can be that it is not confusing counsel diligence for counsel coverup, that it does not demand a standard of conduct beyond that which can reasonably be expected of professionals.

I would urge that as lawyers we not be hesitant in representing our clients, but let us not be hesitant, either, in protecting those who rely, sometimes rather blindly, upon the protections of professional judgment. Corporate law lawyers are paid well, ultimately by society, for doing a professional job and assuming professional responsibility. Let us not, I urge, appear to society fearful and hesitant as we adapt to the emerging responsibilities of this age where consumer is king.

Reinier H. Kraakman, CORPORATE LIABILITY STRATEGIES
AND THE COSTS OF LEGAL CONTROLS

93 YALE L.J. 857 (1984)

Debate continues over how best to tap the private interests of enterprise participants to serve the public interest. In large part, proponents and critics of structural reform in corporate governance remain divided over whether participants within the enterprise or external institutions should define and police "responsible" corporate activity. Yet, questions concerning the self-regulatory potential of the enterprise are not limited to the corporate governance debate: They also surface in modest guise even within the existing framework of corporate regulation, a framework that relies primarily on corporate profit seeking under external legal constraints. In this more limited context, the question becomes how external controls ought to be crafted and enforced, and whom they ought to target. When, for example, can we rely on liability rules directed solely at the corporation to assure compliance with legal norms? When should we impose absolute legal duties and sanctions on individual participants in the firm as well? To analyze these narrower questions of self-regulatory capacity, we must go beyond a simple description of the formal duties that the law imposes on corporate participants. We must also ask how existing legal duties affect the actual incentives of corporate participants, and whether they do so in ways that yield the "right" amount of compliance with legal rules-bearing in mind that enforcing these duties is itself costly.

V.   GATEKEEPER LIABILITY AND ENFORCEMENT INSUFFICIENCY

Enforcement insufficiency occurs when both enterprise and individual penalties fail to elicit sufficient compliance at an acceptable cost. The distinction between enforcement insufficiency and sanction insufficiency is one of degree: Insufficient enterprise sanctions still leave open the possibility of sidestepping constraints on penalties by punishing managers; enforcement insufficiency results only after this alternative has also been exhausted.

Like sanction insufficiency, moreover, enforcement insufficiency is a relative concept. Just as sanctions are "insufficient" only if absolute managerial liability can provide cost-effective deterrence, so enforcement insufficiency exists only when there is a cost-effective enforcement alternative. Because our inquiry focuses on liability rules that operate on a firm's top participants, only one alternative remains: the possibility that civil or criminal liability can induce firm participants outside the circle of controlling managers to discover and prevent offenses. These outsiders are potential gatekeepers. The scope of their liability as gatekeepers depends on the reach of their duties to monitor for and respond to corporate wrongdoing.

General civil and criminal rules of secondary liability such as the aiding-and-abetting and conspiracy doctrines impose a limited form of gatekeeper liability on all firm participants. Yet without the gloss of an explicitly specified duty, these doctrines are default provisions, much like the general rules governing the indemnification of managers. They do not require any affirmative action, but only a passive refusal to facilitate a known ongoing offense. By contrast, true gatekeeper liability joins the risk of absolute liability with an active duty to monitor for offenses. It imposes liability on an entirely new class of innocent gatekeepers (in addition to controlling managers) to reduce enforcement costs, the frequency of offenses, or both.

Top managers themselves are also targets of an enforcement strategy akin to gatekeeper liability when they face absolute liability for delicts initiated by others. Absolute liability triggered by broad supervisory duties falls into this category, as does the startling prospect raised by United States v. Park of imposing strict criminal liability on a large firm's chief executive for corporate delicts-in Park, for unsanitary conditions in distant warehouses. But the paucity of such examples suggests how they differ from true gatekeeper liability. Controlling managers already serve as the firm's chief internal monitors of compliance under a regime of simple enterprise liability. Elevating their supervisory function to a legal duty enforced by personal liability would be useful only if enterprise liability alone failed to induce adequate supervision. If so, however, the question of when to impose such an expanded duty on managers would merely be a special case of the broader question of when to impose absolute liability on managers at all. By contrast, true gatekeeper liability is designed to enlist the support of outside participants in the firm when controlling managers commit offenses, that is, when the firm's internal monitors have failed.

The first requisite for gatekeeper liability is, of course, an outsider who can influence controlling managers to forgo offenses. For this reason, gatekeeper liability has received widest play in response to securities violations and similar "transactional" delicts rather than in response to wrongdoing that occurs wholly within the bowels of the firm. Gatekeepers can be drafted from among the many outsiders who supply specialized expertise to the managers of publicly-held corporations and facilitate their relations with constituencies outside the firm: outside directors, lawyers, accountants, and investment bankers. In fact, most of these influential outsiders have already been tapped for limited enforcement duty. Section 11 of the Securities Act of 1933, for example, imposes a duty on directors, underwriters, and accountants to investigate securities registration statements. Similarly, enforcement actions brought under the federal securities laws during the 1970's have expanded the potential liability of lawyers and accountants who have facilitated-or even failed to halt-clients' delicts. In a parallel development, the accounting standards provisions of the Foreign Corrupt Practices Act of 1977 require firms to institute reliable internal accounting controls and proscribe misleading statements by both officers and directors to the firm's accountants, without regard to scienter.

Despite their disparate roles, moreover, it is easy to see why outside directors, accountants, lawyers, and underwriters are likely targets for a gatekeeper liability strategy. Each has or might have low-cost access to information about firm delicts. Contractually or informally, each already performs a private monitoring service on behalf of the capital markets But most important, each is an outsider with a career and assets beyond the firm. At the very least, these potential gatekeepers face incentives that differ systematically from those of inside managers; in the usual case, they are likely to have less to gain and more to lose from firm delicts than inside managers. Indeed, gatekeeper liability can jeopardize not only the personal interests of individual lawyers and accountants, but also the larger interests and reputations of their respective firms or even of their entire professions.

This extensive reach of gatekeeper liability, in particular, suggests that it generally acts to magnify both the costs of compliance for innocent parties and the benefits of effective deterrence for guilty ones in comparison with liability imposed on controlling managers. Outsiders will be more reluctant than managers to risk personal liability on the firm's behalf. Thus, if these gatekeepers can detect offenses, it will be difficult-or at least very costly-to entice them into a conspiracy. Many offenses will fail because these outsiders prove impossible to corrupt, others will fail because the price of corruption exceeds its potential benefits, and still others will never be attempted in the expectation that they would fail for either reason. But regardless of the mechanism interdicting offenses, whenever potential offenders must employ incorruptible outsiders to gain legitimacy or expertise or to meet a legal requirement, gatekeeper liability will thwart a class of offenses that are unreachable through enterprise-level or managerial sanctions. Of course, firms will also pay for the risk of additional liability in the familiar ways. If outside gatekeepers cannot shift their liability risks, they will charge high risk premiums. In addition, they will have a powerful incentive to lobby for the overinvestment of firm resources in monitoring for offenses and against profitable but risky innocent conduct. In the extreme, they may even withdraw their services entirely from small or risky firms.

There is, however, much more to the economic analysis of gatekeeper liability than is revealed by this rough portrait of costs and benefits. Gatekeeper liability is qualitatively more interventionist and therefore more complex than the simple imposition of absolute liability on controlling managers. Its enforcement potential depends not only on the offense and the level of culpability that triggers personal liability, but also on the choice of gatekeepers and upon the design of their duties. Two problems deserve particular mention.

A.   The Market for Gatekeepers' Services

The first of these concerns is the sensitivity of potential gatekeepers to the risk of personal liability. While outsiders will tend to be more vulnerable to legal risk than insiders, the problem of gatekeeper incentives is actually far more tangled than this generalization implies. Corporate managers, for example, are usually free to control the selection and tenure of outside directors, lawyers, and accountants. Thus, it may be child's play for would-be offenders to select corrupt or captive outsiders who are only too willing to assume personal liability for a price. To evaluate this prospect, we must know a good deal more about managerial incentives in selecting outside participants: What are the incentives to employ reputable law firms and truly independent outside directors, and what are the costs of discharging them?

Similarly, we need to learn more about the specific structure of incentives on the gatekeepers' side of the market. What, for example, are the incentives of individual lawyers and accountants as distinct from the law and accounting firms of which they are members? Although facilitating clients' offenses may be anathema to established firms with deep pockets and venerable reputations, individual members of these firms may face a substantially different set of incentives, especially if derelict clients can aid professional careers, either inside or outside law and accounting firms. When members of established professional firms facilitate clients' offenses, they effectively expropriate and injure the firm's reputation. This element of "firm-specific capital" is among the firm's most valuable assets; it is uninsurable and, unlike the business of particular clients, it cannot be protected by diversifying the firm's clientele. Thus, the conflict of interest between the firm and its individual members turns the familiar problem of dual liability topsy-turvy. The question now becomes whether to extend liability from the individual to the firm even though the firm may be the more costly risk bearer and may also bear de facto legal risk from a loss of reputation even without formal liability.

B. GATEKEEPERS' DUTIES

Detailed analysis of the incentives on each side of the market for gatekeepers' services, however, is only one factor in predicting the potential efficacy of gatekeeper liability and the proper targeting of these liability rules. Another equally tangled problem is the cost-effective design of the potential gatekeepers' legal duties.

The success of gatekeeper liability hinges on the development of legal duties that encourage the detection and interdiction of offenses without overburdening the private relationships that serve as their vehicles. This requires the prudent crafting of circumscribed duties to monitor and to respond that, above all, do not ask too much from their targets. The design of duties is further complicated because potential gatekeepers from outside the firm can rarely perform both the monitoring and interdiction aspects of the enforcement function with equal facility. Thus, at least for complex offenses, gatekeeper strategies must ultimately focus on how enforcement might be exercised by an interacting network of gatekeepers. Once we fit the scope of liability to the enforcement function for individual gatekeepers, we already forgo any recourse to a fixed relationship between the nature of particular conduct and the sanctions imposed. The next step is fitting the duties and risks of individual gatekeepers to one another to create a secondary control system on the foundations of private contract.

For a simple illustration of such a system, consider the roles of outside counsel and board members. Lawyers may be able monitors of most offenses that are likely to surface in the course of legal research and advising, but they are poorly equipped to veto any but a narrow range of illegal transactions that depend on their direct facilitation-for example, the closing of an illegal merger or fraudulent agreement that specifically requires an attorney's legal opinion. By contrast, outside directors may be well positioned to interdict a broad spectrum of offenses, but they are singularly ill equipped to detect offenses in the first instance without expert assistance.Each of these natural weaknesses in enforcement capability must be considered in the design of gatekeepers' duties. One might, for example, impose a response duty on lawyers to report firm delicts to the board; this could exploit the gatekeeping strengths of lawyers and directors in tandem. Similarly, directors might be given the simplified monitoring duty of ensuring that the firm employs reputable outside counsel and of relying on counsel's advice.

Regardless of the structure of gatekeeping duties, however, the discomfiting fact remains that they depend upon private contractual relationships and business conventions that are themselves subject to continuing evolution and renegotiation, perhaps in response to the imposition of greater liability. Changes in the structure and provision of outsiders' traditional services can always alter the enforcement capabilities, individual incentives, and liability risks of potential gatekeepers. The oft-noted (but still undemonstrated) transfer of legal services from outside law firms to the offices of in-house counsel is an obvious example. Where it extends to the responsibilities of gatekeepers, it can reflect both genuine concerns for efficiency and a strategic response to the outside law firm's gatekeeping role.

An analysis of the scope of the director's longstanding statutory duty to monitor securities registration statements may serve to illustrate the limits of effective gatekeepers' liability. The leading judicial opinion construes this statutory duty to extend liability to newly-elected outside directors for failing to inspect personally the disclosure contents of registration statements. This construction accords easily with the capabilities of inside directors, who know the firm well. Yet it appears oddly harsh when applied to those outside directors who lack special insight into the firm's finances, and who might at best be expected to watch for indications that the registration is in reliable hands and that there is nothing suspicious about the behavior or reputation of the firm's managers, auditors, or counsel. To the extent that the Securities Act of 1933 now imposes a duty of personal inspection on all directors, however, the real problem may lie not in its overinclusiveness but in its constricted vision of gatekeeping possibilities.

Viewed broadly, the outside director's duty to inspect the prospectus raises the familiar question of when liability rules should permit risk shifting in a novel way. Allowing outside directors to discharge their duty of personal inspection through reliance on reputable lawyers, accountants, and managers authorizes a new form of risk shifting. Firms can insure their outside directors by employing reputable experts, and their directors will demand such expert coverage just as they require insurance or indemnification for their garden-variety legal risks. As long as the firm's experts, in turn, bear absolute liability for breach of their own gatekeeper duties, the loss of the outside directors' personal monitoring is unlikely to matter. The corollary, of course, is that the liability of experts who are best able to monitor for wrongdoing ordinarily must be absolute unless gatekeepers' liability is imposed solely to assure compensation for the victims of firm wrongdoing.

Thus, we return once again to the general problem of determining the proper allocation of legal risk among the firm and its participants. Gatekeepers' liability, like managerial liability, varies in its effectiveness and cost according to the extent to which, and the forms through which, these parties can shift legal risks. As with the other dimensions of gatekeepers' liability-the selection of gatekeepers and the design of their duties-risk shifting must be tailored to the realities of access to information and of influence over firm conduct for specific offenses.

* * *

John C. Coffee, Jr., THE ATTORNEY AS GATEKEEPER: AN AGENDA FOR THE SEC

103 COLUM. L.REV. 1293 (2003)

I.   WHAT IS A GATEKEEPER?

The term "gatekeeper" has frequently been used to describe the independent professionals who serve investors by preparing, verifying, or assessing the disclosures that they receive. Examples of gatekeepers include: (1) the auditor who provides its certification that the issuer's financial statements comply with generally accepted accounting principles; (2) the debt rating agency that evaluates the issuer's creditworthiness; (3) the securities analyst who communicates an assessment of the corporation's technology, competitiveness, or earnings prospects; (4) the investment banker who furnishes its "fairness opinion" as to the pricing of a merger; and (5) the securities attorney for the issuer who delivers an opinion to the underwriters that all material information of which the attorney is aware concerning the issuer has been disclosed properly. The underwriter in an initial public offering also performs a gatekeeping function, in the sense that its reputation is implicitly pledged and it is expected to perform due diligence services.

Structurally, gatekeepers are independent professionals who are so positioned that, if they withhold their consent, approval, or rating, the corporation may be unable to effect some transaction or to maintain some desired status. For example, institutional investors may be able to purchase the corporation's bonds only if an independent debt-rating agency rates them as being of investment grade. Similarly, a "clean" opinion from an auditor may be required by stock exchanges and the SEC if the corporation is to remain publicly traded. From a law compliance perspective, the existence of the gatekeeper offers an effective strategy for deterrence. Because the gatekeeper will receive little, if anything, from corporate involvement in crime or misconduct, it can be deterred more easily than can the corporation or its managers, who may profit handsomely from crime or who may be tempted to engage in criminal activities to achieve goals or thresholds that allow them to remain in office.

The gatekeeper's relative credibility derives in part from its lesser incentive to lie or dissemble, but even more so from the fact that the gatekeeper in effect pledges reputational capital that it has built up over many years and many clients to secure its representations about the particular client or transaction. At least in theory, a gatekeeper would not rationally sacrifice this reputational capital for a single client who accounts for only a small portion of its revenues. Attorneys resemble gatekeepers in that they usually have reputational capital and are often in a position to block or delay transactions or governmental approvals that are vital to their corporate clients. This is truest in the case of securities attorneys, who could potentially block the effectiveness of a registration statement or the consummation of a merger simply by signaling their displeasure to the SEC. In the past, the SEC has suggested strongly that the attorney who is aware of a disclosure violation has a duty to seek to block or delay the consummation of any transaction, at least until properly-informed shareholder approval is obtained. At times (although inconsistently), the SEC has even said that the attorney has an affirmative obligation to cause the client to comply with the federal securities laws.

Historically, bar associations have resisted these SEC pronouncements, insisting that attorneys owe no mandatory obligations to public investors. The securities bar has, however, been far more equivocal. Although litigators have often asserted (as Evan Davis does in this Symposium) that lawyers owe a duty only to their clients and cannot assume other responsibilities, prominent securities attorneys have long endorsed the idea that they owe a duty to the investor who relies on their work—one that requires them to be skeptical of, and independent from, their client. A classic expression of this view was stated in 1974 by A.A. Sommer, Jr., a long-time leader of the securities bar and at the time an SEC Commissioner. In a speech entitled, "The Emerging Responsibilities of the Securities Lawyer," he succinctly summarized the key elements of this duty:

> I would suggest that in securities matters (other than those where advocacy is clearly proper) the attorney will have to function in a manner more akin to that of auditor than to that of the attorney. This means several things. It means that he will have to exercise a

measure of independence that is perhaps uncomfortable if he is also the close counselor of management in other matters, often including business decisions. It means he will have to be acutely cognizant of his responsibility to the public who engage in securities transactions that would never have come about were it not for his professional presence. It means that he will have to adopt the healthy skepticism toward the representation of management which a good auditor must adopt. It means that he will have to do the same thing the auditor does when confronted with an intransigent client—resign.

In overview, Sommer's definition of the securities attorney's ethical responsibilities stresses precisely the elements that define a gatekeeper: (1) independence from the client; (2) professional skepticism of the client's representations; (3) a duty to the public investor; and (4) a duty to resign when the attorney's integrity would otherwise be compromised.

Of course, other securities attorneys might well disagree with Commissioner Sommer, and his commanding presence in the field does not prove that his policy analysis is inherently correct. But even an ambivalence on the part of securities attorneys about their gatekeeper role contrasts sharply with the unqualified assertions of litigators that attorneys are essentially advocates. The litigators' certainty seems attributable to a "center-of-the-universe" fallacy under which litigators assume that their experience and their typical relationships with clients also necessarily characterize the experiences of other branches of the bar.

* * *

III. Can Attorneys Be Gatekeepers?

How are attorneys different from more classic gatekeepers, such as auditors? Two differences are usually identified.

First, attorneys are not predominantly gatekeepers, as are, in theory, auditors and analysts. Rather, they play multiple roles with respect to the corporate client: (1) advocate; (2) transaction engineer; and (3) disclosure supervisor—or gatekeeper. Critics of the SEC's proposed rules have been quick to assert that imposing gatekeeper-like duties on the attorney would compromise the attorney's loyalty to the client, thereby subordinating the attorney's primary role to the secondary role of gatekeeper.

Second, public policy has uniquely favored free and open communications between the attorney and the client, deeming them to be legally privileged in order to maximize the incentive for the client to communicate freely with the attorney. Once again, critics assert that such communications will "dry up" under the SEC's proposed rules on noisy withdrawal, with the result that the end goal of law compliance could actually be impeded because of reduced communications.

A third and countervailing consideration must also be noted: The other principal gatekeepers are each regulated today by a public body that at least in theory seeks to protect the interests of the public. For example, after Sarbanes–Oxley, auditors are regulated by the Public Company Accounting Oversight Board (PCAOB), which is charged expressly with setting ethical standards for auditors, while securities analysts are subject to regulation by the National Association of Securities Dealers (NASD) and the New York Stock Exchange (NYSE), as self-regulatory bodies monitored by the SEC, and by the SEC itself. Only attorneys stand apart, regulated by private state bar associations. Such guild-like regulation has little incentive to be aggressive, to fund enforcement, or to place the interests of the public above those of its members (as the SEC has complained).

A.   The Multiple Roles of Attorneys

For the sake of argument, let us assume that business lawyers are primarily transaction engineers, who only secondarily oversee the disclosure process. How real is the conflict between these two roles? Unsurprisingly, it has long been the law that an attorney who knowingly files a false disclosure document with the SEC can be held liable by that agency as an "aider and abetter" of the primary violation by the corporate client. Thus, some obligation to play a gatekeeper role already exists. The major difference between current law and a noisy withdrawal obligation is that today an attorney arguably could stand aside and not object when the issuer made a disclosure violation of which the attorney was aware but did not actively assist. If a noisy withdrawal were mandated, however, at least some instances would arise in which the attorney could not remain passive without violating this rule. Thus, the conflict already exists, but, in fairness, it would be exacerbated by subjecting the attorney to gatekeeper duties.

* * *

Of course, Sarbanes–Oxley has restricted such conflicts in the case of the auditor and the analyst. Yet, precisely for this reason, reformers could logically propose a corresponding structural reform for the attorney: To prevent conflicts that compromise the attorney, a corporation might be required to use different counsel for "transaction engineering" tasks than it used for "gatekeeping responsibilities." That is, the corporation could use one law firm to plan and structure a merger and another to handle all disclosure responsibilities pertaining to the merger.

To be sure, this would involve costly duplicative and redundant work. But cost considerations are not necessarily dispositive. For example, in preventing the auditor from serving its client as a consultant, Sarbanes–Oxley may have also precluded the corporate client from similarly realizing cost-efficient synergies. The difference between the auditor and the attorney is then one of degree, not of kind. In all likelihood, the synergies in permitting one law firm to serve as both transaction engineer and disclosure counsel are greater than the synergies in permitting an auditor also to serve as a software consultant. Still, this is debatable on a case-by-case basis. In short, those who point to the multiple roles played by the attorney as a reason for not holding attorneys responsible as gatekeepers are making the same argument unsuccessfully made by auditors prior to Sarbanes–Oxley's severance of auditing from consulting. Possibly, a complete divorce of these multiple (and potentially conflicting) roles is less feasible in the case of attorneys, but if so, this may only suggest that other, less restrictive means of dealing with the same conflicts need to be found. As this Essay suggests, section 307 offers a path to this end.

In some respects, it may even be easier to impose gatekeeper obligations on the attorney than on the auditor. The individual audit partner often has a "one client" practice, at least when the audit partner serves a large firm (such as Enron). Lose that client, and the partner probably has no future with his or her firm. Although a "one client" practice is also possible in the case of partners in a law firm, this pattern has become far less common. General counsel have learned to move their legal business around to foster price competition among law firms; increasingly, recurring and/or less specialized activities are cheaper for the corporate client to internalize by moving such services "in house." In short, because corporations make the same "make or buy" decision with respect to legal services as they do with respect to other commodities and services, the law firm partner has increasingly become a specialist—one with high reputational capital who markets his or her services to multiple clients (for example, the mergers and acquisitions or bankruptcy specialist who typically has a "one shot" relationship with the corporate client and then moves on to the next client). In contrast, neither the auditor nor the investment banking firm has the same "one shot," nonrecurring relationship with its corporate clients that law firms increasingly have. In overview, this "one shot" relationship is precisely the profile of the professional who can best serve as a gatekeeper, because the professional remains more independent of the client and suffers less from a single client's dismissal.

Nonetheless, some argue that the attorney's mindset as an advocate for the client blinds the attorney to signs of illegality. But this only begs the real question: Compared to whom? The auditor or the investment banker has little expertise in spotting or identifying violations of law, while the attorney is far more capable of detecting them. Although it may be true that the attorney does not want to find legal violations, why is that a defense? The more we suspect that attorneys will avert their gaze, the more we need to raise the penalties to deter them from so doing.

The claim that auditors make good gatekeepers and attorneys bad ones is also undercut by the limited empirical evidence. Since the passage of the Private Securities Law Reform Act in 1995, auditors have been under a statutory obligation to report to the SEC any material violations of law that they uncover in the course of their work for publicly held corporate clients. The evidence to date suggests that they have reported such violations on very few occasions. This could conceivably be read to mean that there have been very few such violations to report or, more realistically, that human beings predictably will rationalize and find reasons for avoiding what is not in their self-interest to do. Both attorneys and auditors are subject to this same urge, and hence generalizing the obligation to report so that it applies to the attorney as well as the auditor increases the chance that material violations will come to light. Also, from a deterrence perspective, the corporate client may be more apprehensive that the attorney will report than that the auditor will, either because the attorney may be perceived as more law-abiding or because the attorney is simply better at spotting law violations.

B.   Attorney–Client Communications

The most important argument against imposing gatekeeper obligations on securities attorneys is that attorneys may be less able to communicate freely with their clients if such obligations—and, in particular, a noisy withdrawal requirement—were imposed. In response to this claim, it is first necessary to recognize that the ultimate goal of the law is to achieve law compliance, not to maximize uninhibited communications between the attorney and the client. Client confidentiality is a means to an end, not an end in itself. Thus, the law has long placed some limitations on attorney-client communications (such as the crime/fraud exception).

Still, even with this concession, it remains true that lawyers can counsel most effectively when there is open, relatively unconstrained communication between their clients and themselves. Hence, the practical issue becomes whether gatekeeper obligations would necessarily chill desirable attorney-client communications. The stress here should be on the word "desirable." What would be the likely impact of the SEC's proposed noisy withdrawal standards on such communications? A starting point for this analysis should be the recognition that the client knows little law and will almost always want to know if contemplated action is illegal. From this premise, it follows that the corporate official contemplating prospective action will still inquire of counsel whether the course of action under consideration is lawful. Indeed, the more the government pursues white-collar criminal prosecutions and punitive regulatory actions in the contemporary post-Enron environment, the more likely it is that corporate officers will consult counsel before acting. When, then, will communications be most likely to be chilled? The logical answer is that the officer who has already acted may fear inquiring of an attorney if the officer's conduct was lawful—precisely because the officer fears that the attorney may be under an obligation to report unlawful actions to higher authorities or, indirectly, to the SEC. In short, it is the ex post inquiry by the client of the attorney that is most likely to be chilled.

If one accepts this premise that ex ante communications between counsel and the client are less likely to be chilled than ex post communications, several implications follow. First, the impact of imposing gatekeeper obligations on attorneys may be socially desirable. In a well-known article, Professors Kaplow and Shavell have argued that the case for protecting ex ante communications between attorneys and clients is far stronger than the case for protecting ex post communications. Advice before action leads individuals to comply with the law, they argue, whereas ex post advice does not provide a guide for action; rather, it may simply allow the defendant to discuss defense strategies and means of evasion, thereby reducing the expected penalty costs and encouraging illegality. It is not necessary to accept fully the Kaplow and Shavell analysis, which might limit the attorney-client privilege to ex ante advice, to see that its core distinction between ex ante and ex post advice suggests that we should be more concerned about chilling ex ante communications between attorney and client. Yet this is not what most gatekeeper obligations do; rather, they may induce such communications by making ex post advice less possible.

Second, requiring noisy withdrawals and up-the-ladder reporting also has a deterrent value that is independent of this issue of whether the initial corporate actor will still consult counsel. Few significant actions within a corporation can be taken by a single actor. Decisions made by one person still need to be implemented by others. Thus, even after the initial corporate actor has taken an irrevocable step (and will thereafter be arguably less willing to consult with counsel ex post), other corporate actors must be convinced to cooperate with the initial actor. They will have every incentive to consult with counsel because they are still at the ex ante stage. In turn, knowledge that others are necessarily likely to learn of the original actor's conduct and then to consult with counsel about its legality may deter the original actor. The modern public corporation is embedded with in-house attorneys, and even the possibility that they will report up the ladder should deter some illegal conduct. Accordingly, even if under some conditions there may be less direct communication between corporate actors and counsel, the knowledge that sooner or later counsel is likely to learn ex post (because of the multiple parties likely to consult counsel) may still deter corporate actors ex ante.

Third, this ex ante/ex post distinction also helps clarify when exceptions may need to be created to any obligation on the part of the attorney to report out information relating to violations of the law. The ABA Task Force on Corporate Responsibility recommended this year that some legal roles should be exempted from any obligation to "report out" violations of law, including through a noisy withdrawal. The clearest case arose, it said, when the lawyer "has been engaged by the organization to investigate whether an organizational constituent has committed a material violation of law or a breach of duty to the organization." This setting of internal corporate investigations is, of course, precisely the ex post context. When the corporation's lawyer is functioning in this capacity, the ABA Task Force concluded that the corporation "has an especially compelling need for the ground rules of that investigation to promote open and frank communications between the investigating lawyer and organizational constituents." The ABA Task Force may well be right that greater confidentiality is needed in these circumstances and that a carefully crafted exemption should apply to internal corporate investigations. But to reach this conclusion is in essence to accept the ex ante/ex post distinction and concede that ex ante communications are less likely to be chilled by a limited obligation to report out.

Finally and most importantly, the principal practical effect of imposing gatekeeper obligations on attorneys is that a client who has been advised by an attorney that contemplated action is unlawful now has greater reason to heed that attorney's advice—again precisely to the extent that the client believes that the attorney may be under a legal obligation to report material misconduct (either within the corporation or outside to the SEC). Thus, even if it were true that clients would consult their lawyers less often, this impact could be more than fully offset by the fact that it would become more dangerous to disregard the lawyers' advice. Add to this mix the likelihood that ex ante advice will not be chilled, and the net impact is to increase the attorney's leverage over the client by making it more dangerous to ignore the attorney's advice. If law compliance is the goal, such an impact seems socially desirable. Put simply, the logical remedy for gatekeeper failure is to empower the gatekeeper, and a noisy withdrawal obligation makes it more costly for the client to ignore the lawyer.

IV.   IMPLEMENTING THE GATEKEEPER ROLE OF ATTORNEYS

Although the debate over section 307 to date has been dominated by the issue of noisy withdrawal, the scope of section 307 is far broader. What else can or should the SEC do to make the attorney an effective guardian of the integrity of publicly filed disclosure documents (without imposing obligations that subordinate the attorney's duty of loyalty to the client to this mission)? This Essay will make three proposals: (1) a due diligence obligation; (2) an independence requirement; and (3) an attorney certification requirement. Each is premised on A.A. Sommer's normative claim that the securities attorney must behave in some respects less like an advocate and more like an auditor, but each proposal also recognizes that the attorney cannot undertake an obligation to audit its client.

A.   *The Due Diligence Obligation*

Few norms are less controversial among securities attorneys than that they should perform some due diligence in preparing prospectuses or other disclosure documents. Yet no SEC rule actually requires this. Thus, a logical first step would be for the SEC's Rules of Practice to mandate due diligence by the attorney (within the time realistically available) in the preparation of disclosure documents. Indeed, such an obligation sounds very much like a "minimum standard of professional conduct" that section 307 authorizes. Why? Because it is semantically impossible to assert that an attorney who has behaved in a grossly negligent fashion has behaved "professionally." Interestingly, in its existing Rules of Practice, the SEC already holds auditors to precisely such a standard and asserts the power to suspend or disbar them for merely negligent conduct. If this can be done, then it seems to follow a fortiori, after the enactment of section 307, that the SEC could require attorneys to take reasonable steps to investigate the accuracy of statements made in documents that they prepare. The impact of such a rule is to give fair notice to the attorney that he or she cannot simply rely on the client's assertions, but must perform at least some minimal examination to corroborate those assertions, whose depth and intensity would basically be determined by the profession's own norms and standards.

By no means is it here suggested that negligence should support a private cause of action under Rule 10b–5 against attorneys (or others). But negligence is improper professional conduct, which should in appropriate cases justify the imposition of sanctions under section 307. Such a tradeoff—i.e., public liability but not private liability for negligence— again seems desirable in that it enhances deterrence without threatening insolvency for law firms.

B. Independence

Auditors, of course, must be independent of their client, and SEC rules have long defined tests for auditor independence. Increasingly, a new literature has warned that attorneys are becoming too economically intertwined with their clients, as a result, in part, of the increasing practice of law firms taking (and even demanding) equity stakes in the client in return for professional services. If some level of independence is necessary for an attorney to function as a gatekeeper (as A.A. Sommer, Jr. recognized over a quarter century ago), SEC rules of professional conduct could define these limits. To illustrate, a law firm that holds in its portfolio ten percent of the corporate client's equity (or, alternatively, equity in the client equal to ten percent of its own net asset value) will probably be a poor, or at least a biased, monitor.

Perhaps the context that is most sensitive and would most benefit from such rules is that of internal corporate investigations. Should the corporation's normal outside counsel perform such an investigation? Or should SEC rules define the level of independence necessary to conduct such a sensitive inquiry? Absent SEC action, individual state bar associations will either do nothing (the most likely outcome) or prescribe different and inconsistent standards, thereby creating needless disparities. Uniform standards for corporate internal investigations are desirable and as a practical matter can come only from the SEC. There is no need to offer precise rules here, only to recognize that professionals are expected to be independent of their clients. Accordingly, the SEC should read section 307 to grant it authority to define the point at which the attorney is not sufficiently independent of the client to perform certain sensitive tasks.

C. Attorney Certification

Today, the auditor certifies the firm's financial results, and under Sarbanes–Oxley, senior management certifies that the financial information in periodic reports filed with the SEC "fairly presents in all material respects" the firm's financial condition and results of operations. Even the securities analyst must now certify that its recommendations reflect the analyst's own personal views. Alone, the attorney escapes and need not certify in any way as to the accuracy of the client's disclosures. Yet, traditionally, the attorney is the field marshall of the disclosure process. More importantly, because the auditor's certificate covers only the financial statements that it reviews, no independent professional today expresses any view that the statements made in the textual portions of a Form 10–K or a registration statement are correct or have at least been subjected to a reasonable "due diligence" examination by the professional. Yet increasingly, the most important statements made by a corporate issuer are those set forth in its "Management's Discussion and Analysis of Financial Condition and Results of Operations" (MD & A). If after the Enron-era scandals we are concerned about the quality and reliability of the financial disclosures reaching the market, one of the most obvious, logical, and necessary steps would be to insert a gatekeeper into the disclosure process at exactly this stage and require some professional vetting of the issuer's textual statements.

Still, there remains a problem with this proposal that requires it to be downsized significantly. Put simply, what can the attorney reasonably be asked to certify? After all, the attorney has not audited the client; nor is a law firm organizationally or logistically equipped for any form of inquiry analogous to an audit. Nonetheless, a less onerous form of certification seems possible. Based on the opinions normally delivered by attorneys in registered offerings in the securities market, it would seem justifiable to ask the attorney principally responsible for preparing a disclosure document or report filed with the SEC to certify: (1) that such attorney believes the statements made in the document or report to be true and correct in all material respects; and (2) that such attorney is not aware of any additional material information whose disclosure is necessary in order to make the statements made, in the light of the circumstances under which they were made, not misleading.[56]

In essence, this proposed certification simply tracks the language of Rule 10b–5. Far from intruding significantly into the marketplace, this obligation only generalizes existing practices in the private market. Today, in most public underwritten offerings, issuer's counsel delivers an opinion to the underwriters—sometimes called a "negative assurance" opinion—stating that it is not "aware" of any material information required to be disclosed that has not been disclosed.[57] In this light,

---

56. Issues could arise as to which attorney was principally responsible for preparing a document. The simplest answer to this issue is to require the corporation to disclose the identity of such attorney in the filing and then require that attorney's certification. The real thrust of this proposal is to require the issuer to subject its principal disclosure documents to the review of an attorney who would be subject to SEC sanctions for professional negligence. This author would not require the attorney to be an outside counsel (although others might think that such an additional requirement was also justified).

57. For a description of this standard opinion in registered public offerings, see Richard R. Howe, The Duties and Liabili-

such a negative certification requirement would simply mandate for 1934 Act periodic filings what is already done by the private issuers in the primary market for 1933 Act disclosure documents. The marginal difference is that, in the case of periodic filings under the Securities Exchange Act, there is no private party in a position analogous to the underwriter who can demand such an opinion or certification from the attorney. SEC action would fill this void. The one respect in which this proposal does change current practice is that it would require that some attorney—whether inside or outside the corporation—assume responsibility for supervising the preparation of the disclosure document.[58] Thus, it effectively requires the involvement of a gatekeeper and precludes internal corporate personnel from filing a Form 10–K or Form 10–Q without some review by counsel.

Beyond this structural value, such a requirement would have a profound symbolic and psychological effect on the bar because it would establish the attorney's obligations as a gatekeeper. Potentially, the SEC could go even further and require the certifying attorney responsible for the disclosure document to certify that the attorney believed adequate disclosure had been made "after making such inquiry that the attorney reasonably believed appropriate in the circumstance." This would integrate the certification requirement with the earlier discussed due diligence obligation. As here proposed, either in-house counsel or an outside attorney could provide such certification, but either would be subject to a due diligence obligation.

Admittedly, limits need to be recognized on what an attorney can certify. Because the attorney does not audit its client, the attorney should not be asked to certify the accuracy and completeness of all information disclosed in SEC filings. Thus, the proposal here made requires only a negative certification that the attorney had no reason to

ties of Attorneys in Rendering Legal Opinions, 1989 Colum. Bus. L. Rev. 283, 287. Mr. Howe, a partner at the New York firm of Sullivan & Cromwell, properly observes that "such opinions are not really 'legal opinions' at all in that they do not state any legal conclusion but only say that the attorney believes certain facts to be true." Id. Precisely for this reason, such an opinion is more a pledge of the law firm's reputational capital, which the underwriters demand. The counsel giving such opinion does not purport to conclude that all information required to be disclosed has been disclosed (as an auditor might by analogy), but only that it lacks personal knowledge or belief as to any such failure. The American Bar Association has characterized this type of opinion as a "negative assurance" and finds such opinions to be "unique to securities offerings." See ABA Comm'n on Legal Opinions, Third–Party Legal Opinion Report, Including the Legal Opinion Accord, of the Section of Business Law, 47 Bus. Law.

167, 228 (1991). Although the ABA considers it generally inappropriate for attorneys to request such "negative assurance" opinions from other attorneys, the special context of securities offerings is exempted, reflecting the fact that underwriters consider such an assurance to be necessary to them. That the ABA, as the representative of the bar, "disfavors" such opinions because of the demands they place on the attorney probably only underscores their value.

58. A major question surrounds whether this certification should be given by an inside counsel, such as the general counsel, or an independent outside firm. As noted earlier, the general counsel has a "one client" practice and thus does not make a natural gatekeeper. On the other hand, requiring use of an outside law firm will increase the costs of compliance with SEC disclosure requirements for many corporations.

believe, and did not believe, that the information was materially false or misleading. Legally, such a certification would trigger "aiding and abetting" liability that the SEC could enforce if the attorney knew of the materially false or misleading information, and it could even trigger criminal liability under various federal statutes. But its primary effect is to mandate that an attorney serve as a gatekeeper for investors with respect to important disclosure documents.

Still other rules may be desirable, dealing with more specific problems. This discussion has not been intended to be exhaustive or to offer precise rules, but rather to advance a more general proposition: To the extent that the quality of disclosure declined in the 1990s, the most logical response is to identify a gatekeeper who can be asked to play a more active role in monitoring the issuer's disclosures. This is not a role that attorneys will want to play because it does impose costs on them, but it is a role they may be obliged to play because the social costs of allowing them to escape responsibility are even higher.

IN THE MATTER OF EMANUEL FIELDS

45 S.E.C. 262 (1973)

An order of this Commission that suspends or terminates an attorney's ability to practice is a serious—a very serious—matter for us and for him. Nothing that we say here should be construed as minimizing the gravity of such a step. Yet we think it well to note that the impact of an order by us under our Rule 2(e) is not nearly so devastating as is that of the order of a court barring a man from practicing law at all. The disciplinary sanctions that we impose on lawyers can affect only their capacity to engage in our rather narrow type of practice. A lawyer barred from appearing before us is still free to hold himself out to the world as a lawyer, to practice before all tribunals save this one, and to counsel clients with respect to the infinite variety of legal problems that do not impinge on the area affected by the federal securities statutes. This distinction brings us to what we consider a basic flaw in Field's argument that only the courts of New York which made him a lawyer in the first place can deprive him of the right to practice here. That argument assumes, among other things, that the standards of character and integrity that the New York courts consider adequate or their purposes ought to be and are necessarily controlling here. This fallacious position overlooks the peculiarly strategic and especially central place of the private practicing lawyer in the investment process and in the enforcement of the body of federal law aimed at keeping that process fair. Members of this Commission have pointed out time and time again that the task of enforcing the securities laws rests in overwhelming measure on the bar's shoulders. These were statements of what all who are versed in the practicalities of securities law know to be a truism, i.e., that this Commission with its small staff, limited resources, and onerous tasks is peculiarly dependent on the probity and the diligence of the professionals who practice before it. Very little of a securities lawyer's work is adversary in character. He doesn't work in courtrooms where the pressure of vigilant adversaries and alet judges checks him. He works in his office where he prepares prospectuses, proxy statements, opinions of counsel, and other documents that we, our staff, the financial community, and the investing public must take on faith. This is a field where unscrupulous lawyers can inflict irreparable harm on those who rely on the disclosure documents that they produce. Hence we are under a duty to hold our bar to appropriately rigorous standards of professional honor. To expect this vital function to be performed entirely by overburdened state courts who have little or no contact with the matters with which we deal would be to shirk that duty. As we said in Morris Mac Schwebel, 40 S.E.C. 347, 371 (1960): 'The right to appear and practice before this Commission as an attorney is, like membership in the bar itself, a privilege burdened with condition.'

Tamara Loomis, SEC Gores GC in Sarbanes-Oxley Dust-Up

Legal Times (January 24, 2005)

The Securities and Exchange Commission has a harsh message for in-house lawyers: Fulfill your gatekeeper duties or suffer the consequences.

John Isselmann Jr. learned this lesson last fall, when he became the first general counsel in the post-Sarbanes-Oxley era to be penalized for gatekeeper violations. The SEC's civil case against Isselmann, the former general counsel of Electro Scientific Industries Inc., is a cautionary tale for corporate counsel everywhere.

Stephen Cutler, the SEC's enforcement chief, first put in-house lawyers on notice about the agency's emphasis on gatekeepers in a speech given on Sept. 20, 2004. Cutler defined gatekeepers as 'the sentries of the marketplace'—auditors, directors, and 'the lawyers who advise companies on disclosure standards and other securities law requirements.'

The agency, he added, was 'considering actions against lawyers ... who assisted their companies or clients in covering up evidence of fraud, or prepared, or signed off on, misleading disclosures regarding the company's condition.'

Four days after Cutler's speech, the SEC announced that it had settled its allegations against Isselmann. While the agency has gone after a number of lawyers for their alleged role in a financial fraud, Isselmann's case is unique.

The SEC doesn't claim that he participated in the scheme to fraudulently boost the quarterly financials at ESI, a semiconductor manufacturer based in Portland, Ore.

The agency doesn't even allege that Isselmann knew about the fraud at the company, which reported revenues of $207 million in fiscal year 2004. The SEC says only that the ex-GC failed to communicate material information to ESI's audit committee and outside auditors—information that would have stopped the accounting fraud.

In his settlement with the SEC, Isselmann neither admitted nor denied the agency's allegations. The 37-year-old lawyer agreed to pay a $50,000 civil penalty and consented to a cease-and-desist order. He left ESI in 2003—he says that the company asked him to stay on—and currently does consulting work in Portland. (ESI officials did not respond to requests for comment for this article.)

'Mr. Isselmann failed in his gatekeeper role,' says Patrick Murphy, an enforcement lawyer in the SEC's San Francisco office who supervised the ESI probe. 'He had information that he should have passed on to the board and the company's external independent auditor. If that information had been provided, it would have prevented the financial fraud.'

Isselmann has a different take on the government's case against him: 'Cutler was out there putting the fear of God into lawyers, and he needed an exclamation point. I was that exclamation point.'

Whether the SEC was looking to make an example of Isselmann or not, his case shows how treacherous the GC job can be these days.

The agency alleges that former Chief Financial Officer James Dooley and ex-controller James Lorenz III committed several instances of fraud at ESI. But the SEC doesn't claim that Isselmann was involved in any of the wrongdoing—only that he failed to report a specific incident.

According to the SEC's complaint against Isselmann, Dooley and Lorenz decided late on Sept. 12, 2002, to eliminate $1 million in vested retirement and severance benefits for ESI's employees in Asia. Dooley and Lorenz then fraudulently applied the savings to ESI's bottom line by an accounting move called 'reversing the accrual,' the SEC claims.

Isselmann was not present or consulted when Dooley and Lorenz made their middle-of-the-night decision, according to the SEC's complaint. But Dooley subsequently asked Isselmann to get a written opinion from the company's outside counsel in Japan on whether Japanese law permitted eliminating the benefits. Dooley didn't tell Isselmann that ESI's books had already been altered, the SEC says.

Morrison & Foerster, ESI's Japanese counsel, e-mailed an opinion to Isselmann, stating that the company could not unilaterally terminate the benefits. According to the SEC's complaint, Isselmann tried to raise this point at a disclosure meeting right before the company filed its financial statement, but Dooley objected and cut him off. After the meeting, Isselmann provided Dooley with a copy of the written legal advice. Nevertheless, ESI went ahead and filed a fraudulent statement overstating its quarterly income by 28 percent, the SEC says.

Five months later, according to the agency's complaint, ESI's new CFO told Isselmann how Dooley and Lorenz had decided to eliminate the benefits and reverse the accrual during their Sept. 12 meeting. (Dooley had since been promoted from CFO to chief executive officer.) Isselmann immediately told ESI's audit committee and outside counsel what had happened, the SEC's complaint says. But that wasn't enough for the agency.

The SEC faulted Isselmann for failing to stand up to then-CFO Dooley at the disclosure meeting, and for failing to provide the audit committee with Morrison & Foerster's advice. These failures allowed Dooley and Lorenz to conceal their fraud, the SEC says.

The agency didn't bring a case against ESI, citing the company's 'extraordinary cooperation in the commission's investigation.' But Dooley and Lorenz didn't get off so lightly.

In September, the U.S. Attorney's Office filed a 17-count indictment against the two men, who were fired from ESI in 2003. Prosecutors allege that Dooley and Lorenz made a series of accounting reversals and reclassifications that falsely boosted ESI's earnings by nearly $7 million, allowing the company to hit its financial targets for the first two quarters of its 2003 fiscal year.

Dooley's lawyer, Steven Ungar of Lane Powell Spears Lubersky in Portland, said in a statement that the government's claims against his client 'are false, distorted, and unfairly present only one side of the story.... When the facts are fairly and accurately presented, we are confident that [Dooley] will be fully exonerated.' Lorenz, who has also pleaded not guilty, could not be reached for comment.

For his part, Isselmann says he didn't even realize he'd done anything wrong. 'I didn't fully understand the accounting issues,' says Isselmann.

He explains that at the time, he was just eight years out of law school and had no accounting experience and only a limited securities law background. 'Like many general counsel, I was a generalist—my job was a mile wide and an inch deep. I relied heavily on accounting people like Dooley and outside auditors to flag those issues for me.'

Isselmann says he thought of the Japanese benefits matter as an employment issue, not an accounting issue. He adds that as ESI's only in-house lawyer, 'I didn't have the luxury of focusing on a single e-mail and thinking about it for weeks and weeks.' He says he probably spent an hour and a half in total on the benefits matter.

Ultimately, the SEC charged Isselmann under rule 13b2-2 of the Securities Exchange Act of 1934 with failing to provide a material fact to accountants in connection with an SEC filing. According to Isselmann's lawyer, Melinda Haag, a partner in the San Francisco office of Orrick, Herrington & Sutcliffe, it's essentially a strict liability offense. 'No intent or even negligence needs to be shown,' she says. 'They're saying that [he] should have somehow figured out what was going on.' Haag adds, 'It's a frightening prospect for anyone who holds that gatekeeper position.'

William Baker, a former SEC enforcement chief now in the D.C. office of Latham & Watkins, agrees: 'The SEC is saying, 'Too little, too late." Baker adds, 'Whatever message they're sending, it's a scary one for in-house lawyers.'

C. MATERIALITY

James D. Cox, Robert W. Hillman & Donald C. Langevoort,
SECURITIES REGULATION: CASES AND MATERIALS

(4th ed. 2004)

MATERIALITY ORTHODOXY

Determining what is material is a normative judgment having the same level of precision as determining what the reasonable person would do under the circumstances. In litigation, a fact's materiality is a mixed question of law and fact, so that it arises in pretrial motions as well as at trial. Outside of litigation, considering whether an item is material and thus must be disclosed is frequently an ulcerating experience.

In *Mills v. Electric Auto-Lite Co.*, 396 U.S. 375 (1970), the Supreme Court muddied the waters considerably when in the same paragraph it stated that materiality entails a finding that the information "*might* have been considered important by a reasonable" investor and then it observed that the test required "a significant *propensity* to affect" investors. The Court appeared to embrace two standards for judging materiality, one that tended toward the information's probable influence on investors and the other toward its possible effect. The full impact of the distinction between these standards is illustrated in *TSC Industries, Inc. v. Northway, Inc.*, 426 U.S. 438 (1976), *rev'g* 512 F.2d 324 (1975), involving an allegedly misleading proxy statement circulated in connection with TSC Industries' merger into National Industries. The Seventh Circuit, applying the "might" standard, held that certain omissions were material as a matter of law and granted Northway summary judgment on this issue. The Supreme Court reversed the grant of summary judgment, holding that under its standard of materiality, none of the alleged omissions was materially misleading as a matter of law:

> An omitted fact is material if there is a substantial likelihood that a reasonable shareholder would consider it important in deciding how to vote. This standard is fully consistent with *Mills'* general description of materiality as a requirement that "the defect have a significant propensity to affect the voting process." It does not require proof of a substantial likelihood that disclosure of the omitted fact would have caused the reasonable investor to change his vote. What the standard does contemplate is a showing of a substantial likelihood that, under all the circumstances, the omitted fact would have assumed actual significance in the deliberations of the reasonable shareholder. Put another way, there must be a substantial likelihood that the disclosure of the omitted fact would have been viewed by the reasonable investor as having significantly altered the "total mix" of information made available.

Id. at 449. Virtually all cases involving materiality determinations under the federal securities laws proceed after repeating the Supreme Court's formula as stated in *TSC Industries*.

BASIC INCORPORATED v. LEVINSON, ET AL.

485 U.S. 224, 108 S.Ct. 978, 99 L.Ed.2d 194 (1988)

JUSTICE BLACKMUN delivered the opinion of the Court.

This case requires us to apply the materiality requirement of § 10(b) of the Securities Exchange Act of 1934, (1934 Act) and the Securities and Exchange Commission's Rule 10b–5 in the context of preliminary corporate merger discussions. * * *

I

Prior to December 20, 1978, Basic Incorporated was a publicly traded company primarily engaged in the business of manufacturing chemical refractories for the steel industry. As early as 1965 or 1966, Combustion Engineering, Inc., a company producing mostly alumina-based refractories, expressed some interest in acquiring Basic, but was deterred from pursuing this inclination seriously because of antitrust concerns it then entertained. In 1976, however, regulatory action opened the way to a renewal of Combustion's interest. The "Strategic Plan," dated October 25, 1976, for Combustion's Industrial Products Group included the objective: "Acquire Basic Inc. $30 million."

Beginning in September 1976, Combustion representatives had meetings and telephone conversations with Basic officers and directors, including petitioners here, concerning the possibility of a merger. During 1977 and 1978, Basic made three public statements denying that it was engaged in merger negotiations. On December 18, 1978, Basic asked the New York Stock Exchange to suspend trading in its shares and issued a release stating that it had been "approached" by another company concerning a merger. On December 19, Basic's board endorsed Combustion's offer of $46 per share for its common stock and on the following day publicly announced its approval of Combustion's tender offer for all outstanding shares.

Respondents are former Basic shareholders who sold their stock after Basic's first public statement of October 21, 1977, and before the suspension of trading in December 1978. Respondents brought a class action against Basic and its directors, asserting that the defendants issued three false or misleading public statements and thereby were in violation of § 10(b) of the 1934 Act and of Rule 10b–5. Respondents alleged that they were injured by selling Basic shares at artificially depressed prices in a market affected by petitioners' misleading statements and in reliance thereon.

* * * On the merits * * * the District Court * * *held that, as a matter of law, any misstatements were immaterial: there were no negotiations ongoing at the time of the first statement, and although

negotiations were taking place when the second and third statements were issued, those negotiations were not "destined, with reasonable certainty, to become a merger agreement in principle."

The United States Court of Appeals for the Sixth Circuit * * * reversed the District Court's summary judgment, and remanded the case. The court reasoned that while petitioners were under no general duty to disclose their discussions with Combustion, any statement the company voluntarily released could not be " 'so incomplete as to mislead.' " In the Court of Appeals' view, Basic's statements that no negotiations where taking place, and that it knew of no corporate developments to account for the heavy trading activity, were misleading. With respect to materiality, the court rejected the argument that preliminary merger discussions are immaterial as a matter of law, and held that "once a statement is made denying the existence of any discussions, even discussions that might not have been material in absence of the denial are material because they make the statement made untrue."

* * *

II

* * *

The Court previously has addressed various positive and common-law requirements for a violation of § 10(b) or of Rule 10b–5. The Court also explicitly has defined a standard of materiality under the securities laws, see TSC Industries, Inc. v. Northway, Inc., 426 U.S. 438, 96 S.Ct. 2126, 48 L.Ed.2d 757 (1976), concluding in the proxy-solicitation context that "[a]n omitted fact is material if there is a substantial likelihood that a reasonable shareholder would consider it important in deciding how to vote." Acknowledging that certain information concerning corporate developments could well be of "dubious significance," the Court was careful not to set too low a standard of materiality; it was concerned that a minimal standard might bring an overabundance of information within its reach, and lead management "simply to bury the shareholders in an avalanche of trivial information—a result that is hardly conducive to informed decisionmaking." It further explained that to fulfill the materiality requirement "there must be a substantial likelihood that the disclosure of the omitted fact would have been viewed by the reasonable investor as having significantly altered the 'total mix' of information made available." We now expressly adopt the TSC Industries standard of materiality for the § 10(b) and Rule 10b–5 context.

III

The application of this materiality standard to preliminary merger discussions is not self-evident. Where the impact of the corporate development on the target's fortune is certain and clear, the TSC Industries materiality definition admits straightforward application. Where, on the other hand, the event is contingent or speculative in nature, it is difficult to ascertain whether the "reasonable investor" would have considered the omitted information significant at the time. Merger negotiations, because of the ever-present possibility that the contemplated transaction will not be effectuated, fall into the latter category.

C

Even before this Court's decision in TSC Industries, the Second Circuit had explained the role of the materiality requirement of Rule 10b–5, with respect to contingent or speculative information or events, in a manner that gave that term meaning that is independent of the other provisions of the Rule. Under such circumstances, materiality "will depend at any given time upon a balancing of both the indicated probability that the event will occur and the anticipated magnitude of the event in light of the totality of the company activity." SEC v. Texas Gulf Sulphur Co., 401 F.2d, at 849. Interestingly, neither the Third Circuit decision adopting the agreement-in-principle test nor petitioners here take issue with this general standard. Rather, they suggest that with respect to preliminary merger discussions, there are good reasons to draw a line at agreement on price and structure.

In a subsequent decision, the late Judge Friendly, writing for a Second Circuit panel, applied the Texas Gulf Sulphur probability/magnitude approach in the specific context of preliminary merger negotiations. After acknowledging that materiality is something to be determined on the basis of the particular facts of each case, he stated:

"Since a merger in which it is bought out is the most important event that can occur in a small corporation's life, to wit, its death, we think that inside information, as regards a merger of this sort, can become material at an earlier stage than would be the case as regards lesser transactions—and this even though the mortality rate of mergers in such formative stages is doubtless high." SEC v. Geon Industries, Inc., 531 F.2d 39, 47–48 (1976).

We agree with that analysis.

Whether merger discussions in any particular case are material therefore depends on the facts. Generally, in order to assess the probability that the event will occur, a factfinder will need to look to indicia of interest in the transaction at the highest corporate levels. Without attempting to catalog all such possible factors, we note by way of example that board resolutions, instructions to investment bankers, and actual negotiations between principals or their intermediaries may serve as indicia of interest. To assess the magnitude of the transaction to the issuer of the securities allegedly manipulated, a factfinder will need to consider such facts as the size of the two corporate entities and of the potential premiums over market value. No particular event or factor short of closing the transaction need be either necessary or sufficient by itself to render merger discussions material.[17]

---

17. To be actionable, of course, a statement must also be misleading. Silence, absent a duty to disclose, is not misleading under Rule 10b–5. "No comment" state-

As we clarify today, materiality depends on the significance the reasonable investor would place on the withheld or misrepresented information. The fact-specific inquiry we endorse here is consistent with the approach a number of courts have taken in assessing the materiality of merger negotiations. Because the standard of materiality we have adopted differs from that used by both courts below, we remand the case for reconsideration of the question whether a grant of summary judgment is appropriate on this record.

James D. Cox, Robert W. Hillman & Donald C. Langevoort, SECURITIES REGULATION: CASES AND MATERIALS

(4th ed. 2004)

Is a statement of one's opinion about an event or transaction distinguishable from puffery? Do statements of opinion, such as that the shareholders are receiving a "high" price or that a transaction "is in the stockholders' best interest," relate to material *facts*, so that they fall within the standard strictures of the antifraud provisions? In *Virginia Bankshares, Inc. v. Sandberg*, 501 U.S. 1083, 111 S.Ct. 2749, 115 L.Ed.2d 929 (1991), the Supreme Court provided a qualified yes to the last question without considering the first question. The facts arose from a going-private transaction in which the minority shareholders of First American Bank of Virginia (FABV) were offered $42 per share by the parent corporation. The FABV directors recommended that the stockholders approve the transaction, stating that $42 was a "high value" and a "fair price," even though the directors had received a report that valued the shares at $60 and they were aware that valuing FABV's real estate would, at current market prices, yield a value greater than $42 per share. The plaintiff alleged that the FABV directors acted under pressure from FABV's parent in the hopes of continuing their positions with FABV or one of the other companies controlled by the parent. The majority opinion observed that such opinion statements assume material significance to shareholders: "Shareholders know that directors usually have knowledge and expertness far exceeding the normal investor's

---

ments are generally the functional equivalent of silence. See In re Carnation Co., Exchange Act Release No. 22214, 33 S.E.C. Docket 1025 (1985). See also New York Stock Exchange Listed Company Manual § 202.01, reprinted in 3 CCH Fed.Sec. L.Rep. ¶ 23,515 (1987) (premature public announcement may properly be delayed for valid business purpose and where adequate security can be maintained); American Stock Exchange Company Guide §§ 401–405, reprinted in 3 CCH Fed.Sec.L.Rep. ¶¶ 23,124A–23,124E (1985) (similar provisions).

It has been suggested that given current market practices, a "no comment" statement is tantamount to an admission that merger discussions are underway. See

Flamm v. Eberstadt, 814 F.2d, at 1178. That may well hold true to the extent that issuers adopt a policy of truthfully denying merger rumors when no discussions are underway, and of issuing "no comment" statements when they are in the midst of negotiations. There are, of course, other statement policies firms could adopt; we need not now advise issuers as to what kind of practice to follow, within the range permitted by law. Perhaps more importantly, we think that creating an exception to a regulatory scheme founded on a prodisclosure legislative philosophy, because complying with the regulation might be "bad for business," is a role for Congress, not this Court.

resources, and the directors' perceived superiority is magnified even further by the common knowledge that state law customarily obliges them to exercise their judgment in the shareholders' interest." Id. at 1091. The majority, however, distinguished between objective and subjective falseness. An assertion of "fairness" could be false because the price was not fair or high. The statement could also be false because the directors making it did not believe the price was fair, even if objectively the price was high or even fair. The former is objective falseness and can be the basis of liability. The latter is subjective falseness and not the basis for liability because of its dependence on matters that are not objectively verifiable such that if suit could be based merely on subjective falsehood it would invite strike suits. Because there was objective evidence before the directors that was inconsistent with their professed opinions, the court held that the plaintiff had pled more than a mere subjective disbelief or undisclosed motive. *See, e.g., Shapiro v. U.J.B. Financial Corp.*, 964 F.2d 272 (3d Cir. 1992) (misrepresentation to represent that loan reserves were "solid" and "adequate"); *In re Value-Vision International Inc. Securities Litigation*, 896 F.Supp. 434, 435 (E.D. Pa. 1995) (statement that directors were "confident" financing would be obtained could be shown to be false through garden-variety evidence involving more than defendants' state of mind).

FORWARD-LOOKING INFORMATION

Soft information describes events or activities that will occur, if at all, at some future date. Soft information by definition is inherently uncertain, so that there is every reason to believe its materiality should be assessed by the probability/magnitude standard applied in *Basic*. The Supreme Court, however, expressed no opinion whether the probability/magnitude test should be applied across the board in assessing the materiality of all uncertain events. In considering the scope of the probability/magnitude test, and particularly its application to soft information, the qualities of soft information should be contrasted with so-called historical information: reports on events that have occurred. For example, all accounting-based information in financial statements is essentially historical, reporting on such items as the sales, expenses, and income produced from operations for a period, as well as the assets, liabilities, and equity of the firm as of a specific date in the past. Except for the section for the Management Discussion and Analysis of Financial Condition and Results of Operations, Regulation S-K bears upon events and activities that have transpired within the firm, not those that are likely to occur.

Soft information is important largely because the past is not always prologue in the world of business and finance. That is, historical information, while an accepted basis for extrapolating what is likely to occur in the future, is not nearly as predictive as managers' forecasts. For much of its existence the SEC would not allow registrants to include soft information in their SEC filings because the SEC believed the information was too subjective and inherently unreliable and would be misused by unsophisticated investors. No position has earned the SEC more criticism than its stationing itself between those issuers that wished to disclose their managers' forecasts of future operations and the investment community's insatiable appetite for management forecasts, appraisals, and the like. In 1973, the SEC announced that it had determined to change its policies with respect to soft information, and, in 1978, it assumed its current position, in which it encourages registrants to include projections in SEC filings.

Also important is the SEC's development of Item 303, the Management Discussion and Analysis section of Regulation S-K, examined in the preceding chapter. Item 303 directly requests management to assess the past performance of the business and, importantly, to provide its view of what operations, trends, and forces will affect future operations. At several key points, Item 303 imposes upon management a duty to disclose trends that are likely to affect the firm's financial performance, liquidity, or capital resources as well as the effects of inflation on operations. Even though disclosures such as these necessarily involve a good many subjective judgments, predictive information, and speculation, not only are registrants now encouraged to include such information in their SEC filings, but also in discrete areas such information is actually solicited by Regulation S-K. The full significance of this change in SEC disclosure practices is not so much that it has forced disclosures on unwilling registrants, but that it has removed the SEC opposition from the path of those who wish to include *optimistic* forward-looking information in their filings.

But what of the fact that the distinguishing characteristic of projections and appraisals is that they are seldom accurate? Should the policy choices surrounding soft information be determined on the basis of the relative accuracy of predictions and appraisals? The question posed by soft information is whether resources are better allocated among competing investment opportunities by encouraging the flow of soft information if that additional information is not accurate. To resolve this question upon the slender basis that forecasts or appraisals are untrustworthy overlooks some important considerations. First, it is naive to assume investors accept soft information uncritically. They may, and most likely do, adjust forecasts and appraisals to their own estimates of the possible outcomes. Second, some assumption must be made of the variance between the forecast or appraisal figure and the amount achieved that investors consider material. If the deviance is insignificant in light of the amount that investors have already discounted the forecast or appraisal by the time it was issued, it is difficult to conclude that investors or markets are disserved by the release of soft information. Even if the argument is based upon accuracy, it appears that we are better off by encouraging management to proffer forecasts. Managers are not the only ones that issue forecasts: Security analysts more frequently make published forecasts than do managers, and their forecasts are less accurate than those of managers. *See* Waymire, Additional Evidence on the

Accuracy of Analysts' Forecasts Before and After Voluntary Management Earnings Forecasts, 61 Acct. Rev. 129 (1986).

Finally, since a forecast, prediction, and appraisal each speak of the future, and hence can be expected to deviate from what actually does occur, how do we determine if the forward-looking statement is materially inaccurate when it is made? Does a mere difference between the forecasted or appraised amount and the level ultimately realized mean that the forecast or appraisal is the basis for liability under the securities laws? In *Moss v. Healthcare Compare Corp.*, 75 F.3d 276 (7th Cir. 1996), the company expressed comfort with analysts' forecasts of earnings of $1.20 to $1.25 per share. Two months later the price of the shares lost one-third of their value when the company stated that analysts' estimates of $1.10 per share were too high. In dismissing the suit that was filed within 24 hours after the pessimistic announcement, the court provides the following insight to when a forecast is misleading:

> [C]ases involving forward-looking statements are unique.... [P]redictions of future performance are inevitably inaccurate because things almost never go exactly as planned.... [P]laintiffs must allege "specific facts which illustrate that the company's predictions lacked a reasonable basis.... Projections which turn out to be inaccurate are not fraudulent simply because subsequent events reveal that a different projection would have been more reasonable."

D. PREPARATION OF REGISTRATION STATEMENT UNDER SECURITIES ACT 1933

Carl W. Schneider, Joseph M. Manko & Robert S. Kant,
GOING PUBLIC: PRACTICE, PROCEDURE AND CONSEQUENCES

27 VILL. L. REV. 1 (1981)(updated April 1997)

PREPARING THE REGISTRATION STATEMENT

In preparing the prospectus, which is the most important part of the registration statement, it is essential to focus on the characteristics of the particular business and the industry in which it participates. What are the driving forces that can make the business grow and prosper? What is the company's own game plan for the future? What are the significant macroeconomic and company-specific risks facing the company, the potential impediments to its success? Who are its competitors, what differentiates it from them, and what are its competitive strengths and weaknesses? A good understanding of these points should precede the drafting of the prospectus, although it is likely that the answers will evolve and become more refined as the parties interact throughout the drafting process. It is often useful to review prospectuses of comparable companies, with the caveat that the prospectus of each company must reflect its unique features appropriately.

The "quarterback" in preparing the registration statement is normally the attorney for the company. Drafts are circulated to all concerned. Company counsel is principally responsible for preparing the non-financial parts of the registration statement. The managing underwriter or its counsel may play an active role in drafting various sections of the prospectus, particularly those that will assist in marketing the shares. There are normally at least a few "all hands" drafting sessions prior to filing the registration statement, attended by management personnel of the company, counsel for the company, the company's auditors, representatives of the managing underwriter, and underwriters' counsel. Although the degree of input from each of the participants may differ depending on various factors, such as the quality of the initial draft, the experience level of the participants, the uniqueness of the company, and the particular issues in question, major revisions generally result from these drafting sessions. Close cooperation is required among counsel for the company, the underwriters' counsel, the accountants, and the printer. Unless each knows exactly what the others expect, additional delay, expense, and irritation are predictable.

It is essential for the issuer and all others involved in the financing to perceive correctly the role of company counsel. Counsel normally assists the company and its management in preparing the document and in performing their "due diligence" investigation to verify all disclosures for accuracy and completeness. Counsel often serves as the principal draftsperson of the registration statement. Counsel typically solicits information both orally and in writing from a great many people and exercises judgment in evaluating the information received for accuracy and consistency. Experience indicates that executives often overestimate their ability to give accurate information from their recollections without verification. It shows no disrespect, but merely the professionally required degree of healthy skepticism, when the lawyer insists on backup documentation and asks for essentially the same information in different ways and from different sources.

A lawyer would be derelict in the discharge of his or her professional obligations if the lawyer allowed the client's registration statement to include information that the lawyer knew or believed to be inaccurate, or if the lawyer failed to pursue an investigation further in the face of factors arousing suspicions about the accuracy of the information received. On the other hand, it should be understood that a lawyer generally is not an expert in the business or financial aspects of a company's affairs. The normal scope of a professional engagement does not contemplate that the lawyer will act as the ultimate source to investigate or verify all disclosures in the registration statement or to assure that the document is accurate and complete in all respects. Indeed, in many cases the lawyer would lack the expertise to assume that responsibility. In some instances, the lawyer may lack the technical background even to frame the proper questions and must depend upon the client for education about the nature of the business. Counsel does not routinely check information received against books of original entry or source documents, as auditors do, nor does counsel generally undertake to consult sources external to the client to obtain or verify information supplied by the client.

In the last analysis, the company and its management must assume the final responsibility to determine that the information in the registration statement is accurate and complete. Management cannot properly take a passive role and rely entirely upon counsel to ask the right questions, identify the information to be assembled, verify the information, and prepare the registration statement properly.

Clients may have, quite appropriately, a different expectation of the lawyer's role relating to those parts of the prospectus that deal with primarily "legal" matters, such as descriptions of litigation, legal proceedings, tax consequences of various transactions, interpretation of contracts, and descriptions of government requirements. To the extent that such matters are discussed, it is fair and reasonable that the company rely primarily on its counsel for the accuracy and completeness of the descriptive material in the registration statement, assuming proper disclosure of factual matters has been made to counsel. In addition, company counsel normally renders a formal opinion on the legality of the securities being registered, which is filed as an exhibit to the registration statement. In connection with a common stock offering, the opinion would state that the shares being offered are legally issued, fully paid, and nonassessable.

* * *

It is essential for the lawyers, accountants, and executives to be in close coordination while the prospectus is being written. It frequently occurs that the lawyers and the accountants initially have different understandings as to the structure of a transaction or the proper characterization or effect of an event. These differences may not be readily apparent, even from a careful reading of the registration statement's narrative text together with the financial statements. Lawyers sometimes miss the full financial implication of some important matter unless the accountants are readily available to amplify upon the draft statements and supply background information. The text often is written by counsel before the financial statements are available, based upon counsel's incorrect assumptions regarding the as yet unseen financial statement treatment of a transaction.

* * *

Preliminary Preparation

For the average first offering, a very substantial amount of preliminary work is required that does not relate directly to preparing the registration statement as such. To have a vehicle for the offering, the business going public normally must be conducted by a single corporation or a parent corporation with subsidiaries. In most cases, the business is not already in such a neat package when the offering project commences. It often is conducted by a number of corporations under common ownership, by partnerships, or by combinations of business entities. Considerable work must be done in order to reorganize the various entities by mergers, liquidations, and capital contributions. Even when there is a single corporation, a recapitalization almost always is required so that the company will have an appropriate capital structure for the public offering. A decision must be made regarding the proportion of the stock to be sold to the public. Any applicable state securities, or "blue sky," law limitations on insiders' "cheap stock" should be considered in this context especially if the company has been organized in the relatively recent past.

* * *

In preparing the registration statement, there occasionally are important threshold or interpretive problems that can have a major effect on the preparation process or, indeed, on the feasibility of the offering. It often is possible to discuss such problems with the SEC staff in a pre-filing conference by telephone or in person, although some pre-filing conference requests are denied by the staff. However, decisions to request a pre-filing conference should be made with caution. Among other considerations, once a question has been asked in advance of a filing, there may be no practical alternative other than to wait for the staff's answer, which may delay a filing considerably. Frequently, the decision is made simply to proceed with the filing, resolving the threshold issue on the basis which the company considers most appropriate, in the hope that a satisfactory resolution of the problem (either the issuer's initial solution or some other) will be achieved during the review process.

TIMETABLE

Although businesspersons find it difficult to believe, the average first public offering normally requires two to three months of intensive work before the registration statement can be filed. One reason so much time is required is the need to accomplish the preparatory steps just referred to at the same time the registration statement is being prepared. There are many important and often interrelated business decision to be made and implemented and rarely are all of these questions decided definitively at the outset. Some answers must await final figures, or negotiations with underwriters, and must be held open until the last minute. In many instances, companies first exposed to these considerations will change their minds several times in the interim. Furthermore, drafting of the prospectus normally begins before the financial statements are available. Almost inevitably, some rewriting must be done in the non-financial parts of the prospectus after the financial statements are distributed in order to blend the financial and non-financial sections together. Companies frequently have the frustrating feeling as the deadline approaches that everything is hopelessly confused. They are quite surprised to see everything fall into place at the eleventh hour.

After the registration statement is filed with the Commission, the waiting period begins. It is during this interval that red herrings may be distributed. The Commission reviews the registration statement and finally issues its letter of comments. There is a wide variation in the time required for the SEC to process a registration statement.

* * *

The overall time lapse between the beginning of preparation of a company's first registration statement and the final effective date may well exceed six months. Rarely will it be less than three months.

* * *

LIABILITIES

Under the '33 Act and related statutes, civil and criminal liability may arise from material misstatements or omissions in a registration statement when it becomes effective, including the final prospectus; from failure to comply with applicable registration requirements; from failure to supply a final prospectus in connection with specified activities; and from engaging in fraudulent transactions. Under various provisions, directors, certain officers who must sign the registration statement, underwriters, controlling persons, and experts (such as accountants but normally not attorneys) participating in the registration also may be subject to the same liabilities as are imposed upon the company. The parties named are jointly and severally liable and their potential civil liability is the full sales price of the security.

Under the '33 Act, the company is absolutely liable for material deficiencies in the registration statement irrespective of good faith or the exercise of due diligence. However, certain "due diligence" defenses against liability are available to directors, officers who sign the registration statement, underwriters, experts, and controlling persons if they neither knew of the deficiencies in the registration statement nor had reason to know of them upon the exercise of due diligence. There is still considerable uncertainty in this area. However, any person who is exposed to individual liability under the '33 Act for deficiencies in the registration statement should be thoroughly familiar with its contents. Any such person should realize that it may not be possible to avoid responsibility simply by relying on counsel or some other person to prepare the registration statement. Each person should consult with counsel concerning the scope of his individual responsibility.

Association of the Bar of the City of New York,
Report by the Special Committee on Lawyers'
Role in Securities Transactions

32 Bus. Law. 1879 (1977)

Guideline Four:

The lawyer should assist the issuer, on the basis of information furnished to the lawyer, in reaching its decisions as to what information should be included in the registration statement, how it should be included, and to what extent its omission would raise questions under the 1933 Act—*i.e.,* he should assist the issuer in making judgments as to materiality and compliance with the requirements of the registration form and instructions.

Comment:

(a) Within the confines of the agreed assignment of responsibilities and of a realistic evaluation of the extent to which a lawyer's consideration of essentially non-legal matters is useful to the client and warranted by the circumstances, the lawyer should study documents or otherwise inquire into other matters, not primarily legal in nature and not within counsel's expertise as such, in order to provide himself with a background from which better to assist the issuer in making its decisions.

(b) The determination of "materiality" of a fact or its omission, or of whether there is a material inaccuracy in a statement, involves many questions of fact and judgment. Usually any legal judgment will be based on a factual analysis peculiarly within the knowledge and capability of the management of the issuer. Although a lawyer can be helpful in bringing his experience, interrogation techniques and judgment to bear on questions of materiality, he cannot—and should not—take over from the issuer or other more qualified parties the responsibility for decisions in these gray areas. There will, of course, be matters where the subject involved is primarily a legal issue, or where the facts are so clear that a positive judgment can be made based on administrative regulations or administrative or judicial precedent.

More frequently, however, the lawyer can only give the client the benefit of an experienced judgment which he will often (as a practical matter) have to make without having knowledge of all relevant facts and which must be combined with the business judgment of the client, the underwriters, the auditors and perhaps other experts to enable the client to arrive at a final decision. This is not to say that the lawyer's advice and assistance in these matters (particularly in helping to develop the relevant considerations on which these decisions should be based) may not be extremely valuable to the client. The lawyer must not, however, claim too much for his own ability to give definitive answers to these questions nor should he insist on imposing his judgments in substitution for those of the client when he cannot, as a lawyer, say that his judgment as to materiality in the particular circumstances is clearly correct.

(c) The lawyer should not allow the impression to be created that he will normally "investigate" factual matters covered in a registration statement, personally examining into primary sources or data, or that he can verify the reliability of other persons providing this information. A lawyer does not search the files and records of the issuer to discover, for example, all material contracts or other documents. Except in the case of investigations into certain legal matters (such as due incorporation or valid issuance of securities) which the lawyer undertakes to perform personally rather than to rely on others, the lawyer rarely will go to primary records or other sources but will rely on interrogations of, and reports or compilations prepared by, others including other professionals such as auditors, engineers and other lawyers. Such reliance on others is entirely appropriate. Indeed, in most instances the lawyer will not have the skills and experience to work with and analyze the primary data. By questioning the issuer's officers and the other persons providing the information, the lawyer can secure an understanding of the material provided, the means by which it was prepared, and its relevance and importance, and he can, if appropriate, suggest that further investigation or inquiry be undertaken. He can also attempt to cross-check information which seems subject to doubt for some reason, or otherwise warrants such inquiry, by questioning persons who appear familiar with it. Where, because of suspicious or other unusual circumstances, the lawyer believes special investigation of a particular matter is required, he should take this up with the issuer, and a procedure for such investigation should be decided upon. Such a procedure may include the issuer's assigning specific qualified personnel or retaining outside experts to make a special investigation of underlying primary data.

Guideline Five:

The lawyer should assist in the drafting of the registration statement or portions thereof with the goal that, to the extent feasible, the registration statement says what the lawyer understands the issuer intends it to say, is unambiguous, and is written in a way that is designed to protect the issuer from later claims of overstatement, misleading implications, omissions or other deficiencies due to the manner in which the statements in question have been written. The lawyer should be careful, however, to dispel any impression that his assistance in drafting the registration statement can ensure that it will be free from all misleading, unclear or ambiguous statements.

Comment:

The lawyer's assistance in drafting the registration statement may entail preparation of initial drafts or portions thereof, and discussion and revision of drafts prepared by himself and by others. Such assistance should not be misunderstood as indicating that the lawyer has sufficient knowledge concerning the substantive content of the document that he can or does take responsibility for its accuracy or completeness. The lawyer's drafting services are significant since the manner in which the document is organized and written is of considerable importance; but the lawyer should not delude either himself or the client into regarding the lawyer's drafting or organizing abilities as also giving the lawyer the ability to determine the substantive content of the document.

Guideline Six:

The lawyer should avoid statements in the prospectus which could give a mistaken impression that he has passed upon matters which he has not, or that he takes responsibility for the accuracy and completeness of the prospectus.

Comment:

Normally, except for references to specific opinions given by the lawyer on particular matters which are referred to with the lawyer's consent, the only mention of the lawyer in a prospectus should be to his specific opinion as to the validity of the securities being issued. The lawyer should take care that the use of his name for express purposes is not taken as authorization to rely on it for any other purposes, expressly or impliedly. In this connection, the lawyer should consider the advisability of including the following legend wherever his name appears:

> [The lawyer/law firm] has passed on the validity of the securities being issued [or other specific matters, *e.g.,* status of litigation] but purchasers of the securities offered by this Prospectus should not rely on [the lawyer/law firm] with respect to any other matters.

Such language will serve to ensure that the public does not acquire a mistaken impression as to the lawyer's responsibility for the prospectus, and inclusion of this legend may thus be a useful prophylactic measure. In no event should the lawyer permit his name to be used in connection with a registration statement if he believes the client has engaged him in order to make use of his name and reputation rather than for legal advice and assistance.

ESCOTT v. BARCHRIS CONSTRUCTION CORP.

283 F.Supp. 643 (S.D.N.Y. 1968)

McLEAN, DISTRICT JUDGE.

This is an action by purchasers of 5 1/2 per cent convertible subordinated fifteen year debentures of BarChris Construction Corporation (BarChris). Plaintiffs purport to sue on their own behalf and 'on behalf of all other and present and former holders' of the debentures. * * *

The action is brought under Section 11 of the Securities Act of 1933 Plaintiffs allege that the registration statement with respect to these debentures filed with the Securities and Exchange Commission, which became effective on May 16, 1961, contained material false statements and material omissions.

Defendants fall into three categories: (1) the persons who signed the registration statement; (2) the underwriters, consisting of eight investment banking firms, led by Drexel & Co. (Drexel); and (3) BarChris's auditors, Peat, Marwick, Mitchell & Co. (Peat, Marwick).

The signers, in addition to BarChris itself, were the nine directors of BarChris, plus its controller, defendant Trilling, who was not a director. Of the nine directors, five were officers of BarChris, i.e., defendants Vitolo, president; Russo, executive vice president; Pugliese, vice president; Kircher, treasurer; and Birnbaum, secretary. Of the remaining four, defendant Grant was a member of the firm of Perkins, Daniels, McCormack & Collins, BarChris's attorneys. He became a director in October 1960. Defendant Coleman, a partner in Drexel, became a director on April 17, 1961, as did the other two, Auslander and Rose, who were not otherwise connected with BarChris.

Defendants, in addition to denying that the registration statement was false, have pleaded the defenses open to them under Section 11 of the Act, plus certain additional defenses, including the statute of limitations.* * *

* * * On the main issue of liability, the questions to be decided are (1) did the registration statement contain false statements of fact, or did it omit to state facts which should have been stated in order to prevent it from being misleading; (2) if so, were the facts which were falsely stated or omitted 'material' within the meaning of the Act; (3) if so, have defendants established their affirmative defenses?

Before discussing these questions, some background facts should be mentioned.

At the time relevant here, BarChris was engaged primarily in the construction of bowling alleys, somewhat euphemistically referred to as 'bowling centers.' These were rather elaborate affairs. They contained not only a number of alleys or 'lanes,' but also, in most cases, bar and restaurant facilities.

BarChris was an outgrowth of a business started as a partnership by Vitolo and Pugliese in 1946. The business was incorporated in New York in 1955 under the name of B & C Bowling Alley Builders, Inc. Its name was subsequently changed to BarChris Construction Corporation.

The introduction of automatic pin setting machines in 1952 gave a marked stimulus to bowling. It rapidly became a popular sport, with the result that 'bowling centers' began to appear throughout the country in rapidly increasing numbers. BarChris benefited from this increased interest in bowling. Its construction operations expanded rapidly. It is estimated that in 1960 BarChris installed approximately three per cent of all lanes built in the United States. It was thus a significant factor in the industry * * *.

BarChris's sales increased dramatically from 1956 to 1960. According to the prospectus, net sales, in round figures, in 1956 were some

$800,000, in 1957 $1,300,000, in 1958 $1,700,000. In 1959 they increased to over $3,300,000, and by 1960 they had leaped to over $9,165,000.

For some years the business had exceeded the managerial capacity of its founders. Vitolo and Pugliese are each men of limited education. Vitolo did not get beyond high school. Pugliese ended his schooling in seventh grade. Pugliese devoted his time to supervising the actual construction work. Vitolo was concerned primarily with obtaining new business. Neither was equipped to handle financial matters.

Rather early in their career they enlisted the aid of Russo, who was trained as an accountant. * * * He eventually became executive vice president of BarChris. In that capacity he handled many of the transactions which figure in this case.

In 1959 BarChris hired Kircher, a certified public accountant who had been employed by Peat, Marwick. He started as controller and became treasurer in 1960. In October of that year, another ex-Peat, Marwick employee, Trilling, succeeded Kircher as controller. At approximately the same time Birnbaum, a young attorney, was hired as house counsel. He became secretary on April 17, 1961.

In general, BarChris's method of operation was to enter into a contract with a customer, receive from him at that time a comparatively small down payment on the purchase price, and proceed to construct and equip the bowling alley. When the work was finished and the building delivered, the customer paid the balance of the contract price in notes, payable in installments over a period of years. BarChris discounted these notes with a factor and received part of their face amount in cash. The factor held back part as a reserve.

In 1960 BarChris began a practice which has been referred to throughout this case as the 'alternative method of financing.' In substance this was a sale and leaseback arrangement. It involved a distinction between the 'interior' of a building and the building itself, i.e., the outer shell. In instances in which this method applied, BarChris would build and install what it referred to as the 'interior package.' Actually this amounted to constructing and installing the equipment in a building. When it was completed, it would sell the interior to a factor, James Talcott Inc. (Talcott), who would pay BarChris the full contract price therefor. The factor then proceeded to lease the interior either directly to BarChris's customer or back to a subsidiary of BarChris. In the latter case, the subsidiary in turn would lease it to the customer.

Under either financing method, BarChris was compelled to expend considerable sums in defraying the cost of construction before it received reimbursement. As a consequence, BarChris was in constant need of cash to finance its operations, a need which grew more pressing as operations expanded.

In December 1959, BarChris sold 560,000 shares of common stock to the public at $3.00 per share. This issue was underwritten by Peter Morgan & Company, one of the present defendants.

By early 1961, BarChris needed additional working capital. The proceeds of the sale of the debentures involved in this action were to be devoted, in part at least, to fill that need.

The registration statement of the debentures, in preliminary form, was filed with the Securities and Exchange Commission on March 30, 1961. A first amendment was filed on May 11 and a second on May 16. The registration statement became effective on May 16. The closing of the financing took place on May 24. On that day BarChris received the net proceeds of the financing.

By that time BarChris was experiencing difficulties in collecting amounts due from some of its customers. Some of them were in arrears in payments due to factors on their discounted notes. As time went on those difficulties increased. Although BarChris continued to build alleys in 1961 and 1962, it became increasingly apparent that the industry was overbuilt. Operators of alleys, often inadequately financed, began to fail. Precisely when the tide turned is a matter of dispute, but at any rate, it was painfully apparent in 1962.

In May of that year BarChris made an abortive attempt to raise more money by the sale of common stock. It filed with the Securities and Exchange Commission a registration statement for the stock issue which it later withdrew. In October 1962 BarChris came to the end of the road. On October 29, 1962, it filed in this court a petition for an arrangement under Chapter XI of the Bankruptcy Act. BarChris defaulted in the payment of the interest due on November 1, 1962 on the debentures.

The Debenture Registration Statement

In preparing the registration statement for the debentures, Grant acted for BarChris. He had previously represented BarChris in preparing the registration statement for the common stock issue. In connection with the sale of common stock, BarChris had issued purchase warrants. In January 1961 a second registration statement was filed in order to update the information pertaining to these warrants. Grant had prepared that statement as well.

Some of the basic information needed for the debenture registration statement was contained in the registration statements previously filed with respect to the common stock and warrants. Grant used these old registration statements as a model in preparing the new one, making the changes which he considered necessary in order to meet the new situation.

The underwriters were represented by the Philadelphia law firm of Drinker, Biddle & Reath. John A. Ballard, a member of that firm, was in charge of that work, assisted by a young associate named Stanton.

Peat, Marwick, BarChris's auditors, who had previously audited BarChris's annual balance sheet and earnings figures for 1958 and 1959, did the same for 1960. These figures were set forth in the registration statement. In addition, Peat, Marwick undertook a so-called 'S–1 review,' the proper scope of which is one of the matters debated here.

The registration statement in its final form contained a prospectus as well as other information. Plaintiffs' claims of falsities and omissions pertain solely to the prospectus, not to the additional data.

The prospectus contained, among other things, a description of BarChris's business, a description of its real property, some material pertaining to certain of its subsidiaries, and remarks about various other aspects of its affairs. It also contained financial information. It included a consolidated balance sheet as of December 31, 1960, with elaborate explanatory notes. These figures had been audited by Peat, Marwick. It also contained unaudited figures as to net sales, gross profit and net earnings for the first quarter ended March 31, 1961, as compared with the similar quarter for 1960. In addition, it set forth figures as to the company's backlog of unfilled orders as of March 31, 1961, as compared with March 31, 1960, and figures as to BarChris's contingent liability, as of April 30, 1961, on customers' notes discounted and its contingent liability under the so-called alternative method of financing.

Plaintiffs challenge the accuracy of a number of these figures. They also charge that the text of the prospectus, apart from the figures, was false in a number of respects, and that material information was omitted. Each of these contentions, after eliminating duplications, will be separately considered.

[After an extensive analysis, the Court found that the prospectus was materially false and misleading substantially as the plaintiffs had alleged]

* * *

The 'Due Diligence' Defenses

Section 11(b) of the Act provides that:

'no person, other than the issuer, shall be liable* * * who shall sustain the burden of proof—

(3) that (A) as regards any part of the registration statement not purporting to be made on the authority of an expert he had, after reasonable investigation, reasonable ground to believe and did believe, at the time such part of the registration statement became effective, that the statements therein were true and that there was no omission to state a material fact required to be stated therein or necessary to make the statements therein not misleading; * * * and (C) as regards any part of the registration statement purporting to be made on the authority of an expert (other than himself) * * * he had no reasonable ground to believe and did not believe, at the time such part of the registration statement became effective, that the statements therein were untrue or that there was an omission to state a material fact required to be stated therein or necessary to make the statements therein not misleading .'

Section 11(c) defines 'reasonable investigation' as follows:

> In determining, for the purpose of paragraph (3) of subsection (b) of this section, what constitutes reasonable investigation and reasonable ground for belief, the standard of reasonableness shall be that required of a prudent man in the management of his own property.'

Every defendant, except BarChris itself, to whom, as the issuer, these defenses are not available, and except Peat, Marwick, whose position rests on a different statutory provision, has pleaded these affirmative defenses. Each claims that (1) as to the part of the registration statement purporting to be made on the authority of an expert (which, for convenience, I shall refer to as the 'expertised portion'), he had no reasonable ground to believe and did not believe that there were any untrue statements or material omissions, and (2) as to the other parts of the registration statement, he made a reasonable investigation, as a result of which he had reasonable ground to believe and did believe that the registration statement was true and that no material fact was omitted. As to each defendant, the question is whether he has sustained the burden of proving these defenses. Surprising enough, there is little or no judicial authority on this question. No decisions directly in point under Section 11 have been found.

Before considering the evidence, a preliminary matter should be disposed of. The defendants do not agree among themselves as to who the 'experts' were or as to the parts of the registration statement which were expertised. Some defendants say that Peat, Marwick was the expert, others say that BarChris's attorneys, Perkins, Daniels, McCormack & Collins, and the underwriters' attorneys, Drinker, Biddle & Reath, were also the experts. On the first view, only those portions of the registration statement purporting to be made on Peat, Marwick's authority were expertised portions. On the other view, everything in the registration statement was within this category, because the two law firms were responsible for the entire document.

The first view is the correct one. To say that the entire registration statement is expertised because some lawyer prepared it would be an unreasonable construction of the statute. Neither the lawyer for the company nor the lawyer for the underwriters is an expert within the meaning of Section 11. The only expert, in the statutory sense, was Peat, Marwick, and the only parts of the registration statement which purported to be made upon the authority of an expert were the portions which purported to be made on Peat, Marwick's authority.

* * *

I turn now to the question of whether defendants have proved their due diligence defenses. The position of each defendant will be separately considered.

* * *

BIRNBAUM

Birnbaum was a young lawyer, admitted to the bar in 1957, who, after brief periods of employment by two different law firms and an equally brief period of practicing in his own firm, was employed by BarChris as house counsel and assistant secretary in October 1960. Unfortunately for him, he became secretary and a director of BarChris on April 17, 1961, after the first version of the registration statement had been filed with the Securities and Exchange Commission. He signed the later amendments, thereby becoming responsible for the accuracy of the prospectus in its final form.

Although the prospectus, in its description of 'management,' lists Birnbaum among the 'executive officers' and devotes several sentences to a recital of his career, the fact seems to be that he was not an executive officer in any real sense. He did not participate in the management of the company. As house counsel, he attended to legal matters of a routine nature. Among other things, he incorporated subsidiaries, with which BarChris was plentifully supplied. Among the subsidiaries which he incorporated were Capitol Lanes, Inc. which operated Capitol, Yonkers Lanes, Inc. which eventually operated Yonkers, and Parkway Lanes, Inc. which eventually operated Bridge. He was thus aware of that aspect of the business.

Birnbaum examined contracts. In that connection he advised BarChris that the T–Bowl contracts were not legally enforceable. He was thus aware of that fact.

One of Birnbaum's more important duties, first as assistant secretary and later as full-fledged secretary, was to keep the corporate minutes of BarChris and its subsidiaries. This necessarily informed him to a considerable extent about the company's affairs. Birnbaum was not initially a member of the executive committee, however, and did not keep its minutes at the outset. According to the minutes, the first meeting which he attended, 'upon invitation of the Committee,' was on March 22, 1961. He became a member shortly thereafter and kept the minutes beginning with the meeting of April 24, 1961.

It seems probable that Birnbaum did not know of many of the inaccuracies in the prospectus. He must, however, have appreciated some of them. In any case, he made no investigation and relied on the others to get it right. Unlike Trilling, he was entitled to rely upon Peat, Marwick for the 1960 figures, for as far as appears, he had no personal knowledge of the company's books of account or financial transactions. But he was not entitled to rely upon Kircher, Grant and Ballard for the other portions of the prospectus. As a lawyer, he should have known his obligations under the statute. He should have known that he was required to make a reasonable investigation of the truth of all the statements in the unexpertised portion of the document which he signed. Having failed to make such an investigation, he did not have reasonable ground to believe that all these statements were true. Birnbaum has not established his due diligence defenses except as to the audited 1960 figures.

* * *

GRANT

Grant became a director of BarChris in October 1960. His law firm was counsel to BarChris in matters pertaining to the registration of securities. Grant drafted the registration statement for the stock issue in 1959 and for the warrants in January 1961. He also drafted the registration statement for the debentures. In the preliminary division of work between him and Ballard, the underwriters' counsel, Grant took initial responsibility for preparing the registration statement, while Ballard devoted his efforts in the first instance to preparing the indenture.

Grant is sued as a director and as a signer of the registration statement. This is not an action against him for malpractice in his capacity as a lawyer. Nevertheless, in considering Grant's due diligence defenses, the unique position which he occupied cannot be disregarded. As the director most directly concerned with writing the registration statement and assuring its accuracy, more was required of him in the way of reasonable investigation than could fairly be expected of a director who had no connection with this work.

There is no valid basis for plaintiffs' accusation that Grant knew that the prospectus was false in some respects and incomplete and misleading in others. Having seen him testify at length, I am satisfied as to his integrity. I find that Grant honestly believed that the registration statement was true and that no material facts had been omitted from it.

In this belief he was mistaken, and the fact is that for all his work, he never discovered any of the errors or omissions which have been recounted at length in this opinion, with the single exception of Capitol Lanes. He knew that BarChris had not sold this alley and intended to operate it, but he appears to have been under the erroneous impression that Peat, Marwick had knowingly sanctioned its inclusion in sales because of the allegedly temporary nature of the operation.

Grant contends that a finding that he did not make a reasonable investigation would be equivalent to a holding that a lawyer for an issuing company, in order to show due diligence, must make an independent audit of the figures supplied to him by his client. I do not consider this to be a realistic statement of the issue. There were errors and omissions here which could have been detected without an audit. The question is whether, despite his failure to detect them, Grant made a reasonable effort to that end.

Much of this registration statement is a scissors and paste-pot job. Grant lifted large portions from the earlier prospectuses, modifying them in some instances to the extent that he considered necessary. But BarChris's affairs had changed for the worse by May 1961. Statements that were accurate in January were no longer accurate in May. Grant never discovered this. He accepted the assurances of Kircher and Russo that any change which might have occurred had been for the better, rather than the contrary.

It is claimed that a lawyer is entitled to rely on the statements of his client and that to require him to verify their accuracy would set an unreasonably high standard. This is too broad a generalization. It is all a matter of degree. To require an audit would obviously be unreasonable. On the other hand, to require a check of matters easily verifiable is not unreasonable. Even honest clients can make mistakes. The statute imposes liability for untrue statements regardless of whether they are intentionally untrue. The way to prevent mistakes is to test oral information by examining the original written record.

There were things which Grant could readily have checked which he did not check. For example, he was unaware of the provisions of the agreements between BarChris and Talcott. He never read them. Thus, he did not know, although he readily could have ascertained, that BarChris's contingent liability on Type B leaseback arrangements was 100 per cent, not 25 per cent. He did not appreciate that if BarChris defaulted in repurchasing delinquent customers' notes upon Talcott's demand, Talcott could accelerate all the customer paper in its hands, which amounted to over $3,000,000.

As to the backlog figure, Grant appreciated that scheduled unfilled orders on the company's books meant firm commitments, but he never asked to see the contracts which, according to the prospectus, added up to $6,905,000. Thus, he did not know that this figure was overstated by some $4,490,000.

Grant was unaware of the fact that BarChris was about to operate Bridge and Yonkers. He did not read the minutes of those subsidiaries which would have revealed that fact to him. On the subject of minutes, Grant knew that minutes of certain meetings of the BarChris executive committee held in 1961 had not been written up. Kircher, who had acted as secretary at those meetings, had complete notes of them. Kircher told Grant that there was no point in writing up the minutes because the matters discussed at those meetings were purely routine. Grant did not insist that the minutes be written up, nor did he look at Kircher's notes. If he had, he would have learned that on February 27, 1961 there was an extended discussion in the executive committee meeting about customers' delinquencies, that on March 8, 1961 the committee had discussed the pros and cons of alley operation by BarChris, that on March 18, 1961 the committee was informed that BarChris was constructing or about to begin constructing twelve alleys for which it had no contracts, and that on May 13, 1961 Dreyfuss, one of the worst delinquents, had filed a petition in Chapter X.

Grant knew that there had been loans from officers to BarChris in the past because that subject had been mentioned in the 1959 and January 1961 prospectuses. In March Grant prepared a questionaire to be answered by officers and directors for the purpose of obtaining information to be used in the prospectus. The questionnaire did not inquire expressly about the existence of officers' loans. At approximately the same time, Grant prepared another questionnaire in order to obtain information on proxy statements for the annual stockholders' meeting. This questionnaire asked each officer to state whether he was indebted to BarChris, but it did not ask whether BarChris was indebted to him.

Despite the inadequacy of these written questionnaires, Grant did, on March 16, 1961, orally inquire as to whether any officers' loans were outstanding. He was assured by Russo, Vitolo and Pugliese that all such loans had been repaid. Grant did not ask again. He was unaware of the new loans in April. He did know, however, that, at Kircher's request, a provision was inserted in the indenture which gave loans from individuals priority over the debentures. Kircher's insistence on this clause did not arouse his suspicions.

It is only fair to say that Grant was given to understand by Kircher that there were no new officers' loans and that there would not be any before May 16. It is still a close question, however, whether, under all the circumstances, Grant should have investigated further, perhaps by asking Peat, Marwick, in the course of its S–1 review, to look at the books on this particular point. I believe that a careful man would have checked.

There is more to the subject of due diligence than this, particularly with respect to the application of proceeds and customers' delinquencies.

The application of proceeds language in the prospectus was drafted by Kircher back in January. It may well have expressed his intent at that time, but his intent, and that of the other principal officers of BarChris, was very different in May. Grant did not appreciate that the earlier language was no longer appropriate. He never learned of the situation which the company faced in May. He knew that BarChris was short of cash, but he had no idea how short. He did not know that BarChris was withholding delivery of checks already drawn and signed because there was not enough money in the bank to pay them. He did not know that the officers of the company intended to use immediately approximately one-third of the financing proceeds in a manner not disclosed in the prospectus, including approximately $1,000,000 in paying old debts.

In this connection, mention should be made of a fact which has previously been referred to only in passing. The 'negative cash balance' in BarChris's Lafayette National Bank account in May 1961 included a check dated April 10, 1961 to the order of Grant's firm, Perkins, Daniels, McCormack & Collins, in the amount of $8,711. This check was not deposited by Perkins, Daniels until June 1, after the financing proceeds had been received by BarChris. Of course, if Grant had knowingly withheld deposit of this check until that time, he would be in a position similar to Russo, Vitolo and Pugliese. I do not believe, however, that that was the case. I find that the check was not delivered by BarChris to Perkins, Daniels until shortly before June 1.

This incident is worthy of mention, however, for another reason. The prospectus stated on page 10 that Perkins, Daniels had 'received fees aggregating $13,000' from BarChris. This check for $8,711 was one of those fees. It had not been received by Perkins, Daniels prior to May 16. Grant was unaware of this. In approving this erroneous statement in the prospectus, he did not consult his own bookkeeper to ascertain whether it was correct. Kircher told him that the bill had been paid and Grant took his word for it. If he had inquired and had found that this representation was untrue, this discovery might well have led him to a realization of the true state of BarChris's finances in May 1961.

As far as customers' delinquencies is concerned, although Grant discussed this with Kircher, he again accepted the assurances of Kircher and Russo that no serious problem existed. He did not examine the records as to delinquencies, although BarChris maintained such a record. Any inquiry on his part of Talcott or an examination of BarChris's correspondence with Talcott in April and May 1961 would have apprised him of the true facts. It would have led him to appreciate that the statement in this prospectus, carried over from earlier prospectuses, to the effect that since 1955 BarChris had been required to repurchase less than one-half of one per cent of discounted customers' notes could no longer properly be made without further explanation.

Grant was entitled to rely on Peat, Marwick for the 1960 figures. He had no reasonable ground to believe them to be inaccurate. But the matters which I have mentioned were not within the expertised portion of the prospectus. As to this, Grant, was obliged to make a reasonable investigation. I am forced to find that he did not make one. After making all due allowances for the fact that Bar Chris's officers misled him, there are too many instances in which Grant failed to make an inquiry which he could easily have made which, if pursued, would have put him on his guard. In my opinion, this finding on the evidence in this case does not establish an unreasonably high standard in other cases for company counsel who are also directors. Each case must rest on its own facts. I conclude that Grant has not established his due diligence defenses except as to the audited 1960 figures.

The Underwriters and Coleman

The underwriters other than Drexel made no investigation of the accuracy of the prospectus. One of them, Peter Morgan, had underwritten the 1959 stock issue and had been a director of BarChris. He thus had some general familiarity with its affairs, but he knew no more than the other underwriters about the debenture prospectus. They all relied upon Drexel as the 'lead' underwriter.

Drexel did make an investigation. The work was in charge of Coleman, a partner of the firm, assisted by Casperson, an associate. Drexel's attorneys acted as attorneys for the entire group of underwriters. Ballard did the work, assisted by Stanton.

On April 17, 1961 Coleman became a director of BarChris. He signed the first amendment to the registration statement filed on May 11 and the second amendment, constituting the registration statement in its final form, filed on May 16. He thereby assumed a responsibility as a director and signer in addition to his responsibility as an underwriter.

[The Court summarized the investigation that Coleman and Ballard did before Coleman became a director.]

After Coleman was elected a director on April 17, 1961, he made no further independent investigation of the accuracy of the prospectus. He assumed that Ballard was taking care of this on his behalf as well as on behalf of the underwriters.

In April 1961 Ballard instructed Stanton to examine BarChris's minutes for the past five years and also to look at 'the major contracts of the company.'[23] Stanton went to BarChris's office for that purpose on April 24. He asked Birnbaum for the minute books. He read the minutes of the board of directors and discovered interleaved in them a few minutes of executive committee meetings in 1960. He asked Kircher if there were any others. Kircher said that there had been other executive committee meetings but that the minutes had not been written up.

Stanton read the minutes of a few BarChris subsidiaries. His testimony was vague as to which ones. He had no recollection of seeing the minutes of Capitol Lanes, Inc. or Biel or Parkway Lanes, Inc. He did not discover that BarChris was operating Capitol or that it planned to operate Bridge and Yonkers.

As to the 'major contracts,' all that Stanton could remember seeing was an insurance policy. Birnbaum told him that there was no file of major contracts. Stanton did not examine the agreements with Talcott. He did not examine the contracts with customers. He did not look to see what contracts comprised the backlog figure. Stanton examined no accounting records of BarChris. His visit, which lasted one day, was devoted primarily to reading the directors' minutes.

On April 25 Ballard wrote to Grant about certain matters which Stanton had noted on his visit to BarChris the day before, none of which Ballard considered 'very earth shaking.' As far as relevant here, these were (1) Russo's remark as recorded in the executive committee minutes of November 3, 1960 to the effect that because of customers' defaults, BarChris might find itself in the business of operating alleys; (2) the fact that the minutes of Sanpark Realty Corporation were incomplete; and (3) the fact that minutes of the executive committee were missing.

On May 9, 1961, Ballard came to New York and conferred with Grant and Kircher. They discussed the Securities and Exchange Commission's deficiency letter of May 4, 1961 which required the inclusion in the prospectus of certain additional information, notably net sales, gross

---

23. Stanton was a very junior associate. He had been admitted to the bar in January 1961, some three months before. This was the first registration statement he had ever worked on.

profits and net earnings figures for the first quarter of 1961. They also discussed the points raised in Ballard's letter to Grant of April 25. As to the latter, most of the conversation related to what Russo had meant by his remark on November 3, 1960. Kircher said that the delinquency problem was less severe now than it had been back in November 1960, that no alleys had been repossessed, and that although he was 'worried about one alley in Harlem' (Dreyfuss), that was a 'special situation.' Grant reported that Russo had told him that his statement on November 3, 1960 was 'merely hypothetical.' On the strength of this conversation, Ballard was satisfied that the one-half of one per cent figure in the prospectus did not need qualification or elaboration.

As to the missing minutes, Kircher said that those of Sanpark were not significant and that the executive committee meetings for which there were no written minutes were concerned only with 'routine matters.'

It must be remembered that this conference took place only one week before the registration statement became effective. Ballard did nothing else in the way of checking during that intervening week.

Ballard did not insist that the executive committee minutes be written up so that he could inspect them, although he testified that he knew from experience that executive committee minutes may be extremely important. If he had insisted. he would have found the minutes highly informative, as has previously been pointed out (supra at p. 691). Ballard did not ask to see BarChris's schedule of delinquencies or Talcott's notices of delinquencies, or BarChris's correspondence with Talcott.

Ballard did not examine BarChris's contracts with Talcott. He did not appreciate what Talcott's rights were under those financing agreements or how serious the effect would be upon BarChris of any exercise of those rights.

Ballard did not investigate the composition of the backlog figure to be sure that it was not 'puffy.' He made no inquiry after March about any new officers' loans, although he knew that Kircher had insisted on a provision in the indenture which gave loans from individuals priority over the debentures. He was unaware of the seriousness of BarChris's cash position and of how BarChris's officers intended to use a large part of the proceeds. He did not know that BarChris was operating Capitol Lanes.

Like Grant, Ballard, without checking, relied on the information which he got from Kircher. He also relied on Grant who, as company counsel, presumably was familiar with its affairs.

The formal opinion which Ballard's firm rendered to the underwriters at the closing on May 24, 1961 made clear that this is what he had done. The opinion stated:

'In the course of the preparation of the Registration Statement and Prospectus by the Company, we have had numerous conferences with representatives of and counsel for the Company and with its auditors and we have raised many questions regarding the business of the Company. Satisfactory answers to such questions were in each case given us, and all other information and documents we requested have been supplied. We are of the opinion that the data presented to us are accurately reflected in the Registration Statement and Prospectus and that there has been omitted from the Registration Statement no material facts included in such data. Although we have not otherwise verified the completeness or accuracy of the information furnished to us, on the basis of the foregoing and with the exception of the financial statements and schedules (which this opinion does not pass upon), we have no reason to believe that the Registration Statement or Prospectus contains any untrue statement of any material fact or omits to state a material fact required to be stated therein or necessary in order to make the statements therein not misleading.'

Coleman testified that Drexel had an understanding with its attorneys that 'we expect them to inspect on our behalf the corporate records of the company including, but not limited to, the minutes of the corporation, the stockholders and the committees of the board authorized to act for the board.' Ballard manifested his awareness of this understanding by sending Stanton to read the minutes and the major contracts. It is difficult to square this understanding with the formal opinion of Ballard's firm which expressly disclaimed any attempt to verify information supplied by the company and its counsel.

In any event, it is clear that no effectual attempt at verification was made. The question is whether due diligence required that it be made. Stated another way, is it sufficient to ask questions, to obtain answers which, if true, would be thought satisfactory, and to let it go at that, without seeking to ascertain from the records whether the answers in fact are true and complete?

I have already held that this procedure is not sufficient in Grant's case. Are underwriters in a different position, as far as due diligence is concerned?

The underwriters say that the prospectus is the company's prospectus, not theirs. Doubtless this is the way they customarily regard it. But the Securities Act makes no such distinction. The underwriters are just as responsible as the company if the prospectus is false. And prospective investors rely upon the reputation of the underwriters in deciding whether to purchase the securities.

There is no direct authority on this question, no judicial decision defining the degree of diligence which underwriters must exercise to establish their defense under Section 11.

* * *

The purpose of Section 11 is to protect investors. To that end the underwriters are made responsible for the truth of the prospectus. If they may escape that responsibility by taking at face value representations made to them by the company's management, then the inclusion of underwriters among those liable under Section 11 affords the investors no additional protection. To effectuate the statute's purpose, the phrase 'reasonable investigation' must be construed to require more effort on the part of the underwriters than the mere accurate reporting in the prospectus of 'date presented' to them by the company. It should make no difference that this data is elicited by questions addressed to the company officers by the underwriters, or that the underwriters at the time believe that the company's officers are truthful and reliable. In order to make the underwriters' participation in this enterprise of any value to the investors, the underwriters must make some reasonable attempt to verify the data submitted to them. They may not rely solely on the company's officers or on the company's counsel. A prudent man in the management of his own property would not rely on them.

It is impossible to lay down a rigid rule suitable for every case defining the extent to which such verification must go. It is a question of degree, a matter of judgment in each case. In the present case, the underwriters' counsel made almost no attempt to verify management's representations. I hold that that was insufficient.

On the evidence in this case, I find that the underwriters' counsel did not make a reasonable investigation of the truth of those portions of the prospectus which were not made on the authority of Peat, Marwick as an expert. Drexel is bound by their failure. It is not a matter of relying upon counsel for legal advice. Here the attorneys were dealing with of fact. Drexel delegated to them, as its agent, the business of examining the corporate minutes and contracts. It must bear the consequences of their failure to make an adequate examination.

The other underwriters, who did nothing and relied solely on Drexel and on the lawyers are also bound by it. * * *

The same conclusions must apply to Coleman. Although he participated quite actively in the earlier stages of the preparation of the prospectus, and contributed questions and warnings of his own, in addition to the questions of counsel, the fact is that he stopped his participation toward the end of March 1961. He made no investigation after he became a director. When it came to verification, he relied upon his counsel to do it for him. Since counsel failed to do it, Coleman is bound by that failure. Consequently in his case also, he has not established his due diligence defense except as to the audited 1960 figures.

James D. Cox, Robert W. Hillman & Donald C. Langevoort,
Securities Regulation: Cases and Materials

(4th ed. 2004)

Notes and Questions

1. Insiders and Outsiders. *BarChris* drew a distinction between corporate insiders (management) and outsiders (nonmanagement directors), and in turn between outsiders who have special expertise or involvement in the distribution (e.g., directors who are the company's lawyers or investment bankers) and others. Among these, there seems to be a sliding scale of responsibility based on what can realistically be expected of the particular defendant. At one end of this scale, top managers of the issuer are held to the highest standard of diligence. Another illustration of the sliding-scale approach is found in *Feit v. Leasco Data Processing Equipment Corp.*, 332 F.Supp. 544, 578 (E.D.N.Y. 1971), where the court went so far as to suggest that insiders are virtual "guarantors" of the registration statement.

At the other end of this scale, outside directors and other "peripheral" participants are judged in a more forgiving light—though their duty to investigate remains. Their exposure in turn varies depending upon particular expertise. Here, again, there is an intriguing conceptual question. Is it really consistent with the structure of Section 11(b) to say that for a nonexpertised portion of the registration statement, director *A* may be liable for an inaccuracy because her special expertise (e.g., as an attorney) should have put her on notice that something was wrong, while director *B* is not? Or would it be more consistent to say that director *B* should nonetheless be held liable by virtue of his failure to assure that someone with the requisite expertise did in fact exercise the proper level of care? In other words, does the *BarChris* approach introduce out of whole cloth something of an "expertising" notion (i.e., a right to rely on others) with respect to the entire registration statement? Along this line, consider whether the following more recent statement of due diligence obligations of outside directors is consistent with what *BarChris* seemed to have in mind:

> Since Valentine was an outside director, he was not obliged to conduct an independent investigation into the accuracy of all the statements contained in the registration statement. He could rely upon the reasonable representations of management, if his own conduct and level of inquiry were reasonable under the circumstances. He was reasonably familiar with the company's business and operations. He regularly attended board meetings at which the board discussed every aspect of the company's business. And he reviewed the company's financial statements. He was familiar with the company's development of its new product lines.... He reviewed six drafts of the registration statement and saw nothing suspicious or inconsistent with the knowledge he had acquired as a director. And he discussed certain aspects of the registration statement with management....
>
> Plaintiffs argue that Valentine did not make specific inquiries of the company's management with respect to the representations contained in the prospectus. But he had no duty to do so as long as the prospectus statements were consistent with the knowledge of the company which he had reasonably acquired in his position as a director. He was also given comfort by the fact that the prospectus and the information in it were reviewed by underwriters, counsel and accountants. This met the standard of due diligence and reasonable investigation.

Weinberger v. Jackson, Fed. Sec. L. Rep. (CCH) ¶95,693 (N.D. Cal. 1990).

The sliding-scale approach to due diligence liability does now appear to be codified in Rule 176, which says that in evaluating either reasonable investigation or reasonable grounds for belief, account should be taken of, for example, "[t]he presence or absence of another relationship with the issuer when the person is a director or proposed director" and "[r]easonable reliance on officers, employees and others whose duties should have given them knowledge of the particular facts (in light of the functions and responsibilities of the particular person with respect to the issuer and the filing)."

On diligence generally, *see* R. Haft, Due Diligence in Securities Transactions (2003).

2. *Attorneys' Liability.* Given the central role that they play in the drafting of a registration statement, it seems curious that attorneys are not listed among the potential defendants in an action under Section 11 except to the extent that they are also officers or directors or otherwise treated as "experts." And the courts have held that attorneys are experts only with respect to the discrete portions of the registration statement that operate as legal opinions, for example, that the shares in question have been validly authorized and issued and are nonassessable under state law. E.g., *ZZZZ Best Securities Litigation*, [1989] Fed. Sec. L. Rep. (CCH) ¶ 94,485 (C.D. Cal. 1989); *Ahern v. Gaussoin*, 611 F.Supp. 1465 (D. Or. 1985).

Nor have the courts for the most part been willing to disregard the carefully crafted list of defendants in Section 11(a) by imposing liability on others under a theory such as aiding and abetting. As a result, it is unlikely that the law firm that mistakenly fails to discover material information will be directly liable to investors at all under Section 11.

This does not mean, however, that the firm is safe from liability under the securities laws. There may be some room to argue that liability arises under Section 12(a)(2), considered in the next section. Or suit could be brought against the attorneys under Rule 10b-5, although there the level of culpability for finding a violation is substantially higher—the plaintiff must establish a knowing (or perhaps reckless) involvement in the fraud. As an entirely separate matter, of course, the firm may be liable under a variety of state law theories, including malpractice.

* * *

6. BarChris *Revisited?* Although *BarChris* is still the most frequently noted precedent on the due diligence defense, you should take note of later opinions that suggest a somewhat more lenient attitude toward the responsibilities of underwriters and directors. In *Software Toolworks Securities Litigation*, 789 F.Supp. 1489 (N.D. Cal. 1992), for instance, the court held that the adequacy of a due diligence investigation is a question for the judge, not a jury:

> First, the due diligence defense is a statutory standard; as such, its application to undisputed historical facts should normally be a matter for the judge. This ensures that the administration of the statutory defense benefits from consistency, uniformity and predictability. Second, a decision on the due diligence defense generally affects a class of persons (as opposed to one person), making it in the nature of judicial rule making. Third, knowledge of what constitutes due diligence does not fall within the common experience of jurors, making it instead a

question better suited for the judge. Fourth, leaving the question of what constitutes due diligence to the jury will lead to a battle of experts. While this may be appropriate in some cases, with a question like due diligence, the inquiry does not lend itself to any objective standards. The experts, who basically become paid advocates, will simply express an opinion based on their own subjective viewpoints, which will be biased by their role. The jurors will then be forced to decide between these paid advocates. The resulting uncertainty will increase litigation against deep pocket defendants (such as underwriters) and encourage collusion between plaintiffs and the issuer, who will often be in a precarious financial situation already. These policy implications favor summary judgment as the preferred means of resolution. Finally, treating due diligence as a question of law, once the historical facts are undisputed, will apportion the risk more appropriately, encourage settlement at early stages and lead to more equitable and consistent results.

Id. at 1495–1496. On appeal, the Ninth Circuit agreed that due diligence could be decided as a matter of law (and by means of summary judgment) where the historical facts were undisputed, but only upon determining that no rational jury could find otherwise. It affirmed the lower court's findings for the underwriters as to some matters, but reversed as to others. *See In re Software Toolworks Securities Litigation*, 38 F.3d 1078 (9th Cir. 1994). *See also Weinberger v. Jackson*, [1990–1991 Transfer Binder] Fed. Sec. L. Rep. (CCH) ¶95,693 (N.D. Cal. 1990) (outside director under no duty to make specific inquiries of management so long as the information in the prospectus was consistent with the information he had reasonably acquired during service as a director).

E.   CONTINUOUS DISCLOSURE

IN THE MATTER OF
WILLIAM R. CARTER
CHARLES J. JOHNSON, JR.

47 S.E.C. 471 (1981)

OPINION OF THE COMMISSION

William R. Carter and Charles J. Johnson, Jr. respondents, appeal from the initial decision of the Administrative Law Judge in this proceeding brought under Rule 2(e) of the Commission Rules of Practice. In an opinion dated March 1979, the Administrative Law Judge found that, in connection with their representation of National Telephone Company, Inc. during the period from May 1974 to May 1975, Carter and Johnson willfully violated and willfully aided and abetted violations of Sections 10(b) and 13(a) of the Securities Exchange Act of 1934 (the "Exchange Act") and Rules 10b–5, 12b–20 and 13a–11 thereunder and that they engaged in unethical and improper professional conduct. In light of these findings, the Administrative Law Judge concluded that Carter and Johnson should be suspended from appearing or practicing before the Commission for periods of one year and nine months, respectively.

For the reasons stated more fully below, we reverse the decision of the Administrative Law Judge with respect to both respondents. We have concluded that the record does not adequately support the Administrative Law Judge's findings of violative conduct by respondents. Moreover, we conclude that certain concepts of proper ethical and professional conduct were not sufficiently developed, at the time of the conduct here at issue, to permit a finding that either respondent breached applicable ethical or professional standards. In addition, we are today giving notice of an interpretation by the Commission of the term "unethical or improper professional conduct," as that term is used in Rule 2(e)(1)(ii). This interpretation will be applicable prospectively in cases of this kind.

II.

BACKGROUND OF RULE 2(E)

* * *

B.   The Purpose of Rule 2(e). The Commission promulgated Rule 2(e) pursuant to its general rulemaking powers in order to protect the integrity of its processes. * * *

Rule 2(e) represents a balancing of public benefits. It rests upon the recognition that the privilege of practicing before the Commission is a mechanism that generates great leverage—for good or evil—in the administration of the securities laws. A significant failure to perform properly the professional's role has implications extending beyond the particular transaction involved, for wrongdoing by a lawyer or an accountant raises the spectre of a replication of that conduct with other clients.

Recognition of the public implications of the securities professional's role does not mean that the Commission has, by rule, imposed duties to the public on lawyers where such duties would not otherwise exist.* * * [T]he traditional role of the lawyer as counselor is to advise his client, not the public, about the law. Rule 2(e) does not change the nature of that obligation. Nevertheless, if a lawyer violates ethical or professional standards, or becomes a conscious participant in violations of the securities laws, or performs his professional function without regard to the consequences, it will not do to say that because the lawyer's duty is to his client alone, this Commission must stand helplessly by while the lawyer carries his privilege of appearing and practicing before the Commission on to the next client.

C.   The Operation of Rule 2(e).* * * Subparagraph (1)(i) provides for sanctions upon a finding that a respondent does "not ... possess the requisite qualifications to represent others." The motivating concept is clear: the Commission's processes cannot function effectively without the existence of competent professionals who counsel and assist their clients in securities matters. The same focus is evident in subparagraph (ii), which provides for sanctions if a respondent is "lacking in character or integrity or [has] engaged in unethical or improper professional conduct.''

The operation of subparagraph (iii) of the Rule reflects the same concerns. This provision provides for suspension or disbarment if the Commission finds, after notice of and opportunity for hearing that a respondent has "willfully violated, or willfully aided and abetted the violation of any provision, of the federal securities laws ... or the rules and regulations thereunder." Not every violation of law, however, may be sufficient to justify invocation of the sanctions available under Rule 2(e). The violation must be of a character that threatens the integrity of the Commission's processes in the way that the activities of unqualified or unethical professionals do.

Against that background, we turn to an analysis of respondents' conduct. In our judgment, that conduct presents difficult questions under the applicable legal and professional standards.

III.

RESPONDENTS' CONDUCT

A. National Telephone Company. The conduct at issue in these proceedings occurred in connection with respondents' legal representation of National Telephone Company, Inc. ("National") during the period from mid–1974 through mid–1975. National, a Connecticut corporation with its principal offices located in East Hartford, Connecticut, was founded in 1971 to lease sophisticated telephone equipment systems to commercial customers pursuant to long-term (5–to 10–year) leases. National enjoyed an impressive growth rate in its first three years, increasing its total assets from $320,123 to $19,028,613 and its net income from $2,390 to $633,485 during this period. At the same time, the company's backlog grew from $66,000 to $2,610,000 and the value of equipment leases written by it increased from $255,422 to $13,292,549.

The architect of National's meteoric rise was Sheldon. L. Hart, one of its founders and, at all times relevant to these proceedings, its controlling stockholder. From its incorporation until his resignation on May 24, 1975, Hart was National's chief executive officer, chairman of the board of directors, president and treasurer. National's chief in-house counsel was Mark I. Lurie who, assisted by Brian Kay, was one of respondents' principal contracts with the company.

In large measure, National was a prisoner of its own success. As is commonly the case with equipment leasing companies, the greater part of National's costs in connection with a new lease, including equipment marketing and installation expenses, was incurred well before rental payments commenced. Since rental payments were National's only significant source of revenues, the company's cash flow situation worsened with each new lease, and continued growth and operations could only be sustained through external financing. Between 1971 and 1973, National managed to obtain needed capital from an initial public offering of stock under Regulation A, short-term loans from local banks, and an offering of convertible debentures in September of 1973.

National's last successful effort to secure significant outside financing resulted in the execution, in May and June of 1974, of a $15 million credit agreement (the "Credit Agreement") with a group of five banks. Although the Credit Agreement was not closed (in amended form) until December 1974, the banks were willing to advance substantial sums to National under a variety of demand arrangements prior to the closing. In fact, by the time of the closing on December 20, 1974, these advances totaled some $16.8 million. The Credit Agreement was amended to cover this amount, plus $2.2 million for general corporate purposes and an additional $2 million available only upon the implementation of a special business plan limiting National's business growth if other sources of money could not be located. Unfortunately, funds available under the Credit Agreement, as amended, were not sufficient to finance National's expansion and operations much beyond the closing, and the pressure on National's cash flow continued.

National finally ran out of time in July of 1975, after being unable to secure sufficient external financing after the closing of the Credit Agreement. On July 2, 1975, National was forced to file a petition for an arrangement under Chapter XI of the Bankruptcy Act; in March of 1976 this proceeding was converted into a reorganization under Chapter X of the Bankruptcy Act.

* * *

B. Respondents and Their Law Firm. Carter, an attorney admitted to practice in the State of New York, was born in 1917. He received his law degree from Harvard Law School and has been working for the law firm known as Brown, Wood, Ivey, Mitchell & Petty ("Brown, Wood") since 1945, having become a partner of the firm in 1954. Carter's principal areas of practice have been securities, general corporate and antitrust law.

Johnson, also admitted to practice as an attorney in the State of New York, as well as in the State of Connecticut, was born in 1932. He received his legal education at Harvard Law School and joined Brown, Wood's predecessor firm in 1956, becoming a partner in 1967. Johnson's principal areas of practice have been corporate and securities law.

Kenneth M. Socha worked with Carter and Johnson on a variety of legal matters affecting National, including all of the matters which are the basis of these proceedings. Socha joined Brown, Wood as an associate in 1970 and continued in that capacity during all periods relevant to these proceedings.

* * *

During 1974 and 1975, Brown, Wood, principally through Carter, Johnson and Socha, provided a wide range of legal services to National, including the preparation of a Form S–8 registration statement, proxy materials and an annual report for the company's 1974 annual stock-holders meeting, other Commission filings, press releases and communications to National's stockholders. Johnson was charged with the overall coordination of Brown, Wood's legal efforts on National's behalf and was generally kept aware of progress on all significant projects. In March of 1974, after another Brown, Wood partner left the firm, Johnson asked Carter to assist Socha in working on the Credit Agreement. Thereafter Carter assumed primary responsibility for that project.

In July of 1974, Johnson was elected secretary of National, agreeing to serve in such capacity at Hart's urging. Although his principal duty as secretary was to attend meetings of the board of directors and prepare appropriate minutes, Johnson testified that he attended a total of only four meetings during this period: those of his election on July 1, 1974 and his resignation on May 24, 1975, and two additional meetings which were held on August 19, 1974 and October 15, 1974. The National board of directors held at least three additional meetings during Johnson's tenure as secretary at which he was not present.

* * *

C. Chronology of National's Final Year: May 1974 to May 1975. In order fully to appreciate respondents' role in the events at issue here, it is necessary to set forth the following rather lengthy description of the 12 months immediately preceding public disclosure of the circumstances that led to National's bankruptcy. Except as may be noted below, the record contains ample evidence to support the conclusion that both respondents were aware of the facts and circumstances described.

1. May to August 1974. * * * National's story lies in its unrelenting need to secure ever greater amounts of outside financing. * * *

In May and June of 1974, negotiations with a consortium of five banks, in which Carter, Johnson and Socha were all participants, culminated in the execution of the Credit Agreement, which was dated as of April 30, 1974. * * * As discussed below, the Credit Agreement (as amended) was not formally closed until December 20, 1974, in part because National was unable to satisfy the closing conditions relating to its liquidity and debt-to-net-worth ratios. Ultimately the banks agreed to waive these conditions.

Since the Credit Agreement contemplated that the loans thereunder would be secured by substantially all of National's assets, it was necessary for National to transfer these assets to Systems, a transfer which in turn required the approval of National's stockholders. In order to secure this approval, National called its annual stockholders meeting for June 27, 1974, and Brown, Wood was asked to prepare the proxy materials for this meeting. Carter and Johnson also participated in the preparation of National's 1974 Annual Report. These proxy materials, along with National's 1974 Annual Report, were sent to National's stockholders on June 17 and filed with the Commission on June 19. * * *

National's 1974 Annual Report contained projections of future lease installations which showed, by each quarter, a doubling of annual installations from approximately $13.3 million in fiscal 1974 to approximately $27 million in fiscal 1975. In response to a specific request from Hart, Carter advised National orally and in writing that, in light of Securities Act Release No. 5362 (Feb. 2, 1973), a copy of which Carter sent to Hart, it was permissible to include projections in the Annual Report, but that the assumptions underlying the projections should also be disclosed. Hart ignored this advice and the Annual Report was distributed without assumptions. This incident is the first example the record of Hart's uncooperative reaction to respondents' advice concerning the disclosure demands of the federal securities laws.

* * *

2.   September to December 1974. By early fall of 1974, National's cash needs outstripped its existing financing sources and a severe cash crisis ensued. A meeting between National and its bankers was held on September 11, 1974; neither respondent was present. * * *

At the September 11 meeting with the banks, Hart indicated that the projected equity offering had been ruled out by National's investment bankers, due to deteriorating market conditions. He further reported that National's cash flow problems had caused the company voluntarily to institute a "wind-down" program, effective September 1. * * *

Hart, in fact, had lied to the banks. No wind-down program had been instituted or, as it turned out, would be until almost eight months later, in May of 1975. There is, however, no evidence in the record that respondents were, or ever became, aware of Hart's September 11, 1974 deception.

* * *

In light of his presence at the July 1, August 19 and October 15 board meetings, as well as the October 18 bank meeting, Johnson was well aware of National's cash crisis, its continuing failure to obtain needed financing and its purported "wind-down" program. This, in addition to the well-known depressed state of the credit markets and the fact that National had projected, confirmed and continued to report, without obviously relevant qualifications, rapidly growing sales and earnings, undoubtedly prompted Johnson to instruct Socha to draft a disclosure letter to National's stockholders approximately two days after the October 18 bank meeting.

The proposed stockholders letter, which was reviewed by both Carter and Johnson and sent to the company in early November, was a candid summary of National's financial predicament, noting that National would "in the near future" have to obtain significant financing in addition to the Credit Agreement. * * *

Johnson subsequently told Lurie that this was the type of communication "that a company ... interested in keeping its stockholders advised on a regular basis should be making." Despite this advice, National's management declined to issue the letter. Neither respondent elected to pursue the matter.

* * *

It is important to note, at this point, that both Carter and Johnson must have been aware that, if National were to implement the wind-down plan, the company would have no reasonable opportunity to meet the projections of $27 million in lease installations which were set forth in the 1974 Annual Report and indirectly reconfirmed the company's September 12 letter to its stockholders. The wind-down plan, which Socha summarized in a December 2 memorandum to Johnson, provided that National would not be permitted to enter into any further leases. Obviously, under these circumstances, the company's sales and earnings growth would be halted—short of projected levels.

In early December, Socha received from National a draft of the company's quarterly report to its stockholders for the second fiscal quarter ended September 30, 1974. The report contained a series of graphs, illustrating the successful results of National's operations, but once again made no mention of the dire financial straights in which the company found itself in December. Such an omission was especially significant in light of the disclosure recommendations which Brown, Wood had by then made to National. When Socha inquired whether the use of the graphs had been cleared by Johnson, Lurie informed him that they had. This was not true, as Johnson noted on the copy of the draft report circulated to him by Socha. The quarterly report was mailed as proposed, and neither respondent ever spoke with the company's management about the disclosure problems it presented or about Lurie's misrepresentation to Socha.

It thus appears that, by early December, Carter and Johnson were both fully aware that (1) National was experiencing a cash crisis severe enough to threaten the continued viability of the company if further financing could not be found, (2) when closed, the Credit Agreement, as modified by the Amendment, would not provide the necessary additional financing, (3) National's earlier projections could no longer be achieved if the Credit Agreement's wind-down plan were to be implemented and (4) National's management was unreceptive when confronted with respondents' advice to do close the company's financial problems.

* * *

3. December 1974 to January 1975. In the final days leading to the closing National's "wind-down" plan was renegotiated somewhat and finally emerged with a new name the lease maintenance plan ("LMP").
* * *

At a meeting held on December 11, with Carter and representatives of National and the banks present, final details of the Amendment were negotiated. A draft of the Amendment dated December 13, 1974, which was prepared by White & Case, contemplated an arrangement under which the banks would permit Systems to borrow up to $19 million at any time on or before April 30, 1975. These borrowings were to be secured by the telephone leases and equipment transferred to Systems by National and guaranteed by National. If either (1) National and/or Systems attempted to borrow in excess of $19 million from the existing bank group or (2) National failed to meet a specified liquidity test, National and Systems were acquired to implement the LMP. Their failure to do so in accordance with the provisions of the LMP was an event of default under the Credit Agreement, as modified by the Amendment (the Amended Credit Agreement"), and resulted in all outstanding indebtedness under that Agreement becoming due and payable upon demand.

The December 13 draft of the Amendment for the first time contained a reference to a "lease maintenance plan" and indicated that the LMP was to be attached as an exhibit to the Amendment. The effect of the implementation of the LMP on National's operations and growth would obviously be both dramatic and devastating. Indeed, as one expert called by respondents testified, the LMP was a sort of a holding pattern short of bankruptcy or levy by the creditors." The LMP required National to terminate all sales activities, dismiss all sales personnel, and limit its operations to those necessary to service existing leases. In effect, the company would be transformed into a mere service agency, maintaining existing leases, but writing no new ones. Moreover, the final $2 million of the funds to be provided by the banks was only available until June 30, 1975 and could only be used to implement the LMP, principally by financing the installation of equipment already in inventory to complete existing orders.

* * *

On December 19, the day immediately preceding the closing under the Amended Credit Agreement, at a day-long pre-closing meeting, Hart told Carter that he did not want the terms of the LMP made public or filed with the Commission. Although Carter testified that he could not recall the reason for this request, he speculated that Hart sought not to publicize the LMP because he was concerned that the disclosure of the LMP's effects on the company's business would have a negative impact on the morale of National's sales personnel. After reading the LMP, Carter advised Hart that the LMP would have to be filed with the Commission if it were an exhibit to the Amendment, as originally had been contemplated. However, Carter added that the LMP need not be filed with the Commission or publicized if it were not an exhibit but rather merely referred to in the Amendment. Hart agreed, and the Amendment was modified to delete the LMP as an exhibit.

Also at the December 19 pre-closing conference, Carter reviewed and extensively revised a press release prepared by National announcing the closing of the Amended Credit Agreement. The revised press release was reviewed by all parties at the meeting, including the company's management. No one raised any objections to the revisions proposed by Carter.

On December 20, the Amended Credit Agreement was closed and National immediately borrowed $18 million from the banks. * * *

Whatever the state of Carter's knowledge concerning National's past-due obligations, the record makes it clear that Carter understood that the December 20 financing in no way extricated National from its financial dilemma. At the time of his testimony in the Commission's investigation, Carter stated that he understood that, if National did not obtain significant additional financing, it would soon be "right back in the soup."

Immediately after the closing, National issued the press release that Carter had redrafted the day before. The release stated, in its entirety:

PRESS RELEASE—FOR IMMEDIATE RELEASE

EAST HARTFORD, CONN.,

DECEMBER 20, 1974

National Telephone Company today announced the execution of a $6,000,000 extension of a $15,000,000 Credit Agreement with a group of banks headed by Bankers Trust Company of New York. Included in the $21 million is a contingency fund of $2 million which is available until June 30, 1975 and which may be utilized by the Company only for the purpose of funding a lease maintenance program in the event additional financing is not otherwise available.

Of the $21 million, the Company has borrowed $18 million pursuant to a seven-year term loan, of which approximately $16,500,000 was used to repay outstanding short-term loans. The balance will be used for general operation expenses. Participating in the loans are Bankers Trust Company of New York Mellon Bank N.A. of Pittsburgh, Central National Bank of Cleveland, The Connecticut Bank and Trust Company and The Hartford National Bank and Trust Company of Hartford, Connecticut.

The press release did not discuss either of following matters each of which was then with knowledge of Carter and Johnson.

(1) The precise nature and effects on National's business of the LMP and the likelihood that National would be required to implement the LMP with in a short period of time; and

(2) The substantial limitations placed on National's operations by the Amended Credit Agreement.

It is also apparent from the record that the press release's statement indicating that the balance of the financing remaining after the repayment outstanding bank debt "will be used for general operating expenses" was misleading, in light of the substantial overdue obligations of National then existing.

The second major item of public disclosure concerning the closing was a stockholders letter mailed, without respondents' knowledge, by National on or about December 23. This letter, which was issued in the face of Socha's advice to National that no further public statements should be issued concerning the Amended Credit Agreement unless such statements were cleared by Brown, Wood, contained numerous misstatements and omissions. * * *

Respondents first learned of the letter on December 27, when Brian Kay, who was aware that National had ignored Socha's advice that all public disclosure should be reviewed by them, voluntarily telephoned Socha and dictated the letter to him. Socha thought that the letter's description of the Amended Credit Agreement was "seriously inadequate" and immediately gave a copy of it to Johnson. Carter, too, was consulted. While respondents felt that the letter did not make "adequate disclosure" with respect to the Amended Credit Agreement, they concluded that, when read together with the earlier December 20 press release which Carter had revised, it was not materially false or misleading, and that no corrective action by National was therefore required. Johnson later did, however, orally express his dissatisfaction with the letter to Lurie.

With the close of 1974, the record reveals that respondents were in the uncomfortable position of attempting to provide disclosure advice to an aggressive client whose unreceptive management actively frustrated the giving of advice and ignored what advice managed to get through. It is in the context of this attitude that respondents and National moved into the new year, with the final efforts to save the company and the resulting sharp needs to attend to the company's public disclosure obligations.

4.   January to March 1975. On January 9, 1975, National filed a current report on Form 8–K for the month of December 1974, reporting on the closing under the Amended Credit Agreement. This document was drafted by Carter, who accepted full responsibility for it.

The Amended Credit Agreement, which was attached to the Form 8–K as an exhibit, made frequent reference to the LMP. * * * As previously requested by Hart, however, the LMP itself was not included as an exhibit to the Agreement of the filing; nor was the term "lease maintenance plan" specifically defined or the effects which it would have on the company discussed.

Between the January 9, 1975 filing of National's form 8–K and mid-March, National's financial condition deteriorated even further, to a degree requiring the implementation of the LMP. In addition, the gap between National's public disclosure posture and its private financial condition continued to widen and National's board of directors was becoming increasingly uncomfortable with the situation. There is no indication in the record that either respondent directly or indirectly became aware of the growing seriousness of the situation until a March 17 telephone call from the banks' counsel, described below. * * *

On March 17—nearly one month after the February 20 consultants report, and over six weeks after the LMP had in fact been triggered— Brown, Wood was informed for the first time, by the banks' lawyers, White & Case, that events requiring implementation of the LMP had occurred. The White & Case lawyers had received a telephone call from a vice president of one of the banks informing them of this fact and reporting that no public disclosure had been made by National. The bank vice president also sought White & Case's advice on how to respond to trade creditors of National who were making inquiries to the banks about the company.

During their March 17 conversation, the White & Case lawyers advised Carter that National and its counsel, Brown, Wood, had the responsibility to determine what disclosure, if any, would be appropriate under the circumstances, and they sought assurances that, if proper disclosure were deemed necessary, it would be forthcoming. Carter, who admittedly considered the triggering of the LMP clearly material, assured White & Case that, if what they said were true, Brown, Wood would contact National and "get a statement out." The White & Case lawyers then called the bank's vice president and relayed the content of their conversation with Carter.

On the following day, March 18, Carter telephoned Lurie and informed him of the call from the White & Case lawyers. Lurie neither confirmed nor denied that the LMP had been triggered. Rather he dissembled, stating that the situation was "tight," but adding that, "if they were careful, they would be all right." Carter advised Lurie that, if the LMP had indeed been triggered, the fact should be disclosed publicly, although he did not press Lurie for a definite answer on whether the LMP had in fact been triggered, or on whether National's management was in fact implementing the LMP as required by the Amended Credit Agreement.

Carter informed Johnson both of the telephone call from the banks' lawyers and the subsequent conversations with Lurie. While Johnson's first reaction was to find out what the facts were, neither he nor anyone else at Brown, Wood sought to verify the facts by contacting anyone at National. Nor did they seek to contact anyone outside of National, such as the consulting firm, which they knew had been charged by the parties with responsibility for monitoring National's compliance with the terms of the Amended Credit Agreement.

5.   April to May 1975. * * *

On April 23, 1975 both respondents met with Hart and advised him in no uncertain terms that immediate disclosure was required. In response to Hart's protestations that National would soon obtain additional financing, respondents advised him that these hopes, as well as any negotiations for a waiver of the LMP by the banks, did not serve to excuse National's legal obligation to make prompt disclosure.

Shortly before the April 23 meeting, the vice president of one of the lending banks had written to Hart requesting, among other things, a "written response from your counsel regarding [National's] obligation to make public disclosure regarding significant transactions which may have transpired during the last several months, particularly with regard to the implementing of the lease maintenance plan." Presumably as a result of this request, Hart telephoned Johnson on April 28—only five days after having received the unambiguous and forceful advice that disclosure was required—to request that Johnson issue a legal opinion for the banks to the effect that disclosure of the triggering of the LMP was not necessary. Johnson testified that he replied as follows:

I'm incredulous. I just can't believe this. You sat in my office last week and I told you as clearly and positively and precisely as I could that my advice was that you should disclose that you had gone into the lease maintenance mode.

Ultimately, Hart responded to the bank's request for an opinion of counsel with a letter from National stating that no disclosure had been made because, "in the opinion of the company," none was required.

In late April, after the telephone encounter with Hart described above, Johnson instructed Socha to draft a disclosure document for National to issue, either in its next report to the Commission or in a special letter to the stockholders. In doing so, Johnson specified that the draft should be one that would be "acceptable to a person as emotionally involved as Hart." Both respondents reviewed and approved the draft prepared by Socha and it was forwarded to Hart on or about May 1, with the suggestion that Hart call Carter or Johnson about it.

* * * National did not issue this disclosure document in any form and the record does not indicate any response to Brown, Wood's disclosure advice. Neither respondent questioned anyone at the company about management's failure to make the suggested disclosure.

On May 9, Kay called Socha to seek his approval of a draft of the company's proposed current report on Form 8–K for the month of April. Socha reiterated Brown, Wood's earlier advice that disclosure should be made concerning National's present status under the Amended Credit Agreement and of the event of default that resulted from the company's failure to implement the LMP. Although Kay agreed to include the suggested disclosure, the report actually filed with the Commission did not contain any such disclosure, because Lurie would not permit it.

On May 12, two lawyers from White & Case again called Brown, Wood and talked to Socha. The purpose of their call was to be brought up to date on the progress of public disclosure since their March 17 conversation with Carter. Socha described respondent's repeated advice to National's management with respect to the disclosure matter, since White & Case had informed them of events that had triggered National's obligation to implement the LMP. However, Socha added that, to his knowledge, no such disclosure had been made.

Later the same day, Socha called Kay and asked for a copy of the company's April Form 8–K. Kay replied that Lurie would not permit him to mail a copy to Brown, Wood or to the Commission. The April Form 8–K was eventually filed with the Commission on May 15, 1975. Socha testified that he was required to obtain a copy of it from the Commission.

* * *

The internal and external tensions which had been developing around National came to a head on Saturday afternoon, May 24, at the special meeting of the board of directors in Hartford, Connecticut. Johnson was there, acting as secretary, having been asked to attend by Hart. Also present at the meeting was independent counsel who had been consulted by the outside directors and asked to attend the meeting in the expectation that Johnson would not be there. It was at this meeting that the outside directors learned for the first time that, for over a month, Brown, Wood had been recommending disclosure and Johnson read a draft of the letter which Brown, Wood had sent to Hart on May 1, disclosing that the LMP had been triggered and its effect on the company. One of the nonmanagement directors testified that he had no prior indication that Brown, Wood had been recommending this disclosure to Hart and that when he heard the letter read by Johnson he "was shocked to the core."

At the May 24 meeting, Hart resigned each of his corporate offices, although he remained a director of the company, Johnson prepared a press release which was unanimously approved by the Board and it was decided that Brown, Wood would continue as company counsel. Johnson, however, resigned as secretary of the company.

* * *

IV.

Aiding and Abetting

* * *

In the context of the federal securities laws, [certain legal] principles hold generally that one may be found to have aided and abetted a violation when the following three elements are present:

> 1. there exists an independent securities law violation committed by some other party;

> 2. the aider and abettor knowingly and substantially assisted the conduct that constitutes the violation; and

> 3. the aider and abettor was aware or knew that his role was part of an activity that was improper or illegal.

As noted above, we have no difficulty in finding that National committed numerous substantial securities law violations. * * * [S]ubstantial assistance—is generally satisfied in the context of a securities lawyer performing professional duties, for he is inevitably deeply involved in his client's disclosure activities and often participates in the drafting of the documents, as was the case with Carter. And he does so knowing that he is participating in the preparation of disclosure documents—that is his job.

In this connection, we do not distinguish between the professional advice of a lawyer given orally or in writing and similar advice which is embodied in drafting documents to be filed with the Commission. Liability in these circumstances should not turn on such artificial distinctions, particularly in light of the almost limitless range of forms which legal advice may take. Moreover, the opposite approach, which would permit a lawyer to avoid or reduce his liability simply by avoiding participation in the drafting process, may well have the undesirable effect of reducing the quality of the disclosure by the many to protect against the defalcations of the few.

* * *

It is axiomatic that a lawyer will not be liable as an aider and abettor merely because his advice, followed by the client, is ultimately determined to be wrong. What is missing in that instance is a wrongful intent on the part of the lawyer. It is that element of intent which provides the basis for distinguishing between those professionals who may be appropriately considered as subjects of professional discipline and those who, acting in good faith, have merely made errors of judgment or have been careless.

Significant public benefits flow from the effective performance of the securities lawyer's role. The exercise of independent, careful and informed legal judgment on difficult issues is critical to the flow of material information to the securities markets. Moreover, we are aware of the difficulties and limitations attendant upon that role. In the course of rendering securities law advice, the lawyer is called upon to make difficult judgments, often under great pressure and in areas where the legal signposts are far apart and only faintly discernible.

If a securities lawyer is to bring his best independent judgment to bear on a disclosure problem, he must have the freedom to make innocent—or even, in certain cases, careless—mistakes without fear of legal liability or loss of the ability to practice before the Commission. Concern about his own liability may alter the balance of his judgment in one direction as surely as an unseemly obeisance to the wishes of his client can do so in the other. While one imbalance results in disclosure rather than concealment, neither is, in the end, truly in the public interest. Lawyers who are seen by their clients as being motivated by fears for their personal liability will not be consulted on difficult issues.

Although it is a close judgment, after careful review, we conclude that the available evidence is insufficient to establish that either respondent acted with sufficient knowledge and awareness or recklessness to satisfy the test for willful aiding and abetting liability. Our conclusion in this regard applies to each of the Administrative Law Judge's findings as to respondents' aiding and abetting National's violations of the federal securities laws.

D.   The December Press Release and Form 8–K. In drafting the December press release and Form 8–K, Carter advised National that the provisions of the LMP were not required to be disclosed. There is ample evidence in the record indicating both respondents' knowledge about National's financial condition and the importance of the LMP. Johnson attended the Board meetings held on July 1, August 19, and October 15, 1974 at which the directors emphasized the importance of new financing and reviewed Socha's draft shareholders' letter in October that explained the significance of a proposed informal "wind-down" phase in National's corporate life. Johnson informed Carter of these matters in connection with their joint responsibilities for the representation of National. Carter focused on the details of the LMP when he advised Hart that the document embodying the plan did not have to be filed with the Commission if it were not an exhibit to the Amended Credit Agreement. Respondents were clearly aware of the company's lack of success in raising new capital, and the increasingly critical impact of its negative cash flow.

On the other hand, the record also contains no direct evidence of Carter's knowledge that the details of the LMP were material and we decline to infer such knowledge because of facts in the record on which Carter's erroneous judgment as to its immateriality is claimed to have been based. Carter had been told by Hart and others about numerous potential sources for additional financing. * * *

It is also significant that the December 20 press release, while originally drafted by National's management, was entirely rewritten by Carter in long-hand at the December 19 pre-closing meeting. Having thus revised the document, Carter showed it to all present at the pre-closing and no one suggested any change. In fact, the only comment recalled by Carter was to the effect of, "Boy, that's full disclosure."

In view of the foregoing, we are unable to conclude that it has been demonstrated by sufficient evidence that Carter willfully aided and abetted violations of the securities laws in connection with the December 20 press release and the December Form 8–K.

E.   Subsequent Conduct. The Administrative Law Judge found that, in addition to the violations resulting from the December 20, 1974 press release and the Form 8–K filed on January 8, 1975, National violated the federal securities laws through its continued failure to make adequate disclosures in public statements and Commission filings regarding its deteriorating cash position, its inability to meet earlier growth projections, the triggering of the LMP, and the impact the LMP would have on National. The Administrative Law Judge also found that respondents willfully aided and abetted these violations by failing to ensure that the required disclosures were made or to communicate to National's board of directors concerning management's refusal to make such disclosures. Our review of the record does not reveal a sufficient basis for sustaining respondents' liability as aiders and abettors of these violations.

Respondents' behavior with regard to these violations by National poses an issue that was not present in our earlier discussion of Carter's conduct. There, Carter actively assisted commission of the violations. Here, respondents' behavior was in the nature of inaction and silence.

* * *

When it is impossible to find any duty of disclosure, an aider and abettor should be found liable only if scienter of the high "conscious intent" variety can be found. Where some special duty of disclosure exists, then liability should be possible with a lesser degree of scienter.

Accordingly, in order to sustain the law judge's finding, we must find that respondents either consciously intended to assist National's violation, or that they breached a duty to disclose or act and had some degree of scienter.

On the basis of the record before us, we think that it is a close question, but in the final analysis we are unable to infer that respondents intended to aid the violations by not acting. The level of intent required by this test is higher than that required by some courts to show the appropriate mental state for the third element of aiding and abetting. There, some courts require only that an aider and abettor be "aware" that his role was part of an illegal or improper activity. Here, the test requires a showing that he "intended" to foster the illegal activity. This is a fine distinction, but we think it is an important one.

Our review of the record, which includes respondents' periodic exhortations to Hart to improve the quality of National's disclosure, leads us to believe that respondents did not intend to assist the violations by their inaction or silence. Rather, they seemed to be at a loss for how to deal with a difficult client.

Association of a law firm with a client lends an air of legitimacy and authority to the actions of a client. There are occasions when, but for the law firms's association, a violation could not have occurred. Under those circumstances, if the firm were cognizant of how it was being used and acquiesced, or if it gained some benefit from the violation beyond that normally obtained in a legal relationship, inaction would probably give rise to an inference of intent. This, however, is not such a case, and we find that respondents did not intend to assist the violation by their inaction.

V.

ETHICAL AND PROFESSIONAL RESPONSIBILITIES

A. The Findings of the Administrative Law Judge. The Administrative Law Judge found that both respondents "failed to carry out their professional responsibilities with respect to appropriate disclosure to all concerned, including stockholders, directors and the investing public ... and thus knowingly engaged in unethical and improper professional conduct, as charged in the Order." In particular, he held that respondents' failure to advise National's board of directors of Hart's refusal to disclose adequately the company's perilous financial condition was itself a violation of ethical and professional standards referred to in Rule 2(e) (1)(ii).

Respondents argue that the Commission has never promulgated standards of professional conduct for lawyers and that the Commission's application in hindsight of new standards would be fundamentally unfair. Moreover, even if it is permissible for the Commission to apply—without specific adoption or notice—generally recognized professional standards, they argue that no such standards applicable to respondents; conduct existed in 1974–75, nor do they exist today.

We agree that, in general, elemental notions of fairness dictate that the Commission should not establish new rules of conduct and impose them retroactively upon professionals who acted at the time without reason to believe that their conduct was unethical or improper. At the same time, however, we perceive no unfairness whatsoever in holding those professionals who practice before us to generally recognized norms of professional conduct, whether or not such norms had previously been explicitly adopted or endorsed by the Commission. To do so upsets no justifiable expectations, since the professional is already subject to those norms.

The ethical and professional responsibilities of lawyers who become aware that their client is engaging in violations of the securities laws have not been so firmly and unambiguously established that we believe all practicing lawyers can be held to an awareness of generally recognized norms. We also recognize that the Commission has never articulated or endorsed any such standards. That being the case, we reverse the Administrative Law Judge's findings under subparagraph (ii) of Rule 2(e)(1) with respect to both respondents. Nevertheless, we believe that respondents' conduct raises serious questions about the obligations of securities lawyers, and the Commission is hereby giving notice of its interpretation of "unethical or improper professional conduct" as that term is used in Rule 2(e)(1)(ii). The Commission intends to issue a release soliciting comment from the public as to whether this interpretation should be expanded or modified. [Ed.—The Commission never issued this release]

B. Interpretive Background. Our concern focuses on the professional obligations of the lawyer who gives essentially correct disclosure advice to a client that does not follow that advice and as a result violates the federal securities laws.* * *

While precise standards have not yet emerged, it is fair to say that there exists considerable acceptance of the proposition that a lawyer must, in order to discharge his professional responsibilities make all efforts within reason to persuade his client to avoid or terminate proposed illegal action. Such efforts could include, where appropriate, notification to the board of directors of a corporate client. * * *

We are mindful that, when a lawyer represents a corporate client, the client—and the entity to which he owes his allegiance—is the corporation itself and not management or any other individual connected with the corporation. Moreover, the lawyer should try to "insure that decisions of his client are made only after the client has been informed of relevant considerations." These unexceptionable principles take on a special coloration when a lawyer becomes aware that one or more specific members of a corporate client's management is deciding not to follow his disclosure advice, especially if he knows that those in control, such as the board of directors, may not have participated in or been aware of that decision. Moreover, it is well established that no lawyer, even in the most zealous pursuit of his client's interests, is privileged to assist his client in conduct the lawyer knows to be illegal. The application of these recognized principles to the special role of the securities lawyer giving disclosure advice, however, is not a simple task.

The securities lawyer who is an active participant in a company's ongoing disclosure program will ordinarily draft and revise disclosure documents, comment on them and file them with the Commission. He is often involved on an intimate, day-to-day basis in the judgments that determine what will be disclosed and what will be withheld from the public markets. When a lawyer serving in such a capacity concludes that his client's disclosures are not adequate to comply with the law, and so advises his client, he is "aware," in a literal sense, of a continuing violation of the securities laws. On the other hand, the lawyer is only an adviser, and the final judgment—and, indeed, responsibility—as to what course of conduct is to be taken must lie with the client. Moreover, disclosure issues often present difficult choices between multiple shades of gray, and while a lawyer's judgment may be to draw the disclosure obligation more broadly than his client, both parties recognize the degree of uncertainty involved.

The problems of professional conduct that arise in this relationship are well-illustrated by the facts of this case. In rejecting Brown, Wood's advice to include the assumptions underlying its projections in its 1974 Annual Report, in declining to issue two draft stockholders letters offered by respondents and in ignoring the numerous more informal urgings by both respondents and Socha to make disclosure, Hart and Lurie indicated that they were inclined to resist any public pronouncements that were at odds with the rapid growth which had been projected and reported for the company.

If the record ended there, we would be hesitant to suggest that any unprofessional conduct might be involved. Hart and Lurie were, in effect, pressing the company's lawyers hard for the minimum disclosure required by law. That fact alone is not an appropriate basis for a finding that a lawyer must resign or take some extraordinary action. Such a finding would inevitably drive a wedge between reporting companies and their outside lawyers; the more sophisticated members of management would soon realize that there is nothing to gain in consulting outside lawyers.

However, much more was involved in this case. In sending out a patently misleading letter to stockholders on December 23 in contravention of Socha's plain and express advice to clear all such disclosure with

Brown, Wood, in deceiving respondents about Johnson's approval of the company's quarterly report to its stockholders in early December and in dissembling in response to respondents' questions about the implementation of the LMP, the company's management erected a wall between National and its outside lawyers—a wall apparently designed to keep out good legal advice in conflict with management's improper disclosure plans.

Any ambiguity in the situation plainly evaporated in late April and early May of 1975 when Hart first asked Johnson for a legal opinion flatly contrary to the express disclosure advice Johnson had given Hart only five days earlier, and when Lurie soon thereafter prohibited Kay from delivering a copy of the company's April 1975 Form 8–K to Brown, Wood.

These actions reveal a conscious desire on the part of National's management no longer to look to Brown, Wood for independent disclosure advice, but rather to embrace the firm within Hart's fraud and use it as a shield to avoid the pressures exerted by the banks toward disclosure. Such a role is a perversion of the normal lawyer-client relationship, and no lawyer may claim that, in these circumstance, he need do no more than stubbornly continue to suggest disclosure when he knows his suggestions are falling on deaf ears.

C. "Unethical or Improper Professional Conduct." The Commission is of the view that a lawyer engages in "unethical or improper professional conduct" under the following circumstances: When a lawyer with significant responsibilities in the effectuation of a company's compliance with the disclosure requirements of the federal securities laws becomes aware that his client is engaged in a substantial and continuing failure to satisfy those disclosure requirements, his continued participation violates professional standards unless he takes prompt steps to end the client's noncompliance. The Commission has determined that this interpretation will be applicable only to conduct occurring after the date of this opinion.

We do not imply that a lawyer is obliged, at the risk of being held to have violated Rule 2(e) to seek to correct every isolated disclosure action or inaction which he believes to be at variance with applicable disclosure standards, although there may be isolated disclosure failures that are so serious that their correction becomes a matter of primary professional concern. It is also clear, however, that a lawyer is not privileged to unthinkingly permit himself to be co-opted into an ongoing fraud and cast as a dupe or a shield for a wrong doing client.

Initially, counselling accurate disclosure is sufficient, even if his advice is not accepted. But there comes a point at which a reasonable lawyer must conclude that his advice is not being followed, or even sought in good faith, and that his client is involved in a continuing course of violating the securities laws. At this critical juncture, the lawyer must take further, more affirmative steps in order to avoid the inference that he has been co-opted willingly or unwillingly, into the scheme of non-disclosure.

The lawyer is in the best position to choose his next step. Resignation is one option, although we recognize that other considerations, including the protection of the client against forseeable prejudice, must be taken into account in the case of withdrawal. A direct approach to the board of directors or one or more individual directors or officers may be appropriate; or he may choose to try to enlist the aid of other members of the firm's management. What is required, in short, is some prompt action[77] that leads to the conclusion that the lawyer is engaged in efforts to correct the underlying problem, rather than having capitulated to the desires of a strong-willed, but misguided client.

We recognize, however, that the "best result" is not always obtainable, and that there may occur situations where the lawyer must conclude that the misconduct is so extreme or irretrievable, or the involvement of his client's management and board of directors in the misconduct is so thoroughgoing and pervasive that any action short of resignation would be futile. We would anticipate that cases where a lawyer has no choice but to resign would be rare and of an egregious nature.

D. Conclusion.

As noted above, because the Commission has never adopted or endorsed standards of professional conduct which would have applied to respondents' activities during the period here in question, and since generally accepted norms of professional conduct which existed outside the scope of Rule 2(e) did not, during the relevant time period, unambiguously cover the situation in which respondents found themselves in 1974–75, no finding of unethical or unprofessional conduct would be appropriate. * * *

Richard W. Painter, The Moral Interdependence
of Corporate Lawyers and Their Clients

67 S. Cal. L. Rev. 507 (1994)

V. Carter and Johnson: Legal Responsibility and the Interdependence of Lawyer and Client

If lawyer and client conduct are not always separate and distinct, lawyers in some situations may be legally as well as morally responsible

---

77. In those cases where resignation is not the only alternative, should a lawyer choose not to resign we do not believe the action taken must be successful to avoid the inference that the lawyer had improperly participated in his client's fraud. Rather, the acceptability of the action must be considered in the light of all relevant surrounding circumstances. Similarly, what is "prompt" in any one case depends on the situation then facing the lawyer. Some have argued that resignation is the only permissible course when a client chooses not to comply with disclosure advice. We do not agree. Premature resignation serves neither the end of an effective lawyer-client relationship nor, in most cases, the effective administration of the securities laws. The lawyer's continued interaction with his client will ordinarily hold the greatest promise of corrective action. So long as a lawyer is acting in good faith and exerting reasonable efforts to prevent violations of the law by his client, his professional obligations have been met. In general, the best result is that which promotes the continued, strong-minded and independent participation by the lawyer.

for clients' conduct. Legal responsibility was the subject of the SEC's 1981 Release In re Carter and Johnson. In this Release, the SEC held that lawyers' participation in client conduct may require them to do more than merely advise a recalcitrant client about disclosure requirements. The clearest rational for this holding, although not entirely accepted by the SEC, is that lawyers who knowingly assist clients while they are violating the law may be responsible for their clients' violations even if the lawyers do not want to further the violations.

* * *

Although National and its lawyers sometimes acted independently, the scenario described in the SEC Release reveals a lawyer-client relationship characterized by interdependent decisionmaking. In fact, the lawyers' involvement with National was extensive enough that Johnson became secretary of the company. Moreover, Carter's advice was far from strictly legal, as when he suggested to National that he knew of financing sources outside of the United States. Carter, Johnson, and other lawyers in their firm performed functions attributed * * * to lawyers acting as monitors of management conduct. They used their skills in interpreting and drafting legal language to assist National with SEC filings, including 8–Ks, 10–Ks, and registration statements for new public offerings. They also helped National communicate with shareholders through annual reports and proxy solicitations. Furthermore, Carter and Johnson performed dealmaking functions * * * when they negotiated the new relationship between National and its banks embodied in the ACA. Because National's substantial debt enhanced contractual control of creditors over corporate conduct, the legal language of the ACA dictated the course of National's business.

The Brown, Wood lawyers thus negotiated a business plan for National at the same time they were monitoring disclosure of that plan to shareholders and the SEC. In their monitoring and dealmaking roles, Carter and Johnson may not have wanted to assist National's nondisclosure but they did. Carter told National that the terms of the LMP should be made public but advised Hart how to avoid public disclosure by not attaching the LMP as an exhibit to the ACA filed with National's 8–K. Carter and Johnson criticized Hart's December 23, 1974 mailing to shareholders for not making adequate disclosure, but they also told Hart that corrective action was not required. Meanwhile, Carter and Johnson continued to negotiate with the banks the very restrictions on National's business that were not disclosed to shareholders or the SEC. The message to Hart was clear: His lawyers would tell him what he should do as well as how to avoid doing it and would continue to represent him while he deliberately violated the law.

In re Carter and Johnson also illustrates how lawyers' belief in their independence from client conduct undermines communications between lawyers and clients and may encourage improper client conduct. After Lurie erroneously told Socha that Johnson had approved a draft quarterly report, Johnson merely noted his disapproval on a copy circulated at

Brown, Wood without mentioning his disapproval to National. The presence of the marked up draft in Brown, Wood's files was apparently enough to satisfy Johnson that he had objected to the report, but did not communicate Johnson's view to National. Furthermore, Carter and Johnson distanced themselves from National's conduct by phrasing their legal advice in hypothetical language. Carter told Lurie that if the LMP had been triggered, that fact should be publicly disclosed, and Johnson told Lurie that his proposed disclosure letter should be sent if National was "interested in keeping its stockholders advised on a regular basis." Believing themselves independent from National's conduct, Carter and Johnson did not always insist on finding out the facts and acted as if pure legal advice was sufficient. They disengaged themselves as much as possible from facts bound to put their presumed independence and their clients' asserted independence on a collision course.

Carter and Johnson's legal advice to National thus was undermined by their passivity and presumed independence from the facts. They told National that disclosure was necessary while doing little to learn specifically what needed to be disclosed (the LMP), when it needed to be disclosed, why National's officers were not interested in disclosing it, and what could be done to change National's chosen course of conduct. Instead of zeroing in on the situation to convince their client they were serious, Carter and Johnson sporadically inquired into National's disclosure practices and made some suggestions. When they received no answers or inadequate answers they backpedaled, gave advice on other subjects, and continued negotiating with the banks. Although obtaining information from National become increasingly difficult as the situation deteriorated, Carter and Johnson believed themselves to be so independent from the facts that they could continue to represent a client that would not even tell its own lawyers the truth.

This approach created an aura of uncertainty where there should have been none. If disclosing material facts to stockholders in compliance with the securities laws was something that National might or might not be interested in, perhaps National need not be interested. If the LMP was not important enough for Carter and Johnson to insist on knowing for sure whether it had been implemented, perhaps disclosure of the LMP was not all that important. National may have reasoned that Carter and Johnson, who had been involved with National from its creation, would believe themselves compelled to be certain of important facts and insist that important disclosures be made. Their legal advice, given without complete knowledge, could thus be interpreted as erring on the safe side. Hart, for example, could not have believed that Johnson meant what he said when he told Hart that disclosure was required—Hart's response was to ask Johnson for a legal opinion stating precisely the opposite. Carter and Johnson failed in the first step in getting a client to follow legal advice: getting the client to take their lawyer seriously.

What caused this breakdown in communication? One explanation is that Carter and Johnson, from National's vantage point, appeared to be saying one thing and doing another. A problem with the moral independence theory is that clients do not entirely understand or accept it. When lawyers are active participants in an enterprise, clients may expect lawyers to act as they themselves would—as if their professional reputation depended on that enterprise. Clients may not believe that lawyers who have stood by their side as "friends" when things go well will turn around and deny responsibility when things go badly. Many clients expect more, and this expectation can lead to miscommunication. When a lawyer refuses to confront a client and insist that a wrong be rectified, the lawyer may send an unintended message: The wrong is more theoretical than real and the client's actions are not serious enough to compel correction. Carter and Johnson sent just such a message to National.

The SEC's verdict on these facts was mixed. The Release clearly stated that Carter and Johnson had an obligation to take affirmative steps to correct National's disclosure violations because of their participation in National's conduct, and that the steps Carter and Johnson took were insufficient. The Release pointed to two specific steps Carter and Johnson could have taken: they could have approached other members of National's board of directors or resigned. However, because the SEC believed adequate standards for ethical and professional conduct had not been sufficiently developed at the time, it did not sanction Carter and Johnson under Rule 2(e) of its Rules of Practice, and instead emphatically stated the standard for future conduct:

When a lawyer with significant responsibilities in the effectuation of a company's compliance with the disclosure requirements of the federal securities laws becomes aware that his client is engaged in a substantial and continuing failure to satisfy those disclosure requirements, his continued participation violates professional standards unless he takes prompt steps to end the client's noncompliance. By alluding to lawyers' "significant responsibilities" and faulting lawyers' "participation" in clients' conduct, the SEC here touched on the premise to the moral interdependence theory: The actions of two persons can affect each other to such an extent that it is appropriate to say that both persons are participating in one act. This is so even if the two persons desire different results from their conduct.

What follows? The SEC held that an affirmative obligation to take some corrective action arose out of the lawyers' participation. The Release, however, does not explain why lawyers have such an obligation and resists premising this obligation on lawyers' responsibility for client conduct:

The securities lawyer who is an active participant in a company's ongoing disclosure program will ordinarily draft and revise disclosure documents, comment on them and file them with the Commission. He is often involved on an intimate, day-to-day basis in the judgments that determine what will be disclosed and what will be withheld from the public markets. When a lawyer serving in such a capacity concludes that his client's disclosures are not adequate to comply with the law, and so advises his client, he is "aware," in a literal sense, of a continuing violation of the securities laws. On the other hand, the lawyer is only an adviser, and the final judgment—and, indeed, responsibility—as to what course of conduct is to be taken must lie with the client. Although the lawyer "is an active participant in a company's ongoing disclosure program," and is "involved on an intimate, day-to-day basis in the judgments that determine what will be disclosed," the SEC falls back on a theory of legal responsibility akin to the moral independence theory in allocating final responsibility for conduct.

By mandating enhanced affirmative obligations instead of finding lawyers responsible for client wrongs, the SEC may have sought to avoid confrontation with one of the salient ideological tenants of the bar—the belief that lawyers' and clients' actions are distinct and separable, thereby relieving lawyers from legal or moral responsibility for clients' actions. After hearing the SEC's strong mandate of a lawyer's affirmative obligations, however, the statement that final responsibility for malfeasance lies with the client has a hollow ring. Indeed, without such responsibility being shared by the lawyer it is difficult to imagine the source of these enhanced affirmative obligations.

The SEC's ruling in Carter and Johnson is arguably only supportable by a theory of responsibility broader than that articulated in the Release. When lawyers monitor disclosure of information to regulators and investors, such a theory holds that lawyers assume some responsibility for the flow of accurate information. A litigator's responsibility for the integrity of the adversary system is not the issue; a corporate lawyer's responsibility for the integrity of the financial markets is. Lawyers therefore may be responsible for some actions of their clients that undermine the integrity of the financial markets, even when they have tried to establish their independence by objecting to such conduct. In these situations, the objectionable conduct is imposed by the client upon a compliance or transactional framework designed by the lawyer and so contaminates the framework such that the lawyer has an obligation to repudiate it in its entirety. The lawyer's work has been converted to a fraud from which the lawyer cannot escape responsibility.

INDEPENDENT EXAMINER'S REPORT CONCERNING SPIEGEL, INC., SEC v. SPIEGEL, INC., (N.D. ILL. SEPT. 15, 2003)

[Spiegel is an international multi-channel retailer offering apparel, home furnishings, and other merchandise through catalogs, the internet, and conventional retail stores. Spiegel's domestic base of operations is Chicago, but the ultimate decision-making authority resides in Germany with Michael Otto. who together with his family owns 90% of Spiegel's total equity and 100% of the company's voting shares.

By 1999, Spiegel had, in response to poor sales, adopted an "easy credit" program according to which Spiegel shifted the focus of its credit card portfolio to high risk borrowers, who often could not obtain credit from other sources. During the internet boom of the late 90s, Spiegel removed the risky credit card receivables from its balance sheet by selling them to off-balance-sheet special purpose entities through an asset-backed securitization program. These sales brought Spiegel a short-term return to profitability, and this return to profitability in turn brought Spiegel executives seven-and six-figure performance-based bonuses. But, when the economy faltered, many of the high-risk borrowers defaulted on their credit card payments.

Coupled with poor sales in Spiegel's Eddie Bauer line, the credit card defaults resulted in a rapid decline of Spiegel's financial position. By late 2001, the company had violated the four loan covenants contained in its bank loan agreements. The violations caused hundreds of millions of dollars of long-term debt to become due and lead Spiegel to attempt to renegotiate its financing.

As Spiegel prepared its 2001 10–K. which was due at the end of March 2002, negotiations between Spiegel and its banks continued. KPMG advised Spiegel, that because of Spiegel's inability to conclude the negotiations prior to the 10–K filing deadline, KPMG would have to give Spiegel a "going concern" opinion, which would state that KPMG had serious doubts that Spiegel could continue as a going concern and which Spiegel would have to file with its 10–K. Spiegel felt that a going a going concern opinion would create negative publicity that would cause many suppliers cease or restrict their relationship with Spiegel, cause a substantial decline in Spiegel's stock price, and adversely affect customer sales and employee morale.

On March 25, 2002, the Condor Group, a crisis committee consisting of key domestic management convened in response to Spiegel's economic crisis, discussed several of Spiegel's "life threatening issues" and decided that representatives should immediately fly to Germany to discuss the situation with Otto in Germany. The representatives, including general counsel Robert Sorensen, met with Otto on March 27. In the meeting, the representatives briefed Otto on several financial issues, including concerns over the risky credit card receivables, Spiegel's liquidity situation, and Spiegel's violation of the loan covenants. In particular, Sorensen advised Otto of Spiegel's disclosure obligations under SEC and NASDAQ regulations and identified several issues that "may be considered material and require public disclosure."

Just days after the meeting in Germany, Spiegel decided to withhold its 10–K. Spiegel thus filed a "notification of late filing," which requires that the issuer state "in reasonable detail the reasons why [a form I 0–K] could not be filed within the prescribed time period." Spiegel's response, as drafted by its outside counsel Kirkland & Ellis, was:

> As has been publicly disclosed, the Registrant is not currently in compliance with its 2001 loan covenants and has reached a strategic decision to sell its credit card subsidiary. and as a result the

Registrant is not in a position to issue financial statements for its 2001 fiscal year pending resolution of these issues.

The notification, however, made no mention of the "going concern" opinion. As a result of the notification, Spiegel was granted an extension of its filing deadline until April 15. As with its initial filing deadline, Spiegel failed to meet the extended deadline.

On April 17, NASDAQ issued Spiegel a delisting notice as a result of Spiegel's failure to file it's 10–K, and on April 19, NASDAQ changed the company's stock symbol. On the same day, Spiegel issued a press release that offered little detail. In addition, the press release omitted several facts that Kirkland & Ellis had advised Spiegel to disclose, including Spiegel's efforts to restructure its debt.

As Spiegel's management continued its frenzied efforts to stave of the company's demise, Spiegel's 10–Q became due in mid-May. The company again filed a notification of late filing and repeated the language in its notification for its 10–K. On May *15,* Kirkland & Ellis advised Spiegel that a failure to file its 10–K could result in an SEC enforcement action against Spiegel, its officers and directors, and its controlling shareholder. On May 17, the NASDAQ held a delisting hearing, and after receiving assurances from Spiegel management, NASDAQ deferred delisting until May 28, extending Spiegel even more time to file its 10–K. Spiegel again missed the deadline.

On May 29, Spiegel's general counsel gave Spiegel's audit committee chairman his legal opinion that Spiegel was required to file its form 10–K. The same day, however, Otto "had come to the opinion" that delisting would be preferable to filing a 10–K with a going concern opinion. The next day, NASDAQ informed Spiegel that it would be dclisted and that NASDAQ had determined Spiegel had acted in "willful disregard of the law." In response, Kirkland & Ellis informed Otto that NASDAQ's determination of "willful disregard" increased the risk of an SEC enforcement action.

After receiving word of Kirkland & Ellis' advice, Siegel's Chicago-based management informed Kirkland & Ellis that the management team "was fully prepared to file financial statements today at the risk of being fired, or to be forced to resign in the face of a direct order from the Chairman of the Board to continue with this unlawful behavior."

On May 31, German management held a meeting to discuss the company's decision to withhold its filings. Again, attorney's from Kirkland & Ellis urged the company to file despite the going concern opinion. Attorney's from the German office of White & Case, however, felt that filing was not in Spiegel's best interests. Ultimately, Spiegel's German management decided to continue to withhold Spiegel's filings. Later, Otto recalled Kirkland's advice to file but contends he was not made aware of the extent of the consequences of not filing.]

* * *

Ultimately the SEC filed a civil action against Spiegel, charging that Spiegel violated the federal securities laws by failing to file required periodic reports on Forms 10–K and 10–Q during 2002, by failing to disclose KPMG's advice that Spiegel may not be able to continue as a "going concern," and by failing to disclose other material information and accounting irregularities. Six days after the SEC filed an action against the company, Spiegel filed for Chapter 11 bankruptcy.

* * *

D. Involvement of Spiegel's Professional Advisers

In the present case, the SEC charged Spiegel with fraud, and Spiegel consented (without admitting or denying liability) to a fraud injunction against the company. When a fraud charge hits a public company, the question naturally arises whether its professional advisers could have done anything to prevent this "train wreck" that hurt the company and its shareholders, creditors and employees.

Spiegel's Legal Advisers. In evaluating the performance of Spiegel's lawyers, it is useful to consider rules recently adopted and other rules recently proposed by the SEC under Section 307 of the Sarbanes–Oxley Act, even though these SEC rules were not in effect at the time of the conduct here. Under SEC rules effective August 5, 2003, lawyers representing a public company must report "up the ladder"—as high as the board of directors, if necessary—if the lawyers "become aware" of "evidence" of a "material violation" of federal or state securities law or a material breach of fiduciary duty by the company (or its officer, director, employee or agent). 17 C.F.R. Part 205.

In addition, the SEC has proposed (but not yet adopted) so-called "noisy withdrawal" rules 28 that would require lawyers to assess whether the company has made an "appropriate response within a reasonable time" to the matter the lawyer has reported up the ladder, and if not, whether "substantial injury" to financial interest or property of the issuer or investors has occurred or is likely. An outside attorney must then "withdraw forthwith from representing the issuer," and tell both the company and the SEC that the withdrawal was for "professional considerations." An inside attorney must cease participation in the matter. Both outside and inside attorneys must also disaffirm to the SEC any document the attorney assisted in preparing that "may be" materially false or misleading.

Robert Sorensen joined Spiegel as its general counsel at the end of June 2001. He brought in the firm of *Kirkland & Ellis* as principal outside counsel, in place of Rooks Pins, to provide additional depth in corporate and securities matters. Rooks Pitts continued to represent Spiegel in securitization and other matters. As described above, by mid-May 2002. Kirkland & Ellis had plainly advised Spiegel that it was violating the law by not filing its Form 10–K, and that this illegal act could have serious consequences, including action by the SEC. Sorensen plainly concurred in this advice. The advice reached Spiegel's management, including its president Martin Zaepfel, who was also a member of Spiegel's board committee, which had the power to act for the full board. By the end of May, Zaepfel reported the advice to Michael Otto and Michael Cruesemann, the other two members of the board committee. Kirkland & Ellis also repeated this advice by phone to Spiegel's audit committee at the end of May. Plainly, Kirkland & Ellis and Sorensen reported "up the ladder" to Spiegel's audit committee and its board committee.

However, this was a case where reporting "up the ladder" was not enough. The advice from the lawyers here was rejected by Spiegel's audit and board committees, and the material information that should have reached investors was kept under wraps.

White & Case became involved in Spiegel's affairs as counsel for Spiegel's "sole voting shareholder," Michael Otto and his corporate vehicles. Through its Hamburg partner Urs Aschenbrenner, White & Case "interpreted" for the Otto interests the advice received from Spiegel's U.S. legal advisers, and it clearly played a substant ial role in helping Otto and the Spiegel board committee evaluate that advice. Aschenbrenner consulted with White & Case's New York office on Spiegel issues, and lawyers from the firm's New York office were substantively involved on various Spiegel matters—again as representatives of Spiegel's sole voting shareholder—during much of 2002.

Aschenbrenner began accompanying Cruesemann to meetings with Spiegel's lender banks in Spring 2002, and also attended Spiegel's delisting hearing before Nasdaq on May 17, 2002. On May 31, 2002, the day Spiegel's audit and board committees made the final decision not to file the Form 10–K, Aschenbrenner was invited to be present at the audit committee meeting, and the audit committee had Aschenbrenner phone Kirkland & Ellis on a speakerphone for the committee to get advice. Aschenbrenner was heard to challenge Kirkland & Ellis' advice on the need to file Spiegel's Form 10–K and the consequences of non-filing. In the days following the May 31, 2002 meeting, it appears that neither Aschenbrenner nor his New York partners did anything to express their agreement with Kirkland & Ellis' advice.

Whatever the conclusion as to the lawyers' performance around the time of the May 31, 2002 audit and board committee meetings, the question naturally arises as to what the lawyers did to press Spiegel to make its required SEC filings through the balance of 2002—or otherwise to update, supplement or correct disclosures made in Spiegel's Forms 12b–25 and/or its press releases. There does not appear to be a record of either Kirkland & Ellis or White & Case advising Spiegel of the dire consequences of its continuing failure to file its Form 10–K and make full disclosure to investors after May 31, 2002.

After May 2002, it appears that Spiegel's German directors considered Kirkland & Ellis and Sorensen, along with the rest of Spiegel's U.S. management, to be "black painters"—meaning pessimists who were exaggerating the seriousness of the situation. Over the summer, Cruesemann suggested that Kirkland & Ellis, and perhaps Sorensen, be replaced. The effort to replace Kirkland & Ellis failed only when U.S. management pointed out the cost of bringing in a new firm to draft documentation for the refinancing and other pending matters.

At the same time, while ostensibly still only counsel for Spiegel's sole voting shareholder, White & Case assumed a prominent role in negotiating on Spiegel's behalf with its banks on the refinancing effort, with the OCC on FCNB issues, and with the insurer of the Spiegel securitizations. While still not technically retained as Spiegel's counsel, White & Case clearly enjoyed the confidence of Spiegel's sole voting shareholder, and an effort by White & Case to report "up the ladder" to Spiegel's audit and board committees that it shared the views of the "black painters" Kirkland & Ellis and Sorensen could well have caused Spiegel to comply with its obligations and avoid a fraud charge from the SEC.

As the months went by, Kirkland & Ellis continued to prepare and file Spiegel's Forms 12b–25 providing official notice of Spiegel's failure to file its remaining quarterly reports (Form 10–Q) for the balance of 2002. All of these recited that Spiegel was not filing its periodic reports because it was "not currently in compliance with its 2001 loan covenants and is currently working with its bank group to amend and replace its existing credit facilities," and thus "not in a position to issue financial statements . . . pending resolution of this issue." Of course, as Kirkland & Ellis knew, the real reason why Spiegel was not filing its periodic reports was that it did not want to disclose KPMG's going concern qualification and other material bad facts and circumstances threatening Spiegel's survival.

None of Spiegel's legal advisers withdrew—"noisily" or otherwise— from representing Spiegel. If the SEC's proposed withdrawal rule had then been in effect, the SEC would have been alerted to take action sooner, and investors would have received information they could have acted on to make informed investment decisions about Spiegel. In this case, the absence of a "noisy withdrawal" requirement allowed Spiegel to keep investors and the SEC in the dark.

Spiegel's Accounting Adviser KPMG. KPMG's statutory reporting responsibilities as Spiegel's auditors are contained in Section 10A(b) of the Exchange Act. Section 10A(b) provides that if "in the course of conducting an audit," an accountant becomes aware of a possible "illegal act" defined as "an act or omission that violates any law, or any rule or regulation"—the accountant must assure that the audit committee "is adequately informed" of the illegal act, unless "clearly inconsequential." If the accountant concludes that the act has a material effect on the financial statements, and that the company has failed to take "timely and appropriate remedial action," the accountant must report such conclusions to the board. The company must then notify the SEC of the accountant's report. If the accountant does not get a copy of the company's notice to the SEC, the accountant must resign or give the

SEC a copy of its report. If the accountant resigns, the company must give the SEC a copy of the report.

The accounting profession has imposed similar requirements on itself. Statement on Auditing Standard AU 317.17 requires the auditor to "assure himself that the audit committee, or others with equivalent authority and responsibility, is adequately informed with respect to illegal acts that come to the auditor's attention. ... If senior management is involved in an illegal act, the auditor should communicate *directly* with the audit committee" (emphasis added). AU 317.15 notes that the auditor has a responsibility to evaluate the adequacy of disclosure in the financial statements of the potential effects of an illegal act on the entity's operations. And AU 317 states that an auditor may conclude that withdrawal is necessary "even when the illegal act is not material to the financial statements. Factors that should affect the auditor's conclusion include the implications of the failure to take remedial action, which may affect the auditor's ability to rely on management's representations, and the effects of continuing association with the client."

Here, as required by Section 10A(a), KPMG included in its audit of Spiegel "an evaluation of whether there is substantial doubt about the ability of the issuer to continue as a going concern during the ensuing fiscal year." Having made this statutorily-mandated evaluation, KPMG concluded that there *was* substantial doubt as to Spiegel's ability to continue as a going concern, based on its failure to that date to obtain (i) a viable funding commitment to cover Spiegel's projected cash shortfall, (ii) waiver of Spiegel's loan covenant breaches, and (iii) a binding sale agreement for Spiegel's credit business (already reclassified as a discontinued operation). [KPMG 1–3] And as Spiegel's auditors in the midst of conducting an audit, KPMG had a detailed picture of Spiegel's serious financial difficulties.

With this information, KPMG stood by as Spiegel violated Exchange Act § 13 and Rule 13a–13 by failing to file its 2001 annual report (Form 10–K) on April 15, 2002, violated § 10(b) and Rule 10b–5 by failing to disclose KPMG's own going concern opinion, and failed to disclose other material information concerning its business and serious financial condition. KPMG did not make a report to Spiegel's board, did not resign and did not report the matter to the SEC.

KPMG's articulated reason for inaction is that it saw Spiegel audit committee minutes reciting that Spiegel made its decision not to file its Form 10–K after "consultation with the Company's outside law firm (White & Case)." [SPGL 6071] Pekarek confirmed to KPMG's engagement partner this White & Case consultation. KPMG says that this caused it to believe that White & Case, which it knew was a major U.S. law firm, had given Spiegel a legal opinion that it did not have to file its Form 10–K or make the disclosures relating to its business and financial condition.

As a "Big 4" auditor of public companies, KPMG should have been aware of an illegal act by Spiegel here, based on (i) Spiegel's failure to file its Form 10–K annual report and its subsequent Form 10–Q quarterly reports; (ii) its failure to disclose material information regarding KPMG's own going concern position; and (iii) the Nasdaq delisting of Spiegel. Yet there is no indication that KPMG discussed with Spiegel's audit committee a potential illegal act related to failure to comply with applicable securities laws and rules. There is no indication KPMG bothered to have any discussion with White & Case on this matter. And there is no indication that KPMG sought (or requested Spiegel to seek) an opinion from Spiegel's securities counsel Kirkland & Ellis concerning Spiegel's conduct. KPMG relied on a cryptic reference to a Spiegel consultation with White & Case—not advice from White & Case supporting Spiegel—and failed to gain a complete understanding of the views of either White & Case or Kirkland & Ellis on what on its face appeared to be a clear legal violation by KPMG's audit client Spiegel.

F. SARBANES–OXLEY ATTORNEY RULES

Simon M. Lorne, An Issue-Annotated Version
of the Sox Rules for Lawyer Conduct

Practising Law Institute Corporate Law and Practice Course Handbook Series (2005)

Introduction and Overview

Five provisions of the Sarbanes–Oxley Act of 2002 (SOx) have particular and direct application to the practice by lawyers of their profession:

> Section 303 made it unlawful, "for any officer or director of an issuer, or any other person acting under the direction thereof, to take any action to fraudulently . . . mislead any independent public or certified accountant . . . for the purpose of rendering such financial statements materially misleading."

> Section 307 required the SEC to adopt, within 6 months, minimum standards that would require securities lawyers to report violations up within the organizational client—the "reporting up" rules;

> Section 602 codified, as a part of the Securities Exchange Act of 1934 (Exchange Act), Rule 102(e), formerly Rule 2(e), of the Commission's Rules of Practice, establishing standards for debarring professionals from practicing before the agency.

> Section 806 provided fraud-related "whistleblower" protection for employees of public corporations generally, presumably including employees who are lawyers.

> Section 3(b) generally provided sanctions for violations of SOx or of related rules.

Of these, the rules required by SOx § 307 have clearly generated the greatest consternation within the legal profession, and are the principal focus of these materials. On November 21, 2002, the Commission issued Securities Act Release "Proposed Rule: Standards of Professional Conduct for Attorneys Appearing and Practicing before the Commission in the Representation of an Issuer" (the "Proposing Release"). In that proposal the SEC proposed rules for both "reporting up" and "reporting out," the latter through a process of "noisy withdrawal" that included the attorney's having an obligation under specified circumstances to make a report to the Commission in the event of perceived corporate misconduct that is not rectified to the lawyer's satisfaction. In a number of respects, the proposed rules were broader than required—and quite possibly than permitted—by the statute itself.

On January 29, 2003, the Commission Issued Securities Act Release adopting the "reporting up" rules that that now comprise Part 205 of Title 17 of the Code of Federal Regulations. The new Part 205 rules, although considerably narrowed and improved from what had been proposed, remain in some respects beyond the clear scope of the authorizing statutory language, perhaps impermissibly so, and have embedded within them a number of important uncertainties and ambiguities. When these rules were adopted by the SEC, it deferred action on the more controversial noisy withdrawal proposals, and re-proposed them together with an alternative that would make the superficial distinction of requiring that the issuer, rather than the lawyer, provide the noise to accompany the withdrawal, at least in the first instance. As of this writing, the comment period on the revised "reporting out" proposals has long expired, but the Commission has not yet taken any action on the issue.

I. The New Regulatory Scheme in General

It is not difficult for the typical corporate or securities advisor—presumably, the lawyer most in the Congressional mind when SOx 307 was drafted and adopted—to behave in conformity with the basic thrust of the new "reporting up" rules, erring, as lawyers are wont to do, on the side of conservatism in difficult cases. There are incentives enough in the current environment for lawyers to avoid being present at a scene that they perceive to involve fraudulent client conduct. If what happened in the market to Enron or any of the other major frauds of recent vintage had been anticipated, it would as easily have been anticipated that the lawyers involved in the representation of those companies would encounter financial hurdles well in excess of fees received. The reason those firms proceeded was almost certainly that they did not perceive what now seems all too obvious. And if the fraudulent conduct is not perceived by the lawyers, no amount of rulemaking will be able to deter them from acting on behalf of the perpetrators.

In short, it is entirely plausible to propose that the new rules will not likely affect the behavior of corporate advisors in any meaningful way. They may affect sensitivity to some of the concerns that generated the rules, but in the post-Enron, post-Anderson, post-WorldCom, post-Adelphia, post-Tyco world, such sensitivities were already on high alert.

Rather, the impact of the new rules will most likely be seen in other respects, and recognizing this may be important to considering how the rules will be and should be interpreted. First, the new rules will result in the meting out of additional discipline to lawyers who were (as almost all lawyers are), trying to avoid any relationship to fraudulent conduct, but who ultimately failed in that regard. Such failures, even in a world of high alert, should not be surprising. After all, in every one of the recent large-scale failures it is quite clear that there were a number of sophisticated, buy-side analysts, corporate employees, and others, not facing any conflict of interest, who were fooled by the perpetrators. Perpetrators of large scale fraud succeed because they are good at it—because they are credible in their adamant assurances of success. There is no reason to believe that there will not be some members of the bar who prove to be as susceptible to being misled as some sophisticated investors. But when those frauds surface, and the harsh light of investigation is turned on after the surfacing, there will inevitably be some large number of instances in which it will be perceived after the fact that there were signals that could have been better understood. And in those cases, under the new rules, it will be natural for law enforcers to charge lawyers with responsibility.

Thus, it is in the enforcement context that the interpretive difficulties that inhere in the Part 205 rules will surface. When the SEC's Division of Enforcement encounters an issuer's violation of the securities laws, it will now likely look to see whether there was counsel who (A) knew (or should have known) of the activities in question (B) was "appearing" "before the Commission" "with respect to the issuer" and (C) failed to initiate a process in compliance with the extraordinarily prescriptive mandates of the new rules—as the Division of Enforcement interprets them. If the latter inquiry appears to the Division to so warrant, it will argue that proceedings against the lawyer are appropriate. It is only then that close interpretive attention is likely to be paid to the language of the Part 205 rules. As actions are brought and settled or decided (either of which may bee seen to constitute "precedent" in the view of the Division), authoritative interpretations of the new rules will emerge.

A second respect in which the new rules may affect lawyer behavior relates to the behavior not of corporate advisors, but of other lawyers. As discussed below, the definition of "appearing and practicing before the Commission in the representation of an issuer"—the jurisdictional touchstone—may be quite broadly interpreted. To the extent that it is read to encompass lawyers who are not corporate advisors in the traditional sense, it imposes on them duties that they are simply not used to addressing. Consequently, it may be those lawyers whose practice may be most affected by the rules as they seek to adjust their activities to reflect the new demands.

The new rules will also affect relations between lawyers (internal and external) and the entity's Chief Legal Officer ("CLO"), and between those lawyers collectively and the Board of Directors and its Committees. How those relationships will evolve is difficult of prediction at present, but that evolution will bear the imprint of these rules.

A.   *The Fundamental Principles*

Notwithstanding the significant uncertainties inherent in the new rules, it is important to recognize that the fundamental governing principle of the new lawyer conduct rules is both easily stated and, at least in the absence of the dirty withdrawal obligation, substantially inoffensive:

> When a lawyer becomes aware of inappropriate behavior on the part of a publicly-held client, he or she should make sure that responsible officials at the client are made aware of the behavior, and should monitor the issuer's response. If the improprieties rise to the level of materiality as to the client, and if the client does not deal with them in a reasonable fashion, the lawyer should press the case further up within the organization even, if necessary, as high as the board or a committee of independent directors.

But there is an unfortunate corollary, alluded to in the discussion above:

> The new rules are likely to have their principal effect not so much in guiding lawyer behavior as in establishing the principles under which lawyers will be the object of SEC enforcement actions. As such, there is an inevitable risk that their application will be premised not on the facts as they were understood and anticipated by the lawyers at the time, but on the facts as they will have historically evolved.

Unfortunate, too, is the very detailed and prescriptive nature of the rules as written. Thus, it is not just "a lawyer" whose conduct is affected, but a lawyer "appearing and practicing before the Commission" [a defined phrase] "in the representation of" [a defined phrase] an "Issuer" [a defined term]. Similarly, it is not merely that such a lawyer has a duty to ensure client awareness, to monitor the client response and to be prepared to ensure that decisions purporting to be made for "the corporation" are in fact made by the highest body authorized to speak for it in appropriate circumstances. Rather the duty to take action is triggered under specified circumstances (the receipt of "evidence of a material violation" [defined terms]), and the actions that must be taken—reporting, monitoring, reporting up, etc.—are similarly detailed to a degree that may prove unproductive.

B.   *Thematic Issues*

While many of the issues raised by the new rules are most easily considered in relation to the specific provisions of the rules (and are discussed in that context infra), there are a few issues of an overarching nature that warrant separate discussion.

First, of course, is the message being delivered to the legal profession. Regardless of how well or poorly conceived one thinks SOx to be in general, or Section 307 in particular, one cannot reasonably avoid the conclusion that lawyers are perceived by many to have been nonresponsive to the public need. If Congress can be taken as providing a reasonable proxy for what views are popular in the country, it must be acknowledged that people think lawyers bear some responsibility for allowing the recent spate of frauds to occur. Lawyers were there, it is thought, they should have recognized the fraud—which, of course, looks so obvious in retrospect—and they therefore could, and should, have stopped it. While this public sense of responsibility is not visited on lawyers to nearly the same degree as it is on accountants, it is nonetheless there.

Moreover, notions of client loyalty, confidentiality and the role of counsel in an adversary system have never been well understood by the general populace. How often has every lawyer tried to explain to the uninitiated, with limited success if any, that for the system to work effectively, even the murderer is entitled to have a lawyer to force the state to prove its case? Is it any wonder that corporate counsel, a step removed from the adversary system at its fullest strength, is viewed as failing to satisfy public duties when he or she drafts the documents that are critical to the perpetration of a fraud? While corporate lawyers generally strive to encourage full compliance with the letter and spirit of the law, and almost certainly are an effective voice in improving the social responsiveness of their clients, they cannot expect the public generally to appreciate that role. Such appreciation is even less likely to be forthcoming when there are significant voices within the legal profession itself giving voice to the same sense of public concern.

That recognition carries with it no particular implication for the specific understanding or interpretation of the new rules, other than this: at least in the short term, one cannot expect rule interpretations from a publicly sensitive source (such as the Congress or the SEC) to be particularly accommodating to the relatively subtle and long-term philosophical concerns of many lawyers.

More broadly, some argue that "the problem"—assuming (as has not been legitimately established) that there is significant lawyer responsibility for the chain of frauds that led to SOx—is the consequence of two trends within the profession: (1) increased internalization of the corporate legal function, and (2) balkanization of the external legal function in the form of a broader dispersal of any one client's legal representation among an increasing number of different law firms. The former, it is thought, has led to a reduced degree of expert legal review of the corporation's public reporting—with the underlying premise, as to which no view is expressed here, that securities law expertise is less likely to be resident within the corporation. The latter has arguably created an environment in which, to the extent outside counsel does have the responsibility to review public filings, that counsel necessarily has less familiarity with the events and circumstances generally affecting the entity. As a result, the ability to conduct an effective review is impaired.

Unfortunately, if these trends are indeed the cause of current concern, they are more likely to be exacerbated than ameliorated by the new rules, for the new SOx rules seem likely to increase both internalization and balkanization. As outside firms are in a position in which will have a need to make reports under the conditions specified in the rules, general counsel may decide it is appropriate to control more of the work within the corporation, thereby reducing the risk of unnecessary reports which trigger a time-consuming and expensive investigatory process. For some of the same reasons, outside firms may be less anxious to put themselves in the position of potentially having to file such reports, and may well encourage further internalization. Additionally, general counsel may want to reduce the number of matters being handled by SEC counsel generally—those who are clearly "appearing and practicing before the Commission" and are therefore clearly subject to the reach of the new rules—thereby encouraging balkanization.

From the issuer's perspective (as well as that of the broader society) it may be that the most important aspect of the new rules—particularly if a "dirty withdrawal" provision is adopted—is a reallocation of decision-making authority from clients to lawyers. With the threat of a lawyer's withdrawal or public disclosure, few corporate boards of directors, particularly in a period of increased risk of governmental action and private litigation, will be willing to endorse activities counter to the judgment of counsel, no matter how strongly they believe—even with the advice of other, sophisticated counsel—that corporate counsel is in error. As a result, decisions in most close cases will effectively be made by the lawyers involved. Since lawyers face a very different risk-reward calculus than their clients, even if lawyers were not inherently more risk-averse than their clients (and they generally are), the different risk-reward analysis will lead at the margin to fewer risks being taken. At its most fundamental level, this removal of decision-making from those who bear the consequences of the decisions is counter to elemental principles of capitalism. It is nonetheless an issue . . .

II. The Lawyer Conduct Rules, Simplified, Edited and Re–ordered

The rules that the SEC has adopted are intricate; for most purposes, a fair amount of simplification is useful, and such a simplification is here presented. In this presentation, section references to the rules are inserted for convenience. Defined terms are italicized when consideration of the term's definition may be unusual, or particularly useful or important to an understanding of the regulatory provision. In some instances, the definition, or a relevant portion of it, is then presented as soon as possible without unduly impeding the flow of the rule. In other instances, bracketed information is inserted summarizing portions of the definition. Unless otherwise indicated, the language used is taken directly from the relevant rule; for ease of review, quotation marks are dispensed with.

Inevitably, the process of simplification involves elimination of some items that may be important in some, relatively infrequently encountered, circumstances for the average practitioner. For example, the definition of the term "issuer" is not repeated below as it will seldom be important in practice, but that simplification means that there is no discussion in this section of issuers who have filed, but have not yet withdrawn or had declared effective, a registration statement under the Securities Act (technically included as "issuers"), or of foreign government issuers (specifically excluded from the definition). In any number of such circumstances it will prove true that a precise understanding of the rules' contours will be necessary, and so the rules, as written, must be consulted for responses to specific situations. The version presented here is intended to facilitate an understanding of the rules and the questions they raise. It is typically not intended to provide specific answers to specific questions of application.

The reordered rules in this presentation appear under the following topic heads:

> A.   The lawyer's "reporting up" duty.

> B.   Duties of a chief legal officer on receiving a report of evidence

> C.   Responsive duties of the reporting attorney

> D.   Investigating attorneys:

>> 1.   Subject to the rules

>> 2.   But generally excused from obligations

> E.   Appropriate response ends concern

> F.   Supervising and subordinate attorneys

> G.   Issuer as client

> H.   Qualified Legal Compliance Committees

> I.   Private rights of action

> J.   Permissive disclosure of client confidences

> K.   Sanctions and discipline

> L.   Additional definitions

A. The lawyer's "reporting up" duty.

§ 205.3(b) Duty to report evidence of a material violation. (1) If an attorney, appearing and practicing before the Commission in the representation of an issuer, becomes aware of evidence of a material violation ["material violation" and "evidence of a material violation" are separately defined terms; the definition of the former includes securities law violations and breaches of fiduciary duty] by the issuer or by any officer, director, employee, or agent of the issuer, the attorney shall report such evidence to the issuer's chief legal officer . . . or to both the issuer's chief legal officer and its chief executive officer . . . forthwith.

§ 205.2(a) Appearing and practicing before the Commission:

(1) Means:

(i) Transacting any business with the Commission . . . ;

(ii) Representing an issuer in a Commission . . . proceeding;

(iii) Providing advice in respect of the United States securities laws . . . regarding any document that the attorney has notice will be filed . . . or submitted . . . or incorporated into any [such] document . . . ; or

(iv) Advising an issuer as to whether information or a . . . writing is required . . . to be filed . . . or submitted . . . ; but

(2) Does not include an attorney who:

(i) Conducts the activities . . . other than in the context of providing legal services to an issuer with whom the attorney has an attorney-client relationship; or

(ii) Is a non-appearing foreign attorney.

§ 205.2(e) Evidence of a material violation means credible evidence, based upon which it would be unreasonable, under the circumstances, for a prudent and competent attorney not to conclude that it is reasonably likely that a material violation has occurred, is ongoing, or is about to occur.

B. Duties of a chief legal officer on receiving a report of evidence.

§ 205.3(b)(2) The chief legal officer [who is, by virtue of position, subject to these rules, at least in the Commission's view] . . . shall cause . . . [an] inquiry . . . to determine whether the material violation described in the report has occurred, is ongoing, or is about to occur. If the chief legal officer . . . determines no material violation has occurred . . . he or she shall notify the reporting attorney. . . . Unless the chief legal officer . . . reasonably believes that no material violation has occurred . . . he or she shall take all reasonable steps to cause the issuer to adopt an appropriate response, and shall advise the reporting attorney thereof. In lieu of causing an inquiry . . . , a chief legal officer . . . may refer a report . . . to a qualified legal compliance committee. . . .

C. Responsive duties of the reporting attorney

§ 205.3(b)(3) Unless an attorney who has made a report . . . reasonably believes that the . . . officer . . . has provided an appropriate response within a reasonable time, the attorney shall report the evidence of a material violation to:

(i) The audit committee . . . ;

(ii) Another committee . . . consisting solely of directors who are not employed, directly or indirectly, by the issuer . . . ; or

(iii) The issuer's board of directors (if the issuer's board of directors has no [such] committee. . . .

D. Investigating attorneys:

1. Subject to the rules

§ 205.3(b)(5) An attorney retained or directed by an issuer to investigate evidence . . . shall be deemed to be appearing and practicing before the Commission. . . .

2. But generally excused from obligations

§ 205.3(b)(6) An attorney shall not have any obligation to report evidence of a material violation under this paragraph (b) if:

(i) The attorney was retained or directed by the issuer's chief legal officer (or the equivalent thereof) to investigate such evidence of a material violation and:

(A) The attorney reports the results . . . to the chief legal officer . . .; and

(B) Except where the attorney and the chief legal officer . . . each reasonably believes that no material violation has occurred . . . the chief legal officer . . . reports the results . . . to the issuer's board of directors, a committee thereof . . . or a qualified legal compliance committee; or

(ii) The attorney was retained by the issuer's chief legal officer (or the equivalent thereof) to assert, consistent with his or her professional obligations, a colorable defense on behalf of the issuer . . . in any investigation or . . . proceeding relating to such evidence . . . and the chief legal officer . . . provides reasonable and timely reports . . . to the issuer's board of directors [or] a committee thereof. . . .

§ 205.3(b)(7) An attorney shall not have any obligation to report . . . if such attorney was retained . . . by a qualified legal compliance committee:

(i) To investigate such evidence of a material violation; or

(ii) To assert, consistent with his or her professional obligations, a colorable defense. . . .

E. Appropriate response ends concern.

§ 205.3(b)(8) An attorney who receives what he or she reasonably believes is an appropriate and timely response . . . need do nothing more. . . .

§ 205.3(b)(9) An attorney who does not reasonably believe that the issuer has made an appropriate response within a reasonable time . . . shall explain his or her reasons therefor to the [persons] . . . to whom the attorney reported the evidence. . . .

§ 205.2(b) Appropriate response means a response ... as a result of which the [reporting] attorney reasonably believes:

    (1) That no material violation ... has occurred, is ongoing, or is about to occur;

    (2) That the issuer has ... adopted appropriate remedial measures, including appropriate steps ... to stop ... to prevent ... and to remedy ... any material violation ...; or

    (3) That the issuer, with the consent of the issuer's board of directors, a committee thereof to whom a report could be made ... or a qualified legal compliance committee, has retained or directed an attorney to review the report ... and either:

        (i) Has substantially implemented any remedial recommendations ...; or

        (ii) Has been advised that such attorney may, consistent with his or her professional obligations, assert a colorable defense ... to the reported evidence of a material violation.

F.   Supervising and subordinate attorneys.

§ 205.4(b) A supervisory attorney shall make reasonable efforts to ensure that a subordinate attorney ... conforms to this part. To the extent a subordinate attorney appears and practices ... that subordinate attorney's supervisory attorneys also appear and practice before the Commission.

§ 205.4(c) A supervisory attorney is responsible for complying with the reporting requirements ... when a subordinate attorney has reported ... evidence of a material violation.

§ 205.5(b) A subordinate attorney shall comply with this part....

§ 205.5(c) A subordinate attorney complies ... if the subordinate attorney reports to his or her supervising attorney ... evidence of a material violation....

§ 205.5(d) A subordinate attorney may take the steps permitted or required by § 205.3(b) or (c) if the subordinate attorney reasonably believes that a supervisory attorney to whom he or she has reported ... has failed to comply with § 205.3.

G.   Issuer as client.

§ 205.3(a) An attorney ... owes his or her ... duties to the issuer as an organization....

H.   Qualified Legal Compliance Committees.

§ 205.3(c)(1) If an attorney ... becomes aware of evidence of a material violation ... the attorney may, as an alternative to the reporting requirements of paragraph (b) of this section, report such evidence to a qualified legal compliance committee, if the issuer has previously formed such a committee. An attorney who [so] reports ... has satisfied his or her obligation to report ... and is not required to assess the issuer's response....

(2) A chief legal officer ... may refer a report of evidence of a material violation to a previously established qualified legal compliance committee in lieu of causing an inquiry.... The chief legal officer (or the equivalent thereof) shall inform the reporting attorney that the report has been referred....

§ 205.2(k) Qualified legal compliance committee means a committee of an issuer ... that:

(1) Consists of at least one member of the issuer's audit committee (or ... an equivalent committee of independent directors) and two or more members of the issuer's board ... who are not employed, directly or indirectly, by the issuer ...;

(2) Has adopted written procedures for the confidential receipt, retention, and consideration of any report ...;

(3) Has been duly established ... with the authority and responsibility:

(i) To inform the issuer's chief legal officer and chief executive officer ... of any report of evidence of a material violation (except in the circumstances described in § 205.3(b)(4));

(ii) To determine whether an investigation is necessary ... and, if it determines an investigation is necessary or appropriate, to:

(A) Notify the audit committee or the full board of directors;

(B) Initiate an investigation ...; and

(C) Retain such additional expert personnel as the committee deems necessary; and

(iii) At the conclusion of any such investigation, to:

(A) Recommend, by majority vote, that the issuer implement an appropriate response ...; and

(B) Inform the chief legal officer and the chief executive officer ... and the board ... of the results of any such investigation ...; and

(4) Has the authority and responsibility, acting by majority vote, to take all other appropriate action, including the authority to notify the Commission in the event that the issuer fails in any material respect to implement an appropriate response....

I. Private rights of action.

§ 205.7(a) Nothing in this part is intended to, or does, create a private right of action against any attorney, law firm, or issuer based upon compliance or noncompliance with its provisions.

§ 205.7(b) Authority to enforce compliance with this part is vested exclusively in the Commission.

J. Permissive disclosure of client confidences.

§ 205.3(d) Issuer confidences.

(1) Any report under this section . . . or any response thereto . . . may be used by an attorney in connection with any investigation, proceeding, or litigation in which the attorney's compliance with this part is in issue.

(2) An attorney . . . may reveal to the Commission, without the issuer's consent, confidential information . . . to the extent the attorney reasonably believes necessary:

(i) To prevent the issuer from committing a material violation that is likely to cause substantial injury to the financial interest or property of the issuer or investors;

(ii) To prevent the issuer, in a Commission investigation or administrative proceeding from committing . . . [or] suborning perjury . . . or committing any act proscribed in 18 U.S.C. 1001 that is likely to perpetrate a fraud upon the Commission; or

(iii) To rectify the consequences of a material violation by the issuer that caused, or may cause, substantial injury to the financial interest or property of the issuer or investors in the furtherance of which the attorney's services were used.

K. Sanctions and discipline.

§ 205.6(a) A violation . . . by any attorney . . . shall subject such attorney to the civil penalties and remedies for a violation of the federal securities laws available to the Commission. . . .

§ 205.6(b) An attorney . . . who violates any provision of this part is subject to the disciplinary authority of the Commission, regardless of whether the attorney may also be subject to discipline for the same conduct in a jurisdiction where the attorney is admitted or practices. . . .

§ 205.6(c) An attorney who complies in good faith with the provisions of this part shall not be subject to discipline or otherwise liable under inconsistent standards imposed by any state or other United States jurisdiction. . . .

§ 205.6(d) An attorney practicing outside the United States shall not be required to comply with the requirements of this part to the extent that such compliance is prohibited by applicable foreign law.

L. Additional definitions.

For purposes of this part, the following definitions apply:

§ 205.2(d) Breach of fiduciary duty refers to any breach of fiduciary or similar duty to the issuer recognized under an applicable federal or state statute or at common law. . . .

§ 205.2(i) Material violation means a material violation of an applicable United States federal or state securities law, a material breach of fiduciary duty arising under United States federal or state law, or a similar material violation of any United States federal or state law.

§ 205.2(j) Non-appearing foreign attorney means an attorney:

(1) Who is admitted to practice law in a jurisdiction outside the United States;

(2) Who does not hold himself or herself out ... and does not give legal advice regarding, United States federal or state securities or other laws (except as provided in paragraph (j)(3)(ii) of this section); and

(3) Who:

(i) Conducts activities that would constitute appearing and practicing before the Commission only incidentally to, and in the ordinary course of, the practice of law in a jurisdiction outside the United States; or

(ii) Is appearing and practicing before the Commission only in consultation with counsel ... in a state or other United States jurisdiction.

Michael A. Perino, SEC Enforcement of Attorney Up-the-Ladder Reporting Rules: An Analysis of Institutional Constraints, Norms and Biases

49 Vill. L. Rev. 851 (2004)

* * *

II. Budget and Personnel Constraints at the SEC

In support of rigorous federally based standards of lawyer conduct, Professor [Susan] Koniak has argued elsewhere that state bar authorities are unlikely to reliably enforce ethics rules against 'big-time securities or corporate lawyer[s],' in part because bar authorities are 'notoriously under-funded and under-staffed.' There is little basis for disputing these contentions. Ample empirical evidence supports the view that lawyers at large prestigious firms are rarely the targets of disciplinary proceedings—most state bar disciplinary proceedings involve solo practitioners and small firm lawyers. Money, or the lack thereof, is certainly part of the story. Generally, state bar authorities are on tight budgets and do not have the staff or budgets to pursue complex transactional cases.

Unfortunately for proponents of a substantial SEC role in enforcing professional responsibility standards, the SEC faces similar budgetary constraints despite its recent large increases in budget allocations. The SEC is certainly better funded and has more expertise in securities matters than state bar authorities. But a short review of the resources available to the SEC and its oversight responsibilities in the securities markets suggests that it too may not have sufficient funding to provide the kind of sustained, rigorous oversight of the entire corporate and securities bar that proponents of an active SEC role appear to contemplate ...

Are these budget and staffing problems a thing of the past? I suspect not. While Sarbanes–Oxley did increase the size of the SEC's budget, it is by no means certain in a time of increased budget deficits and shifting spending priorities (i.e., the war on terrorism, Iraq, homeland security) that the SEC can count on those budget increases in the future ...

Will the SEC allocate substantial resources to attorney disciplinary actions? A number of factors suggest that such an allocation is unlikely, at least in the foreseeable future. The SEC faces enormous pressure from Congress and other constituencies to bring enforcement actions involving the primary actors in Enron and other recent scandals; it is reasonable to assume that, at least in the short term, the SEC will concentrate its enforcement resources there ...

It is possible, of course, to argue that vigorously enforcing up-the-ladder reporting rules and requiring noisy withdrawal will actually conserve resources in the long run by effectively enlisting lawyers as additional monitors of client misbehavior. Empirical studies of deterrence strongly suggest that, all other things being equal, increased monitoring (which increases the chances that unlawful activities will be detected) has a greater deterrent impact than enhanced sanctions. As suggested earlier, even if enforcement activity does not increase significantly, the mere presence of Section 307 and the amendments to the ABA Model Rules are likely to cause more lawyers to report evidence of illegal acts up the ladder. But the question remains—is the SEC likely to make disciplining lawyers an enforcement priority? Answering that question requires us to take a somewhat closer look at the institutional features of the SEC as an enforcement agency.

III.   SEC ENFORCEMENT OF ATTORNEY PROFESSIONAL RESPONSIBILITY: A BRIEF ANALYSIS OF INSTITUTIONAL INCENTIVES AND CONSTRAINTS

The case for augmenting the SEC's role in disciplining lawyers is premised largely on the inadequacies of state bar authorities. The standard critique, in addition to highlighting the funding problems previously discussed, paints a picture of generally lax and inconsistent enforcement of professional responsibility standards. When they were first formed, state bar authorities rarely enforced professional responsibility rules. Although disciplinary actions have increased over time, they tend to follow distinct patterns. Most actions are brought against individual lawyers in small law firms or solo practitioners; large firm lawyers are rarely subject to discipline. Most complaints are dismissed with apparently little investigation. The matters in which state bar authorities actually bring disciplinary actions typically involve obvious professional lapses, such as mishandling of client funds. A large percentage of disbarments involve clear-cut cases of lawyer misconduct or unfitness, such as those involving lawyers with felony convictions.

What is most striking about this critique (at least to this securities professor) is that it could equally describe most of the SEC's own history in enforcing professional responsibility standards against attorneys. In a highly condensed form, that history goes something like this. Since its second year of operation (1935), the SEC has had the power under Rule 102(e) of its Rules of Practice to suspend or disbar attorneys from appearing or practicing before the Commission if they engage in improper professional conduct. Like state bar authorities, in the earliest days, the Commission did not exercise its power to discipline attorneys. In the first fifteen years of its existence, Rule 102(e) was used only in disciplinary proceedings against accountants and other non-legal professionals appearing before the Commission. It was not until 1950 that the SEC used Rule 102(e) to suspend an attorney from practicing before the SEC. Throughout the 1950s and 1960s, there was a similar low level of activity.

Things changed in the 1970s. Under the direction of Irving Pollack and his successor as head of the Enforcement Division, Stanley Sporkin, the Commission shifted from generally low to more vigorous enforcement. In those cases which were brought under what the Enforcement Division termed an 'access theory' of securities enforcement, the Commission articulated a vision of Rule 102(e) that is remarkably similar to that expressed by proponents of Section 307. Then, as now, the lawyer was viewed as a gatekeeper who could be enlisted through the threat of disciplinary action to protect shareholders from managerial opportunism. Aggressive access theory enforcement, however, was relatively short-lived and effectively came to an end in the early 1980s. At that point, the SEC reverted to its previous pattern; indeed, it formally took the position that it would only bring Rule 102(e) proceedings against attorneys 'if the alleged misconduct was a violation of established ethical rules at the state level and had a direct impact on the Commission's internal processes.' Since then, nearly all Rule 102(e) proceedings against lawyers have involved actual securities law violations, a pattern that is quite consistent with state bar disciplinary proceedings against lawyers with felony convictions. Like state bar authorities, the SEC has tended to bring these proceedings against solo practitioners or lawyers from small firms. Thus, except for the period of aggressive enforcement in the 1970s, the SEC's enforcement of disciplinary rules against lawyers has looked remarkably similar to state bar authorities' enforcement efforts.

These similarities are not mere coincidence. State bar authorities and the SEC are both bureaucracies that share a common set of cultural norms and institutional constraints. First, from its inception and throughout its history, the SEC has been a lawyer-dominated agency. Lawyer domination does not mean knee-jerk protectionism. It is far too facile to suggest that a lawyer-dominated agency will simply look out for its own and never bring actions against attorneys. At least at the SEC, the historical evidence shows that lawyers do not get a free pass; they are frequently defendants in SEC actions, particularly actions alleging insider trading violations. That being said, however, lawyers' professional norms and experiences are likely to have a profound impact when it comes to enforcing professional responsibility rules that SEC staffers may consider to be outside of the agency's core mission (to protect investors by vigorously enforcing disclosure obligations). Professor Koniak has suggested that client confidentiality and zealous advocacy are 'constitutional' norms for lawyers—core values that lawyers treat as nearly inviolable. As a result, disclosing client fraud is subordinate to the central norm of maintaining confidentiality. The attorney commissioners and staffers, many of whom practiced as securities lawyers before joining the SEC, share the very same professional norms advanced by Professor Koniak.

In this regard, the SEC or state bar authorities are no different from other administrative agencies staffed by professionals. Professionals (not just lawyers, but economists, engineers and others) within agencies often receive incentives (in terms of status, deference and post-government employment opportunities) from 'organized groups of fellow practitioners located outside the agency.' It is, thus, unsurprising that the SEC would vigorously enforce insider trading rules against attorneys because such activity is both at the core of the SEC's investor protection mission and blatantly breaches a lawyer's confidentiality norm. At the same time, finding a plausible interpretation that supports a client's disclosure decision or transaction structure is at the heart of the zealous advocacy norm, and we should not be surprised that the SEC would be less willing to discipline lawyers for that activity.

As lawyers themselves, the SEC staff is also likely to be more acutely attuned to the hindsight bias problem implicated in determining after the fact what a lawyer must have known. Cognitive psychologists have repeatedly found that people reviewing a set of facts ex post consistently exaggerate what could have been anticipated ex ante. In other words, when individuals know an outcome, they tend to believe 'that others should have been able to anticipate events much better than was actually the case.'

Hindsight bias has obvious implications for enforcement of up-the-ladder reporting rules. To be sure, Professor Koniak argues that lawyers never 'know' that their clients are acting improperly, and there is certainly some truth to that position. Lawyers, just like anyone else, can conveniently delude themselves about the existence of improper activities, particularly where they have a strong financial incentive to do so. But it is also true that it is all too easy in hindsight to say that a lawyer 'must have known' of client misbehavior, when, in reality, at the time the lawyer was acting, the facts may have appeared much less clear. Moreover, constructing a positive initial image of a client and then clinging to that initial impression, even in the light of apparently inconsistent evidence, is not necessarily venal. Again, cognitive psychology teaches that once humans (and, despite some suggestions to the contrary, lawyers are human) construct schema (i.e., mental representations used to process incoming data), they are generally reluctant to alter them.

While lawyers at the SEC are not immune from the hindsight bias problem, they are likely to have a greater familiarity with the indeterminate context in which securities lawyers advise clients on, for example, disclosure issues and, therefore, may be reluctant to bring disciplinary proceedings against them. It is, thus, not surprising to see bar officials and SEC enforcement attorneys focusing their disciplinary efforts almost exclusively on the most egregious cases (such as stealing client funds or insider trading), where such uncertainties are less of a concern. And to the extent that the SEC has admonished or disciplined lawyers for reporting failures, it has generally been in cases with compelling facts that strongly suggest lawyer knowledge of client misbehavior.

This implicit recognition of the hindsight bias problem may also explain why the SEC adopted such a convoluted triggering mechanism for up-the-ladder reporting ... If the presence of hindsight bias suggests a significant risk of lawyer discipline in situations in which the lawyer did not know of a client's wrongdoing, then adopting a convoluted and difficult standard is a way of ensuring that discipline will be imposed only in cases in which the lawyer really did know. To be sure, such a standard is a second-best solution. It would be far preferable for enforcement attorneys to assess hindsight bias accurately in individual cases, but expecting that kind of accuracy is unrealistic. Given the drafters' professional norms and the centrality of the confidentiality principle, it is unsurprising to see them adopt a standard that will tend to under- rather than over-discipline attorneys for reporting failures.

In addition to these professional norms, it is also important to recognize that normal prosecutorial preferences will impact SEC enforcement attorneys' decisions whether to bring disciplinary actions. In deciding which cases to bring, the Commission will certainly focus on the potential benefits of enforcement, such as whether enforcement will have an important deterrent impact. Thus, a high-profile case against a prestigious law firm that is likely to generate substantial press coverage has obvious appeal. But that kind of case is a double-edged sword, both because of the downside risk associated with losing a high-profile case and because such cases are likely to require greater staff resources to prosecute. Particularly when it comes to bringing the first test cases, the Commission is likely to have a strong preference for cases in which there is clear evidence that the lawyer violated his or her reporting obligations. In other words, we are likely to continue to see the same pattern we saw before Sarbanes–Oxley—cases in which the violation of the SEC's Rules of Practice is essentially an add-on to a claim that the lawyers were themselves engaged in securities violations.

The same conclusion flows from an analysis of the incentives of the staff enforcement attorneys. As the previously discussed turnover data suggest, typical SEC enforcement staffers are young attorneys who spend only a few years at the SEC before pursuing more lucrative careers in private practice, often at large prestigious law firms. While one way to enhance career advancement within the agency and post-government employment opportunities is to bring high profile cases, attorneys may, quite frankly, be leery of bringing disciplinary proceedings against lawyers from the kind of firms that they hope to join in the future. The reluctance to bring a disciplinary proceeding against a lawyer, however, may be lessened if the subject of the disciplinary proceeding can be portrayed as a rogue attorney who clearly was acting outside the norms of the profession, or if the attorney is a solo practitioner or member of a small firm. Again, it seems that staff attorneys will display the same preferences they have in the past—they will prefer to bring only the most egregious actions, especially if the lawyers involved are from less prestigious firms ...

* * *

IV. CONCLUSION

When it comes to enforcing professional responsibility standards, the SEC and state bar authorities are subject to similar constraints and incentives and exhibit similar norms. As a result, it is reasonable to expect that SEC enforcement of the new lawyer reporting rules will look quite similar to its own past enforcement patterns and the enforcement patterns that state bar authorities exhibit. But incentives, norms and constraints are not outcome-determinative. Bureaucracies can overcome these barriers and change their behavior, broaden their agendas or reconceptualize their missions. Indeed, one need look no further for evidence of such a change than the SEC's own treatment of lawyers in the 1970s. Is such a shift back to vigorous enforcement possible in the future? Anything is possible, but history teaches us that lasting shifts (particularly those that are at odds with agency norms, incentives and constraints) are relatively rare. In this case, past is most likely prologue.

The following chart illustrates the differences and similarities between the ABA Model Rules and the SEC rules under Sarbanes–Oxley.

ABA MODEL RULES AND SEC RULES: A COMPARISON

	ETHICS RULES *	SEC RULES
Coverage	All lawyers	Practicing or appearing before SEC
Source of information	Related to representation	No limitation; may be clarified
State of mind	Know of violation	"Evidence" of material violation; need not be more likely than not

	ETHICS RULES *	SEC RULES
Nature of violation	Violation of duty to organization or of law	Material violation of fed/state securities law; breach of fiduciary duty under fed/state law; or similar violation
Reporting up the ladder	Presumption: must report	Must report and evaluate response
Disclosure outside organization	Model Rules: May Most states: May A few states: Must	May disclose

* Check state bar rules for variations

PROBLEMS

You are completing the 10-K for your client, Sentinel Enterprises, Inc. which is due in five days. Much of your work has been a "cut and paste" job, using material from recent Sentinel filings with the SEC. In these filings, Sentinel has described its only plant (its most valuable asset) as being centrally located in downtown Milton on a large parcel of property that Sentinel "owns in fee simple." That morning, while preparing to contest a recent revaluation of the plant by the county assessor, an associate working with you on the revaluation case told you that a surveying error was made when Sentinel built the plant almost 20 years ago and that the western edge of the plant encroaches by two feet on the property of Sentinel's principal competitor. In three more months, the 20-year period for adverse possession will have run and the encroached upon land will belong to Sentinel. Under local law, the owner of land encroached upon has the option of demanding its fair value or having the encroaching structure promptly removed. To cure the encroachment would render Sentinel's plant inoperable for the better part of a year. Sentinel has asked you how it should proceed.

2. You have drafted the Management's Discussion and Analysis section of Sentinel's 10-K (Item 303 of SEC Regulation S-K). The draft emphasizes some business contingencies that suggest that the company's surprisingly favorable financial results for this year may not be a good indicator of future performance. You believe that this disclosure is necessary, although you have included elaborate qualifiers so as to minimize its potential negative impact. Nevertheless, upon reviewing your draft, both the company's president and general counsel ask you to remove the qualifiers. You resist, stating your belief that the MD&A would be materially false and misleading without them. The general counsel, however, insists on the deletions and says that the document will be filed "her way."

How should you proceed?

3. Your firm is outside counsel for International Development Systems (IDS) whose stock is traded on the New York Stock Exchange. Most of IDS/business comes from major construction projects throughout the world. In recent years, IDS' earnings growth has slowed markedly, although revenues continue to increase. Last year, to compensate for the slow growth, IDS

launched a program to increase activities in Middle Eastern countries. Thus far, the program has been very successful. In its most recent annual report to shareholders IDS said that it is "heralding a new era of substantial growth" that could be used as the basis for a projected rapid earnings growth.

Your firm is preparing a registration statement for the sale of debentures, the proceeds of which will be used to help finance this new growth. In the course of this preparation, you have found correspondence disclosing substantial payments made to foreign nationals that were recorded on the company's books as "sales commissions." IDS' management is aware that the Foreign Corrupt Practices Act bars payments only to "foreign officials." Accordingly, its general counsel has obtained opinions from local law firms in the countries in which such payments were made stating that these payments were not made to government employees. The CEO has admitted to you that the recipients do seem to have "remarkable influence" with the government officials who choose contractors. He has also told you that IDS' efforts would be unsuccessful without these payments.

You believe that these payments must be disclosed in the registration statement and in future 1934 Act periodic and annual reports to the SEC. Although the payments do not clearly violate the Foreign Corrupt Practices Act, you believe that they might constitute a commercial bribe that the SEC would consider material since it reflects on the integrity of management. Moreover, an increasing amount of the company's revenues and its future projections depend on a form of business that is at least questionable.

The CEO is understandably concerned that disclosure will interfere with the proposed financing and with the company's ability to continue its Middle East business successfully. He has asked you to estimate the probability that the failure to disclose would constitute a violation of the securities laws. After some reflection, you conclude that there is an 85% probability that a court would determine that there was a violation. The CEO, after considering the likelihood that the nondisclosure would come to light, the potential damage if it did, and the 15% chance of success on the merits, has determined not to make the disclosure and has instructed you to draft the registration statement accordingly.

How should you proceed?

NOTE: In each of the problems, in analyzing your duties and options, consider the obligations and alternatives that you have under the SEC's rules implementing Sarbanes-Oxley and the extent to which those rules affect your analysis.

Chapter 17

SECURITIES REGULATION: ATTORNEY LIABILITY

The previous chapter dealt with the role of the lawyer in the disclosure system. This chapter explores the ways in which lawyers themselves face liability under the securities laws. Enforcement of these laws is both public and private. The SEC has statutory authority to enforce the securities laws either through actions in federal court or through its own administrative proceedings. Investors who have suffered losses also can bring suit against violators although there are procedural requirements, found primarily in the Private Securities Litigation Reform Act, that restrict their ability to recover. What this chapter makes clear is that lawyers face a real risk of liability for their conduct even if they themselves do not directly make any fraudulent misstatements. The first part of this chapter examines that risk in an SEC action. The second part explores it in a private action.

OVERVIEW OF THE CHAPTER

For lawyers, the greatest risk of liability for a securities law violation comes from SEC enforcement actions rather than private suits. In proceeding against a lawyer, the Commission can bring either judicial or administrative actions and can obtain a wide variety of relief. The Commission also has the power under Rule 102(e) of its Rules of Practice (formerly Rule 2(e)) to bar a lawyer, temporarily or permanently, from practice before the Commission if, among other things, the lawyer has "engaged in unethical or improper professional conduct." This chapter explores he ways in which the SEC has exercised its power, the extent to which a lawyer faces liability in private actions and the SEC rules adopted pursuant to Sarbanes–Oxley.

Attorney Liability

The first part of the chapter presents an overview of the SEC's enforcement process and power, including its disciplinary authority under Rule 102(e). The *Keating, Muething & Klekamp* (KMK) opinion illustrates how the SEC has used this power. In reading the opinion, note that it is not written after a litigated proceeding in which a factual record has been established Rather, it is the result of a settlement in which KMK has consented to the entry of an order without admitting or denying the SEC's allegations. The facts are as the SEC chooses to portray them rather than being drawn from the formal record in the case. Such consents are often the way in which SEC enforcement actions, whether judicial or administrative, are resolved.

Several things are noteworthy in the opinion. First, American Financial Corporation (AFC) represented an unusually large part of KMK's business. In imputing knowledge of AFC's business to the individual KMK lawyers and ultimately to KMK itself, consider whether the SEC is suggesting that KMK should be treated almost as if it were AFC rather than a separate entity. Second, examine the SEC's conclusions carefully. Although the SEC says that it is not dictating what procedures a firm should adopt, is that what the Commission actually does? In her dissent, Commissioner Karmel certainly thinks so. Indeed, her belief that the Commission is acting inappropriately is one of the reasons for her dissent (Section 602 of Sarbanes–Oxley has now mooted her argument that the SEC lacked power to adopt Rule 2(e)). The extent to which the SEC or the states should regulate lawyer conduct, an issue Commissioner Karmel stresses, is a question that runs throughout this chapter. Note that the majority in *KMK* does not address it at all.

The *National Student Marketing Corporation* (NSMC) case is another landmark opinion. The case was significant when it was brought because of the reputations of the law firm defendants. Unlike most SEC actions, this case involved two prestigious law firms who seemingly would have had no motive to engage in the fraud of which they were accused. Because White & Case had already settled Because White & Case had already settled its part of the case with the SEC, the opinion deals solely with Lord, Bissell & Brook but to understand the opinion, you need to examine the conduct of Jay Epley, the White & Case partner, which is integral to what happened.

As with *Carter & Johnson*, try to read the case as if the opinion had not been written and you were in Epley's position. At each step, what would you have done? Would you have postponed the closing, thus creating serious business problems for your client? How would you have reacted to the first telephone call from Peat Marwick? The second phone call? Finally, would you have given the opinion that the closing required absent the comfort letter that might have been relevant to it?

Now consider Lord Bissell & Brook's situation. What more could it have done? Since Interstate could waive the White & Case opinion, how would you have advised Interstate to proceed.? Would you have counseled that the actions of the Interstate officers constituted a valid waiver? If not, what would you have thought needed to be done? In that connection, what was the economic risk to Interstate, its client, if the closing was postponed? And would you have given the required opinion?

In answering the questions relating to both law firms, think back to Langevoort's article in Chapter 9.

In addition to seeking an injunction in federal district court, the SEC has the authority to enter a cease and desist order against a person whom it has found to have violated the securities laws. Although not limited to lawyers, the SEC has used this power against them in several cases. Robert Haft's treatise analyzes those cases and the issues involved in the use of the cease and desist procedure.

The last part of this section deals with Enron. The Enron scandal has given rise to enough issues so that it is the subject of a separate chapter in this book. The excerpt from one of the opinions in the extensive shareholder litigation is included here because it addresses the standard for attorney liability in a securities fraud action.

A moment's reflection will suggest that it is the corporation or corporate officials rather than the lawyer who actually make the fraudulent misstatements or omissions and that they, rather than the lawyer, are the principal actors. The lawyer's role is far more likely to have been in the preparation of the fraudulent documents. Until the Supreme Court's decision in *Central Bank of Denver* v. *First Interstate Bank of Denver*, 511 U.S. 164 (1994), the principal theory for holding a lawyer liable in such a situation was that she had aided and abetted the principal actors' fraud. In *Central Bank*, however, the Court held that aiding and abetting could not be used to establish liability in a securities fraud action (subsequent to *Central Bank*, Congress amended the statute to authorize the SEC to bring an aiding and abetting action but the limitation on private actions remains). Thus, after *Central Bank*, a lawyer could be liable only if she was a primary violator, i.e., seemingly had made the misstatement.

Since the lawyer rarely did so, two theories emerged for determining whether a person who did not actually make the misstatement could be considered a primary violator. In her opinion, Judge Harmon analyzes those theories and ultimately adopts the "substantial participation" test as proposed by the SEC in its amicus curiae brief. Under that test, a person can be a primary violator without actually speaking if she created the misrepresentation on which the plaintiff relied and acted with the requisite scienter.

Enron, of course, involved a major accounting fraud that was manifest in SEC filings and corporate press releases. The plaintiffs alleged that two law firms, Vinson & Elkins and Kirkland & Ellis had participated in writing, reviewing and approving many of those filings and releases and the complaint identified numerous examples of such participation. In deciding defendants' motion to dismiss, Judge Harmon found that the complaint had alleged sufficient facts to establish participation by Vinson & Elkins and thus refused to dismiss the complaint against the firm. She did dismiss the complaint against Kirkland & Ellis. In so doing, she noted that the firm had numerous conflicts of interest and that it might have breached professional ethical standards but she held that the opinions and documents with which Kirkland & Ellis was involved were not intended for the plaintiffs and thus they could not show the requisite reliance. In reading the opinion, it should be clear that Judge Harmon is not deciding that Vinson & Elkins had violated the securities laws. Because this was a motion to dismiss, she accepted plaintiffs' allegations as true solely for that limited purpose. You will study Vinson & Elkins' conduct in greater detail in Chapter 20.

The significance of the opinion lies in the detail in which Judge Harmon explicates the "substantial participation" test and ties Vinson & Elkins to Enron's fraud. Keep in mind, however, that it is only a District Court opinion, that may be reversed on appeal, and that not all courts have accepted the substantial participation theory.

A. ATTORNEY LIABILITY

Enforcement Actions by the SEC

James D. Cox, Robert W. Hillman & Donald C. Langevoort,
Securities Regulation: Cases and Materials

(4th ed. 2004)

ENFORCEMENT ACTIONS BY THE SEC

1. INVESTIGATIONS

a. The Investigatory Process

Each of the acts administered and enforced by the SEC empowers the Commission to investigate whether violations have occurred, are occurring, or are likely to occur. For example, Section 21(a) of the Exchange Act provides that the Commission may, "in its discretion, make such investigations as it deems necessary to determine whether any person has violated, is violating, or is about to violate any provision of" the Act or its rules or regulations. The Commission's Rules of Practice govern the conduct of such investigations. 17 C.F.R. §§ 201.1 et seq. There are many possible causes for the staff to launch an investigation: Its review of filings with the Commission may suggest a disclosure violation has occurred; the staff, as well as self-regulatory organizations, periodically inspects broker-dealers, investment advisers, and investment companies, and such inspections may raise the staff's eyebrows and prompt a further investigation of some matter; news stories, as well as complaints and tips by members of the public, whether they are injured investors or former employees clearing their consciences, are frequent sources for investigations; and market surveillance operations by the Commission and the SROs have been the cause for many of the Commission's investigations of insider trading and market manipulation cases.

The initial investigation by the staff, referred to as an *informal* or *preliminary investigation*, simply entails asking questions of parties involved, without issuing subpoenas or seeking to compel testimony. A preliminary investigation is nonpublic unless the Commission orders that it be public, a step it rarely has taken. The preliminary investigation's success heavily depends upon the voluntary cooperation of the company and individuals that are the object of the investigation. Consider the conflicting tugs on their counsel during the informal investigation:

> Counsel's principal responsibility in the preliminary investigation is to assess tactical considerations for responding to an informal inquiry. Counsel must balance the corporation's interests. On one hand, there is great incentive to provide the information necessary to allay the staff's suspicions of violation without graduating to a formal investigation. Counsel also may be able to quickly eliminate areas of concern and focus the staff's attention on relevant information. On the other hand, counsel may wish to prevent a wholesale disclosure of broadly identified corporate information, and may be forced to make a more limited presentation of information.

Ferrara & Nerkle, Overview of an SEC Enforcement Action, 8 Corp. L. Rev. 306, 307–308 (1985). *See also* Winer & Winer, Effective Representation in the SEC Wells Process, 34 Sec. & Com. Reg. Rept. (Mar. 28, 2001). If the staff's concerns are not satisfied by the information available to it through its informal investigation, it can seek the Commission's authority for a formal investigation, in which the staff is authorized to issue subpoenas and administer oaths. Such authority is embodied in what is known as a *formal order of investigation*. To obtain a formal order, the staff must persuade the commissioners that there is reason to believe that a violation has occurred. The grant of the formal order does not involve the commissioners in either an adjudication or a fact finding: The grant of a formal order reflects no more than the commissioners' support for the staff's view there is reason to believe a violation has occurred, is occurring, or is about to occur.

Once the formal order is granted, the staff has the power to issue subpoenas nationwide against any person or records significant to the investigation. If a person refuses to comply with the subpoena, the SEC staff must apply to the federal district court to enforce the subpoena. An SEC subpoena can be judicially enforced against recalcitrant parties without the staff having to prove probable cause that the securities laws have been violated. *See SEC v. Brigadoon Scotch Distributing Co.*, 480 F.2d 1047 (2d Cir. 1973), *cert. denied*, 415 U.S. 915 (1974). Subpoenas are not enforced, however, if the investigation is not for a proper purpose, the information sought is not relevant to that purpose, the SEC already possesses the information it seeks, or the administrative procedures for issuing the subpoena have not been followed. *See SEC v. Blackfoot Bituminous, Inc.*, 622 F.2d 512, 514 (1980). The ability of the investigation's target to mount challenges to an SEC subpoena is greatly compromised by the Supreme Court's holding that the target of an SEC investigation is not entitled to prior notice when a subpoena is directed toward a third party. *SEC v. Jerry T. O'Brien, Inc.*, 467 U.S. 735, 104 S.Ct. 2720, 81 L.Ed.2d 615 (1984). By and large, the Commission's power to investigate suspected cases of securities law violations is unrestricted.

See SEC v. Brigadoon Scotch Distributing Co., 480 F.2d 1047 (2d Cir. 1973), *cert. denied*, 415 U.S. 915 (1974).

> The Commission must be free without undue interference or delay to conduct an investigation which will adequately develop a factual basis for a determination as to whether particular activities come within the Commission's regulatory authority.

Id. at 1052–1053.

The courts have held with some consistency that, so long as the staff is acting in good faith, its discretion to determine who will be required to testify before it or what documentary information will have to be produced will not be second-guessed. To be sure, constitutional protections apply to SEC investigations. Thus, for example, the Fourth Amendment's guarantee against unreasonable searches and seizures has been interpreted to limit the Commission's ability to make unreasonably burdensome investigatory demands, and the Fifth Amendment's privilege against self-incrimination applies to SEC investigations and proceedings, although that privilege can be raised only by individuals and sole proprietorships and not by corporations and partnerships. (On this point, consider that *Braswell v. United States*, 487 U.S. 99, 108 S.Ct. 2284, 101 L.Ed.2d 98 (1988), held that an officer must produce corporate records, even though those records will incriminate the officer.) During on-the-record testimony, counsel (and perhaps nonlawyer experts, such as accountants, *see SEC v. Whitman*, [1984–1985 Transfer Binder] Fed. Sec. L. Rep. (CCH) ¶ 92,061 (D.D.C. 1985)) is permitted to accompany a witness, but only, according to the Commission's Rules of Practice, to advise the witness and to question him briefly after the staff's examination is finished.

Later materials in this chapter explore the various criminal sanctions that are available for willful violations of the securities laws. It is not unusual for the SEC investigation to occur simultaneously with a criminal grand jury investigation being conducted by the Department of Justice. The SEC's investigatory efforts are not restricted by the simultaneous ongoing criminal investigation, absent a showing of actual prejudice. *See SEC v. Dresser Industries, Inc.*, 628 F.2d 1368 (D.C. Cir.) (en banc), *cert. denied*, 449 U.S. 993 (1980).

b. *Recommendations to the Commission*

Once the staff has completed its investigation, it must return to the Commission for permission to institute any enforcement action. The meeting at which this decision is made is nonpublic, with no right to advance notice or appearance by any named subject. However, as a matter of discretion, the staff generally informs the subjects of the recommendations to the Commission and grants them an opportunity to submit a written statement, referred to as a *Wells submission* (so named because the Commission formally instituted the practice in its Securities Act Release No. 5310 in response to the Advisory Committee on Enforcement Policies, called the Wells Committee, after its chairman). The preparation of a Wells submission is an important, but delicate, undertaking. On the one hand, the opportunity to make a case against the institution of an enforcement proceeding may be valuable, especially for one whose participation is peripheral to the investigation's principal focus. On the other hand, some caution is in order in preparing the Wells submission. The attorney must prepare the submission without knowing the precise nature of the staff's case and without access to all the evidence available to the staff. He may in the course of the submission therefore inadvertently supply the staff with information it had not previously uncovered, and any evidentiary privilege will probably be deemed to have been waived with respect to the information provided to the SEC. *See, e.g., Steinhardt Partners, L.P. v. Steinhardt Partners, L.P.,* 9 F.3d 230 (2d Cir. 1993). But to hold back information may also erode the overall effectiveness of the submission. *See generally* McLucas, Taylor & Mathews, A Practitioner's Guide to the SEC Investigative and Enforcement Process, 70 Temple L. Rev. 53 (1997).

Does the prevailing administrative practice create a structural bias toward institution of an enforcement action once an investigation is under way? Are the Commission's rules fair? For a criticism and recommendations for reform, *see* McLucas, Hamill, Shea, & Dubow, An Overview of Various Procedural Considerations Associated with the Securities and Exchange Commission's Investigative Process, 45 Bus. Law. 625 (1990). At the same time, the SEC is not without limits in using its enforcement powers to establish regulatory policy. Of significance in this regard is a developing line of cases where SEC enforcement actions have been dismissed on the ground the defendant lacked adequate notice that the SEC regarded as a violation the act engaged in by the defendant. Thus in *Upton v. SEC*, 75 F.3d 92 (2d Cir. 1996), the court dismissed the SEC's prosecution of a broker for failing to *continuously* segregate and compute the amount of funds held on behalf of the broker's customers. The SEC's rule mandated *weekly* segregation and computations so that the broker could reasonably argue that it had complied with the requirement by each seventh day segregating the customer's funds and tallying their sum. *Upton* also relied on evidence that industry practice was contrary to the SEC's interpretation of the rule.

Most SEC enforcement proceedings (over 90 percent) are settled, not litigated. Indeed, most staff enforcement recommendations to the Commission are accompanied by offers of settlement by one or more subjects. The reasons for this high rate of settlement vary. From the subject's perspective, litigation itself (even if ultimately successful on the merits) will be expensive and provoke unwanted publicity. Unsuccessful defense, on the other hand, may result not only in the defendant's being immediately sanctioned, but also in its being collaterally estopped from relitigating questions of violation in a subsequent private action whereas settlement has no such collateral effect. From the staff's perspective, there is the severe problem of limited resources; the trial staff is too small to handle more than a fraction of the cases being investigated. Thus, it is often possible to arrive at a settlement whereby the defendant consents to an injunction or other relief without either admitting or denying the underlying violation, allowing the staff to claim a victory without subjecting the defendant to a more demanding sanction and the adverse publicity that frequently accompanies litigation. Conclusions of law and fact that are negotiated by the parties in reaching a settlement are set forth in settlement releases issued by the SEC; these releases are frequently relied on in later SEC enforcement actions as a type of precedent. Thus, settlements create a body of securities law principles that have not been tested through formal rulemaking or litigation proceedings. It should be noted that a clause standard to SEC settlements requires an undertaking on the part of the defendant not to make any public statement denying any allegation in the SEC's complaint or creating the impression the complaint was without factual basis.

There is a wide range of options available to the Commission when it believes some form of action is necessary. The least severe is for the staff to issue a cautionary letter advising the subjects of the investigation that their practices or conduct raises serious questions under the securities laws or constitutes a minor offense. The cautionary letter is not publicly available and is infrequently used.

The Commission sometimes believes it is desirable to give wider publicity to what its investigation has unearthed, even though no further action is to be taken against the investigation's subjects, by publishing a Report of Investigation, which is authorized by Section 21(a) of the Exchange Act. Because the report issued under Section 21(a) generally has some unfavorable observations about the investigated company or individual, emerging from a Commission investigation with a Section 21(a) report is less than a clear victory for the investigation's target.

The SEC's Power to Discipline Professionals

A potent and highly controversial enforcement weapon appears in Rule 102(e)[6] of the Commission's Rules of Practice, which provides that the Commission "may deny, temporarily or permanently, the privilege of appearing or practicing before it in any way to any person who is found by the Commission" after notice and hearing:

(i) not to possess the requisite qualifications to represent others, or

(ii) to be lacking in character or integrity or to have engaged in unethical or improper professional conduct, or

(iii) to have willfully violated, or willfully aided and abetted the violation of any provision of the Federal securities laws ... or the rules and regulations thereunder.

Subparagraph (f) of the Rule provides a nonexclusive definition of *practice*, so that it includes not only transacting business with the

6. In 1995, the SEC Rules of Practice were substantially revised and renumbered. The 1995 amendments to the Rules of Practice carried forward without change former Rule 2(e), renumbering it as 102(e).

Commission but also, more significantly, preparing "any statement, opinion, or other paper by any attorney, accountant, engineer, or other professional or expert" that is included in any document filed with the Commission. As such, not only is this disciplinary proceeding directed at those whose behavior has corrupted the Commission's administrative proceedings—for example, by giving false testimony or concealing evidence—but also, and more importantly, Rule 102(e) reaches the activities of professionals who in the course of rendering a professional service well beyond the Commission's hearing rooms have acted in a dishonest, incompetent, unethical, or unprofessional manner. As interpreted by the Commission, there is little that a securities lawyer does that does not qualify as practice before the Commission.

The Commission is further empowered under Rule 102(e)(3) to *temporarily* suspend without a hearing any person from practicing before the Commission if the person has been permanently enjoined in a Commission action from violating the securities laws or has been found by a court in a Commission action or in a Commission administrative proceeding to have violated or aided and abetted the violation of the securities laws. The suspension under this provision becomes permanent if the person so suspended does not within 30 days petition the Commission for a hearing to consider lifting the suspension. In such a proceeding, the petitioner has the burden of proof.

The sanction provided in Rule 102(e) is a temporary or permanent bar of the respondent from "practicing" before the Commission; again, the scope of the expression "practice" is such that a bar can and has operated to prevent individuals and entire firms from engaging in any work related to a document to be filed with the Commission. For example, the Commission has temporarily barred national accounting firms from assuming Securities Act responsibilities for any new clients even though the audit transgressions it found related only to a small percentage of the total audits undertaken by the firm. *See, e.g.,* Peat, Marwick, Mitchell & Co., Accounting Series Release No. 173 (1975). In imposing the disciplinary sanction under Rule 102(e), the Commission is not required to prove a reasonable likelihood of any further violations as is required in judicial injunctive actions. The length of the bar is guided roughly by how egregious the professional's offense was, so that willful participation in the client's fraudulent scheme has resulted in a lifetime ban from practicing before the Commission, *see, e.g.,* In re James McGovern, Exchange Act Release No. 24,379 (Feb. 22, 1988), whereas less culpable involvement has resulted in bars of five years or less, *see, e.g.,* In re Edward M. Grushko, Exchange Act Release No. 27,253 (Sept. 18, 1989).

Settlement orders under Rule 102(e) as a matter of course are far more encompassing than barring the professional from practicing before the Commission. For example, in In re Edward M. Grushko, Exchange Act Release No. 33,625, the attorney agreed to take 30 hours of continuing legal education courses during each of the five years of his suspension. A common practice among large national accounting firms today is to subject their audit practices and procedures to extensive peer review. The impetus for peer reviews was their inclusion in settlements to Commission Rule 102(e) proceedings against two national accounting firms. *See* In re Laventhol, Krekstein, Horwath & Horwath, Exchange Act Release No. 10,172 (May 23, 1973); In re Touche Ross & Co., Securities Act Release No. 5459 (Feb. 25, 1974).

To what extent does the above amendment address *Checkosky's* condemnation that Rule 102(e)(1)(ii) "yields no clear and coherent standard for violations . . ."?

The disciplinary authority the Commission enjoys under Rule 102(e) is now expressly authorized in Section 4(c) of the Exchange Act. This provision was added by Section 202 of the Sarbanes-Oxley Act. Why does the Commission need the authority to discipline professionals who practice before it? What does this authority add to the other enforcement powers the Commission can wield against professionals?

Sarbanes-Oxley, in addition to legitimizing the power the SEC had long exercised under Rule 102(e), poses some important questions. A further question regards how active the Commission will be in disciplining attorneys under Rule 102(e). The SEC, of course, has other enforcement mechanisms available to it that in appropriate cases will cause it to proceed against an attorney who has violated or contributed to another's violation of the securities laws. *See* In re Jeffrey L. Feldman, 55 S.E.C. Dock. 9 (1993) (cease-and-desist issued against a lawyer whose reckless advice that certain financial instruments were not securities was the "cause" for the sale of unregistered securities). However, before Sarbanes-Oxley, the Commission followed a practice of not instituting a Rule 102(e) proceeding against an attorney unless there has been a prior judicial determination that the lawyer had violated the law in connection with the purchase or sale of securities or bar organization disciplinary determination. Greene, Lawyer Disciplinary Proceedings Before the Securities and Exchange Commission, 14 Sec. Reg. & L. Rep. (BNA) 168 (1982). Why would the Commission so confine its authority to discipline an attorney? After the enactment of Sarbanes-Oxley, the earlier cautious prosecutorial discretion exercised by the Commission with respect to attorneys may well disappear. This possibility is suggested by Section 307 of Sarbanes-Oxley, which directs the SEC to adopt professional standards of conduct. Regardless of Section 307 and the resulting rules of conduct, are there practical reasons for the Commission to be more reluctant to discipline attorneys than accountants under Rule 102(e)? A further consideration is how the SEC's rules of professional conduct will interact with its disciplinary authority under Rule 102(e).

IN THE MATTER OF KEATING, MUETHING & KLEKAMP

Exchange Act Rel. No. 15982 (July 2, 1979)

The Commission deems it appropriate in the public Interest to institute administrative proceedings regarding Keating, Muething &

Klekamp ("KMK"), pursuant to Rule 2(e) of the Commission's Rules of Practice.

Simultaneously with the institution of these proceedings, KMK has submitted an Offer of Settlement, raised in these proceedings. In its Offer of Settlement, which the Commission has determined to accept and which is described in detail below, KMK consents, without admitting or denying the facts, findings or conclusions set forth herein, to the institution of this proceeding and the Issuance of the Order hereinafter set forth.

I

FACTS

A. Background

KMK is a Cincinnati, Ohio law firm currently consisting of eleven partners, eight associates, and one attorney serving as of counsel. The firm is engaged in the general practice of law, including corporate and securities, real estate, labor, leasing, banking and litigation matters. The firm was founded in the late 1950's. From the early 1960's through approximately 1976, KMK served as primary counsel to American Financial Corporation ("AFC")and its subsidiaries, and represented them, including participating significantly, in the preparation and review of such companies' filings with the Commission, including registration statements for the public offering of securities, proxy statements, and annual and periodic reports.

KMK's legal services for AFC and its subsidiaries involved nearly all aspects of AFC's and its subsidiaries' businesses. In this regard, KMK prepared legal documents, rendered legal advice, issued opinion letters, and otherwise rendered a full range of legal services to AFC and its subsidiaries. KMK presently renders substantial legal services to AFC and its subsidiaries, and continues to represent such companies in the preparation and review of their filings with the Commission.

During the relevant time period herein, several partners and associates of KMK participated in certain of the financial transactions with AFC and its subsidiaries which are the subject of the Commission's civil injunctive action against AFC, et al. and this proceeding. In addition, one partner of KMK served on the Board of Directors of the Provident Bank ("Provident"), AFC's 99.9% owned and unconsolidated subsidiary. Another present partner, Donald P. Klekamp ("Klekamp"), from 1972 through December 1974, served on the Board of Directors of American Financial Leasing & Services Co. ("AFLS"), an AFC consolidated subsidiary which filed periodic reports with the Commission. Both Provident and AFLS participated in several of the transactions which are described in this Order, and the partners of KMK who served on the Boards of these Companies served at the time that certain of these transactions occurred.

As a result of a Commission investigation, on July 2, 1979, the Commission filed a civil injunctive action against AFC, Carl H. Lindner ("Lindner"), President, Chairman of the Board and controlling shareholder of AFC, Charles H. Keating, Jr. ("Keating"), former Executive Vice President and Director of AFC, and Klekamp.

B.   Conduct of Respondent

The Commission's concern with the conduct of KMK arises from transactions involving AFC and its subsidiaries. As set forth below, during the relevant periods of time, AFC and AFLS made untrue statements of material facts, and omitted to state material facts, in filings with the Commission relating to certain significant transactions. Because of KMK's involvement with AFC and its subsidiaries, including the participation of various partners in certain of the subject transactions, service by partners of KMK on the Board of Directors of two significant subsidiaries which participated in many of the transactions, and the firm's preparation or review of the subject filings with the Commission, KMK knew or should have known of the material misstatements and omissions in AFC's and AFLS' filings with the Commission.

1.   The Klekamp Transactions

During 1972, Lindner, President, Chairman of the Board and controlling shareholder of AFC, and Keating, Executive Vice President and a Director of AFC, purchased AFC common stock in the open market for Klekamp, a partner of KMK and a director of AFLS from 1972 through December 1974, with funds advanced by AFLS. During this period, Klekamp was engaged primarily in the representation of AFLS and other AFC subsidiaries in leasing, financing and real estate matters. At the time, AFLS was an AFC consolidated subsidiary, and filed reports with the Commission. AFLS' advances for the stock purchases exceeded $1.7 million, and a total of 96,800 shares of AFC common stock was purchased. Subsequent sales of 35,700 shares were made during 1972 and March 1973, leaving a balance of 61,100 shares by the close of the first quarter of 1973. AFLS reported the advances it made to purchase the stock as loans to Klekamp in filings with the Commission.

Based on his initial discussions during the early part of 1972 with Lindner and Keating, Klekamp understood that AFC or an AFC subsidiary would loan him approximately $600,000 to purchase approximately 40,000 shares of AFC common stock, based on market value of the stock at the time. The amount actually advanced in this regard was in excess of $1.7 million, with subsequent reductions of approximately $684,000 through sales of a portion of the stock purchased. While Klekamp learned of these transactions shortly after their occurrence, he apparently did not raise any questions concerning the excess until May 1974. On May 29, 1974, Klekamp met with Lindner and Keating to discuss his personal financial difficulties, and his obligation to AFLS for the advances. Lindner and Keating informed Klekamp that he would not be held responsible for the debt to AFLS. However, AFLS continued to report its advances to Klekamp as a loan in its Annual Report on Form 10–K filed with the Commission for the year ended December 31, 1974. Klekamp did not serve as a director after December 31, 1974.

In December 1975, Klekamp met with certain AFC accounting personnel and a partner of KMK. Klekamp related to these persons the substance of this discussion with Lindner and Keating in 1972 which led to the subsequent stock purchases, and the fact that in excess of $600,000 had been advanced, contrary to this initial understanding of what would occur. He also related the substance of his May 29, 1974 meeting with Lindner and Keating, and the understanding that he would no longer be obligated to AFLS for the advances, which grew out of that meeting. Klekamp was instructed at this December 1975 meeting to transfer the remaining 61,100 shares of AFC common stock to AFC, which he did. In exchange, AFC cancelled the entire indebtedness. The outstanding balance of the indebtedness was approximately $1,326,000 at the time, while the market value of the 61,100 shares was approximately $442,000. The market value of the 61,100 shares on May 29, 1974, at the time that Lindner and Keating relieved Klekamp of the obligation, was approximately $680,000.

The disclosures made by AFLS in its Annual Reports on Form 10–K filed with the Commission for each of the years 1972 and 1973 consisted of one line in a financial schedule to the Annual Reports, which schedule was examined and reported on by AFLS' outside auditors, stating that AFLS had made unsecured loans to Klekamp, the amount thereof, and that the loans were evidenced by a promissory note. Also, the disclosures in AFLS' proxy statements for those years, as set forth below, were incorporated by reference into the 1972 and 1973 Annual Reports. The disclosure by AFLS in its Annual Report on Form 10–K for its 1974 fiscal year consisted of one line in a financial schedule to the Annual Report, which schedule was examined and reported on by AFLS's outside auditors, which contained the same information as the 1972 and 1973 Annual Reports, and under Item 15 of the Annual Report substantially the same information that was disclosed in the 1972 and 1973 proxies of AFLS. AFLS' Proxy Statements filed with the Commission for each of the years ended December 31, 1972 and 1973 disclosed that unsecured loans (stating the amount) had been made to Klekamp, a director of AFLS. Finally, in a Registration Statement on Form S–1 filed by AFLS with the Commission in August 1972, there was no disclosure of the loans to Klekamp or the transactions which gave rise to the loans.

In their Annual Reports on Form 10–K filed with the Commission for the year ended December 31, 1975, both AFC and AFLS disclosed in one line in a financial schedule to the filings, that of the $1,326,000 in outstanding loans by AFLS to Klekamp, $1,079,000 had been collected and $247,000 had been written off during 1975. This was reported despite the fact that the market value of the AFC common stock transferred by Klekamp to AFC in December 1975 in exchange for cancellation of the entire indebtedness was only approximately $442,000, and $680,000 as of May 29, 1974. The $1,079,000 reported as collected represented the cost of the 61,000 shares transferred to AFC. Except through the loans by AFLS, Klekamp did not advance any of his own funds for the purchases of the AFC stock, nor did he receive any of the proceeds from the sales. Finally, Klekamp never paid interest to AFLS on its loans to him.

The above described disclosures by AFC and AFLS were materially inaccurate in that they did not fully describe the facts and circumstances concerning the loans by AFLS and subsequent stock purchases for Klekamp; stated in the financial schedules referred to above that the loans were evidenced by a promissory note when in fact a note was never actually executed; and stated that $1,079,000 had been collected when the market value of the 61,100 shares transferred to AFC was approximately $442,000 at the time of the transfer, and approximately $680,000 on May 29, 1974, the time when Lindner and Keating agreed not to hold Klekamp responsible for his obligation to AFLS.

Klekamp, who was a partner of KMK and a director of AFLS, was aware of all of the facts and circumstances concerning AFLS' advances and the AFC common stock purchases which were made with the advances. In addition, the KMK partner who was principally responsible for preparing AFC's and AFLS' filings with the Commission knew that AFLS had advanced substantial funds to Klekamp. Klekamp did not provide information with respect to these matters to members of the firm preparing AFC's and AFLS' filings with the Commission. Moreover, the attorneys at the firm who participated in the preparation of AFC's AFLS' filings with the Commission relied on the representations by AFC's management concerning the loans to Klekamp, and did not take any steps on their own to verify such information.

The KMK partner who met with Klekamp in December 1975 was made aware of all the relevant facts and circumstances concerning the Klekamp transactions during the meeting. However, he failed to advise the attorneys at the firm who prepared the filings of the knowledge he had obtained concerning the transaction.

2. UDFIC's Sale of the Athens National Bank

In the latter part of 1973, United Dairy Farmers Investment Company ("UDFIC"), an investment company wholly owned and controlled by Lindner and one of his brothers, commenced negotiations with an unrelated party to sell the Athens National Bank ("ANB") of Athens, Ohio, then owned and controlled by UDFIC. In approximately May 1974, UDFIC entered into an agreement with the unrelated party to sell ANB, and the transaction closed in September 1974.

During the course of the negotiations which led to the May 1974 agreement, representatives of the purchaser examined ANB's loan portfolio and learned that ANB had a large number of "out of area" loans totalling approximately $4.8 million to several persons and entities located in the Cincinnati area. The majority of these loans consisted of loans to officers and directors of AFC and its subsidiaries, relatives of such persons, and friends of Lindner and Keating. Further, the borrowers in this group included various partners and associates of KMK, and an investment partnership consisting of KMK partners and associates.

At the time of the purchaser's examination of ANB's loan portfolio, concern was expressed regarding the absence of documentation concerning the large number of "out of area" loans, and the lack of any repayment schedules on such loans. As a condition precedent to the closing of the sale, the purchaser required that the "out of area" loans be eliminated from ANB's loan portfolio. Consequently, ANB informed the various borrowers, including certain KMK partners and associates, that their loans would have to be transferred out of ANB.

The sale of ANB by UDFIC was closed in September 1974, at a sale price of $10 million. From approximately April 1974 through September 1974, Keating and the UDFIC controller caused Provident and AFLS to purchase approximately $3 million of the "out of area" loans in the amount of unpaid principal plus accrued interest. In this regard, Provident purchased approximately $1.8 million of such loans, and AFLS purchased approximately $1.2 million. During the course of the loan transfers, the borrowers, including various partners and associates of KMK, were informed that their loans were being moved to Provident and AFLS. As of April 30, 1979, all of these loans were either paid in full or were current, and no loss had been sustained on such loans.

AFC and AFLS, both of which made periodic filings with the Commission at the time did not make any disclosure of the facts and circumstances concerning UDFIC's sale of ANB and the loan purchases by Provident and AFLS in their Annual Reports on Form 10–K and Proxy Statements filed with the Commission for the year ended December 31, 1974, or in subsequent years. These omissions occurred despite the fact that the two AFC subsidiaries had purchased the loans from a bank owned and controlled by the President and chairman of the Board of AFC to enable him to sell his bank.

Several partners and associates of KMK were aware of the loan takeovers. An express provision in the sale agreement provided for removal of the loans as a condition precedent to the sale of the bank. The agreement specifically listed each of the loans which were eventually taken over by Provident and AFLS, and various attorneys at KMK participated in the preparation and review of the legal documents relating to the sale of ANB, including the sale agreement. In addition to the foregoing, KMK served as counsel for UDFIC and ANB in the transaction which resulted in the sale of ANB. Further, one of the partners of KMK served on the Board of Directors of Provident and another partner of KMK served on the Board of Directors of AFLS. Several partners and associates of KMK and the KMK investment partnership had loans at ANB which were purchased by Provident and AFLS pursuant to the loan takeovers.

Despite the involvement by various members of KMK in the bank sale transaction and loan takeovers as described above, KMK failed to accumulate the information concerning these transactions which was known by the members of the firm, and convey it to the member of the firm who was preparing AFC's and AFLS' filings with the Commission. Those members of the firm preparing the filings with the Commission relied on representations by AFC's and AFLS' management concerning related party transactions, and did little, if any, independent verification of the facts on their own. The ANB transaction was not disclosed as a related party transaction in AFC's or AFLS' filings with the Commission.

3. *The Provident Bank Loans*

Since at least 1972, Provident made and periodically renewed numerous substantial loans which, in certain respects, were made on preferential terms to a group of persons consisting of: (1) officers and directors of AFC and their relatives; (2) officers and directors of AFC's subsidiaries; and (3) various other persons, including attorneys at KMK and other friends of Lindner and Keating (hereinafter collectively referred to as the "Lindner associates and friends"). From 1972 through 1975, the amount of Provident's loans to this group of persons ranged from $5 million to $10 million, and by 1976 reached a peak of approximately $14 million. A large number of these loans were unsecured with no plan of repayment, and interest payments were frequently made through the extension by Provident of additional loans. The proceeds of the majority of these loans were used by the borrowers to purchase AFC securities in the open market and elsewhere.

* * *

Various partners of KMK had knowledge of some of the loans to the Lindner associates and friends, including their own loans, and knew of the terms of such loans which, in certain respects, were preferential. Such information was not conveyed to members of the firm who prepared AFC's filings with the Commission. The persons at the firm preparing the filings relied on representations by AFC's and Provident's management that such loans were made in the ordinary course of business and on comparable terms as with unrelated parties, and did not take sufficient independent steps to determine whether they could rely on such representations.

4. *The Sci–Tek Leases*

In 1971 and thereafter, AFLS entered into various sale and leasebook arrangements with Sci–Tek, Inc. ("Sci–Tek"), a Delaware corporation engaged principally in the electronic data processing business, involving certain computers which cost approximately $5.4 million, and additionally, Sci–Tek borrowed approximately $750,000 from AFLS. AFLS, an AFC consolidated subsidiary sold participations of varying proportions in the leases to Provident and three UDFIC, the Lindner owned partnership, owned banks: ANB of Athens, Ohio; the New Richmond National Bank ("NRNB") of New Richmond, Ohio; and The Security Bank ("Security") of Athens, Ohio.

* * *

In its Annual Report on Form 10–K filed with the Commission for the year ended December 31, 1975, AFLS disclosed that it had agreed to make "advances" to NRNB on account of loans which it had sold to NRNB and which had become delinquent. Such disclosure was materially misleading as it omitted to state that the payments were motivated by the concern for the collateral held by Provident on loans to the purchasers of NRNB.

Various partners and associates of KMK were involved in the preparation and review of the lease documents covering the computers involved in the Sci–Tek transaction, and were involved in the renegotiation of the leases in 1973, and knew of the renegotiation fee. Further, certain attorneys at KMK were in possession of information concerning the renegotiation fee and the indemnification agreements entered into by AFLS and AFC. In addition, one partner of KMK served on the Board of Directors of Provident, and another served on AFLS' Board. Thus, several attorneys at KMK, on a collective basis, had knowledge of all the material facts relating to the Sci–Tek transaction. Despite this knowledge, this related party transaction was omitted from AFC's and AFLS' filings with the Commission.

5.   *Provident's Loans to Purchase the NRNB*

In April 1974, UDFIC, Lindner's investment partnership, entered into an agreement to sell the NRNB, which it owned and controlled, to a group of individual investors unrelated to AFC. The agreement provided that the sales price of $1,650,000 would be payable in three installments, the last of which came due in October 1974. The Purchasers were unable to make the second installment of $675,000 which came due in July 1974, and the sales agreement was amended to provide for payment of the entire balance of the purchase price, plus accrued interest, in September 1974.

* * *

Various attorneys at KMK handled all of the legal matters for Provident, UDFIC and NRNB in connection with the sale of NRNB. This included participation by various attorneys at KMK in the preparation and review of the amended sale agreement which provided for full payment of the purchase price of the bank in September 1974. In connection with the amended agreement, Provident loaned the purchasers the $650,000 referred to above. One of the KMK partners who advised UDFIC and NRNB on the bank sale transaction served on the Board of Directors of Provident. Despite the knowledge within KMK of all the material facts concerning the transaction, including Provident's participation which enabled Lindner, President and Chairman of the Board of AFC, to sell a bank which he owned, the related party transaction was not disclosed in AFC's filings with the Commission.

6.   *Keating Special Compensation*

For his services in assisting with the origination, negotiation and planning in connection with AFC's sale of the Cincinnati Enquirer, formerly an AFC subsidiary, to Combined Communications Corporation in 1975 for approximately $55 million in cash and securities, Keating received special compensation of $600,000. At his request, at the time of payment, the compensation was not paid directly to Keating by AFC but was paid by it through KMK to Keating pursuant to KMK billing and was initially treated by AFC as a legal expense.

The partner of KMK who represented AFC in the preparation and review of filings with the Commission discovered the accounting treatment given Keating's special compensation when such partner was engaged in preparing the proxy statements for the 1976 AFC annual meeting and disclosed such compensation in the proxy materials as required by the proxy regulations.

III

FINDINGS

Based on the foregoing, the Commission finds that during the periods discussed above, KMK did not properly carry out its professional responsibilities with respect to the above described filings of AFC and its subsidiaries with the Commission.

IV

CONCLUSIONS

From the early 1960s through approximately 1976, KMK and its attorneys provided a broad range of legal services to AFC, providing advice and counsel on virtually all aspects of AFC's and its subsidiaries' businesses. As a result, many members of the firm became familiar with the business, operations, and transactions of such companies. In fact, during the relevant time periods, almost every member of KMK was involved in some aspect of AFC's representation. Indeed, KMK derived a large part of its fees, at times ranging from 50 to 80 percent of its billings, from representation of AFC and its subsidiaries.

Almost every member of the firm, including those with responsibility for the filings made with the Commission and the senior partner in charge of the representation of AFC, was aware of one or more of the material transactions by the companies as to which disclosure is deemed by the Commission to have been inadequate or misleading—including the transactions between AFC and certain of its officers and directors and the transactions in which members of KMK were participants. Under these circumstances it is reasonable to conclude that the firm collectively had knowledge of the transactions by virtue of (i) the information which came to the attention of the various members of KMK who worked on legal matters for AFC and its subsidiaries; (ii) the fact that individual partners of KMK served on the Board of Directors of two AFC subsidiaries; and (iii) the participation by various partners of the firm in certain financial transactions with such companies including in certain instances those who participated in drafting the filings described above. This is not a case where a law firm is being held accountable for knowledge or conduct of a few of its members.

There was a division of authority among the partners within the firm concerning, client matters which significantly impaired communications within the firm. One partner was primarily responsible at the firm for the preparation and review of AFC's filings with the Commission; however, other members of the firm had relatively little, if any, contact with this aspect of the firm's representation of AFC, and the information about AFC they possessed was not always provided to the partner in the firm who was primarily responsible for AFC's filings. This was due in part to the lack of comprehensive internal procedures within the firm to gather and evaluate such information in connection with the preparation of AFC's filings with the Commission. Not only did the partners who had the material information fail to communicate that information, the partner responsible for the filings did not take sufficient steps to ascertain information from them or verify information provided by management of AFC concerning the related party transactions, and in other instances the partners failed to appreciate the significance of facts concerning those transactions.

A law firm has a duty to make sure that disclosure documents filed with the Commission include all material facts about a client of which it has knowledge as a result of its legal representation of that client. The Commission does not believe it should dictate to law firms how they should structure their internal procedures to assure that the knowledge possessed by their members and associates is made available to those lawyers in the firm responsible for drafting disclosure documents. But it is clear that substantial additional procedures were required here, for the Commission concludes that KMK failed to carry out its professional responsibilities with regard to the above described filings of AFC and its subsidiaries, when, despite its extensive representation of AFC and the knowledge of the members of KMK relating to material transactions, it did not have a system which assured that the knowledge of the members of the firm was communicated to the persons responsible for preparing disclosure documents so that adequate disclosure of material information—which was within the firm's knowledge—was made.

IV

OFFER OF SETTLEMENT

Respondent has submitted an Offer of Settlement and Undertakings ("Offer") with respect to these proceedings solely for the purpose of settlement only, without admitting or denying the allegations, findings, or conclusions in this Order, and on the understanding that nothing herein constitutes an adjudication with respect to any matter referred to herein. In its Offer of Settlement, Respondent voluntarily undertakes to:

A. Within sixty days after entry of this Order, adopt, maintain, and implement additional internal and supervisory procedures which are reasonably designed to ensure that respondent has adequate procedures with respect to representation in matters involving the federal securities laws handled by respondents and to avoid recurrence of the matters set forth in this Order; and

B. During the sixty day period described in paragraph A, not to accept any legal engagements from new clients which contemplate the filing of registration statements, proxy materials, or annual or other periodic reports, or other filings, with the Commission.

In its Offer, Respondent also admits the jurisdiction of the Commission with respect to it and the matters set forth in this Order and consents to the entry of this Order, ordering Respondent to comply with its undertakings.

VI

ORDER

In view of the foregoing, the Commission deems it appropriate in the public interest that administrative proceedings pursuant to Rule 2(e) of its Rules of Practice be instituted and that Respondent's Offer of Settlement be accepted.

* * *

COMMISSIONER KARMEL, dissenting:

This is another Rule 2(e) disciplinary proceeding which arises from the Commission's efforts to protect investors by articulating and enforcing professional responsibility standards for attorneys. The Commission's authority to promulgate Rule 2(e) is tenuous at best. Since the Commission's program is in aid of its prosecutorial, rather than its rule making or adjudicatory functions, I view it as an invalid exercise of power, particularly where, as here, it is directed at a law firm partnership for conduct which was the basis of an injunction brought by the Commission against an individual partner of the firm and others.

The Commission's regulatory programs are implemented to a significant extent by prosecutorial actions, which may take the form of an injunctive action in the federal district courts, an administrative proceeding before an administrative law judge, or a criminal reference. Even the Commission's adjudicatory function is frequently combined with its prosecutorial function where, as in the instant case, there is a negotiated settlement of an administrative proceeding. As a general policy matter, I believe that it is repugnant to our adversary system of legal representation to permit a prosecutorial agency to discipline attorneys who act as counsel to regulated persons. The frequently made distinction between the lawyer as an adversary versus the lawyer as an advisor cannot and should not be made by an agency with significant prosecutorial responsibilities.

* * *

Although the instant proceeding involves the filing of false or misleading reports with the Commission, it is grounded on findings and conclusions that the internal procedures of a law firm did not meet professional responsibility standards. I interpret this as an effort to regulate the practice of securities laws which I cannot countenance. Furthermore, the Opinion indicates that negligent conduct is a sufficient predicate for a Rule 2(e) proceeding, a standard which I believe is inappropriate, and makes certain statements about an attorney's duty to learn and communicate facts with which I do not agree.

* * *

A primary rationale for so using Rule 2(e) has been that "the task of enforcing the securities laws rests in overwhelming measure on the bar's shoulders" and that given "its small staff, limited resources, and onerous tasks, the Commission is peculiarly dependent on the probity and diligence of the professionals who practice before it." However, Congress did not authorize the Commission to conscript attorneys to enforce their clients' responsibilities under the federal securities laws. Furthermore, institutional limitations alone cannot justify the creation of a new remedy not contemplated by the Congress.

I am firmly convinced that such conscription, or the promulgation and enforcement of regulatory standards of conduct for securities lawyers by the Commission, is very bad policy. It undermines the willingness and ability of the bar to exercise professional responsibility and sows the seeds for government abuse of power.

* * *

Although this matter may involve misconduct by public corporations and by attorneys as active participants in securities law violations, the conduct of their law firm should not be sanctioned as a failure to meet standards of professional responsibility. Ethical and professional standards are peculiarly personal. A law firm should not be held liable in a disciplinary proceeding (as it could be in a damage action) for the conduct of its partners. And in this proceeding, one of the primary wrongdoers was not even a member of the respondent law firm at the time of the events in issue. Whether the Commission has the legal authority to sanction a law firm for the misconduct of its members is even more problematical than its authority to discipline individual attorneys, and I do not believe the facts set forth in this Opinion are a sufficient predicate for such a sanction.

As the Opinion herein indicates, Charles H. Keating, Jr. and Donald P. Klekamp have been permanently enjoined as a result of the same conduct on which this Rule 2(e) proceeding is based. If the terms and conditions of the injunction were insufficient to protect the Commission or the public, further relief should have been requested from the federal court. If additional partners in Keating, Muething & Klekamp could have been held liable for securities law violations, they should have been included in the injunctive action as defendants. Alternatively, a reference could have been made for disbarment proceedings by state authorities. I object to the use of Rule 2(e) to institute a proceeding against the law firm of Keating, Muething & Klekamp for the firm's failure to uncover and report the transactions of its clients and partners.

* * *

I also object to the sanctions imposed herein. These sanctions presume a regulatory authority and expertise concerning the proper way to practice law and manage a law firm which this Commission does not possess. Although the Opinion denies that it is dictating to a law firm how it should operate, the imposition of a sanction for inadequate internal procedures makes that denial hollow. That these sanctions are imposed by consent is irrelevant. They open a Pandora's box of misguided standard-setting regulation.

SECURITIES AND EXCHANGE COMMISSION v. NATIONAL STUDENT MARKETING CORP. ET AL.

457 F.Supp. 682 (D.D.C. 1978)

BARRINGTON D. PARKER, DISTRICT JUDGE:

This opinion covers the final act in a civil proceeding brought by the Securities and Exchange Commission (Commission or SEC) seeking injunctive sanctions against numerous defendants as a result of their participation in alleged securities laws violations relating to the National Student Marketing Corporation (NSMC) securities fraud scheme. The original defendants included the corporation and certain of its officers and directors; the accounting firm of Peat, Marwick, Mitchell & Co. (Peat Marwick) and two of its partners; several officers and directors of Interstate National Corporation (Interstate); the law firm of White & Case and one of its partners; and the law firm of Lord, Bissell & Brook (LBB) and two of its partners. The majority of these defendants are not now before the Court. As discovery progressed during the pre-trial stages of this litigation, NSMC and other principal defendants consented to the entry of final judgments of permanent injunction or otherwise reached a resolution of the charges against them. The only defendants remaining are Lord, Bissell & Brook; its two partners, Max E. Meyer and Louis F. Schauer; and Cameron Brown, a former president and director of Interstate, and presently a director of and consultant to NSMC.

The focal point of the Commission's charges against these defendants is the corporate merger of Interstate with NSMC on October 31, 1969. The principal question presented is whether the defendants violated or aided and abetted the violation of the anti-fraud provisions of the federal securities laws in two instances: (1) consummation of the NSMC merger; and (2) the immediately following sale of newly acquired NSMC stock by former Interstate principals, including certain of the defendants. These transactions are alleged to have occurred despite the prior receipt by the defendants of information which revealed that NSMC's interim financial statements, used in securing shareholder approval of the merger and available to the investing public generally, were grossly inaccurate and failed to show the true condition of the corporation. The information was included in a comfort letter prepared by NSMC's accounts. The Commission contends that these violations demonstrate a reasonable likelihood of future misconduct by the defendants, thereby justifying the requested permanent injunctive relief.

The matter was tried without a jury. After reviewing the extensive record in this case, the Court concludes, for the reasons stated below, that while each of the defendants violated the securities laws in specific instances, the Commission has not fulfilled its obligation of demonstrating a reasonable likelihood that they will do so in the future. Accordingly, the Commission's request for injunctive relief must be denied.

* * *

I. Background

A. *The Companies*

National Student Marketing Corporation was incorporated in the District of Columbia in 1966. The company enjoyed early prosperity; it grew rapidly and experienced a steady increase in assets, sales and earnings. Its common stock, which was registered with the SEC and traded on the over-the-counter market, rose from an initial public offering of $6 per share in the spring of 1968 to a high of $144 per share in mid-December 1969. The financial community held the company and its potential in high regard, and in anticipation of continued high market performance, it was seen as a good "buy" prospect. Its management was considered aggressive, imaginative and capable; if there was a question of its integrity and honesty, it did not surface in the public arena until a later period. During this period, White & Case served as its outside legal counsel, with Marion J. Epley, III, as the partner immediately in charge of the firm's representation. Peat Marwick served as its outside accountant.

Interstate National Corporation, a Nevada corporation, was an insurance holding company. Its principal assets were several wholly-owned subsidiary insurance companies. The company's common stock was traded on the over-the-counter market and owned by approximately 1200 shareholders. Cameron Brown was president, chief executive officer, principal shareholder and a director of the company. Other Interstate principals and directors included Robert P. Tate, chairman of the board; William J. Bach, general counsel; Paul E. Allison, secretary; Louis W. Biegler; and Max E. Meyer. Between board meetings, all management authority was delegated to an executive committee composed of Brown, Tate, Bach, Allison and Biegler. Max E. Meyer, a director and shareholder, was a partner in the Chicago law firm of Lord, Bissell & Brook, which had long represented Interstate and served as its outside legal counsel in all matters relating to the merger of the corporation with NSMC. Meyer, a personal friend and legal advisor to Cameron Brown, served as the contact partner for the Interstate account and was otherwise in overall charge of his firm's representation.Another partner of the firm, Louis F.

Schauer, was also involved in the merger transaction due to his experience in corporate and securities law. Peat Marwick served as Interstate's outside accountant during the period in question.

B. The Merger Negotiations

National Student Marketing Corporation developed a reputation for having a unique and successful marketing network for selling its own and other products to college and high school students. Commencing in 1969, it undertook a highly active program to acquire companies specializing in selling goods and services to students. It was in this connection that NSMC first approached representatives of Interstate.

* * *

[After several meetings, the parties reached] an agreement in principle for the merger. Essentially identical press releases were then issued by the companies, announcing the agreed upon stock exchange ratio, the estimated value of the transaction as $37 million based on the current market value of NSMC stock, and the fact that the transaction represented approximately a 100 percent premium for the Interstate shares based on their market value at the time. Representations were also made in the releases as to NSMC's earnings for the first six months of fiscal 1969, which ended February 28, 1969.

* * *

The Merger Agreement set forth fully the terms and conditions of the understanding between the two corporations. Among other things, both corporations represented and warranted that the information "contained in Interstate's and NSMC's Proxy Statements relating to the transactions contemplated by this Agreement will be accurate and correct and will not omit to state a material fact necessary to make such information not misleading," and that the financial statements included among the provisions "are true and correct and have been prepared in accordance with generally accepted accounting principles consistently followed throughout the periods involved." NSMC specifically referred to its 1968 year-end and May 31, 1969, nine-month financial statements and represented that those statements:

> fairly present the results of the operations of NSMC and its subsidiaries for the periods indicated, subject in the case of the nine month statements to year-end audit adjustments.

The Agreement also provided several conditions precedent to the obligations of the two corporations to consummate the merger. One required the receipt by NSMC of an opinion letter from Interstate's counsel LBB to the effect, Inter alia, that Interstate had taken all actions and procedures required of it by law and that all transactions in connection with the merger had been duly and validly taken, to the best knowledge of counsel, in full compliance with applicable law; a similar opinion letter was required to be delivered from NSMC's counsel to Interstate. Another condition was the receipt by each company of a "comfort letter" from the other's independent public accountants. Each letter was required to state: (1) that the accountants had no reason to believe that the unaudited interim financial statements for the company in question were not prepared in accordance with accounting principles and practices consistent with those used in the previous year-end audited financials; (2) that they had no reason to believe that any material adjustments in those financials were required in order fairly to present the results of operations of the company; and (3) that the company had experienced no material adverse change in its financial position or results of operations from the period covered by its interim financial statement up to five business days prior to the effective date of the merger. Although setting forth these specific conditions to consummation of the merger, the final paragraph of the Agreement also provided that:

> Anything herein to the contrary notwithstanding and notwithstanding any stockholder vote of approval of this Agreement and the merger provided herein, this Agreement may be terminated and abandoned by mutual consent of the Boards of Directors of NSMC and Interstate at any time prior to the Effective Date and the Board of Directors of any party may waive any of the conditions to the obligations of such party under this Agreement.

Finally, the Agreement specified that "(t)he transactions contemplated herein shall have been consummated on or before November 28, 1969."

Both NSMC and Interstate utilized proxy statements and notices of special stockholder meetings to secure shareholder approval of the proposed merger. Interstate's materials included a copy of the Merger Agreement and NSMC's Proxy Statement; the latter contained NSMC's financial statements for the fiscal year ended August 31, 1968, and the nine-month interim financial statement for the period ending May 31, 1969. * * *

The boards of both companies recommended approval of the merger and at special shareholder meetings that approval was secured by large majorities.

In mid-October, Peat Marwick began drafting the comfort letter concerning NSMC's unaudited interim financials for the nine-month period ended May 31, 1969. As issued by NSMC, those financials had reflected a profit of approximately $700,000.

Soon after beginning work on the comfort letter, Peat Marwick representatives determined that certain adjustments were required with respect to the interim financials. Specifically, the accountants proposed that a $500,000 adjustment to deferred costs, a $300,000 write-off of unbilled receivables, and an $84,000 adjustment to paid-in capital be made retroactive to May 31 and be reflected in the comfort letter delivered to Interstate. Such adjustments would have caused NSMC to show a loss for the nine-month period ended May 31, 1969, and the company as it existed on May 31 would have broken even for fiscal 1969. Although Peat Marwick discussed the proposed adjustments with representatives of NSMC, neither the accountants nor NSMC informed Interstate of the adjustments prior to the closing. A draft of the comfort letter, with the adjustments, was completed on October 30 and on the next day, the morning of the closing, it was discussed among senior partners of Peat Marwick.

C. The Closing and Receipt of the Comfort Letter

The closing meeting for the merger was scheduled at 2 p.m. on Friday, October 31, at the New York offices of White & Case. Brown, Meyer and Schauer were present in addition to Interstate directors Bach, Allison and Tate. The representatives of NSMC included Randell, Joy, John G. Davies, their attorney Epley and other White & Case associates.

Although Schauer had had an opportunity to review most of the merger documents at White & Case on the previous day, the comfort letter had not been delivered. When he arrived at White & Case on the morning of the merger, the letter was still not available, but he was informed by a representative of the firm that it was expected to arrive at any moment.

The meeting proceeded. When the letter had not arrived by approximately 2:15 p.m., Epley telephoned Peat Marwick's Washington office to inquire about it. Anthony M. Natelli, the partner in charge, thereupon dictated to Epley's secretary a letter which provided in part:

(N)othing has come to our attention which caused us to believe that:

> 1. The National Student Marketing Corporation's unaudited consolidated financial statements as of and for the nine months ended May 31, 1969:
>
>> a. Were not prepared in accordance with accounting principles and practices consistent in all material respects with those followed in the preparation of the audited consolidated financial statements which are covered by our report dated November 14, 1968;
>>
>> b. Would require any material adjustments for a fair and reasonable presentation of the information shown except with respect to consolidated financial statements of National Student Marketing Corporation and consolidated subsidiaries as they existed at May 31, 1969 and for the nine months then ended, our examination in connection with the year ended August 31, 1969 which is still in process, disclosed the following significant adjustments which in our opinion should be reflected retroactive to May 31, 1969:
>>
>>> 1. In adjusting the amortization of deferred costs at May 31, 1969, to eliminate therefrom all costs for programs substantially completed or which commenced 12 months or more prior, an adjustment of $500,000 was required. Upon analysis of the retroactive effect of

this adjustment, it appears that the entire amount could be determined applicable to the period prior to May 31, 1969.

2. In August 1969 management wrote off receivables in amounts of $300,000. It appears that the uncollectibility of these receivables could have been determined at May 31, 1969 and such charge off should have been reflected as of that date.

3. Acquisition costs in the amount of $84,000 for proposed acquisitions which the Company decided not to pursue were transferred from additional paid-in capital to general and administrative expenses. In our opinion, these should have been so transferred as of May 31, 1969.

2. During the period from May 31, 1969 to October 28, 1969 there has been no material adverse change in the consolidated financial position of National Student Marketing Corporation and its consolidated subsidiaries, or any material adverse change in results of operations of National Student Marketing Corporation and its consolidated subsidiaries as compared with the nine month period ended May 31, 1969 after giving retroactive effect at May 31, 1969 of the adjustments disclosed above.

Epley delivered one copy of the typed letter to the conference room where the closing was taking place. Epley then returned to his office.

Schauer was the first to read the unsigned letter. He then handed it to Cameron Brown, advising him to read it. Although there is some dispute as to which of the Interstate representatives actually read the letter, at least Brown and Meyer did so after Schauer. They asked Randell and Joy a number of questions relating to the nature and effect of the adjustments. The NSMC officers gave assurances that the adjustments would have no significant effect on the predicted year-end earnings of NSMC and that a substantial portion of the $500,000 adjustments to deferred costs would be recovered. Moreover, they indicated that NSMC's year-end audit for fiscal 1969 had been completed by Peat Marwick, would be published in a couple of weeks, and would demonstrate that NSMC itself had made each of the adjustments for its fourth quarter. The comfort letter, they explained, simply determined that those adjustments should be reflected in the third quarter ended May 31, 1969, rather than the final quarter of NSMC's fiscal year. Randell and Joy indicated that while NSMC disagreed with what they felt was a tightening up of its accounting practices, everything requested by Peat Marwick to "clean up" its books had been undertaken.

At the conclusion of this discussion, certain of the Interstate representatives, including at least Brown, Schauer and Meyer, conferred privately to consider their alternatives in light of the apparent nonconformity of the comfort letter with the requirements of the Merger Agreement. Although they considered the letter a serious matter and the adjustments as significant and important, they were nonetheless under some pressure to determine a course of action promptly since there was a 4 p.m. filing deadline if the closing were to be consummated as scheduled on October 31.[20] Among the alternatives considered were: (1) delaying or postponing the closing, either to secure more information or to resolicit the shareholders with corrected financials; (2) closing the merger; or (3) calling it off completely.

The consensus of the directors was that there was no need to delay the closing. The comfort letter contained all relevant information and in light of the explanations given by Randell and Joy, they already had sufficient information upon which to make a decision. Any delay for the purpose of resoliciting the shareholders was considered impractical because it would require the use of year-end figures instead of the stale nine-month interim financials. Such a requirement would make it impossible to resolicit shareholder approval before the merger upset date of November 28, 1969, and would cause either the complete abandonment of the merger or its renegotiation on terms possibly far less favorable to Interstate. The directors also recognized that delay or abandonment of the merger would result in a decline in the stock of both companies, thereby harming the shareholders and possibly subjecting the directors to lawsuits based on their failure to close the merger. The Interstate representatives decided to proceed with the closing. They did, however, solicit and receive further assurances from the NSMC representatives that the stated adjustments were the only ones to be made to the company's financial statements and that 1969 earnings would be as predicted. When asked by Brown whether the closing could proceed on the basis of an unsigned comfort letter, Meyer responded that if a White & Case partner assured them that this was in fact the comfort letter and that a signed copy would be forthcoming from Peat Marwick, they could close. Epley gave this assurance. Meyer then announced that Interstate was prepared to proceed, the closing was consummated, and a previously arranged telephone call was made which resulted in the filing of the Articles of Merger at the Office of the Recorder of Deeds of the District of Columbia Large packets of merger documents, including the required counsel opinion letters, were exchanged. The closing was solemnized with a toast of warm champagne.

Unknown to the Interstate group, several telephone conversations relating to the substance of the comfort letter occurred on the afternoon of the closing between Peat Marwick representatives and Epley. The accountants were concerned with the propriety of proceeding with the closing in light of the adjustments to NSMC's nine-month financials. One such conversation occurred after Epley delivered the unsigned letter to the Interstate participants but before the merger had been consummated. At that time Epley was told that an additional paragraph would

20. The pressure to close on October 31 derived from a public announcement to that effect; it was therefore likely that any delay would have had an adverse impact on the stock of both companies. The 4 p.m. deadline was the closing time of the District of Columbia office where the merger documents were to be filed.

be added in order to characterize the adjustments. The paragraph recited that with the noted adjustments properly made, NSMC's unaudited consolidated statement for the nine-month period would not reflect a profit as had been indicated but rather a net loss, and the consolidated operations of NSMC as they existed on May 31, 1969, would show a break-even as to net earnings for the year ended August 31, 1969. Epley had the additional paragraph typed out, but failed to inform or disclose this change to Interstate. In a second conversation, after the closing was completed and the Interstate representatives had departed, Epley was informed of still another proposed addition, namely, a paragraph urging resolicitation of both companies' shareholders and disclosure of NSMC's corrected nine-month financials prior to closing. To this, he responded that the deal was closed and the letter was not needed. Peat Marwick nonetheless advised Epley that the letter would be delivered and that its counsel was considering whether further action should be taken by the firm.

The final written draft of the comfort letter arrived at White & Case late that afternoon. Peat Marwick believed that Interstate had been informed and was aware of the conversations between its representatives and Epley and of its concern about the adjustments.[23] Because of this belief and especially since the merger had been closed without benefit of the completed letter, Peat Marwick's counsel perceived no obligation to do anything further about the merger. Nonetheless, a signed copy of the final letter was sent to each board member of the two companies, presumably in an effort to underline the accountants' concern about consummation of the merger without shareholder resolicitation.

The signed comfort letter was delivered to the Interstate offices on Monday, November 3. It was first seen and read by Donald Jeffers, Interstate's chief financial officer. He had not been present at the October 31 closing or informed of the adjustments to the interim financials. Concerned, he contacted Brown immediately and read the letter to him. Since a meeting with other Interstate principals was scheduled for the next morning the letter was added to the other matters to be discussed.

The signed letter was virtually identical to the unsigned version delivered at the closing, except for the addition of the following two paragraphs:

Your attention is called, however, to the fact that if the aforementioned adjustments had been made at May 31, 1969 the unaudited consolidated statement of earnings of National Student Marketing Corporation would have shown a net loss of approximately $80,000. It is presently estimated that the consolidated operations of the company as it

---

23. This belief stemmed from representations made by Epley in his telephone conversations with Peat Marwick. From those conversations Peat Marwick received the justifiable impression that counsel for both Interstate and NSMC were aware of the problems engendered by the adjustments and had concluded that the merger could take place nonetheless.

existed at May 31, 1969 will be approximately a break-even as to net earnings for the year ended August 31, 1969.

In view of the above mentioned facts, we believe the companies should consider submitting corrected interim unaudited financial information to the shareholders prior to proceeding with the closing.

The only other change was the reduction in the write-off to receivables from $300,000 to $200,000, making total negative adjustments to NSMC's nine-month financials in the amount of $784,000.

At the meeting the following day, the matter was fully discussed by the former Interstate principals. Of particular concern were the additional "break-even" and "resolicitation" paragraphs. Brown explained what had occurred at the closing and the reasons for the decision to consummate the merger. He called Meyer at LBB, who by that time was also aware of the letter. After some discussion, it was decided that more information was needed. Brown and Jeffers agreed to contact Peat Marwick and Meyer agreed that his firm would contact Epley at White & Case.

On that afternoon, Schauer contacted Epley by telephone. Epley stated that he had not known of the additional paragraphs until after the closing. He added that in any case the additions did not expand upon the contents of the earlier unsigned letter; the "break-even" paragraph simply reflected the results of an arithmetic computation of the effects of the adjustments, and the "resolicitation" paragraph was gratuitous and a matter for lawyers, not accountants. While Schauer disagreed, Epley again responded that the additional paragraphs made no difference and that NSMC regarded the deal as closed.

Brown and Jeffers fared no better with Peat Marwick. That company's representative, Cormick L. Breslin, met briefly with several Interstate representatives on November 4. He could give no information concerning the matter other than that he had not seen a similar letter before and thought it was rather unusual. Later, when contacted again by Brown, Breslin stated that the letter would have to speak for itself and his company would provide no additional information, comment or advice.

Over the next several days the Interstate directors continued their discussion of the matter, consulting frequently with their counsel, Meyer and Schauer. As they viewed it, the available options were to attempt to undo the merger, either permanently or until the shareholders could be resolicited, or to leave things as they were. The attorneys indicated that rescission would be impractical, if not impossible, since Interstate no longer existed and NSMC had indicated that it would oppose any effort to undo the merger. Meanwhile, the market value of NSMC stock continued to increase, and the directors noted that any action on their part to undo the merger would most likely adversely affect its price. By the end of the week, the decision was made to abstain from any action. Thereafter, Brown issued a memorandum to all Interstate employees announcing completion of the merger. No effort was ever made by any of the defendants to disclose the contents of the comfort letter to the former shareholders of Interstate, the SEC or to the public in general.

* * *

E. Subsequent Events

Following the acquisition of Interstate and several other companies NSMC stock rose steadily in price, reaching a peak in mid-December. However, in early 1970, after several newspaper and magazine articles appeared questioning NSMC's financial health, the value of the stock decreased drastically. Several private lawsuits were filed and the SEC initiated a wide-ranging investigation which led to the filing of this action.

II. THE PRESENT ACTION

* * *

The Commission charges Brown and Meyer with responsibility for proceeding with the merger of Interstate and NSMC. Since shareholder approval of the merger was secured in part on the basis of the nine-month financials which the comfort letter indicated were inaccurate, the SEC contends that Brown and Meyer should have refused to close until the shareholders could be resolicited with corrected financials. The Commission also charges the two directors with effecting the sale of NSMC stock following the merger, without first disclosing the information contained in the comfort letter. These allegations clearly constitute charges of principal violations of the antifraud provisions. In addition, Brown is specifically charged with aiding and abetting sales of NSMC stock by Interstate principals through his issuance, with Schauer's assistance, of the Rule 133 letter to NSMC.

Numerous charges, all of which appear to allege secondary liability, are leveled against the attorney defendants. Schauer is charged with "participating in the merger between Interstate and NSMC," apparently referring to his failure to interfere with the closing of the merger after receipt of the comfort letter. Such inaction, when alleged to facilitate a transaction, falls under the rubric of aiding and abetting. Both Schauer and Meyer are charged with issuing false opinions in connection with the merger and stock sales, thereby facilitating each transaction, and with acquiescence in the merger after learning the contents of the signed comfort letter. The Commission contends that the attorneys should have refused to issue the opinions in view of the adjustments revealed by the unsigned comfort letter, and after receipt of the signed version, they should have withdrawn their opinion with regard to the merger and demanded resolicitation of the Interstate shareholders. If the Interstate directors refused, the attorneys should have withdrawn from the representation and informed the shareholders or the Commission. The SEC specifically characterizes the attorneys' conduct in issuing the Rule 133 opinion as aiding and abetting, and because their alleged misconduct with regard to the merger also appears sufficiently removed from the center of that transaction, it too will be considered under a charge of secondary liability. And finally, LBB is charged with vicarious liability for the actions of Meyer and Schauer with respect to the attorneys' activities on behalf of the firm.

* * *

III.   PAST VIOLATIONS

* * *

B.   *Materiality*

* * *

In the present case, the alleged misstatement or omission is the failure to disclose, either to the Interstate shareholders or to the purchasers of the NSMC stock sold by Interstate principals following the merger, the adjustments contained in the unsigned comfort letter delivered at the October 31 closing. Although the defendants contend that the adjustments were not material, and make several arguments in support of that position, the Court concludes that the defendants have misconceived the legal standard of materiality and that the evidence presented clearly demonstrates that the comfort letter adjustments would have assumed "actual significance in the deliberations of the reasonable shareholder" or investor, and were therefore material.

* * *

In a merger transaction such as that presented here, accurate financial information is necessary in order for a shareholder fairly to be able to vote. * * *

* * *

In summary, the Court concludes that the adjustments contained in the unsigned comfort letter would have altered the total mix of information available and would have assumed actual significance in the deliberations of the reasonable Interstate shareholder. Although it is arguable whether the better business decision under the circumstances was to proceed with the merger, the antifraud provisions prohibit such a course of action when a material misrepresentation or omission has occurred, regardless of the business justification for closing the merger. There is no doubt that the adjustments were material, and therefore Brown and Meyer should have refused to proceed with the merger absent disclosure to and resolicitation of the shareholders.

C.   *Scienter*

* * *

After receiving the unsigned comfort letter at the closing, the Interstate representatives immediately expressed concern over the new information; they caucused privately and sought and received various oral assurances from the NSMC representatives. Moreover, the new information included adjustments which were far from insubstantial; they reduced the reported profit of NSMC by several hundreds of thousands of dollars and converted what had been a sizable profit into a net loss. Despite the obvious materiality of this information, especially as demonstrated by their conduct, they made a conscious decision not to disclose it. Such conduct has been found sufficient to meet the scienter requirement.

This knowing failure to disclose does not alone support a finding of scienter here. Also relevant are certain extrinsic factors, such as the presence of trading in the security during the period in question, actions taken by the defendant to remedy his prior actions, the pattern of the defendant's conduct, and any other similar conduct by the defendant. The Commission concedes that none of the defendants has been involved in other misconduct, either before or since the incidents alleged here. Further, the present actions took place within a short period of time, with some pressure on the participants to choose a course of action and proceed.

Nevertheless, it cannot be ignored that Brown and Meyer expected to profit handsomely from the merger and the subsequent stock sales They were in no haste to disseminate the comfort letter information, and in fact they never revealed the adjustments, even after NSMC's year-end audit had been released and their fears of the adjustments being taken out of context should have been assuaged. Finally, although it is difficult to assess their concern with regard to the market value of NSMC stock it is apparent that a major reason for not disclosing the information was the protection of the investments made by Interstate shareholders, including themselves, by avoiding any action which could have a detrimental effect on the price of the stock. These circumstances provide strong additional support for an inference that the defendants acted with scienter.

In any event, to the extent an inference of actual intent to deceive, manipulate, or defraud may be inappropriate, the defendants' actions here clearly constitute "the kind of recklessness that is equivalent to wilful fraud," and which also satisfies the scienter requirement. The failure to disclose the material information in this case was neither inadvertent, nor the product of simple forgetfulness, but instead the result of a conscious decision made by the defendants. In view of the obviousness of the danger that investors would be misled by their failure to disclose the material information, such conduct must be considered reckless.

Accordingly, the Court finds that Brown and Meyer violated s 10(b), Rule 10b–5, and s 17(a) through their participation in the closing of the Interstate/NSMC merger and through their sales of NSMC stock immediately following the merger, in each instance without first disclosing the material information contained in the unsigned comfort letter.

IV. AIDING AND ABETTING

The Court must now turn to the Commission's charges that the defendants aided and abetted these two violations of the antifraud provisions. The violations themselves establish the first element of aiding and abetting liability, namely that another person has committed a securities law violation. The remaining elements, though not set forth with any uniformity, are essentially that the alleged aider and abettor had a "general awareness that his role was part of an overall activity that is improper, and (that he) knowingly and substantially assisted the violation."

The Commission's allegations of aiding and abetting by the defendants, seem to fall into four basic categories: (1) the failure of the attorney defendants to take any action to interfere in the consummation of the merger; (2) the issuance by the attorneys of an opinion with respect to the merger; (3) the attorneys' subsequent failure to withdraw that opinion and inform the Interstate shareholders or the SEC of the inaccuracy of the nine-month financials; The SEC's position is that the defendants acted or failed to act with an awareness of the fraudulent conduct by the principals, and thereby substantially assisted the two violations. The Court concurs with regard to the attorneys' failure to interfere with the closing, but must conclude that the remaining actions or inaction alleged to constitute aiding and abetting did not substantially facilitate either the merger or the stock sales.

As noted, the first element of aiding and abetting liability has been established by the finding that Brown and Meyer committed primary violations of the securities laws. Support for the second element, that the defendants were generally aware of the fraudulent activity, is provided by the previous discussion concerning scienter. With the exception of LBB, which is charged with vicarious liability, each of the defendants was actually present at the closing of the merger when the comfort letter was delivered and the adjustments to the nine-month financials were revealed. Each was present at the Interstate caucus and the subsequent questioning of the NSMC representatives; each knew of the importance attributed to the adjustments by those present. They knew that the Interstate shareholders and the investing public were unaware of the adjustments and the inaccuracy of the financials. Despite the obvious materiality of the information, each knew that it had not been disclosed prior to the merger and stock sale transactions. Thus, this is not a situation where the aider and abettor merely failed to discover the fraud, or reasonably believed that the victims were already aware of the withheld information. The record amply demonstrates the "knowledge of the fraud, and not merely the undisclosed material facts," that is required to meet this element of secondary liability.

The final requirement for aiding and abetting liability is that the conduct provide knowing, substantial assistance to the violation. In addressing this issue, the Court will consider each of the SEC's allegations separately. The major problem arising with regard to the Commission's contention that the attorneys failed to interfere in the closing of the merger is whether inaction or silence constitutes substantial assistance. While there is no definitive answer to this question, courts have been willing to consider inaction as a form of substantial assistance when the accused aider and abettor had a duty to disclose. Although the duty to disclose in those cases is somewhat distinguishable, in that they contemplate disclosure to an opposing party and not to one's client, they are sufficiently analogous to provide support for a duty here.

Upon receipt of the unsigned comfort letter, it became clear that the merger had been approved by the Interstate shareholders on the basis of materially misleading information. In view of the obvious materiality of the information, especially to attorneys learned in securities law, the attorneys' responsibilities to their corporate client required them to take steps to ensure that the information would be disclosed to the shareholders. However, it is unnecessary to determine the precise extent of their obligations here, since it is undisputed that they took no steps whatsoever to delay the closing pending disclosure to and resolicitation of the Interstate shareholders. But, at the very least, they were required to speak out at the closing concerning the obvious materiality of the information and the concomitant requirement that the merger not be closed until the adjustments were disclosed and approval of the merger was again obtained from the Interstate shareholders. Their silence was not only a breach of this duty to speak, but in addition lent the appearance of legitimacy to the closing. The combination of these factors clearly provided substantial assistance to the closing of the merger.

Contrary to the attorney defendants' contention, imposition of such a duty will not require lawyers to go beyond their accepted role in securities transactions, nor will it compel them to "err on the side of conservatism, ... thereby inhibiting clients' business judgments and candid attorney-client communications." Courts will not lightly overrule an attorney's determination of materiality and the need for disclosure. However, where, as here, the significance of the information clearly removes any doubt concerning the materiality of the information, attorneys cannot rest on asserted "business judgments" as justification for their failure to make a legal decision pursuant to their fiduciary responsibilities to client shareholders.

The Commission also asserts that the attorneys substantially assisted the merger violation through the issuance of an opinion that was false and misleading due to its omission of the receipt of the comfort letter and of the completion of the merger on the basis of the false and misleading nine-month financials. The defendants contend that a technical reading of the opinion demonstrates that it is not false and misleading, and that it provides accurate opinions as to Interstate's compliance with certain corporate formalities. Of concern to the Court, however, is not the truth or falsity of the opinion, but whether it substantially assisted the violation. Upon consideration of all the circumstances, the Court concludes that it did not.

Contrary to the implication made by the SEC, the opinion issued by the attorneys at the closing did not play a large part in the consummation of the merger. Instead, it was simply one of many conditions to the obligation of NSMC to complete the merger. It addressed a number of corporate formalities required of Interstate by the Merger Agreement, only a few of which could possibly involve compliance with the antifraud provisions of the securities laws. Moreover, the opinion was explicitly for the benefit of NSMC, which was already well aware of the adjustments contained in the comfort letter. Thus, this is is not a case where an opinion of counsel addresses a specific issue and is undeniably relied on in completing the transaction. Under these circumstances, it is unreasonable to suggest that the opinion provided substantial assistance to the merger.

The SEC's contention with regard to counsel's alleged acquiescence in the merger transaction raises significant questions concerning the responsibility of counsel. The basis for the charge appears to be counsel's failure, after the merger, to withdraw their opinion, to demand resolicitation of the shareholders, to advise their clients concerning rights of rescission of the merger, and ultimately, to inform the Interstate shareholders or the SEC of the completion of the merger based on materially false and misleading financial statements. The defendants counter with the argument that their actions following the merger are not subject to the coverage of the securities laws.

The filing of the complaint in this proceeding generated significant interest and an almost overwhelming amount of comment within the legal profession on the scope of a securities lawyer's obligations to his client and to the investing public. The very initiation of this action, therefore, has provided a necessary and worthwhile impetus for the profession's recognition and assessment of its responsibilities in this area. The Court's examination, however, must be more limited. Although the complaint alleges varying instances of misconduct on the part of several attorneys and firms, the Court must narrow its focus to the present defendants and the charges against them.

Meyer, Schauer and Lord, Bissell & Brook are, in essence, here charged with failing to take any action to "undo" the merger. The Court has already concluded that counsel had a duty to the Interstate shareholders to delay the closing of the merger pending disclosure and resolicitation with corrected financials, and that the breach of that duty constituted a violation of the antifraud provisions through aiding and abetting the merger transaction. The Commission's charge, however, concerns the period following that transaction. Even if the attorneys' fiduciary responsibilities to the Interstate shareholders continued beyond the merger, the breach of such a duty would not have the requisite relationship to a securities transaction, since the merger had already been completed. It is equally obvious that such subsequent action or inaction by the attorneys could not substantially assist the merger. * * *

V. Appropriateness of Injunctive Relief

* * * The crucial question, though, remains not whether a violation has occurred, but whether there exists a reasonable likelihood of future illegal conduct by the defendant, "something more than the mere possibility which serves to keep the case alive." Thus, the SEC must "go beyond the mere facts of past violations and demonstrate a realistic likelihood of recurrence."

* * *

The Commission has not demonstrated that the defendants engaged in the type of repeated and persistent misconduct which usually justifies the issuance of injunctive relief. Instead, it has shown violations which principally occurred within a period of a few hours at the closing of the merger in 1969. The Commission has not charged, or even suggested, that the defendants were involved in similar misconduct either before or after the events involved in this proceeding. Thus, the violations proved by the SEC appear to be part of an isolated incident, unlikely to recur and insufficient to warrant an injunction. The Commission appears to agree, for in the six years since the filing of this action, it has made no attempt to obtain interlocutory injunctive relief against these defendants. Such inaction argues strongly against the need for injunctive relief.

Further, it is difficult to characterize the violations presented here as either "willful, blatant, and often completely outrageous," or as the "garden variety fraud" urged by the Commission. There is no evidence to suggest that these defendants knew about the comfort letter adjustments prior to the receipt of the unsigned comfort letter at the closing; and after receiving the letter, the defendants were under some pressure to determine a course of action, either to proceed with the transactions as scheduled or to abort both the merger and stock sales. Although it has now been found that they unlawfully and with scienter decided to proceed, their actions in this regard hardly resemble the deliberate and well-planned fraudulent scheme frequently found in securities fraud cases.

Finally, the Commission asserts that an injunction is necessary because the professional occupations of the defendants provide significant opportunities for further involvement in securities transactions. It notes that Brown holds positions as a director and as a consultant with NSMC, and that Meyer, Schauer and LBB continue to be involved in various corporate activities, including securities transactions, as part of their legal practice. While these opportunities distinguish the present defendants from those who, because they completely lack such opportunities, should not be subject to the threat of an injunction, they do not alone justify relief. In fact, various circumstances indicate that this factor is not as one-sided as the Commission suggests. Although Brown retains his positions with NSMC, he is in effect virtually retired; the likelihood of his being involved in a securities transaction, other than as an investor, seems quite small. While the attorney defendants are more likely to be so involved, that fact is countered somewhat by their professional responsibilities as attorneys and officers of the court to conform their conduct to the dictates of the law. The Court is confident that they will take appropriate steps to ensure that their professional conduct in the future comports with the law.[75]

After considering the "totality of circumstances" presented here, the Court concludes that the Securities and Exchange Commission has not fulfilled its statutory obligation to make a "proper showing" that injunctive relief is necessary to prevent further violations by these defendants. Accordingly, judgment will be entered for the defendants and the complaint will be dismissed.

IN RE ENRON CORPORATION SECURITIES, DERIVATIVE & ERISA LITIGATION

235 F.Supp.2d.549 (S.D.Tex. 2002)

HARMON, DISTRICT JUDGE.

The above referenced putative class action, brought on behalf of purchasers of Enron Corporation's publicly traded equity and debt securities during a proposed federal Class Period from October 19, 1998 through November 27, 2001, alleges securities violations (1) under Sections 11 and 15 of the Securities Act of 1933 ("1933 Act"), (2) under Sections 10(b), 20(a), and 20A of the Securities Exchange Act of 1934 ("Exchange Act" or "the 1934 Act"), and Rule 10b–5 promulgated thereunder by the Securities and Exchange Commission ("SEC"), and (3) under the Texas Securities Act, Texas Rev. Civ. Stat. Ann. art. 581–33.

Pending before the Court *inter alia* are motions to dismiss pursuant to Rules 8(e)(1), 9(b), and 12(b)(6) of the Federal Rules of Civil Procedure, the Private Securities Litigation Reform Act of 1995 (the "PSLRA"), and *Central Bank of Denver v. First Interstate Bank of Denver,* 511 U.S. 164, 114 S.Ct. 1439, 128 L.Ed.2d 119 (1994), filed by the following accounting firms, law firms, and investment banks/integrated financial services institutions ("secondary actors in securities markets": (1) Canadian Imperial Bank of Commerce ("CIBC")(#615); (2) CitiGroup Inc. (#629); (3) J.P. Morgan Chase & Co.(#632); (4) Vinson & Elkins L.L.P. (#648); (5) Arthur Andersen LLP (#650); (6) Barclays PLC (#653); (7) Credit Suisse First Boston (#658); (8) Kirkland & Ellis (#660); (9) Bank of America Corporation (#664); (10) Merrill Lynch & Co. (#667); (11) Lehman Brothers Holdings Inc. (#679); and (12) Deutsche Bank AG (#716).

---

75. The Commission contends that the defendants' failure to recognize the seriousness of their misconduct, by continuing to maintain that their actions were lawful and proper, demonstrates the need for an injunction. The Court, however, considers the defendants' conduct in this regard as sim- ply putting the SEC to its burden of making a proper showing that injunctive relief is warranted. In the absence of more egregious conduct, such as dilatoriness or bad faith, the defendants will not be penalized for fully defending this action.

In essence Lead Plaintiff's consolidated complaint alleges that these and other named Defendants "are liable for (i) making false statements, or failing to disclose adverse facts while selling Enron securities and/or (ii) participating in a scheme to defraud and/or a course of business that operated as a fraud or deceit on purchasers of Enron's public securities during the Class Period...."

* * *

APPLICABLE LAW

The rapid collapse of Enron Corporation ("Enron") and the resulting scope, variety, and severity of losses are unprecedented in American corporate history. It is not surprising that this consolidated action raises a number of novel and/or controversial issues that the law has thus far not addressed or about which the courts are in substantial disagreement. Lead Plaintiff Regents of the University of California's claims are grounded in securities statutes, but judicial construction of those statutes spans the full spectrum of possibilities. After a careful review of frequently divergent case law and extensive deliberation, the Court applies the following law to the allegations in the consolidated complaint and, where appropriate, explains the bases for its selection.

* * *

II.   Federal Securities Law

A.   Section 10(b) of the 1934 Act and Rule 10b–5

Section 10(b) of the Exchange Act states in relevant part,

It shall be unlawful for any person, directly or indirectly ... (b) To use or employ, in connection with the purchase or sale of any security ... any manipulative or deceptive device or contrivance in contravention of such rules and regulations as the [SEC] may proscribe as necessary or appropriate in the public interest or for the protection of investors.

* * *

c.   Central Bank and Primary Violations

Of substantial relevance to the motions this Court now reviews is the Supreme Court's holding in a 5–4 decision in *Central Bank of Denver, N.A. v. First Interstate Bank of Denver, N.A.*, based on the language and legislative history of the statute, that a private plaintiff may not bring an aiding and abetting claim under § 10(b) and Rule 10b–5. The high court construed the general anti-fraud provision as prohibiting only the making of a material misstatement or a material omission or the commission of a manipulative act; therefore it does not prohibit giving aid to another, who then commits a primary § 10(b) violation. It further emphasized that none of the express private causes of action in both the Securities Act of 1933 and the 1934 Exchange Act imposes liability on one who aids or abets such primary violators. Thus it reasoned, "[t]here is no reason to think that Congress would have attached aiding and abetting liability only to § 10(b) and not to any of the express private rights of action in the Act.'', The court rejected as implausible the argument that silence in the statute constituted an "implicit congressional intent to impose § 10(b) aiding and abetting liability." Furthermore, the Supreme Court pointed out that the critical element for recovery under Rule 10b–5, reliance, would be eliminated if liability were imposed for aiding and abetting. ("Were we to allow the aiding and abetting action proposed in this case, the defendant could be liable without any showing that the plaintiff relied upon the aider and abettor's statements or actions."). Nor did it find that anything in the legislative history "even implies that aiding and abetting was covered by the statutory prohibition on manipulative and deceptive conduct."

* * *

Nevertheless, the Supreme Court did not conclude that secondary actors such as lawyers, accountants, banks, and underwriters were therefore always shielded from § 10(b) and Rule 10b–5 liability:

> Because the text of § 10(b) does not prohibit aiding and abetting, we hold that a private plaintiff may not maintain an aiding and abetting suit under § 10(b). The absence of § 10(b) aiding and abetting liability does not mean that secondary actors in securities markets are always free from liability under the securities Act. Any person or entity, including a lawyer, accountant, or bank, who employs a manipulative device or makes a material misstatement (or omission) on which a purchaser or seller of securities relies may be liable as a primary violator under 10b–5, assuming *all* of the requirements for primary liability under Rule 10b–5 are met . . . . . In any complex securities fraud, moreover, there are likely to be multiple violators. . . .

Furthermore, in *Central Bank* the defendant bank was the indenture trustee for $26 million in bonds issued by a public building authority, some in 1986 and more in 1988. The bonds were secured by landowner assessment liens and contained covenants requiring that the subject land had to be worth at least 160% of the bonds' outstanding principal and interest and that the developer had to give the defendant bank an annual appraisal showing that the value of the land met this requirement. Even though the developer did so in 1998, the bank learned through the underwriter that the appraisal was questionable and that the value of the property securing the 1996 bonds may have declined, a fact confirmed by the bank's own in-house appraiser. Nevertheless the bank continued working with the developer and delayed obtaining an independent review of the developer's valuation of the land while the bank issued more bonds in 1988. Subsequently the building authority defaulted on the bonds and the bond purchasers did not only sue the authority, the bonds' underwriters, and the land developer, but they also sued the bank, but only as "secondarily liable under § 10(b) for its conduct in aiding and abetting the [other defendants'] fraud." The high court examined only the aiding and abetting claim pled against the bank and did not address the question whether the bank might be a primary violator, since the plaintiffs had not alleged such a claim.

In sum, the Supreme Court left it to the lower courts to determine when the conduct of a secondary actor makes it a primary violator under the statute. In the aftermath of *Central Bank,* two divergent standards, the "bright line" test and the "substantial participation" test, have emerged.

Under the "bright line" test, in order for the conduct of a secondary actor to rise to the level of a primary violation, the secondary actor must not only make a material misstatement or omission, but "the misrepresentation must be attributed to the specific actor at the time of public dissemination," i.e., in advance of the investment decision, so as not to undermine the element of reliance required for § 10(b) liability. *Wright v. Ernst & Young LLP,* 152 F.3d 169, 175 (2d Cir.1998), *cert. denied,* 525 U.S. 1104, 119 S.Ct. 870, 142 L.Ed.2d 772 (1999);...For example, according to the investor-plaintiffs' complaint in *Wright,* an outside auditor for BT Office Products, Inc. ("BT"), violated § 10(b) by privately and orally approving false and misleading financial statements that the auditor knew would be passed on to investors. BT subsequently made these statements public during a press release, but represented that the information was unaudited and did not mention Ernst & Young. The district court granted the accounting firm's motion to dismiss based on *Central Bank's* rejection of aiding and abetting liability. On appeal, the Second Circuit affirmed, finding that a contrary result would in effect "revive aiding and abetting liability under a different name, and would therefore run afoul of the Supreme Court's holding in *Central Bank.*" It also required that the defendant, to be liable, must have known or should have known that his representation would be disseminated to investors, although the defendant need not communicate the misrepresentation directly to them. The Second Circuit noted that because in BT's press release BT did not mention Ernst & Young, nor Ernst & Young's private prior approval of the statements made in the press release by BT, the auditor

> neither directly nor indirectly communicated misrepresentations to investors. Therefore, the amended complaint failed to allege that Ernst & Young made "a material misstatement (or omission) on which a purchaser or seller of securities relie[d]." Moreover ... because the press release contained a clear and express warning that no audit had yet been completed, there is no basis for Wright to claim that Ernst & Young had endorsed the accuracy of those results.

The Second Circuit has found that words such as "assisting," "participating in," "complicity in," and synonyms employed throughout a complaint, "all fall within the prohibitive bar of *Central Bank.*" *Shapiro,* 123 F.3d at 720.

* * *

Unlike the Second Circuit, the Tenth Circuit does not require attribution of the alleged misrepresentation to the secondary actor at the time of the statement's dissemination to the public. For instance, the Tenth Circuit in *Anixter,* emphasizing that "[t]he critical element separating primary from aiding and abetting violations is the existence of a representation, either by statement or omission, made by the defendant, that is relied upon by the plaintiff," states,

> Clearly, accountants may make representations in their role as auditor to a firm selling securities. *See, e.g., Herman & MacLean v. Huddleston,* 459 U.S. 375, 103 S.Ct. 683, 74 L.Ed.2d 548 (1983)(defendant accountant found primarily liable for violating § 10(b) based on representations filed with the SEC). Typical representations include certifications of financial statements and opinion letters. *See DiLeo v. Ernst & Young,* 901 F.2d 624, 628 (7th Cir.), *cert. denied,* 498 U.S. 941, 111 S.Ct. 347, 112 L.Ed.2d 312 (1990). An accountant's false and misleading representations in connection with the sale of any security, if made with the proper state of mind and if relied upon by those purchasing or selling a security, can constitute a primary violation. *Central Bank of Denver,* 511 U.S. at 190–91, 114 S.Ct. at 1455; ... There is no requirement that the alleged violator directly communicate misrepresentations to plaintiffs for primary liability to attach.... Nevertheless, for an accountant's misrepresentation to be actionable as a primary violation, there must be a showing that he knew or should have known that his representation would be communicated to investors because § 10(b) and Rule 10b–5 focus on fraud made "in connection with the sale or purchase" of a security.

The less stringent "substantial participation" test provides for primary liability where there is "substantial participation or intricate involvement" of the secondary party in the preparation of fraudulent statements "even though that participation might not lead to the actor's actual making of the statements."

* * *

This Court recognizes that without a clearer definition and a narrowing of the kind of conduct and circumstances required to constitute "substantial participation" or "intricate involvement," the substantial participation test may fail to differentiate between primary liability and aiding and abetting, or even unrestricted conspiracy, and that the area of overlap may be significant under such an expansive test. Until or unless Congress addresses the question that definition appears to be the task of the courts.

The SEC, in the role of *amicus curiae,* has filed a brief in this action that warrants consideration because it addresses the reasons why the bright-line test misses the mark. Brief attached to the SEC's motion for leave, as *amicus curiae,* to submit briefs (instrument #821). The majority of its pleading is a submission filed on behalf of the plaintiffs in a case that was pending in the Third Circuit, but which was settled before that appellate court could review the issue *en banc. Klein v, Boyd,* 949 F.Supp. 280 (E.D.Pa.1996), *aff'd,* ___ F.3d ___, 1998 WL 55245, Fed. Sec. L. Rep. P 90,136 (3d Cir.1998), *rehearing en banc granted, judgment vacated* (Mar. 9, 1998). As framed by the SEC, the issue is,

* * *

> [i]s a person who makes a material misrepresentation, while acting with the requisite scienter, but who does not himself disseminate the misrepresentation to investors, and whose name is not made known to them, only an aider and abettor of the fraud, or is that person a primary violator subject to liability [under § 10(b)]?

More specifically, the issue is whether the phrase, "makes a material misstatement (or omission)," in Rule 10b–5 "means that a law firm or other secondary actor can be primarily liable for a misrepresentation only if it signs the document containing the misrepresentation or is otherwise identified to investors," in other words, does not disclose its identity to investors. The SEC argues that such a person is a primary violator under § 10(b), and in doing so, attacks the "bright line" test as an improper reading of *Central Bank.*

First, the SEC highlights the fact that the Supreme Court's use of the word, "makes," in *Central Bank* does not mandate that an allegedly material misstatement be signed by or attributed to the secondary party so that the secondary party is identified to investors. The statute only makes it unlawful "for any person, directly or indirectly . . . [t]o use or employ . . . any manipulative deceptive device or contrivance" and the interpretation of "makes" must be consistent with that "directly or indirectly" language. The SEC proposes "creates," as opposed to the bright line test's interpretation, "signs," as the appropriate synonym for the term, "makes," in *Central Bank;* the SEC contends that "[a] person who creates a misrepresentation but takes care not to be identified publicly with it, 'indirectly' uses or employs a deceptive device or contrivance and should be liable" under § 10(b). The SEC argues that the bright line test's requirement of identification of the misrepresenter to investors at the time of dissemination

> would have the unfortunate and unwarranted consequence of providing a safe harbor from liability for everyone except those identified with the misrepresentations by name. Creators of misrepresentations could escape liability as long as they concealed their identities. Not only outside lawyers would benefit from such a rule; others who are retained to prepare information for dissemination to investors, including accountants and public relations firms, could immunize themselves by remaining anonymous. Indeed, in-house counsel and other corporate officials and employees could avoid liability for misrepresentations they created, as long as their identities were not made known to the public. In sum, by providing a safe harbor for anonymous creators of misrepresentations, a rule that imposes liability only when a person is identified with a misrepresentation would place a premium on concealment

and subterfuge rather than on compliance with the federal securities laws.

The SEC maintains that "[t]he Supreme Court did not set forth a bright line rule for liability, much less one that turns on whether the identity of a defendant is disclosed." Moreover, under the SEC's construction of the statute, third-party defendants are still substantially protected from frivolous suits by the scienter requirement. *Id.* at 16. As for the element of reliance, the SEC insists that

> [t]he reliance a plaintiff in a securities fraud action must plead is reliance on a misrepresentation, not on the fact that a particular person made the misrepresentation. The Supreme Court stated in *Central Bank* that liability exists where "[a]ny person or entity, including a lawyer, accountant, or bank ... makes a material misstatement (or omission) on which a purchaser or seller of securities relies." ... Thus the Court placed the focus on the misrepresentation, not on the fact that a particular person made it.

The SEC proposes instead the following rule for primary liability of a secondary party under § 10(b): "when a person, acting alone or with others, creates a misrepresentation [on which the investor-plaintiffs relied], the person can be liable as a primary violator ... if ... he acts with the requisite scienter." "Moreover it would not be necessary for a person to be the initiator of a misrepresentation in order to be a primary violator. Provided that a plaintiff can plead and prove scienter, a person can be a primary violator if he or she writes misrepresentations for inclusion in a document to be given to investors, even if the idea for those misrepresentations came from someone else." Furthermore, "a person who prepares a truthful and complete portion of a document would not be liable as a primary violator for misrepresentations in other portions of the document. Even assuming such a person knew of misrepresentations elsewhere in the document and thus had the requisite scienter, he or she would not have created those misrepresentations." Finally, of course, the plaintiff must plead and prove the elements of scienter and reliance.

> Because § 10(b) expressly delegated rule-making authority to the agency, which it exercised *inter alia* in promulgating Rule 10b–5, this Court accords considerable weight to the SEC's construction of the statute since the Court finds that construction is not arbitrary, capricious or manifestly contrary to the statute.

* * *

Furthermore, this Court concludes that not only material misrepresentations, but also the statute's imposition of liability on "any person" that "directly or indirectly" uses or employs "any manipulative or deceptive device or contrivance" in connection with the purchase or sale of security should be "construed 'not technically and restrictively, but flexibly to effectuate its remedial purposes.'"

* * *

This Court finds that the SEC's approach to liability under § 10(b) and Rule 10b–5(b) is well reasoned and reasonable, balanced in its concern for protection for victimized investors as well as for meritlessly harassed defendants (including businesses, law firms, accountants and underwriters), in addition to the policies underlying the statutory private right of action for defrauded investors and the PSLRA. Moreover, it is consistent with the language of § 10b(b), Rule 10b–5, and *Central Bank.* Therefore since the SEC's proposed test is a reasonable interpretation of the text of the statute and serves its underlying policies, the Court adopts and applies it in this litigation to claims under § 10(b) and Rule 10b–5(b).

Central Bank's holding (that there is no cause of action for aiding and abetting under § 10(b) and that "all requirements for primary liability under Rule 10b–5" must be satisfied), 511 U.S. at 191, 114 S.Ct. 1439, affects pleading standards where the plaintiffs allege that a group of defendants participated in a scheme or a course of business to defraud investors under § 10(b) and Rule 10b–5. It is generally agreed that *Central Bank* foreclosed a cause of action merely for conspiracy to violate § 10(b) and Rule 10b–5, in addition to aiding and abetting. *See, e.g* ... Nevertheless, "*Central Bank* does not preclude liability based on allegations that a group of defendants acted together to violate the securities laws, as long as each defendant committed a manipulative or deceptive act in furtherance of the scheme." *Cooper v. Pickett,* 137 F.3d 616, 624 (9th Cir.1997). *Cooper* relied on a key passage in *Central Bank* ...

> The absence of § 10(b) aiding and abetting liability does not mean that secondary actors in the securities markets are always free from liability under the securities Acts. Any person or entity, including a lawyer, accountant, or bank, who employs a manipulative device or makes a material misstatement (or omission) on which a purchaser or seller of securities relies may be liable as a primary violator under 10b–5, assuming *all* of the requirements for primary liability under Rule 10b–5 are met. In any complex securities fraud, moreover, there are likely to be multiple violators. . . .

Thus whether or not the word "conspire" is used, to survive a motion to dismiss, a complaint alleging that more than one defendant participated in a "scheme" to defraud must allege a primary violation of § 10(b) by each defendant.

* * *

Thus secondary actors may be liable for primary violations under an alleged scheme to defraud if all the requirements for liability under Rule 10b–5 have been satisfied as to each secondary-actor defendant and any additional heightened pleading requirements have been met. *Id.* If a plaintiff meets the requirements of pleading primary liability as to each defendant, i.e., alleges with factual specificity (1) that each defendant made a material misstatement (or omission) or committed a manipulative or deceptive act in furtherance of the alleged scheme to defraud,

(2) scienter, and (3) reliance, that plaintiff can plead a scheme to defraud and still satisfy *Central Bank.*

* * *

Lead Plaintiff, using older cases, argues that a defendant that participates in a scheme to defraud is liable for the damages caused by all the other acts taken by participants in a scheme in furtherance of the fraud. In addition to requiring that each participant be a primary violator of the act by itself making a material misrepresentation or omission or using a deceptive device or contrivance to defraud investors, this Court notes that under § 10(b), the PSLRA provides for joint and several liability only if the defendant is found to have knowingly committed the fraud, and otherwise the defendant, if only reckless, is liable only for the percentage of his responsibility for the fraud, i.e., proportionate liability. This express scheme for damages liability seems incompatible with Lead Plaintiff's argument that a participant is liable for damages caused by all participants, known or unknown, in the scheme.

Since the passage of the PSLRA with its procedural hurdles and stringent pleading standards to eliminate strike suits, this country has been overwhelmed with corporate scandals that place Congress' goal in enacting the PSLRA in a much wider perspective. Given the usual recent judicial focus on dismissing frivolous suits under the PSLRA, Judge Robert M. Parker provided balance in his concurrence in *Abrams*, 292 F.3d at 435–36,

> History reminds us of the consequences when financial statements of publicly held companies do not accord with reality. Indeed it was to protect against them that our nation's securities laws were enacted. At the same time we must pay heed to a different set of consequences—those brought about by the overzealous prosecution of specious securities fraud actions. Congress, in passing the Private Securities Litigation Reform Act of 1995, took pains to deter such strike suits. Its findings and legislative history suggest that the cost of protecting against fraud was unduly impairing the efficient operation of lawful business. Today, when applying the PSLRA, courts must keep this policy consideration foremost in mind. But we must also recognize that Congress left unaffected shareholders' right to sue for recompense when they are made the victims of self-dealing and deceit. The PSLRA is a mechanism for winnowing out suits that lack a requisite level of specificity. It was not meant to let business and management run amuck to the detriment of shareholders.

The PSLRA's significance as a protective shield for business must be viewed within the context of the private right of action, granted decades before, to defrauded investors injured by corporate management, auditors, outside counsel, and investment bankers where their conduct allegedly violated the federal securities laws. The Supreme Court has repeatedly emphasized the deterrent value of those private rights of action, which "provide 'a most effective weapon in the enforcement' of the securities laws and are a 'necessary supplement to Commission action.'" Indeed, in adopting the PSLRA, Congress emphasized that "[p]rivate securities litigation is an indispensable tool with which defrauded investors can recover their losses" and that private lawsuits "promote public and global confidence in our capital markets and help to deter wrongdoing and to guarantee that corporate officers, auditors, directors, lawyers and others properly perform their jobs." The importance of this tool has been highlighted by recent disclosures of extraordinary corporate misconduct.

* * *

III. Lead Plaintiff's Allegations in Consolidated Complaint

A. The Scheme, Generally

Lead Plaintiff asserts that Defendants participated in "an enormous Ponzi scheme, the largest in history," involving illusory profits "generated by phony, non-arm's-length transactions with Enron-controlled entities and improper accounting tricks" in order to inflate Enron's reported revenues and profits, conceal its growing debts, maintain its artificially high stock prices and investment grade credit rating, as well as allow individual defendants to personally enrich themselves by looting the corporation, while continuing to raise money from public offerings of Enron or related entities' securities to sustain the scheme and to postpone the collapse of the corporation, a scenario characterized by Lead Plaintiff as "a hall of mirrors inside a house of cards." The consolidated complaint sets out an elaborate scheme of off-the-books, illicit partnerships, secretly controlled by Enron and established at times critical for requisite financial disclosures by Enron in order to conceal its actual financial status. These Enron-controlled entities typically would buy troubled assets from Enron, which Enron would have had difficulty selling in an arm's length transaction to an independent entity and which otherwise would have to be reported on Enron's balance sheet, by means of sham swaps, hedges, and transfers, to record phony profits and conceal debt on Enron's balance sheet. Lead Plaintiff further paints a picture of participation in the scheme by Enron's accountants, outside law firms, and banks, which all were the beneficiaries of such enormous fees and increasing business, as well as investment opportunities for personal enrichment, with the result that their opinions were rubber stamps that deceived investors and the public.

* * *

In sum, the consolidated complaint charges that Defendants caused Enron to violate GAAP and SEC rules in order to overstate Enron's assets, shareholders' equity, net income and earnings per share, and to understate its debt. Defendants also caused Enron to present materially misleading statements in Enron's financial statements (including press releases and SEC filings, such as Form 10–Qs for interim results and Form 10–Ks for annual results), which were incorporated into (Registration Statements and Prospectuses filed during the Class Period). Enron also made misrepresentations about Defendants' manipulations, all concealed by the following numerous, improper accounting ploys: not consolidating illicit SPEs into Enron's financial statements to properly reflect reduced earnings and debt on Enron's balance sheet; improperly accounting for common stock issued to a related-party entity that should have been treated as a reduction in shareholders' equity, but was identified as a note receivable; improperly accounting for broadband transactions; abusing mark-to-market accounting; characterizing loans as forward contracts to conceal Enron's debt; improperly accounting for long-term contracts; failing to record required write-downs for impairment in value of Enron's investments, long-term assets, and its broadband and technology investments in a timely manner; failing to record an aggregate of $92 million in proposed audit adjustments from 1997 until the end of the Class period; failing to disclose related-party transactions; and misstating Enron's debt-to-equity ratio (measured as debt to total capitalization, a figure which rating agencies use to determine a company's credit rating) and ratio of earnings to fixed charges. Even while demonstrating the contrast between Enron's original financial statements and its restatement results, the consolidated complaint notes that many of Defendants' manipulations are not included in the restatement, such as the effects of Enron's abuse of accounting techniques.

Lead Plaintiff describes Enron's "corporate culture" as characterized by "a fixation on the price of Enron stock" and on pushing that price ever higher. Throughout Enron's Houston corporate headquarters, TV monitors constantly displayed the current market price of its stock. A repeated maxim was that managers were always to be "ABCing," i.e., "always be closing" deals to create revenue and profit even if they were questionable. Corporate managers and executives were compensated for closing transactions and placing high values on them, regardless of the economic realities of the deals, to generate profit when "marked to market." There was pressure to do anything necessary to make the numbers, and it was common knowledge that revenues and earnings were being falsified at the direction of top executives. Bonuses went to those who facilitated the company-wide fraudulent behavior. In August 2001, Sherron Watkins, an Enron executive and a former Arthur Andersen accountant, wrote to Kenneth Lay that Enron was "nothing but an elaborate accounting hoax" and that nothing "will protect Enron if these [SPE] transactions are ever disclosed in the bright light of day," while warning that many Enron employees believe, "[W]e're such a crooked company."

In 2001, matters at Enron began to fall apart, according to the complaint. In March 2001, just prior to the end of the quarter, it appeared that Enron would have to take a pre-tax charge against more than $500 million because of a shortfall in the credit capacity of the Raptor SPEs. To avoid the loss and its more dire consequences, Enron, Arthur Andersen, Vinson & Elkins, Kirkland & Ellis and some of the banks "restructured" the Raptors by transferring to them more than $800 million of contracts to receive Enron stock for no consideration;

this transfer was accounted for as an increase in equity and assets, in violation of GAAP. As with so many other previously described contrivances, the transfer allowed the participants in the scheme to continue concealing losses in Enron's merchant investments and kept the alleged Ponzi scheme working. Yet during early 2001, Enron also continued to report record results, certified by Arthur Andersen, and Enron's lawyers and bankers continued to make very positive statements about the business.

* * *

According to the complaint, on July 13, 2001, Jeffrey Skilling told Kenneth Lay that he was going to quit because he knew that the Enron house of cards was crumbling. They and other top Enron officials made up a story that Skilling was resigning for personal reasons to hide the true reason and limit damage to the price of Enron's stock. On August 14, 2001, Fastow, Skilling and other top executives and bankers announced that Skilling, who had only become CEO a few months earlier, was resigning for personal reasons, that his departure did not raise "any accounting or business issues of any kind," that Enron's financial state "had never been stronger" and its "future had never been brighter," that there was "nothing to disclose," that Enron's "numbers look good," that there were "no problems" or "accounting issues," and that the Enron "machine was in top shape and continues to roll on—Enron's the best of the best."

The consolidated complaint quotes Enron management employees in August 2001 complaining to the Board about the fraud Nevertheless, Enron's directors did not investigate or disclose the matters the employees had raised. Instead, according to the consolidated complaint, they brought in Vinson & Elkins to cover up the wrongdoing. Vinson & Elkins issued a whitewash report dismissing these detailed complaints of fraud even though the law firm knew the allegations were true because it was involved in structuring many of the manipulative devices.

* * *

The consolidated complaint charges that Enron's publicly filed reports disclosed the existence of the LJM partnerships, but not the essence of the transactions between Enron and the partnerships, nor the nature or extent of Fastow's financial interests in the partnerships. Instead the disclosures were crafted and approved by Enron's outside Arthur Andersen auditors and counsel (Vinson & Elkins and Kirkland & Ellis) in meetings with Enron top insiders. Moreover, Enron's manipulative devices, contrivances, and related-party transactions were extraordinarily lucrative for Fastow and investors in the LJM partnerships despite the relatively risk-free deals that protected them. Lead Plaintiff quotes a *Newsweek* article from the January 28, 2002 edition: "The key to the Enron mess is that the company was allowed to give misleading financial information to the world for years." Lead Plaintiff concludes that "the scheme to defraud Enron investors was extraordinary in its scope, duration and size," that it "was accomplished over a multi-year period through numerous manipulative devices and contrivances and misrepresentations to investors," and that it "was designed and/or perpetrated only via the active and knowing involvement of Enron's general counsel, Vinson & Elkins, the law firm for the LHM2 entity and its SPEs, Kirkland & Ellis, Enron's accounting firm, Arthur Andersen, and Enron's banks, including JP Morgan, CitiGroup, CS First Boston, Merrill Lynch, Deutsche Bank, Barclays, Lehman Brothers and Bank America." Consolidated complaint at 45.

The Consolidated Complaint at lists the offering documents and describes the kinds of allegedly false and misleading statements in Enron's offering documents for securities offerings from July 7, 1998 through July 18, 2001, which incorporated by reference prior Enron Form 10–Ks and 10–Qs, and which also misstated or misled the public about material matters and failed to disclose the fraudulent activity described above and its resulting deceptive version of Enron's financial status and results. These acts included Enron's deliberate failure to consolidate non-qualifying SPEs, straw transactions with banks, bogus hedging transactions leveraging Enron's own stock equity as credit support, misleading the public about Enron's financial risk management and credit risk, and false statements about its failing nascent businesses that were more conceptual than real, including EBS, EIN, and EBOS.

B.   Defendant–Specific Allegations

* * *

2.   Law Firms

The consolidated complaint claims that Vinson & Elkins, Enron's outside general counsel during the Class Period, and Kirkland & Ellis participated in writing, reviewing, and approving Enron's SEC filings, shareholder reports and financial press releases, and in creating Chewco, JEDI, LJM1, LJM2, and nearly all the related SPEs' transactions. They knew that LJM2's principal purpose was to engage in transactions with Enron and that Enron insiders Fastow, Kopper and Glisan were operating on both sides of the transactions, to virtually insure lucrative returns for the entities' partners.

a.   Vinson & Elkins L.L.P.

Enron was Vinson & Elkins' largest client, accounting for more than 7% of the firm's revenues. Over the years more than twenty Vinson & Elkins lawyers have left the firm and joined Enron's in-house legal department.

The complaint recites a long history of alleged improprieties by Vinson & Elkins as part of the elaborate Ponzi scheme.

The complaint asserts that Vinson & Elkins participated in the negotiations for, prepared the transactions for, participated in the structuring of, and approved the illicit partnerships (Chewco/JEDI and the LJMs) and the SPEs (Raptors/Condor, etc.) with knowledge that they

were manipulative devices, not independent third parties and not valid
SPEs, designed to move debt off Enron's books, inflate its earnings, and
falsify Enron's reported financial results and financial condition at
crucial times. Vinson & Elkins repeatedly provided "true sale" and other
opinions that were false and were indispensable for the sham deals to
close and the fraudulent scheme to continue. Vinson & Elkins also
allegedly drafted and/or approved the adequacy of Enron's press releases,
shareholder reports, and SEC filings, including Form 10Ks and Registration Statements that Vinson & Elkins knew were false and misleading.
Vinson & Elkins also drafted the disclosures about the related party
transactions, which it also knew were false and misleading because they
concealed material facts. It also was involved in structuring and providing advice about the bogus commodity trades utilized by JP Morgan and
Enron with the involvement of Mahonia. Moreover, the firm continually
issued false opinions about the illegitimate business transactions, such as
that they were "true sales." When the scheme began to collapse in
August 2001 and Skilling resigned, whistle-blower Sherron Watkins sent
her August 9, 2001 memorandum warning Kenneth Lay not to use
Vinson & Elkins to handle an investigation of her voiced concerns about
Enron's accounting practices because Vinson & Elkins had a conflict in
that "they provided some 'true sale' opinions on some of the [Condor
and Raptor] deals." Despite Watkins's warning, Vinson & Elkins was
called and allegedly conducted a whitewash investigation of what it knew
were accurate allegations of fraudulent misconduct that also involved
Vinson & Elkins. Vinson & Elkins received over $100 million in legal
fees from Enron.

* * *

Specifically, the complaint asserts that Vinson & Elkins provided
advice in structuring virtually every Enron off-balance sheet transaction
and prepared the transaction documents, including opinions, for deals
involving the following vehicles used to defraud investors and the securities markets: Azurix; Canvasback; CASHco.; Cayco; Condor; Cortez
Energy; EES; Egret; Enron Brazil; Enron Broadband; Enron Global
Power; Firefly; Iguana; JEDI; JEDI/Big River/Little River; JEDI/Condor;
JEDI/Osprey/Whitewing/Condor; JEDI/Whitewing; JEDI II; JEDI I/On-
tario; LJM; LJM/Condor/Raptor; LJM/Brazil Power Plant; LJM2;
LJM2/Chewco; LJM2/Raptors I, II, III, IV; Mahonia Ltd.; Marengo;
Marlin; Newco; Osprey; Red River; Sonoma; Sundance; Wessex; Whitew-
ing; Yosemite; and Yukon. Vinson & Elkins allegedly had to know about
and joined in the fraudulent Ponzi scheme because of its continuing,
intimate involvement in the formation of and transactions with these
blatantly fraudulent entities, created solely to cook Enron's books.

For instance, Lead Plaintiff points to Vinson & Elkins' involvement
in the eleventh-hour formation of Chewco in late 1997 when JEDI's
outside investor withdrew and JEDI had to be restructured or Enron
would have to consolidate JEDI on its books, carry JEDI's debt on its
balance sheet, and lose its ability in the future to continue to generate

profits from an independent SPE. Vinson & Elkins prepared the documents for Chewco's financing and falsified them to make it appear that Chewco was independent of Enron. Because the arrangement had to be completed by year's end, Vinson & Elkins with Kirkland & Ellis drafted a side agreement, dated December 30, 1997, providing for Enron to give the required $6.6 million in cash to fund Chewco by means of clandestine reserve accounts for Big River Funding and Little River Funding. Furthermore, to avoid disclosure of the arrangement, because making Fastow manager of Chewco would necessitate disclosing that interest in Enron's SEC filings and potentially expose the non-arm's-length nature of the whole transaction, Vinson & Elkins, with Fastow, arranged for Michael Kopper to be the manager and thus conceal Enron's financial relationship with Chewco from Enron shareholders. Kopper allegedly objected that there was a conflict of interest because Kopper was also an Enron employee, but the two law firms disregarded his concern. Neither law firm insisted on disclosure of the arrangement in Enron's SEC filings even though the impropriety was obvious. Moreover, Enron continued to use Chewco/JEDI to generate sham profits from 1997 through 2001 in transactions that Vinson & Elkins participated in structuring and providing bogus "true sale" opinions to facilitate, all for the same purpose.

In another example, Vinson & Elkins issued opinions to Enron, Mahonia and JP Morgan stating that the forward sales contracts of natural gas and oil by Enron were legitimate commodities trades when it knew they were a sham, manipulative devices to disguise loans from JP Morgan to Enron so that it would not have to record approximately $3.9 billion of loans as debts on Enron's balance sheet. Physical delivery of the gas and oil was not required or even contemplated.

Similarly Vinson & Elkins participated in the creation of both LJM partnerships and knew the reason for their establishment, i.e., so that Enron could effectuate transactions that it could not otherwise do with an independent entity, such as purchasing Enron assets that Enron otherwise was unable to sell at prices it would never otherwise receive. As discussed previously, LJM2, formed at the critical end of 1999, pursuant to documentation prepared by Vinson & Elkins that allowed the banks to advance 100% of the money needed to fund the partnership in sufficient time to falsify the books for the reporting period. LJM2 was one of the primary manipulative devices to misrepresent Enron's financial results, was also secretly controlled by Enron, and was used to create a number of SPEs, including the Raptors, which in turn served to falsely inflate Enron's profits and conceal its debts. Usually Enron provided the bulk of the capital to set up the SPEs, which the SPEs would then pay to Enron, so that Enron was always at risk. Furthermore Fastow's dual role at Enron and LJM2, by which he could and did self-deal to enrich himself and the other favored investors in the lucrative partnership, rewarded various participants in the Ponzi scheme for their roles. Vinson & Elkins structured a number of critical year-end transactions involving LJM2, including the Collateralized Loan Obligations ("CLOs"),

Nowa Sarzyna power plant, MEGS, LLC, and Yosemite. Typically transactions were timed near the end of financial reporting periods to manipulate, falsify, and artificially inflate Enron's reported financial results while enriching the investors in LJM2. Enron frequently agreed in advance to, and did, buy back the assets after the close of the financial reporting period, always at a profit for the LJM partnerships even if the market value of the assets declined, or the corporation promised to protect the LJM partnerships against any loss. Other transactions that Vinson & Elkins participated in that served as contrivances and manipulative devices to circumvent accounting rules and misrepresent Enron's financial results included the sham hedging transactions involving Rhythms stock and the Raptor SPEs that were funded principally with Enron's own stock to "hedge" against loss of value in Enron's merchant investments.

* * *

As the end of 2000 neared, two of the Raptor SPEs were in danger of unwinding. Vinson & Elkins and Enron then restructured and capitalized them by transferring even more Enron stock to them, only adding to the pressure to keep the price of Enron's stock artificially high. Again in March 2001, Vinson & Elkins restructured the Raptors by transferring more than $800 million of contracts to receive Enron stock before the quarter end. That transfer insured that Enron would not have to take a pre-tax charge of more than $500 million against earnings, and so that it could conceal substantial losses in its merchant investments and remove millions of dollars of debt from its balance sheet, thus keeping the alleged Ponzi scheme afloat.

According to the complaint, Vinson & Elkins was also involved in the New Power transactions. Before the IPO it structured the deal which permitted Enron to take a large phony profit by utilizing LJM2. After the IPO, Vinson & Elkins created Hawaii 125–0, with which, Vinson & Elkins knew, CIBC and several other banks finagled a "total return swap" that guaranteed CIBC's loan of $125 million to the SPE. Disclosures in the following SEC filings, drafted and approved by Vinson & Elkins, concealed material facts about the JEDI/Chewco, LJM, and/or Raptor transactions:

> A. Quarterly Reports (on Form 10–Q) filed on: 8/16/99; 11/15/99; 5/15/00; 8/14/00; 11/14/00; 5/15/01; and 8/14/01.

> B. Annual Reports (on Form 10–K) filed on 3/31/98; 3/31/99; 3/30/00; and 4/02/01.

> C. Annual Proxies filed on: 3/30/99; 5/02/00; 5/01/01.

> D. Report on Form 8–K, filed 2/28/01.

Furthermore, Enron related-party disclosures from Enron's previous Report on Form 10–K and Report on Form 10–Q were incorporated by reference into the following Registration Statements and Prospectuses for Enron securities offerings: the resale of zero coupon convertible senior notes, due 2021, filed 7/25/01; 7.875% notes due 6/15/03, filed

6/2/00; 8.375% notes due 5/23/05, filed 5/19/00; 7% exchangeable notes due 7/31/02, filed 8/11/99; 7.375% notes due 5/15/2019, filed 5/20/99; common stock, filed 2/12/99; 6.95% notes due 7/15/2028, filed 11/30/98; and floating notes due 3/30/00, filed 9/28/98. The disclosures consistently misrepresented that terms of Enron's transactions with related third parties were representative of terms that could have been obtained from independent third parties. Both Sherron Watkins' letter and the Powers' Report concluded that the transactions were not arm's length, lacked true economic import, and were such that no independent third party would have accepted.

* * *

More specifically, the complaint states that in Enron's Reports on Form 10–K for year-end 1997–2000, Vinson & Elkins approved a description of JEDI as an unconsolidated affiliate only 50% owned by Enron. In its Report on Form 10–K filed 3/30/00, Vinson & Elkins drafted and approved the following disclosure: "At December 31, 1999 JEDI held approximately 12 million shares of Enron Corp. common stock. The value of the Enron Corp. common stock has been hedged. In addition, an officer of Enron has invested in the limited partner of JEDI and from time to time acts as agent on behalf of the limited partner's management." These purported disclosures were false and misleading because Chewco, which was not independent of Enron, was not capitalized with outside equity at risk, but was capitalized by JEDI and an Enron guaranty. Enron did not disclose that Chewco was a limited partner of JEDI until Enron announced its catastrophic restatement on 11/8/01. Nor was it disclosed that JEDI's transactions were not true commercial, economic transactions comparable to those of independent third-parties in arm's-length bargains.

The complaint speaks to Vinson & Elkins' alleged false and misleading disclosures about JEDI/Chewco. In March 2001, Enron paid Michael Kopper and his domestic partner, William Dodson, $35 million in a "purchase" of Chewco's limited partnership interest in JEDI so that Kopper could buy Fastow's interest in the LJM partnerships. The deceptive disclosure[95] about the buyout, drafted and approved by Vinson & Elkins for inclusion in Enron's reports on Form 10–Q filed on 5/15/01 and 8/14/01, never stated that it was a deal among some Enron officers, Kopper and Fastow or that it included the $2.6 million gift to Kopper and Dodson. Moreover, the buyout was erroneously characterized as having a net positive effect on Enron's financial statements, when in

---

95. The disclosure was as follows:

In March 2001, Enron acquired the limited partner's interests in an unconsolidated equity affiliate, Joint Energy Development Investments Limited Partnership (JEDI), for $35 million. As a result of the acquisition, JEDI has been consolidated. JEDI's balance sheet as of the date of acquisition consisted of net assets of approximately $500 million, including an investment of 12 million shares of Enron common stock valued at approximately $785 million, merchant investments and other assets of approximately $670 million and third-party debt and debt owed to Enron of approximately $950 million. Enron repaid the third-party debt of approximately $620 million prior to March 31, 2001.

actuality the consolidation of JEDI resulted in a massive reduction in Enron's reported net income and shareholders' equity and a massive increase in its reported debt.

The complaint quotes the Powers' report regarding false and misleading disclosures relating to LJM and the Raptor entities that were drafted and approved by Vinson & Elkins:

> [T]hese disclosures were obtuse, did not communicate the essence of the transactions completely or clearly, and failed to convey the substance of what was going on between Enron and the partnerships. The disclosures also did not communicate the nature or extent of Fastow's financial interest in the LJM partnerships. This was the result of an effort to avoid disclosing Fastow's financial interest and, in some respects, to disguise their substance and import.

Tracking the language in the Powers' report, the complaint asserts that common to all Enron related-party disclosures, drafted and approved by Vinson & Elkins, was concealment of the following material matters known to Vinson & Elkins: (1) that the transactions were not true commercial, economic transactions comparable to those with independent third-parties; (2) the "disclosures" concealed the real substance and effect of the transactions on Enron and on its financial statements, e.g., that the transactions should have been consolidated on Enron's financial statements; and (3) they failed to disclose Fastow's actual financial interest in or compensation from the LJM partnerships. Instead the disclosures in SEC filings through the Class Period gave the impression that each transaction was fair to the company, not contrived, but made at arm's length as it would have been if made with an independent third party. In actuality the transactions, which were controlled only by Enron, Fastow or Kopper through the LJM entities, were bogus, contrived to enrich individual Defendants, and, according to the Powers-led special investigative committee, designed "to accomplish financial results, not achieve *bona fide* economic objectives or to transfer risk."[97] In nearly every transaction, Fastow or Kopper made millions of dollars

---

97. The complaint at 405–06 quotes additional critical passages from the Powers' report:

1. The Powers' report "sharply criticizes the firm for 'an absence of . . . objective and critical professional advice.'"

2. A number of transactions among the SPEs and partnerships "were implemented—improperly, as we are informed by our accounting advisors—to offset losses". They allowed Enron to conceal from the market very large losses resulting from Enron's merchant investments by creating an appearance that those investments were hedged . . . when in fact that third party was simply an entity in which only Enron had a substantial economic stake.

3. Vinson & Elkins "provided advice and documentation" for many of the partnership deals and "assisted Enron with the preparation of its disclosures of related-party transaction in the proxy statements and the footnotes to the financial statements in Enron's periodic SEC filings."

4. Enron's board and management "relied heavily on the perceived approval by Vinson & Elkins of the structure and disclosure of the transactions." It concludes that Vinson & Elkins "should have brought a stronger, more objective and more critical voice to the disclosure process."

while bearing little or no risk, and Enron obtained favorable financial-statement results while bearing all the risk.

* * *

In Enron's report on Form 10–Q, approved by Vinson & Elkins and filed on 8/14/01, a statement "disclosed" that Fastow, "who previously was the general partner of [the LJM] partnerships, sold all of his financial interests . . . and no longer has any management responsibilities for these entities." In actuality, Fastow sold his interest to Kopper, who was also closely connected to and controlled by Enron, so the LJM partnerships were no more legitimate than when Fastow owned them.

The complaint contends that Vinson & Elkins throughout the Class Period drafted and approved as adequate disclosure statements with false and misleading descriptions about related-party transactions using LJM and the Raptors. These include disclosures in Enron's Reports on Form 10–Q filed 8/16/99 and 11/15/99 that only relate to, but fail to identify, the Rhythms transactions:

> In June 1999, Enron entered into a series of transactions involving a third party and LJM Cayman, L.P. (LJM). LJM is a private investment company which engages in acquiring or investing primarily in energy related investments. A senior officer of Enron is managing member of LJM's general partner. The effect of the transactions was (i) Enron amended with the third party certain forward contracts to purchase shares of Enron common stock, resulting in Enron having forward contracts to purchase 3.3. million Enron common shares at the market price on that day, (ii) LJM received 3.4 million shares of Enron common stock subject to certain restrictions and (iii) Enron received a note receivable and a put option related to an investment held by Enron. Enron recorded the assets received and equity issued at estimated fair value. . . . Management believes that the terms of the transactions were reasonable and no less favorable than the terms of similar arrangements with unrelated third parties.

> The complaint charges that this "disclosure" was false and misleading because there was no true third party to give a stamp of legitimacy to the transaction, but only self-dealing: Fastow filled the shoes of the third party, and LJM's general partner was capitalized with Enron stock provided by Enron. Because it did not consolidate LJM, Enron was able to overstate its net income by $95 million in 1999 and by $8 million in 2000.

Similar oblique references are made in inadequate "disclosures" of bogus hedges involving the Raptors, the purported "third parties" that were actually entities created by Enron and LJM2 and capitalized with Enron's stock, while the Raptors' credit capacity was largely determined by the price of Enron stock. In these transactions, LJM2 received its profits and capital from the Raptors up front, before any ostensible hedging took place, so Enron was the only entity left with a stake in the purported counterparty. The complaint quotes from "disclosures" describing the Raptors' transactions with related parties, drafted and approved by Vinson & Elkins, made in Enron's reports on Form 10–Q, filed on 8/14/00 and 11/14/00, on Form 10–K filed on 4/01/01, and references to similar statements in reports on Form 10–Q filed on 5/15/01 and 8/14/01 and in a Proxy filed on 3/17/01. The complaint states that these alleged disclosures were false and misleading because (1) the "share settled options" were purchased by Enron when the transaction was actually based on a future material decrease in the price of Enron's stocks; (2) the disclosures of related party transaction did not disclose that Enron controlled the entities or vehicles; and (3) the transactions were structured to permit LJM2 to receive its profits and capital up front before any hedging (risk of loss), and because Enron carried the ultimate risk of the investment. These concealed matters, if disclosed, would have revealed that Enron was not dealing with valid SPEs and there was no real hedging since the hedges were of Enron investments with the value of Enron stock.

* * *

The complaint asserts that Vinson & Elkins also drafted and approved related-party disclosures concerning Enron's merchant assets sales and purchases that were false and misleading because they hid facts that would have demonstrated that Enron was playing a shell game to falsely inflate its 1999 net income by more than $130 million. The complaint quotes the related-party disclosures in Enron's report on Form 10–K filed on 3/30/00: "In the fourth quarter of 1999, LJM2, which has the same general partner as LJM, acquired, directly or indirectly, approximately $360 million of merchant assets and investments from Enron, on which Enron recognized pre-tax gains of approximately $16 million." Similar disclosures were made in Enron's report on Form 10–K, filed on 4/02/01: "In 1999, the Related Party acquired approximately $371 million, merchant assets and investments and other assets from Enron. Enron recognized pre-tax gains of approximately $16 million related to these transactions." A Proxy filed on 3/27/01 states, "[D]uring 2000, LJM2 sold to Enron certain merchant investment interests for a total consideration of approximately $76 million." Complaint at 423. Lead Plaintiff claims that these disclosures are false and misleading because Enron was merely buying back the same assets and investments that it was selling to Fastow. Sometimes the repurchase of assets was made within months, even before Enron filed its report on Form 10–K on 3/30/00 with the related-party disclosures indicating that Enron was selling the assets. Furthermore, in the third and fourth quarters of 1999, Enron sold seven assets to LJM to rid its balance sheet of debts before the end of the financial reporting period. After the close of the reporting period, Enron bought back five of the seven assets in the transactions referenced, including the sale in 9/99 and subsequent repurchase of Enron's stake in the Cuiaba, Brazil power plant construction; the sale on 12/22/99 and subsequent repurchase of ENA collateralized loan obligations; the sale on 12/21/99 and subsequent repurchase of Enron's interest in the Nowa Sarzyna, Poland power plant construction; the sale on 12/29/99 and subsequent repurchase of Enron's equity interest in MEGS LLC; and the sale in 5–6/00 and subsequent resale of dark fiber (Enron's EBS sold the dark fiber to LJM2 and then resold it for LJM2). The disclosures drafted and approved by Vinson & Elkins did not reveal that in each repurchase, the LJM partnerships profited by millions of dollars, even when the assets had lost value.

The Enron investigative committee led by Dean Powers further found, "The failure to set forth Fastow's compensation from the LJM transactions and the process leading to that decision raise substantial issues." The complaint asserts that Vinson & Elkins knew important facts about Fastow's interest in the LJM transactions but did not reveal them in related-party disclosures drafted and approved by Vinson & Elkins during the Class Period, in spite of specific requirements in SEC regulations that such economic interests be disclosed. Had these facts been disclosed, they would have alerted investors that Fastow and the LJM partnerships were paid to move debt off of Enron's financial statements and not as part of commercial transactions. As a specific example, the complaint focuses on the Rhythms transaction which, before the Proxy was filed on 5/02/00, was terminated by a $30 million payment to Fastow's Swap Sub. Enron's special investigative committee determined that the termination was effected on the following terms: the Rhythms options held by Fastow's Swap Sub. were terminated; Fastow's Swap Sub. returned 3.1 million Enron shares to Enron, but retained $3.75 million in cash received from LJM1; and Enron paid Fastow's Swap Sub. $16.7 million, which included $30 million, plus $500,000 accrued dividends on Enron's stock held by Swap Sub., less $3.75 million in cash in Swap Sub., less $10.1 million in principal and interest on a loan Enron made to Swap Sub. just before the transaction's termination.

The complaint points out that although Sherron Watkins' August 2001 letter to Ken Lay represented that Vinson & Elkins had been involved in the fraud and had a clear conflict of interest, Lay still turned to top Vinson & Elkins partners to find out how to cover up the allegations. Furthermore, Vinson & Elkins despite this obvious conflict, agreed to conduct an investigation into the charges and to issue a letter or report dismissing the allegations of fraud that Vinson & Elkins knew were true. Vinson & Elkins also agreed not to "second guess" the accounting work or judgments of Arthur Andersen and to limit its inquiry to top level executives at Enron. Vinson & Elkins' review took place between August 15 and October 15, 2001.

The complaint also quotes from a letter sent on August 29, 2001 by a management level employee at Enron's EES operation to Enron's Board of Directors detailing concealed losses and misrepresentations at Enron's EES. The complaint claims the letter describing another area of fraud caused "an explosion" at Enron.

* * *

During its investigation, according to the complaint, Vinson & Elkins only interviewed top level executives that Vinson & Elkins knew were involved in the fraud and would deny it. On October 15, 2001 the law firm issued a letter to Enron dismissing all of Sherron Watkins' allegations even though Vinson & Elkins knew they were true from its own involvement. The letter is quoted in part in the complaint [emphasis added by the complaint]:

> You requested that Vinson & Elkins L.L.P. ("V & E") conduct an investigation into certain allegations initially made on an ***anonymous*** basis by an employee of Enron Corp. ("Enron"). Those allegations question the propriety of Enron's accounting treatment and public disclosures for certain deconsolidated entities known as Condor or Whitewing and certain transactions with a related party, LJM, and particularly transactions with LJM known as Raptor vehicles. The anonymous employee later identified herself as Sherron Watkins, who met with Kenneth L. Lay, Chairman and Chief Executive Officer of Enron, for approximately one hour to express her concerns and provided him with materials to supplement her initial anonymous letter....

> In general, the scope of V & E's undertaking was to review the allegations raised by Ms. Watkins' ***anonymous*** letter and supplemental materials to conduct an investigation to determine whether the facts she has raised ***warrant further independent legal or accounting review.***

> By way of background, some of the supplemental materials provided by Ms. Watkins proposed a series of steps for addressing the problems she perceived, which included retention of independent legal counsel to conduct a wide-spread investigation, and the engagement of independent auditors, apparently for the purpose of analyzing transactions in detail and opining as to the propriety of the accounting treatment employed by Enron and its auditors Arthur Andersen L.L.P. ("AA"). ***In preliminary discussions with you, it was decided that our initial approach would not involve the second guessing of the accounting advice and treatment provided by AA, that there would be no detailed analysis of each and every transaction and that there would be no full scale discovery style inquiry. Instead the inquiry would be confined to a determination whether the anonymous letter and supplemental materials raised new factual information that would warrant a broader investigation.***

> * * *

Interviews were also conducted with various Enron personnel based either on their connection with the transactions involving Condor/Whitewing, LJM and Raptor, or because they were identified in materials provided by Ms. Watkins as persons who might share her concerns. Those persons interviewed were: Andrew S. Fastow, Executive Vice President and Chief Financial Officer; Richard B.

Causey, Executive Vice President and Chief Accounting Officer; Richard B. Buy, Executive Vice President and Chief Risk Officer; Greg Whalley, President and Chief Operating Office (formerly Chairman of Enron Wholesale); Jeffrey McMahon, President and Chief Executive Officer, Enron Industrial Markets (formerly Treasurer of Enron); Jordan H. Mintz, Vice President and General Counsel of Enron Global Finance; Mark E. Koenig, Executive Vice President, Investor Relations; Paula H. Rieker, Managing Director, Investor Relations; and Sherron Watkins, the author of the anonymous letter and supplemental materials. Interviews were also conducted with David B. Duncan and Debra A. Cash, both partners with AA assigned to the Enron audit engagement.

* * *

In summary, none of the individuals interviewed could identify any transaction between Enron and LJM that was not reasonable from Enron's standpoint or that was contrary to Enron's best interests . . . .

As stated at the outset, the decision was made early in our preliminary investigation not to engage an independent accounting firm to second guess the accounting advice and audit treatments provided by AA. Based on interviews with representatives of AA and Mr. Causey, all material facts of the Condor/Whitewing and Raptor vehicles, as well as other transactions involving LJM, appeared to have been disclosed to and reviewed by AA. In this regard, AA reviewed the LJM solicitation materials and partnership agreement to assure that certain safeguards were provided that would permit LJM to be a source of third party equity in transactions conducted with Enron. AA likewise reviewed specific transactions between Enron and LJM to assure that LJM had sufficient equity in transaction to justify the accounting and audit principles being applied.

* * *

Enron and AA representatives both acknowledge that the accounting treatment on the Condor/Whitewing and Raptor transactions is creative and aggressive, but no one has reason to believe that it is inappropriate from a technical standpoint. In this regard, AA consulted with its senior technical experts in its Chicago office regarding the technical accounting treatment on the Condor/Whitewing and Raptor transactions, and the AA partners on the Enron account consulted with AA's senior practice committee in Houston on other aspects of the transactions. Enron may also take comfort from AA's audit opinion and report to the Audit Committee which implicitly approves the transaction involving Condor/Whitewing and Raptor structures in the context of the approval of Enron financial statements.

* * *

Notwithstanding the expression of concern in Ms. Watkins' anonymous letter and supporting materials regarding the adequacy of Enron's disclosures as to the Condor/Whitewing and Raptor vehicles (which, to a large extent, reflect her opinion), AA is comfortable with the disclosure in the footnotes to the financials describing the Condor/Whitewing and Raptor structures and other relationships and transactions with LJM. AA points out that the transactions involving Condor/Whitewing are disclosed in aggregate terms in the unconsolidated equity footnote and that the transactions with LJM, including the Raptor transactions, are disclosed in aggregate terms in the related party transactions footnote to the financials.

The concern with adequacy of disclosures is that one can always argue in hindsight that disclosures contained in proxy solicitations, management's discussion and analysis and financial footnotes could be more detailed. *In this regard, it is our understanding that Enron's practice is to provide its financial statements and disclosure statements to V & E with a relatively short time frame with which to respond with comments.*

* * *

Based on the findings and conclusions set forth with respect to each of the four areas of primary concern discussed above, the facts disclosed through our preliminary investigation do not, in our judgment, warrant a further widespread investigation by independent counsel and auditors....

... Finally we believe that some response should be provided to Ms. Watkins to assure her that her concerns were thoroughly reviewed, analyzed, and although found not to raise new or undisclosed information, were given serious consideration.

We have previously reported verbally to Mr. Lay and you regarding our investigation and conclusions and, at your request, have reported the same information to Robert K. Jaedicke, in his capacity of Chairman of the Audit Committee of Enron's Board of Directors. At Dr. Jaedicke's request, we gave a verbal summary of our review and conclusions to the full Audit Committee.[103]

103. The Court observes that this letter alone raises issues of a serious conflict of interest and the propriety of Vinson & Elkins' undertaking this investigation on behalf of Enron. In light of the fact that Enron was Vinson & Elkins' biggest client and of Vinson & Elkins' extensive involvement in the structuring and documenting of the specific transactions with the SPEs that Lead Plaintiff has identified as devices and contrivances manipulated to defraud investors, commentator Roger C. Cramton, evaluating the ethical and legal implications of the law firm's investigation, has opined, "The investigation required V & E to assess objectively, as if it had not been there at all, the soundness and propriety of its prior representations. Thus the situation presented a huge conflict between Enron's presumed interest in an objective investigation and V & E's own interests.... [T]here remains a serious question whether [Enron's] consent was a valid one, and even if it was, whether ... the objective standard that the lawyer reasonably believe the representa-

The complaint recites that although Lay wanted to fire Watkins, he and Vinson & Elkins agreed that discharge would be a mistake and would lead to a wrongful termination suit, disclosing Watkins' allegations about transactions at Enron. So she was shifted to another position at Enron where she would have less exposure to information damaging to Enron.

b. Kirkland & Ellis

The complaint alleges that Kirkland & Ellis actively engaged in the scheme to defraud and course of business that operated as a fraud on Enron investors. Kirkland & Ellis began working with Fastow, Enron, and Vinson & Elkins in the early '90's to create and use off balance sheet investment partnerships and SPEs that allowed Enron to engage in transactions designed to increase or maintain its credit rating by artificially inflating its profits and moving debt off of its balance sheet. The law firm's relationship with Fastow began in the 1980's when Fastow worked for Continental Bank in Chicago and intensified during the Class Period at Enron; in light of this close relationship, Jordon Mintz, Vice President and General Counsel of Enron Global Finance, referred to the firm as "Fastow's attorneys."

tion will not be adversely affected by the lawyer's conflict of interest ... was satisfied." Cramton, 1324 PLI/Corp at 854. Cramton critically observes,

In any event, there remains a serious doubt whether V & E's conflict would not "adversely affect" its performance of the investigation. V & E's opinion letter stated that the Enron transactions it facilitated and approved were "creative and aggressive," suggesting that they went to the outer edge of legality. The letter also concluded that "because of bad cosmetics involving the LJM entities and Raptor transactions, coupled with the poor performance of the merchant investment assets placed in those vehicles and the decline in the value of Enron stock, there is a serious risk of adverse publicity and litigation." It was reasonably foreseeable, as has happened, that the litigation would include V & E as a defendant and that Enron officers, directors, and other co-defendants would defend themselves by blaming V & E for giving poor advice. Under these circumstances, the conflict appears to be too severe to be undertaken: a reasonable lawyer would not believe that his representation would not be adversely affected.

... The adequacy of the investigation is also questionable. V & E interviewed only seven high-level officials, most of whom were directly implicated in the self-dealing and fiduciary violations raised by the Watkins allegations. V & E relied on the denials of wrong doing by those officers and on the fact that none of the persons interviewed could identify a specific transaction that was illegal. Although McMahon, one of those interviewed, mentioned nine lower-level employees who might be good sources of information concerning Fastow's self-dealing, V & E failed to interview any of them. V & E was informed of the "mistake" that was made concerning the failure of the Chewco transaction to meet the required degree of outside equity participation, but never pursued the issue. The investigation as a whole, when compared to the subsequent investigation by the board's special committee, using the services of Wilmer, Cutler & Pickering, appears perfunctory. As the Powers Report stated, the result of the V & E investigation "was largely predetermined by the scope and nature of the investigation and the process employed." It was performed with "insufficient skepticism." ... There is a serious question of whether adequate representation was provided to the entity client, as distinct from satisfying the manager's apparent desire to have a protective document. Id. at 854. Cramton closes with the suggestion that these issues regarding the investigation might provide grounds not only for a malpractice claim against the law firm by Enron, but, along with other allegations, might give rise to a suit by shareholders and employees charging that Vinson & Elkins "participated as a principal along with Enron managers and directors and others in intentional violations of the federal securities acts." Id.

Lead Plaintiff asserts that Enron hand-picked Kirkland & Ellis to provide ostensibly "independent" representation for Chewco, JEDI, LJM1, LJM2, and other SPEs, but in actuality that the firm was selected by Fastow because it was willing to take direction from Fastow and Enron. Along with Arthur Andersen, Vinson & Elkins, and Enron's banks, Kirkland & Ellis under Enron's direction participated in structuring the manipulative devices at the heart of the scheme, including the partnerships and SPEs (LJM1 and 2, Chewco and the Raptors) and their related transactions to present a false picture of Enron's financial condition and results, with the law firm's full knowledge of that purpose. In addition to structuring the entities, Kirkland & Ellis allegedly participated in the monetization of assets, in the preparation of partnership and loan agreements for Chewco, LJM1, and LJM2, and in the offering and sale of partnership interests in LJM2 through private placement memoranda. The firm also allegedly generated false legal opinions about the structure, legality and *bona fides* of the SPEs and their transactions, representing that these were legitimate business deals. The complaint charges that Kirkland & Ellis issued opinions related to numerous transactions and entities, including the following: JEDI I, Big River LLC, Little River LLC, LJM1, LJM2, Raptor I, Raptor II (Timberwolf), Raptor III (Condor), Raptor IV (Bobcat), Honer, Chewco, Bob West Treasure LLC, Cortez LLC, ENA CLO, Yosemite Securities, Southampton Place, Condor, SONR#1 LLC, and SONR#2 LLC. The firm's opinions were essential for effecting the transactions. Nevertheless, because the transactions were shams to inflate Enron's financial performance while favored insiders siphoned off Enron's assets and because the transactions were conducted on terms inconsistent with disclosures being made to investors by Enron, Vinson & Elkins, the banks, and Arthur Andersen, Kirkland & Ellis' opinions were also false. Kirkland & Ellis knew that the SPEs were contrived, manipulative devices that were not independent of Enron, but, like Kirkland & Ellis, acting under the control and direction of Fastow, Kopper, Skilling, Lay and other Enron officials. These Enron insiders directed the SPEs without regard for the legal or economic interests or rights of the SPEs, in whose behalf Kirkland & Ellis was purportedly served as independent counsel. Kirkland & Ellis received tens of millions of dollars in fees for its work, and most of that money was paid directly to it by Enron, even though the law firm was supposed to be representing entities independent of Enron and with economic interests adverse to those of Enron.

More specifically, the complaint asserts that when Enron was unable to find a legitimate buyer for the outside investor's interest in JEDI in 1997 in time for year-end reporting, Kirkland & Ellis, directed by Fastow and Enron, along with Vinson & Elkins, Fastow and Kopper, created Chewco (controlled by Enron and Michael Kopper), Big River Funding and Little River Funding to purchase that stake in JEDI. Kirkland & Ellis did so even though it was supposed to be providing independent representation of Chewco and its equity investors. Kirkland & Ellis knew that Chewco lacked an independent outside investor with a 3% stake, required for independent third-party status for Chewco, and that Barclays' loan of $240 million to Chewco (guaranteed by Enron) and loans to straw parties by means of a $6 million cash deposit with Barclays to provide the money for the equity investment in Chewco, were an improper effort to circumvent that requirement for a valid SPE. Kirkland & Ellis and Vinson & Elkins prepared the documentation for Chewco's financing and falsified the documents to make it appear that Chewco was independent. They also prepared a side agreement, dated 12/30/97, reflecting that Enron would provide the necessary cash to fund Chewco through clandestine reserve accounts for Big River Funding and Little River Funding. The Kopper/Enron side agreement drawn up by the two firms indicates that no outside equity was used to fund Chewco and therefore it was not a viable SPE, but merely a manipulative device to further the fraud.

Kirkland & Ellis did more to conceal the real situation. If, as originally intended, Fastow were to have managerial control of Chewco, that interest would have to be disclosed in Enron's SEC filings and the non-arm's-length nature of the deal would be revealed. Kirkland & Ellis therefore arranged for Kopper, Fastow's subordinate, to manage the SPE.

In addition, during December 1997, Kirkland & Ellis restructured the transaction to avoid disclosure of Enron's financial relationship to Chewco at year end. Kirkland & Ellis converted the general partner of Chewco from a limited liability company to a limited partnership and made Kopper the manager of the general partner instead of Fastow. Although Kopper expressed concern about the conflict of interest because he was simultaneously an Enron employee and the owner of both Chewco's general partner and of the equity of limited partner Big River Funding, Kirkland & Ellis went ahead anyway. Furthermore, Kirkland & Ellis, with Arthur Andersen, Fastow, Kopper and Vinson & Elkins, participated in the concealment of Kopper's managerial position with Chewco by "transferring" Kopper's ownership interest in Big River Funding and Little River Funding to Kopper's domestic partner, Dodson, and completing the purchase of the 50% interest in JEDI by Chewco. Kirkland & Ellis knew that Chewco/JEDI was not a valid SPE, should have been consolidated, and was now available for Enron to use in more non-arm's-length transactions, which the law firm would also help structure from 1998–2001, to create billions of dollars of sham profits for Enron and conceal the true nature of its indebtedness.

Even though Kirkland & Ellis was supposed to be providing independent representation of the LJM partnerships and their SPEs, Kirkland & Ellis participated in creating, structuring, reviewing and approving the two LJM partnerships, which served as manipulative devices for Fastow and others to enrich themselves and for Enron to inflate its financial results. Kirkland & Ellis knew the partnerships were established to allow Enron to effect transactions that it would have been unable to accomplish with independent third-parties. Kirkland & Ellis was involved in transactions between the LJMs and Enron or its affiliates that occurred close to the end of financial reporting periods to perpetuate the alleged Ponzi scheme, including Enron's sale of interests in seven assets near the end of the third and fourth quarters of 1999, five of which Enron bought back after the close of the period as previously agreed among the parties, and on all of which the LJMs made profits even when the value of the assets had declined. The firm participated in June 1999 in structuring LJM1's purchase of an equity interest in Enron's Cuiaba power plant in Brazil, which was burdened with substantial debt that Enron did not want on its balance sheet. Enron sold to LJM1, with a promise to make LJM1 whole, a 13% stake in the Cuiaba plant, effective 9/99, and thus reduced Enron's ownership below the level at which it would have to consolidate its interest, so that Enron could once again "cook its books," but repurchased it in August 2001. The transaction was neither arm's length nor *bona fide*. Kirkland & Ellis also helped structure sham hedging transactions, including in 6/99 the Enron Rhythms stock deal, and transactions involving Enron's merchant assets with the Raptors in 2000–01. Kirkland & Ellis also helped to create the documentation to enable the banks to advance essentially all the money needed to fund LJM2 just before year-end 1999 to avoid reporting a very bad quarter for Enron, as well as to write the offering memorandum for LJM2, with its invitation to benefit from insider self-dealing transactions. In accordance with direction from Enron or Fastow, the firm also helped structure transactions and provided opinions required for year-end deals between LJM2 and Enron before the close of 1999 so that Enron could report strong growth: the CLOs, the Nowa Sarzyna (Poland Power Plant), MEGS LLC, and Yosemite. These deals were then reversed in the first quarter of 2000, reflecting that they were merely manipulative devices and contrivances designed by Kirkland & Ellis and others to manipulate Enron's financial results.

* * *

On March 20, 2000, with Fastow and Kopper, Kirkland & Ellis created a partnership agreement for Southampton Place L.P., with its general partner being Big Doe LLC, and funded it with $70,000 contributed by several Enron employees (Glisan, Mordaunt, Lynn and Patel) for the purpose of acquiring part of the interest held in LJM1 by an existing limited partner. Glisan even objected to Kirkland & Ellis that the transaction should be accounted for as a related-party transaction and should be disclosed. To further the fraudulent scheme, however, the law firm opined that even though these Enron employees were involved, Southampton's transaction with LJM1 and/or Enron did not have to be disclosed.

In May 2000, to generate revenue in Enron's fiber optic business (EBS) so that Enron could meet its earnings estimates for the quarter, when no legitimate purchaser could be found Fastow and Kirkland & Ellis structured a sale of Enron's dark fiber optic cable to LMJ2 for $100 million even though it was not worth even close to that amount. A second deal was effected in the third quarter of 2000 for more than $300 million so that Enron could make its numbers.

During 2000 Kirkland & Ellis and Vinson & Elkins structured increasingly aggressive SPEs to perpetuate the alleged Ponzi scheme. Functioning as both Fastow's personal counsel and as counsel to LJM2, Kirkland & Ellis devised mechanisms for Enron to abuse mark-to-market accounting to create sham income through the four Raptor entities, which were created by Kirkland & Ellis working with Fastow, Arthur Andersen, and Vinson & Elkins. Kirkland & Ellis knew the transactions were structured so that if the value of Enron's stock fell, the SPEs would be unable to meet their obligations and the sham hedges with Enron stock would fail.

In late 2000 and in early 2001, the Raptor SPEs lacked sufficient credit to pay Enron on the hedges and Enron faced having to record a "credit reserve" that would reveal the change in value of its merchant investments. Moreover by year-end 2000 two Raptor SPEs were in danger of coming unwound because of insufficient credit capacity to support their credit obligations. If that happened Enron would have to take a multi-million dollar charge against earnings, which would expose the earlier falsification of Enron's financial results, cause its stock price to plunge, and activate the stock issuance triggers, i.e., precipitate a death spiral for the Ponzi scheme. To avoid this impending catastrophe, Kirkland & Ellis helped restructure and capitalize the Raptor SPEs at the end of 2000 by transferring even more shares of Enron stock to them. Again in 2001, to avoid taking a pre-tax charge against Enron's earnings of more than $500 million because of a credit capacity shortfall by Raptor entities and to conceal substantial losses in Enron's merchant investments, Kirkland & Ellis again helped restructure Raptor vehicles by having Enron transfer to them just before year's end more than $800 million of contracts to receive Enron's stock, with no consideration and in violation of accounting rules.

Kirkland & Ellis also participated in the New Power transaction by involvement in the creation of the Hawaii 125–0 SPE, which the law firm knew was financed by a $125 million "loan" from the banks that were guaranteed against loss through a "total return swap" by Enron.

Finally, Kirkland & Ellis participated in Enron's misleading disclosures. Indeed, near the close of the Class Period, the law firm admitted to a senior Enron employee responsible for preparing Enron's SEC disclosures that there was no precedent for the law firm's rationalization for not disclosing various LJMs and LJM transactions. Kirkland & Ellis reviewed the SEC filings by Enron and knew that the related party transactions were unfair to Enron contrary to its false assertion that the transactions were on terms similar to those it could have obtained with independent third parties. Kirkland & Ellis continued to work on restructuring LJM2 in May 2001 to avoid having to disclose that SPE under Regulation S–K. Indeed throughout the Class Period the law firm evaded or finagled applicable disclosure requests by various means, including having Fastow and Kopper sell some of their ownership interests to others. One senior Enron employee responsible for Enron's SEC disclosures was so suspicious of Kirkland & Ellis that it hired another law firm to review Kirkland & Ellis' work.

* * *

III.   Motions to Dismiss and the Court's Rulings

A.   Defendants' Common Objections

A number of Defendants argue that Lead Plaintiff's allegations that Defendants knew of the Ponzi scheme and yet poured millions of dollars into it or risked their reputations to conceal the scheme merely for fees, payments and profits, and subsequently, once caught in the scheme, shored it up in order to limit their exposure to liability and obtain what payments they could on Enron's debts to them, are inherently irrational, implausible, and/or illogical and the alleged actions are against Defendants' own self-interest. This Court notes that what may have been implausible two or three years ago is hardly so today, in light of a plethora of revelations, investigations, evidence, indictments, guilty pleas, and confessions of widespread corporate corruption and fraud by companies, auditors, brokerage houses, and banks. Lining one's pockets with gold, at the expense of investors, employees, and the public, appears too often to be a dominating ambition, and public scepticism about the market is very prevalent.

The third-party entities have objected with justification to the undifferentiated, boiler-plate allegations repetitively applied to all or many defendants or with generalized references to "the bank defendants" or "the law firm defendants," without the requisite entity-specific and particularized factual allegations for pleading fraud under § 10(b), as required by Rule 9(b) and the PSLRA. They also criticize claims of misconduct based on what are common, legitimate business actions or practices (e.g., loans, commodity swaps, passive investments, underwriting securities offerings, regular working relationships with a company's executives, issuance of analyst reports, and desire to earn profits) that are not inherently improper or fraudulent. This Court responds that the activities must be viewed in context, i.e., within the totality of surrounding circumstances, to determine whether they are merely ordinary and legitimate acts or contrivances and deceptive devices used to defraud. Moreover it is fully aware that more is needed than conclusory allegations to defeat a motion to dismiss under § 10(b) and Rule 10b–5.

Emphasizing the complaint's reliance on language like "assisting," "participating in," "helped," and "complicity in," the motions also argue that, at most, Plaintiff in essence is charging these third-party defendants with aiding and abetting violations that are barred in claims under § 10(b) and Rule 10b–5 by *Central Bank*. Defendants argue that they made no public misrepresentations or omissions in misreporting Enron's financial condition, but point the finger at Enron as the responsible party for any such conduct. Moreover some Defendants have argued that they can only be liable under § 10(b) and Rule 10b–5 for a material misrepresentation or omission.

The Court has indicated its interpretation of and the test it has selected for liability under *Central Bank* and will apply both to determine whether the allegations against each Defendant constitute a primary violation or merely an aiding and abetting violation. See "Applicable Law" section of this memorandum and order. The Court has also indicated that in addition to claims under Rule 10b–5(b), plaintiffs may sue for securities law violations under Rule 10b–5(a) and (c) for conduct other than material misrepresentations or omissions.

* * *

b.   The Law Firms

(i) Vinson & Elkins

Contrary to Vinson & Elkins' contention, the situation alleged in the consolidated complaint is not one in which Vinson & Elkins merely represented and kept confidential the interests of its client, which has "the final authority to control the contents of the registration statement, other filing, or prospectus." Instead, the complaint alleges that the two were in league, with others, participating in a plan, with each participant making material misrepresentations or omissions or employing a device, scheme or artifice to defraud, or engaging in an act, practice or course of business that operated as a fraud, in order to establish and perpetuate a Ponzi scheme that was making them all very rich.

Vinson & Elkins was necessarily privy to its client's confidences and intimately involved in and familiar with the creation and structure of its numerous businesses, and thus, as a law firm highly sophisticated in commercial matters, had to know of the alleged ongoing illicit and fraudulent conduct. Among the complaint's specific allegations of acts in furtherance of the scheme are that the firm's involvement in negotiation and structuring of the illicit partnerships and off-the-books SPEs, whose formation documentation it drafted, as well as that of the subsequent transactions of these entities. It advised making Kopper manager of Chewco so that Enron's involvement in and control of the SPE would not have to be disclosed, drafted "true sales" opinions that Lead Plaintiff asserts were essential to effect many of the allegedly fraudulent transactions. Vinson & Elkins was materially involved in the New Power IPO, and it structured and provided advice on the Mahonia trades, all actions constituting primary violations of § 10(b). In other words, it "effected the very" deceptive devices and contrivances that were the heart of the alleged Ponzi scheme. According to the allegations in the complaint, Vinson & Elkins chose to engage in illegal activity for and with its client in return for lucrative fees. Contrary to the Rules of Professional Conduct, it did not resign and thereby violated its professional principles and ethics. Nevertheless, had Vinson & Elkins remained silent publicly, the attorney/client relationship and the traditional rule of privity for suit against lawyers might protect Vinson & Elkins from liability to nonclients for such alleged actions on its client's (and its own) behalf.

But the complaint goes into great detail to demonstrate that Vinson & Elkins did not remain silent, but chose not once, but frequently, to make statements to the public about Enron's business and financial situation. Moreover in light of its alleged voluntary, essential, material, and deep involvement as a primary violator in the ongoing Ponzi scheme, Vinson & Elkins was not merely a drafter, but essentially a co-author of the documents it created for public consumption concealing its own and other participants' actions. Vinson & Elkins made the alleged fraudulent misrepresentations to potential investors, credit agencies, and banks, whose support was essential to the Ponzi scheme, and Vinson & Elkins deliberately or with severe recklessness directed those public statements toward them in order to influence those investors to purchase more securities, credit agencies to keep Enron's credit high, and banks to continue providing loans to keep the Ponzi scheme afloat. Therefore Vinson & Elkins had a duty to be accurate and truthful. Lead Plaintiff has alleged numerous inadequate disclosures by Vinson & Elkins that breached that duty.

* * *

Vinson & Elkins protests that its purported "whitewash" investigation and report in the wake of Sherron Watkins' August 1999 memorandum were not disclosed to the public until after Enron waived the attorney/client privilege and produced the report for Congressional hearings in 2002, after the Class Period ended, and thus cannot be the basis of a § 10(b) misrepresentation claim by the investors. Nevertheless the investigation and report can serve as the basis of a § 10(b) and Rule 10b–5(a) or (c) claim alleging use of a device, scheme or artifice to defraud or engagement in an act, practice or course of business that operated as a fraud in the perpetuation of the Ponzi scheme.

Furthermore, the complaint references, summarizes, and quotes from the Powers' investigative committee report the negatively critical findings about Vinson & Elkins' substantial and dubious role in the events of the Class Period, as delineated in the complaint, which support Lead Plaintiff's allegations.

For these reasons the Court finds that Lead Plaintiff has stated claims under § 10(b) against Vinson & Elkins.

(ii) Kirkland & Ellis

The Court agrees with Kirkland & Ellis that Lead Plaintiff has only alleged that Kirkland & Ellis represented some of the illicit Enron-controlled, non-public SPEs and partnerships that Enron, but not Kirkland & Ellis, used for transactions (devices or contrivances) to hide its debt and record sham profits, disguising its true financial condition, and performed legal services on their and Enron's behalf. The complaint does not allege that Kirkland & Ellis invested in any partnership or profited from any dealings with Enron other than performing routine legal services for the partnerships. All the assertions against the firm are conclusory and general. While the allegations against Kirkland & Ellis may indicate that it acted with significant conflicts of interests and breached professional ethical standards, unlike its claims against Vinson & Elkins, Lead Plaintiff has not alleged that Kirkland & Ellis exceeded activities would be protected by an attorney client relationship and the traditional rule that only a client can sue for malpractice because it never made any material misrepresentations or omissions to investors or the public generally that might make it liable to nonclients under § 10(b). Any documents that it drafted were for private transactions between Enron and the SPEs and the partnerships and were not included in or drafted for any public disclosure or shareholder solicitation. Any opinion letters that the firm wrote are not alleged to have reached the plaintiffs nor been drafted for the benefit of the plaintiffs. It was not Enron's counsel for either its securities filings or its SEC filings. Thus the Court grants Kirkland & Ellis' motion to dismiss.

Robert J. Haft & Michele H. Hudson, Liability of Attorneys and Accountants for Securities Transactions

(2004–2005 Edition)

Cease-and-desist orders against attorneys: The *Feldman* and *Costanza* cases

In 1990, Section 8A of the Securities Act, Section 21C of the Exchange Act, and analogous Section 9(f) of the Investment Company Act and Section 203(k) of the Investment Advisers Act were added by the Securities Enforcement Remedies and Penny Stock Reform Act of 1990. These sections grant the Commission authority to issue cease-and-desist orders against any person (not limited to regulated persons) that is violating, has violated, or is about to violate any provision of the federal securities laws, and any other person that is, was, or would be a cause of such violation due to an act or omission the person knew or should have known would contribute to such violation.

In 1993, Feldman, a New York attorney, consented to the SEC's issuance of findings and a cease-and-desist order pursuant to Section 8A of the Securities Act. The SEC entered findings that Feldman, in his capacity as an attorney, aided and abetted and caused violations of the registration requirements of Section 5 of the Securities Act, and ordered him to permanently cease and desist from committing or causing any violation or future violations of Section 5. This proceeding represents the first time the SEC has used its cease-and-desist authority to institute proceedings against an attorney in connection with a client's alleged violations.

In 1985, three Pakistani banks contacted Feldman's firm in connection with the offer of rupee-denominated foreign exchange bearer certificates, issued and granted by Pakistan. In June 1985, Feldman's firm was presented with a request to determine what legal restrictions would apply, including restrictions imposed by "exchange or securities authorities," and to make arrangements to comply.

In July 1985, Feldman received a handwritten note from an officer of one of the banks informing him of advice from the Commission staff that registration of the certificates was required, and asking him to determine "precisely what forms need to be filed with the SEC." Nevertheless, Feldman did not take any steps to effect registration. In December 1985 and again in January 1986, Feldman informed the legal department of one Pakistani bank that the offer of the certificates did not involve securities and that their offer and sale did not require approval by the SEC. He advised that only the approval of the New York Superintendent of Banks (NYSB) was required.

After obtaining such approval, the banks commenced sales of the unregistered certificates. In 1986, one of the banks applied to the Office of the Comptroller of the Currency for permission to sell the certificates in the District of Columbia. The OCC responded that the certificates "may be subject to registration under the securities laws," and sent a copy of its response to the NYSB. Feldman wrote to the NYSB arguing that the certificates were not required to be registered under the securities laws. He also reported that one of the banks had requested SEC comments on that question, but had received "no written response." He failed to mention the SEC's oral response. Feldman did not respond to the OCC, advising the bank to abandon its application to sell certificates in D.C., since it would "open a can of worms."

The SEC issued findings that Feldman had "no basis" for his statement that the certificates were not securities and were therefore not covered by the registration requirements of Section 5. In addition to stating that Feldman had no experience in the practice of securities law and that he had notice that the certificates should be registered, the SEC found that he did not perform any legal research prior to reaching his conclusion, or consult with an attorney experienced in securities-related matters.

The Commission essentially held an attorney responsible for a client's noncompliance, based on facts that sound more like negligence and malpractice than aiding and abetting. Arguably, *Feldman* is not based on mere negligence. Feldman may have been more than simply wrong in his advice. He learned of a contrary Commission staff view and did nothing to address the issue, which had been pointedly raised. The allegations also suggest that he was reckless, and that he might be viewed as having taken an active role in furthering the violation. A member of the staff of the Commission stated that the Commission brought the *Feldman* proceeding based on its belief that the attorney "did what he did understanding he was engaged in a course of wrongful conduct and not because he in good faith reached an erroneous conclusion." On the other hand, the "should have known" language in the 1990 cease-and-desist provisions (including Section 8A of the Securities

Act) may support an interpretation that negligence alone suffices, and that is the basis for *Feldman*.

In 1999, the commission commenced another administrative cease and desist order proceeding against Jean Constanza, bond counsel for Orange County, California, in connection with eight note offerings. Constanza settled the proceeding without admitting or denying the Commission's Findings that she negligently participated in drafting municipal offering documents which omitted material information about the risks of the Orange County securities and that she negligently opined that the notes were exempt from federal taxation without disclosing the risks that the notes might lose that status. The Commission held that "Constanza, through negligent conduct, violated sections 17(a)(2) and (3) of the Securities Act in the offer and sale of the Notes."

The Commission's order found that Constanza knew or should have known that the Official Statements omitted material information that "she knew or reasonably should have known ... about the [risky investment] Pools, the Notes' interest rate and [that] the tax exempt status of the Tax Exempt Offerings could have been jeopardized." *Constanza* unambiguously utilized a negligence standard. The SEC staff has publicly made it clear that it intends to pursue other securities offering counsel based on negligence, when such counsel becomes aware of red flags which should trigger a duty to investigate, and, if necessary, disclose.

Since *Carter & Johnson*, the successive General Counsels of the Commission have followed an informal practice of only bringing Rule 2(e) proceedings against attorneys already enjoined or convicted of securities law violations. However, this practice may not survive the Sarbanes-Oxley Act (2002). Apparently, the Office of General Counsel perceives no such restraint with respect to cease-and-desist proceedings against attorneys.

SEC General Counsel David Becker, in response to a hypothetical suggestion at a conference in 2000 that the staff use "cease and desist [proceedings] against attorneys under a negligence standard," reportedly stated that "[i]t may well be something that we ought to think about" and that such a proceeding "could provide a safety valve" in terms of settling cases.

PROBLEMS

1.*   In September 2004, Raven Hill Imports, Inc., a large wine importer whose stock is listed on the NASDAQ Stock Market, filed its annual report on Form 10-K with the SEC. In the MD&A section, Raven Hill stated that based upon (1) its unusually large existing inventory of fine French vintages and (2) orders that it and other importers had received over the past six months signaling a sharp increase in demand for such vintages, Raven Hill expected earnings for the next three quarters to be substantially higher than

* Adapted from James D. Cox, Robert W. Hillman & Donald C. Langevoort, Securities   Regulation: Cases and Materials (4th ed. 2004).

the present quarter. The 10-K was prepared by Raven Hill's outside law firm of which you are a partner on the basis of information supplied by Raven Hill personnel.

Two months later, Raven Hill officers discovered an ongoing scheme of employee theft and misappropriation of inventory in its major warehouse. The scheme was facilitated through the creative piling of boxes in the warehouse and the use of false statements in the inventory control system. One obvious consequence of this scheme is that Raven Hill's inventory was substantially less than announced, and the expectation of an earnings increase is no longer realistic.

What exposure does your law firm and/or the lawyers who prepared the disclosure face?

2. Assume that the senior antitrust partner of your law firm, a lifelong friend of Raven Hill's CEO, is director of Raven Hill and that several senior executive officers of the company were deeply involved in the theft of the wines, constituting about 35% of Raven Hill's total inventory. After a full investigation of the theft, the board has decided that, given the delicate position of the company, Raven Hill should not disclose the involvement of these officers immediately. The board reached this decision because Raven Hill is currently negotiating a line of credit with a major bank. The proceeds from this line of credit had originally been intended to finance expanding Raven Hill's inventory, but, after the theft, it will be used largely to replace the stolen inventory. The officers have agreed to give up their bonuses and stock options and Bill Sanders, formerly vice-president of finance, has taken early retirement at a much reduced pension. Sanders provided all the information that your firm used in preparing the 10-K.

Six years ago, Sanders settled SEC charges that, while an officer with another corporation, he had engaged in insider trading. Without admitting wrongdoing, he disgorged his profits and agreed to enter a drug rehabilitation program to deal with the cocaine problem that had led to his trading. There is evidence that Sanders continues to have a drug problem.

Raven Hill concealed the officers' participation in the theft from your law firm. Indeed, after the theft, you, as senior securities partner, relying totally on representations made by Raven Hill's CEO, prepared a report on Form 8-K which stated that the thefts had been made by low-ranking warehouse personnel.

What exposure do you, your law firm, the lawyer-director and/or any lawyers in the firm who prepared the 10-K and 8-K face?

Chapter 18

NEGOTIATIONS

Lawyers typically spend a lot of time involved in negotiations of one sort or another. Negotiation obviously is a large part of transactional practice. A lawyer in that setting seeks an agreement that maximizes the benefits for her client, while still providing enough rewards for the other party that the deal is attractive to both. In the litigation context, most cases settle. A lawyer's negotiation skills in that setting can be crucial in determining how favorable are the terms of the settlement for her client. Negotiation thus has both adversarial and cooperative features. Each party has to gain enough from an agreement in order to be motivated to enter into it, but each also generally would prefer to derive as many of the benefits as possible for herself.

Negotiators are subject to two main ethical restrictions: that they not make material misrepresentations and that they not fail to disclose material information. Determining when these restrictions are violated, however, can be difficult. With respect to misrepresentation, we expect parties engaged in negotiation to engage in some posturing and some exaggeration of their position. At what point does this kind of behavior cross the line and become fraud and dishonesty? If someone makes a statement on a subject, how complete must it be in order to avoid misleading the other party?

With respect to omissions, when is not disclosing information fraudulent or dishonest? If a party has taken the time and energy to do more research and obtain more information about the subject of the negotiation than has the other party, must she share that information with the other so that she can make an informed decision? Or does that create an undesirable disincentive to engage in such research, which could result in parties entering into agreements that are ill-informed and inefficient?

Ethical rules, contract law, and tort law all regulate behavior in negotiations in various ways. It's also important to keep in mind the potential influence of non-legal considerations on negotiation behavior, such as concern about reputation and the likelihood of future negotiation between the same parties.

OVERVIEW OF THE CHAPTER

The Chapter begins with Model Rule 4.1, which is the rule most directly relevant to negotiations. Note also that the ABA *Ethical Guidelines for Settlement* Negotiations tracks this rule. Rule 4.1 prohibits fraudulent representations, or failures to disclose material information when disclosure is necessary to avoid assisting a client in a criminal or fraudulent act—unless disclosure would violate Rule 1.6. State adoptions of the most recent revisions to Rule 1.6 for the most part negate the impact of the latter qualification. In states with more restrictive confidentiality rules, however, this provision places a lawyer in the awkward position of being at risk of being liable for aiding and abetting fraud under common or criminal law. Furthermore, how do you reconcile Rule 4.1 in such states with Rule 1.2(d), which prohibits a lawyer from assisting a client in committing crime or fraud?

The Chapter then moves on to discussion of tort and contract law doctrines that are applicable to conduct in negotiations. A lawyer may be liable for the tort of fraud if she makes a material misrepresentation in business negotiations, or if she fails to disclose facts that are "basic to the transaction" that the other party reasonably expects to be disclosed. Make sure that you understand each of the excerpts from the various sections of the Restatement of Torts, including the concept of "facts basic to the transaction."

Notice that for a misrepresentation to be material, it generally must relate to a matter that a reasonable person would regard as important to his decision. By contrast, an omission serves as the basis for liability only if the information in question is basic to the transaction, which is a more stringent standard. Why the difference? Consider also that the Comments to the Section on Liability for Nondisclosure suggests that the concept of "facts basic to the transaction" may be expanding, and thus the duty of disclosure becoming more demanding, because of "changing ethical attitudes in many fields of modern business." How is a lawyer to know when such attitudes now require disclosure of information that previously need not have been disclosed?

Even if a lawyer's conduct in negotiations does not constitute fraud, it may permit the other party to void the agreement under contract doctrine. Excerpts from the Restatement of Contract elaborate on this concept. Note that a contract may be voidable due to a misrepresentation either because of the state of mind of the person who made it or because of its importance. Contract law also provides that non-disclosure will be treated as equivalent to a representation that the fact in question does not exist if the other party is mistaken as to a basic assumption of the contract, and if non-disclosure amounts to failure to act in good faith. Does the standard of voidability for non-disclosure track tort liability for non-disclosure? Does the requirement that non-disclosure constitute failure to act in good faith provide any guidance, or is it tautological? Do you think that, akin to tort law, "changing ethical attitudes" are increasing the range of contracts that are voidable for failures to disclose?

Excerpts from two scholars on negotiation follow the material on tort and contract law. Craver's article asserts that all negotiation necessarily involves some deception, and that we do not expect completely open and candid dialogue between negotiating parties. Is he right? If so, how do we determine what forms of deception are permissible and what are not? If we base this on the expectations of the parties, does that risk a downward spiral in which bad behavior lowers expectations, which in turn results in lower standards, which in turn prompts worse behavior, in a vicious cycle?

The excerpt from Strudler suggests one reason why we may not insist on full disclosure in negotiations: that it may dampen incentives of the parties to acquire relevant information. Strudler argues that a party to a negotiation may be entitled to a "deserved bargaining advantage" by virtue of spending time and money obtaining information that increases the value of the object of the bargaining. In these circumstances, he maintains, the person should be granted the equivalent of a property right in the information. This authorizes him to keep the information to himself and to gain a financial return on it.

Do you agree with Strudler? How precisely does he claim that obtaining information about something increases its value? If property becomes more valuable to a person by virtue of the information that she acquires about it, why shouldn't she have to pay more for it? If the information increases the value of the object of bargaining, is it thereby material, so that non-disclosure of it should be grounds for voiding the agreement? Would Strudler agree with how tort and contract law deal with the failure to disclose? What limits would Strudler place on deserved bargaining advantage?

Finally, the Problem that concludes the Chapter deals with negotiations about a corporate merger. It asks that you analyze whether there is a risk of either representations and omissions that might result in sanctions under ethical rules, tort, and contract law.

MODEL RULES: 3.3, 3.4, 4.1, 8.4

A. ETHICAL RULES

Negotiation in transactional matters is governed primarily by Model Rule of Professional Conduct 4.1. That Rule provides that a lawyer shall not knowingly "make a false statement of material fact or law to a third person," or "fail to disclose a material fact to a third person when disclosure is necessary to avoid assisting a criminal or fraudulent act by a client," *unless* the information in question is protected from disclosure by the lawyer's duty of confidentiality under Rule 1.6. As we have seen, that duty is qualified to enable a lawyer to disclose information to prevent or rectify client fraud in certain instances. Comment 1 to the Rule states that misrepresentations can consist of "partially true but misleading statements or omissions that are the equivalent of affirmative false statements."

The American Bar Association *Ethical Guidelines for Settlement Negotiations* addresses negotiations in the litigation context. The Guidelines generally track Rule 4.1. The Committee Notes say that unethical false statements of fact or law may occur when a lawyer: (1) knowingly and affirmatively states a falsehood or makes a partially true but misleading statement that is equivalent to an affirmative false statement; (2) incorporates or affirms the statement of another that the lawyer knows is false; and (3) "in certain limited circumstances" remains silent or fails to disclose a material fact to a third person.[1] The Notes state that the prohibition of false statements of material fact covers "only representations of fact, and not statements of opinion[.]"[2]

With respect to remaining silent, the Committee Notes to the Guidelines state that a lawyer may have a duty of disclosure in at least three situations: (1) she previously made a false statement of material fact or a partially true statement that is misleading by reason of omission; (2) she learns of a client's prior misrepresentation of material fact; (3) she learns that her services have been used in the commission of a crime or fraud by the client. In each such instance, however, disclosure may not violate the duty of confidentiality under the state's version of Rule 1.6 or other ethics rule dealing with confidentiality. The Notes also observe that "even if a lawyer is not subject to discipline for failure to disclose, such failure may be inconsistent with professional practice and may possibly jeopardize the settlement or even expose the lawyer to liability."[3]

B. COMMON LAW

In addition to ethics rules, business lawyers' behavior in negotiations are subject to two bodies of common law: tort and contract. Tort law imposes liability for certain misrepresentations or failures to disclose information that result in financial loss. Contract law provides that, even if conduct does not give rise to tort liability, it may serve as the basis for voiding an agreement and receiving restitution for expenses incurred in reliance on it. Such a remedy may result in considerable cost and inconvenience for the client on whose behalf the offending lawyer negotiated the agreement.

1. TORT

As the selections below from the Restatement (2d) of Torts indicate, the law imposes liability for fraudulent misrepresentation and nondisclosure in certain circumstances. A misrepresentation is fraudulent generally if the person making it knows or believes that matters are not as he

---

1. American Bar Association, Ethical Guidelines for Settlement Negotiations 35 (2002).

2. *Id.*

3. *Id.* at 38.

represents them. The information in question must be material; that is, a reasonable person would regard it as important in making a decision about the matter in question. Certain ambiguous and incomplete representations may be treated as fraudulent if they are misleading.

Tort law is less stringent with respect to failures to disclose information in business transactions. Any nondisclosure that a person knows may justifiably affect the other party's decision creates liability only if the person has a duty to disclose the information. Most relevant to the typical business transaction, such a duty arises with respect to facts that are "basic to the transaction" that the other party reasonably expects to be disclosed. Such an expectation may arise because of the relationship between the parties, the customs of the trade, or other circumstances.

The requirement that a fact be basic to the transaction in order to create liability is a more demanding standard than the requirement that a fact be material. Some facts may be material—that is, highly important—but not go to the "essence" of the transaction. The Comments to Section 551 explain that this rule reflects the view that "superior information and better business acumen are legitimate advantages" in bargaining over business transactions. The Comments do acknowledge, however, that "with changing ethical attitudes in many fields of modern business, the concept of facts basic to the transaction may be expanding and the duty to use reasonable care to disclose the facts may be increasing somewhat."

AMERICAN LAW INSTITUTE, RESTATEMENT OF THE LAW, SECOND, TORTS

§ 525 Liability for Fraudulent Misrepresentation

One who fraudulently makes a misrepresentation of fact, opinion, intention or law for the purpose of inducing another to act or to refrain from action in reliance upon it, is subject to liability to the other in deceit for pecuniary loss caused to him by his justifiable reliance upon the misrepresentation.

§ 526 Conditions Under Which Misrepresentation Is Fraudulent (Scienter)

A misrepresentation is fraudulent if the maker

(a) knows or believes that the matter is not as he represents it to be,

(b) does not have the confidence in the accuracy of his representation that he states or implies, or

(c) knows that he does not have the basis for his representation that he states or implies.

COMMENTS & ILLUSTRATIONS: Comment:

a. The word "fraudulent" is here used as referring solely to the maker's knowledge of the untrue character of his representation. This element of the defendant's conduct frequently is called "scienter" by the courts ...

b. This Section states merely the rules that determine whether a misrepresentation is fraudulently made. In order that a misrepresentation even though fraudulently made, may be actionable, it is necessary that the other conditions stated in § 525 exist.

§ 538 Materiality of Misrepresentation

(1) Reliance upon a fraudulent misrepresentation is not justifiable unless the matter misrepresented is material.

(2) The matter is material if

(a) a reasonable man would attach importance to its existence or nonexistence in determining his choice of action in the transaction in question; or

(b) the maker of the representation knows or has reason to know that its recipient regards or is likely to regard the matter as important in determining his choice of action, although a reasonable man would not so regard it.

§ 527 Ambiguous Representation

A representation that the maker knows to be capable of two interpretations, one of which he knows to be false and the other true is fraudulent if it is made:

(a) with the intention that it be understood in the sense in which it is false, or

(b) without any belief or expectation as to how it will be understood, or

(c) with reckless indifference as to how it will be understood.

COMMENTS & ILLUSTRATIONS: Comment:

a. In its effect the rule stated in this Section is similar to those stated in Clauses (a) and (b) of § 526. A representation that the maker knows to be ambiguous is fraudulent, not only if he believes that it will be understood in the sense in which it is false, but also if he makes it without any belief or expectation as to how it will be understood or with reckless indifference to how it will be understood.

Illustration:

1. A, wishing to sell an antique automobile to B, informs B that it is a Phaeton. "Phaeton" is the name of an obsolete car, manufactured in 1906, models of which are now extremely scarce and therefore valuable. It is also the name of a type of automobile body. The car has a Phaeton type of body but is not a Phaeton make of car. A makes the statement to B, knowing that it can be understood in either sense, without any expectation or belief as to how B will understand it and with indifference as to how he does. The statement is fraudulent.

b. Even though the maker of the statement did not realize the ambiguity of the statement when he made it, if he subsequently becomes aware that as a result of its ambiguity the statement is understood by the recipient in a sense that would make it false, he is under a duty to use reasonable care to disclose to the recipient information to prevent him from being misled by the statement.

§ 529   Representation Misleading Because Incomplete

A representation stating the truth so far as it goes but which the maker knows or believes to be materially misleading because of his failure to state additional or qualifying matter is a fraudulent misrepresentation.

COMMENTS & ILLUSTRATIONS: Comment:

a. A statement containing a half-truth may be as misleading as a statement wholly false. Thus, a statement that contains only favorable matters and omits all reference to unfavorable matters is as much a false representation as if all the facts stated were untrue. Thus a prospectus that accurately states the assets, bonded indebtedness and net earnings of a manufacturing corporation but omits any reference to its floating debt is a false representation of the financial position of the company. So, too, a statement by a vendor that his title has been upheld by a particular court is a false representation if he fails to disclose his knowledge that an appeal from the decision is pending.

b. Whether or not a partial disclosure of the facts is a fraudulent misrepresentation depends upon whether the person making the statement knows or believes that the undisclosed facts might affect the recipient's conduct in the transaction in hand. It is immaterial that the defendant believes that the undisclosed facts would not affect the value of the bargain which he is offering. The recipient is entitled to know the undisclosed facts in so far as they are material and to form his own opinion of their effect. Thus, in the example last given, the fact that the vendor had good grounds for believing that the appeal would fail does not prevent his statement from being a fraudulent misrepresentation.

§ 551   Liability for Nondisclosure

(1) One who fails to disclose to another a fact that he knows may justifiably induce the other to act or refrain from acting in a business transaction is subject to the same liability to the other as though he had represented the nonexistence of the matter that he has failed to disclose, if, but only if, he is under a duty to the other to exercise reasonable care to disclose the matter in question.

(2) One party to a business transaction is under a duty to exercise reasonable care to disclose to the other before the transaction is consummated,

(a) matters known to him that the other is entitled to know because of a fiduciary or other similar relation of trust and confidence between them; and

(b) matters known to him that he knows to be necessary to prevent his partial or ambiguous statement of the facts from being misleading; and

(c) subsequently acquired information that he knows will make untrue or misleading a previous representation that when made was true or believed to be so; and

(d) the falsity of a representation not made with the expectation that it would be acted upon, if he subsequently learns that the other is about to act in reliance upon it in a transaction with him; and

(e) facts basic to the transaction, if he knows that the other is about to enter into it under a mistake as to them, and that the other, because of the relationship between them, the customs of the trade or other objective circumstances, would reasonably expect a disclosure of those facts.

COMMENTS & ILLUSTRATIONS: Comment on Subsection (1):

a. Unless he is under some one of the duties of disclosure stated in Subsection (2), one party to a business transaction is not liable to the other for harm caused by his failure to disclose to the other facts of which he knows the other is ignorant and which he further knows the other, if he knew of them, would regard as material in determining his course of action in the transaction in question. The interest in knowing those facts that are important in determining the advisability of a course of action in a financial or commercial matter is given less protection by the rule stated in this Subsection than is given to the interest in knowing facts that are important in determining the recipient's course of action in regard to matters that involve the security of the person, land or chattels of himself or a third person.

b. The conditions under which liability is imposed for nondisclosure in an action for deceit differ in one particular from those under which a similar nondisclosure may confer a right to rescind the transaction or to recover back money paid or the value of other benefits conferred. In the absence of a duty of disclosure, under the rule stated in Subsection (2) of this Section, one who is negotiating a business transaction is not liable in deceit because of his failure to disclose a fact that he knows his adversary would regard as material. On the other hand, as is stated in *Restatement, Second, Contracts § 303(b)* the other is entitled to rescind the transaction if the undisclosed fact is basic; and under *Restatement of Restitution, § 8*, Comment e, and § 28, he would be entitled to recover back any money paid or benefit conferred in consummation of the transaction.

Comment on Clause (e):

j. *"Facts basic to the transaction."* The word "basic" is used in this Clause in the same sense in which it is used in Comment *c* under *§ 16 of the Restatement of Restitution.* A basic fact is a fact that is assumed by the parties as a basis for the transaction itself. It is a fact that goes to the basis, or essence, of the transaction, and is an important part of the substance of what is bargained for or dealt with. Other facts may serve as important and persuasive inducements to enter into the transaction, but not go to its essence. These facts may be material, but they are not basic. If the parties expressly or impliedly place the risk as to the existence of a fact on one party or if the law places it there by custom or otherwise the other party has no duty of disclosure. (Compare *Restatement, Second, Contracts § 296*).

Illustrations:

3.   A sells to B a dwelling house, without disclosing to B the fact that the house is riddled with termites. This is a fact basic to the transaction.

4.   A sells to B a dwelling house, knowing that B is acting in the mistaken belief that a highway is planned that will pass near the land and enhance its value. A does not disclose to B the fact that no highway is actually planned. This is not a fact basic to the transaction ...

Comment:

k. *Nondisclosure of basic facts.* The rule stated in Subsection (1) reflects the traditional ethics of bargaining between adversaries, in the absence of any special reason for the application of a different rule. When the facts are patent, or when the plaintiff has equal opportunity for obtaining information that he may be expected to utilize if he cares to do so, or when the defendant has no reason to think that the plaintiff is acting under a misapprehension, there is no obligation to give aid to a bargaining antagonist by disclosing what the defendant has himself discovered. To a considerable extent, sanctioned by the customs and mores of the community, superior information and better business acumen are legitimate advantages, which lead to no liability. The defendant may reasonably expect the plaintiff to make his own investigation, draw his own conclusions and protect himself; and if the plaintiff is indolent, inexperienced or ignorant, or his judgment is bad, or he does not have access to adequate information, the defendant is under no obligation to make good his deficiencies. This is true, in general, when it is the buyer of land or chattels who has the better information and fails to disclose it. Somewhat less frequently, it may be true of the seller ...

l. The continuing development of modern business ethics has, however, limited to some extent this privilege to take advantage of ignorance. There are situations in which the defendant not only knows that his bargaining adversary is acting under a mistake basic to the transaction, but also knows that the adversary, by reason of the relation between them, the customs of the trade or other objective circumstances, is reasonably relying upon a disclosure of the unrevealed fact if it exists. In this type of case good faith and fair dealing may require a disclosure.

It is extremely difficult to be specific as to the factors that give rise to this known, and reasonable, expectation of disclosure. In general, the cases in which the rule stated in Clause (e) has been applied have been those in which the advantage taken of the plaintiff's ignorance is so shocking to the ethical sense of the community, and is so extreme and unfair, as to amount to a form of swindling, in which the plaintiff is led by appearances into a bargain that is a trap, of whose essence and substance he is unaware. In such a case, even in a tort action for deceit, the plaintiff is entitled to be compensated for the loss that he has sustained. Thus a seller who knows that his cattle are infected with tick fever or contagious abortion is not free to unload them on the buyer and take his money, when he knows that the buyer is unaware of the fact, could not easily discover it, would not dream of entering into the bargain if he knew and is relying upon the seller's good faith and common honesty to disclose any such fact if it is true.

There are indications, also, that with changing ethical attitudes in many fields of modern business, the concept of facts basic to the transaction may be expanding and the duty to use reasonable care to disclose the facts may be increasing somewhat. This Subsection is not intended to impede that development.

Illustrations:

9. A sells B a dwelling house, without disclosing the fact that drain tile under the house is so constructed that at periodic intervals water accumulates under the house. A knows that B is not aware of this fact, that he could not discover it by an ordinary inspection, and that he would not make the purchase if he knew it. A knows also that B regards him as an honest and fair man and one who would disclose any such fact if he knew it. A is subject to liability to B for his pecuniary loss in an action of deceit.

10. A is engaged in the business of removing gravel from the bed of a navigable stream. He is notified by the United States government that the removal is affecting the channel of the stream, and ordered to stop it under threat of legal proceedings to compel him to do so. Knowing that B is unaware of this notice, could not reasonably be expected to discover it and would not buy if he knew, A sells the business to B without disclosing the fact. A is subject to liability to B for his pecuniary loss in an action of deceit.

11. A, who owns an amusement center, sells it to B without disclosing the fact that it has just been raided by the police, and that A is being prosecuted for maintaining prostitution and the sale of marijuana on the premises. These facts have seriously affected the reputation and patronage of the center, and greatly reduced its monthly income. A knows that B is unaware of these facts, could not be expected to discover them by ordinary investigation and would not buy if he knew them. He also knows that B believes A to be a man of high character, who would disclose any serious defects in the business. A is subject to liability to B for his pecuniary loss in an action of deceit.

12.   A sells a summer resort to B, without disclosing the fact that a substantial part of it encroaches on the public highway. A knows that B is unaware of the fact and could not be expected to discover it by ordinary inquiry, and that B trusts him to disclose any such facts. A is subject to liability to B for his pecuniary loss in an action of deceit.

2.   CONTRACT

Contract law provides that a contract is voidable if agreement to it is obtained by either a fraudulent or material misrepresentation by the other party. Thus, a contract can be voided if a person made representations that he knew or believed were not true, even if they related to matters that were not material. Alternatively, a contract can be voided if a misrepresentation pertains to something material, even if the maker believed that what he was saying was true. Contract law also treats certain failures to disclose as equivalent to representations.

Thus, even if a lawyer is not liable in tort for misrepresentations made in the course of negotiations, those misrepresentations may permit the other party to a transaction to undo it. If this occurs, might the lawyer potentially face any other form of liability? To whom? Keep in mind that an agreement that is potentially voidable under contract doctrine can consist of either a transaction or a settlement of litigation.

AMERICAN LAW INSTITUTE, RESTATEMENT OF THE LAW, SECOND, CONTRACTS

§ 164   When a Misrepresentation Makes a Contract Voidable

(1) If a party's manifestation of assent is induced by either a fraudulent or a material misrepresentation by the other party upon which the recipient is justified in relying, the contract is voidable by the recipient.

COMMENTS & ILLUSTRATIONS: Comment:

a.   Requirements. * * * Three requirements must be met in addition to the requirement that there must have been a misrepresentation. First, the misrepresentation must have been either fraudulent or material. Second, the misrepresentation must have induced the recipient to make the contract. Third, the recipient must have been justified in relying on the misrepresentation. Even if the contract is voidable, exercise of the power of avoidance is subject to the limitations stated in Chapter 16 on remedies.

b.   Fraudulent and non-fraudulent misrepresentation. A representation need not be fraudulent in order to make a contract voidable under the rule stated in this Section. However, a non-fraudulent misrepresentation does not make the contract voidable unless it is material, while materiality is not essential in the case of a fraudulent misrepresentation. One who makes a non-fraudulent misrepresentation of a seemingly unimportant fact has no reason to suppose that his assertion will induce assent. But a fraudulent misrepresentation is directed to attaining that very end, and the maker cannot insist on his bargain if it is attained, however unexpectedly, as long as the additional requirements of inducement and justifiable reliance are met. See Illustration 1. Compare *Restatement, Second, Torts § 538*, which limits liability for fraudulent misrepresentation to cases in which the matter misrepresented is material.

Illustrations:

1. A, seeking to induce B to make a contract to buy a tract of land at a price of $1,000 an acre, tells B that the tract contains 100 acres. A knows that it contains only 90 acres. B is induced by the statement to make the contract. Because the statement is a fraudulent misrepresentation (§ 162(1)), the contract is voidable by B, regardless of whether the misrepresentation is material.

2. The facts being otherwise as stated in Illustration 1, A is mistaken and does not know that the tract contains only 90 acres. Because the statement is not a fraudulent misrepresentation, the contract is voidable by B only if the misrepresentation is material (§ 162(2)).

§ 159 Misrepresentation Defined

A misrepresentation is an assertion that is not in accord with the facts.

COMMENTS & ILLUSTRATIONS: Comment:

a. Nature of the assertion. A misrepresentation, being a false assertion of fact, commonly takes the form of spoken or written words. Whether a statement is false depends on the meaning of the words in all the circumstances, including what may fairly be inferred from them. An assertion may also be inferred from conduct other than words. Concealment or even non-disclosure may have the effect of a misrepresentation under the rules stated in § § 160 and 161. Whether a misrepresentation is fraudulent is determined by the rule stated in § 162(1). However, an assertion need not be fraudulent to be a misrepresentation. Thus a statement intended to be truthful may be a misrepresentation because of ignorance or carelessness, as when the word "not" is inadvertently omitted or when inaccurate language is used. But a misrepresentation that is not fraudulent has no consequences under this Chapter unless it is material. Whether an assertion is material is determined by the rule stated in § 162(2).

§ 162 When a Misrepresentation Is Fraudulent or Material

(1) A misrepresentation is fraudulent if the maker intends his assertion to induce a party to manifest his assent and the maker

(a) knows or believes that the assertion is not in accord with the facts, or

(b) does not have the confidence that he states or implies in the truth of the assertion, or

(c) knows that he does not have the basis that he states or implies for the assertion.

(2) A misrepresentation is material if it would be likely to induce a reasonable person to manifest his assent, or if the maker knows that it would be likely to induce the recipient to do so.

COMMENTS & ILLUSTRATIONS:

Comment:

a. Meaning of "fraudulent." The word "fraudulent" is used in various senses in the law. In order that a misrepresentation be fraudulent within the meaning of this Section, it must not only be consciously false but must also be intended to mislead another. Consequences are intended if a person either acts with the desire to cause them or acts believing that they are substantially certain to result. Thus one who believes that another is substantially certain to be misled as a result of a misrepresentation intends to mislead even though he may not desire to do so ... In order that a fraudulent representation have legal effect within this Chapter, it need not be material. It is, however, essential that it actually induce assent * * *

c. Meaning of "material." * * * There may be personal considerations that the recipient regards as important even though they would not be expected to affect others in his situation, and if the maker is aware of this the misrepresentation may be material even though it would not be expected to induce a reasonable person to make the proposed contract. One who preys upon another's known idiosyncrasies cannot complain if the contract is held voidable when he succeeds in what he is endeavoring to accomplish. Although a nonfraudulent misrepresentation that is not material does not make the contract voidable under the rules stated in this Chapter, the recipient may have a claim to relief under other rules, such as those relating to breach of warranty.

Illustrations:

3. A, while negotiating with B for the sale of A's race horse, tells him that the horse has run a mile in a specified time. A is honestly mistaken, and, unknown to him, the horse has never come close to that time. B is induced by A's assertion to make a contract to buy the horse. A's statement, although not fraudulent, is a material misrepresentation, and the contract is voidable by B under the rule stated in § 164.

§ 161   When Non–Disclosure Is Equivalent to an Assertion

A person's non-disclosure of a fact known to him is equivalent to an assertion that the fact does not exist in the following cases only:

(a) where he knows that disclosure of the fact is necessary to prevent some previous assertion from being a misrepresentation or from being fraudulent or material.

(b) where he knows that disclosure of the fact would correct a mistake of the other party as to a basic assumption on which that party is making the contract and if non-disclosure of the fact amounts to a failure to act in good faith and in accordance with reasonable standards of fair dealing.

(c) where he knows that disclosure of the fact would correct a mistake of the other party as to the contents or effect of a writing, evidencing or embodying an agreement in whole or in part.

(d) where the other person is entitled to know the fact because of a relation of trust and confidence between them.

COMMENTS & ILLUSTRATIONS:

Comment:

* * * *b. Fraudulent or material.* In order to make the contract voidable under the rule stated in § 164(1), the non-disclosure must be either fraudulent or material. The notion of disclosure necessarily implies that the fact in question is known to the person expected to disclose it. But the failure to disclose the fact may be unintentional, as when one forgets to disclose a known fact, and it is then equivalent to an innocent misrepresentation. Furthermore, one is expected to disclose only such facts as he knows or has reason to know will influence the other in determining his course of action. See § 162(2). Therefore, he need not disclose facts that the ordinary person would regard as unimportant unless he knows of some peculiarity of the other person that is likely to lead him to attach importance to them. There is, however, no such requirement of materiality if it can be shown that the non-disclosure was actually fraudulent. If a fact is intentionally withheld for the purpose of inducing action, this is equivalent to a fraudulent misrepresentation.

c. Failure to correct. One who has made an assertion that is neither a fraudulent nor a material misrepresentation may subsequently acquire knowledge that bears significantly on his earlier assertion. He is expected to speak up and correct the earlier assertion in three cases. First, if his assertion was not a misrepresentation because it was true, he may later learn that it is no longer true. Second, his assertion may have been a misrepresentation but may not have been fraudulent. If this was because he believed that it was true, he may later learn that it was not true. If this was because he did not intend that it be relied upon, he may later learn that the other is about to rely on it. Third, if his assertion was a misrepresentation but was not material because he had no reason to know of the other's special characteristics that made reliance likely, he may later learn of such characteristics. If a person fails to correct his earlier assertion in these situations, the result is the same as it would have been had he had his newly acquired knowledge at the time he made the assertion.

C. WHAT'S FAIR?[1]

Charles B. Craver, NEGOTIATION ETHICS: HOW TO BE
DECEPTIVE WITHOUT BEING DISHONEST/HOW TO
BE ASSERTIVE WITHOUT BEING OFFENSIVE

38 S.TEX.L.REV. 713 (1997)

I. INTRODUCTION

Most practicing lawyers are not litigators. They handle family and
property matters, trusts and estates, business transactions, tax liabilities, and similar situations. They almost never participate in judicial or
arbitral adjudications. Most of their interactions with other lawyers
involve negotiations * * * Even litigators rarely participate in formal
adjudications, due to the high financial and emotional costs and the
unpredictable nature of those proceedings. They thus resolve ninety to
ninety-five percent of their cases through direct inter-party discussions
or mediator-assisted settlement talks * * *

Most attorneys feel some degree of professional discomfort when
they negotiate with other lawyers. If they hope to achieve beneficial
results for their clients, they must convince their opponents that those
parties must offer more generous terms than they must actually offer if
agreements are to be generated. To accomplish this objective, lawyers
usually employ some deceptive tactics. Take for example two parties
bargaining over the purchase/sale of a small business. The Seller is
willing to accept $500,000, while the Buyer is willing to pay $575,000.
The Seller's attorney initially indicates that the Seller must obtain
$600,000, with the Buyer's lawyer suggesting that the Buyer cannot go
above $450,000. Once these preliminary offers have been exchanged, the
parties are pleased with the successful way in which they have begun
their discussions. Yet both have begun with position statements designed
to mislead the other side. Have they behaved unethically? Are they
obliged to disclose their true bargaining needs and intentions to preserve
their professional reputations? May they never reject offers they know
their clients will accept?

During their subsequent discussions, the Seller's representative is
likely to embellish the value of the business being sold, while the Buyer's
advocate undervalues that firm. Must the Seller's attorney admit that
the Seller believes that future competition from foreign firms is likely to
diminish the economic value of his company? Must the Buyer's lawyer
disclose the Buyer's innovative plan to enhance the competitive position
and future value of this particular firm? When does the Seller-advocate's
embellishment exceed the bounds of bargaining propriety? To what
extent may the Buyer's representative disingenuously undervalue the
company being discussed? Are the Buyer and Seller representatives

---

1. The title of this section is taken from
an excellent collection of essays on practical
and ethical issues in negotiation, What's

Fair? Ethics for Negotiators (Carrie Menk-
el-Meadow & Michael Wheeler eds., 2004).

ethically obliged to ensure a "fair" price for the business? If the Seller is willing to accept less than the Buyer anticipated or the Buyer is willing to pay more than the Seller imagined, would the lawyer representing the other side be duty bound to disclose this fact and attempt to moderate the other side's "unrealistic" beliefs? * * *

II. Appropriate and Inappropriate Misrepresentations

I frequently surprise law students and practitioners by telling them that while I have rarely participated in legal negotiations in which both participants did not use some misstatements to further client interests, I have encountered few dishonest lawyers. I suggest that the fundamental question is not whether legal negotiators may use misrepresentations to further client interests, but when and about what they may permissibly dissemble. Many negotiators initially find it difficult to accept the notion that disingenuous "puffing" and deliberate mendacity do not always constitute reprehensible conduct.

It is easy to exhort legal practitioners to behave in an exemplary manner when they participate in the negotiation process:

> The lawyer is not free to do anything his client might do in the same circumstances ... The lawyer must be at least as candid and honest as his client would be required to be ... Beyond that, the profession should embrace an affirmative ethical standard for attorneys' professional relationships with courts, other lawyers and the public: The lawyer must act honestly and in good faith. Another lawyer ... should not need to exercise the same degree of caution that he would if trading for reputedly antique copper jugs in an oriental bazaar
> ...
>
> * * * Surely the professional standards must ultimately impose upon him a duty not to accept an unconscionable deal. While some difficulty in line-drawing is inevitable when such a distinction is sought to be made, there must be a point at which the lawyer cannot ethically accept an arrangement that is completely unfair to the other side * * *

Despite the nobility of such pronouncements, others maintain that "pious and generalized assertions that the negotiator must be 'honest' or that the lawyer must use 'candor' are not helpful." They recognize that negotiation interactions involve a deceptive process in which a certain amount of "puffing" and "embellishment" is expected, as the participants attempt to convince their opponents that they must obtain better terms than they must actually achieve.

Observers also note that trustworthiness is a relative concept that is rarely defined in absolute terms, based on different expectations in diverse situations.

Trustworthiness and its outward manifestation—truth telling—are not absolute values. For example, no one tells the truth all of the time, nor is perpetual truth telling expected in most circumstances. To tell the truth in some social situations would be a rude convention. Consequently, when one speaks of the essential nature of trustworthiness and truth telling, one actually is talking about a certain circumstance or situation in which convention calls for trustworthiness or truth telling. Thus, a person considered trustworthy and a truth teller actually is a person who tells the truth at the right or necessary time * * *.

When students or practicing attorneys are asked whether they expect opposing counsel to candidly disclose their true authorized limits or their actual bottom lines at the beginning of bargaining interactions, most exhibit discernible discomfort. They recall the numerous times they have commenced negotiations with exaggerated or distorted position statements they did not expect their adversaries to take literally, and they begin to understand the dilemma confronted regularly by all legal negotiators.

On the one hand the negotiator must be fair and truthful; on the other he must mislead his opponent. Like the poker player, a negotiator hopes that his opponent will overestimate the value of his hand. Like the poker player, in a variety of ways he must facilitate his opponent's inaccurate assessment. The critical difference between those who are successful negotiators and those who are not lies in this capacity both to mislead and not to be misled.

* * * [A] careful examination of the behavior of even the most forthright, honest, and trustworthy negotiators will show them actively engaged in misleading their opponents about their true positions ... To conceal one's true position, to mislead an opponent about one's true settling point, is the essence of negotiation.

* * * Attorneys who believe that no prevarication is ever proper during bargaining encounters place themselves and their clients at a distinct disadvantage, since they permit their less candid opponents to obtain settlements that transcend the terms to which they are objectively entitled.

The schizophrenic character of the ethical conundrum encountered by legal negotiators is apparent in the ABA Model Rules of Professional Conduct, which were adopted by the House of Delegates in August of 1983. Rule 4.1(a) states that "[A] lawyer shall not knowingly ... make a false statement of material fact or law to a third person." This seemingly unequivocal principle is intended to apply to both litigation and negotiation settings. An explanatory Comment under this Rule reiterates the fact that "[a] lawyer is required to be truthful when dealing with others on a client's behalf. ..." Nonetheless, Comment Two acknowledges the difficulty of defining "truthfulness" in the unique context of the negotiation process:

> "Whether a particular statement should be regarded as one of fact can depend on the circumstances. Under generally accepted conventions in negotiation, certain types of statements ordinarily are not taken as statements of material fact. Estimates of price or value placed on the subject of a transaction and a party's intentions as to an acceptable settlement of a claim are in this category..."

If one negotiator lies to another, only by happenstance will the other discover the lie. If the settlement is concluded by negotiation, there will be no trial, no public testimony by conflicting witnesses, and thus no opportunity to examine the truthfulness of assertions made during the negotiation. Consequently, in negotiation, more than in other contexts, ethical norms can probably be violated with greater confidence that there will be no discovery and punishment.

* * * Even though advocate prevarication during legal negotiations rarely results in bar disciplinary action, practitioners must recognize that other risks are created by truly dishonest bargaining behavior. Attorneys who deliberately deceive opponents regarding material matters or who withhold information they are legally obliged to disclose may be guilty of fraud. Contracts procured through fraudulent acts of commission or omission are voidable, and the responsible advocates and their clients may be held liable for monetary damages. It would be particularly embarrassing for lawyers to make misrepresentations that could cause their clients additional legal problems transcending those the attorneys were endeavoring to resolve. Since the adversely affected clients might thereafter sue their culpable former counsel for legal malpractice, the ultimate injury to the reputations and practices of the deceptive attorneys could be momentous. Legal representatives who employ clearly improper bargaining tactics may even subject themselves to judicial sanctions.

Most legal representatives always conduct their negotiations with appropriate candor, because they are moral individuals and/or believe that such professional behavior is mandated by the applicable ethical standards. A few others, however, do not feel so constrained. These persons should consider the practical risks associated with disreputable bargaining conduct. Even if their deceitful action is not reported to the state bar and never results in personal liability for fraud or legal malpractice, their aberrational behavior is likely to be eventually discovered by their fellow practitioners. As other attorneys learn that particular lawyers are not minimally trustworthy, future interactions become more difficult for those persons. Factual and legal representations are no longer accepted without time-consuming and expensive verification. Oral agreements on the telephone and handshake agreements are no longer acceptable. Executed written documents are required for even rudimentary transactions. Attorneys who contemplate the employment of unacceptable deception to further present client interests should always be cognizant of the fact that their myopic conduct may seriously jeopardize their future effectiveness. No short-term gain achieved through deviant behavior should ever be permitted to outweigh the likely long-term consequences of those improper actions.

When lawyers negotiate, they must constantly decide whether they are going to divulge relevant legal and/or factual information to opposing counsel. If they decide to disclose some pertinent information, may they do so partially or is complete disclosure required? They must also determine the areas they may permissibly misrepresent and the areas they may not distort.

A. *Nondisclosure of Information*

Even though Model Rule 4.1(a) states that attorneys must be truthful when they make statements concerning material law or fact, Comment One expressly indicates that lawyers have "no affirmative duty to inform an opposing party of relevant facts." In the absence of special relationships or express contractual or statutory duties, practitioners are normally not obliged to divulge relevant legal or factual information to their adversaries. This doctrine is premised upon the duty of representatives to conduct their own legal research and factual investigations. Under our adversary system, attorneys do not have the right to expect their opponents to assist them in this regard. It is only when cases reach tribunals that Model Rule 3.3(a)(3) imposes an affirmative obligation on advocates "to disclose to the tribunal legal authority in the controlling jurisdiction known to the lawyer to be directly adverse to the position of the client and not disclosed by opposing counsel." No such duty is imposed, however, with respect to pertinent factual circumstances that are not discovered by opposing counsel . . .

B. *Partial Disclosure of Information*

Negotiators regularly use selective disclosures to enhance their positions. They divulge the legal doctrines and factual information beneficial to their claims, while withholding circumstances that are not helpful. In most instances, these selective disclosures are expected by opponents and are considered an inherent aspect of bargaining interactions. When attorneys emphasize their strengths, opposing counsel must attempt to ascertain their undisclosed weaknesses. They should carefully listen for verbal leaks and look for nonverbal signals that may indicate the existence of possible opponent problems. Probing questions may be used to elicit some negative information, and external research may be employed to gather other relevant data. These efforts are particularly important when opponents carefully limit their disclosures to favorable circumstances, since their partial disclosures may cause listeners to make erroneous assumptions.

When I discuss negotiating ethics with legal practitioners, I often ask if lawyers are obliged to disclose information to correct erroneous factual or legal assumptions made by opposing counsel. Most respondents perceive no duty to correct legal or factual misunderstandings generated solely by the carelessness of opposing attorneys. Respondents only hesitate when opponent misperceptions may have resulted from misinterpretations of seemingly honest statements made by them. For example, when a plaintiff attorney embellishes the pain being experienced by a client with a severely sprained ankle, the defense lawyer may indicate how painful broken ankles can be. If the plaintiff representative has said nothing to create this false impression, should he or she be obliged to correct the obvious defense counsel error? Although a respectable minority of respondents believe that an affirmative duty to correct the misperception may exist here—due to the fact plaintiff embellishments may have inadvertently contributed to the misunderstanding—most respondents feel no such obligation. So long as they have not directly generated the erroneous belief, it is not their duty to correct it. They could not, however, include their opponent's misunderstanding in their own statements, since this would cause them to improperly articulate knowing misrepresentations of material fact. * * *

C. Overt Misrepresentation of Information

* * * It is clear that lawyers may not intentionally misrepresent material facts, but it is not always apparent what facts are "material." The previously noted Comment to Rule 4.1 explicitly acknowledges that "estimates of price or value placed on the subject of a transaction and a party's intentions as to an acceptable settlement of a claim" do not constitute material facts under that provision. It is thus ethical for legal negotiators to misrepresent the value their client places on particular items. For example, attorneys representing one spouse involved in a marital dissolution may indicate that their client wants joint custody of the children, when in reality he or she does not. Lawyers representing a party attempting to purchase a particular company may understate their client's belief regarding the value of the goodwill associated with the target firm. So long as the statement conveys their side's belief—and does not falsely indicate the view of an outside expert, such as an accountant—no Rule 4.1 violation would occur.

Legal negotiators may also misrepresent client settlement intentions. They may ethically suggest to opposing counsel that an outstanding offer is unacceptable, even though they know the proposed terms would be accepted if no additional concessions could be generated. Nonetheless, it is important to emphasize that this Rule 4.1 exception does not wholly excuse all misstatements regarding client settlement intentions. During the early stages of bargaining interactions, most practitioners do not expect opponents to disclose exact client desires. As negotiators approach final agreements, however, they anticipate a greater degree of candor. If negotiators were to deliberately deceive adversaries about this issue during the closing stage of their interaction, most attorneys would consider them dishonest, even though the Rule 4.1 proscription would remain inapplicable . . .

III. UNCONSCIONABLE TACTICS AND AGREEMENTS

* * * Many practicing attorneys seem to think that competitive/adversarial negotiators—who use highly competitive tactics to maximize their own client returns—achieve more beneficial results for their clients than their cooperative/problem-solving colleagues—who employ more cooperative techniques designed to maximize the joint return to the parties involved. An empirical study, conducted by Professor Gerald Williams, of legal practitioners in Denver and Phoenix contradicts this notion. Professor Williams found that sixty-five percent of negotiators

are considered cooperative/problem-solvers by their peers, twenty-four percent are viewed as competitive/adversarial, and eleven percent did not fit in either category. When the respondents were asked to indicate which attorneys were "effective," "average," and "ineffective" negotiators, the results were striking. While fifty-nine percent of the cooperative/problem-solving lawyers were rated "effective," only twenty-five percent of competitive/adversarial attorneys were rated effective. On the other hand, while a mere three percent of cooperative/problem-solvers were considered "ineffective," thirty-three percent of competitive/adversarial bargainers were rated "ineffective."

In his study, Professor Williams found that certain traits were shared by both effective cooperative/problem-solving negotiators and effective competitive/adversarial bargainers. Successful negotiators from both groups are thoroughly prepared, behave in an honest and ethical manner, are perceptive readers of opponent cues, are analytical, realistic, and convincing, and observe the courtesies of the bar. The proficient negotiators from both groups also sought to maximize their own client's return. Since this is the quintessential characteristic of competitive/adversarial bargainers, it would suggest that a number of successful negotiators may be adroitly masquerading as sheep in wolves' clothing. They exude a cooperative style, but seek competitive objectives.

Most successful negotiators are able to combine the most salient traits associated with the cooperative/problem-solving and the competitive/adversarial styles. They endeavor to maximize client returns, but attempt to accomplish this objective in a congenial and seemingly ingenuous manner. They look for shared values in recognition of the fact that by maximizing joint returns, they are more likely to obtain the best settlements for their own clients. Although successful negotiators try to manipulate opponent perceptions, they rarely resort to truly deceitful tactics. They know that a loss of credibility will undermine their ability to achieve beneficial results. Despite the fact successful negotiators want as much as possible for their own clients, they are not "win-lose" negotiators who judge their results, not by how well they have done, but by how poorly they think their opponents have done. They realize that the imposition of poor terms on opponents does not necessarily benefit their own clients. All factors being equal, they want to maximize opponent satisfaction. So long as it does not require significant concessions on their part, they acknowledge the benefits to be derived from this approach. The more satisfied opponents are, the more likely those parties will accept proposed terms and honor the resulting agreements.

These eclectic negotiators employ a composite style. They may be characterized as competitive/problem-solvers. They seek competitive goals (maximum client returns), but endeavor to accomplish these objectives through problem-solving strategies. They exude a cooperative approach and follow the courtesies of the legal profession. They avoid rude or inconsiderate behavior, recognizing that such openly adversarial conduct is likely to generate competitive/adversarial responses from their opponents. They appreciate the fact that individuals who employ wholly inappropriate tactics almost always induce opposing counsel to work harder to avoid exploitation by these openly opportunistic bargainers. Legal negotiators who are contemplating the use of offensive techniques should simply ask themselves how they would react if similar tactics were employed against them * * *

IV. Concluding Thoughts

* * * Untrustworthy advocates encounter substantial difficulty when they negotiate with others. Their oral representations must be verified and reduced to writing, and many opponents distrust their written documents. Their negotiations become especially problematic and cumbersome. If nothing else moves practitioners to behave in an ethical and dignified manner, their hope for long and successful legal careers should induce them to avoid conduct that may undermine their future effectiveness.

Alan Strudler, Moral Complexity in the Law of Nondisclosure

45 UCLA L. Rev. 337 (1997)

* * *

I.

Why the Problem of Nondisclosure Is Hard

* * * Plainly not all nondisclosure in negotiation is wrong. Some strategic nondisclosure gets respect in even the best circles. Though speakers seem generally quite squeamish about telling lies, few find it necessary, as a moral matter, or wise, as a strategic matter, to always disclose the whole truth. One of the earlier-known attributions of strategic nondisclosure occurs in the Bible, when God tells Abraham to sacrifice his son, but chooses not to inform Abraham that the demand will be canceled once Abraham sincerely resolves to perform the sacrifice. Presumably, this nondisclosure allowed Abraham to demonstrate a commitment to God that would have been impossible had Abraham known the truth about God's plans. Even by the definition provided in a standard negotiation textbook, God's discussion with Abraham was a negotiation, because they were attempting to reach an agreement on matters in which they had mutually dependent interests.

Most people, in their own negotiations, also engage in strategic nondisclosure, though of a more ordinary sort. Buyer nondisclosure often seems particularly unexceptionable. When confronted by a car salesperson who asks for the most one is willing to pay for a car, for example, one looks for a way to avoid disclosing the truth; disclosure would prompt the salesperson to use that information as part of an argument that the price he offers is good * * *

IV.

Deserved Bargaining Advantages

* * *

A.

Norms in Negotiating

Consider a famous social science experiment called the "ultimatum game," in which two subjects, the "proposer" and the "responder," are given some money (the "stake") on the condition that they reach an agreement about how that money is to be divided. The proposer makes a written offer to the responder about dividing the stake. If the responder accepts the proposer's offer, they keep the money and divide it according to the terms of the agreement; if the responder declines the offer, then neither party receives anything. Proposers' offers tend to be approximately fifty-fifty, and responders usually reject an offer less than twenty percent. Negotiators, then, insist on a fair outcome and will sacrifice financial gain rather than suffer unfairness. This result has surprised social scientists because it conflicts with assumptions of self-interested rationality often used in microeconomic and game-theoretic models. In any case, the results of the ultimatum game conform to an idea often advanced by moral and political philosophers: when distributing goods among people, if there are no relevant differences among them, there is a strong moral presumption that the goods should be distributed equally
* * *

In real-world negotiations, buyers and sellers often differ in their relative circumstances more than do proposers and responders in the ultimatum game. Issues about how to divide a cooperative surplus agreement become acute when the circumstances of buyers and sellers differ in ways relevant to the negotiation. An experimental variant on the ultimatum game, devised by Elizabeth Hoffman and Matthew Spitzer, partially addresses the problem. In Hoffman and Spitzer's experiment, both the proposer and the responder were told that the proposer "earned" his role by scoring well in a contest; the result was that proposers and responders generally settled on giving a share larger than fifty percent of the stake to the proposer. This experiment demonstrates that people think that, as a matter of fairness, earned or otherwise legitimately acquired advantages are relevant differences between negotiators and therefore should play a role in determining the outcome of a negotiation.

In fact, the judgments of Hoffman and Spitzer's experimental subjects seem quite plausible, even if the experimental context is unrealistic. In actual commercial negotiations, people do not earn bargaining advantages by winning a contest. But, people do earn and otherwise acquire bargaining advantages in ways that render it possible for them to fairly claim more than they otherwise could in a negotiation. Consider a typical kind of case that corroborates the judgment of Hoffman and Spitzer's experimental subjects. Jones manufacturers widgets, a component of computers. Smith also manufacturers widgets, which cost just as much to manufacture as do Jones's widgets. But Smith's widgets are of lesser quality than Jones's widgets, and hence, a computer containing Smith's widgets has a worse market value than does a computer containing Jones's widgets. If Acme Computer Company makes a deal with Jones, the deal will likely produce more valuable computers and hence a better selling price for the computers than the corresponding deal Acme might make with Smith. Because Jones brings more value to the bargaining table than Smith, it seems fair for him to insist on more money than Smith could get for a similar transaction. The intuitive plausibility of the idea that Jones can fairly claim more from a deal with Acme than can Smith, together with the results of the Hoffman and Spitzer variant on the ultimatum game, suggest the following simple principle, which I call the deserved advantage principle: other things being equal, the more value one brings to the bargaining table, the more one may fairly insist upon as return.

* * * According to the deserved advantage principle account, a buyer's acquisition of information that increases the value of the object being sold in a negotiation warrants some additional measure of bargaining strength, and a privilege of buyer nondisclosure functions as a prophylactic that protects the buyer in getting a fair return on the valuable information that she brings to the table. The prophylactic operates by granting the buyer a property right in the information she uncovers—a right that gives her discretion not to disclose information. She acquires the property right because she deserves it, not because recognizing the right produces utility. In its recognition that a person may deserve a right to property based on the value he or she produces or uncovers, the deserved advantage principle accords with a host of traditional nonutilitarian, and hence noneconomic, theories of property rights.

Interpreting the deserved advantage principle for cases of precontractual negotiation becomes particularly interesting once one considers the distinctive value that a buyer may bring to the table. Making better widgets, after all, is only one way to bring value to the negotiating table and is therefore only one way to secure a basis for fairly insisting on a larger bargaining return. A very different way of bringing value, more typical of the problems thus far discussed, is by uncovering valuable information. Consider a realistic case. A real estate broker, Joan, learns that a supermarket chain is searching for land to develop. She scours the area for appropriate land, finds a lot, and buys a purchase option from its owner, Fred, without informing him about the interests of the supermarket chain. Presumably, both Joan and Fred are made better off by this transaction; hence, their agreement produces benefits, which must be divided. The property becomes more valuable in Joan's hands, and she deserves something for producing that value. By purchasing the property for a price below that for which she will sell it to the supermarket chain, she may collect what she deserves. But she can do this only if she is able to remain silent and maintain Fred's ignorance about the client to whom she will eventually sell the property. A rule permitting nondisclosure puts Joan in a good position to haggle for a fair return on the value that she brings to the negotiating table. She is in a strong bargaining position because she does not have to disclose, and, according to the deserved advantage principle, she deserves to be in a strong bargaining position because of the value she brings to the bargaining table.

PROBLEM

UScape is a provider of on-line services whose subscriber base has grown over the last eight years to more than twelve million households. An important impetus for this growth has been the company's provision of 100 free trial hours of UScape service through the distribution of free CD–ROMs. UScape's annual revenues have increased over this period by over 700%. In the last three years, however, increasing competition from other on-line services has begun to cut into profit margins from subscriber fees. As a result, UScape has begun to rely more heavily on the sale of on-line advertising as a component of its profits. During this period, advertising has grown from 32% of company profits to more than 58%, with projections for continued increases. A large portion of the advertisers are high-tech companies providing various on-line goods and services for both consumers and other businesses. UScape's ability to meet its revenue targets each quarter has resulted in a share price that has climbed steadily to $31 a share when the company released last quarter's earnings figures. UScape would like to diversity its activities, however, in order to insulate itself from downturns in the high-tech market.

Hourglass (HG) is a large media conglomerate that includes magazine publishing, cable television, and movie production. While profitable, its rate of revenue growth and share price in recent years have lagged behind many of the new Internet companies like UScape. HG is particularly attentive to this development because its managers fear that the new technologies employed by such companies may pose a threat to the traditional media that are the staple of HG's operations. Its management and Board of Directors therefore are on the lookout for ways that HG can jump aboard what seems to be the digital wave of the future.

Initially prompted by their investment bankers, UScape and HG management begin to consider the possibility of merging the two companies. UScape believes that it would gain respectability from its association with a stable media company with a long tradition. More concretely, UScape officials envision that it could use HG's cable lines to provide faster Internet service to its subscribers, and could draw on HG's store of entertainment to stream movies and television over the Internet. From HG's perspective, a merger would be attractive because the company would gain access to potential customers in UScape's large subscriber base, broadening the media through which HG would be able to promote its products. Furthermore, UScape's high-flying stock and revenue growth would boost HG's share price, and enable HG to gain a piece of the stratospheric profits that Internet companies seem to generate.

As officials negotiate a possible combination of the two companies, they agree that the deal will take the form of an exchange of stock. That is, UScape and HG would each exchange shares in their own company for new shares in the combined company. UScape managers press for an exchange ratio whereby its shareholders would end up owning 60% of the new company. Their rationale is that their company's market capitalization (share price x number of outstanding shares) is about $160 billion, which is about twice as much as HG's. They also note that UScape's revenues have increased by 85% over the last two years, far greater than HG's 9% rate of growth. HG negotiators, however, point out that their company would contribute about 75% of the revenues of the combined company, and suggest that share prices of Internet companies are more volatile than those of traditional firms. Eventually, the parties agree in principle on a 55–45 split in favor of UScape. UScape officials thus view the deal as effectively an acquisition of HG by UScape, which will allow them to put their stamp on the new company.

As the parties continue their negotiations, there are three interesting developments. First, UScape has begun to experience a weakening in the market for online advertising. Many of the high-tech companies that tend to be the major purchasers of such advertising are beginning to fall on hard times, which has reduced the demand for advertising. Furthermore, several UScape customers with long-term advertising contracts are claiming that they need to renegotiate them at a lower price in order to remain afloat. UScape thus far has resisted such requests.

The second interesting development is UScape's response to this situation. The company has entered into an agreement with Lunar Computerware to purchase about $250 million of equipment to expand UScape's online network. At the same time, Lunar has agreed to purchase $40 million worth of advertising on UScape over the next three years. Lunar will credit UScape $40 million on its equipment purchase, so that the latter will owe Lunar $210 million. UScape in turn will book the $40 million as advertising revenue, which will enable it to meet its revenue target for the current fiscal year. UScape's outside auditor has concluded that such an arrangement is unconventional, but that nothing in Generally Accepted Accounting Principles forbids recording the $40 million as advertising revenue.

On the HG side, the executives in charge of HG's movie production and distribution business units have made it clear within the company that they will not make movies available to UScape after the merger on terms any more favorable than to other Internet providers. Doing so, they contend, would weaken the HG brand and undermine the profitability of its movie operations. Since these business units are the most profitable within HG, its executives have considerable influence within the company and are likely to be able to prevail after the merger.

You are involved in negotiating the merger on behalf of UScape. You have told your HG counterparts that "advertising revenues look robust for the next fiscal year." Is there any problem with your making this representation?

Should you disclose: (1) the request by several high-tech customers to renegotiate their advertising contracts or (2) the fact that the $40 million in revenues from Lunar represents a credit toward UScape's purchase of equipment from that company?

You are involved in negotiating the merger on behalf of HG. Your UScape counterpart has mentioned in negotiations that UScape is excited about gaining preferential access to HG movies with the merger of the two companies. You say, "We think this is a good deal for everyone," and move on to another subject. Is there any problem in doing this?

Chapter 19

ACCOUNTING AND FINANCIAL REPORTING

Most of the corporate scandals of the early 21st century have involved accounting misconduct in some way. Entire organizations have shut their doors, and powerful people have gone to prison, because numbers on financial statements have been inflated, deflated, or placed in the wrong categories, or those statements did not contain all the information they should have. The lawyer who seeks to protect the interests of her corporate client therefore needs to have at least rudimentary knowledge of accounting and financial reporting.

The material in this chapter describes the system of internal and external financial oversight within the corporation, the responsibilities of high-ranking corporate executives to maintain and attest to the effectiveness of that system, and the most common forms of accounting fraud that tend to be perpetuated. A question that runs through this material is the degree to which a lawyer is responsible for helping ensure the integrity of a company's accounting and financial reporting practices. To what extent can lawyers simply defer to whatever accountants say? When are there enough inconsistencies that a lawyer should conduct further inquiry? Is a corporate lawyer who practices without sufficient knowledge of accounting committing malpractice?

Keep in mind that accountants must first receive from lawyers a conclusion on the legal rights and obligations resulting from a given transaction in order to determine how that transaction should be treated for accounting purposes. At the same time, lawyers may structure transactions in certain ways based on accountants' view of the requirements for recording these transactions on the company's financial statements in a particular way.

OVERVIEW OF THE CHAPTER

The material in this Chapter is intended to acquaint you with the basic concepts of accounting and financial reporting, and to alert you to some of the most common ways in which companies may try improperly to manipulate the financial information that they provide. You should approach it not with the idea of becoming a financial expert, but as someone who will need at least some familiarity with these matters in order to understand a major concern of corporate managers and how your work can be responsive to it. In addition, your ability to ensure that the company is not engaged in fraud will require that you recognize some warning signs that financial misconduct may be occurring.

The Chapter begins with a description of the system that companies need to have in place in order to meet their financial reporting obligations, and the participants that are most important in its operation. The securities laws require that companies submit financial information in both quarterly and annual reports. That information takes the form of both financial statements and narrative description. Make sure that you understand the roles of each key actor in this process: the internal auditors, who are company employees; the outside auditor, which is an independent accounting firm; and the audit committee, composed of directors with no other ties to the company. Pay attention as well to the role of top management and the managers underneath it in furnishing information that eventually will be included in the financial reports.

The excerpt from Bauman, et al. provides an overview of rudimentary accounting concepts and the elements of a company's financial statements. It begins with components of the financial statement of the fictitious Precision Tools Corporation: the Balance Sheet, Income Statement, and Statement of Cash Flows. You should refer periodically to this financial statement as you read the material. The excerpt discusses Generally Accepted Accounting Principles (GAAP), which require that information in financial statements be presented in a certain form. Make sure that you understand the principles that underlie GAAP and the rationales for them. Be aware also that GAAP represents a set of conventions, not a scientifically objective set of requirements.

The excerpt then moves to a discussion of the terms and concepts relevant to the financial statement. Make sure that you understand the difference between cash accounting and accrual accounting, along with the Realization and Matching principles. This will give you a sense of the logic that underlies the presentation of information in the financial statement. Make sure also that you understand the distinctive features and purposes of the Balance Sheet, Income Statement, and Statement of Cash Flows, both for their own sake and because financial misconduct typically take the form of efforts to manipulate one or more of these components. The excerpt provides a detailed description of each of the elements of the Balance Sheet, which you should read while referring back to the Balance Sheet of the Precision Tools Corporation. Finally, the excerpt concludes with a discussion of the Statement of Cash Flows. Refer back to the Precision Tools Statement of Cash Flows as you read this. Note also the suggestion of the kinds of insights that can emerge from comparing a company's Income and Cash Flow Statements.

This material should give you a good foundation for appreciating the remaining material in the chapter. This consists of two pieces that discuss some of the most common forms of accounting and financial reporting manipulation. The article by Henry notes that accounting rules themselves are partly to blame for such manipulation because they give companies wide discretion in making assumptions that can have a significant impact on financial statements. Henry focuses in particular on techniques that corporations can use to affect earnings and cash flow. As you read these, relate them back to the items on the Precision Tools Financial Statement in order to see what kind of differences they can make.

The excerpt from Warren has two important parts. First, it focuses on what has been the most common form of accounting manipulation in recent years: improper revenue recognition. This occurs when companies record revenues from sales before they are entitled to, or count as sales transactions that don't constitute a true exchange of goods or services for revenues. Warren provides a useful catalogue of the various schemes that companies may use to engage in improper revenue recognition.

The second important feature of Warren's article is its discussion of the role of lawyers in the revenue recognition process. He underscores that when recognition of revenue is appropriate is a legal question, centering essentially on when a company has unconditionally surrendered ownership and control of a good or has provided a service that entitles the company to a relatively certain amount of compensation. As Warren declares, this requires lawyers to analyze "contractual performances by their corporate clients, an area that falls squarely within their education, training, and experience."

Warren thus suggests that the modern corporate lawyer must have sufficient familiarity with accounting and revenue recognition practices in order to fulfill her duty to provide competent representation. He argues that the corporate lawyer should undertake "independent, random inquiries" of participants in the sales process and engage in "modified, or short-form due diligence investigation" to confirm the integrity of the revenue recognition process. Is Warren's suggestion consistent with Model Rule 1.13? Does it represent the "cop" role that Nelson and Nielsen describe in Chapter 6? Is the duty of inquiry that Warren proposes feasible? How will a lawyer know that she has done enough?

The Problem asks you to draw on the material on forms of financial fraud to determine if you perceive any red flags that require closer scrutiny of the company's proposed financial statements. You should identify the specific factors that lead you to this conclusion.

MODEL RULES: 1.1, 1.2, 1.13, 8.4

A. CORPORATE ACCOUNTING AND FINANCIAL REPORTING SYSTEMS

Publicly traded companies periodically provide information on their financial condition for review by current and prospective shareholders, creditors, stock analysts, and other interested parties. The financial statements that accompany the corporation's quarterly (10–Q) and annual (10–K) reports to the Securities and Exchange Commission (SEC) furnish the most comprehensive financial portrait of the company. While the statements generally contain a variety of financial information, their most important components are the balance sheet, income statement, and statement of cash flows, all of which are discussed in more detail below in the excerpt from Bauman, et al.

Financial statements are representations that ultimately are attributable to the corporation and its management. Under the Sarbanes–Oxley legislation enacted in 2002, both the Chief Executive Officer (CEO) and Chief Financial Officer (CFO) must certify to the SEC that the financial statements and other financial information included in the 10–K and 10–Q "fairly present in all material respects the financial condition, results of operations, and cash flows" of the company for the period covered by the report. This represents a standard of accuracy and completeness than is broader than compliance with Generally Accepted Accounting Principles (GAAP), which are discussed below.

In addition, management is responsible for preparing the Management's Discussion and Analysis of Financial Conditions and Results of Operations (MD & A) in its 10–K and 10–Q reports to the SEC. The MD & A provides a narrative explanation of the company's financial statements that is supposed to describe the broader context in which those statements should be reviewed. This context consists of those trends, events, and uncertainties that are likely to be material to the company's future performance. It also includes accounting estimates and assumptions that may be material because of the subjectivity and judgment required to account for highly uncertain circumstances.

The preparation and review of the company's financial statements involves three main parties: the company's internal auditors, its outside auditing firm, and the audit committee of the Board of Directors. Each has distinctive responsibilities and obligations.

Internal Auditors

Members of the company's internal auditing program are company employees who work to establish and implement the company's "internal controls" over financial reporting. Such controls involve policies and procedures that are designed to maintain records that accurately reflect a company's transactions. Such records enable the company to prepare its financial statements in accordance with GAAP, and to ensure that all receipts and expenditures have been duly authorized by management. Internal controls help prevent or detect the unauthorized use, acquisition, or disposition of a company's assets that could have a material effect on the financial statements.

Examples of specific control procedures include recording and reconciling account balances, classes of transactions, and assertions in financial statements; controls over significant transactions that are not routine; and procedures for summarizing and adjusting amounts in books and records in a form amenable to depiction in the financial statements. For instance, a company may require the signature of two officials for expenditures above a certain amount, and the presentation of documentation that items have been shipped before the company can record revenue from their sale.

The company must include in its 10–K a report by management that evaluates the effectiveness of the system of internal controls over financial reporting, discloses any "material weaknesses" in that system, and indicates that the company's outside auditor has attested to soundness of this evaluation. In addition, management must on a quarterly basis evaluate and disclose any changes in the internal controls that have materially affected, or are likely materially to affect, the effectiveness of those controls.

Outside Auditor

Once the company has prepared its financial statements in connection with its 10–K, the corporation must have an outside auditor review those statements to determine if they are in accordance with GAAP. Before providing certification of such compliance in the 10–K, the outside auditor must report to the audit committee on the company's "critical accounting policies and practices," and on all alternative accounting treatments of material financial information that have been discussed with management, along with the auditor's view of the preferred treatment.

The audit committee is responsible for hiring and evaluating the work of the company's outside auditor. It also must assess the auditor's independence by examining all relationships between the auditor and the company. In particular, the committee must approve any non-audit work done by the auditor for the company, such as various management consulting functions, to ensure that the desire to continue to receive such work does not compromise the auditor's independence.

The Audit Committee

A combination of Sarbanes–Oxley legislation and SEC and stock exchange rules establish that the audit committee of the Board of Directors bears the major responsibility for ensuring the integrity of a corporation's financial reports. The committee must be comprised entirely of independent directors, and has the authority to hire not only the outside auditing firm, but the committee's own outside legal and financial advisors. In addition, the committee must contain at least one member who is a "financial expert," or explain in its SEC filings why it does not have such a member.

The committee's main duties include the following:

(1) establishing procedures for receiving and responding to complaints from company employees regarding accounting, internal accounting, or auditing matters;

(2) reviewing the outside auditor's annual report on its internal quality control measures, and any material issues raised by the auditor's most recent review of such measures;

(3) discussing with management and the outside auditor the company annual audited financial statements and quarterly statements, and the MD & A;

(4) discussing earnings press releases and financial information and earnings guidance given to analysts and rating agencies;

(5) reviewing with the CEO and the CFO their certifications regarding financial information in the 10–K and 10–Q;

(6) periodically meeting separately with management and the internal and outside auditors;

(7) reviewing with the outside auditor any audit problems or difficulties and management's response;

(8) resolving any disagreements between management and the outside auditor regarding accounting issues;

(9) discussing with management major issues regarding accounting principles and financial statements, including any significant changes in the company's selection or application of accounting principles; and

(10) preparing a report from the committee to be included in the company's annual proxy statement.

Current law thus makes an internal control system the cornerstone of efforts to ensure the integrity of a company's financial reporting, and places ultimate responsibility for the effectiveness of that system on the audit committee.

Collaboration

While no single process describes how all companies perform all the functions described above, corporations generally provide for extensive communication and coordination among management, internal auditors, the outside auditing firm, and the audit committee. As a basis for management's certifications that accompany the 10–K and 10–Q, many companies require "sub-certifications" from lower ranking officials about matters within the business units for which they are responsible. An official may be asked to certify that with respect to his or her unit that the financial information submitted to the company fairly presents the condition of the unit, that there are no material weaknesses in the unit's internal control procedures, that there are no material transactions that have not been properly recorded, and other such representations relevant to the financial affairs of the unit, as well as its compliance with all applicable laws.

Parties involved in meeting their responsibilities with respect to financial reporting generally are in contact with the audit committee during the course of their work, and are expected to alert the committee of any significant issues that arise. Such contact will occur with respect to management's obligation to certify that 10–K and 10–Q reports filed with the SEC are not misleading and that the financial statements contained in them fairly represent the financial condition of the company. The audit committee should have the opportunity to review these certifications and discuss them with management before they are included in the 10–K and 10–Q.

Coordination with management and the committee also is necessary in regard to management's assessment of the effectiveness of the company's internal control system and the existence of any material weaknesses in it, which also requires review by the corporation's outside auditor. In addition, the outside auditor must, prior to certifying the financial statements, report to the audit committee on the company's critical accounting policies and practices, any significant change in the selection of application of accounting principles, and alternative accounting treatments of material items in the financial statements.

The excerpt below from Bauman, et al. provides an overview of basic accounting concepts and financial reports. The excerpt from Warren describes potential abuses with respect to companies' accounting for revenue, or "revenue recognition," which in recent years has been the most significant form of accounting fraud. Warren's article is especially important because it discusses the role of lawyers in monitoring a company's revenue recognition practices.

B.   FINANCIAL STATEMENTS

Jeffrey D. Bauman, Elliott J. Weiss & Alan R. Palmiter,
CORPORATIONS LAW AND POLICY: MATERIALS AND PROBLEMS

(5th ed. 2003)

PRECISION TOOLS, INC.
BALANCE SHEET
(As of December 31)

Assets	2002	2001
Current Assets		
Cash	150,000	275,000
Accounts receivable (less allowance for doubtful accounts)	1,380,000	1,145,000
Inventories	1,310,000	1,105,000
Prepaid expenses	40,000	35,000
Total Current Assets	2,880,000	2,560,000
Fixed Assets		
Land *	775,000	775,000
Buildings	2,000,000	2,000,000
Machinery	1,000,000	935,000
Office equipment	225,000	205,000
Total property, plant and equipment	4,000,000	3,915,000
Less accumulated depreciation	1,620,000	1,370,000
Net Fixed Assets **	2,380,000	2,545,000
Total Assets	5,260,000	5,105,000
Liabilities and Equity		
Current Liabilities		
Accounts payable	900,000	825,000
Notes payable	600,000	570,000
Accrued expenses payable	250,000	235,000
Total Current Liabilities	1,750,000	1,630,000
Long Term Liabilities		
Notes payable, 12.5%, due 12/15/13	2,000,000	2,000,000
Notes payable, 11%, due 7/1/02	—	355,000
Total Liabilities	3,750,000	3,985,000
Stockholders' Equity		
Common stock (1,000 shares authorized and outstanding)		
Paid-in capital	200,000	200,000
Retained earnings	1,310,000	920,000
Total Equity	1,510,000	1,120,000
Total Liabilities and Equity	5,260,000	5,105,000

* The land is in a modern industrial park, and was purchased fifteen years ago for $775,000—the price shown on the balance sheet. A Comparable nearby property recently sold for $975,000. [Ed.]

** The machinery and equipment are in good repair. Depreciation is on a level (straight line) basis over the estimated life of the equipment. The fair market value of the building and equipment combined is about $200,000 more than the amounts shown on the balance sheet. [Ed.]

STATEMENT OF INCOME
(Year Ended December 31)

	2002	**2001**	**2000**
Net sales	7,500,000	7,000,000	6,800,000
Operating Expenses			
Cost of goods sold	4,980,000	4,650,000	4,607,000
Depreciation	250,000	240,000	200,000
Selling and administrative expense *	1,300,000	1,220,000	1,150,000
Research and development	50,000	125,000	120,000
Operating income	920,000	765,000	723,000
Interest expense	320,000	375,000	375,000
Income before taxes	600,000	390,000	348,000
Income taxes	210,000	136,000	122,000
Net Income	390,000	254,000	226,000

* Includes salaries paid to Stern and Starr totaling $130,000 in 2002, and $100,000 in 2001 and $100,000 in 2000, and bonuses totaling $120,000 in 2002, $100,000 in 2001, and $80,000 in 2000.

STATEMENT OF CASH FLOWS
(Year Ended December 31)

	2002	**2001**	**2000**
From Operating Activities			
Net Income	390,000	254,000	226,000
Decrease (Increase) in accounts receivable	(235,000)	(34,000)	(32,000)
Decrease (Increase) in inventories	(205,000)	(28,000)	(3,000)
Decrease (Increase) in prepaid expenses	(5,000)	(3,000)	(3,000)
Increase (Decrease) in accounts payable	75,000	25,000	20,000
Increase (Decrease) in accrued expenses payable	15,000	7,000	5,000
Depreciation	250,000	240,000	200,000
Total from Operating Activities	285,000	461,000	383,000
From Investing Activities			
Sales (Purchases) of machinery	(65,000)	(378,000)	(263,000)
Sales (Purchases) of office equipment	(20,000)	(27,000)	(25,000)
Total from Investing Activities	(85,000)	(405,000)	(288,000)
From Financing Activities			
Increase (Decrease) in short-term borrowings	30,000	(40,000)	(35,000)
Increase (Decrease) in long-term borrowings	(355,000)	—	—
Total from Financing Activities	(325,000)	(40,000)	(35,000)
Increase (Decrease) in Cash Position	(125,000)	16,000	60,000

* * *

"Omigosh, accounting! This is what I went to law school to avoid! If I wasn't so afraid of numbers, I might have gone to B-school. Do I really have to understand this stuff?"

Don't panic! We appreciate that some—perhaps most—law students become apprehensive when they reach this Chapter. But we also are convinced that every business lawyer should have at least a rudimentary grasp of basic accounting concepts and that lawyers practicing in other fields also often will find such knowledge to be extremely useful.

This Chapter is designed to introduce basic accounting concepts to law students who have *no* training in accounting or finance. The Chapter also introduces an approach to accounting that students with training in accounting or finance may find unfamiliar. Most accounting and finance courses are oriented to the informational needs of business owners and managers, who use financial information to keep track of, and exercise control over, the businesses that they own or operate. From the perspective of such owner/managers, the most useful financial statements are those that come as close as possible to presenting the objective truth about the firm's financial status and the results of its operations.

Lawyers, in contrast, more frequently must deal with financial statements in adversarial or quasi-adversarial settings. When a financial statement has been prepared by or on behalf of an opposing party, the lawyer must appreciate the possibility that that statement—even if it has been prepared by a certified public accountant (CPA) who has opined that it presents financial information "fairly" and "in accordance with generally accepted accounting principles" (GAAP)—will in fact represent a subjective and self-serving picture of the opposing party's financial situation.

This possibility exists as a consequence of three fundamental truths relating to the accounting process. First, as concerns financial statements of any complexity, there is no such thing as objective truth. Many judgments are required. Many estimates must be made. Many transactions can be conceptualized in different ways, all of them consistent with GAAP, and then assigned the value most consistent with the conceptualization adopted. In short, although a firm's financial statements always appear precise because they are presented in numerical form, they often reflect numerous, highly subjective judgments. SEC Chairman Harvey Pitt acknowledged this reality when he suggested that every public company should be required to "identify the three, four or five most critical accounting principles upon which [that] company's financial status depends, and which involve the most complex, subjective or ambiguous decisions or assessments." Those companies, he suggested, then should tell investors "concisely and clearly, how these principles are applied, as well as information about the range of possible effects in differing applications of these principles." Harvey Pitt, *How to Prevent Future Enrons* (available at http://www.sec.gov/

news/speech/spch530.htm) (Dec. 11, 2001). *See also* Securities and Exchange Commission Rel. No. 34–45149 (Dec. 12, 2001) (encouraging public companies to provide a "full explanation, in plain English, of their 'critical accounting policies,' the judgments and uncertainties affecting the application of those policies, and the likelihood that materially different amounts would be reported under different conditions or using different assumptions.")

Second, a person preparing a financial statement for use by others often will be inclined to use the flexibility inherent in GAAP to present financial information in a manner that best serves her interests. A divorcing spouse will try to minimize her income and the value of her assets. A person selling a business will attempt to make the business appear as profitable and as free of risks as possible.

Third, CPAs, including many in the largest public accounting firms, have demonstrated that they are willing to use their professional expertise to help their clients understand how the flexibility inherent in GAAP can be exploited to achieve those clients' financial reporting goals. CPAs purport to be dedicated to meeting the public's need for accurate financial information, but accountant's independence often has proven to be open to question. Clients hire—and retain the ability to fire—the CPAs who certify their financial statements. This creates an inherent conflict of interest—a conflict that is exacerbated when accountants generate large amounts of income by also providing consulting services to their audit clients. In addition, in many situations GAAP require firms to make estimates about subjective matters that their CPAs then can accept so long as those estimates are not clearly unreasonable. This creates a business environment in which, for many CPAs, the route to professional and financial success lies not in making rigorous efforts to ensure that clients' financial statements are as objectively accurate as possible but in developing a reputation as an auditor who will help a client paint the financial pictures she wants to paint.* Substantial evidence suggests that the CPA firms that audited the books of Enron, Global Crossing, Waste Management, Xerox, Sunbeam and other large companies charged with financial improprieties in recent years operated in this fashion.

Warren Buffett, the famed investor and chairman of Berkshire Hathaway Inc., noted some time ago that "many managements view GAAP not as a standard to be met, but as an obstacle to be overcome. Too often their accountants assist them.... Even honest and well-intentioned managements sometimes stretch GAAP a bit...." More recently—but well in advance of the accounting scandals brought to light in the early 2000s—Mr. Buffett acknowledged that corporate norms had

---

* This brings to mind an old joke about the CPA who succeeds in securing a new client by coming up with the "right" answer to the client's "killer" question:

Client: "Finally, how much are two plus two?"

CPA: "How much do you want it to be?"

shifted to the point where "stretch[ing] GAAP a bit" had become a pervasive problem:

> What bothers me ... is that people of generally high integrity who you would trust in any situation—you could make them the trustee under your will— ... now ... feel that as the manager of a major company it is up to [them] to play the accounting game, particularly the ones suggested to [them] by [their] very own auditor....

> It is the degree to which the high grade people have either been co-opted or acquiesced or whatever word you want to pick. And that's very tough to cleanse the system of because you don't have good guys and bad guys anymore.

Lawrence A. Cunningham, Ed., *Conversations from the Warren Buffett Symposium*, 19 CARDOZO L.REV. 719, 799 (1997).

Students also should find it useful to obtain a grasp of basic accounting concepts and terminology because that will allow them to better understand many of the cases that follow. Some, such as *Kamin v. American Express* in Chapter 9 and *Francis v. United Jersey Bank* in Chapter 17, directly involve accounting issues. In many others, understanding what gives value to the businesses involved will help students appreciate what really is at stake. Even as concerns this Chapter, if we assume Michael, Jessica and Bernie decide to try to purchase PT's business, some knowledge of accounting would be essential to allow a lawyer to advise them as to the representations and warranties they should seek from Stern and Starr in connection with that transaction.

Contrary to common belief, understanding basic accounting concepts does not require expertise in mathematics. True, as PT's financial statements evidence, accounting information is presented largely in numerical form. But the materials that follow emphasize that, while the numbers in financial statements appear precise, in fact they (i) are the product of a highly conceptual process that involves many subjective judgments; (ii) reflect that process and those judgments, not some sort of scientific truth; and (iii) tell only part of what is important about the subject firm's business, finances and operations.

This last point is significant. The goal of financial statements is to convey information to the user, whether she be an investor, a lender, or a corporate manager. But the information that financial statements provide often tells far less than the entire story. As you read the materials that follow, ask yourself what additional information you would want in order to understand the story that lies behind PT's financial statements. In so doing, you will begin to perform one of a lawyer's most important functions in a business transaction: helping her client ask the right questions.

1. INTRODUCTION TO ACCOUNTING PRINCIPLES

The two basic financial statements are the balance sheet and the income statement. The relationship of these two statements often is described using the analogy of a snapshot and a motion picture. A balance sheet—the "snapshot"—presents a picture of the firm at some given moment, listing all property it owns (its "*assets*"), all amounts it owes (its "*liabilities*"), and the value, at least conceptually, of the owners' interest in the firm (its "*equity*"). An income statement—the "motion picture"—presents a picture of the results of the firm's operations during the period between the dates of successive balance sheets.

Financial statements are produced through a three-stage process. First, a company records in its books information concerning every transaction in which it is involved—the recording and controls stage. Next, in the audit stage, the company (sometimes with the assistance of independent public accountants) verifies the accuracy of the information it has recorded. Finally, in the accounting stage, the company classifies and analyzes the audited information and presents it in a set of financial statements.

MBCA § 16.20 requires corporations to furnish their shareholders with annual balance sheets and income statements, but allows corporations to decide what accounting principles to use when preparing those statements. Most firms, and all public corporations, use generally accepted accounting principles, or "GAAP." GAAP are promulgated—or, more accurately, legislated—by a quasi-public body, the Financial Accounting Standard Board (FASB). The rules adopted by the FASB embody not immutable scientific or mathematical truths, but the (often controversial) judgments and policy preferences of a group of highly-qualified accounting professionals. Moreover, as the perceptions, judgments and preferences of the members of the FASB change over time, so do GAAP governing how information about various kinds of transactions must be presented. This suggests an important insight about accounting: one needs to keep in mind the difference between actual events and how information about those events is presented in financial statements.

Events themselves are real. How an event should be described in a financial statement often is problematic. If information about an event is to be included in a financial statement, GAAP control or limit how that information can be presented. One must understand the more important assumptions and fundamental principles underlying GAAP in order to interpret the information in financial statements. Among the more important of those assumptions and principles are the following:

Separate Entity Assumption: A business enterprise is viewed as an accounting unit separate and distinct from its owners, whether or not it has a separate legal existence.

Continuity Assumption: Unless the facts suggest otherwise, a business enterprise is assumed to be a going concern that will continue in operation for the foreseeable future.

Unit of Measure Assumption: Financial statements report the results of business activity in terms of money and assume that the value of the relevant unit of money—the dollar—remains constant.

Time Period Assumption: To produce useful financial information, the results of business activities must be allocated to discrete time periods—generally one year or some portion of a year—even though most business activities extend over or affect several time periods. How these allocations are made often will have material effects on a firm's financial statements for a given time period.

Cost Principle: Historic cost provides the best basis for recording a transaction, because it can be determined objectively and is verifiable.

Consistency Principle: A firm should consistently apply the same accounting concepts, standards and procedures from one period to the next.

Full Disclosure Principle: Financial statements should include sufficient information, in the statements or in explanatory notes, to ensure full understanding of all material economic information about a firm.

Modifying Principles: (a) *Materiality*—Accounting only needs to be concerned with the accuracy of information that a reasonable decision-maker would consider to be important; where information is immaterial, strict adherence to GAAP is not required. (b) *Conservatism*—Accounting counteracts managers' assumed tendency to present financial information about a firm in the most favorable light possible by mandating, in general, that profits not be anticipated and that probable losses be recognized as soon as possible.

The goals of the accounting process (and of GAAP) include presenting information about a firm's financial position and the results of its operations that (i) is as accurate as possible, (ii) is as reliable as possible, and (iii) can be prepared at reasonable cost. Trade-offs between these goals often are required. For example, one might argue that PT's balance sheet should report the value of its land as $975,000, because a comparable nearby property recently sold for that price, rather than as the $775,000 that PT paid for the land years ago. But in deciding whether to accept this argument, one would need to consider a number of additional questions: How similar are the two pieces of land? Even if they are very similar, should PT be required to determine whether land values have increased or decreased since the other property was sold? Should the value of PT's land be "marked to market" even if no sale of comparable land has occurred recently? What is the best way to determine the market value of PT's land if it has some unique characteristics? Is market value information sufficiently important and sufficiently reliable to justify the cost of obtaining that information? Should the answer to the previous questions depend on whether PT intends to hold the land or sell it? If the land should be valued at its current or estimated market value, should PT's other assets be valued on the same basis? What about its liabilities? Etc., etc., etc.

Three points emerge. First, GAAP consists of a series of conventions, many of which are not immediately intuitive. These conventions serve to resolve potential policy choices as to the most appropriate method of presenting financial information. Second, whatever the shortcomings of GAAP, developing better accounting rules involves complex problems to which there are no easy solutions. Finally, a person who understands GAAP can better appreciate the limitations of the information presented in a firm's financial statements and the additional information that one may need to make decisions relating to that firm.

2. FINANCIAL STATEMENT TERMS AND CONCEPTS

a. How Different Financial Statements Relate

As noted above, the balance sheet often is described as a "snapshot" and the income statement as a "motion picture." The income statement also can be viewed as the "bridge" between successive balance sheets, in that it records whether the firm realized a profit (or incurred a loss) during the period between successive balance sheets. That profit (or loss) then is reflected on the firm's balance sheet as of the end of that period by increasing (or decreasing) the owners' equity account by the amount of that profit (or loss).

The fundamental equation, and thus the balance sheet, represents the conceptual core of a firm's financial statements. Investors and creditors, however, often are more interested in a firm's income statement. They view information about the results of past operations as the best available indicator of a firm's ability to generate profits in the future. Moreover, investors seem to place a very high value on firms whose profits rise steadily.* As one commentator has observed, "if a company reports six straight years of rising profits, Wall Street will cheer. But if it reports five up years and one year of earnings falling only 1%, the company may find itself friendless." Roger Lowenstein, *How to Be a Winner in the Profits Game*, THE WALL ST. J. C1 (April 3, 1997).

Managers, not surprisingly, are sensitive to the way in which many investors evaluate income statements. Moreover, because of the flexibility inherent in GAAP, it is not uncommon for a firm's managers to "massage" their firms' income statement so as to report steady profits or, better yet, steadily rising profits.** In the discussion of financial statement terms and concepts in this and the following section, we note

---

* Recall, from Chapter 2, that most people are risk averse. The more volatile a firm's income, the greater the risk premium investors are likely to demand before investing in that firm—*i.e.*, the less they will be prepared to pay for any given level of anticipated earnings. This gives managers an economic incentive to "manage" the earnings their firm reports to eliminate volatility.

** Burgstahler & Dichev, *Earnings management to avoid earnings decreases and losses*, 24 J. ACCTG. & ECON. 99 (1997), provides compelling evidence that earnings are "managed." One would expect that roughly equal numbers of firms would report earnings just above and just below their previous year's earnings. The authors found, however, that reported earnings form "a striking, nonrandom pattern," with very few firms falling just short of previous year's earnings and many more firms matching or barely exceeding previous year's earnings.

several areas in which GAAP provide opportunities for such "massaging" of financial statement numbers.

The GAAP requirement that most firms use *accrual accounting* to prepare their financial statements is central here. Under the *Realization Principle*, a firm must recognize revenue in the period that services are rendered or goods are shipped, even if payment is not received in that period (and cannot recognize revenue until services are rendered or goods are shipped). Under the *Matching Principle*, a firm must allocate to the period in which revenues are recognized the expenses it incurred to generate those revenues. Consider how these requirements would affect a lawyer who provided $1,000 in services in Year 1, who paid $250 for secretarial support in that year, and whose bill for $1,000 was not paid until Year 2. If the lawyer used *cash accounting*, she would report the $1,000 as earned in Year 2, when payment was received, but deduct the charge for secretarial support in Year 1, when it was paid. Using accrual accounting, which focuses not on the movement of cash but on the performance of services and on matching income to expenses, the lawyer would recognize the $1,000 in income in Year 1 and would also record the $250 secretarial expense in Year 1.

Taken together, the Realization and Matching Principles go a long way toward ensuring that an income statement prepared using accrual accounting presents a conceptually sound picture of the economic results of a firm's operations for a given period. Those principles also limit substantially a firm's ability to manipulate its payment and receipt of cash so as to "manage" the earnings it reports. But because recognition of revenues and recording of expenses are tied to events more difficult to measure than the movement of cash, the Realization and Matching Principles also increase substantially the subjectivity of the information included in accrual basis financial statements. How, for example, should a lawyer record the cost, paid in year 1, of a party to publicize the opening of her office? Is it all as an expense incurred in Year 1, since the lawyer paid it all in Year 1, or should only a portion of the publicity expense be allocated to Year 1 and the remainder deducted in future years so long as the lawyer believes that the publicity will continue to produce benefits for several years?

GAAP addresses this problem of subjectivity, at least in part, by requiring firms to prepare a third financial statement—a *statement of cash flows*—in addition to a balance sheet and an income statement. A firm must use cash, not "income," to pay its bills, repay its debts, and make distributions to its owners. Cash, not "income," must be on hand when the firm needs it. Over a period of many years, a firm's total income and cash flow usually will approximate each other. But over a shorter period of time, income and cash flow may differ substantially.

The statement of cash flows, as its name suggests, reports on the movement of cash into and out of a firm. The statement reflects all transactions that involve the receipt or disbursement of cash, whether they relate to operations or involve only balance sheet accounts such as purchases of plant and equipment, new borrowings, repayment of loans, equity investments, or distributions to equity holders.

b. *Balance Sheet Terms and Concepts*

What follows are brief descriptions of the most important balance sheet accounts. The descriptions also point out instances where the accounting treatment of these and related accounts has an impact on a firm's income statement and highlight areas in which accounting entries often reflect subjective judgments. As you read these descriptions, consider what issues may exist with respect to PT's balance sheet and, where relevant, PT's income and cash flow statements.

1. *Assets* are listed in the balance sheet in the order of their liquidity, beginning with cash, followed by assets that the firm expects to convert to cash in the reasonably near future, and continuing to other assets, such as plant and equipment, that the firm uses in its business.

(A) *Current assets* include cash and other assets which in the normal course of business will be converted into cash in the reasonably near future, generally within one year of the date of the balance sheet. More specifically:

(1) *Cash* is money in the till and money in demand deposits in the bank.

(2) *Marketable securities* are securities purchased with cash not needed for current operations. Most firms use their surplus cash to purchase very liquid securities, such as commercial paper and treasury bills, with a view to generating interest income. Some firms also purchase publicly traded debt and equity securities. Because the value of these securities readily can be determined, GAAP provide that (except where one company owns more than 20% of the stock of another), such securities shall be reported at their fair market value, rather than at their cost. Fluctuations in the value of marketable securities are recorded as income or loss on the reporting firm's income statement.

In recent years, it has become common for firms to invest large amounts in a variety of esoteric financial instruments, either to hedge against fluctuations in interest rates, commodity prices, or other values or to seek trading gains. In general, such instruments also must be "marked to market" as of the date of the balance sheet and the difference between their cost and market value must be recorded as a gain or loss. Where market prices for the goods or services covered by these instruments cannot readily be determined, management is required to make a good faith estimate as of what those prices are. In the case of Enron and a number of other corporations, many of these estimates have proven to be wildly optimistic.

(3) *Accounts receivable* are amounts not yet collected from customers to whom goods have been shipped or services delivered. In recognition of the fact that some customers will not pay their bills, GAAP require that accounts receivable be adjusted by deducting an allowance

(or "reserve") for bad debts. Firms usually compute the bad debt allowance on the basis of past experience. However, if substantial changes have occurred in the nature of a firm's customers, in its business or in the relevant economic environment, the firm's past experience may not be an accurate predictor of future results.*

Losses from extending credit to customers also represent a cost of doing business. Consequently, whenever a firm increases its allowance for bad debts, GAAP require it to record the increase as a charge against income identified as a "bad debt expense."

Notes or loans receivable are somewhat analogous to accounts receivable. They usually represent a very large portion of the assets of firms engaged in financing businesses. Relatively small percentage differences in such firms' allowances for bad debts often will have a major impact on their reported earnings. In a number of instances in recent years, banks and other financial firms, relying on past experience, grossly underestimated the portion of their outstanding loans that borrowers would not repay. As a result, many of those firms continued to report robust annual earnings right up to the time at which many borrowers began to default on their loans. Only then did it become clear that those firms were (and for some time may have been) insolvent.

(4) *Inventory* represents goods held for use in production or for sale to customers. GAAP require inventory to be valued at the lower of cost or market. The value a firm reports for its inventory will affect both the firm's balance sheet and its income statement. Items sold from inventory, called *cost of goods sold* ("COGS"), often represents a firm's largest single expense. Firms that hold a relatively small number of identifiable items in inventory often use the *specific identification method*. They value each inventory item at cost, unless its market value is lower than cost, and compute COGS by adding up the actual cost of all inventory items sold during the relevant period.

Most firms, though, find it impractical to keep track of the cost of each item in inventory. To compute COGS, these firms add their *purchases* during a reporting period to the value of their inventory at the start of the period (called *opening inventory*) and then subtracts the value of their *closing inventory*. By conducting a physical count at the end of an accounting period, a firm can determine the number of items in its closing inventory. The firm then can use one of three methods to value its closing inventory: the *average cost method*, which visualizes inventory as sold at random from a bin; the *first in, first out (FIFO) method*, which visualizes inventory as flowing through a pipeline; and the *last in, first out (LIFO) method*, which visualizes inventory as being added to and sold from the top of a stack.

---

* Similar problems can arise, for similar reasons, in firms that sell goods (such as books) subject to a right of return and record their sales net of an allowance for returns. If the people to whom they are selling or the products they are selling change significantly, past experience may not be an accurate indicator of future results.

In any period in which prices change significantly, the inventory method a firm uses can have a material impact on the value of its inventory account, on COGS, and hence on the firm's reported profits. An added wrinkle is that in many lines of business, the value of inventory sometimes declines as a consequence of technological developments (for example, improvements in personal computers) or changing tastes (as when a line of clothing goes out of style). If the value of items in inventory drops below their cost, GAAP require that the book value of inventory be reduced and that a charge against earnings be recorded for an equivalent amount. A firm's managers usually are best positioned to know whether such a charge is necessary, but may be reluctant to acknowledge that fact.

(5) *Prepaid expenses* are payments a firm has made in advance for services it will receive in the coming year, such as the value of ten months of a one-year insurance policy that a firm purchased and paid for two months before the year ended.

Deferred charges represent a type of asset similar to prepaid expenses, in that they reflect payments made in the current period for goods or services that will generate income in subsequent periods, such as advertising to introduce a new product. Firms sometimes inflate their reported profits by recording as deferred charges (and thus as assets) payments that should be charged against current income because they are unlikely to produce future benefits. A large deferred charge account, and especially a large and growing deferred charge account, usually should provoke further inquiry.

(B) *Fixed assets*, sometimes referred to as *property, plant and equipment*, are the assets a firm uses to conduct its operations (as opposed to assets it holds for sale). Under GAAP, when a firm acquires a fixed asset, it records the asset on its balance sheet at cost. However, because the firm will be using the fixed asset to generate revenue, under the Matching Principle the firm must charge a portion of the fixed asset's cost against the revenues received during the period the fixed asset is in use. This charge, known as a *depreciation expense*, can be computed using any of several formulas and is reflected in regular and periodic charges against income over the useful life of the asset in question. It reduces reported income even though it does not reflect any current outlay of cash—the cash was spent when the asset was acquired. Depreciation expenses also affect a firm's balance sheet; under GAAP, all depreciation expenses accrued with respect to a firm's fixed assets must be added up and recorded, on the asset side of the balance sheet, in an account called *allowance for depreciation* or *accumulated depreciation*, which is then subtracted from the cost of the firm's fixed assets.

The balance sheet value (or *book value*) of a firm's fixed assets—cost less the allowance for depreciation—is not intended to reflect, and usually does not reflect, either the current market value of those assets or what the firm would have to pay to replace them. In times of inflation, the book value of fixed assets often is much lower than either their current value or their replacement value. The book value of fixed assets also can exceed those assets' market value if the assets have become obsolete. In that event, as with inventory, the carrying value of those assets must be written down and earnings must be reduced by an equivalent amount.

(C) *Intangible assets* have no physical existence, but often have substantial value—a cable TV franchise granting a company the exclusive right to service certain areas, for example, or a patent or trade name. GAAP require firms to carry intangible assets at cost, less an allowance for *amortization* (the equivalent of depreciation, applied to intangibles). However, GAAP do not allow a firm to record as an asset the value of an intangible asset a firm has developed or promoted, rather than purchased. Consequently, the value of many extremely well-known and valuable intangible assets, such as the brand names "Coke" and "Pepsi," is not reflected on the balance sheets of the firms that own them.

Similarly, when a firm incurs expenditures for research and development (R & D), GAAP require the firm to treat those expenditures as current expenses and charge them against current revenues. A firm is not allowed to record R & D expenditures as intangible assets or deferred charges even where they have produced discoveries or led to development of products that will enable the firm to generate substantial revenues in future years. In this respect, the accounting system's conservative bias produces balance sheets that understate the value of firm assets. There is also some evidence that this bias leads those managers who are preoccupied with short term earnings to under invest in R & D.

Financial statements sometimes include an intangible asset called *goodwill* which is wholly the product of accounting conventions. Assume one firm acquires another for a price that exceeds the fair market value of the acquired firm's identifiable assets. How should the acquiring firm account for that difference? Under GAAP, it must record the difference as "goodwill." For many years, GAAP also required firms to amortize goodwill over a period of not more than 40 years (*i.e.*, to report an annual expense equal to at least 2.5% of all acquired goodwill), which reduced the acquiring firm's reported earnings. In 2000, GAAP were revised to provide that goodwill should not be amortized.

Now, when a firm acquires another for a price that exceeds the fair market value of the acquired firm's identifiable assets, the acquiror still must record the difference as goodwill, but can carry the goodwill as an asset on its books indefinitely without amortization. (GAAP also were revised to allow firms that had been amortizing previously acquired goodwill to stop doing so and to carry any remaining goodwill on their books indefinitely without further amortization.) However, every firm that has goodwill on its books is required to periodically review the value of its goodwill and to write it off, in whole or in part, if the estimated fair market value of the business unit with which the goodwill is associated drops below the unit's book value.

2. *Liabilities* usually are divided into current liabilities and long-term liabilities.

(A) *Current liabilities* are the debts a firm owes that must be paid within one year of the balance sheet date. Current liabilities often are evaluated in relation to current assets which, in a sense, are the source from which current liabilities must be paid.

(B) *Long-term liabilities* are debts due more than one year from the balance sheet date. Balance sheets usually list fixed liabilities, such as mortgages and bonds, by their maturities and the interest rates they bear. Some long-term liabilities must be estimated. An insurance company, for example, can only estimate the amounts it will have to pay out on the policies it has written. Those estimates usually have a material impact on both the company's balance sheet and its income statement.

In recent years, business firms have developed a variety of techniques for engaging in *off balance sheet financing*—transactions that involve long-term financial obligations, but which, because of their form, are not recorded as liabilities on the balance sheet. GAAP concerning when off balance sheet financing arrangements must be disclosed (generally in footnotes to the reporting firm's balance sheet) are very complex. Investment bankers, lawyers and accountants have created a "cottage industry" of sorts helping firms borrow money through off balance sheet financing arrangements that they do not have to disclose. At the time this book went to press, FASB was in the process of revising the rules that govern off balance sheet financing.

GAAP also are complex with respect to how *contingent liabilities*— such as loan guarantees, warranty obligations, and claims by plaintiffs in civil suits—are to be calculated and when they must be disclosed. Where no claim has yet been asserted, GAAP often do not require any disclosure unless—as is the case with warranties—experience makes clear that some claims will be asserted.

3. *Equity* represents the owners' interest in a firm. The terminology used for equity accounts will vary, depending on whether the firm is a sole proprietorship, a partnership, a LLC or a corporation. Whatever the form, the amount of a firm's equity—also often referred to as its *net worth*—will equal the difference between the book values of the firm's assets and liabilities. (This follows from the fundamental equation. That is, if ASSETS = LIABILITIES + EQUITY, then ASSETS − LIABILITIES = EQUITY.) If the firm's liabilities exceed its assets, equity will be a negative figure.

Corporations' balance sheets generally include two or three equity accounts. Some state laws require corporations to issue stock with some *par* or *stated value*. As explained in more detail in Chapter 9, par or stated value can be established arbitrarily, but once established, it has legal and accounting significance. When a corporation issues stock with a par or stated value, its balance sheet must include a *stated capital* or *legal capital* account for each class of such stock. The amount in each of those accounts is calculated by multiplying the par value of that class of stock by the number of shares issued and outstanding. In a jurisdiction that does not require stock to have par or stated value, no stated capital or legal capital account is necessary.

In economic terms, a corporation's equity has two components. The first, often recorded as *paid-in capital*, reflects the total amount the corporation has received from those who have purchased its stock. (A corporation with par value stock often will divide paid-in capital between accounts entitled "stated capital" and "capital surplus." Terminology varies though, and other account titles sometimes are used.) The second, called *retained earnings* or *earned surplus*, reflects the cumulative results of the corporation's operations over the period since it was formed. Each year, this account increases or decreases in an amount equal to the corporation's net income or net loss. This account also is reduced by an amount equal to any distributions the corporation has made to its shareholders in the form of *dividends* or any amounts the corporation has paid to repurchase its stock.

3. INTRODUCTION TO FINANCIAL ANALYSIS

Managers, investors and creditors use the information in financial statements to engage in financial analysis of the reporting company. Such analysis involves consideration of the relationship between certain data in a firm's current and prior financial statements. It also involves comparison of data derived from a given firm's financial statements with comparable data drawn from the financial statements of other firms engaged in the same or similar businesses. Consider the following types of analyses in connection with PT's financial statements.

a. Cash Flow Analysis

As should be clear by now, "income" is a concept, and computation of a firm's income generally depends on numerous subjective judgments and is heavily influenced by the assumptions underlying GAAP. Cash, on the other hand, is tangible; one can touch, smell and even taste it. More importantly, a company needs cash to pay its bills, repay its debts, and make distributions to its owners.

The sources and uses of a given firm's cash can include its operations, its purchases and sales of fixed assets, and its financing activities. The statement of cash flows reports how much cash a firm has generated and how much it has used in connection with each of these three activities. PT's statement of cash flows shows how that firm has generated and used cash during the prior two years.

Firms frequently report significantly different amounts of income and cash flow for any given year. The disparity most often is attributable, at least in part, to GAAP requirements relating to accounting for fixed assets. Recall that when a firm acquires a fixed asset, it records that asset at cost on its balance sheet and then, over the useful life of that asset, records a portion of its cost as a charge against income—a depreciation expense—on its income statement. That "expense" does not reflect a current disbursement of cash; the cash was spent when the asset was acquired.

As a result, cash flow will be lower than reported income in years in which large amounts of fixed assets are purchased and will be higher than reported income in years in which (non-cash) depreciation expenses are greater than the amounts spent to purchase fixed assets. Look again at PT's income statement and statement of cash flows. Note that the amount PT charges as depreciation expense each year also shows up as a positive entry in the statement of cash flows, while PT's purchases of machinery serve to reduce cash flows.

Changes in the amounts of cash a firm used to provide financing to customers (increases or decreases in accounts receivable), to carry inventory, and to prepay expenses also will affect cash flow from operations, as will increases or decreases in current liabilities. Finally, the cash flow statement reports financing activities: increases and decreases in short- and long-term borrowing, sales and repurchases of equity interests, and distributions to equity holders.

Comparison of a firm's income and cash flow statements often will provide insights into the direction of its business or suggest further inquiries that one might make. Consider the implications when cash flow from operations lags income, for example. Is the shortfall due to rapid growth in the firm's business? If so, is substantial additional financing necessary to sustain that growth? Do increases in inventory and accounts receivable reflect long-term growth in the firm's business, or a short-term effort to pump up reported earnings? If accounts receivable and inventory decreased, does that suggest the firm is managing its current assets more efficiently or that its business is declining? By asking these and similar questions, one can obtain a better understanding of a firm's business than would be the case if one analyzed that firm's balance sheet and income statement alone. Note again that while the financial statements provide a good deal of useful data, it is the user's task to recognize and ask the additional questions that arise from that data.

David Henry, Fuzzy Numbers: Despite the Reforms, Corporate Profits Can Be as Distorted and Confusing as Ever. Here's How the Game is Played

Business Week, October 4, 2004

Construction giant and military contractor Halliburton Co. did something mind-boggling last year: It reported earnings of $339 million, even though it spent $775 million more than it took in from customers. The company did nothing illegal. Halliburton made big outlays in 2003 on contracts with the U.S. Army for work in Iraq—contracts for which it expected to be paid later. Still, it counted some of these expected revenues immediately because they related to work done last year. Investors didn't get the full picture until six weeks later, when the company filed its complete annual report with the Securities & Exchange Commission. Halliburton says it followed generally accepted accounting principles (GAAP).

Maybe so, but after three years of reforms in the wake of corporate scandals, the Halliburton case illustrates that earnings remain as susceptible to manipulation as ever. Why? Because accounting rules give companies wide discretion in using estimates to calculate their earnings. These adjustments are supposed to give shareholders a more accurate picture of what's happening in a business at a given time, and often they do. Bean counters call this accrual accounting, and they have practiced it for decades. By accruing, or allotting, revenues to specific periods, they aim to allocate income to the quarter or year in which it was effectively earned, though not necessarily received. Likewise, expenses are allocated to the period when sales were made, not necessarily when the money was spent.

The problem with today's fuzzy earnings numbers is not accrual accounting itself. It's that investors, analysts, and money managers are having an increasingly hard time figuring out what judgments companies make to come up with those accruals, or estimates. The scandals at Enron, WorldCom, Adelphia Communications, and other companies are forceful reminders that investors could lose billions by not paying attention to how companies arrive at their earnings. The hazards were underscored again Sept. 22 when mortgage-finance giant Fannie Mae said its primary regulator had found that it had made accounting adjustments to dress-up its earnings and, in at least one case, achieve bonus compensation targets. The company said it is cooperating with government investigators. The broader concern is that corporate financial statements are often incomplete, inconsistent, or just plain unclear, making it a nightmare to sort out fact from fantasy. Says Trevor S. Harris, chief accounting analyst at Morgan Stanley: "The financial reporting system is completely broken."

Indeed, today's financial reports are more difficult to understand than ever. They're riddled with jargon that's hard to fathom and numbers that don't track. They're muddled, with inconsistent categories, vague entries, and hidden adjustments that disguise how much various estimates change a company's earnings from quarter to quarter, says Donn Vickrey, a former accounting professor and co-founder of Camelback Research Alliance Inc., a Scottsdale (Ariz.) firm hired by institutional investors to detect inflated earnings.

The upshot: The three major financial statements—income, balance sheet, and cash flow—that investors and analysts need to detect aggressive accounting and get a full picture of a company's value are out of sync with one another. Often, the income and cash-flow statements don't even cover the same time periods. "A genius has trouble trying to get them to tie together because different items are aggregated differently," says Patricia Doran Walters, director of research at CFA Institute, the professional association that tests and certifies financial analysts. "You have to do an enormous amount of guessing to even come close."

Many of the reforms adopted by Congress and the SEC will not remedy the situation. Most are aimed at policing the people who make the estimates rather than the estimates themselves. And some changes have yet to go into effect. No doubt, chief executives and auditing committees are paying closer attention to the numbers, and accounting experts believe there are fewer instances these days of outright fraud. But that's to be expected in a stronger economy. The big question is whether increased scrutiny is yielding more realistic estimates or just more estimates documented by reams of assumptions and rationalizations. We'll only know the answer when the economy begins to falter and corporate earnings come under pressure.

Already, recent academic research suggests that the abuse of accrual accounting is pervasive across a broad swath of companies. And it's enough to goad Wall Street into action. Aware that executives have tremendous opportunity to manipulate the numbers through their estimates, the market is on alert, delving more vigorously than ever into the estimates that go into compiling earnings. Over the past two years, investment banks have beefed up their already complex computer programs to screen thousands of companies to find the cheerleaders who make very aggressive estimates.

As analysts and investors drill deeper into these financials, they're finding some nasty surprises. Accounting games are spreading beyond earnings reports as some companies start to play fast and loose with the way they account for cash flows. That's a shocker because investors always believed cash was sacrosanct and hard to trump up. Now they're discovering that cash is just as vulnerable to legal manipulation as earnings. Companies from Lucent Technologies Inc. to Jabil Circuit Inc. have boosted their cash flow by selling their receivables—what customers owe them—to third parties. Says Charles W. Mulford, accounting professor at Georgia Tech's DuPree College of Management and author of an upcoming book on faulty cash reporting: "Corporate managers, knowing what analysts are looking at, say: 'Let's make the cash flow look better.' So the game goes on." A Lucent spokesman says it sells receivables to raise cash more cheaply than it could by borrowing the money. Jabil did not respond to questions.

Even with Wall Street's heightened scrutiny, many pros think the situation won't improve anytime soon—and it may well get worse. That's because accounting standard-setters at the Financial Accounting Standards Board (FASB) are deep into a drive to require companies to make even more estimates—increasing the potential for further manipulation of their bottom lines. One example: It's requiring companies to estimate changes in the value of a growing list of assets and liabilities, including trade names and one-of-a-kind derivative contracts. Eventually, companies will have to make corresponding adjustments, up or down, to their earnings.

There's some logic in FASB's position. It wants to improve the way changes in the value of corporate assets are reflected in financial statements because they can have a significant impact on a company's value. FASB argues the new estimates should be reliable since many will be based on known market prices. Unfortunately, others will rest on little more than educated guesses that in turn depend on a lot of other assumptions. "When you do that, you reduce the reliability of the numbers, and you open up the doors to fraud," says Ross L. Watts, accounting professor at the William E. Simon Graduate School of Business Administration at the University of Rochester.

FASB is understandably gun-shy about imposing even more rules on businesses. It has spent the last three years, and lots of political capital, trying to put in place requirements to expense the cost of stock options and to limit off-balance-sheet arrangements. But it has come up short by not insisting on financial statements that show in a simple way what judgments have gone into the estimates. FASB Chairman Robert H. Herz doesn't feel any urgency to do so. He argues that investors and analysts aren't yet using all the information they now have. Besides, he adds, he doesn't want to pile too many new requirements on companies. After the recent reforms, Herz says: "Right now, [they] are very tired."

Tired, maybe, but not tired enough to renounce numbers games. Even among execs who wouldn't dream of committing fraud, there are plenty who are ready to tweak their numbers in an effort to please investors. In a Duke University survey of 401 corporate financial executives in November, 2003, two out of five said they would use legal ways to book revenues early if that would help them meet earnings targets. More than one in five would adjust certain estimates or sell investments to book higher income. Faulty accounting estimates by execs caused at least half of the 323 restatements of financial reports last year, according to Huron Consulting Group.

The cost of this obfuscation is high. According to studies of 40 years of data by Richard G. Sloan of the University of Michigan Business School (page 88) and Scott Richardson of the University of Pennsylvania's Wharton School, the companies making the largest estimates—and thus reporting the most overstated earnings—initially attract investors like moths to a flame. Later, when the estimates prove overblown, their stocks founder. They lag, on average, stocks of similar-size companies by 10 percentage points a year, costing investors more than $100 billion in market returns. These companies also have higher incidences of earnings restatements, SEC enforcement actions, and accounting-related lawsuits, notes Neil Baron, chairman of Criterion Research Group, a New York researcher where Richardson consults. "Given the pressure on executives to reach expected earnings, it is not surprising," says Baron.

That's why more portfolio managers are using sophisticated screening to identify companies that make aggressive estimates and those that don't. Sloan and Richardson discovered that if you had sold short the companies with the biggest estimates and bought those with the smallest, you would have beaten the market 37 out of 40 years and by a huge margin—18 percentage points a year before trading costs. Now, Goldman Sachs Asset Management, Barclays Global Investors, and Susquehanna Financial Group, among others, are employing versions of the Sloan–Richardson models to guide their investments. Strategists at brokerages, including Sanford C. Bernstein Research, Credit Suisse First Boston, and UBS have built model portfolios using similar techniques.

Others on Wall Street seek an edge by going even further: They're deconstructing and rebuilding companies' financial reports. Morgan Stanley's Harris recently led an 18–month project aimed at filtering out the effects of accounting rules that can distort results from operations. His team gathered some 2.5 million data points and held countless discussions with analysts of individual companies. In an early test, the exercise determined that Verizon Communications Inc.'s pretax operating profit in 2003 was $13.7 billion rather than the $16.2 billion Morgan Stanley's star telecom analyst had first calculated using GAAP. That's mainly because GAAP allows companies to include estimates for what their pension plans will earn as current profits. A Verizon spokesman said the company has been careful to disclose its assumptions and tell investors how much its pension accounting boosts earnings.

Here are some of the ways companies can legally use accounting rules to inflate—or deflate—the earnings and cash flow they report:

ESTIMATE SALES With the stroke of a pen, companies can use estimates that make it appear as though sales and earnings are growing faster than they really are. Or, if they fear lean times ahead, they can create a cookie jar of revenues they can report later. Hospital companies, such as Health Management Associates Inc., report revenues after estimating discounts they will give to insurers and for charity cases. These discounts are typically two-thirds of list price, so a slight change in what HMA figures they will cost could have a large impact on its income. Vice–President for Financial Relations John C. Merriwether says the company uses conservative estimates.

Getting the revenue right isn't easy. Computer software vendor IMPAC Medical Systems Inc. says three different auditors gave differing opinions on when it could count revenue from certain contracts that included yet-to-be-delivered products. Its latest auditor, Deloitte & Touche, resigned just 10 weeks into the job after declaring that the company had counted revenue from 40 contracts too soon. IMPAC Chairman and CEO Joseph K. Jachinowski says he's asking the SEC how to book the contracts.

PREDICT BAD DEBTS How companies account for customers' bad debts can have a huge impact on earnings. Each quarter they set aside reserves for loan losses—essentially guesses of how much money owed by deadbeats is unlikely to be paid. The lower the estimate, the higher the earnings. On July 21, credit-card issuer Capital One Financial Corp. reported quarterly results that would have been 3 cents a share below Wall Street estimates had it not reduced its reserves, says David A.

Hendler, an analyst at researcher CreditSights. Capital One CFO Greg L. Perlin says the company made the change because it is lending to more credit-worthy customers now.

Sometimes companies on opposite sides of the same deal use different estimates. An example: Reinsurance companies have reserves of about $104 billion to pay claims they expect from property-and-casualty insurers. But the P & C insurers have booked $128 billion in payments they expect to receive from the reinsurers, according to Bijan Moazami, an insurance-industry analyst at Friedman, Billings, Ramsey Group Inc. He says the property-and-casualty companies will cut earnings as it becomes clear they won't collect all the money. Hartford Financial Services Group Inc. and St. Paul Travelers Cos. took such charges this spring, of $118 million and at least $164 million after taxes, respectively. The Hartford said it acted after reviewing its reinsurance arrangements. A St. Paul Travelers spokesman says: "We are comfortable with our estimates."

ADJUST INVENTORY By changing the costs they estimate for inventory that will be obsolete before it can be sold, companies can give their earnings a substantial boost. Vitesse Semiconductor Corp. took inventory expenses of $30.5 million in 2002 and $46.5 million in 2001. In 2003, it took no expenses but wrote off $7.4 million against a previously established reserve for obsolete inventory. Had it not tapped its reserves, the $7.4 million would have come out of current earnings, notes Terry Baldwin, an accounting analyst at researcher Glass Lewis & Co. Instead, Vitesse was able to report earnings of about 2 cents a share more than it could have otherwise. Vitesse's vice-president for finance, Yatin Mody, says the company properly counted the costs in 2002 when it foresaw that the goods were likely to become obsolete because of the telecom bust.

Inventory accounting can produce even more bizarre outcomes. Last year, General Motors Co. reported an extra $200 million in pretax income after using up more inventory than it replaced. In standard last-in, first-out inventory accounting, when the older and less costly goods are sold at today's prices, profits look better. But GM's future earnings could be hit if it needs to replace inventory at higher prices. GM says it properly applied accounting rules to its inventory management.

FORECAST UNUSUAL GAINS OR LOSSES The ability to time big and unusual gains or expenses can give companies plenty of control over their numbers. For 2003, Nortel Networks Corp. reported an earnings rebound when it reversed a portion of the $18.4 billion in charges it had logged for restructuring costs, bad customer debts, and obsolete inventory in the preceding three years. But last Apr. 28, the company said it "terminated for cause" its chief executive, its chief financial officer, and its controller amid an ongoing review and restatement of financial reports. In August, Nortel said it had fired seven more finance officers. Now the company says it had paid out $10 million in executive bonuses based on the trumped-up rebound. Nortel's new managers say they're trying to get the money back and that an independent panel "is examining the circumstances leading to the requirement for the restatements."

MASSAGE CASH Because analysts and investors are focusing on cash flow from operations as an indicator of financial health, those numbers are now a prime target for massaging. Companies have had to report cash flows since 1988, classifying them into one of three categories: operating, investing, and financing. By exploiting loopholes in GAAP rules, they can make their operating cash look a heap better. For example, in their consolidated financial statements, Boeing, Ford, and Harley–Davidson count as cash from operations the proceeds of sales of planes, cars, and bikes that customers bought with money they borrowed from the companies' wholly owned finance subsidiaries. As a result, cash from operations is higher, even though the companies didn't rake in any more of it. In its quarter through March, Boeing Co. reported $268 million in cash from operations that actually reflected what the company classified as investments by Boeing Capital Corp. in loans to customers to buy aircraft. Without the transactions, Boeing would have reported a $363 million drain of operating cash. For all of 2003, such transactions contributed $1.7 billion of Boeing's $3.9 billion in operating cash. The company says it has been preparing its accounts this way for years, and the method conforms to GAAP rules. Boeing began disclosing the amounts in a footnote in mid–2002. Harley–Davidson Inc. Treasurer James M. Brostowitz says its loans are properly disclosed, and analysts can make adjustments as they see fit. A Ford spokesman says the company's accounting complies with GAAP and accurately reflects its business.

The simplest way for companies to pump up their cash is to sell what customers owe them to a third party. Increasingly, companies carve out these receivables from their most creditworthy customers, sell them at a discount, and then present the move as smart capital management that boosts liquidity. Such deals give analysts fits because they are really financing actions. Jabil Circuit sold some receivables in an arrangement with a bank in the two quarters ended in May. That added $120 million, or nearly half of the $275 million of operating cash flow it reported in the period. But Jabil had to sell its receivables at a discount and recognize a $400,000 loss. The company did not provide comments after repeated requests.

Some transactions just keep operating cash flows looking pretty: Companies can use excess cash to buy securities when business is booming and then harvest it by selling them when the business runs cold. In 2003, Ohio Art Co., the tiny maker of Etch–A–Sketch drawing toys, used cash from operations to buy $1.5 million worth of money market funds. It sold them this year, boosting cash flow. CFO Jerry D. Kneipp says the company relied on its auditors in reporting the transactions. Cable company Comcast Corp. reported $85 million in additional operating cash flow in 2003 from sales of securities. Though this move was by the book, it distorted cash flow from operations. Comcast says that before 2002 it counted such proceeds as cash from investments. It changed the way it reports such deals to meet a 2002 FASB standard.

Mergers, too, can cloud the numbers. Consider again the HMA hospital chain. It regularly has a higher ratio of receivables to sales than do its peers—a red flag to analysts because it might be a sign that a company is booking more revenues than it will ever collect. But HMA's Merriwether says the high receivables are explained largely by its steady acquisitions of hospitals, about four a year. With each deal, it has to submit new paperwork to the government and private insurers and wait weeks before they will pay new patients' bills, he says. With a continuous flow of deals, says Sheryl R. Skolnick, an analyst at Fulcrum Global Partners who has recommended selling HMA's stock, "you have no idea what is going on."

One of the quickest, but most fleeting, ways companies can increase cash flow is to shrink their working capital. That can include selling off inventory, pressuring customers to pay quickly, and stalling payments to suppliers. While executives often claim that these moves make the company increasingly powerful and profitable, the opposite may actually be the case. General Dynamics Corp., for example, boasts in its 2003 annual report that it "has proven itself an industry leader in generating strong cash flows, which have enabled it to enhance returns through strategic and tactical acquisitions and share repurchases." Cash generation was "particularly strong" in 2003, it said. But while cash flow from operations rose to $1.7 billion from $1.1 billion the year before, half of the improvement came from slashing inventories in 2003 after adding to them in 2002. While cutting inventory may make sense given the weakened market for planes, it was a one-time cash boost from downsizing a business, not a sign of strong future cash flows. A company spokesman notes that Chairman and CEO Nicholas D. Chabraja told analysts in January that while General Dynamics' cash flow may fluctuate from year to year, it has tracked earnings over the past five years, even as the company was investing for growth in other areas.

The way companies are spinning their cash flows looks to some analysts as worrisome as the press releases announcing "pro-forma" earnings that companies cultivated during the 1990s tech-stock bubble. General Motors, for example, boasted in a Jan. 20 press release that it had "generated" $32 billion in cash in 2003. "That's outrageous," says Marc Siegel, a senior analyst at the Center for Financial Research & Analysis. GM had actually borrowed about half of that money by issuing bonds and convertible securities. The auto maker says it had explained publicly the steps it was taking to get that cash number.

Concentrating too much attention on short-term cash flows can have significant effects. It could discourage companies from making investments that could add to economic growth and boost returns on capital. "They are routinely saying 'no' to valuable projects," laments Campbell R. Harvey of Duke University's Fuqua School of Business. Some stocks, such as Computer Sciences Corp., now tend to move up when they report higher "free cash flow," a measure that looks better when companies scrimp on capital investments. CSC declined to comment. The danger, warns Morgan Stanley's Harris, is that "we can end up inducing people to make wrong economic decisions for appearance purposes. Then the investor will lose." Indeed, CFOs' desire to show high free-cash flow may be one reason corporate investment is now far below average.

THE SOLUTIONS For now, investors are left largely to their own devices to make sense of companies' numbers. Auditors—the first line of defense against financial shenanigans—are under scrutiny by a new oversight board, which is rewriting audit standards. Other accounting reforms have yet to take effect. The requirement in the Sarbanes–Oxley Act of July, 2002, which compels executives and directors of big companies to establish internal controls on bookkeeping and valuations underlying financial reports, won't be in full force until next year. And while the SEC's Corporation Finance Div. has started prodding companies to disclose more of their critical accounting estimates in public filings, the results so far are spotty, and many disclosures are buried in dense text. FASB is talking about revamping the income and cash-flow statements, but not for at least a couple of years.

There's plenty that regulators could do now to improve the quality of financial information. FASB should put aside some of its less pressing projects and turn its full attention to making it easier for investors to get behind companies' earnings numbers. If the form and presentation of financial statements were cleaner and more consistent, investors would be better able to spot accounting tricks. For example, earnings statements could be recast to distinguish between profits that come from selling products from those that come from ever-changing estimates. "You want to understand the subjectivity involved in these different numbers," says the CFA Institute's Walters.

The statement of cash flow needs a lift, too. Regulators must change the mirror-image presentation in which increases in cash show up as negative numbers and decreases as positive. They also have to define more clearly what constitutes an operating, investing, or financing item.

And FASB should make it easier for investors to make reliable comparisons. An obvious and simple step would be for companies to present their statements of cash flows for the same periods as their earnings statements. Even better would be to show the cumulative earnings and cash flows for the previous four quarters as well. Now most companies simply compare the latest quarter's earnings with those for the same quarter a year before, but present a year-to-date statement of cash flows without a comparison. Many financial analysts rearrange company data to highlight meaningful comparisons, but they have to build special spreadsheets for the task, and they need a library of past reports to feed into them. Companies should also clearly display in tables—not just in text—the changes they make in reserves.

With better and more consistent information in financial statements, investors would be able to reward and punish companies based on the quality of their accounting. "Then [investors] would start providing some discipline by discounting stocks when they aren't sure what the numbers are going to be," says Lynn E. Turner, a former SEC chief accountant and now research director at Glass Lewis. What's more, auditors would be on increased alert knowing that investors are looking over their shoulders.

Because companies will be using even more estimates in the future, they'll have even more opportunities to hype their results. To avoid future blowups, investors need a clear picture of a corporation's finances. Investors shouldn't have to wait for another Enron for regulators to tackle these issues.

PUMPING UP THE CASH

Analysts used to believe that cash is a fact and earnings an opinion. Now they're discovering how accounting rules allow companies to massage the presentation of their cash positions, too. Here's what a company can do:

TRADE SECURITIES

Company designates certain stocks or money market accounts it holds as trading instruments

EFFECT: Inflates operating cash flow when the securities are sold; masks the volatility of the business

FREE UP WORKING CAPITAL

Company cuts inventories, delays payments to suppliers, and leans on customers to pay faster

EFFECT: Raises cash flow from operations, but tends to hurt future growth; often reversed in later quarters, depressing cash flow

SELL RECEIVABLES

Company sells customer IOUs for less than face value, booking the cash immediately instead of waiting for customers to pay

EFFECT: Gives cash flow from operations a one-time lift; reduces amount of cash company ultimately receives

TURN TRADE CREDIT INTO CASH

Company lends money to customers to buy its products; resulting sales count as cash from operations, with loans shown as investments

EFFECT: Boosts operating cash flow with company's own money; encourages risky lending practices

SPINNING THE EARNINGS

Even when playing strictly by the book, companies have many ways to inflate or deflate the earnings they report. Here's how:

ESTIMATE SALES

Company estimates the revenues it will receive after allowing for discounts, product returns, and the like

EFFECT: Optimistic adjustments inflate sales and earnings; conservative ones act as a cookie jar that stores earnings for thinner times

PREDICT BAD DEBTS

As it sends out bills, company figures how much it will lose on customers who don't pay

EFFECT: Understating bad debts lowers operating expenses and raises earnings; overstating bad debts gives profits a lift when the estimates are reversed

ADJUST INVENTORY

Company underestimates how much inventory will become obsolete

EFFECT: Lowballing losses on inventory overstates current profits and hurts future results when inventory is finally written off

FORECAST UNUSUAL GAINS OR LOSSES

Company predicts special costs, such as restructurings or special gains

EFFECT: Overestimating one-time expenses cuts earnings now, but banks them for the future; overestimating gains boosts profits, but sets up a potential earnings hit later.

Manning Gilbert Warren III, Revenue Recognition
and Corporate Counsel

56 SMU L. Rev. 885 (2003)

I.   Introduction

Corporate lawyers now work in a world that has become tragically sensitized to executive greed and financial fraud and the consequential damage to our capital markets. The reported corporate accounting frauds during the past five years evidence an epidemic of infectious financial fraud involving an overwhelming number of companies, from the dot.coms to the blue chips. One writer has recently concluded that the executives of "the vast majority of major corporations" have been "artificially inflating their profits." * * * Consequently, corporate counsel should reject any presumption of regularity and stop feigning ignorance when confronted with information that appears, at first blush, to raise accounting issues. All corporate lawyers must familiarize themselves with the various deceptive practices that have led to the downfall of so many publicly-held companies in the last five years. Corporate counsel must understand the mechanisms used in the past to distort corporate earnings in order to recognize the red flags of potential distortion in the future.

During the last five years, earnings restatements by publicly-held companies have increased dramatically. Long considered "a proxy for fraud," these restatements have grown from only three in 1981 to over two hundred last year. The federal government's first in-depth study of earnings restatements, recently concluded by the U.S. General Accounting Office, found that earnings restatements had spiked 145%, from 92 in 1997 to 225 by June 30, 2002, a figure projected to increase to 170% by year-end. Moreover, companies restating their earnings had average market capitalizations of over $2 billion, as compared to an average of $500 million five years ago. The study identified improper revenue recognition as the major cause for these restatements and for the largest resultant decreases in stock prices. The resultant negative impact on the market price of those restating companies' securities, before one even considers the disastrous systemic effect on market prices generally, has been well over $100 billion. These restatements have led to civil and criminal proceedings brought, respectively, by the U.S. Securities and Exchange Commission (SEC) and the U.S. Department of Justice, as well as numerous and well-publicized class actions against these corporations and their officers, directors, accountants, and lawyers. The corporate defendants are not only immature, overly ambitious start-ups, but also are companies once considered among the all-stars of American capitalism, including Xerox, Enron, Global Crossing, WorldCom, Tyco, Qwest Communications, and Rite Aid.

* * * Counsel for publicly-held companies have fought the SEC for years to protect their traditional privileges to establish their own principles of professional responsibility and to regulate themselves. They are now losing that war. Corporate counsel, whether working in-house or externally, have been spotlighted for their role in these financial reporting frauds. In many cases, they have drafted or approved disclosure documents filed with the SEC or press releases and other publicly-disseminated information without fully disclosing their corporate clients' improper revenue recognition practices. In addition, they have negotiated or approved contracts, side agreements, and other documents that were used by corporate insiders to artificially inflate revenues. In some cases, they may have voiced objections to deceptive revenue recognition practices, but, nevertheless, acquiesced in the fraudulent conduct when their advice was not followed.

The SEC has now been joined by Congress in decisive efforts to elevate their standards of behavior. In the Public Company Accounting Reform and Investor Protection Act of 2002, popularly known as the Sarbanes–Oxley Act, Congress has ordered lawyers to tell corporate directors about evidence of corporate fraud. * * * This recently imposed duty to report evidence of fraud, enacted in an environment where most of the fraud has involved deceptive revenue recognition, requires all corporate counsel to have at least the competence of a sophomore accounting major. Without this minimum familiarity with basic accounting principles, corporate lawyers would be marginalized, unable to spot blatant evidence of financial fraud even while standing in its midst.

* * * Because improper revenue recognition has been at the core of many of the current financial scandals and continues to be a major

corporate liability risk, I believe the essential competence required of corporate lawyers must include the ability to recognize the most common deceptive revenue recognition devices and the red flags that indicate the possibility of their occurrence. Corporate counsel must apply these rudimentary skills for the benefit of their organizational clients not only through general vigilance, but also through random due diligence investigations to verify their clients' public disclosures. I will conclude that this enhancement of our competence will not only serve the interests of our corporate clients, but will also preserve what remains of the traditional role of the legal profession in establishing its own principles and standards of professional conduct.

II. Corporate Counsel's Duty of Competence

A. *The Traditional Duty of Competence*

* * * Model Rule 1.1 establishes the lawyer's basic duty of competence. It provides: "A lawyer shall provide competent representation to a client. Competent representation requires the legal knowledge, skill, thoroughness and preparation reasonably necessary for the representation.".... Although this comprehensive duty of competence applies to all lawyers, it imposes particularly intense and difficult obligations on corporate lawyers who represent legally abstract corporate entities.

* * * Model Rule 1.13, by requiring corporate counsel to favor the abstract, artificial corporate entity over its corporate representatives, properly ignores the reality that corporate counsel's professional relationships have been established by and with those corporate representatives. Because the unlawful conduct of these agents will generally be attributed to the corporate principal, the organization's lawyers must fulfill their comprehensive duty of competence in protecting the organization from any harm proposed by its agents. This is the burden imposed by the traditional duty of competence and its related ethical responsibilities. Failure of corporate counsel to satisfy this burden in representing publicly-held corporate clients has substantially contributed to the endemic of financial fraud the country now endures. Congress has recognized this failure and has authorized the codification of this and other aspects of corporate counsel's fundamental ethical duties to their clients.

* * * Competence for corporate lawyers now must include those skills reasonably necessary to fulfill the federally-imposed duty to recognize and report evidence of financial fraud.... By undertaking this federally-imposed duty to report, the lawyer for the publicly-held company implicitly represents to the client that he or she has the requisite competence to perform the lawyer's obligation to recognize and report evidence of financial fraud. If the corporate lawyer fails to develop this competence, personal liability could result.

* * * Because an overwhelming number of corporate scandals in recent years have involved abusive revenue recognition practices, corporate attorneys, in order to fulfill their duty of competence, must be able to understand and recognize the recurrent types of deceptive practices

that have and continue to be used to distort financial information disclosed to the SEC and the securities markets.

C. Corporate Counsel's New Duty of Competence

* * * The SEC's inclusion of basic accounting knowledge in the corporate lawyers' federal duty of competence should not prove particularly onerous. Most of the abusive practices used to perpetrate financial fraud have been remarkably easy to comprehend. It is not at all difficult to develop a familiarity with basic revenue recognition principles and the more common deceptive revenue recognition practices, including the red flags that suggest their occurrence. If corporate lawyers are to perform any meaningful role in the abatement of revenue-related fraud, they must be knowledgeable of its contours. Corporate counsel must be integrally involved in their organizational clients' public disclosure process, and, among other things, should be fully aware of their clients' revenue recognition policies, should independently verify whether those policies are being consistently applied, and should skeptically review all agreements with affiliates, as well as contracts and other arrangements used to generate late-quarter revenues. Corporate counsel's fulfillment of their enhanced duty of competency would markedly improve the mandatory disclosure process and could help restore the public's confidence in publicly-held corporations and their securities.

III. MATERIALITY AND GENERAL REVENUE RECOGNITION PRINCIPLES

A. The Materiality Doctrine

Corporate counsel's development of the requisite competence to detect and report any form of financial fraud must begin with an understanding of the materiality doctrine. After all, the determination of materiality of information is the central issue in satisfying corporate disclosure requirements and in avoiding civil and criminal liabilities under the federal securities laws. Materiality is also the central issue in the public disclosure of corporate financial results and, through its definition and related presumptions, constitutes the predominant principle of revenue recognition. It has long been said that for corporate lawyers, materiality is "the name of the game." They should know that materiality is the name of the game not only for the prose but also for the numbers that publicly-held corporations disclose to the market.

* * * Accountants generally do not have legal training and certainly do not possess the requisite expertise in the application of the securities laws or familiarity with securities fraud case law resolving materiality issues. Accountants (at least those acting without the assistance of securities lawyers) are ill-equipped to make the legal materiality determinations required by the SEC's mandatory disclosure system. Corporate counsel and their clients should not expect accountants to engage in the unauthorized practice of securities law and should not rely on accountants to resolve materiality issues on their own.

Moreover, it is critical that corporate lawyers realize that accounting materiality is substantially distinct from legal materiality. The accounting profession's traditional definition states that information is material if "the magnitude of an omission or misstatement of accounting information, in the light of surrounding circumstances, makes it probable that the judgment of a reasonable person relying on the information would have been changed or influenced by the omission or misstatement." The more obvious contrasts between accounting materiality and legal materiality are the former's focus on the implicitly numerical magnitude rather than the actual significance of the information, its inherent limitation to accounting information, and its reference to the information's probable effect on changing the reasonable person's judgment.

* * * Accountants are generally unaware of the broader context in which legal materiality assessments must be made and are not competent to make those determinations. . . . While acknowledging the non-existence of any authoritative standards for percentage guidelines in assessing materiality, they have stated that common guidelines used by auditors are five to ten percent of income or one percent of total assets or revenues. The large gap between accountants' numerical, quantitative perspective on materiality and lawyers' more broadly contextual, qualitative perspective, may have contributed disastrously to the systemic financial fraud we have recently experienced.

The necessity of legal resolutions for materiality questions becomes equally obvious when one appreciates that the assessment of materiality is far more qualitative than quantitative. This principle obviously flows from the Supreme Court's refusal to adopt bright-line rules for materiality on the basis that any such rules would always be over-inclusive or under-inclusive, given the radically different disclosure contexts in which decisions must be made.

* * * The SEC, in its Staff Accounting Bulletin 99 (SAB 99), reaffirmed its position that no quantitative presumptions should be followed in making materiality determinations. The SEC stated that quantitative standards were not acceptable and had no support under the accounting and auditing literature. The SEC issued this bulletin primarily to remind accountants and others involved in satisfying corporate disclosure obligations that percentage-based rules of thumb were critically deficient. Many accounting professionals have continued to apply a presumption that information that accounts for ten percent or more of a company's total assets, revenues, or net earnings is material, along with a corollary presumption that information that accounts for less than five percent is not material, leaving a materiality purgatory of information that accounts for five to ten percent. According to the SEC, "qualitative factors may cause misstatements of quantitatively small amounts to be material." The SEC was influenced by the Financial Accounting Standards Board's position that "magnitude by itself, without regard to the nature of the item and the circumstances in which the judgment has to be made, will not generally be a sufficient basis for a materiality judgment."

In SAB 99, the SEC identified a number of qualitative factors that could cause misstatements of quantitatively small amounts to be material. These factors included, among others, the following:

- Whether the misstatement masks a change in earnings or other trends,

- Whether the misstatement hides a failure to meet analyst's expectations,

- Whether the misstatement changes a loss into income or vice versa,

- Whether the misstatement concerns an area of the company's business that has been identified as being significant to its operations or profitability,

- Whether the misstatement affects the company's compliance with loan covenants or other contractual requirements,

- Whether the misstatement results in an increase in management's compensation, and

- Whether the misstatement involves concealment of an unlawful transaction.

Each of these factors explains why quality rules quantity in materiality determinations.

The SEC's position in SAB 99 has been highly persuasive in materiality litigation. For example, in Ganino v. Citizens Utilities Co., the defendant corporation, to make up for a revenue loss in 1996, booked $22 million of guaranty fees actually received in 1995. The company allegedly recognized revenues prematurely in order to manage its income trends. Because these fees accounted for only 1.7% of the company's 1996 revenue, the lower court applied the so-called five percent rule to conclude that the misstatements of revenue were immaterial. The Second Circuit, agreeing with SAB 99, reversed. The court held that because the corporation reached its publicly-announced earnings projections through improper revenue recognition, a reasonable investor would have considered the misstatements to have materially altered the total available mix of information about the company.

* * * Despite their inability to apply bright-line rules in making materiality assessments, corporate counsel should, as a practical matter, recognize and apply certain presumptions of materiality. They can be grouped into four categories: (1) information subject to obligatory disclosure under the SEC disclosure rules (the regulatory materiality presumption); (2) information regarding misconduct involving illegality, undisclosed self-dealing, or conduct otherwise bearing on managerial integrity (the integrity issues presumption); (3) information identified by the company as important to assessments of its financial position (the emphasized information presumption); and (4) information strongly related to issues of concern to financial analysts and journalists that have been publicly expressed (the public issues presumption). Although these presumptions are hardly exclusive and are not expressly established by the SEC or the courts, prudent corporate counsel have long used these presumptions both in conducting due diligence in connection with their clients' securities offerings and in resolving materiality issues incident to their clients' periodic reporting obligations, press releases and other public disclosures.

... Corporate counsel who have a developed comprehension of qualitative materiality and the foregoing presumptions of materiality are well-positioned to address revenue recognition issues that regularly confront corporate managers. However, they also must be generally familiar with established principles of revenue recognition.... At the very least, corporate counsel possessing general familiarity with revenue recognition principles will tend to be less deferential and less gullible in confrontations with corporate representatives professing financial or accounting expertise.

B.   General Revenue Recognition Principles

In addition to securing a fundamental grounding in the materiality doctrine, the corporate lawyer must possess at least an elemental understanding of the principles applicable to the financial determination of their corporate clients' revenues. As indicated previously, a large percentage of financial frauds in recent years have involved abusive revenue recognition practices. The appropriate recognition of revenues is largely determined by GAAP. The most important of these accounting principles, and certainly the beginning point for corporate counsel in this area, is that companies must always exalt the substance of a transaction over its form. The SEC has repeatedly emphasized that the best established tenet of GAAP is that transactions must be accounted for in accordance with their substance rather than their form. This is the first cardinal rule, both for corporate lawyers and corporate accountants.

The second cardinal rule for corporate counsel to recognize is that the financial statements of their clients must be prepared in accordance with GAAP or they will be presumed to be misleading under the SEC's Regulation S–X.

* * * If these principles were reduced to their simplest form, all would reiterate the adage, "don't count your chickens before they hatch," perhaps adding, "and before they are unconditionally sold, shipped, delivered, and accepted by creditworthy customers."

For corporate counsel, understanding the SEC's Staff Accounting Bulletin No. 101, Revenue Recognition in Financial Statements (SAB 101), should substantially contribute to their development of the necessary familiarity with revenue recognition principles. The SEC issued this bulletin in late 1999, at least partly in response to the Treadway Commission Committee of Sponsoring Organization's (COSO) report, Fraudulent Financial Reporting: 1987–1997, An Analysis of U.S. Public Companies. The COSO Report concluded that over half of the financial reporting frauds during the ten year period had involved the overstatement of revenue. SAB 101 described the basic framework for recognizing revenues by identifying four bedrock principles, which state that revenue becomes realized or realizable and earned when all of the following criteria are satisfied:

- persuasive evidence of an arrangement exists,
- delivery has occurred or services have been rendered,
- the seller's price to the buyer is fixed or determinable, and
- collectibility is reasonably assured.

According to the SEC's former Chief Accountant, Lynn E. Turner, this general framework "could not be simpler—it is based on the common sense notion that revenue on a sale should not be recognized until the seller has fulfilled its obligations to the buyer under the sale arrangement."

* * * Corporate counsel, in developing their general understanding of revenue recognition principles, could reasonably synthesize SAB 101 and its underlying GAAP as a basic rule that states as follows.

Revenue should only be recognized when:

- the company has persuasive evidence of a firm agreement,
- the company has made a favorable assessment of the buyer's creditworthiness,
- the company has completed the earnings process,
- the company's goods or services have been exchanged for cash or claims to cash,
- the company's goods have been shipped to the buyer and the risks and rewards of ownership have passed to the buyer,
- the company's goods must not be subject to a right of return (unless the amount of future returns can be reasonably estimated and a reasonable reserve for returns has been established),
- the company's right to payment is not otherwise conditional, voidable or cancelable, and
- the company has satisfied the foregoing criteria within the same reporting period.

Corporate counsel should readily observe that this basic rule requires consideration of contractual performances by their corporate clients, an area that squarely falls within their education, training, and experience in handling business transactions. It would be tantamount to malpractice to abdicate their responsibilities as legal experts to corporate accountants and then cower behind those accountants when the corporate client is subsequently charged with financial fraud.

IV. COMMON DECEPTIVE REVENUE RECOGNITION PRACTICES

A general review of the more common deceptive revenue recognition practices will illustrate dramatically how far afield these schemes are from both the four bedrock principles identified by the SEC in SAB 101 and from the basic rule I have distilled from GAAP. Corporate counsel should readily recognize these practices as manipulative devices that raise material issues not only regarding corporate financial statements but also the lack of managerial integrity that permitted their use in the first place. Consequently, these schemes are virtually always accompanied by major breaches of corporate disclosure obligations to publicly disclose the actual use of these schemes, the names of managerial perpetrators and their degree of participation in structuring, executing, and approving these schemes, in addition to the actual revenues that should have been reported had these deceptive devices not been employed. * * *

A. Fictitious Contracts

The creation of fictitious contracts and booking nonexistent revenues from those contracts is the most extreme deceptive revenue recognition device. In order to avoid detection by auditors, corporate personnel often fabricate purchase order forms, shipping documents, and invoices. Where the fabricated contracts involve the sales of goods, corporate personnel may physically conceal the inventory purportedly sold, either by storage at different warehouses or by shipment for storage by third parties who have no obligation to make payment. Of course, this manipulative practice creates phony accounts receivable, often due from either nonexistent customers or from specially created entities that in turn sell goods or services to the company at offsetting prices in what amounts to wash transactions or simple exchanges of checks with no economic substance.

B. Roundtripping

Roundtripping is another commonly used device to create revenue in order to falsely show demonstrable growth in a corporation's business activities. To implement this device, a company simply provides funds to its customers or other third parties to finance their purchases of the company's goods or services without any reasonable expectation that these customers will ever repay those funds. The customer pays for the goods or services with the company's funds, creating revenues for the company, while the customer is not expected to repay the funds advanced by the company to fund the purchase.

C. Unordered Shipments

In order to inflate revenues, a company may ship goods to third parties that never ordered the goods and immediately book revenues represented by the price of those shipments, even though it is highly probable that the products will be returned or, in any event, that the company's invoices will never be paid. * * *

D. Unshipped Orders

In many instances, a company will book revenue on existent orders before shipping the ordered products. In SEC v. Gallo, the SEC alleged that a company's president ordered a sales manager to record the sale of the company's products prior to shipment in order to fraudulently increase the company's revenues. To avoid detection, the president then ordered the chief financial officer to hold the company's books open past the quarter end while the sales manager backdated sales invoices and shipping documents. These practices not only violated GAAP, but also the company's own revenue recognition policy that sales revenues would only be recognized when products were actually shipped. * * *

E.   Misdated Contracts and Related Timing Abuses

Companies have frequently resorted to misdating contracts in order to manipulate the timing of revenue recognition. Companies challenged by quarter-end revenue goals implement this abusive revenue recognition device by backdating contracts, thereby borrowing revenue from the current quarter to inflate revenues for the preceding quarter. In one illustrative case, a company prematurely recognized revenues in one quarter and directed its personnel to misdate packing lists, shipping records, and invoices in order to conceal that shipments were not made until the succeeding quarter.

F.   Consignment Transactions

Although consignment transactions often are legitimate, they are sometimes used by a company as a fraudulent device to improperly recognize revenue. A consignment transaction may be generally described as an arrangement in which the owner of the goods transfers possession, but not title, to those goods to a third party for the purpose of effectuating sales of those goods to others. A company that recognizes revenue on the consignment itself, as opposed to recognizing revenue upon any subsequent sale of the goods, engages in an abusive revenue recognition practice. * * *

G.   Bill and Hold Sales

The bill and hold sales device takes various forms, but may generally be described as a manipulative technique in which the seller retains physical possession of goods ordered by the customer until the customer requests shipment to a designated location. Similar to the unshipped orders device, the company retains the risk and rewards of ownership, but nevertheless books revenue as if it has delivered these products to customers. However, the bill and hold sales device differs because the company does not act unilaterally by booking revenues on unshipped goods, but acts bilaterally pursuant to bill and hold arrangements with various customers. Frequently, the bill and hold arrangement does not involve the customer's contractual commitments to purchase, but a conditional or contingent contract dependent on the customer's acceptance criteria. * * *

I.   Inventory Parking

Inventory parking is a fraudulent scheme in which a company arranges with its distributors to place bogus orders for company products that they do not agree to buy in order to help the company meet its revenue goals. The company then makes a bookkeeping entry, recording the amount of the orders as revenue. In some instances, the product is actually shipped to these purported customers followed by a preauthorized return of the product in subsequent quarters. * * *

J.   Buy–Back Transactions

The buy-back transaction is another frequently used device to create false revenues. In this frequently used arrangement, the seller recognizes revenue on a contract after inducing a purported buyer to purchase the seller's products by promising to repurchase the same products in a subsequent reporting period. * * *

K.   Contingent Sales

Recognition of revenue based on contingent or conditional sales contracts has been used by numerous companies to inflate their quarter-end and year-end sales revenues. Like other abusive devices, this scheme has many variations. Generally, it involves the company's recognition of revenue on contracts that provide for eventual payment only upon the occurrence of various events not subject to its control. For example, the SEC brought an action against officers of Legato Systems, Inc., for recognizing millions of dollars in revenue on orders that were contingent on the customers' ability to resell the products through to end users or contingent on the customer's rights to return the products or to cancel the orders altogether.* * *

L.   Right of Return Contracts

As this designation suggests, right of return or "take back" contracts are contracts providing customers with a right to return products after shipment and delivery. Companies frequently use these types of contracts to induce customers to purchase their products, particularly in situations where a particular product is in its developmental stage or where the customer is a middleman and positioned to demand a right of return if unable to sell the product to end customers. A company that proceeds to recognize revenue on these contracts despite the possibility of return clearly transgresses applicable accounting principles. Unless the company has booked appropriate reserves for the reasonable likelihood of returns, recording revenue on contracts subject to a right of return is blatantly improper.

M.   Try–Buy Contracts

The try-buy contracts device involves a company's practice of recognizing revenues upon delivery of its products to customers on a trial basis. It is a frequently used variant of right of return contracts, and only becomes a mechanism for abuse when a company elects to prematurely recognize revenues. Try-buy contracts are ineligible for such recognition because these sales contracts are incomplete. * * *

N. Inflated Barter Transactions

It is not uncommon for companies to exchange nonmonetary assets, and these exchanges may result in appropriate recognition of revenues if the valuations of the exchanged assets are reasonable. However, a company may act abusively by blatantly overvaluing the assets received while undervaluing the assets transferred in order to recognize exaggerated revenues from the transaction. Under GAAP, in order to recognize revenue from a barter transaction, a company must establish not only the fair value of either the property it transferred or the property it received but also that the ascribed value of the property received reasonably reflects the company's expected actual use of the property. * * *

O. Cookie Jar Reserves

The use of so-called cookie jar reserves to time and inflate revenue recognized by a company has become the subject of increasing scrutiny in recent years by both the SEC and the plaintiffs' bar. A company, in order to develop a resource for smoothing out or otherwise inflating revenues in future reporting periods, may create inflated reserves for future contingencies. If it significantly overreserves for those contingencies, a company will have created a pool of potential revenues available to mask future revenue shortfalls. It can produce these revenues at any time by reducing the reserves. Perhaps the most abusive use of these cookie jar reserves was reflected by the behavior of "Chainsaw Al" Dunlap and his confederates at Sunbeam.

In order to reinforce his reputation as a corporate turnaround wizard, Dunlap caused the creation of exaggerated reserves for unlikely contingencies to provide a source of inflated revenues whenever necessary in the future. By creating excessive reserves in the disastrous year when he came to power, Dunlap positioned himself to inflate Sunbeam's income in the successive year, enabling him to produce the false picture of a rapid turnaround in Sunbeam's financial performance. * * *

P. Channel Stuffing

The term "channel stuffing" refers to a sales practice frequently employed by publicly-held companies to artificially increase revenues to meet Wall Street expectations by inducing their distributors, typically through price cuts, extended payment and delivery terms, and other incentives, to purchase more product than they would have purchased in the normal course of business. Channel stuffing is often compounded by the accompanying use of other deceptive revenue recognition devices, including side agreements providing distributors or other customers with generous rights of return, conditional payment obligations, or cancellation rights. Although channel stuffing allows a manufacturing company to meet financial targets in a given quarter and thus satisfy market expectations, it generally leads to reduced revenues in succeeding periods because distributors would then have a greater supply of inventory than needed to satisfy their own customers' requirements in the ordinary course of business.

* * * The deceptive revenue recognition devices identified above are those that have been the most frequently exposed in recent years by SEC investigations and private securities fraud litigation. Variants of these devices and a host of more creatively fraudulent schemes have been and continue to be exploited to inflate corporate revenues in order to deceive investors and the marketplace. However, the ones I have described should be sufficient to alert the corporate bar that these frauds are being used with impunity, that they involve deception that has little to do with mathematical questions or accounting complexities, and that perhaps no profession is any better equipped than corporate counsel to identify these deceptive practices and report evidence of their use to their corporate clients' highest authorities. This is their federal mandate under the Sarbanes–Oxley Act of 2002, under the ABA Model Rules of Professional Conduct, and under their evolving standards of care.

Corporate counsel obviously must be familiar with each of the commonly used fraudulent revenue recognition schemes if they are to protect the interest of their publicly-held organizational clients. These practices, even apart from their actual impact on reported financial results, may constitute manipulative devices prohibited by federal securities laws. Clearly, corporate counsel must possess a fundamental understanding of their clients' businesses and general familiarity with these abusive practices.

However, they must become better positioned to detect the actual use of these devices. They should undertake independent, random inquiries of their clients' personnel engaged in sales, marketing, and distribution of the clients' goods and services, as well as inquiries of their clients' distributors and other major customers. They should also review contractual arrangements and documentation used by their clients in effecting sales to customers, and, especially, all revenue producing agreements with their clients' affiliates. In making these inquiries, corporate counsel should be particularly vigilant regarding late quarter revenue generation. They must recognize that corporate personnel are subject to mounting pressures to achieve projected results during the final weeks of reporting periods, and, hence, more likely to succumb to fraudulent techniques. This is not to suggest that counsel engage in full-blown due diligence for all periodic reports, press releases, and other public disclosures.

For counsel to be effective professional participants in their corporate clients' disclosure processes, they must engage in a modified, or short-form, due diligence investigation to protect their clients and their clients' shareholder owners from internally generated financial fraud. In implementing this recommended short-form due diligence, corporate counsel will develop the parameters of their clients' random due diligence and thereby set their own standards as professionals representing publicly-held corporations. Should corporate counsel fail to recognize their enhanced responsibilities in the detection, abatement, and disclosure of financial fraud, they and their firms may reap the whirlwind suffered by Arthur Andersen.

PROBLEM

You are an Associate General Counsel for Elektron, a NASDAQ-listed company that manufactures a variety of computer-related equipment. You have been given responsibility for advising the audit committee with respect to its duty to oversee Elektron's financial reporting and internal control system.

In that capacity, you serve as liaison to management and the internal audit staff and the outside auditing firm as they gather material and conduct the analysis that will culminate in the financial statements, MD&A, certifications, and the reports on the internal control system. Your job is to keep the committee abreast of any issues that arise in the course of this process so that it will be aware of any concerns on an ongoing basis.

Among Elektron's major products is a wireless router used in setting up home networks that enable users to connect multiple computers to the Internet via phone or cable lines. Like many high technology companies, Elektron has had trouble in the past two years. Its earnings have been either flat or negative. On January 1, the company brought in Phil Jessup as CEO. Jessup has helped turn around the fortunes of two companies over the past decade, and the Board of Directors announced his appointment with great fanfare. At his press conference, Jessup pledged to have the company post earnings growth by the end of the third fiscal quarter, which is September 30.

At the time that Jessup assumes office, Elektron is engaged in research and development related to a wireless router that company engineers hope will represent a breakthrough in wireless technology. Most wireless routers are susceptible to disruption by the use of household appliances such as cordless telephones and microwave ovens, as well as the placement of computers on separate floors or in rooms with thick walls. Elektron believes that its new Mercury router has the potential to be much less vulnerable than other models to such interference.

Jessup places top priority on, and devotes considerable resources to, accelerating the schedule for the Mercury. By August 1, production begins on the Mercury and the company announces that its "next generation" router will be available for shipment by the second week in September. The company reports that interest is high and orders are brisk. By the end of September, the sales department reports that it has shipped out several hundred thousand dollars worth of the Mercury to distributors. Among the distributors is a company in which a subsidiary of Elektron owns a 20% share in connection with a joint venture between the two enterprises. About 30% of the sales were to this entity.

In connection with the filing of Elektron's 10–Q for the third fiscal quarter ending September 30, the management team and outside auditor discuss with the Mercury project personnel the revenues generated when the company began shipping the Mercury in the last three weeks of the quarter.

Electron's regular practice has been to record revenue when products are shipped to distributors. This revenue is listed as accounts receivable, and is reduced by a reserve amount that reflects the estimated value of the products in each product line that will be returned by customers. The company historically has estimated reserves for routers as about 8% of sales, which is the industry average. If this figure is applied to sales for the third fiscal quarter ending September 30, it would leave Elektron with a decrease in earnings of .1%, despite the fact that the Mercury accounted for the majority of product sales during that quarter.

The head of the Mercury project, however, maintains that the traditional 8% figure is too high, since it reflects customer dissatisfaction with problems in the router that the Mercury has fixed. While he acknowledges that the company does not yet have a track record with the new technology that the Mercury represents, he suggests that the best estimate of the project team is that an average of only 3% of the routers will encounter trouble that leads to recalls. Earnest & Jung (E&J), Elektron's outside auditor for several years, agrees that using a 3% return rate to calculate the loss reserve is appropriate. The head of the Mercury project team submits a "sub-certification" that states, among other things, that the revenue and reserve amount for the Mercury for the third quarter fairly present the financial performance of the Mercury product line during that period.

As a result of this adjustment in the reserve amount, the financial statements included in Elektron's 10–Q indicate that the company enjoyed a 5% increase in earnings during the quarter. The MD&A describes the Mercury, notes that it already has begun to generate considerable revenues, and declares that Elektron expects the innovativeness of the product to produce considerable profits over the next few years. A footnote to the financial statement mentions that the line item representing reserves for expected returns reflects an estimated return rate of 3%.

Management has now presented to the audit committee the MD & A to the 10–Q, along with its certifications that the 10–Q is not misleading and that the financial statements fairly represent the financial condition and results of operations of Elektron. What issues do you believe should be flagged for especially close review by the committee?

Chapter 20

COMPLEX TRANSACTIONS

Lawyers involved in transactional work are involved in providing legal advice and documentation for a wide variety of business activities. These may include the sale, lease, or purchase of assets; lending arrangements with creditors; licensing agreements in which one party permits the other to sell its product in return for a fee and/or a share of the profits; joint ventures between enterprises that otherwise might be competitors; structuring deals to take account of tax and regulatory considerations; and a host of other activities limited only by the imagination of corporate managers, bankers, accountants, management consultants, and lawyers.

Corporate transactions increasingly are large, complex, and multifaceted. Addressing the many legal issues that they raise requires assembling team of lawyers who often are specialists in one area of practice. Each lawyer may work on discrete portions of the deal, but have neither formal responsibility for nor full information about how all the pieces fit together. A given lawyer may regard these other pieces of the puzzle as matters calling for the expertise and judgment of other legal specialists, accountants, or corporate managers. This can raise questions about when it is appropriate for lawyers to rely on others' judgments and when lawyers must inquire further to satisfy themselves that certain assumptions or representations are justified. The inevitable interdependence that complex transactions involve ensures that lawyers will almost always have to make such decisions.

The ethical significance of this situation is that having to make these decisions leaves lawyers potentially vulnerable to the charge that they were in a position to prevent wrongdoing because they should have recognized its warning signs along the way. In hindsight, it may be clear that certain transactions perpetrated a fraud, or were used to manipulate financial reports rather than serve any independent business purpose. A regulatory agency, criminal prosecutor, or jury may find unconvincing the defense that the lawyer bore responsibility for only one part of the deal, or that she assumed that others were in a position to review the entire transaction as a whole. Complex transactional work thus can raise important questions about the fragmentation of responsibility and knowledge in the work life of the modern corporate lawyer.

The Enron scandal provides a good vehicle for exploring these issues in especially stark and visible form. Aside from the company's dramatic and precipitous fall, Enron is notable because the transactions that have been called into question were quite complicated and involved the use of cutting edge financial instruments. Effectuating them required the involvement of outside counsel, inside counsel, company managers, financial experts, and internal and outside accountants.

The material on transactional work in this chapter describes some of the instances in which the Enron Bankruptcy Examiner suggested that Enron's lawyers may have engaged in ethical misconduct. These instances are particularly provocative topics for discussion, because none of them represents a clear-cut case in which we can confidently say that a lawyer deliberately engaged in fraud or helped Enron to do so. Indeed, lawyers whose conduct is at issue may contend that they were simply performing tasks conventionally carried out by transactional lawyers. At the same time, the services of lawyers were essential in enabling Enron to construct fraudulent transactions that drove the company into bankruptcy. The material in this chapter is designed to make you reflect on when we should assign ethical and legal responsibility to lawyers for such an outcome.

MODEL RULES: 1.1, 1.2, 1.3, 1.6, 1.13, 2.1, 8.4

A. ENRON

As background to the discussion of Enron's attorneys and some of the matters on which they worked, this section focuses on what concerns were of particular significance to Enron's business strategy and what kind of culture the company fostered to respond to them. What business pressures did Enron face, how did it attempt to address them, and what effects did this have on organizational culture? How did that culture in turn shape the business opportunities and risks that Enron executives perceived? What was the environment, in other words, in which Enron's inside and outside counsel did their work?

Enron began as a gas pipeline company in the days when natural gas prices were federally regulated. Gas producers explored for gas and pumped it out of fields, then sold it to pipelines at prices set by the federal government. The pipelines then sold gas to local utilities, also at government-regulated rates. Natural gas thus was a relatively sleepy industry, with minimal competition and no market pricing.[1]

By the mid–1980s, the government had deregulated the prices that natural gas producers could charge, and had encouraged pipelines to make their lines available to all gas companies. As a result, local utilities could buy gas directly from producers and then pay pipelines simply for

---

1. Loren Fox, Enron: The Rise and Fall 10 (2003).

transporting the gas. Pipeline companies therefore had to develop separate businesses for gas transportation and gas sales.[2]

Deregulation resulted in much more volatile gas prices for both producers and utilities. Enron tried to hedge this volatility by providing forward contracts to deliver gas to users at specified prices on future dates. This gave natural gas users a measure of predictability by allowing them to lock in maximum prices for the gas they needed to purchase. In these transactions, Enron acted not only as broker, but actually took possession of gas in order to meet its contractual obligations to deliver it. Enron therefore had to hedge its own risk that it might have to acquire gas to meet its commitments at prices higher than the prices it would be receiving under its contracts with utilities. It did so by entering into contracts with gas producers that set the maximum prices that Enron would have to pay.

Enron therefore had to transform itself from a relatively stable company in a regulated industry to an entity that was able to engage in complex estimates of future prices in a volatile natural gas market. In order to do so, it began hiring people with expertise in finance, mathematical modeling, and hedging—employees whose skills and outlook often differed sharply from Enron's traditional workforce of persons who were familiar with the natural gas industry.

The cultural shift at Enron was accelerated when Jeff Skilling arrived in 1990 to become Chief Executive Officer of Enron Finance. As a consultant at McKinsey & Company, Skilling had advised Enron on how it might reposition itself to take advantage of opportunities in the new deregulated environment. As CEO of Enron Finance, he began moving the company away from reliance on physical assets such as pipelines toward an emphasis on holding financial assets—from a gas pipeline company to something more akin to an investment bank.

Under Skilling's prodding, Enron eventually began trading not only gas, but the contracts to buy and sell gas at certain prices. These contracts essentially were derivatives—financial instruments whose prices were based on the underlying price of gas. Most were customized contracts, unregulated by exchanges. Enron sought to use derivatives to lock in maximum and minimum prices, and to seek out profits that came from exploiting the spread between the two. This "freed Enron from having to own assets involved in the production and transportation of natural gas. In theory, instead of owning a portfolio of assets—natural-gas reserves and pipelines—Enron could simply own a portfolio of contracts that would allow it to control the resources it needed."[3]

A crucial step in the transformation of Enron was obtaining permission from the Securities and Exchange Commission to use mark-to-market accounting treatment to establish the value of Enron's gas trading contracts. Traditionally, the assets that these contracts repre-

2. *Id.* at 13.

3. Bethany McLean & Peter Elkind, The Smartest Guys in the Room: The

Amazing Rise and Scandalous Fall of Enron 37 (2003).

sented were carried on the books at historical cost, even if market conditions resulted in increases or decreases in the prices at which they would trade. A company could not recognize the gain from appreciation in the value of such an asset until it actually sold it—until then the gain was only a theoretical possibility on paper.

A different accounting treatment, however, was used by businesses such as the trading units of investment banks, whose assets consist almost entirely of financial instruments that constantly fluctuate in value. These companies are permitted to adjust the value of their assets to reflect current market prices, even if they do not engage in the actual sale or purchase of the assets at those prices. Such an approach ostensibly provides a better picture of the actual financial condition of the company than reliance on the historical cost at which its assets have been acquired.

Ideally, the mark-to-market process is relatively accurate because valuations are based on actual prices in robust trading markets. For contracts based on price movements over a long period, however, or contracts involving assets in thinly traded markets, such price information is either of limited use or unavailable. In these cases, mark-to-market valuation requires the use of mathematical models to predict fluctuations in the price of underlying assets, and thus the anticipated long-term income from various contracts.

Skilling believed that the logic behind mark-to-market accounting applied to Enron's gas contract trading activity—that this treatment provided a better indication of the actual economic value of the company's trading unit. In June of 1991, Enron therefore requested that the SEC permit it to use this accounting approach for its natural gas contracts. In January of 1992 the SEC agreed. Enron ultimately expanded the use of mark-to-market accounting to every portion of its merchant investment business, including profits of private equity and venture capital investments.[4] By 2000, some 35% of Enron's assets received mark-to-market treatment.[5]

One particularly notable feature of mark-to-market accounting is what it permits with respect to booking revenues from long-term contracts. Under conventional accounting, a company recognizes revenues as they are received and calculates profits accordingly. Thus, for instance, if Enron had a ten-year contract to supply natural gas to a utility, it would record the revenues that it received from that contract as the utility made payments over the ten-year period. Under mark-to-market accounting, by contrast, Enron could book the present value of the estimated revenues, and calculate the anticipated profits, for the entire ten-year period immediately when the contract was signed. Any changes in natural gas prices that affected those figures would show up as additional income or losses in later periods. Thus, if Enron expected $200 million in income over the course of a ten-year contract, it could

4. Smartest Guys, at 127.
5. *Id.*

recognize that income on its financial statements as soon as it entered into the contract.

Enron sought to use its natural gas contracts market model as the basis for expansion into trading of other items, such as oil, electricity, timber, broadband, and water. By 1999, Enron Wholesale Business, the trading arm of Enron, accounted for 66% of 1999 Income before Interest and Taxes. At that point, top management at the company regarded trading, deal making, and risk management as Enron's core activities.[6]

This transformation led to an increased emphasis on hiring persons with abstract financial and analytical skills that could be applied to any type of business operation. Ideally, anything could be turned into a commodity that could be traded in a market. As people like Skilling saw it, Enron's business was identifying these commodities, creating a market for them if need be through its own trading activity, and hedging the risks of the market for itself and others. Skilling felt that traditional capital investment in hard assets such as factories and pipelines no longer were the key to good returns. Instead, it was versatile intellectual firepower that maximized performance.

As a result, Enron became an increasingly young, well-compensated culture. By 1999, the average gas pipeline employee had been at Enron for 16 years, while the average capital trading employee had been there for 3–4 years. Furthermore, the Enron's value system began to "divid[e] the world into those who 'got it' and those who didn't." Traders and deal makers were in the first category, and traditional pipeline personnel were in the second.[7] This dichotomy extended beyond the company as well. "Outsiders who came into regular contact with Skilling hungered to be included on the list of those who got it. This was especially true of Wall Streeters, who pride themselves on their smarts."[8] Enron was able when necessary to exploit this pride. As one major investor recounted, "If you asked a question that [Skilling] didn't want to answer, he would dump a ton of data on you. But he didn't answer. If you were brave and said you still didn't get it, he would turn on you. 'Well, it's so obvious,' he'd say. 'How can you not get it?' So the analysts and investors would pretend to get it even when they didn't."[9]

Whatever sense of arrogance traders and deal makers had based on their perceived intellectual superiority was reinforced by their sense of mission. They saw themselves as injecting meritocratic market principles into sleepy industries that for too long had been insulated from the bracing rigor of the market. This was consistent with the animating business spirit of the 1990s, which proclaimed that innovative high-tech companies were rewriting the book for business success. As a result, "[b]ecause the traders thought they were creating a new world, they looked upon existing rules not as guidelines to be respected but as mere

6. Fox at 88.

7. Smartest Guys, at 233.

8. Smartest Guys, at 233.

9. *Id.*

conventions to be gotten around in whatever creative fashion they could devise."[10]

As various markets matured, the entry of other companies tended to erode Enron's competitive advantage and profit margins. The company therefore needed constantly to be on the lookout for opportunities in new markets, where it could enjoy the benefits of being the first entrant at least for awhile. This placed a premium within Enron on creativity and competition among employees to find the next big business idea.

This culture was reinforced by something called the Performance Review Committee (PRC) process—or, more colloquially, "Rank and Yank." The PRC consisted of managers from various business units who met every six months in order to conduct personnel evaluations. Each employee was compared against all other employees in the same business unit on a bell curve in a "forced ranking."[11] This ranking was the basis for one's bonus, which could come to more than a million dollars for some high achievers. More ominously, employees who were ranked in the bottom 10–20% were given six months to improve their ranking by the next PRC review. If they did not, they were fired. As one observer notes, "Inevitably, because of the bell-curve aspect of PRC reviews, internal competition became a part of life at Enron."[12] Managers felt that this was the best way to emphasize the importance of constantly striving for new ideas and never resting on one's laurels.

This system, however, sometimes fostered competition within business units that affected how the company functioned. Originators, for instance, negotiated long-term deals to provide commodities such as natural gas, while traders executed the buy and sell orders that made sure that Enron had the commodities available to meet its obligations. Traders were in charge of calculating "forward price curves," or estimates of the prices at which the commodity would sell in, say, years seven to ten of a ten-year contract. Originators complained that traders adjusted these projections to favor their short-term trading profits at the expense of the longer-term deal. Traders resented the fact that, as they saw it, originators received a windfall at bonus time from mark-to-market accounting simply by getting a customer to sign a contract without assuming responsibility to ensure that Enron was able profitably to perform under it. This infighting "made it more difficult for originators to sign long-term contracts. As a consequence, less business came from long-term contracts and the company had to rely even more on the shorter-term trading operation for profits."[13]

Enron also sought to promote innovation by fostering an entrepreneurial ethos among employees that focused on temporary teams who worked on constantly changing projects, rather than persons who fit into specific positions within an explicit organizational structure. Enron,

10. Smartest Guys, at 216.

11. Fox, at 84.

12. Fox, at 84.

13. Fox, at 85.

according to Skilling, was "like a free market of people."[14] Job assignments could change month to month. Projects were like self-contained jobs; "[o]nce a project was over, it was up to the employee to find work elsewhere within the company."[15] Furthermore, in parts of the company, managers told employees that it would hurt their chances of advancement if they stayed too long on one project.[16] The company started, folded, and reorganized businesses constantly. It spent more than $6 million a year on relocating offices and cubicles.[17] As one former executive put it, "The best way to describe Enron was as a constant job search."[18]

The development of Enron On–Line (EOL), the company's profitable on-line trading operation, reflected the operation of this entrepreneurial culture. Louise Kitchen, the leader of the project, never obtained approval for it from Skilling or Chairman Kenneth Lay. She assembled a team of 350 people by going directly to employees she wanted, not to their bosses. Some managers didn't even know their employees were working on the project.[19] It was not until a month before the launch of the trading program, when versions of it had already been introduced in several European countries, that project leaders even informed Skilling about it. Thus, in keeping with Enron's culture, "even though they were about to spend millions getting EOL off the ground, chew up people's time, and plot radically to change Enron's business model, the coconspirators felt no need to seek approval from Skilling or [CEO and Chairman Kenneth] Lay."[20]

In short, Enron hired smart, ambitious people, granted them autonomy, set them loose in a competitive environment, and then ranked their performances. Skilling sought to position Enron as dot-com with a new business culture of constant change and a flat organizational structure.[21] "Employees who didn't add to profits or at least provide a strategic function were deemed expendable[.]"[22] This resulted in a stressful workplace that had the potential to emphasize the short term. Originators and traders didn't worry about whether the mark-to-market value of deals changed three or four years hence. By then they might be in a different business group and any erosion in the value of their deal wouldn't affect their current PRC ranking.[23]

Understanding the milieu in which Enron's lawyers operated also requires appreciating the company's distinctive business challenges. Enron's role as a market maker, and the company's own predictions to the investment community about its continued growth, required it continually to find and create new markets that enabled it to enjoy first-mover profits from trading and financing activities. Enron needed large

---

14. *Id.* at 89.
15. *Id.* at 88.
16. *Id.* at 89.
17. Smartest Guys, at 120.
18. Smartest Guys, at 121.
19. *Id.* at 222.

20. *Id.*
21. *Id.* at 121.
22. Fox at 87.
23. Fox at 89.

amounts of cash in order to do this. Even though Skilling aspired to an "asset light" strategy in which Enron divested itself of most physical assets, creating new markets often initially required the acquisition or construction of hard assets in order to learn about a business, and then build trading and finance activities around it.[24] Thus, for instance, Enron needed cash to acquire assets such as a public utility in Oregon, timberland in Maine, paper mills in New Jersey and Quebec, and fiber optic cable in various parts of the country. It also built massive power and water projects in places like India and Brazil. The idea was to leverage these assets in order to "build up a complementary financial business."[25]

The problem was that Enron didn't have much cash flow, despite booking large amounts of income based on mark-to-market accounting. The company might be able to record $200 million in income immediately based on the present value of the expected earnings from a contract over its multiple-year duration. That $200 million only came in the door gradually, however, over the life of the contract. As Enron's financial statements declared, the company had considerable "recognized, but unrealized income." The gap between income and actual cash flow thus was a continuing problem, which prevented Enron from using cash to finance most of its growth.

One potential source of financing, of course, was the stock market. Enron likely would be successful in selling additional shares to the public because of its track record. The company, however, didn't want to issue new equity to raise capital. That would lower earnings per share, which would make it harder to hit the earnings targets that the company had indicated to stock analysts.

Finally, Enron didn't want to acquire cash by incurring debt because that would adversely affect its credit rating. In order to continue growth in its trading operations, Enron needed to trade without having to post collateral. This in turn depended on its credit rating for senior unsecured long-term debt. Incurring additional debt could cause that rating to be downgraded. Furthermore, covenants in some of the company's existing loan agreements required Enron to maintain a certain credit rating. Violation of this provision could result in acceleration of Enron's loan obligations.

The result of all this was that Enron's desire to keep its share price high while maintaining its credit rating limited its options for narrowing the gap between its reported income and the cash flow necessary to fuel continued growth.[26]

One reason for attempting to keep Enron's share price remained high was that the company could use its shares as currency to fund its

---

24. Fox at 88.

25. *Id.* at 60.

26. *See generally* U.S. Bankruptcy Court for the Southern District of New York, In re Enron Corporation, et al., Case No. 01–16034 (AJG), Second Interim Report of Neal Batson, Court–Appointed Examiner, January 21, 2003, at 15–36 (hereinafter "Batson Second Report").

growth. Setting and meeting increasing earnings targets was crucial to a high share price. Skilling apparently set quarterly and annual earnings per share targets based solely on what analysts told him was necessary to keep the stock price up, rather than based on analysis of operations of the various business units.[27] Growth numbers thus were imposed on business units from above, with the assumption that the creative and competitive people whom Enron hired would find a way to meet them.

The difficulty with this strategy was that a company built around trading and deal making can't possibly count on steadily increasing earnings, because trading is an inherently risky and volatile business. This is why companies whose business primarily is trading have low stock valuations.[28]

Furthermore, mark-to-market accounting created an earnings treadmill. Marking to market can boost growth rates because it permits booking income from long-term deals immediately. In order for its share price to stay high, a company needs to meet even more ambitious earnings targets for the next quarter. Where would these earnings come from? Enron was not building up a backlog of income, become income from all existing contracts had already been fully recorded. In each quarter, in other words, traders and deal makers "started with a blank page."[29] Enron therefore needed a constant flow of new deals that generated more income that could be booked immediately in the next quarter.

The trading and deal culture that Enron had created was unleashed to find new deals and business opportunities that would accomplish this. In terms of its financial statements, Enron needed transactions that permitted it to: (1) book income and earnings on its income statement as soon as possible (2) remove debt from its balance sheet and (3) book cash flow from operations on its statement of cash flows. These measures would help Enron maintain the favorable financial ratios that were crucial to its stock price and credit rating.[30]

Enron was candid that bolstering the accounting that was the basis for these ratios was more important than the underlying economics of a transaction. As Enron's risk management manual declared:

> "Reported earnings follow the rules and principles of accounting. The results do not always create measures consistent with underlying economics. However, corporate management's performance is generally measured by accounting income, not underlying economics. Therefore, risk management strategies are directed at accounting, rather than economic, performance."[31]

This statement reflects the fact that there is inevitable divergence between accounting treatment and economic substance. Accounting pres-

---

27. Smartest Guys, at 127.

28. *Id.* at 126.

29. Fox, at 42.

30. For a list and short description of these ratios, see Batson Second Report, at 20.

31. Smartest Guys, at 132.

ents a stylized picture of economic activity, whose elements are assembled according to certain conventions. Its traditional conservatism—delay booking income and recognize obligations as soon as possible—may not provide the most accurate reflection of a company's operations and prospects. Furthermore, structuring a transaction one way instead of another can make it eligible for a certain accounting treatment, even though the basic economic characteristics of the transaction are no different.[32] In such instances, the rules themselves provide support and incentives for using form to mask substance. Thus, as two scholars have recently put it, "Accounting information is sufficiently disconnected from underlying economic reality that it presents a distorted and unreliable picture of economic consequences."[33]

Enron was frank in recognizing that stock analysts, investors, and even creditors sometimes take the conventions of accounting as equivalent to the economic reality that the numbers are supposed to represent. As in any instance in which certain variables are taken as indications of performance, gaming the system by manipulating the variables is predictable behavior. This behavior was especially likely near the end of business quarters in which Enron threatened to fall short of its earnings targets. Rather than revise its estimate, the company sent out requests to various business units for creative ways to squeeze out more earnings.[34]

Enron created a free-wheeling culture that it believed was nimble enough to meet its business challenges, but in hindsight failed to put in place effective constraints on it. The company's Risk Assessment and Control (RAC) office, for instance, was supposed to provide an internal review of proposed deals. A Deal Approval Sheet (DASH) was required on each proposed transaction, which summarized the deal, indicated the range of projected returns, and estimated the risks. There was space on the sheet for the signatures of everyone who needed to approve the transaction, and box for RAC to provide its recommendation.[35]

In practice, however, the RAC appeared regularly to shy away from attempting to curb the momentum for any deal. Indeed, Chief Risk Officer Rick Buy said in a promotional video for Arthur Andersen that Enron was a "fast-moving place. You don't want anyone ... [who's]

---

32. Instead of owning an asset such as a manufacturing plant, for instance, a company can enter into a "synthetic lease" whereby it sells the plant to another party and then leases it back. The company then operates the plant as it would if it still owned it. As a result of the change in form, however, the company "will be able to expense the rental payments it makes to the lessor under the synthetic lease, and its balance sheet will not be marred by the appearance of real estate ownership or by the existence of mortgage debt. However, the lessee/corporate user will retain all the tax benefits and burdens of ownership, including the ability to depreciate the real estate assets and obtain any appreciation upon a subsequent purchase of the rental property from the lessor or upon resale to a third party." Anthony J. Luppino, Stopping the Enron End–Runs and Other Trick Plays: The Book–Tax Accounting Conformity Defense, 2003 Colum. Bus. L. Rev. 35, 53 (footnote omitted).

33. Geoffrey A. Manne & E. Marcellus Williamson, Hot Docs vs. Cold Economics, http://papers.ssrn. com/paper.taf?abstract _id=676727

34. Smartest Guys, at 127.

35. Smartest Guys, at 115.

going to slow you down or bog you down or not be value-added ..."[36] Nor did RAC seem to enjoy much respect within in Enron. As one deal originator said, "If a deal had overwhelming commercial support, it got done. I treated [RAC] like dogs, and they couldn't do anything about me." "The corporate culture was such that you never said no to a deal. It was 'how do you make a deal work?' " RAC "didn't want to be seen as someone saying no to a deal."[37] Further undermining RAC's influence was fact that traders and originators sat on the panels that conducted PRC evaluations of RAC personnel.[38]

Attempts by those outside the company to question a transaction also met with stiff resistance. An accountant in Andersen's Professional Standards Group (PSG) in Chicago, for example, had objected to Enron booking a $50 million gain on the sale of an interest in a deal involving Blockbuster. Project Braveheart was a 20–year contract between Enron and Blockbuster to provide video on demand (VOD). Revenue from the project was based on projections about "future DSL use, customer video purchases, the speed of the rollout, market share, expenses, and other factors." As soon as the contract was signed, Enron Broadband sold most of its interest in it to an outside buyer and immediately booked profits from the sale up front.[39]

PSG objected to this accounting treatment, but David Duncan, the accountant in charge of the Enron engagement, did not follow this advice and permitted Enron to recognize the profits. Nonetheless, the Enron Christmas party that year featured a skit that mocked PSG's objection. It depicted Andersen as "The Grinch Who Stole VOD," starring Andersen as the Grinch in "the story of how the mean, heartless auditors tried to ruin the deal[.]"[40]

The evolution of Enron from a gas pipeline company to a trading enterprise using mark-to-market accounting thus created certain challenges and contributed to the emergence of a particular culture within the company. The quest for continuing growth produced pressure for a constant flow of innovative transactions that were high risk but promised high reward, with expert hedging that supposedly minimized the company's exposure. These transactions ideally secured certain outcomes that complied with the technical requirements of accounting rules, notwithstanding some divergence between accounting treatment and economic substance.

Enron's decentralized entrepreneurial culture of multiple fluid project teams provided little systematic oversight by superiors in a conventional organizational hierarchy. Formal review processes were in place, but were buffeted by influences from both above and below in favor of moving deals forward. The project teams themselves were populated by financial whiz kids who ostensibly were creating a new era of capitalism,

36. Smartest Guys, at 116.

37. *Id.* at 116.

38. *Id.* at 117.

39. Smartest Guys, at 293.

40. *Id.* at 296.

and who therefore had little patience for those who failed to understand the intricacies of their transactions.

Finally, the desire to keep the share price high through continued growth in earnings, the use of mark-to-market accounting, and the "Rank and Yank" personnel evaluation process all reinforced a short-term focus within the company. For many, deal origination became the ultimate objective, with much less attention to performance after the contract was signed—in part because Enron was always ready to sell its interest in a project if market conditions were right.

Enron's lawyers thus operated within an environment constituted by "a steady accumulation of habits and values and actions"[41] that shaped their understanding of behavior and events. With that environment in mind, it's time to turn to the attorneys who represented Enron.

B. ENRON'S ATTORNEYS

Enron had a substantial in-house legal department, but also relied extensively on the services of law firms. This section describes the organizational structure within which Enron attorneys operated and some of the major responsibilities that they assumed.[42]

Inside Counsel

James Derrick, a twenty-year veteran of the law firm of Vinson & Elkins (V & E), became Enron's General Counsel in 1991. Derrick regarded Enron's Legal Department as "world-class." Most of its lawyers had between eight and seventeen years of experience when they joined the department. Each of Enron's several business units, such as Enron Energy Services and Enron Global Finance, had its own legal department supervised by a general counsel. Each general counsel reported to the head of the business unit in which he or she served, as well as to Derrick.

Rex Rogers, the Associate General Counsel in Enron's corporate legal department who reported directly to Derrick, was responsible for Enron's compliance with securities laws. Weekly meetings of the general counsels of the major business units occurred in Derrick's office. Eventually, the general counsels of Enron's overseas units participated in these meetings on a monthly basis. Derrick stated that at any given time there were "probably thousands of projects" on which Enron's in-house lawyers were working.

Outside Counsel

Enron retained several outside law firms, but relied most heavily on Vinson & Elkins. The company paid legal fees to V&E of $18.5 million in

---

41. Smartest Guys, at 132.

42. The material in this section is drawn from U.S. Bankruptcy Court for the Southern District of New York, In re Enron Corporation, et al., Case No. 01–16034

(AJG), Final Report of Neal Batson, Court–Appointed Examiner, November 4, 2003, Appendix C: (Role of Enron's Attorneys), at 15–26 (hereinafter "Batson Final Report").

1997, $26.6 million in 1998, $37.8 million in 1999, almost $42.8 million in 2000, and $36.3 million in 2001. During the period relevant to the bankruptcy Examiner's report, the partner at V&E in charge of the relationship with Enron was Joseph Dilg. Periodic advice to Enron on SEC disclosure issues was provided until 1997 by Robert Baird, and afterward by Ronald Astin. Each of these lawyers worked closely on these matters with in-house lawyer Rex Rogers. Several other V&E partners and associates worked on various transactions for Enron. At the height of its work for Enron, V&E derived a little over 7% of its total revenues from this client.

Andrews & Kurth (A&K) began representing Enron on certain "structured finance" transactions, described below, in 1998. A&K partner David Barbour was the primary attorney for these transactions. He was assisted by lawyers who worked on legal opinions for and on tax issues related to these deals. A & K also worked on various other Enron transactions. Enron paid legal fees to A & K of $991,000 in 1997, $2.3 million in 1998, $6.6 million in 1999, $9.7 million in 2000, and $9.2 million in 2001.

C. STRUCTURED FINANCE TRANSACTIONS

Background

The form of transaction that Enron used often to manipulate its financial statements improperly is known as a "structured finance" transaction. In basic terms, this is an arrangement in which a company sells income-generating assets to an affiliated special purpose entity (SPE) in return for a payment from the SPE. The company selling the assets is known as the "originator" because it creates the assets, such as contracts for the receipt of a future stream of payments, that are central to the transaction.[43] The asset may be a set of accounts receivable, an investment in an enterprise, or any other interest that entitles the recipient to future income payments. The SPE purchasing the asset then issues bonds or some other form of security to investors.[44] The issuing SPE receives the proceeds from investors and uses them to pay the seller for the asset. The income from the asset that the issuer owns is earmarked to pay periodic interest to the bondholders and eventually to repay their principal.

Companies use structured finance transactions for legitimate purposes all the time, mainly to lower the cost of borrowing money. A

---

43. *See* Steven L. Schwartz, Bruce A. Markell, & Lissa Lamkin Broome, Securitization, Structured Finance, and Capital Markets 6–7 (2004).

44. In some cases, as in several of the Enron transactions, the entity receiving the assets from the originator may be an affiliate of the originator. This affiliate then transfers the assets to an SPE, which is the entity that issues the securities. In the En-

ron transactions, the affiliate was known as the "sponsor." *See* Batson Second Report, Appendix M (FAS 140 Transactions), January 21, 2003, at 7. *See also* Schwartz, *et al., supra* note ___, at 11–12 (describing a common structured finance transaction in which SPE that receives assets from originator then transfers assets to a second SPE, which issues securities).

company may, for instance, have only a fair credit rating because of the debt that it has outstanding. This means that it must pay a higher interest rate on bonds or for a commercial loan than if its rating were higher. Creating an SPE and selling an income-producing asset to it can result in an entity with a high credit rating, which enables the SPE to borrow funds at a lower rate than could the company on its own. This is because bondholders have security for their loan in the form of the income stream from the asset. The SPE has no other creditors to satisfy with whom the bondholders must compete; its sole asset is pledged to satisfy its obligation to bondholders. When the entity passes the proceeds on to the company from whom it purchased the asset, the effect is that the originating company has been able to obtain funds through proceeds from the sale of the asset more cheaply than if it had incurred debt directly on its own behalf.

If there has been a true sale of the asset from the company to the special entity, the seller can enjoy certain benefits in its financial reports. First, if it sells the asset for a price above the price at which it obtained it, it can book the difference as a gain on its income statement. Second, it can report the proceeds from the sale as cash flow from operating activities. By contrast, proceeds from a loan must be reported as cash flow from financing activities, which investors in the company regard less favorably. Finally, if the asset represents an investment in a company, a gain in the share price of that company is only a paper gain until the investment is actually sold. Selling the asset thus provides a way to "monetize" the investment in a transaction that results in the actual receipt of cash.

Enron's sale of financial assets in structured finance transactions had a major impact on its financial statements. In 2000, for instance, such transactions increased Enron's net income by $351.6 million (36% of total net income); increased cash flow from operations by $1.2 billion (38% of total flow from operations), and kept $1.4 billion in debt associated with the assets off Enron's balance sheet.[45]

Enron's Financial Assets

Enron owned a number of financial assets in the form of interests in various companies, particularly in the energy and telecommunications industries. In order to monetize these assets through sale to an SPE, Enron had to comply with Financial Accounting Standard (FAS) 140.[46] This requires that for the transfer of financial assets to be treated as a sale, the transferor has to surrender control of the assets. Three conditions must be met in order to confirm such surrender. The first of these

---

45. *See* Batson Second Report, at 37.

46. Accounting for Transfers and Servicing of Financial Assets and Extinguishments of Liabilities, Statement of Financial Accounting Standards No. 140 (Financial Accounting Standards Bd. 2000). FAS 140 was preceded by FAS 125, which governed the sale of financial assets prior to April 1, 2001. The two standards are essentially identical with respect to the Enron structured finance issues that the Examiner analyzed.

is that the assets have been "legally isolated" from the transferor.[47] This means that if the transferor were to declare bankruptcy, the assets could not be treated as part of its estate and therefore available to the transferor's creditors. Evidence of this usually takes the form of a "true sale" legal opinion, which opines that the transfer of the assets would be considered a sale rather a loan under relevant state law. In Enron's case, such an opinion would provide assurance to purchasers of the SPE's securities that the income stream from the financial asset could not be used to satisfy the claims of Enron's creditors in case that company filed for bankruptcy. FAS 140 says that whether a true sale has occurred "is largely a matter of law."

Courts look to several factors to determine if a true sale has occurred, such as whether the transferor retains benefits from and risks of holding the asset after the transfer; the actions of the parties after the transfer; the parties' intent; the lender's intent; the amount of the proceeds paid to the transferor compared to the value of the asset transferred; how the transaction was treated for tax and accounting purposes; and how the parties described the transaction.[48] The essence of the inquiry is whether the economic substance of the transaction is consistent with its form; if not, courts are free to disregard its form as a sale.

In Enron's case, if there were not a true sale the transfer would be treated essentially as a loan from the SPE bondholders to Enron, which was secured by the asset in question. In that case, despite their secured status, the bondholders would have to compete with Enron's other creditors for repayment if the company went into bankruptcy. More important from Enron's standpoint, Enron could not record a gain from the transfer of the asset, would have to report the proceeds of the transaction as cash flow from financing activities, and would be required to reflect the debt of the SPE on its books. With few exceptions, Enron asked its outside attorneys to provide an opinion letter that Andersen could use to satisfy FAS 140.

The "Sales" That Weren't

The Enron bankruptcy examiner concluded that Enron had engaged in several supposed FAS 140 transactions in which Enron in fact did not surrender rights and risks with respect to the asset supposedly sold to the SPE. In simplified terms, a typical such Enron transaction proceeded as follows.[49] Enron, directly or through a "Sponsor" entity, transferred a financial asset to an "Asset Limited Liability Company (LLC)." Figure 1, Step 1. This was treated as a capital contribution to the Asset LLC, for

---

47. The other two are that the transferee (or holders of beneficial interests in it) obtains the right to pledge or exchange its interest in the assets, and that the transferor has no right to repurchase or redeem the assets before their maturity. Batson Second Report, Appendix B (Accounting Standards), at 59–60.

48. See Batson Second Report, Appendix C (Legal Standards), at 8–16.

49. See In re Enron Corporation, First Interim Report of Neal Batson, Court–Appointed Examiner, Sept. 21, 2002, pp. 59–63.

which Enron or the Sponsor received a "Class A" interest entitling it to complete voting control over the Asset LLC and a negligible economic interest in it. Enron or the Sponsor also was entitled to a special cash distribution from the LLC in an amount equal to the value of the asset as established by Enron.

The Asset LLC then issued a "Class B" interest to an SPE (which usually took the form of a trust), entitling the latter to all the economic proceeds from the asset held by the former, but no voting rights in the Asset LLC. Figure 1, Step 2. The consideration for the Class B interest was a payment in the amount of the special distribution that the Asset LLC owed Enron or the Sponsor. The SPE then obtained a bank loan, Figure 1, Step 3, for which it used its Class B interest as collateral, and used the proceeds, along with a small equity contribution by a third party (typically an affiliate of the lender), to pay for the Class B interest. Figure 1, Step 4. The amount of the equity generally comprised at least 3% of the purchase price of the Class B interest, plus fees due the lender.

Upon receiving payment from the SPE, the Asset LLC then made the "special distribution" to Enron or its Sponsor as consideration for the asset that ostensibly had been sold to it. Figure 1, Step 5. After giving effect to these transactions, the Asset LLC held the asset, Enron or the Sponsor held voting control over the LLC, and the SPE Trust had an interest in the SPE that entitled it to proceeds from the LLC's asset.

A condition of the bank loan to the SPE to purchase the Class B interest was that Enron would enter into a "Total Return Swap." Under this arrangement, Enron or one of its affiliates agreed to make payments to the SPE or the lender in an amount equal to the SPE's obligation to the lender, which was usually 97% of the purchase price of the asset that had been transferred to the Asset LLC. Enron or its affiliate then was entitled to first priority on the proceeds from the asset up to the amount of its Total Return Swap obligation (and, after any equity holders in the SPE received a return on their investment, any remaining proceeds). The effect of this was to guarantee the SPE's loan from the bank, Figure 1, Step 6, in return for the SPE's Class B interest in the income from the asset. Figure 1, Step 7.[50]

The Examiner found that in five of the six FAS 140 transactions that he reviewed the assets that ostensibly were the source of payment by the SPE to the security holders produced insufficient cash flow to serve this purpose, or may have been difficult to sell on acceptable terms in a genuine arms-length transaction. Enron's guarantee under the Total Return Swap thus "played what appears to be a substantial—if not the decisive—role" in convincing the lenders to advance funds to the SPE.[51]

50. *See* Batson Second Report, Appendix B (Accounting Standards), at 61 (by virtue of the Total Return Swap, "Enron in substance guaranteed the debt" of the SPE).

51. In Re Enron Corp., *et al.*, First Interim Report of Neal Batson, Court—Appointed Examiner, September 21, 2002, at 16 (hereinafter "Batson First Report").

FIGURE 1
ENRON FAS 140 TRANSACTION

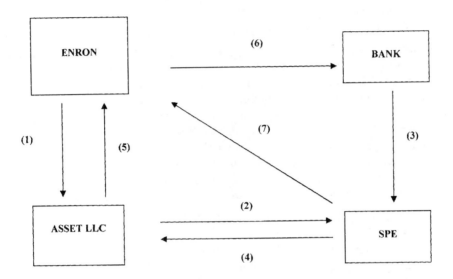

(1)   Enron transfers asset to Asset LLC (True Sale Opinion)
(2)   Asset LLC issues Class B (Income) Interest to SPE (True Issuance Opinion)
(3)   Bank loan to SPE to pay for Class B Interest
(4)   SPE pays Asset LLC for Class B Interest
(5)   Asset special distribution to Enron: (a) Cash   (b) Class A (Voting) Interest
(6)   Enron total return swap effectively guarantees Bank loan to SPE
(7)   SPE transfers class B Interest to Enron

Several features of these deals undermined their compliance with FAS 140. Since Enron retained voting control over the asset, it had not relinquished rights in it. Furthermore, Enron also retained the rewards and risks associated with the asset. By virtue of the Class B interest it obtained in exchange for the Total Return Swap, it would enjoy appreciation in the value of the asset in the form of any increases in income that it generated. If, however, the asset's income stream declined to a level below the amount necessary to cover the bank loan to the SPE, Enron had to make up the difference. In effect, the money used to pay Enron for the "sale" of its asset to the Asset LLC ultimately came from a bank loan that Enron itself guaranteed.

The Examiner concluded that the economic substance of such a transaction as a whole therefore was that Enron had incurred debt, for which the asset served as collateral—not that it had sold an asset to an SPE in a structured finance transaction. In effect, as the Examiner described one of these transactions, Enron "acquire[d] funds in the short term using certain assets, while retaining the opportunity to subsequently re-acquire those assets and sell the assets to a third party" at a more advantageous time.[52] "The economic reality of this transaction thus may be viewed as a bridge loan, as opposed to a sale."[53]

The Examiner came to this conclusion notwithstanding the existence of legal opinions that were issued in connection with these transactions. "In many of the FAS 140 Transactions," the Examiner stated, "legal isolation was not achieved."[54] The legal opinions concluding otherwise, he declared, "were limited in scope and analyzed only certain steps and specific entities, rather than the transaction in its entirety."[55]

To the extent that a transfer of financial assets was not a true sale, Enron was not entitled to book a gain on its income statement from the "sale" of the asset to the Asset LLC, to report the distribution from that entity as cash flow from operating activities, or to avoid listing the bank loan as debt on its balance sheet or in the related footnotes.

Issue One: True Sale vs. True Issuance Opinions

V&E served as counsel to Enron on several FAS 140 transactions that closed in late 1997 and 1998. In each of these transactions, Enron asked V&E to deliver not a "true sale" but a "true issuance" opinion. In terms of the typical transaction described above, a true sale opinion speaks to whether there has been a genuine transfer of an asset from Enron (or an Enron "sponsor") to an Asset LLC in Step 1 of Figure 1. By contrast, a true issuance opinion deals with whether there has been a genuine transfer of a Class B interest in the asset from the Asset LLC to the SPE in Step 2 of Figure 1.[56]

V&E attorneys apparently were puzzled by the request for a true issuance opinion. As an internal V&E memo noted, "[A] 'true issuance' by an [SPE] would accomplish little, in regard to the isolation of its financial assets from the original transferor, if there had not been a true sale or contribution of the financial assets to the [SPE]."[57] As the bankruptcy Examiner stated, "Vinson & Elkins believed, and Vinson & Elkins attorneys testified, that they repeatedly told both Enron and Andersen, that Andersen had asked for the wrong opinion when it requested a true issuance opinion. This was potentially significant because Vinson & Elkins did not believe that it could provide a true sale opinion in some of those transactions as structured."[58]

The response of V&E lawyers to these misgivings was to attempt to confirm that Arthur Andersen understood the difference between a true

---

52. Batson First Report, at 50 n. 129.

53. *Id.*

54. Batson Second Report, at 39.

55. *Id.*

56. Specifically, a true issuance opinion would state that a court would not "recharacterize the issuance of the Class B Membership Interest by [the Asset LLC] as a loan to the [Asset LLC] supported by a security interest in [its] Class B Member-

ship Interest[.]" Batson Final Report, Appendix C, at 35 n. 99.

57. Batson Final Report, Appendix C (Role of Enron's Attorneys), at 31. As an Andersen accountant who worked on Enron matters noted in a memorandum in 2000, "[the] Asset LLC must own the Financial Asset in the first place before it can consider selling it ..." *Id.* at 31 n. 81.

58. *Id.*

sale and true issuance opinion, and that the accountants were comfortable that the latter would satisfy FAS 140. On two transactions known as Sutton Bridge and Riverside, the lawyer had never been asked for a true issuance opinion, nor had any of the V&E partners whom he contacted. He told an Andersen employee that he understood FAS 140 to apply to situations in which assets were bought and sold, not the grant of interests in assets. He questioned whether a true issuance opinion was appropriate, but ultimately provided one in both transactions when he received reassurance from Andersen employees that this is what they wanted. "I mean they were the accountants," he said, "they understood what they wanted and based on what [they] said, I had ... no reason to think that was not reasonable from an accounting criteria standpoint."[59]

On another transaction known as Cornhusker, David Keyes, the V&E lawyer who was asked for a true issuance opinion, didn't know what it was. He told Arthur Andersen that he believed that accountants were asking for the wrong kind of opinion. As Astin testified, this lawyer felt that "from a lawyer's perspective ... what they were asking for was [not] what his reading of the corporate rules required."[60] Keyes also pointed out to Andersen that V&E had added to its opinion the assumption that a court would not recharacterize the transaction in its entirety as a loan. In other words, the opinion assumed that a true sale of the asset to the Asset LLC had occurred prior to the issuance of the Class B interest. When Andersen indicated its understanding of what V&E was providing, the firm issued a true issuance opinion.

Keyes, continued, however, to have concerns about the request for a true issuance opinion. One lawyer working with him on a later transaction indicated in a memo to Dilg that the event in Cornhusker that resulted in recognition of a gain to Enron was the transfer of the asset from an Enron sponsor to the Asset LLC. "This fact suggests," he said, "that for opinion purposes, we and the accountants focused on the wrong part of the transaction."[5] The memo also noted that the characteristics of the transfer to the Asset LLC were such that "virtually all law firms would refuse to give a true sale opinion" for such a transaction.[6]

Eventually, Dilg scheduled a meeting with Enron general counsel Derrick to discuss, among other matters, issues relating to the V&E opinion letters. Dilg focused on two questions. First, was a true issuance opinion sufficient for FAS 140 accounting treatment? Second, did the qualification in V&E's opinion letter that a court would not recharacterize the overall transaction as a loan create any problems with respect to FAS 140? On the latter issue, Dilg's notes for the meeting said, "We are not asked to render accounting advice but qualification we had to take in opinion could be inconsistent with [FAS 140] requirements."[7] Dilg noted that V&E could not remove the qualification from its opinion if asked to.

59. *Id.* at 33 n. 92.

60. *Id.* at 34 n. 8.

5. *Id.* at 37.

6. *Id*, n. 113.

7. *Id.* at 44.

Some time after the meeting, Derrick told Dilg that he had spoken with Rick Causey, Enron's Chief Accounting Officer, who in turn had consulted with high-level Arthur Andersen personnel. The Andersen people told him that the opinions were satisfactory for their purposes. Dilg reported back to V&E lawyers who had raised the issue that both Enron and Andersen understood the nature of the true issuance opinions and felt that there was no problem with them. For Dilg, this information "removed any doubt in my mind" on the question.[61]

Keyes, however, "still was not satisfied, and he continued to raise these same issues in the next FAS 140 Transactions he worked on for Enron[.]"[62] It was not until a transaction named Project Iguana closed in late 1999 that Andersen appeared to have appreciated the true issuance/true sale distinction and the assumption in V&E's true issuance opinion letters that a court would not recharacterize the transaction as a loan. In an internal V&E email, Keyes described a meeting with an Andersen person in which, the lawyer said, the Andersen representative "[f]or the first time . . . really realized that FAS 125 calls for more than what Arthur Andersen has been getting."[63] The lawyer went on to say:

> "I think I am blamed by some of the inside Enron attorneys . . . for drawing this distinction to AA's attention, as it could jeopardize Enron's FAS 125 transactions. The Enron theory is, apparently, that relations with AA must be carefully managed and that AA is a sophisticated organization that can read opinions and draw their own conclusions. I have believed that it is our professional duty to call the attention of a third party recipient to the meaning and scope of our opinion, especially in a situation where we do not believe that the recipient has a correct understanding of what it says in relation to the purpose for which the opinion is requested."[64]

The lawyer later, however, told the Examiner that "I don't think that's a correct statement of legal opinion practice and I–I'm reasonably confident that what I meant was that I shouldn't affirmatively mislead somebody[.]"[65]

The Examiner concluded that V&E possibly could be liable to Enron under Texas law for malpractice and for aiding and abetting breaches of fiduciary duties by Enron officers in connection with its work on the FAS 140 transactions. In several of these transactions, V&E attorneys "rendered true issuance opinions even though those attorneys knew that these opinions did not address the critical issues under FAS 140, as Vinson & Elkins understood those issues."[66] In many cases, the Examiner indicated, the firm knew that Enron was retaining the risks and rewards of the asset supposedly sold, and that Enron was using Total Return Swaps to guarantee repayment of the loans that had been used to finance their "purchase."

61. *Id.* at 46.
62. *Id.* at 47.
63. *Id.* at 47 n. 169.
64. *Id.*
65. *Id.*
66. *Id.* at 179.

With respect to a malpractice claim, the Examiner noted that Texas courts have held that the Texas Disciplinary Rules of Professional Conduct may sometimes be used to aid a fact-finder in determining what a reasonable attorney would have done under the circumstances.[67] For this purpose, the Examiner turned to Texas Rule 1.12, entitled "Organization as Client."[68] This rule, said the Examiner, "is relevant in a situation in which a company's attorney knows that an officer of a company is causing the company to enter into transactions that have an improper purpose."[69]

When an attorney encounters this situation, the rule provides that he or she "shall proceed as reasonably necessary in the best interest of the organization"[70] and "must take reasonable remedial actions."[71] This may consist of asking for reconsideration of the matter, recommending a second legal opinion, and referring the matter to higher authority within the organization, including to the highest authority if the matter is sufficiently serious.[72] If a lawyer fails to take such steps when he or she knows that an officer has committed or intends to commit a legal violation likely to result in substantial injury to the organization,[73] that lawyer does not act as a lawyer of reasonable prudence.[74]

The Examiner noted that V&E "may argue that it had no duty to question the subject matter of a legal opinion requested by an accountant."[75] The firm also could argue that, even though there was no duty to do so, V&E attorneys informed both Andersen and Enron of its belief that Andersen was asking for the wrong opinion, and that V&E obtained assurance that the true issuance opinions were sufficient to satisfy the requirement of FAS 140 that the assets be effectively "legally isolated" from the transferor. V& E could claim that Enron had considered the concerns raised by the firm "and had made an appropriate business decision."[76] "These arguments," stated the Examiner, "present issues of fact for determination by a fact-finder."[77]

Questions

1. Was the question whether a true issuance opinion satisfied FAS 140 an accounting issue or a legal issue? Consider Paragraph 23 of FAS 125, the predecessor to FAS 140:

"The nature and extent of the supporting evidence required for an assertion in financial statements that transferred financial assets have

67. Batson Final Report, Appendix C (Role of Enron's Attorneys), Annex 1 (Legal Standards Applicable to Attorneys, at 9.

68. Texas Disciplinary Rule 1.12: Organization as Client.

69. *Id.* at 10.

70. Texas Rule 1.12(a)

71. *Id.* at 1.12(a).

72. *Id.* at 1.12(c)

73. *Id.* at 1.12(b). The violation also must be related to a matter within the

scope of the lawyer's representation of the organization. *Id.*

74. Batson Final Report, Appendix C (Role of Enron's Lawyers), Annex 1 (Legal Standards Applicable to Attorneys), at 14.

75. *Id.*

76. Batson Final Report, Appendix C, at 183.

77. *Id.* at 180.

been isolated ... depend on the facts and circumstances. All available evidence that either supports or questions an assertion should be considered. That consideration includes making judgments about whether the contract or circumstances permit the transferor to invoke the transfer. It may also include making judgments about [what kind of bankruptcy might be involved], whether a transfer of financial assets would likely be deemed a true sale at law, whether the transferor is affiliated with the transferee, and other factors pertinent under applicable law. [T]he available evidence [must provide] reasonable assurance that the transferred assets would be beyond the reach of the powers of a bankruptcy trustee or other receiver for the transferor or any of its affiliates ... [78]

2. Was it Enron's prerogative as the client, and Andersen's as its agent, to instruct V&E lawyers as to the scope of the work that it wanted V&E to perform? Should V&E have deferred to this instruction as long as Enron and Andersen understood its implications? Or should V&E decline to provide the opinion unless it finds persuasive Andersen's explanation how a true issuance opinion satisfies FAS 140?

3. Was it appropriate for V&E to include in its true issuance opinions the qualification that the opinions assumed that a court effectively would not conclude that a true sale of the asset to the Asset LLC had not occurred? Isn't the precondition for the Asset LLC being able to issue a Class B interest in the asset the LLC's ownership of that asset? Could V&E simply make this assumption, or did it have any obligation to investigate to determine if it was reasonable?

4. Would it be appropriate for V&E to deliver a true issuance opinion in transactions in which it felt that it could not provide a true sale opinion? What if another law firm provided a true sale opinion in the transaction?

5. One of the V&E lawyers working on true issuance opinions suggested that Enron was unhappy with him raising with Andersen the sufficiency of a true issuance opinion "as it could jeopardize Enron's FAS [140] transactions." Enron, said the lawyer, regards Andersen as "a sophisticated organization that can read opinions and draw their own conclusions."

The lawyer went on to say, "I have believed that it is our professional duty to call the attention of a third party recipient to the meaning and scope of our opinions, especially in a situation where we do not believe that the recipient has a correct understanding of what it says in relation to the purpose for which the opinion is requested." The lawyer later recanted this statement during the investigation of Enron. At that point, he said, "I don't think that's a correct statement of legal opinion practice and ... I'm reasonably confident that what I meant was that I shouldn't affirmatively mislead somebody[.]" Which statement is more accurate?

Issue Two: Andrews & Kurth Opinions

Beginning in November 1998, the law firm of Andrews & Kurth (A&K) represented Enron in the majority of the company's FAS 140 transactions. From that month through October 2001, the firm delivered

---

78. Financial Accounting Standard 125, Paragraph 23.

at least twenty-four true sale or true issuance opinion letters in connection with such transactions. In cases in which the firm provided a true issuance opinion, "[u]nlike Vinson & Elkins, Andrews & Kurth did not raise with Enron or Andersen whether or not a true issuance opinion was responsive to the requirements of FAS 125 or FAS 140."[79] In virtually all these transactions, an Enron sponsor transferred an asset to an Asset LLC over which it had voting control. That LLC then issued a Class B interest in the income from the asset to an SPE, which financed the purchase of that interest through a bank loan. In most transactions, Enron entered into a Total Return Swap with the SPE.

The Examiner found that A&K was aware that Enron's goals in these transactions were to raise funds that would not be reflected as debt on its balance sheet and to recognize a gain on its income statement when the sale price of the asset exceeded the value at which Enron was carrying it on its books.[80] He also found that the firm was aware that "the opinions it rendered in the FAS 140 Transactions were critical to Enron's intended accounting treatment."[81]

A&K explicitly recognized in many of its opinions that the Total Return Swap had the characteristics of a guarantee of the loan obtained by the SPE ostensibly to purchase the asset.[82] Furthermore, the bankruptcy examiner noted A&K memos stating that in these transactions "Enron, as a practical matter, retains all the risks and rewards of owning the asset,"[9] and that while the deals "were structured as sales for purposes of accounting treatment, Enron retained full control over its interest ... and commercially the transactions look more like financings."[83] Questioned by the Examiner with respect to the first statement, however, the author of the memo testified that he was "not sure it's completely accurate," because it didn't take into account that the risks were limited to the payment of the debt, and the reward was only any appreciation in the value of the asset that exceeded what was necessary to repay the SPE's security holders.[84]

An additional way in which Enron allegedly sought to retain control of the asset supposedly transferred was to prepay the SPE's loan. This resulted in unencumbering the asset whose income effectively was used to guarantee the loan. It was done by purchasing the equity interest in the SPE and then directing the SPE to pay off the loan and "unwind" the transaction. As a formal matter, the existing SPE equity holder could refuse Enron's offer to purchase its interest. In fact, however, there was never an instance in which Enron made an offer that was not accepted.[85] Indeed, an A&K memo to Enron in March 2000 stated, "In the deals which closed in December we were given very clear instructions that Enron had to be able to prepay and get the assets back at any time. A

79. Batson Final Report, Appendix C (Role of Enron's Lawyers), at 52–53 n. 180.

80. *Id.* at 54–55.

81. *Id.* at 55 (footnote omitted).

82. *Id.* at 58.

9. *Id.* at 56–57.

83. *Id.* at 59 n. 199.

84. *Id.* at 57 n. 192.

85. *Id.* at 59, 60 n. 202.

right to prepay was included in the documents (as for all previous deals)."[86] While the author of this memo clarified to the Examiner that the SPE, not Enron, had the right to prepay, he could not "identify a single instance where Enron desired the facility to be prepaid and it was refused."[87]

The prepayments occurred despite the fact that the FAS 140 transactions provided for an auction of the asset transferred to the SPE (the Class B interest) just before the date on which the SPE had to pay off its obligations to the lender and security holders. Proceeds from the auction were to provide the SPE with funds that would be paid to Enron under the Total Return Swap.[88] A genuine auction would have transferred control of the asset to a party other than Enron or any of its affiliates.

A memo that Enron sent to A&K for revisions, however, stated that "the Auction-related mechanisms will come into play ONLY if the indebtedness is not prepaid by the Sponsor [an Enron affiliate], which is always [Enron] Global Finance's planned means of unwind and has been, with one exception I'm aware of, the actual means of unwind."[89] The memo noted, however, that "this prepayment plan is not memorialized in any deal documentation (and cannot be for financial accounting and legal opinion purposes) [.]"[90]

The Examiner found that A&K was aware as early as November 1998, in connection with the first FAS 140 transactions on which it worked, that "Enron did not intend to transfer the monetized asset to a third party."[91] An A&K memo recounted that the lead Enron attorney assigned to the FAS 140 transactions "did not want to mention the auction in the consent. I said this was okay as long as Enron [was] absolutely confident that there would never in practice be a sale to a third party. [The Enron attorney] said this was correct."[92]

A&K worked on both the FAS 140 transactions and on Enron's steps to unwind them, sometimes simultaneously with respect to the same transaction. Some of the transactions were unwound as soon as about two weeks, four weeks, six weeks, and two months after the transaction transferring the asset had closed.[93] Indeed, in some of the fifteen unwound transactions, the unwinds were effected before the firm issued its true sale or true issuance opinion letter for the original FAS 140 transfer of assets.[94]

The Examiner observed that the ability of Enron to prepay the loan and equity did cause some concern to A&K. In the course of closing an FAS 140 transaction in late 1999, attorneys at the firm asked Enron whether prepayment and sale by Enron about two months after the

86. *Id.* at 59–60.

87. *Id.* at 60 n. 202.

88. *Id.* at 61–62.

89. *Id.* at 61 (emphasis in original). The only exception was an auction in which the purchaser of the asset was an entity controlled by Enron. *Id.* at 62 n. 211.

90. *Id.* at 61.

91. *Id.* at 61 n. 207.

92. *Id.*

93. *See* Table at *id.*, p. 66.

94. *Id.* at 66.

transaction closed would "jeopardize the FASB 125 treatment of the transaction? Does it matter if [the Enron affiliate] *intends* to arrange such a sale and prepay the facility at the time of entering into the FASB 125 transaction?"[95] The Examiner said that he had not seen any evidence that A&K received an answer to this question. He stated, "Andrews & Kurth appeared to think that the answer required an accounting judgment, but the question calls for a legal conclusion."[96]

The Examiner concluded that Enron could have a cause of action against A&K for malpractice based on Texas Rule 1.12 or negligence, as well as for aiding and abetting officers' breaches of their fiduciary duties, in connection with the firm's work on the FAS 140 transactions. A&K, he said, knew of Enron's accounting goals in entering into these transactions, and "also knew that the risks and rewards of owning the assets remained with Enron and that isolation of these assets was not occurring."[97]

Furthermore, A&K assisted Enron in unwinding several of these transactions, and in some cases began work on that project even before delivering the opinion on legal isolation of the assets that was necessary for the transaction to close. "As the number of prepayments and unwinds grew," said the Examiner, "Andrews & Kurth also knew that the transactions were being used by certain officers of Enron to manipulate its financial statements."[98]

The Examiner noted that A&K may argue that it lacked knowledge of wrongful conduct because the prepayments and unwinds were permitted under the transaction documents. Loans "are routinely prepaid prior to their maturity dates or otherwise modified for a variety of legitimate business purposes," the Examiner acknowledged, "but these transactions were supposed to be sales, not loans."[99] A&K also may argue that the opinions were issued "as of" the closing even though they were delivered later, and thus were correct as of their effective dates. The Examiner responded, however, that "the decision to issue an opinion must be made within the context of what the attorneys know about the intent of the parties, and their conduct reveals that intent. Conduct occurring after closing but before delivery of an opinion can reflect on the intent of the parties at closing."[100]

Even if A&K did not have knowledge of wrongdoing, said the Examiner, a fact-finder could conclude that the firm was liable for malpractice based on negligence. This conclusion would be based on a finding that a prudent attorney would have recognized that certain Enron officers did not intend for Enron to relinquish control over the

95. *Id.* at 60. Emphasis appears to be in the original.

96. *Id.* at 60 n. 204.

97. Batson Final Report, Appendix C, Annex 1, at 187.

98. *Id.*

99. *Id.*

100. *Id.*

assets that were transferred and were using the FAS 140 transactions to manipulate the company's financial statements.[101]

Finally, the Examiner found that a fact-finder could conclude that A&K was liable for aiding and abetting Enron officers' breaches of fiduciary duties by lending substantial assistance to those breaches. This consisted of issuing opinions and preparing documents necessary for the transactions to close. A&K may claim that it acted merely as scriveners who memorialized the terms of the deals, but the Examiner noted that "the rendering of just one legal opinion can constitute substantial assistance under some circumstances."[102]

Questions

1.　Why do you think that, unlike V&E, A&K raised no questions about the sufficiency of a true issuance opinion in satisfying FAS 140?

2.　With respect to Enron's prepayment of the SPE loan, was the fact that the SPE equity holder was not legally required to sell its interest to Enron sufficient to allow A&K to provide an FAS 140 opinion letter? At some point, should A&K have concluded that Enron did not intend any of these transactions to transfer assets, and that Enron's effective right to reacquire them was inconsistent with FAS 140?

3.　Would it make any difference to A&K's ability to issue a true sale or true issuance opinion letter if the purported sale of the asset in each FAS 140 transaction occurred immediately prior to the end of a financial reporting quarter and its reacquisition occurred shortly after the end of the quarter?

4.　The Examiner identified statements by A&K that suggest appreciation that the ostensible FAS 140 transactions really weren't sales but loans. He pointed to documents in which A&K lawyers say that the Total Return Swap resembled a loan guarantee, that Enron retained the risks and rewards associated with the assets, and that the deals were structured as sales for accounting purposes but for commercial purposes were more like loans. How could A&K acknowledge this and still give true sale opinions?

D.　RELATED PARTY TRANSACTIONS

Background

Beginning in 1997 and continuing until mid–2001, Enron engaged in twenty-four transactions with special purpose entities (SPEs) created by Enron in which Chief Financial Officer Andrew Fastow and other Enron employees were involved. These entities were known as LJM1 and LJM2. As long as 3% of the equity at risk in the SPE was held by outside investors (and assuming a valid business purpose), these transactions could be treated for accounting purposes as occurring at arms-length between two independent entities. As a result, Enron could book as income any gains that it derived from the transactions. Furthermore, it did not have to reflect on its balance sheet the assets or, especially

---

101.　*Id.* at 188–189.
102.　*Id.* at 188.

important, the liabilities of the SPEs—that is, the SPE did not have to be consolidated into Enron's financial reports.

The examiner concluded that the related party transactions he reviewed "had no business purpose from Enron's perspective, other than to achieve desired financial statement reporting."[103] He estimated that these and other transactions with related party SPEs permitted Enron to overstate its income by $1.5 billion and its equity by the same amount, and to understate its indebtedness by $885 million. Aside from the FAS 140 transactions, the most notable transactions between Enron and the related party SPEs involved hedging, or arrangements in which an SPE purported to indemnify Enron for the loss in value of Enron's investments in other companies.

The discussion below of related party transactions focuses first on two matters with respect to which the Examiner found that Enron's lawyers might be liable for malpractice and/or aiding and abetting breach of fiduciary duty: Enron's purported hedges with the SPEs and the failure to press for adequate disclosure of Fastow's compensation for his involvement in LJM1 and LJM2. The discussion then moves to two matters as to which the Examiner did not find potential attorney liability, but which offer a useful vehicle for analyzing issues that can arise in transactional work. The first of these is possible SPE difficulty in meeting the 3% outside equity requirement, and the second is the "warehousing" of assets by Enron in SPEs.

Issue One: The "Hedges" That Weren't

The hedging transactions took the same general form, with some individual variations. The impetus for them was the fact that Enron had "merchant investments" in companies that it carried on its books at current value, under the mark-to-market method of accounting. To reiterate, under this method if the share price of a company increased, Enron did not need to wait to sell shares at a gain to record an increase in income. Rather, it could reflect the change in price by increasing the value of assets on its balance sheet, and recording the appreciation as income on its income statement. By the same token, any decrease in share price had to be reflected in a reduction in the value of assets on the balance sheet and a loss on the income statement. Enron held a substantial amount of merchant investments in companies whose value was volatile. This created the prospect that Enron's own reported financial performance could vary widely—a condition that would make the stock market nervous and dampen the value of Enron's shares.

Parties facing this prospect can attempt to reduce their risk by entering a "hedging" transaction with another party, typically a large financial institution. For a fee, the institution essentially agrees to compensate a company such as Enron for the decline in the value of certain of its merchant investments. The amount is determined by the difference between the share price at the time of the hedge contract and

---

103. *Id.*

the price at a certain date in the future. With a hedge, while Enron would have to record the decline in the value of its investment in its financial reports, it also would be able to record a gain in the same amount because of its right to this payment. Enron thus would be "held harmless"—it would not be affected one way or other by the decline in the value of the investment. If the share price rose, Enron would pay the hedging party the value of the increase—but it also could record the increase in value in its financial statements. Again, the result is a wash. Through such an arrangement, a company can "lock in" the value of its investments at a given time.

Enron found it difficult to find parties to hedge its risk because many of its investments were in companies for which there was not a substantial and liquid trading market. This was the case, for instance, with many high-tech energy trading and telecommunications companies. The share price of these companies often rose to dizzying heights. They also, however, posed the risk of precipitous declines. Without a party with whom to hedge, Enron could not lock in the high value of the shares. It thus would be fully exposed to the vagaries of the market.

To remedy this situation, Enron decided to create ostensibly independent SPEs with whom it could engage in hedging transactions. In order for the SPE to be treated as a separate entity that did not have to be included in Enron's financial reports, outside investors had to contribute at least 3% of the equity at risk. This contribution, and in some cases other capital, was provided by a partnership managed by Andrew Fastow known as LJM1 or LJM2. The remainder of the capital in most cases was furnished by subsidiaries of Enron.

The SPE then entered into a Total Return Swap with Enron. Under this arrangement, the SPE agreed to pay Enron the amount of any decline in the value of certain investment, while Enron agreed to pay the SPE the amount of any increase. In this way, Enron purported to lock in the value of its investments at the date of the agreement. As the bankruptcy Examiner explained:

> "Accordingly, if the market value of the asset were $100 on the date the hedge became effective and declined to $90 at the end of the next fiscal quarter, Enron would record a $10 decline in the value of the merchant investment on its balance sheet, but it would also record a new $10 price risk management asset on its balance sheet. The net effect on the balance sheet would be $0. The increase and decline would also offset each other on Enron's income statement."[104]

The transactions with the SPEs could serve as true hedges for Enron only if the company suffered no financial impact from a decline in the value of investments that it hedged. This would occur if the SPE was able to compensate Enron for the amount of any decline. In order to cover its potential obligation, the SPE needed capital. The problem was

104. *Id.* at 8.

that investors were unlikely to be interested in contributing funds to the entity because the SPE was unable to hedge its own risks of having to pay compensation to Enron. The very features of the investments that made it nearly impossible for Enron to hedge its investment with a conventional third party—their size, risk, and illiquidity—made it impossible for the SPE to enter into a true hedge with anyone else with respect to its obligations on those same investments. If the SPE did not have enough capital to cover its potential obligations to Enron, however, then Enron obtained no real protection from its hedges with the SPE.

Enron purported to solve this problem primarily by capitalizing the hedging SPE with Enron's own stock. By doing this, however, Enron was effectively hedging with itself—which is no hedge at all. As the Powers Report put it, "The economic reality of these transactions was that Enron never escaped the risk of loss, because it had provided the bulk of the capital with which the SPEs would pay Enron."[105]

The first ostensible hedging transaction with an SPE occurred when Enron established LJM to hedge Enron's investment in a telecommunications company called RhythmsNet Connections. At a later date, Enron established a second SPE known as LJM2, and engaged in several additional purported hedges with LJM2 entities known as the "Raptors."

RhythmsNet

The RhythmsNet transaction involving LJM1 was the first transaction in which Enron entered into a supposed hedge with an SPE. V&E lawyers did not work on structuring this transaction, but did work on discrete aspects of it. The story begins in March 1998, when Enron's broadband unit purchased $10 million shares in an Internet service provider start-up named RhythmsNet Connections. The investment eventually was calculated as a purchase at a sale price of $1.85 per share.[106] In April 1999 Rhythms had an initial public offering (IPO) at a price of $21 per share, and the share price rose sharply afterward. By June 1, 1999, Enron's $10 million investment was worth about $260 million, or $48.50 a share.[107]

Enron treated the Rhythms investment as part of its merchant investment portfolio, which was marked to market under fair value accounting. It thus immediately booked the appreciation in the value of the Rhythms stock as income, which accounted for almost one-third of the company's earnings in 1999.[108] The problem was that this gain was on paper, but not in cash. Indeed, Enron could not convert it to cash for six months. As a condition of being able to buy the pre-IPO Rhythms shares, Enron was prohibited from selling or transferring the ownership risk of the shares to another party.

---

105. Powers Report at 41.

106. Batson Second Report, Appendix L, Annex 2 (Rhythms Transactions), at 2.

107. *Id.* 1.

108. Mimi Schwartz & Sherron Watkins, Power Failure: The Inside Story of the Collapse of Enron 167 (2003).

The company thus was exposed during this period to the risk that the share price of Rhythms would decline, which would lead to the need to book a loss. Enron desired a hedge to lock in the appreciation in the value of the Rhythms stock. It was unlikely, however, to find anyone willing to provide it at anything other than a prohibitive price. Enron held a large portion of the thinly traded stock, which meant that trying to sell the stock could itself depress the price. Furthermore, technology stocks were notoriously volatile, and a precipitous decline in value was a real possibility.

Enron CFO Andrew Fastow told Enron executives that he was willing to create a new SPE to hedge Enron's Rhythms position. This entity was known LJM, and later as LJM1 after Fastow created a second LJM SPE.[109] LJM's general partner was LJM Partners, LP, whose limited partner was Fastow and whose general partner was LJM Partners, LLC. The sole and managing member of the latter entity was Fastow. The upshot of this organizational structure was, as the Examiner put it, that "Fastow owned and controlled the general partner of LJM1."[110] This general partner contributed $1 million to LJM1 through Fastow in return for a 6% interest in it. Figure 2, Step 1. LJM1's two limited partners were entities affiliated with Credit Suisse First Boston and Royal Bank of Scotland. They each contributed $7.5 million in cash to LJM1 and each owned 47% of it. Figure 2, Step 2.

Fastow was not permitted to receive distributions of LJM in the form of Enron stock or proceeds from it. He was, however, was entitled to 100% of all other distributions until he had received (1) $1 million plus the general partner's portion of LJM1's assets and (2) a 25% compound annual rate of return on that amount. Any LJM1 distributions in excess of the latter were to be made 50% to the general partner and 50% pro rata to the limited partners and general partner.[111]

Enron was not a partner in LJM1, but funded it with about 6.7 million Enron shares worth $276 million, in return for $64 million in promissory notes. Figure 2, Step 3. Certain restrictions were placed on LJM1's ability to transfer or hedge these shares. These allowed LJM1 to acquire the shares at a discount of $108 million. This difference between the market value of the shares and LJM1's ostensible obligation to Enron was intended to provide LJM1 the capacity to enter into a hedge with Enron.[112] LJM1 then funded an entity known as Swap Sub. LJM1 formed a wholly-owned entity, SwapCo, and transferred about 32,000 Enron shares to it. Figure 2, Step 5. SwapCo then contributed these shares to Swap Sub in return for becoming Swap Sub's general partner. Figure 2, Step 6.

---

109. LJM were the initials of Fastow's wife and children.

110. Batson Second Report, Appendix L, Annex 2, at 5.

111. *Id.* at 5–6.

112. *Id.* at 8. "Credit capacity is essentially the excess of a[n entity's] asset value over its liabilities." Batson Second Report, Appendix L, Annex 5 (Raptor Transactions), at 5 n. 20.

LJM1 contributed to Swap Sub $3.75 million in proceeds from the sale of about 91,000 of the Enron shares, and about 3.1 million shares of Enron, in return for a limited partnership interest in Swap Sub. Figure 2, Step 4. The market value of these shares was $127 million, with a discounted value of $77 million, which gave Swap Sub credit capacity of about $50 million.[113]

In return for its contributions, Enron received two notes from LJM1 totaling $64 million, with no recourse for Enron against any of the LJM1 partners. In addition, Swap Sub granted Enron a put option under which Enron had the right to require Swap Sub to purchase 5.4 million shares of Rhythms stock at an exercise price of $56.125 per share.[114] Figure 2, Step 7. If Rhythms' share price fell below that figure, Enron would have to record its loss in the value of the investment under mark to market accounting. At the same time, however, even though Swap Sub did not have to make an actual payment until a later time, Enron was entitled immediately to record as income the payment to which it was entitled from Swap Sub, which offset that loss. This ostensibly locked in the appreciation of the Rhythms shares, holding Enron harmless for any decline in value.

The only funds that Swap Sub had available to make its eventual payment to Enron, however, were the Enron shares that it had received either directly or indirectly from LJM1. As a result, "[b]ecause this would be a return of its own property, Enron would never realize any net economic benefit."[115] An additional problem with the arrangement was that, to the extent that Enron's share price might be reduced by the decline in the value of its merchant investments such as Rhythms, a hedging SPE's obligation to Enron would be increasing at the same time as the value of the Enron shares that it had available to satisfy that obligation would be declining. Nonetheless, Enron included the value of the hedge in its financial statements.[116]

113. *Id.* at 9.

114. PriceWaterhouseCoopers eventually provided an opinion that the notes and the put option that Enron

115. received (both for the shares that it contributed to LJM1) was fair consideration. *Id.* at 16.

Batson Final Report, at 115.

116. Another potential problem that the Examiner noted but did not discuss at length is that the lock-up provision that was a condition of Enron's purchase of the pre-IPO Rhythms stock apparently prohibited hedging the investment in the stock. Unless the underwriters waived this provision, Enron's hedge with Swap Sub violated it. Batson Second Report, Appendix L, Annex 2, at 13–14.

FIGURE 2
RHYTHMSNET HEDGE

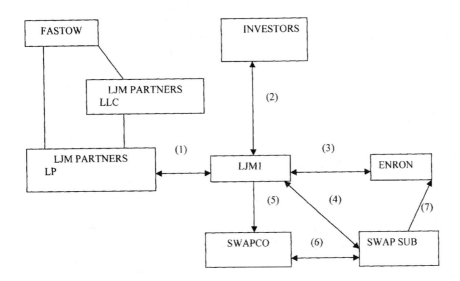

(1) LJM Partners LP contributes $1million cash to LJM1, in return for general partner status

(2) Two outside investors contribute $15 million cash to LJM1, in return for limited partner status and 94% interest

(3) Enron contributes 6.7 million Enron shares worth $276 million, in return for $64 million in promissory notes

(4) LJM1 contributes 3.1 million Enron shares worth $127 million and $3.75 million proceeds from sale of Enron shares to Swap Sub, in return for limited partner status

(5) LJM1 contributes 32,000 Enron shares to wholly-owned SwapCo

(6) SwapCo contributes 32,000 Enron shares it received from LJM1 to Swap Sub, in return for general partner status.

(7) Swap Sub enters into hedge granting Enron a put on 5.4 million RhythmsNet shares at exercise price of $56.125 per share.

The Examiner summarized the net economic effect of the Rhythms hedge in this way:

"Enron's sole motivation for entering into the Rhythms hedging transaction was to impact its income statement to achieve desired financial reporting results. Enron was indifferent as to whether it ever received cash under these hedges in the future because it was marking each option on the Rhythms stock to fair value to offset any losses attributable to declines in the value of the Rhythms stock. The hedges with Swap Sub had no economic benefit to Enron because the sole asset supporting the hedges was the Enron stock held by Swap Sub, which had been contributed by Enron. Upon settling the hedge, all Enron would receive would be the assets that it had contributed (indirectly) to Swap Sub (or their value) less the amount of any compensation paid to LJM1 and its partners."[117]

The law firm of Kirkland & Ellis established LJM1 and represented it in the Rhythms transaction. V&E represented Enron in this matter, but apparently did not participate in the planning or initial structuring of the Rhythms transaction.[118] In-house lawyer Kristina Mordaunt appears to have directed the legal work on the deal. The principal V&E attorneys were Edward Osterberg, John Leggett, and Petrina Chandler. Osterberg and Leggett advised Enron on tax aspects of the transaction, while Chandler acted as the lead transactional lawyer within V&E.[119]

The bankruptcy Examiner concluded that the evidence could support a finding that V&E committed malpractice because it knew that the Rhythms hedge was supported only by Enron's own stock, and thus "was a hedge only for financial statement benefits, lacking any genuine economic substance."[120] He focused specifically on Osterberg, who understood from " 'conversations with people at Enron and the descriptions of the transaction [he] saw' " that the purpose of the project was to hedge Enron's risk on the Rhythms investment.[121] Examiner stated that Osterberg, however, knew that: (1) Enron delivered Enron shares to Swap Sub as consideration for the hedge of Rhythms stock; (2) Enron stock constituted the assets of Swap Sub; and (3) as a result, Enron stock held by Swap Sub was the only thing of value available to meet Swap Sub's hedging obligation to Enron.

The Examiner stated:

"Osterberg therefore possessed all of the facts necessary to an understanding that Enron effectively paid significant value in a transaction in which it had no possibility of obtaining an economic return and that the Rhythms hedge was non-economic in nature and could achieve only accounting benefits. Osterberg testified, however, that during his work on [the project] he neither discussed nor considered whether the Rhythms hedge was economic in nature and did not know how Enron would account for the Rhythms hedge."[122]

Questions

1. Should malpractice be attributed to V&E by virtue of Osterberg's knowledge of the essential features of the Rhythms hedge and his participation in the transaction? Could he claim that he was responsible only for the tax aspects of the deal, and assumed that others focused on the economic substance of the transaction?

2. Could Osterberg avoid liability by maintaining that he did not appreciate the economic significance of the facts that he knew about the

---

117. *Id.* at 36.

118. *Id.* at 117.

119. *Id.*

120. *Id.* at 180.

121. *Id.* at 117–118 (quoting Osterberg sworn statement of Oct. 23, 2003).

122. *Id.* at 180.

Rhythms transaction? Or does a lawyer working on a deal have an obligation to acquire such an understanding? Does it matter if the lawyer is responsible for only one specific aspect of the deal, such as its tax consequences?

3. Suppose that Osterberg asked the main in-house Enron lawyer on the deal whether it constituted a genuine hedge and was assured that it did? What if he consulted Arthur Andersen and received the same answer? If he still had some doubts in either case, should he defer to their judgment?

4. The Enron Board of Directors approved the LJM/Rhythms hedge transaction. The Examiner found, however, that Enron General Counsel Derrick had not "developed an informed understanding of the transaction or performed a substantive analysis of its material terms." He therefore did not adequately advise the Board of the basis upon which its approval of the transaction could be given. If all Osterberg knew was that the Board had approved the deal, could he reasonably resolve any concerns by deferring to the Board's decision?

5. Does a finding of liability in these circumstances create a disincentive for lawyers to attend to anything other than their own narrow portion of a transaction? Or does it prevent them from taking refuge in willful blindness?

Issue Two: Disclosure of Fastow's LJM Compensation

Enron CFO Andrew Fastow served in a management role for the LJM entities in their transactions with Enron, earning several million dollars in addition to his compensation from Enron. In the section of Enron's proxy statements entitled "Certain Transactions," Item 404 of Regulation S–K required Enron to disclose information about transactions over $60,000 between the company and any of its executive officers, including "where practicable, the amount of such person's interest in the transaction."[123] The Examiner concluded that Enron's proxy statements filed in 2000 and 2001 did not satisfy this requirement because they did not include sufficient information about the amount of Fastow's financial interest in Enron's transactions with the LJM entities.[124]

The Examiner opined that Enron might have claims against its in-house counsel because they should have made greater efforts to determine Fastow's compensation for his role in LJM, and should have disclosed the amount both to the Enron Board of Directors and in the company's proxy statement. The lawyers in question were Rex Rogers, who had primary responsibility for securities issues, and Scott Sefton and Jordan Mintz, who were successively General Counsel for Enron Global Finance (EGF), which handled the legal work for the Enron/LJM transactions.

Rogers asked Sefton, and then Mintz, to analyze and draft disclosures relating to Enron's transactions with the LJM entities, since

---

123. 17 C.F.R. 229.404(a).

124. Batson Second Report, Appendix D (Enron's Disclosure of Its SPEs). The Examiner also concluded that Fastow breached his fiduciary duties to Enron with respect to these disclosures. Batson Third Report, Appendix C (Role of Enron's Officers).

lawyers in EGF performed the legal work on these transactions. Because he was the most senior securities attorney at Enron, however, Rogers "actively participated in the analysis and reviewed the disclosure."[125] These lawyers consulted on the disclosure with V&E. The Examiner suggested that Enron also might have a claim against V&E for malpractice based on negligence, because the firm failed to inquire into material facts that were necessary to make an informed judgment about the adequacy of Enron's disclosure.

As part of the proxy statement drafting process, Fastow was required to provide Enron with information about his interest in the LJM transactions in his response to a questionnaire sent annually to directors and officers. As the Examiner put it, "Fastow side-stepped this responsibility."[126] For the 2000 proxy statement, he referred the reader to an Addendum to the questionnaire, which stated that Sefton was preparing a draft disclosure that the attorney would shortly make available. For the 2002 proxy statement, the Addendum said that the nature of Fastow's involvement in the LJM entities was described in Enron's 1999 and 2000 proxy statements. Neither the questionnaire nor the sources to which it referred contained any estimate of the amount of Fastow's financial interest in these transactions. The Examiner concluded that "Mintz took no steps to make Fastow provide a meaningful and responsive answer to the relevant question on the annual D & O Questionnaire, and the Examiner found no evidence showing that Sefton did either."[127]

Efforts to obtain information for the 2001 proxy statement illustrate the concerns of the Examiner with respect to the conduct of the attorneys for Enron. In the course of working on the related party disclosures for that statement, EGF General Counsel Mintz received an email from Ronald Astin of V & E on November 2, 2000 that stated: "As I hope everyone is aware, the 'senior officer'[s] name, and the nature and amount of his interest in the transaction, if quantifiable, will be disclosed in the 2001 proxy.[128] Fastow then told Fastow that Astin had advised him that Enron would have to disclose the compensation that Fastow earned from his general partner position in LJM. Fastow left a voicemail in reply to Mintz, stating his understanding that no disclosure of his compensation was necessary because the earnings that he received from participation in LJM came not from Enron but from LJM's limited partners. He stated, "If that thinking has changed, that's a BIG issue and I need to know about that."[129] Mintz forwarded a transcription of this voicemail to Rogers and copied Astin on it.

A January 2001 conversation with Fastow left Mintz with the understanding that Fastow wanted to avoid disclosing his compensation related to his position with LJM. As Mintz testified, Fastow "told me that if [Enron Chief Operating Officer] Skilling ever found out how

125. Batson Final Report, Appendix C, at 147.

126. *Id.* at 148.

127. *Id.* at 149 (footnote omitted).

128. *Id.* at 150 (footnote omitted).

129. *Id.* at 151 (emphasis in original) (footnote omitted).

much he was making, Skilling would have no choice but to shut down LJM."[130]

Mintz sent an email to Astin and Rogers informing them of this conversation. He asked to meet with them to discuss how to treat the Fastow disclosure issue in the proxy statement. "I think," he said, "that the number one item on our list is to resolve the 'where practicable' language" in connection with AF's interest in the transactions engaged in with Enron by LJM1 and 2." The email went on to say, "I spoke, again, with Andy about this earlier today and he believes (perhaps rightly so) that Skilling will shut down LJM if he knew how much Andy earned with respect to the Rhythm transaction." Mintz closed by saying, "We need to be 'creative' on this point," he said, "within the contours of [SEC regulations] so as to avoid any type of stark disclosure, if at all possible."[131]

Astin testified that when he received this email, he believed that it raised a significant issue for discussion. He had some skepticism, however, about its accuracy, because he had seen Board presentation about the formation of a possible LJM3 entity that referred to Fastow's discussions with Skilling about Fastow's compensation.

Astin, Mintz and Rogers met to discuss the proxy disclosure on January 18, 2001. The testimony is in dispute about what resulted from that meeting. Rogers and Astin testified that the group decided that Mintz would follow up with Fastow and get the necessary factual information. Rogers said that Astin then applied the legal standards to that information. Astin said that he never asked directly, but that the information that Mintz provided led him to infer that there had been no distributions to Fastow in 2000 related to his involvement in LJM. Mintz, on the other hand, denies that he was charged with obtaining additional information from Fastow. He claims that he understood Rogers and Astin to say that the company didn't have an obligation to pursue the issue with the CFO. In any event, no one ever asked Fastow if he had received any such payments, nor did they check LJM's records, which apparently were in the same building as Enron was located.[132]

As the Examiner put it, "Despite lacking this crucial piece of information, preparation of the related party transaction disclosure proceeded."[133] Mintz testified that Astin and Rogers advised him that there was no need to make a disclosure in 2001 regarding the LJM1 Rhythms "hedge." Their argument was that the settlement of this transaction occurred under the original Rhythms agreement, which was entered into in 1999 and disclosed in 2000. Thus, there had been no new Rhythms transaction in 2000 generating income for Fastow that had to be disclosed in the 2001 proxy statement. Mintz said that he "initially disagreed" with this reasoning because he believed that it was possible to calculate and disclose Fastow's interest after the Rhythms transaction

130. *Id.*
131. *Id.*
132. *Id.* at 153.
133. *Id.* at 154.

settled.[134] He eventually, however, accepted the rationale for non-disclosure.[135] He explained the reasoning in a later memo to Fastow in this way:

> At settlement of RhythmsNet it may have been practicable to determine your financial interest. However, no further disclosure was otherwise required of the RhythmsNet transaction in 2000 because settlement occurred under conditions permitted in the original agreement. Thus, there was no new transaction involving LJM1 and Enron in the year 2000 required to be disclosed in this year's proxy[.]"[136]

With respect to Fastow's interest in LJM2, the attorneys concluded that a determination of that interest was "not practicable." This judgment was based on the facts that the Enron/LJM2 transactions had not yet settled, and that Fastow potentially was subject to a requirement to recontribute capital to the LJM2 partnership.[137] In Mintz's memo to Fastow he stated, "We determined it was not practicable to quantify your interest in LJM2 in the most recent Proxy ... based on the existence of multiple open and unmatured transactions making it impossible to compute."[138]

On March 7, 2001, Mintz, Rogers, and Astin met with Enron General Counsel James Derrick to discuss the proxy statement disclosure of related party transactions. Based on the arguments described above, they informed him that no disclosure of Fastow's interest in the LJM transactions with Enron was required, and he accepted their conclusion. The proxy statement was filed on March 27, 2001. The relevant portion of the proxy statement noted that Enron had entered into a number of transactions with LJM2 in 2000, and that Fastow was the managing member of LJM2's general partner. It went on to say, "The general partner of LJM2 is entitled to receive a percentage of the profits of LJM2 in excess of the general partner's portion of the total capital contributed to LJM2, depending upon the performance of the investments made by LJM2."[139]

Mintz's subsequent memo to Fastow indicated that with respect to the LJM1/Rhythms transaction, "the decision not to disclose in this instance was a close call; arguably the more conservative approach would have been to disclose the amount of [your] interest."[140] If the Rhythms transaction had begun and ended in the same year, he told Fastow, "it would have been more difficult to avoid making some additional level of financial disclosure."[141]

134. *Id.*

135. *See id.* at 155 (Mintz, Rogers, and Astin told Derrick in March 2001 that no disclosure was required and that "all involved were comfortable with that position") (footnote omitted).

136. *Id.* at 156.

137. *Id.* at 154–155.

138. *Id.* at 156.

139. *Id.* at 155 n. 696.

140. *Id.* at 156.

141. *I.d* at 156–157.

Mintz circulated a draft of the memo to Rogers and Astin for comments, and Derrick eventually received a copy of it as well. Upon receiving it, Derrick contacted Astin to confirm that he was comfortable with proxy statement, since Derrick had not understood that the determination regarding the disclosure of the LJM1/Rhythms transaction was a "close call."[142] Astin provided such confirmation.

Shortly afterward, without notifying Derrick or Rogers, Mintz sought advice about the related party transactions from the law firm of Fried, Frank, Harris, Shriver & Jacobson. Fried Frank regarded the amount of payments that Fastow had received from LJM as material in determining the adequacy of the disclosures that had been made and those that might be made in the future. The firm concluded that the prior disclosures were incomplete. With respect to Fastow's compensation from LJM2's transactions with Enron, Fried Frank believed that the view that calculating the amount of Fastow's compensation was not "practicable" because the transactions had not yet closed was "too aggressive."[143]

The Examiner found that Enron might have a claim against Rogers and Mintz for malpractice based on violation of Texas Rule 1.12 and breach of fiduciary duty. Rogers knew that Fastow considered the amount of Fastow's interest in the LJM transactions so large that Skilling would shut down the SPEs if he knew about it. Rather than asking Fastow how much this amount was, however, Rogers, Mintz, and Astin focused on why it was not practicable to calculate Fastow's interest. The Examiner notes that Rogers may claim that his responsibility regarding disclosures "was more administrative than substantive," and that he relied on Enron employees, as well as on V&E, with more knowledge of the SPE transactions to review the disclosures.[144] With respect to Mintz, the Examiner found that there was evidence that Mintz was given responsibility to determine whether Fastow received any distributions from LJM transactions in 2000 and, if so, their amount.[145]

Finally, the Examiner found that Enron might have a claim against V&E for malpractice based on negligence in connection with V&E's advice to Enron about disclosure of Fastow's interest in LJM transactions in the 2001 proxy statement. V&E knew of Fastow's characterization of the amount of his compensation from LJM transactions, yet it "never received or insisted upon receiving facts that were sufficiently developed to make an informed legal judgment. No one asked Fastow the simple question: How much money have you received in connection with your LJM activities?"[146] The Examiner noted that the firm might contend that it relied upon Enron's in-house attorneys to determine if it was practicable to calculate the amount of Fastow's interest in LJM matters.

142. *Id.* at 157.
143. *Id.* at 158 (footnote omitted).
144. *Id.* at 192–193.
145. *Id.* at 198–199.
146. *Id.* at 184.

Questions

1. Who was Mintz's client with respect to the disclosure issue?

2. Mintz's approach to disclosure was to be as "creative" as possible in exploring rationales under the regulations for not disclosing Fastow's compensation from participation in LJM. Was this the appropriate approach—just a lawyer trying to be as aggressive as possible to serve his client's interests within the bounds of the law? Or was it inconsistent with his role in ensuring Enron's compliance with the law?

3. Why didn't anyone simply ask Fastow how much compensation he had received from the LJM transactions, as the Examiner suggested?

4. Would Mintz's rationale for not disclosing the compensation from the Rhythms transaction create the possibility for avoiding ever disclosing any compensation from the LJM/Enron transactions by simply entering into an agreement in one year and not settling until the next?

5. If the decision not to disclose was, as Mintz described it, a "close call," should Mintz have resolved it in favor of disclosure?

6. The SEC is understaffed and has limited resources. It reviews only a small number of filings such as proxy statements each year. In presenting the options on disclosure, could Enron lawyers factor into their recommendation an estimate of the likelihood that the SEC would ever review the proxy statement, as well as the likely penalty if it did?

Or does the fact that the probability of detection by the SEC is low impose a greater responsibility on the lawyer to urge her client to abide by the spirit, not just the letter, of the law?

Chapter 21

REGULATORY COUNSELING

Modern corporations are of course subject to considerable regulation on a wide variety of matters. Counsel representing a corporation plays an important role in advising the company of the laws with which it must comply and the penalties for failing to do so. These laws represent the limits within which the client must operate in conducting its business.

In providing advice on legal obligations, counsel also assumes a more subtle and complex responsibility. The meaning of law often is not self-evident, but calls for interpretation. The client may prefer an interpretation that places as few constraints as possible on its freedom of action. To what extent should a lawyer be responsive to this preference when advising the corporation on what the law means? Complete indifference to the client's wishes seems incompatible with the lawyer's duty to advance the client's interest. At the same time, being guided solely by these wishes seems to abandon any pretense of professional independence.

Furthermore, how should the lawyer present the law to the client once she arrives at an interpretation? As a set of rules that carry some intrinsic moral value? Or as a set of obstacles that the lawyer is committed to helping the lawyer avoid as much as possible? Finally, what model of the lawyer's role should the lawyer adopt when considering these questions? The role of the hired gun within the adversary system, on the ground that the company and the government are adversaries? Or the role of a person who has some duty to further respect for the integrity of the legal system, on the ground that there is no judge to take this interest in to account? Are these roles antithetical to one another?

OVERVIEW OF THE CHAPTER

This Chapter contains excerpts from two articles that highlight important issues that arise in determining how lawyers should go about advising corporate clients on their legal obligations. The first is by Stephen Pepper, who argued in Chapter Two that the "hired gun" model of the lawyer's role is justified because it further the autonomy of clients. Pepper notes that knowledge of the law can be used by clients either to follow the law's commands or to avoid them. Truthful information about the law, in other words, can help a client act unlawfully.

This possibility comes into sharp focus when we consider whether information about penalties and enforcement patters are also part of the "law" about which clients are entitled to be informed. Knowledge of penalties may lead a client to conclude that it would be cheaper to violate the law and risk paying the penalty than to comply with it. Awareness of enforcement patterns can furnish a client with an opportunity to arrange activities so as to avoid detection of illegal conduct. If the lawyer provides such information, does she contribute to the idea that the law has only instrumental, rather than intrinsic normative, value?

Pepper considers some possible criteria that may help determine when a lawyer should and should not provide information about the law that she suspects the client will use to violate it and/or avoid detection. One is that the lawyer should provide advice only when it is not likely to lead to "prohibited" conduct that society has indicated it will not tolerate, as opposed to conduct that merely exposes one to the obligation to pay damages or penalties. Another is the distinction between the substance of the law and the manner of its enforcement. While each criterion has some intuitive appeal, Pepper demonstrates that it also poses some difficulties. Ask yourself if you agree with his assessment of these difficulties. If so, are there other alternatives that might do the job?

Ultimately, Pepper suggests that counseling affords an opportunity for the lawyer to inquire into, rather than simply assume, the client's goals or desires. Consider the application of this idea in the context of corporate representation. Is it improper for a lawyer to assume that the main objective of her corporate client is to maximize profits? If she is inclined to heed Pepper's suggestion, how will the conversation go between the lawyer and the corporate manager? If the manager makes it clear that the company wants to use the lawyer's information to push or exceed the limits of the law, how should the lawyer respond?

The excerpt from Cynthia Williams examines in more detail the idea of "law as price"—that is, that legal commands merely indicate the costs of engaging in behavior that the law prohibits. If we think back to the excerpt from Robert Rosen in Chapter 9 on the increasing prevalence of risk management in corporate operations, we can see that the cost of failing to obey the law can be treated as simply one particular type of risk to add to the analysis. Williams argues that the "law as price" approach regards the goal of regulation as inducing "efficient investment in compliance," just as law and economics treats the goal of tort law as encouraging efficient levels of care or contract damages as promoting efficient breach of contract. On this view, society is indifferent to whether a party chooses to comply with the law or to violate it and pay the penalty.

Williams argues that this approach to legal compliance is fundamentally misguided. At the most fundamental level, the notion of efficient violation of law does not conform to the law and economics model. Companies do not violate the law and then admit it so that they are subject to the appropriate penalty. Rather, those that deliberately engage in non-compliance attempt to escape detection. Even if we take efficiency as the objective of all regulation, this course of action is not efficient.

Furthermore, Williams contends, proponents of the "law as price" model admit that there is a small subset of law that *does* have intrinsic normative force and should not be the subject of deliberate calculation. This is the group of behaviors that we regard as morally wrong, such as murder and theft. Because of the strong moral judgments they evoke, however, we need binding legal commands least with respect to this type of behavior. Where we need them most, argues Williams, is in regulatory law, which is technically complex and not easily amenable to judgments based on broad moral consensus.

The subject that Williams discusses may seem a bit theoretical at times, but it has profound ramifications. There is no way that regulators and law enforcement personnel can effectively monitor all corporations to ensure that they comply with the law. Even if there were, we might not prefer such an intrusive state presence. Most legal compliance in society occurs voluntarily, at least partly out of respect for the law as such. What are the likely consequences if that respect is eroded? Do you agree with Williams that the "law as price" approach contributes to such erosion? If so, do you believe that how lawyers present legal advice plays any role in this process? If you do, how should lawyers go about providing such advice? Williams acknowledges that not every law is equally important, and that regarding some laws as merely establishing prices for violations is less justified in some cases more than others. If you agree, how is a lawyer to determine how to classify a given law?

The first problem presents a situation in which you could structure activities in a way that might enable a bank to circumvent prohibitions on money laundering of proceeds from illegal activity. The problem effectively asks if you would suggest this structure in response to requests from banking managers for ways to minimize the risk of tapping into a market for banking services that likely involves customers engaged in illegal conduct. Is the risk that the bank might be breaking the law a business consideration that is for risk managers rather than the lawyer?

The second problem is drawn directly from the excerpt from Pepper. It asks whether it is appropriate for the lawyer to inform the client about Environmental Protection Agency enforcement patters if this information may lead the client to violate limits on the discharge of pollution.

MODEL RULES: 1.2, 2.1, 3.1, 8.4

Stephen L. Pepper, Counseling at the Limits of the Law: An
Exercise in the Jurisprudence and Ethics of Lawyering

104 Yale L.J. 1545 (1995)

I. Introduction

A. *Summary of the Problem*

The primary job of the lawyer is to give the client access to the law
in its multitude of facets. The litigator provides access to the dispute
resolution mechanisms that are our civil and criminal courts and to the
substantive law that they apply; the "deal maker" provides access to the
structuring aspects of the law, regimes of contract, corporate law,
securities, property, and trust; the family law lawyer and the estate
planner provide access to systems of law that include both court resolution and structuring by legal mechanisms; and so on with all sorts of law
and lawyers. Each of these functions combines the lawyer's knowledge of
the law with the client's need for or ability to profit from access to that
law. This is true across the spectrum of law, whether procedural or
substantive; whether concerning the mechanics and structures of various
legal devices such as contracts, deeds, and trusts, or the legal entities
that can be formed from combinations of such structures (a corporation
or set of corporations, for example, or a condominium, the limited
partnership that builds it, and the condominium association that will
manage it).

The client often wants or needs to understand what the law is in
order to evaluate options and make decisions about his or her life, and
the most common function of lawyers (across specializations and areas of
practice) is to provide that knowledge. Knowledge of the law, however, is
an instrument that can be used to follow the law or to avoid it. Knowing
that the speed limit is fifty-five miles per hour on an isolated, rarely
patrolled stretch of rural highway will lead some to drive at or below
fifty-five, but will lead others to drive at sixty-three miles per hour or
faster. Similarly, knowing that the only penalty for engaging in unfair
labor practices is back pay and reinstatement for individual harmed
employees can lead the employer/client either to avoid such practices or
to engage in them intentionally. Knowledge of the law thus is two-edged.
When the lawyer is in a situation in which the client may well use the
relevant knowledge of the law to violate the law or avoid its norms, what
ought the lawyer to do?

* * * Our legal system is premised on the assumption that law is
intended to be known or knowable, that law is in its nature public
information. The "rule of law" as we understand it requires promulgation. (Consider for a moment the alternative possibility of secret
"law.") And one fundamental, well-understood aspect of the lawyer's
role is to be the conduit for that promulgation. In a complex legal
environment much law cannot be known and acted upon, cannot func-

tion as law, without lawyers to make it accessible to those for whom it is relevant. Thus, in our society lawyers are necessary for much of our law to be known, to be functional. The traditional understanding is that lawyers as professionals act for the client's benefit in providing that access to the law. Under this understanding, lawyers do not function as law enforcement officers or as judges of their clients in providing knowledge of the law; the choices to be made concern the client's life and affairs, and they are therefore primarily the client's choices to make.

The limits on the assistance lawyers may provide to their clients have commonly been articulated and thought of as the "bounds of the law." The lawyer may not become an active participant in the client's unlawful activity, and does not have immunity if she becomes an aider and abettor of unlawful conduct. The difficulty arises in deciding whether providing accurate, truthful information about the law—the core function of lawyering—can also be considered active assistance in violation of the law in situations in which the lawyer knows the information may well lead to or facilitate the client's unlawful conduct . . .

B. A Range of Examples

The lawyer is confronted with concrete situations, and to understand the lawyer's awkward position it helps to approach the problem in context. I present now a range of examples, starting with two extremes and then moving to the large middle ground.

Breach of Contract. At one end of the continuum is advice about conduct that most lawyers would not categorize as "unlawful," but to which the law applies a sanction. Advice about breach of contract is the paradigm. The dominant modern understanding of contract law is that one is free to breach a contract, but may thereafter be required to pay compensatory damages. Absent very unusual circumstances, there will be no punishment. Although it is unclear whether the law regards intentional breach of contract as normatively wrong, whether such conduct is "contrary to law," it is clear that the message of the law is that breach of contract is not prohibited. Rather, it is conduct that may entail a cost imposed by the law. Not only do lawyers feel free to give this advice (which may well encourage or facilitate breach of contract), but it would probably be malpractice to fail to give it when relevant to the client's situation or to advise that breach of contract is prohibited by the law.

The Burdens of Civil Litigation. A closely connected example concerns advice about the costs and delays involved in the law's procedures. In counseling the client concerned about the legal consequences of a contemplated breach of contract, should the lawyer inform the client about the substantial burdens imposed upon the person who wants to collect compensatory damages for breach of contract? Should the lawyer inform the client of the three-year delay created by the current docket situation of the relevant court? Should the lawyer inform the client of the evidentiary burdens (or problems) the plaintiff may face in proving existence of the contract, breach, and damages? Should the lawyer inform the client of the probability that these burdens will lead the person to whom he is contractually obligated to accept a substantially discounted amount to settle the claim rather than litigate? If the lawyer concludes that this information will lead the client to breach the contract, should the lawyer refrain from giving the information? Or is it malpractice to fail to give it?

Criminal Conduct Involving Harm to Third Parties. At the other end of the spectrum is legal advice the client may use for clearly criminal conduct involving concrete harm to third parties. The classic example is the client who asks which South American countries have no extradition treaty with the United States covering armed robbery or murder.

Criminal Procedure. What do you advise the lawyer whose childless, middle-aged, male client has just asked whether it is true that police and judges in the community consider children under ten to be incompetent to testify in sexual abuse cases? (Assume it is true.) A more timely example is the defendant in a murder case being informed by the lawyer that the maximum penalty for jury tampering is six months in prison and a $1000 fine. Or imagine the client who consults the lawyer concerning the legality of and penalties for euthanasia. If the facts in the euthanasia situation are sufficiently sympathetic to make the advice relevant, may the lawyer inform the client of the possibilities of prosecutorial discretion and jury nullification?

Examples from the Broad Middle Ground. Assume an Environmental Protection Agency water pollution regulation, widely publicized to relevant industries, prohibiting discharge of ammonia at amounts greater than .050 grams per liter of effluent. The client owns a rural plant that discharges ammonia in its effluent, the removal of which would be very expensive. The lawyer knows from informal sources that: (1) violations of .075 grams per liter or less are ignored because of a limited enforcement budget; and (2) EPA inspection in rural areas is rare, and in such areas enforcement officials usually issue a warning prior to applying sanctions unless the violation is extreme (more than 1.5 grams per liter). Is it appropriate for the lawyer to educate the client concerning these enforcement-related facts even though it may motivate the client to violate the .050 gram limit?

A second, well-known example is the client who wants to file a tax return reporting a favorable outcome based upon an arguable interpretation of the law. The lawyer is confident the IRS would challenge the client's return if it became aware of this interpretation and would be highly likely to succeed in the event of litigation. If that were to occur, the penalties would likely be only the tax due plus interest. The lawyer knows that in the past the audit rate for this type of return has been less than two percent, and knows that this fact is likely to lead this client to take the dubious position on her return. Ought the lawyer to communicate this information to the client?

C. Law and Lawyering: Predictions, Manipulation, and Norms

From the perspective of the dominant American understanding of law—taught in the law schools and practiced in the law offices—the enforcement-related facts in the last two examples would be considered part of the "law," and thus appropriate information to convey to an interested client. This is an instrumental view of the law, which casts its net wide in defining "law" and in attempting to aid clients in their encounters with the law, whether the law functions in the particular circumstance primarily to limit or to empower the client. The American lawyer is likely to view law as a complex process embedded in human interaction and taking place over time. Written provisions, while an important part of law, are only a part. Human actors, from the potential plaintiff in the contract action, through the budget makers who limit the EPA's enforcement budget and the IRS' audit budget, to the prosecutor and the judge, make decisions throughout the process that affect clients as much as written provisions. Part of the lawyer's job is to take account of and predict as well as possible the way both the written law and the conduct of legal actors will impact on the client's situation ...

[This approach] empowers the client and gives the client the benefit of a sophisticated, realistic understanding of the processes of law. But as the hypotheticals show, it is not a view without costs. Under this lens, the law seems to transmute from a knowable limit to a rather amorphous thing that is dependent upon the client's situation, goals, and risk preferences.

If the law becomes generally perceived as merely indicating a potential cost, a penalty that one is free to incur and to discount by the probability of its enforcement, then structuring our common life together through law becomes vastly more difficult and requires vastly more resources. For example, consider the last two situations, environmental regulation and tax. To the extent the client is led to perceive enforcement as a part of law, or, one might say, led to reduce law to the probability of enforcement, the power and effectiveness of the law as written, of the law as norm, has been reduced. Such a conflation of law with enforcement may be the untoward result of legal advice to the client under this "legal realist" view of the law. And the recently dominant jurisprudential trend in the law schools—law and economics—substantially reinforces this effect of legal realism by perceiving legal limits and rules as just another "cost," and clients as "profit maximizers," simply Holmes' "bad man" dressed in modern clothes.

The lawyer giving legal advice to a client who may use that advice to violate the law or its norms thus stands at an awkward moral focal point. Under the traditional understanding, she has not been delegated the legal authority to judge or police her clients. To the contrary, her role has been defined as serving her clients: to provide access to that public good that is the law; to equalize power and opportunity by making available to all citizens knowledge (and hence the power) of the law. But the modern lawyer's legal realist (and law-and-economics) view of the law may lead the client to respect the law less; to choose to violate the law and chance the consequences.

II.   LEGAL ADVICE WITHIN THE BOUNDS OF THE LAW: SOME GUIDING DISTINCTIONS

I present below a series of distinctions that might assist a lawyer in deciding what information about the law to give to the client, and what not to give * * *

B.   The Distinction Between Law as "Cost" and Law as "Prohibition" (the Criminal/Civil Line)

Legal provisions can convey at least three rather different messages. First, the law can tell you that if you want to accomplish *x,* you will have to do *a, b,* and *c* in certain prescribed ways. If you want to create a contract, you will have to have an offer, an acceptance, and consideration. If you want to create a corporation, the necessary actions are prescribed by statute. Second, the law can indicate that some specific conduct will have certain prescribed negative consequences; that some specific conduct creates liability for certain costs or penalties. Failure to comply with a valid contractual obligation renders one liable for some of the damages caused to the promisee and to a limited class of third parties. A corporation that fails to conduct its business as required by the state of incorporation, by not holding required annual meetings, for example, may forfeit some of the benefits of being a corporation, such as limited liability.

Third, the law can indicate that certain conduct is prohibited and will not be tolerated by society. A person who murders or steals will be punished by being forcibly removed from society for some period of time, in part to demonstrate how serious society is about the prohibition and in part to prevent repetition of the violation. Legal provisions in the first two categories indicate that some conduct is favored and some disfavored, and legal consequences will reflect the differences, but the third category involves a different and stronger message.

The ethical line for legal advice could be based on this distinction. Under such a rule or guide, a lawyer could not give legal advice in a context in which that advice is likely to lead to conduct prohibited by law, but such advice could be given in a context in which it is likely to lead to conduct to which the law only attaches a cost or penalty. The distinction between criminal and civil law is traditionally understood as distinguishing the prohibited from the tolerated, the prohibited from the "merely" wrongful.

1.   The Ends of the Spectrum

The principal advantage of this distinction lies in its apparent congruence with accepted legal culture and practice at both ends of the range of examples. Holmes' "bad man" understanding of contract law has become so descriptively accurate that few would contest the notion of a "right" to breach a contract, and where a citizen has a right, it is difficult to envision a rule of lawyers' ethics that would prohibit a lawyer from informing the client of that right or a malpractice rule that would allow a lawyer to choose to leave the client in ignorance of a right she might profit from exercising. At the other end of the spectrum, it is hard to countenance the notion that a citizen (client) has a "right" to murder or steal, as long as she is willing to accept the law's penalty if she is caught. The dominant legal rules and culture are certainly in accord with this perception. Legal advice that facilitates such criminal conduct may be prohibited by the current versions of lawyers' ethics, and the lawyer is more likely to face tort liability for providing such legal advice than for withholding it.

Even at the ends of the range the distinction is not without problems, however. Breach of contract can cause serious harm, and our society (and perhaps our law) perceive some level of normative obligation not to breach contracts. It is not pleasant to contemplate a legal regime in which the primary message of the law as transmitted through lawyers is that breaching contracts is perfectly acceptable if it is to one's economic advantage to do so after having calculated potential compensatory damages as a cost, discounted by the probability and expense of enforcement by the promisee. This is perhaps just another example of the two-edged nature of law with which we began: all law, not just breach of contract, can be used to harm or to wrong. Here, however, the law has specifically recognized the harm and the wrong and has placed a cost or penalty on it. (Is it inaccurate to refer to the sanction as a "penalty" because compensatory damages only include the cost of the damages one's "wrong" has caused, and there is no additional sum whose only purpose is to discourage the conduct? Note that torts are normally considered "wrongs," but are ordinarily "punished" only with "compensatory" damages.)

At the other end of the spectrum, [consider the person whose elderly parent is terminally ill and in great pain, who asks about the legality of consensual euthanasia]. Here we have contemplated murder, surely one of the core examples that makes the criminal/civil distinction intuitively plausible, yet the notion that the client has a "right" to know the law under which her behavior will be judged and the procedures through which that law will be applied does not seem so far-fetched. To prohibit the lawyer from giving the advice means that the prosecutor has lawful discretion to apply the law to the facts in a fully contextualized, nuanced fashion and to choose not to prosecute; the jury has power to choose not to apply the law at all if it finds that the facts and justice lead that way; but the lawyer must keep the client in ignorance of these aspects of the legal system regardless of the specific facts of the situation.

2. *The Middle Range of the Spectrum*

The intuitive appeal of the criminal/civil distinction as applied to limiting lawyer advice about the law is substantially weaker when the examples come from the middle range. In that category, I would include nonobvious or nontraditional crimes, much regulatory law, and torts.

Indiscriminate usage of the criminal sanction creates a problem for drawing our line between civil and criminal wrongs. To the extent that conduct is criminalized when it is not intuitively obvious that the conduct involves a serious moral wrong, the justification for the criminal/civil distinction becomes obscure. The criminal sanction is supposed to announce that we are particularly serious about a legal rule, that we really *mean* a particular act is *prohibited*. But when applied to conduct that in no obvious way involves serious moral wrongdoing, the question irresistibly pushes up: why are we so serious about this? If no persuasive reason is available, we are reduced to the circular, positivist, formal justification: because it's *criminal*.

A few years after the national speed limit of fifty-five miles per hour was imposed, the reason for the rule—conserving gasoline—no longer seemed to be a strong national priority. Imagine the small trucker in a spacious, flat western state who wants to reimburse his drivers for fines imposed for driving between fifty-five and seventy miles per hour. He has asked his lawyer if it is permissible to do so and if he could deduct such reimbursement as an expense of the business. Or imagine a retailer just within the border of a state with a Sunday closing law, in competition with stores just across the state line, who asks his lawyer about the penalties for remaining open. The lawyer finds out that the penalty is a criminal fine of only twenty-five dollars per Sunday. In such situations, is the message sent by the law that the conduct is prohibited, that it is disfavored and comes with a cost, or some mixture that is difficult to interpret?

This problem is particularly pervasive in major areas of regulatory law administered by agencies. Here much conduct is "prohibited" by law, but the sanction can either be civil or criminal, at the discretion of the administrative agency, and civil enforcement is the norm, with criminal enforcement unusual. In our water pollution example, this would mean that the lawyer does not even know which side of the criminal/civil line she is on until the agency has chosen to act and draw that line in relation to the client's conduct.

A final problem with the criminal/civil line is contemplated tortious conduct. Nineteenth-century tort opinions speak of negligent conduct not only as wrongful in a strong normative sense, but also often as if it were forbidden. The thrust of the shift in tort thinking over the last eighty years or so has been to drain tort law of much of its normative content, to move away from a focus on the "wrongfulness" of the conduct of defendant and plaintiff and toward allocation of the costs of accidental injury on the bases of compensation, loss spreading, and efficiency. Where the language of the courts once seemed to assimilate tortious conduct to criminal conduct, the language of much torts scholarship and at least some judicial opinions now seems to assimilate tortious conduct to breach of contract. One is free to be negligent so long as one is willing to pay compensatory damages to persons injured by that negligence. Tort law is *civil* law. Tortious conduct is not prohibited, but it may, after litigation, result in the imposition of an obligation to pay damages. And thus it would seem that the client is free to commit torts, has a right to commit torts (unless stopped by injunction), and the lawyer has an obligation to educate him about all this if the circumstances make it relevant.

Imagine: The owner of a small chain of run-down motels has discovered that his twenty-year-old water heaters, all identical in make and model, are starting to malfunction and release scalding hot water with no warning. There is no way to know which one will go next. The owner does not have funds to replace all the units, and he already carries so much debt that financing to remedy the problem is unavailable. He has consulted his lawyer for legal advice concerning his obligations. The severity and foreseeability of potential injuries to guests using the showers probably make further use of the water heaters negligent, but the probability of suit is unclear because neither the injured party nor his or her lawyer will have reason to know of the pattern of malfunction absent suit and discovery. Also, the client's liability insurance is sufficient to cover likely compensatory damages. The lawyer knows that the client is very attached to his business, and that he may have no realistic option to avoid injuries except to close down—at least temporarily—and this is likely to be fatal to the enterprise. The client is free to commit the tort—has a right to commit the tort—and, under the criminal/civil dichotomy, the lawyer is free (and possibly obligated) to give the advice likely to lead to that result * * *

C.   The Law/Enforcement Distinction

Is a distinction between law and enforcement of law the solution to the problem of legal advice that may facilitate unlawful conduct? The lawyer's obligation to provide access to the law could be considered to be fulfilled by informing the client concerning substantive law. The line would then be drawn at information about the various contingencies involved in the future application of that substantive law to the client's facts: advice about the enforcement rules or practices that might reveal to the authorities a violation of the substantive law and the legal procedures through which any enforcement or penalties would be applied would be out of bounds. The constraints that channel application of the substance of the law to the client would be information the lawyer could not convey to the client. To the extent the problem is the perception of law as cost—the conflation of law with enforcement—this seems the most direct answer for the lawyer giving advice.

Imagine that lawyers have access to a bulletin board behind the counter at the police station with a weekly list of the frequency of patrol of city neighborhoods by day and time. The client, previously represented by a lawyer on burglary charges, wants to know the frequency for Chez Ultra neighborhood, Sunday, 2–4 a.m. Intuitively we know the lawyer ought not to supply this information. The law/enforcement dichotomy provides an explanation. The two-percent audit rate information in our tax return hypothetical appears to be directly analogous under the law/enforcement dichotomy, which would disallow this more generally accepted legal advice. The distinction also provides a plausible answer to the water pollution hypothetical, disallowing any advice beyond the written .050 gram per liter limit.

[According to the] law/enforcement distinction, [whether a law actually is ever enforced is] not something the lawyer could communicate to the client. Likewise, the sanction for law violation, whether it be conceived as "cost" or as "prohibition," falls on the "enforcement" side of the dichotomy and would therefore be out of bounds for lawyer advice. Distinguishing between "law" and "enforcement," while intuitively attractive, thus presents significant difficulties[.]

1. The Problem of Disentangling Civil Law from Enforcement

Imagine being asked to advise a client with a contract or tort problem, but being unable to discuss the nature of the sanctions or the mechanisms of enforcement for breach of contract or for tortious conduct. Could one communicate to the client the nature of contract or tort without telling her how they are enforced; without describing the nature of a civil lawsuit and civil damages? What would the lawyer say? Could you tell the client that breach of contract is "prohibited" by the law, or is "unlawful"? Could you characterize tortious conduct as "prohibited" or "unlawful"? Or are those characterizations sufficiently inaccurate that you would be misleading the client in giving such advice? The distinction between civil and criminal law is fundamental, and to a large extent it is a difference in the nature and mechanisms of enforcement. If discussion of future consequences is out of bounds, it becomes truly difficult to imagine the lawyer's discussion with the client in the area of civil law.

Return to the situation of the client who owns the run-down motels with water heaters likely at some point in the future to seriously injure a customer. If it is not criminal under these circumstances to proceed with business at the motels, it would be misleading to tell the owner that the law "prohibits" further use of the water heaters, or that further use is "illegal" or "unlawful." And informing the client only that the conduct is "negligent" doesn't tell him much if he hasn't been to law school. To communicate adequately to the client the nature of liability for negligence will require the attorney to provide some account of a civil lawsuit and civil damages. But once one is conveying the nature of a civil lawsuit and civil damages, one has entered the area of enforcement, and that is not acceptable under the guideline we are considering.

The situation becomes even clearer if we imagine giving advice about the obligations of contract to one who is either contemplating entering a contract or contemplating breach of an existing contract. To convey that breach of contract is "prohibited" by the law (is "illegal" or "unlawful") is to suggest to the client that society does not tolerate breach of contract. This would be very misleading, however, because the regime of contract law clearly does tolerate breach. (Some would argue that on occasion it encourages breach.) The message of contract law is nuanced, one might even say, conflicted.

Perhaps the example of bankruptcy makes the point most forcefully. What is bankruptcy law other than an elaborate set of procedures dealing with both the enforcement and the extinguishment of debt? If discussion and explanation of these procedures and their consequences is out of bounds for the lawyer, bankruptcy law could not function as intended.

It seems, then, that disentangling civil law from enforcement simply is not possible. That may be, of course, an underlying part of the fundamental problem we are examining. But it also suggests the law/enforcement distinction is not as useful for lawyers as it first appears ...

* * *

4. Intended and Unintended Lax Enforcement

The water pollution hypothetical raises another problem with distinguishing between enforcement and law. It is possible that a disparity between a written rule and the way it is enforced is intended government policy, and thus amounts to a *de facto* amendment of the law by a governmental actor with the power to make such a change. On the other hand, it is also possible that the lax enforcement is not a matter of policy, but rather results from unintended circumstances such as budget limits, incompetence, or happenstance.

Imagine two possible reasons why enforcement inspections might be rare in rural areas. First, it might be that rural water tends to be significantly cleaner than urban water (at least in regard to ammonia) and that pollution, if it is occurring, is far less likely to be harmful in the rural environment than in the urban environment. Multiple sites discharging the same pollutant are also far less likely. These facts may have been known when discharge limits for the particular effluent were promulgated, but more detailed regulation defining "urban" as opposed to "rural" and articulating differential limits for the two types of area, or otherwise more accurately calibrating the limit to the environmental context, may not have been feasible. The agency thus may have framed the limit with the most typical area and the most serious harms in mind, with the intention of exercising regulatory discretion to fine tune the regulation to different areas and conditions. The regulation was promulgated with knowledge that it was intended more for urban areas than rural, and the enforcement disparity known to the lawyer might well be part of the regulator's policy. Alternatively, the .05 gram ammonia limit may be the regulator's best judgment as to the amount sufficiently likely to cause significant harm regardless of the presence of other effluents or multiple sites. The less frequent testing in rural areas may be attributed solely to insufficient funds for enforcement, and the fact that it is less expensive to test in the urban areas.

In the first situation, it is meaningful to say that the .05 limit is not "really" the legal limit in rural areas. The source of law—the regulatory agency—has intentionally made the law-as-enforced different from the law-as-written for reasons related to its legal mission. (The situation is akin to the desuetude example where prosecutors refuse to enforce an anachronistic statute.) Since the harm the agency is to prevent is unlikely to occur in the rural area, even over the .05 limit, the agency has tailored the law through enforcement decisions. Such intentional use of enforcement policy for substantive reasons appears to break down the "law/enforcement" distinction; enforcement is part of the "real" law here. When, however, lax enforcement is based simply upon cost, incompetence, or inadvertence, rather than substantive reasons, the "law/enforcement" distinction retains meaningful content.

If the lawyer knows the reasons for a significant differential between the law-as-written and the law-as-enforced, then the "law/enforcement" distinction might be used in deciding what information to convey to the client. Frequently, however, the lawyer does not know. Absent information, ought the lawyer to assume that such a differential is not substantively based? Or, is it more likely the case that in most such decisions substantive and cost factors are mixed in a complicated way? Is it likely that enforcement policy is usually partly law—that is, partly assessment of what is more and less important, more and less wrongful, and so on—and partly "just" enforcement? If the latter is true, the utility of the "law/enforcement" distinction is substantially diluted.

In sum, the distinction between law and enforcement has significant intuitive attraction. A citizen's access to the law ought not mean access to the means to evade the law; and distinguishing law from enforcement of the law appears to speak to that difference. Our exploration of the possible ways of framing and applying the distinction, however, reveals substantial difficulties. The distinction will assist a lawyer's understanding of the situation, but these difficulties render a thorough analysis complex and problematic * * *

IV. COUNSELING AND CHARACTER

A. *Four Premises*

For the lawyer who has worked her way through all of the above, what guidance is there? The law tells her that she *may* discuss the legal consequences of all potential conduct with the client, but does not tell her that she must. The * * * distinctions developed above provide a process to assist analysis, a mode for initiating, testing, and refining intuition. But they rarely yield a specific or concrete answer, presenting instead a picture of the complexity and difficulty of the problem. In sum, they usually provide significant clarification, but only partial guidance.

Aside from the lawyer's own devices and intuition, are there other premises or foundations that can provide guidance? Several such bases were mentioned * * *, and a summary of these places to start may be helpful at this point. The first premise is that law is a public good that is intended to be available for individuals to use in leading their lives. In other words, the fundamental purpose of law is to be available to guide conduct. This means that a client has a clear interest in, and perhaps even an entitlement to, knowledge of the law that governs her. The second premise is that the primary function of lawyers as professionals is to assist their clients, and a core part of that role is to provide access to law that is otherwise inaccessible to most lay clients. (A corollary of this premise is that judging or policing clients is not a primary lawyer role, although it may be appropriate at some margins.) The third premise is that a lawyer's assistance to a client is bounded by the limits of the law; a lawyer should not assist a client in unlawful conduct.

In the context of the situations considered in this Article, these three premises suggest a fundamental problem: determining the weight of the client's entitlement to knowledge of the law and balancing it against the weight of society's interest in preventing lawyers from assisting in the violation of law and legal norms. My own sense is that the notion of "secret law" is incompatible with a conception of citizens as free and equal and the government as the servant of the people. This understanding is subject, however, to the considerable difficulties and complexities of deciding what counts as "law" under what sorts of situations, which we have been examining. It is also subject to those considerations that may well justify [failure to inform the client of] some enforcement policies and practices. [These] complicate any reckoning of the balance. Limited by that very substantial caveat, I would still maintain that our democratic constitutional order presumes that persons do have something approaching a "right" to know "the law" that purports to govern them. (The notion of keeping the knowledge from them implies, disturbingly, someone or some institution on high deciding who is to know what about the law.)

In my opinion the first two premises therefore justify a rebuttable presumption that it is generally appropriate for the lawyer to educate the client concerning the law, and that is a significant starting point for the lawyer pondering what to do. The third premise and the distinctions explored in Part II strongly suggest, however, that there are occasions when that presumption is rebutted, and the client does not have the "right" to be informed of the law—or law-related information—that will govern or judge his conduct. These three premises taken together essentially restate our basic problem. Reformulated as a rebuttable presumption in favor of the client learning relevant law and legal considerations, they suggest a beginning orientation (or bias), but they do not provide a methodology for determining when the lawyer should decide the presumption has been rebutted.

Reconsider for a moment (1) the motel owner and (2) the party negotiating a long-term contract and contemplating the possibility of breaching it several years down the line. A thoughtful application of the * * * distinctions to each of these situations does not yield determinate guidance as to what legal information ought to be conveyed or withheld. Where does the lawyer turn next? Two observations related to the premises mentioned above seem apposite. First, although the lives of lawyer and client have come together here, the lawyer ought to remember that it is the client's life that is primarily involved. It is the client who owns and has invested much of his life in the motels; it is the client who will be making the choice about whether to continue in business with the defective water heaters. It is the client who will or will not enter into the long-term contracts, with or without the secret intention or inclination to breach (and maybe with breach as just one of several planned possibilities). This suggests that the decision to be made is primarily the client's, and that withholding arguably "legal" information is wrong. On the other hand, there is, in each case, a potential victim to consider, a third party who may be significantly harmed by the client. Communicating only the law as expansively understood (the legal realist view) too often amounts (from the client's perspective) to encouragement to engage in wrongful conduct contrary to legal norms. Thus, communicating only the law too often functions as assistance in unlawful conduct that may injure a third party.

I would therefore add a fourth foundation, a premise that will provide a different kind of perspective on the problem and will draw us toward a different kind of process for resolving it. That premise is that the lawyer ought not assume her client's goals or desires. She ought not assume that the client desires the maximum possible wealth or freedom. She ought not assume her client is Holmes' "bad man, who cares only for the material consequences which [legal] knowledge enables him to predict." The way to avoid such disrespectful assumptions is to talk to the client, to explore with the client his situation, desires, and preferences, and to discuss how the law impacts or interacts with all of these. This strategy points toward the process of dialogue and counseling, an approach to the problem that supplements the factor analysis developed over the course of this Article. When confronted with situations raising the issues discussed in this Article, the lawyer ought not just think and analyze. In addition, the lawyer ought to *talk* with the client.

Does the client negotiating the contract really intend to breach it in three years? Or is she merely curious about that possibility? By conversing with her about the obligations contracts may entail aside from the law, and about the injuries she might be imposing upon the relying promisee, a lawyer may both learn and reveal pertinent information, and may also help the client shape her intentions and conduct. Similarly, the conversation with the motel owner may explore how severe an impact a serious burn can have on an accident victim, how important continued operation of the business is to the owner, and how these two relate. The more the lawyer learns from the client, the more she will know concerning how real her dilemma is. If it turns out that the client may use information about the law to violate it, she will have gained more information, more nuance, to assist her in an analysis of how she ought to proceed. In addition, such a conversation may itself alter the preferences or intentions of the client (and the lawyer), and thus may expand the possibilities.

Cynthia A. Williams, Corporate Compliance
With the Law in the Era of Efficiency

76 N.C.L. Rev. 1265 (1998)

I. Introduction

Fifteen years ago, Professor (now Judge) Frank Easterbrook and Professor Daniel Fischel set out the following proposition about corporate law compliance: "Managers have no general obligation to avoid violating regulatory laws, when violations are profitable to the firm ... We put to one side laws concerning violence or other acts thought to be malum in se."

That statement, asserted in a footnote, was elaborated upon only briefly, again in a footnote:

> "[M]anagers do not have an ethical duty to obey economic regulatory laws just because the laws exist. They must determine the importance of these laws. The penalties Congress names for disobedience are a measure of how much it wants firms to sacrifice in order to adhere to the rules; the idea of optimal sanctions is based on the supposition that managers not only may but also should violate the rules when it is profitable to do so."

Easterbrook and Fischel's view of corporate compliance with the law, which I call the "efficient breach" view, has obvious intellectual connections to some aspects of law and economics and to the theory of efficient breach of contract, expanded to include efficient breach of public law. While many people might view Easterbrook and Fischel's theory of "efficient breach of public law" as lacking a sound legal and political foundation, a more plausible view (but one that is also flawed) is that of "efficient investment in compliance." That view suggests the maximum amount of money a firm should invest in order to comply with the law is determined by the maximum penalty for violations of a particular law, since it would be economically inefficient to invest more in compliance than one risks in fines.

In this Article, I argue that the conception of law underlying "efficient breach" is similar to the conception underlying "efficient compliance," and that both understate the significance of law in a similar way, treating vast realms of law as simply a pricing scheme or set of tariffs on behavior. I call the underlying conception of law, which I am criticizing in this Article, the "law-as-price" view of law, and I assert that both efficient breach and efficient compliance theories of corporate law compliance derive in important (yet different) ways from the law-as-price conception of law. Under this penalty-driven approach to law, what is of paramount importance about law are the penalties, either because the penalties form the basis for determining whether to obey the law or not (efficient breach), or because they form the basis for determining the law's importance and how much money a corporation should spend on compliance efforts (efficient compliance). Moreover, under the efficient breach theory a corporation may purchase the "right" to violate the law by simply risking paying the penalty * * *

A corollary of the tendency to treat sanctions as prices is a distinctly voluntaristic approach to law: a theory that posits one realm of true "mandatory" law, establishing limits on behavior, and a separate realm of "voluntary" law, setting out suggestions of desired behavior and a pricing scheme for the "right" not to meet those suggestions * * *

[T]he theory criticized here suggests that firms have a choice between meeting the standards of the law or deliberately violating the law and paying the penalties. Yet this Article uses the phrase risking paying the penalties. There is probably not a single example in modern history in which a firm decided to discharge pollutants over regulated levels, for instance, and then immediately wrote a polite letter to the Environmental Protection Agency (the "EPA") enclosing a check for the penalties due; or churned securities accounts and then promptly "remitted the balance due and owing on all penalties thereby accumulated" to the affected securities owners' accounts and/or the government. These things do not happen, in part because there are no clear and socially acceptable mechanisms for "paying the price" (since these are not, in fact, prices). Rather, part of the calculation to violate the law includes a calculation of the probability that the violation will go undetected; or if detected, that it will go unprosecuted for any one of a plethora of reasons; or if prosecuted, that liability will not be established; or if liability is established, that the penalty will be lower than the profits obtained; or that the penalty will not be upheld on appeal in any event. Moreover, the probabilities at each of these stages can be, and in many cases will be, driven downward by actions by the corporation and the corporation's lawyers. So, although the theory may treat the question as one of "violat[ing] a law deliberately and pay[ing] the penalty," the reality is that of risking paying a penalty at best.

II.   THEORIES ABOUT THE MEANING OF LAW

A.   Law-as-Limit

One of the first debates engendered by the ALI Corporate Governance Project was with respect to section 2.01, "The Objective and Conduct of the Corporation." Crudely put, this was a debate between those who envisioned the corporation simply as an economic actor and those who envisioned it as both an economic and social actor. The latter camp prevailed (at least in 1984), and in so doing articulated what I will call the traditional view of law-as-limit.

Thus, while subsection (a) of section 2.01 adopts wealth-enhancement as the primary object of the corporation, subsection (b) recognizes certain constraints on wealth-enhancement, including a mandatory obligation to comply with the law, a permissive power to take ethical considerations appropriate to the responsible conduct of the business into account, and a permissive power to make charitable contributions. The law-compliance obligation of section 2.01(b)(1), which is imposed on the corporation itself in favor of the shareholders, is distinct from any fiduciary duties owed by the officers or directors to the shareholders or the corporation, or duties owed by the corporation to the state or other third parties. Rather, section 2.01(b)(1) imposes a new, specifically corporate law obligation on the corporation to obey the law, whether profits are enhanced thereby or not.

In adopting the general law compliance obligation, the commentary and illustrations to the ALI Principles explicitly rejected the law-as-price theory of law. The commentary suggests that while cost/benefit analysis may be proper when used by the legislature to make determinations about what the law should be, once that determination is made, "cost-benefit analysis [about] whether to obey the rule is out of place." One example illustrating this antipathy to cost/benefit thinking about law compliance is a public trucking company with annual revenues of approximately $5–7 million, which instructs its drivers to drive at seventy-five miles per hour (at a time when the speed limits were fifty-five miles per hour) because the relevant corporate decision-maker determines that this will increase the company's net earnings by $400,000–$500,000 annually. The Reporter concludes, not surprisingly, that this decision represents a violation of section 2.01(b)(1) * * *

Since the general law compliance obligation is comparable to the obligation of any individual to comply with the law, the commentary to section 2.01(b)(1) recognizes that there are certain limited instances in which compliance is not required, such as under the doctrines of necessity or desuetude. But the commentary also shows that these concepts are to be construed narrowly. For instance, the commentary gives the example of a public utility that, despite diligent efforts, is unable to complete a modification of its plant in time to meet an air quality standard, where non-compliance would not threaten the health or safety of the community, and the only alternative to continuing to operate while the modifications are being made is a shut-down that would black out the community. This example of necessity posits attempted compliance and assumes that ultimately the plant will be successful in meeting the air quality standards; it does not contemplate profit-maximizing calculations by a rational actor as the basis for non-compliance ...

As was remarked above and has been extensively discussed elsewhere, the ALI Corporate Governance Project was highly controversial, and early drafts were severely criticized by both the business community and academics within the law and economics movement. As a result, there were dramatic changes between the black-letter law proposed in earlier drafts and that in the ALI Principles as ultimately adopted by the ALI membership in 1992. Section 2.01 emerged virtually unscathed in this process, though, as did its concept of the law-as-limit. What changed dramatically, however, were the board's fiduciary duties and the enforcement mechanisms, including the potential for derivative liability, adopted to effect this concept of law and corporate responsibility. At least in theory, though, the ALI concept of the law is a frankly normative one, rejecting the notion that the penalties for violating even the quintessentially regulatory, malum prohibitum laws, such as those establishing speed limits, can be treated simply as a cost of doing business.

B. Law-as-Price

Two of the most explicit academic proponents of the law-as-price view of law have been Judge Frank Easterbrook (formerly a law professor at The University of Chicago and now a judge on the Seventh Circuit Court of Appeals) and Professor Daniel Fischel. Easterbrook and Fischel recognize a narrow subset of laws that truly prohibit certain actions, a subset they would confine to violence and actions that are mala in se; beyond that, their concept of the law is as a pricing mechanism, or tax upon various activities. Their concept of law incorporates the theory of "optimal sanctions," which assumes that "[t]he principal task in designing remedies is to establish the optimal level of violations." Thus, "[t]he law establishes a price for the violation, and people then must decide how to respond to the schedule of penalties." The major structural elements of their theory are those of conservative law and economics, built upon a positivist jurisprudential foundation laid down by Oliver Wendell Holmes.

One central tenet of Easterbrook and Fischel's view is that of rational-choice theory, which is also a central tenet of law and economics. Rational-choice theory is a general theory of decision-making. It posits that people are rational, self-interested, utility maximizers using cost/benefit analysis to make decisions; it has been applied to numerous types of decisions, including decisions about obeying the law. Further, rational-choice theory, as applied to law compliance, asserts that the costs of legal sanctions can be treated like prices in a theory of supply and demand affecting law compliance. The law-as-price view of law is, in essence, rational-choice theory interpreted not simply as a descriptive claim about how people respond to legal sanctions, but as two, distinct normative claims.

The first normative claim is * * * that the sanctions for violating the law can be treated as the price to be paid for the "right" to violate the law. Inherent in this view of law is the legal voluntarism claim: that particularly with respect to regulatory law, a person can either conform to the law or violate it while accepting the known consequences, and that either choice is an acceptable means for an individual or corporation to fulfill its obligations as a citizen. The second normative claim is that since people and corporations will, and possibly should, make decisions about compliance with law based on a "rational actor's" calculations of costs and benefits, their expectations about the likely outcome of violating the law or investing a certain amount in compliance ought to be recognized as settled expectations upon which they may legitimately rely.

Professor Daniel Fischel provided some greater amplification about the intellectual derivation of the law-as-price theory in an article in the Vanderbilt Law Review. The article was published in 1982, at a time when there was a collision between the "Reagan revolution" of deregulation and free-market theory and the previous decade's vigorous academic and social debate over corporate social responsibility. In the Vanderbilt Law Review article, Fischel defended the shareholder wealth-maximizing norm against the claim that "managements' single-minded dedication to profit maximization is inconsistent with social welfare" * * *

Fischel recognized, however, that there will be situations involving negative externalities, such as pollution, in which firms "may impose costs on others without providing compensation," or involving types of behavior, such as "sensitive foreign payments," in which some would argue that profit-maximizing was inconsistent with social welfare. According to Fischel, these types of situations were best addressed by changing the laws, rather than by re-evaluating the corporate purpose to de-emphasize profit-maximizing, because when laws restricting pollution or prohibiting foreign payments or anticompetitive behavior are violated, "an argument could be made that a breakdown in accountability has occurred." But, he suggested, "even here the situation is more complicated than may first appear," and he argued that:

Because many laws can be violated inadvertently or by subordinates, the costs of preventing violations may far exceed the gains from avoiding violations. A firm may also find it advantageous to violate a law deliberately and pay the penalty for the same reason that an individual in some cases may prefer to breach a contract and pay damages. Because the gains from breach or violation presumably exceed the social costs (as reflected in the penalty), compliance with the statute or contract is undesirable from a personal as well as a social perspective * * *

Another aspect of the law-as-price view of law that is directly derived from rational-choice theory is the tendency to determine whether to obey the law by reference to the likelihood of actually having to pay a penalty for noncompliance, and so discounting penalties by the likelihood of detection and successful enforcement of violations. One articulation of this idea is found in David Engel's article An Approach to Corporate Social Responsibility. In that article, Engel defines "corporate voluntarism" or "corporate altruism" (and with it "corporate social responsibility") as instances when corporations "pursue social ends where this pursuit conflicts with the presumptive shareholder desire to maximize profit." Engel's premise is that public corporations should pursue only those goals supported by a broad and clearly signaled social consensus, and that while pursuing profit-maximizing is supported by such a consensus, pursuing other social goals is not. Among the social goals that Engel considers for which corporations might forego profit-making is "altruistic" corporate obedience to the law, or complying with the substantive standards of the law even when the corporation can escape a liability rule because of non-detection or non-prosecution. The way Engel poses the question is to ask whether a corporation, having determined that it is profitable to violate a given law (given the potential penalty, as discounted by the risks of detection and successful prosecution), should nonetheless act to forbear violating that law based on a cost/benefit calculation using the non-discounted penalty, which Engel assumes equals the full social costs that the corporation's behavior would impose.

Note, however, the narrowness of Engel's position: What is defined as altruism is not even "voluntary" obedience to the substantive standards of the law, but rather the corporation's use of a non-discounted penalty in its cost/benefit analysis. Even posed this narrowly, Engel finds no persuasive evidence that society clearly signals that it wants corporations to act "altruistically" in this manner. So, he concludes, while we may want corporations "at least some times—to obey, for example, substantive criminal laws—or to spend money to keep lower echelon employees within the laws—beyond the point dictated by profit-maximization," there is no way for society to signal when it wants such "corporate voluntarism."

Engel's article also sets out the argument for the "efficient investment in compliance" paradigm. Looking at the particular context of crime, Engel first argues that it is not true that "we criminalize only those acts that we do not want performed in the society at all—regardless of cost." Rather, "[i]n an emergency, or where the costs of law-obedience are otherwise high enough, we do not view the laws against trespass or larceny or burglary or even homicide as absolutes." So instead of enumerating all of the justifiable "violations," the legislature allows discretion with respect to the penalty; the penalty indicates how much society cares about certain categories of violations. Engel then applies this principle to the corporate context and asserts that "the argument that the socially optimal level of crime is zero seems particularly infirm in the corporate context." This is because reducing corporate crime involves the special costs of corporate law-compliance expenditures, except in the rare instances in which the board actively conducts or condones a pattern of criminal activity. And, with respect to law-compliance expenditures,

> "[I]t is not plausible to argue that every substantive crime represents a legislative judgment that every corporation should spend an infinite amount on an internal auditing system to ensure that none of its employees engages in the prohibited conduct. And yet as soon as the argument is diluted at all from this proposition, a moralistic approach to the meaning of substantive criminal law gives no guidance as to how much a corporation should spend to reduce lower-echelon crime."

The additional guidance on how much a corporation should spend on law compliance, according to Engel, is found in the penalty levels:

> "This is not in itself to suggest . . . that it is necessarily appropriate or desirable for corporate management to shape its conduct entirely with a calculated view to legislative penalty levels . . . But it is meant to say that not all violations are socially undesirable; and that if some are undesirable without being clearly signaled to the corporation by the penalty level, then they must be clearly signaled in some other way or the corporation will not know it should avoid them."

In Easterbrook and Fischel's writing, and in Engel's, one thus sees articulated a number of the premises of the law-as-price view of law, including (1) equating breaches of mechanisms of public-law ordering (statutes and regulations) with breaches of mechanisms of private-law ordering (contract); (2) explicit interpretation of the penalties for violation of the law as prices or as taxes on behavior; (3) an assumption that the penalties for violating the law equal the social costs of the harm thereby imposed; (4) development of the concept of efficient investment in law compliance; (5) reduction of the concept of the law as a system of limiting individual freedom and structuring behavior; and (6) elevation of the values of efficiency and individual self-interest over the values of democratic authority, community, and social cohesion * * *

IV. A Developing Jurisprudence I: Efficient Breach in the Law

* * *

B. The Law-as-Price Concept Inherent in Efficient Breach of Public Law Is Fundamentally Ironic

* * * [There is a] fundamental irony in the law-as-price position. According to these views, there is a narrow realm of positive law that truly commands obedience: law that prohibits mala in se actions, such as those constituting violence; * * * actions that are deemed morally reprehensible by a clear social consensus; * * * and actions that involve criminal or moral norms * * * Often these will be the same thing. All other law, and in particular most regulatory law, is law as cost: "[C]onduct to be penalized in some legal fashion, but which the citizen is still free to choose to do."

In other words, the only law that is binding operates when law is not actually necessary to set the necessary standards of behavior. If the behaviors that are prohibited are wrongful in their very nature, then we do not need law to establish the standards of behavior. We do not need laws against murder to tell us that murder is wrong, nor, in general, do we need laws against rape or kidnapping or child abuse or arson or burglary to communicate the necessary standards of behavior. These things are obviously wrong whether we have laws to define them as wrong or not because these are actions in which there is a "clear societal consensus" that they involve "a serious and substantial moral wrong."

Where we need law most, though, given the highly complex, sophisticated, and technological post-industrial nature of society today, is where the law-as-price view of the law would make law impossible: precisely within the broad ambit of regulatory law. There, we definitely need binding law to structure interactions so that there is a level playing field among competitive economic enterprises, so that persons are treated fairly and with respect, and so that industrial practices include considerations of human and environmental health and safety. It is precisely because the issues addressed by regulatory law are so technically complex—composed of interrelated webs of harm, causation, and subtle externalities—and not amenable to determination by reference to obvious moral precepts, that regulatory law is critical.

Should airlines maintain their aircraft by a thorough operational review every twenty flights or every one hundred flights? Who knows, but in our society we have empowered a technically expert administrative agency, the FAA, with at least a partial mandate to protect passenger safety, to make that decision and to impose its decision on every industry participant. Should industrial plants discharge ammonia at a level of .050 grams per liter of effluent or at a level of .060 grams per liter? Who knows, but we have empowered the EPA to study the issue, to consider the economic and health effects of permitting discharges of various levels of ammonia, and to make a binding decision. It is precisely because "most of us would not have an immediate answer" about "whether or not it is wrong to discharge .060 grams of ammonia per liter of water effluent" that we need a rule developed by experts who are not self-interested, and we need that rule to be recognized as binding by all industry participants. Therefore, by denying the mandatory nature of regulatory law, the law-as-price view denies us law precisely where we need it most: in the regulatory arena, where there is not a social consensus, where there is not an obvious moral component to the standards the law sets, and where humanistic concerns and economic self-interest collide most acutely.

C.   Society Is Not Indifferent Concerning Whether Firms Choose Compliance with the Law Versus Risking Paying the Penalty

In addition to that fundamental irony at the core of the law-as-price theory, there is another serious problem with the theory: the implicit (and in some cases explicit) premise that society is indifferent concerning whether firms choose compliance with the law rather than risking paying the penalty, or even that society is benefited by this approach to law, is demonstrably false.

The efficient breach concept of statutory and regulatory law, which is based on an understanding of law as a series of prices established for the "right" to violate the law, has evolved as a direct extension of the efficient breach of contract theory. Both Easterbrook and Fischel, separately and writing together, make this derivation explicit. Yet their argument fails to acknowledge the significant differences between breach of contract and breach of public law. While Pepper suggests that "Holmes' "bad man" understanding of contract law has become so descriptively accurate that few would contest the notion of a "right" to breach a contract," this insight about private law, even if it were true, says nothing about whether one also has a "right" to breach public, statutory law simply by assuming a similar Holmesian equivalence between performance and paying damages. Admittedly, there is a surface plausibility to the analogy, since a number of influential jurisprudential traditions emphasize a contractarian understanding of social and political relationships. Yet the analogy ultimately underestimates the differences between breach of contract and breach of statutory law; it also underestimates the extent to which performance of statutory obligations is far superior, from a social viewpoint, to risking paying penalties.

Thus, contract law is a species of private, voluntary law; absent duress, no one is required to enter into most contracts. These are voluntarily undertaken obligations and usually confined to mechanisms of economic exchange. Even Holmes recognized that the voluntary nature of contract law is important in our view of breach of contract. Public law, on the contrary, is not voluntary in this same sense: one takes on the obligations of citizenship (which include following the law) simply by virtue of enjoying the benefits of society; it is impossible to live in a society without enjoying those benefits, and thereby being required to fulfill the correlative obligations. Indeed, following the law has traditionally been thought of as the absolute minimum component of a citizen's duty to her society.

Related to this point is one based on the underlying norms or values of contract law, as opposed to public, statutory law. These norms point in different directions and are effectuated by a different relationship between the individual and her society. Thus, the underlying norms of contract law are autonomy and individualism: "[T]he contract paradigm expresses the basic norm that individuals should be able to agree between and among themselves how to allocate resources." Absent unusual circumstances, society, through the auspices of the courts, will not even enter into the relationship, at least not so far as judging the fairness of the terms of the contract or whether parties should or should not engage in the underlying terms of exchange.

In contrast, the underlying norm of regulation is that of social obligation and responsibility, and the process is one of society, through the legislature and administrative agencies, setting out what constitutes minimally acceptable behavior. There is no obvious reason why conclusions from a paradigm that effectuates individual freedom should apply at all to a paradigm that effectuates the processes of social control— control that is necessary, given the size of the population, in order to maintain any realm of individual freedom * * *

[G]iven the significant differences between "efficient breach of contract" and "efficient breach of public law," society is still the net loser under the Easterbrook/Fischel view of the law even if there is compensation, given the nature of many of the types of harm caused by failing to comply with one's statutory and regulatory obligations. Since the harm caused by breach of contract is primarily economic, it can often be fully compensated by monetary damages. Significantly, when money damages will not equally compensate a promisee, the courts demand specific performance. In the realm of public law, specific performance of statutory obligations is always far superior to having putative defendants paying penalties when the harm to be avoided is not primarily economic. Even in those instances in which the harm to be avoided by a particular statute is purely economic, statutory compliance will usually be preferable. A number of examples can best illustrate these points.

1. Violations of Laws Regulating Economic Harm

The overtime provisions of the Fair Labor Standards Act ("FLSA") establish the general rule that employees must be compensated at not less than one and one-half times their regular rate of pay for all hours worked in excess of forty hours in a single work week. These overtime provisions do not apply to professional, managerial, or administrative employees, as those terms are defined in regulations issued by the Secretary of Labor. Recently, the Employer Policy Foundation, which is an employer-sponsored policy institute in Washington, D.C., issued a report estimating that employees would be paid an additional $19 billion a year if violations of these overtime rules were not so common. While the U.S. Department of Labor initiates 20,000 cases a year challenging overtime violations and wins settlements for employees in ninety percent of them, the extent of the problem clearly overwhelms the Department's enforcement capabilities.

A number of points can be made about this example, which is an instance in which the harm to be avoided is purely economic. First, employers are not "efficiently" breaching the law and paying the penalties. They are violating the law and not paying either the penalties or overtime legitimately owed to their employees absent enforcement actions. This should more properly be called stealing or cheating, rather than "efficient breach of law." Moreover, it cannot be argued that this is a law that, through the processes of desuetude, has become "not law." Society has established a labor standard and, through the auspices of the Department of Labor, is attempting to enforce it; in setting that standard the economic interests of employers were no doubt well represented and seriously considered. Certainly the extent of Labor Department enforcement is constrained by the number of investigators. Yet it would be quite a cynical argument to suggest that the low level of investigators is indicative of an underlying lack of seriousness about enforcement of this law that borders on desuetude. Rather, there is a limit to how many resources our society can spend to enforce any of its laws, given all the other competing priorities for the use of funds. To a very great extent, society needs to rely upon a reservoir of law-abidingness as an "enforcement" tool. To the extent that the efficient breach theory undermines that reservoir and legitimizes violations of law, it is to be condemned
* * *

[I]n many instances, there is a clear economic incentive for employers to violate the law, since the damages are usually money owed for the prior two years' overtime (or three years for a willful violation) and the delays in getting a judgment can be considerable (which, given the time value of money, operates to the employer's benefit). In most instances, employers can violate these laws with impunity, notwithstanding the social consensus, as expressed in the statute, that non-professional employees ought not to be required to work overtime without appropriate compensation. Since most employers who violate these laws are merely risking paying penalties, not actually paying them, the ultimate effect of this "efficient breach of law" is wrongfully to redistribute $19 billion per year from workers (who are also consumers) to employers. These kinds of uncompensated distributions from employee to employer ought not be dignified under the rubric of increasing efficiency.

2. *Violations of Laws Regulating Non–Economic Harm*

In many (and perhaps most) instances the harm to be prevented by a statute or regulatory enactment is not purely economic; in such cases "specific performance" is even more obviously superior to the risk of paying penalties, or even paying the penalties. Speed limits are one such type of law. Pepper's writing would suggest that speed limits are the essence of a malum prohibitum law, firmly located in the realm of law-as-price. In contrast, in commentary to section 2.01 the ALI stated that it would not be permissible for the relevant decision-maker at a trucking firm to instruct its drivers to exceed the speed limit by twenty miles per hour in order to save $400,000–500,000 per year (although that message of section 2.01 was significantly qualified, as discussed above). In other words, according to the ALI the penalties for violating speed limits are not to be treated as simply another cost of doing business. When the underlying policy goals animating speed limits are examined, it is evident that the unqualified ALI exhortatory position is correct.

Thus, setting speed limits is not simply an economic decision or a revenue-generating device for local taxing authorities, although economics plays a part and speed limits can seem to be a revenue-generating device in certain states on certain holiday weekends. In setting speed limits, the primary goal is obviously safety: the higher the speed limit, the higher the fatality rate in serious automobile accidents. A secondary goal is to reduce the environmental impact of driving: driving fifty-five miles per hour instead of sixty-five results in reduced gasoline consumption, which in turn reduces air pollution. Reducing air pollution produces corollary health benefits. And during the 1970s, reducing gasoline consumption was also tied to the policy goal of reducing American dependence on foreign oil.

Moreover, in setting speed limits, the legislature and various administrative agencies balance the economic costs of lower speed limits (including increased transportation time to ship goods) with the social benefits of safety, health, and environmental protection. It is reasonable to assume that the economic interests of corporate entities are well-represented in the legislative and administrative-agency process as a general matter. So, for individual corporations to determine that they will violate the law because the potential costs to them of compliance are outweighed by the potential costs and benefits of violation creates a "double-counting" problem: the legislature has already considered the costs to industry of regulatory compliance in making its determination. In a democracy, if the corporation disagrees with the legislature, there are ways to seek to change that determination short of economic vigilantism. Because general compliance with the law will promote the legislative goals of safety, health, and environmental protection, general compliance is far superior to general non-compliance coupled with some percentage of people paying traffic tickets to various local authorities.

The argument that compliance is socially preferable to paying penalties is even stronger with respect to statutes and regulations that seek to prevent harms that are primarily non-economic, such as health or safety statutes (the Occupational Safety and Health Act being a prime example), environmental statutes (the Clean Air Act or the Clean Water Act, for instance) or civil rights statutes (such as the Americans with Disabilities Act or the Civil Rights Act). The purposes of these statutes are to promote health, safety, dignity, equality, and environmental protection; they are not simply alternative types of revenue-raising devices. Compensation ex post for an arm lost or a daughter killed in an industrial accident or a water table that is lethal or a human spirit that is heavy with being judged as a type and not as an individual is better than no compensation at all, but it is a distinct second-best alternative to being the beneficiary of good faith efforts to comply fully with the protective goals of the law ex ante. While the costs of these "intangible" harms can be given an economic value for purposes of compensation ex post, to confuse the economic value of after-the-fact compensation with the actual human (and environmental) costs of non-economic harm is like an occupant of Plato's cave confusing the shadows of reality for the real thing.

Even if the analogy between breaching a contract and breaching a public law were a good one—and it is not, for the reasons identified above—"specific performance" of statutory obligations is always superior to risking penalties, even when the underlying statute aims at preventing economic harm (because of distributional effects), but in particular when the underlying statute seeks to prevent various kinds of non-economic harm that are badly compensated, if at all, in money.

Taking this "moralistic approach to the meaning of . . . law," must one then argue that every law is equally important? On one interpretation, what the "law-as-prohibition" versus "law-as-cost" approach seems to be getting at is the obviously correct idea that some laws are more important than other laws. So, are OSHA regulations requiring posting of inspection information, or a Delaware statute requiring corporations to keep a list of their current shareholders available in Delaware for shareholders to inspect and copy, as important as FAA regulations governing commercial airline maintenance and equipment requirements? And are each of these laws as important as laws prohibiting murder?

Of course not. It is not a necessary corollary to an argument that the penalties for violations of the law cannot be treated as a price tag for the right to violate the law that one assume every law is equally important. The importance of a law is determined by its purposes and the harm it seeks to prevent or ameliorate. A law seeking to prevent an immediate death is obviously of paramount importance because of the irrevocability of the harm. Laws such as airline maintenance requirements seeking to prevent a very small possibility of death or serious injury are somewhat less important (although still extremely important), since some huge proportion of individuals will "beat the odds" no matter how bad airline maintenance becomes. The law on corporate shareholders' lists is less important still (except perhaps to shareholders and institutions ready and willing to engage in proxy contests), and the

OSHA posting requirements are less important than each of the others, since failure to post required information is not, in itself, likely to result in an injury or illness.

And yet to recognize that there is a range of importance of law does not mean that there is a range of permissible fidelity to the law that goes to zero, simply because one is willing to risk the imposition of a penalty. Unless a law explicitly and clearly imposes a tax or tariff on behavior, even the most objectively unimportant, purely administrative law with no distributive, health, safety, environmental, or existential implications (hereinafter "unimportant law") establishes a minimum standard of behavior that may not be overcome by a corporate or individual actor's private economic benefit (assuming the underlying political system is worthy of fidelity). That is the ideal. The vagaries and imperfections of human beings being what they are, the ideal will never be fully realized. And yet we ought not to sully our ideals about law by undermining the meaning of law ab initio, turning it into a price tag, available to be risked by anyone who can afford it, and then, further to undermine the ideal, dignify that erosion by calling disobedience "efficient" and suggesting that it is to society's benefit.

Note

The federal indictment of individuals in connection with certain KPMG tax shelter opinions alleged that a KPMG executive urged the firm not to register the shelters as required by the Internal Revenue Service because "the IRS penalties applicable to a failure to register would be dwarfed by the lucrative fees KPMG stood to collect from selling unregistered tax shelters." United States District Court, Southern District of New York, United States v. Stein, et al., Sealed Indictment 05 Crim. 888, August 24, 2005, at 25. The indictment further alleged, "Moreover, KPMG's office of general counsel, among others, advised that by deciding not to register tax shelters, KPMG risked criminal prosecution, but ... advised that KPMG's tax leadership could nevertheless 'make a business decision to not register the activity as a tax shelter.'" *Id.* at 26. Was counsel's approach to registering the shelters with the IRS defensible? Does it make any difference whether there was any doubt if the shelters had to be registered? Would the existence of an argument against the IRS that was virtually certain to lose but was not frivolous mean that the decision whether to register was essentially a business judgment?

PROBLEMS

1. You are an attorney in the legal department of Megabank. You work in the Private Banking section of the bank, which provides various banking and financial services for high-wealth individuals. As with every section of the bank, Megabank treats Private Banking as an independent profit center whose performance is evaluated both quarterly and annually. As a result, managers in Private Banking and other Megabank sections are continually working on projects to develop new products and services to enhance profitability. Every section proposal to Megabank upper management for a new product or service must be accompanied by a risk analysis, which

describes both the potential benefits of the proposal and its financial, legal, and other risks. As part of the Private Banking team, you assist the financial professionals in the section with this process by helping them structure proposals in a way that minimizes legal risk.

The head of the Private Banking team and her top assistants have focused in recent months on what they believe is an untapped source of lucrative profits from high-wealth individuals in South America, especially Colombia. Both the number of the individuals and the assets that they control have grown significantly in the last few years, and projections are that this will continue for some time. Employees within the section have begun to analyze the financial rewards and risks of moving into this market. The head of Private Banking has asked you to analyze the legal risks of doing so, and to consider ways in which that risk could be minimized.

You regard the main legal risk as violation of the Money Laundering Control Act (MLCA), which prohibits any person from knowingly engaging in a financial transaction that involves the proceeds of a "specified unlawful activity." 18 U.S.C. 1956–57. Such activities include terrorism, drug trafficking, and foreign crimes involving bribery and misappropriation of funds. In furtherance of this provision, all banks are required to conduct a "due diligence" review before accepting new wealthy foreign clients. 31 U.S.C. 5318(h). The bank must compile basic background information on each client for whom an account is opened, with respect to matters such as the individual's source of wealth and the expected value and volume of transactions in the account. You suspect that a not insignificant amount of the wealth accumulated by individuals in this region in recent years reflects proceeds from drug trafficking. As a result, you conclude that Megabank's direct solicitation of accounts from and provision of private banking services to high-wealth individuals would create a very high risk of violating the MLCA.

You could, however, devise an alternative that would reduce the risk to the bank. The Bank of Fredonia (BoF) is a bank in Fredonia, a country with relatively lax banking laws. Megabank periodically involves BoF as a partner in various syndicated loans, and refers some international business to the bank. Megabank could propose to BoF that it form a South American private banking subsidiary that would accept accounts from and provide services to high-wealth individuals in this part of the world. BoF would own 51% of the subsidiary, and Megabank would enter into a partnership with an outside individual, which would own the remaining 49%. The partnership would be entitled to receive 60% of the dividends from the subsidiary, which would constitute its sole source of income. Megabank's interest in the partnership would entitle it to 99% of its income but no voting power. The outside individual would have voting control over the partnership and be entitled to 1% of its profits. Because it would have no control over the partnership and the outside party would contribute the amount to it necessary to satisfy the relevant accounting rules, the partnership would not be treated as a part of Megabank. In addition to receiving 40% of the dividends of the subsidiary, BoF would benefit from assurance of a steady future stream of business opportunities from Megabank.

This arrangement would carry significantly less legal risk than if Megabank were directly to provide private banking services. First, it would be contestable whether the bank was involved in any "transaction" involving private banking under the MLCA by virtue of simply being entitled to 99% of the partnership's income. Second, even if Megabank were treated as being involved in such a transaction, it would be able to claim that it was not "knowingly" involved in any transaction involving proceeds from drug trafficking. Fredonia law prevents banks in that country from disclosure of client information to any outside party. Megabank thus would be unaware of the source of the dividends paid to the partnership that constitutes that entity's income.

How do you advise the Megabank Private Banking team?

* * *

2. Consider the question posed in the excerpt from Professor Pepper:

"Assume an Environmental Protection Agency water pollution regulation, widely publicized to relevant industries, prohibiting discharge of ammonia at amounts greater than .050 grams per liter of effluent. The client owns a rural plant that discharges ammonia in its effluent, the removal of which would be very expensive. The lawyer knows from informal sources that: (1) violations of .075 grams per liter or less are ignored because of a limited enforcement budget; and (2) EPA inspection in rural areas is rare, and in such areas enforcement officials usually issue a warning prior to applying sanctions unless the violation is extreme (more than 1.5 grams per liter). Is it appropriate for the lawyer to educate the client concerning these enforcement-related facts even though it may motivate the client to violate the .050 gram limit?"

Chapter 22

TAX PRACTICE

Tax practice provides a good example of an arena in which the issues raised in the previous Chapter on regulatory counseling are highly salient. How aggressively lawyers for corporations are willing to press for advantage under the tax code has consequences not simply for their clients but for society as a whole. As the Internal Revenue Service (IRS) observes, "tax advisors play a critical role in the Federal tax system, which is founded on principles of compliance and voluntary self-assessment. The tax system is best served when the public has confidence in the honesty and integrity of the professional providing tax advice." 31 CFR Part 10: Regulations Governing Practice Before the Internal Revenue Service. The IRS can audit only a small fraction of tax returns, and many people would be uneasy if it controlled enough resources to engage in close monitoring of every single taxpayer. A sense of the legitimacy of the system thus is crucial to the voluntary compliance that undergirds the tax system–and what lawyers do can affect that perception of legitimacy.

Many practitioners maintain that the tax bar historically has recognized and responded to this responsibility. Its members have provided advice that has been based not only on the literal language of the tax code, but on appreciation of its spirit–that is, the underlying purposes of its various provisions. To the extent this is true, many tax lawyers have rejected the unqualified hired gun model of law practice in favor of one that include some measure of social obligation.

Developments in recent years have placed some pressure on this professional self-understanding. One example has received much recent publicity and is the main focus of this chapter: the provision of legal opinions on tax shelters. Corporations operating in intensely competitive markets have sought every source of advantage, and reducing their effective tax rate is one way to gain an edge. Accounting firms and other entities have responded by developing and marketing new tax shelter "products" consisting of transactions designed to lower taxes. Lawyers play a key role in this process. Those who market and purchase these products rely on lawyers' formal opinions that the tax treatment of the transactions in question likely will withstand any challenge by the IRS. Law firms facing an increasingly competitive market for legal services find that providing these opinions can be quite lucrative. This means that a client that fails to receive a favorable legal opinion about a tax product may well be able to shop around for another law firm that will not have qualms about furnishing one.

There is enough complexity and ambiguity in the tax code that a lawyer intent on rationalizing the delivery of a certain tax opinion often will have no trouble doing so. In addition, creative minds can devise transactions whose individual steps each comply with the literal language of the code. Historically, informal norms of good faith may have constrained abuse of the discretion that such features of the code provide. A less homogeneous and more competitive legal profession, however, as well as modern skepticism about the defensibility of substantive value judgments, may be eroding the effectiveness of those norms. If so, will this also erode public confidence in the legitimacy of the tax system?

Despite its technical nature, tax practice therefore raises profound questions of professional ethics and social policy. There may be no better vehicle for examining the tensions inherent in the lawyer's role, how economic and social changes in the profession are shaping those tensions, and the implications of shifts in lawyers' self-understanding for society as a whole.

OVERVIEW OF THE CHAPTER

As the introduction has indicated, this Chapter uses the provision of legal opinions for tax shelters as the vehicle for exploring ethical issues in tax practice. As background, the Chapter begins with a short overview of IRS regulation of the conduct of tax practitioners in what is known as Circular 230. Much as the SEC rules governing securities lawyers adopted under Sarbanes–Oxley, these regulations reflect ethical provisions designed to be sensitive to the distinctive characteristics of a particular practice specialty.

The Chapter then moves to a report from the Department of Treasury that provides background on the impact of tax shelters, their typical characteristics, and the legal rules and doctrines available to respond to them. There follows a discussion of provisions in Circular 230 that deal specifically with tax shelter opinions. These provisions reflect recent revisions designed to tighten controls over such opinions in the wake of complaints about tax shelter abuses. As your read these rules, ask yourself how well they are likely to serve this purpose. Consider also the potential impact of IRS discipline for lawyers in firms who have some administrative responsibility for the firm's tax practice.

The article by Braverman offers a case study of a particular lawyers involved in both marketing tax shelters and providing legal opinions on them. Make sure that you understand why assuming these roles constituted an ethical violation. The article also notes the ostensible distinction between tax practitioners and tax shelter practitioners, the latter representing a new generation of lawyers more willing to take aggressive positions on behalf of clients. One difference between the two, suggests Braverman, is that in traditional tax practice the client has a business purpose that it wants to achieve, and approaches the lawyer about the most advantageous way to structure it for tax purposes. By contrast, those involved in tax shelter products approach corporations and convince them to engage in transactions that will achieve a certain tax outcome. Why is the first scenario appropriate but the second not? Why isn't reducing a company's effective tax rate a legitimate business purpose? Is providing a tax shelter product any different from suggesting any other way that a company can improve its profitability?

Finally, the Bankman excerpt discusses two different roles that lawyers may play with respect to tax shelters. The first is preparation of an opinion that tax treatment of a transaction more likely than not will be upheld if challenged. The second is serving as advisor to a client about the wisdom of using a particular tax shelter. Bankman suggests that lawyers playing the latter role sometimes are skeptical about tax shelters. They may believe that tax shelters are deceptively marketed, may believe that the benefits from a shelter are overstated, may regard those who market shelters and who provide opinions on them as competitors for tax advice, or may have doubts about the social value of shelters. Bankman says, however, that most such misgivings "are kept from clients and do not directly affect behavior." Should they? If so, why don't they? Should a legal opinion that the shelter more likely than not will withstand challenge obviate the need for corporate counsel to make her own assessment of the risk to the client?

The Problem at the end of the Chapter describes a tax shelter and asks that you assume the two roles that Bankman has identified. First, what is your advice to your corporate client about purchasing the shelter? In answering this question, focus mainly on the IRS tax shelter rule described in the Chapter that permits a taxpayer to avoid an accuracy-related penalty if it acts in good faith. Facts 1–3 at the end of the Problem are especially relevant to this issue. Consider also whether you should recommend use of the shelter even if the company may be liable for a penalty. How should you go about analyzing this question? Finally, ask whether general corporate concerns beyond whether the company pays a penalty are relevant to the decision.

The second question asks you to assume the role of a law firm that has been approached about providing a legal opinion to prospective purchasers of the shelter. How do the IRS rules on tax shelter opinions affect your decision? Other considerations?

MODEL RULES: 1.2(d), 2.1, 8.4

A. TAX SHELTERS

One of the most controversial areas of tax practice is the provision of opinions by lawyers in connection with tax shelters. For purposes of most opinions subject to Circular 230, a tax shelter is an arrangement "a significant purpose of which" is to avoid or evade federal income tax. 31 CFR10.35(b)(2)(C).

Estimates are that the federal government annually loses several billions of dollars in tax revenues as a result of tax shelters. The following report by the U.S. Department of the Treasury elaborates on the impact of tax shelters, their typical characteristics, and the legal provisions that are available to address them.

U.S. DEPARTMENT OF THE TREASURY

THE PROBLEM OF CORPORATE TAX SHELTERS: DISCUSSION, ANALYSIS AND LEGISLATIVE PROPOSALS

July 1999

* * *

III.   Reasons for Concern

There are several reasons to be concerned about the proliferation of corporate tax shelters. These concerns range from the short-term revenue loss to the tax system, to the potentially more troubling long-term effects on our voluntary income tax system.

Short-Term Revenue Loss

Corporate tax shelters reduce the corporate tax base, raising the tax burden on other taxpayers.

Disrespect for the Tax System

Corporate tax shelters breed disrespect for the tax system–both by the people who participate in the tax shelter and by others who perceive unfairness. A view that well-advised corporations can and do avoid their legal tax liabilities by engaging in these tax-engineered transactions may cause a "race to the bottom." If unabated, this could have long-term consequences to our voluntary tax system far more important than the short-term revenue loss we are experiencing.

The New York State Bar Association recently noted the "corrosive effect" of tax shelters: "The constant promotion of these frequently artificial transactions breeds significant disrespect for the tax system, encouraging responsible corporate taxpayers to expect this type of activity to be the norm, and to follow the lead of other taxpayers who have engaged in tax advantaged transactions."

Complexity

Piecemeal legislative remedies complicate the Code and call into question the viability of common law tax doctrines. In the past few years alone, nearly 30 narrow statutory provisions have been adopted responding to perceived abuses.

Uneconomic Use of Resources

Significant resources, both in the private sector and in the Government, are currently being wasted on this uneconomic activity. Private sector resources used to create, implement, and defend complex sheltering transactions could be better used in productive activities. Similarly, the Congress (particularly the tax-writing committees and their staffs), the Treasury Department, and the IRS must expend significant resources to address and combat these transactions.

The *ACM Partnership v. Commissioner* case alone cost the Federal Government over $2 million to litigate. In addition, there are a number of docketed cases involving almost identical shelter products.

Peter Cobb, former Deputy Chief of Staff to the Joint Committee on Taxation, recently stated: "You can't underestimate how many of America's greatest minds are being devoted to what economists would say is totally useless economic activity."

IV. CHARACTERISTICS OF CORPORATE TAX SHELTERS

Because corporate tax shelters take many different forms and utilize many different structures, they are difficult to define with a single formulation. A number of common characteristics, however, can be identified that are useful in crafting an approach to solving the corporate tax shelter problem.

Lack of economic substance. Professor Michael Graetz recently defined a tax shelter as "a deal done by very smart people that, absent tax considerations, would be very stupid." This definition highlights one of the most important characteristics common to most corporate tax shelters—the lack of any significant economic substance or risk to the participating parties. Through hedges, circular cash flows, defeasements and the like, the participant in a tax shelter is insulated from any significant economic risk.

Inconsistent financial accounting and tax treatments. There is a current trend among public companies to treat corporate in-house tax departments as profit centers that strive to keep the corporation's effective tax rate (*i.e.*, the ratio of corporate tax liability to book income) low and in line with that of competitors. Accordingly, in most recent corporate tax shelters involving public companies, the financial accounting treatment of the shelter item has been inconsistent with the claimed Federal income tax treatment.

Tax-indifferent parties. Many recent shelters have relied on the use of "tax-indifferent" parties—such as foreign or tax-exempt entities–who participate in the transaction in exchange for a fee to absorb taxable income or otherwise deflect tax liability from the taxable party.

Marketing activity. Promoters often design tax shelters so that they can be replicated multiple times for use by different participants, rather than to address the tax planning issues of a single taxpaper. This allows the shelter "product" to be marketed and sold to many different corporate participants, thereby maximizing the promoter's return from its shelter idea.

Confidentiality. Similar to marketing, maintaining confidentiality of a tax shelter transaction helps to maximize the promoter's return from its shelter idea–it prevents expropriation by others and it protects the efficacy of the idea by preventing or delaying discovery of the idea by the Treasury Department and the IRS. In the past, promoters have required prospective participants to sign a non-disclosure agreement that provides for million dollar payments for any disclosure of the "proprietary" advice. The 1997 Act addressed this feature to some extent.

Contingent or refundable fees and rescission or insurance arrangements. Corporate tax shelters often involve contingent or refundable fees in order to reduce the cost and risk of the shelter to the participants. In a contingent fee arrangement, the promoter's fee depends on the level of tax savings realized by the corporate participant. Some corporate tax shelters also involve insurance or rescission arrangements. Like contingent or refundable fees, insurance or rescission arrangements reduce the cost and risk of the shelter to the participants.

High transaction costs. Corporate tax shelters carry unusually high transaction costs. For example, the transaction costs in the *ASA* case ($24,783,800) were approximately 26.5 percent of the purported tax savings (approximately $93,500,000).

V.　Present Law Applicable to Shelters

The tax consequences of a particular business transaction generally are determined through the application of mechanical rules (primarily Code and regulatory provisions). However, certain standards under current law may be invoked to challenge the legitimacy of a transaction where a literal application of the mechanical rules to the facts produces technical tax results that are unreasonable or unwarranted. In addition, certain procedural provisions generally enacted in response to the individual tax shelters of the 1970s and 1980s apply.

Anti-abuse rules. In connection with a highly complex statutory or regulatory regime, the Treasury Department has issued several broad-based regulatory anti-abuse rules intended to prevent manipulation of the mechanical rules in a manner that circumvents the overall purposes of the regime. These anti-abuse rules limit the need for even more complicated mechnical rules that would otherwise be necessary to address particular fact patterns. One commentator has declared that regulatory anti-abuse rules potentially are "a path toward a coherent solution" to the problem of tax shelters.

Statutory grants of broad authority. Congress has enacted several general provisions granting the Secretary of the Treasury broad authority to reallocate income and deductions to require the proper reflection of income. These grants of authority were considered necessary by Congress to empower the Secretary to curb inappropriate activities. These include [authority to disallow certain losses, prescribe a change of method of accounting if necessary to reflect income clearly, and reallocate income and deductions between related entities if necessary to prevent tax evasion or clearly reflect income].

Judicial doctrines. Courts have created, developed and re-interpreted various broad common law doctrines to address unreasonable or unwarranted tax benefits, including:

(1) Substance-over-form. Under the substance-over-form doctrine, the IRS and the courts may recharacterize a transaction in accordance with its substance, if "the substance of the transaction is demonstrably contrary to the form." For example, a taxpayer cannot label what is, in essence, equity as debt and thereby secure an interest deduction. As one commentator recently has written, "standards must govern the factual characterization of relationships and arrangements to some extent, and the Commissioner must have the ability to challenge the taxpayer's description of the relevant facts–otherwise the taxpayer's advantage would be insurmountable."

(2) Step transaction doctrine. The step transaction doctrine is a relatively common application of the substance-over-form doctrine. Under the doctrine, formally separate steps may be treated as one transaction for tax purposes (rather than giving tax effect to each separate step), if integration more accurately reflects the underlying substance.

(3) Business purpose. The business purpose doctrine requires that a taxpayer have a business reason–other than the avoidance of federal taxes–for undertaking a transaction or series of transactions. In the Supreme Court's decision in *Gregory v. Helvering*, the Court articulated the doctrine: "The legal right of the taxpayer to decrease the amount of what otherwise would be his taxes, or altogether avoid them, by means which the law permits, cannot be doubted. But the question for determination is whether what was done, apart from tax motive, was the thing which the statute intended."

(4) Economic substance. Under this doctrine, tax benefits may be denied if the tax benefits arise from a discrete set of transactions that do not meaningfully alter the taxpayer's economic position. The economic substance doctrine can be applied by comparing the taxpayer's pre-tax profit to its tax benefits from a transaction. Many commentators believe that the economic substance doctrine is the superior standard to evaluate the legitimacy of a purported business transaction for a variety of reasons.

* * *

B. TAX SHELTER OPINIONS

Lawyers provide opinions that are intended to provide various levels of assurance to potential participants in tax shelters that the IRS will accept the parties' characterization of a transaction and permit the taxpayer thereby to reduce its tax obligation. The most significant benefit from a legal opinion is that a taxpayer may be able to avoid the imposition of a penalty even if the IRS disallows an arrangement that it concludes was entered into mainly to avoid taxes.

The IRS is authorized to levy an "accuracy-related" penalty of 20% of the tax underpayment in most cases, which may rise to 40% in certain cases. A taxpayer may avoid a penalty upon a showing "that there was reasonable cause for, and the taxpayer acted in good faith with respect to" the amount of underpayment. 26 CFR 1.6664–4(a).

Special rules determine whether a corporate taxpayer acted with reasonable cause and good faith. First, there must be "substantial authority" for the position that the taxpayer took. *Id.* at 1.6666–4(f)(2)(i)(A). Second, the corporation must have reasonably believed that the tax position was more likely than not correct. *Id.* at 1.6664–4(f)(2)(i)(B). As a basis for such belief, the corporation may reasonably rely in good faith on the opinion of a professional tax advisor that states that there is a greater than 50% likelihood that the tax position will be upheld if challenged by the IRS. *Id.* at 1.6664–4(f)(2)(i)(B)(2). In arriving at its reasonable belief, the corporation may not take into account the possibility that its tax return will not be audited. *Id.* at 1.6664–4(f)(2)(i)(B).

IRS regulations specifically govern the issuance of tax shelter opinions on which a corporate taxpayer may rely. 31 C.F.R. 10.35. A practitioner must use reasonable efforts to identify and ascertain the facts. She may not base her opinion on any factual assumptions that she knows or should know are incorrect or incomplete, nor on any unreasonable factual representations by the taxpayer or anyone else. "For example, a practitioner may not rely on a factual representation that a transaction has a business purpose if the representation does not include a specific description of the business purpose or the practitioner knows or should know the representation is incorrect or incomplete." 31 CFR 10.35(c) (1)(iii). The opinion must identify in a separate section all factual representations of the taxpayer on which the practitioner has relied.

A tax shelter opinion must include a conclusion as to the likelihood that the taxpayer will prevail on the merits on each significant federal tax issue considered in the opinion. If the lawyer cannot say that the likelihood of prevailing on a specific issue is more likely than not, the opinion must "prominently disclose" this. *Id.* at 10.35(e)(4)(1). With respect to any such issue, the opinion cannot serve as the basis for avoidance of a penalty by the taxpayer. Finally, if the opinion is a "marketed opinion" that will be used by someone other than the practitioner to promote a tax shelter, the practitioner can only issue the opinion if the likelihood of prevailing on each significant federal tax issue is more likely than not. *Id.* at 10.35(c)(3)(iv).

Any practitioner who has authority for overseeing a firm's provision of tax advise must take reasonable steps to ensure that the firm has adequate procedures in effect to ensure compliance with the requirements for issuing tax shelter opinions. Such a practitioner will be subject to discipline for failure to do so "through willfulness, recklessness, or gross incompetence." *Id.* at 10.36(1). In addition, such practitioner will be subject to discipline if she knows or should know that anyone in the firm has engaged in a "pattern or practice" of noncompliance with the regulations on tax shelters, and "fails to take prompt action to correct the noncompliance." *Id.* at 10.36(2).

The American Bar Association (ABA) also has provided some guidance on the issuance of tax shelter opinions. ABA Formal Opinion 82–346 states that "[t]he lawyer rendering a tax shelter opinion which he knows will be relied upon by third persons ... functions more as an advisor than as an advocate." The Opinion says that a lawyer engages in dishonesty if he "accepts as true the facts which the promoter tells him, when the lawyer should know that a further inquiry would disclose that these facts are untrue." A lawyer also is dishonest by "[r]ecklessly and consciously disregarding information strongly indicating that material facts expressed in the tax shelter opinion are false or misleading[.]"

The following two readings elaborate on the role of lawyers in providing tax shelter opinions.

Paul Braverman, HELTER SHELTER

The American Lawyer
December 2003

James Haber made a business proposal to Paul Daugerdas in 1997. Haber is president of The Diversified Group, Incorporated [DGI], a New York company that makes and sells tax shelters. At the time, Daugerdas was a partner in the tax department at Chicago's Altheimer & Gray. The two had known each other since the early 1990s.

Haber had an idea for a tax shelter that he wanted Daugerdas to help create. Daugerdas expressed interest. Haber sent him some materials about the shelter so he could "get comfortable" with the deal.

The two subsequently entered into a business arrangement, described by Haber this way: Daugerdas would work with Haber to develop and sell the shelter, eventually called COBRA. Daugerdas would then write opinion letters for the buyers, giving them legal backing for the deal. The pair would split the profits fifty-fifty. When asked later what Daugerdas thought about the arrangement, Haber recalled, "I believe he said 'that sounds reasonable' to him, because he is 'a reasonable man.' He often said that."

The venture seems to have been a success. In 1997 Haber wrote to Daugerdas: "I want to express my sincere and heartfelt gratitude for the manner in which we have worked together over the past year. I greatly appreciate the mutual respect and trust that we have developed for each other, and look forward to greater successes with you in the future."

But in 2000 DGI sued Daugerdas, claiming that he was using DGI's idea but not giving DGI its cut. Daugerdas, who had since moved to Jenkens & Gilchrist, responded that no agreement prohibited him from using the shelter, adding that it was based on a nonproprietary strategy that anyone familiar with the tax code could figure out.

Defining Daugerdas's role became a key issue in the case. At his deposition, Haber referred to Daugerdas as both his "marketing partner" and his lawyer. "We would have conversations at least weekly, maybe more frequently, in which we would discuss where we were in the marketing of that particular idea," testified Haber.

For his part, Daugerdas denied that he was either a "tax shelter salesman" or DGI's lawyer. Any money he made on the deal, he testified, was from fees paid by people for whom he wrote opinion letters.

The case settled in 2001 after a payment by Jenkens's malpractice carrier, and most of the case file was sealed. Last summer The American Lawyer asked Judge Shira Scheindlin of the Southern District of New York to unseal the record. The motion was granted. This article is based, in part, on documents obtained as a result of that motion.

It's no wonder Haber wanted a piece of the action. Daugerdas's efforts resulted in the sale of at least 600 COBRA-style shelters while he was at Jenkens. Sources at the Internal Revenue Service and the U.S. Department of Justice, both of which are investigating Daugerdas, estimate that the fees he charged ran into the hundreds of millions. Some of those fees were paid to Treasurex Financial, Ltd., a corporation controlled by Daugerdas that, he would later testify, no one at Jenkens knew about at the time.

Several of the people who bought a COBRA [which stands for Currency Options Bring Reward Alternatives] are now suing Daugerdas and Jenkens, claiming that the shelter was a mere gimmick cooked up to avoid taxes, not the kind of legitimate technique they had been assured would pass muster in court. The IRS says that a COBRA is the "same or substantially similar" to an earlier, discredited shelter. Independent experts who reviewed Jenkens's own descriptions of the shelter at the request of The American Lawyer reached the same conclusion.

The plaintiffs also allege that Daugerdas, because he had a stake in both making and selling shelters, violated his professional ethics when he advised them to buy it. Ethics experts contacted by The American Lawyer, relying on materials prepared by the IRS and the plaintiffs, reached similar conclusions.

The government is looking into Daugerdas's actions as well. For more than a year, the IRS has been serving summonses [the rough equivalent of subpoenas from other agencies] on Jenkens, seeking the names of people who bought a COBRA. The firm has refused to provide those names, and the matter is currently in federal court in Illinois. The IRS is also trying to find out if Jenkens has been complying with rules that require tax shelter promoters to register their products and keep lists of their clients.

The litigation risks facing the firm were magnified in September when the firm's malpractice insurance carrier filed a declaratory judgment action, claiming that it's not liable for any further damages arising out of the tax shelter controversy.

A firm spokesman said Daugerdas declined repeated requests for an interview. The spokesman said that Daugerdas "continues to believe the tax advice was sound." He added that the private lawsuits are "without merit" and that the attorney-client privilege requires the firm to resist the IRS's summonses, but the firm refused to discuss any particulars regarding Daugerdas's tax work.

Before the mid–1990s, lawyers in big firms such as Jenkens didn't work on tax shelters. To this day, traditional tax practitioners scorn the practice, casting shelter lawyers as salespeople peddling a dubious product. They try to draw a sharp line between that business and their own work-giving individualized advice about corporate transactions. Tax shelter lawyers are "a different breed, different by experience, temperament, reputation, and calling," is the way Peter Canellos of Wachtell, Lipton, Rosen & Katz, a leader of the old school, put it in a 2001 article in the Southern Methodist University Law Review.

But a new generation of tax lawyers has blurred the line. They work closely with tax shelter "promoters"-accounting firms, investment banks, and insurance companies-to organize and sell shelters. They may still be a minority of the tax bar, but their number has been growing steadily since the mid–1990s, and they now occupy positions of prominence at top firms. DGI, for example, worked on tax shelters with Sidley Austin Brown & Wood and Proskauer Rose, as well as Altheimer and Jenkens.

It would be hard to overstate the magnitude of their work. Shelters have become commonplace, spreading beyond the Fortune 500 companies that have been using esoteric tax schemes for the past decade, to smaller companies and wealthy individuals. A recent report by an IRS consultant estimated that illegal tax shelters cost the government $14–18 billion in lost revenue in 1999.

Daugerdas is a leading figure in this new generation. Former partners of his at Altheimer [since defunct] and Jenkens paint the picture of an aggressive lawyer who has been working to transform the once-staid tax practice since 1994, when he left accounting giant Arthur Andersen LLP and joined Altheimer.

At the time Daugerdas made the jump, most of the shelters being sold were fairly conservative. The customers were mostly major corporations, and they had in-house legal staff and outside counsel on retainer to review any proposed deals. Those lawyers tended to shy away from aggressive schemes, and their reluctance to sign off on cutting-edge maneuvers usually killed the sale, because a company wouldn't close a deal without a favorable opinion letter from tax counsel. And if its regular tax counsel refused, a corporation usually had difficulty finding another firm to write an opinion. As a rule, big-firm lawyers wouldn't give opinions to companies with whom they didn't have a relationship.

The reluctance of others was a business opportunity for Daugerdas. When he joined Altheimer, the firm had a traditional tax practice, where tax lawyers handled the relevant end of business transactions that originated elsewhere in the firm. That work had little appeal for Daugerdas, according to former Altheimer partners. "He was interested in the business-generation side of the business, and in project-oriented billing, not charging by the hour," says former Altheimer managing partner Laurence Bronska.

Daugerdas changed the focus to a "tax products" practice. A products practice essentially inverts the customary lawyer-client relationship, where a client needing legal advice or services goes to a lawyer who charges for his or her time. The "products" lawyer creates something, then goes looking for someone to buy it. Accountants had been doing this for years, but the practice put Altheimer on the cutting edge among law firms. Daugerdas eventually became chairman of the tax department.

The new practice meant a new, aggressive approach to marketing. Referring to one shelter sold by Daugerdas while he was at Altheimer in 1996, which involved the short sale of securities from the U.S. Department of the Treasury, Haber testified:

The Internal Revenue Service issued two revenue rulings directly on point in 1995 relevant to the use of Treasuries and the short sale of Treasuries in transactions similar to the one that Paul was using. So, from a marketing perspective, he was marketing directly opposed to revenue rules. It is my understanding that if he is not the only [lawyer] in the country that would have rendered a more likely than not tax opinion involving the short sale of the Treasuries, then he certainly was, then he was certainly within only two or three that would have.

A lawyer gives a "more likely than not" opinion if he or she believes a court is likely to approve the shelter. Sheldon Pollack, a professor of business law at the University of Delaware and a leading expert on tax shelters, reviewed a description of the shelter in an opinion by Judge Scheindlin. "Daugerdas took a position directly contrary to that of the IRS, as well as an old decision of the Supreme Court from 1940," says Pollack. "And he claims it was 'more likely than not' that the investor would prevail if challenged by the tax authorities? Amazing."

Questions raised about the shelter's legitimacy also touch on what his accusers say were Daugerdas's multiple roles. Daugerdas, they say, acted as both lawyer and promoter, and the dual role resulted in conflicts of interest. However that claim is decided, the DGI material makes clear that Daugerdas has been performing the same roles for many years. According to sworn testimony by DGI president Haber, Daugerdas was working with DGI to create and sell shelters, then writing opinion letters for the buyers, as far back as 1996.

An opinion letter is an essential part of virtually every tax deal. Generally speaking, there are two types. One is written by a lawyer working for the taxpayer who uses the shelter. It is written at the close of the deal and specifies the tax treatment that person should expect to receive [i.e., it's "more likely than not" that a court will approve the shelter]. It's these letters that are the source of much of the controversy surrounding Daugerdas. The second type of opinion is written by a lawyer hired by a promoter to help build the shelter. Called a "marketing letter," it not only gives the lawyer's view about the validity of the shelter, it is also used as a sales tool with potential buyers.

Until a few years ago, it was unheard of for the same lawyer to write both a marketing letter and a final opinion letter. Ethics experts contacted by The American Lawyer say the practice improperly conflates the role of "lawyer" with that of "promoter."

Daugerdas made a lot of money at Altheimer, but his work made the firm's leaders nervous. So when he began agitating for more, Altheimer didn't fight hard to keep him. "He was entitled to a lot more than he got," says one former partner. "But, to their credit, firm management had qualms about his practice."

In 1998, according to Jenkens chairman William Durbin, Jr., Daugerdas and some other Altheimer lawyers read an article in The National Law Journal that billed Jenkens as the fastest-growing firm in the country. They called the firm, and a few months later Jenkens's Chicago office was born. At some point, DGI opened a Chicago office in the same building. Among the lawyers making the jump from Altheimer were Donna Zak Guerin and Erwin Mayer. Along with Daugerdas, they are the central figures in Jenkens's tax shelter practice, according to the IRS. They also declined requests for interviews.

Former Jenkens partners Stephen Fox of Dallas and Keith McGlamery of Washington, D.C., say the firm knew Daugerdas's practice was unusual, and that there were concerns about potential liabilities when he was hired. But after discussions pro and con, the firm decided to go ahead. Firm chairman Durbin confirms that Daugerdas received "special attention," but declines to offer specifics.

From the start, Daugerdas was the focal point of the Chicago office. "The office was built on his visions, his ideas," says Michael Nutter, who was an associate in the office and is now with Michael Best & Friedrich. Until last spring Daugerdas was the managing shareholder in Chicago. He has also identified himself as the head of the Structured Investment Practice and the Tax & Estate Planning Group, although a firm spokesman says he doesn't currently hold any of those positions.

Daugerdas, a resident of the fancy North Shore suburb of Wilmette, not only set the business agenda, he was also the office's most visible personality; a big, gregarious guy with strong opinions and a willingness to express them. He pushed for a commitment to pro bono work and was very active in local charities, such as the Make–A–Wish Foundation of Illinois, where he is chairman of the board. He frequented charity auctions and gave purchases to associates, recalls Nutter, who once received a pair of courtside seats to a Chicago Bulls basketball game.

Soon after Daugerdas got to Jenkens, according to his testimony, he started selling a shelter he called COBRA. [Slight variations on the same shelter go by different names. DGI, which claimed it had invented the shelter, called it Option Partnership Strategy. According to the IRS, they're both similar to a discredited transaction it calls "son of BOSS," which in turn is a variation on Bond and Option Sales Strategy.

COBRA was a team effort. Members included accountants Ernst & Young, L.L.P.; KPMG L.L.P.; and BDO Seidman, LLP, according to the IRS. On board to handle the necessary currency options was Deutsche Bank Securities Inc. These firms weren't clients of Daugerdas, they were copromoters, according to E&Y partner Robert Coplan. E&Y has been named as a defendant in each of the suits brought against Jenkens. In an unrelated action, that firm recently entered into a $15 million settlement with the IRS after an investigation of its tax shelter work.

The division of labor was clear, according to E&Y's Coplan: Daugerdas was responsible for creating the shelter, and he took lead responsibility for putting each one together. The accountants were salespeople. Daugerdas had been selling the shelter before E&Y got involved, according to Coplan. And each time one was sold, Jenkens created the necessary entities and filed the paperwork, according to Coplan and people who bought the shelters. The division of labor was also reflected in the fees—3 percent of the promised business loss for Daugerdas, 1.5 percent to the accounting firm.

COBRA was a hit. The shelter is designed to offset capital gains, and many people were getting big ones, thanks to the tech explosion and the late–1990s stock market bubble. The accounting firms were perfectly situated to identify those customers.

Details are available about 11 shelters, as a result of the IRS investigation and the lawsuits filed against Jenkens and Daugerdas. Those 11 shelters were supposed to produce business losses totaling $173.8 million. To get those deductions, the buyers, all of whom say they never met or even spoke to Daugerdas or any other Jenkens lawyer, paid him a total of about $5 million in fees.

Those numbers represent a small fraction of Daugerdas's tax shelter business. Between 1999 and 2002 Daugerdas handled at least 600 shelters, according to an audit Jenkens conducted of its files pursuant to an IRS summons, and the IRS says it has "reason to believe" he handled 100 more on top of that. Those shelters generated hundreds of millions in fees and billions of dollars in tax savings, according to sources at the IRS, which is currently questioning the legitimacy of those savings.

David Deary of Shore Deary in Dallas and Blair Fensterstock of New York have, between them, spoken with about 70 of these COBRA buyers. Both have suits pending against Daugerdas and Jenkens. The lawyers tell remarkably similar stories when talking about people who bought the shelter:

Buyers were required to use Jenkens, the firm that created the shelter. E&Y insisted that each sign a confidentiality agreement not to disclose the marketing materials to anyone except "internal personnel," a group that didn't include independent tax lawyers. For Jenkens, people who wanted to use COBRA were a captive market.

They each received a nearly identical opinion letter. Like most shelters, once the COBRA structure was completed and a template opinion letter was written, setting up each additional shelter required little new work.

They each paid a fee to Jenkens equal to 3 percent of the promised tax loss.

Henry Camferdam is a typical plaintiff. Now represented by Deary in a suit against Daugerdas and Jenkens, Camferdam is an Indiana businessman who sold his software company in August 1999 for about $70 million. A few months later, he got a call from an E&Y representative who told him that the firm had a plan that would make that capital gain disappear. Camferdam agreed to a meeting at the E&Y offices in Indianapolis.

When he arrived, the first order of business was the execution of very restrictive confidentiality agreements. "They acted like it had been cooked up in an underground lab in North Dakota. They were paranoid about somebody else finding out about it," says Camferdam. He was then shown an hour-long PowerPoint presentation extolling the virtues of a COBRA, and he was given a form to fill out, asking how much of a loss he wanted to create.

Camferdam says he was initially skeptical. But E&Y had been acting as auditors and consultants for him and his company for years. "I knew them, I trusted them," he says. A key selling point, says Camferdam, was that the shelter was backed up by an opinion from a leading law firm-Jenkens. The E&Y representatives told him that the opinion would be "insurance" in the case of an audit, meaning that he wouldn't be penalized if the IRS disallowed the shelter. Brown & Wood [now Sidley Austin Brown & Wood] would supply a second opinion "just to make sure."

Camferdam says he hadn't heard of Jenkens, but there was never a question about which law firm to use. Like most COBRA buyers, Camferdam didn't have a large legal staff or a team of tax lawyers on retainer to review the transaction. [Few lawyers could understand the mind-numbingly complex details of the transaction, anyway.] He says E&Y refused to let a tax specialist from Camferdam's regular firm, Indianapolis's Ice Miller, even look at the shelter. Nor would they let him make copies of the paperwork to take with him.

A few days after seeing the presentation, Camferdam again met with the E&Y representatives, signed all the necessary paperwork, and the deal was under way. A few weeks later, he wired slightly more than $2 million to Jenkens.

As Camferdam describes the sales pitch, what's most remarkable is what he says he was not told. He was not told that Jenkens was offering an opinion about a shelter that it had created. He was not told that the firm had entered into a cooperative business arrangement with E&Y and Deutsche Bank that depended on the sale of those shelters for its success. He says he never met or spoke with Daugerdas or any other Jenkens lawyer.

Like Camferdam, the approximately 70 people who have consulted with Deary and Fensterstock say they've never had contact with a Jenkens lawyer. That fact is proving troublesome for the firm. Last June the firm tried to use the attorney-client privilege to fend off an IRS summons served on Wachovia Corporation seeking the identity of CO-BRA users. North Carolina federal district court judge Lacy Thornburg rejected the argument, ruling that Jenkens "merely sold a package [to the plaintiffs], which contained a description of the transaction and a memorandum as to the potential tax consequences. . . . Nor is there any evidence that any individual taxpayer ever had so much as a conversation with an attorney at J&G."

Camferdam's deal was a small piece of a big problem. The amount of money tied up in tax shelters grew throughout the 1990s. In 1998 Stanford Law School professor Joseph Bankman created a bit of a stir when Forbes quoted his estimate that the government was losing $10 billion in revenue per year to illegal shelters. In 2000 Treasury secretary Lawrence Summers said that "abusive tax shelters are the most serious problem in the U.S. tax system."

Around that time the IRS began receiving anonymous, plain-paper packages. Inside were promoters' marketing materials, sent to tip off the agency about illegal shelters. An investigation began in 2000, but because it depended on voluntary cooperation from promoters, it didn't get far, according to Roland Barral, counsel to the IRS and the man in charge of the promoter side of the investigation.

In 2002 the IRS gave up on the idea of voluntary cooperation and began serving summonses. More than 100 promoters have been served, including five to eight law firms, Jenkens among them. The IRS wants to know, first, whether the firms are complying with rules that required promoters to register their shelters and keep lists of their clients. Second, the agency tried to find their clients and collect taxes that may have been wrongfully avoided.

E&Y was one of the firms that got a summons. In June 2002 the firm wrote to Camferdam, telling him that the IRS wanted the names of everyone who bought a COBRA. Did he have any objection? He did, as a matter of fact, and told the firm not to release the information. But a few months later, E&Y did so, anyway.

That December, Camferdam was notified that the IRS would be auditing his 1999 return, an audit that is ongoing today. He says the IRS told him that it's likely to declare the shelter invalid, and he may be liable for back taxes, interest, and possibly penalties.

[Camferdam may find some company down at the IRS office. Promoters often use their own shelters. A firm spokesman would only say that Daugerdas declined to discuss his personal tax returns.]

Also in December 2002, Camferdam sued Daugerdas, Jenkens, E&Y, Sidley, and others, seeking reimbursement of the $6 million in fees he had paid for a COBRA. Like the other plaintiffs, he has alleged conspiracy and racketeering by Jenkens, and is seeking treble damages under the Racketeer Influenced and Corrupt Organizations Act. He's also seeking reimbursement of any penalties and interest he is forced to pay the IRS.

Camferdam might find some sympathy from an influential source-Senator Chuck Grassley [R–Iowa], the Senate's leading proponent of tax shelter reform. In an interview about the state of enforcement, Grassley notes that the current regime leans heavily on taxpayers and lets promoters off too easily. Although he didn't refer specifically to Camferdam or Jenkens, Grassley did complain about "lawyers who sell illegitimate shelters, then go running off into the woods like snake-oil salesmen, leaving the taxpayer holding the bag."

Camferdam's suit, like virtually all pending tax shelter litigation, turns on whether the shelters had "economic substance" and a "nontax business purpose." Those judicial doctrines are designed to make sure that, even if a shelter manages to tiptoe through the tax code's technicalities, it won't be considered legitimate if it's just a ploy concocted to avoid taxes.

Most shelters today involve purely financial instruments. In that context, "economic substance" is synonymous with risk-a deal has economic substance if there's a chance that the taxpayer could lose his or her investment. Camferdam alleges that the result of his investment in currency options was preordained, hence there was no risk, hence the shelter was no good.

That issue may ultimately be decided in a courtroom. In the meantime, The American Lawyer asked professors Bankman and Pollack to review a summary of the transaction prepared by Jenkens. Both believe that the shelter lacks economic substance, as does the IRS and a chorus of former Treasury officials and private practitioners. Camferdam couldn't lose money, they say, because his investment was almost perfectly hedged. And although E&Y promised him that he could make money on the deal, that possibility was so remote-especially given the fees he paid Daugerdas and the other promoters-that no reasonable person would have done it if not for the tax benefits. In truth, say the experts, a COBRA is about nothing but saving taxes.

The professors say this conclusion was inescapable after the IRS issued notices in 1999 and 2000 holding that the shelters known as BOSS and son of BOSS were "abusive" and invalid. Referring to COBRA, Bankman says, "This is just son of BOSS in slightly different dress."

Nonetheless, one of the plaintiffs says he received a positive opinion about a COBRA in 2001. It's not clear when, if ever, Daugerdas stopped issuing those opinions. In February 2003 B. John Williams, Jr., chief counsel for the IRS, told a tax panel of the Chicago Bar Association that he was "very concerned" that promoters were still selling son of BOSS-style shelters. Williams, who has since left the IRS and joined Shearman & Sterling in Washington, D.C., could not be reached for comment.

Jenkens's Durbin refuses to address the pending litigation over COBRA, saying only that it's "without merit." He adds that the tax code is ambiguous, and that the IRS is punishing people who took advantage of that ambiguity.

In addition to attacking the shelter itself, Camferdam alleges that Daugerdas's relationships with the accounting firms and Deutsche Bank compromised his independence, leaving him unfit to render an opinion about it.

The American Lawyer asked experts on legal ethics to review materials prepared by the IRS and the private litigants. On the basis of those documents, they concluded that Daugerdas violated the applicable rules of professional ethics. Given his participation in the joint marketing effort with the accounting firms and investment bank, they say, Daugerdas had a stake in the business of making and selling shelters. As described, that stake conflicts with the duty he owed to clients who sought his advice on whether the shelter worked. "Pretty outrageous stuff," says Tanina Rostain of New York Law School, who has written on ethics and tax shelters.

At a minimum, say the experts, a great deal of disclosure was called for. "If Jenkens created the shelter, it's opining on its own work," says Mary Daly, an ethics professor at Fordham Law School. "If you were the client, wouldn't you want to know that?"

Tax lawyers divide the world in two-the tax bar and the tax shelter bar-as if the twain have never met. "Two cultures," is how Andrew Berg of Debevoise & Plimpton describes it. In that view, one culture gives considered, individualized advice about corporate transactions; the other writes what Barral of the IRS describes as "cookie-cutter" opinions that are nothing more than thinly veiled contrivances to justify a promoter's questionable schemes.

The line, however, isn't as bright as the old guard would like to think. Daugerdas may have been an early adopter, but an increasing number of lawyers have followed him. The secrecy surrounding the tax shelter business makes it hard to know who and how many. Shelters are marketed to a select group. The first step in virtually any shelter deal is the execution of very restrictive confidentiality agreements. And no one involved in a shelter transaction-seller, buyer, or lawyer-has any interest in having the IRS find out about it.

When asked for an estimate, one old-line tax lawyer says about 20 firms in The Am Law 100 are doing tax shelter work. Stanford's

Bankman puts the number closer to ten: "But you have to remember, the line has moved for everybody. Every firm, even if it hasn't stepped over the line as it's drawn today, is still doing work it wouldn't have done ten years ago."

Barral says while relatively few law firms are actually promoting shelters, many more firms are in bed with shelter promoters, and the work has compromised their independence. Grassley refers to it as "collusion" among law firms, accounting firms, and investment banks.

In those rare instances when secrecy is lifted, a surprising roster of lawyers can be found. DGI, for example, worked with Sidley and Proskauer, as well as Jenkens. A privilege log produced by the company shows communications with Davis Polk & Wardwell; Skadden, Arps, Slate, Meagher & Flom; Piper Marbury [now Piper Rudnick]; and Mintz, Levin, Cohn, Ferris, Glovsky and Popeo. Davis Polk did not return phone calls seeking comment, and the other firms denied that they ever represented DGI.

An early example of the changed nature of the tax bar was the controversy surrounding a shelter used by Colgate–Palmolive Company in 1989. As with COBRA, big promoters were involved-Price Waterhouse [now PriceWaterhousCoopers] and Merrill Lynch & Co., Inc. Big law firms were also involved-King & Spalding wrote a marketing letter for Merrill [author Mark Kuller, now with McKee Nelson, calls it a "technical memorandum"]; Skadden defended Colgate when the IRS challenged the shelter. And, as with COBRA, the IRS found that the shelter lacked economic substance. Eleven of the shelters were sold. Some of the taxpayers settled with the IRS, some are still in court.

Why are major firms doing the tax work they used to turn away? Some responsibility lies with clients. In the 1990s corporate financial officers became more comfortable with aggressive tax positions. They balanced the upside-savings that could run into the hundreds of millions of dollars-against minimal risk of an audit. Taking an aggressive position became known as "playing the audit lottery," and the financial types knew the odds were stacked in their favor. They also knew that if they lost, there was little chance they'd be penalized. All they had to show was a "reasonable basis" for their position, and an opinion letter from a major law firm was almost always enough to meet that burden. Opinion letters became known as "get out of jail free cards."

So they began to ask their lawyers to take more and more aggressive positions. The requests came with an implicit threat: "If you won't do it, I'll go down the street to someone who will." The number of firms willing to say no dwindled. And as the sale of shelters moved downmarket, to smaller companies and individuals, the pool of potential customers increased. Lawyers moved to meet the demand.

The move was made easier by the lack of deterrence from the IRS. As the number of shelters grew in the 1990s, the IRS budget was being cut, its enforcement powers curtailed. Since 1992, the number of IRS tax investigations has fallen by 37 percent, and the number of prosecutions for tax crimes is down by more than half, according to a study by Syracuse University's Transactional Records Access Clearinghouse.

But there's little doubt that money is the biggest motivator. Tax shelter work is "premium billing" par excellence. Compared with traditional by-the-hour work, astonishing amounts of money can be made. Not only can fees reach into the millions for each deal, but once a shelter is put together and a template opinion letter is written, additional deals can be done as fast as they can be sold. When asked to estimate the fees Daugerdas brought in during his time at Jenkens, people at the IRS, Justice Department, and elsewhere put the number in the hundreds of millions of dollars. And the work isn't hard to find. Lots of tax lawyers get lots of calls from shelter promoters, asking them to work on their deals.

Where all that money went is another question. In 1999 Daugerdas was a new lawyer, in a new office, far from Jenkens's Dallas headquarters. Former partners McGlamery and Fox say that Daugerdas negotiated a special compensation arrangement when he joined the firm, and his revenue was tracked separately. According to them, as few as three people may have been privy to the details.

Some of those fees were paid to Treasurex, an Illinois corporation of which Daugerdas is the president. At his deposition, Daugerdas said that nobody at either Altheimer or Jenkens knew about Treasurex, agreeing with the statement that "it just wasn't something that needed to be disclosed."

The DGI case file contains five invoices with Treasurex letterhead mailed to DGI in 1998 and 1999 totaling $2.67 million. Those charges relate to a deal that took place about the time Daugerdas moved from Altheimer to Jenkens. When asked about it, he testified: "Treasurex acted as an intermediary and arranged a buyer and a seller to come together and was compensated for that. As part of the same transaction, one law firm I was associated with did corporate legal work on behalf of the purchaser, and another law firm I was associated with rendered a tax opinion to the purchaser."

But during the DGI v. Daugerdas case, Haber made the following declaration: "At no time did Diversified receive services from Treasurex. At no time did Daugerdas suggest to Diversified that he was performing services on behalf of Treasurex."

Durbin would say only that Treasurex is an "internal matter" and that the issue has been resolved.

Durbin also defends Jenkens's financial performance. According to the *2003 Am Law 100* survey, the firm lost 69 lawyers, and revenue dropped 5 percent from the previous year. Since those numbers were compiled, dozens more lawyers have left. Those who were interviewed say their move wasn't a result of the controversy surrounding Daugerdas, but a barrage of headlines, civil suits, and government investigations isn't much of a selling point, to either clients or potential laterals.

Durbin says the reduction in firm size is part of a strategic plan, and the firm's revenue and profits are exceeding projections.

Those declining numbers, along with the litigation and government investigations, have prompted much speculation about the survival of the firm among former Jenkens partners and observers of the Dallas legal scene. That speculation is likely to intensify when word gets out that its malpractice insurance carrier, Executive Risk Indemnity Inc., brought a declaratory judgment action against the firm in federal court in Illinois at the end of September. The insurer claims that it's not liable for any damages arising from the firm's tax shelter work. It argues, first, that the policy has already been drawn on for the DGI v. Daugerdas settlement and, second, the policy doesn't cover the firm if it has to reimburse its customers for tax penalties and interest.

Attention has focused on the tax shelter controversy ever since Enron Corp.'s aggressive schemes were made public early this year, and the controversy surrounding Jenkens has helped keep it in the spotlight. It has also highlighted the weakness of the enforcement regime, and the need for reform.

Existing enforcement procedures are so toothless, they must look like an invitation to a lawyer considering tax shelter work. Current rules require a promoter to register certain transactions and keep lists of customers who use them. But if a promoter has a "good faith" belief that his or her shelter is different, the disclosure rules don't apply. For a tax shelter lawyer, drawing those fine distinctions is as easy as finding a free drink in Vegas.

Efforts at improvement have repeatedly run into what Senator Grassley calls "powerful K Street interests"-lobbyists for the law firms, accounting firms, and investment banks. Bills to strengthen the economic substance doctrine, to increase disclosure, and to stiffen penalties have all died on Capitol Hill. For years Grassley has been pushing a measure that would crack down on illegal shelters, but it was rejected as recently as last spring.

Some progress, however, may be in the works. Grassley's bill has once again cleared the Senate Finance Committee [for the fourth time] and will soon be considered by the full Senate. Grassley says action is expected by March. And new IRS rules tightening the disclosure requirements have taken effect.

But the new rules may cause problems of their own. Hundreds of thousands of new disclosures will pour in, according to Stanford's Bankman. For the IRS, the abusive shelters will be needles in a haystack, he says. In addition, lawyers and other promoters are likely to shift their efforts to devising shelters that avoid the disclosure requirements. Bankman compares them to a bunch of underground chemists trying to design a new recipe for Ecstasy that skirts existing drug laws.

Of course, audits, penalties, and fines aren't the front line in the fight against tax cheating. In our system, people and corporations are expected to pay their fair share of taxes voluntarily, and most do. But the belief that it's the right thing to do is eroding, according to a recent IRS study. Daugerdas's practices certainly aren't helping matters.

Joseph Bankman, THE NEW MARKET IN CORPORATE TAX SHELTERS

83 TAX NOTES 1775 (1999)

* * *

B. THE ROLE OF TAX LAWYERS

1. Writing the tax shelter opinion. The most prominent role for tax lawyers acting in capacity as lawyers (rather than promoters) in the shelter industry is as opinion writers. Most shelters come with more-likely-than-not opinions. * * * [T]he opinion provides insurance against tax penalties; more speculatively, it also provides psychological support to executives and their advisors.

The opinion writing process is by all accounts odd, in large part because the law is so ill-defined. Virtually all tax shelters comply with the literal language of a relevant (and perhaps the most relevant) statute, administrative ruling, or case. The issue presented is whether the result is so at odds with economic reality and/or tax theory that it ought to be trumped by a competing legal rule. Frequently, the only competing legal rule is one encapsuled, perhaps, in common law doctrines such as business purpose, substance over form, step transaction, and sham transaction. As discussed more fully in part III of this report, these doctrines are by their nature analytically elusive (some might describe these doctrines in harsher terms) and are interpreted only in a few cases.

Adding to the difficult of opinion writing is the required translation of legal analysis into the language of the more-likely-than-not opinion. "Deciding whether a close question is 51 percent likely to go to a client or 49 percent can drive you crazy," says one practitioner.

A common issue opinion writers wrestle with is how much weight to give the recent decisions in ACM and ASA Investerings. ACM is the first case to decide the fate of one of the more recent variety of corporate tax shelters, and one of only a few cases in the past decade to discuss common law doctrines such as business purpose and economic substance. "You can guess how David Laro (the Tax Court judge in the case) will rule on the deal, but what about the next judge?" asks one practitioner.

Given the ambiguity in law and standards, it is not surprising that tax lawyers vary dramatically in their estimation of a given shelter. One might imagine that the variance would primarily be a function of the lawyer's implicit interpretive theory: a literalist would find the opinions easy to write; a lawyer who believes in a more purposive interpretation of legal rules would find the task harder. In fact, attorneys with similar interpretive theories and therefore similar levels of "tax aggressiveness" often have different estimations of the possibility of success of a given tax shelter. Attorneys from one firm may refuse to give a more likely than not opinion, while attorneys from another firm find the same opinion easy to write. The firm that gives the opinion may generally have the reputation of a more aggressive firm, but not always. The legal ambiguity and hence variance in perception of a given shelter, together with the different attitudes lawyers bring to interpretive issues make it easy for a shelter promoter to obtain a more likely than not opinion: all the promoter has to do is to "shop" the opinion to more than one firm. Eventually, the promoter will find a lawyer who will give the opinion.

Some lawyers offer a more cynical explanation for the ease by which promoters get more likely than not opinions on the more aggressive tax shelters. Opinion writing is interesting work, and promoters generally don't question how many hours it takes to get a desired opinion. For lawyers under billing pressure, tax shelter work can be a godsend. "You break your back for a firm, month after month," one partner reports, "and next month the firm is going to ask 'What have you done for me lately?' Then a Merrill Lynch comes to you—maybe for the first time—to ask you for an opinion. You know that if you give the client what it wants, there is more work in the future. It's a real temptation."

More commonly, lawyers report that the pressure to "deliver" an opinion comes from the dynamics of the promotion and opinion writing process. A lawyer might first write an opinion on a tax product that assumes some genuine nontax business purpose or investment. The product, with opinion, is then pitched to clients who like the tax results but wish to reduce the real investment and business risk. The promoter wishes to accommodate the client, and the lawyer is asked to modify the opinion to bless the revised deal. At this point, the lawyer is aware that a number of parties have already sunk considerable time and expense into considering the deal, that the business purpose doctrine is analytically elusive and that there is no sharp dividing line between sufficient and insufficient business purpose. The temptation to at least compromise, giving the revised opinion if the parties will accept some business risk (but less risk than in the deal as originally envisioned) is strong.

Most lawyers take opinion writing seriously, in part because of ethical norms, and in part because an opinion is a semi-public document, shown to other lawyers, and reflects on its authors competence and good faith. For the most part, however, lawyers who write opinions do not worry about legal liability. In theory, a company that purchased a shelter that was successfully challenged in court could sue an opinion writer. In practice, a necessary condition of a suit—judicial rejection of a shelter—is itself rarity. Moreover, companies that purchase shelters do not rely on promoter-supplied opinions for legal analysis but instead use in-house and outside advisors to evaluate the merits of a shelter position. As noted earlier, the primary function of a tax opinion is to insulate companies that purchase the shelter from penalties. An opinion succeeds in this function by its very existence. The tacit understanding of the nature of an opinion makes it less likely that an opinion writer will be sued, and makes reliance in a suit harder to establish. Finally, the "more likely than not" standard and the confused nature of the tax law work against any potential liability. "It really comes down to a malpractice standard, notes one tax lawyer. You opine the likelihood of success is 51–49 but it turns out that maybe it really was 45–55. Is being 6 points off malpractice?"

However profitable it is to write opinions, and whatever the temptation that profit provides, there is more to be made in developing and promoting the shelters. Investment bankers who develop and market tax shelters can earn seven-figure incomes; promoters in tax shelter boutiques can do at least as well. Those in the industry who merely evaluate or write opinions on shelters are acutely aware of the pay differential. Many have at some time or another toyed with the idea of moving from advisor to promoter. The tax shelter market induces the same feeling of envy for tax lawyers that the mergers and acquisitions market induces for corporate lawyers.

Promoters evince skepticism as to the ability of the average tax lawyer, however talented, to step into their shoes, and justify their compensation in market terms. "We tell our outside counsel that we take the entrepreneurial risk and reap the entrepreneurial rewards," says one promoter.

2. Lawyers as outside advisors. The tax shelter market has more purchasers than sellers; consequently, most tax lawyers hear of and participate in the market only when a company they advise is considering a shelter investment. Quite obviously, tax lawyers acting as outside advisers differ widely in their attitudes and behavior toward shelters. Some may enjoy the light a tax shelter sheds on a hitherto unexplored flaw in the tax system, or on more general structural flaws in the system, enjoy dealing with promoters, regard the government or current tax law with disdain or contempt, and for these and other reasons think positively of shelters. In general, however, tax lawyers in their capacity as outside counsel seem to regard shelters negatively. Any attribution of this negative attitude is necessarily speculative. However, anecdotal evidence suggests the following factors drive the tax lawyers to their position.

First, lawyers acting as outside advisor regard many if not most shelters as deceptively marketed and (somewhat less common) as "bad deals." The deceptive marketing complaint is most often addressed to the "more likely than not" opinions that accompany the shelters, and/or the statements of the promoter as to the legal support for the shelter position. As noted above, "opinion shopping" can produce a more likely than not opinion for a shelter most tax lawyers believe would have only a slight chance of surviving IRS challenge. An irresistible practice of outside counsel in the industry (to the extent permitted by confidentiality concerns) is to share stories and engage in a sort of one-upmanship as to who has seen the most unrealistic legal opinion.

Many tax lawyers also believe that the economic consequences of a shelter are often overstated. A particular shelter, for example, may require a client to sink funds into an equipment lease transaction. The lease transaction will invariably be described as one that produces a reasonable economic return. Lawyers often doubt this assumption. (Since one of the requirements for meeting a successful challenge is that the shelter have a prospect of producing some economic return, skepticism over economic consequences is related to skepticism over legal consequences.)

Some (though by no means all) outside counsel are upset at the ethics of tax shelter work. One lawyer states, "You feel like asking some of these promoters whether their momma knows what they spend their time doing." Outside counsel that would not put the matter in such stark terms may still be upset at the lack of social utility of shelters. Many tax lawyers would prefer to structure "real deals" than do shelter work.

Other factors influence some but perhaps not most tax lawyers. Some tax lawyers, for example, are bothered by what might best be described as the aesthetic concerns. Tax shelters get the "wrong" answers—that is, answers that are inconsistent with a coherent vision (that some feel exists, or should exist) of the tax law. In addition, the opinions that accompany the shelters are inelegant and poorly written, as well as exaggerated. Other tax lawyers are bothered by the fact that shelters—even shelters they are asked to advise on—represent competition for their tax-advice services from accounting firms and investment banks. "When I started out, I was the tax adviser," reports a former tax lawyer (turned investment banker). Then I realized my clients were getting their advice from the investment banks and accounting firms and shelter promoters. I thought, I've lost my role." Still other lawyers may feel most comfortable, consciously or unconsciously, giving conservative advice; helping clients avoid risk rather than profit form an attractive risk. Finally, the great salaries of shelter promoters, noted above, may add a soupon of envy to the outside adviser's attitude.

Most of the above attitudes are kept from clients and do not directly affect behavior. While tax lawyers are quick to criticize overly optimistic opinion letters or promoter representations, they are extremely careful to keep their attitudes regarding ethics to themselves. (It goes without saying that feelings of competition and the like go unmentioned.)

But the negative position of tax lawyers, combined with a sense of the appropriate role of an outside adviser, does introduce a somewhat negative spin in client presentations, which in turn acts as a partial brake on tax shelter purchases. For example, on a dollars and cents basis, a shelter that comes with a more likely than not opinion letter is virtually certain to be a good investment for a client. Lawyers in their advisory roles may be reluctant to point this out. Lawyers as advisors are unlikely to bring a particular tax shelter, or shelters in general, to a client's attention.

Of the above factors driving outside counsel attitudes, this reluctance may be most closely tied to ethical norms: a shelter may be attractive at the core only because of the audit lottery, and most advisers will shy away from being too explicit about any cost benefit analysis that hinges on audit odds. In part, too, the reluctance reflects an unwillingness to be seen pushing any particular product. The reluctance may also be pegged to uncertainty as to the client's response to the ethics of the investment. The reluctance may finally reflect lack of initiative or time of many counsel, who are more comfortable responding to articulated needs (e.g., structuring a particular deal) than coming up with unrelated tax suggestions.

It is interesting to compare this response, however, to the more enthusiastic response outside counsel might have to a very aggressive use of a particular case or ruling in a transaction on which they are already working. And whatever the causes of the current outside counsel response to shelters, the response is certain to be much different if and to the extent that firms develop and market tax products.

PROBLEM

You are Associate General Counsel responsible for tax matters in ABC Corporation. ABC operates in a fiercely competitive market with low barriers to entry and low profit margins. The company has just sold a subsidiary for a gain of $150 million, and faces the prospect of paying taxes on that amount. Clark & Simmons (C&S), ABC's outside auditor, is aware of the sale and approaches the CFO of your company about a transaction it has devised to shield most of the $150 million gain from taxation. C&S has sold this tax shelter to other companies, including some of ABC's competitors.

The transaction would work as follows. XYZ Corporation, a foreign company not subject to U.S. taxes, owns securities consisting of options to purchase interests in certain investment funds. XYZ's "basis" in the securities–the amount it paid for them—is $160 million, but the securities currently are worth only $10 million because of the poor performance of the investment funds. XYZ would contribute the securities to ABC in exchange for $11 million in nonvoting stock in ABC. Because XYZ is contributing the securities in exchange for ABC stock, the tax code allows ABC to succeed to XYZ's $160 million basis in the securities. When ABC sells the securities in the market the following day for $10 million, it therefore can claim a $150 million loss on the sale. This loss can be used to offset the $150 million gain from ABC's sale of its subsidiary. In sum, ABC would be paying $11 million for $10 million worth of securities and $150 million worth of losses, or a net of $1 million for $150 million in losses.

The CFO has asked for your recommendation whether ABC should avail itself of the C&S tax shelter. Among the facts that may be relevant in your deliberations are the following:

    1.   The law firm of Shield & Shelter has issued an opinion that the tax treatment of the transaction more likely than not will be upheld if challenged by the IRS.

    2.   You are skeptical that the tax treatment more likely than not would be upheld for this transaction. You would put the odds of prevailing if challenged at about one in three.

3. Based on past experience, the likelihood that the transaction would attract notice by the IRS and trigger an audit is about 20%. C&S recommends that ABC engage in several other securities transactions around the same time so that the purchase from XYZ does not stand out. If ABC does so, the odds that the transaction would attract notice and trigger an audit is about 10%.

4. The company's current effective tax rate is 35%, which means that it ordinarily would owe $52.5 million in tax on its gain from the sale of the subsidiary. If the company is found to have substantially understated its tax liability and is assessed a 20% penalty, it will owe an additional $10.5 million.

5. Clark & Simmons will charge $10 million for arranging the transaction. It says that it and Shield and Shelter will defend the tax treatment if it is challenged, with a cap on combined fees of $1 million.

6. C&S is required to register the tax shelter with the IRS and to maintain a list of investors in it.

Please lay out your analysis and recommendations for the CFO. Focus on: (1) whether the company is likely to be able to avoid an accuracy-related penalty under IRS tax shelter rules if the shelter is disallowed, (2) whether the company should purchase the shelter even if it may be liable for such a penalty, and (3) whether any considerations beyond the penalty are relevant to your analysis.

7. Suppose that you are head of the tax practice at Shelter & Shield. Your firm has long sought to do legal work for C&S, but for the most part has been unsuccessful. Before beginning to market the tax shelter, C&S approaches you with a request for an opinion from your firm to provide to prospective purchasers of the shelter. How do you respond to this request? Focus on: (1) how the IRS tax shelter opinion rules affect your decision and (2) any other considerations that you think are relevant.

Chapter 23

REGULATORY COMPLIANCE

Ensuring corporate compliance with applicable regulatory provisions is a crucial undertaking. Violation of the law can expose the company to civil sanctions by regulatory agencies, both derivative and direct actions by shareholders against the company and its managers, and criminal prosecution. In addition, there may be collateral consequences such as being barred from the receipt of government contracts, which can deal a serious blow to companies such as defense contractors, health care organizations, and others.

Companies nowadays try to avoid, or at least minimize, these risks by establishing regulatory compliance programs. This is a process in which lawyers typically are heavily involved. These programs are designed to educate employees about relevant legal regulations, monitor conduct to ensure that it complies with these provisions, provide mechanisms for detecting and reporting legal violations, and determining appropriate responses to illegal behavior. A company with a program that is deemed effective in promoting compliance may receive lenient treatment under the Federal Organizational Sentencing Guidelines if it is prosecuted for the criminal activity of any of its employees.

The next four chapters are designed as a sequence. This chapter deals with regulatory compliance. Chapter 24 then discusses the conduct of an internal investigation when there is suspicion that an officer or other employee has engaged in illegal behavior notwithstanding the company's compliance program. Chapter 25, on Criminal Prosecution, reflects escalation of the stakes. It deals with questions of ethics and judgment that are relevant to prosecutors in deliberating on possible criminal charges against a corporation and/or its managers. The existence of an effective compliance program is one factor that a prosecutor may take into account in considering whether to bring criminal charges against the company. Finally, Chapter 26, on Criminal Defense, addresses the situation in which the government has decided that it will prosecute the company and/or its managers. It examines the ethical issues that arise in defending against such charges.

OVERVIEW OF THE CHAPTER

The chapter begins with a discussion of the Federal Organizational Sentencing Guidelines, which have been one of the main incentives for the establishment of corporate regulatory compliance programs. While no longer mandatory, those Guidelines are likely to remain influential as a factor in sentencing decisions. Note the features of a program that are relevant to determining whether it is effective, and thus can serve as the basis for leniency in sentencing for corporate criminal activity. The excerpt from the *Caremark* case that follows reflects a second impetus for creation of a compliance program: the perceived possibility of director liability for failure to do so. *Caremark* indicates that directors may have an obligation to institute a corporate information gathering and reporting system to alert them to legal violations even in the absence of any indication that such violations have occurred. Caremark has generated considerable commentary and some anxiety. Make sure that you read the opinion closely so that you are clear about precisely what it does and does not say.

The excerpt from Williams, Kastner, & Gibbs fleshes offers an example of what provisions a compliance program might include in order to prevent illegal activity by employees of companies that operate in the health care industry. As such, it fleshes out the more general characteristics of an effective program as described in the Sentencing Guidelines. Note the variety of laws applicable to health care companies and hospitals, some of which are general and some of which are specific to health care. Ask yourself how effective the provisions that are set forth are likely to be in preventing violation of these laws.

Finally, the SEC action in the *Gutfreund* case deals with a scandal that brought down a powerful Wall Street chief executive and tarnished the investment bank that he headed. Note that the problem was not the original violation of Treasury regulations by the Salomon Brothers trader, but the failure of top management to respond adequately to it. The case involves in part application of regulations applicable to the company as a broker-dealer, and thus is an example of the significance of industry-specific legal obligations. It also is more generally instructive, however, as a case study of culpable inaction by corporate management.

Make sure that you are clear about both the nature of the original violation and the sequence of events after top officials learned of it. Focus in particular on Feuerstein, Salomon's general counsel. What should he have done differently? Why do you think he acted as he did? What is the basis for the SEC's determination that he was a "supervisor" who had an obligation to respond to the misbehavior? Do you agree with the SEC's reasoning?

Finally, the first problem requires you to draw mainly upon the Organizational Sentencing Guidelines and the example from the health care industry to determine what would be an effective compliance program for your corporate client. The second problem asks you to consider how you should proceed once a compliance program reveals that a violation has occurred.

MODEL RULES: 1.2, 1.6, 1.13, 2.1

A. FEDERAL ORGANIZATIONAL SENTENCING GUIDELINES

In a large organization with thousands of employees, monitoring regulatory compliance can be difficult and challenging. Since 1991, the Federal Organizational Sentencing Guidelines have provided an incentive for companies to establish regulatory compliance programs. While those Guidelines are no longer mandatory after a Supreme Court decision in early 2005, judges are likely to continue to consult and take them into account in sentencing. The Guidelines provide that if an organization has in place an "effective compliance and ethics program," it is eligible for mitigation of punishment for a criminal offense attributable to the organization. Such mitigation includes both reductions in fines avoidance of ongoing judicial oversight of the company as a result of being placed on probation. If an organization of 50 or more employees at the time of sentencing "does not have an effective program to prevent and detect violations of the law," the court *must* impose probation.

The Guidelines state that an effective compliance and ethics program requires that an organization: (1) exercise due diligence to prevent and detect criminal conduct and (2) promote an organizational culture that encourages ethical conduct and commitment to compliance with the law. This requires at a minimum the following features:

1) Standards and procedures to prevent and detect criminal conduct;

2) The organization's governing authority is knowledgeable about the program and exercises reasonable oversight regarding its implementation and effectiveness;

3) Specific high-level personnel are assigned overall responsibility for the program;

4) Specific individuals have day-to-day operational responsibility for the program and report periodically to high-level personnel on its effectiveness. Such individuals must be given adequate resources, authority, and direct access to high-level personnel in order to enable them to carry out these obligations;

5) The organization conducts effective training programs designed to inform its managers, employees, and agents of the requirements of the program;

6) The organization takes reasonable steps to ensure compliance with the program, including monitoring and auditing to detect criminal conduct;

7) The organization periodically evaluates the effectiveness of the program;

8) The organization has and publicizes a system whereby employees and agents may report or seek guidance about potential or actual criminal conduct without fear of retaliation;

9) The program is promoted through appropriate incentives to comply with it, and the institution of discipline for engaging in criminal conduct and for failing to take reasonable steps to prevent or detect it;

10) The organization takes reasonable steps to respond to criminal conduct and to prevent further similar conduct, including modifying as necessary the program;

11) The organization periodically assesses the risk of criminal conduct and takes appropriate steps to revise the features of its program to reduce the risk of such conduct.

The Guidelines establish a rebuttable presumption that the organization did not have in place an effective compliance and ethics program if a person with "substantial authority" within the organization "participated in, condoned, or was willfully ignorant of" the criminal offense. Such persons are defined as those who "within the scope of their authority exercise a substantial measure of discretion in acting on behalf of an organization."

B. LEGAL COMPLIANCE PROGRAMS

IN RE CAREMARK INTERNATIONAL INC. DERIVATIVE LITIGATION

698 A.2d 959 (Del. Ch. 1996)

ALLEN, CHANCELLOR

Pending is a motion pursuant to Chancery Rule 23.1 to approve as fair and reasonable a proposed settlement of a consolidated derivative action on behalf of Caremark International, Inc. ("Caremark"). The suit involves claims that the members of Caremark's board of directors (the "Board") breached their fiduciary duty of care to Caremark in connection with alleged violations by Caremark employees of federal and state laws and regulations applicable to health care providers. As a result of the alleged violations, Caremark was subject to an extensive four year investigation by the United States Department of Health and Human Services and the Department of Justice. In 1994 Caremark was charged in an indictment with multiple felonies. It thereafter entered into a number of agreements with the Department of Justice and others. Those agreements included a plea agreement in which Caremark pleaded guilty to a single felony of mail fraud and agreed to pay civil and criminal fines. Subsequently, Caremark agreed to make reimbursements to various private and public parties. In all, the payments that Caremark has been required to make total approximately $250 million.

This suit was filed in 1994, purporting to seek on behalf of the company recovery of these losses from the individual defendants who constitute the board of directors of Caremark. The parties now propose that it be settled and, after notice to Caremark shareholders, a hearing on the fairness of the proposal was held on August 16, 1996. . . .

A motion of this type requires the court to assess the strengths and weaknesses of the claims asserted in light of the discovery record and to evaluate the fairness and adequacy of the consideration offered to the corporation in exchange for the release of all claims made or arising from the facts alleged. The ultimate issue then is whether the proposed settlement appears to be fair to the corporation and its absent shareholders. * * *

I. Background

For these purposes I regard the following facts, suggested by the discovery record, as material. Caremark, a Delaware corporation with its headquarters in Northbrook, Illinois, was created in November 1992 when it was spun-off from Baxter International, Inc. ("Baxter") and became a publicly held company listed on the New York Stock Exchange. The business practices that created the problem pre-dated the spin-off. During the relevant period Caremark was involved in two main health care business segments, providing patient care and managed care services. As part of its patient care business, which accounted for the majority of Caremark's revenues, Caremark provided alternative site health care services, including infusion therapy, growth hormone therapy, HIV/AIDS-related treatments and hemophilia therapy. Caremark's managed care services included prescription drug programs and the operation of multi-specialty group practices.

A.　Events Prior to the Government Investigation

A substantial part of the revenues generated by Caremark's businesses is derived from third party payments, insurers, and Medicare and Medicaid reimbursement programs. The latter source of payments are subject to the terms of the Anti–Referral Payments Law ("ARPL") which prohibits health care providers from paying any form of remuneration to induce the referral of Medicare or Medicaid patients. From its inception, Caremark entered into a variety of agreements with hospitals, physicians, and health care providers for advice and services, as well as distribution agreements with drug manufacturers, as had its predecessor prior to 1992. Specifically, Caremark did have a practice of entering into contracts for services (*e.g.*, consultation agreements and research grants) with physicians at least some of whom prescribed or recommended services or products that Caremark provided to Medicare recipients and other patients. Such contracts were not prohibited by the ARPL but they obviously raised a possibility of unlawful "kickbacks." * * *

B.　Government Investigation and Related Litigation

In August 1991, the HHS Office of the Inspector General ("OIG") initiated an investigation of Caremark's predecessor. Caremark's predecessor was served with a subpoena requiring the production of documents, including contracts between Caremark's predecessor and physicians (Quality Service Agreements ("QSAs")). Under the QSAs, Caremark's predecessor appears to have paid physicians fees for monitoring patients under Caremark's predecessor's care, including Medicare and Medicaid recipients. Sometimes apparently those monitoring patients were referring physicians, which raised ARPL concerns. In March 1992, the Department of Justice ("DOJ") joined the OIG investigation and separate investigations were commenced by several additional federal and state agencies

C. Caremark's Response to the Investigation

* * * Throughout the period of the government investigations, Caremark had an internal audit plan designed to assure compliance with business and ethics policies. In addition, Caremark employed Price Waterhouse as its outside auditor. On February 8, 1993, the Ethics Committee of Caremark's Board received and reviewed an outside auditors report by Price Waterhouse which concluded that there were no material weaknesses in Caremark's control structure. n3 Despite the positive findings of Price Waterhouse, however, on April 20, 1993, the Audit & Ethics Committee adopted a new internal audit charter requiring a comprehensive review of compliance policies and the compilation of an employee ethics handbook concerning such policies.

The Board appears to have been informed about this project and other efforts to assure compliance with the law. * * *

D. Federal Indictments Against Caremark and Officers

On August 4, 1994, a federal grand jury in Minnesota issued a 47 page indictment charging Caremark, two of its officers (not the firm's chief officer), an individual who had been a sales employee of Genentech, Inc., and David R. Brown, a physician practicing in Minneapolis, with violating the ARPL over a lengthy period. According to the indictment, over $1.1 million had been paid to Brown to induce him to distribute Protropin, a human growth hormone drug marketed by Caremark. The substantial payments involved started, according to the allegations of the indictment, in 1986 and continued through 1993. Some payments were "in the guise of research grants", and others were "consulting agreements." The indictment charged, for example, that Dr. Brown performed virtually none of the consulting functions described in his 1991 agreement with Caremark, but was nevertheless neither required to return the money he had received nor precluded from receiving future funding from Caremark. In addition the indictment charged that Brown received from Caremark payments of staff and office expenses, including telephone answering services and fax rental expenses. * * *

Subsequently, five stockholder derivative actions were filed in this court and consolidated into this action. The original complaint, dated August 5, 1994, alleged, in relevant part, that Caremark's directors breached their duty of care by failing adequately to supervise the conduct of Caremark employees, or institute corrective measures, thereby exposing Caremark to fines and liability. * * *

E. Settlement Negotiations

* * * Caremark began settlement negotiations with federal and state government entities in May 1995. In return for a guilty plea to a single count of mail fraud by the corporation, the payment of a criminal fine, the payment of substantial civil damages, and cooperation with further federal investigations on matters relating to the OIG investigation, the government entities agreed to negotiate a settlement that would permit Caremark to continue participating in Medicare and Medicaid programs. * * *

Settlement negotiations between the parties in this action commenced in May 1995 as well, based upon a letter proposal of the plaintiffs, dated May 16, 1995. These negotiations resulted in a memorandum of understanding ("MOU"), dated June 7, 1995, and the execution of the Stipulation and Agreement of Compromise and Settlement on June 28, 1995, which is the subject of this action. n13 The MOU, approved by the Board on June 15, 1995, required the Board to adopt several resolutions, discussed below, and to create a new compliance committee. The Compliance and Ethics Committee has been reporting to the Board in accord with its newly specified duties. * * *

F. The Proposed Settlement of this Litigation

In relevant part the terms upon which these claims asserted are proposed to be settled are as follows:

1. That Caremark, undertakes that it and its employees, and agents not pay any form of compensation to a third party in exchange for the referral of a patient to a Caremark facility or service or the prescription of drugs marketed or distributed by Caremark for which reimbursement may be sought from Medicare, Medicaid, or a similar state reimbursement program;

2. That Caremark, undertakes for itself and its employees, and agents not to pay to or split fees with physicians, joint ventures, any business combination in which Caremark maintains a direct financial interest, or other health care providers with whom Caremark has a financial relationship or interest, in exchange for the referral of a patient to a Caremark facility or service or the prescription of drugs marketed or distributed by Caremark for which reimbursement may be sought from Medicare, Medicaid, or a similar state reimbursement program;

3. That the full Board shall discuss all relevant material changes in government health care regulations and their effect on relationships with health care providers on a semi-annual basis;

4. That Caremark's officers will remove all personnel from health care facilities or hospitals who have been placed in such facility for the purpose of providing remuneration in exchange for a

patient referral for which reimbursement may be sought from Medicare, Medicaid, or a similar state reimbursement program;

5. That every patient will receive written disclosure of any financial relationship between Caremark and the health care professional or provider who made the referral;

6. That the Board will establish a Compliance and Ethics Committee of four directors, two of which will be non-management directors, to meet at least four times a year to effectuate these policies and monitor business segment compliance with the ARPL, and to report to the Board semi-annually concerning compliance by each business segment; and

7. That corporate officers responsible for business segments shall serve as compliance officers who must report semi-annually to the Compliance and Ethics Committee and, with the assistance of outside counsel, review existing contracts and get advanced approval of any new contract forms.

II. LEGAL PRINCIPLES

A. *Principles Governing Settlements of Derivative Claims*

As noted at the outset of this opinion, this Court is now required to exercise an informed judgment whether the proposed settlement is fair and reasonable in the light of all relevant factors. On an application of this kind, this Court attempts to protect the best interests of the corporation and its absent shareholders all of whom will be barred from future litigation on these claims if the settlement is approved. The parties proposing the settlement bear the burden of persuading the court that it is in fact fair and reasonable.

B. *Directors' Duties To Monitor Corporate Operations*

The complaint charges the director defendants with breach of their duty of attention or care in connection with the on-going operation of the corporation's business. The claim is that the directors allowed a situation to develop and continue which exposed the corporation to enormous legal liability and that in so doing they violated a duty to be active monitors of corporate performance * * *

1. Potential liability for directoral decisions: Director liability for a breach of the duty to exercise appropriate attention may, in theory, arise in two distinct contexts. First, such liability may be said to follow *from a board decision* that results in a loss because that decision was ill advised or "negligent". Second, liability to the corporation for a loss may be said to arise from an *unconsidered failure of the board to act* in circumstances in which due attention would, arguably, have prevented the loss. The first class of cases will typically be subject to review under the director-protective business judgment rule, assuming the decision made was the product of a *process* that *was either* deliberately considered in good faith or was otherwise rational. . . . Where a director *in fact exercises a good*

faith effort to be informed and to exercise appropriate judgment, he or she should be deemed to satisfy fully the duty of attention * * *

2. Liability for failure to monitor: The second class of cases in which director liability for inattention is theoretically possible entail circumstances in which a loss eventuates not from a decision but, from unconsidered inaction. Most of the decisions that a corporation, acting through its human agents, makes are, of course, not the subject of director attention. Legally, the board itself will be required only to authorize the most significant corporate acts or transactions: mergers, changes in capital structure, fundamental changes in business, appointment and compensation of the CEO, etc. As the facts of this case graphically demonstrate, ordinary business decisions that are made by officers and employees deeper in the interior of the organization can, however, vitally affect the welfare of the corporation and its ability to achieve its various strategic and financial goals. If this case did not prove the point itself, recent business history would. Recall for example the displacement of senior management and much of the board of Salomon, Inc.; the replacement of senior management of Kidder, Peabody following the discovery of large trading losses resulting from phantom trades by a highly compensated trader; or the extensive financial loss and reputational injury suffered by Prudential Insurance as a result its junior officers misrepresentations in connection with the distribution of limited partnership interests. Financial and organizational disasters such as these raise the question, what is the board's responsibility with respect to the organization and monitoring of the enterprise to assure that the corporation functions within the law to achieve its purposes?

Modernly this question has been given special importance by an increasing tendency, especially under federal law, to employ the criminal law to assure corporate compliance with external legal requirements, including environmental, financial, employee and product safety as well as assorted other health and safety regulations. In 1991, pursuant to the Sentencing Reform Act of 1984, the United States Sentencing Commission adopted Organizational Sentencing Guidelines which impact importantly on the prospective effect these criminal sanctions might have on business corporations. The Guidelines set forth a uniform sentencing structure for organizations to be sentenced for violation of federal criminal statutes and provide for penalties that equal or often massively exceed those previously imposed on corporations. The Guidelines offer powerful incentives for corporations today to have in place compliance programs to detect violations of law, promptly to report violations to appropriate public officials when discovered, and to take prompt, voluntary remedial efforts.

In 1963, the Delaware Supreme Court in *Graham v. Allis–Chalmers Mfg. Co.,* addressed the question of potential liability of board members for losses experienced by the corporation as a result of the corporation having violated the anti-trust laws of the United States. There was no claim in that case that the directors knew about the behavior of subordinate employees of the corporation that had resulted in the liability. Rather, as in this case, the claim asserted was that the directors *ought to have known* of it and if they had known they would have been under a duty to bring the corporation into compliance with the law and thus save the corporation from the loss. The Delaware Supreme Court concluded that, under the facts as they appeared, there was no basis to find that the directors had breached a duty to be informed of the ongoing operations of the firm. In notably colorful terms, the court stated that "absent cause for suspicion there is no duty upon the directors to install and operate a corporate system of espionage to ferret out wrongdoing which they have no reason to suspect exists." The Court found that there were no grounds for suspicion in that case and, thus, concluded that the directors were blamelessly unaware of the conduct leading to the corporate liability.

How does one generalize this holding today? Can it be said today that, absent some ground giving rise to suspicion of violation of law, that corporate directors have no duty to assure that a corporate information gathering and reporting systems exists which represents a good faith attempt to provide senior management and the Board with information respecting material acts, events or conditions within the corporation, including compliance with applicable statutes and regulations? I certainly do not believe so. I doubt that such a broad generalization of the *Graham* holding would have been accepted by the Supreme Court in 1963. The case can be more narrowly interpreted as standing for the proposition that, absent grounds to suspect deception, neither corporate boards nor senior officers can be charged with wrongdoing simply for assuming the integrity of employees and the honesty of their dealings on the company's behalf.

A broader interpretation of *Graham v. Allis Chalmers*—that it means that a corporate board has no responsibility to assure that appropriate information and reporting systems are established by management—would not, in any event, be accepted by the Delaware Supreme Court in 1996, in my opinion. In stating the basis for this view, I start with the recognition that in recent years the Delaware Supreme Court has made it clear—especially in its jurisprudence concerning takeovers, from *Smith v. Van Gorkom* through *QVC v. Paramount Communications*—the seriousness with which the corporation law views the role of the corporate board. Secondly, I note the elementary fact that relevant and timely *information* is an essential predicate for satisfaction of the board's supervisory and monitoring role under Section 141 of the Delaware General Corporation Law. Thirdly, I note the potential impact of the federal organizational sentencing guidelines on any business organization. Any rational person attempting in good faith to meet an organizational governance responsibility would be bound to take into account this development and the enhanced penalties and the opportunities for reduced sanctions that it offers.

In light of these developments, it would, in my opinion, be a mistake to conclude that our Supreme Court's statement in *Graham* concerning "espionage" means that corporate boards may satisfy their obligation to be reasonably informed concerning the corporation, without assuring themselves that information and reporting systems exist in the organization that are reasonably designed to provide to senior management and to the board itself timely, accurate information sufficient to allow management and the board, each within its scope, to reach informed judgments concerning both the corporation's compliance with law and its business performance.

Obviously the level of detail that is appropriate for such an information system is a question of business judgment. And obviously too, no rationally designed information and reporting system will remove the possibility that the corporation will violate laws or regulations, or that senior officers or directors may nevertheless sometimes be misled or otherwise fail reasonably to detect acts material to the corporation's compliance with the law. But it is important that the board exercise a good faith judgment that the corporation's information and reporting system is in concept and design adequate to assure the board that appropriate information will come to its attention in a timely manner as a matter of ordinary operations, so that it may satisfy its responsibility.

Thus, I am of the view that a director's obligation includes a duty to attempt in good faith to assure that a corporate information and reporting system, which the board concludes is adequate, exists, and that failure to do so under some circumstances may, in theory at least, render a director liable for losses caused by non-compliance with applicable legal standards. I now turn to an analysis of the claims asserted with this concept of the directors duty of care, as a duty satisfied in part by assurance of adequate information flows to the board, in mind.

III. ANALYSIS OF THIRD AMENDED COMPLAINT AND SETTLEMENT

A. *The Claims*

On balance, after reviewing an extensive record in this case, including numerous documents and three depositions, I conclude that this settlement is fair and reasonable. * * *

1. Knowing violation for statute: Concerning the possibility that the Caremark directors knew of violations of law, none of the documents submitted for review, nor any of the deposition transcripts appear to provide evidence of it. * * *

2. Failure to monitor: Since it does appears that the Board was to some extent unaware of the activities that led to liability, I turn to a consideration of the other potential avenue to director liability that the pleadings take: director inattention or "negligence". Generally where a claim of directorial liability for corporate loss is predicated upon ignorance of liability creating activities within the corporation, as in *Graham* or in this case, in my opinion only a sustained or systematic failure of the board to exercise oversight—such as an utter failure to attempt to assure a reasonable information and reporting system exits—will establish the lack of good faith that is a necessary condition to liability. Such a

test of liability—lack of good faith as evidenced by sustained or systematic failure of a director to exercise reasonable oversight—is quite high. But, a demanding test of liability in the oversight context is probably beneficial to corporate shareholders as a class, as it is in the board decision context, since it makes board service by qualified persons more likely, while continuing to act as a stimulus to *good faith performance of duty* by such directors.

Here the record supplies essentially no evidence that the director defendants were guilty of a sustained failure to exercise their oversight function. To the contrary, insofar as I am able to tell on this record, the corporation's information systems appear to have represented a good faith attempt to be informed of relevant facts. If the directors did not know the specifics of the activities that lead to the indictments, they cannot be faulted.

The liability that eventuated in this instance was huge. But the fact that it resulted from a violation of criminal law alone does not create a breach of fiduciary duty by directors. The record at this stage does not support the conclusion that the defendants either lacked good faith in the exercise of their monitoring responsibilities or conscientiously permitted a known violation of law by the corporation to occur. The claims asserted against them must be viewed at this stage as extremely weak.

B.   The Consideration for Release of Claim

The proposed settlement provides very modest benefits. Under the settlement agreement, plaintiffs have been given express assurances that Caremark will have a more centralized, active supervisory system in the future. Specifically, the settlement mandates duties to be performed by the newly named Compliance and Ethics Committee on an ongoing basis and increases the responsibility for monitoring compliance with the law at the lower levels of management. In adopting the resolutions required under the settlement, Care mark has further clarified its policies concerning the prohibition of providing remuneration for referrals. These appear to be positive consequences of the settlement of the claims brought by the plaintiffs, even if they are not highly significant. Nonetheless, given the weakness of the plaintiffs' claims the proposed settlement appears to be an adequate, reasonable, and beneficial outcome for all of the parties. Thus, the proposed settlement will be approved.

* * *

Note

The features of a corporate compliance program will vary depending on the kinds of regulations to which a company is subject and the risks that are typical of the industry in which it operates. Thus, for instance, a chemical company will need, among other things, a program designed to ensure compliance with environmental laws, while a computer software firm will want to have measures to prevent theft of intellectual property. In addition, both companies should have in place programs to ensure compliance with more generally applicable laws, such as those prohibiting employment discrimination.

Rather than discuss compliance programs on a general level, the most useful way to gain a sense of what they involve is to examine compliance measures established to address the kinds of misconduct that are specific to companies in a particular industry. The following excerpt discusses some of the problems that can arise in the health care industry and suggests how a compliance program should be structured to minimize their occurrence.

Williams, Kastner & Gibbs PLLC, CORPORATE ACCOUNTABILITY AND COMPLIANCE IN HEALTH CARE—WILL HEALTH CARE BE THE NEXT ENRON?

MONDAQ BUSINESS BRIEFING, August 9, 2004

INTRODUCTION

In recent years, the government has devoted substantial resources to respond to health care fraud and abuse. The increase in governmental prosecutorial activity in the health care industry can be traced to two significant trends. Concern over waste, fraud and abuse has become more prevalent, prompting the Department of Justice to identify the eradication of health care fraud as its number two priority, right behind violent crime. In addition, employees are becoming increasing aware of the economic benefits of becoming a "whistleblower." The qui tam provisions of the False Claims Act entitles individuals who bring violations of the Act to the attention of the government to a significant percentage of any recovery.

The Office of Inspector General ("OIG") of the Department of Health and Human Services ("HHS") is encouraging the health care community to prevent and reduce fraud and abuse in federal health care programs by providing voluntary guidance on effectively implementing and monitoring a compliance program. In the last several years, the OIG has issued compliance program guidance directed at several segments of the health care industry. The best way for a health care organization to mitigate risk is to implement an effective compliance program. . . .

I. Overview of Statutory Schemes Regulating Fraud and Abuse

A. Introduction.

There are a multitude of Federal statutory schemes aimed at preventing waste, fraud and abuse in the health care industry. The prime areas of governmental concern include:

1. Additional costs to Federal health care programs;

2. Quality of care;

3. Access to care;

4. Patients' freedom of choice;

5. Competition; and

6. Health care providers abuse of professional judgment.

A common thread running through each of the federal statutes is that the bottom line is always about money-wrongful receipt of state or Federal funds, the presentment of a false claim for reimbursement, or improper relationships with referral sources (resulting in kickbacks/discounts). Many of the statutory schemes impose criminal as well as stiff civil penalties.

The government's enforcement efforts have resulted in a multi-billion dollar recovery. In 2003 alone, over $2 billion was recovered. In fiscal year 2003, whistle-blowers recovered over $319 million in rewards under the Act. Between 1995 and 2003, over $8 billion has been recovered. Six billion dollars has been recovered as a result of whistle-blower cases. * * *

The following is a sample of the DOJ's largest recoveries during 2003 for fraud and abuse in health care:

—$641 million from HCA Inc. (formerly known as Columbia/HCA and HCA—The Healthcare Company) for cost report fraud, the payment of kickbacks to physicians and overbilling Medicare for HCA's wound care centers. This settlement concluded litigation in numerous qui tam lawsuits as well as separate investigations initiated by the government. Along with an earlier civil settlement and criminal guilty plea reached in 2000, as well as a related administrative settlement with HHS, HCA has paid the United States $1.7 billion, with whistleblowers receiving a combined share of $154 million-by far, setting record recoveries both by the United States and whistle-blowers.

—$382 million from Abbott Laboratories and its Ross Products Division. Abbott's conduct resulted in the first combined civil settlement and criminal conviction arising from "Operation Headwaters," an undercover investigation by the Federal Bureau of Investigation, the U.S. Postal Inspection Service and the Office of the Inspector General for HHS, in which federal agents created a fictitious medical supplier known as Southern Medical Distributors. During its operation, various manufacturers, including Ross, offered kickbacks to undercover agents to purchase the manufacturers' products and then advised them how to fraudulently bill the government for those items. In addition to federal Medicare and Medicaid recoveries, the states recovered $18 million in state Medicaid funds in connection with the federal government's claims and an additional $14.5 million on claims the states pursued alone. Abbott subsidiary C G Nutritionals also paid $200 million in criminal fines. * * *

The net result of the increased focus on health care fraud and abuse is that organizations must understand the strucures and regulations and how to avoid or, at a minimum, mitigate risks. [The excerpt below describes some of the bases for corporate liability in the health care industry].

B.   False Claims Act.

The Civil False Claims Act, 31 U.S.C. Para. Para. 3729–3733, ("FCA") a Civil War-era statute, prohibits the knowing submission of false or fraudulent claims to the federal government. The FCA was not originally enacted to address health care fraud. Nonetheless, FCA is the legal basis most often used to bring a case against a health care provider for the submission of false claims to a Federal health care program. Numerous other fraud statutes are tied to the FCA.

The FCA prohibits knowingly presenting (or causing to be presented) to the Federal Government a false or fraudulent claim for payment or approval. Additionally, it prohibits knowingly making or using (or causing to be made or used) a false record or statement to get a false or fraudulent claim paid or approved by the Federal Government or its agents, like a carrier, other claims processor, or State Medicaid program. * * *

False Claim—A "false claim" is a claim for payment for services or supplies that were not provided specifically as presented or for which the provider is otherwise not entitled to payment. Examples of false claims for services or supplies that were not provided specifically as presented include, but are not limited to:

—a claim for a service or supply that was never provided;

—a claim indicating the service was provided for some diagnosis code other than the true diagnosis code in order to obtain reimbursement for the service (which would not be covered if the true diagnosis code were submitted);

—a claim indicating a higher level of service than was actually provided;

—a claim for a service that the provider knows is not reasonable and necessary; or

—a claim for services provided by an unlicensed individual;

retaliation to be "any action harmful to any person" who reported "any federal offense."

* * *

D.   Criminal Penalties for Acts Involving Federal Health Care Programs under 42 U.S.C. Para. Para. 1320a–7b.

1.   False Statement and Representations

It is a crime to knowingly and willfully:

(1) make, or cause to be made, false statements or representations in applying for benefits or payments under all Federal health care programs;

(2) make, or cause to be made, any false statement or representation for use in determining rights to such benefit or payment;

(3) conceal any event affecting an individual's initial or continued right to receive a benefit or payment with the intent to fraudulently receive the benefit or payment either in an amount or quantity greater than that which is due or authorized;

(4) convert a benefit or payment to a use other than for the use and benefit of the person for whom it was intended;

(5) present, or cause to be presented, a claim for a physician's service when the service was not furnished by a licensed physician;

(6) for a fee, counsel an individual to dispose of assets in order to become eligible for medical assistance under a State health program, if disposing of the assets results in the imposition of an ineligibility period for the individual.

2. Anti–Kickback Statute

It is a crime to knowingly and willfully solicit, receive, offer, or pay remuneration of any kind (e.g., money, goods, services):

—for the referral of an individual to another for the purpose of supplying items or services that are covered by a Federal health care program; or

—for purchasing, leasing, ordering, or arranging for any good, facility, service, or item that is covered by a Federal health care program.

The statute prohibits the solicitation or receipt of any remuneration for a prohibited purpose, which places both parties to a prohibited "kickback" transaction at equal risk. The statute covers transactions involving any of the federal health programs. . . .

Examples

1. Dr. X accepted payments to sign Certificates of Medical Necessity for durable medical equipment for patients she never examined.

2. Home Health Agency disguises referral fees as salaries by paying referring physician Dr. X for services Dr. X never rendered to the Medicare beneficiaries or by paying Dr. X a sum in excess of fair market value for the services he rendered to the Medicare beneficiaries. . . .

F. Health Care Fraud under 18 U.S.C. Para. 1347.

Under 18 U.S.C. Para. 1347, it is a crime to knowingly and willfully execute (or attempt to execute) a scheme to defraud any health care benefit program, or to obtain money or property from a health care benefit program through false representations. Note that this law applies not only to Federal health care programs, but to most other types of health care benefit programs as well. * * *

Examples

1. Dr. X, a chiropractor, intentionally billed Medicare for physical therapy and chiropractic treatments that he never actually rendered for the purpose of fraudulently obtaining Medicare payments.

2.   Dr. X, a psychiatrist, billed Medicare, Medicaid, TRICARE, and private insurers for psychiatric services that were provided by his nurses rather than himself. * * *

H.   False Statements Relating to Health Care Matters under 18 U.S.C. Para. 1035.

Under 18 U.S.C. Para. 1035, it is a crime to knowingly and willfully falsify or conceal a material fact, or make any materially false statement or use any materially false writing or document in connection with the delivery of or payment for health care benefits, items or services. Note that this law applies not only to Federal health care programs, but to most other types of health care benefit programs as well.

The penalty may include the imposition of a fine, imprisonment of up to 5 years, or both.

Example

Dr. X certified on a claim form that he performed laser surgery on a Medicare beneficiary when he knew that the surgery was not actually performed on the patient. * * *

II.   Corporate Compliance in Healthcare

A.   Overview.

* * * Organizations must understand the fraud and abuse statutes, recognize activities that may run afoul of these statutes and implement effective compliance programs aimed at mitigating risk and reducing unlawful conduct.

B.   Compliance Programs: Prevention is Key

The best way to avoid encountering the adverse consequences of increased enforcement against overpayments, fraud and abuse is to prevent the potentially unlawful conduct in the first place. This means an effective compliance program. The OIG has developed and issued voluntary compliance program guidance directed at [sectors in the health care industry]. * * *

The OIG believes there are seven essential elements to an effective compliance program for any organization, whether a hospital or clinic, or a pharmaceutical manufacturer. The seven elements are modeled on the seven steps of the Federal Sentencing Guidelines. At a minimum, all compliance programs aimed at reducing health care fraud and abuse should include the following seven elements:

1.   The development and distribution of written standards of conduct, as well as written policies and procedures that promote the hospital's commitment to compliance (e.g., by including adherence to compliance as an element in evaluating managers and employees) and that address specific areas of potential fraud, such as claims development and submission processes, code naming and financial relationships with physicians and other health care professionals.

2. The designation of a chief compliance officer and other appropriate bodies, for example, a corporate compliance committee charged with the responsibility of operating and monitoring the compliance program and who report directly to the CEO and the governing body;

3. The development and implementation of regular, effective education and training programs for all affected employees;

4. The maintenance of a process, such as a hotline, to receive complaints, and the adoption of procedures to protect the anonymity of complainants and to protect whistle blowers from retaliation;

5. The development of a system to respond to allegations of improper/illegal activities and the enforcement of appropriate disciplinary action against employees who have violated internal compliance policies, applicable statutes, regulations or federal health care program requirements;

6. The use of audits and/or other evaluation techniques to monitor compliance and assist in the reduction of identified problem area;

7. The investigation and remediation of identified systemic problems and the development of policies addressing the non-employment or retention of sanctioned individuals.

C.   Compliance Programs for Hospitals.

On February 23, 1998, the OIG issued a publication on compliance program guidance for hospitals. The guidance was provided to assist hospitals in implementing compliance programs to address the prevention, detection and resolution of conduct that does not conform to federal and state law, as well as the hospital's own ethical and business policies.20 Each hospital should tailor its own compliance program to the unique risks of its organization. The OIG has identified the following risk areas that hospitals should be specifically aware of in considering written policies and procedures concerning regulatory exposure. [Some] areas of concern include the following:

1. Billing for items or services not actually rendered;

2. Providing medically unnecessary services;

3. Upcoding—The practice of using a billing code that provides a higher payment rate than the billing code that actually reflects the service furnished to the patient. * * *

7. Duplicate billing;

8. False costs reports;

9. Unbundling—The practice of submitting bills piecemeal or in fragmented fashion to maximize the reimbursement for various tests or procedures that are required to be billed together and therefore at a reduced cost * * *

13.   Hospital incentives that violate the anti-kick-back statute or other similar federal or state statute or regulation * * *

17.   Knowing failure to provide covered services or necessary care to members of a health maintenance organization * * *

Hospitals should have specific policies in place to comply with anti-kickback statutes and the * * * physician self-referral law, in particular:

1.   All of the hospital's contracts and arrangements with referral sources comply with all applicable statutes and regulations;

2.   The hospital does not submit or cause to be submitted to the Federal health care programs claims for patients who were referred to the hospital pursuant to contracts and financial arrangements that were designed to induce such referrals in violation of the anti-kickback statute, * * * physician self-referral law or similar Federal or State statute or regulation; and

3.   The hospital does not enter into financial arrangements with hospital-based physicians that are designed to provide inappropriate remuneration to the hospital in return for the physician's ability to provide services to Federal health care program beneficiaries at that hospital.

Compliance programs guide the hospital's governing body including boards of directors or trustees, chief executive officer, managers, other employees and physicians and other health care professionals in the efficient management and operation of a hospital. * * *

The health care industry operates in a heavily regulated environment with multiple risk areas. There are unique challenges for health care organization directors, especially in light of the increased oversight and focus on health care fraud and abuse. Failure to comply with federal and state statutes and regulations can be devastating for a health care organization since federal and state-sponsored health care programs play a significant role in paying for health care. In addition to criminal and civil monetary penalties, health care providers found to have defrauded federal health care programs may be excluded from participation in these programs. The crippling effect of financial penalties and exclusion from federal programs may be the death knell for some organizations. The focus on "corporate responsibility" places additional pressure on health care organization directors to implement and carry out effective corporate compliance programs. * * *

III.   Discussion on Reform and the Future

The benefits of enhanced corporate governance and compliance are more than mitigating risk and reducing fraud and abuse. Compliance programs foster a sense of investor and public trust. An effective compliance program, which outlines policies and procedures for recognizing and reducing risk of health care fraud and abuse, increases trust and confidence among employees, staff, and directors (all levels of the organization).

IN THE MATTER OF JOHN H. GUTFREUND, THOMAS W. STRAUSS, AND JOHN W. MERIWETHER, RESPONDENTS

Securities and Exchange Commission
51 S.E.C. 93 (1992)

I.

The Commission deems it appropriate and in the public interest that public administrative proceedings be and they hereby are instituted against John H. Gutfreund, Thomas W. Strauss, and John W. Meriwether pursuant to Section 15(b) of the Securities Exchange Act of 1934 ("Exchange Act").

* * *

IV.

On the basis of this Order and the Respondents' Offers of Settlement, the Commission finds the following:

A. FACTS

1. Brokerage Firm Involved

Salomon Brothers Inc ("Salomon") is a Delaware corporation with its principal place of business in New York, New York. At all times relevant to this proceeding, Salomon was registered with the Commission as a broker-dealer pursuant to Section 15(b) of the Exchange Act. Salomon has been a government-designated dealer in U.S. Treasury securities since 1939 and a primary dealer since 1961.

2. Respondents

John H. Gutfreund was the Chairman and Chief Executive Officer of Salomon from 1983 to August 18, 1991. He had worked at Salomon since 1953.

Thomas W. Strauss was the President of Salomon from 1986 to August 18, 1991. During that time period, Strauss reported to Gutfreund. He had worked at Salomon since 1963.

John W. Meriwether was a Vice Chairman of Salomon and in charge of all fixed income trading activities of the firm from 1988 to August 18, 1991. During that period, Meriwether reported to Strauss. During the same period, Paul W. Mozer, a managing director and the head of Salomon's Government Trading Desk, reported directly to Meriwether.

3. Other Individual

Donald M. Feuerstein was the chief legal officer of Salomon Inc and the head of the Legal Department of Salomon until August 23, 1991. From 1987 until August 23, 1991, the head of Salomon's Compliance Department reported directly to Feuerstein.

4. Summary

In late April of 1991, three members of the senior management of Salomon—John Gutfreund, Thomas Strauss, and John Meriwether— were informed that Paul Mozer, the head of the firm's Government Trading Desk, had submitted a false bid in the amount of $3.15 billion in an auction of U.S. Treasury securities on February 21, 1991. The executives were also informed by Donald Feuerstein, the firm's chief legal officer, that the submission of the false bid appeared to be a criminal act and, although not legally required, should be reported to the government. Gutfreund and Strauss agreed to report the matter to the Federal Reserve Bank of New York. Mozer was told that his actions might threaten his future with the firm and would be reported to the government. However, for a period of months, none of the executives took action to investigate the matter or to discipline or impose limitations on Mozer. The information was also not reported to the government for a period of months. During that same period, Mozer committed additional violations of the federal securities laws in connection with two subsequent auctions of U.S. Treasury securities.

The Respondents in this proceeding are not being charged with any participation in the underlying violations. However, as set forth herein, the Commission believes that the Respondents' supervision was deficient and that this failure was compounded by the delay in reporting the matter to the government.

5. The Submission of Two False Bids in the February 21, 1991 Five–Year U.S. Treasury Note Auction

For a considerable period of time prior to the February 21, 1991 auction, the Treasury Department had limited the maximum bid that any one bidder could submit in an auction of U.S. Treasury securities at any one yield to 35% of the auction amount. On February 21, 1991, the Treasury Department auctioned $9 billion of five-year U.S. Treasury notes. Salomon submitted a bid in its own name in that auction at a yield of 7.51% in the amount of $3.15 billion, or 35% of the auction amount.[3] In the same auction, Salomon submitted two additional $3.15 billion bids at the same yield in the names of two customers: Quantum Fund and Mercury Asset Management. Both accounts were those of established customers of Salomon, but the bids were submitted without the knowledge or authorization of either customer. Both bids were in fact false bids intended to secure additional securities for Salomon. Each of the three $3.15 billion bids was prorated 54% and Salomon received a total of $5.103 billion of the five-year notes from the auction, or 56.7% of the total amount of securities sold at that auction.

---

3. The Treasury Department adopted the 35% limitation in July of 1990 after Salomon submitted several large bids in amounts far in excess of the amount of securities to be auctioned. . . . The Salomon bids which led to the adoption of the 35% bidding limitation were submitted at the direction of Paul Mozer. Mozer was angered by the adoption of the new bidding limitation and he expressed his disagreement with the decision to adopt the new rule to officials at the Treasury Department and in several news articles. * * *

After the auction results were announced, Paul Mozer, then a managing director in charge of Salomon's Government Trading Desk, directed a clerk to write trade tickets "selling" the $1.701 billion auction allocations received in response to the two unauthorized bids to customer accounts in the names of Mercury Asset Management and Quantum Fund at the auction price. Mozer at the same time directed the clerk to write trade tickets "selling" the same amounts from those accounts back to Salomon at the same price. These fictitious transactions were intended to create the appearance that the customers had received the securities awarded in response to the unauthorized bids and had sold those securities to Salomon.

Under Salomon's internal procedures, the trade tickets written by the clerk resulted in the creation of customer confirmations reflecting the purported transactions. Mozer directed the clerk to prevent the confirmations from being sent to either Mercury Asset Management or Quantum Fund. As a result, the normal procedures of Salomon were overridden and confirmations for the fictitious transactions were not sent to either Mercury Asset Management or Quantum Fund.

6. The Submission of a bid in the February 21, 1991 Auction by S.G. Warburg and the Treasury Department's Investigation of That Bid and the Salomon False Bid

In the February 21, 1991 five-year note auction, S.G. Warburg, a primary dealer in U.S. Treasury securities, submitted a bid in its own name in the amount of $100 million at a yield of 7.51%. The 7.51% yield was the same yield used for the unauthorized $3.15 billion Mercury bid submitted by Salomon. At the time the bids were submitted, S.G. Warburg and Mercury Asset Management were subsidiaries of the same holding company, S.G. Warburg, PLC. Because the unauthorized Mercury bid was for the maximum 35% amount, the submission of the $100 million bid in the name of S.G. Warburg meant that two bids had apparently been submitted by affiliated entities in an amount in excess of 35% of the auction.

The submission of the bids was noticed by officials of the Federal Reserve Bank of New York and brought to the attention of officials of the Treasury Department in Washington, D.C. The Treasury Department officials did not know that one of the bids had been submitted by Salomon without authorization from Mercury. Because the bids were to be significantly prorated, officials of the Treasury Department decided not to reduce the amount of either bid for purposes of determining the results of the February 21, 1991 auction. The Treasury Department began to review whether the relationship between S.G. Warburg and Mercury Asset Management was such that the bids should be aggregated for determination of how the 35% limitation should be applied to those entities in future auctions.

After reviewing facts concerning the corporate relationship between Mercury Asset Management and S.G. Warburg, the Treasury Department determined to treat the two firms as a single bidder in future auctions of U.S. Treasury securities. The Treasury Department conveyed that decision in a letter dated April 17, 1991 from the Acting Assistant Commissioner for Financing to a Senior Director of Mercury Asset Management in London. The April 17 letter noted that a $3.15 billion bid had been submitted by Salomon on behalf of Mercury Asset Management in the five-year U.S. Treasury note auction on February 21, 1991, and that S.G. Warburg had also submitted a bid in the same auction, at the same yield, in the amount of $100 million. The letter noted that Mercury Asset Management and S.G. Warburg were subsidiaries of the same holding company and stated that the Treasury Department would thereafter "treat all subsidiaries of S.G. Warburg, PLC as one single entity for purposes of the 35 percent limitation rule." Copies of the letter were sent to Mozer and to a managing director of S.G. Warburg in New York.

7. Receipt of the April 17, 1991 Treasury Department Letter by Salomon

Mozer received the April 17 letter during the week of April 21, 1991. On April 24, he spoke with the Senior Director at Mercury Asset Management who had also received the April 17 letter. Mozer told the Senior Director that the submission of the $3.15 billion bid in the name of Mercury Asset Management was the result of an "error" by a clerk who had incorrectly placed the name of Mercury on the tender form. Mozer told the Senior Director that he was embarrassed by the "error," which he said had been "corrected" internally, and he asked the Senior Director to keep the matter confidential to avoid "problems." The Senior Director indicated that such a course of action would be acceptable. The Mercury Senior Director was not aware that the submission of the bid was an intentional effort by Salomon to acquire additional securities for its own account.

8. Mozer's Disclosure to John Meriwether of the Submission of One False Bid

Mozer then went to the office of John Meriwether, his immediate supervisor, and handed him the April 17 letter. When Meriwether was finished reading the letter, Mozer told him that the Mercury Asset Management bid referred to in the letter was in fact a bid for Salomon and had not been authorized by Mercury. After expressing shock at Mozer's conduct, Meriwether told him that his behavior was career-threatening, and he asked Mozer why he had submitted the bid. Mozer told Meriwether that the Government Trading Desk had needed a substantial amount of the notes, that there was also demand from the Government Arbitrage Desk for the notes, and that he had submitted the false bid to satisfy those demands.

Meriwether then asked Mozer if he had ever engaged in that type of conduct before or since. Mozer responded that he had not. Meriwether told Mozer that he would have to take the matter immediately to Thomas Strauss. Mozer then told Meriwether of his conversation with the Mercury Senior Director in which he had told that individual that the bid was an "error" and had asked him to keep the matter confidential. Meriwether listened to Mozer's description of the conversation, but did not respond. He then gave the letter back to Mozer and Mozer left the office.

9. Discussions Among Senior Management

Meriwether then called Thomas Strauss. Strauss was not in, but he returned Meriwether's call later that day. Meriwether told Strauss that Mozer had informed him that he had submitted an unauthorized customer bid in an auction of U.S. Treasury securities. Strauss indicated that they should meet to discuss the matter first thing the next morning.

Meriwether met with Strauss at 9:15 a.m. the following morning, April 25, in Strauss' office. Prior to the meeting, Strauss had arranged for Donald Feuerstein, the firm's chief legal officer, to attend, and Feuerstein was in Strauss' office when Meriwether arrived. Meriwether began the meeting by describing his conversation with Mozer the previous day. He told Strauss and Feuerstein that Mozer had come to him and had informed him that he had submitted an unauthorized customer bid in an auction of U.S. Treasury securities. He said that he had informed Mozer that his conduct was career-threatening and that Mozer had denied that he had ever before or since engaged in that type of conduct. He indicated that Mozer had received a letter from the Treasury Department inquiring about the bid and that Mozer had shown him a copy of that letter. Meriwether also reported that Mozer had said that he had submitted the bid to satisfy demand for the securities from the Government Trading Desk and from Salomon's Government Arbitrage Desk. Finally, he told Strauss and Feuerstein that Mozer had informed him that he had contacted an individual at Mercury Asset Management who had also received the letter from the Treasury Department. Meriwether indicated that Mozer had told that individual that the submission of the bid was an error, and had attempted to persuade him not to inform the government of that fact.

When Meriwether was finished, Feuerstein said that Mozer's conduct was a serious matter and should be reported to the government. Feuerstein asked to see a copy of the April 17 letter. Meriwether returned to the trading floor and retrieved the letter from Mozer. He then returned to Strauss' office and provided the letter to Feuerstein. After some discussion about the letter, Strauss said he wanted to discuss the matter with Gutfreund, who was then out of town, and the meeting ended.

A meeting was then held early the following week, on either Monday, April 29 or Tuesday, April 30, with Gutfreund. The meeting was attended by Meriwether, Feuerstein, Strauss and Gutfreund and was held in Strauss' office. Meriwether summarized his conversation with Mozer. Meriwether also indicated that he believed that the incident was an aberration and he expressed his hope that it would not end Mozer's career at Salomon.

After Meriwether's description, Feuerstein told the group that he believed that the submission of the false bid was a criminal act. He indicated that, while there probably was not a legal duty to report the false bid, he believed that they had no choice but to report the matter to the government. The group then discussed whether the bid should be reported to the Treasury Department or to the Federal Reserve Bank of New York. The hostile relationship that had developed between Mozer and the Treasury Department over the adoption of the 35% bidding limitation in the Summer of 1990 was noted, as was the role of the Federal Reserve Bank of New York as Salomon's regulator in the area of U.S. Treasury securities, and the group concluded that the preferable approach would be to report the matter to the Federal Reserve Bank of New York. The meeting then ended.

At the conclusion of the meeting, each of the four executives apparently believed that a decision had been made that Strauss or Gutfreund would report the false bid to the government, although each had a different understanding about how the report would be handled. Meriwether stated that he believed that Strauss would make an appointment to report the matter to Gerald Corrigan, the President of the Federal Reserve Bank of New York. Feuerstein stated that he believed that Gutfreund wanted to think further about how the bid should be reported. He then spoke with Gutfreund the next morning. Although the April 17 letter had been sent from the Treasury Department, Feuerstein told Gutfreund that he believed the report should be made to the Federal Reserve Bank of New York, which could then, if it wanted, pass the information on to the Treasury Department. Strauss stated that he believed that he and Gutfreund would report the matter in a personal visit with Corrigan, although he believed that Gutfreund wanted to think further about how the matter should be handled. Gutfreund stated that he believed that a decision had been made that he and Strauss, either separately or together, would speak to Corrigan about the matter.

Aside from the discussions referred to above regarding reporting the matter to the government, there was no discussion at either meeting in late April about investigating what Mozer had done, about disciplining him, or about placing limits on his activities.[5] There was also no discussion about whether Mozer had acted alone or had been assisted by others on the Government Trading Desk, about whether false records had been created, about the involvement of the Government Arbitrage Desk, which Mozer had said had sought securities from the auction, or about what had happened with the securities obtained pursuant to the bid. Similarly, there was no discussion about whether Salomon had violated the 35% bidding limitation by also submitting a bid in its own name.

For almost three months, no action was taken to investigate Mozer's conduct in the February 21 auction. That conduct was investigated only

---

5. Sometime after the meetings in late April, Meriwether informed Mozer that a decision had been made to report the false bid to the government.

after other events prompted an internal investigation by an outside law firm, as is discussed below. During the same period, no action was taken to discipline Mozer or to place appropriate limitations on his conduct. Mozer's employment by Salomon was terminated on August 9, 1991, after an internal investigation had discovered that he had been involved in additional improper conduct.

Each of the four executives who attended the meetings in late April placed the responsibility for investigating Mozer's conduct and placing limits on his activities on someone else. Meriwether stated that he believed that, once he had taken the matter of Mozer's conduct to Strauss and Strauss had brought Feuerstein and Gutfreund into the process, he had no further responsibility to take action with respect to the false bid unless instructed to do so by one of those individuals. Meriwether stated that he also believed that, though he had the authority to recommend that action be taken to discipline Mozer or limit his activities, he had no authority to take such action unilaterally. Strauss stated that he believed that Meriwether, who was Mozer's direct supervisor, and Feuerstein, who was responsible for the legal and compliance activities of the firm, would take whatever steps were necessary or required as a result of Mozer's disclosure. Feuerstein stated that he believed that, once a report to the government was made, the government would instruct Salomon about how to investigate the matter. Gutfreund stated that he believed that the other executives would take whatever steps were necessary to properly handle the matter. According to the executives, there was no discussion among them about any action that would be taken to investigate Mozer's conduct or to place limitations on his activities.

10. Violations After Disclosure by Mozer to Management

After Mozer's disclosure of one unauthorized bid on April 24, 1991, he submitted two subsequent unauthorized bids in auctions of U.S. Treasury securities.

a. The April 25, 1991 Five–Year U.S. Treasury Note Auction

On April 25, 1991, the U.S. Treasury auctioned $9 billion of five-year U.S. Treasury notes. Salomon submitted a bid in that auction for $3 billion, just under the maximum 35% amount of $3.15 billion. Salomon also submitted a $2.5 billion bid in the name of Tudor Investment Corporation ("Tudor"). A bid of only $1.5 billion had been authorized by Tudor, however, and the tender form submitted by Salomon was thus false in the amount of $1 billion. The bid by Salomon in its own name and the unauthorized portion of the Tudor bid totalled $4 billion, or 44.4% of the auction amount. * * *

b. The May 22, 1991 Two–Year U.S. Treasury Note Auction

On May 22, 1991, the U.S. Treasury auctioned $12.255 billion of two-year U.S. Treasury notes. Salomon submitted a $2 billion bid in that auction on behalf of Tiger Management Corporation ("Tiger"). A bid of only $1.5 billion had been authorized by Tiger, and the tender form submitted by Salomon was thus false in the amount of $500 million....

With the securities received in response to its own bid, the $500 million of notes received in response to the unauthorized portion of the Tiger bid, and the extra $485 million received as a result of the failure accurately to disclose the firm's net long position, Salomon received a total of $5.185 billion of the two-year notes from the auction, or 42.3% of the auction amount.

The activities described above with respect to the April 25, 1991 and the May 22, 1991 auctions of U.S. Treasury securities violated Sections 10(b) and 17(a) of the Exchange Act and Rules 10b–5, 17a–3, and 17a–4 thereunder. There is no evidence that the respondents or Feuerstein knew of the submission of the false bids in the February 21, April 25 and May 22, 1991 auctions.

11. The Delay In Reporting the False Bid to the Government

There was no disclosure to the government of the false bid in the February 21, 1991 auction prior to August 9, 1991, when the results of the internal investigation were first made public.

In mid-May, after it had become clear to Feuerstein that the false bid had not yet been reported, Feuerstein met with Gutfreund and Strauss and urged them to proceed with disclosure as soon as possible. He was told by both that they still intended to report the matter. Feuerstein also learned from the in-house attorney who worked with the Government Trading Desk of a proposal by Mozer that Salomon finance in excess of 100% of the amount of the two-year U.S. Treasury notes auctioned on May 22, 1991. Feuerstein expressed his disapproval of the proposal to the attorney. Feuerstein believed that Mozer's support for this proposal, his submission of the unauthorized bid in the February auction, and his conduct during the Summer of 1990 which led to the adoption of the 35% bidding limitation combined to indicate that he had an "attitudinal problem." Prior to leaving for Japan on May 23, 1991, Feuerstein spoke with Strauss and conveyed these concerns to him. He also again discussed with Strauss his belief that the bid should be reported to the government as soon as possible. Feuerstein also spoke with Gutfreund in early June and again urged him to report the matter to the government.

Strauss and Gutfreund also discussed the matter of reporting the bid on several occasions during this period. On at least one occasion, Strauss also urged Gutfreund to decide how to handle the matter and to proceed with disclosure to the government. Gutfreund indicated on these occasions that he still intended to report the false bid to the government. Gutfreund stated that he believed, however, that the false bid was a minor aberration, and that the reporting of the bid was not a matter of high priority.

As noted above, in the auction on May 22, 1991 for two-year U.S. Treasury notes, Salomon and two customers bid for and received approximately 86% of the two-year notes. On May 23, reports appeared in the press concerning rumors of a possible "squeeze" in the May two-year issue. On May 30, press reports mentioned Salomon by name in connection with a rumored short squeeze in the two-year notes.

In early June, Strauss spoke by telephone with a senior official of the Treasury Department. Strauss told the official that the firm was aware of the Department's interest in the May 22, 1991 auction and was willing to discuss the matter with the Department. Following Strauss' call, Gutfreund arranged to meet with officials of the Treasury Department to discuss Salomon's role in the May 22, 1991 auction.

On June 10, 1991, Gutfreund met with an Under Secretary of the Treasury and other Treasury Department officials in Washington, D.C. During the meeting, Gutfreund told the Treasury Department officials that he believed that the firm had acted properly in connection with the May 22, 1991 auction, and he indicated that the firm would cooperate with any inquiries by the Department into the matter. While the focus of the discussion at the meeting was the May 22, 1991 auction, Gutfreund did not disclose to the Treasury Department officials that he knew that a false bid had been submitted in the February 21, 1991 five-year note auction by the head of the firm's Government Trading Desk, the same individual responsible for the firm's activities in connection with the May two-year note issue.

On June 19, Meriwether, Strauss and Gutfreund met to discuss the allegations concerning the May 22, 1991 two-year note auction. At that meeting, Strauss and Gutfreund decided that disclosure of the unauthorized customer bid in the February 21, 1991 auction should be delayed until more information could be obtained about Salomon's activities in the May two-year note auction. No decision was made about how much time should elapse before a report was made. While Gutfreund and Strauss were under the general impression that someone in the legal department was reviewing the May 22, 1991 auction, there was not any discussion about any specific efforts or inquiries that would have to be undertaken before a report could be made. There were also no efforts or inquiries underway at that time to investigate Mozer's conduct in the February 21, 1991 auction. Feuerstein was not informed of or present at the meeting and was not informed of the decision to delay the disclosure.

For the next several weeks, there was not any further consideration of reporting the unauthorized bid in the February 21, 1991 auction to the government. Some discussion about limiting Mozer's activities did occur in late June with respect to the auction for June two-year U.S. Treasury notes. On the day of the auction, Strauss and Gutfreund told Mozer that he should not bid in an aggressive or high-profile manner in the auction because of the attention which had been focused on Salomon's role in the May two-year auction.

12. The Internal Investigation

In early July, Salomon retained a law firm to conduct an internal investigation of the firm's role in the May 22, 1991 two-year note auction. On July 2, a lawyer with that law firm had received a call from the general counsel of a brokerage firm who indicated that an FBI agent and a representative from the Antitrust Division of the Department of Justice had made a request to speak with representatives of the firm about the May two-year note auction. Before agreeing to be retained by the firm, the lawyer indicated that he wished to determine whether Salomon, which was a regular client of the firm, also wanted representation in connection with the matter. The lawyer then spoke with employees of Salomon and was told that Salomon might wish to be represented in connection with the matter and that the firm should hold itself available. Prior to that time, in late June of 1991, Salomon had received inquiries from the Commission and from another government agency concerning activities in the two-year U.S. Treasury notes auctioned on May 22, 1991. Several days after the lawyer contacted Salomon, Feuerstein decided to retain the law firm and directed that it begin an internal investigation of the firm's activities in the May 22, 1991 two-year note auction.

At the time the law firm was retained, it was asked only to investigate facts concerning the May two-year notes. The law firm was not informed of the false bid submitted in the February 21, 1991 auction. On July 8, attorneys from the law firm began interviewing employees on the Government Trading Desk at Salomon. The interviews were attended by several attorneys from the law firm and by the in-house attorney working with the Government Trading Desk. Sometime during the week of July 8, the attorneys learned that one of Salomon's customers in the May two-year note auction, Tiger Management Corporation, had apparently sold $500 million of a $2 billion auction award to Salomon on the day of the auction at the auction price, and that trade tickets for the transaction did not exist.

On July 12, attorneys from the law firm interviewed Thomas Murphy, who was then the head trader on the Government Trading Desk. In connection with questions about customer authorization for the $500 million portion of the $2 billion Tiger award sold to Salomon on the day of the auction, Murphy was asked whether there had been similar types of problems in the past. Murphy said that he could not answer the question without speaking to the Salomon attorney who was present. Murphy and the attorney then left the room. When they returned, Murphy did not answer the question but continued with the interview.

When the interview was over, Feuerstein met with the attorneys from the law firm for a previously-scheduled status meeting. During that meeting, Feuerstein and the attorneys discussed the questions concerning authorization for the $500 million portion of the Tiger award. Feuerstein then informed the attorneys that Salomon had submitted an unauthorized customer bid in the February 21, 1991 five-year note auction. The attorneys and Feuerstein agreed that the scope of the internal investigation should be broadened, and a decision was made that the law firm would expand the investigation to include a review of all auctions for U.S. Treasury notes and bonds since the July 1990 adoption by the Treasury Department of a 35% bidding limitation.[8]

On the following Monday, July 15, the attorneys from the law firm began the expanded internal investigation agreed upon at the meeting. During the review that was conducted between July 15 and early August, the law firm discovered a $1 billion false bid in the December 27, 1990 auction of four-year U.S. Treasury notes, a second $3.15 billion false bid in the February 21, 1991 auction, a $1 billion false bid in the February 7, 1991 auction of thirty-year U.S. Treasury bonds, the failure to disclose the $485 million when-issued position in the May 22, 1991 auction, and questions concerning customer authorization for the bid submitted in the name of Tudor in the April 25, 1991 auction. The results of the internal investigation were reported to Feuerstein on August 6 and to other members of senior management of Salomon, including Gutfreund, Strauss, and Meriwether, on August 7.

On August 9, 1991, after consultation with and review by outside counsel, Salomon issued a press release stating that it had "uncovered irregularities and rule violations in connection with its submission of bids in certain auctions of Treasury securities." The release described several of the violations and stated that Salomon had suspended two managing directors on the Government Trading Desk and two other employees.

In telephone conversations on August 9, 1991 in which they reported on the results of the internal investigation, Gutfreund and Strauss disclosed to government officials for the first time that the firm had known of a false bid in a U.S. Treasury auction since late April of 1991. On August 14, 1991, Salomon issued a second press release which publicly disclosed for the first time that Gutfreund, Strauss and Meriwether had been "informed in late April by one of the suspended managing directors that a single unauthorized bid had been submitted in the February 1991 auction of five-year notes."

On Sunday, August 18, at a special meeting of the Board of Directors of Salomon Inc, Gutfreund and Strauss resigned their positions with Salomon and Salomon Inc, and Meriwether resigned his position with Salomon. On August 23, 1991, Feuerstein resigned his position as Chief Legal Officer of Salomon.

13. The Commission's Action

Following an intensive investigation, on May 20, 1992, the Commission filed a complaint in U.S. District Court for the Southern District of New York charging Salomon and its publicly-held parent, Salomon Inc, with numerous violations of the federal securities laws. Among other things, the complaint charged that Salomon had submitted or caused to

---

8. Feuerstein also told the lawyers that he had advised senior management that for business reasons the false bid should be reported to the government. He then asked the lawyers to research the question of Sa-lomon's legal duty to report the false bid. Several weeks later, the law firm advised Salomon that, based on the research it had conducted, it was unable to provide any conclusive answer to the question.

be submitted ten false bids in nine separate auctions for U.S. Treasury securities between August of 1989 and May of 1991. The false bids alleged in the complaint totalled $15.5 billion and resulted in the illegal acquisition by Salomon of $9.548 billion of U.S. Treasury securities. The complaint alleged that submission of the bids allowed Salomon repeatedly to circumvent the limitations imposed by the Treasury Department on the amount of securities any one person or entity may obtain from auctions of U.S. Treasury securities.

Simultaneously with the filing of the action, Salomon and Salomon Inc consented, without admitting or denying the allegations of the complaint, to the entry of a Final Judgment of Permanent Injunction and Other Relief. The Judgment required, among other things, that Salomon pay the amount of $290 million, representing a payment of $190 million to the United States Treasury as civil penalties and asset forfeitures and a payment of $100 million to establish a civil claims fund to be administered by a Fund Administrator appointed by the Court.

On May 20, 1992, the Commission also instituted and settled, pursuant to an Offer of Settlement submitted by Salomon, an administrative proceeding against the firm pursuant to Section 15(b) of the Exchange Act. In that proceeding, the Commission found that Salomon had failed, in connection with the facts described in this Order, reasonably to supervise a person subject to its supervision with a view to preventing violations of the federal securities laws.

B. FINDINGS

1. *Legal Principles*

Section 15(b)(4)(E) of the Exchange Act authorizes the Commission to impose sanctions against a broker-dealer if the firm has:

failed reasonably to supervise, with a view to preventing violations [of federal securities laws], another person who commits such a violation, if such person is subject to his supervision.

Section 15(b)(6) of the Exchange incorporates Section 15(b)(4)(E) by reference and authorizes the Commission to impose sanctions for deficient supervision on individuals associated with broker-dealers.

The principles which govern this proceeding are well-established by the Commission's cases involving failure to supervise. The Commission has long emphasized that the responsibility of broker-dealers to supervise their employees is a critical component of the federal regulatory scheme. As the Commission stated in Wedbush Securities, Inc.: "In large organizations it is especially imperative that those in authority exercise particular vigilance when indications of irregularity reach their attention."

The supervisory obligations imposed by the federal securities laws require a vigorous response even to indications of wrongdoing. Many of the Commission's cases involving a failure to supervise arise from situations where supervisors were aware only of "red flags" or "suggestions" of irregularity, rather than situations where, as here, supervisors were explicitly informed of an illegal act.

Even where the knowledge of supervisors is limited to "red flags" or "suggestions" of irregularity, they cannot discharge their supervisory obligations simply by relying on the unverified representations of employees. Instead, as the Commission has repeatedly emphasized, "[t]here must be adequate follow-up and review when a firm's own procedures detect irregularities or unusual trading activity...." Moreover, if more than one supervisor is involved in considering the actions to be taken in response to possible misconduct, there must be a clear definition of the efforts to be taken and a clear assignment of those responsibilities to specific individuals within the firm.[19]

2. The Failure to Supervise

As described above, in late April of 1991 three supervisors of Paul Mozer—John Meriwether, Thomas Strauss, and John Gutfreund—learned that Mozer had submitted a false bid in the amount of $3.15 billion in an auction of U.S. Treasury securities. Those supervisors learned that Mozer had said that the bid had been submitted to obtain additional securities for another trading area of the firm. They also learned that Mozer had contacted an employee of the customer whose name was used on the bid and falsely told that individual that the bid was an error. The supervisors also learned that the bid had been the subject of a letter from the Treasury Department to the customer and that Mozer had attempted to persuade the customer not to inform the Treasury Department that the bid had not been authorized. The supervisors were also informed by Salomon's chief legal officer that the submission of the false bid appeared to be a criminal act.

The information learned by the supervisors indicated that a high level employee of the firm with significant trading discretion had engaged in extremely serious misconduct. As the cases described above make clear, this information required, at a minimum, that the supervisors take action to investigate what had occurred and whether there had been other instances of unreported misconduct. While they could look to counsel for guidance, they had an affirmative obligation to undertake an appropriate inquiry. If they were unable to conduct the inquiry themselves or believed it was more appropriate that the inquiry be conducted by others, they were required to take prompt action to ensure that others in fact undertook those efforts. Such an inquiry could have been conducted by the legal or compliance departments of the firm, outside counsel, or others who had the ability to investigate the matter adequately. The supervisors were also required, pending the outcome of such an investigation, to increase supervision of Mozer and to place appropriate limitations on his activities.

19. Supervisors who know of wrongdoing cannot escape liability for failure to supervise simply because they have failed to delegate or assign responsibility to take appropriate action.

The failure to recognize the need to take action to limit the activities of Mozer in light of his admitted misconduct is particularly troubling because Gutfreund and Strauss did place limitations on Mozer's conduct in connection with the June two-year U.S. Treasury note auction at a time when they thought the firm had not engaged in misconduct, but press reports had raised questions about the firm's activities. Although they had previously been informed that a serious violation had in fact been committed by Mozer, they failed for over three months to take any action to place limitations on his activities to deal with that misconduct.

The need to take prompt action was all the more critical in view of the fact that the potential unlawful conduct had taken place in the market for U.S. Treasury securities. The integrity of that market is of vital importance to the capital markets of the United States, as well as to capital markets worldwide, and Salomon occupied a privileged role as a government-designated primary dealer. The failure of the supervisors to take vigorous action to address known misconduct by the head of the firm's Government Trading Desk caused unnecessary risks to the integrity of this important market.

To discharge their obligations, the supervisors should at least have taken steps to ensure that someone within the firm questioned other employees on the Government Trading Desk, such as the desk's clerk or the other managing director on the Desk. Since the supervisors were informed that Mozer had said that he submitted the false bid to obtain additional securities for another trading desk of the firm, they should also have specifically investigated any involvement of that area of the firm in the matter. The supervisors should also have reviewed, or ensured that others reviewed, documentation concerning the February 21, 1991 auction. Such a review would have revealed, at a minimum, that a second false bid had been submitted in the auction and that false trade tickets and customer confirmations had been created in connection with both false bids. Those facts would have raised serious questions about the operations of the Government Trading Desk, and inquiries arising from those questions might well have led to discovery of the additional false bids described above. For instance, two of the other false bids, those submitted in the December 27, 1990 and February 7, 1991 auctions, involved the same pattern of fictitious sales to and from customer accounts and the suppression of customer confirmations used in connection with the February 21, 1991 auction. Inasmuch as Mozer had admitted to committing one apparently criminal act, the supervisors had reason to be skeptical of Mozer's assurances that he had not engaged in other misconduct.

Each of the three supervisors apparently believed that someone else would take the supervisory action necessary to respond to Mozer's misconduct. There was no discussion, however, among any of the supervisors about what action should be taken or about who would be responsible for taking action. Instead, each of the supervisors assumed that another would act. In situations where supervisors are aware of wrongdoing, it is imperative that they take prompt and unequivocal action to define the responsibilities of those who are to respond to the wrongdoing. The supervisors here failed to do that. As a result, although there may be varying degrees of responsibility, each of the supervisors bears some measure of responsibility for the collective failure of the group to take action.

After the disclosure of one unauthorized bid to Meriwether, Mozer committed additional violations in connection with the submission of two subsequent unauthorized customer bids. Had limits been placed on his activities after the one unauthorized bid was disclosed, these violations might have been prevented. While Mozer was told by Meriwether that his conduct was career-threatening and that it would be reported to senior management and to the government, these efforts were not a sufficient supervisory response under the circumstances. The supervisors were required to take action reasonably designed to prevent a repetition of the misconduct that had been disclosed to them. They could, for instance, have temporarily limited Mozer's activities so that he was not involved in the submission of customer bids pending an adequate review of what had occurred in the February 21, 1991 auction, or they could have instituted procedures to require verification of customer bids.

Under the circumstances of this case, the failure of the supervisors to take action to discipline Mozer or to limit his activities constituted a serious breach of their supervisory obligations. Gutfreund, Strauss and Meriwether thus each failed reasonably to supervise Mozer with a view to preventing violations of the federal securities laws.[20]

As Chairman and Chief Executive Officer of Salomon, Gutfreund bore ultimate responsibility for ensuring that a prompt and thorough inquiry was undertaken and that Mozer was appropriately disciplined. A chief executive officer has ultimate affirmative responsibility, upon learning of serious wrongdoing within the firm as to any segment of the securities market, to ensure that steps are taken to prevent further violations of the securities laws and to determine the scope of the wrongdoing. He failed to ensure that this was done. Gutfreund also undertook the responsibility to report the matter to the government, but failed to do so, although he was urged to make the report on several occasions by other senior executives of Salomon. The disclosure was made only after an internal investigation prompted by other events. Gutfreund's failure to report the matter earlier is of particular concern because of Salomon's role in the vitally-important U.S. Treasury securities market. The reporting of the matter to the government was also the only action under consideration within the firm to respond to Mozer's actions. The failure to make the report thus meant that the firm failed to take any action to respond to Mozer's misconduct.

20. Salomon did not have established procedures, or a system for applying those procedures, which together reasonably could have been expected to detect and pre-vent the violations. The affirmative defense provisions of Section 15(b)(4)(E) thus do not apply in this case.

Once improper conduct came to the attention of Gutfreund, he bore responsibility for ensuring that the firm responded in a way that recognized the seriousness and urgency of the situation. In our view, Gutfreund did not discharge that responsibility.

Strauss, as the President of Salomon, was the official within the firm to whom Meriwether first took the matter of Mozer's misconduct for appropriate action. As its president, moreover, Strauss was responsible for the operations of Salomon as a brokerage firm. Though he arranged several meetings to discuss the matter, Strauss failed to direct that Meriwether, Feuerstein, or others within the firm take the steps necessary to respond to the matter. Even if Strauss assumed that Meriwether or Feuerstein had taken the responsibility to address the matter, he failed to follow-up and ascertain whether action had in fact been taken. Moreover, it subsequently became clear that no meaningful action was being taken to respond to Mozer's misconduct. Under these circumstances, Strauss retained his supervisory responsibilities as the president of the brokerage firm, and he failed to discharge those responsibilities.

Meriwether was Mozer's direct supervisor and the head of all fixed-income trading activities at Salomon. Meriwether had also been designated by the firm as the person responsible for supervising the firm's fixed-income trading activities, including the activities of the Government Trading Desk.

When he first learned of Mozer's misconduct, Meriwether promptly took the matter to senior executives within the firm. In so doing, he took appropriate and responsible action. However, Meriwether's responsibilities did not end with communication of the matter to more senior executives. He continued to bear direct supervisory responsibility for Mozer after he had reported the false bid to others within the firm. As a result, until he was instructed not to carry out his responsibilities as Mozer's direct supervisor, Meriwether was required to take appropriate supervisory action. Meriwether's efforts in admonishing Mozer and telling him that his misconduct would be reported to the government were not sufficient under the circumstances to discharge his supervisory responsibilities.

C. Donald M. Feuerstein

Donald Feuerstein, Salomon's chief legal officer, was informed of the submission of the false bid by Paul Mozer in late April of 1991, at the same time other senior executives of Salomon learned of that act. Feuerstein was present at the meetings in late April at which the supervisors named as respondents in this proceeding discussed the matter. In his capacity as a legal adviser, Feuerstein did advise Strauss and Gutfreund that the submission of the bid was a criminal act and should be reported to the government, and he urged them on several occasions to proceed with disclosure when he learned that the report had not been made. However, Feuerstein did not direct that an inquiry be undertaken, and he did not recommend that appropriate procedures, reasonably designed to prevent and detect future misconduct, be instituted, or that other limitations be placed on Mozer's activities. Feuerstein also did not inform the Compliance Department, for which he was responsible as Salomon's chief legal officer, of the false bid.

Unlike Gutfreund, Strauss and Meriwether, however, Feuerstein was not a direct supervisor of Mozer at the time he first learned of the false bid. Because we believe this is an appropriate opportunity to amplify our views on the supervisory responsibilities of legal and compliance officers in Feuerstein's position, we have not named him as a respondent in this proceeding. Instead, we are issuing this report of investigation concerning the responsibilities imposed by Section 15(b)(4)(E) of the Exchange Act under the circumstances of this case.

Employees of brokerage firms who have legal or compliance responsibilities do not become "supervisors" for purposes of Sections 15(b)(4)(E) and 15(b)(6) solely because they occupy those positions. Rather, determining if a particular person is a "supervisor" depends on whether, under the facts and circumstances of a particular case, that person has a requisite degree of responsibility, ability or authority to affect the conduct of the employee whose behavior is at issue. n24 Thus, persons occupying positions in the legal or compliance departments of broker-dealers have been found by the Commission to be "supervisors" for purposes of Sections 15(b)(4)(E) and 15(b)(6) under certain circumstances.

In this case, serious misconduct involving a senior official of a brokerage firm was brought to the attention of the firm's chief legal officer. That individual was informed of the misconduct by other members of senior management in order to obtain his advice and guidance, and to involve him as part of management's collective response to the problem. Moreover, in other instances of misconduct, that individual had directed the firm's response and had made recommendations concerning appropriate disciplinary action, and management had relied on him to perform those tasks.

Given the role and influence within the firm of a person in a position such as Feuerstein's and the factual circumstances of this case, such a person shares in the responsibility to take appropriate action to respond to the misconduct. Under those circumstances, we believe that such a person becomes a "supervisor" for purposes of Sections 15(b)(4)(E) and 15(b)(6). As a result, that person is responsible, along with the other supervisors, for taking reasonable and appropriate action. It is not sufficient for one in such a position to be a mere bystander to the events that occurred.

Once a person in Feuerstein's position becomes involved in formulating management's response to the problem, he or she is obligated to take affirmative steps to ensure that appropriate action is taken to address the misconduct. For example, such a person could direct or monitor an investigation of the conduct at issue, make appropriate recommendations for limiting the activities of the employee or for the institution of appropriate procedures, reasonably designed to prevent and detect future misconduct, and verify that his or her recommendations, or acceptable alternatives, are implemented. If such a person takes appropriate steps but management fails to act and that person knows or has reason to know of that failure, he or she should consider what additional steps are appropriate to address the matter. These steps may include disclosure of the matter to the entity's board of directors, resignation from the firm, or disclosure to regulatory authorities.[26]

These responsibilities cannot be avoided simply because the person did not previously have direct supervisory responsibility for any of the activities of the employee. Once such a person has supervisory obligations by virtue of the circumstances of a particular situation, he must either discharge those responsibilities or know that others are taking appropriate action.

V. ORDER

In view of the foregoing, the Commission deems it appropriate and in the public interest to impose the sanctions specified in the Offers of Settlement submitted by John H. Gutfreund, Thomas W. Strauss, and John W. Meriwether.

Accordingly, IT IS HEREBY ORDERED that:

A. John H. Gutfreund be, and he hereby is:

(i) ordered to comply with his undertaking not to associate in the future in the capacity of Chairman or Chief Executive Officer with any broker, dealer, municipal securities dealer, investment company or investment adviser regulated by the Commission; and

(ii) ordered to pay to the United States Treasury a civil penalty aggregating $100,000 pursuant to Section 21B(a)(4) of the Exchange Act;

B. Thomas W. Strauss be, and he hereby is:

(i) suspended from associating with any broker, dealer, municipal securities dealer, investment company or investment adviser for a period of six (6) months; and

(ii) ordered to pay to the United States Treasury a civil penalty aggregating $75,000 pursuant to Section 21B(a)(4) of the Exchange Act;

C. John W. Meriwether be, and he hereby is:

(i) suspended from associating with any broker, dealer, municipal securities dealer, investment company or investment adviser for a period of three (3) months; and

---

26. Of course, in the case of an attorney, the applicable Code of Professional Responsibility and the Canons of Ethics may bear upon what course of conduct that individual may properly pursue.

(ii) ordered to pay to the United States Treasury a civil penalty aggregating $50,000 pursuant to Section 21B(a)(4) of the Exchange Act.

By the Commission.

* * *

PROBLEMS

1. You are the general counsel of Diversified Corporation, which is a holding company for several service industries. Diversified has recently acquired Reviva, a smaller company engaged in the manufacture of various cosmetics and personal care products at plants in Jacksonville, Florida and Charleston, South Carolina. Reviva will now be a division of Diversified. To this point, it has been a privately held company with only modest operations. Reviva holds several valuable patents, however, and Diversified plans to rely on these in substantially expanding its manufacturing activity.

In light of this acquisition, Diversified for the first time will be subject to various environmental regulations. The Board of Directors therefore requests that the company establish a program to ensure Diversified's compliance with environmental law by the time that the acquisition is completed. The CEO asks that you oversee this project. You establish an Environmental Compliance Working Group headed by your top assistant, Diversified's Deputy General Counsel. The Group is to submit to you for discussion a draft proposal for such a program.

One month later, you receive the a report on the draft compliance program. The program designates an attorney in the General Counsel's as the "compliance attorney" responsible for all environmental compliance issues. An engineer in each of Reviva's two manufacturing plants is designated as the "compliance officer" for that plant, responsible for ensuring that company operations in the plant conform to all environmental provisions. In order to inaugurate the program, the compliance attorney will visit each plant for a day and provides an overview for the compliance officer of all pertinent environmental regulations. The compliance officer has the discretion to determine how best to delegate authority within the plant in order to ensure adherence to environmental laws. As statutes are amended, regulations are issued, and cases are decided, the compliance attorney sends a memo to each compliance officer describing these developments.

Each compliance officer is required to submit an annual report to the compliance attorney that confirms that the plant is operating consistently with applicable environmental provisions. He or she also is instructed to call the compliance attorney if any questions arise or if there is any reason to believe that the plant may be in violation of any environmental directive. If necessary, the attorney will visit the plant to resolve any of these issues. At the end of each fiscal year, the compliance attorney draws on the annual reports from the compliance officers to prepare an annual report to you that in turn goes to the Board of Directors. The report certifies that the company is in compliance with its environmental obligations. The report to the Board generally does not describe any of the problems that have arisen during the year unless they jeopardize the company's compliance status at the time of the report. The compliance attorney is also responsible for preparing quarterly reports to the Environmental Protection Agency (EPA) that attest that the company is in compliance with environmental laws. You and the compliance attorney are the signatories on these reports, although the compliance attorney is the one who puts the relevant data together and determines whether the company is in compliance.

What comments do you have on the draft proposal before you recommend to the CEO that it be presented to the Board?

2. Diversified has adopted what you regard as an effective environmental compliance program. The company's plants in Jacksonville and Charleston have recently begun using a new chemical in the manufacturing process that is on the list of substances designated as hazardous by the Environmental Protection Agency (EPA). The Comprehensive Environmental Response, Compensation, and Liability Act (CERCLA) at 42 U.S.C. § 9603 requires that release of any such substance at or above a certain level be reported to the agency. Failure to comply with this provision can subject offenders to criminal fine and imprisonment for up to three years. Persons subject to the reporting obligation are high-level company management and persons in charge of the facilities where such discharge occurred. You are not included in either of these categories.

Appropriate personnel at each plant monitor the amount of discharge of the new chemical when it is first introduced, and conclude that it is below the level requiring a report. Shortly thereafter, however, changes in the production process increase the discharge to an amount that must be reported. Through inadvertence, these changes are not communicated to compliance personnel for a month. When they are, testing reveals that for the last month the substance has been discharged at each plant in an amount greater than permitted by statute. When you are informed of this, you direct the managers of each plant to suspend use of the new production process pending further instructions.

You report to management the release of the substance and the duty to report it under CERCLA. The senior vice-president immediately contacts each plant manager and directs him continue refraining from using the new production process until purchase of equipment that will reduce its discharge to a lawful level. Each plant manager and compliance officer is directed to confirm in writing to you that the equipment has been purchased and installed, and to submit tests indicating that discharge is below the level that must be reported, before resumption of the new production process. Company scientists conduct further tests and express the opinion that the discharge thus far has caused no serious harm to the river in which the chemical has been released.

Management is reluctant to report the offense. The regional administrator of the EPA has recently announced a "zero tolerance" policy regarding release of hazardous substances, and has indicated that she will use heavy fines to make examples of companies who are responsible for such releases. Management fears that the company will be subject to a financial penalty that could place a serious strain on it. Officials maintain that the problem has been addressed without the need to involve the EPA, and that the involvement of the agency would just complicate things and subject the company to unwarranted strict monitoring of its operations.

What are the alternatives that you might recommend and what are the risks of each?

Chapter 24

INTERNAL INVESTIGATIONS

When corporate officers or directors get wind of possible misconduct by persons within the corporation, the audit committee or Board of Directors often commissions an internal investigation to ascertain the facts and determine the company's potential legal exposure. A corporation may ask that an internal investigation be conducted by either inside counsel or an outside law firm. Generally speaking, the more widespread the alleged misconduct and the higher it may reach into executive ranks, the more likely outside lawyers will be asked to undertake the investigation.

Sometimes an investigation will occur without anyone outside the corporation being aware of any possible wrongdoing. Once the results of the investigation are reported to the appropriate corporate authority, the company must then decide whether and on what terms to approach regulators and/or law enforcement agencies with the information.

Other times, an agency such as the Securities and Exchange Commission or the Department of Justice will inform the corporation that wrongdoing may possibly have occurred within the company. In such cases, the corporation may agree to conduct an investigation at the agency's behest and to turn over the results of that inquiry to the agency. In return for such cooperation, a corporation may gain lenient treatment by the government. The chapter on Criminal Prosecution describes in more detail the Justice Department's views on factors that are relevant in evaluating a company's cooperation.

Internal investigations raise a host of questions calling for the exercise of both ethical and practical judgment. Investigators and corporate management must contend with issues such as clarifying the identity of the client, conflicts of interest, confidentiality, corporate lines of authority, and the circumstances under which internal investigations effectively should be treated as being conducted on behalf of the government. Internal investigations, in other words, can be a minefield for lawyers.

OVERVIEW OF THE CHAPTER

The chapter begins with a general overview by Foley Lardner of the steps in an internal investigation and the decisions that must be made at each juncture. Note that the first question to confront is whether circumstances warrant conducting an investigation at all. Among the other key issues are document collection and preservation, the process for interviewing witnesses, the ability to preserve the confidentiality of any material generated during the investigation, whether to commit findings and conclusions to writing in a report, and what remedial action is appropriate.

The *Hart* case illustrates the consequences of counsel's failure to clarify to a witness that counsel represents the corporate entity rather than the individual employee. Make sure that you understand precisely under what circumstances this can occur and what the impact of such failure will be. Ask yourself what might inhibit lawyers conducting investigations from being forthright about the identity of the client they represent. Consider also how best to make this clear in light of the risks of doing so.

The *Westinghouse* case that follows provides an extensive discussion of when a company will be deemed to have waived attorney-client privilege and work product protection by furnishing the report of an internal investigation to the government. What seems to be a corporation's main concern about a finding of waiver? Does the court seem sympathetic to this concern? Should it be? Note also the difference between what constitutes a waiver of the privilege and of work product protection. Do you agree with the *Westinghouse* court's analysis of the latter issue? Companies claim that a narrow conception of waiver is necessary in order to encourage corporations to undertake internal investigations. Do you think that is true?

The last two articles in the chapter discuss a phenomenon that seems to have become more common in recent years. This is corporate conduct of an internal investigation at the behest of a governmental agency that suspects wrongdoing, and which may even be conducting its own parallel investigation. As the Longstreth article observes, in such cases lawyers involved in the investigation represent the corporation's board of directors, but also anticipate turning over the results of the inquiry to the government.

Furthermore, as the Department of Justice "Thompson memo" contained in the next Chapter describes, uncovering and disclosing to authorities incriminating evidence against corporate individuals can help the corporate entity avoid prosecution. Longstreth notes that this represents a departure from past practice, in which the company and its employees often presented a united front and the lawyer "jousted with the government and sought to limit the flow of information." The Berenson article describes one consequence of this state of affairs: employees who lie to lawyers conducting internal investigations may be subject to criminal prosecution for lying to the government.

As you read these last two articles, think about whether what they describe represents a useful way to ferret out wrongdoing that in the past too often was concealed by corporations with significant resources—or whether it represents government overreaching. Consider also whether a company's pledge to turn over the results of its investigation can create any potential conflicts for the lawyer who performs the inquiry.

The first problem places you in the role of a lawyer requested to conduct an internal investigation, and effectively asks that you consider what action is appropriate at each step of that investigation. The second problem asks to what extent the company that has authorized the investigation will be able to preserve attorney-client privilege or work product protection for the material generated during the investigation.

MODEL RULES: 1.3, 1.6, 1.7, 1.13,4.1, 4.2, 4.3

Foley & Lardner, CONDUCTING INTERNAL INVESTIGATIONS

UNITED STATES MONDAQ BUSINESS BRIEFING, January 14, 2005

In the current regulatory environment, companies [frequently] * * * conduct[ ] internal investigations focused on potential wrongdoing. U.S. laws and law enforcement agencies increasingly expect that companies will police their own conduct and report potential misconduct to the appropriate federal law enforcement agency. * * *

There is no standard definition of the term "internal investigation." For [our] purposes, we mean to include the full range of information-gathering activities that a company engages in upon learning of possible wrongdoing. In some instances, the internal investigation may appropriately be limited to a few interviews and the gathering and review of a limited number of documents. In other instances, the internal investigation will require a far-reaching and comprehensive search for documents, the review of vast quantities of documents and other records, and extensive interviews of large numbers of witnesses. * * *

What follows is a thumbnail discussion of seven steps for conducting internal investigations from the initial stages, to document collection, to corrective action and government disclosure.

I. DECIDING WHETHER TO INITIATE AN INTERNAL INVESTIGATION

The initial issue to be considered upon uncovering potential wrongdoing is whether an internal investigation is warranted. If it appears that the government has already initiated an investigation or that one is probable, then the case for undertaking an internal investigation is likely to be compelling. When faced with a government investigation, it is almost always in the best interests of the company to gather information to enable the company to respond effectively to the government's investigation.

There are several respects in which information gathered during an internal investigation can assist in forming an effective response to a government investigation. The internal investigation may uncover persuasive evidence from which the company can argue either that no violative conduct occurred or that the matter otherwise does not warrant prosecution. The results of the internal investigation can assist the company in deciding whether to attempt to settle the government investigation. The results of the internal investigation might assist the company in persuading the government to agree to a settlement that the company finds acceptable. Disclosing the results of the investigation can assist the company in persuading the government either that no government investigation is necessary or, more likely, that the government investigation need be far less extensive and disruptive than it might otherwise be. Evidence gathered in the internal investigation can also assist in preparing witness testimony. The internal investigation might uncover evidence that refreshes a witness's recollection so that the witness recalls exculpatory events or appears more credible than might otherwise be the case. In addition, an internal investigation might enable the company to develop themes that are helpful to the company and that place the alleged misconduct in an appropriate context. * * *

The case for an internal investigation is also likely to be compelling if private litigation has been commenced or is probable. An internal investigation can greatly assist a company in mounting an effective response to a private action. For example, in response to an allegation of discrimination, a prompt and effective investigation followed by appropriate remedial action can assist the company in successfully asserting an affirmative defense[.] Similarly, the extent, if any, to which the company may be exposed to punitive damages in a private action may be affected by whether a company conducted a prompt and effective investigation in response to indications that an employee or agent may have engaged in misconduct. * * *

Determining whether to undertake an internal investigation is more difficult where the government has not yet initiated an investigation and where it appears improbable that the government will initiate an investigation or that a private action will be brought. Internal investigations can have a number of negative consequences to a company. They can be expensive and disruptive. They can distract the energy of management and create morale problems. They can uncover wrongful conduct that might otherwise never have become known. Moreover, the process of conducting an internal investigation can increase the likelihood that information regarding possible misconduct will reach the government and/or the press. Accordingly, in the absence of a government investigation or the threat of a lawsuit, management might hesitate to authorize an internal investigation.

There are a number of reasons why management nevertheless often authorizes internal investigations even when it does not appear that the government has initiated an internal investigation or is likely to do so. First, the willingness and capacity to conduct internal investigations in response to red flags is an important component of an effective compliance program. Company personnel are likely to take a company's procedures and policies less seriously if they learn that the company does not pursue indications of wrongdoing. For example, if employees observe both that company personnel routinely make improper payments to foreign officials in order to secure business for the company and that senior management appears indifferent to these payments, employees will be more likely to ignore company policies prohibiting such payments.

Second, senior management has an obligation to take steps when confronted with indications of wrongful conduct. Recent case law indicates that members of the board of directors might be personally liable for fines, penalties and losses incurred by a company as a result of unlawful conduct by the company or its employees unless the directors have "assured themselves that information and reporting systems exist in the corporation that are reasonably designed to provide to senior management and to the board itself timely, accurate information sufficient to allow management and the board, each within its scope, to reach informed judgments concerning both the corporation's compliance with the law and its business performance. * * *" In re Caremark International, Inc. Derivative Litigation, 698 A.2d 959, 967 (Del. Ch. 1996). * * *

In bringing an enforcement action against senior officials of a major securities dealer, Salomon Brothers, Inc., the Securities and Exchange Commission ("SEC") took the position that supervisors have a duty to gather information in response to red flags:

Even where the knowledge of supervisors is limited to "red flags" or "suggestions" of irregularity, they cannot discharge their supervisory obligations simply by relying on the unverified representations of employees. Instead, as the Commission has repeatedly emphasized, "t here must be adequate follow-up and review when a firm's own procedures detect irregularities or unusual trading activity. * * *"

In this particular case, the SEC sanctioned senior officials of Salomon Brothers on the grounds, among others, that upon receiving information that an irregularity had occurred, they failed to "take action to investigate what had occurred and whether there had been other instances of unreported misconduct."

Third, and perhaps most importantly, companies recognize that even where it does not appear that the government has commenced or is likely to commence an investigation, future developments might result in a government investigation. In that event, for the reasons set forth above, the information gathered during the internal investigation is likely to assist the company in responding effectively to the government's later investigation and in preparing the company's defenses.

II. STAFFING THE INVESTIGATION

Once the decision is made to conduct an internal investigation in response to a red flag or other indication of wrongdoing, a decision must be made regarding who will conduct the investigation. In many instances, indications of possible wrongdoing can be quickly addressed and resolved by company personnel without the involvement of outside counsel. In certain cases, company personnel have the experience and expertise necessary to obtain the information and can do so with less disruption and expense to the company than outside counsel can. For example, the human resource department often has the skills and expertise necessary to investigate allegations of employment discrimination or sexual harassment. Similarly, the internal audit department might have the skills and expertise necessary to investigate allegations of theft or embezzlement. * * *

* * * There are a number of reasons why companies sometimes choose outside counsel to conduct an investigation. First, outside counsel often are hired because of a perception that they are more independent than company employees. This perception of greater independence can be important for a number of reasons. If the subject matter of the investigation implicates senior management or the legal department, the independence of the outside law firm might provide the board of directors additional comfort in relying on the results of the investigation. In matters that pose a potentially serious threat to the company, it often is appropriate to retain outside counsel. In determining whether the investigation is sufficiently serious to warrant the retention of outside counsel, companies consider the title and prominence of the individuals whose conduct will likely be the subject of the investigation, the potential financial exposure to the company, and the extent that the subject matter of the investigation is likely to result in law enforcement activity and/or substantial media coverage. In order to heighten both the reality and the perception that the investigation was independent, responsibility for overseeing outside counsel is sometimes assumed by the Board of Directors, the Audit Committee, or by a special committee consisting of independent members of the board of directors. This is especially appropriate where the investigation potentially involves conduct by the senior management of the company.

A second reason for utilizing outside counsel is the need to dedicate substantial resources to responding promptly to a red flag or other indication of possible wrongdoing. It often is difficult for even large companies to pull a team of employees from ongoing tasks and devote them to an internal investigation.

A third reason for utilizing outside counsel is the possibility that members of the legal department will have relevant knowledge or that the conduct of the legal department will become an issue. For example, retaining outside counsel might be appropriate if the legal department had been consulted with respect to the transaction or activity at issue and had advised the client concerning the matter.

A fourth reason for utilizing outside counsel is the reality that specialized outside counsel might have the experience and expertise to conduct the particular investigation more effectively or more efficiently than company personnel who do not specialize in this particular type of investigation. In addition, to the extent that the subject matter of the investigation is likely to result in interaction with a law enforcement or regulatory agency, it is often useful for a company to be represented by counsel who is familiar with that agency. Similarly, if there is likely to be litigation, it often is appropriate to retain counsel with relevant litigation and trial experience.

A fifth reason for utilizing outside counsel is a desire to increase the likelihood that the results of internal investigation will be protected by the attorney-client privilege and the work product doctrine. While both the attorney-client privilege and the work product doctrine can apply to the work of an in-house attorney, a court is less likely to find that a business purpose was the primary purpose behind the investigation if the investigation was conducted by outside counsel. * * *

If outside counsel is retained to conduct the internal investigation, the company should assign an employee to act as a liaison between the company and the outside counsel. The liaison can be an invaluable resource regarding background information regarding the company, its history, its operations, and its recordkeeping practices. The liaison can assist outside counsel in identifying individuals and departments that are likely to possess relevant information. The liaison can facilitate the interview process by making the initial introductions between the outside counsel and the company employees with relevant knowledge. In terms of supervision of the investigation, it is usually appropriate for the Legal Department or for other senior company officials to supervise the work of outside counsel, though in some instances, outside counsel should report to the Audit Committee or a special committee of the Board of Directors. Reporting to the Audit Committee or a special committee is especially appropriate in matters where it is important to establish the independence of outside counsel and its investigation. * * *

III.   DEFINING THE SCOPE OF THE INVESTIGATION AND DEVELOPING AN ACTION PLAN

* * * At the outset of the investigation, the company should issue a charter setting forth the mandate pursuant to which the internal investigation is being conducted. This charter can consist of one or more of: a resolution of the Board of Directors; a resolution of the Audit Committee; an engagement letter; or a memorandum issued by senior management or the General Counsel. The charter should instruct the investigators to conduct a confidential internal investigation, define the scope of the investigation, authorize the investigators to inform company personnel that they are instructed to cooperate in the investigation, and specify (if appropriate) that the investigation is being conducted in anticipation of litigation and for the purpose of obtaining legal advice. Because some courts cease to protect attorney work product once the litigation relating to the work product has been concluded, the charter should be drafted broadly enough to cover all conceivable litigation likely to arise, including securities class actions, derivative actions, and related commercial litigation. Such a charter forces the company to focus on the scope of the

internal investigation and will assist the company in successfully seeking the protection of the attorney-client privilege and the work product doctrine in the event that discovery is sought for documents generated in connection with the investigation. * * *

The scope of the investigation should be constantly reevaluated as information is gathered and analyzed. While the initial red flags or indications of possible wrongdoing might have warranted an investigation of limited scope, the investigation might uncover information that warrants a substantial expansion of the scope of the investigation. * * * It is important that an internal investigation be conducted quickly, efficiently and effectively, especially if the company anticipates that the government may initiate its own investigation. In many circumstances, the government will not defer its investigation pending completion of the company's internal investigation. Factors that the government considers in evaluating whether to defer its investigation include: (1) the amount of time expected to elapse during the company's internal investigation; (2) the nature of the suspected violation and whether it is potentially ongoing; (3) whether the internal investigation is being conducted by outside counsel; and (4) whether the government will be permitted to see all of the notes and records compiled during the internal investigation. * * *

The action plan should describe the documents to be gathered and identify who should be responsible for gathering the documents. The plan should also identify the witnesses to be interviewed, the nature of the questions to be posed during the interviews, and where the witnesses will be interviewed. * * *

One important issue that often arises in developing an action plan is the extent, if any, to which the investigators should contact third party witnesses. In many instances, third parties are likely to possess information significant to the investigation. For example, in an investigation involving revenue recognition, customer personnel might have significant information regarding when sales contracts were executed and whether the sales contracts were accompanied by any side agreements. On the other hand, contacting third parties might endanger the confidentiality of the investigation or jeopardize the company's relationship with the third party. In many instances, an investigative plan can be developed that will enable the investigators to obtain the information they need while minimizing the associated risks.

IV. GATHERING DOCUMENTS

Documents are a key part of almost all internal investigations. * * *

As soon as the company becomes aware of allegations of wrongful conduct, it should consider suspending normal document retention procedures in order to ensure that company personnel do not destroy or otherwise dispose of documents relating to the transaction or the incident that is the subject of the investigation. For example, the legal department might circulate to appropriate personnel a memorandum instructing personnel not to destroy or discard specified categories of documents. Such a memorandum is especially appropriate where the company is aware that the government has already initiated an inquiry or investigation. While communicating the importance of not destroying relevant documents, the memorandum should disclose only as much information regarding the matter under investigation as the recipient needs to know. It is important to consider the possibility that the company may be discarding or overwriting computerized information in the ordinary course of business as back up media are rotated and reused, and tapes are recycled, electronic media storage devices are replaced, and new software is loaded.

A diligent search should be taken to locate and secure the documents that relate to the subject transaction or incident. * * *

In conducting its document search, the company must limit its reliance on individuals who might have participated in the suspected underlying misconduct. In some instances, it is best to have counsel show up at the critical locations and search for relevant documents without prior warning so that the individuals involved in the suspected underlying misconduct will not have an opportunity to destroy or discard significant documents. * * *

V. Interviewing Witnesses

Interviews are also a key aspect of the investigation process. Along with documents, interviews are the primary source of the information that will be gathered during the investigation. In addition, interviews present an important opportunity for the investigators to assess the credibility of the witness.

Counsel should interview all company personnel likely to have knowledge regarding the relevant transaction or the alleged violation. * * *

At the outset of each interview, counsel should inform the witness that: (1) senior management (or the board of directors or a special committee of the board of directors) has authorized counsel to state that company employees should cooperate in the investigation; (2) counsel are attempting to determine the truth relating to the matter and the surrounding circumstances; (3) counsel are not asking the witness to provide untruthful or misleading information to any government investigators; and (4) the witness should not destroy or discard any documents relevant to the investigation. If the investigators are attorneys they should also: (1) identify their client, and state they do not represent the individual witness; (2) explain that they are seeking information to assist in providing legal advice and services to the company; (3) indicate that, in order to protect the privileged nature of the interview, it is important that the witness keep the substance of the interview confidential from anyone other than counsel; and (4) state that the company controls the privileges associated with the investigation and has the sole right to determine whether to waive those privileges and disclose the substance of the interview to the government. If the company has already agreed to disclose to the government information obtained in the interview, counsel should advise the witness of this agreement.

This is a delicate part of the interview. In communicating this information to the witness, counsel should be sensitive to the danger that these communications will cause undue alarm on the part of the witness and thereby impede the ability of the company to gather the necessary information. * * *

Both the notes of the interview and the memoranda summarizing the interview should be marked as "confidential," and should note (if true) that they reflect the attorney's mental impressions and are not a substantially verbatim record of the interview. The notes should clearly reflect that the investigators made the appropriate statements to the witness (as discussed above) at the outset of the interview. The interview memoranda should contain and intertwine the attorney's mental impressions and explicit strategy because such memoranda are more likely to be protected as opinion work product under the work product doctrine. In drafting interview memoranda, the investigator should be conscious of the possibility that the memoranda will ultimately be disclosed to prosecutors or to counsel for a plaintiff litigating against the company. * * *

* * * While it would be improper and illegal to instruct a witness not to talk to U.S. government officials, it is appropriate to discuss with the witness that the witness has the right to decline to answer questions without first contacting the company or consulting with an attorney. In conducting the interview, investigators should be careful not to attempt to influence the witness's answers. To the extent possible, the investigators should avoid telling one witness what another witness has told them or otherwise educating the witness regarding the transaction, although it will often be necessary to refresh the witness's recollection regarding facts of which the witness once had knowledge. * * *

In many cases, former employees will be among the key witnesses. The interview of a former employee might be protected by attorney-client privilege if the witness is being interviewed regarding information obtained when the witness was an employee of the company represented by counsel. While the law is not completely settled, a number of courts have held that the attorney client privilege can apply to communications between a former employee of a company and counsel to a company, at least if the former employee had been employed by the company when the relevant conduct occurred.

VI.   Preparing A Report Of The Investigation

* * * Careful consideration should be given to whether some or all portions of the investigation should be reduced to writing. Reducing the report to writing can offer a number of benefits. Written reports often contain substantially more content and more precise analysis, and are easier for company management to digest, than oral reports. The Board of Directors may feel more comfortable relying on a written report than

on an oral report. If disclosed to the government, a written report can help persuade the government that a thorough investigation had been conducted and either no wrongful conduct occurred or that government action is otherwise not warranted.

There are also a number of problems associated with reducing a report to writing. The process of writing a report can be expensive. If disclosed to the government or to others outside the corporation, the written report can be used against the company. Production of the written report is likely to jeopardize the privileges associated with the investigation. In subsequent litigation, adversaries will seek to discredit the report by identifying arguable omissions or inaccuracies in the report.

Careful consideration should also be given to whether the company should disclose the results of the investigation to the government. Under some circumstances, companies have a legal obligation to report to the government or otherwise disclose that they have engaged in conduct that is unlawful. The New York Stock Exchange requires that member firms promptly report to the NYSE whenever the member, or any employee associated with the member, has violated any provision of any securities laws or regulations or any rules of a self-regulatory organization or has engaged in conduct inconsistent with just and equitable principles of trade. NYSE Rule 351. Under some circumstances a publicly owned corporation may have an obligation under the federal securities laws to disclose in its periodic reports or on a Current Report on Form 8–K a violation of law that is material to the operations or financial condition of the company. * * *

In a criminal context, self-reporting can increase the likelihood of the company's obtaining lenient treatment. As set forth above, a number of government law enforcement agencies have formal programs that offer leniency to companies that report violations before the government begins an investigation. Absent such a program, prosecutors may nevertheless exercise their discretion and decide not to prosecute a company that has voluntarily reported a violation. * * *

If the company decides to make some disclosure to the government, it might attempt to limit the extent of the disclosure. In some circumstances, the government might agree that it is sufficient if the company identifies the nature and extent of the offense and the individual(s) responsible for the criminal conduct. In general, however, the government will often press to see both the report of the internal investigation and/or the materials generated and collected in connection with the investigation. Outside legal counsel should always be consulted prior to making a disclosure to the government.

If the company decides to disclose a written report to the government, there is a substantial risk that all of the company's privileges with respect to the investigation will be deemed waived. A majority of the courts addressing the issue have held that disclosure of a report to a law enforcement agency waives any privileges that would otherwise attach to the report under U.S. law. * * *

In any event, steps should always be taken to protect the investigation and any written investigation materials from discovery. Any documents or other written materials prepared as part of an investigation should be marked privileged and confidential, and their distribution should be limited.

VII. Taking Corrective Action Based On The Investigation

The company must assess what corrective action, if any, should be taken in light of the information gathered during the internal investigation. Throughout the course of the investigation, counsel and the company should be alert to whether there might be an ongoing, recurring or other prospective violation of law or of the company's policies and procedures. If it appears that there might be an ongoing or recurring violation, then the company should take measures necessary to prevent any further violations. These measures can consist of instituting new procedures, instituting new training sessions, and/or disseminating compliance materials.

Furthermore, the company should consider whether any employee and/or agent should be disciplined and whether the investigation has revealed any areas in the compliance program that should be enhanced. * * *

[Any] sanction should reflect the seriousness of the offense, the extent to which the employee has been put on notice that the conduct at issue was contrary to company policy, and the need to protect the company from future violations. * * *

Disciplinary action that results in the termination of the employee responsible for alleged misconduct may lead to the employee bringing a lawsuit for wrongful discharge. Courts differ as to the legal standard to be applied in determining whether the disciplined employee has a cause of action against the company. Compare Cotran v. Rollins Hudig Hall International, Inc., 17 Cal. 4th 93, 69 Cal. Rptr.2d 900; 948 P.2d 412 (1998) and Sanders v. Parker Drilling Company, 911 F.2d 191 (9th Cir. 1990) (applying Alaska law). In Cotran, a company had terminated an employee after finding that the employee had sexually harassed certain fellow employees. The terminated employee sued his former employer alleging that he had been terminated without just cause. The trial court ruled that the issue was whether the employee had actually engaged in the alleged sexual harassment, found that the terminated employee had not engaged in sexual harassment, and held that the employee had therefore been terminated without just cause. The Supreme Court held that the employee had been terminated with just cause as long as at the time of the decision to terminate the employment, the employer, acting in good faith and following an investigation that was appropriate under the circumstances, had reasonable grounds for believing plaintiff had done so. 17 Cal. 4th at 109. In Sanders, two employees of Parker Drilling

Co. informed Parker's safety managers that several fellow employees were routinely smoking marijuana on the job and during break periods. The company asked for and obtained written statements from the two employees stating this accusation. The company then confronted the plaintiffs who denied using drugs. Based on this information, Parker terminated the plaintiffs. The Ninth Circuit held that to carry its burden of showing just cause for termination, Parker had the burden of showing that the discharged employees had engaged in the alleged prohibitive conduct and that Parker's subjective good faith belief that it possessed good cause was insufficient. 911 F.2d at 194–95.

Finally, a company considering remedial action should consider taking additional remedial steps, such as making compensatory payments to individuals or entities that were overbilled; making job offers to job applicants against whom the company had discriminated; and correcting disclosure statements that have been released to the investing public.

UNITED STATES v. HART

1992 WL 348425 (E.D. La. 1992)

Mentz, District Judge.

Before the Court is the Government's Motion to Compel Defendants to Establish an Attorney–Client Privilege. Based upon evidence presented by the Government and defendants, David Walters and Craig Van der Voort, at an evidentiary hearing, the Court finds that defendants are entitled to invoke an attorney-client privilege so as to prevent disclosure of statements made by them to attorneys Ben Gill and Pauline Hardin.

FACTS

In October, 1991, subpoenas were issued by a federal grand jury, sitting in the Eastern District of Louisiana, for certain documents from the Little Rock office of A.J. Gallagher & Co. Later, two officers of the Little Rock office, Walters and his superior Jack Cowell, were summoned to produce documents and appear before the grand jury. The grand jury was investigating the payment of consulting fees to M.W. Hart by Gallagher on behalf of St. Tammany Parish. Upon learning of the grand jury investigation, the head office of Gallagher directed Ben Gill, the corporate counsel of Gallagher, to investigate. Gill interviewed several employees. Over the next several months, Gill had two telephone conversations and one meeting with defendant Walters and several telephone conversations and meetings with defendant Van der Voort. During the course of these interviews, Gill did not inform either defendant whether the company would assume their defense or whether they should employ their own counsel throughout the interviews. It was not until a February 1, 1992 meeting with Walters and a February 7, 1992 telephone conversation with Van der Voort, that Gill informed each defendant that he should get separate counsel.

Also, around December 16, 1991, Pauline Hardin and her firm were hired as local counsel for the corporation. Hardin met with Walters and had a telephone conversation with Van der Voort. Hardin testified that she told Walters that she represented the corporation and was not his attorney. Walters and Van der Voort each testified that Hardin never said she represented the corporation and not them. Van der Voort testified that he considered Hardin as an extension of Ben Gill. Jack Cowell, who was also interviewed by Hardin, testified that Hardin never told him that she represented the corporation and not him.

Defendants have claimed an attorney-client privilege as to their conversations with Gill and Hardin. The Government claims that the only attorney-client privilege belongs to the corporation which has waived the privilege as to the investigation of this matter conducted by its attorneys.

Analysis

The Court considers that defendants' belief that their conversations with Gill and Hardin were confidential was reasonable, based on the circumstances surrounding their discussions with Gill and Hardin. An attorney-client privilege attaches to communications between a client and his attorney where at least an implied relationship exists between them. This relationship "hinges upon the client's belief that he is consulting a lawyer in that capacity and his manifested intention to seek professional legal advice." The relationships must be established by more than the individual clients' mere subjective belief that they are represented individually by the attorney, jointly with the corporation.

In support of their belief that they were being individually represented by Gill and Hardin, the defendants point to the indemnification provision set forth in Article VII of the By–Laws of A.J. Gallagher & Co., wherein the corporation promises to:

> "indemnify any person who was or is a party or is threatened to be made a party to any threatened, pending or completed action, suit or proceeding, whether civil, criminal, administrative or investigative (other than action by or in the right of the corporation) by reason of the fact that he is or was a director, officer, employee or agent of the corporation or is or was serving at the request of the corporation as a director, officer, employee or agent of another corporation, partnership, joint venture, trust or other enterprise, against expenses (including attorneys' fees), judgments, fines and amounts paid in settlement actually and reasonably incurred by him in connection with such action, suit or proceeding if he acted in good faith and in a manner he reasonably believed to be in or not opposed to the best interests of the corporation, and, with respect to any criminal action or proceeding, had no reasonable cause to believe his conduct was unlawful."

Pat Gallagher, President of the corporation, stated that his general policy was that the company would protect its employees in the case of civil or criminal proceedings involving the employees.

While the indemnification provision is not dispositive of the attorney-client privilege issue, in the absence of any advice by Gill or Hardin to the contrary, defendants were justified in believing that Gill and Hardin were there to protect their individual interests as well as those of the corporation.[1] Also significant is the fact that the communications between the defendants and Gill and Hardin were initiated, not by the defendants, but by Gill and Hardin as part of a "factfinding" mission.

Given this background, defendants reasonably believed that, during their conversations with Gill and Hardin, they were clients of Gill and Hardin, that they were communicating with them in their capacities as lawyers, and that they were providing legal services to them in their individual capacities, jointly with the corporation. This Court finds that defendants, Walters and Van der Voort, are entitled to assert an attorney-client privilege as to all communications made to Ben Gill and Pauline Hardin in the course of Gill's and Hardin's investigation, preventing disclosure of those communications until such time as defendants choose to waive this privilege.

Accordingly,

IT IS ORDERED that all communications between corporate counsel, Ben Gill and Pauline Hardin, and the defendants, David Walters and Craig Van der Voort, are protected by the attorney-client privilege belonging to Walters and Van der Voort.

WESTINGHOUSE ELECTRIC CORP. v. REPUBLIC OF THE PHILLIPPINES

951 F.2d 1414 (3d. Cir. 1991)

BECKER, CIRCUIT JUDGE.

This petition for a writ of mandamus requires us to resolve an important issue that has divided the circuits: whether a party that discloses information protected by the attorney-client privilege and the work-product doctrine in order to cooperate with a government agency that is investigating it waives the privilege and the doctrine only as against the government, or waives them completely, thereby exposing the documents to civil discovery in litigation between the discloser and a third party. The issue arises in an action brought by the Republic of the Philippines (the "Republic") and its National Power Corporation ("NPC") against Westinghouse Electric Corporation and its wholly-owned subsidiary, Westinghouse International Projects Company (collec-

---

1. The Court notes that, under Rule 1.13(d) of the ABA Model Rules of Professional Conduct, Gill and Hardin should have informed the defendants at the inception of their conversation that any revelations made by them might not be covered by the privilege in the event that Gill decided that they should obtain separate counsel, which he ultimately did advise.

tively "Westinghouse"). The Republic and the NPC allege that Westinghouse obtained a large power plant contract in the Philippines by bribing a henchman of former President Ferdinand Marcos. Their complaint charges that Westinghouse and others tortiously interfered with and conspired to tortiously interfere with the fiduciary duties that President Marcos owed to the Philippine people and to the NPC. The complaint seeks damages on a variety of theories.

During discovery, the Republic sought certain documents generated during an internal investigation conducted by Westinghouse's outside counsel. The investigation was a response to an investigation by the Securities and Exchange Commission ("SEC") into allegations that Westinghouse had obtained contracts by bribing foreign officials. Westinghouse disclosed the documents in question to the SEC in order to cooperate with the agency's investigation. Westinghouse later disclosed the same documents, as well as other, related documents, to the Department of Justice ("DOJ") in order to cooperate with an investigation conducted by the DOJ. Westinghouse's petition for mandamus follows the district court's ruling that the disclosures effected a complete waiver of the attorney-client privilege and the work-product doctrine, thus rendering the documents available to the Republic in discovery.

For the reasons that follow, we hold that by disclosing documents to the SEC and to the DOJ, Westinghouse waived both the attorney-client privilege and the work-product doctrine with respect to those documents. * * *

I. Factual Background

A. The Contract

In the mid–1970s, Westinghouse sought and obtained the prime contract to construct the first Philippine nuclear power plant and to ready it for use on a turnkey basis. As part of Westinghouse's efforts to procure the contract, it retained as its "special sales representative" Herminio T. Disini, a Philippine businessman and close friend and associate of then-President Marcos. Disini agreed to promote Westinghouse's interests with the NPC, which was the Philippine government agency responsible for electric power generation and for contract negotiations on the power plant project. Westinghouse received the prime contract for the power plant. Several years later, newspaper articles appeared in the Philippine and American press, charging that the company had procured the contract by passing bribes to Philippine government officials through Disini.

B. The SEC Investigation and Westinghouse's Disclosures Pursuant Thereto

In January 1978, shortly after the appearance of the press reports concerning Westinghouse's alleged misconduct in connection with the Philippine nuclear plant, the SEC commenced an investigation into whether Westinghouse had violated United States securities laws by making illegal payments to obtain the contract. In March 1978, Westinghouse retained the law firm Kirkland & Ellis to conduct an internal investigation into whether company officials had made improper payments. In the course of the internal investigation, which lasted until November 1978, Kirkland & Ellis produced two letters reporting its findings.

The law firm, at the behest of Westinghouse, showed the SEC investigators one of the letter reports and, in addition, orally presented its findings to the agency. Kirkland & Ellis did not supply the SEC with any of the documents underlying the presentation and the report, and the SEC agreed not to retain the report. Westinghouse asserts that in disclosing to the SEC the results of the Kirkland & Ellis investigation, it relied upon the SEC's confidentiality regulations, as well as the Eighth Circuit's decision in *Diversified Industries, Inc. v. Meredith, 572 F.2d 596 (8th Cir. 1977)* (en banc), as creating a reasonable expectation of continuing confidentiality for the materials shown to the SEC.

In 1980, the SEC served subpoenas on Disini, based on allegations that he had engaged in illegal activities relating to the award of the prime contract for the power plant. Thereafter, counsel for Westinghouse and for Disini entered into a joint defense agreement, under which they agreed to exchange—and to maintain confidentiality with respect to—privileged information and work product. Counsel for Disini, the law firm Baker & McKenzie, subsequently began negotiating with the SEC on his behalf. As a result, the accounting firm Coopers & Lybrand was retained to perform audits tracing the funds that Westinghouse had paid to Disini. Coopers & Lybrand summarized the results of these audits in a report that Disini made available to the SEC, which in turn agreed to keep the contents of the report confidential and neither to copy nor to retain it. Pursuant to their joint defense agreement, Disini provided Westinghouse with a copy of the Coopers & Lybrand report. The SEC discontinued its investigation of Westinghouse in April 1983.

C. The Department of Justice Investigations and Westinghouse's Disclosures Pursuant Thereto

In 1978, the DOJ began to investigate Westinghouse. The DOJ's investigation explored whether Westinghouse had made illegal payments to obtain contracts not only in the Philippines, but also in other countries. * * * The DOJ's investigation ended when Westinghouse entered into a plea agreement concerning payments that the company admitted making in order to obtain business in Egypt.

In 1986, after Marcos was deposed as President of the Philippines, the DOJ reactivated its 1978 investigation of Westinghouse's conduct in procuring the turnkey contract on the Philippine nuclear plant. A grand jury subpoenaed the Kirkland & Ellis letters reporting the results of Westinghouse's internal investigation, as well as all documents accumulated in connection with that investigation. In an effort to preserve its attorney-client privilege and work-product protection, Westinghouse moved to quash the subpoena. After entering into a confidentiality agreement with DOJ ... Westinghouse disclosed the subpoenaed documents to the grand jury. According to Westinghouse, this agreement, which was itself confidential, provided

> "that the [DOJ] review at Westinghouse counsel's office (but not keep copies of) attorney-client privileged and work product protected materials in the Kirkland & Ellis files, that the information contained therein would not be disclosed to anyone outside of the DOJ, and that such review of the Kirkland & Ellis documents would not constitute a waiver of Westinghouse's work product and attorney-client privileges."

The DOJ's investigation is apparently still ongoing (at least the record does not indicate the contrary).

D.　The Republic's Investigation

In 1987, the Republic initiated its own investigation into the contract-procurement activities of Westinghouse and a second company, Burns & Roe Enterprises, Inc., a New Jersey corporation that had obtained the architecture and engineering contract on the power plant project and that also had secured the services of Disini as a "special sales representative." The Republic's Presidential Commission on Good Government (the "PCGG"), the government entity charged with investigating Westinghouse's and Burns & Roe's conduct, subsequently entered into an agreement with the DOJ, denominated the "Agreement on Procedures for Mutual Legal Assistance" (the "Agreement").

The Agreement, which is still in force, provides that the PCGG and to the DOJ will exercise their best efforts to provide one another with information and materials relevant to their concurrent investigations that can be used in any subsequent criminal, civil, and administrative proceedings. Under the Agreement, the PCGG and the DOJ also have undertaken to maintain confidentiality as to all correspondence concerning shared information.

II.　Procedural History

A.　The Current Proceedings

In December 1988, the Republic and the NPC [filed a fifteen-count complaint] against Westinghouse and Burns & Roe in the district court for the District of New Jersey. * * *

Pursuant to a clause in its contract with the NPC, Westinghouse moved to stay the action pending arbitration.... [T]he district court stayed all claims except (1) the claim that Westinghouse, along with Burns & Roe, tortiously interfered with Marcos's performance of the fiduciary duties that he owed to the Philippine people and (2) the claim that the two defendants conspired to prevent Marcos from performing his fiduciary duties to the Philippine people and to the NPC.

In the course of discovery on these two claims, the Republic requested that Westinghouse produce the documents that it had made available to the SEC and to the DOJ. Westinghouse objected to this discovery request, invoking both the work-product doctrine and the attorney-client privilege. Westinghouse sought, in turn, to discover documents that the Republic had shared with the DOJ under the Agreement. The Republic resisted, asserting that these documents were protected by the work-product doctrine.

The magistrate judge supervising discovery concluded that Westinghouse had waived its attorney-client privilege regarding the documents it disclosed to the SEC and to the DOJ because at least in adversarial situations, once disclosure has been made to a government agency, any privilege is lost, notwithstanding any confidentiality agreement between Westinghouse and the government. He therefore ruled that Westinghouse must identify and produce all documents disclosed to the DOJ and to the SEC, although he invited Westinghouse to appeal this ruling to the district court.

The magistrate judge further held that the documents that Westinghouse had requested from the Republic were protected by the work-product doctrine and therefore were not subject to discovery. The magistrate judge reasoned that, because the DOJ is an *ally* of the Republic, the latter, by sharing information with the agency, had not subverted the principles of the adversary system in which the work-product doctrine is grounded. The magistrate judge also reasoned that the sharing of information between the DOJ and the Republic was "highly unlikely" to lead to the disclosure of the information to adversaries.

B.   *The District Court's Opinion*

The district court affirmed both rulings * * *

IV.   THE ATTORNEY-CLIENT PRIVILEGE AND THE SELECTIVE WAIVER THEORY

The central question regarding Westinghouse's attorney-client privilege claim is the validity of the celebrated and controversial selective waiver[7] theory fashioned by the Eighth Circuit in *Diversified Industries, Inc. v. Meredith, 572 F.2d 596 (8th Cir. 1978)* (en banc), and resoundingly rejected by the D.C. Circuit in *Permian Corp. v. United States, 214 U.S. App. D.C. 396, 665 F.2d 1214 (D.C. Cir. 1981),* and subsequent cases. In *Diversified,* the Eighth Circuit held that disclosure of material protected by the attorney-client privilege to the SEC during a formal investigation constituted only a selective waiver of the privilege, and that

---

7. Although the rule in *Diversified* is often referred to as the "limited waiver rule," we prefer not to use that phrase because the word "limited" refers to two distinct types of waivers: selective and partial. Selective waiver permits the client who has disclosed privileged communications to one party to continue asserting the privilege against other parties. Partial waiver permits a client who has disclosed a portion of privileged communications to continue asserting the privilege as to the remaining portions of the same communications.

therefore the material could not be discovered in subsequent civil litigation.

It is often stated that the purpose of the attorney-client privilege is to encourage "full and frank communication between attorneys and their clients." Full and frank communication is not an end in itself, however, but merely a means to achieve the ultimate purpose of the privilege: "promoting broader public interests in the observance of law and administration of justice." The Supreme Court recognized this underlying rationale for the privilege long ago, when it stated:

> "[The attorney-client privilege] is founded upon the necessity, in the interest and administration of justice, of the aid of persons having knowledge of the law and skilled in its practice, which assistance can only be safely and readily availed of when free from the consequences or the apprehension of disclosure."

Hunt v. Blackburn, 128 U.S. 464, 470, 9 S. Ct. 125 , 32 L. Ed. 488 (1888) (quoted in *Upjohn, 449 U.S. at 389*).

Because the attorney-client privilege obstructs the truth-finding process, it is construed narrowly. The privilege "protects *only* those disclosures—necessary to obtain informed legal advice—which might not have been made absent the privilege." Accordingly, voluntary disclosure to a third party of purportedly privileged communications has long been considered inconsistent with an assertion of the privilege. As one commentator cogently explained:

> "If clients themselves divulge such information to third parties, chances are that they would also have divulged it to their attorneys, even without the protection of the privilege. Thus, once a client has revealed privileged information to a third party, the basic justification for the privilege no longer applies . . ."

Comment, *Stuffing the Rabbit Back into the Hat: Limited Waiver of the Attorney–Client Privilege in an Administrative Agency Investigation, 130 U Pa L Rev 1198, 1207 (1982)*. Consequently, it is well-settled that when a client voluntarily discloses privileged communications to a third party, the privilege is waived.

When disclosure to a third party is necessary for the client to obtain informed legal advice, courts have recognized exceptions to the rule that disclosure waives the attorney-client privilege. For example, courts have held that the client may allow disclosure to an "agent" assisting the attorney in giving legal advice to the client without waiving the privilege. Courts have also held that the client may disclose communications to co-defendants or co-litigants without waiving the privilege. These exceptions are consistent with the goal underlying the privilege because each type of disclosure is sometimes necessary for the client to obtain informed legal advice.

Westinghouse in essence asks that we recognize another exception to the waiver doctrine, one designed to accommodate voluntary disclosure to government agencies. In this regard, we note preliminarily that numerous cases have applied the traditional waiver doctrine to communications disclosed to government agencies.

In *Diversified*, the Eighth Circuit departed from the traditional waiver doctrine by recognizing an exception for voluntary disclosures made in cooperation with SEC investigations. The court's explanation for its departure consists, in its entirety, of the following sentence: "To hold otherwise may have the effect of thwarting the developing procedure of corporations to employ independent outside counsel to investigate and advise them in order to protect stockholders, potential stockholders and customers."

In rejecting *Diversified*, the D.C. Circuit observed that it could not see how the availability of a selective waiver "would serve the interests underlying the [attorney-client privilege]." The court reasoned that selective waiver "has little to do with" the privilege's purpose—protecting the confidentiality of attorney-client communications in order to encourage clients to obtain informed legal assistance. Id. The court explained that while voluntary cooperation with government investigations "may be a laudable activity, ... it is hard to understand how such conduct improves the attorney-client relationship." The court then advanced a second reason for rejecting the selective waiver rule, stating:

> "The client cannot be permitted to pick and choose among his opponents, waiving the privilege for some and resurrecting the claim of confidentiality to obstruct others, or to invoke the privilege as to communications whose confidentiality he has already compromised for his own benefit.... The attorney-client privilege is not designed for such tactical employment."

We find the first part of the D.C. Circuit's reasoning persuasive. The Eighth Circuit's sole justification for permitting selective waiver was to encourage corporations to undertake internal investigations.... [S]elective waiver does not serve the purpose of encouraging full disclosure to one's attorney in order to obtain informed legal assistance; it merely encourages voluntary disclosure to government agencies, thereby extending the privilege beyond its intended purpose. Moreover, selective waiver does nothing to promote the attorney-client relationship; indeed, the unique role of the attorney, which led to the creation of the privilege, has little relevance to the selective waiver permitted in *Diversified*.

The traditional waiver doctrine provides that disclosure to third parties waives the attorney-client privilege unless the disclosure serves the purpose of enabling clients to obtain informed legal advice. Because the selective waiver rule in *Diversified* protects disclosures made for entirely different purposes, it cannot be reconciled with traditional attorney-client privilege doctrine. Therefore, we are not persuaded to engraft the *Diversified* exception onto the attorney-client privilege. Westinghouse argues that the selective waiver rule encourages corporations to conduct internal investigations and to cooperate with federal investigative agencies. We agree with the D.C. Circuit that these objectives, however laudable, are beyond the intended purposes of the attorney-client privilege, and therefore we find Westinghouse's policy arguments irrelevant to our task of applying the attorney-client privilege to this case. In our view, to go beyond the policies underlying the attorney-client privilege on the rationale offered by Westinghouse would be to create an entirely new privilege.

* * * [W]e do not think that a new privilege is necessary to encourage voluntary cooperation with government investigations. Indeed, no such privilege was established at the time Westinghouse decided to cooperate with the SEC and the DOJ. When Westinghouse first disclosed privileged materials to the SEC, only one court of appeals had adopted the selective waiver rule. By the time Westinghouse made its disclosures to the DOJ, another court of appeals had trenchantly rejected the selective waiver rule. We find it significant that Westinghouse chose to cooperate despite the absence of an established privileged protecting disclosures to government agencies. We also note that many other corporations also have chosen to cooperate with the SEC despite the lack of an established privilege protecting their disclosures.

Our rejection of the selective waiver rule does not depend, however, on the second reason the D.C. Circuit gave in *Permian* for rejecting *Diversified*. Generally, the "fairness doctrine" is invoked in partial (as opposed to selective) disclosure cases. This case involves selective, rather than partial, disclosure. The courts and commentators disagree about whether there is anything unfair about selective disclosure. Here is it unnecessary to decide the question. We need not find unfairness to the Republic in order to find waiver because we have concluded already that the attorney-client privilege protects only those disclosures necessary to encourage clients to seek informed legal advice and that Westinghouse's disclosures were not made for this purpose.

Westinghouse further contends, however, that the SEC's regulations concerning confidentiality and the stipulated court order memorializing the confidentiality agreement between Westinghouse and the DOJ must be regarded as preserving the attorney-client privilege with respect to the information disclosed because of Westinghouse's expectations of confidentiality engendered thereby. We reject Westinghouse's argument that it did not waive the privilege because it reasonably expected that the SEC and the DOJ would maintain the confidentiality of the information that it disclosed to them.

Even though the DOJ apparently agreed not to disclose the information, under traditional waiver doctrine a voluntary disclosure[15] to a third party waives the attorney-client privilege even if the third party agrees not to disclose the communications to anyone else. We also note that the agreement between Westinghouse and the DOJ preserved Westing-

---

15. We consider Westinghouse's disclosure to the DOJ to be voluntary even though it was prompted by a grand jury subpoena. Although Westinghouse originally moved to quash the subpoena, it later withdrew the motion and produced the documents pursuant to the confidentiality agreement. Had Westinghouse continued to object to the subpoena and produced the documents only after being ordered to do so, we would not consider its disclosure of those documents to be voluntary.

house's right to invoke the attorney-client privilege only as to the DOJ—and does not appear in any way to have purported to preserve Westinghouse's right to invoke the privilege against a different entity in an unrelated civil proceeding such as the instant case.

Moreover, even if Westinghouse could preserve the privilege by conditioning its disclosure upon a promise to maintain confidentiality, no such promise was made here regarding the information disclosed to the SEC. As Westinghouse emphasizes, SEC regulations in effect at the time of Westinghouse's disclosures to that agency provided that the SEC would maintain confidentiality as to information and documents obtained in the course of any investigation. We do not think, however, that these regulations justified a reasonable belief on Westinghouse's part that the attorney-client privilege would be preserved with respect to the Kirkland & Ellis letter and the other information disclosed to the SEC. As the Republic observes, the very regulations on which Westinghouse relies explicitly provided that information obtained in the course of a non-public investigation must be made a matter of public record and provided upon request if the disclosure of the confidential information was "not contrary to the public interest." * * *

V. Westinghouse's Claim for Protection Under the Work-Product Doctrine

Westinghouse also argues that the work-product doctrine shields the documents that it disclosed to the SEC and to the DOJ from the Republic. Once again, Westinghouse's argument requires us to choose between positions taken by the Eighth and D.C. Circuits. In order to evaluate those positions, however, we must begin with a review of the purpose underlying the work-product doctrine.

The purpose of the work-product doctrine differs from that of the attorney-client privilege. As we have explained, the attorney-client privilege promotes the attorney-client relationship, and, indirectly, the functioning of our legal system, by protecting the confidentiality of communications between clients and their attorneys. In contrast, the work-product doctrine promotes the adversary system directly by protecting the confidentiality of papers prepared by or on behalf of attorneys in anticipation of litigation. Protecting attorneys' work product promotes the adversary system by enabling attorneys to prepare cases without fear that their work product will be used against their clients.

A disclosure to a third party waives the attorney-client privilege unless the disclosure is necessary to further the goal of enabling the client to seek informed legal assistance. Because the work-product doctrine serves instead to protect an attorney's work product from falling into the hands of an adversary, a disclosure to a third party does not necessarily waive the protection of the work-product doctrine. Most courts hold that to waive the protection of the work-product doctrine, the disclosure must enable an adversary to gain access to the information.

We agree that the purpose of the work-product doctrine requires us to distinguish between disclosures to adversaries and disclosures to non-adversaries. We also find Westinghouse's argument that the DOJ and the SEC were not its adversaries to be without merit. Unlike a party who assists the government in investigating or prosecuting another, Westinghouse was the target of investigations conducted by the agencies. Under these circumstances, we have no difficulty concluding that the SEC and the DOJ were Westinghouse's adversaries.

The more difficult question is whether Westinghouse's disclosure to these two adversaries waives the protection of the work-product doctrine as against the Republic. Even though the courts generally agree that disclosure to an adversary waives the work-product doctrine, they disagree over the reasons behind this principle and thus, over its application to specific circumstances. * * *

We hold that Westinghouse's disclosure of work product to the SEC and to the DOJ waived the work-product doctrine as against all other adversaries. As we explained at page 1424, parties who have disclosed materials protected by the attorney-client privilege may preserve the privilege when the disclosure was necessary to further the goal underlying the privilege. We require the same showing of relationship to the underlying goal when a party discloses documents protected by the work-product doctrine. In other words, a party who discloses documents protected by the work-product doctrine may continue to assert the doctrine's protection only when the disclosure furthers the doctrine's underlying goal.

Two considerations inform our formulation of this standard for waiving the work-product doctrine. First, we are mindful of the general principle that evidentiary privileges are to be strictly construed. Second, the work-product doctrine recognizes a *qualified* evidentiary protection, in contrast to the absolute protection afforded by the attorney-client privilege. The protection of the work-product doctrine, unlike that of the attorney-client privilege, may be overcome by a showing of substantial need, and "like other qualified privileges, [it] may be waived." These two considerations persuade us that the standard for waiving the work-product doctrine should be no more stringent than the standard for waiving the attorney-client privilege.

Applying this standard here, we hold that Westinghouse's disclosures to the SEC and to the DOJ waived the protection of the work-product doctrine because they were not made to further the goal underlying the doctrine. When a party discloses protected materials to a government agency investigating allegations against it, it uses those materials to forestall prosecution (if the charges are unfounded) or to obtain lenient treatment (in the case of well-founded allegations). These objectives, however rational, are foreign to the objectives underlying the work-product doctrine. Moreover, an exception for disclosures to government agencies is not necessary to further the doctrine's purpose; attorneys are still free to prepare their cases without fear of disclosure to an adversary as long as they and their clients refrain from making such disclosures themselves. Creating an exception for disclosures to government agencies may actually hinder the operation of the work-product doctrine. If internal investigations are undertaken with an eye to later disclosing the results to a government agency, the outside counsel conducting the investigation may hesitate to pursue unfavorable information or legal theories about the corporation. Thus, allowing a party to preserve the doctrine's protection while disclosing work product to a government agency could actually discourage attorneys from fully preparing their cases.

We also reject Westinghouse's argument that it did not waive the work-product protection because it reasonably expected the agencies to keep the documents it disclosed to them confidential. Even if we had found that the agencies had made such an agreement, it would not change our conclusion. * * *

VI. CONCLUSION

For the foregoing reasons, we conclude that Westinghouse waived the attorney-client privilege and the work-product doctrine when it disclosed otherwise protected documents to the SEC and to the DOJ. Therefore, the district court did not commit clear error in ordering Westinghouse to produce the disputed material. Accordingly, the petition for a writ of mandamus will be denied.

Andrew Longstreth, DOUBLE AGENT: IN THE NEW ERA OF INTERNAL INVESTIGATIONS, DEFENSE LAWYERS HAVE BECOME DEPUTY PROSECUTORS

THE AMERICAN LAWYER, February 2005

In 2001 an anonymous letter arrived at the Securities and Exchange Commission. The letter raised questions about accounting practices at Symbol Technologies, Inc., and cited two fraudulent transactions. Those transactions, the letter alleged, were "just the tip of the iceberg of how Symbol management continues to manipulate and improperly handle their business accounting."

The SEC notified Symbol, which quickly asked one of its regular outside firms, Clifford Chance, to conduct an internal investigation. But when the firm reported its findings, the government wasn't satisfied. "We told the company they needed to do better," says George Stepaniuk, an assistant regional director for the SEC's Northeast regional office. Not long after that meeting in the spring of 2002, Symbol's general counsel, Leonard Goldner, with the approval of the audit committee, retained Andrew Levander, then of Swidler Berlin Shereff Friedman [he's now a partner at Dechert]. Though Swidler had no longstanding relationship with the company, Goldner and Levander had been partners before Goldner went in-house. And Levander, a former federal prosecutor, had plenty of experience with internal investigations ranging from uncovering lies made by Datascope Corp. to the Food and Drug Administration to unraveling a basketball point shaving scandal at Tulane University.

So he wasn't surprised when he encountered resistance at Symbol. A handful of employees allegedly hid key documents and encouraged others to stonewall his probe-just as they had with Clifford Chance. But the two investigations had one crucial difference: Levander ferreted out the alleged obstructionists and asked the company's board of directors to fire them. "I always feel discomfort [about firing people]," says Levander. "But you do what you have to do." [Lawyers from Clifford Chance declined to comment on their investigation. A firm spokesperson noted that Clifford Chance's investigation, which was conducted before Sarbanes–Oxley passed, was limited to responding to the allegations made in the anonymous letter to the SEC. He also noted that, as alleged by the government, former Symbol executives misled and lied to Clifford Chance.]

In the Symbol case, Levander found himself serving several masters. Symbol's board was Levander's client. But the SEC and federal prosecutors from New York's Eastern District, who were running a parallel criminal investigation, were just as interested in his findings. "I was told by the SEC I had better do a better job, or they would be taking testimony from employees for the next two years," Levander says. After two months of negotiating, Symbol agreed to share Levander's finding with the feds.

The move paid off for his client. Since Levander's 18–month investigation concluded last year, six Symbol executives, including general counsel Goldner, Levander's former partner, have pled guilty to charges arising from the investigation into accounting fraud. Six other Symbol executives are to stand trial in July on charges they engaged in fraudulent practices that inflated reports of Symbol's revenue by more than $200 million over three years. As a result of the company's effective investigation and cooperation, the U.S. attorney's office announced last June that it would not charge Symbol with criminal wrongdoing.

In many ways, the Symbol case typifies the new era of corporate criminal investigations-and the fundamental shifts that are taking place in the corporate defense practice. While working to uncover wrongdoing, the investigating lawyer used to present a united front on behalf of both the corporation and its employees. The lawyer jousted with the government and sought to limit the flow of information. Today, the investigating lawyer essentially acts as a fact-finder with a badge-the newest [and highest-paid] government agent. He [or she] conducts hundreds of interviews, scans company computers for damaging e-mails, rummages through the CFO's wastebasket, and then hands potential evidence over to the government.

This work can form the spine of an indictment. For example, last year during a hearing in the case against former WorldCom, Inc., CEO Bernard Ebbers, his lawyers asked prosecutors from the Southern District of New York to provide more details about the charges against their client. David Anders, an assistant U.S. attorney, referred them to the internal investigation report done by the firm now known as Wilmer Cutler Pickering Hale and Dorr. "[The defense attorneys] don't need to search through all of the discovery," said Anders, "because they have a road map, literally, [of] the charges here through the Wilmer report."

And prosecutors continue to push the boundaries. Last year prosecutors in the Eastern District of New York charged the former CEO of Computer Associates International with, among other things, obstruction of justice for lying to the company's attorneys from Wachtell, Lipton, Rosen & Katz who were investigating the company. In other cases, prosecutors have called internal investigators to testify as government witnesses.

This shift in roles has been in motion since at least the early 1990s, when companies under investigation regularly began waiving the attorney-client privilege in order to avoid prosecution. The practice has accelerated since the Enron Corp. scandal. The effect has pitted company against individual. To avoid prosecution-and a prolonged drag on share prices-companies now readily waive the privilege as a way of distancing themselves from any officer or employee under suspicion of wrongdoing. That suits the government, which is often more than willing to trade a corporation's immunity for individual scalps.

Market and regulatory skepticism toward corporate America has fueled the demand for internal investigations. Just 36 days after World-Com announced it would restate earnings by $3.8 billion in June 2002, President George Bush signed the sweeping Sarbanes–Oxley Act. The legislation assigned more liability for the company's well-being to the board of directors. Now, any whiff of wrongdoing can compel nervous board members to call in their own private prosecutor. This is more than paranoia or window-dressing: In January ten former WorldCom board members agreed to pay $18 million out of their own pockets to settle a shareholder suit.

Most internal investigations remain private or at least out of the headlines. But it has become a booming practice area for many law firms. New York attorney general Eliot Spitzer's investigation of the insurance industry is one of the latest events to set off internal probes. Levander, among others, has been hired to work on one. Anxious corporate boards like to hire former prosecutors like Levander, counting on their reputations with law enforcement agencies. It's a competitive field. Dozens of Am Law 200 firms market internal investigations on their menu of services. That's why it helps to have a star on board like Mary Jo White at Debevoise & Plimpton, Dan Webb at Winston & Strawn, or Robert Fiske, Jr., at Davis Polk & Wardwell. All are former U.S. attorneys.

The first call for help often goes to William McLucas at Wilmer. The former SEC enforcement chief has brought in two of the biggest internal investigations for his firm. In documenting the affaires Enron and WorldCom, Wilmer billed $3.88 million and $12.32 million, respectively.

These investigations can strain regular client-outside counsel relations. They're expensive, and they can expose a company's business practices to inquiry. Because parts of an investigation can end up in the government's hands, lawyers interviewing company employees are required to give what are known as Upjohn warnings, named after a 1981 U.S. Supreme Court case. Counsel must advise individuals that they represent the corporation, not them; that the privilege of the interview belongs to the company; and that the company could decide to waive the privilege in the future. Skadden, Arps, Slate, Meagher & Flom partner David Zornow says that in many cases today it's a "foregone conclusion that the company will turn over materials to the government."

Sometimes those warnings are not so well received. "Internal investigations can be a diplomatic challenge," says Sharon Nelles, a partner at Sullivan & Cromwell. "Investigating employees and officers of your clients can put you in the difficult position of walking into the room, giving them Upjohn warnings, asking hard questions, and proceeding to go through their drawers and walk away with their papers."

Those situations can be made easier when a firm with no ties to the company is conducting the investigation. It can also eliminate conflict-of-interest questions. Some lawyers say the emphasis on independence is a legacy of Vinson & Elkins's inadequate investigation of its longtime client Enron. "I'm not saying that in the past the inquiries were done with a wink and a nod," says Wilmer's McLucas. "I just don't think [that in the past] you have had the market and regulatory skepticism that now means if there are problems, there may be risk for everyone. It has to be a credible process."

The government—the real prosecutors—can be very demanding. For instance, in the Symbol case, the government clearly expected an aggressive inquiry and was disappointed by the results Clifford Chance presented. "How and why Swidler was able to find things that Clifford Chance was not able to find out is not something I can comment on," says Stepaniuk of the SEC.

From the beginning of its probe, Clifford Chance had told the SEC that Symbol was committed to full cooperation. As part of that effort, the company designated its senior vice president of finance, Michael DeGennaro, to act as a liaison between Clifford Chance and Symbol. DeGennaro, a certified public accountant, had formerly been an audit partner with Symbol's primary outside audit firm.

According to the SEC, the accountants helping Clifford Chance with its investigation wanted to review the ten largest invoices the company sent out in the fourth quarter of 2000. To identify those invoices, the accountants relied on DeGennaro. Their conclusion, which Clifford Chance presented to the SEC at a March 2002 meeting: No evidence of accounting fraud existed for that quarter.

But according to the SEC, that conclusion was skewed because DeGennaro had given the accountants an inaccurate list of invoices. Not long after that March meeting, the SEC made its displeasure clear, and Symbol hired Levander to conduct another investigation. Levander says that both the SEC and the U.S. attorney's office immediately asked the company to waive the attorney-client privilege. Levander was able to stall a decision for a couple of months while he got the lay of the land, though he says both offices kept pressing for the waiver. Ultimately, Symbol's board of directors decided to enter into an arrangement with the government in which both sides agreed to share information related to their investigations. To protect itself from third-party litigants, Levander says, Symbol asked the government to sign a confidentiality agreement in which the government would not consider any information it received as a waiver of the attorney-client and work-product privilege [see "The Consequences of Cooperation," page 72]. The government would get what it wanted-access to the findings of the investigation-while Symbol would theoretically be able to keep those findings privileged.

Levander's inquiry into Symbol's accounting didn't get far in its first few months. A handful of employees were allegedly doctoring documents, delaying access to databases, and holding back information. After conducting dozens of interviews, Levander identified DeGennaro as one of the ringleaders ordering the obstruction. So, in September 2002, Levander asked the board to fire him. [DeGennaro's lawyer, Michael Sommer at McDermott Will & Emery, says his client "worked diligently and professionally" to assist both investigations. Sommer also says that "the notion that [DeGennaro] was secretly undermining those investigations is silly."]

After DeGennaro was dismissed, Levander's investigation began to make progress. As promised, Symbol cooperated fully and gave the government practically everything but the keys to company headquarters in Holtsville, New York. Throughout Levander's investigation, Symbol shared the substance of hundreds of interviews with current and former employees and customers, made witnesses available, and handed over more than a half-million pages of company documents and hundreds of thousands of restored e-mail and voicemail messages.

Could the SEC and the U.S. attorney's office have achieved the same results without Levander's investigation? Maybe. But it likely would have taken government investigators several additional months, if not years, to obtain the same information. Still, like many lawyers who do these investigations, Levander would rather not be looked at as a government agent. For one thing, that title wouldn't go over well with most clients. He does acknowledge, though, that this is far from normal defense work. "I like to think I do it in a fair way," he says. "But clearly [it's] a different role."

While the emphasis—and consequences—have changed, corporations have been investigating themselves and reporting the results to the government for decades. After the Watergate scandal exposed companies making illegal campaign contributions, the SEC began an inquiry into corporate slush funds. That inquiry later expanded to a broader investigation of payments made to bribe foreign and domestic officials.

Limited government resources became an issue. Stanley Sporkin [a former federal judge and now a partner at Weil, Gotshal & Manges], who ran the probe as head of SEC enforcement, says that about 65 companies were initially charged with securities violations. More might have been charged, but Sporkin's staff wasn't big enough to investigate and sue every company under suspicion.

So Sporkin started a voluntary disclosure program. It allowed companies to avoid penalty by conducting their own investigations. The SEC didn't promise anything in return, but if it deemed an investigation's quality to be satisfactory, the company could make a disclosure and avoid charges.

The idea was risky. If the investigations turned out to be white-washes, Sporkin would have looked like a fool. One of the first companies to come forward was Gulf Oil Corporation. Sporkin remembers explaining his predicament to the company's lawyers, including John McCloy of Milbank, Tweed, Hadley & McCloy.

"I said, 'My neck is on the line if this doesn't work,' "recalls Sporkin.

But according to Sporkin, the Gulf Oil report prepared by McCloy was "one of the greatest reports you could ever find." It detailed exactly how and who at the company orchestrated the illegal activities. Many other reports did the same. In total, Sporkin says, the voluntary program resulted in more than 650 companies conducting investigations and admitting wrongdoing.

Other government bodies later adopted the same idea. The U.S. Department of Defense started a program in the 1980s that encouraged defense contractors to report fraud. In the early 1990s the U.S. Department of Justice antitrust division revised a corporate leniency program that gave incentives to companies to disclose violations and cooperate with the government.

But it was not always in the company's interest to divulge the contents of their internal investigations. And it certainly wasn't always expected that a company would share them with the government. Robert Bennett at Skadden, Arps has been probing troubled clients for more than 30 years. But until the mid-to-late 1990s, his investigations were usually for the company's eyes only. They weren't often seen or judged by prosecutors or regulators. "When you were doing an internal investigation, you fought hard not to disclose it [to the government]," says Bennett.

Today lawyers operate under the premise that their internal investigation findings will be turned over to the government. Prosecutors in the Southern District of New York have helped lead this change. In the

1990s one new factor they considered when weighing the adequacy of a company's cooperation was its willingness to waive the corporation's attorney-client privilege. By 1999, the Department of Justice adopted that principle in the Holder memo, named after then-deputy attorney general Eric Holder, Jr. The so-called Thompson memo [named after former deputy attorney general Larry Thompson], written in 2003, reinforced those ideas.

The memos have rankled the defense bar. While the Thompson memo states clearly that prosecutors should not require a waiver when deciding whether to prosecute a company, defense lawyers complain that it has become a requirement in reality.

Defense lawyers also point to the federal sentencing guidelines and the SEC's model guidelines for cooperation as tools that prosecutors and regulators have used to obtain privileged materials. If privileged materials are routinely passed to the government, they argue, the flow of information at companies could slow down. That could impede the effectiveness of any investigation, which would prevent shareholders from learning critical information about the company. "You want company officers and directors to talk to their outside and inside lawyers," explains Mary Jo White, former U.S. attorney for the Southern District of New York. "If what becomes the rule of the road-that everything you say will be turned over to the government-that will chill communications."

Prosecutors and regulators don't see cause for concern. David Kelley, U.S. attorney for the Southern District of New York, professes to strongly believe in the sanctity of the attorney-client privilege, and says the private bar's worries about it being waived are overblown. Kelley maintains that his office rarely asks a company to waive its attorney-client privilege. His prosecutors are like Joe Friday, he says: just interested in the facts. And the disclosure of those facts ultimately helps shareholders. "Companies are saying that the government has to stay out of these things," he says. "Our goal is good corporate governance. We wouldn't be there if we didn't need to be there."

To "be there," though, the government needs help. In a speech last September, SEC enforcement director Cutler acknowledged his agency's resource deficit. "While we've been the beneficiaries of significant budget increases in the last three years," he said, "we're still quite small when you consider the breadth of our 'beat'-more than 12,000 public companies, 7,200 broker-dealers, 8,200 investment advisers, and 35,000 mutual funds." So prosecutors and regulators increasingly rely on the defense bar. Last year, for example, the SEC's investigation of possible accounting improprieties at Royal Ahold N.V. would have been a lot tougher, if not impossible, without the help of Wilmer. Royal Ahold voluntarily expanded its own internal probe from the United States to 17 operating companies in ten countries and arranged for staff to be interviewed by the SEC in the U.S. and abroad. Wilmer devoted more than 50 lawyers to the task. Morvillo, Abramowitz, Grand, Iason & Silberberg also worked on the investigation in the U.S. In October the SEC announced that it would not seek civil penalties from the company, partly because of Ahold's extensive internal investigation and cooperation.

Internal investigators don't just gather evidence for the government. Sometimes they have to testify, too. "A lot of us are uneasy about that prospect," says Kirby Behre, a white-collar criminal defense lawyer at Paul, Hastings, Janofsky & Walker. And with good reason. Consider the attack on David Boies during the closing remarks of Mark Swartz's criminal trial. The former chief financial officer of Tyco International Ltd., Swartz was accused of abusing the company's loan program and stealing from the company through payments not approved by the board of directors. Tyco's board hired Boies to conduct an internal investigation into the company's accounting.

Swartz's lawyer, Charles Stillman of Stillman & Friedman, attempted to portray Boies as beholden to the company and the district attorney's office in Manhattan. In his closing argument, Stillman reminded the jury that Boies's firm, Boies, Schiller & Flexner, had collected $30 million in legal fees from Tyco over a 19–month period [for work in the investigation and for representing Tyco in civil litigation against Swartz and the former CEO, Dennis Kozlowski].

Boies had testified that his firm had regularly consulted with prosecutors about the case, and Stillman implored the jury to question the reliability of Boies's statements. "Ask yourselves in light of that testimony whether Mr. Boies has a bias," said Stillman before the prosecution objected. "I would suggest it's almost as if the district attorney called one of its prosecutors sitting at their table to the stand to refute Mark Swartz's testimony." [Boies did not return two messages to his office.]

Robert Jossen also learned what it's like to take the stand. When the former general counsel of Rite Aid Corporation, Franklin Brown, was on trial for allegedly conspiring to manipulate earnings at Rite Aid, Jossen was called as a witness for the prosecution. Jossen, then at Swidler Berlin and now a partner at Dechert, had been hired by Rite Aid's audit committee in November 1999 to look into the company's financial statements. During the course of his investigation, he interviewed Brown and wrote a memo about the conversation. The memo was entered into evidence at trial.

Much of Jossen's testimony focused on what Brown had told him during that interview. But on cross-examination, Brown's lawyer, Reid Weingarten of Steptoe & Johnson, also spent time on the processes of Jossen's internal investigation, seemingly aiming to question its reliability. Jossen testified that he had not written down verbatim what Brown said in the interview, and that no court reporter or tape recorder had been used. He also stated that he and a colleague had collaborated to write the memo of the interview and that they did not share the contents with Brown.

Weingarten also asked Jossen to confirm that he was hired by the audit committee. At one point Weingarten asked Jossen if during his investigation he ever had concerns about being "viewed as new management's hatchet man." Jossen replied, "Absolutely not."

"No defense lawyer likes to do that," says Jossen about testifying as a prosecution witness. "It was not a pleasant experience. It was probably the least enjoyable experience I have had. But to some extent, when you sign on to do one of these, if the company decides it wants to cooperate with the government, that comes with the territory."

Where does the current status of investigations leave corporate officers? In need of their own counsel. Circling the wagons doesn't work anymore. In Den of Thieves, an account of the insider trading scandals during the late 1980s, author James Stewart [an alumnus of The American Lawyer] reported that famed lawyer Edward Bennett Williams made an impassioned plea to James Dahl, one of Michael Milken's colleagues. Williams, who was already representing Milken in the government's investigation, wanted to be Dahl's lawyer, too. He told Dahl, "We'll beat these sons of bitches, but we have to remain on the inside of the tent pissing out."

That type of coordination on the defense side is now hard to find, and individuals bear a heavy burden in the current era of internal investigations. If an employee speaks to the company's lawyers, he or she risks having any statements turned over to the government. Employees who refuse to speak risk being fired and branded criminal. As the practice of internal investigations has matured, this dynamic has caused some concern in the defense bar. "If something bad happens, okay," says Charles Stillman. "But I think they should analyze their case. They should stand up [to the government]." But sometimes it's just more effective to toss out the weakest-or the most culpable-and hope that their meat will satisfy the hunger of the proverbial wolves.

Alex Berenson, CASE EXPANDS TYPE OF LIES PROSECUTORS WILL PURSUE

THE NEW YORK TIMES, May 17, 2004

Until last month, lying to your own company's lawyers was not a crime.

Now it is.

Defense lawyers and civil libertarians are expressing alarm at the government's aggressive use of obstruction of justice laws in its investigation of accounting improprieties at Computer Associates, the giant software company. Some of the lawyers also criticize the handling of the case by Wachtell, Lipton, Rosen & Katz, a prominent law firm that the company hired to investigate the charges on its behalf.

On April 9, three former executives at the company pleaded guilty to obstruction charges tied to lies they told to Wachtell, whose investigation was led by John F. Savarese, a former federal prosecutor who also represented Martha Stewart before her trial this year.

The Computer Associates executives were never accused of lying directly to federal investigators or a grand jury. Their guilty pleas were based on the theory that in lying to Wachtell they had misled federal officials, because Wachtell passed their lies to the government. When the federal investigation became public in February 2002, the company promised to cooperate fully with the prosecutors.

Tim Lynch, director of the Cato Institute's Project on Criminal Justice, said he was quite surprised that Judge I. Leo Glasser had accepted the guilty pleas. An executive who lies to his company's lawyers should be fired, not prosecuted, he said. Prosecutors are stretching the law, he believes, in a way that Congress did not intend.

"If an employee is speaking to an internal investigator, the only sanction for lying to or misleading an internal investigator is discharge from your company," Mr. Lynch said. "It's improper to let these private investigators assume some set of quasi-governmental status which is very unclear to people. The bottom line is that it's not a crime."

Prosecutors disagree with Mr. Lynch's assessment, saying that the executives knew that their testimony would be turned over to the government and that they needed to tell the truth.

Defense lawyers say the case vividly reveals the potential traps that mid-and high-level executives face during internal corporate investigations, which have become increasingly common.

Prosecutors now demand that companies give up any claim of legal privilege and turn over whatever information they have uncovered internally to avoid a companywide indictment that could devastate the corporation, lawyers say. Though employees are usually warned that their answers are not protected by attorney-client privilege, they may not have the same reservations about lying to their own lawyers that they would have to federal agents.

At the same time, company employees cannot assert a right against self-incrimination during an internal investigation: if they refuse to answer questions, they can be fired. So managers may feel they have little choice but to lie, especially if senior executives are also lying.

Usually, obstruction charges cover behavior like destroying documents or pressuring witnesses not to testify. There are also laws that make lying to federal officials a crime even for people who are not under oath. Perjury laws bar lying in court.

In addition to the obstruction charges, the Computer Associates executives pleaded guilty to securities fraud. Two of the executives face up to 10 years in federal prison for the obstruction and securities fraud; the third, Ira H. Zar, the former chief financial officer, could serve up to 20 years.

All three men are now cooperating with prosecutors in hopes of receiving significantly shorter sentences, giving them a strong incentive to plead guilty to the charges rather than contest them in court. In March, a former midlevel executive at Dynegy, the natural gas trading company, was sentenced to 24 years in prison after a jury found him guilty of accounting fraud. That sentence has unnerved many executives who face white-collar crime charges, encouraging them to plead guilty in return for lighter sentences, defense lawyers say.

The Computer Associates investigation, which began more than two years ago, is being jointly conducted by prosecutors in Brooklyn and the Securities and Exchange Commission. The inquiry is now focusing on Sanjay Kumar, who resigned last month as chief executive; Mr. Kumar remains at the company as chief software architect, although he has no day-to-day management responsibilities. His lawyers say he has done nothing wrong.

In their guilty pleas, the executives depicted a broad conspiracy at the company to lie to Wachtell and to slow the government's investigation. Just because those lies were told through lawyers rather than by the executives directly does not excuse them, said Roslynn R. Mauskopf, United States attorney for the Eastern District of New York.

"Zar and other indicted C.A. officers made false statements to C.A.'s attorneys that were intended to—and did in fact—obstruct justice," Ms. Mauskopf said.

"That the false statements were passed along to the government through attorneys does not blunt the obstructers' intent or the effect of their actions. To conclude otherwise would have the perverse effect of creating a safe harbor for individuals who carry out their obstruction through attorneys."

But Kirby Behre, a defense lawyer in Washington, said that lawyers are becoming "almost extensions of the government" because of the increasing pressure to cooperate with investigations. "I think that's something a lot of us as criminal defense lawyers feel a bit uncomfortable about."

"There used to be a time when an internal investigation was an internal investigation to figure out whether there was wrongdoing. Part 1 was figuring out what happened, and Part 2 was figuring out whether it could be defended," said a lawyer for a Computer Associates executive who has pleaded guilty. The lawyer insisted on not being identified because his client has not yet been sentenced.

"The government won't accept that any more. An internal investigation has to be an absolute search for the truth and an absolute capitulation to the government."

Using those criteria, some lawyers expressed doubts about whether Mr. Savarese and Wachtell did a good job.

In February 2002, after the criminal inquiry was publicly disclosed, Computer Associates hired Wachtell to conduct an internal investigation into its accounting practices. By that time, employees had already publicly disclosed problems with Computer Associates' financial statements, including its practice of backdating sales to meet its quarterly goals.

The practice was common at Computer Associates and widely known among employees, and had been mentioned prominently in a New York Times article in May 2001. Computer Associates has now admitted backdating more than $2 billion in revenue in 1999 and 2000.

But the executives apparently were willing to take the risk of lying to Wachtell about the practice. In their pleas, the men depicted a widespread conspiracy among the company's top management to mislead the firm.

Harvey Silverglate, a criminal defense lawyer in Boston who was not involved in the case, said Mr. Savarese should have investigated the company more aggressively.

"Any experienced criminal lawyer has a very good idea when he's being lied to early on," Mr. Silverglate said. In fact, prosecutors made progress in their investigation despite the executives' lies, and after the audit committee of Computer Associates' board hired a second law firm to conduct its own internal investigation in the summer of 2003, the conspiracy quickly crumbled.

Internal investigations are very lucrative for law firms, which may not want to anger their clients by pressing too hard for the truth, Mr. Silverglate said. As a result, they can put both individual executives and the company that hired them at risk.

"They look at themselves as servants of these corporate people," he said. "They do the bidding of the client, and what they're really doing is the bidding of the government."

Mr. Savarese did not return repeated calls for comment.

Along with the Computer Associates case, he had difficulty with another case that ultimately hinged on obstruction. Mr. Savarese represented Ms. Stewart last year, although not at her trial. In March a jury found Ms. Stewart guilty of obstruction of justice for lying to federal investigators about the reason she sold 3,928 shares of ImClone Systems. In both the Stewart and Computer Associates cases, investigators have charged that defendants impeded their investigations.

PROBLEMS

1. You are a junior partner at the law firm of Hatch & Burriss, which does most of the intellectual property and antitrust work for the computer company Cyberquest. A more senior partner at the firm calls you into his office to participate in a meeting with Cyberquest's regulatory compliance officer. The officer says that the most recent periodic internal audit of the company has raised concern that an employee or employees may have been engaged in illegal price-fixing activity with respect to a line of computer components.

Cyberquest would like your firm to conduct an internal investigation to determine if this suspicion is well-founded. If it is, the company will consider notifying the Department of Justice. Under the Department's antitrust amnesty program, the first company to inform DOJ of an antitrust violation and cooperate in the investigation of it may receive lenient treatment by the government. Only the first company to come forward, however, is eligible for amnesty. If Hatch & Burriss reports that there is evidence of price-fixing, Cybrerquest officials plan to discuss whether it would be in the best interest of the company to report it so as to take advantage of the amnesty program. The more senior partner at the firm asks you to conduct the internal investigation.

The first person whom you are able to interview is John Wallace, Cyberquest's marketing director for computer components. You tell him that Cyberquest officials are concerned that there may have been some activity by employees that runs the risk of violating antitrust laws, and that you have been asked to investigate this possibility. You say that you would like him to tell you whatever he knows about the pricing of the components so that the company can determine if any problem has occurred and can rectify it. Wallace appears somewhat nervous. He tells you that he is not aware of anything that would lead him to believe that there has been any illegal activity.

You next interview Cynthia Schultz, Wallace's assistant in the computer component marketing division. You begin by telling her what you told Wallace, and then asks if she has any information relating to possible price-fixing. She is noticeably nervous. She asks whether the company has to turn over whatever information it gathers to the government. "Cynthia," you respond, "what you tell me is privileged information. That means that the government has no right to force me to disclose what you say to me."

Schultz appears to be relieved at your response. She then to tell you that the chief purchasing officer of Exton, a major Cyberquest customer, has recently announced that Exton plans to be significantly more aggressive in seeking volume discounts for purchases of computer components. If successful, such a policy could substantially reduce profit margins on computer components, which are an important source of revenue for Cyberquest.

Schultz says that she and Wallace had a series of conversations about the Exton initiative with their counterparts at Zenon Corporation, the company's main competitor. In these discussions, the four employees agreed to "hold the line" by refusing to offer any volume discounts. Since the two companies together have the overwhelming share of the market for the main components used by Exton, such coordination would ensure a stable level of profits for company. Schultz tells you that she and Wallace are the only two Cyberquest employees who participated in this arrangement, and that they have taken steps to conceal it from those higher in the company chain of command.

Based on the information you gain from Schultz, your firm advises Cyberquest that it notify the Department of Justice that: (a) it believes that company employees may have engaged in antitrust violations in conjunction with Zenon Corporation and (b) it is prepared to turn over the results of your investigation to the Department. The company accepts this advice.

On the basis of the information contained in your investigation, John Wallace and Cynthia Schultz are charged with the crime of price-fixing, and Wallace also is charged with obstruction of justice for his denial of illegal activity during your interview with him. Schultz has now recanted her story, and the Zenon employees deny engaging in price-fixing. Are there ways in which your conduct of the investigation could be subject to question in a way that might jeopardize the prosecutions of Wallace and Schultz? If so, what could you have done differently?

2. Shortly after the Justice Department brings its charges, Exton learns from independent sources of the alleged price-fixing activity by your company and Zenon. It institutes a civil antitrust suit against you both. When it learns that your company has provided a report of its internal investigation to the Justice Department, it moves to obtain the report and the underlying information on which it is based. How should its motion be decided?

Chapter 25

CRIMINAL PROSECUTION

Corporate lawyers don't serve as criminal prosecutors. It is helpful, however, for corporate counsel to understand the considerations that a prosecutor takes into account in deciding whether to prosecute a corporation or its members. Recent years have seen an increasing willingness to bring criminal charges in response to conduct that in the past might have been subject only to civil sanctions.

Those charges may be brought not only against individuals, but against corporate entities themselves. As a result of a conviction, a corporation may be ordered to pay a substantial fine, may be precluded from bidding on work for the government or participating in government reimbursement programs, and may be placed on probation under the supervision of a court. Furthermore, the effect of a criminal conviction on a company's reputation may be devastating. Indeed, as the fall of the Arthur Andersen accounting firm illustrates, even an indictment may be enough to sound the death knell for a business enterprise.

Prosecutors therefore wield substantial power. Much of that power consists of exercises of discretion behind closed doors, and thus occurs without significant external review. For this reason, society must depend to a large degree on a prosecutor's internalized sense of constraint as protection against government abuse. Special ABA rules have been adopted to guide prosecutors in carrying out their duties, and federal and state prosecutors' offices have their own guidelines and policies setting forth the boundaries of acceptable behavior. Prosecutors at least in theory resemble thus resemble lawyers guided by William Simon's contextual model of the lawyer's role described in Chapter 2. As the ABA declares, the duty of the prosecutor "is to seek justice, not merely to convict."

OVERVIEW OF THE CHAPTER

The chapter begins with the ABA Standards that deal with the Prosecution Function. These Standards, along with those relating to the Defense Function described in the next chapter, have prompted the revision of the criminal codes in many states. They also regularly are cited in federal court opinions. The standards complement, rather than displace, the ethical rules of each state bar, to which prosecutors and defense lawyers remain subject.

Pay particular attention to Standard 3–1.9, which relates to the criteria for bringing criminal charges. Section (a) of that Standard is intended to constrain the prosecutor's discretion when charges are not supported by probable cause, and when there is insufficient admissible evidence to support a conviction. While the portion relating to the absence of probable cause is framed in the advisory form of "should," note that Model Rule 3.8(a) says that a prosecutor "shall" refrain from bringing charges in such an instance.

By contrast, the second portion of Section (a) also is worded in terms of "should," but has no Model Rule counterpart. The prosecutor therefore is encouraged not to bring charges without sufficient admissible evidence to support a conviction, but is not forbidden from doing so. Does such a provision serve any purpose if it effectively leaves the decision up to the prosecutor?

The excerpt from Webb, Molo, and Hurst provide an overview of the criminal liability of both corporations and their employees. Notice how expansively the criteria for liability of the corporation are interpreted. A business organization can be liable even if an employee acts against express company policy, for instance, and if at least part of the motivation is to benefit the corporation. Take note also of how the concept of collective knowledge is used to respond to the difficulties of ascribing a state of mind to a legal fiction such as a corporation. Finally, the excerpt provides a useful example of how penalties are calculated under the Federal Sentencing Guidelines. Even though those Guidelines no longer are mandatory, they still will likely be influential in judges' sentencing decisions.

The "Thompson Memo," named after then-Deputy Attorney General Larry Thompson, elaborates on an earlier statement of Department of Justice policy regarding prosecution of business organizations. The Memo notes that, while factors relevant to prosecution of individuals may be relevant, there are additional factors that are distinctive to the prosecution of organizations. As you read the factors, note that one relates to a subject that we covered in an earlier chapter: the adequacy of a company's legal compliance program. Make sure that you are clear about what each of the factors involves and how it might militate for or against prosecution.

The consideration that has received perhaps the most attention is the degree of the company's cooperation in furthering investigation of wrongdoing and identification of culpable individuals. The Memo makes clear that the Department is especially concerned that cooperation be genuine and not illusory. Read carefully what a prosecutor may take into account in determining the sincerity of a corporations' cooperation. The Memo describes these as necessary in order to surmount the difficulty of determining from outside the organization its lines of authority and responsibility. Note in particular that a corporation's willingness to advance attorneys' fees to employees, or its issuance of a directive to decline an interview, in some circumstances may be interpreted as impeding an investigation and protecting culpable employees. Ask yourself whether the Memo's expectations reflect a practical response to the difficulty of determining corporate criminal activity, or whether it goes too far by compromising the interests of corporate employees.

The next excerpt describes a practice in which prosecutors have engaged with increasing frequency in recent years: entering into a deferred prosecution agreement with a corporation whose employees allegedly have engaged in criminal activity. Make sure that you understand precisely the conditions to which a company agrees in entering into such an agreement, as well as the circumstances in which the government might prefer a deferred rather than immediate prosecution of the corporation. Finally, a short Note describes the limits on the prosecution's ability to interview employees of the corporation without the consent of corporate counsel.

The first problem initially focuses on the interaction of two ABA Standards that deal with the charging decision and conduct during plea bargains. It then requires consideration of a third Standard that relates to public statements. The second problem essentially asks you to consider the factors described in the Thompson Memo in deciding whether to bring criminal charges against a corporate entity.

MODEL RULES: 3.6, 3.8, 4.1, 4.2

AMERICAN BAR ASSOCIATION STANDARDS RELATING TO THE ADMINISTRATION OF CRIMINAL JUSTICE, THE PROSECUTION FUNCTION

(1992)

Standard 3–1.2   The Function of the Prosecutor

* * *

(b) The prosecutor is an administrator of justice, an advocate, and an officer of the court; the prosecutor must exercise sound discretion in the performance of his or her functions.

(c) The duty of the prosecutor is to seek justice, not merely to convict * * *

Standard 3–1.4   Public Statements

(a) A prosecutor should not make or authorize the making of an extrajudicial statement that a reasonable person would expect to be disseminated by means of public communication if the prosecutor knows or reasonably should know that it will have a substantial likelihood of prejudicing a criminal proceeding.

Standard 3–1.9   Discretion in the Charging Decision

(a) A prosecutor should not institute, or cause to be instituted, or permit the continued pendency of criminal charges, when the prosecutor knows that the charges are not supported by probably cause. A prosecutor should not institute, cause to be instituted, or permit the continued pendency of criminal charges in the absence of sufficient admissible evidence to support a conviction.

(b) The prosecutor is not obliged to present all charges which the evidence might support. The prosecutor may in some circumstances and for good cause consistent with the public interest decline to prosecute, notwithstanding that sufficient evidence may exist which would support a conviction. [The prosecutor may consider factors such as]:

(i) the prosecutor's reasonable doubt that the accused is in fact guilty;

(ii) the extent of the harm caused by the offense;

(iii) the disproportion of the authorized punishment in relation to the particular offense or the offender . . .

(vi) cooperation of the accused in the apprehension or conviction of others . . .

(f) The prosecutor should not bring or seek charges greater in number or degree than can reasonably be supported with evidence at trial or than are necessary to fairly reflect the gravity of the offense.

Standard 3–4.1   Availability for Plea Discussions

* * *

(c) A prosecutor should not knowingly make false statements or representations as to fact or law in the course of plea discussions with defense counsel or the accused.

Note on Charging Decisions

It's worth noting that ABA Model Rule 3.8 provides that a prosecutor "shall" refrain from prosecuting a case that is not supported by probably cause. This goes beyond the reference to probable cause in ABA Prosecution Standard 3-3.9(a) above. The combination of the two rules thus prohibits bringing charges that are not supported by probable cause, and advises against, although not prohibiting, bringing charges that are not supported by sufficient admissible evidence to support a conviction.

Dan K. Webb, Steven F. Molo & James F. Hurst, Understanding and Avoiding Corporate and Executive Criminal Liability

49 Business Lawyer 617 (1994)

Introduction

The Scope of This Article

Potential criminal liability is, or should be, a concern for all business organizations and the lawyers representing them. Expanding theories of liability, increasing penalties under the Federal Sentencing Guidelines, and new requirements to minimize liability have made compliance with the law far more complex than simply trying to do the right thing. * * *

Reasons for Concern

Expanding Liability

In the last two decades, the increase in criminal and regulatory investigations and prosecutions of corporations has been staggering. In a recent nationwide survey of over 200 general counsel, forty-two percent revealed that their corporation had been the target of a federal investigation. (1) The number of federal criminal convictions has gone from a few dozen per year to more than 300 per year. (2) Corporations now routinely are held criminally accountable for the misdeeds of their directors, managers, supervisors, independent contractors, and lowest-level employees—even when the agent or employee acted contrary to established corporate policy. Additionally, corporate executives increasingly are held personally accountable along with the corporation. The areas of taxation, securities issuance and financing, antitrust, purchasing and sales, environmental safety, worker safety, government contracts, campaign contributions, and international transactions are rife with issues that create potential criminal exposure for a corporation as well as for those who run it.

Many of the fundamental principles governing the imposition of corporate criminal liability are entrenched in the common law and have been part of our legal fabric for years. What has changed, however, is Congress' expanding "criminalization" of business regulatory offenses and prosecutors' increasing willingness to bring criminal charges in matters that traditionally were left to the civil courts. * * *

PRINCIPLES OF CORPORATE CRIMINAL LIABILITY

Historical Development

English Common Law

Under historical common law principles of criminal accountability, a party could not be convicted of a crime unless he or she possessed a criminal state of mind. Because a corporation cannot form any state of mind, much less a criminal state of mind, early English common law cases held that corporations could not be held criminally liable. Besides, the English courts reasoned, corporations could not be imprisoned.

Development of Vicarious and Strict Liability

This began to change in the mid-1800s with the development of the doctrines of vicarious and strict liability. The doctrine of vicarious liability allowed an employee's acts and intent to be imputed to the corporation for purposes of tort liability. In imposing vicarious liability, courts recognized that a corporation can act only through its agents and concluded that there is nothing inequitable about imposing corporate liability for an agent's tortious acts performed on the corporation's behalf. The doctrine of strict liability, which evolved as an attempt to address many social ills inherent to modern industrialized society, allows the imposition of liability in certain circumstances without the need to prove any particular state of mind. Strict liability generally reflects overriding public welfare and safety concerns.

Extending the Law to Impose Criminal Liability

With the evolution of vicarious and strict liability in the mid-1800s, courts began to impute the criminal liability of an employee to a corporation. Courts eventually found that corporations could be held accountable even for the specific intent crimes of its employees. As the affairs of modern corporations have become increasingly complex, the spectrum of problems that can result in criminal prosecution has grown.

Imposing Corporate Criminal Liability

Executives often are surprised to learn that a corporation can be held criminally liable for the acts of even the lowest-level employee, even when the employee was acting contrary to express directions. Generally, a corporation can be held criminally liable for its agent's criminal act if two elements are satisfied. First, the conduct must occur within the scope of the agent's authority. Second, the agent must undertake the conduct, in part, for the benefit of the corporation.

Scope of Authority

The "scope of authority" does not mean that the corporation actually must have authorized the agent to commit illegal acts. Rather, the requirement means that the agent committed the acts in the course of exercising his or her ordinary and authorized duties—for example, a salesman agreeing with competing salesmen to fix prices or a truck driver illegally dumping waste. The focus of this analysis is on the function delegated to the employee and whether the employee's conduct falls within that general function. So long as the employee committed the acts within the scope of his or her general duties, a corporation can be held liable for those acts, even if they were contrary to express corporate policy. Accordingly, corporate codes of conduct—while beneficial for sentencing and useful to deter misconduct—generally do not define the scope of an employee's authority and do not provide a defense to criminal liability.

For the Benefit of the Corporation

The "for the benefit of the corporation" requirement is satisfied if the agent's conduct was intended, at least in part, to benefit the corporation. So long as the agent intended to confer some direct or ancillary benefit on the corporation, the requirement is met—even if the employee's conduct was motivated primarily by personal gain and even if the corporation never ultimately realized the intended benefit. As a practical matter, an agent will satisfy the "for the benefit of the corporation" requirement easily, except in situations when the corporation is truly a victim, such as in an embezzlement or many kickback schemes.

An Example of the "For the Benefit of the Corporation" Requirement: United States v. Automated Medical Laboratories

In United States v. Automated Medical Laboratories, the head of a corporation's Food and Drug Administration regulation compliance office instructed his employees to falsify and fabricate records to conceal various regulatory deficiencies. The corporation later was convicted for regulatory violations. On appeal, the corporation argued that the head of the compliance office instigated the unlawful practices to benefit himself—not the corporation—citing the manager's ambitious nature and desire to ascend the corporate ladder. The United States Court of Appeals for the Fourth Circuit rejected this argument, noting that the manager "was clearly acting in part to benefit the corporation since his advancement within the corporation depended on the corporation's) well-being and its lack of difficulties with the FDA."

Imputing the Acts of Agents to the Corporation

A corporation can be held criminally liable for the acts of any of its agents—as that term is understood under recognized principles of agency. Thus, determining precisely whose acts may give rise to corporate criminal liability can be a function of the limits of agency law. In general, however, the types of agents whose conduct might create corporate liability may be categorized as follows: (i) individuals directly associated with the corporation, such as directors, officers, and employees; (ii) subsidiaries; and (iii) independent contractors.

Individuals Directly Associated With the Corporation

Officers and Directors

Because officers and directors sit atop the corporate hierarchical pyramid, courts naturally impute their acts to the corporation. In essence, these people are the corporation's alter-ego; more than any other agent, they embody the corporation. Accordingly, courts have found that a wide array of acts of directors and officers have been sufficient to hold the corporation liable. For example, courts imputed corporate liability when a president instructed various employees to collect kickbacks from prospective purchasers, when an officer made unlawful payments to union officials, and when officers falsified invoices submitted to various governmental bodies in connection with federal construction projects.

Managers and Supervisors

Corporations also can be held criminally liable for the acts of nonexecutive middle managers and supervisors. Based on the fundamental principles of accountability discussed supra, courts generally have refused to recognize any limitation of liability based on job title or description. The focus, again, is on the agent's authority. For example, courts have imputed corporate liability when the branch manager of a motion picture company willfully and contumaciously violated an antitrust consent decree, When a mid-level manager coordinated bid rigging and customer allocation practices between two companies in violation of the Sherman Act, and when managers responsible for a corporation's compliance with Food and Drug Administration regulations instructed other employees to falsify and fabricate records to conceal violations.

Low-Level Employees

Even the acts of the lowest-level employees may be imputed to the corporation, provided the acts occur within the scope of the employee's authority. Accordingly, courts have imputed corporate liability when clerical employees of a retail eye-wear chain conspired to falsify Medicare claims, when a hotel chain's local purchasing agent participated in a boycott violative of the Sherman Act even though such actions were contrary to general corporate policy and express instructions to the employee, when a salesman for a car dealership obtained automobile loans for customers by misrepresenting financial information submitted to a bank, and when bid rigging activities in state road paving contracts were perpetrated by two lower-level employees without the knowledge of any corporate officers despite a long-standing corporate policy against such activities.

Subsidiaries

The general rules governing corporate liability also apply when the corporation's agent is a division or subsidiary of the corporation. This may hold true even where a corporation acquired the subsidiary after the illegal conduct began. Once the parent acquires the subsidiary, the parent has an obligation to supervise its conduct and assure that it complies with all applicable laws. Accordingly, courts have imputed criminal liability of the subsidiary to the parent from the time of the acquisition forward. As Professor Brickey points out, this is particularly relevant in light of the recent frenzy of corporate mergers and acquisitions.

Independent Contractors

Courts have held that agency relationships as distinct as principal and independent contractor are sufficient to impute criminal liability from the agent to the corporation. For example, in United States v. Parfait Powder Puff Co., a corporation was held liable when its independent contractor violated section 301(a) of the Federal Food, Drug, and Cosmetic Act by failing to properly place finished goods in appropriately labeled containers. The court held the principal corporation criminally liable for this mislabeling because it delegated its authority to the contractor to perform that task and received the benefit of the contractor's acts. Accordingly, a corporation should assume that it will be held accountable for acts committed by an independent contractor within the scope of authority provided to the contractor to accomplish the ends of the principal corporation.

Criminal Liability Despite Compliance Program

Although there are many benefits of an effective compliance program, it usually will not provide an absolute legal defense to criminal liability. Generally, as indicated supra, even when an employee acts contrary to compliance program policies and specific directives, the corporation can be held criminally liable.

Policy Behind the Rule

While this may seem unfair, public policy considerations support the rule. The rationale typically advanced for imposing liability, notwithstanding a corporation's precautionary measures and instructions to employees, is that criminal laws prohibit and forbid certain acts. In general, the prohibited acts pose a serious threat to the public well-being. If a corporation could raise an absolute defense by showing that it used due care to attempt to prevent the offense, the criminal law in question would be changed from one of prohibition to one merely requiring due care. This would leave the public without the degree of protection intended by the law's drafters. Moreover, a corporation can be held liable only when the agent acted within his or her authority and for the benefit of the corporation; thus there is a rationale for penalizing the corporation that stood to benefit from the criminal acts and granted the agent authority to act on its behalf.

Limited Contrary Authority

While the weight of federal authority follows the general rule, some limited contrary authority exists, primarily the United States Court of Appeals for the Sixth Circuit's decision in Holland Furnace Co. v. United States.[45] Holland Furnace indicates that in limited circumstances the violation of explicit directives might be a defense. Holland Furnace Company was indicted for selling a replacement furnace that could have been repaired, in violation of certain wartime regulations. The sale was based on dishonest representations by the salesman concerning the irreparability of the homeowner's furnace. The court, however, considered the evidence of a strict compliance policy that included the periodic issuance of bulletins and warnings to salesmen to stay strictly within the bounds of the regulations or risk being fired. The court noted the "emphatic admonition of the corporation to its agents" and held that it would not impose liability "on the facts of that case." While this case raises some hope and provides room for argument, Holland Furnace has not been cited frequently to reverse corporate convictions on this basis. The weight of authority holds that a corporation can be held criminally liable for its employees' actions taken in contravention of explicit corporate directives.

Collective Knowledge Doctrine

Given the often complex and decentralized nature of many corporations, it is sometimes difficult, if not impossible, to prove that any single

---

45. 158 F.2d 2 (6th Cir. 1946).

corporate agent acted with the necessary intent and knowledge to commit an offense. Under the judicially created "collective knowledge" doctrine, however, this will not preclude a corporation's conviction. That doctrine deems a corporation's knowledge to be the combined knowledge and intent of all of its employees. Thus, even if no single employee has the intent and knowledge necessary to commit a crime, the corporation can be convicted on the basis of its employees collective knowledge and intent. * * *

Personal Criminal Liability of Officers and Directors, Managers, and Subordinate Employees

Individuals who are agents of a corporation also may be held personally liable for crimes committed in the course of their corporate duties. Individual liability generally arises in one of three ways: (i) the agent participates directly in the commission of a crime; (ii) the agent aids or abets the commission of the crime; or (iii) the agent fails to prevent the crime by not properly controlling or supervising subordinates.

Direct Participation in the Crime

An individual is not allowed to hide behind the corporate shield by contending that, because he or she committed a criminal act as part of his or her job, the corporation alone should accept responsibility for the offense. Incorporation subjects the corporate enterprise to the laws of the state but does not relieve the individuals participating in the corporation from liability under the same laws. For courts to hold otherwise would allow individuals to avoid criminal liability merely by incorporating. Thus, corporate agents are individually responsible for their criminal acts.

For purposes of determining individual accountability, the corporation and the individual are distinct. Although they may be prosecuted together, their guilt is assessed independently. In fact, courts have upheld verdicts in which a corporation was convicted but its employees were acquitted, even though the acts of the employees formed the basis of the charge against the corporation.

Aiding and Abetting Liability

Aiding and abetting, or accomplice, liability occurs where a party facilitates the commission of a crime by doing some affirmative act or by knowingly failing to act. Federal law recognizes no distinction between those acting directly and those who merely aid and abet a crime; both are equally culpable. Instructing or authorizing another to commit a criminal act is sufficient to impose accomplice liability. The touchstone is some effort, through action or inaction, to bring about the fruition of the criminal conduct. The accomplice need not have the capacity to commit the crime himself or herself so long as the party he or she aided can be prosecuted directly for the crime.

Failure to Supervise. The "Responsible Corporate Officer" Doctrine

Individual corporate agents may be held liable for failing to prevent the commission of corporate crimes under what is known as the "responsible corporate officer" doctrine. Under this doctrine, a corporate officer can be convicted for the criminal acts of subordinates—even if the officer lacks criminal intent and has no actual knowledge of the specific wrongdoing. To convict the officer, the government must show simply that by reason of his or her "responsible relation to the situation," the officer had the power to correct or prevent the criminal violations and failed to do so.

The Seminal "Responsible Corporate Officer" Doctrine Case: United States v. Park

The seminal case on the responsible corporate officer doctrine is United States v. Park.[71] In Park, the United States Supreme Court held that the president of a food retailer had a duty to implement measures to prevent violations of the federal Food, Drug and Cosmetic Act (FDCA). Rodents infested food at a warehouse run by Acme Markets, Inc., a retailer. While both the company and its president, Park, were charged with violating the Act, the company pled guilty but Park stood trial. The pivotal issue on which the jury was instructed was "whether Park held a position of authority and responsibility in the business of Acme Markets." The Court upheld Park's conviction, finding that in light of his responsible relation to the situation, guilt was attributable to him "even if he did not consciously do wrong" and did not "personally participate in the situation."

Scope of Doctrine's Application

Courts have extended criminal liability under the responsible corporate officer doctrine to directors and officers under a broad array of federal criminal statutes, including the Federal Hazardous Substances Act, the Sherman Act, the Economic Stabilization Act of 1970, the Occupational Safety & Health Act, the Federal Water Pollution Act, and other state and federal statutes.

Doctrine's Applicability to Knowledge and Intent Crimes

Some question exists about whether the responsible corporate officer doctrine can be applied to crimes that require a showing of knowledge or specific intent. Park does not resolve this issue because that case dealt with a strict liability crime under the FDCA. . . .

PUNISHING THE BUSINESS ORGANIZATION

* * *

The Organizational Sentencing Guidelines

Purpose of the Guidelines

The Organizational Guidelines are "designed so that the sanctions imposed upon organizations * * * will provide just punishment, ade-

---

71. 421 U.S. 658 (1975).

quate deterrence, and incentives for organizations to maintain internal mechanisms for preventing, detecting, and reporting criminal conduct."

Recommended Sentences

A corporation's sentence under the Guidelines may have three components: (i) a remedial order; (ii) a criminal fine; and (iii) probation. The nature of the crime and the victims will determine which components comprise the sentence. * * *

EXAMPLES

A few examples will help clarify the steps taken to calculate a convicted corporation's criminal fine.

Example One: Antitrust Violation

Assume that in an effort to increase profits, PRICEFIX, Inc. and three other computer chip manufacturers tacitly agree to fix their prices. Over the course of five years working under the illegal agreement, PRICEFIX sells $20 million worth of computer chips. At that point, the government investigates the matter, and PRICEFIX is convicted in federal court of one count of price fixing.

Remedial Order and/or Disgorging Profits

Before it sets a fine, if possible, the court will issue a remedial order. For instance, the court may order PRICEFIX to pay restitution to its customers over the last five years. Also, to ensure that PRICEFIX does not pay part of its fine with its illegal profits, the court will add to the fine any illegal profits not paid as restitution or by way of other remedial measures.

Offense Level

To determine PRICEFIX's fine under the Guidelines, the first step is to calculate its offense level. According to the calculations outlined in section 2R1.1, which is the section pertaining to price fixing, PRICE-FIX's offense level is 15.

Base Fine

The next step is to calculate PRICEFIX's base fine. As noted, a base fine is the highest of the pecuniary gain to the organization, the pecuniary loss knowingly caused by the offense, or the fine listed under the Offense Level Fine Table corresponding to the applicable offense level for price fixing. It is safe to assume, according to the Guidelines commentary explaining section 2R1.1, that pecuniary loss caused by the price fixing agreement is greater than the pecuniary gain to PRICEFIX. Pecuniary loss caused by PRICEFIX's offense is $4 million—20% of "the volume of commerce done by defendant in goods" according to section 2R1.1(d)(1). Under the Offense Level Fine Table, based on an offense level of 15, PRICEFIX's base fine would be only $125,000. Thus, because it is higher than both the pecuniary gain to PRICEFIX and the Offense Level Fine Table listing, the $4 million pecuniary loss is PRICEFIX's base fine.

Culpability Score, Fine Range, and Sentence

Like all organizations, PRICEFIX starts with a culpability score of 5. Assuming no aggravating or mitigating factors apply, according to the multiplier table, PRICEFIX must pay anywhere from its base fine to twice its base fine—anywhere from $4 million to $8 million. Unless the court finds it appropriate to depart from the Guidelines, PRICEFIX's fine ultimately will be in that range. . . .

Circumstances Warranting Probation

The Guidelines list many and varied circumstances when a court must order a term of probation, including: (i) when probation appears necessary to prevent future criminal conduct; (ii) when probation appears necessary to secure payment of restitution or the fine imposed; or (iii) when the organization engaged in similar misconduct within five years prior to sentencing. Most Significantly, though, a court must impose probation if at the time of sentencing, an organization having 50 or more employees does not have an effective program to prevent and detect violations of the law."

Conditions of Probation

The conditions of probation authorized by the Guidelines can be debilitating, demeaning, and expensive. In fact, the Guidelines grant courts fairly broad authority to closely monitor a convicted company. As one former prosecutor remarked in 1990:

> "the next time a nominee for a federal judgeship appears for Senate confirmation, the Judiciary Committee should add to the list of legal qualifications whether the candidate can run General Motors, or Alcoa, or Nynex. If the U.S. Sentencing Commission's draft guidelines for corporate criminal sanctions become law . . . . the judge might wind up managing a major corporation."

When imposing probation, and depending on the circumstances, the court may order the corporation to: (i) "publicize," at its own expense, the nature of the offense, its conviction, the sentence imposed, and the steps it will take to prevent further transgressions; (ii) develop and implement an effective compliance program; (iii) notify its employees and shareholders of its conviction, punishment, and new compliance program; periodically report to the court any new criminal prosecution, civil litigation, administrative proceeding, or governmental investigation involving the corporation; (v) submit to "regular or unannounced examinations of its books and records;" and (vi) allow the interrogation of its officials. If the court finds it necessary to ensure the payment of a deferred portion of a fine or restitution, it also may order the corporation to report its financial condition and the results of business operations regularly to the court or a court-appointed expert, whose bills would be paid by the corporation.

PENALTY FOR VIOLATING PROBATION

If the corporation violates any term of its probation, the court "may extend the term of probation, impose more restrictive conditions of probation, or revoke probation and resentence the organization." For the most pervasive and serious violations, the court can appoint a master or trustee to ensure compliance with court orders....

CONCLUSION

The issues surrounding corporate criminal liability are complex and rapidly evolving. The stakes are high and the opportunity for a mistake is great even when a corporation acts with the best intentions. Prudence requires that a corporation seeking to avoid the devastating consequences of a criminal prosecution of the company or its employees obtain competent advice from experienced counsel before a problem arises.

MEMORANDUM [January 20, 2003]

TO: **Heads of Department Components**
            United States Attorneys

FROM: **Larry D. Thompson**
            Deputy Attorney General

SUBJECT: Principles of Federal Prosecution of Business Organizations

As the Corporate Fraud Task Force has advanced in its mission, we have confronted certain issues in the principles for the federal prosecution of business organizations that require revision in order to enhance our efforts against corporate fraud. While it will be a minority of cases in which a corporation or partnership is itself subjected to criminal charges, prosecutors and investigators in every matter involving business crimes must assess the merits of seeking the conviction of the business entity itself.

Attached to this memorandum are a revised set of principles to guide Department prosecutors as they make the decision whether to seek charges against a business organization. These revisions draw heavily on the combined efforts of the Corporate Fraud Task Force and the Attorney General's Advisory Committee to put the results of more than three years of experience with the principles into practice.

The main focus of the revisions is increased emphasis on and scrutiny of the authenticity of a corporation's cooperation. Too often business organizations, while purporting to cooperate with a Department investigation, in fact take steps to impede the quick and effective exposure of the complete scope of wrongdoing under investigation. The revisions make clear that such conduct should weigh in favor of a corporate prosecution. The revisions also address the efficacy of the corporate governance mechanisms in place within a corporation, to ensure that these measures are truly effective rather than mere paper programs.

Further experience with these principles may lead to additional adjustments. I look forward to hearing comments about their operation in practice. * * *

Federal Prosecution of Business Organizations[1]

I. Charging a Corporation: General

A. General Principle: Corporations should not be treated leniently because of their artificial nature nor should they be subject to harsher treatment. Vigorous enforcement of the criminal laws against corporate wrongdoers, where appropriate results in great benefits for law enforcement and the public, particularly in the area of white collar crime. Indicting corporations for wrongdoing enables the government to address and be a force for positive change of corporate culture, alter corporate behavior, and prevent, discover, and punish white collar crime.

B. Comment: In all cases involving corporate wrongdoing, prosecutors should consider the factors discussed herein. First and foremost, prosecutors should be aware of the important public benefits that may flow from indicting a corporation in appropriate cases. For instance, corporations are likely to take immediate remedial steps when one is indicted for criminal conduct that is pervasive throughout a particular industry, and thus an indictment often provides a unique opportunity for deterrence on a massive scale. In addition, a corporate indictment may result in specific deterrence by changing the culture of the indicted corporation and the behavior of its employees. Finally, certain crimes that carry with them a substantial risk of great public harm, e.g., environmental crimes or financial frauds, are by their nature most likely to be committed by businesses, and there may, therefore, be a substantial federal interest in indicting the corporation.

Charging a corporation, however, does not mean that individual directors, officers, employees, or shareholders should not also be charged. Prosecution of a corporation is not a substitute for the prosecution of criminally culpable individuals within or without the corporation. Because a corporation can act only through individuals, imposition of individual criminal liability may provide the strongest deterrent against future corporate wrongdoing. Only rarely should provable individual culpability not be pursued, even in the face of offers of corporate guilty pleas.

Corporations are "legal persons," capable of suing and being sued, and capable of committing crimes. Under the doctrine of *respondeat superior*, a corporation may be held criminally liable for the illegal acts of its directors, officers, employees, and agents. To hold a corporation

---

1. While these guidelines refer to corporations, they apply to the consideration of the prosecution of all types of business organizations, including partnerships, sole proprietorships, government entities, and unincorporated associations.

liable for these actions, the government must establish that the corporate agent's actions (i) were within the scope of his duties and (ii) were intended, at least in part, to benefit the corporation. In all cases involving wrongdoing by corporate agents, prosecutors should consider the corporation, as well as the responsible individuals, as potential criminal targets.

Agents, however, may act for mixed reasons—both for self-aggrandizement (both direct and indirect) and for the benefit of the corporation, and a corporation may be held liable as long as one motivation of its agent is to benefit the corporation. In *United States v. Automated Medical Laboratories*, 770 F.2d 399 (4th Cir. 1985), the court affirmed the corporation's conviction for the actions of a subsidiary's employee despite its claim that the employee was acting for his own benefit, namely his "ambitious nature and his desire to ascend the corporate ladder." The court stated, "*Partucci* was clearly acting in part to benefit AML since his advancement within the corporation depended on AML's well-being and its lack of difficulties with the FDA." Similarly, in *United States v. Cincotta*, 689 F.2d 238, 241–42 (1st Cir. 1982), the court held, "criminal liability may be imposed on the corporation only where the agent is acting within the scope of his employment. That, in turn, requires that the agent be performing acts of the kind which he is authorized to perform, and those acts must be motivated—at least in part—by an intent to benefit the corporation." Applying this test, the court upheld the corporation's conviction, notwithstanding the substantial personal benefit reaped by its miscreant agents, because the fraudulent scheme required money to pass through the corporation's treasury and the fraudulently obtained goods were resold to the corporation's customers in the corporation's name. As the court concluded, "Mystic—not the individual defendants—was making money by selling oil that it had not paid for."

Moreover, the corporation need not even necessarily profit from its agent's actions for it to be held liable. In *Automated Medical Laboratories*, the Fourth Circuit stated:

[B]enefit is not a "touchstone of criminal corporate liability; benefit at best is an evidential, not an operative, fact." Thus, whether the agent's actions ultimately redounded to the benefit of the corporation is less significant than whether the agent acted with the intent to benefit the corporation. The basic purpose of requiring that an agent have acted with the intent to benefit the corporation, however, is to insulate the corporation from criminal liability for actions of its agents which be inimical to the interests of the corporation or which may have been undertaken solely to advance the interests of that agent or of a party other than the corporation.

770 F.2d at 407 (emphasis added; quoting *Old Monastery Co. v. United States*, 147 F.2d 905, 908 (4th Cir.), cert. denied, 326 U.S. 734 (1945)).

II. Charging a Corporation: Factors to Be Considered

A. General Principle: Generally, prosecutors should apply the same factors in determining whether to charge a corporation as they do with respect to individuals. *See* USAM § 9–27.220, *et seq.* Thus, the prosecutor should weigh all of the factors normally considered in the sound exercise of prosecutorial judgment: the sufficiency of the evidence; the likelihood of success at trial,; the probable deterrent, rehabilitative, and other consequences of conviction; and the adequacy of noncriminal approaches. *See* id. However, due to the nature of the corporate "person," some additional factors are present. In conducting an investigation, determining whether to bring charges, and negotiating plea agreements, prosecutors should consider the following factors in reaching a decision as to the proper treatment of a corporate target:

1. the nature and seriousness of the offense, including the risk of harm to the public, and applicable policies and priorities, if any, governing the prosecution of corporations for particular categories of crime (*see* section III, *infra*);

2. the pervasiveness of wrongdoing within the corporation, including the complicity in, or condonation of, the wrongdoing by corporate management (*see* section IV, *infra*);

3. the corporation's history of similar conduct, including prior criminal, civil, and regulatory enforcement actions against it (*see* section V, *infra*);

4. the corporation's timely and voluntary disclosure of wrongdoing and its willingness to cooperate in the investigation of its agents, including, if necessary, the waiver of corporate attorney-client and work product protection (*see* section VI, *infra*);

5. the existence and adequacy of the corporation's compliance program (*see* section VII, *infra*);

6. the corporation's remedial actions, including any efforts to implement an effective corporate compliance program or to improve an existing one, to replace responsible management, to discipline or terminate wrongdoers, to pay restitution, and to cooperate with the relevant government agencies (*see* section VIII, *infra*);

7. collateral consequences, including disproportionate harm to shareholders, pension holders and employees not proven personally culpable and impact on the public arising from the prosecution (*see* section IX, *infra*); and

8. the adequacy of the prosecution of individuals responsible for the corporation's malfeasance;

9. the adequacy of remedies such as civil or regulatory enforcement actions (*see section X, infra*).

B. Comment: As with the factors relevant to charging natural persons, the foregoing factors are intended to provide guidance rather than to mandate a particular result. The factors listed in this section are intended to be illustrative of those that should be considered and not a complete or exhaustive list. Some or all of these factors may or may not apply to specific cases, and in some cases one factor may override all others. The nature and seriousness of the offense may be such as to warrant prosecution regardless of the other factors. Further, national law enforcement policies in various enforcement areas may require that more or less weight be given to certain of these factors than to others.

In making a decision to charge a corporation, the prosecutor generally has wide latitude in determining when, whom, how, and even whether to prosecute for violations of Federal criminal law. In exercising that discretion, prosecutors should consider the following general statements of principles that summarize appropriate considerations to be weighed and desirable practices to be followed in discharging their prosecutorial responsibilities. In doing so, prosecutors should ensure that the general purposes of the criminal law—assurance of warranted punishment, deterrence of further criminal conduct, protection of the public from dangerous and fraudulent conduct, rehabilitation of offenders, and restitution for victims and affected communities—are adequately met, taking into account the special nature of the corporate "person."

III. Charging a Corporation: Special Policy Concerns

A. General Principle: The nature and seriousness of the crime, including the risk of harm to the public from the criminal conduct, are obviously primary factors in determining whether to charge a corporation. In addition, corporate conduct, particularly that of national and multi-national corporations, necessarily intersects with federal economic, taxation, and criminal law enforcement policies. In applying these principles, prosecutors must consider the practices and policies of the appropriate Division of the Department, and must comply with those policies to the extent required.

B. Comment: In determining whether to charge a corporation, prosecutors should take into account federal law enforcement priorities as discussed above. *See* USAM § 9–27–230. In addition, however, prosecutors must be aware of the specific policy goals and incentive programs established by the respective Divisions and regulatory agencies. Thus, whereas natural persons may be given incremental degrees of credit (ranging from immunity to lesser charges to sentencing considerations) for turning themselves in, making statements against their penal interest, and cooperating in the government's investigation of their own and others' wrongdoing, the same approach may not be appropriate in all circumstances with respect to corporations. As an example, it is entirely proper in many investigations for a prosecutor to consider the corporation's preindictment conduct, *e.g.*, voluntary disclosure, cooperation, remediation or restitution, in determining whether to seek an indictment. However, this would not necessarily be appropriate in an antitrust investigation, in which antitrust violations, by definition, go to the heart of the corporation's business and for which the Antitrust Division has therefore established a firm policy, understood in the business community, that credit should not be given at the charging stage for a compliance program and that amnesty is available only to the first corporation to make full disclosure to the government. As another example, the Tax Division has a strong preference for prosecuting responsible individuals, rather than entities, for corporate tax offenses. Thus, in determining whether or not to charge a corporation, prosecutors should consult with the Criminal, Antitrust, Tax, and Environmental and Natural Resources Divisions, if appropriate or required.

IV. Charging a Corporation: Pervasiveness of Wrongdoing Within the Corporation

A. General Principle: A corporation can only act through natural persons, and it is therefore held responsible for the acts of such persons fairly attributable to it. Charging a corporation for even minor misconduct may be appropriate where the wrongdoing was pervasive and was undertaken by a large number of employees or by all the employees in a particular role within the corporation, *e.g.*, salesmen or procurement officers, or was condoned by upper management. On the other hand, in certain limited circumstances, it may not be appropriate to impose liability upon a corporation, particularly one with a compliance program in place, under a strict *respondeat superior* theory for the single isolated act of a rogue employee. There is, of course, a wide spectrum between these two extremes, and a prosecutor should exercise sound discretion in evaluating the pervasiveness of wrongdoing within a corporation.

B. Comment: Of these factors, the most important is the role of management. Although acts of even low-level employees may result in criminal liability, a corporation is directed by its management and management is responsible for a corporate culture in which criminal conduct is either discouraged or tacitly encouraged. As stated in commentary to the Sentencing Guidelines:

Pervasiveness [is] case specific and [will] depend on the number, and degree of responsibility, of individuals [with] substantial authority ... who participated in, condoned, or were willfully ignorant of the offense. Fewer individuals need to be involved for a finding of pervasiveness if those individuals exercised a relatively high degree of authority. Pervasiveness can occur either within an organization as a whole or within a unit of an organization.

USSG § 8C2.5, comment. (n. 4).

V. Charging a Corporation: The Corporation's Past History

A. General Principle: Prosecutors may consider a corporation's history of similar conduct, including prior criminal, civil, and regulatory enforcement actions against it, in determining whether to bring criminal charges.

B. Comment: A corporation, like a natural person, is expected to learn from its mistakes. A history of similar conduct may be probative of a corporate culture that encouraged, or at least condoned, such conduct, regardless of any compliance programs. Criminal prosecution of a corporation may be particularly appropriate where the corporation previously had been subject to non-criminal guidance, warnings, or sanctions, or previous criminal charges, and yet it either had not taken adequate action to prevent future unlawful conduct or had continued to engage in the conduct in spite of the warnings or enforcement actions taken against it. In making this determination, the corporate structure itself, *e.g.*, subsidiaries or operating divisions, should be ignored, and enforcement actions taken against the corporation or any of its divisions, subsidiaries, and affiliates should be considered. *See* USSG § 8C2.5(c) & comment. (n. 6).

VI. Charging a Corporation: Cooperation and Voluntary Disclosure

A. General Principle: In determining whether to charge a corporation, that corporation's timely and voluntary disclosure of wrongdoing and its willingness to cooperate with the government's investigation may be relevant factors. In gauging the extent of the corporation's cooperation, the prosecutor may consider the corporation's willingness to identify the culprits within the corporation, including senior executives; to make witnesses available; to disclose the complete results of its internal investigation; and to waive attorney-client and work product protection.

B. Comment: In investigating wrongdoing by or within a corporation, a prosecutor is likely to encounter several obstacles resulting from the nature of the corporation itself. It will often be difficult to determine which individual took which action on behalf of the corporation. Lines of authority and responsibility may be shared among operating divisions or departments, and records and personnel may be spread throughout the United States or even among several countries. Where the criminal conduct continued over an extended period of time, the culpable or knowledgeable personnel may have been promoted, transferred, or fired, or they may have quit or retired. Accordingly, a corporation's cooperation may be critical in identifying the culprits and locating relevant evidence.

In some circumstances, therefore, granting a corporation immunity or amnesty or pretrial diversion may be considered in the course of the government's investigation. In such circumstances, prosecutors should refer to the principles governing non-prosecution agreements generally. *See* USAM § 9–27.600–650. These principles permit a non prosecution agreement in exchange for cooperation when a corporation's "timely cooperation appears to be necessary to the public interest and other means of obtaining the desired cooperation are unavailable or would not be effective." Prosecutors should note that in the case of national or multi-national corporations, multi-district or global agreements may be necessary. Such agreements may only be entered into with the approval of each affected district or the appropriate Department official. *See* USAM § 9–27.641.

In addition, the Department, in conjunction with regulatory agencies and other executive branch departments, encourages corporations, as part of their compliance programs, to conduct internal investigations and to disclose their findings to the appropriate authorities. Some agencies, such as the SEC and the EPA, as well as the Department's Environmental and Natural Resources Division, have formal voluntary disclosure programs in which self-reporting, coupled with remediation and additional criteria, may qualify the corporation for amnesty or reduced sanctions.[2] Even in the absence of a formal program, prosecutors may consider a corporation's timely and voluntary disclosure in evaluating the adequacy of the corporation's compliance program and its management's commitment to the compliance program. However, prosecution and economic policies specific to the industry or statute may require prosecution notwithstanding a corporation's willingness to cooperate. For example, the Antitrust Division offers amnesty only to the first corporation to agree to cooperate. This creates a strong incentive for corporations participating in anti-competitive conduct to be the first to cooperate. In addition, amnesty, immunity, or reduced sanctions may not be appropriate where the corporation's business is permeated with fraud or other crimes.

One factor the prosecutor may weigh in assessing the adequacy of a corporation's cooperation is the completeness of its disclosure including, if necessary, a waiver of the attorney-client and work product protections, both with respect to its internal investigation and with respect to communications between specific officers, directors and employees and counsel. Such waivers permit the government to obtain statements of possible witnesses, subjects, and targets, without having to negotiate individual cooperation or immunity agreements. In addition, they are often critical in enabling the government to evaluate the completeness of a corporation's voluntary disclosure and cooperation. Prosecutors may, therefore, request a waiver in appropriate circumstances.[3] The Department does not, however, consider waiver of a corporation's attorney-client and work product protection an absolute requirement, and prosecutors should consider the willingness of a corporation to waive such protection when necessary to provide timely and complete information as one factor in evaluating the corporation's cooperation.

Another factor to be weighed by the prosecutor is whether the corporation appears to be protecting its culpable employees and agents. Thus, while cases will differ depending on the circumstances, a corporation's promise of support to culpable employees and agents, either through the advancing of attorneys fees,[4] through retaining the employ-

---

2. In addition, the Sentencing Guidelines reward voluntary disclosure and cooperation with a reduction in the corporation's offense level. *See* USSG § 8C2.5)g).

3. This waiver should ordinarily be limited to the factual internal investigation and any contemporaneous advice given to the corporation concerning the conduct at issue. Except in unusual circumstances, prosecutors should not seek a waiver with respect to communications and work product related to advice concerning the government's criminal investigation.

4. Some states require corporations to pay the legal fees of officers under investigation prior to a formal determination of

ees without sanction for their misconduct, or through providing information to the employees about the government's investigation pursuant to a joint defense agreement, may be considered by the prosecutor in weighing the extent and value of a corporation's cooperation. By the same token, the prosecutor should be wary of attempts to shield corporate officers and employees from liability by a willingness of the corporation to plead guilty.

Another factor to be weighed by the prosecutor is whether the corporation, while purporting to cooperate, has engaged in conduct that impedes the investigation (whether or not rising to the level of criminal obstruction). Examples of such conduct include: overly broad assertions of corporate representation of employees or former employees; inappropriate directions to employees or their counsel, such as directions not to cooperate openly and fully with the investigation including, for example, the direction to decline to be interviewed; making presentations or submissions that contain misleading assertions or omissions; incomplete or delayed production of records; and failure to promptly disclose illegal conduct known to the corporation.

Finally, a corporation's offer of cooperation does not automatically entitle it to immunity from prosecution. A corporation should not be able to escape liability merely by offering up its directors, officers, employees, or agents as in lieu of its own prosecution. Thus, a corporation's willingness to cooperate is merely one relevant factor, that needs to be considered in conjunction with the other factors, particularly those relating to the corporation's past history and the role of management in the wrongdoing.

VII. Charging a Corporation: Corporate Compliance Programs

A.   General Principle: Compliance programs are established by corporate management to prevent and to detect misconduct and to ensure that corporate activities are conducted in accordance with all applicable criminal and civil laws, regulations, and rules. The Department encourages such corporate self-policing, including voluntary disclosures to the government of any problems that a corporation discovers on its own. However, the existence of a compliance program is not sufficient, in and of itself, to justify not charging a corporation for criminal conduct undertaken by its officers, directors, employees, or agents. Indeed, the commission of such crimes in the face of a compliance program may suggest that the corporate management is not adequately enforcing its program. In addition, the nature of some crimes, *e.g.*, antitrust violations, may be such that national law enforcement policies mandate prosecutions of corporations notwithstanding the existence of a compliance program.

their guilt. Obviously, a corporation's compliance with governing law should not be considered a failure to cooperate.

B. Comment: A corporate compliance program, even one specifically prohibiting the very conduct in question, does not absolve the corporation from criminal liability under the doctrine of *respondeat superior. See United States v. Basic Construction Co.*, 711 F.2d 570 (4th Cir. 1983) ("a corporation may be held criminally responsible for antitrust violations committed by its employees if they were acting within the scope of their authority, or apparent authority, and for the benefit of the corporation, even if... such acts were against corporate policy or express instructions."). In *United States v. Hilton Hotels Corp.*, 467 F.2d 1000 (9th Cir. 1972), *cert. denied*, 409 U.S. 1125 (1973), the Ninth Circuit affirmed antitrust liability based upon a purchasing agent for a single hotel threatening a single supplier with a boycott unless it paid dues to a local marketing association, even though the agent's actions were contrary to corporate policy and directly against express instructions from his superiors. The court reasoned that Congress, in enacting the Sherman Antitrust Act, "intended to impose liability upon business entities for the acts of those to whom they choose to delegate the conduct of their affairs, thus stimulating a maximum effort by owners and managers to assure adherence by such agents to the requirements of the Act."[5] It concluded that "general policy statements" and even direct instructions from the agent's superiors were not sufficient; "Appellant could not gain exculpation by issuing general instructions without undertaking to enforce those instructions by means commensurate with the obvious risks." *See also United States v. Beusch*, 596 F.2d 871, 878 (9th Cir. 1979) ("[A] corporation may be liable for the acts of its employees done contrary to express instructions and policies, but ... the existence of such instructions and policies may be considered in determining whether the employee in fact acted to benefit the corporation."); *United States v. American Radiator & Standard Sanitary Corp.*, 433 F.2d 174 (3rd Cir. 1970) (affirming conviction of corporation based upon its officer's participation in price-fixing scheme, despite corporation's defense that officer's conduct violated its "rigid anti-fraternization policy" against any socialization (and exchange of price information) with its competitors; "When the act of the agent is within the scope of his employment or his apparent authority, the corporation is held legally responsible for it, although what he did may be contrary to his actual instructions and may be unlawful.").

While the Department recognizes that no compliance program can ever prevent all criminal activity by a corporation's employees, the critical factors in evaluating any program are whether the program is adequately designed for maximum effectiveness in preventing and detecting wrongdoing by employees and whether corporate management is enforcing the program or is tacitly encouraging or pressuring employees to engage in misconduct to achieve business objectives. The Department has no formal guidelines for corporate compliance programs. The fundamental questions any prosecutor should ask are: "Is the corporation's

---

5. Although this case and *Basic Construction* are both antitrust cases, their reasoning applies to other criminal violations.
* * *

compliance program well designed?" and "Does the corporation's compliance program work?" In answering these questions, the prosecutor should consider the comprehensiveness of the compliance program; the extent and pervasiveness of the criminal conduct; the number and level of the corporate employees involved; the seriousness, duration, and frequency of the misconduct; and any remedial actions taken by the corporation, including restitution, disciplinary action, and revisions to corporate compliance programs. Prosecutors should also consider the promptness of any disclosure of wrongdoing to the government and the corporation's cooperation in the government's investigation. In evaluating compliance programs, prosecutors may consider whether the corporation has established corporate governance mechanisms that can effectively detect and prevent misconduct. For example, do the corporation's directors exercise independent review over proposed corporate actions rather than unquestioningly ratifying officers' recommendations; are the directors provided with information sufficient to enable the exercise of independent judgment, are internal audit functions conducted at a level sufficient to ensure their independence and accuracy and have the directors established an information and reporting system in the organization reasonable designed to provide management and the board of directors with timely and accurate information sufficient to allow them to reach an informed decision regarding the organization's compliance with the law. *In re: Caremark,* 698 A.2d 959 (Del. Ct. Chan. 1996).

Prosecutors should therefore attempt to determine whether a corporation's compliance program is merely a "paper program" or whether it was designed and implemented in an effective manner. In addition, prosecutors should determine whether the corporation has provided for a staff sufficient to audit, document, analyze, and utilize the results of the corporation's compliance efforts. In addition, prosecutors should determine whether the corporation's employees are adequately informed about the compliance program and are convinced of the corporation's commitment to it. This will enable the prosecutor to make an informed decision as to whether the corporation has adopted and implemented a truly effective compliance program that, when consistent with other federal law enforcement policies, may result in a decision to charge only the corporation's employees and agents.

Compliance programs should be designed to detect the particular types of misconduct most likely to occur in a particular corporation's line of business. Many corporations operate in complex regulatory environments outside the normal experience of criminal prosecutors. Accordingly, prosecutors should consult with relevant federal and state agencies with the expertise to evaluate the adequacy of a program's design and implementation. For instance, state and federal banking, insurance, and medical boards, the Department of Defense, the Department of Health and Human Services, the Environmental Protection Agency, and the Securities and Exchange Commission have considerable experience with compliance programs and can be very helpful to a prosecutor in evaluating such programs. In addition, the Fraud Section of the Criminal

Division, the Commercial Litigation Branch of the Civil Division, and the Environmental Crimes Section of the Environment and Natural Resources Division can assist U.S. Attorneys' Offices in finding the appropriate agency office and in providing copies of compliance programs that were developed in previous cases.

VIII. Charging a Corporation: Restitution and Remediation

A. General Principle: Although neither a corporation nor an individual target may avoid prosecution merely by paying a sum of money, a prosecutor may consider the corporation's willingness to make restitution and steps already taken to do so. A prosecutor may also consider other remedial actions, such as implementing an effective corporate compliance program, improving an existing compliance program, and disciplining wrongdoers, in determining whether to charge the corporation.

B. Comment: In determining whether or not a corporation should be prosecuted, a prosecutor may consider whether meaningful remedial measures have been taken, including employee discipline and full restitution. A corporation's response to misconduct says much about its willingness to ensure that such misconduct does not recur. Thus, corporations that fully recognize the seriousness of their misconduct and accept responsibility for it should be taking steps to implement the personnel, operational, and organizational changes necessary to establish an awareness among employees that criminal conduct will not be tolerated. Among the factors prosecutors should consider and weigh are whether the corporation appropriately disciplined the wrongdoers and disclosed information concerning their illegal conduct to the government.

Employee discipline is a difficult task for many corporations because of the human element involved and sometimes because of the seniority of the employees concerned. While corporations need to be fair to their employees, they must also be unequivocally committed, at all levels of the corporation, to the highest standards of legal and ethical behavior. Effective internal discipline can be a powerful deterrent against improper behavior by a corporation's employees. In evaluating a corporation's response to wrongdoing, prosecutors may evaluate the willingness of the corporation to discipline culpable employees of all ranks and the adequacy of the discipline imposed. The prosecutor should be satisfied that the corporation's focus is on the integrity and credibility of its remedial and disciplinary measures rather than on the protection of the wrongdoers.

In addition to employee discipline, two other factors used in evaluating a corporation's remedial efforts are restitution and reform. As with natural persons, the decision whether or not to prosecute should not depend upon the target's ability to pay restitution. A corporation's efforts to pay restitution even in advance of any court order is, however, evidence of its "acceptance of responsibility" and, consistent with the practices and policies of the appropriate Division of the Department entrusted with enforcing specific criminal laws, may be considered in determining whether to bring criminal charges. Similarly, although the inadequacy of a corporate compliance program is a factor to consider when deciding whether to charge a corporation, that corporation's quick recognition of the flaws in the program and its efforts to improve the program are also factors to consider.

IX. Charging a Corporation: Collateral Consequences

A. General Principle: Prosecutors may consider the collateral consequences of a corporate criminal conviction in determining whether to charge the corporation with a criminal offense.

B. Comment: One of the factors in determining whether to charge a natural person or a corporation is whether the likely punishment is appropriate given the nature and seriousness of the crime. In the corporate context, prosecutors may take into account the possibly substantial consequences to a corporation's officers, directors, employees, and shareholders, many of whom may, depending on the size and nature (e.g., publicly vs. closely held) of the corporation and their role in its operations, have played no role in the criminal conduct, have been completely unaware of it, or have been wholly unable to prevent it. Prosecutors should also be aware of non-penal sanctions that may accompany a criminal charge, such as potential suspension or debarment from eligibility for government contracts or federal funded programs such as health care. Whether or not such non-penal sanctions are appropriate or required in a particular case is the responsibility of the relevant agency, a decision that will be made based on the applicable statutes, regulations, and policies.

Virtually every conviction of a corporation, like virtually every conviction of an individual, will have an impact on innocent third parties, and the mere existence of such an effect is not sufficient to preclude prosecution of the corporation. Therefore, in evaluating the severity of collateral consequences, various factors already discussed, such as the pervasiveness of the criminal conduct and the adequacy of the corporation's compliance programs, should be considered in determining the weight to be given to this factor. For instance, the balance may tip in favor of prosecuting corporations in situations where the scope of the misconduct in a case is widespread and sustained within a corporate division (or spread throughout pockets of the corporate organization). In such cases, the possible unfairness of visiting punishment for the corporation's crimes upon shareholders may be of much less concern where those shareholders have substantially profited, even unknowingly, from widespread or pervasive criminal activity. Similarly, where the top layers of the corporation's management or the shareholders of a closely-held corporation were engaged in or aware of the wrongdoing and the conduct at issue was accepted as a way of doing business for an extended period, debarment may be deemed not collateral, but a direct and entirely appropriate consequence of the corporation's wrongdoing.

The appropriateness of considering such collateral consequences and the weight to be given them may depend on the special policy concerns discussed in section III, *supra.*

X.   Charging a Corporation: Non-Criminal Alternatives

A.   General Principle: Although non-criminal alternatives to prosecution often exist, prosecutors may consider whether such sanctions would adequately deter, punish, and rehabilitate a corporation that has engaged in wrongful conduct. In evaluating the adequacy of non-criminal alternatives to prosecution, *e.g.,* civil or regulatory enforcement actions, the prosecutor may consider all relevant factors, including:

  1.   the sanctions available under the alternative means of disposition;

  2.   the likelihood that an effective sanction will be imposed; and

  3.   the effect of non-criminal disposition on Federal law enforcement interests.

B.   Comment: The primary goals of criminal law are deterrence, punishment, and rehabilitation. Non-criminal sanctions may not be an appropriate response to an egregious violation, a pattern of wrongdoing, or a history of non-criminal sanctions without proper remediation. In other cases, however, these goals may be satisfied without the necessity of instituting criminal proceedings. In determining whether federal criminal charges are appropriate, the prosecutor should consider the same factors (modified appropriately for the regulatory context) considered when determining whether to leave prosecution of a natural person to another jurisdiction or to seek non-criminal alternatives to prosecution. These factors include: the strength of the regulatory authority's interest; the regulatory authority's ability and willingness to take effective enforcement action; the probable sanction if the regulatory authority's enforcement action is upheld; and the effect of a non-criminal disposition on Federal law enforcement interests. *See* USAM §§ 9–27.240, 9–27.250.

XI.   Charging a Corporation: Selecting Charges

A.   General Principle: Once a prosecutor has decided to charge a corporation, the prosecutor should charge, or should recommend that the grand jury charge, the most serious offense that is consistent with the nature of the defendant's conduct and that is likely to result in a sustainable conviction.

B.   Comment: Once the decision to charge is made, the same rules as govern charging natural persons apply. These rules require "a faithful and honest application of the Sentencing Guidelines" and an "individualized assessment of the extent to which particular charges fit the specific circumstances of the case, are consistent with the purposes of the Federal criminal code, and maximize the impact of Federal resources on crime." *See* USAM § 9–27.300. In making this determination, "it is appropriate that the attorney for the government consider, *inter alia,* such factors as the sentencing guideline range yielded by the charge, whether the penalty yielded by such sentencing range ... is proportional to the seriousness of the defendant's conduct, and whether the charge achieves such purposes of the criminal law as punishment, protection of the public, specific and general deterrence, and rehabilitation." *See* Attorney General's Memorandum, dated October 12, 1993.

XII.   Plea Agreements with Corporations

A.   General Principle: In negotiating plea agreements with corporations, prosecutors should seek a plea to the most serious, readily provable offense charged. In addition, the terms of the plea agreement should contain appropriate provisions to ensure punishment, deterrence, rehabilitation, and compliance with the plea agreement in the corporate context. Although special circumstances may mandate a different conclusion, prosecutors generally should not agree to accept a corporate guilty plea in exchange for non-prosecution or dismissal of charges against individual officers and employees.

B.   Comment: Prosecutors may enter into plea agreements with corporations for the same reasons and under the same constraints as apply to plea agreements with natural persons. *See* USAM §§ 9–27.400– 500. This means, *inter alia*, that the corporation should be required to plead guilty to the most serious, readily provable offense charged. As is the case with individuals, the attorney making this determination should do so "on the basis of an individualized assessment of the extent to which particular charges fit the specific circumstances of the case, are consistent with the purposes of the federal criminal code, and maximize the impact of federal resources on crime. In making this determination, the attorney for the government considers, inter alia, such factors as the sentencing guideline range yielded by the charge, whether the penalty yielded by such sentencing range * * * is proportional to the seriousness of the defendant's conduct, and whether the charge achieves such purposes of the criminal law as punishment, protection of the public, specific and general deterrence, and rehabilitation." *See* Attorney General's Memorandum, dated October 12, 1993. In addition, any negotiated departures from the Sentencing Guidelines must be justifiable under the Guidelines and must be disclosed to the sentencing court. A corporation should be made to realize that pleading guilty to criminal charges constitutes an admission of guilt and not merely a resolution of an inconvenient distraction from its business. As with natural persons, pleas should be structured so that the corporation may not later "proclaim lack of culpability or even complete innocence." *See* USAM §§ 9- 27.420(b)(4), 9–27.440, 9–27.500. Thus, for instance, there should be placed upon the record a sufficient factual basis for the plea to prevent later corporate assertions of innocence.

A corporate plea agreement should also contain provisions that recognize the nature of the corporate "person" and ensure that the principles of punishment, deterrence, and rehabilitation are met. In the corporate context, punishment and deterrence are generally accomplished by substantial fines, mandatory restitution, and institution of appropriate compliance measures, including, if necessary, continued judicial oversight or the use of special masters. *See* USSG §§ 8B1.1, 8C2.1, *et seq.* In addition, where the corporation is a government contractor, permanent or temporary debarment may be appropriate. Where the corporation was engaged in government contracting fraud, a prosecutor may not negotiate away an agency's right to debar or to list the corporate defendant.

In negotiating a plea agreement, prosecutors should also consider the deterrent value of prosecutions of individuals within the corporation. Therefore, one factor that a prosecutor may consider in determining whether to enter into a plea agreement is whether the corporation is seeking immunity for its employees and officers or whether the corporation is willing to cooperate in the investigation of culpable individuals. Prosecutors should rarely negotiate away individual criminal liability in a corporate plea.

Rehabilitation, of course, requires that the corporation undertake to be law-abiding in the future. It is, therefore, appropriate to require the corporation, as a condition of probation, to implement a compliance program or to reform an existing one. As discussed above, prosecutors may consult with the appropriate state and federal agencies and components of the Justice Department to ensure that a proposed compliance program is adequate and meets industry standards and best practices. *See* section VII, *supra.*

In plea agreements in which the corporation agrees to cooperate, the prosecutor should ensure that the cooperation is complete and truthful. To do so, the prosecutor may request that the corporation waive attorney-client and work product protection, make employees and agents available for debriefing, disclose the results of its internal investigation, file appropriate certified financial statements, agree to governmental or third-party audits, and take whatever other steps are necessary to ensure that the full scope of the corporate wrongdoing is disclosed and that the responsible culprits are identified and, if appropriate, prosecuted. *See* generally section VIII, *supra.*

Vanessa Blum, A Nightmare Deferred

Corporate Counsel, June 2005

Federal prosecutors scored a major victory in March with the fraud conviction of Bernard Ebbers, the former CEO of WorldCom, Inc. But even as the government prepares for more trials of individual executives, it's taking a different approach with companies accused of cooking the books. Prosecutors are increasingly willing to put criminal charges against corporations on hold, if the businesses agree to spill the beans on their employees.

In the past six months alone, the U.S. Department of Justice has announced such arrangements—known as deferred prosecution agreements—with six companies, including American International Group,

Inc., Computer Associates International Inc., Monsanto Co., and Time Warner Inc.

While deferred prosecution isn't an all-out win for a business caught in the government's crosshairs, it's certainly preferable to trial and potential ruin. Sullivan & Cromwell partner Robert Giuffra, for example, is happy with the deferral deal that he helped negotiate for Computer Associates. "It's an excellent way for prosecutors to satisfy their objectives without imposing serious collateral consequences," Giuffra says. Computer Associates acknowledged that employees had routinely backdated contracts and wrongly recorded income in order to meet earnings expectations.

Criminal indictments against corporate entities have been rare, but they've generally led to a company's collapse, as happened with Drexel Burnham Lambert in the late 1980s and Arthur Andersen more recently. Andersen was already on the rocks when the government indicted it in 2002 for destroying records related to its accounting work for Enron Corp. Andersen's indictment and subsequent conviction hastened its fall, however, putting 28,000 people out of work.

Though Justice officials stand by their decision to indict Andersen, the firm's fate has become a cautionary tale for both sides at the negotiating table. In 2003, then-deputy AG Larry Thompson formally endorsed the use of deferred prosecution in exchange for a company's cooperation. His memo to U.S. attorneys, which outlined the principles for prosecuting business entities, came to be known simply as the Thompson memo. In the two years since it was drafted, no corporation has been charged with a major corporate fraud investigation outside a negotiated deferral deal.

After the March 15 conviction of Ebbers, Attorney General Alberto Gonzales issued a statement pledging to continue the work of the Corporate Fraud Task Force, created in the wake of the Enron scandal. However, Gonzales also signaled that the department is sensitive to business concerns.

"The president's Corporate Fraud Task Force will continue to work to ensure justice for the workers and shareholders who lost billions of dollars to this fraud," Gonzales said. "We will also continue to work with those corporate leaders and CEOs whose exemplary ethical standards and transparent business models have helped build and fortify a nation's trust in our economy."

A typical deferred prosecution agreement includes a formal indictment, but the government agrees to delay prosecution in return for the company's cooperation. Furthermore, the Justice Department requires a business to accept responsibility for illegal conduct by its employees; step up internal compliance programs; and provide investigators with nearly unfettered access to internal records. If the company fulills its obligations, Justice will drop all charges at the end of an agreed-upon probation period.

According to Timothy Coleman, "We are encouraging prosecutors out there to be innovative, to be creative, to think about possibilities for resolving corporate investigations other than the binary decision—indict company or decline prosecution." Coleman is senior counsel to current deputy AG James Comey, Jr.

Prosecutors insist that deferred prosecution doesn't let misbehaving corporations off the hook. "This can be a way to get better results more quickly," says Andrew Hruska, the chief assistant U.S. attorney who oversaw the government's case against Computer Associates. "We're getting the sort of significant reforms you might not even get following a trial and conviction."

Plus, Hruska says that deferred prosecution agreements are structured with an enormous penalty if a business falls short on its end of the bargain. Each agreement includes a lengthy statement of criminal allegations that the company agrees not to contest should the case ever be activated. "The ultimate enforcement mechanism is that at the end of the deferral period, it is up to the U.S. attorney's office to determine whether the company satisfactorily lived up to [its] end of the deal," Hruska says. "If the answer is no, then the Justice Department has a statement of facts sufficiently incriminating that a prosecutor could put in as Exhibit A, and that would pretty much be the end of the case."

While deferred prosecution may be an acceptable deal from the company's standpoint, it's considerably less appealing for the business's employees. That's because most deferral deals require companies to assist in the prosecution of individual defendants by providing documents, waiving legal privileges, and making employees available to testify.

This stacks the deck against individual defendants, according to David Zornow, who represents Stephen Richards, a former Computer Associates executive facing criminal charges. "It undermines the adversarial system of justice," says Zornow, a partner at Skadden, Arps, Slate, Meagher & Flom. "I think the Justice Department has ample tools to bring to their investigations already."

Note: Prosecutor Contact with Corporate Employees

Model Rule 4.2 provides that a lawyer "shall not communicate about the subject of the representation with a person the lawyer knows to be represented by another lawyer in the matter" without the consent of that person's lawyer. In the early and mid–1990s the Justice Department took the position that the Supremacy Clause precluded federal prosecutors and their agents from being subject to state ethics rules. A particular concern of the Department was that its undercover agents be able to contact persons suspected of involvement in organized crime activities who were represented by the organization's lawyers. In 1998, however, Congress enacted 28 U.S.C. 530B, which provides that an attorney for the Government carrying out duties in a particular state is subject to that state's ethical rules "to the same extent and in the same manner as other attorneys in that state."

Comment 7 to Rule 4.2 describes the organization's employees who are deemed to be represented by the organization's counsel for purposes of the Rule. It states that the Rule prohibits contact with "a constituent of the organization who supervises, directs, or regularly consults with the organization's lawyer concerning the matter or has authority to obligate the organization with respect to the matter or whose act or omission may be imputed to the organization for purposes of civil or criminal liability." Former constituents, however, are not regarded as represented by the organization's counsel, although the consent of their individual counsel is required if they have one.

There is some variation among the states regarding which constituents are treated as represented by organizational counsel under Rule 4.2. The District of Columbia departs perhaps most significantly from the Model Rule. D.C. Rule 4.2 effectively confines organizational employees covered by the rule to those who have "the authority to bind" the organization with respect to the representation to which the lawyer's contact relates. A lawyer may communicate with other organizational employees without the consent of the organization's lawyer, but must disclose to those employees the lawyer's identity and the fact that he or she represents a client with a claim against the employer.

PROBLEMS

1. You are an Assistant U.S. Attorney in the U.S. Attorney's Office for the District of Columbia. A former employee in Safetech Corporation's office of government affairs, James Jones, has approached you with allegations that the company's executive vice-president for government affairs, Richard Garp, arranged for the payment of a $350,000 bribe to the chief purchasing officer at the Department of Homeland Security in return for the award of a contract for $25 million worth of identity-recognition technology that will be used as in security programs at airports and federal office buildings. Jones says that Safetech's technology actually still has some bugs in it that make it less reliable than some other competitors' products, but that the alleged bribe secured the contract for the company. He also says that he has heard that Garp made the payment at the direction of Safetech chief executive officer Warren Thorpe, who in fact offered suggestions about how to route the money so as to attract the least suspicion.

Jones says that although he has no direct evidence of this scheme, there are enough rumors about it at the company that he believes there is something to it. He says that he decided to come forward with all this information because his superiors in the government affairs office never appreciated his talents and unfairly persecuted him for petty offenses. Your investigation reveals that Jones and Garp once were very good friends, but that Jones was recently fired for having a drinking problem and for submitting false expense receipts.

You commence an investigation and obtain evidence that you believe would support an indictment of Garp for bribery. While your investigation leads you to suspect strongly that CEO Thorpe knew of and participated in the bribe, you are unable to find any evidence that would support charging him.

Given the importance of public confidence in the integrity of the government's anti-terrorism efforts, you would like very much to prosecute Thorpe in order to send the strongest possible message to the highest levels of corporate America. In your plea bargaining negotiations with Garp, however, it is clear that he is unwilling to accept a deal that would involve him implicating Thorpe because Thorpe is a powerful executive with many friends and extensive contacts in the industry.

Jones then brings you a tape recording of a conversation with himself and Garp in which Garp expressed anguish over his 19-year old son's drug problems. His son has been arrested a couple of times for drug possession, and served a brief period of time in jail for his second offense. In the taped conversation, Garp confides to Jones that he has learned that his son has now moved beyond drug use to selling drugs. Garp clearly is despondent about this turn of events. Not only does it insinuate his son more deeply into the drug culture, but if he were caught he would face twenty-five years in jail because of the gravity of the offense and his prior record.

You know that the tape would be inadmissible at trial, since Jones did not obtain Garp's permission before taping the conversation. You initiate an investigation into the activities of Garp's son, but that produces no additional evidence. Some of your colleagues nonetheless suggest that threatening to bring narcotics sale charges against Garp's son might make the father willing to accept a plea bargain that included his incrimination of Thorpe.

Should you make this threat in plea negotiations with Garp? What about simply indicating to him that you will inform the press that you are conducting an investigation into allegations of drug sales by his son?

2.   Suppose that you raise the possibility of an indictment of Garp's son and he agrees to provide evidence incriminating Thorpe. Thorpe and Safetech then plead guilty to bribery. The Safetech audit committee cooperates with your office in developing detailed monitoring procedures for the company's dealing with the Department of Homeland Security. The Board of Directors also sends out a directive emphasizing the company's insistence that all employees are expected to comply with all laws and regulations applicable to their activities and will be disciplined for failure to do so. Safetech also hires a new outside auditing firm and establishes a hotline that persons can use to report suspected illegal activity by employees.

Two years later, the company receives allegations that salespersons in the Phoenix office have been paying bribes to the United States Postal Service (USPS) in order to induce officials to purchase computerized mail-sorting equipment for post offices in the Phoenix area. Some 65% of salespersons' annual compensation is based on commissions, and each month the company ranks and circulates the sales figures for each office. An internal Safetech investigation confirms that payments are being made and that the office director has been aware of this practice. The company informs the USPS of the results of its investigation and fires the offending employees.

Safetech has made its internal investigation report available to you and has waived any privileges that otherwise would apply to communications regarding the matter. You have decided to prosecute the employees for bribery. Should you also bring a prosecution against the company?

Chapter 26

CRIMINAL DEFENSE

The so-called "white collar" criminal defense bar has expanded tremendously in recent years in response to more extensive pursuit of criminal charges for corporate misconduct. Most white-collar criminal defense lawyers will say that their most successful cases are those that no one hears about. This is because of the reputational damage to a corporation or its managers that can occur even from a criminal indictment, regardless of the eventual outcome of the case. Criminal defense lawyers with corporate clients thus seek first and foremost to persuade a prosecutor not to bring charges. This means that many of the most critical tasks a corporate criminal defense lawyer performs, and perhaps most of the ethical issues she confronts, occur when a criminal investigation is imminent or underway. This also means that many of the choices that she makes will not be subject to judicial review, nor known fully by the government.

Another distinctive feature of white collar criminal defense is the considerable amount of resources typically available to defendants and their lawyers. As Chapter 2 on the Lawyer's Role indicated, the hired gun model is seen by many people as most justified in the case of the criminal defense lawyer. The rationale is that assuming this role protects both vulnerable clients and society in general against the massive power of the state. Does this justification hold when the imbalance in power is the reverse–when, say, the defendant is a multinational corporation or its wealthy chief executive and the prosecutor has to operate within significant budgetary constraints? Do concerns about individual liberty and dignity apply when the defendant is a legal fiction? Does the Thompson Memo set forth in the previous chapter indicate that government still has powerful leverage notwithstanding limited resources? Does the sensitivity of corporate entities and managers to public opinion magnify that leverage? More generally, do corporate criminal lawyers serve to limit power or to reinforce it? Or both?

OVERVIEW OF THE CHAPTER

The chapter begins with excerpts from the ABA Standards for the criminal defense function. Note that Standard 4–1.2 states that the lawyer's duty is solely to the client, which contrasts with the Standards' description of the prosecution function. The excerpt from Webb, Molo and Hurst provides a short overview of defense counsel's involvement in the indictment process. As it indicates, counsel sometimes has the opportunity to make a written submission to the government that presents an argument for not indicting the client.

The excerpt from Mann elaborates on the ways in which white-collar criminal defense work differs from defense work with respect to street crime. The lawyer may be called in even before an investigation has begun, and often has a greater ability to learn the facts of the case than the government investigator and prosecutor. Furthermore, because time and resources usually are not scarce, "each case is individually cultivated with great care." The defense lawyer usually will have several opportunities to argue the innocence of her client before the government decides whether to issue an indictment.

Mann suggests that the chief strategy of the defense attorney in this context is to control information. This means keeping potentially incriminating documents away from the government and preventing clients and witnesses from sharing information with the prosecutor. He maintains that, given certain ethical constraints, this often is done by indirection rather than direct instruction. Take careful note of the various scenarios that can unfold as part of this process. When does a lawyer cross the line and assist a client in unlawfully withholding evidence by virtue of the advice that she provides? Is providing information with a wink and a nod but disclaiming responsibility for what the client does consistent with the lawyer's ethical obligations? If so, is it consistent with moral accountability? Or does the hired gun model immunize the corporate criminal defense lawyer from such accountability?

Finally, the excerpt from Subin asks whether it is ethical for the criminal defense lawyer to attempt to create reasonable doubt by suggesting an alternative account of events that she knows is false. Subin argues that the defense lawyer should mount a vigorous attack on the sufficiency of the state's evidence, but should draw the line at presenting a false defense. Does this distinction make sense, in light of the fact that a lawyer who knows that her client is guilty may nonetheless have the client plead not guilty? If you reject Subin's argument, how do you deal with ABA Defense Standard 4–7.7(a), which states that defense counsel in closing argument should not "mislead the jury as to the inferences it may draw?"

The first problem asks you to draw on both this chapter and the chapter on criminal prosecution to determine if the company should cooperate with the government investigation or mount a vigorous defense. One thing to consider in addressing this question is whether the company is in a position to engage in the kind of information control that Mann describes. What would you need to know to answer this, and how appropriate would you regard that strategy? The second problem asks you to draw on the excerpt from Subin in deciding what kind of a defense to present on behalf of your client, who is a corporate officer.

MODEL RULES: 1.2, 1.3, 1.13, 3.3, 3.4

AMERICAN BAR ASSOCIATION STANDARDS FOR CRIMINAL JUSTICE, THE DEFENSE FUNCTION
(1992)

Standard 4–1.2 The Function of Defense Counsel
* * *

(b) The basic duty defense counsel owes to the administration of justice and as an officer of the court is to serve as the accused's counselor and advocate with courage and devotion and to render effective, quality representation * * *

Standard 4–1.4 Public Statements

Defense counsel should not make or authorize the making of an extrajudicial statement that a reasonable person would expect to be disseminated by means of public communication if defense counsel knows or reasonably should know that it will have a substantial likelihood of prejudicing a criminal proceeding.

Standard 4–4.3 Relations with Prospective Witnesses

(a) Defense counsel, in representing an accused, should not use means that have no substantial purpose other than to embarrass, delay, or burden a third person, or use methods of obtaining evidence that violate the legal rights of such a person * * *

Standard 4–6.2 Plea Discussions
* * *

(c) Defense counsel should not knowingly make false statements concerning the evidence in the course of plea negotiations with the prosecutor * * *

Standard 4–7.6 Examination of Witnesses
* * *

(d) Defense counsel should not ask a question which implies the existence of a factual predicate for which a good faith belief is lacking.

Standard 4–7.7 Argument to the Jury

(a) In closing argument to the jury, defense counsel may argue all reasonable inferences from the evidence in the record. Defense counsel should not intentionally misstate the evidence or mislead the jury as to the inferences it may draw * * *

(c) Defense counsel should not make arguments calculated to appeal to the prejudices of the jury * * *

* * *

Dan K. Webb, Steven F. Molo & James F. Hurst, Understanding and Avoiding Corporate and Executive Criminal Liability

49 Business Lawyer 617 (1994)

* * *

Defense Counsel's Role in the Indictment Process

White collar indictments normally result from lengthy government investigations—usually lasting months and sometimes years—that rarely are kept secret. Thus, a corporation or a business executive almost never will be surprised by an indictment; the indictment will be a long-feared prospect. At the first sign of a government investigation, the corporation should advise outside counsel with experience in criminal matters, thus allowing sufficient time for efforts to stave off an indictment.

Meeting with Prosecutors

Defense counsel can influence the indictment decision. While counsel inevitably will have contact with the prosecutors throughout the investigation, counsel should request to meet with the prosecutors before the final indictment decision is made. Prosecutors almost always agree to such meetings, at a minimum as a courtesy, but also because pre-indictment meetings sometimes provide the government with valuable information about weaknesses in its case and even defense strategy. Prosecutors typically are not eager to bring indictments when serious obstacles to a conviction exist or when innocence is likely.

Moreover, defense counsel's arguments can sway a prosecutor in a close case. Among other possibilities, counsel can argue that the evidence is insufficient to obtain a conviction, that any violation was merely technical or inconsequential, or that the conduct was the aberrant conduct of a rogue employee in a corporation's otherwise law-abiding existence.

Written Submissions

Depending on the circumstances of the case, counsel even may choose to commit his or her arguments to writing in a pre-indictment submission. Some defense counsel balk at the use of such submissions, contending that they only provide a road map of defense strategy upon indictment. Primarily for that reason, whether to provide a written submission is a delicate decision—one that turns on the facts of each case. As a general rule, however, providing a written submission is the better course of action whenever defense counsel believes that a reasonable chance to avoid indictment exists. Indeed, given the stakes in most white collar prosecutions, counsel should seize any reasonable opportunity to avoid the disaster of an indictment.

Appealing the Indictment Decision

If, despite counsel's best efforts, the line prosecutor decides to indict, defense counsel should consider appealing the prosecutor's decision to a higher authority within the prosecutor's office—the First Assistant, the United States Attorney, or a group of supervisors. If the indictment decision was truly a close call, and depending upon the nature of the case, most prosecutors will not object to a request to have a superior review the decision. Some crimes, RICO violations for example, require approval by Main Justice in Washington, D.C. before an indictment can be returned. Counsel should be aware that while an appeal is not necessarily a waste of time in all circumstances, the opinion of the line prosecutor who developed the case will receive significant deference.

Kenneth Mann, DEFENDING WHITE-COLLAR CRIME
A PORTRAIT OF ATTORNEYS AT WORK

(1985)

* * *

STRATEGIC ISSUES

Imagine that three years ago you cheated on your income tax. Today you are being subjected to a routine civil audit by the Internal Revenue Service, and you are asking yourself, "How am I going to explain that cash bonus I left off my tax return?" This audit, you learn later, has turned into a criminal investigation. You are like many other persons investigated for white-collar crimes each year: you now need a defense attorney. And you need that attorney to achieve results such as these:

- In October 1980, the U.S. Attorney in a major city (the chief prosecutor in the federal district) closed a fraud investigation of an industrial equipment manufacturer that had falsified records to inflate losses and obtain tax benefits. This large company was also making illegal payments to congressional representatives to obtain influence over pending legislation. After many months of work, the defense attorneys had been successful in convincing the U.S. Attorney that his office could not carry out a successful prosecution of the officers of the company or of the company itself.

- In July 1979, defense attorneys traveled to Dallas. Texas, to meet with IRS criminal investigators investigating one of the largest oil producers in the world. Their objective was to prove that certain questionable tax writeoffs did not constitute a fraud on the U.S. Treasury. They failed to convince the investigators not to send the case to the Department of Justice with a recommendation for prosecution. But later they were successful in meetings with officials in the tax fraud division of the department. The case was closed without public knowledge.

• In the spring of 1978, defense attorneys in another firm accompanied subpoenaed corporate officers to an interview at the Securities and Exchange Commission (SEC). The officers had conducted an international scheme for hiding income in foreign banks. After careful coaching by their defense attorneys, the officers were able to talk their way around the questions asked by the SEC officials. And after opposing and quashing subpoenas for documents, the defense attorneys succeeded in putting an end to the investigation.

• In the same week, the attorneys who appeared before the SEC also handled the case of a used car salesman under investigation for turning back odometers to reduce the mileage of cars sold. No appearance was made by these attorneys before any investigator or court in this matter, but advice they gave to the client was critical to the case being closed at the field investigation stage.

These four investigations are representative of a broad range of cases in the United States that we have come to call white-collar crimes. The cases are prosecuted under such statutes as tax fraud, securities fraud, bribery, false statements, mail fraud, wire fraud, and conspiracy to defraud the United States. In the late sixties and the decade of the seventies these crimes came to be identified as a major social problem. It is now conventional wisdom that they cause the loss of billions of dollars a year to the public, which is victimized by individual swindlers and by corporations and corporate officers carrying out complex schemes of deception.

But the cases exemplified in these paragraphs are not only typical instances of white-collar crime. They are also distinctive because defense attorneys intervened early in the criminal process—while the investigation was taking place—and stopped governmental action before an official criminal charge was made. The attorneys used one or a number of defense strategies that are distinctive to white-collar crime. And they were able to provide clients whom they knew to be guilty with protection from what could have been the most damaging event of their careers and family lives—the public revelation of a criminal accusation through the issuance of an indictment. They represent a special characteristic of the adversarial criminal process: the potential for early action by a defense attorney to prevent the issuance of a formal criminal charge.

The white-collar crime defense attorney is zealous in his advocacy of his client's interest, often rejecting government overtures to negotiate and compromise. In contrast to the attorney handling street crime, his time is not a scarce resource, and each case is individually cultivated with great care. In white-collar cases, the defense attorney is usually called in by the client to conduct a defense before the government investigation is completed and in some cases even before it begins. The defense attorney employs his own investigators, who are experts in accounting and finance, as well as a staff of legal researchers. He learns thoroughly the details of the case, usually having a greater ability to do this than the government investigator and prosecutor. This attorney, in distinct contrast to the attorney handling street crime, has a number of opportunities to argue the innocence of his client before the government makes a decision to issue an indictment. A plea agreement may be an important element in the final disposition of the white-collar case, but the compromise that leads to a plea agreement is the result of a carefully managed process of adversary interaction in which cooperation with the government plays little or no part. And in many cases the guilty plea is followed by a second period of intensive advocacy—at the time of sentencing—where compromise and negotiation again remain conspicuously absent. But above all, and this is the central theme of the white-collar crime defense function, the defense attorney works to keep potential evidence out of government reach by controlling access to information.

The Information Control Defense and the Substantive Defense

The defense attorney's adversaries are the government agents who decide whether a criminal charge should be made—government investigators and, eventually, prosecutors. To prevent issuance of an indictment, the attorney must keep these persons from concluding that the client has done something that warrants criminal prosecution. The central strategy question for the attorney is how to accomplish this end, and this applies in all cases, irrespective of whether the attorney's client has in fact committed a crime, or whether it is a white-collar or a street crime.

In making a substantive defense, the defense attorneys studied had a distinctive role because they were handling white-collar cases. Rather than waiting until trial or until the immediate pretrial period when plea negotiations usually take place, these defense attorneys had an opportunity to make a substantive defense before a charge was made. While attorneys in other types of cases also make opportunities for adversary argument before charging, in white-collar cases there is typically a series of institutionalized settings for conducting precharge adversarial proceedings on questions of substantive criminal responsibility. Substantive legal argument before the charge decision is a routinized pattern of defense advocacy in white-collar cases.

The substantive defense is not, however, the initial defense strategy for a competent attorney. The defense attorney's first objective is to prevent the government from obtaining evidence that could be inculpatory of his client and used by the investigator or prosecutor to justify issuance of a formal criminal charge. Instead of preparing legal argument, the defense attorney first devotes himself to keeping evidence out of any prospective adversary forum in which legal argument about the client's criminal responsibility might take place. This action is crucial to prevent issuance of a criminal charge. I call this task information control and the defense strategy built on these actions an information control defense.

Information control entails keeping documents away from and preventing clients and witnesses from talking to government investigators, prosecutors, and judges. It will become evident as I describe defense attorneys handling actual cases of white-collar crime that information control is not the conventional advocacy task of substantive argument in which the defense attorney analyzes a set of facts and argues that a crime is not proved. It occurs before the substantive defense and is in some ways a more important defense. If successful, it keeps the raw material of legal argument out of the hands of the government, it obviates argument about the substantive legal implications of facts about crime, and it keeps the government ignorant of evidence it needs in deciding whether to make a formal charge against a person suspected of committing a crime. And, even if a formal charge is made, it keeps facts about a crime out of the arena of plea negotiations and out of the courtroom if a trial takes place. For these reasons, information control lies at the very heart of the defense function, preventing the imposition of a criminal sanction on an accused person who has committed a crime, as well as on the rare one who has not.

Attorneys act in two different ways to control information. First, they oppose their adversaries in quasi-judicial and court settings. In one situation, the attorney argues to a judge in court or to an investigator in an office that a subpoena for documents is improper because, for instance, it is overburdensome or vague. In another situation, the attorney argues that information already seized by the government should not be admissible evidence because of government misbehavior in making the seizure. The essential feature of these information control arguments is their focus on the behavior of the opposing party, directly by convincing that party not to press the request or indirectly through the sanction of a judge or other decisionmaker. The legal rules used to support these attempts to control information are communicated to the opposing party. For instance, the defense attorney argues that the law of search and seizure prohibits the government from taking the documents. The prosecutor argues that the law permits him to do so. In these contexts, the government has the opportunity to rebut the defense position with its own arguments about what the applicable legal rules require. I will call this adversarial information control.

Second, the defense attorney uses an information control strategy that focuses on the potential source of inculpatory information, rather than on the behavior of the adversary seeking to gain access to the source. The defense attorney's aim is to instruct the client or third party holding inculpatory information how to refrain from disclosing it to the government and, if necessary, to persuade or force him to refrain. The legal justification supporting such information control actions is usually not communicated to the adversary. The setting of this action is typically concealed, behind the attorney-client confidentiality privilege or in private attorney-witness meetings, and concealment is often essential to success of the information control action. When this kind of information control is undertaken, the opposing party has no or little opportunity to rebut it using legal argument. I will call this managerial information control.

When an attorney in a meeting in his office advises a client about to be questioned by a government agent to "avoid answering that question, and if pushed, tell him that you have to examine your books before responding," the target of control is the client and the aim is information control. The attorney has acted on the client and the information in the client's possession, in a setting concealed from the adversary. If the client handles the situation well, he may successfully avoid prosecution or avoid or delay raising of an issue where this result may be important to other defense efforts. Managerial information control focuses on what the attorney does to manage the disposition of information sources.

Information control as a defense strategy is not exclusive to whitecollar cases. In many kinds of criminal cases, defense attorneys move to exclude illegally seized evidence, an adversarial control device, and they engage in pretrial coaching of witnesses, a managerial control device. What is distinctive in whitecollar cases is the centrality of information control strategies to defense work: they are fundamental modus operandi constituting a basic defense plan, rather than merely tactics in a broader strategy.

Information Control and Ethical Problems

When an attorney decides that his main defense strategy will be to keep information out of the forum of legal argument, a fundamental ethical question emerges: "How far," he must ask himself, "can I go in my effort to keep facts from being revealed to my opponent?" This problem is a common one for attorneys who handle cases early in an investigation and are presented with opportunities to influence clients, witnesses, and the disposition of documents. The attorney must determine the proper standard of conduct when faced with two goals that may conflict with each other, one compelling him to create maximum control over information, the other to avoid committing an offense himself while attempting to help his client.

The attorney is mandated by the principles of the adversary system to be zealous in pursuing the interest of his client and to resolve doubt in his client's favor. A critical question then is how close to the margin of legitimate action he can go before violating ethical proscriptions. He must decide, for instance, how much he can help clients to understand which documents not to turn over to the government, when the relevant ethical rule states that an attorney shall not "conceal or knowingly fail to disclose that which he is required by law to reveal," or "knowingly make a false statement of law or fact," or "counsel or assist his client in conduct that [he] knows to be illegal or fraudulent"; and he must decide how far to go in secreting information he receives about a client's ongoing crimes or new crimes committed to cover up past crimes, when the relevant ethical rules state that the attorney shall "not knowingly reveal a confidence or secret of his client," but that he "*may* reveal the intention of his client to commit a crime and the information necessary to prevent the crime" (emphasis added). He must decide whether he can influence a client to persuade his employees, associates, or other persons to keep silent, when the relevant ethical rule states that an attorney "shall not give advice to a person who is not represented by a lawyer other than the advice to secure counsel, if the interests of such persons are or have a reasonable possibility of being in conflict with the interest of his client."

The defense attorneys studied here demonstrate particular behaviors when faced with these questions. How they act is significant for understanding the nature of criminal defense practice. But many opportunities for information control found in these criminal cases are also found in cases of civil litigation, where attorneys often represent clients whose objective of winning is dependent on concealing information from an adversary. A civil case for damages caused by fraud or misrepresentation brought by a stockholder against corporate executives requires that the attorney ask himself the same question: How far do I go in facilitating compliance with a discovery request made by the plaintiff against my client? How actively do I seek out the real facts and reveal them to my adversary? Or how far can I go in influencing my client not to cooperate or in bringing pressure to bear against witnesses who otherwise might weaken or destroy my case? While certain elementary rules about how the litigation is carried out are different in the civil cases, the ethical and moral dilemmas faced by attorneys handling criminal and civil litigation are fundamentally similar. The advocate must weigh his commitment to the client against his commitment to the court, to the public, and to truth and justice. Providing the best available defense to a client—in a criminal case as well as a civil case—requires an acute sense of how to approach as close as possible to the margin of legitimate action, without going over it. I assess how these issues are resolved in the context of white-collar crime defense practice. But it would not be reaching too far to say that this assessment is applicable to any litigating attorney facing difficult issues of information control.

Client Disclosures to Attorneys

Legal Advice and Lack of Inquiry

The attorney's desire not to know is perhaps most significant in the area of subpoena and summons compliance. The government is often dependent on documents to establish proof. Government investigative policy and in many cases Constitutional doctrine make search-and-seizure investigative techniques impermissible for obtaining documents. The investigator's use of subpoenas and summonses allows long periods of time for an answer, putting the attorney in a position where intentional avoidance of inquiry—by the attorney into the client's compliance with a government request for documents—yields a substantial defense strategy.

Here is an archetype scenario of the attorney in the inquiry avoidance role; a subpoena is issued by a court calling for the client to produce all documents related to a certain transaction. Upon receipt, the client takes the subpoena to an attorney and asks, "How do I proceed?" In the characteristic case of avoidance, the attorney begins by explaining to the client what is called for by the subpoena and what significance certain types of documents would have for the course of the investigation. He will not blandly ask the client what documents currently exist but will explain to the client what the subpoena indicates about the subject and scope of the investigation. Some attorneys go one step further and explain to the client what kinds of documents could be used against the client "*if* they exist." For example, the attorney says, "The government is trying to establish that officers in the corporation had knowledge of the improper evaluation of assets before the public distribution of the prospectus; if there are any documents which show such knowledge, these may be used by the prosecution as evidence for an indictment. Or if there is any document which indicates that an officer requested certain financial analyses that were not made, this may also be problematic." In this fashion, an attorney educates a client as to what constitutes a potentially adverse document. Subsequently, the client takes several weeks to conduct an independent search.

In many instances, such a discussion is the last detailed consideration of the type and possible existence of the requested documents. The client is later asked to report to the attorney whether any such documents were found. And then he is instructed how to make a formal reply on the date of appearance before the prosecutor to answer the subpoena. An attorney who is avoiding inquiry will not ask, "Did such documents ever exist?" or "Was document X or document Y found?" His interaction with the client is likely to be limited to a narrower question: "Do you have anything to present in response to the subpoena?" An attorney who was preparing to accompany his client to a U.S. Attorney's office to make a formal response to a subpoena explained his mission this way.

> The client's going to meet me here and then we are going down to Foley Square [location of U.S. Attorney's office in the Southern District of New York]. I'm not going to ask him whether he has all the books and records that have been requested. The assistant [U.S. Attorney] will do the asking. The only thing I'm going to do is to warn him about—explain to him—the dangers of a perjury charge. It's then up to him to handle the response.

In fact, the attorney explained to the client in detail how to answer the prosecutor's oral questions testing compliance with the subpoena, *after* the client said that he did not have anything to present. "You do not," said the attorney, "state anything more than 'The documents do not exist.' You do not say what kind of a search you made, or how you defined the nature of the documents you were looking for. All you have to say is that you read the subpoena and did not find anything that was described therein."

Another attorney was asked directly about the attorney-client relationship in IRS summons compliance procedures. He stated:

> There are many cases in which one would surmise that documents summoned from the client existed at the time the summons was issued. My function in this procedure is a very limited one. I, of course, do not want the client convicted of an obstruction of justice charge, and I do warn him of the dire consequences of such a happening. But in the end it is the client's choice. I have no doubt that clients destroy documents. Have I ever "known" of such an occurrence? No. But you put two and two together. You couldn't convict anyone on such circumstantial evidence, but you can draw your own conclusion.

Still another attorney summed up the same views when he replied to an associate who seemed to think that a client was not being completely honest: "What you are trying to tell me is that the client is not telling the truth. What I am saying is that the response is credible. We are not law enforcement agents."

These interview comments represent the widespread view that it is not the attorney's task to enforce his client's compliance with the law. His obligation—even if it is an obligation not met all the time by all attorneys—is to refrain from actively facilitating or knowingly taking part in law violations. It is not a defense attorney's obligation to go into the corporate and personal records or send associates to conduct a search. Nor is it his obligation to find out what happened to missing documents. The attorney's limited role in this particular procedure is to serve his client by educating him. In addition to describing the evidentiary value of different types of documents, the attorney educates the client in the legal significance of the subpoena: "The language in the subpoena encompasses documents of type A, B, and C, but not documents of type X, Y, and Z; you can legally refuse to hand over this document but not that." Or the attorney makes independent legal conclusions: "The subpoena is overburdensome or excessive in scope and you can object to its enforcement." In essence, the attorney draws two diagrams for the client. One shows the client what is required by law and the language of the subpoena to be disclosed. The other shows the client which kind of documents are adverse to his interest and which are not. This is a passive role in which the attorney intentionally avoids proactive inquiry. The action—determination of whether the document exists and compliance or noncompliance—is left to the client.

Principles of the Adversary System

The legal profession is central to the operation of information control aspects of the adversary system. Without legal representation and counsel, the parties to a dispute are adrift before the law, unable to take advantage of its rights and trapped by its obligations. The attorney stands, for the most part, in his client's shoes, bearing no more and often less of an obligation to disclose information relevant to the client's actions. When information acquisition is an issue, the attorney exercises for the client his right to specificity and proper timing of a request, his right to application of the rule of relevancy, and his right to be protected by the privilege against self-incrimination. In other ways, the defense attorney educates his client about legal protection of information sources and the penalties of the law for behavior constituting a breach of information control limits. The adversary system thus creates a broad range of information control rights and opportunities, as well as obligations. The defense attorney is an expert in their use and is therefore formally attributed a key role in how information is managed.

The Ethical Rules

When an attorney learns that a client to whom he has given legal counsel has intentionally not turned over documents in violation of a subpoena, he is not required to take remedial action unless he learns of this from a third party. In relation to the client, the attorney's information control capacity remains in full force, meaning that the attorney's obligation is governed by the former rule that allows but does not require the attorney to take remedial action. The ABA *Code* permits the attorney to collaborate in the client's design, in the sense that the attorney has no obligation to rectify a fraud committed on an adversary or court when the client has "used" expertise provided to him by the attorney.

If information control is permitted in these two situations, it is prohibited in a third, and that is when the attorney would actively take part in concealment for which there is no affirmative privilege or actively take part in misrepresentation. This prohibition is set out specifically in the ABA rule that requires the attorney to refrain from *knowingly* engaging in conduct that would assist his client in defrauding an adversary or court, which includes a prohibition on knowing participation in misrepresentation and illegal concealment. On one level, these rules express the obvious: an attorney cannot advise the client to engage in illegal behavior, such as advising a client not to turn over documents properly requested or advising a client to change a document or misstate a factual situation when he knows that this will misrepresent the truth.

The Problem of Knowing Participation in Illegal Information Control

We can now focus on the major ethical problem presented by the cases and defense strategies reported here: at what point does the attorney cross the line between the second situation above, that in which the attorney becomes aware after the fact that the client has misused his expertise, and the third situation, that in which the attorney knowingly causes the client's misrepresentation or illegal concealment? In other words, when does an attorney representing a client *know* that he is assisting his client in committing fraud on an adversary or court?

The answer to this question depends on how attorneys are supposed to interpret the term *knowing*. The ABA *Code* is ambiguous. It states that an attorney must *know* that he is causing a client to act illegally before he will be held responsible, but there are few authoritative decisions on what constitutes knowing participation by an attorney. If the standard stated by the following case correctly interprets the law, then attorneys would be held responsible for a large range of illegal acts of concealment carried out by their clients.

> The effort to distinguish between a suggestion of a possible course of action . . . and advice or counsel . . . is without force or basis. The precise form of the words in which the advice is couched is immaterial. The question is: has the lawyer conveyed to the client the idea that by adopting a particular course of action he may successfully defraud someone or impede the administration of justice? If a bank official, who had . . . robbed his bank, should call upon a lawyer . . . and ask for his suggestion as to what he should do, could that lawyer escape responsibility by saying to his client, "Have you thought about . . . going to . . . Argentina, where you are not likely to be traced for a long time?" instead of saying directly "I advise you to . . . run away?"

This statement of the governing standard of conduct was *obiter dictum* in the context of the case decided because the attorney/defendant had openly advised a fraudulent course of action. Nonetheless, the statement is quoted in the commentary to the Proposed Model Rules of Professional Conduct of the ABA to support an interpretation of the ABA *Code* that would mandate counsel to avoid indirectly facilitating a client's illegal behavior. In the same commentary, however, competing propositions are also set out. They state that the "standard does not impose a general duty to investigate the client's purposes" and that "a lawyer does not violate this standard by giving advice on a doubtful question concerning conduct later found to be criminal." Taken together, the existing rule and the cases interpreting it give an attorney little concrete sense of what is meant by *knowing* facilitation and what behavior is meant to be prohibited.

The question can be stated in another way: Is the attorney to be held responsible only for words and actions that explicitly constitute advice or assistance in illegal conduct, or must the attorney be held to a standard that imputes to him knowledge of the reasonably foreseeable actions of a client? Or, as a third possibility, is some intermediate standard—what is called in the criminal law willful blindness or conscious avoidance—to apply to the attorney? The third standard attributes to the attorney only consequences that are more than *reasonably* foreseeable but not merely those that are explicitly advised.

This question is open to debate on the part of the legal profession. What is not open to debate, and this must be one of the major conclusions of this research, is that defense attorneys have adopted a role in representing clients that excuses them from knowledge of the causal connection between what they say and what their clients do, where the clients' actions are not more than a reasonable possibility. While the attorney often knows that his client, after meeting with him, is going to illegally alter or conceal a document, he does not have "legal knowledge" of a causal connection between the counsel provided and the client's action. The attorney is morally knowledgeable, which may disturb him, but he is instrumentally ignorant.

One response to what I have described could be a rule requiring that attorneys take responsibility for all the *reasonably foreseeable* actions of their clients. Such a rule would make an attorney responsible for the client's fraudulent actions that followed on counsel received from the attorney, when the attorney could have concluded that the client was reasonably likely to act in that way. But there are major problems in such a rule. One can ask whether every client would not fall within this category. Is it not always reasonably foreseeable that a person who learns that a document he holds will result in his going to prison may destroy it rather than turn it over to a government prosecutor? If it is not always reasonably foreseeable, how is an attorney to distinguish the clients to whom this does apply from those to whom it does not? Can an attorney be saddled with this responsibility and still give legitimate and effective advice?

If the answers to these questions lead one to the conclusion that a standard of reasonable foreseeability is inappropriate, there is a much stronger argument for promulgating an intermediate standard of responsibility, which would define "advising the client to do an illegal act" as applying in situations where the client has made obvious to the attorney (that is, more than reasonably foreseeable) the likelihood of illegal action. This rule removes much of the stultifying effect on legal counsel associated with the stricter rule, while mandating the attorney to evaluate his client's intentions and to prevent, on proper forewarning, the client's misuse of legal counsel.

If an intermediate standard does or should apply, then this standard must be spelled out by specific legislation. The existing ambiguity in the ABA *Code* promotes a situation in which even the well-intentioned attorney falters in pursuing effective self-regulation. On the one hand, he properly feels compelled to provide every legitimate advantage to his client. That, after all, is what the client is paying for. On the other hand, he also feels compelled not to exceed the margin of proscribed conduct. In attempting to find the proper dividing line, the well-intentioned attorney is ineffectively guided, the wavering attorney is ineffectively warned, and the cynical, devious attorney is provided with excuses. There is, then, a pressing need for greater rule specificity.

Note: Information Control and Ethical Rules

The excerpt from Mann refers to the ABA Code of Professional Responsibility, which has been superceded in most states by versions of the ABA Model Rules of Professional Conduct. The Model Rules relevant to his discussion of information control, however, are similar to the Code provisions that he discusses.

Model Rule 3.4(a) says that a lawyer may not counsel or assist anyone to obstruct unlawfully access to evidence or unlawfully alter, destroy, or conceal any material "having potential evidentiary value." The term "unlawfully" refers to provisions of state or federal law. As comment 2 to the Rule states, "Applicable law in many jurisdictions makes it an offense to destroy material for purpose of impairing its availability in a pending proceeding or one whose commencement can be foreseen." Federal law is similar, as is described in more detail in Chapter 28 on Civil Litigation.

Model Rule 3.4(b) says that a lawyer may not counsel or assist a witness to testify falsely. Of particular relevance to corporate lawyers, however, Rule 3.4(f) permits a lawyer to advise employees of a client to refrain from giving information to anyone, as long as the lawyer believes that the person's interests will not be adversely affected by the failure to cooperate. Comment 4 says that this is based on the idea that the employees "may identify their interests with those of the client."

Violations of Model Rule 3.4(a) and 3.4(b) can constitute violations of Model Rule 1.2(d), which prohibits a lawyer from counseling or assisting a client to engage in a crime or fraud. They also can be the basis for aiding and abetting liability under tort or criminal law.

THE CRIMINAL LAWYER'S "DIFFERENT MISSION": REFLECTIONS ON THE "RIGHT" TO PRESENT A FALSE CASE

Harry I. Subin
Georgetown Journal of Legal Ethics
Summer, 1987

I. THE INQUIRY

This article attempts to define the limits on the methods a lawyer should be willing to use when his or her client's goals are inconsistent with the truth. * * *

I am now concerned with a related but knottier question concerning the proper limits on the lawyer's loyalty to the client: Should the criminal lawyer be permitted to represent a client by putting forward a defense the lawyer knows is false? * * *

Presenting a "false defense," as used here, means attempting to convince the judge or jury that facts established by the state and known to the attorney to be true are not true, or that facts known to the attorney to be false are true. While this can be done by criminal means— e.g., perjury, introduction of forged documents, and the like—I exclude these acts from the definition of false defense used here. * * *

My concern, instead, is with the presently legal means for the attorney to reach a favorable verdict even if it is completely at odds with the facts. The permissible techniques include: (1) cross-examination of truthful government witnesses to undermine their testimony or their credibility; (2) direct presentation of testimony, not itself false, but used to discredit the truthful evidence adduced by the government, or to accredit a false theory; and (3) argument to the jury based on any of these acts. * * *

* * *

II.   Truth Subversion in Action: The Problem Illustrated

A.   *The accusation*

About fifteen years ago I represented a man charged with rape and robbery. The victim's account was as follows: Returning from work in the early morning hours, she was accosted by a man who pointed a gun at her and took a watch from her wrist. He told her to go with him to a nearby lot, where he ordered her to lie down on the ground and disrobe. When she complained that the ground was hurting her, he took her to his apartment, located across the street. During the next hour there, he had intercourse with her. Ultimately, he said that they had to leave to avoid being discovered by the woman with whom he lived. The complainant responded that since he had gotten what he wanted, he should give her back her watch. He said that he would.

As the two left the apartment, he said he was going to get a car. Before leaving the building, however, he went to the apartment next door, leaving her to wait in the hallway. When asked why she waited, she said that she was still hoping for the return of her watch, which was a valued gift, apparently from her boyfriend.

She never did get the watch. When they left the building, the man told her to wait on the street while he got the car. At that point she went to a nearby police precinct and reported the incident. She gave a full description of the assailant that matched my client. She also accurately described the inside of his apartment. Later, in response to a note left at his apartment by the police, my client came to the precinct, and the complainant identified him. My client was released at that time but was arrested soon thereafter at his apartment, where a gun was found. No watch was recovered.

My client was formally charged, at which point I entered the case. At our initial interview and those that followed it, he insisted that he had nothing whatever to do with the crime and had never even seen the woman before. He stated that he had been in several places during the night in question: visiting his aunt earlier in the evening, then traveling to a bar in New Jersey, where he was during the critical hours. He gave the name of a man there who would corroborate this. He said that he arrived home early the next morning and met a friend. He stated that he had no idea how this woman had come to know things about him such as what the apartment looked like, that he lived with a woman, and that he was a musician, or how she could identify him. He said that he had no reason to rape anyone, since he already had a woman, and that in any event he was recovering from surgery for an old gun shot wound and could not engage in intercourse. He said he would not be so stupid as to bring a woman he had robbed and was going to rape into his own apartment.

I felt that there was some strength to these arguments, and that there were questionable aspects to the complainant's story. In particular, it seemed strange that a man intending rape would be as solicitous of the victim's comfort as the woman said her assailant was at the playground. It also seemed that a person who had just been raped would flee when she had the chance to, and in any case would not be primarily concerned with the return of her watch. On balance, however, I suspected that my client was not telling me the truth. I thought the complaining witness could not possibly have known what she knew about him and his apartment, if she had not had any contact with him. True, someone else could have posed as him, and used his apartment. My client, however, could suggest no one who could have done so. Moreover, that hypothesis did not explain the complainant's accurate description of him to the police. Although the identification procedure used by the police, a one person ''show up,'' was suggestive, the woman had ample opportunity to observe her assailant during the extended incident. I could not believe that the complainant had selected my client randomly to accuse falsely of rape. By both her and my client's admission, the two had not had any previous association.

That my client was probably lying to me had two possible explanations. First, he might have been lying because he was guilty and did not see any particular advantage to himself in admitting it to me. It is embarrassing to admit that one has committed a crime, particularly one of this nature. Moreover, my client might well have feared to tell me the truth. He might have believed that I would tell others what he said, or, at the very least, that I might not be enthusiastic about representing him.

He also might have lied not because he was guilty of the offense, but because he thought the concocted story was the best one under the circumstances. The sexual encounter may have taken place voluntarily, but the woman complained to the police because she was angry at my client for refusing to return the valued wrist watch, perhaps not stolen, but left, in my client's apartment. My client may not have been able to admit this, because he had other needs that took precedence over the particular legal one that brought him to me. For example, the client might have felt compelled to deny any involvement in the incident because to admit to having had a sexual encounter might have jeopardized his relationship with the woman with whom he lived. Likewise, he might have decided to ''play lawyer,'' and put forward what he believed to be his best defense. Not understanding the heavy burden of proof on the state in criminal cases, he might have thought that any version of the facts that showed that he had contact with the woman would be fatal because it would simply be a case of her word against his.

I discussed all of these matters with the client on several occasions. Judging him a man of intelligence, with no signs of mental abnormality,

I became convinced that he understood both the seriousness of his situation, and that his exculpation did not depend upon maintaining his initial story. In ensuring that he did understand that, in fact, I came close enough to suggesting the "right" answers to make me a little nervous about the line between subornation of perjury and careful witness preparation, known in the trade as "horseshedding." In the end, however, he held to his original account.

B.   The Investigation

At this point the case was in equipoise for me. I had my suspicions about both the complainant's and the client's version of what had occurred, and I supposed a jury would as well. That problem was theirs, however, not mine. All I had to do was present my client's version of what occurred in the best way that I could.

Or was that all that was required? Committed to the adversarial spirit reflected in Justice White's observations about my role, I decided that it was not. The "different mission" took me beyond the task of presenting my client's position in a legally correct and persuasive manner, to trying to untrack the state's case in any lawful way that occurred to me, regardless of the facts.

With that mission in mind, I concluded that it would be too risky to have the defendant simply take the stand and tell his story, even if it were true. Unless we could create an iron-clad alibi, which seemed unlikely given the strength of the complainant's identification, I thought it was much safer to attack the complainant's story, even if it were true. I felt, however, that since my client had persisted in his original story I was obligated to investigate the alibi defense, although I was fairly certain that I would not use it. My students and I therefore interviewed everyone he mentioned, traveled and timed the route he said he had followed, and attempted to find witnesses who may have seen someone else at the apartment. We discovered nothing helpful. The witness my client identified as being at the bar in New Jersey could not corroborate the client's presence there. The times the client gave were consistent with his presence at the place of the crime when the victim claimed it took place. The client's aunt verified that he had been with her, but much earlier in the evening.

Because the alibi defense was apparently hopeless, I returned to the original strategy of attempting to undermine the complainant's version of the facts. I demanded a preliminary hearing, in which the complainant would have to testify under oath to the events in question. Her version was precisely as I have described it, and she told it in an objective manner that, far from seeming contrived, convinced me that she was telling the truth. She seemed a person who, if not at home with the meanness of the streets, was resigned to it. To me that explained why she was able to react in what I perceived to be a nonstereotypical manner to the ugly events in which she had been involved.

I explained to my client that we had failed to corroborate his alibi, and that the complainant appeared to be a credible witness. I said that in my view the jury would not believe the alibi, and that if we could not obtain any other information, it might be appropriate to think about a guilty plea, which would at least limit his exposure to punishment. The case, then in the middle of the aimless drift towards resolution that typifies New York's criminal justice system, was left at that.

Some time later, however, my client called me and told me that he had new evidence; his aunt, he said, would testify that he had been with her at the time in question. I was incredulous. I reminded him that at no time during our earlier conversations had he indicated what was plainly a crucial piece of information, despite my not too subtle explanation of the elements of an alibi defense. I told him that when the aunt was initially interviewed with great care on this point, she stated that he was not with her at the time of the crime. Ultimately, I told him that I thought he was lying, and that in my view even if the jury heard the aunt's testimony, they would not believe it.

Whether it was during that session or later that the client admitted his guilt I do not recall. I do recall wondering whether, now that I knew the truth, that should make a difference in the way in which the case was handled. I certainly wished that I did not know it and began to understand, psychologically if not ethically, lawyers who do not want to know their clients' stories.

I did not pause very long to ponder the problem, however, because I concluded that knowing the truth in fact did not make a difference to my defense strategy, other than to put me on notice as to when I might be suborning perjury. Because the mission of the defense attorney was to defeat the prosecution's case, what I knew actually happened was not important otherwise. What did matter was whether a version of the "facts" could be presented that would make a jury doubt the client's guilt.

Viewed in this way, my problem was not that my client's story was false, but that it was not credible, and could not be made to appear so by legal means. To win, we would therefore have to come up with a better theory than the alibi, avoiding perjury in the process. Thus, the defense would have to be made out without the client testifying, since it would be a crime for him to assert a fabricated exculpatory theory under oath. This was not a serious problem, however, because it would not only be possible to prevail without the defendant's testimony, but it would probably be easier to do so. Not everyone is capable of lying successfully on the witness stand, and I did not have the sense that my client would be very good at it.

There were two possible defenses that could be fabricated. The first was mistaken identity. We could argue that the opportunity of the victim to observe the defendant at the time of the original encounter was limited, since it had occurred on a dark street. The woman could be made out to have been in great emotional distress during the incident.

Expert testimony would have be adduced to show the hazards of eyewitness identification. We could demonstrate that an unreliable identification procedure had been used at the precinct. On the other hand, given that the complainant had spent considerable time with the assailant and had led the police back to the defendant's apartment, it seemed doubtful that the mistaken identification ploy would be successful.

The second alternative, consent, was clearly preferable. It would negate the charge of rape and undermine the robbery case. To prevail, all we would have to do would be to raise a reasonable doubt as to whether he had compelled the woman to have sex with him. The doubt would be based on the scenario that the woman and the defendant met, and she voluntarily returned to his apartment. Her watch, the object of the alleged robbery, was either left there by mistake or, perhaps better, was never there at all.

The consent defense could be made out entirely through cross-examination of the complainant, coupled with argument to the jury about her lack of credibility on the issue of force. I could emphasize the parts of her story that sounded the most curious, such as the defendant's solicitude in taking his victim back to his apartment, and her waiting for her watch when she could have gone immediately to the nearby precinct that she went to later. I could point to her inability to identify the gun she claimed was used (although it was the one actually used), that the allegedly stolen watch was never found, there was no sign of physical violence, and no one heard screaming or any other signs of a struggle. I could also argue as my client had that even if he were reckless enough to rob and rape a woman across the street from his apartment, he would not be so foolish as to bring the victim there. I considered investigating the complainant's background, to take advantage of the right, unencumbered at the time, to impeach her on the basis of her prior unchastity. I did not pursue this, however, because to me this device, although lawful, was fundamentally wrong. No doubt in that respect I lacked zeal, perhaps punishably so.

Even without assassinating this woman's character, however, I could argue that this was simply a case of a casual tryst that went awry. The defendant would not have to prove whether the complainant made the false charge to account for her whereabouts that evening, or to explain what happened to her missing watch. If the jury had reason to doubt the complainant's charges it would be bound to acquit the defendant.

How all of this would have played out at trial cannot be known. Predictably, the case dragged on so long that the prosecutor was forced to offer the unrefusable plea of possession of a gun. As I look back, however, I wonder how I could justify doing what I was planning to do had the case been tried. I was prepared to stand before the jury posing as an officer of the court in search of the truth, while trying to fool the jurors into believing a wholly fabricated story, i.e., that the woman had consented, when in fact she had been forced at gunpoint to have sex with the defendant. I was also prepared to demand an acquittal because the state had not met its burden of proof when, if it had not, it would have been because I made the truth look like a lie. If there is any redeeming social value in permitting an attorney to do such things, I frankly cannot discern it.

* * *

C. *The Lawyer as Trier of Fact—When Does the Lawyer "Know" the Truth?*

* * *

Assuming for the moment that criminal lawyers should be concerned with the truth, there appears to be no reason why the standards applied to them should be different from those applied to others. If those others, ultimately juries, are to be asked to find facts on the basis of probabilities determined in accordance with the rules of the legal system, then it would seem that lawyers should be required to do so as well. As I shall describe more fully below, the process of applying the rules for evaluation of evidence by the lawyer must obviously be somewhat different than for the jury. The established legal standards for determining facts, however, should be the same. Put in the terms used by lawyers in arguing their cases, the test is this: Given the available evidence, and subjecting that evidence to adversarial testing, has the proponent of the evidence met the burden of proof required in a particular kind of case?

The "case" under discussion here is the theory to be offered by the defense to rebut the prosecution's evidence. I am suggesting that the defense attorney has the duty to "judge" that theory, i.e., to determine whether it is adequately supported in fact. To do that, he or she must consider as objectively as possible the state's evidence, and, as is the attorney's responsibility, investigate both that case and the client's story, subjecting both cases to cross-examination.

Given that the attorney is not the trier of fact in the case but the representative of the defendant, it seems appropriate that the lawyer be directed to apply a burden of proof in favor of the client. Because there is a strong societal interest in providing the defendant the opportunity to state a case, the presumption should be strong. It would seem, therefore, that the attorney should be permitted to offer a defense unless he or she "knew" beyond a reasonable doubt that the defense was false.

Applying this standard to the case under discussion, I would conclude that I "knew" beyond a reasonable doubt that the proposed consent defense was false. My client's admission of guilt was, of course, an important factor. It should, however, neither be dispositive in and of itself, nor necessary to the determination. As some clients make false denials, some—albeit undoubtedly not as many—accuse themselves falsely, or at least incorrectly. In either case, other evidence should be sought and weighed. Here there was nothing in the client's account to support a consent defense, and there was ample evidence that force was used, in that both said the intercourse took place at gunpoint.

If as the defense attorney I should have been concerned with the truth, then it seems to me that on the basis of the analysis just given, I should not have been permitted to present the consent defense. Precisely how I should be permitted to represent my client I will discuss shortly. First, however, it is necessary to question whether it is relevant that the lawyer fashion the defense in accordance with what he or she knows to be true.

IV. DOES THE TRUTH MATTER? APPRAISING THE DIFFERENT MISSION

* * *

Two principal arguments have been advanced to explain why the needs of the adversary system permit the attorney to assert a defense not founded upon the truth. The first is that a false defense may have to be asserted to protect the defendant's right in a particular case right to have a defense at all. The second argument is that it may be necessary to subvert the truth in a particular case as a way of demonstrating the supremacy of the autonomous individual in the face of the powerful forces of organized society.

A. *Subverting the Truth to Protect the Defendant's Right to a Defense*

The most commonly offered justification for a right to undermine a truthful case is that if there were no such right, the guilty defendant would effectively be deprived of a defense. All defendants, it is asserted, are entitled to have the state prove the case against them, whether they are factually innocent or guilty. If the spurious defense were not allowed it would be impossible to represent persons who had confessed their guilt to their lawyers, or who, in accordance with rules of the sort I advanced in the last section, were "found" guilty by them. * * *

If it were true that a false defense must be allowed to assure that the guilty defendant has a defense, it would seem to follow that presently established constraints on the defense attorney representing a guilty person, let alone an innocent person against whom the state had incriminating evidence, should be removed. An exception to the criminal laws prohibiting the deliberate introduction of false evidence would have to be adopted. Some have argued that a criminal defendant has a right to commit perjury, and that the defense attorney has a concomitant duty not to interfere with such testimony, or for that matter with even more extraordinary means of prevailing at trial.

The notion of a right to commit perjury, however, has been forcefully rejected by the courts and by the organized bar, albeit less forcefully. I suggest, however, that it cannot logically be rejected by those who espouse the Different Mission theory in defense of subverting the truth. If the right to mount a defense is paramount, and if the only conceivable defense which the guilty defendant can mount involves the defendant, or his or her witnesses committing perjury, and the defense attorney arguing that that perjury is true, then it follows that the restraints of the penal law should not be conceded to be applicable.

The resolution of this apparent conflict in values cannot sensibly be to immunize the defense attorney and defense witnesses from the operation of these criminal laws in the very context for which they were principally designed. Nor is it to defend the utterly arbitrary line we have drawn between deliberately offering perjured testimony and deliberately attempting to create false "proof" by offering truthful but misleading evidence, or by impeaching a truthful witness. Instead, it is to recognize that the right to put forward a defense is limited, not absolute.

* * *

It may help to explain this position by positing the defense function as consisting of two separate roles, usually intertwined but theoretically distinct. One enlists the attorney as the "monitor" of the state's case, whose task it is to assure that a conviction is based on an adequate amount of competent and admissible evidence. The lawyer as monitor is a kind of quality inspector, with no responsibility for developing a different product, if you will, to "sell" to the jury. The other attorney role involves the attorney as the client's "advocate," whose task is to present that different product, by undermining the state's version of the facts or presenting a competing version sufficient at least to establish a reasonable doubt about the defendant's guilt. The monitor's role is to assure that the state has the facts to support a conviction. The advocate attempts to demonstrate that the state's evidence is not fact at all. Where, as in most cases, the facts are in doubt, or where the state's case is believed or known to be based upon mistaken perceptions or lies, the defense attorney quite properly plays both roles. Having monitored the state's case and found it factually and legally sound, however, should he or she be permitted to act as advocate and attempt to undermine it? I submit that the answer to that is no, and that the defendant's rights in cases of this kind extend only as far as the monitoring role takes the attorney. The right in question, to have the state prove guilt beyond a reasonable doubt, can be vindicated if the attorney is limited to good faith challenges to the state's case; to persuading the jury that there are legitimate reasons to doubt the state's evidence. It may on occasion be more effective for the attorney to use his or her imagination to create doubts; but surely there cannot be a right to gain an acquittal whenever the imagination of one's attorney is good enough to produce one.

* * *

V. ACCOMPLISHING THE DEFENSE ATTORNEY'S DIFFERENT MISSION—MORALLY

I propose a system in which the defense attorney would operate not with the right to assert defenses known to be untrue, but under the following rule:

It shall be improper for an attorney who knows beyond a reasonable doubt the truth of a fact established in the state's case to attempt to refute that fact through the introduction of evidence, impeachment of evidence, or argument.

In the face of this rule, the attorney who knew there were no facts to contest would be limited to the "monitoring" role. Assuming that a defendant in my client's situation wanted to assert his right to contest the evidence against him, the attorney would work to assure that all of the elements of the crime were proven beyond a reasonable doubt, on the basis of competent and admissible evidence. * * *

Applying these principles to my rape case, I would engage fully in the process of testing the admissibility of the state's evidence, moving to suppress testimony concerning the suggestive "show-up" identification at the precinct, and the gun found in the defendant's apartment after a warrantless search, should the state attempt to offer either piece of evidence. At the trial, I would be present to assure that the complainant testified in accordance with the rules of evidence.

Assuming that she testified at trial as she had at the preliminary hearing, however, I would not cross-examine her, because I would have no good faith basis for impeaching either her testimony or her character, since I "knew" that she was providing an accurate account of what had occurred. Nor would I put on a defense case. I would limit my representation at that stage to putting forth the strongest argument I could that the facts presented by the state did not sustain its burden. In these ways, the defendant would receive the services of an attorney in subjecting the state's case to the final stage of the screening process provided by the system to insure against unjust convictions. That, however, would be all that the defense attorney could do.

* * *

VI. CONCLUSION

* * *

If this proposal seems radical, consider that it is essentially an adaptation of what today is the principal function of the defense attorney in every criminal justice system of significance in this nation. That function is not to create defenses out of whole cloth to present to juries, but to guide the defendant through a process that will usually end in a guilty plea. It will so end, at least when competent counsel are involved, very frequently because the defense attorney has concluded after thorough analysis that there is no answer to the state's case. If that role can be played in out of court resolution of the matter there seems to be no reason why it cannot be played in court, when the defendant insists upon his right to a trial. The important point is that the right to a trial does not embody the right to present to the tribunal any evidence at all, no matter how fictitious it is.

If lawyers in the case I have described drew the line at presenting the kind of defense I was planning to present, nothing much about the system would change directly. Given the dearth of trials of any kind, whether dealing with real factual disputes or with figments of the lawyer's imagination, the most we might expect would be the conviction of some defendants whose acquittals are due to the ability of their lawyers to manipulate the truth. I believe, however, that the indirect rewards of a greater devotion to truth would be substantial. Criminal lawyers pay a great price for acquiescing in the description of the defense attorney's function that Justice White exemplifies in United States v. Wade. The fact is that not only Supreme Court justices, but trial judges, prosecutors, law enforcement agents, witnesses, defendants and the public at large seem to share the impression of the defense attorney as a person unconcerned with the truth and therefore not to be trusted, little more than the alter ego, if not alter id, of his or her client. It is, I know, uncomfortable for many criminal lawyers to be seen this way, and it may well disserve most of their clients most of the time. There may be no way accurately to measure that proposition, but I believe that many more defendants have suffered because their attorneys, seen as truth manipulators or worse, have not been able to obtain information from adversaries or hostile witnesses which would be useful in structuring a good faith defense, or to have their arguments taken seriously by judges or juries, than have profited by the successful false defense. Perhaps, then, our clients suffer as much as we do from our assumption of that part of the mission that defense lawyers need not undertake.

Note: Ability of Corporation to Restrict Access to Employees

As noted earlier, Model Rule 3.4(f) provides that a lawyer may not "request a person other than a client to refrain from voluntarily giving relevant information to another party unless" that person is, *inter alia*, "an employee or other agent of a client" and the lawyer "reasonably believes that the person's interest will not be adversely affected by refraining from giving such information." Comment 4 to the Rule says that the rationale for this provision is that "the employees may identify their interests with those of the client." A lawyer may, however, be guilty of obstruction of justice if she bribes, intimidates, or otherwise "corruptly persuades" an employee from providing information to the government in a criminal investigation, 18 U.S.C. 1510, or in an official proceeding. 18 U.S.C. 1512(b). If the employee is represented by separate counsel, of course, Rule 4.2 prohibits the company's lawyer from contacting the employee without the consent of her lawyer.

Requesting employees not to cooperate with the government thus may constitute part of a criminal defense strategy for the corporation. At the same time, however, the company must consider whether it will benefit more from cooperation with the government by encouraging employees to provide information.

PROBLEMS

1. You are the general counsel of WellCare, a company that operates hospitals, nursing homes, and outpatient clinics throughout the United

States. In recent years, a growing percentage of the patients in these facilities are covered by Medicare. WellCare submits claims for reimbursement of costs in treating these patients according to a formula established by federal law.

Four years ago, the official at WellCare in charge of Medicare reimbursement was prosecuted and convicted of fraud for directing the company's facilities to inflate treatment costs in filing Medicare claims. WellCare itself was unable to avoid prosecution because of the high office held by the culpable manager and the scope of the fraud. It did, however, receive lenient treatment by cooperating with federal prosecutors and promising to establish a more effective system of internal controls to prevent and detect fraud in the filing of reimbursement claims with the federal government. The company paid a $1 million fine, and was permitted to continue to participate in the Medicare program.

You have now been contacted by officials from the Department of Justice and the Department of Health and Human Services. They notify you that, acting on an anonymous tip, they have been conducting an investigation into what appears to be systematic inflation of treatment costs for Medicare claims for outpatient surgery in WellCare facilities in the Southeastern United States, especially in Florida. David Custiss, the WellCare manager for the Southeastern Region, has been cooperating with federal authorities. He has told them that WellCare has overbilled the Medicare program several million dollars in the region over the past two years. Custiss says, however, that he was directed to engage in this practice by two high-level company officials: Chief Financial Officer Linda Lowe and Senior Vice-President for Outpatient Facilities Dennis Magill.

The prosecutors say that Custiss is emphatic in his insistence that he acted at the direction of Lowe and Magill. They tell you that they would like WellCare to cooperate with their investigation in order to identify the wrongdoers and bring them to justice. They say that they cannot commit to forgoing prosecution of WellCare itself at this point, but that this is a possibility depending on what the investigation uncovers.

You immediately notify WellCare Chief Executive Officer Russell Rodriguez. Rodriguez expresses serious concern that if Lowe and Magill are culpable, WellCare likely will be prohibited from participating in any government health care reimbursement program because of their high positions within the company and the company's prior violation. This would deal a fatal blow to WellCare's ability to remain in business. Rodriguez calls the chair of the Board of Directors, briefly describes the situation, and says that there needs to be a special meeting of the Board of Directors as soon as possible.

The next day, four of the seven members of the Board of Directors are present at a meeting at WellCare headquarters, and the other three are linked to the meeting via telephone conference call. You describe your conversation with the DOJ and HHS officials. Rodriguez then expresses his concerns about the company being able to continue participating in government reimbursement programs because of WellCare's prior prosecution and Lowe's and Magill's high positions within the company.

It is clear that Board members regard the prospect of preclusion from government programs as the most serious issue. Some members favor full cooperation with the government's effort to identify culpable corporate employees. Others argue that the company's best hope is to act vigorously to defend Lowe and Magill, on the theory that Custiss is a rogue employee. The latter alternative would involve arranging for each of them to obtain their own lawyer, with the company entering into a joint defense agreement with them. WellCare also would advance Lowe and Magill their attorney's fees, as the company is permitted to do under its by-laws. If the two ultimately are found to have engaged in illegal activity, the company is authorized to seek to recoup those expenses from them.

Rodriguez and the Board then look to you for your advice. How do you advise them? Is there any additional information that you would regard as relevant in deciding which course of action WellCare should take?

2. Assume the same facts as described above, except that Custiss has identified only Lowe as the official who directed him to inflate Medicare claims. Suppose that you are Lowe's lawyer. Lowe tells you that she has been under tremendous personal and professional pressure over the last two years. She has gone through a painful and expensive divorce and child custody contest, which has drained her finances. In addition, WellCare's profits have fallen because of increased competition from other health care providers and managed care limitations on insurance reimbursements. Lowe therefore has suffered a reduction in compensation and has been fearful that she might be let go if the company's performance does not improve. She admits that, faced with these pressures, she instructed Custiss to "supplement" WellCare's Medicare reimbursement requests by a certain percentage in the Southeastern region. She says that she left the details of how to do this to Custiss.

Lowe says that she is terrified of going to jail. You tell her that she probably has little leverage avoiding jail time through a plea bargain, because she has no higher-level officials whom she can implicate in the wrongdoing. As a result, you and she agree that her best strategy is to resist prosecution as strenuously as possible.

Lowe tells you that there is material that could be used to discredit Custiss in the eyes of prosecutors. Three years ago, he took a six week-long medical leave of absence to deal with depression and related psychological problems that had resulted in some erratic behavior on his part. Since that time, he has been on medication that appears to have controlled his condition. Nonetheless, some co-workers do not like his style or personality, and he has detractors who likely would be willing to declare that he is "a loner" and "paranoid." Those same co-workers also are prepared to state that Custiss has been "obsessive" about falling profits in the Southeastern region and was "desperate" to find something that would halt the reversal. Finally, Lowe says that it would be easy for friends of hers in the accounting department to review Custiss's expense reports carefully and find some discrepancies, since no one is ever able fully to document every single expense for which he or she seeks reimbursement.

The combined portrait of Custiss that could emerge from all this information is that he is somewhat mentally unstable, tends to go off on his own, has a history of being dishonest with respect to expense reimbursements—in short, that he is the kind of person who easily could be a "rogue" employee who engages in misconduct on his own. Concern about the impeachability of Custiss thus might give prosecutors pause in bringing charges against Lowe.

How do you proceed?

Chapter 27

MERGERS AND ACQUISITIONS

For some lawyers, mergers and acquisition work is as glamorous, exciting and lucrative as the practice of law can get. Huge corporate transactions are on the front page of major newspapers. Those who are involved in such transactions charge very high fees to represent bidders, targets and white knights in hotly contested tender offers. The bar is small, highly specialized and highly publicized. What could be better?

True as that picture may be for some, it is by no means complete. Most mergers are negotiated rather than contested. Most corporations are smaller rather than larger. And stories about most deals, if they are published at all (and many are not) appear in the business pages of local newspapers rather than the Wall Street Journal.

The lack of immediate glamor, however, does not make the work less interesting. Uncontested mergers require the full panoply of a lawyer's skills. Indeed, merger and acquisition practice (or "M & A" as it is known) warrants a book of its own.* The ethical questions that arise in such a practice, however, do not differ substantially from other areas of corporate law and thus are not treated separately in this chapter.

Tender offers and leveraged buyouts are different because they raise potential conflicts of interest that directly affect the lawyer's role. We know that a corporation is a bloodless entity consisting of numerous constituent parts—its shareholders, managers, creditors and employees, to name just a few. If, as Model Rule 1.13 provides, the "organization" (the corporation in this case) rather than any of its constituents is the client, to whom does the lawyer owe a duty when the constituencies conflict? And when there is a conflict, how can a lawyer determine the best interests of "the corporation?"

OVERVIEW OF THE CHAPTER

The chapter consists of two sets of materials. The first tells the story of the battle between Seagram and DuPont for control of Conoco. As you read it, note how important a role the lawyers play in the events that

---

* Which it has. *See* James C. Freund, Anatomy of a Merger (1976).

1114

unfold (several of the lawyers were students of one of the authors of this book) and how closely intertwined legal and business advice become as the contest becomes more heated.

The second part of the chapter is a play that is built around a leveraged buyout. The play (actually a video that, unfortunately, cannot be included with this book but is highly recommended for use in this exercise) focuses on the conflicts of interest facing the lawyers in the transaction. The ethical issues that the play raises are quite complex but they should be familiar to you by now. The play is divided into five acts (in the best tradition of classical tragedy). Each part is preceded by a factual summary of events, some of which contain background information that is not directly developed in the play itself. The script is then followed by the ethical issues that the play has just raised.

MODEL RULES: 1.4, 1.5, 1.6, 1.7, 1.9, 1.10, 1.13, 1.16

Philip B. Heymann & Lance Liebman, The Social Responsibilities of Lawyers: Case Studies

(1998)

D. Lawyers for Wall Street

M & A: The Conoco Takeover*

If anyone had told Martha Solinger the day she graduated from Georgetown University Law Center in 1980 that in less than one year she would play an active role in one of the world's largest corporate takeovers, she would have doubled over with laughter. And if that prescient someone had informed the 25-year-old graduate that she would labor 45 out of 47 straight days her first "real" summer at a New York law firm on securities litigation—and love every minute of it—her smiles would have flashed to a look of skepticism, if not outright scorn. "I had that liberal orientation, you know, same as lots of others at law school," she says now from her quarters at Dewey, Ballantine, Bushby, Palmer & Wood. "I thought all of this corporate litigation was a lot of crap." Outside of a course in corporations and another in tax, until she came to Dewey, Ballantine, her only knowledge of Wall Street came from a subway map of Lower Manhattan.

So when she entered her office that early day in May 1981, Martha Solinger did not automatically turn to the back section of *The Wall Street Journal* to scan for "tombstone" ads, those squared-off bits of somber block print that serve as the corporate world's billboard of just-hatched deals. If she had, she might have spotted one curious notice. A pipsqueak Canadian oil company named Dome Petroleum Ltd. announced that it was attempting to buy a piece of the ninth largest U.S. oil concern, Conoco, by purchasing some of the company's common stock. Maybe it is just as well that her mind was not drawn. For all but a

---

* This case is based on journalistic accounts of the Conoco takeover dispute and on interviews with some of the lawyers who participated.

handful of cognoscenti, the offer seemed absurd, sort of like Calgary declaring war on the United States and demanding Washington, Oregon, and the rest of the Great Northwest, not a battle you expected to hear a lot from that summer—let alone be inducted to fight in.

Dome, after all, had made it known that it was not really trying to buy Conoco. It just wanted to twist Conoco's arm into surrendering its Canadian subsidiary, Hudson's Bay Oil & Gas, to Dome. But in corporate takeover wars, looks beguile. The Dome offer signaled the beginning of a fight that would eventually conscript 300 lawyers, spill millions of dollars in legal fees, and crunch hundreds of thousands of billable hours before it would come to a truce at the end of the summer.

How did the fate of a company with 41,000 employees worldwide and $18 billion in revenues come to rest in the hands of people like first-year associate Solinger and other associates and partners at law firms around the country? That is one question this case study seeks to answer. Along the way the case looks for answers to a few other questions, including: (1) What exactly do lawyers do—and not do—in these takeovers? (2) Does anyone benefit from their frantic activities? (3) Are they worth the fees these companies lavish on them?—and perhaps the most important, considering the broken evenings, canceled dinners, littered vacation plans, sleepless nights, and tension-filled days, all for the bidding of large corporations—(4) why do so many do it, and do it so proudly?

Long Hot Summer

The last thing Conoco Chairman Ralph Bailey wanted to do that May day was sell to the upstarts from Dome a big piece of the company he had spent his life helping to build. But unlike all other decisions he had reached over the years involving Conoco's assets, he knew this one might not be his to make. By offering to buy up some of Conoco's stock at a premium, a sum higher than the current market price, Dome was bypassing Bailey's authority over Conoco and appealing directly to the company's shareholders.

Wall Street professionals dub this move a "hostile" tender offer. The term, however, refers only to relations between the chief executives of the predator and prey. If you happen to own Conoco shares when the company is trading at $49.875, as it was that day, you probably do not harbor much hostility toward someone who offers to pay you $65 for some of those very same shares. Most stocks move up or down in quarter- and eighth-of-a-dollar increments. The Dome offer represented a chance to make a quick 30 percent killing for all stockholders, especially the pension and mutual fund managers who, through their investments in Conoco common stock, were the real majority "owners" of the company. For most shareholders, who bet on a company's stock the way touts wager on horses—trying to pick the one with the best possible payoff, not the one that is the prettiest, or the most kindly managed—"hostile" certainly is a misnomer.

But that is not the way Conoco executives viewed it. Until May 6, the company's status as a publicly held corporation meant little more than having to pay lawyers to file reports to the Securities and Exchange Commission, hosting a noisy shareholder meeting once a year, and sending out a batch of splashy yearbooks annually. Executives answered only to each other and to the board of directors.

After May 6, the roles suddenly changed. Everyone from the widows and orphans who had held the stock for years to the quick-buck speculators who had snapped up Conoco on takeover rumors before the offer was made became the real decision-makers. It is as if army generals suddenly faced elections for the first time, and the other side was offering privates money to vote against them.

Company officers who work their way up the corporate ladder may meet this kind of challenge to their authority once in their lives, if ever. They cannot turn to their in-house counsel. Their lawyers may be schooled well in oil and gas, as were Conoco's, but they know little about takeovers. So executives must turn to outsiders, corporate lawyers and investment bankers, to figure out what to do.

There were more than 650,000 lawyers and 14,500 banks in the United States, but only a handful of each knew enough about corporate mergers to be of use to Conoco's management at that moment. Chief executives know all about this scarcity. About 300 of them, including at that time Conoco, pay one law firm, Skadden, Arps, Slate, Meagher & Flom, a retainer of between $25,000 and $150,000 per year just to be sure the New York law firm will be on their side if an offer strikes. So Bailey's first move, naturally, was to call Joseph Flom, Skadden's leader and one of the best-known merger and acquisition (M & A) specialists in the country. The 60-year-old lawyer agreed to meet with Conoco's management the next day.

Besides Skadden, Conoco turned to its regular counsel, Dewey, Ballantine, which had performed the large bulk of Conoco's corporate work over the years. Leonard Larrabee, a 53-year-old senior partner at Dewey, and Conoco's attorney at the firm, learned of the troubles facing his largest client when Conoco's in-house counsel phoned him at the Yale Club in midtown Manhattan, where he was attending the firm's monthly dinner.

Larrabee knew that Conoco had retained Skadden. But in takeover situations the usually resolute lines between the personnel of each firm blur into one united team. Larrabee instantly realized that Russel "Cap" Beatie, Jr., a fiery securities litigation partner, might spur some creative thinking. "I left the firm dinner, came back to the downtown office, picked up my papers and got hold of Cap," recalls Larrabee. "I had to track him down at a Ranger hockey game." Both agreed to journey to Conoco's Stamford, Connecticut, headquarters for the next day's meeting.

Legal takeover specialists work in tandem with investment bankers in corporate merger practice. These bankers do not solicit deposits or handle checking accounts, like savings and loans or commercial banks. They help companies raise money by structuring and selling a company's stock and bonds. Only about a half-dozen firms, all in New York, have carved out expertise in large scale M & A work. Like law firms, top M & A talent is scarce. Conoco chose Morgan Stanley, Conoco's regular investment banker for a host of financings in past years. Morgan Stanley, as is the custom in all takeovers, immediately called in its own regular counsel, Davis Polk & Wardwell, to advise the firm on the matter. Davis Polk's Peter Bator, until his death in 1984 one of the firm's leading corporate lawyers, was dispatched to Stamford to join Morgan's, Skadden's, and Dewey's representatives.

In an era when it seems that no company is too large to be swallowed and the likes of U.S. Steel and Texaco are taking buyout precautions, it is difficult to imagine now what that first meeting between Conoco and the experts must have been like. Even as recently as 1981, executives of companies on the scale of Conoco did not worry about golden parachutes, shark repellants, and all the other merger paraphernalia that make up take-over defense. Conoco's brass did not suspect that Dome's offer to buy 20 percent of its shares through a tender offer would amount to much. And they certainly figured that at least one of the hired guns in the room would be able to shoot down Dome's offer before it did any damage. But that judgment, recalled Bator in an interview shortly before his death, is precisely what lawyers and investment bankers get paid to worry about.

From the beginning, Morgan's corporate finance people, who, as part of their job, try to predict how shareholders will react to the prices of different offers, feared that Dome's offer might provoke disaster for their client. They fretted even though Dome's stated goal was the much less ambitious plan to swap a piece of Conoco for its real target, Conoco's Canadian subsidiary.

"Morgan Stanley advised us that unless something else happened, something unforeseen, then Dome Petroleum was likely to get far more of Conoco's stock than was subscribed for," Bator recalled. "There was a great deal of skepticism about that advice in Conoco headquarters that day. There was general disbelief in those circles that Morgan could be right in its evaluation. They [Conoco's managers] couldn't believe that they would be held in such low esteem by their stockholders. They still suffered from a romantic illusion that they had loyal institutional shareholders. They had wined and dined them, even taken them out on fishing trips, and, on the whole, they had done a very good job at shareholder relations. They assumed that people wouldn't tender for less than the value of the company"—a value Conoco's management pegged at much higher than the current market price and substantially higher than Dome's $65 offer.

Nor could the lawyers gathered that day allow Conoco's management to believe that even the best of hired guns would necessarily triumph over their rivals, especially if the shootout were to take place in a federal court. "In tender offer litigation, members of the target company invariably sue with the hope that it will strike a quick death blow to the potential acquirer and win the whole deal," said one of the key litigators on the case. "But anybody with any brain at all advises the board that the likelihood of winning a knockout punch is negligible. Having given them that advice, you go forward and do your best."

With that sobering wisdom dispensed, the lawyers dissolved their own firm allegiances and re-combined in corporate and litigation ranks, with Skadden's Flom heading up the former, and Dewey's Beatie running the latter. Both teams shared one goal: keeping Conoco independent by finding a way to beat back Dome's 20 percent offer. Each used his respective tools honed through years of practice. For Flom, that meant trying to negotiate, perhaps with another Canadian company that might be interested in purchasing Conoco's northern subsidiary, or, if things proved as dire as Morgan Stanley's prognosis, with Dome itself, trying to hammer out better terms than Dome had offered already. For Beatie, that meant suing to stop the offer, not so much to defeat Dome in court, but more to buy time for the investment bankers to create a better deal.

These attorneys approach their work differently. Flom is solitary. Other than Bator, a self-described sounding board for Flom's ideas during all of the Conoco events, and Robert Greenhill, the senior Morgan managing director on the deal, Flom tended to seek his own counsel. "I operate a little peculiarly," says Flom about his methods. "I go to these meetings by myself. I don't bring along a lot of others." How does he communicate information back to other members of his firm, let alone with teammates from other firms on deals? "Badly," he says with a laugh. "But people here have a way of finding out what is going on. It filters down." The loner approach is not all Flom's doing. Corporate work on large mergers at first entails concentrated meetings either with high-level executives in individual strategy sessions or in large board meetings. Neither lends itself to armies of associates, says Flom.

But litigation, on the other hand, is exactly the opposite: it is people intensive. Staffing a big securities law case excites Cap Beatie, who has since left Dewey to open his own firm. He likes to choose and discard associates as if he were in an aggressive schoolyard pick-up game. For this matter Beatie drew on some of his more experienced associates and, as he remembers now, he decided to dip deep into the ranks, all the way down to a first-year associate, someone who had already showed sparkle on two earlier assignments: Martha Solinger.

A Game of Low-Percentage Arguments

Solinger's view from the bottom up provides a unique vision of what a junior litigator can—and cannot—do in a takeover battle. No matter how savvy a first-year associate may be, her role is decidedly small-picture. For example, Solinger knew from the beginning that she would not be the lawyer who would depose Dome's flamboyant chairman, Jack

Gallagher, with the hope of tripping him up, getting him to spill out something that could later come to haunt him in court. That assignment, grilling the top manager of the acquiring firm, perhaps the most coveted in a takeover battle, typically goes to the partners in charge of litigation, as it did here. Nor would she necessarily be deciding which arguments would be made, once they got into court. That would be the province of Beatie, with input from Flom.

But finding the right court to sue Gallagher—that is a matter that fits an associate's research skills. Beatie asked Solinger to find out which state, of all the states in which Conoco operated, would have the most favorable anti-takeover statute. There they would make their first stand. "We knew that most of the states' statutes wouldn't be upheld if Dome were to challenge them," she says now. "They would probably be found to be unconstitutional or to be preempted by federal law. But I started reading all of the statutes, and you could tell that some looked better than others for us. I thought the statute in Louisiana (where Conoco had a large refinery) looked particularly good because, unlike most of the vague anti-takeover statutes of the day, this one was specific, and it was directed at natural resources, oil and gas, an area traditionally regulated by states. That was perfect for us, and it gave us hope."

Solinger informed the higher-ups of the good news and got to work plumbing what Conoco would need to fight Dome's preliminary injunction motion (which, if granted, would block Conoco's efforts to utilize the state's anti-takeover statute) in Louisiana federal court. She produced a discussion level draft that was considered by mid-level associates and partners at both Skadden and Dewey.

All agreed that they needed more information, and Solinger arranged with Kurt Koegler, a Skadden partner, to fly to New Orleans to meet with state regulators to find out if their reading of the statutes was correct. "They had spoken together constantly by phone all week," recalled one lawyer who knew both attorneys. "But it wasn't until they got on the plane together that day that Kurt learned that Martha was only a first-year associate, just out of law school. He just fainted dead when he learned she was so young. But they worked great together."

Solinger said that after their day-long meetings they returned and decided to write two briefs, one saying that they were right because of the law and the other saying they were right because the regulators agreed with them. They found they needed additional support for their arguments and jetted back to Louisiana for more affidavits. They ended up going back to Louisiana not just once but twice that week. "I went back three times in five days altogether," she recalls. It was all for naught. Conoco lost the motion to block the merger—Dome's motion to dismiss was granted.

In most legal disputes, when a federal judge boots you out of court summarily, you have to question whether it is not worth caving in and telling your client to forget it. But, as one defense litigator explained, this defeatist attitude does not even get an airing in takeover battles.

"From the viewpoint of the target, this is a life or death situation. People who run companies in these situations will pay anything to anyone who can give them hope. Chief executive officers see this as a fight to the death. Consequently, anything with even the most remote chance of success is done." Takeover litigation, the lawyer said, "is not a game of high percentage arguments. Don't get me wrong. It is not that you are filing totally idiotic lawsuits. It is just that you are more likely to make an argument that would not hold up in some other situations."

That logic brought Conoco's lawyers to the next confrontation— Oklahoma, another state with massive Conoco operations and one in which Conoco's defenders were hoping to find a judge who would be open-minded about enjoining a takeover for disclosure reasons, a plea judges in the securities-litigation-weary northeast look upon with increasing skepticism.

This time Solinger was assigned a question that read like something out of a corporations class hypothetical. She was asked to research why Dome should be allowed to purchase 20 percent of Conoco, become its largest shareholder, and then act contrary to its newfound fiduciary responsibilities to Conoco's shareholders by cutting a deal that benefitted only Dome's interests. Did Dome owe a fiduciary duty not to act in its self-interest by foisting its opinions on the rest of Conoco's shareholders?

"It was like *Perlman v. Feldmann*,"* she says, citing that venerable corporations class warhorse. "We ended up phrasing it in disclosure language, saying that the deal would not be arms-length. Dome had a particular intention, but had not disclosed it. It was sort of a bizarre claim," she says. And for that reason it was not pushed hard by local counsel in court and merited only a couple of pages in the brief.

Instead, Conoco pushed arguments questioning Dome's ability to pay for the acquisition without running afoul of Federal Reserve margin rules. "We proved pretty conclusively that Dome's debt would increase dramatically, and the company wouldn't be able to handle it," one of the defense lawyers said. Nevertheless, none of the arguments found favor with Oklahoma federal judge Lee West, and he sent everyone packing to New York in a hurry. It was a judgment that still has a key defense litigator stewing. "The trial judge took what I consider to be a knee-jerk attitude of many federal courts these days and said, 'We don't want to interfere with tender offers. Let the shareholders vote and just tell me if there is anything grossly misleading. If not, so long.' "

Another defender pointed out that Conoco's arguments that day have been borne out by subsequent events. "At the time the company was practically insolvent, but its bankers kept saying 'how much more money do you want?' " the lawyer said. Those optimistic bankers and heady talk of oil cascading to $40 or $50 a barrel on new shortage fears had Dome's stock selling for about $20 a share at the time. Not much

---

* *Perlman v. Feldmann*, 219 F.2d 173 (2d Cir. 1955), *cert. denied*, 349 U.S. 952 (1955).

after the Conoco deal, Conoco lawyers' doomsday scenario came true for the Canadians. The company went broke, could not meet its interest payments, and the stock plummeted to $3. Dome exists now only because of Canadian government intervention. "I feel vindicated about it everyday," says Solinger.

Meanwhile, the corporate team was faring no better. "Because Conoco's management was skeptical about the Dome thing as a major threat, I am not sure that efforts to find an alternative solution were pursued as hard as possible," recalled Bator. "Our activities at this stage were basically sitting in on the councils of war, seeing what interest could be elicited in finding a buyer for Hudson's Bay," he continued. "I spent a lot of time in Canada doing a lot of work with oil companies, hoping to interest them. We looked at the obvious [acquirers], anyone who could have an interest, and made presentations to them. But Conoco wanted too much from any prospective buyer. All that can be said of these efforts now is that they were too little, too late. We saw it is a real threat that Dome could buy 25 to 30 percent of Conoco. And if the offer was oversubscribed, then Gallagher would reserve the right to acquire real control of the company. The scarey part of all of this is that Dome was riding terribly high at the time. I thought fair warning had been given, but it was not really believed. Conoco, in other words, was on the thin edge of being bought by Dome Petroleum."

The Seagram Caper

Morgan Stanley's view of what shareholders would do, and not that of Conoco's management, proved prescient. When the tender expiration date was reached, Dome, which had set out to acquire only 20 percent of Conoco, ended up with 52.9 percent of the company's shares, an amount equal to control. But because of the structure of its offer, Dome would have to revise its agreement before it could begin to purchase any of the tendered shares in excess of 20 percent. As the bad news set in with Conoco's management, the lawyers and bankers reached the conclusion that it was time to make a deal with Dome.

Speed was paramount, because the over-subscription of Dome's offer left 32.9 percent of Conoco's stock floating free, available for anyone who was willing to offer a price slightly higher than Dome's. That loose block could be used as a start to buy up the rest of Conoco before Dome could arrange the credit to do so itself.

At any given moment there are lots of companies with millions of dollars in cash that managers do not want to pour back into their own companies or disburse as dividends to their shareholders. Often it is because they feel they can get a better return on their money from an investment in another industry.

Joseph E. Seagram & Sons, a behemoth Canadian distiller, was one of those companies. Flush with $2.3 billion in cash from the disposition of an oil and gas property, it was prowling for coal companies when Dome's all-too-successful bid was made. Seagram's management moved swiftly to find out if Conoco would make a deal with them rather than Dome. And so the second round, "the Seagram Caper," as Bator called it, began.

It is not easy to reconstruct what happened next, not because no one remembers, but because everybody remembers differently, and many remembrances are couched in bitterness. Several points, however, are clear.

The first is that Seagram came to Stamford at the end of May with the idea of making some sort of deal to purchase a substantial block of Conoco shares directly from Conoco or from the market. The offer was meant to be "friendly," in the merger sense of the word, meaning not unilateral, but with the blessing of Conoco management. We are sure of that, in part, because Seagram hired Goldman, Sachs & Co. as its investment banker for the negotiations and Goldman is the only investment bank with a stated policy against doing hostile takeovers. We also know, however, that at the same time Conoco was sitting down in discussions with Seagram, Conoco's officers were also dealing with Dome and a third company, Cities Service, which it hoped to acquire so as to make Conoco too big to be taken over.

Seagram, on Saturday, May 30, proposed that it buy 35 percent of Conoco's stock, and agreed not to purchase any more—a standstill agreement—for a set number of years. Conoco countered that perhaps 25 percent was a more suitable figure. Before an agreement could be reached, Bailey suspended discussions until the next day. Unbeknownst to Seagram, Bailey then flew to Cities Service headquarters in Oklahoma to prospect for a better deal with that midwest oil company. "We knew that Ralph Bailey—apparently on his own—was playing footsie with Cities," says Bator. "But it was fairly clear that if Dome stayed around, then Seagrams would too."

With Friends Like These . . .

On Sunday, May 31, Seagram's officers were ready to make a deal. So were the officers of Dome. Bailey, who flew back late the night before, placed Seagram's officials in one room and Dome's in another. Flom and Greenhill worked the two different rooms, moving quickly from one prospective suitor to another. The halls between the two suites were lined with associates, both lawyers and bankers, most of whom remained in the dark about the discussions that surrounded them.

"You could tell that Flom and Greenhill were doing a tag-team," said one associate who spent the weekend waiting for board meetings to break up. "But you didn't have much of an idea of what was going on." While Conoco officials debated the very existence of their corporation, the associates outside did their very best to stay awake and beat the tedium. "We played endless hours of liars' poker," said one, referring to a makeshift poker game based on the serial numbers of dollar bills. "We would do anything to keep ourselves busy while we waited for these people to reach a decision."

The hold-up? As Bator explains, "The basic problem was schizophrenia in Conoco on the whole relationship with Seagram. They were needed and essential if Dome stayed in and tried to buy. But if [Conoco] could get rid of Dome as a stockholder, then obviously Seagram's role as a preferred majority shareholder didn't seem that marvelous."

The resolution came later that Sunday when Conoco agreed to trade its subsidiary to Dome in return for the 20 percent of the stock Dome had acquired and $245 million in cash. The move immediately cooled negotiations between Seagram and Conoco about the remaining large block of shares up for grabs.

Seagram still put forward its friendly standstill offer. But with the Cities option maturing, Conoco could afford to put Seagram on hold. When, two weeks later, the Cities deal became a real possibility, thus freeing Conoco from its schizophrenic paralysis, the Conoco board of directors rejected the Seagram bid. At the same meeting Conoco's board took action to protect Bailey's job with a golden parachute. No matter what happened to Conoco, Bailey would get his current annual salary of $637,766 until 1989. But if he decided he could not work well with whoever his new boss might be, he could walk out of his job and get all of the money due—$5 million—in one chunk.

After the Seagram rejection, Dewey partner Larrabee recalls: "We began working around the clock to hammer out the Cities Service matter." But they misjudged Seagram's response to their actions. One day after its rejection at the hands of Conoco's board, Seagram began buying Conoco's stock in the open market. Trading activity was so great that, on Friday June 19, the New York Stock Exchange stopped trading and demanded that Conoco offer an explanation about what was going on with its stock.

The company complied with a bland statement explaining that it had received an offer from a U.S. subsidiary of a foreign corporation to purchase its shares, and that it was holding preliminary discussions about a possible merger with a "major corporation." Neither Seagram nor Cities Service was mentioned.

Cities and Conoco steamed toward a deal that night. Both sides agreed to a stock-for-stock swap with the arrangement hinging on the companies' current stock prices the next day. As the finishing touches were being applied, Seagram struck like a lightning bolt. "I was working on the press release to announce the merger," recalls Larrabee, "when someone rushed in with the news from the stock ticker that Seagram was making a hostile bid for Conoco." Conoco's stock price jumped immediately in reaction to the news, thus scuttling the Cities deal because the stock for stock pricing ratio was now hopelessly distorted. "It got put on the sideburner," said Larrabee. And it never moved to the front again.

There is still much speculation about why Seagram took its unilateral plunge. It had pledged not to go hostile to both Conoco and its investment banker, who subsequently resigned from the deal in accordance with its policy not to do hostile takeovers. One reason given at the time was that Seagram's management felt taken in by Conoco's behind-the-back negotiations with Cities. Board meeting minutes released later as part of discovery reflected that sentiment.

Bator, for one, says he felt that the lawyers and bankers on his side simply played too much hardball. "I think Seagram was pressured too hard," he recalled. "If Seagram hadn't been strung along, would they have considered an unfriendly tender? That's relatively unlikely. They were played for a chump. The terms Conoco wanted were simply too onerous. It would have been a nonsensical deal for [Seagram]. I believe now that if Seagram had not been pushed to extremes in the deal then [they] wouldn't have acted like this. Clearly it's the biggest single reason why Conoco was unable to stay independent."

Flom quickly dismisses Bator's history of the event. He notes one unassailable truth: Seagram would later agree to the same sort of deal that Bator said was too tough for them to accept with Conoco. "It was the Conoco directors that didn't want to do it," Flom reminds about the breakdown that led Seagram to go hostile.

Conoco's March to the Sea

Up until Seagram's surprise attack, Conoco's defensive team had waged a restrained war, reflecting the client's belief that the 25th largest industrial concern in the country ultimately would not succumb to an acquirer. But Seagram's $2.5 billion bid to purchase 35 million Conoco shares at $73 per share (approximately 40.7 percent of all shares outstanding) changed all that. Now the defenders were unleashed, and younger lawyers got to see first-hand why companies fall over one another to retain Joe Flom.

With lawyers from Dewey and Skadden waiting for orders, Flom ticked off idea after idea about how Conoco could either stop Seagram or temporarily derail the company until Morgan Stanley's people could come up with a more friendly suitor. Some of the more promising tactics that came to Flom's mind immediately, associates say, included:

- possible violations of state statutes that forbid wholesale liquor sellers such as Seagram from owning alcoholic beverage retailers, such as Conoco, which sold liquor at some of its gas stations;

- possible damages to Conoco's extensive network of foreign oil contracts because of a merger with Seagram (Seagram's chief business, liquor, found no favor with abstinent Moslems, and Seagram's boss, Edgar Bronfman, was president of the World Jewish Congress and a long-time supporter of Israel); and

- congressional disapproval of a transaction that would allow Canadians to raid American natural resources while the Canadians were erecting barriers to American entry into their markets.

How did these ideas, normally the product of several days of thinking, germinate so quickly in Flom's mind? "First of all," he answers, "those ideas don't come from the sky. I've got a little bit of experience and I do a lot of listening to clients. The clients, you see, know their businesses far better than you will get to know them during the short time you are on these matters. So if you listen to them—instead of them just listening to you—they will tell you what you can use. You don't know all of the implications of the merger like they do. You find out some of your best ideas from them. But not one of these is like an apple that falls from the sky and hits you on the head. That's not the way it works." Anybody, he insists, can come up with winning ideas in a short time. But in takeovers, the winners "come up with them in 15 minutes."

Flom's quarter of an hour's worth of ideas did not take long to put in place. Within a short time, *The Wall Street Journal* ran a story about letters from the governments of Dubai—an oil-rich state in the United Arab Emirates—and Norway containing threats of oil supply cutoffs if Seagram were to take an interest in Conoco. Hearings soon opened in the House of Representatives about Canadian ownership. Representatives questioned whether Canadians should be allowed to bid on federal leases.

Meanwhile, Skadden and Dewey people went to work trying to employ "tied house" statutes—state laws designed to keep wholesalers from competing with retailers—to stop Seagram. Finding out which states had the strongest tied-house statutes was a perfect assignment for an eager associate, and once again Solinger drew it. "There were at least 20 states to start," she says. Once they were isolated she and other associates corralled local counsel in each state to check up on the possibilities. "Many statutes fizzled out quickly, as the local lawyers said, 'forget it, they won't hold up,'" she says. But five states looked good: Florida, Alabama, Iowa, Missouri, and North Carolina. Solinger took charge of keeping track of the potential litigation or regulatory activity in each state.

While Conoco's defense team was placing these indirect roadblocks, the litigators also attacked Seagram's hostile move head-on in a federal district court in New York. Before Judge Edward Weinfeld, Conoco sought $1 billion in damages and a temporary restraining order blocking Seagram from purchasing any shares. Beatie pressed three contentions: Seagram broke its word by going hostile; the Canadian company's actions caused Conoco to lose a good business opportunity in its scuttled merger with Cities Service; and a Seagram takeover would raise various disclosure claims, including the fact that Seagram had not informed shareholders that its move would violate the tied-house statutes in states across the country.

Shopping the Company

At the same time Beatie was preparing to file his suit, efforts by the corporate half of Conoco's defense team were beginning to bear fruit. From the moment that the Conoco fracas began brewing, Morgan Stanley people started doing what they do best: valuation studies of the company's worth. Most companies fighting hostile bids hope things never get to the stage where these studies have to be used. A company must lay its soul bare to the investment bankers, only to have the information turn up in the hands of any company, including rivals, that might have an interest in purchasing the target.

The value study had another purpose, more central to law than to business. It is the document that corporate directors rely on when they assess the price of a tender offer with an eye toward its possible endorsement or rejection. For directors, who are the natural targets of suits by disgruntled shareholders if they reject a potential acquirer's price as too low, the valuation study and the quality of the name on that survey may be the only protection against a lawsuit. Conoco's board members knew that they had to be sensitive to such charges. Even though 11 out of 15 of the board members were "independent" (they had other jobs and were not salaried executives of Conoco), so many executives fight scorched earth battles to stay in office that almost all directors are wary of simply rejecting an offer with the usual "not in the shareholders' interests" excuse.

The valuation study showed that, without much doubt, the value of Conoco's assets exceeded $100 per share. Thus, even though Seagram's $73-a-share offer might look good to shareholders who bought in at a much lower price, the offer looked much too low to Conoco's directors. Morgan's study also showed another problem: the fine print of the offer. As is the case with most tender offers, the actual share price bandied about—in this case $73—had little to do with what shareholders might get after the smoke cleared. Seagram was not offering to buy. all of the shares, just 41 percent, enough to get control of the company and no more. If Seagram were offered everybody's shares, all stockholders would have their shares "pro-rated," meaning that Seagram would purchase only 41 percent of their shares. The rest would be returned to the market, at who knows what price—certainly much lower than the $73 premium Seagram was willing to pay, and possibly as low as the pre-Dome price of $50. That boded poorly for the 600 institutions that owned 62 percent of the company's stock, and it was those stockholders, among others, that the directors were paid to protect. With this information in hand, the Board again rejected a Seagram offer.

With that turndown, Morgan's people were free to "shop the company," Wall Street parlance for a corporate firesale. Despite Conoco's giant size, investment bankers know that there is almost always a buyer for a profitable company. Morgan had shopped enough companies in the past to know that it must do it scientifically so as not to overlook potential buyers. Using a sophisticated computer filled with information from just about every company in the world, Morgan analysts began winnowing. Which companies had enough assets to command a credit line big enough to swallow Conoco? Plug in a minimum asset number. Which companies would not suffer from earnings dilution if they printed up stock to make the purchase? Plug in earnings per share data. Which companies had such strong cash flow that they would not blink at shelling out billions? Insert a cash flow. Once programmed with these kinds of data, the computer can spit out a list of potential buyers. Morgan's people could then pitch Conoco in the same way that any salesperson offers his or her wares—except this purchase would come with a multi-billion dollar pricetag.

At the same time Morgan was drawing up its list, Conoco's chairman was getting discreet inquiries on his own. One of them, according to a prospectus filed later, was from the chairman of Du Pont, the nation's largest chemical company and an industrial concern with assets about equal to Conoco's. Du Pont said it just wanted to know if Conoco needed help. It was the beginning of a $7.54 billion shotgun marriage.

The Best Seat in the House

July Fourth weekend for most is a celebration, three days of picnics, barbecues, and fireworks in the midst of a hot summer. Unless you worked on Conoco. During those three days, meetings often began before 8 a.m. and never quit before midnight. Beach plans, summer houses, and in Peter Bator's case even his own birthday party became casualties (although the *Journal* reported several days later that Bator had managed to drop in to the festivities for ten minutes). The only concession to the holiday: "we got to wear jeans," says Solinger.

As if the near round-the-clock Conoco dealings were not enough for most mortals, the irrepressible Flom was negotiating another acquisition simultaneously, as counsel for Texasgulf in its talks with acquirer Société Nationale Elf Acquitane. Fortunately, the shuttle was not too arduous; Texasgulf shared the same industrial park quarters with Conoco.

And the spirit of the Fourth was not totally missing. "I had the best seat in the house for the Macy's fireworks," says Skadden partner Richard Easton. Unfortunately for him, it was from the 57th floor of One Chase Manhattan Plaza, in the offices of Cravath, Swaine & Moore (representing Du Pont), where he was holed up all night with five lawyers.

Once Du Pont declared its intentions, negotiations centered on three points: (1) developing a financial package that would allow Du Pont to afford Conoco without destroying its balance sheet, (2) structuring a merger proposal that pleased Du Pont's shareholders while winning over Conoco's in the face of competing tenders, and (3) finding a way to steer its offer through government shoals and put it into effect on time.

The first two points were largely the province of Cravath and First Boston—the new investment bankers on the scene, Du Pont's selection—with a team headed by M & A specialists Joseph Perella and lawyer-turned-banker Bruce Wasserstein. In a situation with a competing offer, the two most important considerations are mastering the maze of federal takeover laws that govern the time periods for the offers and gauging what might look attractive to investors. The first, obviously, was Cravath's job. Investment bankers know the second because, in addition to their function as deal makers, they also, through their large institutional trading desks and sales forces, know what buyers want. Together, Cravath and First Boston hammered out a complicated agreement that would give shareholders an option to take cash, or stock if they wished the tax-free status that comes from a stock-for-stock swap. Shareholders tendering to Du Pont would get $87.50 in cash for 40 percent of their stock and 1.6 Du Pont shares for the rest, the stock valued at $82 on the day of the announcement. It was a combination with parts borrowed from a host of previous deals but, taken together, was quite novel.

Friendly deals may insure the cooperation of the target's management. But when management does not wield a large portion of a company's shares, as was the case with Conoco, that friendliness may not be enough to sell the deal to the market. So, as a security blanket, the lawyers and bankers devised an option for Du Pont that would allow the chemical company to buy 15.9 million unissued Conoco shares, also at $87.50 each. No other suitor would have such an option. However, with an offer that was $9 higher than Seagram's at the time, such an option seemed to be an excess of caution.

The third key factor, the speed of the deal, is solely the work of lawyers. Well-run companies like Du Pont, with a solid credit status, can line up $7 billion over a weekend, even when it is a national holiday. But when it comes to filing a complicated registration statement and getting SEC and antitrust approval, lawyers must compress what would normally take several months of work into just a few days.

The job of creating this registration statement and shepherding it through all the relevant agencies fell to Skadden, Dewey, Ballantine, and a team of lawyers from Du Pont's counsel, Cravath, Swaine & Moore. Meanwhile, it was, once again, the job of Dewey, Ballantine litigators to buy time, as these corporate lawyers went to work.

Registration statements take on larger-than-life proportions during takeovers because, besides being necessary for SEC clearance, they act as fodder for opposing litigators to create deal-threatening problems. As Dewey's Larrabee explains: "You can't bring frivolous suits, but these tender offer documents are sometimes put together in tremendous haste and sometimes they turn out to have information that is not correctly stated. So, first you decide if the tender offer price that is being offered is too low. Then you climb all over the other guy's documents." To the trained eye, the document's mass can be filled with 10b-5 actions for fraud and manipulation.

Patience, Humility & Caffeine

Much gets written about powerhouse corporate lawyers who, as dealmakers, play a role in determining which companies live or die. Most corporate lawyering is not as glamorous. Work on the Du Pont registration statement typified what it takes to be a great corporate lawyer: care, writing skills, patience, humility, and an ability to go without sleep for long periods of time without complaining. How else could eight to ten people work together around-the-clock to write a 191-page book that contains fluid prose, no typos, and no credit for its authors?

Partner Alan Stephenson served as the lead lawyer for Cravath in negotiating and structuring the registration statement issues, coordinating all of the parties, and making sure that the statement fairly represented the wishes of everyone involved. Colleague and partner George Lowy did the actual drafting. The group worked almost non-stop for two straight weeks. Rich Easton, the Skadden partner, who was at that time an associate, cannot recall having dinner with his wife during the whole period, and more than once he would trudge home to Larchmont as dawn emerged, not to catch a few hours of sleep, but to take a cold shower, button down a new shirt, and head back to the office.

At 6 a.m. on the morning of July 15, just two weeks after Du Pont came in, Lowy, the oldest attorney on the deal, was the only one still standing—and still drafting. He had included several dozen chapters with information ranging from the nature of the offer to the size of the fees the investment bankers would receive. After he put the finishing touches on the document, he decided to file it personally at the SEC in Washington. Luckily he did. Upon arrival, he was told by the clerk that the filing fee check was $1.71 shy of the mark. "I had to take it from my pocket," says Lowy. "I even had to borrow a penny from the clerk."

Lowy stayed in Washington for some time, shooting down red flags raised ostensibly by the SEC's Corporate Finance Division but provided principally by Seagram's lawyers, who were climbing all over the statement. The registration process is wide open, with the SEC not only tolerating comments from opposing lawyers but seeking them out to aid disclosure. The Seagram people wanted the SEC to raise eyebrows about the so-called "lock-up" option, allowing Du Pont to buy 15 percent of Conoco's not-yet-minted shares. But Lowy reminded the SEC's staff that it recently had embraced that type of arrangement. He made sure to secure a waiver from the division for the option. With a document chock full of red marks, Lowy bounded back to New York for a few more tense nights at the printer, making revisions and having them proofed by associates, a common task for bleary-eyed junior people. But through Cravath's efforts, the SEC approval was achieved.

When Friendship Is Not Enough

Despite the euphoria of the initial filing commencing Du Pont's offer, discouraging news seemed to lurk everywhere. First, while Du Pont was filing, Seagram upped its bid to $85 a share, signalling its intention to remain competitive with Du Pont. Du Pont immediately countered to $95 a share and bumped up the back end of its deal to 1.7 Du Pont shares. But its stock price was sagging badly, bringing down the value of the whole offer.

Second, the federal rules involving merger waiting periods had an inexplicable quirk that clearly favored Seagram's type of bid. To let the government, either through the Federal Trade Commission or the Justice Department's Antitrust Division, study the anti-competitive nature of cash tender offers, the Hart-Scott-Rodino Act of 1978 provides that one or the other agency has 15 days to approve the bid, with a proviso that ten more days can be added if additional information is needed.

But if your offer contains a mixture of stock and cash, as did Du Pont's, the approval period doubles in length to 30 days. Seagram filed its Hart-Scott application June 22, and was approved for purchasing stock on July 8—the same day that Du Pont began the filing process. However the Williams Act, which regulates tender offers, states that companies that bump up their offers must wait an additional ten days after each bump before they can purchase shares. Seagram's raise thus set back its bid ten days in its race with Du Pont. But unlike Seagram, Du Pont faced antitrust questioning under Hart-Scott. For an energy-intensive company like Du Pont, buying Conoco would mean potentially violative vertical integration.

A dizzying flurry of events soon followed. First, Judge Weinfeld dealt Du Pont's attempt a severe setback on July 16 when he angrily dismissed Conoco's action against Seagram. It was just one in a series of 12 defeats the defense team suffered that summer, but it was a bitter one. One of the litigators later reflected on how defensive takeover litigation has fallen into disrepute with judges and academics. "It's easy for some airhead to say that the litigation we filed is stupid and counterproductive and if it has no chance then why bother to file it. They tell you they would be embarrassed to file some of this stuff. But if you would only litigate those matters you were absolutely certain you would win, you would be a pisspoor litigator." As for the skein of defeats on behalf of Conoco, the lawyer said: "I look at it this way. I was shot at 12 times, got a dozen bullet holes in me and I still lived to fight again."

The day after Weinfeld's dismissal, Mobil, the second largest U.S. oil company, which had been rumored to be interested in Conoco from the moment Seagram surfaced, struck with a $90 a share cash offer for 50 percent of the company. The offer was lower than most Wall Street analysts expected. However, because it was a cash deal, it could be approved under Hart-Scott in 15 days, thus potentially freeing Mobil to purchase shares on July 31, a week before Du Pont would be able to buy. Of course, such a short period would be relevant only if Mobil could clear all antitrust objections; otherwise, Mobil could be stuck with an additional information request, keeping Mobil's bid back for another ten days.

Then, on July 23, Seagram raised its bid to $92 in cash and announced it would begin purchasing shares tendered on July 31, also a full week before Du Pont could hope to begin buying its tendered shares.

At this point, with all the offers on the table, the fight moved from the legal and financial spheres to the world of public relations. Each offer had its strengths and weaknesses. It was now up to lawyers on each side to exploit them.

When Joe Flom talks about what it means to be a good business lawyer, he frequently cites three qualities that all must have: good legal sense, some business savvy, and a flair for public relations. "Takeover work is multi-disciplinary," he says. "All of these things are mixed together." Flom's firm started its public relations campaign against Mobil with an all-out attack on the antitrust implications of merging the nation's number two and number nine oil companies. The campaign was designed only in part to scare the Justice Department into action. The real goal was to make the large institutional holders wary of tendering to Mobil and then ending up with nothing if the government were to clamp down on that merger.

Skadden filed a private antitrust suit in Washington against Mobil, figuring correctly that Mobil would have to waste a day removing the case to New York. "We were hoping that it might throw Mobil off-guard to file down there," says antitrust partner William Pelster, who headed up Skadden's foray. "We also wanted out of the Southern District where we had already lost once before. It bought time. We had to do that because we were not yet up to speed on the oil industry."

Pelster used the time to set up a ten-attorney drafting crew. The hours were incredible. "Let's see," says Pelster, leafing through his red lawyer's diary for the period, "hmmm, Saturday, 18 hours; Sunday, 19 hours; then 18, 20, 21, 21. It did go on like that for a long time." The going was not easy because Mobil's lawyers put up a stonewall to discovery attempts. "We asked for a bunch of specific documents, and all we got back were 10-k's, which contain information no different from Mobil's annual reports. Pelster quickly broke down the antitrust issues into coal, pipe-line, refining, jet fuel, and retail gas overlaps. Partners then divvied up all of the areas except one, coal, which went to Robert Zimet, a senior associate with much securities litigation experience.

Zimet does not deny that for an associate just a few months away from a partnership decision, getting the coal draw was a good sign. But it was not the first time he had been given large responsibility for an important discrete matter, and he approached it as an old hand.

Zimet immediately secured the talents of the two associates who worked next door to him and went to work researching everything he could find out about coal. "It didn't look like it going in, but there were significant overlap issues involving coal," he recalls. "It was fascinating for me because it was a lesson in business. I got to learn about an industry that I knew absolutely nothing about before I went into this. I hadn't studied anything about coal since junior high, when you find out the difference between anthracite and bituminous."

After that Zimet focused on formulating a discovery strategy. He noticed the depositions of those in coal from Mobil and he defended Conoco's coal people. Then he scouted the country for experts in the field. It was a process he had done many times before but, he points out, the skills needed are not taught in law school. "You can only learn this by observing what lawyers more senior to you and their adversaries do," he says. "You learn from their successes and their failures. You learn how to look at annual reports and spot the problem areas. You learn how to track down the experts. You develop a sort of mental checklist, a cookbook on how to approach each of these."

Zimet says that despite some of the longest days he has spent at the firm, he felt "galvanized" by the activity. "You want to be involved in all phases of one of these big cases," he says. "You want to find out what is going on at all times. You wander into other lawyers' offices, just to try to get an awareness. You bump into partners and ask what is happening." Zimet finished up his section of the brief on time. He says he felt "very proud" of both his team and the final product, even though his section, along with almost all of the other antitrust issues, never got an airing in court.

With the brief writing underway, Pelster turned his attention toward smoothing any government objections to Du Pont's merger and creating a few for Mobil to deflect. "We were trying to agitate," he recalls. At that moment the Federal Trade Commission and Justice were locked in a turf war over which department should scrutinize the cases. FTC had built up expertise in the oil business over the years, but William Baxter, then the new antitrust division chief, was eager to assert his authority and stamp Justice with his philosophy. He grabbed the matter.

At first, Skadden people thought such interest on the part of a Justice official boded poorly not only for Mobil but for Du Pont itself. Negotiations for Du Pont's antitrust clearance centered on a Conoco joint venture agreement with Monsanto, Du Pont's archrival in the chemicals business. Surprisingly, the staff talks, also attended by a Covington and Burling attorney, went exceptionally well. Justice seemed to be willing to accede to the merger if Du Pont bought out Monsanto, thus ending the joint venture.

So Skadden turned its attention toward warning Justice of the evils of a merger between number two and number nine. Skadden bolstered its ranks by adding William Mulligan, an antitrust expert and former federal district judge turned Skadden partner, to the negotiations. And it brought in Harvard antitrust professor Philip Areeda as a paid consultant. A meeting between Baxter and these experts was arranged.

"At first he just glowered a lot," says Pelster of Baxter at the meeting. He kept saying "show me, show me," after everything Skadden's team said would be anticompetitive. Areeda discussed some foreign supply restrictions, but Baxter did not seem bothered. He then raised some extensive joint venturing problems, pointing out that the oil market was less competitive than it looked. Baxter expressed some interest and acted a trifle concerned. But Pelster did not think the session went very well. "It was a depressing meeting," he would summarize later.

Nevertheless, the next day, Justice approved Du Pont for immediate clearance, provided it would work out the Monsanto problem. But it asked for additional information from Mobil. The effect on Mobil's bid was devastating. Even though it seemed that Mobil would probably get through clearance in the next ten days, there were no guarantees. The offer lost credibility. It seemed that everything that Skadden had been saying all along about the antitrust hang-ups of Mobil's offer had been right. Mobil's bid suddenly had too much risk in relation to its reward. Although Mobil raised its price to $105 right before the call for additional information, the largest player was looking more and more like Goliath to Seagram's David.

Six Packs and Crown Sevens

While Du Pont's effort to show antitrust violations in a Mobil-Conoco merger was building to a climax, Seagram was within days of being able to begin purchasing the shares tendered to its offer. No one was sure how many shares had already been attracted to Seagram. But the opportunity for a quick pay-out—Seagram was readying checks to be sent out Saturday night—was a terrific lure. What Du Pont needed was some sort of last-minute impediment to Seagram's cash-on-the-barrel-head campaign. It got its wishes with the now-ready tied house litigation.

Solinger, charting the progress of the tied house suits, was in constant contact with local counsel. "Our Florida attorney told us they had a good chance of prevailing there, so our Florida lawyers drafted papers for state court. Our lawyer chartered a plane that Thursday afternoon from Miami to fly to Tallahassee. He would call me from each place, you know, 'Now I'm at the airport. Now I am at the court house.' " The Miami lawyer, from the Florida office of Stroock & Stroock & Lavan, convinced state judge John Rudd in an ex parte discussion in chambers that the $7-billion merger should be put on hold because Conoco sold six packs at Florida gas stations. But because the Florida lawyer needed time to post the necessary bond for the suit, Solinger said the announcement of Conoco's sub rosa victory had to wait until the next day, Friday—the day before Seagram would be allowed to purchase shares.

It came as a crucial blow to Seagram. Their attorneys were enraged by the ex parte action and lashed out that Friday morning to Judge Weinfeld, imploring him to overturn the Florida ruling. Weinfeld, too, was livid. But he cautioned that he could not touch a Florida state court's judgment. He did, however, warn that he would not tolerate further secret actions on behalf of clients. The warning came too late. As Seagram's people that afternoon convened an open hearing in Florida and got Judge Rudd to recant his TRO, the exact same scenario was unfolding in North Carolina. A state court judge once again blocked the Seagram purchase plan because Conoco sold liquor in his state's gas stations. "By the time they found out about it," says Solinger "the judge was on a boat somewhere in some North Carolina river."

Seagram's people, however, were up to the challenge. As the American Lawyer later reported, an associate at Simpson, Thacher & Bartlett, Seagram's attorneys, had taken the precaution of incorporating both in New York and Delaware the Seagram paper subsidiary doing the bidding, just in case diversity would be needed down the road against a suit by Conoco, a Delaware company. That shrewd precaution gave Seagram the right to take the matter to the emergency federal judge who is always available on a 24-hour basis in each district. Seagram prevailed later that evening, but once again not before Du Pont could create uncertainty and confusion about Seagram's offer. The TRO was not lifted until long after the close of Friday's market. Most Wall Streeters had already fled their offices for the weekend without considering whether to deliver their shares to Seagram because they presumed that the North Carolina order would last at least until Monday, and no checks would be sent out Saturday night.

Robert Myers, a litigation partner at Dewey, defended the ex parte dealings in this fashion: "Whether you are required or not to notify opposing counsel about such discussions is only a matter of state law. Sure, it was an elbow in the eye and probably does not meet everybody's expectation of what a good guy is. But these two companies were in a life and death struggle. From our standpoint, we did nothing inappropriate. I'm friends with a lot of lawyers from Simpson Thacher, but that doesn't mean they are going to get special consideration."

Where Wall Street Hits Madison Avenue

With investors now facing all three competing bids, all with confusing deadlines and prices that seemed to change with every day of trading, the contenders took to the newspapers to wage a war of words. Within one page of each other, in *The Wall Street Journal* and *The New York Times,* giant full-page ads appeared stating each company's case. "Seagram is paying $92 in cash. Quickly," screamed the ad for the distiller. "No Maybes." Mobil's advertisement urged all Conoco shareholders: "You must act now."

But it was Conoco's ad, in the form of a letter from Chairman Bailey, with simple "Important" stamped where the letterhead should be, that would prevail. It ticked off reason after reason why Du Pont made the most sense politically, economically, and legally. To highlight the antitrust hazards of the Mobil offer, Conoco switched to bold print to say that possible intervention by the government "makes it questionable whether the Conoco shareholders would ever get paid under the Mobil offer." It also noted in boldface that "All Conoco directors have tendered or are tendering their shares to Du Pont," in an attempt to show institutions that Du Pont was the favored hand. While the letter bore Bailey's signature, most of the input was Flom's. "Looking back, I would have to say the thing I was most proud of in Conoco was the ad," he said. "It was the best thing I did on the deal. It hit a lot of themes, and I think it was most effective. The public relations people, they hardly changed a word, maybe just a line or two," he says with a smile.

Whether it was the ad campaign or the lawsuits or just Conoco's antitrust baiting, the message was working. By the time Seagram began mailing checks that weekend, Du Pont could lay claim to 48 million shares, about 56 percent of those outstanding. By contrast, Seagram had pulled in about 17 million shares, mostly those of the arbitrageurs, quick-trading specialists who buy shares on news of a takeover and then tender to whoever pays the quickest and most sure profit. Often these "arbs," as they are known, can hold hostage a whole deal because they represent such a large part of the pool of outstanding shares by the time the final bidding begins. But here the pool was simply too great, drowning the arbs in a sea of more important institutional holders—all of whom seemed smitten by Du Pont's bid.

At that point, however, because tendering is not synonymous with purchasing, the war could not be considered over. Because of the quirk in the federal timing rules, shareholders who had tendered to Du Pont could still withdraw their shares from Du Pont's pool if another bidder pleased them more.

With the price of Du Pont's stock eroding almost daily, because of fears of what Du Pont's increased debt and diluted stock would do to the company's future earnings-per-share figures, the back end of Du Pont's offer—the exchange of stock—was looking more and more dubious. At one point it was possible to take Seagram's $92 and go out and buy two shares of Du Pont's stock, far better than the 1.6 shares you would get if you held on for some indefinite period of time before Du Pont could begin purchasing.

I Will Sue You and Raise You Twice

For Mobil, Du Pont's late purchase date was enough of a hope to merit one last chance at Conoco. On Monday August 3, Mobil raised its bid to $115. The bump was vital; Mobil had only gotten 2 million shares so far, way below its rivals, even with its higher offering price, because institutions feared possible antitrust action. Mobil also tried one last legal foray.

Michael Mitchell, a 46-year-old Skadden litigator, remembers well how things unfolded. He had been brought into the case one week before, to help defend depositions of high-level Conoco officers. At around lunch time he had begun the defense of Chairman Bailey when he learned that Mobil had just gone into federal court in the Southern District to seek a temporary restraining order to block Du Pont's bid. The application ostensibly represented Mobil's counter-claim to Du Pont's antitrust case, but it was obviously a last ditch attempt to stop Du Pont from its imminent purchase of the shares in its pool. At 5 p.m., Mitchell found himself standing before Federal District Court Judge Lawrence Pierce, prepared to defend Du Pont against anything that Mobil could throw at him.

A transcript of the hearing shows that the judge must not have read a newspaper, or at least the financial pages of one, anytime during the summer. He admitted being unsure of who brought the case and even who the parties involved were. Sanford Litvack, a partner at Donovan, Leisure, Newton & Irvine, the New York law firm that represented

Mobil, tried to explain that he thought Du Pont should be restrained because its lock-up option was manipulative. He urged that the deal be put on ice for a few days—just long enough to get Mobil out of the clutches of Justice's Antitrust Division, so both could be considered equally.

To an uninitiated judge, Litvack had one compelling argument on his side. It did not seem right that Du Pont should be offering roughly $1 billion less than Mobil and yet still be able to walk off with the prize. What he did not know was, judging by the way the market was acting, Mobil could be offering double what Du Pont was prepared to pay and nobody would be nibbling as long as the antitrust hold-up lurked.

Mitchell stuck to the facts and the law, explaining why they were in court in the first place and how Mobil had had plenty of time to press its action before that crucial moment. Further, he pointed out that not a single case supported Mobil's position. Thomas Barr, a Cravath litigator, followed up, again trying to answer a bewildered judge's questions about how the federal takeover rules interacted with the suit.

A victory was imperative for Du Pont. "It would have been like a bank panic if that judge had said, 'Maybe let's take a week and decide this thing,' " Cravath's Stephenson said later. "The capital at that point just runs to the safest offer, whether it be $92 or $95, anything just so it works."

A look at Pierce's opinion issued the next day shows that the Conoco litigators had prevailed—the opinion matched almost word-for-word Mitchell's brief filed earlier that day. Pierce found that Mobil had failed to show that a TRO refusal would harm Mobil more than a TRO would damage Du Pont. "Mobil entered the bidding contest for Conoco knowing that it would be subjected to waiting periods," he noted. The next day, August 4, Mobil breathed two more gasps: raising its bid to $120 and filing an appeal. Both were for naught. Du Pont announced it was moving its bid up to $98 a share and that it had reached agreement with Monsanto to buy out that chemical firm's end of the joint-venture agreement, thus clearing away any Hart-Scott problems and allowing it, at last, to close the gate on the millions of tendered shares.

Champagne corks popped that night for 200 lawyers, investment bankers, executives, chauffeurs, typists, and messengers at Du Pont's Wilmington, Delaware, headquarters. The next day Du Pont purchased 55 percent of Conoco's shares and exercised its option for 15.9 million others, giving it 62 percent of Conoco. Mobil threw in the towel, directing its shares to Seagram, and the Canadian liquor company in turn swapped its 27,885,000 Conoco shares for 20 percent of Du Pont. This time, Seagram signed the standstill agreement and consented to sit, docile, on Du Pont's board. Three months and $7.54 billion later, the deal was over.

Characters

Martha Solinger—Associate, Dewey, Ballantine

Ralph Bailey—Conoco's Chairman

Joseph Flom—Partner, Skadden, Arps

Leonard Larrabee—Partner, Dewey, Ballantine

Russel "Cap" Beatie—Partner, Dewey, Ballantine

Peter Bator—Partner, Davis Polk

Robert Greenhill—Senior Managing Director, Morgan Stanley

Jack Gallagher—Dome's Chairman

Kurt Koegler—Partner, Skadden, Arps

Richard Easton—Associate, Skadden, Arps

Joseph Perella—Investment Banker, First Boston

Bruce Wasserstein—Investment Banker, First Boston

Alan Stephenson—Partner, Cravath, Swaine & Moore

George Lowy—Partner, Cravath, Swaine & Moore

William Pelster—Partner, Skadden, Arps

Robert Zimet—Associate, Skadden, Arps

William Baxter—Assistant Attorney General for the Antitrust Division

Robert Myers—Partner, Dewey, Ballantine

Michael Mitchell—Partner, Skadden, Arps

Epilogue

Since Du Pont swallowed Conoco in 1981, "The Deal" has been knocked out of the record books first by Texaco-Getty and then by Socal-Gulf. But for many of those involved, that torrid summer epitomized all that is exciting about the practice of law. As Dewey partner Myers put it: "There were some who might have had qualms about working so hard, but there is only one Conoco in people's lives. Each morning you would pick up the *Times* and read about something you were working on." This kind of work, he says, "is not the kind of thing where people want to sneak off and play golf. We were at the heart of it. It was a once in a lifetime experience."

Solinger agrees, even though she spent 45 out of 47 days in June and July at the office, billing about 300 hours a month. She says she would not have had it any other way. Although she was often the only woman in the room for much of the Conoco negotiations, the ratio did not bother or intimidate her. She laughs now at some of the more blatant forms of sexism she saw and heard during the deal, including constant apologies for the use of four letter words in her presence. She says she never felt excluded from any of the hard work or the camaraderie.

Was it all worth it? For the lawyers, the payoff, besides psychic rewards, was handsome. Skadden reportedly received $4 million for its efforts, the top draw of all the law firms. Such a sum, however, is much smaller than the fees the investment bankers racked up for their work. Unlike lawyers, who bill by the hour, the bankers can command a percentage of the deal. Thus First Boston, which came in more than a month after Skadden, got .2 percent of the deal for its work: $15,080,000. Morgan Stanley made about the same from Conoco. Neither firm employed one-fourth as many professionals as Skadden.

Are these fees justified in relation to the spoils of the lawyers who toiled side-by-side with them throughout the period? To Solinger, an associate who got her regular first-year salary whether she billed 300 hours or 150, the sums seemed outrageous. "I can't see why they are able to draw 10 times what we earn," she says.

But Cravath's Lowy says he is not cynical about the differences. "We get paid what I think we should get paid. What is just is what the market will bear," he says. "Perhaps lawyers are undercompensated, but I think we make out well enough. I know that First Boston's contribution was absolutely critical, at least as critical as any lawyer's role." Flom agrees: "We do fine." Bankers, he says, have a lot more overhead, including a much larger support system than lawyers have. "And," he adds, "their risk opinions (analyzing the pluses and minuses of making deals) are very meaningful."

For Du Pont, the results of the merger are mixed. On the one hand, oil prices, far from shooting up, have leveled off, making the purchase appear expensive compared to where oil prices seemed to be heading at the time. On the other hand, Du Pont's stock has performed well since the merger relative to other chemical companies, so the market perceives the merger to have made some sense.

How about the shareholders who ended up paying those fees? Do they benefit from the thousands of hours put in by these firms? Du Pont's shareholders saw their stock fall rapidly but then retrace its steps to wind up at around pre-Conoco merger levels. But how about the shareholders of Conoco whom the rules are designed to protect? One defense lawyer, who prefers to stay anonymous, thinks they made out the best of all. "One of the worst of the arguments I hear from airhead academics is that litigation hurts shareholders. Well, if we hadn't filed all of those suits, then Conoco would have gone for $65 a share instead of $98. Some ass on your law review wrote soon after that there should be no resistance attempts once an offer is made, because that is what is supposed to be best for shareholders. That guy doesn't have the first idea of what he is talking about."

Sure, the lawyer admits, there must be a better way to settle these fights. But all ways he can think of would interfere with the ultimate rights of the shareholders to get the best price. Until a better method is created, he says, the Conoco way will be the standard. Do you agree?

CONFLICTS OF INTEREST IN CORPORATE TRANS-ACTIONS: THE LEVERAGED BUYOUT OF THE HARRIS CHEMICAL COMPANY

Commerce Clearing House & Center on Professionalism of
the University of Pennsylvania Law School (1989)

PART I: THE LEVERAGED BUYOUT BEGINS

The Founder Dies

Walter Harris, the founder and chairman of the board of the Harris Chemical Company, died last spring. With his death speculation on Wall Street mounted as to the future of the company.

As a young man Harris, a native of Louisville, Kentucky, travelled north to earn his Ph.D. in chemistry. Brilliant and inventive, he remained there as a research chemist for a major northeastern chemical company. Although admired and well rewarded, Harris was frustrated by his lack of control over the direction of his work in the large corporate environment. Determined to be master of his own fate, he returned to Louisville to start his own fledgling operation.

Harris Chemical started small, manufacturing printers inks and related products. The company struggled in the early years—especially since Harris was more interested in scientific research than in management and marketing.

Eventually his research paid off. From his work with carbon black, Harris developed a toner of high quality to be used in the burgeoning copy machine business. Named Copy-Rite, this product was an immediate financial success. With the profits the company built a top quality physical plant and purchased large tracts of undeveloped real estate on the outskirts of Louisville to hold for possible future expansion. The lion's share of the revenues generated by Copy-Rite, however, went back into the creative end of the business. The research and development department was the soul of Harris Chemical Company.

Harris and his staff continued their work with carbon black and activated charcoal. The work with carbon black led to the development of optical paints. These deep black non-reflecting paints were used for optical equipment and for camouflaging military equipment and aircraft. The company began to receive military contracts—another profitable venture.

More recently the continued research with activated charcoal has uncovered its usefulness as a purifying agent for biotechnological drugs. This has been an important scientific breakthrough of which the company is proud. The current market for these agents is small, so their manufacture will not be profitable short-term. The unavailability of purifying agents, however, would be a blow to the emerging biotechnological drug industry and to the patients who would benefit from those drugs.

Harris's daughter, Lee, grew up immersed in the family business. She, too, got her Ph.D. in chemistry and returned to Louisville to work at Harris Chemical. Sometime after Lee Harris became involved in the business the family decided to take the company public. By the time Harris Chemical Company became a public corporation, it had three divisions: (1) Copy-Rite (toner, printers inks, and related supplies); (2) Optipaint (optical paint); and (3) Purifax (drug purifying agents).

After 35 years at the helm of the company, Walter Harris retired as chief executive officer. He remained as chairman of the board and Lee Harris became the CEO. Under Lee Harris's management the company's stock continued to be traded in the over-the-counter market. Lee Harris began to think, however, that the shares of the company were trading at a lower price than was justified by the success of the company. At the same time the budget for research and development—the heart of the company—was gradually being eroded by the pressure to assure adequate dividends for the public shareholders. Two unwanted tender offers had been successfully resisted, but the battles were unsettling. Given the upsurge in hostile takeovers and the increasing number of institutional investors and individual entrepreneurs looking for short-term profit, Harris understood that Harris Chemical—with its valuable resources and dependable cash flow—would continue to be a target.

Harris began to consider taking the company private again. If she and a few trusted executives could buy back the company, perhaps she could retain the now-threatened control of the company. Since the stock price on the market was so low, offering the shareholders a higher-than-market price would be fair to the shareholders and would still constitute a good investment for the buyout group.

Her resolve strengthened when her father died and Wall Street deal makers identified the company as an ideal candidate for breakup or merger.

Outside Counsel Introduces the Investment Banker

The story begins as Lee Harris calls the company's law firm, Oldham and Keiser, to further investigate taking the company private. The Oldham firm is the largest in Louisville and one of the oldest. The founder, Martin Keiser, helped Walter Harris start up the company. In the early days of the representation Keiser brought in a young associate named Jack Oldham to help on the account. Harris Chemical at that time was struggling and Oldham invested some of his own funds in the company. Upon Mr. Keiser's retirement, Oldham became the chair of the firm's corporate department and Harris Chemical's chief outside lawyer. Both the law firm and the company have prospered.

Lee Harris confers with Oldham. Neither Harris nor the rest of her management group owns a majority of the stock. Nor do they have a great deal of excess cash. Oldham therefore advises considering a leveraged acquisition. He recommends talking to Torberg Investment Associates, a Wall Street investment banking firm specializing in leveraged buyouts. Although Harris is concerned about bringing a New York firm into Louisville business, Oldham assures her that they are the best and she can encourage them to use local banks and financial institutions to obtain a substantial portion of the financing. Harris retains Torberg Investment Associates.

Arthur Torberg meets with Harris to sketch out a tentative proposal to offer the Board of Directors. The stock is currently selling at $20 a share. They propose to offer $30 a share thereby giving the shareholders a 50% bonus on their stock, but still remaining within what the group believes is a reasonable value range for the stock. The management group tentatively plans to put up about 10% of the bid price in cash. The rest of the bid price will then be borrowed against the company's assets, with 50 to 70% being in the form of secured bank loans and the remaining 20 to 40% from junk bonds sold to insurance companies and pension funds, among others. Rounding up the financing would be the primary responsibility of the Torberg firm.

The Wall Street Law Firm Enters

Arthur Torberg is interested. He likes the looks of the company. The management group, while not terribly sophisticated in corporate finance, seems intelligent and solid. Torberg calls Jason Flynn, partner in the large Wall Street law firm of Resnick and Morris, whom Torberg has often used in this kind of deal.

Torberg tells Flynn that he has a deal he wants him to do. He explains that Harris, the CEO of a prosperous Louisville chemical company, and a small management group want to make a proposal to the Board to buy out the company. Torberg wants to join in the proposal. Torberg would like Flynn to do the legal work necessary to accomplish the deal.

Scene 1: Introduction to Players in the LBO Drama

LEE HARRIS, looking earnest, is jogging through a pastoral setting in the early morning.

Announcer

And that's the top of the business news for Tuesday, May 2nd. This is Business Forum.

Walter Harris, founder and chairman of the Board of the Harris Chemical Company, died last week. Today Wall Street is asking whether the death of Harris also spells the demise of his company.

Harris Chemical is best known as the manufacturer of Copy-Rite, a high quality toner used in copy machines. Copy-Rite provides the financial underpinnings of the company. But the soul of Harris Chemical lies in its research and development department.

The Harris labs have created a string of brilliant scientific products over the years—the latest being in the exciting new field of biotechnology.

When Harris retired as chief executive officer in 1981, his daughter Lee Harris became CEO. With the founder's death, speculation has mounted as to the direction of the company.

Reflecting that uncertainty, trading in Harris Chemical stock has been active in the last week. Wall Street deal makers believe that the company is an ideal candidate for breakup or merger.

Lee Harris has refused comment since her father's death. A friend of the family said that Ms. Harris "feels as though Wall Street is dancing on her father's grave."

And now let's look at yesterday's stock market activity. Stock prices were mixed yesterday. . . .

————

Harris Chemical Company, a publicly held corporation headquartered in Louisville, Kentucky, has become a takeover target.

Fearing for the company's future, Lee Harris, Chief Executive Officer of Harris Chemical, decides to take action to prevent a takeover.

Jack Oldham, who has represented Harris Chemical and the Harris family for many years, suggests a leveraged buyout by a management group. To help arrange the financing he introduces Harris to Jason Flynn, a New York lawyer specializing in mergers and acquisitions, to "do the deal." Flynn is a partner in a large Wall Street law firm with offices in six cities.

Scene 2: Outside Counsel Introduces Investment Banker

As scene opens, LEE HARRIS is sitting at her desk working. Her telephone buzzes; she picks up the phone and exchanges a few words with her secretary who is apparently telling her that TORBERG and OLDHAM have arrived.

Harris

Yes?

(Listening) Yes, send them in.

HARRIS rises from her desk, goes to the office door, opens it and greets OLDHAM and TORBERG. As they shake hands and engage in introductory chatter, they move toward the seating group and eventually sit down.

Harris

Hello, gentlemen. Please come in.

Oldham

Lee, I'd like you to meet Arthur Torberg. Arthur, as you know is the head of Torberg Associates, one of the finest investment banking firms in New York.

Arthur, this is Lee Harris.

Harris

(graciously)

(extending her hand to Torberg) Pleased to meet you. I appreciate your coming down here.

Torberg

Glad to come. I've heard about your company for years and I'm eager to learn more about it.

(nodding toward Oldham) Jack was good enough to come out in this rainstorm to pick me up at the airport.

(They all sit down.)

Oldham

Yes, it gave me an opportunity to fill Arthur in a little about the company.

Harris

(smiling affectionately at Oldham)

Well, there's no one better to tell you about our company than Jack Oldham. Jack's law firm helped my father start this company and Jack himself has been our lawyer for years.

Well, where shall we start?

Torberg

Why don't you start by telling me exactly what you have in mind?

Harris

(slowly and thoughtfully)

Well, as you know, my father died recently. His death set off an avalanche of rumors about the fate of our company—about takeovers— and so forth. All this speculation worries me, but it's really just pushing me in a direction I was already heading.

Our company has always prided itself on creating new products. A perfect example of this is our new drug purifying agents. They're taking a long time to develop and they're not going to be profitable for a while, but they've got a great future. We've learned to be patient.

Oldham

(breaking in)

Unfortunately, stockholders are not always so patient.

(with pride) I'm a stockholder myself—started investing when I was a young associate here.

(shaking himself back to the subject) Well, that's beside the point—in recent years Lee and the Board have felt a lot of pressure to increase dividends. That's resulted in a cut in the R & D budget.

Then, of course, I told you about the unfriendly tender offers we've had.

Harris

(interrupting)

Yes, with Jack's help we fought them off, but it was draining. These fights take us away from running the company.

Anyway, to get to the point, I've decided to buy the company back. I've spoken with a few other members of management who've agreed to join me.

Jack tells me your firm is the best there is in doing leveraged buyouts. Can you help us out with that?

Scene 3: Wall Street Law Firm Enters

Scene opens with full screen shot of ARTHUR TORBERG at checkout counter of Louisville hotel making a phone call. Changes to split screen when JASON FLYNN answers the phone.

Torberg

Jason, Arthur Torberg here.

(Pause)

Torberg

Fine, fine. Listen, Jason. I'm in a hurry. I'm in Louisville, Kentucky. I'm about to catch a cab to the airport.

But I wanted to tell you. I've got a deal out here I want you to do. I'm down here looking at the Harris Chemical Company. Do you know it?

Flynn

Harris? Is that the one where the Chairman of the Board died? I've been reading about it in the Journal.

Torberg

Yeah, that's the one. Well, the daughter—she's the CEO—and a couple of management types—wanna do a buyout. We're gonna round up the financing. You're our man for the legal work. Let's have lunch when I get back to New York and I'll give you the details.

Flynn

Sounds interesting. Who's representing the company?

Torberg

Oldham and Keiser in Louisville. Jack Oldham—one of the senior partners there—set this up for me. He's represented the firm forever.

Flynn

Oh, yes, I know them. Biggest firm in Louisville—(sarcastically) "pillars of the bar."

Torberg

Maybe, but they don't know anything about this game. I checked; they've never done any big deals.

Flynn

What about the management group? Who do they have?

Torberg

Harris says she wants to use her general counsel, Sam Hirsch. He's part of the buyout group. You're gonna have to draft the proxy statement, though. Hirsch doesn't know how to do it.

In fact, you're going to have to take the lead in this whole deal. Everyone else is an amateur. I want you to fly down here and get this done right.

Flynn

What are the fee arrangements?

Torberg

(hesitating)

Well, uh.

(Formally) The management group has agreed to indemnify us for all our fees, including attorneys fees.

(Clears his throat) They were a little shocked at your hourly rate. Louisville lawyers don't bring down quite so much. We thought maybe you could, uh, discount it a bit if the deal doesn't work, say 70%, then charge a premium, say ... 175%, when the deal goes through.

We'll talk about it when I get back.

Flynn

(hesitating) This isn't going to be like Summit Foods, is it, where the deal cratered out and the company never picked up the expenses? If you remember correctly, I had to do some arm-twisting just to get paid.

Torberg

(heartily)

Don't worry. This deal will work; you'll see to that.

Oh, here's my cab. Gotta go.

ISSUES FOR PART I

ISSUE 1.   Role of Outside General Counsel

Jack Oldham, Harris Chemical's outside general counsel, introduces Lee Harris, the CEO, to the investment banker who will assist her in effectuating the management buyout. Before this introduction he apparently advised her of the possibility of such a leveraged transaction.

(a) Is there a problem with his doing so?

(b) Must he inform the Board of the MBO plans, even if Harris is not ready to make disclosure to the Board?

(c) After his meeting with Harris and Oldham, Torberg tells Flynn that Oldham will represent the "company" in this transaction. Even if Oldham can go on representing the company in day-to-day corporate business after having put the LBO in motion, can he also represent the company (or the Board) in the buyout transaction itself?

ISSUE 2.   Lawyer as Investor in Client Corporation

Oldham owns stock in his corporate client—the Harris Chemical Company.

(a) How does stock ownership affect his representation of the company in general? Is it inconsistent with being counsel to the company, or, does it more clearly align his and the company's interests?

(b) Specifically, does his status as a shareholder make his advice to Harris to engage in a leveraged buyout suspect? How does it affect his ability to represent the Board of Directors as it decides whether to accept the buyout offer?

(c) Does the amount of stock he owns affect the answer to these questions?

ISSUE 3.   Fees: Lawyer with a Stake in the Deal

(a) Lawyer's Own Interests: The fee arrangement proposed gives Jason Flynn a stake in the outcome of the deal. If the deal falls through, his fee is to be discounted to 70%; if the LBO is successful, he is to receive a large premium. With such an arrangement Flynn clearly has a stake in the outcome of the deal. What are the potential dangers in such a fee arrangement?

(b) Contingent Fee: Is this arrangement a contingent fee that must meet the requirements of Model Rule 1.5 (c)? If so, or even if not, what disclosures should be made and to whom? Should the terms of this arrangement be embodied in a writing?

(c) Indemnity Arrangement: Are there any concerns raised by the fact that the management buyout group has agreed to indemnify the investment banker for its fees, including the attorneys fees?

ISSUE 4.   Representation Arrangements in a Friendly Transaction

The management buyout group and the LBO firm intend to cooperate in doing the leveraged acquisition of Harris Chemical. Arthur Torberg has told Flynn: "... you're going to have to take the lead in this whole deal. Everyone else here is an amateur." What does it mean to take the lead?

(a) Whom does Flynn represent? Since both Harris and Torberg want to do the deal, can Flynn act as the "lawyer for the deal" or the "lawyer for the situation"? Where two or more clients have the single goal of cooperatively completing a transaction such as this one, is it appropriate for one lawyer to handle the work to accomplish the goal?

What are the risks and benefits of such an arrangement?

(b) Structuring the Representation: Whether Flynn intends to engage in a common representation or to act as Torberg's lawyer, what must he tell the clients when he flies down to "get this done right"?

[These questions are asked at this point simply as food for thought in reading the next section. The references on those issues are listed under Issue 5 below.]

PART II: JASON FLYNN: LAWYER FOR THE TRANSACTION?

The Wall Street Lawyer Meets the CEO

Jason Flynn flies to Louisville to begin the process of accumulating the information necessary for the proxy statement.

He meets with Lee Harris. Although not a sophisticated Wall Street player, she, as her father before her, has been running a well-managed and prosperous business for many years. Furthermore, being a chemist herself, Harris knows the substance of the business. It is clear to Flynn that her heart and her money are all tied up in this company.

Harris takes her responsibility to the shareholders seriously, but she also resents what she perceives as interference with the real work of the company by the problems of fighting off tender offers and keeping the dividends high enough.

Scene 4: Wall Street Lawyer Meets CEO

LEE HARRIS and JASON FLYNN sitting at table. They are concluding a meeting. FLYNN is packing his briefcase.

Harris

(looking somewhat harried)

I'll be so relieved when this buyout is done and I can get back to running the company. Our biotech division really needs a lot of support. I'm very grateful that you'll be in charge of putting this deal together.

Flynn

Well, thank you.

(pauses, then carefully) But, of course, there will be certain matters for which you may need separate counsel.

Harris

(alert)

Like what?

Flynn

Well, for example, the engagement letter and perhaps certain other matters that may have to be settled between your group and Torberg's firm.

Harris

(brushing him off) Oh, that, that's no problem. Sam Hirsch can take care of that. He's our General Counsel and part of the group. He's never done a buyout before, but with your guidance, I'm sure he can draft whatever you need.

Flynn

It's not what I need . . . .

Harris

(interrupting and becoming more cheerful)

And with Jack Oldham taking care of the Board, we ought to be able to work this out pretty efficiently.

Flynn

(looks uncomfortable and as if he is about to say something, but he doesn't)

Harris

(goes on, looking at some notes in front of her)

Here's another thing. I spoke with Torberg about this, but I'd like your input, too. It's about putting together the financing group. Torberg wants a New York bank to take the lead. I really wanted to use our local banks, but I've begun to think he's right about the primary lender. This may be a little "rich" for one of our banks. We'll still use the locals, but I think one New York bank would be o.k. Do you have any suggestions?

Flynn

That seems right to me—to use a New York bank to take the lead. (Pausing slightly) Our firm represents Mercantile Midland. I'd be glad to introduce you to their people. My partner Charlie James does a lot of their work.

Harris

(rather too enthusiastically)

That would be great. If your firm could handle the bank's work, too, it would make it move quickly.

Flynn

(hesitating)

Well, normally, we wouldn't represent two parties in a deal.

Harris

(looking displeased and interrupting)

Oh, please, don't tell me we need more lawyers. That would only hold up the deal.

Flynn

(continuing haltingly)

. . . well, maybe—in the interests of moving this along—we could screen Charlie from our part of the deal—and if we could get consent from both you and the bank for the representation—it should work.

ISSUES FOR PART II

ISSUE 5. Jason Flynn: Lawyer for the Transaction?

Now we have seen the first Louisville meeting. Jason Flynn met with CEO Lee Harris to begin the process of accumulating information necessary for the proxy statement. Harris has not hired an outside law firm to represent the buyout group. She intends to rely on Sam Hirsch, her general counsel and member of the group, to watch over the deal. In the scene just watched, Hirsch was not present.

Let's go back to some of those questions we considered before this scene.

(a) Whom does Flynn represent? Perhaps more importantly now, whose lawyer does Lee Harris think he is?

Can Flynn act as "lawyer for the deal" or "lawyer for the situation"? Where two or more clients have the single goal of cooperatively completing a transaction such as this one, is it appropriate for one lawyer to handle the work to accomplish the goal? Do the Model Rules of Professional Conduct or the Model Code of Professional Responsibility permit such an arrangement?

(b) Structuring the Representation: Has Jason Flynn handled his definition of the role properly?

(i) If he is Torberg's lawyer, did he make that clear to Lee Harris and should he have met with Harris alone (without Hirsch)?

(ii) If this is a joint representation, did he explain that arrangement clearly—to Harris and to Torberg?

ISSUE 6. Multiple Representation: Mercantile Midland

In this scene Jason Flynn, upon being asked for suggestions by Lee Harris, recommends Mercantile Midland bank, one of his firm's clients, as a possible source of financing. Several questions arise.

(a) First, is there any reason for Flynn not to introduce Mercantile to Harris? Suppose it is customary practice for Flynn to recommend Mercantile in such transactions and that Mercantile in turn uses the law firm's services and recommends that others do the same. Must there be additional disclosures?

(b) Second, can Flynn's partner James represent Mercantile in this transaction? Does walling-off James help resolve the conflict problem? What kind of consent, if any, must be obtained, and from whom?

(c) Suppose, however, that Flynn and James decide it is wiser for James not to represent Mercantile on this particular transaction. James nevertheless has represented, and will continue to represent, Mercantile on similar financing with other companies. Does that create problems for Flynn's representation of the Harris group in negotiations with Mercantile?

(d) How much weight should be given to Harris's plaint: "Oh, please, don't tell me we need more lawyers. That would only hold up the deal?" How many lawyers can you have in a transaction without debilitating the entire project?

ISSUE 7. House Counsel's Dilemmas

Sam Hirsch was not present at this meeting between Harris and Flynn. This seems to indicate that he wishes to take a back seat to Flynn's control of the transaction. Whether he acts as a front line player or only comes in from the bench when called, what kind of professional responsibility dilemmas might he face in his triple role as (a) general counsel for Harris Chemical, (b) lawyer to the buyout group and (c) member of the buyout group?

(a) Can Hirsch be a member of the MBO group?

(b) If Hirsch continues to serve as general counsel, can he also be counsel to the buyout group?

(c) Hirsch has no expertise in the area of leveraged acquisitions. Is he competent to represent the buyout group?

PART III: CONFLICTS EMERGE

Investment Banker Seeks Short-Term Gain

One outside event begins to worry Torberg, although it does not worry Harris. Congress has begun to hold hearings on the feasibility of continuing the production of certain types of conventional military equipment and aircraft. The optical paint division of Harris has been relying for its profitability in large measure on military contracts. If this equipment line is cut back, contracts for this division will decrease and so will profits. The stock price of Harris Chemical dips slightly as these hearings begin.

Harris does not worry because she's seen ups and downs in all the divisions of the company. She knows it is a strong company and it will bounce back from a loss of military contracts. She also knows that there are many other potential applications for optical paint; the R&D department in fact is now engaged in developing several. Although profits may dip in the short term, she is confident that in the long run their new applications will create an upsurge in profits.

Torberg Investment Associates, on the other hand, wants to put together a profitable transaction now. It cannot afford to wait a few years for the development of future products.

Scene 5: Investment Banker Seeks Short-Term Gain

Scene opens with split screen shot of JASON FLYNN and ARTHUR TORBERG sitting at their desks working. Flynn's telephone rings and he absentmindedly answers it.

Flynn

Jason Flynn.

Torberg

Jason—Arthur. Say, I've got a couple of problems with this Harris deal.

Flynn

What are they?

Torberg

Well, first, there are these damned Congressional hearings. It looks like that Senate committee might discontinue the Stealth bomber. If that happens, Harris's military contracts are gonna get cut back and there go the profits for the Optipaint division. The stock started to slip as soon as the hearings started.

Flynn

Harris says she's not concerned about these hearings. You know that the Copy-Rite division is very strong. It can go on supporting the whole company indefinitely.

Torberg

I know, but overall profits will go down. And it won't be as easy to restructure the company after the deal is done. We'll still be able to sell off that biotech division, of course, but our option to sell Optipaint might go down the drain.

Flynn

Well, Harris says ...

Torberg

(impatiently interrupting)

I know what Harris says, but she doesn't seem to realize that we have to sell these divisions. Regardless of her pipe dreams, we've gotta change the deal. First, our offering price is too high and so is the percentage of the deal we're gonna leverage. Harris has to put more cash up front.

And, with the stock slipping, the financing may be tougher to round up, so we need a bigger percentage for our work. Can't you stick in an extra clause for advisory fees?

Flynn

Well, that may be difficult for Harris ....

Torberg

(interrupting again)

Here's another thing. Harris is giving us a hard time about those local banks. You know what a hometown booster she is. We're happy with Mercantile Midland, of course, but we've got commitments to other lenders here in New York. Can't you talk Harris into forgetting the local banks? She seems to trust you.

Scene 6: CEO Seeks Long-Term Stability

Scene opens with split screen shot of JASON FLYNN and LEE HARRIS at their desks talking on the phone.

Harris

Hello, Jason. This is Lee Harris.

Flynn

Hi, Lee. How are you?

Harris

Oh, I'm fine. But Torberg's been worrying me.

Flynn

(looking apprehensive)

Why?

Harris

Well, this deal has changed so much from our original plan. Torberg keeps trying to get more for himself and pushing us to give up more.

And all this panic about the military contracts is ridiculous. Sure their loss would depress profits in that division for a while, but over the long run we'll get them back. We've got plenty of new products in the R&D pipeline.

Flynn

Yes, I know, but you've got to understand Torberg's position . . . .

Harris

(interrupting) Understand Torberg? Torberg certainly doesn't understand this company. He's always talking instant profits. He even mentioned selling off Optipaint and Purifax because they weren't not making as much as Copy-Rite. I think I talked him out of that. That's not the way we operate here. We're in this for the long term. Our stockholders understand that.

Flynn

Yes, but you're buying the company back from them.

Harris

Well, yes, but . . . I'm very suspicious of Torberg's motives. And I hold him responsible for these New York arbitrage firms coming in to buy up stock. If we don't get this deal done fast, we'll be walking right into the hostile tender offer we've been trying to avoid.

Flynn

Lee, we're moving as fast as we can.

Harris

Oh, I don't blame you. But I am concerned about what to tell the Board's special committee; I'm just not comfortable with Torberg. Do you think we should talk to another LBO firm?

Flynn

(taken aback)

I can't advise you about another firm. That would put me in an impossible situation. Torberg brought me into this and we represent his firm. I think you should speak directly to Torberg. I think you could work things out with him.

ISSUES FOR PART III

ISSUE 8. Conflicts Emerge

The potential conflicts between Harris and Torberg have begun to emerge as actual conflicts. Although they began by sharing the objective of completing a successful buyout, their reasons for doing so were different. Torberg, who had no previous connection with Harris Chemical, had a profit motive. Harris, while also undoubtedly wishing to profit from the deal, had another more personal motive—to protect and maintain the company as it had always been run.

In addition to their conflicting motivations, they also have conflicting ideas on the nature of the company after the transaction is finished. Torberg plans to break up the company; Harris wants to keep it intact.

Furthermore Harris has indicated that she may speak to another LBO firm.

(a) Lawyer as Intermediary: As an intermediary there will always be rough spots. Are these the kind of rough spots that Flynn ought to try to work out as lawyer for the transaction? Should he try to bring them together? Or is it so rough that he must withdraw?

The remaining issues are also raised in the next section. Think about them now and after you have read the next scene.

(b) Conflicts: Torberg asks Flynn to "lean on" Harris with respect to advisory fees and the local banks. Should Flynn do this? Does the answer to this question depend on whether Flynn is Torberg's attorney or lawyer for the deal? If this is in fact a joint representation, what must Flynn say to Torberg?

Harris seeks advice contrary to Torberg's interest—whether she should talk to another LBO firm. Should, or can, Flynn advise her on this subject?

(c) Confidentiality: Torberg has given Flynn a confidence (we'll sell off assets) and so has Harris (I'm suspicious of Torberg). How must Flynn handle these confidences? How do confidentiality obligations differ in a joint representation?

(d) Counseling: Does Flynn have an obligation to disabuse Harris of her "pipe dreams" about keeping the company together and about revitalized R&D? If it is a joint representation? If he is Torberg's lawyer? At what point should such counseling take place, or have taken place?

PART IV: CONFLICTS ESCALATE

SEVERAL DAYS LATER

Scene 7: CEO Shares a Confidence

Harris

(discouraged)

I don't know which way this deal is going now. I just want to make sure we're doing the best thing for the company and the shareholders.

(carefully) I did have a talk with an investment firm here in town. They told me that, with all the debt we'll have after the buyout, we're going to have a hard time finding enough money for R & D. Torberg never discussed that with me, and neither did you. Why didn't you tell me that?

Flynn

(avoiding her question)

Have you told Torberg about this meeting?

Harris

No.

Flynn

I'll have to tell Torberg. I'm his lawyer.

Harris

You're my lawyer, too. I've relied on you all along in this deal. I've trusted you with all our company's information. That's why I'm trusting you with this.

Flynn

Then you'll have to tell Torberg. If you don't, I'll have to withdraw from this deal.

Harris

(backing off)

No, no. You're overreacting. Nothing's really happened. Can't you just wait a couple of days. We're still leaning toward Torberg. We just wanted to do a little comparison shopping.

Flynn

(slowly)

Well, I'm not scheduled to talk to Torberg until Thursday. I suppose I could wait until then.

Harris

Fine. Just keep drafting. You know the deal better than anybody. Besides, if you do withdraw, Torberg will know something's up as surely if you told him.

Scene 8: CEO Considers Other Options

THURSDAY MORNING

Scene opens in the early morning with HARRIS coming into her home from the outside wearing her jogging clothes. FLYNN is in his office in New York.

The phone rings and HARRIS picks it up.

Harris

Hello.

Flynn

It's Jason. What's going on?

Harris

(considerably more distant than in previous conversations)

Good morning, Jason. I did speak with Torberg about our talks with the other investment bank. Needless to say, he was not pleased.

We haven't made a final decision about bringing the other group in yet.

Flynn

(coolly)

Until you've made that decision I'm in a rather awkward position. Should I go forward with the drafting?

Harris

Of course. You've gone too far to turn back. I'm not going to pay to educate another lawyer.

(sarcastically) You've run up a hell of a bill already.

Flynn

(reluctantly)

All right. What does the other investment firm propose?

Harris

(cautiously)

As I said, we've made no final decision about that. I will give you that information when and if we do.

Scene 9: Investment Banker Threatens Withdrawal

LATER THAT MORNING

Flynn

Arthur, I spoke with Harris this morning and she was very noncommital about her talks with the local LBO firm.

Torberg

(gruffly)

Yeah, I bet.

Flynn

Then I got a call from Sam Hirsch—her inside lawyer. He was asking questions that could only mean that he's doing something behind our backs—maybe even setting up a deal with the local firm. I gave him what he wanted, but this has put me in a hell of a spot.

Torberg

If they screw us by trying to bring those local guys into this, we'll get out. I've had about enough of this home town crap. I'm sure as hell not going to share this deal with some two-bit investment bankers from Louisville, Kentucky.

Flynn

Now, wait a minute. If you're serious about the possibility of getting out, we're going to have to warn them about that.

Torberg

Not now. Just keep drafting and get this thing done.

ISSUES FOR PART IV

ISSUE 9. Counseling

Until her conversation with the local LBO firm, Harris was still operating under unrealistically optimistic illusions about the financial ability of the company to engage in research and development with the debt obligations incurred as a result of the buyout.

As lawyer for the transaction—or as lawyer for Torberg—what are Flynn's obligations when he realizes her misunderstanding? Should he have counseled her about this? When?

ISSUE 10. Confidentiality

Because Harris is relying on Flynn to carry out the transaction, she reveals confidential information to him that would be significant to Torberg—the talks with the other LBO firm. What obligation does receipt of this information place on Flynn?

ISSUE 11. Withdrawal as Intermediary?

At this point it is abundantly clear that Flynn is being used as a tool by both sides as their hostilities escalate. Is it possible for Flynn to stay in and try to hold things together? Is he able in this situation to maintain his independent judgment as a lawyer or is he simply being pushed around by the two clients?

PART V: THE LAW FIRM'S DILEMMA

Multi-Office Firm: The Left Hand Knoweth Not What the Right Hand Doeth

Flynn's firm has recently merged with a medium-sized Denver law firm. Resnick and Morris now has six offices—in New York, Albany, Washington, Denver, Los Angeles and London. As a part of the merger process the Denver firm prepared a "Client Status Report" describing its client base. Information from the Report was entered into Resnick and Morris's computer to determine whether any litigation or transaction adverse to these new clients existed. Flynn read the Report and was pleased with the Denver firm's client profile. He welcomed the addition of clients such as Progressive Petroleum Products, a large mid-western conglomerate. The billing partner, Grace Santos, had written in the Report that she did "general corporate representation, including mergers and acquisitions and investment counseling." She had listed some of the transactions she had handled in the last several years.

Because of the difficulties of communication between geographically dispersed offices, Resnick and Morris holds annual partners meetings in New York. At a cocktail party preceding a partners' dinner, Flynn and Santos are chatting.

Scene 10: Multi-Office Firm: The Left Hand Knoweth Not What the Right Hand Doeth

Partners are drinking and chatting. The mood is festive but restrained. It is a "business" cocktail party.

Santos

Hello, Jason. I'm Grace Santos from the Denver office. We met just after our firms merged last year.

Flynn

Yes, of course. Nice to see you again, Grace.

Santos

Great party here.

Flynn

Thanks. Now that the firm is so big, this is about the only way to meet all the partners. By the way, Grace, I read the Client Status Report that you did for us before the merger. You've brought some very nice clients to the firm.

Santos

Thank you.

Flynn

I notice that you represent Progressive Petroleum Products. Seems to be an up and coming company. What do you do for them?

Santos

Oh, general corporate work, some acquisitions. They started out with just petroleum products, but in the last couple of years they've started to diversify. Last year they picked up a lumber company in the northwest. I did that deal for them.

Flynn

Good. Anything on the front burner now?

Santos

Well, I may be about to do another acquisition. PPP has a lot of excess cash and they've been looking around for a few potential targets. Yesterday they may have decided on a nice little chemical company in Louisville, Kentucky. They already had some stock in it and they're about to go over 5%. I think we'll be making a tender offer soon.

FLYNN chokes on his drink.

ISSUES FOR PART V

ISSUE 12. Adverse Representation

Jason Flynn's law firm has recently merged with a Denver firm. A client of the Denver firm—Progressive Petroleum Products (PPP) is about to make a tender offer for the Harris Chemical Company. Such an offer will be in direct competition with the buyout offer. Both PPP and Torberg Associates are long-standing clients of the two offices.

What can be done to resolve this conflict? The firm and Santos and Flynn appear to have four options. Which of these should they choose:

(1) withdraw from all clients—PPP and Torberg/Harris;

(2) withdraw from PPP but continue Torberg/Harris;

(3) withdraw from Torberg/Harris but continue PPP;

(4) continue representing all clients?

ISSUE 13. Interplay of Conflicts and Confidentiality

Assume that the resolution of the conflict is that only Santos withdraws. If Santos is no longer representing PPP, what may or must Flynn do? Can he now tell Torberg and Harris about the imminent offer? Or does the receipt of confidential information allow or require Flynn to withdraw from representation?

ISSUE 14. Law Firm Management

What type of conflict management system could the firm have used to avoid such a problem? Is it feasible to expect Santos, or any other lawyer, to send out a conflicts memo every time a client invests in, or even discusses acquiring, another company? If a conflicts check must await a decision to acquire, is there any way to prevent this dilemma? At what point in the identification of targets—or in the progress of a transaction—must potential adverse interests or even participants be run through the system?

What procedures should a firm have for handling multiple simultaneous representations? How frequently must a conflicts check be updated? What is the effect of coding on the effectiveness of the conflicts system?

What steps must a law firm take before merging with another firm or before making lateral hires from other firms, corporations or government agencies to avoid conflicts problems?

Should large multi-office, multi-city law firms be treated differently from smaller one-office, one-city law firms for purposes of conflict of interest rules?

PART VI: THE DEAL DISINTEGRATES

CEO Reneges

The firm conflicts committee resolves the conflict by telling Santos that she cannot represent PPP in this matter. Santos refers the matter to another Denver firm.

Progressive Petroleum Products approaches the special committee of the Board with a proposed tender offer of $33 a share. They give the Board 48 hours to respond.

Harris is distraught. She sees her company slipping from her grasp. The dream she had to get back control of the company and continue the creation of new products is fading.

Unbeknownst to Flynn, Harris starts talking with PPP. PPP is interested in a straight acquisition rather than a leveraged buyout. Harris discusses her vision of the future of Harris Chemicals. She explains how the extreme profitability of the Copy-Rite division has allowed the company to engage in research and development and she describes the new products that are in various stages of readiness in the R&D pipeline. She explains her commitment to supporting the non-profitable purifying agents for biotechnological drugs by the more than ample profits of the other divisions. She stresses that the potential pullback in military contracts is only a temporary profit gap that will soon be filled by other military applications or other civilian optical paint products.

PPP likes Harris and her ideas. They like the way she's managed the company in the past. They have enough cash and profitability to be able to afford a little high-prestige dabbling in biotechnological drugs and research and development. They offer Harris a nice package of personal compensation and benefits as well as an agreement to allow her a certain amount of time to run the company according to her vision. They agree to allow the company to keep its name.

Harris sees this as her only way now to retain any control over her company and to have enough money to keep up the R & D. She recommends to the special committee of the Board that it accept the PPP offer rather than the LBO proposal.

Scene 11: CEO Reneges

LEE HARRIS is seated at her desk dictating into a hand-held dictaphone a memorandum to the Board of Directors. She is surrounded by papers. As she dictates, she occasionally pauses to think and write.

Harris

The Special Committee of the Board of Directors has asked my recommendation on two proposals pending before the Committee.

The first proposal is from the Harris Acquisition Group in which I have been a primary investor. The Group's proposal is to do a leveraged buyout of the Company. The second proposal is from Progressive Petroleum Products which has made a tender offer for the purpose of making a straight acquisition of the Company.

New paragraph. A comparison of the terms of the two proposals snows the following. PPP has agreed to honor the commitment of the company to research and development. PPP has agreed to allow the Harris Chemical Company to retain its name . . . .

After thorough and, I might add, painful consideration of the merits of the two proposals, I have come to the following conclusion.

New paragraph. The long-term goals of the Harris Chemical Company can best be met by accepting the proposal of Progressive Petroleum Products.

HARRIS TURNS OFF HER DICTAPHONE AND PUTS HER HEAD DOWN.

Scene 12: Investment Banker Declares War

THE NEXT DAY

It is late at night. FLYNN is in his study looking tired and discouraged. TORBERG is still working in his office looking disheveled and angry.

Torberg

(enraged)

We've put too much into this to get out now. We'll reverse our strategy. We're going to take this company over ourselves. We'll outbid PPP. Start drawing up the documents right now.

Flynn

I can't do that. I can't oppose Harris directly; and I can't oppose PPP.

Torberg

You have to. You're the only one who knows this deal inside and out. For God's sake, you're our lawyer—not Harris's. And you're not representing PPP, you're representing us. We'll be set back a millenium if you get out now.

Flynn

No, I've got to withdraw. I should never have let this go on.

Torberg

You have to. You're the only one who knows this deal inside and out. For God's sake, you're our lawyer—not Harris's. And you're not representing PPP, you're representing us. We'll be set back a millenium if you get out now.

Flynn

No, I've got to withdraw. I should never have let this go on.

Torberg

You never told me it would come to this. You can drop Harris, but you can't walk out on me. I've relied on you; you're my lawyer.

ISSUES FOR PART VI

ISSUE 15.   Withdrawal: A Hardship Exception?

The supposedly friendly transaction between the CEO and the LBO firm turns hostile. By the end of the videotape Harris has decided to abandon the buyout, but Torberg is determined to continue. Can Flynn continue to represent Torberg after he decides to oppose Harris?

If Flynn is forced to withdraw Torberg will be severely prejudiced because the transaction is so far advanced and must be accomplished quickly. Should the hardship to his client justify a decision by Flynn not to withdraw? Should there be an explicit hardship exception to the mandatory withdrawal rules?

ISSUE 16.   Effect of Lawyer Ineptitude on Clients

Evaluate the effect of Flynn's apparent ineptitude in handing this situation on all the parties involved in this transaction.

ISSUE 17.   Flynn's Professional Obligations: Recapitulation

When did Flynn go wrong? Or was he simply trapped by circumstances beyond his control?

What steps could Flynn have taken as the deal began to turn sour to salvage the situation so that his ultimate withdrawal from the deal would not have been necessary?

Chapter 28

CIVIL LITIGATION

At any given moment, a corporation is likely to be involved in perhaps hundreds of lawsuits. The largest component of the increase in litigation in society over the past few decades involves suits between business organizations. In addition, of course, consumers, current and future employees, tort victims, and shareholders in both direct and derivative actions all may be parties in litigation with the corporation.

The overwhelming percentage of cases settle rather than go to trial. Decisions made in the pretrial phase of a lawsuit can powerfully shape the willingness of parties to settle and the terms on which they do so. What motions are made and how discovery is conducted are especially important. The material in this chapter therefore focuses on Rule 11 motions for sanctions against opposing attorneys and on duties to preserve evidence as topics that raise significant strategic and ethical issues for lawyers involved in corporate representation.

OVERVIEW OF THE CHAPTER

The excerpt from Rhode and Luban sets forth the relevant provisions of Rule 11, which deals with the integrity of pleadings, motions, and other documents filed with a court. As they note, the rule is designed to address three abuses dealing with the presentation of filings in litigation: filings made for an improper purpose, that are unwarranted by law, or that assert or deny factual claims without adequate support.

As you read the provisions of the Rule, one thing to keep in mind is how the current Rule adopted in 1994 differs from the prior version enacted in 1983. Sanctions against a lawyer now are discretionary, for instance, whereas they were mandatory from 1983–1994. In addition, the current Rule contains a "safe harbor" provision, which permits a party who is served with notice of the intention to file a motion for Rule 11 sanctions has twenty-one days in which she can withdraw the filing that is being challenged without incurring any penalty. These provisions reflect concern that parties previously were using Rule 11 motions for strategic purposes, which resulted in considerable satellite litigation. Do the changes made in 1994, however, undermine the effectiveness of Rule 11 as a deterrent?

The *Garr* case provides an example of when a court concludes that investigation of allegations in a pleading are so inadequate as to warrant Rule 11 sanctions. Note that the court acknowledges that an attorney need not personally verify the basis for each allegation, but may reasonably rely on others in some cases. One consideration in evaluating the reasonableness of such reliance, says the court, is the amount of time available to the lawyer. How much guidance does this provide a lawyer on what she must do in order to avoid Rule 11 sanctions?

The disagreement between the majority and the dissent in *Garr* raises another issue. The dissent argues that if a claim turns out to be meritorious, a court should not inquire further into the adequacy of the lawyer's investigation prior to filing the complaint. By contrast, the majority quotes another court: "A shot in the dark is a sanctionable event, even if it somehow misses the mark." The difference in opinion reflects a disagreement about the function of Rule 11. Is it designed to monitor attorney conduct, as the majority suggests? Or is it intended to weed out nonmeritorious cases from the court system, as the dissent suggests?

As the prosecution of the Arthur Andersen accounting firm indicates, document preservation and destruction has become a major corporate concern. The material on this topic begins with a description of the criminal statutes that are relevant to this topic. Keep in mind that the basis for such prosecution can be a failure to preserve potentially relevant documents not only when a legal proceeding is underway, but when such a proceeding, or even simply an investigation, can be reasonably anticipated. Companies thus need to weigh their legitimate desire to destroy material in order to avoid drowning in paper or filling up computer space with the obligation to consider the potential future legal relevance of that material. Note also that the legal proceedings or investigation in question can be civil, and need not be criminal, for criminal sanctions to apply to the failure to preserve material of potential evidentiary value.

The common law doctrine of spoliation also can be used to sanction the failure to preserve potentially relevant material in pending or reasonably foreseeable litigation. The *Zubulake* case discusses the criteria for imposition of this sanction. The case also is notable for two other reasons. First, it provides an extensive discussion of a company's obligation to preserve material in electronic form. Second, it elaborates in some detail the steps that counsel for a company must take in order adequately to meet its duty to ensure that the company meets its obligation. As *Zubulake* and the *Morgan Stanley* case discussed in the note that follows illustrate, the sanction for violation of a discovery obligation can be severe: the entry of an adverse inference order against the offender. Such an order may result in an instruction that the jury is to conclude that the other party has proven one or more of its allegations.

The first problem asks you to consider whether filing a complaint on behalf of a corporate client would risk Rule 11 sanctions under the circumstances. The second problem requires you to determine whether criminal or common law spoliation sanctions could be imposed on the company for failure to preserve material with potential evidentiary value.

MODEL RULES: 3.1, 3.3, 3.4

A. RULE 11

Deborah L. Rhode & David Luban, LEGAL ETHICS

(4th ed. 2004)

The core of * * * Rule [11 as amended in 1994] reads:

By presenting to the court (whether by signing, filing, submitting, or later advocating) a pleading, written motion, or other paper, an attorney ... is certifying that to the best of the person's knowledge, information, and belief, formed after an inquiry reasonable under the circumstances—

(1) it is not being presented for any improper purpose, such as to harass or to cause unnecessary delay or needless increase in the cost of litigation;

(2) the claims, defenses, and other legal contentions therein are warranted by existing law or by a nonfrivolous argument for the extension, modification, or reversal of existing law or the establishment of new law;

(3) the allegations and other factual contentions have evidentiary support or, if specifically so identified, are likely to have evidentiary support after a reasonable opportunity for further investigation or discovery; and

(4) the denials of factual contentions are warranted on the evidence or, if specifically so identified, are reasonably based on a lack of information or belief.[1]

The rule is directed at three abuses of the litigation process:

● presenting paper for an *improper purpose* (subsection 1, quoted *supra*);

● presenting paper that is *unwarranted by law* (subsection 2); and

● presenting paper that makes or denies *factual claims* without appropriate support (subsections 3 and 4). By signing, filing, submitting, or later advocating the paper, an attorney or party

---

1. Fed. R..Civ.P. 11(b) (1994).

certifies that he has made a reasonable inquiry into the factual and legal basis of the paper.

Moreover, the Committee Notes to the rule explain that an attorney may be sanctioned for "insisting on a position after it is no longer tenable." Thus, if subsequent research or factual investigation reveals that the paper is insufficiently supported by law or fact, even though reasonable inquiry at the time of the filing did not reveal the insufficiency, the attorney must withdraw the paper or face sanctions. Typically, an adversary will move for Rule 11 sanctions, but a court can order sanctions on its own initiative.

Several other features of the rule are worth noting:

First, sanctions are discretionary—courts need not sanction lawyers who violate the rule.

Second, section (c)(1)(A) of the rule creates a so-called "safe harbor" provision: when adversaries move for sanctions, parties have twenty-one days to withdraw or modify the paper with no penalty. Alternatively, parties can take their chances and do neither if they believe that the unmodified paper does not violate Rule 11.

Third, the current version no longer favors monetary sanctions paid to the adversary * * * [I]f they are monetary, the fine will generally be paid to the court * * * unless payment to the adversary is warranted for purposes of deterrence. Fed.R.Civ.P. 11(c)(2)(1994).

Fourth, Rule 11(c)(1)(A) provides that "[a]bsent special circumstances, a law firm shall be held jointly responsible for violations committed by its partners, associates, and employees." * * *

Sixth, the rule permits so-called "fishing expeditions," where a plaintiff alleges wrongdoing without much evidence, hoping and intending to develop the evidence through the discovery process. Clearly, there is some point to forbidding such expeditions * * *

To most commentators and courts, however, a categorical prohibition on fishing expeditions seemed excessively harsh, particularly in actions where a plaintiff is required to show that the defendant knew or was aware of certain facts, or that the defendant had engaged in a conspiracy. These include securities, fraud, antitrust, RICO, and employment discrimination cases. Typically, the plaintiff will need some kind of "smoking gun" from the defendant's own files. In such cases, a fishing expedition becomes a practical necessity, because the crucial evidence can be found only through discovery after the complaint has been filed. The current version of Rule 11 recognizes these difficulties ...

GARR v. U.S. HEALTHCARE, INC.

22 F.3d 1274 (3d. Cir. 1994)

GREENBERG, CIRCUIT JUDGE.

I. INTRODUCTION

... This action arose in the aftermath of an article in the Wall Street Journal published on November 4, 1992, entitled "U.S. Healthcare Insiders Sold Stock Before Last Week's 17% Price Decline." The article recited that U.S. Healthcare, Inc. insiders, including Leonard Abramson, its chairman and president, had been heavy sellers of its stock before a 17% two-day drop in its price in the week before publication of the article. The article indicated the drop had been precipitated by disappointing earnings.

James R. Malone, Jr., a member of the Haverford, Pennsylvania, law firm of Greenfield & Chimicles, who read the article on the morning it was published, was interested in its contents because his firm specialized in securities litigation. Indeed, in an extraordinary allegation, not denied by Malone, U.S. Healthcare in the Rule 11 proceedings charged that Greenfield & Chimicles maintained a list of corporate stockholders available to become plaintiffs in securities litigation.[1] Robert K. Greenfield was on that list.[2] It is undisputed that after Malone read the article he examined a "representative sampling of stories relating to U.S. Healthcare," as well as a report on background information on the company. He also obtained considerable other information about U.S. Healthcare, including filings it had made with the Securities and Exchange Commission.

Malone does not contend that at the time that he was doing this research he had a client who had expressed any interest in the article to him. Rather, Malone was seeking to generate a lawsuit. Thus, in the pithy words of the district court, "having a case but no client," he called Greenfield who lives in Florida to discuss the U.S. Healthcare situation. Malone described the Wall Street Journal article to Greenfield and established that he owned stock in U.S. Healthcare. Malone asked Greenfield whether he would like Greenfield & Chimicles to file a suit on his behalf if the firm believed that there had been actionable wrongdoing, and Greenfield answered affirmatively. Within hours Malone determined that a certain class of U.S. Healthcare stockholders had "a legitimate and cognizable legal claim" stemming in part from the insiders' stock sales.

Events continued to unfold rapidly on November 4, 1992, for on that day Malone prepared and filed a class action complaint on behalf of Greenfield under section 10(b) of the Securities Exchange Act of 1934. *15 U.S.C. § 78j(b).* The gravamen of the complaint was that U.S. Healthcare and Abramson had issued false and misleading statements which were filed with the Securities and Exchange Commission and which caused Greenfield and the stockholder class to purchase U.S. Healthcare stock at artificially inflated prices. The complaint asserted controlling

---

1. This arrangement reverses the traditional regime which contemplates that the client start the steps towards formation of an attorney-client relationship by seeking legal representation.

2. Robert K. Greenfield is not related to the Richard D. Greenfield of Greenfield & Chimicles.

person liability against Abramson under section 20 of the Securities Exchange Act. *15 U.S.C. § 78t.* In the complaint, Malone recited that Greenfield fairly and adequately could represent the interest of the class of stockholders on whose behalf the action was being brought. Inasmuch as Malone mailed the complaint to Greenfield on November 4, 1992, Malone filed it before Greenfield received it. Obviously Malone did not think it important for Greenfield to see the complaint before it was filed even though Malone regards Greenfield as a distinguished retired corporate attorney.

On November 5, 1992, Malone on behalf of Allen Strunk filed a second class action against U.S. Healthcare and Abramson. The Strunk action repeated the allegations word for word from the Greenfield case except that the name of the plaintiff and the number of shares he owned were changed. Malone filed this action after Fred Taylor Isquith, an attorney in New York, contacted him and asked him to represent Strunk.

Malone and Strunk's New York lawyers were not the only attorneys interested in the U.S. Healthcare situation. On November 4, 1992, appellant Arnold Levin of the Philadelphia firm of Levin, Fishbein, Sedran & Berman, also read the Wall Street Journal article. Levin and his firm have what he characterized as "a long-standing professional relationship" with Greenfield & Chimicles, and Levin had a high regard for Greenfield & Chimicles' ethical standards and skill in handling federal securities law suits. On November 4, 1992, after Levin had read the article, Malone called him to discuss the merits of bringing a section 10(b) action against U.S. Healthcare and Abramson. Malone mentioned the Wall Street Journal article, and said he had done research into whether a section 10b action could be brought. Malone also told Levin that he had prepared such a complaint. Levin requested that Malone fax him a copy of the complaint, and Malone promptly did so. Levin then read the Greenfield complaint and reread the Wall Street Journal article and concluded, as he set forth in his affidavit, that "based upon my experience and understanding from the two documents," and in "reliance on the integrity of the pre-filing investigation of Greenfield & Chimicles," the section 10(b) action had merit.

There was even more interest in the U.S. Healthcare situation for on November 4, 1992, appellant Harris J. Sklar, a Philadelphia attorney in individual practice, also read the article. According to his affidavit, Sklar discussed the possibility of bringing an action against U.S. Healthcare with his client Scott Garr who was a U.S. Healthcare stockholder, and Garr authorized Sklar to bring the case on a class action basis. Sklar, however, saw the need to obtain co-counsel and consequently called Levin, as he had worked with him in the past. Levin then told Sklar of his dealings with Malone, and Levin and Sklar discussed the possibility of a suit.... On November 6, 1992, Levin and Sklar filed that complaint which replicated the Greenfield and Strunk complaints except that the names of the plaintiffs and the number of shares they owned were changed. * * *

* * * On November 6, 1992, the same day that Levin and Sklar filed the Garr complaint, U.S. Healthcare and Abramson moved in the district court for the imposition of sanctions pursuant to Rule 11 in the Greenfield, Strunk, and Garr actions * * *

* * * In their brief, U.S. Healthcare and Abramson explained the basis for the motion in detail. They asserted that Malone, Levin, and Sklar failed to conduct "even the most cursory factual and legal investigation" of the case and that if they had done so they would have determined that the complaints had no basis in fact or law. The brief indicated that the three complaints demonstrated the "all too familiar pattern of an instant class action lawsuit based on newspaper reports followed by a covey of cut and paste copycat complaints."

* * * On November 8, 1992, Robert K. Greenfield finally read the complaint, and at that time came to the realization that he had made a mistake in bringing the action because he knew of no basis for it and because his son had substantial business dealings with U.S. Healthcare. Thus, he directed Malone to withdraw the complaint. When U.S. Healthcare and Abramson learned of Robert K. Greenfield's position, they supplemented their motion for Rule 11 sanctions to assert that Malone had failed to make a reasonable inquiry into whether Greenfield fairly and adequately could protect the interests of the plaintiff class ...

Thereafter, the district court filed its reported opinion of February 4, 1993. After setting forth the background of the case at length, the court found that Malone could not be sanctioned under Rule 11 with respect to the accuracy of the information on which he had predicated the Greenfield complaint because his inquiry into the underlying facts "was reasonable under the circumstances." *146 F.R.D. at 125.* However, the court found that Malone had violated Rule 11 with respect to the allegation in the complaint that Greenfield fairly and adequately could protect the interests of the class. *146 F.R.D. at 125–26.* But it also found that it could not say that Malone had made an inadequate inquiry into Strunk's ability fairly and adequately to protect the class. Accordingly, as Malone's factual inquiry into the merits of the case against U.S. Healthcare and Abramson had been reasonable, the court did not impose sanctions in the Strunk action.

The district court next discussed whether sanctions should be imposed on Levin and Sklar. In this regard the court pointed out that Levin cited our opinion in *Lewis v. Curtis, 671 F.2d 779 (3d Cir.), cert. denied, 459 U.S. 880, 103 S. Ct. 176, 74 L. Ed. 2d 144 (1982),* in which we indicated that reliance on an article in the Wall Street Journal is not based "on an insubstantial or meaningless investigation" and that plaintiffs and their attorneys "need not make further expenditures to prove independently that which may be read with some confidence of truthfulness and accuracy in a respected financial journal." The court observed that Lewis was decided under *Fed. R. Civ. P. 23.1* and that we have never applied that case under Rule 11. It then held that Rule 11 imposes a "non-delegable duty upon the signing attorney to conduct his own independent analysis of the facts and law which form the basis of a pleading or motion," citing *Pavelic & LeFlore Marvel Entertainment Group, 493 U.S. 120, 125–27, 110 S. Ct. 456, 459–60, 107 L. Ed. 2d 438 (1989)*. The court rejected Levin's argument that he could rely on the integrity of the investigation by Greenfield & Chimicles, and it therefore ruled that Sklar could not rely on that investigation either. Ultimately the court held "that Levin and Sklar sought to act more quickly than fulfilling their duty would have allowed" and that "Levin['s] and Sklar's inquiry, or lack thereof, was unreasonable under the circumstances and a violation of Rule 11." *146 F.R.D. at 122–28.*

The court provided for the following sanctions. It required that Malone, Levin, and Sklar pay all of U.S. Healthcare's and Abramson's reasonable costs and attorney's fees incurred to that time, that the Greenfield and Garr complaints be dismissed without prejudice, and that the matter be referred to the Disciplinary Board of the Supreme Court of Pennsylvania for an investigation into whether the conduct of Malone, Levin, and Sklar constituted a violation of the Pennsylvania Rules of Professional Conduct.

* * *

II. Discussion

Insofar as significant here, Rule 11 provides that:

The signature of an attorney or party constitutes a certificate by the signer that the signer has read the pleading, motion, or other paper; that to the best of the signer's knowledge, information and belief formed after reasonable inquiry it is well grounded in fact and is warranted by existing law or a good faith argument for the extension, modification, or reversal or existing law, and that it is not interposed for any improper purpose, such as to harass or cause unnecessary delay or needless increase in the cost of litigation.[6]

The signer's signature on a pleading, motion, or other paper certifies the signer has done three things: (1) read the pleading, motion, or paper; (2) made a reasonable inquiry into the contents of the pleading, motion, or other paper and concluded that it is well grounded in fact and warranted in law; and (3) has not acted in bad faith in signing the document. * * *

A signer's obligation personally to comply with the requirements of Rule 11 clearly does not preclude the signer from any reliance on information from other persons. For example, no one could argue fairly that it would be unreasonable for an attorney to rely on witnesses to an accident before bringing a personal injury action. After all, the accident hardly can be reconstructed for the benefit of a plaintiff's attorney. Similarly, an attorney is not always foreclosed from relying on information from other persons. Thus, in CTC Imports and Exports, we stated

6. None of the parties contends that the amendments to Rule 11 effective December 1, 1993, are germane here. Thus, we do not discuss them.

that a determination of whether there has been "a reasonable inquiry may depend on ... whether [the signer] depended on forwarding counsel or another member of the bar." *951 F.2d at 578* (quoting Notes of Advisory Committee on Rules, 1983 Amendment, *Fed. R. Civ. P. 11*, reprinted at *97 F.R.D. 165, 199*). Furthermore, as we recognized in CTC Imports and Exports, inasmuch as the standard under Rule 11 is "fact specific," the court must consider all the material circumstances in evaluating the signer's conduct. *951 F.2d at 578.*

It is also important to observe that when the court examines the sufficiency of the inquiry into the facts and law, it must avoid drawing on the wisdom of hindsight and should test the signer's conduct by determining what was reasonable when the document was submitted. * * *

There is also a temporal element in a determination of whether an inquiry was reasonable. Thus, we have recognized that a factor in ascertaining the reasonableness of the signer's inquiry is the amount of time available to investigate the facts and law involved. *Bradgate Assocs., 999 F.2d at 752; CTC Imports and Exports, 951 F.2d at 578.* Accordingly, if a client comes into an attorney's office for an initial consultation concerning a possible case one day before the statute of limitations will run, the attorney might be justified in filing a complaint predicated on an inquiry which would be inadequate if the attorney had more time for investigation. On the other hand, an attorney with a great deal of time to file a document might be expected to make a more comprehensive inquiry than an attorney working under severe time constraints. * * *

Application of the foregoing principles requires us to affirm....

We do not doubt that sometimes it is difficult to reconcile the tension between the requirement that a signer personally discharge the Rule 11 obligations and the acknowledgement that a signer may rely on an other party's inquiry in some cases. But this appeal presents no difficulties. Malone's declaration described the scope of his inquiry in great detail. He obtained a representative sampling of stories regarding U.S. Healthcare and a "disclosure" report giving a great deal of financial information regarding U.S. Healthcare, including five-year figures showing sales, net income, earnings per share, and growth rate. He also considered financial ratios and examined forms filed with the Securities and Exchange Commission showing trading in U.S. Healthcare stock by insiders. In fact, in the district court's view, Malone's inquiry was inadequate only as to Greenfield's status as the class representative.[7]

On the other hand, Levin and Sklar relied only on the Wall Street Journal article, the Greenfield complaint, and Malone. They made no effort to examine the numerous materials Malone assembled, and they cannot justify their failure to have done so. They do not contend that

---

7. Malone obtained this information rapidly through the use of computer infor-   mation retrieval services.

Malone would not at their request have sent the materials to them. Alternatively, we see no reason why they could not have seen the materials by travelling the short distance from their offices in Philadelphia to Malone's office in Haverford, a Philadelphia suburb. We also point out that the documents on which Malone relied were all accessible to the public so that Levin and Sklar could have obtained them themselves.

Furthermore, there were no time constraints requiring Levin and Sklar to file the Garr complaint on an expedited basis. The Wall Street Journal article was published on November 4, 1992, and Levin and Sklar filed the Garr complaint two days later. Levin and Sklar do not contend that they were confronted with a statute of limitations problem compelling immediate action. * * *

We also point out that Levin and Sklar have advanced no other reason why the Garr complaint had to have been filed within two days of the publication of the article. They do not contend, for example, that the Garrs needed emergency relief, nor do they suggest that U.S. Healthcare or Abramson might have evaded process or concealed assets if the suit had not been filed so quickly. While at oral argument the suggestion was made that class actions are brought quickly so that the attorney filing the case may control the litigation, we would not regard that reason as in any way detracting from the reasonable inquiry otherwise required under Rule 11.

At bottom, there is no escape from the conclusion that Levin and Sklar abdicated their own responsibilities and relied excessively on Malone contrary to Rule 11. Furthermore, they did not rely on Malone only as to some small portion of the case. Rather, they relied on his inquiry to justify the entire cause of action. Indeed, they filed the complaint Malone had prepared, changing only the name of the plaintiffs and the number of shares owned. We recognize that it could be argued that it would have been pointless for Levin and Sklar to make an inquiry into the merits of the case sufficient to satisfy Rule 11 as Malone already had done so. Yet Rule 11 requires that an attorney signing a pleading must make a reasonable inquiry personally. The advantage of duplicate personal inquiries is manifest: while one attorney might find a complaint well founded in fact and warranted by the law, another, even after examining the materials available to the first attorney, could come to a contrary conclusion. Overall, we conclude that the Rule 11 violation in this case is so clear that even on a plenary review, we would uphold the sanctions imposed on Levin and Sklar. Accordingly, under the deferential abuse of discretion standard, we certainly must affirm the district court's determination that sanctions were required.

* * *

III.　Conclusion

The orders of February 5, 1993, and July 6, 1993, will be affirmed.

ROTH, CIRCUIT JUDGE, dissenting:

Although I share the majority's view that Levin and Sklar's conduct fell far short of the ideal, I do not share its belief that Rule 11 sanctions are appropriate in this situation. Instead, I believe that, when a court finds that an attorney has filed a meritorious complaint, the court should not go on to inquire whether the attorney conducted an adequate investigation prior to filing the complaint. I therefore respectfully dissent.

Except for changes in the named plaintiffs and the number of shares they owned, the complaint filed by Levin and Sklar on behalf of the Garrs was identical to the complaints filed by Malone on behalf of Greenfield and Strunk. As the majority notes, the district court did not dismiss the Strunk complaint, thereby implicitly finding that on its face it stated a valid claim. Presumably, had the district court not determined that Levin and Sklar violated Rule 11, it would not have dismissed the Garr complaint. Thus it is safe to assume that the district court believed that the Garr complaint on its face was meritorious.

In holding that the imposition of sanctions was appropriate in this case, the majority relies on the following statement in an opinion from a district court in another circuit: "A shot in the dark is a sanctionable event, even if it somehow hits the mark." *Vista Mfg., Inc. v. Trac-4, Inc., 131 F.R.D. 134, 138 (N.D.Ind. 1990)*. Though this statement has the virtue of being colorful, as the basis of the majority's reasoning it suffers from three flaws. First, Vista does not support the majority's position; despite the quoted statement the court imposed no sanctions. Second, in relying on Vista the majority overlooks apparent statements of law to the contrary by the Vista court's own circuit, the Seventh, and by the Second Circuit. Finally, the majority's conclusion that the Vista rule is necessary to further the purposes of Rule 11 is the product of an incomplete analysis of both the policies animating Rule 11 and the impact of that rule on the effectiveness of Rule 11. I shall address these latter two points in turn.

The Seventh Circuit, a very aggressive court in terms of enforcing Rule 11 * * * observed pre-Vista that for purposes of Rule 11 "an attorney takes a frivolous position if he fails to make a reasonable inquiry into facts (which later prove false) or takes a position unwarranted by existing law or a good faith argument for its modification." *Magnus Elecs. v. Masco Corp. of Indiana, 871 F.2d 626, 629 (7th Cir.),* cert. denied, *493 U.S. 891 (1989).* * * *

Indeed, this court has remarked that we "have interpreted [Rule 11's] language to prescribe sanctions, including fees, only in the 'exceptional circumstance' * * * where a claim or motion is patently unmeritorious or frivolous." *Doering v. Union County Bd. of Chosen Freeholders, 857 F.2d 191, 194 (3d Cir. 1988)*(citation omitted). Taken as a whole, these cases support the notion that sanctions are inappropriate where, as here, there was a reasonable basis for a complaint even if the attorney filing it failed adequately to inquire into the existence of that basis.

I believe the majority is mistaken in asserting that this rule would frustrate the purposes of Rule 11. The Supreme Court has stated that

> "the central purpose of Rule 11 is to deter baseless filings in the District Court and thus, consistent with the Rule Enabling Act's grant of authority, streamline the administration and procedure of the federal courts.... Although the rule must be read in light of concerns that it will spawn satellite litigation and chill vigorous advocacy ... any interpretation must give effect to the rule's central goal of deterrence. *Cooter & Gell v. Hartmarx Corp., 496 U.S. 384, 110 S. Ct. 2447, 2454, 110 L. Ed. 2d 359 (1990)."*

Similarly, the Advisory Committee indicated that the purpose of Rule 11 is "to discourage dilatory or abusive tactics and to help streamline the litigation process by lessening frivolous claims or defenses." Notes of the Advisory Committee on Rules, 1983 Amendment, *Fed. R.Civ.P. 11*, reprinted in *97 F.R.D. 165, 200 (1983)*.

On the whole, the goals of deterring abuses of the system and streamlining litigation would be better served by the standard I advocate. Because the vast majority of "shots in the dark" will not hit their target, almost all of them will be subject to sanction. I find it difficult to believe that this slightly reduced probability of sanction will encourage lawyers to take blind shots. The deterrent function of Rule 11 to prevent baseless filings will not be undermined by not sanctioning when a complaint on its face does have merit. As the Second and Seventh Circuits have implicitly recognized, the best evidence of an inadequate investigation will often be the fact that a complaint states a frivolous claim. Without that evidence, the inquiry becomes considerably more speculative.

Moreover, in cases in which the complaint states a meritorious claim, we must consider whether we want to encourage a secondary line of inquiry into the adequacy of the attorney's research. I believe that opening up such a line of attack, which will require courts to engage in pure speculation in the worst case and will lead to a waste of the court's time and resources in the best case, will create a greater clog in the courts' efficient functioning than will the failure to sanction the rare case of the successful shot in the dark.

The majority is eager to sanction counsel in this case because it believes sanctions are necessary to discourage the indiscriminate filing of lawsuits. As I have pointed out above, it is unlikely that the majority's rule would have a greater effect in this regard than my standard. Ironically, however, the majority's approach will encourage the indiscriminate filing of motions for sanctions. This case, in which the motion for sanctions was prepared before defendants had even seen the Garr complaint and was waiting at the courthouse for the complaint to be filed, provides a perfect example of the sort of behavior that the majority's reasoning will encourage. Were the court to hold that facially meritorious but inadequately investigated complaints are not subject to sanction, defendants would have less incentive to file such motions. * * *

Simply stated, I believe that the majority, in its eagerness to uphold sanctions against the inexcusable behavior by the attorneys in this case, overlooks the fact that its holding will frustrate rather than further the goals of Rule 11. I would reverse the district court's imposition of Rule 11 sanctions against Levin and Sklar.

* * *

B. DOCUMENT PRESERVATION AND DESTRUCTION

Corporations generate billions of pages of documents and a comparable amount of information in electronic form on an ongoing basis. Much of this material becomes outdated or useless over time. Any company that hopes to operate efficiently must adopt a document retention policy. This policy instructs employees how long they must preserve various types of documents and when it is appropriate to destroy them. The periodic purge conducted according to this policy is perfectly appropriate. The policy should also indicate, however, when material that ordinarily would be destroyed under the policy must be preserved because it may be relevant to legal proceedings. As the material below describes, failure to preserve such material can be costly, resulting in criminal or civil sanctions.

Corporate civil litigation typically involves large amounts of documents. When companies must preserve and when they may destroy documents is an important issue in litigation. Parties involved in current or anticipated legal proceedings have an obligation to retain material that may be relevant in those proceedings.

1. CRIMINAL STATUTE

The most serious sanction for violation of the duty to preserve possible evidence is criminal prosecution. For instance, 18 U.S.C. 1503 provides that anyone who "corruptly ... influences, obstructs, or impedes, or endeavors to impede, the due administration of justice" may be fined up to $5,000 and/or imprisoned up to five years. Liability under this statute requires that there be a pending legal proceeding. An ongoing investigation, even one that is highly likely to result in institution of a formal legal proceeding, is insufficient to create liability. *United States v. Baum, 32 F.Supp.2d 642 (S.D.N.Y. 1999); United States v. Smith, 729 F.Supp. 1380 (D.D.C. 1990).* Impaneling a grand jury may constitute such a proceeding; when this has occurred, the grand jury may not need to have issued a subpoena for Section 1503 to apply. *United States v. Gravely, 840 F.2d 1156, 1160 (4th Cir. 1988). But see United States v. Ellis, 652 F.Supp. 1451, 1453 (S.D. Miss. 1987)*(refusing to find proceeding pending where grand jury had been impaneled but no subpoena had been issued). The documents in question need not be material or even admissible, but simply need be relevant. *United States v. Siegel, 152 F.Supp. 370, 375 (S.D.N.Y. 1957), aff'd 263 F.2d 530 (2d Cir. 1959).* In order to be liable, an actor must have "knowledge that his actions are likely to affect a judicial proceeding." *United States v. Aguilar, 515 U.S. 593, 599, 115 S.Ct. 2357, 132 L.Ed.2d 520 (1995).* A violation of Section 1503 can occur not only with respect to criminal proceedings, but can include the willful destruction of documents in pre-trial discovery in civil litigation. *United States v. Lundwall, 1 F.Supp.2d 249 (S.D.N.Y. 1998).* Violating Section 1503 is punishable by fine and imprisonment up to five years.

18 U.S.C. Section 1512(b) imposes criminal liability on anyone who "corruptly persuades" or "cause[s] or induce[s]" another person to "alter, destroy, mutilate, or conceal an object with intent to impair the object's integrity or availability for use in an official proceeding." Section 1512(f) provides that an official proceeding need not be pending or about to be instituted. A defendant can be liable if he induces another to destroy or alter evidence to impair its integrity or availability in an investigation that the defendant has reasonable cause to believe may be about to commence. *See, e.g., United States v. Conneaut Indus., 852 F.Supp. 116 (D.R.I. 1994).* 18 U.S.C. Section 1512(c)(1) imposes liability on anyone who himself who corruptly alters, destroys, or conceals evidence, or attempts to do so, with intent to impair its availability for use in an official proceeding.

Finally, Congress enacted 18 U.S.C. Section 1519 under the Sarbanes-Oxley legislation. It states that anyone who "knowingly alters, destroys, mutilates, conceals, covers up, falsifies, or makes a false entry in any record [or] document ... with the intent to impede, obstruct, or influence the investigation or proper administration" of any matter within the jurisdiction of a federal agency or bankruptcy courts subject to fine and/or imprisonment up to 20 years. The legislative history indicates that there need not be a pending or imminent proceeding, but only a possible future investigation. 148 Cong. Rec, S7418 (daily ed. July 25, 2002) (statement of Senator Leahy).

Note

In the case excerpted below, the Supreme Court reversed the conviction of the Arthur Andersen accounting firm for obstruction of justice in connection with its destruction of material relating to the firm's work for Enron Corporation. The Court found that the jury had been erroneously instructed that it could find a violation of 18 U.S.C. 1512(b) without finding that Andersen had acted "dishonestly," and that it could convict even if the accounting firm "honestly and sincerely believed that its conduct was lawful." The Court also held that the jury had not been instructed that it had to find that corrupt persuasion was exerted to destroy documents relevant to a particular proceeding. As you read the excerpt, consider whether the jury reasonably could have found Andersen guilty if it had been properly instructed.

ARTHUR ANDERSEN LLP v. UNITED STATES

125 S.Ct. 2129 (2005)

CHIEF JUSTICE REHNQUIST DELIVERED THE OPINION OF THE COURT.

As Enron Corporation's financial difficulties became public in 2001, petitioner Arthur Andersen LLP, Enron's auditor, instructed its employees to destroy documents pursuant to its document retention policy. A jury found that this action made petitioner guilty of violating *18 U.S.C. §§ 1512(b)(2)(A)* and *(B)*. These sections make it a crime to "knowingly use intimidation or physical force, threaten, or corruptly persuade another person * * * with intent to * * * cause" that person to "withhold" documents from, or "alter" documents for use in, an "official proceeding." The Court of Appeals for the Fifth Circuit affirmed. We hold that the jury instructions failed to convey properly the elements of a "corrupt persuasion" conviction under *§ 1512(b)*, and therefore reverse.

Enron Corporation, during the 1990's, switched its business from operation of natural gas pipelines to an energy conglomerate, a move that was accompanied by aggressive accounting practices and rapid growth. Petitioner audited Enron's publicly filed financial statements and provided internal audit and consulting services to it. Petitioner's "engagement team" for Enron was headed by David Duncan. Beginning in 2000, Enron's financial performance began to suffer, and, as 2001 wore on, worsened. On August 14, 2001, Jeffrey Skilling, Enron's Chief Executive Officer (CEO), unexpectedly resigned. Within days, Sherron Watkins, a senior accountant at Enron, warned Kenneth Lay, Enron's newly reappointed CEO, that Enron could "implode in a wave of accounting scandals." She likewise informed Duncan and Michael Odom, one of petitioner's partners who had supervisory responsibility over Duncan, of the looming problems.

On August 28, an article in the Wall Street Journal suggested improprieties at Enron, and the SEC opened an informal investigation. By early September, petitioner had formed an Enron "crisis-response" team, which included Nancy Temple, an in-house counsel. On October 8, petitioner retained outside counsel to represent it in any litigation that might arise from the Enron matter. The next day, Temple discussed Enron with other in-house counsel. Her notes from that meeting reflect that "some SEC investigation" is "highly probable."

On October 10, Odom spoke at a general training meeting attended by 89 employees, including 10 from the Enron engagement team. Odom urged everyone to comply with the firm's document retention policy. He added: " 'If it's destroyed in the course of [the] normal policy and litigation is filed the next day, that's great. . . . We've followed our own policy, and whatever there was that might have been of interest to somebody is gone and irretrievable.' " On October 12, Temple entered the Enron matter into her computer, designating the "Type of Potential Claim" as "Professional Practice—Government/Regulatory Investigation." Temple also e-mailed Odom, suggesting that he " 'remind the engagement team of our documentation and retention policy.' "[1]

On October 16, Enron announced its third quarter results. That release disclosed a $1.01 billion charge to earnings. The following day, the SEC notified Enron by letter that it had opened an investigation in August and requested certain information and documents. On October 19, Enron forwarded a copy of that letter to petitioner.

On the same day, Temple also sent an e-mail to a member of petitioner's internal team of accounting experts and attached a copy of the document policy. On October 20, the Enron crisis-response team held a conference call, during which Temple instructed everyone to "make sure to follow the [document] policy." On October 23, Enron CEO Lay declined to answer questions during a call with analysts because of "potential lawsuits, as well as the SEC inquiry." After the call, Duncan met with other Andersen partners on the Enron engagement team and told them that they should ensure team members were complying with the document policy. Another meeting for all team members followed, during which Duncan distributed the policy and told everyone to comply. These, and other smaller meetings, were followed by substantial destruction of paper and electronic documents.

On October 26, one of petitioner's senior partners circulated a New York Times article discussing the SEC's response to Enron. His e-mail commented that "the problems are just beginning and we will be in the cross hairs. The marketplace is going to keep the pressure on this and is going to force the SEC to be tough." On October 30, the SEC opened a formal investigation and sent Enron a letter that requested accounting documents.

Throughout this time period, the document destruction continued, despite reservations by some of petitioner's managers. On November 8, Enron announced that it would issue a comprehensive restatement of its earnings and assets. Also on November 8, the SEC served Enron and petitioner with subpoenas for records.[2] On November 9, Duncan's secretary sent an e-mail that stated: "Per Dave—No more shredding. . . . We have been officially served for our documents." Enron filed for bankruptcy less than a month later. Duncan was fired and later pleaded guilty to witness tampering.

In March 2002, petitioner was indicted in the Southern District of Texas on one count of violating §§ *1512(b)(2)(A)* and *(B)*. The indictment

1. That policy provided for retention "only of information which is relevant to supporting our work" on an engagement, and for the destruction of all other material, including draft work papers—Eds.

2. The following day, Temple left a voicemail with the Enron engagement team informing it of the subpoena and of the need to preserve material relevant to it, as well as to a lawsuit filed against Andersen and another suit reported in the press. On November 10, Temple elaborated on this message by sending an email to Duncan and others with the instruction to "take all necessary steps to preserve all of the documents and materials already in existence," and to ensure that "nothing is done to destroy or discard any of the information and materials now in your possession."– Eds.

alleged that, between October 10 and November 9, 2001, petitioner "did knowingly, intentionally and corruptly persuade ... other persons, to wit: [petitioner's] employees, with intent to cause" them to withhold documents from, and alter documents for use in, "official proceedings, namely: regulatory and criminal proceedings and investigations." A jury trial followed, [and] the jury returned a guilty verdict. The District Court denied petitioner's motion for a judgment of acquittal.

The Court of Appeals for the Fifth Circuit affirmed * * *

"Document retention policies," which are created in part to keep certain information from getting into the hands of others, including the Government, are common in business. It is, of course, not wrongful for a manager to instruct his employees to comply with a valid document retention policy under ordinary circumstances.

Acknowledging this point, the parties have largely focused their attention on the word "corruptly" as the key to what may or may not lawfully be done in the situation presented here. *Section 1512(b)* punishes not just "corruptly persuading" another, but *"knowingly* ... corruptly persuading" another. (Emphasis added.) ...

* * * "Knowledge" and "knowingly" are normally associated with awareness, understanding, or consciousness. "Corrupt" and "corruptly" are normally associated with wrongful, immoral, depraved, or evil. Joining these meanings together here makes sense both linguistically and in the statutory scheme. Only persons conscious of wrongdoing can be said to "knowingly ... corruptly persuade." And limiting criminality to persuaders conscious of their wrongdoing sensibly allows *§ 1512(b)* to reach only those with the level of "culpability ... we usually require in order to impose criminal liability."

The outer limits of this element need not be explored here because the jury instructions at issue simply failed to convey the requisite consciousness of wrongdoing. Indeed, it is striking how little culpability the instructions required. For example, the jury was told that, "even if [petitioner] honestly and sincerely believed that its conduct was lawful, you may find [petitioner] guilty." The instructions also diluted the meaning of "corruptly" so that it covered innocent conduct.

The parties vigorously disputed how the jury would be instructed on "corruptly." The District Court based its instruction on the definition of that term found in the Fifth Circuit Pattern Jury Instruction for *§ 1503*. This pattern instruction defined "corruptly" as " 'knowingly and dishonestly, with the specific intent to subvert or undermine the integrity' " of a proceeding. The Government, however, insisted on excluding "dishonestly" and adding the term "impede" to the phrase "subvert or undermine." The District Court agreed over petitioner's objections, and the jury was told to convict if it found petitioner intended to "subvert, undermine, or impede" governmental factfinding by suggesting to its employees that they enforce the document retention policy.

These changes were significant. No longer was any type of "dishonesty" necessary to a finding of guilt, and it was enough for petitioner to have simply "impeded" the Government's factfinding ability. As the Government conceded at oral argument, " 'impede' " has broader connotations than " 'subvert' " or even " 'undermine,' " and many of these connotations do not incorporate any "corruptness" at all. The dictionary defines "impede" as "to interfere with or get in the way of the progress of" or "hold up" or "detract from." By definition, anyone who innocently persuades another to withhold information from the Government "gets in the way of the progress of" the Government. With regard to such innocent conduct, the "corruptly" instructions did no limiting work whatsoever.

The instructions also were infirm for another reason. They led the jury to believe that it did not have to find *any* nexus between the "persuasion" to destroy documents and any particular proceeding. In resisting any type of nexus element, the Government relies heavily on § 1512(e)(1), which states that an official proceeding "need not be pending or about to be instituted at the time of the offense." It is, however, one thing to say that a proceeding "need not be pending or about to be instituted at the time of the offense," and quite another to say a proceeding need not even be foreseen. A "knowingly ... corrupt persauder" cannot be someone who persuades others to shred documents under a document retention policy when he does not have in contemplation any particular official proceeding in which those documents might be material. * * *

For these reasons, the jury instructions here were flawed in important respects. The judgment of the Court of Appeals is reversed, and the case is remanded for further proceedings consistent with this opinion.

Question

Was there enough evidence to convict Arthur Andersen if the jury had been given the Fifth Circuit Pattern instruction that to act corruptly the defendant must act "knowingly and dishonestly, with the specific intent to subvert or undermine the integrity" of a proceeding, and that it must do so with a particular proceeding in mind?

2. COMMON LAW

The doctrine of spoliation provides another form of sanction for the failure to preserve potentially relevant evidence. It authorizes a court to impose penalties in the course of a civil proceeding. As the case below describes, the widespread existence of evidence in electronic form can impose distinctive obligations on counsel to ensure that clients preserve potentially relevant information.

ZUBULAKE v. UBS WARBURG

2004 WL 1620866 (S.D. N.Y. 2004)

Shira A. Scheindlin, U.S.D.J.:

* * *

I. INTRODUCTION

This is the fifth written opinion in this case, a relatively routine employment discrimination dispute in which discovery has now lasted over two years. Laura Zubulake is once again moving to sanction UBS for its failure to produce relevant information and for its tardy production of such material. In order to decide whether sanctions are warranted, the following question must be answered: Did UBS fail to preserve and timely produce relevant information and, if so, did it act negligently, recklessly, or willfully?

This decision addresses counsel's obligation to ensure that relevant information is preserved by giving clear instructions to the client to preserve such information and, perhaps more importantly, a client's obligation to heed those instructions. Early on in this litigation, UBS's counsel—both in-house and outside—instructed UBS personnel to retain relevant electronic information. Notwithstanding these instructions, certain UBS employees deleted relevant emails. Other employees never produced relevant information to counsel. As a result, many discoverable e-mails were not produced to Zubulake until recently, even though they were responsive to a document request propounded on June 3, 2002.[3] In addition, a number of e-mails responsive to that document request were deleted and have been lost altogether.

Counsel, in turn, failed to request retained information from one key employee and to give the litigation hold instructions to another. They also failed to adequately communicate with another employee about how she maintained her computer files. Counsel also failed to safeguard backup tapes that might have contained some of the deleted e-mails, and which would have mitigated the damage done by UBS's destruction of those e-mails.

The conduct of both counsel and client thus calls to mind the now-famous words of the prison captain in *Cool Hand Luke:* "What we've got here is a failure to communicate." Because of this failure by *both* UBS and its counsel, Zubulake has been prejudiced. As a result, sanctions are warranted.

II. FACTS

The allegations at the heart of this lawsuit and the history of the parties' discovery disputes have been well-documented in the Court's

---

3. *See Zubulake v. UBS Warburg LLC, 217 F.R.D. 309, 312 (S.D.N.Y. 2003)* ("*Zubulake I*") (quoting Zubulake's document request, which called for "all documents concerning any communications by or be- tween UBS employees concerning Plaintiff," and defining "document" to include "without limitation, electronic or computerized data compilations."

prior decisions, familiarity with which is presumed. In short, Zubulake is an equities trader specializing in Asian securities who is suing her former employer for gender discrimination, failure to promote, and retaliation under federal, state, and city law.

A. Background

Zubulake filed an initial charge of gender discrimination with the EEOC on August 16, 2001. Well before that, however—as early as April 2001—UBS employees were on notice of Zubulake's impending court action. After she received a right-to-sue letter from the EEOC, Zubulake filed this lawsuit on February 15, 2002.

Fully aware of their common law duty to preserve relevant evidence, UBS's in-house attorneys gave oral instructions in August 2001—immediately after Zubulake filed her EEOC charge—instructing employees not to destroy or delete material potentially relevant to Zubulake's claims, and in fact to segregate such material into separate files for the lawyers' eventual review. This warning pertained to both electronic and hard-copy files, but did *not* specifically pertain to so-called "backup tapes," maintained by UBS's information technology personnel. In particular, UBS's in-house counsel, Robert L. Salzberg, "advised relevant UBS employees to preserve and turn over to counsel all files, records or other written memoranda or documents concerning the allegations raised in the [EEOC] charge or any aspect of [Zubulake's] employment." Subsequently—but still in August 2001—UBS's outside counsel met with a number of the key players in the litigation and reiterated Mr. Salzberg's instructions, reminding them to preserve relevant documents, "including e-mails." Salzberg reduced these instructions to writing in e-mails dated February 22, 2002—immediately after Zubulake filed her complaint—and September 25, 2002. Finally, in August 2002, after Zubulake propounded a document request that specifically called for e-mails stored on backup tapes, UBS's outside counsel instructed UBS information technology personnel to stop recycling backup tapes. *Every* UBS employee mentioned in this Opinion (with the exception of Mike Davies) either personally spoke to UBS's outside counsel about the duty to preserve e-mails, or was a recipient of one of Salzberg's e-mails....

C. The Instant Dispute

The essence of the current dispute is that during the re-depositions required by *Zubulake IV*, Zubulake learned about more deleted e-mails and about the existence of e-mails preserved on UBS's active servers that were, to that point, never produced. In sum, Zubulake has now presented evidence that UBS personnel deleted relevant e-mails, some of which were subsequently recovered from backup tapes (or elsewhere) and thus produced to Zubulake long after her initial document requests, and some of which were lost altogether. Zubulake has also presented evidence that some UBS personnel did not produce responsive documents to counsel until recently, depriving Zubulake of the documents for almost two years.

* * *

III. LEGAL STANDARD

Spoliation is "the destruction or significant alteration of evidence, or the failure to preserve property for another's use as evidence in pending or reasonably foreseeable litigation." "The determination of an appropriate sanction for spoliation, if any, is confined to the sound discretion of the trial judge, and is assessed on a case-by-case basis." The authority to sanction litigants for spoliation arises jointly under the Federal Rules of Civil Procedure and the court's inherent powers.

The spoliation of evidence germane "to proof of an issue at trial can support an inference that the evidence would have been unfavorable to the party responsible for its destruction." A party seeking an adverse inference instruction (or other sanctions) based on the spoliation of evidence must establish the following three elements: (1) that the party having control over the evidence had an obligation to preserve it at the time it was destroyed; (2) that the records were destroyed with a "culpable state of mind" and (3) that the destroyed evidence was "relevant" to the party's claim or defense such that a reasonable trier of fact could find that it would support that claim or defense.

In this circuit, a "culpable state of mind" for purposes of a spoliation inference includes ordinary negligence. When evidence is destroyed in bad faith (*i.e.,* intentionally or willfully), that fact alone is sufficient to demonstrate relevance. By contrast, when the destruction is negligent, relevance must be proven by the party seeking the sanctions.

In the context of a request for an adverse inference instruction, the concept of "relevance" encompasses not only the ordinary meaning of the term, but also that the destroyed evidence would have been favorable to the movant. "This corroboration requirement is even more necessary where the destruction was merely negligent, since in those cases it cannot be inferred from the conduct of the spoliator that the evidence would even have been harmful to him." This is equally true in cases of gross negligence or recklessness; only in the case of *willful* spoliation does the degree of culpability give rise to a presumption of the relevance of the documents destroyed.

IV. DISCUSSION

In *Zubulake IV,* I held that UBS had a duty to preserve its employees' active files as early as April 2001, and certainly by August 2001, when Zubulake filed her EEOC charge. Zubulake has thus satisfied the first element of the adverse inference test. As noted, the central question implicated by this motion is whether UBS and its counsel took all necessary steps to guarantee that relevant data was both preserved and produced. If the answer is "no," then the next question is whether UBS acted wilfully when it deleted or failed to timely produce relevant information—resulting in either a complete loss or the production of responsive information close to two years after it was initially sought. If UBS acted wilfully, this satisfies the mental culpability prong of the adverse inference test and also demonstrates that the deleted material was relevant. If UBS acted negligently or even recklessly, then Zubulake must show that the missing or late-produced information was relevant.

A. Counsel's Duty to Monitor Compliance

In *Zubulake IV,* I summarized a litigant's preservation obligations:

"Once a party reasonably anticipates litigation, it must suspend its routine document retention/destruction policy and put in place a "litigation hold" to ensure the preservation of relevant documents. As a general rule, that litigation hold does not apply to inaccessible backup tapes (*e.g.,* those typically maintained solely for the purpose of disaster recovery), which may continue to be recycled on the schedule set forth in the company's policy. On the other hand, if backup tapes are accessible (*i.e.,* actively used for information retrieval), then such tapes *would* likely be subject to the litigation hold."

A party's discovery obligations do not end with the implementation of a "litigation hold"—to the contrary, that's only the beginning. Counsel must oversee compliance with the litigation hold, monitoring the party's efforts to retain and produce the relevant documents. Proper communication between a party and her lawyer will ensure (1) that all relevant information (or at least all sources of relevant information) is discovered, (2) that relevant information is retained on a continuing basis; and (3) that relevant non-privileged material is produced to the opposing party.

1. Counsel's Duty to Locate Relevant Information

Once a "litigation hold" is in place, a party and her counsel must make certain that all sources of potentially relevant information are identified and placed "on hold," to the extent required in *Zubulake IV.* To do this, counsel must become fully familiar with her client's document retention policies, as well as the client's data retention architecture. This will invariably involve speaking with information technology personnel, who can explain system-wide backup procedures and the actual (as opposed to theoretical) implementation of the firm's recycling policy. It will also involve communicating with the "key players" in the litigation, in order to understand how they stored information. In this case, for example, some UBS employees created separate computer files pertaining to Zubulake, while others printed out relevant e-mails and retained them in hard copy only. Unless counsel interviews each employee, it is impossible to determine whether all potential sources of information have been inspected. A brief conversation with counsel, for example, might have revealed that Tong maintained "archive" copies of e-mails concerning Zubulake, and that "archive" meant a separate on-line computer file, not a backup tape. Had that conversation taken place, Zubulake might have had relevant e-mails from that file two years ago.

To the extent that it may not be feasible for counsel to speak with every key player, given the size of a company or the scope of the lawsuit, counsel must be more creative. It may be possible to run a system-wide keyword search; counsel could then preserve a copy of each "hit." Although this sounds burdensome, it need not be. Counsel does not have to review these documents, only see that they are retained. For example, counsel could create a broad list of search terms, run a search for a limited time frame, and then segregate responsive documents. When the opposing party propounds its document requests, the parties could negotiate a list of search terms to be used in identifying responsive documents, and counsel would only be obliged to review documents that came up as "hits" on the second, more restrictive search. The initial broad cut merely guarantees that relevant documents are not lost.

In short, it is *not* sufficient to notify all employees of a litigation hold and expect that the party will then retain and produce all relevant information. Counsel must take affirmative steps to monitor compliance so that all sources of discoverable information are identified and searched. This is not to say that counsel will necessarily succeed in locating all such sources, or that the later discovery of new sources is evidence of a lack of effort. But counsel and client must take *some reasonable steps* to see that sources of relevant information are located.

2. Counsel's Continuing Duty to Ensure Preservation

Once a party and her counsel have identified all of the sources of potentially relevant information, they are under a duty to retain that information (as per *Zubulake IV*) and to produce information responsive to the opposing party's requests. *Rule 26* creates a "duty to supplement" those responses. Although the *Rule 26* duty to supplement is nominally the party's, it really falls on counsel. As the Advisory Committee explains,

> "Although the party signs the answers, it is his lawyer who understands their significance and bears the responsibility to bring answers up to date. In a complex case all sorts of information reaches the party, who little understands its bearing on answers previously given to interrogatories. In practice, therefore, the lawyer under a continuing burden must periodically recheck all interrogatories and canvass all new information."

To ameliorate this burden, the Rules impose a continuing duty to supplement responses to discovery requests *only* when "a party[,] or more frequently his lawyer, obtains actual knowledge that a prior response is incorrect. This exception does not impose a duty to check the accuracy of prior responses, but it prevents knowing concealment by a party or attorney."

The *continuing* duty to supplement disclosures strongly suggests that parties also have a duty to make sure that discoverable information is not lost. Indeed, the notion of a "duty to preserve" connotes an ongoing obligation. Obviously, if information is lost or destroyed, it has not been preserved.

The tricky question is what that continuing duty entails. What must a lawyer do to make certain that relevant information—especially electronic information—is being retained? Is it sufficient if she periodically re-sends her initial "litigation hold" instructions? What if she communicates with the party's information technology personnel? Must she make occasional on-site inspections?

Above all, the requirement must be reasonable. A lawyer cannot be obliged to monitor her client like a parent watching a child. At some point, the client must bear responsibility for a failure to preserve. At the same time, counsel is more conscious of the contours of the preservation obligation; a party cannot reasonably be trusted to receive the "litigation hold" instruction once and to fully comply with it without the active supervision of counsel.

There are thus a number of steps that counsel should take to ensure compliance with the preservation obligation. While these precautions may not be enough (or may be too much) in some cases, they are designed to promote the continued preservation of potentially relevant information in the typical case.

First, counsel must issue a "litigation hold" at the outset of litigation or whenever litigation is reasonably anticipated. The litigation hold should be periodically re-issued so that new employees are aware of it, and so that it is fresh in the minds of all employees.

Second, counsel should communicate directly with the "key players" in the litigation, *i.e.,* the people identified in a party's initial disclosure and any subsequent supplementation thereto. Because these "key players" are the "employees likely to have relevant information," it is particularly important that the preservation duty be communicated clearly to them. As with the litigation hold, the key players should be periodically reminded that the preservation duty is still in place.

Finally, counsel should instruct all employees to produce electronic copies of their relevant active files. Counsel must also make sure that all backup media which the party is required to retain is identified and stored in a safe place. In cases involving a small number of relevant backup tapes, counsel might be advised to take physical possession of backup tapes. In other cases, it might make sense for relevant backup tapes to be segregated and placed in storage. Regardless of what particular arrangement counsel chooses to employ, the point is to separate relevant backup tapes from others. One of the primary reasons that electronic data is lost is ineffective communication with information technology personnel. By taking possession of, or otherwise safeguarding, all potentially relevant backup tapes, counsel eliminates the possibility that such tapes will be inadvertently recycled.

3.   *What Happened at UBS After August 2001?*

As more fully described above, UBS's in-house counsel issued a litigation hold in August 2001 and repeated that instruction several times from September 2001 through September 2002. Outside counsel also spoke with some (but not all) of the key players in August 2001. Nonetheless, certain employees unquestionably deleted e-mails. Although many of the deleted e-mails were recovered from backup tapes, a number of backup tapes—and the e-mails on them—are lost forever. Other employees, notwithstanding counsel's request that they produce their files on Zubulake, did not do so.

a. UBS's Discovery Failings

UBS's counsel—both in-house and outside—repeatedly advised UBS of its discovery obligations. In fact, counsel came very close to taking the precautions laid out above. *First,* outside counsel issued a litigation hold in August 2001. The hold order was circulated to many of the key players in this litigation, and reiterated in e-mails in February 2002, when suit was filed, and again in September 2002. Outside counsel made clear that the hold order applied to backup tapes in August 2002, as soon as backup tapes became an issue in this case. *Second,* outside counsel communicated directly with many of the key players in August 2001 and attempted to impress upon them their preservation obligations. *Third,* and finally, counsel instructed UBS employees to produce copies of their active computer files.

To be sure, counsel did not fully comply with the standards set forth above. Nonetheless, under the standards existing at the time, counsel acted reasonably to the extent that they directed UBS to implement a litigation hold. Yet notwithstanding the clear instructions of counsel, UBS personnel failed to preserve plainly relevant e-mails.

b. Counsel's Failings

On the other hand, UBS's counsel are not entirely blameless. "While, of course, it is true that counsel need not supervise every step of the document production process and may rely on their clients in some respects," counsel is responsible for coordinating her client's discovery efforts. In this case, counsel failed to properly oversee UBS in a number of important ways, both in terms of its duty to locate relevant information and its duty to preserve and timely produce that information.

With respect to locating relevant information, counsel failed to adequately communicate with Tong about how she stored data. Although counsel determined that Tong kept her files on Zubulake in an "archive," they apparently made no effort to learn what that meant. A few simple questions—like the ones that Zubulake's counsel asked at Tong's re-deposition—would have revealed that she kept those files in a separate *active* file on her computer.

With respect to making sure that relevant data was retained, counsel failed in a number of important respects. *First,* neither in-house nor outside counsel communicated the litigation hold instructions to Mike Davies, a senior human resources employee who was intimately involved in Zubulake's termination. *Second,* even though the litigation hold instructions were communicated to Kim, no one ever asked her to produce her files. And *third,* counsel failed to protect relevant backup tapes; had they done so, Zubulake might have been able to recover some of the e-mails that UBS employees deleted.

In addition, if Varsano's deposition testimony is to be credited, he turned over "all of the e-mails that [he] received concerning Ms. Zubulake." If Varsano turned over these e-mails, then counsel must have failed to produce some of them.

In sum, while UBS personnel deleted e-mails, copies of many of these e-mails were lost or belatedly produced as a result of counsel's failures.

c. Summary

Counsel failed to communicate the litigation hold order to all key players. They also failed to ascertain each of the key players' document management habits. By the same token, UBS employees—for unknown reasons—ignored many of the instructions that counsel gave. This case represents a failure of communication, and that failure falls on counsel and client alike.

At the end of the day, however, the duty to preserve and produce documents rests on the party. Once that duty is made clear to a party, either by court order or by instructions from counsel, that party is on notice of its obligations and acts at its own peril. Though more diligent action on the part of counsel would have mitigated some of the damage caused by UBS's deletion of emails, UBS deleted the e-mails in defiance of explicit instructions not to.

Because UBS personnel continued to delete relevant e-mails, Zubulake was denied access to e-mails to which she was entitled. Even those e-mails that were deleted but ultimately salvaged from other sources (*e.g.*, backup tapes or Tong and Kim's active files) were produced 22 months after they were initially requested. The effect of losing potentially relevant e-mails is obvious, but the effect of late production cannot be underestimated either * * * I therefore conclude that UBS acted wilfully in destroying potentially relevant information, which resulted either in the absence of such information or its tardy production (because duplicates were recovered from Kim or Tong's active files, or restored from backup tapes). Because UBS's spoliation was willful, the lost information is presumed to be relevant.

B. Remedy

Having concluded that UBS was under a duty to preserve the e-mails and that it deleted presumably relevant e-mails wilfully, I now consider the full panoply of available sanctions. In doing so, I recognize that a major consideration in choosing an appropriate sanction—along with punishing UBS and deterring future misconduct—is to restore Zubulake to the position that she would have been in had UBS faithfully discharged its discovery obligations. That being so, I find that the following sanctions are warranted.

First, the jury empanelled to hear this case will be given an adverse inference instruction with respect to e-mails deleted after August 2001, and in particular, with respect to e-mails that were irretrievably lost when UBS's backup tapes were recycled. No one can ever know precisely what was on those tapes, but the content of e-mails recovered from other sources—along with the fact that UBS employees wilfully deleted e-mails—is sufficiently favorable to Zubulake that I am convinced that the contents of the lost tapes would have been similarly, if not more, favorable.

Note that I am *not* sanctioning UBS for the loss of the tapes (which was negligent), but rather for its *willful* deletion of e-mails. Those e-mails happen to be lost forever because the tapes that might otherwise have contained them were lost.

Second, Zubulake argues that the e-mails that *were* produced, albeit late, "are brand new and very significant to Ms. Zubulake's retaliation claim and would have affected [her] examination of every witness . . . in this case." Likewise, Zubulake claims, with respect to the newly produced e-mails from Kim and Tong's active files, that UBS's "failure to produce these e-mails in a timely fashion precluded [her] from questioning any witness about them." These arguments stand unrebutted and are therefore adopted in full by the Court. Accordingly, UBS is ordered to pay the costs of any depositions or re-depositions required by the late production. *Third;* UBS is ordered to pay the costs of this motion.

Finally, I note that UBS's belated production has resulted in a self-executing sanction. Not only was Zubulake unable to question UBS's witnesses using the newly produced e-mails, but UBS was unable to prepare those witnesses with the aid of those e-mails. Some of UBS's witnesses, not having seen these e-mails, have already given deposition testimony that seems to contradict the newly discovered evidence. For example, if Zubulake's version of the evidence is credited, the e-mail from Davies acknowledging receipt of Zubulake's EEOC charge at 11:06 AM on August 21, 2001, puts the lie to Davies' testimony that he had not seen the charge when he spoke to Orgill—a conversation that was reflected in an e-mail sent at 2:02 PM. Zubulake is, of course, free to use this testimony at trial.

These sanctions are designed to compensate Zubulake for the harm done to her by the loss of or extremely delayed access to potentially relevant evidence. They should also stem the need for any further litigation over the backup tapes.

* * *

V. Conclusion

In sum, counsel has a duty to effectively communicate to her client its discovery obligations so that all relevant information is discovered, retained, and produced. In particular, once the duty to preserve attaches, counsel must identify sources of discoverable information. This will usually entail speaking directly with the key players in the litigation, as well as the client's information technology personnel. In addition, when the duty to preserve attaches, counsel must put in place a litigation hold and make that known to all relevant employees by communicating with them directly. The litigation hold instructions must be reiterated regularly and compliance must be monitored. Counsel must also call for employees to produce copies of relevant electronic evidence, and must arrange for the segregation and safeguarding of any archival media (*e.g.*, backup tapes) that the party has a duty to preserve.

Once counsel takes these steps (or once a court order is in place), a party is fully on notice of its discovery obligations. If a party acts contrary to counsel's instructions or to a court's order, it acts at its own peril.

UBS failed to preserve relevant e-mails, even after receiving adequate warnings from counsel, resulting in the production of some relevant e-mails almost two years after they were initially requested, and resulting in the complete destruction of others. For that reason, Zubulake's motion is granted and sanctions are warranted. UBS is ordered to:

> 1. Pay for the re-deposition of relevant UBS personnel, limited to the subject of the newly-discovered e-mails;

> 2. Restore and produce relevant documents from Varsano's August 2001 backup tape;

> 3. Pay for the re-deposition of Varsano and Tong, limited to the new material produced from Varsano's August 2001 backup tape; and

> 4. Pay all "reasonable expenses, including attorney's fees," incurred by Zubulake in connection with the making of this motion.

In addition, I will give the following instruction to the jury that hears this case:

> You have heard that UBS failed to produce some of the e-mails sent or received by UBS personnel in August and September 2001. Plaintiff has argued that this evidence was in defendants' control and would have proven facts material to the matter in controversy.

> If you find that UBS could have produced this evidence, and that the evidence was within its control, and that the evidence would have been material in deciding facts in dispute in this case, you are permitted, but not required, to infer that the evidence would have been unfavorable to UBS.

> In deciding whether to draw this inference, you should consider whether the evidence not produced would merely have duplicated other evidence already before you. You may also consider whether you are satisfied that UBS's failure to produce this information was reasonable. Again, any inference you decide to draw should be based on all of the facts and circumstances in this case....

VI. Postscript

The subject of the discovery of electronically stored information is rapidly evolving. When this case began more than two years ago, there was little guidance from the judiciary, bar associations or the academy as to the governing standards. Much has changed in that time. There have been a flood of recent opinions—including a number from appellate courts—and there are now several treatises on the subject.[121] In addition, professional groups such as the American Bar Association and the Sedona Conference have provided very useful guidance on thorny issues relating to the discovery of electronically stored information * * *[122]

Now that the key issues have been addressed and national standards are developing, parties and their counsel are fully on notice of their responsibility to preserve and produce electronically stored information. The tedious and difficult fact finding encompassed in this opinion and others like it is a great burden on a court's limited resources. The time and effort spent by counsel to litigate these issues has also been time-consuming and distracting. This Court, for one, is optimistic that with the guidance now provided it will not be necessary to spend this amount of time again. It is hoped that counsel will heed the guidance provided by these resources and will work to ensure that preservation, production and spoliation issues are limited, if not eliminated.

Note: Document Preservation and Destruction

In Coleman Holdings, Inc. v. Morgan Stanley & Co., Inc., Case no. CA 03–5045 AI (Fla. Cir. Ct., Palm Beach Co., March 23, 2005), the court entered an especially notable adverse inference instruction as a remedy for the wrongful failure of Morgan Stanley to comply with its discovery obligations.

The case involved an allegation by Ronald Perelman, controlling shareholder of Coleman, that Morgan Stanley had worked with Sunbeam to falsify Sunbeam's financial statements, and thereby overstate the value of Sunbeam's stock, when Perelman sold Coleman to Sunbeam in 1998. Sunbeam purchased Coleman in part with Sunbeam stock. Perelman alleged that misrepresentation of the value of that stock caused him to receive considerably less than full value for his sale of Coleman.

The court found that Morgan Stanley had "deliberately and contumaciously violated numerous discovery orders", id. at 16, including the destruction of e-mails. It was critical of both the company and its outside law firm, at one point describing the response of the latter as its "usual stonewall tactic." Id. at p. 7. As a remedy for the violation, the court ordered that the jury was to be instructed that Morgan Stanley had colluded with Sunbeam to

---

121. See Michael Arkfeld, Electronic Discovery and Evidence (2003); Adam I. Cohen & David J. Lender, Electronic Discovery: Law and Practice (2004).

122. See Memorandum from Gregory P. Joseph & Barry F. McNeil, *Electronic Discovery Standards—Draft Amendments to ABA Civil Discovery Standards* (Nov. 17, 2003), available at http://www.aban-et.org/litigation/taskforces/electronic/document.pdf; The Sedona Conference, *The Sedona Principles: Best Practices Recommendations & Principles for Addressing Electronic Document Production* (January 2004), available at http://www.thesedona-conference.org/publications_html.

commit fraud as the plaintiff had alleged. That left Coleman with the burden of showing only that it had relied on Morgan Stanley, and had suffered damages as a result of that reliance. Two months later, the jury awarded Perelman $604.3 million in actual damages and $850 million in punitive damages.

In light of the potentially serious consequences for the failure to preserve documents, two practitioners suggest:

> "[A]ll corporations should strongly consider adopting a written document retention policy ... [C]orporations should make the fulfillment of their document retention obligations a higher priority than destroying documents, and should consider retaining more rather than fewer electronic documents. To be certain, corporations have legitimate interests in discarding documents that are no longer needed to manage the business ... In today's compliance environment, however, the destruction of documents is subject to second-guessing and attendant downside risks. Moreover, a document retention policy with the goal of eliminating 'bad' documents in advance of litigation is a quixotic and self-defeating enterprise. A document retention policy should begin from the opposite perspective: what documents should and must be *retained*."[1]

PROBLEMS

1. You are the general counsel for Xis Corp., a company in the Silicon Valley that manufactures various parts used in high-speed computers. Xis was started by two college classmates of yours five years ago. They deliberately have sought to create a family-friendly workplace in which employees are given the opportunity to tailor their schedules to meet obligations such as the need to care for children, spouses, companions, or parents. The company provides a generous health benefits package as part of this policy. The founders of the company, John Taylor and Susan Marks, have been committed to demonstrating that corporations can be both profitable and humane toward its employees.

Xis is just now beginning to achieve a respectable market share in a very competitive market. It plans an initial public offering (IPO) within the next week. The capital gained from this offering is sorely needed to enable the company to make investments in research that will preserve its profitability over the next few years while adhering to its family-friendly work policy.

About two weeks ago, two disgruntled, Aaron Roberts and Brenda Cook, decided to leave Xis to form their own firm, RC Technologies. It is unclear exactly what their company will be manufacturing, but the founder of Xis are concerned that the new firm will compete with Xis in several product markets. In particular, they fear that the new company will be producing integrated circuits, since Roberts and Cook are talented engineers who played an important role in developing this product for Xis. Xis officials are worried that the prospect of serious competition will threaten the attractive-

---

1. David Priebe & Diane Holt Frankle, *Five Tenets of a Written Document Reten-*   *tion Policy*, 18 Insights 2 (2004).

ness of Xis to investors just when the company is preparing to launch its IPO.

Taylor and Marks want you to file a lawsuit against RC Technologies alleging that Roberts and Cook will be appropriating Xis trade secrets and infringing its patents in developing products for the new company. They have no direct evidence of this. They insist, however, that Roberts and Cook "must be" planning to do this, since it would allow their new firm quickly achieve profitability by capitalizing on the former employees' area of expertise. They observe that Roberts and Cook left Xis because they felt that the company's employment philosophy reduced profits available to compensate them at a level that they felt was appropriate. They observe that the two former employees would love to cut into Xis' market share. In any event, they say, filing the suit will keep Roberts and Cook preoccupied, require them to incur expenses defending the suit, and will deter venture capitalists from investing in RC Technologies. They emphasize that the suit needs to be filed immediately, before the new company can threaten the success of the Xis IPO.

What do you do?

2.   You are the general counsel at Medicraft, a publicly traded company that develops and sells medical devices. The company has been working on a lightweight portable dialysis machine, tentatively called the Dialafriend, that can be used at home and on travels. The company has indicated to investors and analysts that it is encouraged by progress on the machine, and expects to begin production within the next six months. Largely in anticipation of this development, Medicraft's share price has been steadily increasing.

Medicraft scientists now have indicated to company officials that they have run into a snag with the machine. They are not certain whether the problem arises from the way that the machine has been constructed, or whether there is a more fundamental defect in its basic design. They state that they are hopeful that there is no design defect and that the problem can be fixed by retooling a part of the hardware. Even if this is the case, Medicraft would not be able to bring the Dialafriend on to the market any sooner than 18 months from now. If there is a design defect, however, it would take much longer. Indeed, it is possible that the entire project would have to be scrapped. Members of the project team are divided about which alternative is most likely.

Medicraft's CEO calls a meeting to discuss what he will say in his regularly scheduled conference call with stock analysts. There is agreement that the company needs to "get out in front" of the issue by indicating that it will not be able to meet its six-month target for introducing the Dialafriend. Beyond that, there are varying opinions about how optimistic or pessimistic the CEO should try to be in managing the expectations of the market.

You and the company's public affairs officer agree to assume responsibility for drafting a "script" for the CEO to follow in his call with analysts. The discussion turns to the wording of that script. In the course of the discussion, you review the notes of the meeting that participants have been taking. The Chief Financial Officer is the most pessimistic of the group. He has jotted down "Product in trouble—may have to take a hit, cut our losses, and move on to a different product." You suggest to him that this is too bleak an outlook at his point. He shrugs, and says, "Maybe."

The meeting eventually adjourns, with you and the press officer promising to circulate a draft of the script later that day. As participants are leaving, you remind them of Medicraft's document retention policy. That policy requires that employees destroy any notes of meetings when a document later is prepared that summarizes the meeting and any actions to be taken as a result of it. You circulate the draft script later that day, and a final version is in place by the time that the CEO speaks with analysts three days later.

In his conference call, the CEO says that there has been an "unexpected hitch" in development of the Dialafriend that could delay its introduction for as long as a year. He says that he has the utmost confidence in the problem-solving ability of Medicraft's scientists, and that he is optimistic that they will eventually make the Dialacraft a breakthrough medical device. He says that Medicraft is committed to being certain that all its products are safe and effective, and that analysts and investors should "just hold on" until the Dialacraft meets this standard. The company's share price dips slightly after the call, but then begins a slow but steady increase.

In the next six months, things take a bad turn with the Dialafriend project. After repeated test problems, scientists indicate that they are likely to come to the conclusion that the machine has a basic design flaw. As one scientist says to you and other top company officials, "It looks like we'll probably have to scrap the project and go back to the drawing board."

A couple of days after you get this information, you participate in a regular meeting of the Medicraft's Information Technology committee on document retention, to which you are an advisor. The committee adopted a detailed policy two years ago, but there is some concern that not all employees are following it. You suggest sending out an urgent reminder within the company that summarizes the policy and requests that everyone review documents in their possession and take immediate steps to comply with the policy. One point that should be emphasized in the reminder, you suggest, is that notes of all meetings should be destroyed as soon as a document is prepared that summarizes the meeting.

Two days later, scientists confirm that the Dialafriend project should be shut down. The CEO schedules a conference call with analysts and breaks the news that Medicraft reluctantly has concluded that it will have to discontinue work on the Dialafriend. The company is optimistic, he says, that its scientific expertise will result in the development of other innovative products in the future. Medicraft's share price takes a sharp dive.

A week later, a shareholder class action is filed against Medicraft. Plaintiffs contend that the CEO misled investors in the conference call six months ago when he expressed confidence in bringing the Dialafriend to market despite being aware that the machine potentially had a fatal design defect.

In discovery, plaintiffs request all material prepared in connection with the analyst conference call at issue. Medicraft produces the "script" prepared as a result of the meeting. The company also discovers that the Vice-

President for Marketing has handwritten notes of the meeting, which Medicraft also produces. Plaintiffs' counsel observes that these notes indicate that four other corporate officials attended the meeting. Counsel asks for their notes as well. The company responds that those notes were destroyed pursuant to Medicraft's document retention policy.

At his deposition, the Medicraft CFS testifies that he had not destroyed his notes of the meeting in accordance with the company's document policy after a memo on the meeting was prepared. He did so, however, when he received the recent reminder about the policy.

Plaintiffs then claim that Medicraft has engaged in spoliation of evidence by destroying the notes of the meeting relating to the first analyst conference call, and asks for appropriate relief. How is this issue likely to be decided? If for the plaintiffs, what form of relief might they obtain?

Could criminal charges be filed against anyone for their conduct?

Chapter 29

SHAREHOLDER LITIGATION

The complexities of identifying the corporate lawyer's client can become magnified when shareholders sue the corporation. Such lawsuits may take the form of class actions, in which shareholders sue *qua* shareholders, or derivative actions, in which shareholders purport to represent the interests of the corporation. We have already seen in an earlier chapter how the law of attorney-client privilege has sought to accommodate the fact that shareholders have a unique status with respect to the corporation, which can require that they have access to otherwise privileged information.

This chapter focuses primarily on shareholder derivative litigation, although it is useful to keep in mind that shareholder class actions and derivative suits often may be filed simultaneously with respect to the same events. Derivative litigation raises important ethical issues based on the fact that such litigation generally does not involve a standard relationship between attorney and client, in which the lawyer as fiduciary takes her instruction from the client. In addition, the fact that the corporation formally is both plaintiff and defendant in a derivative suit, and that its interests and those of individual corporate directors and officers may be either aligned or in conflict, creates additional complications for lawyers involved in these lawsuits. The materials in this chapter provide an overview of the questions raised by this distinctive form of legal action.

OVERVIEW OF THE CHAPTER

As you read the materials in this chapter, keep in mind the unique structure of the derivative suit and the incentives (both positive and negative) that this structure creates. Most claims that directors have breached their fiduciary duties must be maintained as a derivative suit rather than a direct action. Nevertheless,because recovery goes to the corporation rather than the shareholders, they have little incentive to bring such a suit. The principal incentive is that of the plaintiff's attorney who, if successful, usually will receive a substantial fee for her efforts. The conflicts that arise from the incentive structure of a derivative suit are the principal focus of this chapter.

John C. Coffee, Jr. explores these conflicts in considerable depth. Using economic theory, he analyzes how plaintiff's counsel's interest often diverges from that of the corporation whose rights are actually being asserted. Counsel will receive a fee only if there is a recovery and will get nothing if the suit is unsuccessful. In addition, the corporation can and will indemnify the defendants' substantial litigation expenses but only if there has not been a finding of a breach of fiduciary duty. The economic consequences of these factors is to create a large incentive by both defendants and plaintiff's counsel to settle the litigation rather than risk losing the suit and receiving nothing.

The remainder of the chapter deals with some of the procedural mechanisms that have been created to deal with the structural problems that the derivative suit creates. Although the materials focus on Delaware law, you should be aware that other jurisdictions, particularly those that have adopted the Model Business Corporation Act, treat these mechanisms differently. Demand and the Special Litigation Committee both ensure that the plaintiff shareholder is not able to usurp completely the role of directors in the governance of the corporation simply by bringing a derivative suit. Judicial approval of the fairness of a settlement and the award of attorneys fees provide a way to protect the corporation's interest when the parties and their attorneys may have incentives not to do so. The extent to which these mechanisms work and the desirability of a derivative suit as a check on corporation management are questions that you should consider throughout the chapter.

MODEL RULES: 1.2, 1.5, 1.7, 1.13, 3.1

Jeffrey Bauman, Lewis D. Soloman, Donald E. Schwartz and Elliott J. Weiss, CORPORATIONS LAW AND POLICY: MATERIALS AND PROBLEMS

(4th 1998)

A derivative suit is an action on behalf of another "person" brought by one who has an interest in that person but is not its normal decision maker * * * In the typical derivative suit, a shareholder is allowed to assert the corporation's rights on the theory that the board of directors, which is charged with that responsibility, has failed to do so. Any recovery from the derivative suit belongs to the corporation, the real party in interest, rather than to the plaintiff-shareholder. Plaintiff's counsel, who plays a major role in initiating derivative suit litigation, receives a fee from the corporation on the theory that she is entitled to compensation for conferring a benefit on the corporation.

The modern derivative suit originated from mid-19th century English equity and trust theory, as a means of allowing shareholders to challenge management abuses * * * American courts adopted and refined the derivative suit, focusing from the start on the relationship between corporate directors and shareholders.

The stockholder-plaintiff in a derivative suit acts in a representative capacity for all the injured shareholders. Indeed, F.R.C.P. 23.1 requires that the plaintiff must "fairly and adequately represent the interests of the shareholders * * * similarly situated in enforcing the rights of the corporation." Courts stress the obligations that fall on a stockholder when she initiates a derivative suit. The Supreme Court has characterized the stockholder as assuming "a position, not technically as a trustee perhaps, but one of a fiduciary character. He sues, not for himself alone, but as representative of a class comprising all who are similarly situated." *Cohen v. Beneficial Industrial Loan Corp., 337 U.S. 541, 549, 69 S.Ct. 1221, 93 L.Ed. 1528 (1949).* Having assumed that role, the plaintiff cannot later abandon it for personal benefit. * * *

1. THE PARTIES' INCENTIVES

To understand fully the policy issues that derivative suits raise, one must appreciate the economic incentives of the principal players in these suits and the conflicts that these incentives create. Because any recovery in a derivative suit goes to the corporation, the nominal shareholder-plaintiff receives no direct pecuniary benefit from successful litigation; her benefit comes from an increase in the corporation's stock price attributable to the recovery. Thus, the plaintiff wants to maximize the size of that recovery, an interest shared by the corporation itself. The defendant, usually a senior executive or director, seeks to minimize her costs, which consist of monies paid in judgment or settlement and attorneys' fees. As in any contingent fee litigation, plaintiffs counsel will receive a fee if the suit results in a favorable judgment or a settlement; she earns nothing if the plaintiff loses. The size of the fee generally will be based either on the time spent on the litigation or on a percentage of the total recovery.

Unlike most litigation in which the plaintiff's gain comes at the defendant's expense, a derivative suit is not a zero-sum game; in fact both plaintiff *and* defendant can recover many of their litigation costs from the corporation. The defendant in a derivative suit, particularly if she is a director, is not like a defendant in other actions. * * * [U]nder most state corporate laws, a corporation may indemnify a director for her expenses in a derivative suit if she has not been *adjudged* to have breached her duty to the corporation and otherwise meets the standards for indemnification. These expenses include attorneys' fees, which can be substantial, and, in some jurisdictions, even the amounts paid in settlement. Thus, a risk-averse defendant has a strong incentive to agree to a relatively small settlement and be indemnified for substantially all her expenses rather than risk an adverse judicial decision. To the extent that the monetary settlement is reduced through the inclusion of non-pecuniary relief, the defendant's economic risk is lessened still further. Because indemnification usually is paid by insurance which the corporation purchases at its own expense, a settlement may result in the shareholders paying part of the cost of the defense, notwithstanding that the defendant may have breached her duty to the corporation.

Similarly, the plaintiff in a derivative suit is not like most plaintiffs, and her relationship with her lawyer is not like most lawyer-client relationships in contingent fee litigation. In most litigation, counsel must operate within the bounds set by her client. When the client tells counsel to litigate, counsel litigates; when the client prefers to settle, the lawyer settles. By contrast, the shareholder in a derivative suit has only a nominal economic interest and usually gives no directions. Additionally, in most contingent litigation the client knows she has been injured and seeks out a lawyer; in the derivative suit, it is not uncommon for the lawyer to seek out the client and advise her of the wrong that has occurred. Indeed, one commentator has called plaintiff's counsel "the engine that drives the derivative action." John C. Coffee, Jr., *American Law Institute's Corporate Governance Project: Remedies: Litigation and Corporate Governance: An Essay on Steering Between Scylla and Charybdis,* 52 GEO.WASH.L.REV. 789, 800 (1984). Finally, in a derivative suit, the lawyer has far more at stake than the plaintiff shareholder. Thus, plaintiff's counsel has an incentive to agree to settlements that shareholders collectively might view as inadequate, in order to assure that she receives a fee for her work.

Some of the problems described above are present in any form of contingent litigation. They are more troublesome here because of the representative nature of the derivative suit. Nuisance suits are not peculiar to the corporate setting. Nevertheless, in order to discourage abuses by people purporting to act on the corporation's behalf, the law has singled out derivative suits for the imposition of special procedural restrictions and judicial oversight. Among other things, this chapter examines the reasons for these restrictions, how they operate, and how to evaluate their efficacy and desirability. The class action is another tool of shareholder litigation, but it is a device with broader applicability and will not be examined here.

2. RATIONALES FOR THE DERIVATIVE SUIT

The original rationale for the derivative suit appears to have been compensatory; the corporation has been harmed by the defendant's acts and can be made whole if the defendant pays the appropriate damages. There are, however, several problems with such a rationale. First, because the recovery goes to the corporation, whose shareholder body is changing constantly, those who were shareholders when the wrong occurred and have subsequently sold their shares at a price which reflects that wrong do not share in the subsequent recovery. Similarly, those who purchased at the depressed price receive a windfall when the recovery ultimately occurs.

A second problem is that the amount of the corporate injury may not be the same as that suffered by the shareholders. As Professors Coffee and Schwartz have noted: "... [F]or legal purposes, the corporation's loss is a historical concept, measured by accounting conventions and limited to injuries that have actually occurred; in contrast, the shareholder's loss may be greater, because in a securities market that discounts future possibilities, predictions of future loss are immediately converted into a present decline in share values." [citation omitted] Still another problem with the compensatory rationale is that because the corporation pays indemnification [to directors for certain liability] and the plaintiff's attorneys fees, the corporation can never be fully compensated for the wrong, particularly when the suit is filed.

Coffee and Schwartz argue that deterrence rather than compensation should be the principal rationale for the derivative suit. However, as they recognize, there are also serious problems with the deterrence rationale. To begin with, the plaintiff is cast in the role of a "bounty hunter," seeking a reward for assuring that the deterrence function has been performed. Indeed, the role of plaintiff in a deterrence system is such that anyone, regardless of the nature of her interest in the corporation, could pay it. Moreover, even if it were possible to limit appropriate plaintiffs, the litigation costs that the corporation incurred might exceed its recovery. The excess could [always be] rationalized as necessary to achieve the desired level of deterrence. * * *

A more serious question is whether derivative suits, whatever their rationale, actually improve corporate governance through their effects on corporate managers' behavior. Sampling a number of shareholder suits, including both derivative and class-action proceedings, [Professor Roberta] Romano concluded that "shareholder litigation is a weak, if not ineffective, instrument of corporate governance." [citation omitted] Plaintiffs rarely prevail in derivative lawsuits, and any monetary settlement is extremely small on a per share basis (recovery is significantly higher for class actions than derivative suits). Negotiated settlements sometimes include changes in board structure or composition, but Romano argues that these changes usually are cosmetic, so that even indirect benefits from derivative suits are minimal. Shareholder suits do not deter managers from improper actions, because insurance and indemnification provisions normally cover their expenses. Romano suggests that the main beneficiaries of shareholder suits are the attorneys who collect fees for pursuing them.

Questions as to the underlying rationale and incentives of derivative suits are of more than academic interest; they also raise issues of practicality and public policy. * * * To what extent is the derivative suit appropriately viewed as an effective weapon in the arsenal of corporate governance or, rather, is the old appellation, "strike suit," still appropriate?

* * *

John C. Coffee, Jr., Understanding the
Plaintiff's Attorney: The Implications of
Economic Theory for Private Enforcement
of Law Through Class and Derivative Actions

86 Colum. L. Rev. 669 (1986)

Introduction

Probably to a unique degree, American law relies upon private litigants to enforce substantive provisions of law that in other legal systems are left largely to the discretion of public enforcement agencies. This system of enforcement through "private attorneys general" is most closely associated with the federal antitrust and securities laws and the common law's derivative action, but similar institutional arrangements have developed recently in the environmental, "mass tort," and employment discrimination fields. The key legal rules that make the private attorney general a reality in American law today, however, are not substantive but procedural—namely, those rules that establish the fee arrangements under which these plaintiff's attorneys are compensated. Inevitably, these rules create an incentive structure that either encourages or chills private enforcement of law. * * *

I. The Incentive to Litigate in Class and Derivative Actions

In those areas of litigation where a client cannot closely monitor or control the plaintiff's attorney's conduct, the plaintiff's attorney's incentives will shape important litigation decisions. * * *

A. Principal and Agent: Who's in Control?

In theory, a fundamental premise of American legal ethics is that clients, not their attorneys, should define litigation objectives. Yet, in the context of class and derivative actions, it is well understood that the actual client generally has only a nominal stake in the outcome of the litigation.... [O]ur legal system has long accepted, if somewhat uneasily, the concept of the plaintiff's attorney as an entrepreneur who performs the socially useful function of deterring undesirable conduct. This acceptance is manifested in a variety of ways: by permitting the attorney to advance the expenses of the litigation and receive reimbursement only if successful; by sometimes permitting the attorney to settle a class or derivative action over the objections of the actual client who is serving as representative of the class; and by allowing the use of fee formulas that view "the lawyer as a calculating entrepreneur regulated by calculating judges." Thus, although our law publicly expresses homage to individual clients, it privately recognizes their limited relevance in this context.

Although this legal structure is largely unparalleled in other common law systems, it has its obvious advantages. First, it enables clients who are dispersed or have suffered relatively small injuries to receive legal representation without incurring the substantial transaction costs of coordination. Absent such a system, a classic "free rider" problem would arise because litigation is a form of "public good" in which the benefits of an action accrue to persons who are not required to bear their share of the action's costs. This means that litigation would be predictably underfunded, from the clients' perspective, if the clients had to take collective action. Second, because the attorney as private enforcer looks to the court, not the client, to award him a fee if successful, the attorney can find the legal violation first and the client second. In principle, this system should encourage the attorney to invest in search costs and seek out violations of the law that are profitable for him to challenge, rather than wait passively for an aggrieved client to arrive at his door. Thus, the attorney becomes a "bounty hunter"—or, less pejoratively, an independent monitoring force—motivated to prosecute legal violations still unknown to prospective clients.

However, this system also creates the potential for both opportunism and overenforcement. The first of these dangers arises because, in economic terms, there are high "agency costs" associated with class and derivative actions * * *

The second danger—overenforcement—arises because the unconstrained attorney may be motivated to sue where the client would not. Although the rational plaintiff's attorney would consider only the immediate payoff, the client may be concerned about the longer-term effects of litigation. For example, a plaintiff's attorney might commence a derivative suit against a corporation's officers and directors for a negligent business decision whenever the expected settlement would justify a fee that covered the attorney's opportunity costs. The shareholders, however, might rationally fear that such litigation would make directors excessively risk averse in the long-run. Similarly, in other contexts, shareholders may fear reprisals or counterclaims which could produce liabilities that are not borne by the plaintiff's attorney. Finally, overenforcement might result when a court awards attorney's fees based primarily on the time expended by the attorney, because such a fee formula creates an incentive to continue litigating a case well past the point at which the marginal costs of such effort equal the marginal returns generated thereby.

What happens when client control is so weak as to make the attorney virtually an independent entrepreneur? In some areas of contemporary litigation, the pattern is typically one of the lawyer finding the client, rather than vice versa. A principal characteristic of these areas is that plaintiff's attorneys typically have low search costs. That is, plaintiff's attorneys can discover the existence of potentially meritorious legal claims at low cost to themselves. As an entrepreneur who is compensated only when successful, the plaintiff's attorney bears the costs of failure and seeks to minimize those costs by free riding on the monitoring efforts of others * * * For example, a dramatic market decline in a corporation's stock value may lead the plaintiff's attorney to infer the existence of previously undisclosed and material adverse information. The plaintiff's attorney will thus be motivated to search for a securities law violation. The mass tort, such as an airplane crash or a toxic disaster, provides another obvious example. Similarly, a publicized takeover attempt may lead to a "greenmail" transaction, the adoption of a "poison pill," or some other defensive measure by the board of directors of a target corporation, thereby indicating the potential for a derivative suit.

Empirical evidence suggests that such dramatic, highly visible events underlie most securities class actions and derivative suits. The data confirm a basic fact about enterpreneurial plaintiff's attorneys: they gravitate to those areas where search costs are lowest. Thus, an entrepreneurially motivated system of private enforcement is likely to work well in areas where search costs are low, but considerably less well where such costs are high and the attorney must invest significant funds before discovering legal violations.

Once the plaintiff's attorney has decided to bring suit, identifying and securing a nominal client is often only a necessary procedural step that seldom poses a substantial barrier for the experienced professional. In the securities and derivative suit areas, there are well-known individuals who possess broad (but thin) securities portfolios and have served as the lead plaintiff in numerous previous class actions. * * * When the client is neither a potentially valuable witness nor a co-investor in the action, his role may often be only that of a "ticket of admission" by which the plaintiff's attorney can join the caucus of attorneys who gather to organize a class action.

As a normative matter, such a description of the attorney-client relationship may seem offensive to those accustomed to viewing the relationship as a fiduciary one. Yet for analytical purposes, one better understands the behavior of the plaintiff's attorney in class and derivative actions if one views him not as an agent, but more as an entrepreneur who regards a litigation as a risky asset that requires continuing investment decisions. Furthermore, a purely fiduciary perspective is misleading because it assumes that the client's preferences with respect to when an action should be settled are exogenously determined, when, in fact, they are largely influenced by the fee award formula adopted by the court. * * *

III. THE PLAINTIFF'S ATTORNEY'S INCENTIVES: TOWARD AN ACONOMIC MODEL

* * *

D. The Problem of Collusion: Litigation As a Non-Zero Sum Game

The principal-agent problem that is endemic to class and derivative actions implies that there are three sets of interests involved in these actions: those of the defendants, the plaintiffs, and the plaintiff's attorneys. Often, the plaintiff's attorneys and the defendants can settle on a basis that is adverse to the interests of the plaintiffs. At its worst, the settlement process may amount to a covert exchange of a cheap settlement for a high award of attorney's fees. Although courts have long recognized this danger and have developed some procedural safeguards intended to prevent collusive settlements, these reforms are far from adequate to the task.

Indeed, in some areas, the law seems almost to have institutionalized a process which ensures that a case will be settled on a basis that need not closely reflect the litigation odds. The derivative action supplies the best example. Under well-established rules, the corporation pays the plaintiff's attorney's fees when the action produces a substantial benefit to the corporation. Correspondingly, the corporation is permitted to indemnify defendant corporate officials for their legal expenses incurred in connection with a derivative action. Many large corporations have adopted by-laws authorizing such indemnification to the full extent permitted by law, and virtually every corporation listed on a national securities exchange purchases liability insurance for its corporate officials covering such legal expenses. Restrictions exist, however, on the availability of both insurance and indemnification: typically, the corporation may not indemnify a defendant's litigation expenses when he has been "adjudicated" to have breached a duty to the corporation. Also, as a matter of both law and insurance contract provisions, insurance does not cover liability for fraud or unfair self-dealing. Hence, powerful pressures to settle exist because each side can assure itself that its legal fees will be reimbursed in the wake of a settlement. The defendants will avoid being "adjudicated" to have breached a duty and can characterize the nature of the liabilities so as to permit insurance to recover these payments.

Of course, the defendants' settlement calculus must also include any payments they must make to the corporation. However, this payment may be trivialized or rendered nonexistent if certain forms of settlement, which are attractive to both sides, can be arranged. Recent precedents have approved wholly nonpecuniary settlements in which the defendants did not contribute any cash or property to the settlement fund. Instead, the only relief received by the corporation was therapeutic: disclosures were made, by-laws were revised, and new board procedures were adopted. The availability of these bloodless settlements gives rise to a set of circumstances in which it can appear economically irrational not to settle. By settling, neither side loses anything, and both recoup their legal expenses from the corporation (and thus indirectly from the shareholders).

Notwithstanding this logical description of how the principal adversaries can settle collusively at the expense of the shareholders, experienced litigators will dispute the accuracy of this account. They will respond that in their entire experience they have never seen anyone offer or agree to swap a high fee award for a low recovery. Indeed, this response is probably accurate, because there is one further nuance that must be understood in order to comprehend settlement dynamics. This factor involves the impact of the now prevailing method of awarding attorney's fees. The lodestar formula n130 compensates the attorney based essentially on the time the attorney expends on the action, rather than simply awarding the attorney a percentage of the recovery.... [T]he lodestar formula enables collusion to occur on an implicit, rather than explicit, basis. Collusion becomes structural, not actual, because the fee award is no longer a simple function of the recovery.

To see this, consider the position of a plaintiff's attorney who invests a year's effort in preparing a case for trial. Assume the case has an expected value to the class of $ 4,000,000 (meaning that the plaintiffs would reject any lesser settlement and take their chances at trial). Assume further that the attorney historically would have received a fee award of $ 1,000,000 based on a percentage of the recovery benchmark of twenty-five percent, but that today the attorney is instead compensated based on the time reasonably expended on the action. Assume finally that on the eve of trial, the attorney has already expended sufficient time to justify a $ 1,000,000 fee award on an hourly basis, and that there is also a substantial litigation risk that the judgment (if the attorney goes to trial) will be adverse to his side (in which case the attorney will receive nothing).

If defendants now offer a settlement of only $ 2,000,000, there is little reason for the attorney to decline this settlement, even though the plaintiffs would prefer to hold out for $ 4,000,000. That is, when fees are based on the lodestar formula, the plaintiff's attorney receives the same fee award under the proposed settlement as if the plaintiffs had won a much larger victory at trial. In addition, the attorney avoids the substantial risk of an adverse decision. Indeed, if the attorney won a $ 10,000,-000 verdict at trial, he would gain little incremental benefit because the time expended in trying the case probably would not materially enhance the fee award, but the attorney would have had to accept a significant risk that his substantial investment of time would go uncompensated. In effect, under the lodestar formula, a plaintiff's attorney shares his clients' downside risk, but not their upside gain, by rejecting a settlement and proceeding to trial.

Of course, the plaintiff's attorney may procrastinate and seek to build up the expected fee award from $ 1,000,000 to, say, $ 1,250,000. This obvious incentive for delay under the lodestar formula, which would not arise under a percentage of the recovery formula, helps explain the popular impression that it produces makework and padded bills. Nonetheless, the critical point is that the formula produces de facto collusion that each side can rationalize. The defendant's counsel has every reason to make a low settlement offer. Similarly, defense counsel can happily oblige the plaintiff's attorney's procrastination while the latter builds up the fee to the maximum level that the court will allow. The plaintiff's attorney can rationalize a low settlement on any of a variety of grounds: the risk of an adverse verdict, the suspected hostility of the court, the impact of delay on the class, or the increased expenses for the class if the action continues. At no point must either side actually link the fee award and the settlement size in their negotiations—the law does this for them by tying fee awards to hours billed rather than settlement size. Once the plaintiff's attorney is able to estimate the fee award simply by computing the hours expended, he does not need a collusive offer from the defendant, but merely their acquiescence in a strategy that maximizes the interests of both sides. In short, under the lodestar formula, actual collusion is replaced by structural collusion. * * *

CONCLUSION

Whether called a "private attorney general" or a "bounty hunter," the plaintiff's attorney in class and derivative actions has long been a controversial figure. Claims that such actions disproportionately result in extortionate or collusive settlements are not new, but an understanding of why such outcomes may occur requires that we move beyond character assassination and identify those legal rules that permit the parties to settle on a basis unrelated to an action's litigation odds. Here, the cost differential thesis, portfolio theory, and the claim that the lodestar formula invites structural collusion all have some explanatory power, with the last explanation seeming much the most powerful. * * *

Private enforcement of law has its inevitable flaws, which are largely rooted in the principal-agent problems that attend class and derivative litigation. These problems are only aggravated so long as we repress the fact that the plaintiff's attorney is different from other attorneys, both in terms of the extent of the conflict and the potential for opportunism. Once this is recognized, the basic goal of reform should be to reduce the agency costs incident to this attorney-client relationship.

Convenient and comforting as it is to view the attorney only through th[e] nostalgic lens of fiduciary analysis, a fixation on this mode of analysis is likely to blind us to the real issues relating to the incentives and misincentives that the law today creates for the plaintiff's attorney. Sadly, to call a lawyer a fiduciary is too often to end the analysis, not begin it.

* * *

The Demand Requirement

The ability of shareholders to bring a derivative action on behalf of the corporation obviously is in tension with the business judgment rule. Whether the corporation should bring a lawsuit ordinarily is a matter for the board to decide. The law seeks to resolve this tension by requiring that prior to bringing a derivative suit, shareholders must make a demand on the directors to sue to correct the alleged wrong to the corporation. The response of the board to this demand is then subject to review under the business judgment rule.

Shareholder demand is excused in Delaware, however, when it would be futile. The case below describes the criteria for determining futility, which, if satisfied, permit shareholders to bring a derivative action without making demand on the board.

RATTNER v. BIDZOS

2003 WL 22284323 (Del. Ch. 2003)

Noble, Vice Chancellor

Court of Chancery Rule 23.1 requires that, in derivative actions, "the complaint shall ... allege with particularity the efforts, if any, made by the plaintiff to obtain the action the plaintiff desires from the directors or comparable authority and the reasons for the plaintiff's failure to obtain the action or for not making the effort." The demand requirement embodied in Court of Chancery Rule 23.1 is an acknowledgement that a shareholder's prosecution of a derivative action necessarily impinges upon the power and autonomy of a board of directors to manage the affairs of the corporation, including whether or not to pursue a cause of action belonging to the corporation. The hurdle of proving demand futility also serves an important policy function of promoting internal resolution, as opposed to litigation, of corporate disputes and grants the corporation a degree of control over any litigation brought for its benefit....

A critical requirement of Court of Chancery Rule 23.1 is that the complaint must allege *with particularity* the reasons for demand excusal.

"Those pleadings must comply with stringent requirements of factual particularity that differ substantially from the permissive notice pleadings governed solely by Chancery Rule 8(a). Rule 23.1 is not satisfied by conclusory statements or mere notice pleading.... What the pleader must set forth are particularized factual statements that are essential to the claim.... A prolix complaint larded with conclusory language ... does not comply with these fundamental pleading mandates."

In considering whether a derivative plaintiff has satisfied Court of Chancery Rule 23.1, I am confined to reviewing the well-pled allegations of the complaint. While I am unable to accept cursory contentions of wrongdoing in light of the obligation to plead facts with particularity, I must accept as true all well-pled allegations of fact in the complaint, and all reasonable inferences from non-conclusory allegations contained in the complaint must be drawn in favor of the plaintiff. With these principles in mind, I turn to the question of whether Rattner has pleaded with particularity that demand upon the Board would be futile and, thus, is excused. * * *

The business judgment rule and demand excusal are "inextricably bound." When a derivative suit challenges decisions made by directors in accordance with their managerial authority, "stockholder plaintiffs must overcome the powerful presumptions of the business judgment rule before they will be permitted to pursue the derivative claim." However, it is also recognized that the business judgment rule only operates in instances of action by the board of directors or a conscious decision to refrain from acting. The business judgment rule has no role in the case of inaction by the board of directors. From this dichotomy, two overlapping yet different tests have been developed to determine whether demand is excused.

If a derivative suit challenges a decision made by a board of directors, then demand futility is properly evaluated under that test announced in *Aronson v. Lewis.* Under the *Aronson* test, "to determine whether demand would be futile, the Court must determine whether the particular facts, as alleged, create a reason to doubt that: '(1) the directors are disinterested and independent' or '(2) the challenged transaction was otherwise the product of a valid exercise of business judgment.'" Thus, *Aronson* adopted a two-pronged analysis for determining whether demand is futile: the first prong inquires into the independence and disinterestedness of the directors, and the second prong focuses on the substantive nature of the challenged transaction and the directors' approval thereof.

The parties, however, agree that, here, because Rattner does not challenge any particular action undertaken by the Board as a whole, the standard established in *Rales v. Blasband* governs the determination of demand futility. Thus, under the *Rales* test,

> "a court must determine whether or not the particularized factual allegations of a derivative stockholder complaint create a reasonable doubt that, as of the time the complaint is filed, the board of directors could have properly exercised its independent and disinterested business judgment in responding to a demand. If the derivative plaintiff satisfies this burden, then demand will be excused as futile."

Because there has been no action or decision by a board of directors, a premise of the *Aronson* test, that of the application of the business judgment rule, is lacking, and accordingly it is under the *Rales* test that the fundamental right of boards of directors to manage the affairs of corporations is recognized. Thus, in examining "whether the board that would be addressing the demand can impartially consider its merits without being influenced by improper considerations," the focus is upon the disinterestedness and the independence of a majority of the board of directors in responding to a demand.

Under the *Rales* test, demand is excused if the particularized facts of the Amended Complaint create a reasonable doubt that, at the time the original complaint was filed, a majority of the Board could have exercised disinterested and independent business judgment in responding to Rattner's demand. Rattner does not challenge the independence of any Director Defendant; thus, the inquiry turns to the disinterestedness of the Director Defendants at the time this action was filed. Directors are considered [not] disinterested for purposes of determining demand futility when they "appear on both sides of a transaction [or] expect to derive any personal financial benefit from it in the sense of self-dealing, as opposed to a benefit which devolves upon the corporation or all stockholders generally." Directorial interest may also be said to exist when "'a corporate decision will have a materially detrimental impact on a director, but not on the corporation and the stockholders.'"

Often, as is the case here, a derivative suit essentially asks the directors to authorize a suit against themselves and, thus, to act against their own personal interests.

> "The conundrum for the law in this area is well understood. If the legal rule was that demand was excused whenever, by mere notice pleading, the plaintiffs could state a breach of fiduciary duty claim against a majority of the board, the demand requirement of the law would be weakened and the settlement value of so-called "strike suits" would greatly increase, to the perceived detriment of the best interests of stockholders as investors. But, if the demand excusal

test is too stringent, then stockholders may suffer as a class because the deterrence effects of meritorious derivative suits on faithless conduct may be too weak."[4]

Except in "egregious circumstances," the "mere threat" of personal liability does not constitute a disabling interest for a director considering a derivative plaintiff's demand. "However, a 'substantial likelihood' of personal liability prevents a director from impartially considering a demand." It is this difference, between a "mere threat" of personal liability and (i) "a substantial likelihood" of personal liability or (ii) a "mere threat" in "egregious circumstances," as addressed in the context of the first prong of *Aronson* and the test established in *Rales*, that accommodates and balances the competing policy concerns of adequately policing boards of directors while guarding against strike suits.

The Special Litigation Committee

Even if demand is excused, the Board of Directors may be able to regain control of the litigation by appointing a disinterested Special Litigation Committee (SLC) to investigate the allegations and determine whether to pursue or dismiss the action that has been filed by the shareholders. The Committee's decision does not enjoy deference under the business judgment rule, however. The excerpt below describes the standard of review of a motion by an SLC to dismiss a shareholder suit in which demand had been excused because the Board was not disinterested with respect to the decisions subject to challenge.

ZAPATA CORP. v. MALDONADO

430 A.2d 779 (Del. 1981)

[In this case, Zapata Corporation took actions that benefited certain officers and directors who held options to purchase company stock. Plaintiff filed a derivative suit, with respect to which demand was excused because a majority of the directors held options and benefited from the decision under review. Four years later, the Zapata Board appointed two new directors and named them to a special committee to review the allegations. The committee retained counsel in its investigation, concluded that the suit should be dismissed, and filed a motion to do so. The lower court held that the company lacked the power to compel dismissal of a properly filed derivative suit. The Delaware Supreme Court held that the board could legally delegate its authority to a committee of disinterested directors to determine if continuation of the litigation was in the company's best interest. The Court then set forth the standard for determining whether to defer to the committee's decision].

First, the Court should inquire into the independence and good faith of the committee and the bases supporting its conclusions. Limited discovery may be ordered to facilitate such inquiries. The corporation

---

4. Guttman v. Huang, 823 A.2d 492, 500 (Del. Ch. 2003).

should have the burden of proving independence, good faith and a reasonable investigation, rather than presuming independence, good faith and reasonableness. If the Court determines either that the committee is not independent or has not shown reasonable bases for its conclusions, or, if the Court is not satisfied for other reasons relating to the process, including but not limited to the good faith of the committee, the Court shall deny the corporation's motion. If, however, the Court is satisfied . . . that the committee was independent and showed reasonable bases for good faith findings and recommendations, the Court may proceed, in its discretion, to the next step.

The second step provides, we believe, the essential key in striking the balance between legitimate corporate claims as expressed in a derivative stockholder suit and a corporation's best interests as expressed by an independent investigating committee. The Court should determine, applying its own independent business judgment, whether the motion should be granted. This means, of course, that instances could arise where a committee can establish its independence and sound bases for its good faith decisions and still have the corporation's motion denied. The second step is intended to thwart instances where corporate actions meet the criteria of step one, but the result does not appear to satisfy its spirit, or where corporate actions would simply prematurely terminate a stockholder grievance deserving of further consideration in the corporation's interest. The Court of Chancery of course must carefully consider and weigh how compelling the corporate interest in dismissal is when faced with a non-frivolous lawsuit. The Court of Chancery should, when appropriate, give special consideration to matters of law and public policy in addition to the corporation's best interests.

If the Court's independent business judgment is satisfied, the Court may proceed to grant the motion, subject, of course, to any equitable terms or conditions the Court finds necessary or desirable.

A Special Litigation Committee bears the burden of persuasion on any motion to dismiss a suit, and must establish that there is no material issue of fact calling its independence into doubt in order for the motion to be granted. In *In re Oracle Corp. Derivative Litigation*, 824 A.2d 917 (Del. Ch. 2003), the court reviewed the motion of an SLC to dismiss actions alleging insider trading by certain corporate officers and directors. The court denied the motion on the ground that the two members of the Committee were Stanford professors who were being asked to investigate fellow directors who also had important ties to Stanford. Among those directors were another professor at the University who had taught one of the SLC members and who served on a committee at Stanford with that member; a Stanford alumnus who had "directed millions of dollars to Stanford during recent years," *id.* at 920, had a conference center at Stanford named for him, and had contributed over half million dollars to the Stanford Law School, with which one SLC member was affiliated; and the company CEO, who had donated millions to Stanford and was considering making donations of his home and for a scholarship program to the University. The Court emphasized that the issue was not the "good faith" or "moral probity" of the Committee members. *Id.* at 947. Rather, the members "were not situated to act with the required degree of impartiality", *id.*, because they were put in the position of having to "consider accusing a fellow professor and two large benefactors of their university" of criminal conduct. *Id.* at 921.

One observer has suggested that recent cases such as *Oracle* indicate that the Delaware courts "have begun to look harder at personal relationships that go beyond potential economic gain in determining the independence of officers and directors." A. Gilchrist Sparks, *Trends in the Delaware Corporate Law: Director Liability and Indemnification*, 1405 PLI/Corp. 331, 335 (2004). Keep in mind, however, that the court's inquiry into the independence of a Special Litigation Committee is more searching that its review of the independence of the Board in the demand futility context. *See, e.g., Beam v. Stewart*, 845 A.2d. 1040 (Del. 2004) (affirming dismissal of derivative suit, rejecting claim of demand futility because plaintiffs failed to allege with sufficient particularity how directors' personal friendships with defendant created reasonable doubt regarding their independence).

Settlement

Federal Rules of Civil Procedure 23 and 23.1 and comparable state provisions require judicial approval of any settlement, compromise, discontinuance, or dismissal of a derivative suit or shareholder class action. Approval of a settlement, in turn, requires the court to find that the terms of the settlement are "fair and reasonable." Moreover, the court must also determine the appropriate fee for the plaintiff's attorney. In theory, then, when evaluating a settlement, the court can address any problems arising from the potentially divergent interests of the shareholder-plaintiff and her attorney.

Federal Rules of Civil Procedure 23 and 23.1 and comparable state provisions require that parties must obtain approval from the court of any settlement, compromise, discontinuance, or dismissal of a derivative suit or shareholder class action. The court in these proceedings also must determine appropriate attorneys' fees. These rules offer at least an opportunity for the court to address any problems arising from the potentially divergent interests of plaintiffs and their attorneys in such cases.

> Jeffrey Bauman, Elliott J. Weiss and Alan
> R. Palmiter, CORPORATIONS LAW AND
> POLICY: MATERIALS AND PROBLEMS
>
> (5th ed. 2003)

2. Judicial Review of Settlements

Shareholder-plaintiffs rarely participate in settlement negotiations. It is up to the court to decide whether to approve a settlement that typically has been negotiated by plaintiffs' attorneys without input from the "clients" they represent. * * * The proponents of a settlement bear the burden of convincing the court that it is fair. In most cases, that determination will depend largely on the adequacy of the amount being recovered when compared to the potential recovery were plaintiff to succeed at trial. In making this evaluation, the court will discount the potential recovery at trial by the risk factors inherent in any litigation and the time value of money over the period during which recovery will be delayed. Most courts look to a list of factors similar to those enumerated by the Delaware Supreme Court in *Polk v. Good, 507 A.2d 531, 536 (Del. 1986):*

> * * * (1) the probably validity of the claims, (2) the apparent difficulties in enforcing the claims through the courts, (3) the collectibility of any judgment recovered, (4) the delay, expense, and trouble of litigation, (5) the amount of compromise as compared with the amount and collectibility of a judgment, and (6) the views of the parties involved, pro and con.

Evaluation of a settlement becomes more difficult when it involves nonpecuniary benefits to the corporation of the plaintiff class. For example, settlements of derivative suits may involve agreements to add outside directors to the board, to create more independent audit, compensation, or nominating committees, or to require managers to surrender stock options * * * [Professor Roberta] Romano reports that approximately one-half of the derivative suits settlements [that she] studied included structural relief and only about one-fifth included monetary relief. Although settlements calling for improved governance mechanisms may reduce the prospect of future wrongdoing, they raise a separate problem: in the words of the A[merican] L[aw] I[nstitute], "such therapeutic relief can sometimes represent a counterfeit currency by which the parties can increase the apparent value of the settlement and thereby justify higher attorney's fees for plaintiff's counsel, who is often the real party in interest." To deal with this problem, the ALI recommends that the court review the value of non-pecuniary relief both when evaluating the settlement and when computing plaintiff's counsel fees. ALI Principles of Corporate Governance Section 7.14, Comment c.

American Law Institute, Principles of Corporate Governance: Analysis and Recommendations

Part VII.   Remedies

Chapter 1.   The Derivative Action
Analysis and Recommendation

§ 7.17.   PLAINTIFF'S ATTORNEY'S FEES AND EXPENSES

A successful plaintiff in a derivative action should be entitled to recover reasonable attorney's fees and other reasonable litigation expenses from the corporation, as determined by the court having jurisdiction over the action, but in no event should the attorney's fee award exceed a reasonable proportion of the value of the relief (including nonpecuniary relief) obtained by the plaintiff for the corporation.

Comment:

a. Comparison with present law. The rule is firmly established that a plaintiff who has conferred a substantial benefit on the corporation is entitled to recover reasonable expenses, including attorney's fees, from the corporation in whose name the action is brought. Most American jurisdictions today follow the "lodestar" method of computing the attorney's fee, which essentially rewards the plaintiff's attorney for time reasonably expended in the action. However, Delaware decisions and a recent Supreme Court case have indicated that in "common fund" cases, such as the derivative action, it may sometimes be more appropriate to award a percentage of the recovery. In light of this lack of consensus, Section 7.17 does not direct the court to use either the lodestar or its chief rival, the percentage-of-the-recovery formula, as the basis for the fee award.

Instead, the only admonition of § 7.17 is that the fee, however computed, should not exceed a reasonable percentage of the total recovery. This limitation recognizes that in some cases the settlement dynamics can result in overstating the "benefit" in order to justify a fee award. Over the long run, allowing the award of an attorney's fee on the basis of such cosmetic benefits would encourage the filing of non-meritorious claims and can expose the corporation to a greater risk of frivolous litigation than would prevail if closer judicial scrutiny were given to the value of the benefit received by the corporation. Thus, although § 7.17 does not require that the benefit be a tangible one ... it does require that the benefit be susceptible to sufficient valuation as to permit the court to relate the fee award to it. * * *

d. Substantial benefit and nonpecuniary relief. The "substantial benefit" test for determining when a plaintiff's attorney has been sufficiently "successful to justify an award of attorneys' fees" looks to whether the action had an impact "more than technical in its consequence" and achieved "a result which corrects or prevents an abuse which would be prejudicial to the rights and interests of the corporation or affect the enjoyment or protection of an essential right to the stockholder's interest." [citation omitted] Thus, the mere fact that there has been a judgment or settlement does not alone establish that it constituted a substantial benefit. For example, a judgment or settlement simply delaying a shareholders' meeting or requiring additional notices might accomplish relatively little of value. On the other hand, such a standard is forward-looking in the sense that future protection and avoidance of continuing abuse deserves judicial consideration in the fee determination. Thus, a judgment establishing an important precedent or principle that will be of continuing value to all shareholders merits an enhanced fee, in part because shareholders hold diversified portfolios and will benefit from the decision's impact on other corporations.

Case law has long recognized that nonpecuniary relief to the corporation can constitute a "substantial" benefit. * * * Under Section 7.17, the requisite "substantial benefit" can consist of nonpecuniary relief, but the court must attempt to place a value on this relief in order to apply the percentage ceiling on attorneys' fees mandated by Section 7.17, at least when the nonpecuniary relief constitutes a substantial portion of the relief obtained by the settlement.

* * *

SULLIVAN v. HAMMER

1990 WL 114223 (Del. Ch. 1990)

MEMORANDUM OPINION ON THE APPROVAL OF A STOCKHOLDER DERIVATIVE AND CLASS ACTION SETTLEMENT

The settlement of this stockholder derivative and class action suit must be approved because, on balance, the claims asserted would likely be dismissed before or after a trial because they all fall within the ambit of the business judgment rule and although the benefit to be received by the corporation and its stockholders from the settlement is meager, it is adequate considering all the facts and circumstances.

I

On April 25, 1989 defendant Occidental Petroleum Corporation ("Occidental") mailed to its stockholders a Proxy Statement for the Company's 1989 annual meeting, which reported that a Special Committee of Occidental had approved a proposal to provide financial support for The Armand Hammer Museum of Art and Cultural Center ("the Museum"). The Museum is to be located adjacent to and be physically integrated with Occidental's Los Angeles headquarters building, the Occidental Petroleum Center. Dr. Armand Hammer, who is over 90 years old, is the founder and Chairman of the Board of Occidental.

The Proxy Statement referred to the financial support that Occidental would provide to the Museum, including: (a) funding construction costs estimated at approximately $ 50 million and granting the Museum a 30-year rent-free lease in the Occidental Petroleum Center; (b) funding an annuity for the Museum, at an estimated after-tax cost of $ 24 million; and (c) granting the Museum an option to purchase the Museum complex and the Occidental Petroleum Center at the end of the 30-year lease term for $ 55 million, their estimated fair market value at that time. * * *

Plaintiffs filed this action asserting class and derivative claims on May 9, 1989. The complaint alleges, inter alia: (1) that Occidental's Proxy Statement failed to disclose certain material facts; (2) that Occidental's expenditures and commitments with respect to the Museum and its obligations to the Armand Hammer Foundation pursuant to Dr. Hammer's employment contract constitute a gift and waste of corporate assets; (3) that certain individual defendants (directors of Occidental) had breached their duty of care in authorizing these expenditures; (4) that Dr. Hammer had breached his duty of loyalty by causing Occidental to make these expenditures for his personal benefit; and (5) that the remaining individual defendants had aided and abetted Dr. Hammer. The complaint sought injunctive, declaratory, rescissory and other equitable relief. * * *

Previously, on May 2, 1989, an action had been commenced in this Court captioned Kahn v. Occidental Petroleum Corporation, et al., (the "Kahn" action) alleging claims substantially similar to those in this action. * * *

On May 9, 1989, plaintiff's counsel accepted defendants' invitation to enter into settlement discussions and between May 24, 1989 and June 3, 1989, met to discuss a possible settlement. * * * Plaintiffs' counsel made an effort to include Mr. Kahn's New York counsel in the settlement negotiations but were rebuffed.

On May 12, 1989, Occidental issued a supplement to its Proxy Statement. Plaintiffs concede that the supplemental disclosures provided the corrective disclosures the Sullivan and Levitan complaints sought.

On June 3, 1989 * * * the parties entered into a written Memorandum of Understanding setting forth the general terms of a proposed settlement of the litigation * * * On June 9, 1989, the plaintiff in Kahn filed a motion to enjoin defendants from proceeding to complete the settlement. This Court by written decision dated July 19, 1989 denied Kahn's preliminary injunction motion. That opinion did indicate, however, several areas of concern that the Court thought should be addressed before the settlement was submitted to the Court for approval.

On August 4, 1989, a Special Committee of Occidental's Board of Directors retained former Chancellor Grover C. Brown of the law firm of Morris, James, Hitchens & Williams as its independent counsel to review the merits of the actions taken by the Board of Occidental and to advise the members of the Special Committee with respect to any financial support to be given by Occidental to the Museum. On October 6, 1989, Occidental's Board of Directors delegated to the Special Committee the additional authority to approve or disapprove the proposed settlement agreement in this action after consulting with and considering the advice of its independent counsel.

The Special Committee reexamined the proposal for the financial support by Occidental to the Museum. Also, through its independent counsel, the Special Committee met with and discussed possible settlement of the litigation with counsel for the plaintiff in the Kahn action, as well as counsel for plaintiffs in this action. The Special Committee subsequently, and for the first time, formally approved the challenged charitable contributions. Furthermore, the Special Committee was advised by its special counsel regarding the litigations and determined that, in its opinion, it was in the best interests of Occidental to agree to the proposed settlement presented in this action.

Since the Court's July 19, 1989 opinion, counsel for plaintiffs also engaged in further negotiations with the defendants, the Special Committee and its counsel on the aspects of the settlement. Plaintiffs' counsel asserted that he evaluated or reevaluated the challenged transactions, the relative strength of plaintiffs' complaint, the activities of the Special Committee and the claims made by Kahn and various others opposing settlement of this litigation. * * *

II

Despite this Court's expressed displeasure with the settlement efforts, as set forth in its July 19, 1989 opinion in Kahn, the settlement now before the Court is only slightly changed from the June 3, 1989 Memorandum of Understanding. The proposed Settlement, inter alia, provides:

(1) The Museum building shall be named the "Occidental Petroleum Cultural Center Building" with the name displayed appropriately on the building.

(2) Occidental shall be treated as a corporate sponsor by the Museum for as long as the Museum occupies the building.

(3) Occidental's contribution of the building shall be recognized by the Museum in public references to the facility.

(4) Three of Occidental's directors shall serve on the Museum's Board (or no less than one-third of the total Museum Board) with Occidental having the option to designate a fourth director.

(5) There shall be an immediate loan of substantially all of the art collections of Dr. Hammer to the Museum and there shall be an actual transfer of ownership of the collections upon Dr. Hammer's death or the commencement of operation of the Museum whichever later occurs.

(6) All future charitable contributions by Occidental to any Hammer-affiliated charities shall be limited by the size of the dividends paid to Occidental's common stockholders. At current dividend levels, Occidental's annual contributions to Hammer-affiliated charities pursuant to this limitation could not exceed approximately 3 cents per share.

(7) Any amounts Occidental pays for construction of the Museum in excess of $ 50 million and any amounts paid to the Foundation upon Dr. Hammer's death must be charged against the agreed ceiling on limitations to Hammer-affiliated charities.

(8) Occidental's expenditures for the Museum construction shall not exceed $ 50 million, except that an additional $ 10 million may be expended through December 31, 1990 but only if such additional expenditures do not enlarge the scope of construction and if such expenditures are approved by the Special Committee. Amounts in excess of $ 50 million must be charged against the limitation on donations to Hammer-affiliated charities.

(9) Occidental shall be entitled to receive 50% of any consideration received in excess of a $ 55 million option price for the Museum property or 50% of any consideration the Museum receives from the assignment or transfer of its option or lease to a third party.

(10) Plaintiffs' attorney fees in this action shall not exceed $ 1.4 million.

III

* * * [T]he settlement in the Court's opinion leaves much to be desired.

The Court's role in reviewing the proposed Settlement, however, is quite restricted. If the Court was a stockholder of Occidental it might vote for new directors, if it was on the Board it might vote for new management and if it was a member of the Special Committee it might vote against the Museum project. But its options are limited in reviewing a proposed settlement to applying Delaware law to the facts adduced in the record and then determining in its business judgment whether, on balance, the settlement is reasonable.

Delaware law clearly favors the voluntary settlement of litigation. It is neither necessary nor desirable for the Court to try the case or to decide any of the issues on the merits prior to determining whether a settlement should be approved. Rather, the Court must look to the facts and circumstances upon which the claim is based, and the possible defenses thereto, and must then exercise its own business judgment and determine the overall reasonableness of the settlement. In short, it is the function of the Court to decide whether the proposed settlement is fair and reasonable in light of the factual and legal circumstances of the case. * * *

The Delaware Supreme Court recently [stated] in *Barkan v. Amsted Industries, Inc., Del. Supr., 567 A.2d 1279, 1285 (1989)*:

"The strength of claims raised in a class action lawsuit helps to determine whether the consideration received for their settlement is adequate and whether dismissal with prejudice is appropriate. Thus, if the Chancellor were to find that the plaintiff class was being asked to sacrifice a facially credible claim for a small consideration, he would be justified in rejecting a settlement as unfair. Conversely, where the Chancellor finds that the plaintiff's potential challenges have little chance of success he has good reason to approve the proposed settlement."

The Court must therefore consider the benefit to the class and whether the benefit is reasonable when compared to the range of potential recovery.

IV

The potential for ultimate success on the merits here is, realistically, very poor. The business judgment rule, as consistently reiterated by the

Delaware Supreme Court, stands as an almost impenetrable barrier to the plaintiffs. * * *

The plaintiffs have not shown any facts which would show that the directors have any self-interest in the transaction either from a personal financial interest or from a motive for entrenchment in office. Nor is there any evidence in the record showing that the members of the Special Committee are in fact dominated by Dr. Hammer or anyone else.

The record also shows that the directors and the Special Committee gave due consideration to the transaction.

It is therefore highly probable that, in deciding a motion to dismiss or for summary judgment or after trial, this Court would find that the decisions of the directors are entitled to the presumption of propriety afforded by the business judgment rule.

This Court, therefore, must review the claims of plaintiffs against a presumption that the acts of the directors are valid.

V

First to be reviewed is the claim that the compensation being paid to Dr. Hammer constitutes a waste of corporate assets. While there is a limit to executive compensation, courts have always been hesitant to substitute their judgment for the directors in ascertaining whether executive compensation is rational.

On the present record it is obvious that plaintiffs would have a most difficult burden to establish that the compensation being paid to Dr. Hammer is a waste of corporate assets. It is therefore highly probable that plaintiffs would be unsuccessful on this claim.

VI

This court's role in reviewing the gift by Occidental Petroleum Corporation to the Museum is also severely limited.

The test of whether a corporation may make a charitable gift is its reasonableness. It is clear that the Museum qualifies as a charity. From the present record it is also clear that the present gift (as now limited) is within the range of reasonableness.

It is therefore reasonably probable that plaintiffs would also fail to prevail on this claim.

VII

Against this background of weakness of plaintiffs' claims, the Court must weigh the consideration being received by the class.

While the consideration to be received by the class is speculative, I find, on balance, in the exercise of my business judgment, that it is adequate to support the settlement.

Plaintiffs' claim that "the proposed settlement: (1) reinforces and assures Occidental's identification with and meaningful participation in the affairs of the Museum; (2) reinforces and protects the charitable nature and consequences of Occidental's gifts by securing prompt delivery and irrevocable transfer of the art collections to the Museum; (3) imposes meaningful controls upon the total construction costs that Occidental will pay, which have already forced the reduction of the construction budget by $ 19.4 million; (4) places meaningful restrictions upon Occidental's future charitable donations to Hammer-affiliated entities and avoids increases in posthumous payments to the Foundation or any other designated recipient after Dr. Hammer's death; (5) restores to Occidental an equitable portion of any appreciation of the properties in the event the Museum exercises its option and disposes of the properties or transfers its option for value; and (6) guarantees that the art collections will continue to be located in the Los Angeles area and remain available for the enjoyment of the American public rather than dissipated into private collections or sold abroad." Obviously the value of these benefits is speculative.

Plaintiffs, in justifying their request for attorney fees, submitted an affidavit of Kenneth A. Budenstein of Duff & Phelps Financial Consulting Co. in which it is claimed that the monetary value of having the Museum Building called the "Occidental Petroleum Cultural Center Building" is approximately $ 10 million.

Although the Court views this estimate with a good deal of skepticism, it seems clear that Occidental will receive good will from the gift and will be able to utilize the adjacent Museum in the promotion of its business purposes.

I therefore find that the benefit to the stockholders of Occidental is sufficient to support the settlement and is adequate, if only barely so, when compared to the weakness of plaintiffs' claims.

IX

Last to be considered is plaintiffs' request to be awarded $ 1.4 million in counsel fees.

Plaintiffs concede that while there are other factors to be considered, the primary factor to be considered is the benefits achieved by the litigation. Plaintiffs claim that:

> "The settlement here provides three forms of benefits which support a substantial award of attorneys' fees. First, the settlement has generated a monetary benefit by reducing the amount Occidental would have otherwise expended on the construction of the museum by nearly $ 20 million. Second, the settlement provides substantial non-monetary benefits that have been quantified by a competent expert (e.g. naming the building for Occidental; division of sale proceeds). Third, other tangible and substantial non-monetary benefits have been conferred, including corrective disclosure and limitation of charitable contributions."

I find the value of the benefits to be highly speculative and the methodology of the expert to not be entirely persuasive.

After considering all the facts and circumstances * * * I find that the award of counsel fees and reimbursable costs must be reduced to $ 800,000, in part, because: 1) the value of the benefit is significantly less than plaintiffs claim; 2) the possibility of success, when suit was filed (as plaintiffs now concede) was weak; 3) the benefit achieved is meager ... and 4) the relatively short time the plaintiffs' counsel devoted to the case.

* * *

As the court in Sullivan indicates in its opinion, it previously had denied the Kahn plaintiffs' motion to enjoin settlement negotiations between defendants and the Sullivan plaintiffs. *Kahn v. Occidental Petroleum*, 1989 WL 79967 (Del. Ch. 1989). In the opinion denying that motion, however, the court had commented that "[t]he acts of defendants in approaching the attorney in the later-filed Sullivan action and ignoring the counsel in the first-filed Kahn suit concerning possible settlement, and then negotiating settlement without advising the Kahn counsel" raised the "spectre of ... possible overreaching[.]" The court observed, "I increasingly suspect that in some cases plaintiffs' counsel seem to be primarily motivated by the huge counsel fees now being generated in class and stockholder derivative actions and that defendant corporations are often willing to pay the fees to obtain a res judicata bar to claims against the corporation."

The court also noted in its opinion denying the motion for injunction that "[a]mong the troublesome issues which will have to be addressed at any settlement hearing" is "the failure of the Special Committee appointed by the directors to hire its own counsel and advisors[.]" As the opinion approving the settlement notes, the Special Committee retained special counsel to advise it with respect to the corporation's contributions to the museum and the disposition of the litigation before it submitted the settlement for approval.

Attorney Conflict of Interest Issues

As we have seen, in a derivative action, the corporation is the nominal plaintiff but also is a defendant. It is being sued to compel it to bring an action against its co-defendants, who are directors and/or officers who are alleged to have caused it injury. Since any recovery from individual defendants found liable would go to the corporation, the corporate and individual defendants have potentially conflicting interests. At the same time, the corporation and individual defendants have congruent interests if the corporation resists the plaintiffs' suit because it does not wish to pursue a cause of action against the individuals. Does the potential conflict prevent regular corporate counsel from representing both the corporate and individual defendants in a derivative suit? Or does the potential alignment of interests permit dual representation until a conflict actually arises? Unfortunately, as one court has put it, "as a general matter, the case law is not uniform on the issue of joint representation of the corporation and individual defendants" in this situation. *Bell Atlantic Corp. v. Bolger*, 2 F.3d 1304 (3d Cir. 1993).

One line of cases and commentary maintains that corporate counsel may never represent both the corporate and individual defendants in a derivative action. *See, e.g., In re Oracle Securities Litigation*, 829 F.Supp. 1176 (N.D. Cal. 1993); *Messing v. FDI, Inc.*, 439 F.Supp. 776 (D.N.J. 1977); *Cannon v. U.S. Acoustics*, 398 F.Supp. 209, 216–217 (N.D. Ill. 1975), aff'd in relevant part per curiam, 532 F.2d 1118 (7th Cir. 1976). 13 William M. Fletcher, Fletcher Cyclopedia of the Law of Private Corporations, Section 6205, at 442 (perm. rev. ed. vol. 1991; Charles J. Greves, Practice Tips: The Unique Issues in Shareholder Derivative Litigation, 25 Los Angeles Lawyer 16 (December 2002). The concern about such representation is that the interests of the corporation may not receive adequate consideration. Regular counsel is accustomed to working with and treating directors and officers as the voice of the company, and often develops personal relationships with them. As one court suggested, when directors and officers are defendants in the derivative action, it seems likely that counsel "would be reluctant to recommend that the corporation take any position adverse to these men, individual defendants for whom he works on a day-to-day basis and who control his future with the corporation." *Oracle*, 829 F.Supp., at 1189. This scenario is especially an issue with respect to in-house counsel, although regular outside counsel also might be subject to the same subtle influences.

Another concern about dual representation is that counsel will have obtained confidential information from the individual clients in the course of representing the company. She has an obligation to keep this information confidential from parties who might use it to these clients' disadvantage, such as the corporation. While this theoretically is a legitimate concern, as a practical matter it arguably will be of less concern in a derivative suit. It is likely that in this type of case information has been and will be shared between the corporation and the individual defendants. *See Cannon*, 398 F.Supp. at 216–217.

A second approach to dual representation in the derivative context is to prohibit it when plaintiffs allege fraud, intentional misconduct, or self-dealing. *See Musheno v. Gensemer*, 897 F.Supp. 833 (M.D. Pa. 1995); *Forrest v. Baeza*, 58 Cal.App.4th 65, 67 Cal.Rptr.2d 857 (Cal. App. 1997); *Lewis v. Shafer Stores Co.*, 218 F.Supp. 238 (S.D.N.Y. 1963). *See also Bell Atlantic v. Bolger*, 2 F.3d 1304, 1317 (3d Cir. 1993) (prohibiting dual representation when such allegations are made, "except in patently frivolous cases"). One court suggests that this position reflects the fact that allegations of breaches of the duty of loyalty traditionally have been regarded as more serious than allegations of breaches of the duty of care. *Bolger*, 2 F.3d at 1317. That court went on to say that separate representation should be required "in cases where the line is blurred between duties of care and loyalty." *Id.* Another court has held that separate representation is required when derivative plaintiffs allege fraud and self-dealing, even when an independent committee of the corporation has determined that the company should not pursue legal action against the individual defendants. *Musheno*, 897 F.Supp. at 837.

The Model Rules of Professional Conduct appear to follow this second approach, which focuses on the nature of the plaintiffs' allegations. Comment 13 to Model Rule 1.13 says that a derivative action "may be brought nominally by the organization, but usually is, in fact, a legal controversy over management of the organization." Comment 14 states: "Most derivative actions are a normal incident of an organization's affairs, to be defended by the organization's lawyer like any other suit." If, however, "the claim involves serious charges of wrongdoing by those in control of the organization, a conflict may arise between the lawyer's duty to the organization and the lawyer's relationship with the board. In those circumstances, Rule 1.7 governs who should represent the directors and the organization." When separate representation is required, the practice is that corporate counsel will represent the individual defendants because of her familiarity and past experience with them. *See Musheno*, 897 F.Supp. at 837; *Cannon*, 398 F.Supp. at 220; *Oracle*, 829 F.Supp. at 1189.

Finally, the American Law Institute's *Restatement (Third) of the Law Governing Lawyers (2000)* provides that a lawyer may represent both the corporate and individual defendants in a derivative action if the company's disinterested directors conclude that there is no basis for the claim. *Id. at Section 131, Comment g.* Because of the potential for conflict, such dual representation requires the consent of all clients; in the case of the corporate client, this means "responsible agents not named and not likely to be named in the case." *Id.* The Comment to Section 131 says that "if the advice of the lawyer acting for the organization was an important factor in the action of the officers and directors that gave rise to the suit, it is appropriate for the lawyer to represent, if anyone, the officers and directors and for the organization to obtain new counsel."

PROBLEM

Starcrest Corporation is a public company founded by the Adams family in 1935. Its common stock is listed on the New York Stock Exchange. Starcrest constructs, owns and operates hotels and restaurants throughout the United States. It has built many of these hotels and restaurants after acquiring the raw land on which they sit.

In 1955, Starcrest sold 60% of its stock to public investors. Members of the Adams family continue to own the remaining 40%. Elizabeth Adams, the president and chief executive officer, owns 25% and other family members who are not active in the business own the remaining 15%. The board of directors consists of Elizabeth Adams; Paul Baker, the chief financial officer; Robert Crown, the vice-president for sales; Linda Diamond, the general counsel; and Michael Brown, Ruth Grey and Robert White, each of whom is a prominent business executive having no other connections with Starcrest. Baker and Crown have been officers for more than ten years. Diamond joined Starcrest two years ago. Prior to that, she was a senior associate in its principal outside law firm in which she devoted most of her time to Starcrest's work.

Many years ago, Elizabeth inherited a large tract of raw land from a distant uncle. Until recently, she had paid little attention to this land. Now, however, Starcrest is considering building another hotel in the area where the land is situated. Although she knew very little about real estate, conversations with her uncle's lawyer (who specialized in probate work) convinced her that the land was worth $10 million. For the next 30 days, she sought to sell the land privately to sophisticated buyers, none of whom offered more than $5 million. Somewhat daunted, she next listed the land with a real estate broker for a thirty-day period at price of $7.5 million, but received no offers.

In early March, at Elizabeth's request, Patricia Jones, the head of the Corporation's real estate department, appraised the land as a possible site for a new hotel. After examining other nearby sites, none of which seemed as suitable for a new hotel, Jones concluded that the land was worth the *$7.5 million* Elizabeth had been seeking. On March 15, Elizabeth offered to sell the land to Starcrest for $7.5 million. She accompanied her offer with a copy of Jones' appraisal. She did not disclose that she had unsuccessfully tried to sell the land before offering it to the Corporation because she did not believe that this information was material to the board of directors in making its decision.

In response to the offer, the board of directors established a committee consisting of Brown, Grey and Diamond to evaluate the offer. Because none of the committee members were experts in real estate, they hired an outside consultant who opined that the land might conceivably be worth *$7.5* million but that he wouldn't pay that price. The committee also obtained a formal appraisal from an outside appraiser which valued the land at $5 million.

In June, relying primarily on Jones' appraisal and that of its outside appraiser, the committee recommended that the Corporation offer to purchase the land for $6.5 million, a price that Elizabeth had indicated she was willing to accept. The committee's report set out in detail the procedures it had followed and the basis for the recommendation. Grey dissented from the recommendation on the grounds that there was insufficient evidence to justify paying more than $5 million. The board accepted the committee's recommendation by a vote of 4–1. Grey again dissented and White did not attend the meeting at which the decision was made. Elizabeth did not participate in any of the deliberations of either the committee or the board of directors and did not vote on the transaction.

On Diamond's advice, the Corporation submitted the transaction to the shareholders for ratification at the annual meeting in October. The proxy statement disclosed all the information available to the board of directors and the process by which the board reached its decision. At the meeting, the shareholders ratified the transaction with Elizabeth and other Adams family members voting. 54% of the outstanding stock voted in favor; 22% opposed.

Two years after Starcrest acquired the land from Elizabeth surveys disclosed the existence of a previously undiscovered geological fault that made it economically unfeasible for Starcrest to build the planned hotel.

After considerable effort, Starcrest sold the land for $2.5 million, incurring a loss of at least $4 million.

1. a. Harry Patterson is a retired attorney who owns a few shares of stock in many public companies, including 10 shares of the stock of Starcrest. Harry has agreed to serve as a named plaintiff in many previous shareholder suits. Pamela Gilbert, the partner who has been plaintiffs counsel in many such suits, recently advised Harry that it would be possible to assert numerous claims against Elizabeth and the Starcrest board of directors alleging breaches of their fiduciary duties. Harry told Pamela that he did not need to know the details of the allegations and authorized her to file such claims as she thought had merit.

Is it appropriate for Pamela to accept the representation on his basis'? Who is Pamela's client? How will Pamela be compensated for her work'? What conflicts does Pamela have in proceeding further'? Do your answers depend on who initiated the discussion about possible litigation'?

b. In a derivative suit, would Harry be required to make demand on the Starcrest board of directors or would he be able to establish demand futility with respect to the claims in the action?

2. a. You are an attorney in the law firm that advised the Starcrest board of directors in connection with the purchase of the land from Elizabeth. In a derivative suit against Elizabeth and the Starcrest board of directors, whom if anyone, can you represent?

b. Assume that the lawsuit has been filed but that no pre-trial discovery has occurred. Prior to the court's ruling on various preliminary motions, Pamela approaches you and proposes a settlement on the following terms:

1. Elizabeth will repurchase the land for $3.5 million. If she is able to sell the land for more than that amount within one year, she will pay Starcrest 1/3 of the difference between her sale price and the *$3.5 million*. In no event, however, will she pay more than an additional $500,000.

2. The board of Starcrest will create a special negotiating committee consisting solely of independent directors which will be required to approve any subsequent contracts between Starcrest and its officers and directors.

3. Starcrest will pay attorneys' fees of $850,000 to Pamela and Starcrest will support Pamela's request to the court for that amount.

How do you respond? What is the likelihood that the court will approve the settlement? What additional information is the court likely to request before deciding on the fairness of the settlement? In answering these questions, consider who you are most likely to be representing and how that representation will affect your answers.

Chapter 30

TRANSNATIONAL LAW PRACTICE

The tremendous growth of transnational corporations, global markets, and law firms with offices in several different countries means that on any given matter a lawyer may have to address both domestic and foreign law considerations. Different countries have different rules on what constitutes the practice of law, and in many countries only specified persons may provide certain kinds of legal services. Furthermore, there is no uniform set of ethical rules for lawyers practicing in the transnational arena. The closest approximation to such uniformity is the code of conduct governing lawyers in European Union countries who work on matters involving more than one member country. Finally, lawyers must determine which body of substantive law governs the matters on which they are working. Lawyers engaged in transnational practice thus often must attempt to navigate largely uncharted waters.

OVERVIEW OF THE CHAPTER

First, read Model Rule 8.5, which we encountered in the Chapter on Multistate Practice. Take note of Comment 7, which reflects a recent revision to the Comments. It states: "The choice of law provision applies to lawyers engaged in transnational practice, unless international law, treaties, or other agreements between competent regulatory authorities in the affected jurisdictions provide otherwise." Notwithstanding this provision, some uncertainty remains with regard to transnational practice because not all states have adopted this change, foreign countries are not bound by it, and the Rule itself contains some ambiguity with respect to lawyers not engaged in practice before a tribunal.

The excerpt from Carroll describes the different roles that a lawyer may be called upon to play when engaged in transnational practice, and compares the requirements that various countries have established in order to practice law in those jurisdictions. Carroll observes that there is little coordination among countries in responding to the increasing amount of transnational practice. As you read this excerpt, consider how a United States lawyer playing each of the roles that Carroll describes would have to do to practice in the countries that the excerpt discusses.

A short Note on Multi–Disciplinary practice organizations follows Carroll, which describes how the affiliation of lawyers with large accounting firms has created professional service organizations that provide a significant amount of transnational legal services. Make sure that you understand the Model Rule provision that effectively bar integrated lawyer and non-lawyer organizations in the United States. The excerpt from Frank then describes a notable effort to harmonize the ethical regulation of cross-border practice in Europe: the European Union Code of Conduct for lawyers (CCBE). The CCBE is interesting both as an example of an effort to coordinate regulation among countries, as well as a basis for comparison with respect to the substantive rules that it contains. Finally, the *Pancotto* case illustrates the considerations that courts take into account in addressing choice of law questions for matters that involve more than one country.

The first problem asks you to analyze the respective impact of United States, French, and CCBE ethical rules that all potentially apply to a situation involving transnational practice. The second problem requires you to draw on *Pancotto* in determining which law should govern a lawsuit involving parties and activities with connections both to the United States and Spain.

MODEL RULES: 1.7, 5.4, 5.5, 8.5

A. OVERVIEW OF TRANSNATIONAL PRACTICE

Wayne J. Carroll, INNOCENTS ABROAD: OPPORTUNITIES AND CHALLENGES FOR THE INTERNATIONAL LEGAL ADVISER

34 VAND. J. TRANSNAT'L L. 1097 (2001)

I. INTRODUCTION

The legal profession in most countries developed with a traditional focus on the needs of the average citizen. Only in rare instances did lawyers need much more than knowledge of the local law, as legal norms were applied in a "jurisdictionally mutually exclusive" manner. The concept of overlapping legal systems conflicted with the concepts of the nation-state and sovereignty. Times have changed. Along with the globalization of trade and expanded communication has come the need for advisers to combine local legal paradigms with those from multiple, often international, sources. Lawyers and legal practices have recognized these trends and an internationalization of the practice is already underway. Similarly, educational institutions realize that they need to modify traditional curricula to prepare future lawyers for global practice. But are the regulatory authorities sufficiently adapting to these changes? This Article argues that some are not and looks at one factor in the equation, namely admission requirements and restrictions.

* * *

II. SETTING THE STAGE: INTERNATIONAL AND TRANSNATIONAL LEGAL ADVISING

The demand for international legal advice takes up an increasingly larger part of legal services as a whole. Many, if not most, of the practitioners of international and transnational legal services are in large commercial firms. Over the past few years, many large commercial firms have merged with firms in other countries in an attempt to offer seamless global legal services. Smaller firms have also banded together— more frequently through informal alliances—to extend international legal services to their clients.

* * * The following categories help to distinguish the roles a lawyer may have to assume in international practice.

A. Advising Foreign Clients on Domestic Law in the "Domestic Tongue"

Clients having business in or personal connections to a jurisdiction other than their home jurisdiction(s) often consult lawyers in the other jurisdiction for advice on local law. The only real "international" element in this picture is that the client happens to come from a jurisdiction outside the one in which the advising lawyer generally practices. The actual work of the lawyer changes little. They resort to the usual sources for addressing the particular legal issues, rely on similar situations encountered before with domestic or foreign clients, and advise accordingly in the usual tongue of the local jurisdiction.

In dealing with foreign clients, the main difference from the standard advising scenario often entails dealing with cultural nuances or dispelling misperceptions foreign clients might have regarding the domestic legal system. Aside from the cultural sensitivity aspect, this type of legal practice is, for the most part, indistinguishable from practice in the normal domestic context. Generally for this type of legal practice, the only prerequisites are those mandated by the jurisdiction for the provision of legal advice, namely admission to the local legal profession. For most jurisdictions, this involves a combination of legal study and passing of a professional examination.

B. Advising Clients on Domestic Law in a "Foreign Tongue"

* * * In providing advice in a foreign language, the adviser by necessity must often equate both factual and legal concepts from two or more legal systems. The adviser might do this directly, based upon his or her own understanding of and familiarity with the foreign legal system and language, or indirectly, by means of supervising and reviewing the work done by legal translators.

From the client's perspective, the fact that the advice is given in its native or primary tongue reduces the "comprehension risk," from both a linguistic and a legal/conceptual point of view. The legal concepts, albeit from a "foreign,"—those existing or arising under a legal system other than the one of the adviser's normal jurisdiction—legal system, are being analyzed, discussed, and presented outside of their natural conceptual environment but within their and their client's natural linguistic environment. At the end of the day, the client relies upon the information communicated to him in his native or requested language, and the lawyer is potentially liable for the accuracy of this advice.

Certain practice areas are more likely to be affected by globalization than others. Immigration law has always had an inherent international component to it. Other practice areas, such as divorce and estate planning, take on an added international dimension for those clients with family in other countries. For the multilingual lawyer, practicing in these areas enables him to better serve the needs of the client and sometimes to act as a liaison between cultures, both legal and general. The significance of this type of practice is growing as the size of the local immigrant population in many countries increases. In addition to the normal admission requirements, language ability is an added practical requirement for this type of practice.

C. Advising Clients on Foreign or International Law in the "Domestic Tongue"

As barriers to travel, trade, and communication have fallen, clients are now increasingly confronted with foreign legal systems. Here it is useful to make a distinction between "international law"—supranational law—and "foreign law"—the domestic law of a foreign jurisdiction. The former is often subdivided into "public international law," the law of nations, and "private international law," a layer of supranational law applicable to domestic parties resting above domestic law. Both are generally considered part of the respective domestic legal system. "Foreign law," on the other hand, generally refers to the national legislation, case law, and regulations of a foreign jurisdiction. Non-locally admitted lawyers are not permitted to give advice regarding it. Although this law also includes supranational law, including that jurisdiction's interpretation of international law, the term mainly refers to the strictly "homegrown" law. In practice, the line can often become blurred.

D. Advising Clients on Foreign or International Law in a "Foreign Tongue"

Although less common in the United States than in Europe and other regions, some legal practitioners also offer advice on legal issues outside of their original jurisdiction of admission and in a language that may not be their native or primary one. Although this is perhaps the narrowest group of legal practitioners, their numbers are growing. These practitioners and their firms emphasize the global nature of their legal practice, implicitly de-emphasizing the importance of geographic boundaries or, for that matter, the related legal systems.

As in section B above, the relevant regulatory requirement is admission to local practice in the jurisdictions in which the individual or firm advises, and the practical requirement is language ability. Aside from the attendant right to advise on public international law through local admission, the question arises under what authority a locally-admitted lawyer may opine on foreign law. Even if the lawyer is fluent in the language and intimately familiar with a particular foreign jurisdiction, few are actually dually-qualified. This is changing, however, as lawyers take advantage of increased liberalization by becoming fully admitted practitioners in another jurisdiction. Until then they are left to deal with the vagaries of the existing rules covering temporary or ancillary interjurisdictional practice.

III.   Existing Requirements and Barriers to Practice: The U.S. and EU Compared

* * * The reasons why a lawyer might wish to expand his or her practice could be personal, professional, or a combination of both. The lawyer may be asked to or decide to follow a client to a new jurisdiction, for example. Although temporarily practicing the law of a foreign jurisdiction is tolerated to a certain extent, most countries restrict the volume of such local work a lawyer may accept without obtaining full admission to the local bar and associating with local counsel. And even these rules are not consistently applied across jurisdictions or even within a jurisdiction. The only safe solution for the practitioner is to become fully admitted to the local legal profession. Unfortunately, this is often not possible. The approaches of the United States and the European Union—both for domestic and foreign lawyers—are compared and contrasted below.

A.   The U.S. Admission Requirements

1.   Locally-Trained Lawyers

Most states in the United States have similar requirements for admission to the local legal profession. A uniform test, the Law School Admission Test (LSAT), is required by almost all law schools. Law is a graduate degree program, though there are no particular requirements concerning which subject or subjects an applicant to law school must have majored in at the undergraduate level * * *

Following completion of the legal education program ... one may sit for the local bar examination. Half of this examination consists of a harmonized multiple-choice section, while the other half is made up of a number of essays testing the nuances of state law. Almost all applicants for admission must pass a standardized test in professional ethics, and a few states even have a full day of testing covering these topics * * *

2.   Treatment of Other U.S.–Admitted Lawyers

Once a lawyer is admitted in one U.S. jurisdiction he generally faces reduced restrictions to obtain full admission to another U.S. jurisdiction. In a few states, admission in one state generally suffices to gain admission to the local legal profession in other states. Some states will recognize a lawyer's qualification upon a showing of a certain number of years of practice, but others may still require the lawyer to complete the bar examination, or at least a part of it. In some states, the body charged with regulatory oversight of the legal profession has discretion to accept, or not to accept, a lawyer's educational and practice experience in reviewing an application for admission on motion.

3. Treatment of Foreign–Trained Lawyers

Most lawyers, at least those from W[orld] T[rade] O[rganization] Member States, are able to apply for Foreign Legal Consultant status, thereby opening the door to practice their local law under the home legal professional designation. In general, this entails the verification of home country qualifications, the provision of information regarding past practice experience and the intent to practice local law, the obligation to register with the local authority and become subject to its ethical rules, and the duty to report changes in personal or professional status, in particular anything affecting the authorization to practice law. Foreign lawyers wishing to practice local law are generally treated the same as out-of-state lawyers. Some states have special rules that may be more or less restrictive than those covering their U.S. colleagues. * * *

[The American Bar Association also has adopted a Model Rule for Temporary Practice by Foreign Lawyers, modeled on Model Rule 5.5 dealing with Multijurisdictional Practice. The Model Rule provides that a lawyer not admitted in the United States does not engage in the unauthorized practice of law in a U.S. jurisdiction when she performs services on a temporary basis in one of several circumstances: (1) in association with a lawyer admitted to practice in the jurisdiction who actively participates in the matter; (2) that are reasonably related to a pending or potential proceeding before a tribunal outside the United States in which the lawyer is authorized to appear; (3) that are reasonably related to a pending or potential alternative dispute resolution proceeding if the lawyer's services arise out of or are reasonably related to her practice in a jurisdiction in which she is admitted to practice; (4) that are performed for client who resides or has an office in a jurisdiction in which the lawyer is admitted to practice; (5) that arise out of or are reasonably related to a matter that has a substantial connection to a jurisdiction in which the lawyer is authorized to practice; or (6) in a matter governed primarily by international law or the law of a jurisdiction outside the United States.—*Eds.*]

B. The Admission Requirements within the European Union

1. Locally–Trained Lawyers

Within the European Union, law is treated as an undergraduate subject. The curriculum for law reflects this; the first year consists of general classes in philosophy, political science, and government. In the later years, courses delve deeper into the material of the law. Following the completion of the law curriculum, the graduates may apply to sit for the state exam or exams. As in the United States, external review courses for the exam(s) have become a standard part of the legal education in the European Union, filling in gaps in the traditional curriculum and approach to legal education.

Many EU countries also have a practical training period as a prerequisite for admission to the local legal profession. Though there is no counter-part training requirement in the United States, most U.S. law students do seek training opportunities during their period of study. Once an applicant has completed the necessary educational requirements and taken and passed the state examination(s), he may apply to the local court for admission to the local legal profession. Generally, there is a formal step akin to the U.S. swearing-in requirement. Thus, as in the United States, the traditional steps to the legal profession in the European Union involve both an educational component and a testing component. The total time required ranges from four or five years in Spain to up to seven or eight years in countries such as Germany.

The legal profession in many EU countries is much more fragmented than in the United States. Once admitted, the status and professional title of the lawyer depends upon the capacity in which he practices law—for example, as in-house counsel, private practitioner, or in government service. In short, the legal profession in many EU countries is much more fragmented than in the United States. * * * [T]he discussion [here] focuses on the respective equivalent of the U.S. private practitioner.

Until recently, the practice of lawyers in many EU countries was restricted to the region of the local court in which they were formally admitted. For certain practices, such as litigation, this meant that local colleagues would have to represent clients in that jurisdiction. For the most part, these restrictions have been abolished, so that once a lawyer is admitted in an EU country, he may practice throughout the [country].

2. Treatment of EU–Trained Lawyers

[Directives 89/48 and 98/5 of the European Parliament and the Council of the European Union set forth the conditions under which a lawyer admitted to the bar in a country that is a member of the European Union (the "home state") may be permitted to practice law in another member country (the "host state") on terms identical to lawyers admitted to the host state.[1] The lawyer must either pass an examination or have three years' practice experience in her home state in order to attain this status. Doing so permits the lawyer to give advice on her home state law, the host state law, the law of the European community, and international law.[2] While engaged in practice in the host state, the lawyer is subject to its ethical rules.[3] The effect of these Directives is to reduce dramatically barriers to the flow of legal services among countries that are members of the European Union.—Eds.]

3. Treatment of non-EU–Trained Lawyers

Lawyers from outside the European Union have also enjoyed benefits from the loosening of restrictions on admission to the local legal

---

1. European Parliament and Council Directive 89/48, 1989 O.J. (L 19) 16; European Parliament and Council Directive 98/5, 1998 O.J. (L 77) 36.

2. Directive 98/5, Article 5.1.

3. *Id.* at Article 5.1.

profession. As in the United States, though, this liberalization has not been applied consistently across the Member States. Instead, EU restrictions on admission to the local legal profession represent a patchwork of liberalization. This seems to contradict the EU law principle that Directives—the legal basis for much of the liberalization—be implemented consistently throughout the European Union.

a. Liberal Regimes

Countries like England and Wales, Ireland, and France permit foreign lawyers to take a special qualification examination in order to be admitted to local practice. The Qualified Lawyers Transfer Test (QLTT) is a conversion test that enables lawyers qualified in certain countries outside England and Wales, as well as UK and common law Barristers, to qualify as solicitors * * *

France also paints an interesting picture regarding the treatment of non-EU lawyers. Just ten or fifteen years ago, U.S. lawyers could practice U.S. law in France without significant restrictions; eventually they expanded into French law as well. As the numbers grew, the French tightened the rules and introduced an examination requirement in January 1992. Anyone who had been practicing in France up to that point since 1971 as conseil juridique could be grandfathered in. When the examination was first offered in 1996 there were immediate complaints from the small circle of participants, mainly regarding the broad scope of the test. The ABA got involved and argued to the Paris bar that the so-called Article 100 Examination was "unnecessarily burdensome." It requested that the test be made "reasonably related to the applicant's intended practice" and that the French ensure that preparation courses be made readily available. Finally, it requested that the test be made available in the other WTO languages—English or Spanish—in addition to French * * *

b. Restrictive Regimes

Germany represents the small minority of EU countries that do not make any concessions to foreign lawyers. Although, as required by EU legislation, they do offer an examination for foreign lawyers to prove their knowledge of the national law, they do not open this examination to lawyers hailing from outside the European Union. Thus, the only alternative for aspirants for admission to the local legal profession in such countries is to complete the full educational program, a seven or eight year endeavor. For most practitioners, this is simply not feasible, especially given that there is next to no opportunity to pursue legal education in the evening. The requirement thus constitutes a practical bar to entry for those lawyers coming from outside the European Union.

* * *

VI. Conclusion

The market for legal services is calling for more expertise of transnational and international legal issues. To date the legal status of lawyers "dabbling" in legal systems other than that of the jurisdiction of their original or subsequent admission has been a murky area. Recognizing the inevitability and sometimes even the utility of having lawyers capable of opining across legal systems, regulators have gradually begun to accept the practice, provided that the competence of the lawyer is guaranteed and the interests of the client protected. More thought must be given to true cross-system advising scenarios and the related rules applicable thereto.

Increasingly, more than temporary or ancillary advising is sought. Little attention has been paid to the topic of dual or multiple admissions, though with the increased mobility and developments in communication of society, both the opportunity and need for cross-system knowledge and experience will grow. And behind the "closed shop" approach of the restrictive regimes lurks a real danger. The failure of regulators and bar associations to confront such jurisdictions could give rise to a precedent justifying discriminatory treatment of other foreign service providers. If so, much of the progress made in liberalizing such sectors could begin to unravel. The regulators have their work cut out for them in terms of guaranteeing a level playing field worldwide and orienting the admissions rules to reflect the nuances of international legal advising.

* * *

Note: Non-Lawyer Professional Service Firms

It is not only law firms that provide transnational legal services. In some parts of the world, especially in Europe, large accounting firms have become substantially involved in the provision of such services. To some extent, this reflects the fact that many countries do not have a unified legal profession, but a set of different occupations authorized to provide specific types of services that lawyers provide in the United States. Persons in many of these occupations are permitted to affiliate or share fees with nonlawyers, and accounting firms have hired them to furnish these services.[4]

Accounting firms have become a major force in the legal services market in Europe, however, primarily by contractually affiliating with law firms. In these arrangements, the accounting and law firm each formally agrees to work together to provide a variety of professional services to clients. Each firm remains formally separate, and each agrees to refer clients to each other on a non-exclusive basis. The law firm, however, typically identifies its affiliation with the accounting firm on its letterhead and business cards, and in its advertising. The law firm also agrees to purchase goods and services from the accounting firm such as staff, communications technology, office space, and office equipment.[5] In a few countries, law firms and accounting firms can go even further,

---

4. Mary C. Daly, *Monopolist, Aristocrat, or Entrepreneur? A Comparative Perspective on the Future of Multidisciplinary Partnerships in the United States, France, Germany, and the United Kingdom After the Disintegration of Andersen Legal*, 80 Wash. U. L.Q. 589, 607 (2002) (describing accounting firm employment of French conseil juridique, as opposed to avocat).

5. *Id.* at 596–598.

combining into a single integrated professional services firm, generally known as multi-disciplinary partnerships (MDPs).[6]

MDPs are flatly prohibited by ethical rules in the United States. In addition, contractual affiliations between accounting and law firms generally have not caught on, perhaps in part because of uncertainty about whether the two firms would be regarded as sufficiently separate under most state ethical rules. Model Rule 5.4(a) forbids a lawyer or law firm from sharing legal fees with a nonlawyer; Rule 5.4(b) prohibits a lawyer from forming a partnership with a nonlawyer if any of the activities of the partnership consist of the practice of law; and Rule 5.4(d) says that a lawyer may not practice with or in the form of a professional organization authorized to practice law for a profit if a nonlawyer owns any interest in the organization or serves as a director or officer in it. In addition, Rule 5.5(a) prohibits a lawyer from assisting anyone unauthorized practice in a jurisdiction, and the professional services firm would be deemed to be engaged in such practice as an organization that contains nonlawyers.

In 1999, the American Bar Association Commission on Multidisciplinary Practice recommended that ethical rules be amended to permit lawyers and nonlawyers to merge into MDPs, subject to certain conditions. This proposal, and a more modest one submitted a year later, was rejected by the ABA House of Delegates. It is unclear how much pressure there will be for law and accounting firm affiliations or mergers in the wake of the collapse of Arthur Andersen and the myriad scandals involving accounting firms in recent years. As a major scholar and reporter for the ABA Commission on MDPs concludes, however:

> Three observations can be made without qualification: first, that the demand for cross-border legal services remains strong and will continue to grow; second, that before Andersen's collapse, the legal networks affiliated with the Big Five were on the verge of becoming formidable competitors in certain sectors of the marketplace for cross-border legal services; and third, that the Final Four will generously support their affiliated law firm networks to advance the long-term goal of enabling the member firms to increase their marketplace share at the expense of traditional law firms.[7]

* * *

B. ETHICAL RULES

Lauren R. Frank, ETHICAL RESPONSIBILITIES AND
THE INTERNATIONAL LAWYER: MIND THE GAPS

2000 U. ILL. L. REV. 957

I. INTRODUCTION

With the proliferation of a global market and many American businesses taking advantage of economic opportunities abroad, the

---

6. *Id.* at 613.

7. *Id.* at 634 (footnotes omitted).

American legal profession similarly has expanded. American lawyers are following their clients abroad, broadening their legal services to provide counsel to clients uncertain how to proceed in a foreign environment ...

Yet American firms are not only expanding globally to meet the needs of existing clients but are searching for new clients as well. The economic recession in the United States during the late 1980s forced several firms to look for new markets and business opportunities in Japan, Eastern and Western Europe, and Central America. This trend was mirrored by events in those regions making legal inroads much more accessible: the opening up of Japan to foreigners, the collapse of communism and the introduction of capitalism in Eastern Europe, the increasing strength of the European Union, and the signing of NAFTA promoting free trade between the United States and Mexico.

These growing numbers of American lawyers practicing abroad face many of the same legal and ethical issues as their domestic counterparts, issues invariably addressed in the practice of law. The foreign environments in which American lawyers practice, however, engender additional and sometimes greater ethical questions, stemming from the different laws, customs, and traditions they encounter daily. Moreover, each foreign jurisdiction promulgates its own rules of professional conduct, and these rules can differ markedly from jurisdiction to jurisdiction. In short, pitfalls abound for the inexperienced.

Effective overseas representation thus cannot be drawn solely from a law school education and on-the-job training. Rather, lawyers working in the international arena must be cognizant of the unique ways foreign countries structure their legal systems and ethical codes, often in manners entirely divergent from the American model—differences rooted in cultural, political, and social traditions ...

B. Common v. Civil Law Systems

Closely related to the issue of cultural differences are the different legal systems in which international lawyers practice. Specifically, many European nations, such as France and Spain, utilize a civil law model, where codified law and tradition, and not case law precedent, form the backbone of judicial review. This difference from the American (and British) common law system has important ethical ramifications for lawyers working in both systems.

In a civil law system, judges focus entirely on the written law in which customs and traditions are codified. Lawyers present only relevant law to the judge; there is no arguing by analogy to other cases, as in American courts. The civil law, or civilian, lawyer has less leeway to present facts subjectively, and some commentators interpret this limitation as leaving the civil law lawyer with less power in society and less freedom of action within the legal system than the common law counterpart.

The civil law system thus has been characterized as "inquisitorial," while the common law has been deemed litigious and adversarial. The civilian lawyer is more than merely her client's representative; she is also part of the system of law, as evidenced by the lawyer's wearing of legal robes when she appears in court. The common law lawyer, in contrast, wears no robe. She is set off from the judge, suggesting she is not there to cooperate with the judge but rather to present zealously her client's case. Although in theory an officer of the court, the common law lawyer is less a part of the system and more a hired advocate for the client * * *

II. ETHICAL RULES AND THE TRANSNATIONAL LAWYER

* * *

B. *European Community Code of Conduct*

In Europe today, an integrated market for the practice of law is quickly becoming workable, the result of several economic, historical, social, and political factors functioning together. More narrowly, the principal impetus is financial, and as the European Union moves closer to creating an integrated internal market, more and more legal assistance will be needed to structure and oversee the various transactions that now reach from one country to another and form the backbone of this increased activity.

Moreover, European law firms have expanded into a cross-border practice within the Community and elsewhere in Europe in the past decade. This expansion has mirrored that of large international accounting firms, providing clients with "easier communication with key advisors," "the application of uniform standards of service," and "reliable assurances of quality control." Cross-border practice has similarly been facilitated by important changes made to the laws of several key countries regarding regulations of foreign lawyers and domestic lawyers practicing in foreign countries.

Paralleling Europe's cross-border growth has been the CCBE.[1] The organization was founded in 1960 to address the problems and opportunities for the legal profession stemming from the 1957 Treaty of Rome that created the European Economic Community (EC or EEC). Its role is to "provide a forum for the interchange of views and information among its member bodies, as well as to represent the legal profession to the EEC Commission and before the Court of Justice." The CCBE has no binding legislative authority per se, but its recommendations are accorded much deference.

The CCBE's primary task was to draft a legal ethics code for EC lawyers working in and/or with other Community countries and lawyers. The CCBE Code was promulgated on October 28, 1988, in Strasbourg, France, to address these issues and provide a guide for lawyers and countries working within the EC. Although other laws of the EC had

---

1. [The acronym stands for the original name of the organization, Conseil des Bar-   reaux de la Communaute Europe—*Eds.*]

addressed the mechanics of cross-border practice, little mention was made of legal ethics rules and the potential difficulties occurring when lawyers are subject to two divergent ethical codes—the code of the lawyer's home country and the code of the country in which the lawyer is working. To fill this gap, the then-twelve Member States of the EC, working together under the CCBE's rubric, adopted a common code with two applications: (1) to all transnational activities between EC lawyers, including all work with lawyers of Member States other than their own and (2) to the professional activities of lawyers in a Member State other than their own. Creating the Code avoided the possibility of each country being forced to recognize [many]different codes, the details of which might only be partially understood, if at all, by foreign lawyers ...

The Code, although not binding law, is not a "purely advisory document" either. In fact, the Code's authors intended it to be adopted by the Member States. Rule 1.3 of the Code calls for the parties to adopt it as "enforceable rules as soon as possible in accordance with national or Community procedures in relation to the cross-border activities of the lawyer in the European Community." Most Member States have adopted the Code.

The Code utilizes a structure similar to that of the ABA's Model Rules, setting forth black letter rules that are mandatory principles, as opposed to mere guidelines for permissible conduct. Yet the Code is not a panacea; in some instances, it does no more than serve as a conflicts of law code, determining which state's ethical regulations to use, rather than creating one overarching legal ethics code acceptable to all. Nonetheless, the Code's value in regulating cross-border lawyering is unquestioned. Although the United States is not a party to the EC and, therefore, not subject to the CCBE Code, the Code is instructive as it, in conjunction with each European state's own national code, delineates the parameters of ethical behavior for lawyers practicing in Europe.

* * *

C. SELECTED SECTIONS OF THE CCBE CODE

1.2   The Nature of Rules of Professional Conduct

1.2.1   * * * The failure of the lawyer to observe these rules must in the last resort result in a disciplinary sanction.

1.3   The Purpose of the Code

1.3.1   The continued integration of the European Union * * * and the increasing frequency of the cross-border activities of lawyers within the European Economic Area have made necessary in the public interest the statement of common rules which apply to all lawyers from the European Economic Area * * * in relation to their cross-border practice.

1.3.2   * * * After the rules in this Code have been adopted as enforceable rules in relation to his cross-border activities the lawyer will remain bound to observe the rules of the Bar or Law Society to which he belongs to the extent that they are consistent with the rules in this Code.

1.5   Field of Application Ratione Materiae

* * * Cross-border activities shall mean:

(a) all professional contacts with lawyers of Member States other than his own;

(b) the professional activities of the lawyer in a Member State other than his own, whether or not the lawyer is physically present in that Member State.

2.1   Independence

2.1.1   The many duties to which a lawyer is subject require his absolute independence, free from all other influence, especially as may arise from his personal interests or external pressure. Such independence is as necessary to trust in the process of justice as the impartiality of the judge. A lawyer must therefore avoid any impairment of his independence and be careful not to compromise his professional standards in order to please his client, the court or third parties.

2.1.2   This independence is necessary in non-contentious matters as well as in litigation. Advice given by a lawyer to his client has no value if it is given only to ingratiate himself, to serve his personal interests or in response to outside pressure.

2.3   Confidentiality

2.3.1   * * * The lawyer's obligation of confidentiality serves the interest of the administration of justice as well as the interest of the client. It is therefore entitled to special protection by the State.

2.3.2   A lawyer shall respect the confidentiality of all information that becomes known to him in the course of his professional activity.

2.3.2   The obligation of confidentiality is not limited in time.

3.2   Conflict of Interest

3.2.1   A lawyer may not advise, represent or act on behalf of two or more clients in the same matter if there is a conflict, or a significant risk of a conflict, between the interests of those clients.

* * *

3.2.3   A lawyer must also refrain from acting for a new client if there is a risk of a breach of confidence entrusted to the lawyer by a former client or if the knowledge which the lawyer possesses of the affairs of the former client would give an undue advantage to the new client.

3.2.4   Where lawyers are practicing in association, [these provisions] shall apply to the association and all its members.

3.3 Pactum de Quota Litis

3.3.1 A lawyer shall not be entitled to make a pactum de quota litis.

3.3.2 [A pactum de quota litis is] an arrangement between a lawyer and his client entered into prior to final conclusion of a matter to which the client is a party, by virtue of which the client undertakes to pay the lawyer a share of the result * * *

4.1 Applicable Rules of Conduct in Court

A lawyer who appears, or takes part in a case before a court or tribunal in a Member State, must comply with the rules of conduct applied before that court or tribunal.

5.1 Corporate Spirit of the Profession

5.1.1 The corporate spirit of the profession requires a relationship of trust and cooperation between lawyers for the benefit of their clients and in order to avoid unnecessary litigation and other behaviour harmful to the reputation of the profession. It can, however, never justify setting the interests of the profession against those of the client.

5.9 Disputes Amongst Lawyers in Different Member States

5.9.1 If a lawyer considers that a colleague in another Member State has acted in breach of a rule of professional conduct he shall draw the matter to the attention of his colleague.

5.9.2 If any personal dispute of a professional nature arises amongst lawyers in different Member States they should if possible first try to settle it in a friendly way.

5.9.3 A lawyer shall not commence any form of proceedings against a colleague in another Member State on matters referred to in 5.9.1 or 5.9.2 above without first informing the Bars of Law Societies to which they both belong for the purpose of allowing both Bars or Law Societies concerned an opportunity to assist in reaching a settlement.

* * *

Note: The CCBE Code

One notable feature of the CCBE Code is that it defers in its definition of lawyers to individual Member States, some of whom do not include in-house corporate counsel as members of the legal profession. As Professor Laurel Terry, a leading observer notes, "Many European countries take the position that an employed lawyer, who by definition has only one client, cannot maintain the required independent professional judgment and is, in essence, in a permanent conflict of interest situation. These countries therefore specifically exclude employed lawyers or house counsel from their definition of lawyer."[1] If a lawyer in

---

1. Laurel S. Terry, *An Introduction to the European Community's Legal Ethics Code, Part I: An Analysis of the CCBE's* *Code of Conflict*, 7 Geo. J. Legal Ethics 1, 20 (1993).

such country accepts a position, she must suspend her membership in the bar for the duration of such employment.

The CCBE Code also is notable for its generality and brevity. As Professor Terry has commented, "This leanness is understandable. It is a truism that American lawyers have a different style of lawyering than European lawyers; Americans are accustomed to more detail and specification than is used in Europe. Europeans have revealed a concern to avoid overly-detailed provisions."[2] A commentary on the CCBE expresses the philosophy behind this approach:

> Codes can create an environment in which certain standards are encouraged. Codes, themselves, however, have limitations. They have more often a dissuasive effect than a positive impetus. They help us to avoid rather than to fulfill. They are attempts to capture on paper an approved pattern of behavior, a desired moral climate, an answer to all questions of conduct—which cannot be adequately captured on paper. Codes are helpful only if the value judgments on which they rest are sound, the distinctions which they make are clear and the means by which they are applied are effective.[3]

Professor Terry also suggests that the disinclination in the CCBE to provide as detailed ethical rules as in the United States may reflect a view of the lawyer as inevitably having to exercise discretion for the purpose of maintaining more independence from the client than is the norm in the United States.[4] For instance, the general conflict of interest provision in the CCBE is less elaborate than in the Model Rules and has no explicit provision for consultation with the client. "[T]he CCBE Code simply does not have the plethora of rules which tell the lawyer how to behave when face with situations which may tempt the lawyer."[5] Rather, it relies on the lawyer to determine the most appropriate course of action in light of her responsibilities as an independent professional.

* * *

D. CHOICE OF LAW ISSUES

PANCOTTO v. SOCIEDADE de SAFARIS de MOCAMBIQUE, S.A.R.L

422 F.Supp. 405 (N.D. Ill. 1976)

MARSHALL, DISTRICT JUDGE.

The plaintiff, Rosemary Pancotto, has brought this diversity action to recover damages for a personal injury she sustained in 1973 while on a hunting safari in Mozambique. Pending for decision is the motion of

---

2. *Id.* at 16.

3. Cross-Border Practice Compendium, ch. 4, at 14 (Dorothy Margaret Donald-Little ed., 1991).

4. Terry, *An Introduction*, at 46–55.

5. *Id.* at 55.

defendant Sociedade de Safaris de Mocambique (Safrique), to apply the law of Mozambique to the substantive issues in the action, and for a determination of the relevant Mozambique law ... [A] federal court sitting in diversity applies the conflicts law of the state in which it sits. Thus our task regarding the first part of defendant's motion is to determine and apply the Illinois choice of law rule.

Illinois modified its choice of law rules for tort cases in *Ingersoll v. Klein, 46 Ill.2d 42, 262 N.E.2d 593 (1970)*. "In our opinion, the local law of the State where the injury occurred should determine the rights and liabilities of the parties, unless Illinois has a more significant relationship with the occurrence and the parties, in which case, the law of Illinois should apply." *Id. at 45, 262 N.E.2d at 595.*

The first step in the choice of law analysis is to isolate the substantive legal issues and determine whether the various states' tort rules conflict. If a potential conflict is discovered, the next step is to examine the contacts with the states, evaluating the importance of each contact in relation to the legal issues of the case. Finally, under the Illinois choice of law rule, the law of the state or country of the place of injury is followed, unless Illinois is more significantly interested in the resolution of a particular legal issue.

I. THE DEFENDANT'S LIABILITY

Defendant's motion identifies the two substantive legal issues to be addressed by this choice of law analysis, each of which will be considered in turn: (1) the defendant's liability; and (2) the appropriate measure of damages. A cursory look at the defendant's materials outlining Mozambique law indicates that the standard of care there was different from Illinois'. Briefly, the Mozambique standard of care upon which defendant relies was the "diligence with which a law abiding male head of a family would act." Portuguese Civil Code, Art. 487(2). Although this standard of care bears an analytical similarity to Illinois' reasonable man standard, it may be more or less demanding of an alleged wrongdoer. This putative difference could lead to a different result if Mozambique rather than Illinois law is applied. Consequently, we are faced with a true conflict of laws and must evaluate the parties' contacts with the two states to determine which law should control.

Ingersoll refers us to what is now *Restatement (Second) of Conflicts of Laws § 145* (1971), for a listing of the contacts to be evaluated in determining which jurisdiction is most significantly concerned with the liability of the alleged tortfeasor. The first of these is the place where the injury occurred. The parties do not dispute that plaintiff sustained her injuries in Mozambique. Mrs. Pancotto accompanied her husband and sons on a hunting safari directed by defendant. She was taking pictures of other members of the hunting party when a swamp buggy driven by a Safrique employee ran into her.

The place of injury has an interest in applying its own tort principles to discourage harmful behavior within its borders. This interest in controlling the tortfeasor's conduct is strongest when the alleged tort is intentional. If the harmful contact is unintentional, however, the interest of the place of injury is attenuated. Realistically, the negligent tortfeasor is not affected by a state's civil liability laws because he does not premeditate before he acts. Nonetheless, to the extent that such conduct is shaped by legal standards, Mozambique was, at the time of the alleged wrong, interested in the choice of the standard of care to be imposed upon the defendant.

The second contact listed in the Restatement is the place of the conduct which caused injury, which is again clearly Mozambique. The interest of the jurisdiction where the conduct occurred is similar if not identical to that of the place of injury. Again, however, Mozambique's valid interest in controlling harmful conduct assumes less importance when the alleged tortfeasor was not governed by conscious reference to a behavioral standard.

The Restatement's third contact is the domicile or place of business of the parties. This consideration refers us to both Illinois law and that of Mozambique. The plaintiff's domicile, Illinois, is interested in compensating both the victim and her creditors. Mozambique, on the other hand, as the defendant's domicile and principal place of business, is concerned that defendant's conduct conforms to its standards, and may also have an interest in insulating a domiciliary from liability.

The Restatement's final contact point is the place where the parties' relationship is centered. The relationship here has an international flavor. The safari was arranged in large part by intercontinental telephone calls and cables. In addition, certain employees of the defendant visited the plaintiff's husband in Illinois approximately three times prior to the safari, although the parties dispute the business as opposed to personal significance of the visits. Regardless of the nature of the Illinois contacts, they obviously were preparatory to an extended, well-planned interaction in Mozambique. Plaintiff's ultimate presence in that country was hardly fortuitous. In short, although the relationship had international aspects, it can fairly be characterized as centering in Mozambique.

These contacts and the state interests evoked by them indicate that both Illinois and Mozambique are interested in the resolution of the liability issue. Both jurisdictions' interests are significant. The numerous Mozambique contacts highlight that government's interest in controlling the conduct of those who take action within its borders, and the interest in affording the protection of its laws to its domiciliaries. Illinois, on the other hand, has a strong interest in seeing that its residents are adequately compensated for tortious injuries. The Illinois interest, although based upon a single contact, cannot for that reason be automatically dismissed as less significant. A contact assumes significance only in view of the legal issue to which it relates. Our evaluation of the contacts indicates that both Illinois and Mozambique are validly interested in the resolution of the issue of defendant's liability, and we hesitate to characterize either jurisdiction's interest as more significant.

In general, the Illinois courts have chosen their own law rather than the law of the place of injury only if the majority of the significant contacts were in Illinois, and the tort's occurrence in the foreign state was fortuitous. Given that both states here may assert significant although distinct interests in the outcome of the liability issue, the Illinois choice of law rule directs the application of the law of the place of injury, Mozambique.

We now turn to a determination of the Mozambique law governing liability for the acts of misconduct alleged in the complaint.

Rule 44.1 gives district courts wide discretion in the materials to which they may resort to determine the content of foreign law. The defendant has provided copies of the relevant sections of the Portuguese Civil Code, both in that language and in translation. In addition, defendant offers the affidavit of Mr. Marcel Molins, an expert witness conversant with the law of Portugal, who comments upon the law pertinent to the issues of liability and damages. Regarding liability, these combined resources indicate that Portuguese law sets out two standards for liability, either of which might apply to the facts alleged in the complaint. The first standard seems to be a rough equivalent, allowing for cultural differences, of the common law reasonable man standard. Under this standard, "[fault] is judged, in the absence of another legal criterion, by the diligence with which a law-abiding male head of a family would act in the face of the circumstances of each case." Art. 487(2). The injured person carries the burden of proving that the opposing party was at fault as measured by this standard, unless there is a legal presumption of fault. Art. 487.

A second standard may be available, however, under the facts alleged here. As in the United States, in Mozambique liability was sometimes imposed without regard to fault. Under the Portuguese Civil Code this concept is called objective liability, and appears to be theoretically equivalent to our concept of strict liability in tort. Under the Portuguese Code, the operation of a land vehicle is considered inherently hazardous. Thus, Art. 503(1) provides that "[one] who has effective control of a vehicle for travel on land and uses it for his own purposes or by means of an agent, is chargeable for the damage originating in the risks inherent in the vehicle, even though it is not in movement." A Safrique employee was operating the swamp buggy at the time of Mrs. Pancotto's injury. Mr. Molins admits that the available Mozambique case law does little to clarify the meaning and application of the term "for his own purposes." But, on the record as presently constituted, a fact finder could find that the vehicle was "for travel on land", was under the control of Safrique, and was used "by means of an agent" in which event it would appear that defendant would be liable for risks inherent in the vehicle, *i.e.*, striking a pedestrian.

Without further testimony on the matter, we are not prepared to decide at this time which standard of liability would be applied by a Mozambique court. We also need edification on the question whether the common law reasonable man standard and the Mozambique "male head of a family" standard are equivalents or whether the latter imposes a greater or lesser standard of care than does the former. Therefore, in preparation for trial the parties are directed to submit supplemental materials addressing these issues.

II. THE MEASURE OF DAMAGES

A brief look at Mozambique's and Illinois' laws on recoverable damages reveals an acute conflict. Illinois permits recovery for medical expenses due to the injury, and, *inter alia*, compensation for the injury itself, for disfigurement, and for pain and suffering. In contrast, Art. 508 of the Portuguese Civil Code limits liability for travel accidents to 600 contos, or approximately $6,600 in United States dollars. This limit is not inflexible, however. A Mozambique court may apparently, in its discretion, award damages to the full extent of the plaintiff's out-of-pocket loss, although the typical recovery is less generous. And, under Mozambique law, the plaintiff recovers nothing for pain and suffering, disfigurement, or loss of enjoyment of life as she might under Illinois law.

The defendant argues that the Illinois choice of law rule dictates the application of Mozambique law to this issue also. And, in fact, the analysis of the two jurisdictions' interests in the measure of damages leads to such a result. As the place of conduct, injury, defendant's domicile, and the place where the parties' relationship centered, Mozambique has a strong interest in the resolution of this issue. As plaintiff's domicile and the place where the consequences of the injury are felt, Illinois is concerned that plaintiff receives compensation. Plaintiff, however, contends that the application of Mozambique's damage limitation would be so grossly repugnant to Illinois' public and constitutional policy of providing a remedy for all injuries that an Illinois court would refuse to follow Mozambique law, even if the *Ingersoll* rule would normally dictate its application.

With no Illinois cases in point, the parties discuss certain cases in which the New York courts have faced similar contentions. Of these, *Rosenthal v. Warren, 475 F.2d 438 (2d Cir. 1973),* is the closest factually to the case here. As a federal court sitting in New York, the *Rosenthal* court was concerned with the proper application of New York's choice of law rule, which differs from the Illinois rule. Despite this difference in orientation, *Rosenthal* points out the important factors to consider in determining whether the forum state's public policy should overrule the law of a foreign jurisdiction.

The plaintiff's decedent in *Rosenthal* was domiciled in New York. Accompanied by the plaintiff, his wife and later his executrix, the decedent traveled to Boston for medical treatment by a physician domiciled in Massachusetts. The decedent died while recuperating in a Massachusetts hospital after surgery performed by the physician. The decedent's wife subsequently sued the physician and the hospital in a New York state court.

The defendants argued that the Massachusetts wrongful death statute, with its $50,000 limit on damages, should apply. The court rejected Massachusetts' statute in favor of New York's full compensation policy. Before doing so, the court confronted and thoroughly analyzed the factors militating against the forum's application of its own public policy. First, the court considered whether the defendants had patterned their conduct upon the Massachusetts statute. A doctor does not, however, ordinarily think of wrongful death limitations before performing surgery; consequently the doctor could not claim he acted in reliance upon a Massachusetts behavioral standard. Second, the court considered whether the defendants would be unfairly surprised by the application of New York law. Neither the doctor nor the hospital had a strictly local clientele or practice. Consequently it could not be said that they justifiably expected to be affected only by Massachusetts law. Third, the court considered whether defendants had purchased insurance in reliance upon the Massachusetts limitation. The defendants' policies, however, made no distinction between recoveries for personal injuries and recoveries for wrongful death. As a result, the defendants could not convincingly argue that they relied upon the Massachusetts limit. Finally, the court evaluated the policy behind the Massachusetts limitation to determine whether application of the New York law would frustrate an important Massachusetts interest. Finding that the few remaining wrongful death limitations are vestiges of the mistaken view that a common law action for wrongful death did not exist, the court declined to apply an archaic and unjust policy, particularly in view of its own policy to assure just and fair compensation for the victims of tortious conduct.

In short, *Rosenthal* indicates that the defendant's reliance, and principles of fundamental fairness and governmental policy should be balanced in determining whether the forum's measure of damages, grounded upon a strong public policy, may be applied against a foreign defendant.

Applying these principles to the factual context here yields some similar conclusions. The tort alleged in the complaint is unintentional, rendering any argument of behavioral reliance untenable. And, as in *Rosenthal*, the defendant here anticipated and welcomed, if not solicited, business contacts with persons outside the jurisdiction. The last two *Rosenthal* considerations, however, are not so easily dismissed. Defendant's counsel has submitted an affidavit attesting that defendant told him it carries no insurance * * * [T]he lack of insurance suggests that defendant relied upon Mozambique's damage limitation. Moreover, although a New York court can confidently characterize wrongful death limitations as an archaic minority rule, we have no knowledge of the status of damage limitations for personal injury actions in the world community of nations.

Despite these countervailing considerations, our educated prediction is that the Illinois courts would refuse to enforce the Portuguese limitation as unreasonable and contrary to Illinois public policy. Illinois' public policy is found in its Constitution, laws, judicial decisions, and also in its customs, morals, and notions of justice. There is perhaps no more compelling Illinois public policy than one expressed in the state's Constitution, which provides that every person should find a certain remedy in the law for injuries to his person. Ill. Const. Art. I, § 12. On occasion, the Illinois courts have accepted reasonable limits on recoveries for personal injuries, as for example in the Dram Shop Act and the Wrongful Death Act. Ill.Rev.Stat. ch. 43, § 135; ch. 70, §§ 1, 2 (1973).[4] But as the Illinois Supreme Court noted in its recent decision invalidating Illinois' medical malpractice law, these statutes created actions unknown at common law. Thus, the courts were not disturbed when the newly created right was accompanied by a limited remedy. But if the right existed at common law, damage limitations without a *quid pro quo* have been disfavored. Moreover, the damage limitations incorporated into Illinois legislation have been more consistent with potential out-of-pocket loss. The Dram Shop Act limits damages to $20,000, Ill.Rev.Stat. ch. 43, § 135; the recently voided malpractice act carried a $500,000 limit.

Of course, we are not dealing here with a law of Illinois, but one from a foreign country. Recently liberated from foreign rule, the economic and social conditions in Mozambique are quite different from those in Illinois. Recognizing such international disparities, the court in *Ciprari v. Servicos Aereos Cruzeiro, 245 F.Supp. 819 (S.D.N.Y. 1965),* applied the Brazilian Code, which limited damages to an amount less than $100. The court, however, emphasized the unique justifications for the limitation, which applied only to accidents involving Brazil's national airline. In particular, the court cited Brazil's public policy of protecting the financial integrity of an infant national industry, and the overtones of national security in Brazil's special interest in the national airline. *245 F.Supp. at 824–25.* On the contrary, no exceptional national concern is asserted here. Instead, the damage limitation is general, applying to all injuries sustained in travel accidents. The parties have cited no public policy to be advanced by the law and we hesitate to speculate on the question.

In the absence of an articulated national policy, the final inquiry is whether the application of the Illinois law would unfairly prejudice the defendant. Although the defendant is a Mozambique corporation, its trade is international in scope. Safrique allows travel agencies to use its name in advertisements for sporting magazines with national circulation. If Safrique induces residents of other countries to visit Mozambique and profits from the excursions, it is hardly unfair to require Safrique to compensate its clients for tortious injuries inflicted by Safrique employees. Concomitantly, Safrique cannot claim that its clients' residencies

---

4. In respect to wrongful death, the limitation has now been removed. Ill.Rev.Stat. ch. 70, §§ 1, 2 (1975).

take it by surprise. Indeed, Safrique deliberately engages in a business which thrives on international tourism.

A final aspect of the question of prejudice involves counsel's allegation that defendant carries no liability insurance. Safrique's failure to obtain insurance, however, is not alleged to have been motivated by the Mozambique damage limitation. Without supplemental affidavits, this neglect is as easily attributed to oversight as to a calculated business decision that it might cost more in premiums than to directly compensate a victim to the statutory limit.

In conclusion, although the Illinois choice of law rule indicates the application of Mozambique's law to the substantive issues in this action, we feel the Illinois courts would refuse to enforce the Mozambique policy of providing a remedy for personal injuries. Foreign substantive law is not unenforceable simply because it differs from our own law, but because the differences are against public policy. The refusal to enforce a foreign law should not be lightly made. But when no justification is offered for a policy which contravenes a sound public policy of the forum, and the defendant is not unfairly surprised, we believe that the Illinois courts would decline to apply the foreign limitation.

PROBLEMS

1. Bell & Ferris (B&F) is a law firm based in New York with offices in the United States and abroad. Its Delaware office currently represents Alpha Corporation in a private antitrust suit that has been filed in Wilmington, Delaware. Janet Stevens, a B&F partner in that office, is lead counsel on that case. Alpha is a United States automobile company incorporated in Delaware with several United States and foreign subsidiaries in which it holds a majority interest.

Alpha has approached Omega, a Dutch holding company, about purchasing one of Omega's majority-owned subsidiaries, OmegaFrance. Omega-France is an small automobile company involved in the development and manufacture of hybrid vehicles that run in part on energy sources other than fossil fuels. The company currently has two plants in France, and plans to add one in Spain in the near future. OmegaFrance hopes eventually to produce vehicles that run entirely on alternative energy sources, although that day is several years away.

Alpha believes that the acquisition of OmegaFrance would give it a foothold in the hybrid automobile market. It regards Europe as an especially lucrative market for such automobiles, and projects that there will be a very high future demand in Europe for vehicles that run completely on sources other than fossil fuels. Omega, on the other hand, has concluded that OmegaFrance's current profitability does not fit its business strategy. It therefore would like to divest itself of the French subsidiary.

B&F's Paris office has done some work for Omega in the past. The company now turns to B&F partner David Rousseau, a member of the French bar, to represent it in the negotiations for the sale of OmegaFrance to Alpha. Rousseau agrees. At the first negotiating session in Amsterdam, the Alpha representative objects to Rousseau's representation of Omega. He claims that B&F has a conflict of interest because it represents Alpha in the antitrust suit in Delaware. B&F's Paris office regards Omega as a valuable client, and wishes to continue to represent the company. Rousseau maintains that there is no conflict, and refuses to withdraw.

Delaware has adopted most of the Model Rules of Professional Conduct verbatim, including Rules relating to conflicts of interest and Rule 8.5. Comment 7 to Rule 1.7, relating to concurrent conflicts, says, "Directly adverse conflicts can also arise in transactional matters. For example, if a lawyer is asked to represent the seller of a business in negotiations with a buyer represented by the lawyer, not in the same transaction but in another, unrelated matter, the lawyer could not undertake the representation without the informed consent of each client." Comment 7 to Rule 8.5 says, "The choice of law provision applies to lawyers engaged in transnational practice," unless international law, treaties or other agreements provide otherwise.

French National Bar Council Harmonised Practice Rule Rule 4.1 deals with concurrent conflicts. It provides that a lawyer may not "advise represent or act on behalf of two or more parties in the same matter if there is a conflict between their interests," or if there is a serious risk of such a conflict. Rule 4.3 states, "When lawyers practise in a group structure, the provisions relating to conflicts of interest shall apply to the group as a whole and to all of its members." The French bar rules contain no provision addressing choice of law in cases involving bar rules other than those of France.

Finally, the CCBE Code addresses concurrent conflicts in Section 3.2.1: "A lawyer may not advise, represent, or act on behalf of two or more clients in the same matter if there is a conflict, or a significant risk of a conflict, between the interests of those clients." Section 3.2.4 states: "Where lawyers are practising in association," the conflict of interest rules "shall apply to the association and all its members." CCBE Code section 1.3.1 provides that the CCBE Code applies to all lawyers in the European Union (EU), of which France and the Netherlands are members, "in relation to their cross-border practice" within the EU. Lawyers in member states are required to follow their country's bar rules "to the extent that they are consistent with the rules in this Code." Section 1.3.2.

What, if any, legal recourse, does Alpha have in attempting to remove or have B&K withdraw as counsel for Omega in the sale of OmegaFrance to Alpha?

2.   You are an attorney in the litigation department of Worldwide Insurance Group (WIG), a major insurer of business corporations. One of WIG's policyholders is Bluestone Corporation, a manufacturer of computer components whose headquarters is in New Jersey. Bluestone recently made a shipment of $1 million worth of components to Oliva Corporation, a customer in Spain. The shipment was insured by WIG. The components were flown by overnight delivery service to Madrid, and then loaded on a truck for same-day delivery to Oliva's plant about an hour outside Madrid. On the way to the plant, the truck was involved in a major collision with a large sport utility vehicle (SUV). The driver of the truck escaped serious injury, but the truck was totaled, and the computer components it was carrying were completely destroyed. The driver of the SUV was at fault.

Tests indicate that he had a level of alcohol in his system above the threshold for liability for driving under the influence of alcohol.

WIG has paid the insurance claim by Bluestone for the $1 million in components that were destroyed in the accident. As a result, it has succeeded to any legal rights that Bluestone may have against any party in connection with the accident. Unfortunately, the driver of the SUV has minimal income and assets.

You learn, however, that shortly before the accident the driver had sampled several of the wines during one of the public tours at a nearby winery, La Festival, which accounted for the alcohol in his system. La Festival exports wine to the United States and other countries and has an office in New York. You therefore sue the winery in a diversity action in federal court in New Jersey, asking for $1 million in damages.

Such a cause of action against establishments that serve alcohol to persons who foreseeably will be operating motor vehicles is recognized in New Jersey and some other states. It also is recognized in Spain, but recovery is limited by statute to what is the current equivalent of US$50,-000. In adopting such a limitation, the Spanish parliament explicitly stated that the purpose of this provision is to preserve the viability of the Spanish wine industry, which is important to both the country's economy and its traditions.

New Jersey law regarding choice of law is similar to the Illinois law described in the *Pancotto* case. You contend that New Jersey law should govern the suit, while the winery insists that Spanish law should apply. Who should prevail?

†